CASSELL'S COMPACT ENGLISH DICTIONARY

REVISED BY ARTHUR L. HAYWARD

ETYMOLOGICAL AND PRONOUNCING

WITH APPENDICES CONTAINING

Foreign phrases and words in English use

Pronunciation of proper names

Abbreviations

British and Metric weights

and measures

CASSELL · LONDON

CASSELL & COMPANY LTD
an imprint of
Cassell and Collier Macmillan Publishers Ltd
35 Red Lion Square,
London WC1R 4SG
Sydney, Toronto, Johannesburg
Auckland
and an affiliate of
Macmillan, Inc., New York

———

First new and revised edition 1956
2nd edition 1960
3rd edition 1962
4th edition 1963
5th edition 1965
6th edition 1966
7th edition 1968
7th edition, 2nd impression 1969
7th edition, 3rd impression 1970
7th edition, 4th impression 1972
7th edition, 5th impression 1975
I.S.B.N. 0 304 91815 6

Printed in Great Britain by
Butler & Tanner Ltd,
Frome and London
1274

COMMON ABBREVIATIONS

(For Complete List of Abbreviations see page 472)

a., adjective.
adv., adverb.
A.F., Anglo-French.
Am., American.
Ang.-Ind., Anglo-Indian.
Ang.-Ir., Anglo-Irish.
Ang.-Lat., Anglo-Latin.
Arab., Arabic.
A.-S., Anglo-Saxon.
aux. v., auxiliary verb.

Bibl., Bible, biblical.
Bot., Botany.

c., *circa*, about.
Celt., Celtic.
Chem., Chemistry.
colloq., colloquially.
comb. form., combining form.
conj., conjunction.
cp., compare.

Dan., Danish.
dat., dative.
Dut., Dutch.

e.g., *exempli gratia*, for example.
Eng., English.
etym., etymology.
Eur., European.

F., French.
f., feminine.
fam., familiar, familiarly.
fig., figuratively.
Flem., Flemish.
Fris., Frisian.
fut., future.

G., German.
Gael., Gaelic.
gen., genitive.
Goth., Gothic.
Gr., Greek.

Heb., Hebrew.
Hind., Hindustani.

Icel., Icelandic.
i.e., *id est*, that is.
imper., imperative.
Ind., India, Indian.
int., interjection.
intr., intransitive.

Ir., Irish.
It., Italian.

L., Latin.
L.G., Low German.

M.E., Middle English.
M.F., Middle French.
M.G., Middle German.

n., noun.
neut., neuter.
nom., nominative.
Norm., Norman.

obj., objective.
O.F., Old French.
O.H.G., Old High German.
O.L.G., Old Low German.
O.S., Old Saxon.

pass., passive.
pl., plural.
Port., Portuguese.
p.p., past participle.
pref., prefix.
pres. p., present participle.
pret., preterite.
pron., pronoun.

r., reflexive.
ref., referring, reference.
Rus., Russian.

Sansk., Sanskrit.
Sc., Scottish.
sing., singular.
Slav., Slavonic.
Sp., Spanish.
suf., suffix.
Swed., Swedish.

Teut., Teutonic.
tr., transitive.

v., verb.
v.i., verb intransitive.
viz., *videlicet*, namely.
v.r., verb reflexive.
v.t., verb transitive.

W., Welsh.
*, Obsolete.

KEY TO PRONUNCIATION

VOWELS

a	as in	far (far).
ă	,,	fat (făt).
ā	,,	fate (fāt).
aw	,,	fall (fawl).
ä	,,	fair (fär).
e	,,	bell (bel).
ĕ	,,	her (hĕr).
ē	,,	beef (bēf).
i	,,	bit (bit).
ī	,,	bite (bīt).

o	as in	not (not).
ō	,,	no (nō).
ô	,,	north (nôrth).
oo	,,	food (food).
u	,,	bull (bul).
ŭ	,,	sun (sŭn).
ū	,,	muse (mūz).
ou	,,	bout (bout).
oi	,,	join (join).

A dot placed over a, e, o, or u (ȧ, ė, ȯ, ů,) signifies that the vowel has an obscure, indeterminate, or slurred sound as in :.

advice (ȧd-vīs'), current (kŭr'ėnt), notion (nō'shůn).

CONSONANTS

" s " is used only for the sibilant " s " (as in " toast," tōst,) the sonant " s " (as in " toes ") is printed " z " (tōz).

" c " (except in the combinations " ch " and " *ch* "), " q " and " x " are not used.

b, d, f, h (see the combinations below), k, l, m, n (see *n* below), p, r, t, v, z, and w and y when used as consonants, have their usual values.

ch	as in	church (chĕrch).
ch	,,	loch (lo*ch*).
g	,,	get (get).
j	,,	join (join).
hw	,,	white (hwīt).

n	as in	cabochon (ka-bō-sho*n*').
sh	,,	shawl (shawl).
zh	,,	measure (mezh'ůr).
th	,,	thin (thin).
th	,,	thine (*th*īn).

The accent (') follows the syllable to be stressed.

CASSELL'S COMPACT
ENGLISH DICTIONARY

A

a (ā, à), **an** (ăn) [A.-S. *an*, one], *a.* The indefinite article. *A*, before words beginning with a consonant, *h* aspirate, the sound of *yu*, and before *one*; *an*, sometimes used before *h* unaccented, *an historian*.

ab- (1) L. *ab*], *pref.* Off, from, away, apart, as in *abrogate, abuse*.

ab- (2) [L. *ad*, to], *pref.* To, as in *abbreviate*.

aback (à-băk') [A.-S. *onbœc*]. *adv.* Backwards; behind; by surprise.

abacus (ăb'à-kŭs) [Gr. *abax-akos*, tablet], *n.* A counting-frame made of beads sliding on wires; (*Arch.*) a flat stone crowning the capital of a column.

abaft (à-baft') [A.-S. *bœftan*], *adv., prep.* Towards the hinder part of a ship; behind.

abandon (à-băn'dòn) [O.F. *abandoner*, from *à bandon*, at liberty; low L. *bandum*, proclamation], *v.t.* To give up, forsake; surrender oneself unreservedly. *n.* Careless freedom of manner. **abandoned**, *a.* Deserted; profligate. **abandonment**, *n.* The act of abandoning.

abase (à-bās') [O.F. *abaissier*, late L. *bassus*, low], *v.t.* To humble, degrade. **abasement**, *n.* State of humiliation.

abash (à-băsh') [O.F. *esbaïr*, to express amazement], *v.t.* To put to shame or confusion. **abashment**, *n.*

abate (à-bāt') [O.F. *abatre*, to beat down], *v.t.* To diminish, lessen. *v.i.* To become less. **abatement**, *n.* Deduction.

abattoir (a-ba-twar') [F.], *n.* A public slaughter-house.

abbacy (ăb'à-si), *n.* The office of an abbot. **abbatial** (à-bā'shi-ăl), *a.* **ab'bé** [F.], *n.* A R.C. ecclesiastic without a cure. **ab'bess**, *n.* A lady superior of a nunnery.

abbey (ăb'ĭ) [O.F. *abeie*], *n.* A monastery; the church attached.

abbot (ăb'ŏt) L. *abbas*, Syriac, *abbā*, father], *n.* The superior of a monastery.

abbreviate (à-brē'vi-āt) [L. *abbreviāre*], *v.t.* To shorten, abridge. **abbrevia'tion**, *n.* **abbre'viator**, *n.*

abdicate (ăb'di-kāt) [L. *dicāre*, to declare], *v.t.* To resign. *v.i.* To relinquish a throne or other dignity. **abdica'tion**, *n.* The act of abdicating.

abdomen (ăb-dō'měn) [L.], *n.* The trunk between the thorax and pelvis; the belly. **abdominal** (ăb-dŏm'-), *a.*

abduct (ăb-dŭkt') [L.], *v.t.* To take away (esp. a woman or child) by guile or force. **abduction**, *n.* A taking away of a child, wife, or ward by fraud or force.

abeam (à-bēm') [A.-S.], *adv.* (*Naut.*) At right angles to the keel.

abed (à-bĕd') [A.-S.], *adv.* Gone to bed.

aberrant (ăb-er'ànt) [L. *errāre*, wander], *a.* Wandering from the right way; deviating from type. **aberra'tion**, *n.*

abet (à-bet') [O.F.] *v.t.* To encourage or aid; to instigate (in a bad sense). **abetment**. *n.* abettor, *n.*

abeyance (à-bā'àns) [O.F. *abeance*], *n.* The state of being held back; dormancy.

abhor (ăb-hôr') [L. *horrēre*, to bristle, shudder], *v.t.* To loathe, shrink from with horror. **abhorrence**, *n.* **abhorrent**, *a.* Exciting loathing.

abide (à-bīd') [A.-S.], *v.i.* To dwell in a place; to remain firm. *v.t.* To await; tolerate. **abiding**, *a.*

abigail (ăb'i-gāl) [Heb.], *n.* A waiting-maid (1 Sam. xx. 5).

ability (à-bil'i-ti) [O.F. *ablete*], *n.* Power, capacity; (*pl.*) intellectual gifts.

abiogenesis (à-bi-ō-jen'e-sis), *n.* Spontaneous generation.

abject (ăb'jekt) [L. *jacere*, to cast], *a.* Servile, degraded. **abjectly**, *adv.*

abjure (ăb-joor') [L. *jurāre*, to swear], *v.t.* To retract on oath. *v.i.* To take an oath of abjuration. **abjuration**, *n.*

ablative (ăb'là-tiv) [L. *lātus*, p.p. of *fero*, I bear], *n.* The case in Latin, etc., expressing separation or instrumentality.

ablaze (à-blāz') [A.-S.], *adv.* or *a.* On fire.

able (ābl) [L. *habilis*, handy], *a.* Having sufficient power, skill, resources, etc., to do something indicated; gifted, vigorous, active. **ably** (āb'li), *adv.*

-able, *suff.* Fit, suitable for.

ablution (à-bloo'shùn) [L. *luere*, to wash], *n.* The act of washing or purifying.

abnegate (ăb'nē-gāt) [L. *negāre*, to deny], *v.t.* To deny, refuse, abjure. **abnegation** (-gā'shùn), *n.* Renunciation.

abnormal (ăb-nôrm'ăl) [L. *norma*, rule], *a.* Not according to type. **abnormal'ity**, *n.* Irregularity, deformity. **abnormally**, *adv.* **abnor'mity**. *n.* Departure from rule.

aboard (à-bôrd') [Fr. *à bord*], *adv.* In a ship or boat.

abode (à-bōd') [ABIDE], *n.* A habitation.

abolish (à-bol'ish) [L. *olēre*, to grow], *v.t.* To do away with, cancel. **aboli'tion**. *n.*

aboli'tionist, *n.* One who favoured the abolition of slavery.

abominate (à-bom'ĭ-nāt) [L. *abŏmināri*, to dislike], *v.t.* To detest, hate exceedingly. abominable, *a.* abomina'tion, *n.*

aborigines (ăb-ō-rĭj'ĭ-nēz) [L. *origine*, beginning], *n.pl.* The original inhabitants of a country. aborig'inal, *a.* Indigenous, *n.* An original inhabitant, esp. of Australia.

abort (à-bôrt') [L. *orīri*, to arise, grow], *v.t.* To make abortive. abortion, *n.* The production of the fœtus before the time; anything which does not come to maturity. abortive, *a.*

abound (à-bound') [L. *abundāre*, to overflow], *v.i.* To be rich (in). abounding, *a.*

about (à-bout') [A.-S.], *prep.* Around, surrounding; near in time, space, number, quantity, or quality; on the point of; concerning, in connection with. *adv.* Nearly.

above (à-bŭv') [A.-S.], *prep.* Over; at a higher point; in excess of. *adv.* Overhead. above-board, *adv.* Openly.

abrade (à-brād') [L. *rādere*, to scrape], *v.t.* To rub or wear away by friction.

abrasion (à-brā'zhŭn) [L. *abrāsio*], *n.* A rubbing away.

abreast (à-brest') [A.-S.], *adv.* Side by side; up to the standard (of).

abridge (à-brij') [O.F. *abregier*], *v.t.* To shorten, epitomize. abridgment, *n.*

abroad (à-brawd') [A.-S.], *adv.* At large; out of doors; in a foreign country.

abrogate (ăb'rō-gāt) [L. *rogāre*, to ask], *v.t.* To repeal. abroga'tion, *n.*

abrupt (à-brŭpt') [L. *abruptus*, broken off], *a.* Very steep; disconnected; sharp in manner.

abscess (ăb'ses) [L. *abscessus*], *n.* A gathering of pus in a tissue of the body.

abscond (ăb-skond') [L. *condere*, to hide], *v.i.* To go away secretly.

absent (ăb'sĕnt) [L. *abesse*, to be away], *a.* Away from a place; wanting; inattentive to passing events. absence, *n.* absent', *v.r.* To keep oneself away. absentminded, *a.* Inattentive. absentee', *n.* One who is habitually absent, esp. a landlord from his estate. absenteeism, *n.* Habitual absence from work.

absinthe (ăb'sinth) [F.], *n.* A liqueur flavoured with wormwood.

absolute (ăb'-sŏ-loot) [L. *absolūtus*], *a.* Independent; self-existent; arbitrary, despotic; perfect; (*Gram.*) applied to a case determined by any other word in a sentence; (*Chem.*) free from mixture.

absolution (ăb-sŏ-loo'shŭn), *n.* Remission, forgiveness; the pardon of sins by a priest after confession.

absolutism (ăb'sŏ-lu-tizm), *n.* Despotic government. absolutist, *a.* Pertaining to despotism.

absolve (ăb-solv') [L. *solvere*, to loosen], *v.t.* To pardon, acquit; pronounce forgiveness of sins to a penitent.

absorb (ăb-sôrb') [L. *sorbēre*, to suck up], *v.t.* To drink in. absorbent, *a.*

absorption (ăb-sôrp'shŭn) [L *absorptio*], *n.* The act of absorbing. absorptive, *a.*

abstain (ăb-stān') [L. *tenēre*, to hold], *v.i.* To refrain (from). abstainer, *n.* One who refrains, esp. from intoxicants.

abstemious (ăb-stē'mĭ-ŭs) [L.], *a.* Sparing, esp. in use of food and drink.

abstention (ăb-sten'shŭn), *n.* The act of abstaining. ab'stinence, *n.* Refraining, esp. from some indulgence.

abstract (ăb-străkt') [L. *abstractus*], *v.t.* To take away, remove; to consider apart from other things; to epitomize, summarize. ab'stract, *a.* Separated from particular things, ideal; not concrete. *n.* An epitome. abstracted, *a.* Absent-minded.

abstraction (ăb-străk'shŭn), *n.* The act of separating or taking away; being engrossed in thought; an abstract idea.

abstruse (ăb-stroos') [L. *trūdere*, to push], *a.* Recondite. abstruseness, *n.*

absurd (ăb-sĕrd') [L. *surdus*, deaf], *a.* Contrary to reason; nonsensical. absurdity, *n.*

abundance (à-bŭn'dàns) [L. *abundantia*, ABOUND], *n.* Plenteousness. abundant, *a.* Ample.

abuse (à-būz') [L. *ūtī*, to use], *v.t.* To misuse; to reproach coarsely. abuser, *n.* abuse (à-būs'), *n.* Improper treatment; a corrupt custom; scurrilous language. abusive, *a.*

abut (à-bŭt) [O.F. *abouter* (à, to, *but*, end)], *v.t.* To border upon. abutment, *n.* That which borders; a pier or wall against which an arch rests.

abysm (à-bizm') [O.F. *abisme*], *n.* A poetical form of abyss. abys'mal, *a.* Profound, immeasurable.

abyss (à-bĭs') [L. *abyssus*, bottomless], *n.* A vast depth, chasm, or cavity; primeval chaos; (*fig.*) anything profound and unfathomable. abyssal, *a.*

ac- [L. AD], *pref.* As in *accord, acquire*.

-ac [Gr. *-akos*], *suf.* Pertaining to, *e.g. demoniac.*

acacia (à-kā'shà) [Gr. *akakia* (*akē*, a point, thorn)], *n.* A genus of trees.

academy (à-kăd'ē-mǐ) [Gr. *akadēmeia* (the garden at Athens where Plato taught)], *n.* A place for higher education; a society for promoting literature, science or art. academ'ic, *a.* Professorial, theoretical, unpractical. academicals, *n. pl.* Cap and gown. academically, *adv.* academic'ian, *n.* A member of an academy, esp. Royal Academy.

acanthus (à-kăn'thŭs) [Gr. *akanthos*, a thorn], *n.* The plant bear's-breech; (*Arch.*) an ornament resembling its foliage.

accede (ăk-sēd') [L. *cēdere*, to come], *v.i.* To agree to, assent; to come to (an office or dignity). ac'cess, *n.* Admission to; means of approach; increase. access'ible, *a.* Capable of being approached; easy of access. accessibil'ity, *n.* accessibly, *adv.* accession (ăk-sesh'un), *n.* Going or coming to; agreeing or consenting to; an addition, improvement. access'ory, *a.* Contributive; accompanying; guilty, not as the chief actor, but by assisting or concealing the offender. *n.* An accomplice; any secondary accompaniment.

accelerate (ăk-sel'ĕr-āt) [L. *celer*, swift], *v.t.* To hasten; to increase the velocity of; to bring nearer in point of time. accelera'tion, *n.* accelerator, *n.* A device fitted to motor-cars for allowing the engine to run at an accelerated speed.

accent (ăk'sĕnt) [L. *accentum* (*cantus*, singing)], *n.* Prominence given to a syllable; manner of speaking peculiar to an individual, locality, etc.; a mark used to direct the stress of the voice; (*pl.*) words, language. **accent'**, *v.t.* To lay stress upon a syllable or word, or passage of music. **accen'tual**, *a.* (*Prosody*) Accented verse as distinguished from that governed by quantity. **accen'tuate**, *v.t.* To emphasize. **accentua'tion**, *n.*

accept (ăk-sĕpt') [L. *capere*, to take], *v.t.* To take what is offered; agree to. **acceptable**, *a.* acceptance. The act of receiving; agreement to terms; an accepted bill of exchange; the subscription to a bill of exchange. **accepta'tion**, *n.* Favourable reception; the recognized sense of an expression. **accep'tor**, *n.*

accidence (ăk'si-dĕns) [L. *accidentia*], *n.* That part of grammar which deals with the inflection (*i.e.* the *accidents*) of words.

accident (ăk'si-dĕnt) [L. *cadere*, to fall], *n.* An unexpected event proceeding from an unknown cause; a mishap. **acciden'tal**, *a.* Occurring unexpectedly; adventitious; *n.* (*Mus.*) Sharps, flats, or naturals occurring before particular notes.

acclaim (ă-klām') [L. *clāmāre*, to shout], *v.t.* To applaud loudly, welcome with enthusiasm. *v.i.* To shout applause. **acclama'tion**, *n.*

acclimatize (ă-klī'mà-tīz) [F. *à*, to, *climat*, climate], *v.t.* To habituate to a new climate. **acclimatiza'tion**, *n.*

acclivity (ă-kliv'i-ti) [L. *clivus*, a slope], *n.* An upward slope.

accolade (ăk-kō-lād') [F.], *n.* The ceremony of conferring knighthood; (*Mus.*) a brace uniting several staves.

accommodate (ă-kom-'mō-dāt) [L. *accommodāre*], *v.t.* To make suitable, to fit; to bring into harmony; to supply or furnish; to supply lodging. **accommodating**, *a.* Obliging, complying. **accommoda'tion**, *n.* Adjustment, compromise: supplying a want; a loan; lodging.

accompaniment (à-kŭm'pàn-i-mĕnt) [F. *accompagnement*], *n.* Something attendant upon another thing; (*Mus.*) the part performed by instruments accompanying the voice. **accompanist**, *n.* (*Mus.*) The performer who plays the accompaniment.

accompany (à-kŭm-pà-ni) [F. *accompagner*], *v.t.* To go with, escort; to exist along with. *v.i.* (*Mus.*) To play the accompaniment.

accomplice (à-kom'plis) [L. *com-*, together, *plicāre*, to fold], *n.* A partner in crime.

accomplish (à-kom'plish) [late L. *accomplēre*], *v.t.* To complete, fulfil, achieve. **accomplished**, *a.* Having the attainments perfecting one for good society. **accomplishment**, *n.*

accord (à-kōrd') [L. *cor*, *cordis*, heart], *v.t.* To cause to agree, to adjust, grant. *v.i.* To agree, to be in harmony. *n.* Agreement, harmony. **accordance**, *n.* **accordant**, *a.* **according**, *part.a.* and *adv.* Agreeing, corresponding (to); agreeably with. **accordingly**, *adv.*

accordion (à-kōr'di-ón) [It. *accordare*, to

tune], *n.* A small keyed instrument in which the notes are produced by bellows acting on metal reeds.

accost (à-kost') [late L. *accostāre*]. *v.t.* To approach, to address; to solicit.

accouchement (a-koosh'màn) [F.], *n.* Confinement, lying-in. **accou'cheur**, *n.* A man midwife. **accoucheuse'**, *n.* A midwife.

account (à-kount') [L. *com-*, together, *putāre*, to reckon], *v.t.* To compute, count; to regard as, deem. *v.i.* To give a reason, explanation, or answer. *n.* Statement showing the balance, register of debit and credit; advantage, behalf, sake; narrative. **accountable**, *a.* Liable to be called on to render an account. **accountant**. *n.* One who keeps or inspects accounts. **accountant-general**, *n.* **accountancy**, *n.*

accoutre (à-koo'tér) [med. F. *accoustrer*], *v.t.* To array in military dress. **accoutrements**, *n.* Outfit.

accredit (à-kred'it), *v.t.* To sanction; send with credentials.

accretion [L. *accrētus*], *n.* Increase by external additions; a part added.

accrue (à-kroo') [O.F. *acreue*, growth]. *v.i.* To increase; to come to.

accumulate (à-kū'mū-lāt) [L. *accumulāre*, to heap up], *v.t.* To pile one thing on another; to amass. *v.i.* To grow by additions. **accumula'tion**, *n.* **accu'mulative**, *a.* **accumulator**, *n.* An apparatus for the storage of electricity.

accurate (ăk'ū-ràt) [L. *accūrātus*, from *cūra*, care], *a.* Careful, exact. **accurately**, *adv.* **accuracy**, *n.*

accursed (à-kĕr'sĕd) [A.-S.], *a.* Lying under a curse; detestable; excommunicated.

accusative (à-kū'zà-tiv) [F. *accusatif*], *a.* Belonging to the objective case.

accuse (à-kūz') [L. *causa*, cause, law-suit], *v.t.* To charge with a crime, etc., to indict. **accuser**, *n.* **accusa'tion**, *n.* **accu'satory**, *a.*

accustom (à-kŭs'tòm) [O.F. *acostumer*], *v.t.* To make familiar by use. **accustomed**, *a.*

ace (ās) [L. *as*, a unit], *n.* The single point on cards or dice; a trifle; an airman who has brought down ten or more hostile aircraft; a man of first rank in sport, etc.

-aceous, *suf.* Of the nature of, *e.g.* crustaceous, cretaceous, farinaceous, filaceous.

acerbity (à-sĕr'bi-ti) [L. *acerbus*, bitter], *n.* Sourness; harshness of speech, etc.

acetic (à-sē'tik) [L. *acētum*, vinegar], *a.* Pertaining to vinegar, sour. **ac'etate**, *n.* A salt of acetic acid.

acetylene (à-set'i-lēn), *n.* A gas composed of carbon and hydrogen.

ache (āk) [A.-S. *acan*], *v.i.* To suffer pain or distress. *n.* Continuous pain.

achieve (à-chēv') [F. *à chef*, to a head], *v.t.* To accomplish; to bring about by effort. **achievement**, *n.*

achromatic (ăk-rō-măt'ik) [Gr. *a-*, not, *chrōma*, colour], *a.* Colourless.

acid (ăs'id) [L. *acidus*, sour], *a.* Tart, sharp to the taste. *n.* A sour substance. **acid'ity**, *n.* Sourness. **acid'ify**, *v.t.* To render acid. **acid'ulous**, *a.* A little acid. **acidulated**, *a.* Rendered slightly acid.

-acious, *suf.* Abounding in, characterized by, *e.g. loquacious, tenacious.*

-acity, *suf.* The quality of; forming nouns from adjectives in -ACIOUS.

acknowledge (ăk-nol'ĕj) [A.-S. *acknowe, cnáwan,* to know], *v.t.* To own the truth of, admit; recognize the authority of. **acknowledgment,** *n.* Recognition, admission; receipt; expression of gratitude.

-acle, *suf.* Diminutive of nouns, *e.g. pinnacle.*

acme (ăk'mē) [Gr. *akmē,* an edge], *n.* The highest point, the culmination.

acolyte (ăk'ō-lĭt) [Gr. *akolouthos,* a follower], *n.* An inferior officer in the R.C. Church; an attendant.

aconite (ăk'ō-nĭt) [Gr. *akonīton*], *n.* The common monk's-hood or wolf's-bane.

acorn (ā'kŏrn) [A.-S. *æcern*], *n.* The fruit of the oak.

acotyledon (á-kot-ĭ-lē'dŏn) [Gr. *a-,* not, *kotule,* a cup], *n.* A plant without distinct seed-lobes. **acotyledonous,** *a.*

acoustic (á-kou'stĭk) [Gr. *akouein,* to hear], *a.* Pertaining to the ear or hearing. **acousti'cian,** *n.* One skilled in acoustics. **acoustics,** *n.* The science of sound and of the phenomena of hearing; the sounding properties of an auditorium.

acquaint (á-kwănt') [L. *cognitum,* known], *v.t.* To inform, to communicate intelligence. **acquaintance,** *n.* The state of knowing a person or thing; a person whom one knows. **acquaintanceship,** *n.*

acquiesce (ăk-wi-es') [L. *acquiēscere*], *v.i.* To submit to; accept tacitly, to concur in. **acquiescence,** *n.* **acquiescent,** *a.*

acquire (á-kwīr') [L. *quærere,* to seek], *v.t.* To obtain. **acquirement,** *n.* A personal attainment. **acquisi'tion,** *n.* The act of acquiring; the object acquired; a gain, acquirement. **acquis'itive,** *a.*

acquit (á-kwit') [late L. *aquitāre*], *v.t.* To release from a charge, etc. *v.r.* To discharge the duties of one's position. **acquittal,** *n.* Discharge from arrest, a promise, debt, or other obligation; performance. **acquittance,** *n.* A receipt.

acre (ā'kĕr) [A.-S. *æcer,* a field], *n.* A superficial measure containing 4,840 square yards; tilled or enclosed land. **acreage,** *n.* The area of land in acres.

acrid (ăk'rĭd) [L. *ácer ácris,* pungent], *a.* Sharp to the taste; irritating.

acrimony (ăk'ri-mô-ni) [L. *ácrimōnia,* sharpness], *n.* Bitterness of temper or manner. **acrimo'nious,** *a.*

acrobat (ăk'rō-băt) [Gr. *akrobatos*], *n.* A performer of daring gymnastic feats; a rope-dancer. **acrobat'ic,** *a.*

acropolis (á-krop'ō-lis) [Gr.], *n.* The citadel of a Greek town, especially that of Athens.

across (á-kraws')[A.-S.], *adv.* or *prep.* Transversely, from side to side, athwart.

acrostic (á-kros'tik) [Gr. *acro,* on the top, *stichos,* a row], *n.* A verse composition in which the initial letters of the lines constitute a word.

act (ăkt) [L. *actus,* a doing, from *agere,* to do], *n.* That which is done, a deed; a principal division of a play; a law or edict of a legislative body. *v.t.* To play the part of; impersonate. *v.i.* To exert power; carry out a purpose; behave; to perform as an actor. **acting,** *a.* Performing dramatically; doing temporary duty. *n.* Action; dramatic performance. **actor, actress,** *n.*

actinic (ăk-tĭn'ĭk) [Gr.], *a.* Pertaining to rays. **ac'tinism,** *n.* The property in rays of light by which chemical changes are produced; the radiation of light or heat.

action (ăk'shŭn) [F. *action,* L. *ac·iōnem,* n. The state or condition of doing; activity; anything done; a battle; the mechanism of an instrument; gesture; the main subject of a play, etc.; a legal process or suit. **actionable,** *a.* Furnishing ground for an action at law.

active (ăk'tiv) [*activus*], *a.* Possessed of power of acting; agile; busy; denoting action. **activ'ity,** *n.*

actual (ăk'tū-ál) [L. *actuālis*], *a.* Real, existing. **actual'ity,** *n.*

actuary (ăk'tū-á-ri) [L. *actuārius,* accountkeeper], *n.* One skilled in statistics, esp. connected with insurance.

actuate (ăk'tū-āt) [med. L. *actuātus*], *v.t.* To put in action, furnish the motive of.

acumen (á-kū'mĕn) [L. *acuere,* to sharpen], *n.* Shrewdness, keen penetration.

acute (á-kūt') [L. *acuere,* to sharpen], *a.* Sharp, penetrating; quick to perceive minute distinctions; piercing (of pain); the accent ('); (*Med.*) attended with violent symptoms; (*Geom.*) less than a right angle.

-acy, *suf.* Forming nouns of quality, state, condition, etc.; *e.g. fallacy, infancy.*

ad-, *pref.* Signifying motion towards, direction to, adherence, etc.; *e.g. adduce, adhere, adjacent, admire.*

adage (ăd'áj) [L. *adagium*], *n.* A proverb; a pithy maxim.

adagio (á-da'ji-ō) [It.], *adv.* (*Mus.*) Slowly, gracefully.

adamant (ăd'á-mánt) [Gr. *a-,* not, *damaō,* I tame], *n.* A stone of impenetrable hardness; loadstone, diamond. *a.* Intensely hard; unfeeling. **adaman'tine,** *a.*

adapt (á-dăpt') [L. *aptare,* from *aptus,* fit], *v.t.* To adjust to, to remodel. **adaptable,** *a.* **adapta'tion,** *n.*

add (ăd) [L. AD-, to, *dare,* to put], *v.t.* To put together, unite, put into one total; annex. **addition** (á-dish'ŭn), *n.* The process of adding, the thing added. **additional,** *a.* Supplementary.

addendum (a-den'dŭm) [L.], *n.* A thing to be added, an addition, an appendix.

adder (ăd'ĕr) [A.-S. *nædre*], *n.* The common viper.

addict (á-dĭkt') [L. *addictus*], *v.t.* To apply habitually, to habituate. *v.r.* To make oneself a slave to (a vice); *n.* (ăd'ĭkt). A slave to a vice. **addicted,** *part.a.* Given over to, prone. **addiction,** *n.*

addle (ădl) [A.-S. *adela,* mire, filth], *a.* Putrid, as an egg. (*fig.*) idle, vain, confused, *v.t.* To confuse (mentally). *v.i.* To become putrid (as an egg). **addleheaded,** *a.* Muddle-headed.

address (á-dres') [F. *adresser*], *v.t.* To direct a communication to; speak to; write the address or direction on; make suit to; apply (oneself) to. *n.* A discourse; the name of the place where one lives; tact;

skill; bearing in conversation; (pl.) court-ship. **addressee'**, n. One to whom a communication is addressed.

adduce (á-dūs') [L. dūcere, to lead], v.t. To bring forward as a proof, to cite.

-ade, suf. Forms nouns from verbs, etc., e.g. cannonade, brigade, lemonade, parade.

adenoid (ăd'ĕn-oid) [Gr. adēn, an acorn], a. Glandular. pl.n. A spongy growth at the back of the nose.

adept (á-dept') [L. adeptus, one who has attained], n. One completely versed in any science or art.

adequate (ăd'ĕ-kwăt) [L. adœquātus, made equal], a. Equal to, sufficient. **adequacy**, n. Adequateness, sufficiency.

adhere (ád-hēr') [L. hœrēre, to stick], v.i. To stick to, to remain attached to. **adherence**, n. **adherent**, a. Sticking to. n. A partisan.

adhesion (ád-hē'zhŭn) [F. adhésion], n. The act or state of sticking to or joining. **adhesive**, a. Able to adhere, sticky.

adhibit (ád-hĭb'it) [L. habēre, to hold], v.t. To append, use, employ. **adhibit'ion**, n. Application, use.

adieu (á-dū') [F.], int. and n. God be with you; good-bye.

adipose (ăd'i-pōs) [L. adeps, fat], a. Pertaining to fat, fatty.

adit (ăd'it) [L. aditus], n. Approach, entrance.

adjacent (ád-jā'sĕnt) [L. AD-, jacēre, to lie], a. Lying near to; neighbouring.

adjective (ăd'jĕk-tiv) [L. adjectivus], n. A part of speech joined to nouns to define their signification. **adjecti'val**, a.

adjoin (ád-join') [O.F. ajoindre], v.t. To be contiguous to. **adjoining**, a.

adjourn (ád-jĕrn') [O.F. ajorner], v.t. To put off or defer till a later period; to postpone. v.i. To cease for the time being. **adjournment**, n.

adjudge (ád-jŭj') [O.F. ajūger], v.t. To award by a judicial decision, to condemn.

adjudicate (ád-joo'di-kāt) [L. jūdicāre, to judge], v.t. To judge, pronounce sentence. v.i. To sit as a judge. **adjudica'tion**, n. **adju'dicator**, n.

adjunct (ăd'jŭnkt) [L. jungere, to join], n. Any thing joined to another; an attribute. a. Added to. **adjunctive**, a. Joining.

adjure (ád-joor') [L. jūrāre, to swear, put to an oath], v.t. To charge upon oath, or upon pain of the divine displeasure. **adjura'tion**, n.

adjust (ád-jŭst') [L. AD-, juxta, near], v.t. To arrange; to fit, accommodate, settle. **adjustment**, n.

adjutant (ăd'ju-tănt) [L. adjutans], n. An officer who assists the commanding officer; a gigantic Indian stork.

administer (ăd-min'is-tĕr) [L. ministrāre, to minister], v.t. To manage; to tender, as an oath, to supply. **administra'tion** n. The act of administering, the executive functions of government; the executive. **admin'istrative**, a. **administrator**, n. One who administers; (Law) one who manages the estate of an intestate.

admiral (ăd'mir-ăl) [O.F. amiral, Arab. amir, a prince], n. The commander of a fleet or a division of a fleet. **Admiralty**, n. The Government department that deals with the Navy; the building where they transact business.

admire (ád-mir') [L. mīrāri, to wonder], v.t. To regard with wonder and pleasure; to have a high opinion of. **admirable** (ăd'mir-ábl), a. Worthy of admiration, excellent. **admirably**, adv. **admira'tion**, n. Wonder excited by anything pleasing. **admirer**, n.

admit (ád-mit') [L. mittere, to send], v.t. To let in; accept as valid; acknowledge. **admittance**, n. **admiss'ible**, **admittable**, a. Fit to be considered as evidence; qualified for entrance. **admissibil'ity**, n. **admiss'ion**, n. **admittedly**, adv. Agreed.

admixture (ád-miks'tūr) [L. admiscere; MIX], n. An alloy; a foreign element.

admonish (ád-mon'ish) [L. monēre, to advise], v.t. To reprove gently; caution. **admonisher**, n. **admon'ishment**, n. **admoni'tion**, n.

ado (á-doo') [Scand.], n. Trouble, fuss.

adolescent (ăd-ò-les'ént) [L. adolēscere, to grow up], a. Growing up to maturity. n. A person in the age of adolescence. **adolescence**, n. The period between childhood and maturity.

Adonis (á-dō'nis)[A beautiful youth of Gr. legend], n. A beau, dandy.

adopt (á-dopt') [L. optāre, to choose], v.t. To take into relationship (as heir, candidate, etc.); to embrace (a principle, cause, etc.). **adoption**, n. **adoptive**, a. Due to or by reason of adoption.

adore (á-dôr') [L. ōrāre, to pray], v.t. To pay divine honours to; to regard with the utmost respect. **adorer**, n. A worshipper, admirer. **adorable**, a. **adora'tion**, n. Divine worship; homage.

adorn (á-dôrn') [L. ornāre, to deck], v.t. To ornament, embellish. **adornment**, n. A decoration, ornament.

adrenalin (á-dren'á-lin) [L. renes, kidneys], n. (Med.) A substance used to stop bleeding.

adrift (á-drift') [DRIFT], adv. Floating at random; swayed by chance influence; at loose.

adroit (á-droit') [F. à, to, droit, right], a. Dexterous, ready in resource.

adulate (ăd'ū-lāt) [L. adūlārī, to flatter], v.t. To fawn upon, flatter servilely. **adulation**, n. **adulatory**, a.

adult (á-dŭlt') [L. adultus], a. Grown up, full-grown. n. One grown to maturity.

adulterate (á-dŭl'tĕr-āt) [L. adulterāre, to corrupt], v.t. To debase a thing by mixing with it a baser substance. **adultera'tion**, n.

adultery (á-dŭl'tĕr-i) [L. adultērium], n. Illicit sexual intercourse on the part of a married person. **adulterer**, **adulteress**, n. **adulterous**, a.

adumbrate (ăd'ŭm-brāt) [L. adumbrāre, to cast a shadow], v.t. To shadow forth, indicate faintly. **adumbra'tion**, n.

advance (ăd-vans') [O.F. avancer], v.t. To bring or move forward; promote; supply on credit. v.i. To move forward, to progress. n. The act of moving forward; promotion; a rise (in price); payment beforehand, a loan. **advanced**, a. **advancement**, n. Preferment.

advantage (ăd-van'tăj) [F. *avantage*], n. Favourable condition or circumstance; gain, superiority. v.t. To benefit; promote the interests of. advanta'geous, a.

Advent (ăd'vĕnt) [L. *venire*, to come], n. The Incarnation; the Second Coming of Christ; the four weeks before Christmas; a coming.

adventitious (ăd-vĕn-tish'ŭs) [L. *adventicius*, coming from abroad], a. Not properly pertaining to; accidental.

adventure (ăd-ven'chŭr) [O.F. *aventure*], n. Hazard; an enterprise in which risk is incurred; a speculation. v.t. To risk, to hazard. adventurer, n. adventuress, n. A woman who seeks to gain social position by false pretences. adventurous, a. Fond of adventure; daring, rash.

adverb (ăd'vĕrb) [L. *verbum*, word], n. A word qualifying a verb, an adjective, or another adverb. adver'bial, a.

adversary (ăd'vĕr-săr-i) [L. *adversarius*, see ADVERSE], n. An opponent, a foe.

adverse (ăd'vĕrs) [L. towards, *vertere*, to turn], a. Acting in a contrary direction; hostile; opposite in position. adver'sity, n. Misfortune.

advert (ăd-vĕrt), v.t. To turn attention to, refer to. advertence, n. Attention, notice, regard.

advertise (ăd'vĕr-tīz) [F. *avertissement*], v.t. To give notice of; make publicly known; to further sales of a commodity by means of public announcements. v.i. To give public notice. adver'tisement, n. advertiser, n.

advice (ăd-vīs') [L. *visum*, seen], n. Opinion as to course of action; formal notice.

advise (ăd-vīz') [late L. *advisāre*], v.t. To counsel; to inform. advi'sedly, adv. With mature deliberation. advisable, a. Proper, befitting. advisory, a. Having power to advise.

advocate (ăd'vŏ-kăt) [L. *vocāre*, to call], n. One who defends or promotes a cause; an intercessor. v.t. To plead in favour of, recommend. advocacy, n.

advowson (ăd-von'zŏn) [L. *advocationem*], n. The right of presentation to a benefice.

adze (ădz) [A.-S. *adesa*], n. An axe with an arched blade at right angles to the handle.

ægis (ē'jis) [L.], n. A shield; protection, a protective influence.

æon (ē'ŏn) [Gr. *aiōn*], n. An age of the universe; a period of immense duration.

aerate (ā'ĕr-āt) L. *aēr*, air] v.t. To charge with air or other gas. aerated, part.a. Charged with air or carbonic acid gas; effervescent.

aerial (ā-ēr'i-ăl) [L. *aēr*, air], a. Belonging to the air; airy, thin; immaterial. n. (*Radio*) An exposed wire that catches or transmits electro-magnetic waves.

aerie, aery (ā'ĕr-i), eyrie, eyry (ī'ri) [med. L. *aeria*], n. The nest of a bird of prey, esp. an eagle; the brood of such birds.

aero- [L. *aēr*, the air], *comb. form*. Pertaining to the air, e.g. aeroplane, aeronaut.

aerobatics (ār-ō-băt'iks), n.pl. Aerial acrobatics; stunting in an aeroplane.

aerodrome (ār'ō-drōm) [Gr. *dromos*, race, race-course], n. A station for aeroplanes.

aerodynamics (ār-ō-dī-năm'iks) [DYNA-MICS], n. The science which treats of gases in motion.

aerolite (ā'ĕr-ō-līt) [Gr. *lithos*, a stone], n. A meteoric stone.

aeronaut (ā'ĕr-ō-nawt) [Gr. *nautēs*, a sailor], n. One who sails or floats in the air; a balloonist. aeronautics, n. The science or art of aerial navigation.

aeroplane (ār'ō-plān), n. A flying machine fitted with one or more fixed planes that are supported by the air.

aerostatics (ā-ĕr-ō-stăt'iks) [Gr. *statikos*, causing to stand], n. The science which treats of air at rest; aeronautics.

æsthete (ēs'thēt) [Gr. *aisthētes*, one who perceives], n. One who professes a special appreciation of the beautiful. æsthetic, a. æstheticism, n. Devotion to the study of the beautiful. æsthetics, n. The theory or philosophy of the perception of the beautiful.

ætiology (ē-ti-ol'ō-ji) [Gr. *aitia*, a cause], n. An account of or assignment of a cause; the philosophy of causation. ætiological (ēt-i-ō-loj'ik-ăl), a.

afar (à-far') [A.-S.], adv. From, at, to a distance.

affable (ăf'ăbl) [L. *affābilis*], a. Courteous, benign. affability (ăf-à-bil'i-ti), n.

affair (à-fār') [F. *à*, to, *faire*, to do], n. Any kind of business; a love intrigue; (*pl.*) business; finances.

affect (à-fekt') [L. *facere*, to do, act], v.t. To tend towards, aim at; to fancy, like; to feign, pretend, to exert an influence upon. affec'ted, a. Pretending to what is not natural or real. affectation, n. Artificiality, pretence, assumption of airs. affecting, a. Touching; exciting emotion.

affection (à-fek'shŭn) [F.], n. Feeling, disposition, love, malady, disease. affectionate, a. Of a loving disposition.

affiance (à-fī'ăns) [L. *fidus*, faithful], n. Plighting of faith, betrothal.

affidavit (ăfĭdă'vit) [late L., *affidāre*, to make oath], n. A voluntary affirmation sworn before a person qualified to administer an oath.

affiliate (à-fil'i-āt) [L. *filius*, a son], v.t. To adopt, to receive as a son; to assign (an illegitimate child) to its father. affilia'tion, n.

affinity (à-fin-i-ti) [L. *finis*, end, border], n. Relationship; attraction, and its object.

affirm (à-fĕrm') [L. *firmus*, strong], v.t. To assert positively or confidently. v.i. To make a solemn affirmation in lieu of oath. affirma'tion, n. That which is affirmed. affirm'ative, a. Containing an affirmation; confirmatory.

affix (à-fiks') [med. L. *affixāre*], v.t. To fasten, annex. n. (ăf'fiks), An addition; a syllable added to a word.

afflation (à-flā'shŭn) [L. *flāre*, to blow], n. The act of blowing or breathing upon; inspiration. afflatus, n. Inspiration.

afflict (à-flikt') [L. *fligere*, to strike], v.t. To inflict pain on. affliction, n. Calamity, trouble; ailment.

affluent (ăf'lu-ĕnt) [L. *fluere*, to flow], a. Flowing, wealthy. n. A tributary. affluence, n. Abundance, wealth.

afford (à-förd') [A.-S. *ge-*, *forthian*, to

further], *v.t.* To yield the means; to be able to bear the expense of.

afforest (à-for'èst), *v.t.* To convert into forest. **afforesta'tion,** *n.*

affray (à-frā')[O.F.*effreēr*],*v.t.*To frighten. *n.* Commotion; a fight.

affright (à-frīt')[A.-S. *ā-*, intens., *fyrhtan,* to frighten], *v.t.* To frighten, to terrify. *n.* Fright, terror.

affront (à-frŭnt') [L. *frontem,* forehead], *v.t.* To insult. *n.* An insult; contemptuous or rude treatment.

afield (à-fēld') [A.-S.], *adv.* To or in the field; at a distance.

afire (à-fīr'), *adv.* and *a.* On fire.

afloat (à-flōt') [M.E. *on flote*], *a.* or *adv.* Floating; aboard ship; solvent; current.

afoot (à-fut'), *n.* On foot; in motion.

afore (à-fōr')[A.-S.], *adv.* Before. **afore-said,** *a.* Said or mentioned before. **aforethought,** *a.* Premeditated.

afraid (à-frād') [*p.p.* of AFFRAY], *pred.a.* Impressed with fear; terrified.

afresh (à-fresh')[A.-S.], *adv.* Again, anew, freshly.

African (âf'ri-kàn) [L. *Africa*], *a.* Pertaining to Africa. *n.* A native of Africa, or of African race.

Afrikaner (âf-ri-kä'nèr) [Dut.], *n.* and *a.* One born in South Africa of white parents whose mother tongue is Afrikaans. **Afrikaans,** *n.* The S. African Dutch language.

Afro-American (âf-rō-à-mer'i-kan), *n.* and *a.* An American Negro of African descent.

aft (aft) [A.-S.], *a.* or *adv.* Towards the stern of a vessel; abaft.

after (af'tèr) [A.-S.], *adv., prep.,* and *conj.* In the rear; behind; in pursuit of; following (in time). *a.* Later, subsequent. **after-birth,** *n.* The placenta. **aftermath,** *n.* Grass which springs up after a first crop has been mown; a sequel. **afternoon,** *n.* Between midday and evening. **afterthought.** Reflection after the act; a belated explanation. **afterwards,** *adv.* At a later period.

again (à-gān')[A.-S.], *adv.* A second time, once more, in addition.

against (à-gànst'), *prep.* In opposition to, opposite to, in contrast to; in contact with.

agamic (à-găm'ik) [Gr. *a-,* not; *gamos,* marriage], *a.* (*Zool.*) Characterized by absence of sexual action.

agate (ăg'àt) [Gr. *achatēs*], *n.* A variegated form of silica, used for seals, etc.

age (āj) [O.F. *aage*], *n.* A period or the duration of life; maturity, senility; an epoch; an æon. *v.i.* To grow old, **aged** (ājd, ā-jèd), *a.* Of a certain age, old.

-age, *suf.* Forms abstract or collective nouns, *e.g. baronage, courage;* notes act of doing or thing done, *e.g. passage, voyage.*

agenda (à-jen'dà) [L. *agere,* to do], *n.pl.* Things to be done; business to be transacted; a list of these.

agent (ā'jènt) [L. *agere,* to do], *n.* One who or that which exerts power; a deputy. **agency,** *n.* The business of an agent; causative action.

agglomerate (à-glom'èr-āt) [L. *glomus,* a ball], *v.t.* To heap up into a mass. **agglomera'tion,** *n.*

agglutinate (à-gloo'tin-āt)[L.*gluten,* glue], *v.t.* To cause to adhere. *a.* Glued together; (*Philol,*) consisting of simple words, or roots, combined into compounds. **agglutina'tion,** *n.*

aggrandize (ăg'ràn-dīz) [F. *agrandir,* to greaten], *v.t.* To enlarge; to make great, to exalt. **aggran'dizement,** *n.*

aggravate (ăg'rà-vāt) [L. *gravāre,* to make heavy],*v.t.* To intensify; (*colloq.*) to provoke, irritate. **aggravating,** *a.* Provoking. **aggrava'tion,** *n.*

aggregate (ăg'rè-gāt) [L. *grex gregis,* a flock], *v.t.* To collect together, bring into a whole. *a.* Collected together. *n.* A mass formed by union; the total. **aggregation,** *n.* The act of collecting together; an aggregate.

aggression (à-gresh'ŭn) [L. *aggressāre, gradior,* I walk], *n.* An unprovoked attack or injury. **aggress'ive,** *a.* **aggress'or,** *n.* One who begins a quarrel.

aggrieve (à-grēv') [L. *gravis,* heavy], *v.t.* To cause grief, pain, or injustice to.

aghast (à-gast')[A.-S.], *a.* Terrified, taken aback.

agile (ăj'īl) [L. *agilis,* nimble], *a.* Quick, nimble, active. **agility** (à-jil'iti), *n.*

agio (ăj'i-ō) [It.], *n.* (*Fin.*) Difference in value between currencies. **agiotage,** *n.* Money-changing.

agitate (ăj'i-tāt)[L.*agitātus*],*v.t.* To shake or move briskly; to excite. *v.i.* To bring forward a question for public discussion. **agita'tion,** *n.* Commotion; public excitement. **agitator,** *n.* One who excites political agitation.

aglow (à-glō')[A.-S.], *adv.* In a glow.

agnate (ăg'nàt) [L. *gnātus,* born], *a.* Related on the father's side; hence, allied, akin.

agnomen (ăg-nō'men)[L.(*g*)*nōmen,* name], *n.* An additional name.

agnostic (àg-nos'tik) [Gr. *agnōstos,* ignorant of], *n.* One who denies that man can know anything of God or have any knowledge except of phenomena. **agnosticism,** *n.*

ago (à-gō')[*a-,* forth GO], *a.* and *adv.* Gone by, since.

agog (à-gog') [O.F. *en gogues*], *adv.* In a state of expectation; astir.

-agogue [Gr. *agōgos,* leading], *comb. form.* A leader, as in *demagogue, pedagogue.*

agony (ăg'ò-ni) [Gr. *agōnia,* contest], *n.* Anguish of mind; a paroxysm; the death struggle. **agonizing,** *a.*

agrarian (àgràr'i-àn) [L. *agrārius*], *a.* Pertaining to landed property or cultivated land. **agrarianism,** *n.* Political agitation concerning land or land-tenure.

agree (à-grē') [O.F. *agréer*], *v.i.* To be of one mind; to coincide; to suit. **agreeable.** *a.* Pleasant; favourable; conformable. **agreement,** *n.* Mutual understanding; a contract legally binding.

agriculture(ăg'ri-kŭl-tūr)[L. *ager,* field], *n.* The science and art of cultivating the soil. **agricultural,** *a.* **agriculturist,** *n.* One engaged in agriculture. **agrimotor,** *n.* Motor tractor used in agriculture.

aground, *adv.* and *a.* Stranded.

ague (ā'gū)[O.F.], *n.* A malarial fever.

ahead, *adv.* and *a.* In advance; forward.

ahoy (á-hoi'), *int.* (*Naut.*) Used in hailing.

aid (ād) [O.F. *aider*], *v.t.* To assist, help. *n.* Help, succour.

aide-de-camp (ā′dė-coṅ) [F.], *n.* An officer attending a general.

aigrette (ā′grėt) [F.], *n.* The egret; a tuft of feathers like the egret's; a spray of gems worn on the head.

ail (āl) [A.-S. *eglan*], *v.i.* To be in pain or trouble. **ailment**, *n.* Sickness.

aileron (ā′le-ron) [Fr. wing-tip], *n.* (*Av.*) Hinged portion on the rear edge of the wing-tip of an aeroplane, used for control.

aim (ām) [O.F. *aësmer*], *v.t.* To direct; endeavour; point at with a weapon. *v.i.* To take aim; form plans. *n.* The point aimed at; design. **aimless**, *a.*

air (âr) [Gr. *aër*], *n.* The atmosphere; a light breeze; manner, mien; haughtiness (*usu. in pl.*); a tune. *v.t.* To ventilate, show off. **aircraft**, *n.* Collective term for all types of flying machines. **aircraft carrier**, *n.* (*Navy*) A vessel designed to house and service aircraft, with a deck they can take off from and alight upon. **air field**, *n.* Field for aircraft to land upon and take off from. **air-force**, *n.* The strength of a country in military aircraft. **air letter**, *n.* Single-sheet letter of regulation form sent by air-mail at a reduced rate. **air-lift**, *n.* Organized use of aircraft for transport where surface travel is not possible. **air-mail**, *n.* Aerial post. **airplane**, *n.* An aeroplane. **airport**, *n.* A station for passenger aircraft. **air raid**, *n.* An attack by hostile aircraft. **air-ship**, *n.* A dirigible balloon carrying its own motive power. **air-tight**, *a.* So tight as to prevent the passage of air. **air-worthy**, *a.* Passed as fit for flying. **airing**, *n.* Exposure to the free action of the air, or to a fire; a walk or ride in the open air. **airy**, *a.* airily, *adv.* **airiness**, *n.*

aisle (īl) [L. *âla* (*axilla*), wing], *n.* A lateral division of a church.

ajar (á-jar′) [A.-S. *on cerre*, on the turn], *adv.* Partly open, as a door.

akimbo (á-kim′bō) [?], *adv.* With hands resting on hips and elbows turned outwards.

akin (á-kin′), *a.* Allied by blood.

-al, *suf.* Belonging to, capable of, like, *e.g. annual*, *equal*; forming substantives, *e.g. canal*, *hospital.*

alabaster (ǎl′á-bas′tér) [O.F. *alabastre*], *n.* Gypsum, white or delicately shaded.

alack (á-lǎk′), *int.* Expressing grief. **alackaday**, *int.*

alacrity (á-lǎk′ri-ti) [L. *alacer*, brisk], *n.* Eagerness; vivacity, cheerful ardour.

alamode (a-la-mōd′) [F., in the fashion], *adv. and a.* Fashionable. *n.* A thin black silk. **alamode beef**, *n.* Beef stewed by a savoury method.

alarm (á-larm′) [O.F. *alarme*], *n.* A warning of danger; terror and surprise. *v.t.* To rouse to a sense of danger. **alarming**, *a.* **alarmist**, *n.* One who creates panic.

alarum (á-lǎr′ům), *n.* (*poet.*) An alarm; an alarm-clock or watch.

alas (á-las′) [O.F. *a*, ah! *las*! wretched], *int.* Expressive of sorrow, grief, pity, etc.

albatross (ǎl′bá-tros) [Arab. *al, quadras*, the pelican], *n.* The largest sea-bird.

albeit (awl-bē′it), *conj.* Although.

albert (ǎl′bėrt) [*Albert*, Prince Consort], *n.* A short watch-chain.

albino (ǎl-bē′nō) [L. *albus*, white], *n.* A human, animal, or plant in which the colour pigment is absent, resulting in an abnormally light colour.

album (ǎl′bŭm) [L. *albus*, white], *n.* A blank book for the insertion of autographs, etc.

albumen (ǎl-bū′mén) [L.], *n.* The white of egg; (*Bot.*) the substance between the skin and embryo of many seeds. **albuminous**, *a.*

alchemy (ǎl′kė-mi) [Arab. *al, kimia*], *n.* The chemistry of the Middle Ages, the search for the philosophers' stone, etc. **alchemist**, *n.*

alcohol (ǎl′kô-hol) [Arab. *al,* the, *koh′l*, powder to stain the eyelids], *n.* Pure spirit, spirits of wine; any intoxicating liquor. **alcohol′ic**, *a.* **al′coholism**, *n.*

alcove (ǎl′kōv) [Arab. *alquobbah*, the vault], *n.* A vaulted recess; a bower.

alder (awl′dér) [A.-S.], *n.* An English tree growing in moist places.

alderman (awl′dér-mán) [A.-S. *ealdor*, a chief], *n.* A civic dignitary next below the mayor.

alderney (awl′dér-ni) [name of island], *n.* A breed of cattle common in the Channel Islands.

ale (āl) [A.-S. *ealu*], *n.* An intoxicating liquor made by fermenting malt. **ale-house**, *n.* A tavern licensed to sell ale.

alert (á-lėrt′) [F. *alerte*], *a.* Watchful, sprightly.

alfalfa (ǎl-fǎl′fá) [Sp.], *n.* (*Bot.*) Lucerne.

alfresco (al-fres′kō) [It.], *adv. and a.* In the open air, open-air.

alga (ǎl′gá) [L.], *n.* (*pl.* algæ) A seaweed.

algebra (ǎl′jė-brá) [Arab. *al-jebr*, the reunion of parts], *n.* Universal arithmetic, in which letters stand for quantities, and signs represent arithmetical processes. **algebra′ic**, *a.* Relating to algebra.

alias (ā′li-ǎs) [L.], *adv.* Otherwise (named or called). *n.* An assumed name.

alibi (ǎl′i-bī) [L. elsewhere], *n.* The plea that one was "elsewhere"; (*Amer.*) an excuse.

alien (ā′li-én) [L. *alienus*, a stranger], *a.* Of foreign extraction; repugnant to; incongruous with. *n.* A foreigner. **alienable**, *a.* That may be alienated. **alienate**, *v.t.* To transfer to another. **alienation**, *n.* The act of alienating; mental derangement. **alienism**, *n.* The treatment and study of mental disease. **alienist**, *n.* One skilled in alienism.

alight (1) (á-līt′) [A.-S. *ālīhtan*], *v.i.* To get down, dismount, to settle on.

alight (2) (á-līt′) [A.-S. *onlīhtan*, to shine upon], *a.* On fire; illuminated.

alike (á-līk′) [A.-S. *onlic, lie, likel*, *a.* Similar. *adv.* Equally, in the same manner.

aliment (ǎl′i-mént) [L. *alere*, to nourish], *n.* Nutriment, food; support. **alimen′tal**, *a.* **alimen′tary**, *a.* **alimenta′tion**, *n.*

alimony (ăl'ĭ-mŏni) [L. *alimōnia*], *n.* The part of a husband's income allowed for a wife's support on legal separation.

aline, align (à-līn') [F. *aligner*], *v.t.* To range in line. **alinement,** *n.*

aliquot (ăl'ĭ-kwot) [L. *aliquot*, several, so many], *a.* Pertaining to a number contained an exact number of times by a given number.

alive (à-līv') [A.-S. *on life*], *adv.* and *a.* Living; in operation; lively.

alkali (ăl'kà-lĭ) [Arab. *al-qalī*], *n.* A chemical compound which is soluble in water and capable of neutralizing acids. **al'kaline,** *a.*

all (awl) [A.-S. *eal*], *a.* The whole. *n.* The whole, everything, every one. *adv.* Wholly, completely. **all but;** Almost. **all in all;** All things in all respects. **at all;** In any respect; whatever.

Allah (ăl'à) [Arab.], *n.* The name of God in the religion of Islam.

allay (à-lā') [A.-S.], *v.t.* To quiet, abate, alleviate.

allege (à-lej') [O.F. *esligier*], *v.t.* To adduce as an authority, plead as an excuse; to affirm positively. **allega'tion,** *n.* A specific charge.

allegiance (à-lē'jàns) [O.F. *ligeance*], *n.* A subject's obligation to his sovereign.

allegory (ăl'ē-gŏ-ri) [Gr. *allegoria*], *n.* Description of one thing under the image of another; an emblem. **allegor'ic,** *a.*

allegro (ăl-ā'grō) [It.], *adv.* Briskly, quickly.

allergy (ăl'er-ji) [Gr. *allos*, other; ENERGY], *n.* (*Med.*) Abnormal response to food or other substance innocuous to most people. **allergic,** *a.*

alleviate (à-lē'vĭ-āt) [L. *levāre*, to lift], *v.t.* To lessen, mitigate. **allevia'tion,** *n.*

alley (ăl'lĭ) [O.F. *alee* (*aller*, to go)], *n.* A narrow street.

alliance (à-lī'àns) [O.F. *aliance*], *n.* The state of being allied; a treaty or league.

alligator (ăl'lĭ-gā-tòr) [Sp. *el lagarto*, the lizard], *n.* Large Saurian from America and China.

alliterate (à-lĭt'ĕr-āt) [L. *litera*, a letter], *v.i.* To commence with the same sound. **allitera'tion,** *n.* **alliterative,** *a.*

allocate (ăl'ō-kāt) [L. *locāre*, to place], *v.t.* To assign, allot. **alloca'tion,** *n.*

allocution (ăl-ō-kū'shùn) [L. *loqui*, to speak], *n.* A formal address (*esp.* by the Pope).

allodium (à-lō di-ùm) [O. Frankish, *al*, all, *ōd*, estate], *n.* Landed property held in absolute ownership. **allodial,** *a.*

allopathy (à-lop'à-thi) [Gr. *allos*, other, -PATHY], *n.* The treatment of disease by inducing an action of a different kind; ordinary medical practice, as opposed to homœopathy. **allop'athist,** *n.*

allot (à-lot') [A.-F. *aloter*], *v.t.* To distribute, assign as one's share. **allotment,** *n.* The act of allotting; the share assigned; a small plot of land let for cultivation.

allow (à-lou') [O.F. *alouer*], *v.t.* To admit; permit; concede; give credit for. **allowable,** *a.* **allowance,** *n.* Permission; fixed quantity or sum allowed.

alloy (à-loi') [O.F. *aleier*, to combine], *n.*

A mixture of metals; an amalgam; any base admixture.

allspice (awl'spīs), *n.* The pimento berry, tasting of cinnamon, cloves, and nutmeg.

allude (à-lood') [L. *lūdere*, to play], *v.i.* To hint at. **allusion,** *n.* A reference to anything not directly mentioned; a hint. **allusive,** *a.*

allure (à-loor') [O.F. *alurer*], *v.t.* To tempt by the offer of some real or apparent good; to entice. **allurement,** *n.*

alluvium (à-loo'vĭ-ùm) [L. *luere*, to wash], *n.* Earth, stones, etc., washed away and deposited elsewhere by flowing water.

ally (à-lī') [L. *ligāre*, to bind], *v.t.* To unite by treaty, marriage, etc. (al'ĭ) *n.* One united by treaty or agreement; something akin to another.

almanac (awl'mán-ăk) [F. *almanach*], *n.* A register of the days of the year, with astronomical and other data.

almighty (awl-mī'ti) [A.-S.], *a.* Omnipotent; possessed of unlimited power.

almond (a'mŏnd) [Gr. *amygdalē*], *n.* The nut of the almond-tree; the almond-tree.

almoner (ăl'mŏn-ĕr, a'mŏn-ĕr) [O.F. *aumoner*], *n.* A distributor of alms; a hospital official.

almost (awl'mōst), *adv.* Nearly, wellnigh.

alms (amz) [A.-S. *œlmœsse*], *n.* Anything given out of charity to the poor. **almshouse,** *n.* A house for poor persons endowed by charity.

aloe (ăl'ō) [Gr. *aloē*], *n.* A plant with bitter juice; (*pl.*) a purgative drug.

aloft (à-loft') [Icel.], *adv.* On high; (*Naut.*) in the rigging, at the mast-head.

alone (à-lōn') [M.E.], *a.* Single, by oneself. *adv.* Only, solely.

along (à-long') [A.-S.], *adv.* Lengthwise; in progressive motion. *prep.* By the side of, from end to end. **alongshore,** *adv.* Along and on the shore. **alongshoreman,** *n.* Fisherman engaged in coastal fishing. **alongside,** *adv.* By the side of.

aloof (à-loof') [M.E. *loof*, see LUFF], *adv.* At a distance from; (*Naut.*) to windward.

aloud (à-loud'), *adv.* Loudly; with a loud voice; audibly.

alp (ălp) [L. *Alpes*], *n.* A high mountain; (*fig.*) a formidable obstacle. **Alpine,** *a.* **Alps,** *n.pl.* The mountain ranges of Switzerland.

alpaca (ăl-păk'à) [Sp.], *n.* The llama of Peru; cloth made from its wool.

alpenstock (ăl'pĕn-stok) [G. *Alpen, stock*, STICK], *n.* A long stick shod with iron, used in mountaineering.

alpha (ăl'fà) [Gr.], *n.* The first letter of the Greek alphabet; (*Astron.*) the chief star in a constellation. **alpha and omega;** The beginning and the end.

alphabet (ăl'fà-bet) [Gr. *alpha, bēta,* A, B], *n.* The letters of a language arranged in order; alphabet'ic, *a.*

already (awl-red'ĭ), *adv.* Beforehand, before some specified time.

also (awl'sō), *adv.* and *conj.* Likewise, in like manner, besides; in addition.

altar (awl'tàr) [L. *altus*, high], *n.* A sacrificial block or place of sacrifice; the communion-table. **altar-screen,** *n.* The reredos.

alter (awl'tẽr) [F. *altérer*], *v.t.* To cause to vary or change; to modify. *v.i.* To undergo change. **altera'tion**, *n.*

altercate (awl'tẽr-kāt) [L. *altercāri*], *v.i.* To dispute hotly. **alterca'tion**, *n.*

alternate (awl'tẽr-nāt) [L. *alternāre*, to do by turns], *v.t.* To arrange or perform by turns. *v.i.* (*Elec.*) To change from positive to negative and back again in turns. **alter'nate**, *a.* Done or happening by turns. **alter'nately**, *adv.* **alternating current**, *n.* (*Elec.*) Electric current that changes from positive to negative regularly and frequently. **alterna'tion**, *n.* The act of alternating; the state of being alternate. **alter'native**, *a.* Offering a choice of two things. *n.* Either of two things which may be chosen. **alter'natively**, *adv.*

although (awl-thō'), *conj.* Though, however.

altitude (ăl'tĭ-tūd) [L. *altus*, high], *n.* Vertical height; elevation of an object above its base; elevation of a heavenly body above the horizon.

alto (ăl'tō) [It., high], *n.* The highest male voice; a singer of this, and the part sung.

altogether (awl-tȯ-geth'ẽr), *adv.* Wholly, completely; on the whole.

altruism (ăl'tru-izm) [F. *altruisme*], *n.* Devotion to the good of others. **altruist**, *n.* **altruis'tic**, *a.*

alum (ăl'ŭm) [L. *alumen*], *n.* A double sulphate containing aluminium and an alkali.

aluminium (ăl-ū-min'ĭ-ŭm), *n.* A white, sonorous, ductile metal not subject to oxidation. **aluminous**, *a.*

alumnus (à-lŭm'nŭs) [L., foster-child], *n.* A student in relation to his place of education.

always (awl'wāz) [A.-S.], *adv.* All the while; uninterruptedly; while one lives.

am (ăm) [A.-S.], *1st sing. pres. ind. of v.* to be.

amain (à-mān') [A.-S.], *adv.* Energetically, violently, in full force, at full speed.

amalgam (à-măl'găm) [F.], *n.* A mixture of a metal with mercury; a compound of different things. **amalgamate**, *v.t.* To combine. *v.i.* To blend, to merge into one. **amalgama'tion**, *n.*

amanuensis (à-măn-ū-en'sis) [L.], *n.* (*pl.* -ses). One employed to write what another dictates; a secretary.

amaranth (ăm'à-rănth) [Gr. *a-*, not, *marainein*, to wither], *n.* An imaginary flower supposed never to fade.

amass (à-măs') [F. *amasser*], *v.t.* To make into a heap; collect together.

amateur (ăm'à-tẽr) [F.], *n.* One who cultivates anything as a pastime, not as a profession. **amateur'ish**, *a.* Indifferently executed (of painting, writing, etc.).

amative (ăm'à-tiv) [L. *amāre*, to love], *a.* Disposed to loving.

amatory (ăm'à-tȯ-ri) [L. *amātor*, a lover], *a.* Pertaining to love.

amaze (à-māz') [A.-S.], *v.t.* To overwhelm with wonder, to bewilder. **amazement**, *n.* **amazing**, *a.*

amazon (ăm'à-zŏn) [Gr. *a-*, not, *mazos*, breast], *n.* A female warrior; a masculine woman; a virago. **amazo'nian**,

a. Pertaining to the fabled Amazons, or to the river Amazon.

ambassador (ăm-băs'à-dȯr) [F. *ambassadeur*], *n.* A minister representing his country at a foreign court. **ambassador'ial**, *a.*

amber (ăm'bẽr) [Arab. *anbar*, ambergris], *n.* A yellowish translucent fossil resin.

ambergris (ăm'bẽr-grēs) [F. grey amber], *n.* A morbid secretion from the intestines of the cachalot or spermaceti whale.

ambidexter (ăm-bĭ-dek'stẽr) [L. *ambi-* both, *dexter*, right-handed], *a.* Using both hands with equal facility. *n.* One who can do this; (*Law*) one who accepts bribes from both sides. **ambidextrous**, *a.*

ambient (ăm'bĭ-ĕnt) [L.], *a.* Surrounding, investing.

ambiguous (ăm-big'ū-ŭs) [L. *ambiguus*, doubtful], *a.* Of doubtful meaning, equivocal. **ambigu'ity**, *n.*

ambit (ăm'bĭt) [L.], *n.* Bounds, scope.

ambition (ăm-bĭsh'ŭn) [L. *ambitiōnem*, soliciting for votes], *n.* A desire for power, superiority, etc.; the object of such desire. **ambitious**, *a.* **ambitiously**, *adv.*

ambivalence (ăm-bĭv'à-lens) [L. *ambo*, both, *valens*, being worth], *n.* (*Psych.*) The simultaneous working in the mind of two incompatible wishes. **ambivalent**, *a.*

amble (ămbl) [L. *ambulāre*, to walk], *v.i.* To move (as a horse) by lifting the two feet on one side alternately with those on the other; to move easily. *n.* The pace described; an easy pace.

ambrosia (ăm-brō'zi-à) [Gr. *a-*, not, *brotos*, mortal], *n.* The fabled food of the gods. **ambrosial**, *a.*

ambulance (ăm'bū-lāns) [L. *ambulāre*, to walk], *n.* A hospital which follows an army in the field; a vehicle, wheeled stretcher, etc., for wounded or invalids.

ambuscade (ăm-bŭs-kād') [F. *embuscade*, see AMBUSH], *n.* An ambush.

ambush (ăm'bush) [O.F. *embusche*, from L. *in*, in, *boscus*, a bush, thicket], *n.* Concealment of forces to entrap an enemy; any lying in wait. *v.t.* To waylay.

ameliorate (à-mē'li-ȯr-āt) [L. *melior*, better], *v.t.* To make better; to improve. **ameliora'tion**, *n.*

amen (ā-men') [Heb., certainly; verily], *int.* Truly, verily; so be it.

amenable (à-mēn'àble) [F. *amener*], *a.* Liable to be called to account; easy to lead. **amenabil'ity**, *n.* Tractableness.

amend (à-mend') [L. *ex-*, *menda*, fault], *v.t.* To alter (a person or thing) for the better; to formally alter (a bill or resolution). **amendment**, *n.* A change for the better; reformation; something added to a bill or motion; correction of error. **amends**, *n.* Reparation, compensation.

amenity (à-mē'ni-ti) [L.], *n.* The quality of being pleasant or agreeable; something which possesses this quality.

amerce (à-mẽrs') [A.F. *à merci*, at the mercy of the court], *v.t.* To punish by fine. **amerciable**, *a.* **amercement**, *n.*

Amerind (ăm'ẽr-ind), *n.* (*Ethn.*) Indian of either of the American continents. **Amerindian**, *a.*

amethyst (ăm'ĕ-thĭst) [Gr. *amethustos*], *n.* A violet-blue variety of crystalline quartz. **amethystine**, *a.*

amiable (ā'mĭ-ǎbl) [O.F.], *a.* Kindly disposed, lovable. **amiabil'ity**, *n.*

amicable (ăm'ĭk-ǎbl) [L. *amicus*, friend], *a.* Friendly; resulting from friendliness. **amicabil'ity**, *n.* **amicably**, *adv.*

amice (ăm'ĭs) [L. *amictus*], *n.* A square piece of white linen worn on the shoulders by a priest saying Mass.

amid, amidst (à-mĭdst') [A.-S. *on middan*, in the middle], *prep.* In the midst; **among. amidships**, *adv.* In the middle of a ship.

amiss (à-mĭs') [A.-S.], *a.* Faulty, unsatisfactory. *adv.* Wrongly, astray.

amity (ăm'ĭ-tĭ) [F. *amitié*], *n.* Friendship, concord, mutual good feeling.

ammonia (à-mō'nĭ-à) [L. *sal ammōniac*], *n.* A pungent volatile alkaline gas obtained from sal ammoniac; spirit of hartshorn. **ammoniac**, *a.* **ammo'niated**, *a.* Combined with ammonia. **ammonal**, *n.* An explosive composition.

ammonite (ăm'ō-nīt) [med. L. *cornu Ammonis*, horn of Ammon], *n.* A spirally curved fossil shell-fish.

ammunition (ăm-ū-nĭsh'ŭn) [F. *munition*], *n.* Powder, shot, shell, etc.; offensive missiles generally.

amnesia (ăm-nē'zhà) [Gr.], *n.* Loss of memory.

amnesty (ăm'nĕs-tĭ) [Gr. *amnēstos*, forgotten], *n.* A general overlooking or pardon.

amoeba (à-mē'bà) [Gr. *amoibē*, change], *n.* A microscopic organism, consisting of a single extensile and contractile protoplasmic cell. **amoebæ'an**, *a.*

among, amongst (à-mŭngst') [A.-S., *on gemange*, in a crowd], *prep.* Mingled with, in the number of; surrounded by.

amoral (à-mor'ǎl), *a.* Not concerned with morals; non-moral.

amorous (ăm'ŏr-ŭs) [L. *Amŏr*, love], *a.* Naturally inclined to sexual love; relating to love. **amorously**, *adv.* **amorousness**, *n.*

amorphous (à-môr'fŭs) [Gr. *a-*, not, *morphē*, form], *a.* Shapeless; ill-arranged.

amortize (à-môr'tĭz) [Fr. *amortir*, to bring to death], *v.t.* (*Fin.*) To extinguish by a sinking fund. **amortization**, *n.*

amount (à-mount') [O.F. *à mont*, to a mountain], *v.t.* To run into an aggregate by accumulation of particulars; to mount up to; to be equivalent to. *n.* The sum total, result, significance; a (numerical) quantity.

amour (à-moor') [F.], *n.* A love affair; an amorous intrigue.

ampere (ăm-pâr') [French electrician, A. M. Ampère (1775-1836)], *n.* The unit by which an electric current is measured.

ampersand (ăm-pér-sănd') [*and per se*, "and" standing by itself], *n.* The sign "&".

amphi-, *comb. form.* Both; of both kinds, *e.g. amphibia.*

amphibia (ăm-fĭb'ĭ-à [Gr. *bios*, life], *n.pl.* Animals which can live either on land or in the water. **amphibian**, *a.* Pertaining to amphibia. *n.* Any animal of the amphibia. **amphibious**, *a.* **amphibious** warfare, *n.* Hostilities in which land and sea forces co-operate.

amphitheatre (ăm-fĭ-thē'à-tér), *n.* An oval or circular building with rising rows of seats round an open space; a gallery in a theatre, above the boxes.

ample (ămpl) [L. *amplus*], *a.* Large, wide, fully sufficient. **amply**, *adv.* **am'plify**, *v.t.* To enlarge or dilate upon. **amplifica'-tion**, *n.* Extension; diffuseness. **amplifier**, *n.* (*Rad.*) Instrument in a receiving set to magnify sound. **am'plitude**, *n.* Extent, greatness, abundance.

amputate (ăm'pū-tāt) [L. *amputāre*, to lop off], *v.t.* To cut a portion from an animal body. **amputa'tion**, *n.*

amuck (à-mŭk) [Malay, *amoq*], *adv.* in to run amuck: To attack indiscriminately.

amulet (ăm'ū-lĕt) [L. *amulētum*, a talisman], *n.* A thing worn as a preservative against sickness, witchcraft, etc.

amuse (à-mūz') [F. *à*, to, *muser*, stare], *v.t.* To please with anything light and cheerful; to entertain. **amusement**, *n.* That which amuses; play, diversion. **amusing**, *a.* Entertaining, laughable.

an-, *pref.* (1) A.-S. *an*, *on*, prep., as in *anent*, *anon*; (2) L. *ad-* before *n*., as in *annex*, *announce*; (3) Gr. *an-*, *a-*, not, as in *anæsthetic*.

-an [L. *-ānus*], *suf.* Of, belonging to, pertaining to, *e.g. human*, *publican*, *Christian*, *European*, etc.

ana-, an- [Gr., upon up, backwards], *pref.* As in *anachronism*, *analogy*, *aneurysm*.

-ana [L., neut. pl. of *-anus*, see **-AN**], *suf.* Sayings of, anecdotes concerning, as in *Shakespeariana*, *Virgiliana*.

Anabaptist (ăn-à-băp'tĭst), *n.* One who rebaptizes, or maintains that only adults should be baptized.

anachronism (à-năk'rŏn-ĭzm) [Gr. *anachronizein*, to refer to a wrong time], *n.* The reference of an event, etc., to a wrong period; anything out of date.

anaconda (ăn-à-kon'dà) [Sinhalese, *henakandāya*], *n.* A python; a large South American boa.

anæmia (à-nē'mĭ-à) [Gr. *haima*, blood], *n.* Want of blood. **anæmic**, *a.*

anæsthesia (ăn-ĕs-thē'zĭ-à) [Gr. **AN**-, *aisthanomai*, to feel], *n.* Loss of feeling. **anæsthet'ic**, *n.* A substance which produces anæsthesia.

anagram (ăn'à-grăm) [Gr. **ANA**-, *graphein*, to write], *n.* A word or sentence formed by transposing the letters of another word or sentence.

analgesia (ăn-ăl-jē'zĭ-à) [Gr. painlessness], *n.* (*Med.*) Loss of sensibility to pain.

analogue (ăn'à-log) [Fr. from Gr. *analogon*], *n.* An analogous word or thing, a parallel. (*Nat. Hist.*) A part which agrees with another in function but not in origin.

analogy (à-năl'ō-jĭ) [Gr. **ANA**-, *logos*, word, relation], *n.* Similitude of relations, similarity. **anal'ogous**, *a.* Presenting some resemblance.

analyse (ăn'à-lĭz) [Gr. **ANA**-, *luein*, to loosen], *v.t.* To resolve into its constituent elements; examine minutely. **anal'ysis**, *n.* (*pl.* **-ses**) The process of analysing. **an'alyst,** *n.* One who analyses. **analyt'ic,** *a.* Pertaining to analysis.

anarchy (ăn'ár-ki) [Gr. AN-, *archos,* ruler], *n.* Absence of government; disorder, lawlessness. **anar'chic, -al,** *a.* Pertaining to anarchy. **an'archist,** *n.* One opposed to all forms of government.

anathema (á-năth'ĕ-má) [Gr. ANA-, *tithnai,* to put], *n.* A formal curse or excommunication. **anath'ematize,** *v.t.* To excommunicate, curse.

anatomy (á-năt'ó-mi) [Gr. *anatomē,* cutting up], *n.* The art of dissecting an organized body so as to discover its structure, and interrelation of its parts; the science of its structure. **anatom'ic, -al,** *a.* **anat'omize,** *v.t.* To dissect. **anat'omist,** *n.* One who is skilled in anatomy.

-ance, *suf.* Noting state or action, as *distance, fragrance, parlance, riddance.*

ancestor (ăn'sĕs-tór) [L. *antecessor,* one who goes before], *n.* One from whom descent is derived. **ancestress,** *n.* A female ancestor. **ances'tral,** *a.* **ancestry** *n.* A line of ancestors.

anchor (ăng'kŏr) [A.-S. *ancor*], *n.* A heavy hooked iron instrument used to grapple a ship aground and prevent her drifting. *v.t.* To secure by an anchor; to fix firmly. *v.i.* To come to anchor; take up a position. **an'chorage,** *n.* A place suitable for anchoring.

anchoret, anchorite (ăng'kŏ-rīt) [Gr. ANA-, *khōreein,* to withdraw, retire], *n.* A hermit; a person of solitary habits. **anchoress, ancress,** *n.* A female anchorite.

anchovy (ăn-chō'vǐ) [Sp.], *n.* A small fish of the herring family.

ancient (ān'chĕnt) [O.F. *ancien*], *a.* Of or belonging to long-past time; antiquated. *n.* Flag; standard-bearer. *n.pl.* Those who lived in former (esp. Classical) times.

ancillary (ăn-sil'ăr-ǐ) [L. *ancilla,* a maid], *a.* Subservient, auxiliary.

and (ănd) [A.-S.], *conj.* The copulative which joins words and sentences.

andante (an-dan'tĕ) [It.], *adv.* (*Mus.*) Moderately slow, *n.* A moderately slow movement or piece.

andiron (ănd'îrn) [O.F. *andier*], *n.* A horizontal bar on short legs, placed on each side of the hearth to support logs in a fire.

anecdote (ăn'ĕk-dōt) [Gr. AN-, *ekdotos,* published], *n.* The relation of an isolated biographical fact; a short tale.

anemometer (ăn-e-mom'ĕ-tĕr) [Gr. *anemos,* wind; meter], *n.* A wind gauge.

anemone (á-nem'ó-ni) [Gr. wind-flower], *n.* A genus of plants with brilliantly coloured flowers; the wind-flower.

anent (á-nent') [A.-S. *on,* in, *efen,* even, equal], *prep.* Concerning, in respect of.

-aneous [L.], *suf.* Belonging to, *e.g.* extraneous, instantaneous.

aneroid (ăn'er-oid) [Gr. *nēros,* wet], *n.* A barometer which measures the pressure of the air by its action on the lid of a metallic box.

aneurysm (ăn'ū-rizm) [Gr. ANA-, *eurunein,* to widen], *n.* A morbid dilatation in an artery.

anew (á-nū') [A.-S.], *adv.* Again; afresh.

angel (ān'jĕl) [A.-S. *œngel,* Gr. *angelos,* a messenger], *n.* A messenger from God; a guardian or attendant spirit; an old English gold coin (value 6*s.* 8*d.* to 10*s.*). **angel'ic,** *a.* **angelically,** *adv.*

angelica (ăn-jel'ik-á) [med. L. *herba angelica*], *n.* A plant used in medicine, and as a sweetmeat.

angelus (ăn'jĕ-lŭs) [opening of *Angelus domini*], *n.* A short devotional exercise in the R.C. Church in honour of the Incarnation; the bell rung as a signal to say the Angelus.

anger (ăng'gĕr) [Icel. *angr,* sorrow], *n.* Rage, passion, excited by a sense of wrong, *v.t.* To make angry, to enrage. **angry,** *a.* **angrily,** *adv.*

angina (ăn-jī'ná) [L. *angere,* to strangle], *n.* Quinsy; angina-pectoris, a disease of the heart.

angle (ăng'gĕl) [A.-S. *angel,* fish-hook, Gr. *ankōn,* a bend], *n.* A corner; the inclination of two lines towards each other; the space between them; a fish-hook. *v.i.* To fish with rod and line; to try to elicit or get by craft. **angler,** *n.* One who fishes with a baited hook. **angling,** *n.* The art of fishing with rod and line; (*fig.*) trying to find out by craft.

Anglican (ăng'gli-kăn) [med. L. *Anglicānus*], *a.* English (as opposed to Roman); of or belonging to the English Church; esp. High Church. *n.* A member of the High Church school in the Church of England. **Anglicanism,** *n.* The teachings and practices of the High Church party in the Church of England.

anglice (ăng'gli-sē) [L.], *adv.* In English.

Anglo- [*comb. form* of English, of or connected with England of the English]. **Anglo-Catholic, n.,** *a.* Anglican. **Anglo-Indian, n., a.** An Englishman born in India or long resident there; one of mixed blood. **Anglomania, n.** Excessive fondness for English manners and customs. **Ang'lophobe, n.** A hater of England or the English. **Anglopho'bia, n.**

Angora (ăng-gŏr'á) [town in Asia Minor], *n.* A goat with long silky hair; the hair, or fabric made therefrom; a long-haired cat; a breed of rabbit with long fur.

anguish (ăng'gwish) [O.F. *anguisse,* the sense of choking], *n.* Excessive pain or distress of body or mind.

angular (ăng'gŭ-lár) [L. *angulāris*], *a.* Having angles or sharp corners; bony, lacking in plumpness; stiff, formal. **angular'ity, n.**

anigh (á-nī') [A.-S.], *adv.* and *prep.* Near; near to.

aniline (ăn'i-lēn) [Sansk. *nīlas,* blue], *n.* A chemical base used in dyeing, originally obtained from indigo, now chiefly from coal-tar.

animadvert (ăn-i-măd-vĕrt') [L. *animus,* the mind, *ad,* to, *vertere,* to turn], *v.i.* To direct attention to; to criticize. **animadversion, n.** Criticism, reproof.

animal (ăn'i-mál) [L. *anima,* breath], *n.* A being possessing life, sensation, and the power of voluntary motion; one of the lower animals, esp. a quadruped. *a.* Of or belonging to animals; carnal. **an'imalism, n.** The theory which views mankind as merely animal; sensuality.

animalcule (ăn-i-măl'kūl) [L. *animalculum*], *n.* A small animal invisible to the naked eye. **animalcular**, *a.*

animate (ăn'i-māt) [L. *animāre*], *v.t.* To give life or spirit to; to vivify, stir up. **animated**, *part.a.* Full of life or spirits. **anima'tion**, *n.* Vitality, vivacity.

animism (ăn'im-izm) [L. *anima*], *n.* The doctrine that a soul is the basis of life; the attribution of a living soul to inanimate objects and to natural phenomena.

animosity (ăn-i-mos'i-ti) F. *animosité*], *n.* Enmity showing itself in action.

animus (ăn-i-mŭs) [L. mind, spirit, passion], *n.* Spirit, actuating feeling, usually of a hostile character; animosity.

anise (ăn'is) [Gr. *anison*, dill], *n.* A plant cultivated for its seeds. **aniseed**, *n.* The seed of the anise, used as a carminative.

anker (ăng'kėr) [Dut.], *n.* A measure of nearly nine imperial gallons.

ankle (ăngkl) [A.-S. *ancléow*], *n.* The joint uniting the foot to the leg. **anklet**, *n.* An ornament or band for the ankle.

anna (ăn'á) [Hind. *ana*], *n.* An East Indian coin; one-sixteenth of a rupee.

annals (ăn'álz) [L. *annus*, year], *n.pl.* An annual narrative of events; historical records. **annalist**, *n.* One who writes annals.

anneal (á-nēl') [A.-S. *onælan*], *v.t.* To temper glass or metals by intense heat, and slow cooling. **annealing**, *n.* The burning of metallic colours into glass, etc.

annex (á-neks') [L. AD-, *nectere*, to bind], *v.t.* To unite to, add on to; to take possession of. **annexa'tion**, *n.* **annexe** (á-neks'), *n.* A subsidiary building.

annihilate (á-nī'hil-āt) [L. AD-, *nihil*, nothing], *v.t.* To reduce to nothing; blot out of existence. **annihila'tion**, *n.* Complete destruction.

anniversary (ăn-i-vėr'sá-ri) [L. *annus*, year, *versus*, turned], *n.* The annual return of a date, or its celebration.

annotate (ăn'ō-tāt) [L. AD-, *notāre*, to mark], *v.t.* To make notes or comments upon. **annota'tion**, *n.* **annotator**, *n.*

announce (á-nouns') [L. AD-, *nuntiāre*, to report], *v.t.* To make known, proclaim; to declare officially. **announcement**, *n.*

annoy (á-noi') [O.F. *anoier*, to molest], *v.t.* To trouble, to put to inconvenience by repeated acts. **annoyance**, *n.* The act of annoying; that which annoys.

annual (ăn'ū-ál) [L. *anndlis*, yearly], *a.* Happening every year; done in a year; (*Bot.*) lasting but a single season. *n.* A book published every year; a plant which lives for a year only. **annually**, *adv.*

annuity (á-nū'i-ti) [F. *annuité*], *n.* An investment insuring fixed annual payments; the payment. **annuitant**, *n.* One who receives an annuity.

annul (á-nŭl') [L. *nullus*, none], *v.t.* To render void, cancel. **annulment**, *n.*

annular (ăn'ū-lár) [L. *annulus*, ring], *a.* Ring-shaped, ringed. **annula'tion**, *n.*

annunciate (á-nŭn'shi-āt), *v.t.* To announce, bring tidings. **annuncia'tion**, *n.* The act of announcing; the announcement of the Incarnation by the angel Gabriel to the Virgin Mary.

anodyne (ăn'ō-dīn) [Gr. *an-*, not, *odunē*,

pain], *a.* Assuaging pain or distress, soothing. *n.* A medicine, or anything, which does this.

anoint (á-noint') [L. *in-*, *unctus*, smeared], *v.t.* To smear with oil, esp. as a religious ceremony; to consecrate with oil. **anointed**, *a.*

anomaly (á-nom'á-li) [Gr. AN-, *ōmalos*, even], *n.* Irregularity; deviation from established order. **anomalous**, *a.*

anon (á-non') [A.-S. *on ân*, in one moment], *adv.* Thereupon; in a little while.

anonymous (á-non'i-mŭs) [Gr. AN-, *onoma*, name], *a.* Nameless; of unknown or unavowed authorship. **anonym'ity**, *n.*

another (á-nŭth'ėr) [A.-S.], *pron.* and *a.* An other one; a different one; any other.

anserine (ăn'ser-īn) [L. *anserinus*], *a.* Pertaining to a goose; silly.

answer (an'sėr) [A.-S. *andswaru*, a reply], *n.* A reply to a charge, question, etc.; a solution of a problem. *v.t.* To reply to; to be suitable to; to be opposite to. *v.i.* To suit, correspond. **answerable**, *a.* Liable to be called to account; capable of being answered.

ant (ănt) [A.-S. *œmette*], *n.* A small, social, hymenopterous insect; an emmet.

ant- [ANTI-], *pref.* Against, as in *antagonist*, *Antarctic*.

antagonist (ăn-tăg'ó-nist) [Gr. ANTI-, against, *agōnizesthai*, to struggle], *n.* An opponent. **antagonism**, *n.* Opposition. **antagonis'tic**, *a.*

Antarctic (ănt-ark'tik), *a.* Opposite to the Arctic; belonging to the southern pole or circle.

ante- [L.], *pref.* Before, as in *antedate*.

antecede (ăn-te-sēd') [L. *antecēdere*, to go before], *v.t.* To precede. **antecedence**, *n.* A going before; (*Astron.*) an apparent motion contrary to the true motion. **antecedent**, *a.* Going before in time, prior, presumptive. *n.* That which goes before; the word to which a relative refers; (*pl.*) past circumstances.

antechamber (ăn'te-), *n.* An anteroom.

antediluvian (ăn-tē-di-loo'vi-án) [ANTE-, L. *dilŭvium*, flood], *a.* Pertaining to the period before the Flood; (*fig.*) antiquated.

antelope (ăn'tė-lōp) [late Gr. *antholops*], *n.* A ruminant akin to the deer and goat.

antemeridian (ăn-tē-mer-id'iăn), [ANTE-, MERIDIAN], *a.* Pertaining to the forenoon.

antenatal (ăn-te-nā'tál), *a.* Happening or existing while in the uterus.

antenna (ăn-ten'á) [L., sail-yard], *n.* (*pl.* -æ). The palp or feeler of insects.

antenuptial (ăn-tē-nŭp'shi-ál), *a.* Happening before marriage.

antepenult (ăn-tē-pēn-ŭlt') [ANTE-, L. *pœne*, almost, *ultimus*, latest], *a.* Pertaining to the last syllable but two.

anterior (ăn-tēr'i-ŏr) [L.], *a.* Going before, preceding, prior. **anterior'ity**, *n.*

anteroom (ăn'tė-rum), *n.* A room forming an entrance to another.

anthelmintic (ăn-thel-min'tik) [Gr. *anth*, against; *helmins*, worm], *a.* (*Med.*) Remedial against worms.

anthem (ăn'thėm) [A.-S. *antefn*, Gr. *antiphōna*], *n.* A hymn in alternate parts; a portion of Scripture set to music.

anther (ăn'thẽr) [Gr. *anthēra*, flowery], *n.* The pollen-bearing organ of plants.

anthology (ăn-thŏl'ŏ-ji) [Gr. *anthologia*, a gathering of flowers], *n.* A collection of poems (esp. a famous Greek collection) or literary extracts. **anthologist,** *n.* The compiler of an anthology.

anthracite (ăn'thrȧ-sīt) [Gr. *anthrax*, coal, carbon], *n.* Non-bituminous coal, burning with intense heat and with little flame.

anthrax (ăn'thrăks), *n.* The splenic fever of sheep and cattle (communicable to man).

anthropo- [Gr. *anthrōpos*, a man], *comb. form.* Human; pertaining to man or mankind. **anthropoid** (ăn'thrŏ-poid), *a.* Resembling man; of human form. *n.* One of the higher apes. **anthropoph'agous** [-PHAGOUS], *a.* Man-eating, cannibal.

anthropology (ăn-thrŏ-pol'ŏ-ji), *n.* The study of man, or mankind, in the widest sense. **anthropolog'ical,** *a.* **anthropometry,** *n.* Scientific measurement of the human body.

anthropomorphous (ăn-thrŏ-pŏ-môr'fŭs) [ANTHROPO-, Gr. *morphē*, form], *a.* Possessed of a form resembling that of man. **anthropomor'phism,** *n.* The attribution of human character to the Deity. **anthropomor'phic,** *a.*

anti- [Gr.], *pref.* Opposite, against, instead of, as in *antibilious; antiseptic.*

anti-biotic (ăn-ti-bī-ot'ik), *n.* (*Biol.*) A chemical agent produced by living organisms, capable of killing bacteria, such as penicillin.

antibody (ăn'ti-bo'di), *n.* (*Med.*) Substance produced in the blood capable of counteracting toxins.

antic (ăn'tik) [L. *antiquus*, ancient], *a.* Odd, whimsical. *n.* (*Usually in pl.*) An odd trick; a ludicrous gesture.

Antichrist (ăn'ti-krīst), *n.* A personal antagonist of Christ spoken of in the N.T.

anticipate (ăn-tis'i-pāt) [L. *anticipātus,* taken before], *v.t.* To forestall; to cause to happen earlier; to look forward to; to deal with before the proper time. **anticipant,** *a.* Anticipating, expecting. **anticipa'tion,** *n.* The act of anticipating; expectation, presentiment. **anticipa'tory,** *a.*

anticlimax (ăn-ti-klī'măks), *n.* A decrease in impressiveness; bathos.

anticyclone (ăn'ti-sī-klōn), *n.* The rotatory outward flow of air from an atmospheric region of high pressure. **anticyclon'ic,** *a.*

antidote (ăn'ti-dōt) [ANTI-, Gr. *didōmi,* I give], *n.* A counteracting medicine; anything intended to counteract evil.

antimacassar (ăn-ti-mȧ-kăs'sȧr), *n.* A removable covering for the backs of chairs, sofas, etc.

antimony (ăn'tim-ŏ-ni) [med. L.], *n.* A bright bluish-white brittle metal, used in the arts and in medicine. **antimo'nial,** *a.* Pertaining to or containing antimony.

antinomy (ăn-tin'ŏ-mi) [Gr. *antinomia*], *n.* Contradiction between two laws; conflict of authority; intellectual contradiction.

antipathy (ăn-tip'ȧ-thi) [ANTI-, Gr. *pathein*,

to suffer], *n.* Hostile feeling towards; aversion, dislike. **antipathet'ic,** *a.*

antiphlogistic (ăn-ti-flŏ-jis'tik), *a.* (*Med.*) Allaying inflammation; cooling.

antiphon (ăn'ti-fon) [Gr. *anti-*, in return, *phōnē*, voice], *n.* A sentence sung by one choir in response to another; an anthem. **antiph'onal,** *n.* A book containing antiphons. **antiphony,** *n.* Opposition of sound; alternate chanting.

antipodes (ăn-tip'ŏ-dēz) [ANTI-, Gr. *pous,* foot], *n.pl.* Those who dwell directly opposite to each other on the globe; places on the surface of the globe diametrically opposite. **antip'odal, antipode'an,** *a.*

antipope (ăn'ti-pōp), *n.* A pope elected in opposition to one canonically chosen.

antiquary (ăn'ti-kwȧr-i) [L. *antiquārius*], *n.* A student, collector, or vendor of antiques. **antiquar'ian,** *a.* Pertaining to the study of antiquities. *n.* An antiquary. **antiquarianism,** *n.*

antiquate (ăn'ti-kwāt) [L. *antiquātus*], *v.t.* To make old or obsolete; (*in p.p.*) made out of date, old-fashioned, or disused.

antique (ăn-tēk') [F., L. *antiquus*], *a.* Ancient, old-fashioned, antiquated, *n.* A relic of antiquity. **antiq'uity,** *n.* The state of being ancient; ancient times; manners, customs, etc., of ancient times.

antirrhinum (ăn-ti-rī'nŭm) [Gr. *anti-*, instead of; *rhinos*, nose], *n.* (*Bot.*) Snapdragon.

antiscorbutic (ăn-ti-skôr-bū'tik), *a.* Of use against scurvy.

anti-Semitism, *n.* Hostility to Jews as a race.

antiseptic (ăn-ti-sep'tik) [ANTI-, Gr. *sēptos,* decayed], *a.* Counteracting growth of bacteria.

antithesis (ăn-tith'e-sis) [ANTI-, Gr. *thesis,* a setting], *n.* (*pl.* -ses). Opposition or contrast between words, clauses, or ideas; a counter-proposition. **antithe'tic,** *a.* Pertaining to antithesis; sharply opposed.

antler (ănt'lẽr) [O.F. *antoillier*], *n.* A branch of the horns of a stag or deer.

antonym (ăn'tŏ-nim) [Gr. *anti-*, instead of; *onuma*, name], *n.* Term expressing the reverse of some other term.

anus (ā'nus) [L., a ring], *n.* The lower orifice of the intestinal tube.

anvil (ăn'vil) [A.-S. *onfilti*], *n.* The iron block on which smiths hammer and shape their work; a bone in the ear.

anxiety (ăng-zī'ĕ-ti) [L. *anxietas*], *n.* The state of being anxious; trouble, solicitude.

anxious (ănk'shŭs) [L. *anxius* (*angere*, to choke)], *a.* Troubled about some uncertain event. **anxiously,** *adv.*

any (en'i) [A.-S. *ænig*], *a* and *pron.* One indefinitely; whichever, whatever. **anybody,** *n. or pron.* Any person, any one; a person of no importance. **anyhow,** *adv.* and *conj.* At any rate; in any case; at haphazard. **anything,** *n.* and *pron.* Any thing (in its widest sense). **anywhere,** *adv.* In any place.

Anzac (ăn'zăk) [initials Australian and New Zealand Army Corps], *n.* Soldier in these forces in World War I.

aorta (ā-ôr'tȧ) [Gr. *aortē (aeirein,* to lift)],

n. The largest artery in the body, proceeding from the left ventricle of the heart.

apace (à-pās') [A.-S.], *adv.* At a quick pace.

apanage (ăp'à-năj) [O.F. *apaner*, to nourish], *n.* Lands, etc., for the maintenance of a royal house; a perquisite.

apart (à-pärt') [F. *à part*], *adv.* To one side.

apartheid (à-ärt'-hāt), *n.* The doctrine of racial segregation practised in S. Africa.

apartment (à-pärt'mĕnt) [L. AD-, *partire*, to divide], *n.* A portion of, or single room in, a house; (*pl.*) lodgings. **apartment house,** *n.* (*Am.*) Block of flats.

apathy (ăpà-thǐ) [Gr. *a-*, not, *pathein*, to suffer], *n.* Absence of feeling; indifference. **apathet'ic,** *a.*

ape (āp) [A.-S. *apa*], *n.* A tailless monkey; a servile imitator. *v.t.* To imitate or mimic. **a'pish** (ā'), *a.*

aperient (à-pēr'ǐ-ent), **aper'itive** [L. *aperire*, to open], *a.* Laxative, *n.* A purgative medicine.

aperitif (à-per'ǐ-tēf) [Fr.], *n.* Short alcoholic drink taken as an appetizer.

aperture (ăp'ĕr-tûr), *n.* An opening, gap.

apex (ā'peks) [L.], *n.* (*pl.* apices or apexes). The summit of anything.

aphæresis (à-fēr'ē-sis) [Gr. *apo-*, away, *airein*, to take], *n.* The removal of a letter or syllable at the beginning of a word.

aphasia (à-fā'zhǐ-à) [Gr. *a-*, not, *phēmi*, I speak], *n.* Loss of the power of articulate speech.

aphelion (à-fē'lǐ-ŏn) [Gr. *aph-*, *hēlion*, away from the sun], *n.* (*pl.* -ia). The point most distant from the sun in an orbit.

aphis (āf'is) [mod. L.], *n.* (*pl.* aph'ides, āf'ǐ-dēz). The plant-louse, very destructive to vegetation. **aphid'ian,** *a.*

aphorism (ăf-ō-rizm) [Gr. *aphorismos*, a definition], *n.* A maxim or wise precept.

aphrodisiac (ăf-rō-dǐz'ǐ-ăk) [Gr. *aphrodisiakos*], *a.* Exciting venereal desire. *n.* Drug doing this.

apiary (ā'pǐ-àr-ǐ) [L. *apis*, bee], *n.* A place where bees are kept.

apiculture (ā'pǐ-kŭl-tûr) [L. *apis*, a bee, CULTURE], *n.* Bee-keeping; bee-rearing.

apiece (à-pēs'), *adv.* For or to each, severally.

aplomb (a-plon) [F., perpendicular], *n.* Self-possession, coolness.

apo- [Gr.], *pref.* Away, detached, separate, as in *apology, apostrophe.*

apocalypse (à-pok'à-lips) [Gr. *kaluptein*, to cover], *n.* The last book of the N.T., the Revelation. **apocalyp'tic,** *a.*

apocrypha (à-pok'rǐ-fà) [Gr. *kruptein*, to hide], *n.* Books included in the Septuagint and the Vulgate, but not reckoned genuine by the Jews, nor inserted in the Authorized Version of the Bible. **apocryphal,** *a.* Mythic, fabulous.

apogee (ăp'ō-jē) [Gr. *gaia*, earth], *n.* The point in an orbit which is at the greatest distance from the earth; (*fig.*) the culmination.

apologia (ă-pol-ō'jà) [L. from Gr], *n.* Vindication, formal defence.

apologue (ăp'ō-log) [Gr. *logos*, speech], *n.* A moral fable.

apology (à-pol'ō-jǐ) [Gr. *legein*, to speak], *n.* A defence; vindication; excuse. **apologet'ic,** *a.* Excusing, explanatory. **apologetics,** *n.pl.* Defensive argument, esp. in defence of Christianity. **apol'ogist,** *n.* One who defends or apologizes by speech or writing. **apol'ogize,** *v.i.* To make an apology.

apophthegm (ăp'ō-them) [Gr. *phthengesthai*, to speak], *n.* A terse pointed saying. **apophthegmatic** (ăp-ō-theg-măt'ik), *a.* Sententious, pithy.

apoplexy (ăp'o-plek-si) [Gr. *apoplēssein*, to cripple with a blow], *n.* A sudden loss of sense and motive power, generally caused by effusion on the brain. **apoplec'tic,** *a.* Predisposed to apoplexy.

apostasy (à-pos'tà-si) [Gr. *apostasia, stasis*], *n.* Renunciation of principles—religious, moral, political, etc.

apostate (à-pos'tāt) [as prec.], *n.* One who apostatizes. *a.* Unfaithful to creed or principles. **apostatize,** *v.i.* To abandon one's principles or party.

apostle (à-posl') [Gr. *apostolos*, a messenger], *n.* One of those appointed by Christ to preach the gospel; the leader of a reform. **apostolate** (à-pos'tō-lāt), *n.* The office of apostle. **apostol'ic,** *a.*

apostrophe (à-pos'trō-fē) [Gr. *apostrephein*, to turn away], *n.* An address to one person in particular, or to the absent or dead; the sign ('), denoting contraction or the possessive case. **apostrophize** (à-pos'trō-fīz), *v.t.*

apothecary (à-poth'ē-kàr-ǐ) O.F. *apotecaire*, late L. *apothēcārius*, a storekeeper], *n.* A druggist or pharmaceutical chemist.

apotheosis (à-poth-ē-ō'sis) [APO-, Gr. *theoō*, I deify], *n.* Deification; transformation into a god or saint.

appal (à-pawl') [O.F. *apalir*, to grow pale], *v.t.* To terrify; to dismay. **appalling,** *a.*

apparatus (ăp-à-rā'tǔs) [L. AD-, *parāre*, to prepare], *n.* Equipment, means; scientific instruments; materials for critical study.

apparel (à-păr'él) [O.F. *apareiller*, to dress], *n.* Dress, attire; to adorn, embellish, trick out. *v.t.* To clothe; to fit out.

apparent (à-păr'ĕnt) [O.F. L. *appārēntem*, come into sight], *a.* Visible; plain, obvious. **apparently,** *adv.*

apparition (ăpà-rish'ŭn) [F., from L.; see APPEAR], *n.* A strange appearance; a spectre.

appeal (à-pēl') [O.F. *apeler*], *v.i.* To refer to a superior authority; to invoke aid, pity, etc.; to have recourse to. *n.* Reference or recourse to another; the right of appeal. **appealing,** *a.* Suppliant.

appear (à-pēr') [L. AD-, *pārēre*, to come into sight], *v.i.* To become visible; come before the public; to seem. **appearance,** *n.* The act of appearing; the thing seen; aspect; (*pl.*) the aspect of circumstances.

appease (à-pēz') F. *à*, to, *pais*, peace), *v.t.* To quiet, pacify.

appellant (à-pel'ănt), *n.* One who appeals to a higher tribunal or authority. **appella'tion,** *n.* A name, designation. **appel'lative,** *a.* Common as opposed to proper; designating a class.

append (à-pend') [L. AD-, *pendere*, to hang], *v.t.* To hang to or upon; to add or subjoin. **appendage,** *n.* **appendant,** *a.*

appendix (ȧ-pen'diks), *n.* (*pl.* **appendices**, **-dixes**). An adjunct; a supplement to a book; (*Physiol.*) a small prolongation of any organ, esp. the vermiform appendix of the intestine. **appen'-dici'tis**, *n.* Inflammation of this.

appertain (ăp-ėr-tān') [L. *pertinēre*, to pertain], *v.i.* To belong to; relate to.

appetite (ăp'ė-tīt) [L. *petere*, to seek], *n.* Desire to satisfy the natural functions; desire for food. **appetize**, *v.t.* To give an appetite to; to make (one) feel hungry.

applaud (ȧ-plawd') [L. *plaudere*, to clap], *v.i.* To express approbation, esp. by clapping. *v.t.* To praise in an audible and significant manner. **applause**, *n.* Praise loudly expressed.

apple (ăpl) [A.-S.], *n.* The fruit of the apple-tree; the pupil of the eye.

Appleton layer [Sir E. Appleton], *n.* Layer in the upper atmosphere reflecting radio waves.

appliance (ȧ-plī'ȧns), *n.* The act of applying; anything applied as a means to an end.

applicable (ap'lik-abl), *a.* Capable of being applied; fit, suitable, appropriate.

applicabil'ity, *n.* **applicant**, *n.* **applica'tion**, *n.* The act of applying; thing applied; request; close attention.

apply (ȧ-plī) [L. AD-, *plicāre*, fold together, fasten], *v.t.* To lay on, put close to; to employ, devote; to adapt, conform to. *v.i.* To be relevant; to have recourse (to); to study. **applied**, *a.* Practical.

appoint (ȧ-point') [F. *à*, to, *point*, the point], *v.t.* To decree, ordain; nominate; make an appointment; to grant. **appoint'ment**, *n.* That which is appointed or fixed; an engagement; (*pl.*) equipment, accoutrements.

apport (ăp'ôrt) L. *apportare*, to bring], *n.* In Spiritualism a material object brought without material agency.

apportion (ȧ-pôr'shŭn), *v.t.* To divide in suitable proportion. **apportionment**, *n.*

apposite (ăp'ō-zit) [L. *pōnere*, to place], *a.* Fit, appropriate. **appositely**, *adv.* **appositeness**, *n.* **apposi'tion**, *n.* The act of putting side by side; juxtaposition; (*Gram.*) the placing together of two nouns, one being a complement to the other. **appositional**, *a.*

appraise (ȧ-prāz'), *v.t.* To set a price on; to value.

appreciate (ȧ-prē'shi-āt) [L. *pretium*, a price], *v.t.* To form an estimate of value; to estimate aright; to esteem highly. *v.i.* To rise in value. **appreciable**, *a.* **appreciably**, *adv.* To an appreciable extent. **apprecia'tion**, *n.* Estimate; adequate recognition; rise in value. **appre'ciative**, *a.* Esteeming favourably.

apprehend (ăp-re-hend') [L. *prehendere*, to seize], *v.t.* To take hold of; to seize, to arrest; conceive mentally; to dread; to anticipate. *v.i.* To understand. **apprehensible**, *a.* **apprehension**, *n.* The act of laying hold of or arresting; the mental faculty which apprehends; fear of what may happen. **apprehensive**, *a.*

apprentice (ȧ-pren'tis) [O.F. *aprentis*, from *apprendre*, to learn, see prec.], *n.* One bound by indentures to serve for a term of years in order to learn some trade or craft. *v.t.* To bind as an apprentice. **apprenticeship**, *n.*

apprise (ȧ-prīz') [F. *appris*], *v.t.* To inform, bring to the knowledge of.

apprize (ȧ-prīz') [O.F. *aprisier*, to appraise], *v.t.* To estimate the worth of.

approach (ȧ-prōch') [L. *propius*, nearer], *v.i.* To come or draw nearer; to approximate. *v.t.* To come near to; to resemble. *n.* The act of drawing near; resemblance; avenue, access. **approachable**, *a.*

approbation (ăp-rō-bā'shŭn), *n.* Approval, commendation, praise.

appropriate (ȧ-prō'pri-āt) [L. *proprius*, one's own], *v.t.* To take as one's own; to devote to a special purpose. *a.* Suitable, fit, becoming; set apart for a particular use. **appropriately**, *adv.* **appropria'tion**, *n.* **appropriator**, *n.*

approve (ȧ-proov') [L. *probāre*, to test, try], *v.t.* To esteem, pronounce as good; to sanction, confirm. *v.i.* To express or feel approbation. **approval**, *n.* Approbation, sanction. **approver**, *n.* One who approves; one who confesses and gives evidence against his associates.

approximate (ȧ-proks'i-māt) [L. *proximus*, very near], *v.i.* To draw or bring near. *a.* Very close to; closely resembling; **approxima'tion**, *n.*

appurtenance (ȧ-pėr'tėn-ȧns), *n.* That which appertains to something else; an adjunct, appendage. **appurtenant**, *a.* Pertaining to, pertinent.

apricot (ā'pri-kot) [L. *præcox*, early ripe], *n.* A stone-fruit allied to the plum.

April (ā'pril) [L. *Aprīlis* (prob. from *aperire*, to open)], *n.* The fourth month of the year.

apron (ā'prŏn) [O.F. *naperon*, a large cloth], *n.* A garment worn in front to protect the clothes, or as part of a distinctive dress, *e.g.* of bishops, Freemasons.

apropos (a'prō-pō) [F. *à propos*], *adv.* Seasonably; by the way; as suggested by. *a.* Opportune; to the point.

apse (ăps) [Gr. *apsis*, fastening, felloe of a wheel], *n.* A semi-circular, dome-roofed recess in a building.

apsis (ăp'sis), *n.* (*pl.* **apsides**, ăp-sī'dēz). One of two points at which a planet is at its greatest and least distance from the body round which it revolves. **ap'sidal**, *a.* Of the shape of an apse or apsis.

apt (ăpt) [L. *aptus*], *a.* Suitable; having a tendency to; quick. **ap'titude**, *n.* Fitness, suitability; proneness to. **aptly**, *adv.* **aptness**, *n.*

apterous (ăp'tėr-ŭs) [Gr. *a-*, not, *pteron*, a wing], *a.* Wingless.

aqua (ăk'wȧ) [L.], *n.* Water, liquid. **aqua-vitæ**, *n.* Unrectified alcohol.

aquamarine (ă-kwȧ-mȧ-rēn') [L. seawater], *n.* A bluish-green variety of beryl.

aquarium (ȧ-kwār'i-ŭm), *n.* A tank or vessel in which aquatic plants and animals are kept alive.

aquat'ic, *a.* Pertaining to water; living, growing in or near water.

aqueduct (ăk'wė-dŭkt) [L. *aquæ*, of water,

ductus, conveyance], *n.* A conduit, esp. one raised on pillars or arches, for the conveyance of drinking-water.

aqueous (ā'kwē-ŭs), *a.* Containing, formed in, or deposited from water; watery.

aquiline (ăk'wi-lin) [L. *aquila,* an eagle], *a.* Pertaining to an eagle; eagle-like (esp. of noses), hooked.

ar- [AD-], *pref.,* as in *arrest, arrogate.*

-ar (1) [L.], *adj. suf.* Belonging to, of the nature of; *e.g. angular, lunar. n. suf.* Thing pertaining to; *e.g. altar, exemplar.*

-ar (2) [O.F.], *suf.* Agent; *e.g. bursar, vicar, liar.*

Arab (ăr'ăb), *n.* A native of Arabia; an Arabian horse. *a.* Arabian. **arabesque'** [F.], *a.* Arabian in design; fantastic. *n.* Surface decoration composed of flowing lines fancifully intermingled. **Ara'bian,** *a.* Pertaining to Arabia. *n.* An Arab, a native of Arabia. **Ar'abic,** *a.* Pertaining to Arabia, or to its language. *n.* The language.

arable (ăr'ăbl) [L. *arāre,* to plough], *a.* Capable of being ploughed; fit for tillage.

arachnid (á-răk'nid) [Gr. *arachne,* spider], *n.* (*Zool.*) One of the class containing spiders, scorpions, and mites.

Aramaic (ăr'à-mā'ik), *a.* Of or belonging to Aram; applied to the northern branch of the Semitic family of languages, including Syriac and Chaldee. *n.* Syriac.

arbiter (ar'bi-tẽr) [L.], *n.* A judge; an umpire; one who can decide according to his absolute pleasure. **arbit'rament,** *n.* Power or liberty of deciding; the decision or award given by arbitrators. **ar'bitrary,** *a.* Determined by one's own will; capricious; absolute. **arbitrariness,** *n.*

arbitrate (ar'bi-trāt) [L. *arbitrari,* to give judgment], *v.t.* To hear and judge as an arbitrator; to decide, act as an arbitrator or umpire. **arbitra'tion,** *n.* The determining of a dispute by means of an arbiter. **ar'bitrator,** *n.* **arbitress,** *n.*

arbor'eal (ar-bôr'ē-ăl) [L. *arbor,* a tree], *a.* Pertaining to trees; living in trees. **arbores'cent,** *a.* Having tree-like characteristics; branching like a tree. **ar'boriculture,** *n.* The systematic culture of trees and shrubs.

arbour (ar'bôr) [L. *herba,* a tree, herb, grass, assim. to *arbor*], *n.* A bower formed by trees or shrubs, lattice-work, etc.

arbutus (ar'bū-tŭs) [L.], *n.* An evergreen shrub, the strawberry-tree.

arc (ark) [L. *arcus,* a bow], *n.* A portion of a circle or other curve; the luminous bridge between two carbon poles when an electric current is sent through them.

arcade (ar-kād') [It. *arcata,* arched], *n.* A series of arches; a walk arched over; a covered passage.

Arcadian (ar-kā'di-ăn) [L.], *a.* Pertaining to Arcadia, the ideal region of rural happiness; hence, ideally rustic or pastoral.

arcanum (ar-kā'nŭm) [L. *arcēre,* to shut up], *n.* (*usually in pl.* arcana) A mystery; an elixir.

arch (1) (arch) [L. *arca,* a chest (confused with *arcus,* a bow)], *n.* A curved structure, the parts supporting each other by mutual pressure; a vault, a curve. *v.t.* To cover with or form into an arch; to overarch, span.

arch (2) (arch), *a.* Clever, cunning, mirthfully mischievous or waggish. **archly,** *adv.* **archness,** *n.*

arch-, archi- (ar'ki-) [Gr. *archos,* chief], *pref.* Chief, principal; leading, pre-eminent; first; *e.g. archangel, archbishop.*

archæo- [Gr., *archaios,* ancient], *pref.* Pertaining to past time; primitive.

archæology (ar-kē-ol'ŏ-ji), *n.* The study of antiquities, esp. prehistoric remains. **archæological,** *a.* **archæol'ogist,** *n.*

archaic (ar-kā'ik) [Gr. *archaios,* old], *a.* Pertaining to antiquity; antiquated. **ar'chaism,** *n.* An old-fashioned habit; an obsolete expression; affectation of ancient style.

archangel (ark'ān-jĕl), *n.* An angel of the highest rank. **archangel'ic,** *a.*

archbishop (arch-bish'ŏp), *n.* A chief bishop; the spiritual head of an archiepiscopal province. **archbishopric,** *n.*

archdeacon (arch'dē-kŏn) [Gr. *archidiakonos*], *n.* A dignitary next below a bishop. **archdeaconry,** *n.* The portion of a diocese over which an archdeacon exercises jurisdiction.

archduke (arch'dūk), *n.* The title of the sons of the former Emperors of Austria.

archer (ar'chẽr) [O.F. *archier*], *n.* A bowman; (*Astron.*) the constellation Sagittarius. **archery,** *n.* The act or art of shooting with bows and arrows.

archetype (ar'kē-tip), *n.* The primitive model or pattern on which anything is formed.

archidiaconal (ar-ki-dī-ăk'ŏn-ăl), *a.* Pertaining to or holding the office of an archdeacon.

archiepiscopal (ar-ki-ē-pis'kŏ-păl) [Gr. *archiepiskopos*], *a.* Of or pertaining to an archbishop or archbishopric.

archimandrite (ar-ki-măn'drit) [Gr. *archi-,* chief, *mandra,* an enclosure, monastery], *n.* The superior of a monastery in the Greek Church.

archipelago (ar-ki-pel'à-gō) [ARCHI-, Gr. *pelagos,* sea], *n.* The Ægean Sea; any sea or water studded with islands.

architect (ar'ki-tekt) [ARCHI-, Gr. *tektōn,* a builder], *n.* One who plans and designs buildings and superintends their erection.

architecture (ar'ki-tek-tyŭr), *n.* The art of building edifices; architectural work; style of building; construction. **architec'tural,** *a.*

architrave (ar'ki-trāv) [ARCHI-, L. *trabs,* a beam], *n.* The part of the entablature that rests immediately on the column; ornamental moulding round a door or window.

archive (ar'kiv) [Gr. *archeion,* public office], *n.* (*usually in pl.*) Historical records officially preserved. **archivist** (ar'ki-vist), *n.* One who has charge of archives.

archway (arch'wā), *n.* An arched entrance or vaulted passage.

Arctic (ark'tik) [Gr. *arktikos,* belonging to the Great Bear (*arktos,* bear)], *a.* Pertaining to the region within the Arctic Circle, *i.e.* the parallel of the globe 23° 28' distant from the North Pole, which is its centre. *n.* The Arctic regions.

arcuate (ar'kū-āt) [L. *arcus*, bow], *a.* Curved like a bow; arched.

ardent (ar'dent) [O.F. *ardant*, L. *ardēre*, to burn], *a.* On fire; fierce, eager, zealous. ardency, *n.* ardently, *adv.*

ardour (ar'dŏr), *n.* Fierce heat; flame; heat of passion; warmth of emotion.

arduous (ar'dū-ùs) [L. *arduus*, steep, difficult], *a.* Involving much labour; difficult, laborious, energetic. arduously, *adv.*

area (âr'ê-à) [L.], *n.* Any clear or open space; the sunken, partly enclosed court giving access to the basement of some houses; superficial extent; a tract of country.

areca (âr'ê-ká) [Tamil *adai*, clustering, *kāy*, nut], *n.* A genus of palms.

arena (à-rē'ná) [L. *arēna*, *harēna*, sand], *n.* The sand-strewn floor of an amphitheatre where combats took place; an amphitheatre; a field of conflict, sphere of action. arena'ceous, *a.* Sandy; in the form of sand.

argent (ar'jènt) [L. *argentum*], *n.* Silver (esp. in heraldry). *a.* Resembling silver; silvery-white. argentif'erous, *a.* Producing silver. ar'gentine, *a.* Silvery.

argil (ar'jil) [Gr. *argillos*, white clay], *n.* White clay, potters' earth. argilla'ceous, *a.* Clayey.

argon (ar'gŏn) [Gr. *a-*, not, *ergon*, work], *n.* An inert gaseous constituent of the atmosphere.

Argonaut (ar'gŏ-nawt) [Gr. *argonautēs*], *n.* One of the legendary heroes who sailed in the *Argo* to seek the Golden Fleece; (*Zool.*) the paper-nautilus.

argosy (ar'gŏ-si) [prob. It. *una Ragusea* (*nave*), a Ragusan (ship)], *n.* A large merchant-vessel; a richly-laden ship.

argot (ar'gō) [F.], *n.* Thieves' slang; the phraseology of a class; slang generally.

argue (ar'gū) [L. *arguere*, to prove], *v.t.* To discuss, debate; to exhibit or convince by logical methods, to evince. *v.i.* To bring forward reasons, to discuss, dispute. arguable, *a.* Capable of being argued. argument, *n.* Reason, demonstration; process of reasoning; debate; a summary; the subject of a discourse. argumen'tative, *a.* Pertaining to argument; disputatious.

aria (a'ri-à) [It.], *n.* An air; song for one voice.

Arian (âr'i-àn), *a.* Pertaining to Arius. *n.* A follower of Arius of Alexandria (4th cent.), who denied that Christ was consubstantial with the Father. Arianism, *n.*

arid (âr'id) [L. *ārēre*, to dry], *a.* Dry, parched; barren, bare; (*fig.*) uninteresting. aridity (à-rid'i-ti), aridness (âr'id-nês), *n.* Dryness, drought.

aright (à-rīt') [A.-S.], *adv.* Rightly, properly.

arise (à-rīz') [A.-S. *a-*, intens., *rīsan*], *v.i.* (arose, arisen). To assume an upright position, to get up; to appear, to come into notoriety; to originate.

aristocracy (âr-is-tok'rá-si) [Gr. *aristos*, the best, *kratia*, rule], *n.* Government by the best citizens or nobles; a state so governed; the nobility; (*fig.*) the best of any class. ar'istocrat, *n.* A noble; a member of an aristocracy. aristo-cra'tic, *a.*

arithmetic (â-rith'mê-tik) [Gr. *arithmeein*, to count], *n.* The science of numbers; computation by figures. arithmet'ical, *a.* arithmet'ically, *adv.* arithmetician (-tish'án), *n.* One skilled in arithmetic.

-arium [L.], *suf.* Thing connected with, used for, place for; as *aquarium*, *herbarium*.

ark (ark) [A.-S.], *n.* A chest; a large flat-bottomed ship; a sacred repository.

arm (arm) [A.-S.], *n.* The upper limb of the human body, from the shoulder to the hand; a sleeve; a projecting branch, as of the sea; the parts of a yard on each side of the mast; a weapon; a branch of the military service; (*pl.*) war; the military profession; armour; heraldic bearings. *v.t.* To furnish or equip with arms; to prepare for war. armful, *n.* As much as the arm or arms can hold.

armada (ar-mā'dà) [Sp.], *n.* An armed fleet, esp. that sent by Philip II of Spain against England in 1588.

armadillo (ar-mà-dil'ō) [Sp.], *n.* (*pl.* -os). A small burrowing edentate S. American animal, encased in bony armour, and capable of rolling itself into a ball.

armaments (ar'mà-mentz) [L.], *n. pl.* Munitions of war.

armature (ar'mà-tūr), *n.* A piece of soft iron placed in contact with the poles of a magnet to preserve and increase its power.

armed (armd), *a.* Equipped with weapons or armour; prepared for war; equipped with anything required for action or defence.

Armenian (ar-mē'ni-àn), *a.* Pertaining to Armenia. *n.* A native of Armenia; the language.

armistice (ar'mis-tis) [F. from L. *arma*, arms, *-stitium*, from *sistere*, to stop], *n.* A cessation of arms for a stipulated time during war; a truce.

armlet (arm'lèt), *n.* A small band worn on the arm.

armory (ar'mŏ-ri) [O.F. *urmoier*, to blazon], *n.* The science of heraldry. armorial (ar-môr'i-àl), *a.*

armour (ar'mŏr) [O.F. *armure*], *n.* Defensive covering; heraldic bearings. *v.t.* To furnish with protective covering, esp. ships, tanks, etc. armoured, *a.* Clad in armour; ironclad. armoured car, train, etc., *n.* Vehicle, etc., protected by steel plates. armoured column, *n.* (*Mil.*) Force equipped with armoured vehicles, tanks, etc. armourer, *n.* A maker of arms; a non-commissioned officer in charge of the arms of a regiment, ship, etc. armoury, *n.* Place for keeping arms, an arsenal.

armpit (arm'pit), *n.* The hollow under the arm at the shoulder.

army (ar'mi) [F. *armée*], *n.* Men organized for land warfare; a host.

arnica (ar'ni-ká) [?], *n.* A vegetable tincture used for bruises, sprains, etc.

aroma (à-rō'má) [Gr. *arōma*, a spice], *n.* An agreeable odour or smell; a subtle pervasive quality. aromat'ic, *a.*

around (á-round´), *prep.* Surrounding; round about. *adv.* All round.

arouse (á-rouz´), *v.t.* To raise, awaken; to excite, stimulate.

arpeggio (ar-pej´yō) [It.], *n.* (*Mus.*) Chord produced by playing notes in rapid succession instead of simultaneously.

arraign (á-rān´) [L. AD-, *ratio-ōnem*, reason], *v.t.* To cite before a tribunal; to accuse, charge with fault, find fault with, **arraignment**, *n.* Accusation, charge.

arrange (á-rānj´) [O.F. *à*, to, *rangier*, to range], *v.t.* To draw up in order; to adjust, settle; to plan circumstances in readiness. *v.i.* To make a settlement. **arrangement**, *n.* Settlement, disposition; a grouping of things in a particular way; (*pl.*) preparations.

arrant (ăr´ant), *a.* Notorious, downright, thorough.

arras (ăr´ás), *n.* Tapestry made at Arras; wall hangings.

array (á-rā´) [A.-F. *arayer*], *v.t.* To marshal, dress up, deck. *n.* Order, esp. of battle, troops.

arrear (á-rēr´) [O.F. *arere*, backward], *n.* The state of being behindhand; (*pl.*) that which is unpaid.

arrest (á-rest´) [L. AD-, *restāre*, to stay], *v.t.* To stop; to stay (legal proceedings, etc.); to apprehend, seize by authority. *n.* A stoppage; seizure, detention.

arrive (á-rīv´) [L. AD, *rīpam*, to shore], *v.i.* To come to, reach, attain. **arrival**, *n.* The act of coming to a destination, etc; one who has arrived.

arrogance (ăr´ō-gáns), *n.* The act or quality of being arrogant; undue assumption. **arrogant** (ăr´ō-gánt), *a.* Assuming too much; insolent, haughty.

arrogate (ăr´ō-gāt) [L. *arrogātus*], *v.t.* To put forth unduly exalted claims or baseless pretensions.

arrow (ăr´ō) [A.-S. *arewe*], *n.* A slender, straight missile shot from a bow. **arrow-root**, *n.* A nutritious starch.

arsenal (ar´sen-ál) [Arab. *dār*, house, *al*, the, *çinā'ah*, art, trade], *n.* A place for the manufacture and (or) storage of weapons and ammunition.

arsenic (ar´sé-nik) [Arab. *az-zernikh* (*al*, the, *zernikh*, orpiment], *n.* A brittle, very poisonous semi-metallic element. **arsen'ical**, *a.*

arson (ar´sŏn) [L. *arsus*, burnt], *n.* The wilful setting on fire of property.

art (art) [L. *ars artem*], *n.* Skill, workmanship; skill applied to subjects of taste; the practical application of science; rules for putting principles into practice; craft, artifice; (*pl.*) the subjects in a university course; the faculty concerned with such subjects. **fine arts**: Pursuits in which the mind or imagination is chiefly engaged, as painting, music, sculpture, etc. **artful**, *a.* Characterized by art or skill; crafty, cunning. **artfulness**, *n.* **artless**, *a.* Uncultured, natural; guileless, simple.

artefact (art´é-făkt) [L. *ars*, art; *factus*, made], *n.* (*Archæol.*) Man-made stone implement.

artery (ar´tér-i) [Gr. *arteria*], *n.* A large pulsating vessel conveying blood from the heart; a main channel. **arter'ial**, *a.*

Pertaining to, contained in, or resembling an artery; ramifying. **arterial road**, *n.* Special road for swift traffic between large towns.

Artesian (ar-tē´zhán) well [F. *Artésien*, from *Artois*], *n.* A well made by boring through an upper retentive stratum to a water-bearing stratum, the water rising by natural pressure.

arthritis (ar-thrī´tis) [Gr. *arthron*, a joint, -ITIS], *n.* Disease of the joints.

artichoke (ar´ti-chōk) [It. *articiocco*], *n.* A composite plant of which the receptacle and fleshy bases of the scales are eaten as a vegetable. **Jerusalem artichoke**, *n.* A species of sunflower, the tuberous roots of which are edible.

article (ar´tikl) [L *articulus*, a little joint], *n.* A point of faith or duty; a prose composition, complete in itself; an item, detail; a provision in an agreement, statute, etc.; a thing; the adjectives *a*, *an*, *the*, considered as separate parts of speech; (*pl.*) a formal agreement; terms, conditions.

articulate (ar-tik´ū-lāt), *v.t.* To divide sounds into words and syllables; to utter distinctly; to join together in proper order; to joint. *v.i.* To utter intelligible sounds; speak distinctly. **artic'ulated**, *a.* Jointed. **articula'tion**, *n.* Articulate sound, utterance, speech; a joint or jointed structure.

artifice (ar´ti-fis) [L. *ars artis*, art, *facere*, to make], *n.* Human skill; trickery; a contrivance or trick. **artif'icer**, *n.* A craftsman. **artificial** (-fish'ál), *a.* Made or produced by art; affected in manner. **artificial'ity**, *n.*

artillery (ar-til´ér-i) [O.F. *artiller*, to fortify, equip], *n.* Guns and cannon with their equipment; troops trained in gunnery.

artisan (ar-ti-zăn´) [F.], *n.* One trained to practise a manual art.

artist (ar´tist) [F.], *n.* One who practises any of the fine arts, especially painting; any artistic producer or performer. **artiste** (ar-tēst´) [F.], *n.* A public performer, actor, dancer, musician, acrobat, etc.; a highly proficient cook, hairdresser, etc. **artis'tic**, *a.* Pertaining to art or artists. **artistically**, *adv.*

arum (âr´ŭm) [Gr. *aron*], *n.* A genus of plants, containing the cuckoo-pint.

Aryan (âr´l-án) [Sansk. *ārya*, noble], *a.* Belonging to an ancient race of northern Europe or Central Asia.

as (ăz) [A.-S. *eal swá*, all so], *adv.* and *conj.* In the same manner or degree; thus; while; since, because, that. *rel. pron.* That, who, which.

asafœtida (ăs-á-fet'i-dá) [L. *asa*, mastic, *fœtida*, stinking], *n.* A gum with a strong smell of garlic.

asbestos (ăz-bes'tòs) [Gr. *a-*, not, *sbestos*, from *sbenunai*, to quench], *n.* A variety of hornblende, of fibrous structure, practically incombustible.

ascend (á-send´) [L. AD-, *scandere*, to climb], *v.i.* To rise, to be raised; to slope upwards; to proceed from a lower to a higher plane; to go back in order of time; to come above the horizon. *v.t.* To climb or go up to a higher position, or to the summit or source of; to mount. **ascend'-ancy, ascend'ency,** *n.* Controlling influence; governing power. **ascend'ant, ascend'ent,** *a.* Rising; predominating.

ascension (à-sen'shŭn), *n.* The act of ascending; the ascent of Christ to Heaven; the rising of a celestial body. **ascent** (à-sent'), *n.* The act or process of ascending; upward motion; a slope.

ascertain (ås-er-tān') [O.F.], *v.t.* To find out by investigation or experiment; to make sure of. **ascertainable,** *a.*

ascetic (à-set'ik) [Gr. *askētikos*, given to exercises], *a.* Severely abstinent, austere; practising rigorous self-discipline. *n.* An early hermit who practised rigorous self-denial and mortification, any person given to this. **ascetical,** *a.* **asceticism** (à-set'i-sizm), *n.*

ascribe (à-skrib') [L. AD-, *scribere*, to write], *v.t.* To attribute, impute, assign.

Asdic (as'dik) [initials Allied Submarine Detection Investigation Committee], *n.* (*Naut.*) Device for detecting the location of submarines.

aseptic (à-sep'tik), *a.* Not liable to putrefaction. *n.* An aseptic substance.

ash (1) (ăsh) A.-S. *æsce*], *n.* The remains of anything burnt; (*pl.* ashes) the remains of a cremated body, a symbol of grief or repentance. **Ash-Wednesday,** *n.* The first day of Lent (when the foreheads of the people were sprinkled with ashes). **Ashes, The,** *n. pl.* Symbolic term for the winning of the season's Test Matches between England and Australia. It dates from 1882. **ashy,** *a.* Composed of ashes; whitish-grey; pale.

ash (2) (ăsh) [A.-S. *æsc*], *n.* A forest tree with tough, close-grained wood, its wood. **ashamed** (à-shāmd'), *a.* Affected with shame, abashed by consciousness of error or guilt.

ashen (ăsh'en), *a.* The colour of ashes; pertaining to the ash or made of its wood. **ashlar** (ăsh'lår) [O.F. *aiseler*], *n.* Squarehewn stone.

ashore (à-shôr'), *adv.* To the shore; on the shore; on land.

Asian (ā'shàn), *a.* Pertaining to Asia. *n.* Member of an Asiatic race.

Asiatic (ā-shi-ăt'ik), *a.* Pertaining or belonging to Asia. *n.* A native of Asia.

aside (à-sīd'), *adv.* At or towards one side, away. *n.* Something spoken so as to be audible only to the person addressed.

asinine (ăs'in-īn) [L. *asinus*, an ass], *a.* Having the character of an ass; stupid.

ask (ask) [A.-S. *ascian*], *v.t.* To request, question, solicit; to state a price required; to invite. *v.i.* To make a request; to inquire.

askance (à-skăns'), **askant** (à-skănt') [?], *adv.* Obliquely, sideways.

askew (à-skū), *adv.* Askance; in an oblique direction. *a.* Oblique, awry.

aslant (à-slant'), *adv.* Slantingly, obliquely. *prep.* In a slanting direction.

asleep (à-slēp'), *adv.* and *pred.a.* In or into a state of sleep.

aslope (à-slōp') [A.-S. *aslopen*], *a.* Sloping, oblique. *adv.* With a slope, aslant.

asp (ăsp) [Gr. *aspis*], *n.* A small venomous hooded serpent, the Egyptian cobra.

asparagus (à-spăr'a-gŭs) [Gr. *asparagos*], *n.* A plant, the tender shoots of which are eaten.

aspect (ăs'pekt) [L. *aspectus*, beheld], *n.* Look, view; way of looking; direction in which something is turned; appearance.

aspen (as'pĕn) [A.-S. *æspe*], *n.* The trembling poplar, remarkable for its quivering leaves.

asperity (à-sper'i-ti) [L. *asper*, rough], *n.* Roughness; a rugged excrescence; harshness of sound; bleakness; acrimony.

asperse (à-spērs') [L. *aspersus*, sprinkled], *v.t.* To strew upon, besprinkle; to defame. **aspersion,** *n.* Calumny, slander.

asphalt (ăs'fält) [Gr. *asphalton*], *n.* A dark form of bitumen or an artificial substitute used for paving, etc.

asphodel (ăs'fô-del) [Gr. *asphodelos*], *n.* A mythical undying flower.

asphyxia (ăs-fiks'i-à) [Gr. *a-*, not, *sphuzein*, to pulsate], *n.* Stoppage of the pulse; suspended animation; suffocation. **asphyxial,** *a.* **asphyxiate,** *v.t.* To suffocate.

aspic (ăs'pik) [F.], *n.* A savoury dish of game, etc., with hard-boiled eggs, in jelly.

aspirate (ăs'pi-rāt), *v.t.* To pronounce with a full breath; to prefix the sound of *h.* *a.* Aspirated; pronounced with a breathing. *n.* The sound of *h.* **aspira'tion,** *n.* The act of breathing, aspiring, or aspirating; steadfast desire.

aspire (à-spīr') [L. *ad-, spirāre*, to breathe], *v.i.* To desire eagerly; to seek to attain. **aspiring,** *a.* Eagerly desirous of some high object, ambitious. **aspiringly,** *adv.* **aspir'ant,** *a.* Aiming at a higher position. *n.* A candidate.

ass (ăs) [A.-S. *assa*], *n.* A quadruped allied to the horse, but smaller, with long ears and a tufted tail; (*fig.*) a stupid, obstinate fellow.

assagai (ăs'à-gī) [Arab. *azzaghayah*], *n.* A slender lance of hard wood.

assail (à-sāl') [L. AD-, *salīre*, to leap], *v.t.* To attack violently; to dash against. **assailable,** *a.* **assailant,** *n.* One who assails.

assassin (à-săs'in) [Arab. *hashshāshīn*, hashish-eaters], *n.* One who kills by surprise (generally for other than private motives). **assassinate,** *v.t.* To murder by sudden violence. **assassina'tion,** *n.*

assault (à-sawlt'), *n.* A violent attack; a charge on a fortified post; (*Law*) a threatening word or act. *v.t.* To assail; to make a violent onset or attack on.

assay (à-sā') [O.F. *assai*, L. *exagium* (*ex, out, agere,* to drive, deal)], *n.* Trial, examination; determination of the quantity of metal in an ore, alloy, etc. *v.t.* To try, test; to determine the purity of alloys, etc. *v.i.* To attempt, endeavour. **assayer,** *n.*

assemble (à-sembl') [L.AD-, *simul*, together], *v.t.* To call or bring together into one mass or heap. *v.i.* To meet or come together; to gather. **assemblage,** *n.* A gathering, a concourse. **assembly,** *n.* People met together for some common purpose; a deliberative, legislative, or religious body.

assent (à-sent') [L. *sentīre*, to feel], *v.i.* To sanction (something proposed); to admit (a statement) as true. *n.* Sanction, acquiescence.

assert (à-sĕrt') [L. *serere*, to join, bind], *v.t.* To affirm, declare positively; to insist on a right, etc. **assertion**, *n.* The act of asserting a claim or right; a positive statement. **assertive**, *a.*

assess (à-ses') [L. *sedĕre*, to sit], *v.t.* To fix the amount of a tax, etc.; to value property for the purpose of taxation; to estimate. **assessable**, *a.* Capable of being or liable to be assessed. **assessment**, *n.* The amount assessed; a scheme of rating or taxation; estimation, appraisal. **assessor**, *n.* One who advises a judge on technical points.

assets (ăs'ets) [A.-F. *asetz*, L. *ad satis*, sufficiency], *n.pl.* Goods sufficient to satisfy debts; the effects of an insolvent debtor; property in general.

asseverate (à-sev'ĕr-āt) [L. *sevĕrus*, serious], *v.t.* To affirm with solemnity. **asseveration**, *n.*

assiduous (à-sĭd'ū-ŭs), *a.* Constant in application; diligent. **assiduously**, *adv.* **assidu'ity**, *n.*

assign (à-sīn') [L. *signāre*, to mark], *v.t.* To allot, designate for a specific purpose; to transfer, surrender. *n.* One to whom a property or right is transferred. **assignable**, *a.* Capable of being transferred. **assignation** (ăs-ĭg-nā'shŭn), *n.* The act of assigning; definite appointment for a meeting, esp. an illicit meeting of lovers. **assignee** (ăs-ĭ-nē'). An agent, a representative; (*Law*) one to whom an assignment is made. **assignment** (à-sīn'mĕnt), *n.* The act of assigning; allocation; legal transference; the instrument effecting such transference; the right or property transferred. **assignor** (ăs-ĭ-nŏr'). One who transfers a right or property.

assimilate (ă-sĭm'ĭ-lāt) [L. *similis*, like], *v.t.* To make like to; to digest; to incorporate. *v.i.* To become similar; to be incorporated in the substance of a living organism. **assimila'tion**, *n.*

assist (à-sist') [L. *sistere*, to place], *v.t.* To help, support, further. *v.i.* To give help or aid. **assistance**, *n.* Help, support, succour. **assistant**, *n.*

assize (à-sīz') [F. *asseoir*, to sit at], *n.* A statute regulating weight and price, hence standard of quantity, price, or quality, esp. of bread and ale; (*pl.*) sessions held periodically by judges in each county for the administration of justice.

associate (à-sō'shi-āt) [L. *sociāre*, to join], *v.t.* To join for a common purpose; to combine. *v.i.* To keep company or have familiar intercourse with. *a.* Connected, allied; in the same category. *n.* An ally, colleague; member of an association. **associa'tion**, *n.* The act of associating; a society for the promotion of some common object; fellowship.

assoil (à-soil') [L. *ab-, solvere*, to loosen], *v.t.* To absolve.

assonant (ăs'ŏ-nănt) [L. *sonāre*, to sound], *a.* Rhyming in the accented vowels, but not in the consonants.

assort (à-sŏrt') [F. *à, to, sorte*, sort], *v.t.* To arrange or dispose in sorts or lots. *v.i.* To suit, to agree, match. **assortment**, *n.* A collection of things assorted.

assuage (à-swāj') [L. *suavis*, sweet], *v.t.* To allay, mitigate, lessen the violence of. **assuagement**, *n.* Mitigation.

assume (à-sūm') [L. *sūmere*, to take], *v.t.* To take upon oneself; to arrogate, claim; take for granted. *v.i.* To be arrogant; to claim more than is due. **assumed**, *a.* Usurped; taken for granted. **assumedly**, *adv.* assuming, *a.* Arrogant, haughty. **assump'tion**, *n.* The act of assuming; the thing assumed; supposition; ascent to Heaven, esp. of the Virgin Mary (commemorated Aug. 15).

assure (à-shoor') [L. *sēcūrus*, safe], *v.t.* To make secure, give confidence to, insure the payment of compensation in case of loss. **assurance** (à-shoor'ăns), *n.* Act of assuring; positive declaration; security; audacity, impudence; insurance. **assured**, *a.* Safe; made certain.

aster (as-, ăs-tėr) [Gr. *astēr*, a star], *n.* A genus of plants.

asterisk (ăs'tėr-isk) [Gr. *asteriskos*], *n.* A printers' mark (*) used to call attention to a note, etc.

astern (à-stėrn'), *adv.* In, at, or towards the hinder part of a ship.

asteroid (ăs'tėr-oid) [Gr. *astēr*, star], *n.* (*Astron.*) A minor planet between the orbits of Mars and Jupiter.

asthma (ăs'mà) [Gr. *azein*, to breathe hard], *n.* A disease of respiration characterized by cough, wheezing, and constriction of the chest. **asthmat'ic**, *a.*

astigmatism (à-stig'mà-tizm) [Gr. *a-*, not, *stigma*, point], *n.* A defect of the eye which prevents the convergence of rays of light at a point on the retina. **astigmat'ic**, *a.*

astir (à-stėr'), *adv.* and *pred.a.* In motion; in excitement; out of bed.

astonish (à-ston'ish) [O.F. *estoner*, to amaze], *v.t.* To strike with sudden wonder; to surprise. **astonishing**, *a* astonishingly, *adv.* **astonishment**, *n.*

astound (à-stound') [M.E. *astoned*], *v.t.* To strike with amazement. **astounding**, *a.*

astrakhan (ăs-trà-kăn'), *n.* A fine kind of furry lamb's wool, from Astrakhan and Persia.

astral (ăs'tràl) [Gr. *aster*, a star], *a.* Pertaining to the stars. **astral body**, *n.* A spiritual body which occultists claim to be able to project to a distance.

astray (à-strā') [prob. O.F. *estraié*, strayed], *adv.* and *pred.a.* Out of the right way.

astride (à-strid'), *adv.* and *pred.a.* With legs apart or on either side. *prep.* Astride of.

astringent (à-strinj'ĕnt) [L. *stringere*, to bind], *a.* (*Med.*) Contracting muscular fibre; binding, styptic. **astringency**, *n.*

astrology (à-strol'ŏ-ji) [Gr. *astron*, star, *logia*, -LOGY], *n.* The art of foretelling pretended events from the position of the stars; their occult influence on human affairs. **astrologer**, *n.* One versed in this.

astronaut (ăs'-trō-nawt), *n.* One borne into space beyond the earth's atmosphere in a projectile.

astronomy (à-stron'ŏ-mi) [Gr. *astron*, star,

nemein, to arrange], *n*. The science which treats of the phenomena of the heavenly bodies, and of the earth in relation to them. **astronomer**, *n*. One versed in this. **astronom′ical**, *a*.

astute (á-stūt′) [L. *astūtus*, crafty], *a*. Acute, shrewd, cunning. **astuteness**, *n*.

asunder (á-sŭn′dẽr) [A.-S. *onsundran*], *adv*. Apart, separately, in different pieces.

asylum (á-sī′lŭm) [Gr. *asūlos*, inviolable], *n*. A place of refuge, a sanctuary; an institution affording relief and shelter to the afflicted, the destitute, or the insane.

at (ăt) [A.-S. *æt*], *prep*. Denoting nearness in time, space, etc.

atavism (ăt′á-vizm) [L. *atavus*, an ancestor], *n*. Reversion to some ancestral peculiarity. **atavis′tic**, *a*.

ate (et), *pret*. [EAT].

-ate [L.], *suf*. (1) Forming nouns of office or function, *e.g. curate, aldermanate;* participial nouns, *e.g. delegate, mandate;* salts of acids, *e.g. acetate, carbonate;* (2) participial adjectives, *e.g. desolate, situate;* and other adjectives formed by analogy, *e.g. roseate, ovate;* (3) forming verbs, *e.g. separate, isolate*.

atelier (átel′iā) [F.], *n*. A workshop, studio.

atheism (ā′thē-izm) [Gr. *a-*, not, *theos*, God], *n*. Disbelief in God. **atheist**, *n*. One who disbelieves, or denies, the existence of God. **atheis′tic**, *a*.

athirst (á-thẽrst′) [A.-S. *ofthyrst*], *a*. Thirsty, oppressed with thirst; (*fig.*) eager.

athlete (ăth′lēt) [Gr. *athlētēs* (*athlein*, to contend)], *n*. One trained to perform feats of strength and activity; a powerful, vigorous man. **athlet′ic**, *a*. Pertaining to contests requiring strength and activity; muscular, robust. **athletics**, *n*. Physical exercises by which muscular strength is developed.

athwart (á-thwôrt′), *prep*. From side to side of, across. *adv*. Transversely, crosswise, awry.

-atic, *suf*. Forming adjectives, *e.g. aquatic*.

-atile, *suf*. Forming adjectives chiefly denoting possibility or quality, *e.g. volatile*.

-ation, *suf*. Forming abstract nouns from verbs, *e.g. agitation, appreciation*.

-ative, *suf*. Forming adjectives, *e.g. demonstrative, representative*.

atlas (ăt′lás) [Gr. *Atlas*, fabled to uphold the universe], *n*. A collection of maps in a volume. **atlante′an**, *a*. Of colossal size.

atmosphere (ăt-mó-sfēr) [Gr. *atmos*, vapour, *sphaira*, a ball], *n*. The gaseous envelope surrounding the earth or a heavenly body; (*fig.*) mental or moral environment. **atmospher′ic**, **-ical**, *a*. **atmospherics**, *n.pl.* (*Rad.*) Electro-magnetic waves in the ether.

atoll (á-tol′, ăt′ŏl) [Maldive], *n*. A coral island, a reef surrounding a lagoon.

atom (ăt′ŏm) [Gr. *atomos*, indivisible], *n*. The smallest conceivable portion of anything; a body incapable of further division, one of the supposed ultimate particles of matter. **atom bomb**, *n*. Bomb in which the explosion is due to atomic energy. **atom′ic**, *a*. **atomic energy**, *n*. (*Phys.*) Energy liberated when the power emanating from the

atomic structure of all elements is released. **atomizer**, *n*. A spray for disinfecting, etc.

atone (á-tōn′) [AT ONE], *v.i.* To make expiation or satisfaction. **atonement**, *n*. Expiation, amends, reconciliation; the Redemption.

atop (á-top′), *adv*. On or at the top.

atrabilious (ăt-rá-bil′i-ús) [L. *ātra bīlis*, black bile], *a*. Melancholy, splenetic, bitter-tempered. **atrabiliar**, *a*.

a-trip (á-trip′), *adv*. Just drawn out of the ground at right angles to it (of an anchor); hoisted as high as possible (of the topsails).

atrocious (á-trō′shŭs) [L. *atrox*], *a*. Savagely and wantonly cruel, fierce, violent; characterized by heinous wickedness. **atrociously**, *adv*. **atrocity** (á-tros′i-ti), *n*. Excessive cruelty; an atrocious act.

atrophy (ăt′rô-fi) [Gr., *a-*, not, *trephein*, to nourish], *n*. A wasting of the bodily organs through want of nourishment or disease. *v.i.* To waste away.

attach (á-tăch′) [O.F. *atachier*], *v.t.* To fasten on, connect; to seize, arrest. *v.i.* To adhere to. **attaché** (á-tăsh′ā) [F.], *n*. One attached to the suite of an ambassador. **attaché case**, *n*. Case for carrying papers, etc. **attachment**, *n*. The act of attaching; means by which a thing is attached; connexion; fidelity, affection; a thing attached.

attack (á-tăk′) [F. *attaquer*], *v.t.* To fall upon with force of arms; to assail by hostile words, etc.; to begin a work. *n*. The act of attacking; an onset, an assault; violent abuse; fit of illness.

attain (á-tān′) [L. AD-, *tangere*, to touch], *v.i.* To arrive at some object. *v.t.* To reach, gain; arrive at; accomplish. **attainment**, *n*.

attainder (á-tān′dẽr) [O.F. *ataindre*], *n*. The extinction of civil rights for some crime; the act or process of attainting a criminal; the state of being so attainted. **attaint′**, *v.t.* To condemn or subject to attainder; to accuse.

attar (ăt′ár) [Pers. *′atar*, essence], *n*. Fragrant essence, esp. of roses.

attempt (á-temt′) [L. *tentāre*, to strive after], *v.t.* To try, endeavour; to attack; to make trial of. *n*. An endeavour; an effort as contrasted with attainment.

attend (á-tend′) [L. *tendere*, to stretch], *v.t.* To turn the thoughts towards; to accompany, wait upon; to be present at. *v.i.* To pay attention, be in attendance; to wait upon or for a person. **attendance**, *n*. **attendant**, *a*. Accompanying. *n*. One who attends or accompanies.

attention (á-ten′shŭn), *n*. The act, state, or mental faculty of attending; an act of courtesy or love (*often pl.*); military attitude of readiness. **attentive**, *a*. Heedful; polite, courteous. **attentively**, *adv*. **attentiveness**, *n*.

attenuate (á-ten′ū-āt) [L. *tenuis*, thin], *v.t.* To make thin or slender; to dilute.

attest (á-test′) [L. *testis*, a witness], *v.t.* To testify (esp. in a formal manner); to put a person on his oath. *v.i.* To bear witness. *n*. Evidence, attestation. **attesta′tion**, *n*. The act of attesting;

formal confirmation; the administration of an oath. attes'tor, *n.*

Attic (1) (ăt'ik) [Gr. *Attikos*], *a.* Of or belonging to Attica or its capital, Athens; classical, refined; witty. *n.* A native of Attica; the Attic dialect.

attic (2) (ăt'ik) [F. *attique*], *n.* A room in the top story of a house.

attire (ȧ-tīr') [O.F. *atirer*], *v.t.* To dress; to array. *n.* Dress, clothes.

attitude (ăt'i-tūd) [It. *attitudine*], *n.* Posture; disposition of things; behaviour indicating opinion and sentiment. attitu'dinize, *v.i.* To pose; to behave affectedly.

attorney (ȧ-tẽr'ni) [O.F. *atorné*], *n.* A qualified practitioner in the Common Law courts, who prepares the case for counsel; a solicitor of the Supreme Court.

attract (ȧ-trăkt') [L. *tractus*, drawn], *v.t.* To draw to or cause to approach; to allure. *v.i.* To exert the power of attraction, to be attractive. attractable, *a.* That may be attracted. attraction, *n.* The action or power of attracting; that which attracts. attractive, *a.*

attribute (ăt'ri-būt) [L. *tribuere*, to give], *n.* A quality ascribed to any person or thing, as an essential characteristic; a characteristic; an attributive word. attribute (ȧ-trib'ūt), *v.t.* To ascribe; to impute as belonging or due to. attributable, *a.* attribu'tion, *n.*

attrition (ȧ-trish'ŭn) [L. *terere*, to rub], *n.* The act or process of rubbing away; abrasion.

attune (ȧ-tūn'), *v.t.* To put in tune, or make tuneful; render accordant.

auburn (aw'bẽrn) [O.F. *auborne*, L. *alburnus*, whitish], *a.* Ruddy brown; golden brown.

auction (awk'shŭn) [L. *auctus*, increased], *n.* A public sale in which each bidder offers a higher price than the preceding. *v.t.* To sell by auction. auctioneer', *n.* A person who sells by auction.

audacious (aw-dā'shŭs) [L. *audax*, daring], *a.* Bold, spirited; impudent, shameless. audaciously, *adv.* audac'ity, *n.* Courage; impudence.

audible (aw'dibl) [L. *audīre*, to hear], *a.* Capable of being heard. audibil'ity, *n.*

audience (aw'dyĕns), *n.* The act of hearing; an assemblage of hearers; reception at a formal interview.

audit (aw'dit) [L. *audītus*, hearing], *n.* An official examination of accounts. *v.t.* To examine officially and pronounce as to the accuracy of (accounts). auditor, *n.* One of an audience; one appointed to audit accounts. auditor'ium, *n.* The part of a building occupied by the audience. au'ditory, *a.* Pertaining to the organs of hearing; perceived by the ear.

auger (aw'gẽr) [A.-S. *nafugār*], *n.* A tool like a very large gimlet, for boring holes.

aught (awt) [A.-S. *āwiht*], *n.* Anything whatever; a whit, a jot, or tittle. *adv.* In any respect.

augment (awg-ment') [L. *augēre*, to increase], *v.t.* To make larger in number, degree, etc.; to extend, enlarge; to prefix a grammatical inflexion to. *v.i.* To increase; to become greater. augmenta'-tion, *n.* augmen'tative, *a.* Having the power or quality of augmenting; increasing the force of a word (of an affix); extending the force of an idea (of a word).

augur (aw'gŭr) [L.], *n.* An official among the Romans who foretold future events from omens; a soothsayer, a diviner. *v.t.* To prognosticate from omens; to betoken, portend. *v.i.* To forbode, anticipate. au'gury, *n.* The art or practice of the augur; an omen.

august (aw-gŭst') [L. *augustus*, honoured], *a.* Majestic, stately, inspiring reverence. August (aw'gŭst), *n.* The eighth month of the year. Augustan, *a.* Pertaining to the time of Augustus Cæsar (B.C. 27–A.D. 14), when Latin literature reached its highest development; classical.

auk (awk) [Swed. *alka*, a puffin], *n.* A northern sea-bird with rudimentary wings.

aulic (aw'lik) [Gr. *aulikos*], *a.* Pertaining to a royal court; courtly.

aunt (ant) [O.F. *aunte*], *n.* The sister of one's father or mother; one's uncle's wife.

aura (aw'rȧ) [Gr. breath], *n.* A subtle emanation from any body.

aural (aw'rȧl) [L. *auris*, ear], *a.* Pertaining to the ear.

aureate (aw'rē-ȧt) [late L. *aureātus*, golden], *a.* Golden, gold-coloured; (*fig.*) splendid.

aureola (aw-rē'ō-lȧ) [L. golden], *n.* The crown of virgins, martyrs and doctors; an aureole. au'reole, *n.* The gold disk surrounding the head in early pictures, denoting glory; a nimbus, glory.

auricle (aw'rikl) [L. dim. of *auris*, ear], *n.* The external ear; the two upper cavities of the heart. auric'ula, *n.* A garden flower allied to the primrose. auric'ular, *a.* Pertaining to the sense of hearing, or to an auricle of the heart.

auriferous (aw-rif'ẽr-ŭs) [L. *aurum*, gold, *-fer*, producing], *a.* Yielding gold.

aurora (aw-rōr'ȧ) [L.], *n.* The Roman goddess of dawn; morning twilight; dawn; illumination of the night sky common within the polar circles, called aurora borealis or aurora australis, as it is seen near the North or South Pole.

auscultation (aws-kŭl-tā'shŭn) [L. *auscultāre*, to listen], *n.* The act of listening esp. with the stethoscope to the sounds made by the internal organs.

auspices (aw'spi-sēz) [L. *auspicies*], *n.* Omens drawn from the actions of birds; a prognostication; (*fig.*) patronage, protection. auspic'ious, *a.* Auguring good fortune; conducive to prosperity.

austere (aw-stẽr') [Gr. *austĕros*, dry, harsh], *a.* Severe, stern, rigorous; rough to the taste; simple, unadorned. ·auster'ity, *n.*

austral (aw'strȧl) [L. *auster*, south wind], *a.* Pertaining to the south; southern.

autarchy (aw'tar-ki) [AUTO-, *archein*, to rule], *n.* Absolute sovereignty.

autarky (aw'tar-ki) [Gr. *autarkein*], *n.* Self-sufficiency.

authentic (aw-then'tik) [Gr. *authentikos*, vouched for], *a.* Of undisputed origin, genuine; really proceeding from its professed source. authenticate, *v.t.* To render authentic; to establish the truth or credibility of. authentic'ity, *n.*

author (aw'thŏr) [L. *auctor* (from *augere*, to make to grow)], *n.* The originator of anything; the composer of a literary work. authoress, *n.* A female author. authorship, *n.* The profession of a writer of books; the origin of a literary work.

authority (aw-thor'ĭ-tĭ) [L. *auctoritātem*], *n.* Legitimate power to command or act; a person or body exercising this power; weight of testimony, credibility; the author or source of a statement; the standard work on any subject; an expert. authoritarian, *n.* One who places obedience to authority above personal liberty. authoritative, *a.* Commanding; possessed of or founded ●n authority. authoritatively, *adv.* au'thorize, *v.t.* To empower; to sanction; to justify, afford just ground for; to make or prove legitimate; to vouch for, confirm. authorized, *a.* authoriza'tion, *n.*

auto- [Gr. *autos*, self], *comb. form.* Self; by oneself; one's own, independently.

autobiography (aw-tŏ-bī-og'rȧ-fĭ), *n.* A memoir of one's life, written by oneself. autobiographer, *n.* One who writes an account of his own life. autobiograph'ic, autobiograph'ical, *a.* autobiograph'ically, *adv.*

autocracy (aw-tok'rȧ-sĭ) [Gr. *krateein*, to rule], *n.* Absolute government. au'tocrat, *n.* A sovereign of uncontrolled authority. autocrat'ic, *a.*

autocycle, *n.* Push-bicycle with motor attachment.

auto-da-fé (aw-tŏ-da-fā) [Port., action for the faith], *n.* The burning of a heretic.

autograph (aw'tŏ-gräf) [Gr. *graphein*, to write], *n.* A person's own handwriting, esp. his signature.

automatic (aw-tŏ-măt'ĭk) [Gr. *automatos*, acting of itself], *a.* Self-acting; having the power of movement within itself; carried on unconsciously. autom'atism, *n.*

automaton (aw-tom'ȧ-tŏn) [Gr., neut. of *automatos*], *n.* (*pl.* -ata). Mechanism simulating human or animal action; one whose actions are merely mechanical.

automobile (aw-tŏ-mō-bēl') [L. *mōbilis*, moving], *n.* A motor-car.

autonomy (aw-ton'ŏ-mi) [Gr. *nomos*, law], *n.* The right of self-government; an independent community. auton'omous, *a.* Possessing autonomy.

autopsy (aw'tŏp-sĭ) [Gr. *opsis*, sight], *n.* Personal observation; dissection; postmortem examination.

autosuggestion, *n.* Suggestion arising from oneself, esp. hypnotic or morbid suggestion.

autumn (aw'tŭm) [L. *autumnus*], *n.* The season between summer and winter. autum'nal, *a.*

auxiliary (awg-zil'ĭ-ȧ-rĭ) [L. *auxilium*, help], *a.* Helping; subsidiary to; an auxiliary verb. *n.* One who or that which helps; a verb used in the conjugation of other verbs; (*pl.*) foreign troops in the service of a nation at war.

avail (ȧ-vāl') [O.F. *vail*, 1st pers. pres. sing. of *valoir*, to be worth], *v.i.* To be of use, or advant*r*ge; to be helpful, effectual,

sufficient. *v.t.* To be of use (to). available, *a.* Capable of being used; at one's disposal.

avalanche (ăv'ȧ-lansh) [Swiss-F., from *avaler*, to descend to the valley], *n.* A mass of snow, ice, and debris sliding from the upper parts of a mountain.

avarice (ăv'ȧ-ris) [L. *avārus*, greedy], *n.* Excessive craving after wealth; eager desire to get and keep. avaric'ious, *a.*

avast (ȧ-vast') [prob. Dut.], *int.* (*Naut.*) Stay! Stop!

avatar (av-ȧ-tar') [Sansk. *avatara*, descent], *n.* The descent or incarnation of a deity; (*fig.*) manifestation, phase.

avaunt (ȧ-vawnt') [F., before], *int.* Be off! Away with you! Begone!

ave (a'vi, ā'vi)[L., hail!], *int.* Hail! Welcome! *n.* A prayer beginning Ave Maria; a shout of welcome or adieu.

avenge (ȧ-venj') [O.F. ȧ, to, *vengier*, revenge], *v.t.* To vindicate by punishing a wrong-doer; to inflict punishment on account of. avenger, *n.*

avenue (ăv'ė-nū) [F., *avenir*, to come to], *n.* A means of access or approach; a broad alley bordered with trees.

aver (ȧ-vĕr') [L. *verum*, truth], *v.t.* To assert positively; to declare. averment, *n.* The act of averring; affirmation.

average (ăv'er-ȧj) [F. *avarie*], *n.* A quantity intermediate to several different quantities; a mean; the rate, proportion, degree, quantity, or number generally prevailing. *a.* Medium, ordinary. *v.t.* To calculate the average; to take the ordinary standard.

averse (ȧ-vĕrs') [L. *a-*, *ab-*, away, *vertere*, to turn], *a.* Feeling dislike; unwilling, disinclined. aversely, *adv.* averseness, *n.* aversion, *n.* Disinclination, repugnance; an object of dislike.

avert (ȧ-vĕrt'), *v.t.* To turn from or away (used esp. of something feared or threatened); to ward off.

aviary (ā'vi-ȧri) [L. *avis*, a bird], *n.* A large cage or building for birds.

aviation (ā-vi-ā'shŭn), *n.* The art of flying, or of travelling in the air by mechanical means. aviator, *n.* A person skilled in managing flying-machines.

avid (ăv'id) [L. *avidus*, greedy], *a.* Greedy, ardently desirous. avid'ity, *n.*

avocation (ăv-ō-kā'shŭn) [L. *ā-*, *ab-*, away, *vocāre*, to call], *n.* Ordinary employment, calling, business.

avoid (ȧ-void') [O.F. *es-*, out, *vuidier*, to void], *v.t.* To shun; keep away from; evade. avoidable, *a.* avoidably, *adv.*

avoirdupois (ăv'ėr-de-poiz) [O.F. *avoir* (*aveir*) *de pois*, things of weight], *n.* The system of weights based on the unit of a pound of 16 ounces.

avouch (ȧ-vouch') [L. *vocāre*, to call], *v.t.* To affirm, guarantee; to avow.

avow (ȧ-vou'), *v.t.* To own, admit; to state, declare. avowal, *n.* An open declaration. avowed, *a.* Acknowledged.

avuncular (ȧ-vŭng'kū-lȧr) [L. *avunculus*, a maternal uncle], *a.* Pertaining to an uncle, or (*slang*) to a pawnbroker.

await (ȧ-wāt') [O.N.F. *awaitier*, to lie in wait for], *v.t.* To wait for, look out for, expect; to be in store for.

awake (á-wāk´) [A.-S.], *v.i.* To wake from sleep; to become alive to (anything); to become active or alert. *v.t.* To arouse from sleep, or from lethargy or inaction; to excite to action. *a.* Not asleep; vigilant, aware of, alive to (some object). **awaken,** *v.t.* To awake.

award (á-wôrd´) [A.-F. *awarder*], *v.t.* To adjudge, to assign judicially. *n.* The decision of judge or umpire.

aware (á-wâr´) [A.-S. *gewær*], *a.* Apprised, conscious; watchful, vigilant.

away (á-wā´) [A.-S. *onweg*, on the way], *adv.* Implying motion from; absent, in the other direction; constantly; straightway. Used elliptically as a verb, Be off!

awe (aw) [Icel. *agi*], *n.* Dread mingled with veneration; solemn, reverential wonder. **awesome,** *a.* Full of awe.

awful (aw-ful), *a.* Inspiring awe; sublime; dreadful, fearful, appalling; (*colloq.*) frightful, terrible; often as a mere intensive. **awfully,** *adv.*

awhile (á-whil´) [A.-S. *āne while*], *adv.* For some time; for a little.

awkward (awk´wárd) [M.E. *awk*, contrary, untoward, -WARD], *a.* Unhandy; lacking dexterity, ill adapted for use; embarrassed.

awl (awl) [A.-S. *æl*], *n.* A small tool used for making holes in leather.

awn (awn) [Icel. *ögn*, chaff], *n.* The beard of corn and grasses.

awning (aw´ning) [?], *n.* A covering of canvas or other material used as a protection from sun or rain.

awry (á-rī), *adv.* Obliquely, crookedly; amiss. *a.* Distorted; wrong.

axe (ăks) [A.-S. *æx*], *n.* A sharp-edged iron instrument with a wooden handle, for hewing or chopping.

axillar, axillary (ăk´sil-ár, -ár-i), [L. *axilla*, an armpit], *a.* Pertaining to the armpit.

axiom (ăk-si-óm) [Gr. *axioō*, I esteem], *n.* A self-evident proposition, assented to as soon as enunciated. **axiomat´ic,** *a.* Self-evident, containing an axiom or axioms; full of maxims.

axis (ăk´sis) [L., the axle], *n.* (*pl.* axes). A real or imaginary straight line round which a body revolves or its parts are arranged; the second cervical vertebra, or the process on it by which it articulates with the skull. **Axis, The,** *n.* (*Pol.*) Political collaboration between Nazi Germany and Fascist Italy, 1935-43.

axle (ăksl) [Icel. *öxull*, L. *axis*], *n.* The bar on which a wheel revolves, or which revolves with the wheel; the axle-tree. **axle-tree,** *n.* The bar connecting wheels, on the ends of which they revolve.

ay, aye (1) (ī) [?], *adv., int.* Yes. *n.* An affirmative vote; (*pl.*) those who vote in the affirmative.

ayah (ī´á) [Indian vernacular *āya*], *n.* A native Hindu nurse or lady's-maid.

aye (2) (ā) [M.E. *ay* (cogn. with Gr. *aei*)], *adv.* Always, ever, on all occasions.

azalea (á-zā´lē-á) [Gr. *azaleos*, dry], *n.* A genus of shrubby plants with showy flowers.

azure (ăzh´ér, ăzh´ūr) [Pers. *lāzhward*, lapis lazuli], *n.* The deep blue of the sky.

B

baa (ba) [Imit.], *n.* The bleat of a sheep. *v.i.* To cry or bleat as a sheep.

babble (băbl) [from *ba ba*, the earliest attempts of a child to speak], *v.i.* To utter indistinct sounds; to prattle; to make inarticulate sounds (of streams, birds, etc.). *v.t.* To prate; to utter idly. *n.* Shallow, foolish talk; confused murmur, as of a brook. **babbler,** *n.*

babe (bāb) [prob. from obs. *baban*, imit. from childish speech], *n.* A baby.

babel (bā´bél) [Heb., confusion], *n.* Noisy confusion, tumult, disorder.

baboo (ba´boo) [Hind. *babu*], *n.* A term corresponding in Bengal to English *Mr.*; an Indian clerk who writes English.

baboon (bá-boon´) [?], *n.* A large monkey with dog-like snout.

baby (bā´bi), *n.* An infant; a child in arms; (*fig.*) a foolish, childish person. **babyhood,** *n.* **babyish,** *a.*

baccara, baccarat (băk´á-ra) [F.], *n.* A game of cards.

bacchanal (băk´á-nál) [L. (*Bacchus*, the god of wine)], *a.* Pertaining to Bacchus, characterized by drunken revelry. *n.* A drunken reveller. **bacchanalian,** *a.* Bacchanal, *n.* A drunken reveller.

bachelor (băch´él-ór) [O.F. *bacheler*], *n.* An unmarried man; one who has taken the university degree below master or doctor. **bachelorhood, bachelorship,** *n.*

bacillus (bá-sil´ús) [late L., a little rod], *n.* (*pl.* bacilli). Microscopic rod-like bacteria, found in diseased tissue.

back (băk) [A.-S. *bæc*], *n.* The hinder part of the human body and the corresponding part in the lower animals; the hinder part of anything, the rear; (*Football*) one of the players who defends the goal. *adv.* In a direction to the rear. *v.t.* To furnish with a back; to be at the back of; to support, second, uphold; to bet in favour of; to mount; to countersign, endorse; to push or cause to move back. *v.i.* To retreat. **backbite,** *v.t.* and *i.* To slander or speak ill of. **backbiter,** *n.* **backbone,** *n.* The spine; a main support; strength of character, firmness. **backer,** *n.* One who supports, by money or credit; one who bets on a horse or an event. **background,** *n.* The ground or surface behind the chief objects of contemplation; the setting; (*fig.*) inferior position; obscurity. **backroom boys,** *n.pl.* (*Coll.*) Scientists who work in the background, unrecognized and unknown. **backslide,** *v.i.* To fall into wrong-doing or false opinions after conversion; to relapse. **backslider,** *n.* **backstage,** *n.* (*Theat.*) Behind the scenes. **backstairs,** *n.pl.* Stairs at the back of a house; private stairs for use of servants, etc. *a.* Clandestine, underhand, scandalous. **backstays,** *n.pl.* Ropes or stays extending with a slant aft from the mast-heads to the sides of the ship. **backwoods,** *n.pl.* Remote, uncleared forest land. **backwoodsman,** *n.* A settler in these; a man living remote from everyday life. **backing,** *n.* Support, esp. financial.

backgammon (băk-găm'ŏn), *n.* A game for two, played on a table with draughtsmen and dice.

backward, -wards (băk'wård, -z), *adv.* Towards the back; behind; towards past time or a worse state or condition; in reverse order. **backward,** *a.* Directed to the back or rear; reversed, reluctant, unwilling; behind in progress.

bacon (bā'kŏn) [O.H.G. *bacho,* buttock, ham], *n.* The back and sides of a pig, cured by salting and drying.

bacterium (băk-tēr'ĭ-ŭm) [Gr. *baktērion,* a little stick], *n.* (*pl.* bacteria). Microscopic fission fungi, rod-shaped and unicellular; found in decomposing infusions of organic bodies. **bacterial,** *a.* **bacteriol'ogy,** *n.* The scientific study of bacteria. **bacteriol'ogist,** *n.* **bacteriological warfare,** *n.* Dropping of disease bacteria among hostile troops or in enemy country.

bad (băd) [?], *a.* (comp. worse, superl. worst). Not good, worthless; evil, wicked. **baddish,** *a.* Rather bad. **badly,** *adv.* (comp. worse, superl. worst). In a bad manner; evilly; unskilfully; (*colloq.*) very much. **badness,** *n.*

badge (băj) [?], *n.* A distinctive sign or token worn.

badger (băj'ĕr) [?], *n.* A burrowing, nocturnal quadruped. *v.t.* To tease.

badinage (băd'ĭ'nazh) [F., from *badiner,* to jest], *n.* Light raillery; banter.

badminton (băd'mĭn-tŏn) [country seat of Duke of Beaufort], *n.* A game resembling lawn-tennis, played with shuttlecocks.

baffle (băfl) [perh. F. *bafouer,* to hoodwink], *v.t.* To frustrate, elude, thwart. *n.* (*Acous.*) A rigid appliance that regulates the distribution of sound waves from a producer. **baffling,** *a.*

bag (băg) [?], *n.* A small sack or other flexible receptacle; a game-bag, the result of a day's sport. *v.t.* To put into a bag; (*slang*) to catch, take. *v.i.* To swell as a bag; hang loosely. **bagpipe,** *n.* A musical instrument consisting of a windbag and several reed-pipes into which the air is pressed.

bagatelle (băg-ă-tel') [It. *bagatella,* a trifle], *n.* A trifle, a trumpery amount; a game played on a nine-holed board, with nine balls and a cue.

baggage (băg'ăj) [O.F. *bagage;* It. *baga,* a wine-skin], *n.* Portable belongings esp. of an army or for use on a journey; (*hum.*) a saucy girl.

bail (bāl) [O.F. *bail,* safe keeping], *n.* The release of a prisoner from custody on security; the security, or those who give it; guarantee; (*Cricket, pl.*) the crosspieces laid on the top of the wicket. *v.t.* To procure the liberation of by giving sureties; to release on bail. To empty a boat of water. **bail out,** *v.i.* (*Av.*) To jump from an aeroplane in the air and descend by parachute. **bailee** (bā-lē'), *n.* One to whom goods are entrusted.

bailey (bā'lĭ) [?], *n.* The outer court of a feudal castle.

Bailey bridge [name of inventor], *n.* A steel bridge of standard parts for rapid erection and transport.

bailiff (bā'lĭf), *n.* A sheriff's officer who executes writs and distrains; an agent or steward.

bairn (bârn) [A.-S.], *n.* A child.

bait (bāt) [Icel. *bita,* to bite], *v.t.* To furnish (a hook, trap, etc.) with real or sham food; to allure; to give food to a horse; to worry, harass.' *v.i.* To stop on a journey for rest or refreshment. *n.* An attraction put on a hook, etc.

baize (bāz) [F. *baies,* chestnut-coloured], *n.* A coarse woollen stuff like flannel.

bake (bāk) [A.-S. *bacan*], *v.t.* To cook by dry heat, in an oven or on a heated surface; to harden by fire or the sun's rays. *v.i.* To cook food by baking; to undergo the process; to become dry and hard by heat. **baker,** *n.* One whose occupation is to bake. **bakery,** *n.* A baker's establishment.

bakelite (bā'ke-līt) [L. H. *Baekeland,* inventor], *n.* Protected trade name of synthetic resin used for insulating purposes, plastics, etc.

balance (băl'ăns) [L. *bi,* two, *lanx,* a flat plate], *n.* A pair of scales, or any instrument for weighing; a regulator for clocks, etc.; equipoise, equality of weight or power; the amount necessary to make two unequal amounts equal; the difference between the debtor and creditor side of an account; an impartial state of mind. *v.t.* To weigh; compare by weighing; bring to an equipoise. *v.i.* To be in equipoise; to oscillate. **balancer meal,** *n.* Poultry meal with nutritive ingredients.

balcony (băl'kŏ-nĭ) [It. *balcone*], *n.* A platform projecting from a wall.

bald (bawld) [?], *a.* Without hair upon the crown of the head; bare; destitute of ornament or grace. **bald-faced,** *a.* Having the face marked with white. **baldly,** *adv.* In a bald manner; shamelessly, inelegantly. **baldness,** *n.*

baldachin, -quin (bawld'ă-kin) [It.], *n.* Canopy over an altar.

balderdash (bawl'dĕr-dăsh) [?], *n.* A confused speech or writing.

bale (1) (bāl) [A.-S. *bealo*], *n.* Evil, calamity; pain, misery. **baleful,** *a.*

bale (2) (bāl) [O.F. *bale*], *n.* A package of goods, wrapped and ready for transportation.

balk, baulk (bawk) [A.-S. *balca,* a ridge], *n.* A ridge of land left unploughed; a beam of timber; the part of a billiard table behind a transverse line; an obstacle, a hindrance, disappointment. *v.t.* To check, hinder; to disappoint, evade, frustrate. *v.i.* To turn aside.

ball (1) (bawl) [M.E. *balle*], *n.* A spherical body of any dimensions.

ball (2) (bawl) [F. *bal*], *n.* A social assembly for dancing.

ballad (băl'ăd) [O.F. *balade*], *n.* A popular song; a simple spirited poem telling a story.

ballade (bă-lad') [F., see prec.], *n.* A poem consisting of three eight-lined stanzas, rhyming a b a b b c b c, each having the same line as a refrain, and with an envoy of four lines.

ballast (băl'ăst) [Scand. *bar*, bare, *last*, load], *n.* Heavy substances placed in the bottom of a ship to keep her steady; gravel or other material laid as foundation for a road; that which tends to give intellectual or moral stability.

ballet (băl'ā) [F.], *n.* A dramatic representation, consisting of dancing and pantomime.

ballistics (bă-lis'tiks) [Gr. *ballein*, to throw], *n.pl.* The science of projectiles.

balloon (bă-loon') [It. *ballone*, a large ball], *n.* A spherical or pear-shaped bag of light material, which when filled with heated air or hydrogen rises and floats, often with a car attached capable of containing several persons. **balloon barrage**, *n.* A line or series of captive balloons employed as a defence against hostile aircraft. **ballooning**, *n.* The practice of making balloon ascents; aeronautics. **balloonist**, *n.*

ballot (băl'ŏt) [It. *ballotta*], *n.* A ball used for voting; a paper used to give a secret vote; the system of secret voting. *v.i.* To vote secretly.

balm (bam) [L. *balsamum*], *n.* Balsam; fragrant gum of certain trees; anything which soothes; fragrance; several fragrant garden herbs. *v.t.* To anoint with balm; to soothe, assuage. **balmy**, *a.* **balminess**, *n.*

balsam (bawl'săm), *n.* A vegetable resin with a strong fragrant odour; a medicament made with oil or resin for anointing wounds or soothing pain; anything of healing or soothing qualities.

baluster (băl'ŭs-tĕr) [Gr. *balaustion*, flower of the pomegranate (from supposed resemblance to its calyx tube)], *n.* A small column forming part of a series called a **balustrade**; a **banister**; **balustrade'**, *n.* A range of balusters supporting a coping or rail.

bamboo (băm-boo') [?], *n.* A giant tropical grass; the stem of such grass used as a stick, etc.

bamboozle (băm-boozl') [?], *v.t.* To mystify for purposes of fraud; to cheat.

ban (băn) [A.-S. *bannan*, to summon], *v.t.* To curse, anathematize; to interdict, proscribe. *n.* A public proclamation; an interdict; a formal anathematization or prohibition, proscription, outlawry; (*pl.*, *now spelt* BANNS) proclamation of intended marriage.

banal (bă'năl, băn'al) [F.], *a.* Commonplace, trite, petty. **banal'ity**, *n.* A commonplace; triviality.

banana (bă-nä'nă) [native name in Guinea], *n.* A tropical tree, or its fruit.

band (bănd) [O. Teut. *bindan*, to bind], *n.* That which binds, confines, or restrains; a collar or ruff; a bond, tie, uniting influence; an assemblage of men or animals; a company of musicians trained to play together. **bandbox**, *n.* A light box for holding collars, hats, millinery, etc. **band brake**, *n.* A flexible brake that grips the periphery of a drum or wheel. **band-master**, *n.* The leader of a band of musicians. **band-saw**, *n.* An endless

steel saw, running rapidly over wheels. **bandsman**, *n.* A member of a band of musicians. **band-stand**, *n.* An elevated platform for musicians.

bandage, *n.* A strip used to bind up wounds, fractures, etc.; the operation of bandaging; (*Arch.*) a tie or bond. *v.t.* To bind up with a bandage.

bandanna (băn-dăn'ă) [Hind. *bāndhnū*, a mode of spot dyeing], *n.* A coloured silk handkerchief with white spots.

bandeau (băn'dŏ) [F.], *n.* (*pl.* **-eaux**). A narrow fillet for the head.

bandit (băn'dit) [It. *bandito*], *n.* (*pl.* **banditti**, **bandits**). An outlaw; a brigand.

bandoleer, **-lier** (băn-dŏ-lēr') [Sp. *bandolera*], *n.* A shoulder-belt with loops to receive cartridges.

bandy (băn'di) [?], *v.t.* To beat, toss, or throw to and fro; to give and take. *n.* Hockey. *a.* Crooked, bent.

bane (băn) [A.-S. *bana*, a murderer], *n.* Poison; that which causes ruin; destruction, woe. **baneful**, *a.*

bang (băng) [Icel. *banga*, to beat], *v.t.* To beat with hard blows; to slam (a door), fire, beat (drum, cymbals) with a loud noise. *n.* A resounding blow, a thump; a sudden explosive noise.

bangle (băng'gel) [Hind. *bangri*, wristring], *n.* A ring-bracelet.

banish (băn'ish) [O.F. *banir*], *v.t.* To condemn to exile; to expel. **banishment**, *n.* Exile, expatriation.

banister (băn'is-tĕr), *n.* A shaft supporting a hand-rail; (*pl.*) the whole railing protecting the outer side of a staircase.

banjo (băn'jŏ) [Negro], *n.* A stringed musical instrument, played with the fingers. **banjoist**, *n.*

bank (1) (băngk) [M.E. *banke*, a bench], *n.* A mound with steeply sloping sides; a shelving elevation of sand, etc., in the sea or in a river; the margin of a river; a long flat-topped mass, as of snow, cloud, etc.; the ground at the top of a coal-mine. *v.t.* To confine within, or strengthen with, banks. *v.i.* (*Aeroplaning*) To incline inwards at a high angle in turning.

bank (2) (băngk) [F. *banque*, It. *banca*, a bench], *n.* An establishment which receives money on deposit from customers and invests it; (*Gaming*) the money which the proprietor of the table, or player who plays against the rest, has before him. *v.t.* To deposit in a bank.

banker (băngk'er), *n.* A proprietor, partner, or manager of a bank; one who keeps the bank at a gaming-table; the dealer in certain card-games.

bankrupt (băngk'rŭpt) [It. *banca rotta*, bank broken], *n.* One judicially declared an insolvent debtor. *a.* Insolvent; (*fig.*) without credit; at the end of one's resources. *v.t.* To render (a person) bankrupt; to reduce to beggary or discredit. **bankruptcy**, *n.*

banner (băn'ĕr) [O.F. *baniere*, standard, Goth. *bandwa*, sign, token], *n.* A standard used as a rallying-point in battle; an ensign bearing a device or emblem.

bannock (băn'ŏk) [Gael.], *n.* A flat round cake baked on an iron plate over the fire.

banns (bănz), *n.pl.* Proclamation in church of an intended marriage.

banquet (băng'kwĕt) [F. dim. of *banc*, bench], *n.* A ceremonial feast, followed by speeches. *v.t.* To entertain at a sumptuous feast. *v.i.* To feast luxuriously.

banshee (băn'shē) [Ir. *bean sidhe*, woman of the fairies], *n.* A supernatural being, supposed by Irish peasantry to wail round a house when one of the inmates is about to die.

bantam (băn'tăm) [*Bantam* in Java], *n.* A small, very pugnacious, domestic fowl. **bantam-weight,** *n.* A boxer not exceeding 8 st. 4 lb.

banter (băn'tĕr) [?], *v.t.* To ridicule good-humouredly; to chaff. *v.i.* To indulge in good-natured raillery. *n.* Chaff.

banting (băn'ting) [originator W. Banting (1797–1878)], *n.* Reduction of obesity by dieting.

baptism (băp'tizm), *n.* The act of baptizing; admission into the Christian Church, etc. **baptismal** (-tiz'măl), *a.* Conferred at baptism. **Baptist,** *n.* One who holds that baptism should be administered only to adults and by immersion. **bap'tistry,** *n.* The place where baptism is administered.

baptize (băp'tīz) [Gr. *baptizein* (*baptein*, to dip)], *v.t.* To sprinkle with or immerse in water as a sign of admission into the Christian Church; to christen.

bar (1) (bar) [O.F. *barre*], *n.* A piece of solid material, long in proportion to breadth; a transverse piece in a gate, window, grate, etc.; a connecting piece; a straight stripe, a broad band; an ingot; a hindrance or obstruction; a bank of silt at the mouth of a river or harbour; a barrier, esp. that at which prisoners stand during trial; the profession of a barrister; barristers collectively; the counter in an hotel or place of refreshment, across which liquors, etc., are sold; the room containing this; (*Mus.*) a vertical line across the stave dividing a composition into parts of equal duration; the portion contained between two such lines. *v.t.* To fasten with bars; to take exception to; to hinder, to prevent, exclude. **barmaid, barman,** *n.* A woman or man who serves at the bar of an hotel, etc.

bar (2) [Gr. *baros*, weight], *n.* The unit of atmospheric pressure; the weight of a column of mercury standing at 29·531 in. or 750·06 millimetres.

barb (1) (barb) [L. *barba*, beard], *n.* The appendages on the mouth of certain fishes; a recurved point, as in a fish-hook or arrow, or on barbed wire; a sting.

barb (2), *n.* A fine breed of horse originally from Barbary.

barbarian (bar-bâr'iăn) [L. *barbaria*], *n.* A savage; one destitute of pity or humanity. *a.* Uncivilized, cruel, inhuman. **barbaric** (-bâr'ik), *a.* Pertaining to barbarians. **bar'barism,** *n.* barbarity (-bâr'i-ti), *n.* Inhumanity, cruelty. **barbarous** (bar'bà-rŭs) [Gr. *barbaros* (prob. imit. of unintelligible speech)], *a.* Foreign in speech, barbarian; hence, harsh-sounding; uncivilized, uncultured.

barbel (bar'bĕl) [L. *barba*, beard], *n.* A European freshwater fish.

barber (bar'bĕr) [L. *barbātŏr*, from *barba*, beard], *n.* One who shaves and cuts beards and hair.

barberry (bar'bĕr-i) [late L. *barbaris*], *n.* A shrub bearing red acid berries.

barbette (bar-bet') [F., dim of *barbe*, beard], *n.* A mound of earth, or a platform in a warship, on which guns are mounted.

barbican (bar'bi-kăn) [O.F. *barbacan*], *n.* An outer fortification designed as a cover to the inner works.

barcarole (bar'kà-rōl) [It. *barcaruola*, a boat song], *n.* A song sung by the Venetian gondoliers.

bard (bard) [Gael.], *n.* A Celtic minstrel who celebrated heroic achievements; a poet. **bardic,** *a.* **bardish,** *a.*

bare (bâr) [A.-S. *bœr*], *a.* Naked; destitute of natural covering as fur, leaves, soil, etc.; with head uncovered as a mark of respect; unarmed; unsheathed; ill-furnished, empty; (*fig.*) mere, unsupported; unadorned. *v.t.* To strip, make bare. **barefaced,** *a.* Impudent, shameless. **barely,** *adv.* Nakedly; hardly, scarcely.

bargain (bar'găn) [O.F. *bargaine*, a chaffering], *n.* An agreement between parties concerning a sale; the thing sold; an advantageous purchase. *v.i.* To haggle; to make an agreement for purchase or sale.

barge (barj) [O.F.], *n.* A flat-bottomed freight-boat used on canals or rivers; a large, ornamental state or pleasure boat. *v.i.* (*slang*) To lurch (into). **bargee** (bar-jē'), *n.* A member of a barge's crew.

baritone (băr'i-tōn) [Gr. *barus*, heavy, *tonos*, tone], *n.* A male voice intermediate between bass and tenor; a singer having such a voice. *a.* Having this compass.

bark (1) (bark) [A.-S. *beorcan*], *v.i.* To utter a sharp cry, like a dog's. *n.* The sharp, explosive cry of dogs.

bark (2) (bark) [Scand.], *n.* The exterior covering of a tree. *v.t.* To strip the bark from a tree; to graze, abrade (shins, elbows, etc.).

bark (3), **barque** (bark) [F.], *n.* A small sailing vessel; (**barque**) a three-masted vessel, with fore and main masts square-rigged and mizen fore-and-aft rigged.

barley (bar'li) [A.-S. *bœrlic*], *n.* The grain or the plant of the genus *Hordeum*, a hardy, awned cereal. **barley-corn,** *n.* A grain of barley; the third part of an inch.

barm (barm) [A.-S. *beorma*], *n.* The frothy scum which rises to the surface of malt liquor in fermentation; yeast.

Barmecide (bar'me-sīd) [character in *Arabian Nights*], *n.* One who gives illusory benefits. **Barmecide feast,** *n.* Short commons.

barn (barn) [A.-S. *bern*], *n.* A covered building for the storage of grain, etc. **barnstormer,** *n.* Strolling player; a mouthing actor.

barnacle (bar'năkl) [O.F. *bernaque*], *n.* The barnacle-goose; a small crustacean attached by a stalk; (*fig.*) a constant attendant. **barnacle-goose,** *n.* A wild goose.

barnacles (bar'năklz) [O.F. *bernac*, flat-nosed], *n.pl.* A twitch put on the nostrils of a horse while being shod; an instrument of torture; (*slang*) a pair of spectacles.

barograph (băr'ō-gräf) [Gr. *baros*, weight, -GRAPH], *n.* An aneroid barometer recording the variations of atmospheric pressure.

barometer (bá-rom'ě-těr), *n.* An instrument for measuring atmospheric pressure, indicating probable weather change and altitudes reached. baromet'ric, *a.*

baron (băr'ŏn) [O.F. *barun*], *n.* A member of the lowest rank of nobility; a title of the judges of the Court of Exchequer. **baroness** (băr'ō-nes), *n.* The wife of a baron. baro'nial, *a.* bar'ony, *n.* The lordship, rank, or dignity of a baron; in Scotland a large manor.

baronet (băr'ō-net), *n.* An hereditary titled order of commoners ranking next below barons. **baronetcy** *n.* The title or rank of a baronet.

barouche (bá-roosh') [L. *birotus*, two-wheeled], *n.* A four-wheeled carriage with a movable top.

barrack (băr'ăk) [F. *baraque*], *n.* A building used to house troops (*usu. in pl.*); any large building resembling barracks. *v.i.* (*slang*) to cheer ironically.

barrage (bar'áj) [F.], *n.* The formation of an artificial dam to raise the water in a river; the bar or dam so formed; a storm of projectiles.

barrator (băr'á-tor) [O.F. *barateor*, a fraudulent dealer], *n.* One who stirs up litigation or discord; **barratry,** *n.* Fraud or criminal negligence on the part of a master of a ship; the offence of vexatiously exciting or maintaining law-suits.

barrel (băr'ĕl) [F. *baril*], *n.* A cylindrical wooden vessel bulging in the middle and with flat ends; the capacity or contents of such a vessel; the tube of a firearm; a revolving cylinder round which a chain or rope is wound.

barren (băr'ĕn) [O.F. *baraine*], *a.* Incapable of producing, esp. offspring or fruit; (*fig.*) fruitless, unprofitable; uninventive, dull. **barrenly,** *adv.* barrenness, *n.*

barricade (băr'i-kād') [Sp. *barricada* (*barrica,* a barrel)], *n.* A makeshift rampart thrown up to obstruct an enemy; any obstruction. *v.t.* To block or defend with a barricade.

barrier (bar'i-ěr) [A.-F. *barrere,* L. *barra,* bar], *n.* That which hinders approach; a fence, railing, limit, boundary.

barrister (băr'is-těr) [F. *barre* (the *bar* was a division in the Inns of Court)], *n.* A lawyer practising as an advocate at the bar; a counsellor-at-law.

barrow (1) (băr'ō) [A.-S. *bearwe,* from *beran,* to carry], *n.* A small hand-cart with one wheel and two handles.

barrow (2) (băr'ō) [A.-S. *beorg*], *n.* A prehistoric grave-mound, a tumulus.

barter (bar'těr) [O.F. *bareter,* to cheat], *v.t.* To exchange commodities. *v.i.* To traffic by exchanging one thing for another. *n.* Traffic by exchange. barterer, *n.*

basalt (băs'awlt) [L. *basaltes*], *n.* A dark-coloured, compact igneous rock often found in columnar form. basaltic, *a.*

base (1) (bās) [F. *bas,* late L. *bassus,* short], *a.* Low, occupying a low position; unworthy, despicable; inferior in quality; counterfeit; base-born, *a.* Born out of wedlock. baseness, *n.*

base (2) (bās) [F. *base,* L. and Gr. *basis* (*bainein,* to stand)], *n.* The lowest part on which a thing rests; fundamental principle, groundwork; a pedestal; a starting-post; that line or place from which a combatant draws reinforcements of men, ammunition, etc.; (*Chem.*) that with which an acid combines to form a salt; (*Gram.*) the original stem of a word; the datum or basis for any process of reckoning measurement or argument. *v.t.* To make a foundation for; to lay on a foundation; (*fig.*) to found, secure. **basal,** *a.* baseless, *a.* Without foundation; groundless. **basement,** *n.* The lowest inhabited story of a building, esp. when below the ground level. **basic,** *a.* Fundamental. Basic English, *n.* A selection of 850 fundamental words to form a common first step in English.

bashful (băsh'fŭl), *a.* Shamefaced, shy; characterized by excessive modesty. bashfully, *adv.* bashfulness, *n.*

basilica (bá-sil'í-ká) [Gr. *basilikě,* royal house], *n.* A large oblong building with double colonnades and an apse; a church built on this plan. basilican, *a.*

basilisk (băs'i-lisk) [Gr. *basiliskos,* kingly], *n.* A fabulous reptile, said to be hatched by a serpent from a cock's egg, whose look and breath were reputed fatal.

basin (băsn) [O.F. *bacin*], *n.* A hollow (*usu.* circular) vessel for holding water; a bowl; a dock, a land-locked harbour; the tract of country drained by a river and its tributaries; a hollow.

basis (bā'sis), *n.* (*pl.* bases) The base, fundamental principle, groundwork.

bask (bask) [O. Scand. *bathask,* to bathe oneself], *v.i.* To expose oneself to the sun; (*fig.*) to sun oneself in love, good fortune, etc.

basket (bas'kĕt) [?], *n.* A receptacle of plaited osiers, twigs, etc. (*Arch.*) the vase of a Corinthian column with its carved foliage. basket-work, *n.* Wickerwork.

bas-relief (bas'rě-lēf) [It. *basso-rilievo*], *n.* Low relief; sculpture in which the figures project only slightly.

bass (1) (băs), *n.* Bast.

bass (2) (bās) [earlier *base* BASE (1)], *n.* The lowest part in harmonized musical compositions; the deepest male voice; one who sings the bass part.

bass (3), **basse** (băs) [A.-S. *bars*], *n.* A sea-fish, common in European waters.

basset (băs'et) [F. dim. of *basse,* low], *n.* A short-legged dog used to drive foxes and badgers from their earths.

bassinet (băs-i-net') [F.], *n.* A hooded, oblong wicker basket used as a cradle; a perambulator.

bassoon (bá-soon') [F. *basson*], *n.* A wooden double-reed instrument, the bass to the clarinet and oboe.

bast (băst) [A.-S. *bæst*], *n.* The inner bark of the lime; any similar fibrous bark; a rope, mat, etc., made from this.

bastard (băs'tárd) [O.F. *bast,* pack-saddle],

B

n. An illegitimate child; anything spurious; an old Spanish wine. *a.* Born out of wedlock; spurious, not genuine.

baste (1) (băst) [?], *v.t.* To moisten (a roasting joint) with gravy, etc.; to beat with a stick, thrash, cudgel.

baste (2) (băst) [O.F. *bastir*], *v.t.* To sew lightly, tack, fasten together with long stitches.

bastinado (băs-ti-nā'dō) [Sp.], *n.* An Oriental punishment inflicted with a stick on the soles of the feet. *v.t.* To beat with a stick.

bastion (băs'ti-ŏn) [F.], *n.* A projecting work at the angle or in the line of a fortification, having two faces and two flanks.

bat (1) (băt) [?], *n.* A wooden club with a cylindrical handle and broad blade used to strike the ball at cricket, etc.; to wink. *v.i.* To take an innings as batsman. **batsman**, *n.* One who uses the bat at games.

bat (2) (băt) [M.E. *bakke*, from Icel. *blaka*, to flutter], *n.* A small nocturnal mouse-like mammal, having the digits extended to support a membrane by means of which it flies.

bat (3) (băt) [F. *bât*, a pack-saddle], *n.* (*only in combination*) A pack-saddle. **bat-horse**, *n.* A sumpter-horse carrying officers' baggage. **batman**, *n.* The military servant of an officer.

batch (băch) [A.-S. *bacan*, to bake], *n.* As much bread as is produced at one baking; sort, lot, set, crew.

bate (băt), *v.t.* To diminish; to humble; to moderate, restrain; deprive, remove. *v.i.* To fall away, decrease.

bath (1) (bath) [A.-S. *bœth*], *n.* A washing or immersing; the water or other fluid used for bathing; the vessel for containing this; a room or building for bathing in. *v.t.* To wash or put (*usu.* a child) in a bath. **bath brick**, *n.* A preparation of calcareous earth (found near Bath, Somerset) used for cleaning metal. **bath chap**, *n.* A small pig's cheek cured. **bath-room**, *n.* An apartment containing a bath. **Order of the Bath**, *n.* The second oldest order of chivalry in Britain.

bath (2) (băth) [Heb.], *n.* An ancient Hebrew liquid measure, about 6½ gallons.

bathe (băth) [A.-S. *bathian*], *v.t.* To immerse in a bath. *v.i.* To take a bath. *n.* The act of taking a bath (esp. in the sea, a river, etc.). **bather**, *n.* One who bathes, esp. in sea or river.

bathos (bă'thos) [Gr., depth], *n.* Ridiculous descent from the sublime to the commonplace; anticlimax. **bathet'ic**, *a.*

bathymetry (bă-thim'et-ri) [Gr. *bathos*, deep; *metry*], *n.* The art or method of taking deep sea soundings. **bathyscafe**, *n.* Submersible craft fitted for deep-sea observations.

bating (bā'ting), *prep.* Leaving out of the question; excepting.

batiste (bă-tēst') [F.], *n.* A cambric; a fine fabric resembling this.

baton (băt'ŏn) [F.], *n.* A staff; a truncheon as a badge or symbol of authority; the wand used by a conductor in beating time.

Batrachia (bă-trā'ki-ă) [Gr. *batrachos*, frog], *n.pl.* An order of reptiles including those breathing by gills, and of Amphibia which have gills and tail only in the larval stage. **batrachian**, *a.* Pertaining to the Batrachia. *n.* Any individual of the Batrachia.

battalion (bă-tăl'yŏn) [F. *bataillon*, *batailler*, to battle], *n.* A main division of an army; the tactical and administrative unit of infantry, generally about 1000 strong on a war footing.

batten (1) (bătn), *n.* A piece of wood from 1 to 9 ins. wide and ½ to 2¼ ins. thick; a scantling, ledge. *v.t.* To fasten or strengthen with battens. **batten down**; (*Naut.*) To close down the hatches.

batten (2) (bătn) [cp. Dut. *baten*, to avail, to profit], *v.i.* To feed on gluttonously, grow fat; to thrive, prosper; to revel in.

batter (băt'ér) [O.F. *batire*, to beat], *v.t.* To strike repeatedly; to impair by beating or rough usage; to subject to crushing attack, esp. with artillery; to bombard. *n.* A mixture of several ingredients well beaten together; a soft pudding; liquid mud; a blow. **battering-ram**, *n.* An ancient military engine used for battering down walls.

battery (băt'ér-i) [F. *batterie*], *n.* An assailing by blows; pieces of artillery for combined action, with their men, traction, and equipment; the fortified work, or the part of a ship, in which artillery is mounted; a ship's guns; an apparatus forming a source of electric energy.

battle (bătl) [O.F. *batayle*, L. *battuere*, to beat], *n.* A fight between opposing armies or forces; fighting, hostilities, war. *v.i.* To fight, to contend (with or against). **battle-cry**, *n.* A war-cry, a slogan. **battle-dress**, *n.* (*Mil.*) Loose-fitting uniform of blouse and trousers. **battle-royal**, *n.* A free fight, a general row. **battle-ship**, *n.* A warship adapted by armament for line of battle as opposed to a cruiser.

battledore (bătl'dŏr) [?], *n.* A light racket used to strike a shuttlecock.

battlement (bătl'mént) [O.F.], *n.* A parapet with embrasures, on the top of a building, originally for defence.

battue (ba-too') [F., beaten], *n.* Driving game from cover by beating the bushes; a shoot on this plan; (*fig.*) a beat up, wholesale slaughter.

bauble (bawbl) [O.F. *baubel*, a child's plaything], *n.* A jester's short stick having a head with ass's ears carved at the end of it; a thing of no value.

bawbee (baw-bē') [?], *n.* An old Scots copper coin equivalent to about a half-penny.

bawl (bawl) [med. L. *baulāre*, to bark], *v.i.* To cry loudly, bellow. *n.* A loud, prolonged shout or cry.

bay (1) (bā) [F. *baie*], *n.* An arm of the sea extending into the land with a wide mouth; a recess or opening in a wall; a main compartment; an internal recess in a room formed by the outward projection of the walls; part of a ship between decks. **bay-window**, *n.* An angular window structure forming a recess in a room.

bay (2) (bā) [O.F. *abai*, barking; *aboi*, *aboyer*, to bark], *n.* Barking; the position of a hunted animal defending itself at close quarters. *v.i.* To bark hoarsely. *v.t.* To bark at; to bring to bay.

bay (3) (bā) [L. *bāca*, berry], *n.* The bay-tree or bay-laurel; (*pl.*) its leaves or twigs woven into a garland for a conqueror or poet; (*fig.*) fame, renown. **bay-tree**, *n.* The bay, *Laurus nobilis*.

bay (4) (bā) [F. *bai*, L. *badius*], *a.* Reddish-brown, approaching chestnut. *n.* A horse of that colour.

bayonet (bā'ō-nĕt) [prob. from *Bayonne*], *n.* A weapon attachable to the muzzle of a rifle, converting it into a kind of pike. *v.t.* To stab with a bayonet.

bazaar (bă-zar') [Pers. *bāzār*], *n.* An Oriental market-place, where goods are offered for sale; a sale of articles for benevolent purposes; a repository.

be (bē) [A.-S. *bēon*], *inf.*, *pres. subj.* and *imper. v.* To exist, to have a real state or existence; to become, to remain, continue (commonly used as a copula, asserting connexion between the subject and the predicate).

be- [A.-S.], *pref.* About, by; *e.g.* (1) *besmear*, to smear all over, *bedaub*, to daub about, *before*, about the front of, *besiege*, to sit around; (2) making intransitive verbs transitive or reflective; *e.g. bemoan*, *bethink*; (3) forming verbs from nouns or adjectives, as *befool*, *benumb*; (4) having a privative force, as in *behead*, *bereave*; (5) compounded with nouns, signifying to call this or that, as *bedevil*, *belady*; (6) intensive, *e.g. becrowd*, *bedrug*; (7) making adjectives, *e.g. bejewelled*, *bewigged*.

beach (bēch) [?], *n.* A sandy or pebbly seashore; the strand on which the waves break. **beach-comber**, *n.* A long wave rolling in from the ocean; a settler in the Pacific Islands; a loafer.

beacon (bē'kŏn) [A.-S. *bēacen*], *n.* A signal-fire on an eminence; a conspicuous hill; watch-tower; lighthouse.

bead (bēd) [A.-S. *biddan*, to pray], *n.* A small globular perforated body for threading on a string; a bead-like drop of a liquid, a bubble; the front sight of a gun; a narrow semi-circular moulding; (*pl.*) a necklace; a rosary. **beading**, *n.* Bead-moulding. **beady**, *a.* Small and bright like beads.

beadle (bēdl) [A.-S. *bydel*, a herald], *n.* A messenger or usher of a court; a petty officer of a church, parish, etc.

beagle (bēgl) [?], *n.* A small hunting dog.

beak (bēk) [F. *bec*], *n.* The bill of a bird; anything pointed like this; a promontory; a spout; (*slang*) a police magistrate. **beaked**, *a.*

beaker (bē'kẽr) [Icel. *bikarr*], *n.* A large wide-mouthed drinking-vessel.

beam (bēm) [A.-S.], *n.* A large, long, squared piece of timber, esp. a support for rafters or a deck; the part of a balance from which the scales are suspended; the pole of a carriage; the main trunk of a stag's horn; a ray or collection of rays of light; a bright look, a smile; the width of a boat. *v.t.* To radiate, to emit in rays. *v.i.* To send forth rays of light, to shine radiantly. **beam transmission**, *n.* (*Rad.*) A system of sending short-waves within a limited angle for reception in a particular zone.

bean (bēn) [A.-S. *bēan*], *n.* The kidney-shaped seed in long pods of *Faba vulgaris* and allied plants; the other seeds resembling these. **bean-feast**, *n.* An annual outing originally given by employers to their workmen; children's outing.

bear (1) (bâr) [A.-S. *bera*], *n.* A mammal belonging to the genus *Ursus*; a rough unmannerly man; two northern constellations, the Great and Little Bear; (*Stock Ex.*) one who sells stock for future delivery in the belief that prices will fall. *v.i.* To speculate for a fall in stocks. *v.t.* To produce a fall in the price of (stock, etc.). **bear-garden**, *n.* A place in which bears were kept and baited; hence, a rude, turbulent assembly. **bearish**, *a.* Bear-like; rough, uncouth. **bearskin**, *n.* The skin of a bear; the tall fur cap worn by the Foot Guards.

bear (2) (bâr) [A.-S. *beran*], *v.t.* (*past bore*, *p.p. borne*). To carry, bring; to sustain, support the weight of; to be responsible for, suffer, endure; to give birth to, produce, yield. *v.i.* To behave; to be patient; to imply, to have relation to; to incline, take a certain direction (as to the point of the compass) with respect to something else. **bearable**, *a.* **bearably**, *adv.* **bearer**, *n.* One who or that which bears, carries, or supports; one which assists to carry a corpse to the grave or to hold the pall; one who holds or presents a cheque; the holder of any rank or office. **bearing**, *n.* Endurance, toleration; mien, carriage, manner; connexion; a support for moving parts of any machine; a part of a machine that bears the friction; (*Her.*) a charge, a device; (*Naut.*) the direction in which an object lies from a vessel; (*pl.*) relative position. **bearing-rein**, *n.* A fixed rein for holding a horse's head up.

beard (bērd) [A.-S.], *n.* The hair on the lower part of a man's face; the barb of an arrow; the awn of grasses. *v.t.* To oppose with resolute effrontery; to set at defiance. **bearded**, *a.* **beardless**, *a.*

beast (bēst) [L. *bestia*], *n.* Any of the inferior animals as distinguished from man; a domestic animal, esp. oxen or cattle; (*fig.*) a brutal or objectionable person. **beastly**, *a.* **beastliness**, *n.*

beat (bēt) [A.-S. *bēatan*], *v.t.* (*past beat*, *p.p.* beaten). To strike with repeated blows, to thrash, to strike, as bushes, in order to rouse game, to mix by beating; to dash against (of water, wind, etc.); to conquer, overcome; to tread, as a path. *v.i.* To pulsate, throb; to move rhythmically; (*Naut.*) to make way against the wind. *n.* A stroke or blow; a pulsation, throb; an assigned space traversed at intervals by patrols, police, etc., hence, sphere, range; (*Mus.*) the rise or fall of the hand in regulating time. **beaten**, *a.* Subjected to repeated blows; defeated, vanquished, exhausted. **beater**, *n.* One who or that which beats, a man employed to rouse game. **beating,** *n.* The action of striking repeated blows, corporal castigation; pulsation, throbbing; overthrow, defeat; (*Naut.*) sailing against the wind.

beatify (bē-ăt'ĭ-fī) [L. *beātus,* happy, *facere,* to make] *v.t.* To pronounce (by the Pope) that the deceased is in enjoyment of heavenly bliss, the first step towards canonization. **beatific** (bē-à-tif'ik), *a.* **beatification** (bē-ăt-ĭ-fĭ-kā'shŭn), *n.* The act of rendering blessed or of beatifying. **beatitude** (bē-ăt'ĭ-tūd), *n.* Supreme felicity; the special blessedness announced in the Sermon on the Mount.

beau (bō) [F. *beau,* fine, pretty], *n.* (*pl.* beaux, bōz) A fop, a dandy; a sweetheart. **beau-ideal** (bō-ĭ-dē'ăl), *n.* The highest conceivable type of excellence.

beauteous (bū'tē-ŭs), *a.* Endowed with beauty, beautiful. **beauteousness,** *n.* **beautiful,** *a.* Possessing the attributes that constitute beauty; palatable, delicious; *n.* One who or that which is beautiful; the abstract notion of the qualities constituting beauty. **beautify** (bū'tĭ-fī), *v.t.* To make beautiful.

beauty (bū'tĭ) [O.F. *biaute*], *n.* That quality which gives the eye intense pleasure; that characteristic which gratifies the intellect or the moral feeling; a beautiful woman, feature, or characteristic; embellishment, grace, charm.

beaver (1) (bē'vėr) [A.-S. *beofer*], *n.* An amphibious rodent with broad tail, soft fur, and habits of building huts and dams; its fur, or a hat made of it.

beaver (2) (bē'vėr) [O.F. *bavière,* bib], *n.* The lower part of the visor of a helmet; (*slang*) a beard.

becalm (bē-kam'), *v.t.* To render calm or still; to deprive (a ship) of wind.

because (bē-koz'), *conj.* By cause or reason of, on account of, for; inasmuch as.

beck (1) (bek), *n.* A bow or curtsy; a nod, a gesture.

beck (2) (bek) [Icel. *bekkr*], *n.* A brook, rivulet; a mountain or moorland stream.

beckon (bek'ón) [A.-S. *bēacnian,* a sign, BEACON], *v.i.* To make a signal by a gesture or nod. *v.t.* To summon or signal to by a motion of the hand, a nod, etc.

become (bē-kŭm') [A.-S.], *v.i.* To change to; to come into existence; (*copulative*) to come to be. *v.t.* To be suitable to, to befit, to be proper to or for; to look well upon. **becoming,** *a.* Befitting, suitable; in harmony or keeping with; graceful in conduct.

bed (bed) [A.-S.], *n.* A thing to sleep upon; the resting-place of an animal, the flat surface on which anything rests; a plot of ground in a garden; the channel or bed of a river or the sea-bottom; the foundation of a road or railway; the bottom layer or support on which a mechanical structure or machine is laid; a horizontal course in a wall; (*Geol.*) a stratum, a layer of rock; a layer of oysters. *v.t.* To put in bed; to plant in a bed or beds; to fix in a stratum or course; to place in a matrix of any kind, to embed. *v.i.* To go to bed. **bed-clothes,** *n.pl.* bedding, *n.* Mattresses and bed-clothes; litter for domestic animals; a bottom layer or foundation. **bedpost,** *n.* One of the upright supports of a bedstead. **bed-ridden,** *a.* Confined to bed through age or sickness. **bed-rock,** *n.* (*Geol.*) The rock underlying superficial formations; hence, bottom, foundation, fundamental principles. **bedroom,** *n.* A sleeping apartment. **bedside,** *a.* Pertaining to the sick-chamber. **bed-sore,** *n.* A sore produced by long lying in bed. **bedstead,** *n.* The framework on which a bed is placed. **bedtime,** *n.* The usual hour for going to bed.

bedaub (bē-dawb'), *v.t.* To daub over.

bedeck (bē-dek'), *v.t.* To adorn.

bedew (bē-dū'), *v.t.* To moisten or sprinkle with dew-like drops.

bedizen (bē-dizn'), *v.t.* To deck out gaudily. **bedizenment,** *n.*

Bedlam (bed'lăm), *n.* The Bethlehem Hospital, a lunatic asylum; a scene of wild uproar. *a.* Of or belonging to a madhouse. **bedlamite,** *n.* A madman, a lunatic.

Bedouin (bed'u-in) [Arab. *badawīn,* wandering (*badw,* a desert)], *n.* A nomadic Arab, as distinguished from one living in a town. *a.* Pertaining to the wandering Arabs; nomad.

bedraggle (bē-drăg'l), *v.t.* To soil by trailing in the mire.

bee (bē) [A.-S. *bēo*], *n.* A social insect, partially domesticated for the wax and honey it produces; (*fig.*) a busy, productive worker. **beehive,** *n.* A receptacle for housing bees. **bee-line,** *n.* The shortest route between two places. **bee-skep,** *n.* A straw beehive. **beeswax,** *n.* The wax secreted by bees for their cells. *v.t.* To rub or polish with beeswax. **beeswing,** *n.* The second crust, a fine filmy deposit in an old port wine; old port.

beech (bēch) [A.-S. *bēce*], *n.* A well-known forest tree with smooth bark, and yielding nuts or mast; its wood. **beechmast,** *n.* The fruit of the beech-tree. **beechen,** *a.*

beef (bēf) [O.F. *boef,* ox], *n.* The flesh of the ox used as food; an ox (*usu. in pl.,* beeves), esp. one fatted for the market. **beef-tea,** *n.* The nutritive juice extracted from beef by simmering. **Beefeater,** *n.* A Yeoman of the Guard, instituted in 1485; a warder of the Tower of London. **beefy,** *a.* Like beef; fleshy; stolid.

beer (bēr) [A.-S. *bēor*], *n.* A malt liquor prepared by brewing, ale and stout. **beery,** *a.* Like beer; under the influence of beer; fuddled.

beet (bēt) [A.-S. *bēte*], *n.* A plant used (red) as a salad, and (white) in sugar-making, cultivated for its esculent root.

beetle (1) (bētl) [A.-S. *bitela,* from *bitan,* to bite], *n.* A coleopterous insect, the upper wings of which have been converted into hard wing-cases, the under ones being used for flight, if it is able to fly.

beetle (2) (bētl) [A.-S. *bytel,* O. Teut. *bautan,* to beat], *n.* A heavy wooden mallet for ramming and crushing operations. *v.i.* To jut out, to hang over. *a.* Projecting, overhanging, scowling. **beetle-brow,** *n.* A projecting brow. **beetling,** *a.* Jutting, overhanging, prominent.

befall (bė-fawl') [A.-S. *befeallan*], *v.t.* To happen to. *v.i.* To happen.

befit (bė-fit'), *v.t.* To be suitable to or for; to become; to be incumbent upon. befitting, *a.*

befog (bė-fog'), *v.t.* To confuse.

before (bė-fōr') [A.-S. *beforan*], *prep.* In front of (in time, space, rank, or degree); under the cognizance, influence, or impulsion of; in preference to. *adv.* Ahead, in front; beforehand. *conj.* Earlier than; rather than. beforehand, *adv.* In anticipation, in advance, before the time. beforetime, *adv.* Formerly.

befriend (bė-frend'), *v.t.* To favour, help.

beg (beg) [?], *v.i.* To ask for alms. *v.t.* To supplicate in charity; to ask earnestly, entreat. beggar, *n.* One who lives by obtaining alms; one in indigent circumstances; (*colloq.*) fellow; *v.t.* To reduce to want; to impoverish. beggarly, *a.* beggary, *n.* The state or condition of an habitual beggar; extreme indigence.

beget (bė-get') [A.-S. *begitan*], *v.t.* To engender, generate, procreate. begetter, *n.* One who begets; an originator.

begin (bė-gin') [A.-S. *beginnan*], *v.i.* To come into existence, to start. *v.t.* To be the first to do, to do the first act of, to enter on, commence. beginner, *n.* One who originates or is the first to do anything; a young learner or practitioner. beginning, *n.* The first cause, the origin; the first state or commencement.

begone (bė-gon'), *imper.v.* Get you gone, go away, depart.

begonia (bė-gō'ni-a) [Michael *Begon* (1638-1710)], *n.* A genus of ornamental plants.

begrudge (bė-grŭj'), *v.t.* To grudge; to envy (a person) the possession of.

beguile (bė-gīl'), *v.t.* To deceive, cheat, to deprive of by fraud; to charm away tedium. beguilement, *n.* beguiler, *n.* beguiling, *a.* Deceiving, charming.

begum (bē'gŭm) [Hind.], *n.* A queen, princess, or lady of high rank in India.

behalf (bė-haf') [A.-S. *be healfe*, by the side], *n.* Interest, lieu, stead.

behave (bė-hāv'), *v.r.* To conduct, demean. *v.i.* To conduct oneself; (*colloq.*) to conduct oneself well, to display good manners. behaviour (bė-hā'vyėr), *n.* Outward deportment, carriage; manners, demeanour; the way in which a thing acts. behaviourism, *n.* (*Psych.*) The objective study of behaviour under stimuli.

behead (bė-hed'), *v.t.* To cut the head off.

behemoth (bē'hė-moth) [Heb., from Egypt. *p-ehe-mau*, water-ox], *n.* The animal described in Job xl. 15-24, probably the hippopotamus.

behest (bė-hest') [A.-S. *behæs*], *n.* A command; an injunction.

behind (bė-hīnd') [A.-S. *behindan*], *prep.* At the back of; later than. *n.* The back part of a person or garment; the posteriors. behindhand, *a.* Tardy.

behold (bė-hōld') [A.-S. *bihaldan*], *v.t.* To see, view; to consider. *v.i.* To look. *int.* Lo! beholden, *a.* Indebted, under obligation of gratitude (with *to*).

behoof (bė-hoof') [A.-S. *behōf*], *n.* Advantage, use, profit, benefit.

behove (bė-hŏv') [A.-S. *bihōvian*], *v.t.* To befit, to be due to. *v.i.* To be needful to, incumbent.

being (bē'ing), *n.* The state of existing; lifetime; essence; a thing or person existing. *a.* Existing, present. *conj.* Seeing that, since.

belabour (bė-lā'bŏr), *v.t.* To cultivate with labour, labour at; to beat, to thrash.

belated (bė-lā'ted), *a.* Benighted; too late, behind time.

belay (bė-lā') [A.-S. *belecgan*, to lay, envelop], *v.t.* To fasten a running rope by winding it round a cleat or belaying-pin. belaying-pin, *n.* (*Naut.*) A stout pin to which running ropes may be belayed.

belch (belch) [A.-S. *bealcan*], *v.i.* To eject wind by the mouth from the stomach. *n.* An eructation.

belcher (bel'chėr) [Jim *Belcher*, pugilist (1781-1811)], *n.* A blue and white spotted neckerchief.

beldam (bel'dàm), *n.* An old woman; a hag, a witch.

beleaguer (bė-lē'gėr) [Dut. *be-*, around, *leger*, a camp], *v.t.* To besiege, invest.

belfry (bel'fri) [O.F. *berfrei*, M.H.G. *bercfrit* (*berc*, protection, *fride*, peace), a protecting tower], *n.* A bell-tower; the chamber for the bells in a church-tower.

Belial (bē'li-ál) [Heb. *b'li-yaal*, worthlessness], *n.* Satan.

belie (bė-lī') [A.-S. *belēogan*], *v.t.* To tell lies about, to misrepresent.

belief (bė-lēf') [BE-, A.-S. *lēafa*], *n.* The mental operation of accepting as true; the thing so believed; opinion, persuasion.

believe (bė-lēv') [A.-S. *gelēfan*], *v.t.* To give credence to; have confidence in, or reliance on, to accept as true; be of opinion that. *v.i.* To think, to have, or exercise, faith. believable, *a.* Capable of being believed, credible. believer, *n.* One who believes; a Christian. believing, *a.* Exercising belief or the virtue of faith.

belike (bė-līk'), *adv.* Possibly, perhaps.

belittle (bė-litl'), *v.t.* To make little; to depreciate.

bell (bel) [A.-S.], *n.* A hollow metallic body emitting a clear musical sound when struck by a hammer; the cry of a buck at rutting time. *v.i.* To bellow (of stags). bell-buoy, *n.* A buoy to which a bell is attached, rung by the motion of the waves. bell-founder, -founding, -foundry, *n.* The caster, the casting, and the manufactory of bells. bellman, *n.* A public crier who attracts attention by ringing a bell. bell-metal, *n.* An alloy of copper and tin, usually with a little zinc, used for bells. bell-pull, *n.* A cord or handle by which a bell is rung. bell-wether, *n.* The sheep that wears a bell and leads a flock; (*fig.*) a leader.

belladonna (bel-à-don'à) [It., a fine lady], *n.* Deadly nightshade.

belle (bel) [F., from L. *bellus*, fine, pretty], *n.* A beautiful woman; a reigning beauty.

belles-lettres (bel-letr) [F.], *n.pl.* Polite literature, the humanities.

bellicose (bel'i-kos) [L. *bellicosus* (*bellum*, war)], *a.* Warlike; inclined to fighting.

belligerent (bĕ-lij'ẽr-ĕnt) [L. *bellum*, war, *gerere*, to wage], *a.* Pertaining to the carrying on of war. *n.* A nation or individual engaged in war. **belligerence**, *n.* The state of being at war.

bellow (bel'ō) [A.-S. *bellan*], *v.i.* To emit a loud hollow sound (as a bull); to bawl. *n.* The roar of a bull, or a similar sound.

bellows (bel'ōz) [M.E. *belu* (pl. *belwes*), a bag], *n.pl.* An apparatus for supplying a strong blast of air to a fire or wind instrument; the expansible portion of a camera.

belly (bel'i) [A.-S. *bœlg*, a leather bag, *balgan*, to swell out], *n.* That part of the body containing the stomach and bowels; anything protuberant. *v.t.* To cause to swell out, to render protuberant. *v.i.* To swell or bulge out, to become protuberant.

belong (bĕ-long') [M.E. *bilongen*], *v.i.* To pertain; to be the property, attribute, duty, concern, or business of; to be connected with. **belonging**, *n.* One's property (*usu. in pl.*).

beloved (bĕ-lŭvd', -lŭv'ĕd), *a.* Loved greatly. *n.* One greatly loved.

below (bĕ-lō'), *prep.* Beneath; under in place, down stream from; inferior; unworthy of. *adv.* In or to an inferior position; on earth (as opp. to heaven); in hell (as opp. to earth); down stream.

belt (belt) [A.-S.], *n.* A strip of leather or other material, worn as a girdle; a broad strip or stripe; a flat endless strap passing round two wheels, and communicating motion. *v.t.* To encircle, fasten, invest, or thrash with a belt. **belted**, *a.* Wearing a belt, esp. as a mark of rank or distinction. **belting**, *n.* Material for belts; (*Mech.*) a belt or system of belts.

belvedere (bel've-dẽr) [It. *bel*, fine; *vedere*, to see], *n.* An erection commanding a fine view.

bemoan (bĕ-mōn') [A.-S. *bimœnan*], *v.t.* To moan over, deplore. *v.i.* To lament.

bemuse (bĕ-mūz'), *v.t.* To make confused or dazed, as by drinking.

bench (bench) [A.-S. *benc*], *n.* A long wooden seat; a seat where judges sit in court, hence judges or magistrates collectively; a tribunal; a carpenter's or other mechanic's work-table. **bencher**, *n.* One of the senior members of an Inn of Court. **bench-mark**, *n.* An ordnance survey mark.

bend (bend) [A.-S. *bendan*], *v.t.* To curve, deflect, direct to a certain point; (*fig.*) to subdue; (*Naut.*) to fasten, tie into a knot; aim (a weapon). *v.i.* To assume the form of a curve; to stoop; to submit. *n.* A curve, flexure; a turn in a road.

beneath (bĕ-nēth') [A.-S. *be-*, by, *neothan*, below], *prep.* Below, under; unworthy of. *adv.* In a lower place, below.

benediction (ben-ė-dik'shŭn) [L. *benedictio*], *n.* A blessing.

benefaction (ben-ė-făk'shŭn) [L. *benefactio*], *n.* The conferring of a benefit; a benefit conferred.

benefactor (ben-ė-făk'tõr), *n.* One who gives another help or friendly service. **benefactress**, *n.*

benefice (ben'ė-fis) [L. *beneficium*], *n.* An ecclesiastical living.

beneficent (bĕ-nef'i-sĕnt), *a.* Kind, generous; characterized by benevolence. **beneficence**, *n.* **beneficial** (-fish'ál), *a.* Advantageous; serviceable, remedial. **beneficiary**, *n.* One who receives a benefit, favour.

benefit (ben'ė-fit) [L. *benefactum*], *n.* A favour, benefaction; profit, advantage. *v.t.* To do good or be of advantage or profit to. *v.i.* To derive advantage. **benefit of clergy**, *n.* (*Law*) An obsolete privilege granted to clergy and such as could read whereby they were exempt from the sentence of secular courts.

benevolent (bĕ-nev'ō-lĕnt) [L. *bene volens*, well wishing], *a.* Kind, charitable, generous. **benevolently**, *adv.* **benevolence**, *n.*

benighted (bĕ-nī'tĕd), *p.p.* Overtaken by night. *a.* Ignorant; uncivilized.

benign (bĕ-nīn') [L. *benignus*], *a.* Kind-hearted, gracious; favourable. **benignly**, *adv.* **benignant** (bĕ-nig'nȧnt), *a.* Gracious, kind, benevolent. **benignity**, *n.*

benison (ben'i-zòn) [O.F. *beneison*], *n.* A blessing, a benediction.

bent (1), *n.* Inclination, disposition.

bent (2) [A.-S. *beonet*], *n.* Stiff, rush-like grass.

benthos (ben'thos) [Gr., depths of the sea], *n.* (*Zool.*) Animal and plant life on the ocean bed.

benumb (bĕ-nŭm') [A.-S. *benumen*], *v.t.* To render numb; to deaden.

benzene (ben'zēn), *n.* An aromatic hydrocarbon used for illuminating and for removing grease-spots.

benzoin (ben'zō-in) [Arab. *lubān jāwi*, Javanese frankincense], *n.* A resin used in medicine and in perfumery; a camphor obtained from bitter-almond oil. **benzoic** (ben-zō'ik), *a.* Pertaining to or derived from benzoin. **benzol, benzole, *n.*** Benzene. **benzoline, *n.*** Impure benzene.

bequeath (bĕ-kwēth') [A.-S. *becwethan*], *v.t.* To leave by will; transmit to future generations. **bequest**, *n.* A legacy.

bereave (bĕ-rēv') [A.-S. *berēafian*], *v.t.* To deprive, rob, or spoil of anything. **bereavement**, *n.* The state of being bereaved; loss by death.

beret (be'rā) [Fr.], *n.* A round, brimless cap fitting the head fairly closely.

bergamot (bẽrg'à-mot) [*Bergamo*, Italy], *n.* An orange which yields a fragrant essential oil; the oil; a mint which yields a similar oil; a coarse kind of tapestry; a juicy kind of pear.

beriberi (ber'i-ber-i) [Cingalese *beri*, weakness], *n.* A disease prevalent in India and Japan, characterized by paralysis and dropsy.

berlin (bẽr-lin') [capital of Prussia], *n.* A fine wool for knitting, embroidery, etc.

berry (ber'i) [A.-S. *berige*], *n.* A small fleshy fruit containing many seeds; one of the eggs of a lobster.

berserk, -er (bẽr'sẽrk, -ẽr) [Icel. *berserkr*, prob. bear-coat], *n.* A Norse warrior possessed of preternatural strength and fury; a bravo. *a.* Filled with rage.

berth (bẽrth) [?], *n.* A place for a ship; a room, a situation, or a sleeping-place on board ship; a sleeping-place in a rail-

way carriage; a situation of any kind. *v.t.*
To moor; to furnish with a berth.

beryl (ber'il) [Gr. *bērullos*], *n.* A gem like
the emerald, but lighter in colour.

beseech (bė-sēch') [BE-, M.E. *sechen, seken*],
v.t. To implore, entreat. **beseeching,** *a.*

beseem (bė-sēm'), *v.t.* To be fit, proper
for, or becoming to.

beset (bė-set') [A.-S.], *v.t.* To surround,
invest; to fall upon.

beside (bė-sīd') [A.-S. *be sīdan*], *prep.* By
the side of, in comparison with; hard by;
wide of. **besides,** *prep.* In addition to. *adv.*
Moreover, over and above; otherwise.

besiege (bė-sēj') [M.E. *bisegen*], *v.t.* To
invest; to crowd round; to assail importunately. **besieger,** *n.*

besmirch (bė-smėrch'), *v.t.* To soil, sully.

besom (bē'zŏm) [A.-S. *besma*], *n.* A
broom made of twigs.

besotted, *a.* Muddled, infatuated.

bespeak (bė-spēk') [A.-S. *besprecan*], *v.t.*
To arrange for, order beforehand; to
betoken. **bespoke,** *p.p.* Ordered beforehand.

besprinkle (bė-sprinkl'), *v.t.* To sprinkle
or scatter over.

best (best) [A.-S., superl. of GOOD], *a.* Of
the highest excellence. *adv.* [superl. of
WELL]. In the highest degree. *n.* The
best thing; the utmost. *v.t.* To get the
better of; to cheat, outwit.

bestial (bes'ti-ăl) [L. *bestiālis*], *a.* Pertaining to or resembling beasts; brutish,
obscene. **bestial'ity,** *n.* **bestially,** *adv.*

bestir (bė-stėr'), *v.t.* To rouse into activity.

bestow (bė-stō), *v.t.* To lay up; to provide
with quarters; to expend; to give as a
present. **bestowal,** *n.* Disposal; gift.

bestrew (bė-stroo'), *v.t.* To strew over.

bestride (bė-strīd'), *v.t.* To sit upon with
the legs astride.

bet (bet), *n.* A wager staked upon a
contingent event. *v.t.* To stake upon
a contingency. *v.i.* To lay a wager.

betake (bė-tāk'), *v.r.* To commit oneself
to any course of action.

betel-nut, *n.* The nut of the areca palm.

bethink (bė-think'), *v.t.* To recollect. *v.i.*
To consider, collect one's thoughts.

betide (bė-tīd') [M.E. *betiden*], *v.t.* To
happen to. *v.i.* To happen.

betimes (bė-tīmz'), *adv.* In good time.

betoken (bė-tōkn') [M.E. *bitacnen*], *v.t.* To
be a type of; to foreshow.

betray (bė-trā') [M.E. *betraien*], *v.t.* To
deliver up treacherously; to be false to;
to lead astray. **betrayal,** *n.* **betrayer,**
n. A traitor.

betroth (bė-trŏth'), *v.t.* To contract in an
engagement to marry. **betrothal,** *n.*
The act of betrothing; the state of being
betrothed; affiance. **betrothed,** *n.* A
person engaged to be married.

better (bet'ėr) [A.-S., comp. of GOOD], *a.*
Superior, more excellent; greater in
degree; improved in health. *adv.* [comp.
of WELL]. In a more excellent or more
desirable manner; more correctly; with
greater profit. *n.pl.* Social superiors.
v.i. To improve.

between (bė-twēn') [A.-S. *be, by, twēon,*
twain], *prep.* In, along, or across a place,
space, or interval of any kind; inter-

mediate in relation to; related to both
of; in shares among.

betwixt (bė-twikst') [A.-S. *betweox*], *prep.*
and *adv.* (*archaic*) Between.

bevel (bevl') [F. *beveau*], *a.* Oblique,
slanting. *n.* A tool for setting off angles;
a slope from the right angle. *v.t.* To cut
away to a slope. *v.i.* To slant.

beverage (bev'ėr-ăj) [O.F. *bevrage*], *n.*
Drink; liquor for drinking.

bevy (bev'i) [?], *n.* A flock of larks or
quails; a herd of roes; a company.

bewail (bė-wāl'), *v.t.* To wail over, lament
for. *v.i.* To express grief. **bewailing,** *n.*
Loud lamentation.

beware (bė-wâr') [M.E. *be war*, be cautious,
A.-S. *wœr*, wary], *v.i.* To be wary, on
one's guard; to take care.

bewilder (bė-wil'dėr), *v.t.* To perplex,
confuse. **bewildering,** *a.* Causing one
to lose his way, physically or mentally.
bewilderment, *n.* The state of being
bewildered.

bewitch (bė-wich'), *v.t.* To practise witchcraft; to charm, to fascinate.

bey (bā) [Turk. *bēg*], *n.* A Turkish governor.

beyond (bė-yond') [A.-S. BE-, *geond,* across],
prep. On or towards the farther side of;
past; exceeding in quantity, surpassing
in quality or degree. *adv.* Farther away.

bezel (bez'ĕl) [O.F. *bisel*], *n.* A sloping
edge; an oblique side of a cut gem; the
groove by which a jewel is held.

bezique (bė-zēk') [F. *besigue*], *n.* A game
of cards.

bi- [L., double], *pref.* Twice; doubly; every
two, once in every two. **biang'ular,** *a.*
Having two angles. **bicar'bonate,** *n.* A
carbonate containing two equivalents of
carbonic acid to one of a base. **bicus'-
pid.** *a.* Having two points or cusps. *n.*
One of the premolars. **bien'nial,** *a.*
Happening every two years, lasting two
years. *n.* A biennial plant.

bias (bī'ás) [F. *biais*, obliquity], *n.* A weight
placed in a bowl to impart oblique
motion; the motion; inclination, prejudice. *adv.* Obliquely, awry. *v.t.* To
cause to incline to one side; to prejudice.

bib (bib) [L. *bibere*, to drink], *n.* A cloth
worn under a child's chin. **bibber,** *n.*
A tippler.

Bible (bībl) [Gr. *biblia*, writings], *n.* The
Christian sacred writings. **biblical**
(bib'li-kǎl), *a.* **biblicist, biblist** (bib'list),
n. One who takes the Bible as the only
rule of faith; a biblical student.

biblio- [Gr. *biblion*, a book], *comb. form,*
pertaining to books. **bibliography,** *n.*
The methodical study of books, editions,
authorship, etc.; a systematic list of
books on any subject. **bibliographer,** *n.*
bibliographical, *a.* **bibliology,** *n.* Scientific study of books; biblical study.
bibliomania, *n.* A mania for collecting
books. **bibliophile,** *n.* A lover or fancier
of books.

bibulous (bib'û-lŭs) [L. *bibulus* (*bibere*)], *a.*
Given to tippling.

bicentenary (bi-sent'ė-nár-i), *a.* Pertaining
to two hundred years. *n.* The two
hundredth anniversary.

biceps (bī'seps), *n.* The large muscle in
front of the upper arm and of the thigh.

bicker (bik'er) [M.E. *bikere*], *v.i.* To dispute, wrangle; (*fig.*) to move rapidly to and fro. **bickering**, *n.* Altercation.

bicycle (bī'sĭkl), *n.* A two-wheeled velocipede, with the wheels one behind the other, propelled by the rider. *v.i.* To ride on a bicycle. **bicyclist**, *n.*

bid (bid) [A.-S. *beodan*, to offer, and *biddan*, to beg], *v.t.* To command; to invite; to offer. *v.i.* To make an offer at an auction. *n.* An offer of a price. **bidder**, *n.* One who makes an offer at an auction. **bidding**, *n.* Invitation, command.

bide (bīd) [A.-S. *bīdan* (cp. Dut. *beiden*, O.H.G. *bītan*)], *v.t.* To await. *v.i.* To abide, stay; to remain.

bier (bēr) [A.-S. *bēr* (*beran*, to bear)], *n.* A stand on which a corpse is placed, or on which the coffin is borne to the grave.

bifurcate (bī'fūr-kāt) [L. *furca*, a prong], *v.i.* To divide into two branches. *a.* Divided thus. **bifurca'tion**, *n.* Division into two parts; the point of division; one of the branches.

big (big) [?], *a.* Large or great in bulk; grown up; pompous, pretentious. **big game**, *n.* Hunter's name for the larger mammals. **bigness**, *n.* The quality of being big. **big-wig**, *n.* A man of importance.

bigamy (big'ā-mĭ) [BI-, Gr. *gamos*, marriage], *n.* Marriage with a second person while a legal spouse is living. **bigamist**, *n.* **bigamous**, *a.*

bight (bīt) [A.-S. *byht*], *n.* A bend; a small bay; the loop of a rope.

bigot (big'ŏt) [?], *n.* One unreasonably and intolerantly devoted to some creed, system, or party. **bigoted**, *a.* **bigotry**, *n.* The mental condition, etc., of a bigot.

bijou (bē'zhoo) [F.], *n.* (*pl.* bijoux). A jewel, a trinket; anything small and pretty.

bikini (bĭ-kē'nĭ) [Pacific island], *n.* (*Am.*) A style of beach garment; a swim suit.

bilateral (bī-lăt'ēr-ăl), *a.* Having or pertaining to two sides.

bilberry (bil'bĕr-ĭ) [cp. Dan. *böllebœr*], *n.* The whortleberry, blaeberry.

bilboes (bil'bōz) [?], *n.pl.* A long iron fetter, with sliding shackles for the feet.

bile (bīl) [L. *bīlis*, bile, anger], *n.* A bitter yellowish fluid secreted by the liver; (*fig.*) anger, choler. **bil'iary**, *a.* Pertaining to the bile. **bilious** (bil'yŭs), *a.* Produced or affected by bile; peevish, ill-tempered. **biliousness**, *n.*

bilge (bilj), *n.* The bulging part of a cask; (*Naut.*) the bottom of a ship's floor. *v.i.* (*Naut.*) To spring a leak; to bulge or swell. **bilge-water**, *n.* The foul water that collects in the bilge of a ship.

bilingual (bī-ling'gwăl) [L. *lingua*, tongue], *a.* In or pertaining to two languages.

bilk (bilk) [?], *v.t.* To cheat, defraud; to evade payment of, elude.

bill (1) (bil) [A.-S. *bile*], *n.* The horny beak of birds; a beak-like projection; a kind of halberd; a bill-hook. *v.i.* To lay the bills together (as doves). **bill-hook**, *n.* A heavy knife with hooked end, for chopping brushwood, etc.

bill (2) (bil) [A.-F. and M.E. *bille*, late L. *billa*, corr. of *bulla*, a sealed writing], *n.*

A statement of account; promissory note; draft of a proposed Act of Parliament; an advertisement distributed or posted up. *v.t.* To announce by, or cover with bills or placards; to put into a programme. **bill of fare**, *n.* A menu.

billet (1) (bil'et) [A.-F. *billette*, dim. of prec.], *n.* A ticket requiring a householder to furnish food and lodgings for a soldier; the quarters so assigned; a situation, appointment. *v.t.* To quarter (soldiers).

billet (2) (bil'et) [F. *billette*, dim, of *bille*, a log of wood], *n.* A small log for firing; a wedge or ingot of gold or silver.

billiards (bil'yărdz) [F. *billard*, a little stick], *n.pl.* A game in which three balls are driven about on a special table with a cue. **billiard-cue**, *n.* A tapering stick used to drive the balls.

Billingsgate (bil'ingz-gāt) [London fish-market], *n.* Scurrilous abuse.

billion (bil'i-ŏn, bil'yŏn) [BI-, *million*], *n.* A million millions, (in France and America) a thousand millions.

billow (bil'ō) [Icel. *bylgja*], *n.* A great swelling sea-wave. *v.i.* To surge; to rise in billows. **billowy**, *a.*

billy [*Austral.*], *n.* Combined kettle and teapot.

bimetallic (bī-mē-tăl'ik), *a.* Pertaining to bimetallism. **bimet'allism**, *n.* The employment of two metals (gold and silver) in currency at a fixed ratio, and as standard coin.

bin (bin) [A.-S. *binn*], *n.* A receptacle for corn, bread, wine, etc.

binary (bī'nȧ-rĭ) [L. *bīnārius*], *a.* Consisting of a pair or pairs; double, dual.

bind (bīnd) [A.-S. *bindan*], *v.t.* To tie or fasten; to confine; to cover, secure, or strengthen, by means of a band; to tie up; to cause to cohere; to make costive; to oblige, engage. *v.i.* To cohere; grow stiff and hard; to be obligatory. **binder**, *n.* **binding**, *a.* Obligatory. *n.* The act of binding; the act or art of book-binding; a book-cover, braid or other edging. **bindweed**, *n.* A climbing plant, esp. *Convolvulus.*

bingo (bing'gō), *n.* The game of lotto.

binnacle (bin'ȧkl) [formerly *bittacle*, L. *habitāculum*, a dwelling-place], *n.* The case in which the ship's compass is kept.

binocle (bin'ŏkl) [L. *bīnī*, two each, *oculi*, eyes], *n.* A telescope with tubes for both eyes. **binoc'ular**, *a.* Suited for use by both eyes. *n.* A binocle; binocular microscope.

binomial (bī-nō'mi-ăl) [L. *nomen*, a name], *n.* An expression consisting of two terms united by the signs + or -.

bio- [Gr. *bios*, life], *comb. form.* Pertaining to life or living beings. **bio-chemistry**, *n.* The chemistry of living things. **biogen'esis**, *n.* The doctrine that life originates only from life; the science of the origin of life.

biograph (bī'ō-gräf), *n.* An early name for the cinematograph.

biography (bī-og'rȧ-fĭ), *n.* The history of a person; literature dealing with personal history; biographer, *n.* A writer of biography. **biograph'ic, -al**, *a.* Pertaining to biography.

biology (bī-ol'ŏ-ji), *n.* The science of life in all its phases. **biolog'ic,** *a.* Pertaining to biology. **biol'ogist,** *n.*

biped (bī'ped) [L. *pes pedis*, foot], *n.* An animal having only two feet.

biplane (bī'plān), *n.* An aeroplane with two planes, one above the other.

birch (bērch) [A.-S. *birce*], *n.* A northern forest tree, with slender limbs and thin, tough bark; its wood; a birch-rod. *v.t.* To chastise with a birch-rod; to flog. **birching,** *n.* A flogging.

bird (bērd) [A.-S. *brid*], *n.* Any feathered vertebrate animal. **bird-lime,** *n.* A viscous substance used to snare birds. *v.t.* To smear or catch with bird-lime. **bird's-eye,** *a.* Resembling a bird's eye; seen from above, as by a bird. *n.* A tobacco.

biretta (bi-ret'ä) [It. *berretta*], *n.* A square cap worn by clerics.

birth (bērth) [M.E. *byrthe*, O. Teut. *beran*, to bear], *n.* The act of bringing forth, bearing offspring, or being born; that which is brought forth; parentage, extraction. **birthday,** *n.* The day on which one was born, or its anniversary. **birthmark,** *n.* A blemish formed on the body at or before birth. **birthplace,** *n.* The place at which one was born. **birth-rate,** *n.* The percentage of births to the population. **birthright,** *n.* Rights belonging to an eldest son or to a person as a human being.

biscuit (bis'kit) [O.F. *bescoit*, L. *bis coctus*, twice cooked], *n.* Thin flour-cake baked until it is highly dried; pottery baked in an oven before glazing.

bisect (bī-sekt') [L. *sectum*, cut], *v.t.* To divide into two equal parts. *v.i.* To fork. **bisection,** *n.*

bishop (bish'ŏp) [A.-S. *biscop*, L. *episcopus*, an overlooker], *n.* An ecclesiastical dignitary presiding over a diocese; a piece in chess; a drink of wine, oranges, and sugar. **bishopric** [A.-S. *bisceoprice* (*rice*, dominion)], *n.* The diocese, jurisdiction, or office of a bishop.

bismuth (bis'muth) [G.], *n.* A reddish-white metallic element used in medicine.

bison (bī'sŏn) [O.Teut. *wisand*], *n.* The wild ox; the American buffalo.

bisque (bisk), *n.* Unglazed white porcelain used for statuettes; a stroke allowed to the weaker player at tennis, etc.

bissextile (bis-sek'stil) [L.], *a.* Pertaining to leap-year. *n.* Leap-year.

bistre (bis'tĕr) [F.], *n.* A brown pigment.

bit (bit) [A.-S. *bite*], *n.* A bite, the act of biting; a small portion, morsel, fragment; the iron part of the bridle inserted in the mouth of a horse; the movable boring-piece in a drill.

bitch (bich) [A.-S. *bicce*], *n.* The female of the dog and of allied species.

bite (bīt) [A.-S. *bītan*], *v.t.* To seize, cut, crush anything with the teeth; to affect with severe cold, cause to smart; to wound with reproach or sarcasm; to hold fast, as a screw. *n.* The act of biting; wound made by the teeth; a mouthful. **biting,** *a.* Sharp, acrid, pungent; stinging, sarcastic.

bitt (bit) [?], *n.* A post fixed in pairs in the deck of a ship for fastening cables. **bitter end,** *n.* The loose end of a belayed rope; (*fig.*) the last extremity.

bitter (bit'ĕr) [A.-S. *biter*], *a.* Sharp or biting to the taste; acrid, harsh; piercingly cold; distressing. **bitterly,** *adv.* **bitterness,** *n.* **bitter-sweet,** *a.* Sweet or pleasant with a bitter after-taste.

bittern (bit'ĕrn) [M.E. *bitore*], *n.* A wading bird smaller than a heron and of the same family.

bitumen (bi-tū'mĕn) [L.], *n.* Mineral pitch, asphalt; a highly inflammable hydrocarbon, as naphtha, petroleum, etc. **bituminous,** *a.*

bivalve (bī'vălv), *a.* Having two shells which open and shut. *n.* A mollusc whose shell is in two connected portions. **bival'vular,** *a.*

bivouac (biv'u-ăk) [F.], *n.* A temporary encampment in the field without tents, etc. *v.i.* To camp in the open.

bizarre (bi-zar') [F.], *a.* Odd, whimsical; of discordant style; irregular. **bizar'rerie,** *n.* Grotesqueness, eccentricity.

blab (blăb) [?], *v.t.* To tell indiscreetly; to betray. *v.i.* To talk indiscreetly, tell secrets, tattle.

black (blăk) [A.-S. *blæc*], *a.* Intensely dark (the opposite of white); destitute of light; gloomy, dirty; atrociously wicked; disastrous. *n.* The darkest colour; a Negro; mourning garments; a minute particle of soot. *v.t.* To blacken; to blacklead. **black art,** *n.* Witchcraft. **blackamoor,** *n.* A Negro. **blackball,** *n.* Vote of rejection in a ballot. *v.t.* To vote against, exclude. **black-beetle,** *n.* The cockroach. **blackberry,** *n.* The common bramble; its fruit. **blackbird,** *n.* A British song-bird, *Turdus merula*. **blackboard,** *n.* A board used by teachers to write and draw on. **black cap,** *n.* A British bird, with the top of the head black, esp. the black-cap warbler, *Curruca atricapilla*. **black-cock,** *n.* The male of the black grouse. **blacken,** *v.t.* To make black, to darken; to sully, to defame. **blackguard** (blăg'ard), *n.* A low, worthless fellow; a rough. *a.* Scurrilous, abusive. *v.t.* To revile in scurrilous language. **blackguardism,** *n.* **blacking,** *n.* A composition for giving a shining black polish to boots, harness, etc. **blacklead** (blăk-led'), *n.* Plumbago or graphite, used for pencils and metal-polish. **black-letter,** *n.* The Old English or Gothic character. **black-list,** *n.* A list of persons who have incurred censure or punishment. **blackmail,** *n.* A payment extorted by intimidation. *v.t.* To levy blackmail on. **black market,** *n.* Illegal buying and selling of rationed goods. **blackness,** *n.* **black-out,** *n.* The shading of artificial light that might be visible from the air. **black sheep,** *n.* A bad character, a vicious person. **blacksmith,** *n.* A smith who works in iron. **blackthorn,** *n.* The sloe; a stick or cudgel of its wood.

bladder (blăd'ĕr) [A.-S. *blædre*], *n.* A sac in the body which receives the urine; any similar membranous bag.

blade (blād) [A.-S. *blæd*], *n.* A leaf, esp.

the expanded part; any broad, flattened part, as of a bat, oar, etc.; the cutting part of a knife, sword, etc.; a sword; a dashing, reckless fellow.

blaeberry (blä′bėr-i) [Icel. *blā*, dark blue], *n.* The bilberry or whortleberry.

blame (blām) [O.F. *blasmer*], *v.t.* To censure, reproach; to hold responsible. *n.* The expression of censure; responsibility. **blameable,** *a.* Deserving blame; culpable. **blameless,** *a.* **blameworthy,** *a.* Deserving blame.

blanch (blanch) [F.], *v.t.* To whiten, bleach, make pale. *v.i.* To lose colour; to become white.

blancmange (blä-monzh) [F.], *n.* A dish of corn-flour, etc., boiled to a jelly with milk, and flavoured.

bland (blănd) [L. *blandus*, agreeable], *a.* Mild, gentle. **blandly,** *adv.*

blandish (blăn′dish) [L. *blandīrī*, to flatter], *v.t.* To coax, cajole. **blandishment,** *n.*

blank (blăngk) [F. *blanc*, white], *a.* Empty; not written or printed on; confused, nonplussed; downright; (of verse) unrhymed. *n.* A vacant space, a void; a lottery ticket that draws no prize. **blankly,** *adv.* **blank cheque,** *n.* A signed cheque with the amount not filled in; a commission without limitations.

blanket (blăng′kėt) [O.F. *blankete*], *n.* A heavy, loosely-woven woollen stuff, used for bed-coverings, horse-wrappers, etc. *v.t.* To cover with or as with a blanket; to take the wind out of the sails of (a yacht) by passing to windward. **wet blanket,** *n.* A person who is a damper to conversation or enjoyment.

blare (blâr) [imit.], *v.i.* To bellow; to sound as a trumpet. *n.* Trumpet sound; roar.

blarney (blar′ni) [place-name], *n.* Flattering speech; cajolery. *v.t.* To wheedle, cajole.

blasé (bla′zā) [F.], *a.* Dulled in emotion; worn out; used-up.

blaspheme (blăs-fēm′) [Gr. *blasphemos*, evil-speaking], *v.t.* To utter profane language against (God or anything sacred); to abuse. *v.i.* To utter blasphemy, to rail. **blas′phemous,** *a.* **blas′phemy,** *n.*

blast (blast) [A.-S. *blæst*], *n.* A violent gust of wind; the sound of a trumpet; pernicious or destructive influence; a blowing by an explosive. *v.t.* To blow or breathe on so as to wither; to blight, to ruin; to blow up with an explosive; to curse. **blasted,** *a.* Blighted, confounded, cursed. **blast furnace,** *n.* Furnace into which a current of air is introduced to assist combustion.

blatant (blā′tănt) [?], *a.* Bellowing like a beast; clamorous. **blatancy,** *n.*

blaze (1) (blāz) [A.-S. *blæse*], *n.* A bright flame; a glow of bright colour; an outburst of splendour or of passion. *v.i.* To burn with a bright flame; to shine.

blaze (2) (blāz) [Icel. *blesi*], *n.* A white mark on the face of a horse or ox, or made on a tree by chipping off bark. *v.t.* To mark (a tree).

blaze (3) (blāz) [Icel. *blāsa*, to blow], *v.t.* To proclaim; to blazon.

blazer (blā′zėr), *n.* A flannel jacket of bright colour.

blazon (blā′zòn) [F. *blason*, a coat of arms], *n.* A coat of arms. *v.t.* To describe heraldically; to publish vauntingly.

bleach (blēch) [A.-S. *blǣcan*], *v.t.* To make white or lighter. *v.i.* To grow white; to become pale or colourless. **bleacher,** *n.*

bleak (blēk) [A.-S. *blāc*], *a.* Bare of vegetation; cold, desolate, cheerless.

blear (blēr) [?], *a.* Dim with rheum; dull, indistinct. *v.t.* To make (the eyes) dim; to blur with tears.

bleat (blēt) [A.-S. *blǣtan*], *v.i.* To cry like a sheep. *v.t.* To say feebly and foolishly. *n.* The cry of a sheep, etc.

bleed (blēd) [A.-S. *blēdan*], *v.i.* To emit or run with blood (sap, resin, etc.); to feel acute mental pain. *v.t.* To draw blood from; to extort money from; **bleeder,** *n.* (*Path.*) Person affected with hæmophilia. **bleeding,** *n.* Hæmorrhage; letting blood. *a.* Running with blood.

blemish (blem′ish) [O.F. *blesmir*], *v.t.* To tarnish, sully. *n.* A defect.

blench (blench) [A.-S. *blencan*], *v.i.* To shrink back, turn aside, flinch.

blend (blend) [A.-S. *blandan*], *v.t.* To mix, to mingle. *v.i.* To become mingled; to pass imperceptibly into each other. *n.* A mixture of various qualities (of teas, wines, tobacco, etc.).

bless (1) (bles) [A.-S. *blētsian*], *v.t.* To consecrate, invoke God's favour on; to render happy or wish happiness to. **blessed, blest,** *a.* Consecrated; worthy of veneration. *n.* (*collect.*). The saints in heaven. **blessedness,** *n.* **blessing,** *n.*

blether (bleth′ėr) [Icel. *blathr*, nonsense], *v.i.* To talk nonsense. *n.* Voluble nonsense.

blight (blīt) [?], *n.* A disease caused in plants by fungoid parasites, smut, aphides, etc.; any obscure malignant influence. *v.t.* To affect with blight; to exert a baleful influence on. **blighter,** *n.* A scamp, blackguard; an obnoxious person.

blind (blind) [A.-S.], *a.* Unseeing; sightless; admitting no light, having no outlet; destitute of understanding or foresight. *n.* Blind persons collectively; a window-screen; a pretence, a pretext. *v.t.* To deprive of sight; to make dim. **blindfold,** *v.t.* To cover the eyes, esp. with a bandage; *a.* Having the eyes bandaged. **blindly,** *adv.* **blindness,** *n.* **blind alley,** *n.* A street, road, etc., walled up at one end.

blink (blingk) [A.-S. *blencan*], *v.i.* To open and shut the eyes; to look unsteadily; to wink. *v.t.* To shut the eyes to; to shirk. *n.* A glimmer, twinkle; a glance. **blinkers,** *n.* Leather screens to prevent a horse from seeing sideways.

bliss (blis) [A.-S. *blis*], *n.* Happiness of the highest kind; the perfect joy of heaven.

blister (blis′tėr) [M.E.], *n.* A pustule on the skin containing a watery fluid; a similar swelling on metal, paint, etc.; a thing applied to raise a blister. *v.i.* To rise in blisters. *v.t.* To raise blisters on.

blithe (blīth) [A.-S. *blīthe*], *a.* Gay, merry, sprightly. **blithely,** *adv.*

blizzard (bliz′ård) [?], *n.* A furious storm of snow and wind.

bloat (blōt) [M.E. *bloat, blote,* see next], *v.t.*

To cause to swell; to make conceited. *v.i.* To swell; to grow turgid. bloated, *a.* Swollen, puffy; puffed up with pride.

bloater (blō'tĕr) [M.E. *blote*, soft, soaked], *n.* A herring partly cured by steeping in dry salt and smoking.

bloc (blok) [F.], *n.* (*Pol.*) A combination of parties or of nations.

block (blok) [F. *bloc*, G. *block*], *n.* A solid mass of wood, stone or any material; the piece of wood on which criminals were beheaded; a compact group of houses; a mould on which a thing is shaped; a pulley, or system of pulleys; an obstruction or its effects. *v.t.* To enclose; to stop up, obstruct; to impede progress; to shape a hat on the block; (*Cricket*) to stop a ball without attempting to hit it. **blockhead**, *n.* A stupid, dull person. **block-house**, *n.* A detached fort with loopholes for musketry. **blockish**, *a.* Stupid, dull; rough. **block-letters**, *n.pl.* Writing with capital letters only. **block system**, *n.* (*Rail.*) A method of signals to prevent collisions.

blockade (blok-ād'), *n.* The investment of a place so as to compel surrender by starvation or prevent communication with the outside. *v.t.* To subject to a blockade; to block up, to obstruct. **blockade-runner**, *n.* A vessel that attempts to run into a blockaded port.

blond. **blonde** (blond) [F.], *a.* Having light hair and a fair complexion. *n.* One who has this.

blood (blŭd) [A.-S. *blōd*], *n.* The red fluid circulating through the bodies of vertebrates; analogous fluid in invertebrates; lineage, descent; slaughter; the guilt of murder. **blood donor**, *n.* One who gives blood for transfusion. **blood-horse**, *n.* A horse of good breed or pedigree. **bloodhound**, *n.* A hound remarkable for keenness of scent; (*fig.*) a detective, spy. **bloodless**, *a.* Without blood; spiritless. **blood-money**, *n.* Money paid for information leading to conviction on a capital charge. **blood-poisoning**, *n.* A diseased condition set up by septic matter in the blood. **blood pressure**, *n.* (*Med.*) Pressure of blood on the walls of the containing arteries. **blood-relation**, *n.* A relation by descent, not merely by marriage. **bloodshed**, *n.* The act of shedding blood; murder; slaughter in war. **bloodshot**, *a.* Suffused with blood (of the eye). **blood-stone**, *n.* A variety of quartz with blood-like spots of jasper. **blood-sucker**, *n.* (*fig.*) An extortioner. **bloodthirsty**, *a.* Eager to shed blood. **bloodthirstiness**, *n.* **blood transfusion**, *n.* (*Med.*) Transference of blood from a healthy person to one whose blood is deficient in quantity or quality. **blood-vessel**, *n.* An artery or vein in which blood circulates. **bloody**, *a.*

bloom (bloom) [Icel. *blōm*, a blossom], *n.* A blossom, flower; the delicate dust on plums, grapes, etc.; flush, glow, perfection. *v.i.* To come into flower; to be at the highest point of perfection or beauty. **blooming**, *a.* Flourishing; bright, lustrous. **bloomy**, *a.* Full of blooms, flowery.

bloomer (bloo'mĕr) [Mrs. *Bloomer* (1850)], *n.* Short skirt and loose trousers gathered round the ankles for women.

blossom (blos'ŏm) [A.-S. *blōstma*], *n.* A flower; the mass of flowers on a fruit-tree. *v.i.* To put forth flowers, to bloom.

blot (blot) [?], *n.* A stain of ink or other discolouring matter, a cancellation, a blemish, disfigurement, defect, a fault. *v.t.* To spot or stain with ink, etc., to obliterate, to dry with blotting-paper; to disfigure, sully. *v.i.* To make blots, become blotted. **blotter**, *n.* A pad or book for absorbing superfluous ink from paper after writing; a blotting-pad. **blotting-paper**, *n.* Absorbent paper for drying up ink.

blotch (bloch), *n.* A pustule, boil; a clumsy daub; blotched, blotchy, *a.*

blouse (blouz) [F.], *n.* A loose upper garment belted at the waist.

blow (1) (blō) [A.-S. *blāwan*], *v.t.* To make a current of air, or send one from the mouth; to pant, to sound (a trumpet, etc.); to eject water and air (as cetaceans). *v.t.* To drive a current of air upon, to impel by wind; to inflate with air; to put out of breath, to sound a wind instrument; to taint by depositing eggs upon (as flies); to shatter by explosives. *n.* A blowing, a breath of fresh air; an egg (of a flesh-fly). **blow-fly**, *n.* The meat-fly. **blow-hole**, *n.* An air-hole; (*pl.*) the spiracles of a cetacean. **blower**, *n.* **blowy**, *a.*

blow (2) (blō) [A.-S. *blōwan*], *v.i.* To blossom. *n.* The state of blossoming; bloom.

blow (3) (blō) [?], *n.* A stroke with the fist or a weapon; a severe shock; a sudden calamity.

blubber (blŭb'ĕr), *n.* The fat underlying the skin in whales, etc.; blubber, blub, *v.i.* To cry noisily. **blubbing**, *n.*

bludgeon (blŭj'ŏn) [?], *n.* A short, thick stick, sometimes loaded.

blue (bloo) [O.F. *bleu*], *a.* Of the colour of the cloudless sky or deep sea; dressed in or coloured blue; (*fig.*) miserable, low-spirited; learned, pedantic (of women). *n.* One of the primary colours; a man who plays for his University in sport. *v.t.* To make blue; to treat with laundress's blue. **blueness**, *n.* **bluey**, **bluish**, *a.* **bluishness**, *n.* **blue bell**, *n.* The harebell of Scotland; the wild hyacinth of England. **blue-blooded**, *a.* Aristocratic. **blue-book**, *n.* An official report of Parliament or the Privy Council; **blue-bottle**, *n.* The meat-fly or blow-fly. **bluejacket**, *n.* A sailor in the British Navy. **bluestocking**, *n.* A woman affecting learning or literary tastes. **blue water**, *n.* The open sea.

bluff (1) (blŭf) [?], *a.* Having a broad, flattened front; blunt, outspoken. *n.* A cliff or headland with a broad, precipitous front. **bluffness**, *n.*

bluff (2) (blŭf) [?], *n.* An excuse, a blind; bluffing at cards; empty talk. *v.t.* To hoodwink; to make one's adversary believe one's hand, or position, etc., is stronger than it is.

blunder (blŭn'dĕr) [?], *v.i.* To err grossly or stupidly; to flounder, stumble. *v.i.*

To mismanage. *n.* A gross mistake, a stupid error. **blunderer,** *n.*

blunderbuss (blŭn'dẽr-bŭs) [Dut. *donderbus,* thunder-gun], *n.* A short, large-bored gun.

blunt (blŭnt) [?], *a.* Dull, obtuse; without edge or point; abrupt, unpolished. *v.t.* To make less sharp; to deaden, dull. *v.i.* To become blunt. **bluntness,** *n.*

blur (blẽr) [?], *n.* A smear, blot, misty effect. *v.t.* To smear; to stain, render indistinct.

blurb (blẽrb), *n.* Synopsis or puff of a book, usu. printed on the jacket.

blurt (blẽrt) [imit.], *v.t.* To utter abruptly.

blush (blŭsh) [A.-S. *āblisian*], *v.i.* To become red in the face; to be ashamed; to bloom. *n.* The reddening of the face.

bluster (blŭs'tẽr), *v.i.* To make a loud boisterous noise like the wind; to swagger, boast. *n.* Boisterous, blowing, inflated talk, swaggering. **blusterer,** *n.*

boa (bō'à) [L.], *n.* A large serpent; a long fur or feather tippet worn by women.

boar (bôr) [A.-S. *bār*], *n.* The uncastrated male of the swine. **boarish,** *a.* Swinish, brutal; cruel.

board (bôrd) [A.-S. *bord*, plank, table], *n.* A long piece of timber, moderately broad and thick; a flat slab of wood; a table; a frame on which chess, draughts, etc., are played; layers of paper, etc., pasted together; a table, esp. for meals; food served at table, one's keep, or money in lieu of keep; a council, or its members; (*pl.*) the stage. *v.t.* To furnish or cover with boards; to provide with daily meals (and usu. with lodgings); to go on a ship, embark. *v.i.* To have one's meals (and usu. lodging) at another's house. **boarder,** *n.* One who lives in the house of another; one who boards an enemy's ship. **boarding-house,** *n.* A house in which board may be had. **boarding-school,** *n.*

boast (bōst) [?], *n.* Vainglorious assertion, a brag; an occasion of pride. *v.i.* To brag, to praise oneself, speak ostentatiously. *v.t.* To extol, to speak of with pride. **boaster,** *n.* **boastful,** *a.*

boat (bōt) [A.-S. *bāt*], *n.* A small vessel, generally undecked; applied also to large vessels, passenger steamers, etc. *v.t.* To transport in a boat. *v.i.* To take boat, to row in a boat. **boat-hook,** *n.* A pole with an iron point and hook, used to push or pull a boat. **boat-house,** *n.* A house by the water in which boats are kept. **boatman,** *n.* A man who lets out, rows, or sails a boat for money. **boatswain,** **bos'n** (bōsn), *n.* A ship's officer who has charge of the rigging, cables, stores, etc.

bob (bob) [?], *n.* A weight at the end of a cord, pendulum, etc.; a bunch of hair, short curl; the docked tail of a horse; a shake, jog; a set of changes in bell-ringing; (*colloq.*) a shilling *v.i.* To have a short jerking motion; to curtsy.

bobbin (bob'in) [F. *bobine*], *n.* A wooden pin on which thread for making lace, etc., is wound; a reel, spool.

bobby sox (*Amer.*), *n.pl.* Ankle socks worn by young girls. **bobby soxer,** *n.* An adolescent girl.

bode (bōd) [A.-S. *boda,* a messenger], *v.t.*

To foretell, presage, forebode. *v.i.* To portend (well or ill). **boding,** *a.*

bodice (bod'is), *n.* A corset; a vest worn over the corset.

bodkin (bod'kin) [?], *n.* A tool for piercing holes; needle for leading a tape through a hem; person squeezed between two others.

body (bod'i) [A.-S. *bodig*], *n.* The material frame of animals; the trunk; the upper part of a dress; the main or central part; a collective mass of persons, things, doctrines, etc.; matter, substance, as opposed to spirit; a person, society, corporation, military force; strength, substantial quality. *v.t.* To clothe with a body; to embody. **body-guard,** *n.* A guard for the person of a sovereign or dignitary; retinue, following. **bodiless,** *a.* **bodily,** *a.* Pertaining to the body or physical nature; corporeal. *adv.* Corporeally united with matter, wholly, entirely.

Boer (boor) [Dut., farmer], *n.* A South African of Dutch birth or extraction.

boffin (bof'in), *n.* (*R.A.F. slang*) A scientist employed in the Service.

bog (bog) [Ir. *bogach*], *n.* A marsh, morass; wet, spongy soil. **boggy,** *a.* **bog-oak,** *n.* Oak found preserved in bogs. **bogtrotter,** *n.* An Irishman.

bogey (bō'gi) [Col. *Bogey,* an imaginary person], *n.* (*Golf*) A fair score or allowance for a good player.

boggle (bogl) [?], *v.i.* To start with fright; to hesitate, make difficulties; to bungle.

bogie (bō'gi) [?], *n.* A long, low truck on four small wheels; a plate-layer's trolley.

bogus (bō'gŭs) [?], *a.* Sham, spurious.

bogy (bō'gi) [?], *n.* A spectre, bugbear.

bohea (bō-hē') [*Bu-i* hills, in China], *n.* A kind of black tea.

Bohemian (bō-hē'mi-àn) [*Bohemia,* **-AN**], *a.* Pertaining to Bohemia, its people, or language; characteristic of gipsies or of social bohemians. *n.* A native or inhabitant of Bohemia; a gipsy; one who leads a free, irregular life, despising social conventionalities. **bohemianism,** *n.* The habits or conduct of a social bohemian.

boil (1) (boil) [O.F. *boillir,* L. *bulla,* a bubble], *v.i.* To bubble by the action of heat; to reach the temperature at which liquids become gas; to be cooked boiling; (*fig.*) to be agitated with passion. **boiler,** *n.* One who boils; a vessel in which a thing is boiled, or in which water is converted into steam; a tank for heating water; a vessel for boiling clothes, a copper. **boiling,** *a.*

boil (2) (boil) [A.-S. *bȳl*], *n.* A hard, inflamed, suppurating tumour.

boisterous (bois'tẽr-ŭs) [?], *a.* Stormy, noisy; tumultuous, rudely violent. **boisterously,** *adv.* **boisterousness,** *n.*

bold (bōld) [A.-S. *beald*], *a.* Daring, confident, fearless; striking; audacious, forward; steep, prominent. **bold-faced,** *a.* Impudent, shameless. **boldly,** *adv.* Impudently; with effrontery. **boldness,** *n.* Courage, enterprise; effrontery.

bole [Icel. *bolr*], *n.* The trunk of a tree.

bollard (bol'ärd) [**BOLE**], *n.* A large post on a dock for securing cables.

Bolshevism (bol'she-vizm) [Rus. *bolsheviki,*

majority party], *n.* The doctrine of proletarian rule, as inaugurated in Russia under Lenin in 1917. **Bolshevist, Bolshevik,** *n.* An adherent of this doctrine.

bolster (bōl'stér) [A.-S.], *n.* A long under-pillow; a pad or cushion. *v.t.* To support with a bolster; to aid, abet. **bolstering,** *n.* Prop, support.

bolt (1) (bōlt) [A.-S.], *n.* A short thick arrow; a discharge of lightning; a bar for fastening a door; a screw-headed metal pin for holding objects together; that portion of a lock which forms the fastening; a sudden flight; a measure of woven fabric (usu. 30 yards). *v.t.* To shut or fasten by means of a bolt; to swallow without chewing. *v.i.* To start suddenly forward or aside; to run away, desert. **bolter,** *n.* One that bolts or runs; a horse given to bolting.

bolt (2), **boult** (bōlt) [O.F. *bulter*], *n.* A sieve for separating bran from flour. *v.t.* To pass through a bolt; to examine. **bolting-cloth,** *n.* A fine cloth used in sifting meal.

bolus (bō'lŭs) [Gr. *bōlus*, a clod, lump], *n.* A large pill; anything unpalatable.

bomb (bom) [Gr. *bombos*, a humming sound], *n.* An explosive usually dropped from the air or thrown by hand. *v.t.* To attack with bombs. **bombard** (bom-bard'), *v.t.* To attack with shot and shell; to assail with arguments or invective. *n.* The earliest form of cannon. **bombardier** (bom-bár-dēr'), *n.* A non-commissioned artillery officer ranking as corporal. **bombard'ment,** *n.* The act of bombarding. **bomber,** *n.* (*Av.*) An aircraft designed for dropping bombs.

bombast (bom'bàst) [O.F. *bumbace*], *n.* Inflated speech, high-sounding words. **bombas'tic,** *a.*

bona fide (bō'nà fī'dē) [L.], *adv.* In good faith. *a.* Genuine.

bonanza (bō-năn'zà) [Sp. prosperity], *n.* A rich mine; a run of luck.

bon-bon (bon'bon) [F.], *n.* A sweetmeat.

bond (bond), *n.* That which binds or confines, restrains or cements, impedes or enslaves; a binding agreement; a mode of disposing bricks in a wall; (*Law*) a binding agreement, esp. a deed by which one person binds himself to pay a certain sum to another; a debenture. (*pl.*) chains, imprisonment, captivity. *v.t.* To put into a bonded warehouse; to mortgage; to bind or connect (as bricks). **bonded,** *a.* Bound by a bond; put in bond. **bondage** (bon'dàj), *n.* Slavery, captivity; subjection, restraint. **bondsman,** *n.* A slave; a surety.

bone (bōn) [A.-S. *bàn*], *n.* The hard parts of the skeleton and the substance of which it consists; articles made of bone; (*pl.*) mortal remains; dice; castanets. *a.* Of or pertaining to bone; made of bone. **bony,** *a.* **bone-shaker,** *n.* Early form of bicycle with metal or wooden tires.

bonfire (bon'fīr), *n.* A large fire in the open at public rejoicings, etc.; a fire for burning rubbish.

bonhomie (bon'ó-mē') [F. *bon*, good, *homme*, man], *n.* Good-nature, geniality.

bon mot (bon-mō) [F.], *n.* A witticism.

bonnet (bon'ét) [O.F. *bonet*, stuff of which caps were made], *n.* A head-covering without a brim; a protective covering to a machine, motor engine, etc.

bonny (bon'ĭ) [?], *a.* Beautiful, healthy-looking. **bonnily,** *adv.*

bonus (bō'nŭs) [L. good], *n.* Something over and above what is due; a premium; an extra dividend.

bonze (bonz) [Jap. *bonzō*], *n.* A Buddhist priest in Japan, China, etc.

booby (boo'bĭ) [Sp. *bobo*, a blockhead], *n.* A stupid fellow, a dunce; a gannet.

boogie-woogie (boo'gi-woo'gi), *n.* (*Mus.* and *Dancing*) A jazz style of a rhythmic and percussive nature based on 12-bar blues.

book (buk) [A.-S. *bōc*], *n.* A collection of sheets printed, written on, or blank, bound in a volume; a division of a literary composition; (*Turf*) bets on a race or at a meeting taken collectively. *v.t.* To enter or register in a book; to obtain by payment in advance (a seat at a theatre, etc.). **book-account,** *n.* A register of debit or credit in a book. **booked,** *a.* Registered, entered in a book; (*slang*) caught, engaged. **book-debt,** *n.* A debt entered in an account book. **booking,** *n.* Registry in a book. **booking-office,** *n.* An office where railway or other tickets are issued, goods booked to be forwarded, etc. **bookish,** *a.* Learned, studious; acquainted with books only. **book-keeper,** *n.* One who keeps accounts in a merchant's office, etc. **book-maker,** *n.* A professional betting-man. **book-plate,** *n.* A device pasted in a book to show the ownership. **book-worm,** *n.* A worm which eats holes in books; (*fig.*) one always poring over books.

boom (1) (boom) [imit.], *n.* A deep, resonant sound, as of artillery, etc.; (*fig.*) a sudden demand for a thing; a rapid burst of commercial activity and prosperity. *v.i.* To make a loud, deep, resonant sound; to rush with violence, as a ship in full sail; (*fig.*) to become very popular, prosperous or active. *v.t.* To utter with a booming sound; (*fig.*) to force on public attention or into great activity, etc.

boom (2) (boom) [Dut. *boom*, a tree], *n.* A long spar to extend the foot of a sail; a line of floating spars forming an obstruction.

boomerang (boo'mĕ-răng) [Austral.], *n.* A native Australian missile weapon, so constructed that, thrown forward, it returns to the rear of the thrower.

boon (1) (boon) [Icel. *bōn*], *n.* A petition; a favour, gift; a blessing.

boon (2) (boon) [F. *bon*, good], *a.* Jolly, convivial.

boor (boor), *n.* A rustic; a rude, ill-bred fellow. **boorish,** *a.* **boorishness,** *n.*

boot (1) (boot) [O.F. *bote*], *n.* A leather covering for the foot reaching above the ankle; an instrument of torture applied to the leg and foot; a receptacle under driver's or guard's seat in a coach, etc. *v.t.* To put boots on. **booted,** *a.* Having boots on; (*slang*) kicked out. **boot-jack,**

n. A board with a crotch to retain the heel while the boot is being pulled off. **boot-last, -tree,** *n.* A block inserted into a boot to stretch it or keep it in shape. **boots,** *n.* A male servant at an hotel.

boot (2) (boot) [A.-S. *bōt* (*bētan*, to help)], *n.* Profit, advantage. **to boot:** Into the bargain. *v.i.* To avail, to be of use. **bootless,** *a.* Profitless, unavailing.

booth (booth) [M.Dan. *bōth*], *n.* A stall, tent, or other temporary erection; a temporary structure for voting in at elections

booty (boo'tï) [M.Dut. *būte*, booty], *n.* Spoil taken in war; plunder. **to play booty,** *v.i.* To join with confederates to cheat another player; to play to lose.

booze (booz) [M.E. *bousen*, to drink deeply], *n.* Drink; a drinking bout. *v.i.* To drink to excess. **boozy,** *a.*

borage (bûr'aj) [O.F. *borrace*], *n.* A hairy, blue-flowered plant.

borax (bôr'ăks) [Arab. *būrāq*], *n.* A native salt used as a solder, and as a detergent. **borac'ic,** *a.* Pertaining to, or derived from, borax.

border (bôr'dêr) [O.F. *bordure*], *n.* Edge, margin; frontier; an ornamental edging. *v.t.* To put a border or form a boundary to. *v.i.* To lie on the border; to be contiguous. **borderer,** *n.* **borderland,** *n.*

bore (1) (bôr) [A.-S. *borian*], *v.t.* To perforate or make a hole through; to weary with twaddle or dullness. *v.i.* To make a hole; to push a horse, boat, or other competitor out of the course. *n.* A hole made by boring; the diameter of a tube; a tiresome person, a wearisome twaddler. **borer,** *n.* One who or that which bores.

bore (2) (bôr) [prob. Icel. *bāra*, a billow], *n.* A tidal wave of great height and velocity.

borecole (bôr'kōl) [Dut.], *n.* A variety of winter cabbage, kail.

boredom (bôr'dŏm), *n.* The behaviour of bores; the condition of being wearied by a bore; bores collectively.

born (bôrn), *p.p.* and *a.* Brought into the world; brought forth, produced.

borough (bûr'ŭ) [A.-S. *burh*], *n.* A town with a municipal corporation, or which sends a representative to Parliament. **borough English,** *n.* (*Law*) An old custom whereby the youngest son inherits lands, etc.

borrow (bor'ō) [A.-S. *borgian*], *v.t.* To obtain as a loan; to adopt, assume.

Borstal system (bôr'stăl) [name of village nr. Rochester], *n.* A method of treating juvenile offenders by education.

borzoi (bôr'zoi) [Rus.], *n.* A Russian wolfhound.

bosh (bosh) [Turk.], *n.* Empty talk, folly.

bosky (bos'kï), *a.* Bushy, woody.

bosom (buz'ŭm) [A.-S. *bŏsm*], *n.* The breast (esp. of a woman); the seat of emotions, repository of secrets. *a.* Much beloved; confidential.

boss (1) (bos) [O.F. *boce*], *n.* A protuberance; an ornamental knob; a miss, bad shot. *v.t.* To miss, bungle. *v.i.* To make a miss. **boss-eyed,** *a.* Afflicted with a squint; having but one eye, or with one eye damaged.

boss (2) (boss) [Dut. *baas*, master], *n.* A foreman, manager; a political dictator. *v.t.* To manage, direct, control.

bot, bott (bot) [?], *n.* A parasitic worm; (*pl.*) a disease caused by these in horses, cattle, and sheep.

botanic (bŏ-tăn'ĭk), **-al** [Gr. *botanikos*, pertaining to plants], *a.* Pertaining to botany. **bot'anist,** *n.* **bot'any,** *n.* The science which treats of plants.

botch (boch) [?], *n.* A clumsy patch; a bungle. *v.t.* To mend or put together clumsily. **botcher,** *n.* A bungler.

both (bōth) [Icel. *bāthir*], *a.* and *pron.* The one and the other, the two. *adv.* As well the one as the other; equally in two cases.

bother (both'êr) [?], *v.t.* To tease, vex, to annoy. *v.i.* To make a fuss, worry oneself; to take trouble. *n.* Worry, disturbance, fuss. **bothera'tion,** *n.*

bothy, bothie (both'ï) [?], *n.* A hut.

bottle (botl) [O.F. *boteile*], *n.* A vessel (usu. of glass) with a narrow neck for holding liquids; its contents. *v.t.* To put into bottles; to restrain, repress. **bottle-green,** *n.* Dark green. **bottle-holder,** *n.* A second at a prize-fight, **bottle-washer,** *n.* A general factotum.

bottom (bot'ŏm) [A.-S. *botm*], *n.* The lowest part of anything; the bed of a body of water; the farthest point of a recess, gulf, etc.; a ship as receptacle for cargo. *v.t.* To put a bottom to; to sound, fathom. **bottomless,** *a.* **bottommost,** *a.* **bottomry,** *n.* Borrowing money on the security of a ship.

botulism (bot'ū-lizm) [L. *botulus*, sausage], *n.* Poisoning by a ptomaine found in decomposed meat, esp. sausages.

boudoir (boo'dwar) [F., from *bouder*, to sulk], *n.* A lady's private apartment.

bough (bou) [A.-S. *bōg*, shoulder], *n.* A large arm or branch of a tree.

boulder (bōl'dêr) [M.E. *bulderston*], *n.* A large rounded block of stone.

boulevard (bool'var) [F.], *n.* A broad street planted with trees.

bounce (bouns) [?], *n.* A recoil, leap, spring; swagger, self-assertion. *v.i.* To bound like a ball; to spring suddenly forth; to come or go unceremoniously; to talk big. **bouncer,** *n.*

bound (1) (bound) [F. *bondir*], *n.* A leap, spring, rebound. *v.i.* To leap, to spring; to bounce. **bounder,** *n.* (*Slang*) An ill-bred, vulgar, pushful man.

bound (2) (bound) [O.F. *bonde*], *n.* A limit, a boundary. *v.t.* To set bounds to; to confine. **boundless,** *a.* Without bounds. **boundary,** *n.* A mark indicating limit; the limit thus marked.

bound (3) (bound) [*past and p.p.*, BIND], *a.* Under obligation; certain (*with inf.*; (*Books*) in a cover. **bounden,** *a.* Bound; obliged.

bound (4) (bound) [M.E. *boun*], *a.* Starting, destined.

bounty (boun'tï) [O.F. *bonté*], *n.* Gracious liberality; a premium for recruits, or to encourage commerce or industry. **bounteous,** *a.* Full of bounty; liberal. **bountiful,** *a.* Liberal, munificent; plenteous.

bouquet (bu-kā') [F.]. *n.* A nosegay, bunch of flowers; perfume of wine.

bourgeois (boor'zhwa) [F.], *n.* A citizen; one of the mercantile or shop-keeping class. *a.* Middle-class as distinguished from working-class; *(fig.)* commonplace, unintellectual. **bourgeoisie** (-zē'), *n.* The middle class.

bourne, bourn (boorn) [F. *borne*], *n.* A bound, limit, goal.

bout (bout) [?], *n.* A round, a set-to; a spell of work, drunkenness, etc.

bovine (bō'vin) [L. *bovīnus*], *a.* Of or resembling oxen; sluggish; dull, stupid.

bow (1) (bō) [A.-S. *boga*], *n.* A weapon for discharging arrows; a rainbow; a curve; an ornamental knot; the appliance with which instruments of the violin family are played. *v.t.* To play with the bow on the violin, etc. **bow-legged,** *a.* Having the legs curved outwards. **bowshot,** *n.* The distance to which an arrow can be shot. **bowstring,** *n.* The string by which a bow is stretched. *v.t.* To strangle with a bowstring.

bow (2) (bou) [A.-S. *būgan*], *v.i.* To bend forward as a sign of assent, salutation, etc.; to bend under a yoke. *v.t.* To cause to bend; to incline; to crush. *n.* An inclination of the head, as a salute.

bow (3) (bou), *n.* The rounded fore-end of a ship or boat; the rower nearest this. **bowline** (bō'lin), *n.* A rope fastened to a sail to make it stand close to the wind. **bowsprit** (bō'sprit) *n.* A spar running out from the bows of a vessel.

bowdlerize (boud'lér-iz) [Thomas *Bowdler* (1754–1825), who expurgated Shakespeare], *v.t.* To expurgate (a book). **bowdleriza'tion,** *n.*

bowel (bou'él) [O.F. *boel*], *n.* One of the intestines; *(pl.)* the entrails, intestines; the seat of tender emotions; compassion.

bower (bou'ér) [A.-S. *būr*, a chamber], *n.* A boudoir; an arbour; [BOW (3)] a small anchor carried at the bow.

bowl (1) (bōl) [A.-S. *bolla*], *n.* A hollow, rounded vessel for holding liquids.

bowl (2) (bōl) [F. *boule*, L. *bulla*, a bubble], *n.* A solid, slightly biased ball used to play with; *(pl.)* a game with bowls. *v.i.* To play at bowls; to roll a bowl along the ground; to deliver the ball at cricket. *v.t.* To cause to roll or run along the ground; to deliver (as a ball at cricket); to strike the wicket and put a man out.

bowler (bō'lér), *n.* A low-crowned stiff felt hat; one who plays at bowls; the player who delivers the ball at cricket.

bow-window, *n.* A bay-window.

box (1) (boks) [A.-S.], *n.* A genus of evergreen shrubs; box-wood; a receptacle adapted for holding solids, not liquids; its contents; a compartment in a theatre, tavern, etc., or for animals in a stable; the driver's seat on a coach. *v.t.* To enclose in or furnish with a box. **boxcloth,** *n.* A tough, closely-woven cloth. **box-office,** *n.* An office in a theatre, etc., for booking seats. **box spanner,** *n.* *(Mech.)* A tubular spanner with the ends shaped to fit the nuts, and turned by a bar inserted into a transverse hole.

box (2) (boks) [?], *n.* A blow with the open hand on the side of the head. *v.t.* To strike with the open hand. *v.i.* To fight with fists or gloves. **boxer,** *n.*

boy (boi) [?], *n.* A male child; a native labourer. **boyhood,** *n.* The state of being a boy; the time when one is a boy. **boyish,** *a.* Boy Scout, *n.* Member of an organization founded in 1908 for the development in boys of good citizenship and character.

boycott (boi'kōt) [Capt. *Boycott* 1832–97)], *v.t.* To combine to ostracize (a person); to refuse to have dealings with. *n.* The action of boycotting.

brace (brās) [O.F. *brace*, Gr. *brachiōn*, the arm], *n.* That which clasps, tightens, supports; a couple, a pair; a tool used by carpenters for boring; a rope attached to a yard for trimming the sail; *(pl.)* straps to support the trousers. *v.t.* To gird or bind; to tighten or strengthen, to fill with energy or firmness. **bracing,** *a.* Imparting tone or strength.

bracelet (brās'lét) [F.], *n.* An ornamental ring or band for the wrist or arm.

brachy- [Gr. *brachus*, short], *comb. form.* Short. **brachycephalic** (brăk-i-sē-făl'ik) [Gr. *kephalē*, head], *a.* Short-headed.

bracken (brăk'én) [Swed. *brāken*], *n.* The brake-fern, *Pteris aquilina.*

bracket (brăk'ét) [L. *braccœ*, breeches], *n.* A support fixed to a wall; a mark enclosing a word or words.

brackish (brăk'ish) [Dut. *brak*], *a.* Partly fresh, partly salt; saline.

brad (brăd) [M.E. *brod*], *n.* A thin, flattish nail. **brad'awl,** *n.* A small boring-tool.

brae (brā) [Icel. *brā*], *n.* A slope, hill.

brag (brăg) [?], *n.* A boast; a game of cards. *v.i.* To boast. **braggadocio** (brăg-á-dō'shi-ō), *n.* An empty boaster; empty boasting. **brag'gart,** *n.* A boastful fellow. *a.* Given to bragging.

braid (brād) [A.-S. *brœgd*, trick, deceit], *n.* A narrow woven band; a woven fabric for trimming, etc. *v.t.* To intertwine, plait; to trim or bind with braid.

brail (brāl) [O.F.], *n.* A rope used to furl sails and tent-bottoms.

braille (brāl) [Louis *Braille* (1809–52)], *n.* A system of writing for the blind.

brain (brān) [A.-S. *brœgen*], *n.* The convoluted mass of nervous substance contained in the skull; the seat of thought, etc., centre of sensation; intellectual power. *v.t.* To dash out the brains of. **brainless,** *a.* **brainy,** *a.* Acute, clever. **brain wave,** *n.* Sudden inspiration, a good notion.

braise (brāz) [F. *braise*, hot charcoal], *v.t.* To cook in a tightly-closed pan.

brake (1) (brāk), *n.* Bracken.

brake (2) (brāk) [O.Dut. *bracke*, a flax-brake], *n.* A large wagonette.

brake (3) (brāk) [?], *n.* An appliance to check motion of a wheel; a brake-van. *v.t.* To retard by means of a brake. **brake-van,** *n.* A railway carriage containing a brake.

brake (4) (brāk) [perh. M.L.G. *brake*, tree-stumps], *n.* A mass of brushwood, a thicket. **braky,** *a.* Full of brake; rough.

bramble (brămbl) [A.-S. *brembel*], *n.* The blackberry, or allied thorny shrub.

bran (brăn) [O.F.], *n.* The husks of ground corn.

branch (branch) [F. *branche*], *n.* A limb of a tree, esp. from a bough; any analogous offshoot or subdivision. *v.i.* To shoot out into branches; to diverge, divide, to ramify. *v.t.* To divide into branches.

brand (brănd) [A.-S.], *n.* A piece of burning wood; a mark made with a hot iron, an instrument for burning a mark; a trade-mark, a particular kind of manufactured article; a sword; a stigma; class, quality. *v.t.* To mark with a brand; to imprint on the memory; to stigmatize. **brand-new**, *a.* As if just from the furnace, quite new.

brandish (brăn'dish) [F. *brandir*], *v.t.* To wave or flourish about. *n.* A flourish.

brandy (brăn'di) [Dut. *brande-wijn*, burnt or distilled wine], *n.* A spirit distilled from wine.

brass (bras) [A.-S. *bræs*], *n.* A yellow alloy of copper and zinc; anything made of this; effrontery, impudence. *a.* Made of brass. *v.t.* To coat with brass. **brass hat**, *n.* (*colloq.*) A staff officer. **brass tacks**, *n.pl.* (*colloq.*) Facts and not words. **brassy**, *a.* Resembling brass; impudent, shameless; pretentious. *n.* A wooden golf club faced with brass.

brassard (brăs'ärd) [F.], *n.* A badge for the arm.

brassière (brăs'i-âr) [F.], *n.* A bodice for supporting the bust.

brat (brăt) [?], *n.* A child (in a slighting sense).

bravado (bră-va'dō) [Sp.], *n.* (*pl.* -oes) An insolent menace; ostentatious defiance.

brave (brāv) [F.], *a.* Daring, courageous; noble; gay; excellent. *n.* A warrior. *v.t.* To defy, challenge; to meet with courage. *v.i.* To swagger, show off. **bravery**, *n.* Courage; display, finery.

bravo (bra'vō) [It.], *n.* (*pl.* -oes) A hired assassin, a desperado; a cry of approval, a cheer. *int.* Capital! well done!

bravura (bră-voo'ră) [It.], *n.* Brilliance of execution.

brawl (brawl) [?], *v.i.* To quarrel noisily, create a disturbance; to babble (as running water). *n.* A noisy quarrel, disturbance, tumult. **brawler**, *n.* **brawling**, *a.*

brawn (brawn) [O.F. *braon*, flesh for roasting], *n.* Muscle; the flesh of a boar; pig's head collared or potted. **brawny**, *a.* Muscular, strong, hardy. **brawniness**, *n.*

bray (1) (brā) [O.F. *breier*], *v.t.* To pound small; to beat fine.

bray (2) (brā) [O.F. *braire*], *v.i.* To make a discordant noise like an ass. *n.* The cry of the ass; a harsh, grating sound.

braze (brāz) [O.F. *braser*], *v.t.* To solder with an alloy of brass and zinc; to cover or ornament with brass.

brazen (brā'zĕn) [A.-S. *bræsen*], *a.* Made of or resembling brass; shameless, impudent. *v.t.* To face impudently; to harden, make shameless. **brazen-faced**, *a.* Impudent, shameless. **brazenly**, *adv.*

brazier (1) (brā'zi-êr), *n.* A worker in brass.

brazier (2) (brā'zi-êr) [F. *braise*, live coals], *n.* A large pan to hold lighted charcoal.

breach (brēch) [A.-S. *brice*], *n.* The act of breaking; a gap; violation of a law;

alienation, quarrel. *v.t.* To make a gap in.

bread (bred) [A.-S.], *n.* Food made of flour or meal kneaded into dough, generally with yeast, and baked. **bread-crumb**, *n.* A fragment of the soft part of bread. **bread-fruit**, *n.* The farinaceous fruit of a South Sea tree, *Artocarpus incisa.*

breadth (bredth) [A.-S. *brædu*], *n.* Measure from side to side; liberality, tolerance.

break (brāk) [A.-S. *brecan*], *v.t.* (*past* broke, earlier brake, *p.p.* broken, broke) To part by violence; to rend apart, rupture, disperse; to subdue, tame; to ruin financially; to cashier, reduce to the ranks; to disable, exhaust the strength or resources of; to interrupt, intercept, lessen the force of; to transgress, violate. *v.i.* To separate into portions; to burst forth; to decline in health; to change direction, as a ball at cricket; to make the first stroke at billiards; to alter (as a boy's voice). *n.* The act of breaking; an opening, gap; interruption; the twist of a ball at cricket; (*Billiards*) a number of points scored continuously. **breakdown**, *n.* Downfall, collapse; failure resulting in stoppage. **breakfast** (brek'-făst), *n.* The first meal in the day, *v.i.* To take breakfast; *v.t.* To provide with or entertain at breakfast. **break-neck**, *a.* Endangering the neck, hazardous. **breakwater**, *n.* A pier, wall, mole, etc., to protect shipping. **breakable**, *a.* Capable of being broken. **breakage**, *n.* The act of breaking; damage from breaking; the thing broken. **breaker**, *n.* One who or that which breaks; a heavy wave breaking against rocks, or in passing over shallows.

bream (brēm) [O.F. *bresme*], *n.* A freshwater fish.

breast (brest) [A.-S. *brēost*], *n.* The forepart of the body; one of the organs for the secretion of milk in women; the upper fore-part of a coat, etc.; the affections. *v.t.* To apply or oppose the breast to; to stem, oppose. **breast-bone**, *n.* The sternum, to which certain ribs are attached. **breast-summer**, **bressummer** (bres'ŭm-êr), *n.* A beam supporting the front of a building.

breath (breth) [A.-S. *bræth*], *n.* The air drawn in and expelled by the lungs; the act of breathing; a single respiration; a very slight breeze; an exhalation; a rumour, whisper. **breathless**, *a.*

breathe (brēth), *v.i.* To inhale or exhale air; to live; to take breath; to move or sound like breath. *v.t.* To inhale or exhale (as air); to utter with vehemence (with *out*); to express; to allow breathing space to; to blow into. **breathing**, *a.* Living; life-like. *n.* Respiration; a respite; an aspirate.

breech (brēch) [A.-S. *brēc*], *n.* (*pl.* breeches, brich'ĕz). The hinder part of anything; the portion of a gun behind the bore; (*pl.*) an outer garment worn by men from the loins to the knees. *v.t.* To clothe with breeches. **breech-loader**, *n.* A firearm loaded at the breech.

breed (brēd) [A.-S. *brēdan*], *v.t.* To give birth to; to raise (cattle, etc.); to yield, produce; to engender, to educate, to bring up. *v.i.* To be pregnant; to produce offspring; to come into being. *n.* A line of descendants from the same stock; family, race. **breeder**, *n.* One who breeds cattle. **breeding**, *n.* Deportment, good manners.

breeze (brēz) [Sp. *brisa*, the N.E. wind], *n.* A light wind; a disturbance, a row. **breezy**, *a.* Exposed to breezes, windy; lively, brisk, jovial. **breeziness**, *n.* breeze block, *n.* A brick or block made of cinders and cement.

Bren gun (bren) [two first letters each of *Brno* and *En*field], *n.* (*Mil.*) A type of light machine-gun.

breve (brēv), *n.* A sign (˘) used to mark a short vowel; (*Mus.*) a note equal to two semibreves.

brevet (brĕ-vet′) [F., dim of *bref*, a letter], *n.* An official document conferring certain privileges; (*Mil.*) a warrant conferring rank on an officer without pay. *a.* Honorary, nominal.

breviary (brē′vi-à-ri) [L. *breviārium*], *n.* (*R.-C. Ch.*) A book containing the prayers for the canonical hours.

brevier (bre-vēr′), *n.* (*Print.*) A small size of type.

brevity (brev′i-ti) [L. *brevitas-tātem*], *n.* Briefness, shortness; conciseness.

brew (broo) [A.-S. *bréowan*], *v.t.* To make (beer, ale, etc.); (*fig.*) to contrive, to bring about. *v.i.* To make beer, etc., by boiling, fermenting, etc.; to be in preparation. *n.* The action, process or product of brewing; the quantity brewed. **brewer**, *n.* One who brews malt liquors. **brewery**, **brew-house**, *n.*

bribe (brīb) [O.F.], *n.* A gift offered to one to influence his judgment or conduct; an inducement. *v.t.* To influence action or opinion thus. *v.i.* To practise bribery. **bribery**, *n.* The act of giving or receiving bribes.

bric-à-brac (brik′à-bràk) Fancy ware, curiosities.

brick (brik) [F. *brique*, a fragment], *n.* A block of moulded and baked clay used in building; a brick-shaped loaf; (*slang*) a good fellow. *v.t.* To construct with bricks; to imitate brickwork in plaster. **brickbat**, *n.* A broken piece of brick. **bricklayer**, *n.* One who sets bricks.

bridal (brī′dàl) [A.-S. *brȳd-ealo*, wedding-feast], *n.* The nuptial ceremony or festival; a marriage.

bride (brīd) [A.-S. *brȳd*], *n.* A woman newly married or on the point of being married. **bridegroom** [A.-S. *guma*, man], *n.* A man about to be married, or recently married. **bridesmaid**, *n.* An unmarried woman who attends on the bride at her wedding.

bridge (1) (brij) [A.-S. *brycg*], *n.* A structure over a river, road, etc., to carry a road or path across; the upper bony part of the nose; the bar over which the strings are stretched in a violin, etc. *v.t.* To span or cross with a bridge.

bridge (2) (brij), *n.* A card game developed from whist. **auction-**, **contract-bridge**, *n.* Developments of bridge.

bridle (brīdl) [A.-S. *brīdel*], *n.* A head-

stall and bit for a horse; a curb, check, restraint. *v.t.* To put a bridle on; to control with a bridle; to hold in, check. *v.i.* To hold up the head in pride, scorn, or resentment (with *up*). **bridle-hand**, *n.* The left hand, which holds the reins. **bridle-path**, *n.* A horse-track not wide enough for vehicles.

brief (brēf) [O.F. *bref*], *a.* Short in duration; concise; curt. *n.* A papal letter; a summary given to counsel in charge of a case. *v.t.* To instruct or retain (a barrister) by brief; to furnish with essential information in order to perform a task. **briefless**, *a.* Having no briefs; without clients.

brier (brī′ér) [A.-S. *brēr*, F. *bruyère*, heath], *n.* A thorny or prickly shrub, esp. of a wild rose; the white or tree heath, *Erica arborea*; a tobacco-pipe made from its root.

brig (brig), *n.* A square-rigged vessel with two masts.

brigade (bri-gād′) [It. *brigata*, a ʒɔɛp], *n.* A large subdivision of an army. **brigadier** (brig-à-dēr′), *n.* An officer in command of a brigade; rank above that of colonel.

brigand (brig′ånd) [F.], *n.* A robber, bandit, outlaw.

brigantine (brig′àn-tēn) [It. *brigantino*, a pirate-ship], *n.* A two-masted vessel brig-rigged on the foremast and schooner-rigged on the mainmast.

bright (brīt) [A.-S. *beorht*], *a.* Emitting or reflecting abundance of light; shining; cheerful, sanguine, clever. *adv.* Brightly. **brighten**, *v.t.* To make bright. *v.i.* To become bright; (*weather*) to clear up. **brightly**, *adv.* **brightness**, *n.*

brill (bril) [?], *n.* A sea-fish.

brilliant (bril′yànt) [F. *brillant*], *a.* Shining, sparkling; distinguished; clever and successful. *n.* A diamond of the finest cut; the smallest type. **brilliance**, **brilliancy**, *n.* **brilliantly**, *adv.*

brim (brim) [?], *n.* The upper edge of a vessel, body of water, etc.; the rim of a hat.

brimstone (brim′stòn) [M.E. *bren*, to burn, STONE], *n.* Sulphur.

brindled (brindld) [?], *a.* Tawny, streaked with bars of darker hue.

brine (brīn) [A.-S. *brȳne*], *n.* Water strongly impregnated with salt. **briny**, *a.*

bring (bring) [A.-S. *bringan*], *v.t.* To cause to come with oneself; to carry, conduct, prevail upon, influence, persuade.

brink (bringk) [Scand.], *n.* The edge of a precipice, pit, etc.; the margin of water.

briquette (bri-ket′) [F.], *n.* A block of compressed coaldust.

brisk (brisk) [?], *a.* Lively, animated; stimulating, bracing. **briskly**, *adv.*

brisket (bris′kĕt) [?], *n.* That part of the breast next to the ribs; a joint of meat.

bristle (brisl) [A.-S. *byrst*], *n.* A short, stiff, coarse hair, particularly of swine; a stiff hair on plants. *v.i.* To stand erect (as hair); to show defiance, etc.; to be thickly beset (with difficulties, dangers, etc.). **bristly**, *a.*

Britain (brit′àn) [Celtic *Britto*, *Brython*, name of the people], *n.* England, Wales, and Scotland. Britannia (bri-tăn'yá), n. Britain personified. Britannia metal, n. A white alloy of tin, copper, and antimony. British, a. Briton (brit'òn), n. A native of Britain.

brittle (britl) [A.-S. *brēotan*, to break], a. Liable to be broken, fragile.

broach (brōch) [F. *broche*, a spit], n. A roasting-spit; a mason's chisel, a boring-bit. v.t. To pierce (as a cask), so as to allow liquor to flow; to make public.

broad (brawd) [A.-S. *brād*], a. Wide, extended across; extensive; of wide range; tolerant, liberal; rustic, coarse; free in style or effect. n. A freshwater lake, formed by the broadening of a river. adv. In breadth; broadly, widely. **broadcast,** a. Scattered by the hand (as seed); (*fig.*) widely disseminated. n. A radio transmission. v.t. To disseminate widely, esp. by radio. **broadcaster,** n. One who does this, esp. by radio. **broadcasting,** n. Transmitting by radio; broadcast sowing. **broaden,** v.i. To become broader, to spread. v.t. To make broader. **broadness,** n. Coarseness, indelicacy. **broadsheet,** n. A large sheet printed on one side only. **broadside,** n. The side of a ship above the water; a volley from all the guns on one side of a ship of war; a broadsheet. **broadsword,** n. A cutting sword with a broad blade.

brocade (brō-kad') [Sp. *brocado*], n. Silken stuff with raised figures.

broccoli (brok'ó-li) [It. *broccolo*, a sprout], n. A variety of cauliflower.

brochure (brō-shoor') [F.], n. A pamphlet.

brock (brok) [A.-S. *broc*], n. A badger.

brogue (brōg) [Ir. *brōg*, shoe], n. A rough shoe of untanned leather; dialectal pronunciation, esp. Irish.

broil (1) (broil) [It. *broglio*, confusion], n. A tumult, disturbance, contention.

broil (2) (broil) [?], v.t. To cook on a gridiron. v.i. To be very hot; to be subjected to heat.

broken (brō'kèn) [*p.p.*, BREAK], a. In pieces; crushed, humbled; violated; interrupted, ejaculatory; bankrupt, ruined. **broken-down,** a. Decayed; worn-out; ruined.

broker (brō'kèr) [M.E. and A.-F. *brocour*], n. An agent, factor, middleman; one licensed to appraise and sell distrained goods. **brokerage,** n.

bromine (brō'min, -mīn) [Gr. *brōmos*, a stench], n. A non-metallic element with a strong, irritating odour. **bromide,** n. A combination of bromine with a metal or a radical; (*colloq.*) a platitude.

bronchi, **bronchia** (brong'ki, -ki-á) [L., from Gr. *bronchos*, *bronchia*], n.pl. The main divisions of the windpipe. **bronchial,** a. **bronchi'tis,** n. Inflammation of the bronchia.

bronco (brong'kō) [Sp., rough, rude], n. Half-tamed horse of the western U.S.A. **bronco-buster,** n. Man who tames a bronco.

bronze (bronz) [L. *Brundusīnium*, made at Brindisi], n. A brown alloy of copper and tin, with a little zinc or lead; a brown colour; a work of art in bronze. v.t. To give a bronze-like appearance

to; to brown. v.i. To become brown or tanned.

brooch (brōch), n. An ornamental clasp with a pin, for fastening.

brood (brood) [A.-S. *brōd*], n. Birds hatched at one time; offspring; lineage; (*contemp.*) a swarm, crowd. v.i. To sit on eggs; to hang close over (as clouds); to meditate moodily. **broody,** a.

brook (1) (bruk) [A.-S. *brōc*], n. A small stream.

brook (2) (bruk) [A.-S. *brūcan*], v.t. To endure, support, put up with.

broom (brum) [A.-S. *brōm*], n. A shrub with yellow flowers; a besom for sweeping, orig. made of broom. v.t. To sweep with a broom. **broomstick,** n.

broth (broth) [A.-S.], n. The liquor in which meat, etc., has been boiled.

brother (brŭth'èr) [A.-S. *brōthor*], n. (*pl.* brothers, brethren). A son of the same parents; one of the same community, city, church, order, profession, etc.; a fellow-man. **brother-in-law,** n. The brother of one's husband or wife, one's sister's husband. **brotherhood,** n. The relationship of a brother; an association for mutual service. **brotherly,** a. Becoming to a brother; fraternal. adv. Fraternally.

brougham (broom) [Lord *Brougham* (1778-1868)], n. A four-wheeled, one-horsed carriage.

brow (brou) [A.-S. *brū*], n. The ridge over the eye; the forehead; the edge or top of a hill. **brow-beat,** v.t. To bear down arrogantly; to bully.

brown (broun) [A.-S.], a. Of a dusky colour tinged with red; dusky, dark. n. A colour produced by a mixture of red, black, and yellow. **brown study,** n. Reverie, day-dream. **browned off,** adv. (*slang*) Disappointed, bored, "fed up".

brownie (brou'ni) [BROWN], n. A benevolent domestic spirit. **Brownie,** n. A junior Girl Guide.

browse (brouz) [F.], v.t. To nibble; (*fig.*) to read in a desultory way.

bruise (brooz) [A.-S. *brȳsan*], v.t. To injure, discolour, by a blow from something blunt and heavy without breaking skin or bone; to pound, grind up. n. An injury caused thus; a contusion. **bruiser,** n. A prize-fighter.

bruit (broot) [F., noise], n. Noise, tumult, report. v.t. To rumour, noise abroad.

brunette (broo-net') [F.], n. A darkish woman. a. Brown-haired.

brunt (brŭnt) [?], n. The shock or stress of an attack, danger, or crisis.

brush (brŭsh) [O.F. *brosse*], n. Brushwood; an instrument for sweeping or scrubbing, white-washing, painting, smoothing the hair, etc.; a bushy tail, as of a fox; a skirmish. v.t. To sweep or scrub with a brush; to remove by brushing; to touch lightly, as in passing. v.i. To move with a sweeping motion; to pass lightly over. **brushwood,** n. A thicket, underwood; loppings. **brushy,** a. Rough, shaggy.

brusque (broosk) [F.], a. Rough, unceremonious. **brusqueness,** n.

brussels sprouts (brŭs'èls) [Brussels, capital of Belgium], n.pl. Small sprouts springing from the stalk of a variety of cabbage.

brute (broot) [L. *brūtus*, stupid], *n.* An irrational animal; a beast; a brutal person; the animal nature in man. **brutal**. *a.* Resembling a brute; savage, unrefined, sensual. **brutal'ity**, *n.* **bru'talize**, *v.t.* To render brutal. **brutish**, *a.* Like a brute; bestial.

bubble (bŭbl) [imit.], *n.* A vesicle of liquid filled with air or other gas; a cavity in ice, glass, etc.; a cheat, fraud, swindling project. *v.i.* To rise in bubbles; to make a noise like bubbling water.

buccaneer (bŭk-å-nēr') [F. *boucanier*], *n.* A pirate, filibuster. *v.i.* To act the part of a buccaneer.

buck (bŭk) [A.-S. *bucc*], *n.* The male of the fallow-deer, goat, etc.; a gay, dashing young fellow. *v.i.* To buck-jump. **buck-hound**, *n.* A small variety of the staghound. **buck-jumper**, *n.* A horse given to jumping with the feet drawn together and the back arched.

bucket (bŭk'ét) [?], *n.* A vessel with a handle for drawing or carrying liquids; as much as a bucket will hold. **bucket shop**, *n.* Office of unofficial stock-brokers.

buckle (bŭkl) [O.F. *bocle*], *n.* A link of metal for fastening straps, etc.; a twist; the state of being twisted. *v.t.* To fasten with a buckle; to bend, twist; to prepare (oneself) resolutely. *v.i.* To be put out of shape.

buckler (bŭk'lér) [O.F. *bucler*], *n.* A small round shield.

buckram (bŭk'råm) [O.F. *boucaran*], *n.* Strong, coarse linen cloth, stiffened with gum. *a.* Made of buckram; starched, stiff, precise.

buckwheat (bŭk'hwēt) [*beechwheat*, from shape of seeds], *n.* A cereal plant.

bucolic (bū-kol'ik) [Gr. *boukolos*, herdsman], *a.* Pastoral, rustic.

bud (bŭd) [?], *n.* The germ of a branch, flower or leaf; something undeveloped. *v.i.* To put forth buds; begin to grow.

Buddha (bud'å) [Sansk. *buddha*, enlightened], *n.* Gautama, the founder of Buddhism. **Buddhism**, *n.* The religious system founded in India in the 5th cent. *B.C.* **Buddhist**, *n.* A follower of Buddha. *a.* Connected with Buddhism.

budge (bŭj) [F. *bouger*, to stir], *v.i.* To move from one's place. *v.t.* To cause (something heavy) to move.

budgerigar (bŭj'ér-i-gar) [abor. Austral.], *n.* (*Zool.*) The Australian green parakeet.

budget (bŭj'ét) [F. *bougette*], *n.* A small leather bag or its contents; a bundle, collection of news; an estimate of receipts and expenditure. *v.i.* To prepare an estimate (for).

buff (bŭf) [F. *buffle*, buffalo], *n.* Soft leather prepared from buffalo hide or other skin; the colour of this, light yellow; the bare skin.

buffalo (bŭf'å-lō) [Gr. *boubalos*], *n.* A wild ox; the American bison.

buffer (bŭf'ér) [O.F. *buffe*, a blow], *n.* An apparatus for counteracting the effect of a concussion; a fellow.

buffet (1) (bŭf'ét) [O.F. *bufet*], *n.* A blow

a cuff; a disaster, misfortune. *v.t.* To strike with the hand; to contend with.

buffet (2) (bŭf'ét) [F.], *n.* A cupboard or sideboard; (buf'å) a refreshment bar.

buffoon (bŭf-oon') [F. *bouffon*], *n.* One who indulges in low jests. **buffoonery**, *n.*

bug (bŭg) [?], *n.* A blood-sucking, evil-smelling insect.

bugbear (bŭg'bär) [W. *bwg*, a ghost], *n.* A hobgoblin; an imaginary object of terror.

buggy (bŭg'i) [?], *n.* A light, four-wheeled, one-horse vehicle.

bugle (būgl) [O.F. *bugle*, a wild ox], *n.* A hunting-horn, orig. of horn; a small trumpet for military signals; a slender glass bead. **bugler**, *n.*

build (bild) [A.-S. *bold*, a house], *v.t.* (*past* and *p.p.* built). To construct, make by putting together parts and materials; to establish. *v.i.* To erect a building; make a nest. *n.* Mode of construction; shape, figure. **builder**, *n.* **building**, *n.*

bulb (bŭlb) [Gr. *bolbos*, onion], *n.* A subterranean bud sending roots below and leaves above; a spherical swelling; an electric globe. **bulbous** (bŭl'bŭs), *a.* Bulb-shaped.

bulge (bŭlj) [O.F. *boulge*], *n.* The protuberant part of a cask; a swelling. *v.i.* To swell irregularly; be protuberant.

bulk (bulk) [Icel. *bulki*, a heap], *n.* Magnitude of three dimensions; the main mass. *v.i.* To appear relatively big; to amount. **bulky**, *a.* Large.

bulkhead (bŭlk'hed) [?], *n.* An upright partition dividing a ship into compartments.

bull (1) (bul) [A.-S. *bule*, *bellan*, to bellow], *n.* The uncastrated male of cattle, applied also to the male of the elephant, whale, etc.; (*Stock Exchange*) one who speculates for a rise (cp. BEAR); a bull's-eye. *v.t.* To speculate for or produce a rise in (stocks, etc.). **bulldog**, *n.* A powerful breed of dog. **bulldozer**, *n.* (*Eng.*) A power-operated machine with a large blade, employed for removing obstacles, levelling ground, etc. **bullfinch**, *n.* An English song-bird with handsome plumage. **bull's-eye**, *n.* The centre of a target; a sweetmeat; a lantern with a hemispherical lens.

bull (2) (bul) [L. *bulla*, a seal], *n.* A leaden seal appended to a Papal edict; the edict.

bull (3) (bul) [?], *n.* A ludicrous contradiction in terms.

bullet (bul'ét) [F. *boulette*], *n.* A ball or cone of lead, etc. used in small fire-arms.

bulletin (bul'é-tin) [It. *bulletino*], *n.* An official report.

bullion (bul'yôn) [F.], *n.* Uncoined gold and silver.

bullock (bul'ôk) [A.-S. *bulluc*], *n.* A castrated ox.

bully (bul'i) [?], *n.* A blustering fellow; a cowardly tyrant, swashbuckler. hired ruffian. *v.t.* To treat in a tyrannical manner. **bully beef**, *n.* Tinned beef.

bulrush (bul'rŭsh) [?], *n.* A tall rush with a brown head, growing in water.

bulwark (bul'wårk) [Dut. *bolwerk*], *n.* A rampart or fortification; shelter, protection; the sides of a ship which rise above the upper deck.

bumble-bee (bumbl'bē) [imit.], *n.* A large bee.

bump (bŭmp) [onomat.], *n.* A dull, heavy blow; a swelling; a touch in a bumping-race. *v.t.* To cause to strike forcibly or hurt by striking against something; to hit (against). *v.i.* To strike heavily; to collide. **bumper**, *n.* A glass filled to the brim; the fender of a motor-car. **bumpy**, *a.* Full of lumps; uneven.

bumpkin (bŭmp'kin) [?], *n.* A country lout; a clumsy, thickheaded fellow.

bumptious (bŭmp'shŭs). *a.* Self-assertive.

bun (bŭn) [?], *n.* A small sweet cake; a ball of hair at the back of the head.

bunch (bŭnch) [?], *n.* A cluster, tuft, lot, collection. *v.t.* To tie up or form into a bunch. *v.i.* To grow into a cluster.

buncombe (bŭng'kŭm) [*Buncombe*, N. Carolina], *n.* Humbug, clap-trap.

bundle (bŭndl) [O.Teut. *bindan*, to bind], *n.* Things bound together; a package, parcel; a group of characteristics.

bung (bŭng) [L. *puncta*, an orifice], *n.* A large cork stopper for a bung-hole. *v.t.* To stop with a bung. **bung-hole**, *n.* The hole through which a cask is filled.

bungalow (bŭng'gá-lō) [Hind. *bānglā*, of Bengal], *n.* A lightly-built one-storied house.

bungle (bŭng'gĕl) [?], *v.t.* To botch; to manage clumsily. *v.i.* To act clumsily or awkwardly. *n.* Botching; mismanagement. **bungler**, *n.* **bungling**, *a.*

bunion (bŭn'yŏn) [?], *n.* A swelling on the joint of the great toe.

bunk (bŭngk) [?], *n.* A recess serving for a bed; a sleeping-berth. *v.i.* To run away, to make off.

bunker (bŭng'kẽr) [?], *n.* (*Naut.*) a coal-bin; an obstruction on a golf-course.

bunkum [BUNCOMBE].

bunny (bŭn'ĭ) [?], *n.* A childish name for a rabbit.

bunting (bŭn'ting) [?], *n.* A group of birds allied to the larks; stuff of which flags are made; a flag.

buoy (boi) [O.F. *boie*], *n.* An anchored float indicating shoals, etc.; a float to sustain a person in the water. *v.t.* To mark with a buoy. **buoy'ancy**, *n.* Ability to float; power of resisting or recovering from depression; light-heartedness. **buoy'ant**, *a.*

bur, burr (bẽr) [M.E.], *n.* The prickly envelope of the burdock; the husk of the chestnut.

burden, burthen (bẽr'dĕn, -*th*ĕn) [A.-S. *byrthen*], *n.* Something borne or carried; a load; the gist of a composition; tonnage; a refrain. *v.t.* To load; to oppress, encumber. **burdensome**, *a.* Hard to bear; grievous.

burdock (bẽr'dok), *n.* A coarse plant with prickly flower-heads.

bureau (bū-rō') [F.], *n.* (*pl.* -eaux). A writing-table with drawers; an office, Government department.

bureaucracy (bū-rok'rásĭ), *n.* Government by officials; centralization of government; officialism. **bureaucrat'ic**, *a.*

burgee (bẽr-jē) [?], *n.* A swallow-tailed flag.

burgess (bẽr'jĕs) [BOURGEOIS]. *n.* A citizen possessing full municipal rights.

burgher (bẽr'gẽr), *n.* A citizen, burgess.

burglar (bẽrg'lár) [Ang.-Lat. *burglātor*], *n.* One who breaks into a house after sunset to thieve. **burglarious** (-lär'ĭ-ŭs), *a.* burglary, *n.* **burgle**, *v.* To commit burglary.

burgomaster (bẽr'gō-mas-tẽr) [Dut.], *n.* A chief magistrate in Holland or Flanders.

burial (ber'ĭ-ál) [A.-S. *byrgels*, a tomb], *n.* The act of burying; a funeral.

burin (bũr'ĭn) [F.], *n.* The cutting-tool for engraving on copper.

burke (bẽrk) [W. *Burke* (1792–1829), murderer], *v.t.* To smother, hush up.

burlesque (bẽr-lesk') [F.], *a.* Mock-serious or mock-heroic. *n.* Mockery, grotesque imitation. *v.t.* To travesty.

burly (bẽr'lĭ) [M.E. *burliche*], *a.* Stout, lusty, corpulent. **burliness**, *n.*

burn (1) (bẽrn) [A.-S. *bærnan*], *v.t.* (*past* and *p.p.* burnt, burned). To consume, or injure by fire; to treat with heat; to corrode, eat into, cauterize. *v.i.* To be on fire; to shine, glow, to rage, be inflamed. *n.* The effect of burning; a burnt place. **burner**, *n.* That part of a lamp, etc., from which the flame issues. **burning**, *a.*

burn (2) (bẽrn) [A.-S. *burna*], *n.* A brook.

burnish (bẽr'nish) [O.F. *brunir*, to brown], *v.t.* To polish, esp. by rubbing. *n.* Gloss, lacquer. **burnisher**, *n.*

burr (bẽr) [?], *n.* A bur; the rough edge left on metal after punching, etc. *v.t.* To pronounce with a rough sounding of the *r*.

burrow (bũr'ō) [?], *n.* A hole made by rabbits, foxes, etc., for a dwelling-place. *v.i.* To excavate a burrow.

bursar (bẽr'sár) [L. *bursa*, purse], *n.* A treasurer of a college; one who holds a bursary. **bursary**, *n.* An exhibition in a university or school.

burst (bẽrst) [A.-S. *berstan*], *v.t.* To break or rend asunder with suddenness and violence. *v.i.* To be broken suddenly from within; to rush forth with force. *n.* A sudden and violent breaking forth.

bury (ber'ĭ) [A.-S. *byrgan*], *v.t.* To inter, to consign to the grave or to obscurity.

busby (bŭz'bĭ) [?], *n.* The fur-covered cap worn by Hussars, Artillerymen, and the Royal Engineers.

bush (bush) [Icel. *buskr*], *n.* A thick shrub; a thicket; uncleared land. **bushman**, *n.* Aborigines living in Cape Colony; one who lives in the Australian bush. **bush-ranger**, *n.* One who has taken to the bush as a highwayman. **bushy**, *a.* Abounding with bushes; growing like a bush.

bushel (bush'ĕl) [O.F. *boissel*], *n.* A dry measure of capacity (8 gals.).

business (biz'nĕs) [A.-S. *bisigness*], *n.* Trade, profession; duty, concern; bargaining; a particular matter demanding attention; a commercial establishment; (*Theat.*) action as distinct from speech.

busk (bŭsk) [M.F. *busque*], *n.* A stiffening bone or plate in a corset.

buskin (bŭs'kin) [O.F. *bousequin*], *n.* A boot reaching nearly to the knee worn by actors in Athenian tragedy.

bust (bŭst) [F. *buste*], *n.* The head, shoulders, and breast of a person sculptured; the upper front part of the body.

bustard (bŭs'tård) [L. *avis tarda*, slow bird], *n.* A large bird allied to the plovers and the cranes.

bustle (bŭsl) [?], *n.* Activity with noise and excitement; stir, fuss; a pad worn by women below the dress at the back. *v.i.* To make a show of activity. *v.t.* To hurry, to cause to work hard.

busy (biz'l) [A.-S. *bysig*], *a.* Fully occupied; closely engaged, diligent; officious, meddlesome. *v.r.* To occupy oneself. **busybody**, *n.* An officious meddler.

but (bŭt) [A.-S. *bútan*], *prep.* Except, barring. *conj.* Yet still; except that; nevertheless, however. *adv.* Only.

butcher (buch'ér) [O.F. *bochier*], *n.* One who slaughters and sells the flesh of domestic animals for food. *v.t.* To put to death in a wanton or sanguinary fashion. **butchery**, *n.*

butler (bŭt'lér) [O.F. *bouteillier*], *n.* A servant in charge of the wine, etc.

butt (1) (bŭt) [?], *n.* The hinder or blunter end of a tool, weapon, etc.; the square end of a piece of timber.

butt (2) (bŭt) [O.F. *boute*, a cask], *n.* A large cask; 126 galls. of wine, or 108 galls of beer.

butt (3) (bŭt) [F. *but*, a goal], *n.* A target; the mound behind targets, the shelter for the marker; (*pl.*) a shooting-range; an object for ridicule, etc.

butt (4) (bŭt) [O.F. *boter*, to push], *v.t.* To strike, thrust, or push with the head.

butter (bŭt'ér) [A.-S. *butere*], *n.* The fatty portion of milk solidified by churning. *v.t.* To spread with butter; (*fig.*) to flatter grossly. **buttercup**, *n.* The yellow-flowered ranunculus. **butterfly**, *n.* An insect with erect wings and knobbed antennæ; a giddy or fickle person.

buttery (bŭt'ér-I) [O.F. *bouteillerie*, buttery], *n.* A room in which liquor and provisions are kept.

buttock (bŭt'ŏk), *n.* One of the protuberant parts of the rump.

button (bŭt'ón) [O.F. *boton*], *n.* A disk used for fastening or ornamenting the dress; a small bud; a small fastener, catch, etc.; a knob actuating electrical apparatus. *v.t.* To fasten, furnish, or secure with buttons. **buttonhole**, *n.* A slit to admit a button; a small bouquet for the buttonhole of a coat.

buttress (bŭt'rês) [?], *n.* A structure built against a wall to strengthen it.

buxom (bŭk'sóm) [A.-S. *búgan*, to bend], *a.* Plump and comely.

buy (bī) [A.-S. *bycgan*], *v.t.* To purchase; to procure by means of money; to gain by bribery. **buyer**, *n.*

buzz (bŭz) [onomat.], *n.* A hum like that of a bee; a confused noise; bustle; rumour. *v.i.* To make a noise like humming or whirring. *v.t.* To spread abroad secretly. **buzz-saw**, *n.* A circular saw.

buzzard (bŭz'árd) [O.F. *busard*], *n.* A kind of falcon.

by (bī) [A.-S.], *prep.* Near, at, beside, via; through (as author, cause); during, not later than; concerning. *adv.* Near at hand; in reserve; past. *a.* Side, secondary; private, secret. **by-election**, *n.* An election caused by the death or resigna-

tion of a member. **bygone**, *a.* Past. *n.* A past event; (*pl.*) the past; past injuries. **by-lane**, *n.* A lane lying off the main road. **by-law**, *n.* A statute made by a local authority; rules adopted by a society. **by-line**, *n.* (*Newspaper*) Line naming the writer of what follows. **by-pass**, *n.* A pipe passing round a tap or valve. **bypath**, *n.* A private or unfrequented path. **by-play**, *n.* Action carried on aside, while the main action is proceeding. **by-product**, *n.* A secondary product. **by-road**, *n.* A road little frequented. **bystander**, *n.* An onlooker, eye-witness. **by-street**, *n.* An out-of-the way or unfrequented street. **byword**, *n.* A common saying; an object of general contempt.

bye (bī), *n.* (*Cricket*) A run scored when the ball passes the batsman; (*Golf*) holes left over and played as a new game; a goal at lacrosse; an odd man after pairs have been drawn. [For compounds see BY.]

byre (bīr) [A.-S., a hut], *n.* A cow-house.

Byzantine (bi-zăn'tīn) [L. *Byzantinus*], *a.* Pertaining to Byzantium (Constantinople).

C

cab (kăb) [short for F. *cabriolet*], *n.* A public vehicle drawn by one horse; the covered part of a locomotive.

cabal (ká-băl'), *n.* A small body of persons closely united for some secret purpose; a clique. *v.i.* To intrigue secretly.

cabaret (kăb'á-rā) [F.], *n.* A restaurant where musical turns are given.

cabbage (kăb'áj) [F. *caboche*, great head], *n.* The plain-leaved, hearted varieties of *Brassica oleracea*.

cabin (kăb'in) [F. *cabane*], *n.* A hut, temporary shelter; a room or compartment in a ship. *v.t.* To coop in.

cabinet (kăb'i-nêt), *n.* A small room; a piece of furniture in which to keep curiosities, etc.; a council, council chamber; a committee of the principal members of the British Government.

cable (kābl) [L. *caplum*], *n.* A strong rope; the rope or chain to which an anchor is fastened; a line for submarine telegraphs. *v.t.* To send (a message) by cable. **cablegram**, *n.* A message by submarine cable.

caboose (ká-boos') [?], *n.* Cook's galley; (*Am. rly.*) the guard's van.

cache (kăsh) [F. *cacher*, to hide], *n.* A hole in the ground in which provisions, ammunition, etc., are hidden.

cachet (kăsh'ā) [F.], *n.* A paper capsule for administering medicine; a sign of authenticity.

cachinnation (kăk-in-ā'shŭn) [L. *cachinnáre*], *n.* Loud or immoderate laughter.

cackle (kăkl) [M.E. *kakelen*], *n.* The sound made by a hen; idle chatter. *v.i.* To make a noise like a hen after laying an egg; to chatter in a silly manner.

caco- [Gr. *kako-*, evil, bad], *comb. form.* (*Path.*) Bad, malformed, evil to the senses.

cacophony (kà-kof'ô-ni) [Gr. *kakophōnos*, harsh-sounding], *n.* A rough, discordant style. cacoph'onous, *a.* Harsh-sounding, discordant.

cactus (kăk'tŭs) [Gr. *kaktos*], *n.* A succulent spiny plant.

cad (kăd), *n.* A low, vulgar, ill-mannered fellow. caddish, *a.*

cadaverous (kà-dăv'ér-ŭs) [L. *cadăver*, a corpse], *a.* Corpse-like; deathly pale.

caddie (kăd'i), *n.* (*Sc.*) A lad or man attending on a golfer.

caddis (kăd'is) [?], *n.* The larva of the may-fly, etc.

caddy (kăd'i) [Malay *kātī*, a weight of 1⅓ lb.], *n.* A small box in which tea is kept.

cade (kăd) [Gr. *kados*, a pail, cask], *n.* A barrel of 600 herrings or 1000 sprats.

cadence (kā'déns) [L. *cadere*, to fall], *n.* The sinking of the voice at the end of a sentence; modulation, intonation; rhythm. *v.t.* To put into rhythmical measure.

cadenza (kà-den'zà) [It.], *n.* (*Mus.*) A flourish at the close of a movement.

cadet (kà-det') [Prov. *capdet*], *n.* A younger son, younger branch of a family; a pupil in a military or naval academy.

cadge (kăj) [?], *v.t.* To get by begging, cadger, *n.* One who cadges; a huckster hawker; a beggar.

caduceus (kà-dū'sē-ŭs) [L.], *n.* The winged staff of Mercury.

caesura (sē-zū'rà) [L. *caesere*, to cut], *n.* A pause about the middle of a line of poetry.

café (kăf'ā) [F.], *n.* A coffee-house; restaurant. caffeine (kăf'ê-īn), *n.* A vegetable alkaloid derived from the coffee and tea plants.

cage (kăj) [L. *cavus*, hollow], *n.* An enclosure wholly or partly of wire, wicker-work, or iron bars, etc.; a prison; the lift used in mines. *v.t.* To confine. cagey (kā'ji), *a.* (*Am. slang*) Cautious, shrewd.

cairn (kârn) [Gael.], *n.* A pyramidal heap of stones, as a grave-mound, landmark, etc.

cairngorm (kârn-gôrm) [Gael.], *n.* A brownish rock crystal from the Cairngorm mountains, Scotland.

caisson (kăs'ón, kā-soon') [F.], *n.* An ammunition-chest; a water-tight chamber used in laying foundations under water or for raising sunken vessels.

caitiff (kā'tif) [L. *captivus*], *n.* A despicable, cowardly fellow. *a.* Cowardly, base.

cajole (kà-jōl') [F.], *v.t.* To beguile by flattery; to wheedle, coax. cajolement, cajolery, *n.*

cake (kăk) [Icel. *kaka*], *n.* A composition of flour, butter, sugar, etc., baked; a flat mass of food or any solidified or compressed substance. *v.t.* To make into a cake. *v.i.* To assume a cake-like form.

calabash (kăl'à-băsh) [Sp. *calabaza*], *n.* A gourd or pumpkin; its dried shell.

calamity (kà-lăm'i-ti) [L. *calamitas*], *n.* Extreme misfortune, disaster. calamitous, *a.* Causing or characterized by great distress or unhappiness.

calc- [G. *kalk*, L. *calx -cis*], *comb. form.*

(*Geol.*) Lime. calc-spar, *n.* Calcareous spar.

calcareous (kăl-kār'i-ŭs) [L.], *a.* Of the nature of lime or limestone.

calceolaria (kăl-sē-ô-lār'i-à) [L. *calceolus*, dim. of *calceus*, a shoe], *n.* Slipperwort, a plant with slipper-like flowers.

calcine (kăl'sin) [L. *calcinăre*], *v.t.* To reduce to quick-lime or powder by heat; to desiccate by heat; to burn to ashes. *v.i.* To undergo calcination. calcina'-tion, *n.*

calcium, *n.* The metallic base of lime.

calculate (kăl'kū-lāt) [L. *calculāre*], *v.t.* To reckon up, estimate; to ascertain by mathematical process; to adjust, to arrange. *v.i.* To reckon, form an estimate; to rely (upon). calculated, *a.* Pre-arranged; cold-blooded; well adapted (to). calculable, *a.* That may be calculated. calcula'tion, *n.* The act of reckoning or computing; the result of this; estimate, inference. calculator, *n.* A person or mechanical contrivance that calculates; tables for use in calculating.

calculus (kăl'kū-lŭs) [L., a pebble], *n.* (*pl.* -li) A stony, morbid concretion formed in various organs of the body; (*Math.*) a method of calculation.

Caledonian (kăl-ê-dō'ni-àn) [L. *Caledonia*, N. Britain], *a.* (*poet.*) Pertaining to Scotland. *n.* A Scotsman.

calefactory (kăli-fak'tóri) [L. *calēre*, to be warm, *facere*, to make], *a.* Producing or communicating heat.

calendar (kăl'én-dàr) [L. *calendārium*, an account-book], *n.* A register of the months, weeks, and days of the year; an almanac; a chronological catalogue of documents with digests of the contents.

calender (kăl'én-dér) [L. *cylindrus*, roller], *n.* A rolling-machine for making cloth or paper glossy. *v.t.* To glaze by passing between rollers.

calends (kăl'éndz) [L.], *n.* The first day of any month in the old Roman calendar.

calf (1) (kaf) [A.-S. *cealf*], *n.* (*pl.* calves) The young of the cow, and of some large animals, as of the elephant, whale, etc.; leather from calfskin.

calf (2) (kaf) [Icel. *kālfi*], *n.* (*pl.* calves) The thick fleshy part of the leg behind.

calibre (kăl'i-bér) [F. *calibre*], *n.* The internal diameter of the bore of a gun.

calico (kăl'i-kō) [*Calicut*, Malabar], *n.* White or unbleached cotton cloth.

caliph (kā'lif) [Arab. *khalīfah*, successor], *n.* The chief ruler in Mohammedan countries, the successor of Mohammed. caliphate (kăl'i-fāt), *n.* The office, dignity, or dominion of a caliph.

call (kawl) [Icel. *kalla*], *v.t.* To name, to designate, describe as; to summon, to cite, invoke; to rouse from sleep; to ring up by telephone. *v.i.* To cry aloud, shout; to pay a short visit. *n.* A loud cry; a supplication; the cry of an animal or bird; a short visit; an invitation, summons, a signal on a bugle, etc.; justification, occasion. call-boy, *n.* A boy who calls actors for the stage. calling, *n.* Habitual occupation; a vocation; a solemn summons to duty, etc.

calligraphy (kà-lig'rà-fi) [Gr. *kallos*, beauty,

-GRAPHY], *n.* The art of beautiful hand-writing.

callipers (kăl'ĭ-pĕrz) [*calibre-compasses*], *n.pl.* Compasses for measuring convex bodies or calibres.

callisthenics (kăl-ĭs-then'ĭks) [Gr. *kallos*, beauty, *sthenos*, strength], *n.pl.* Gymnastics (esp. for girls) productive of strength and grace.

callous (kăl'ŭs) [L. *callōsus*, hard], *a.* Hardened, indurated; unfeeling. callos'-ity, *n.* **callus** (kăl'ŭs), *n.* Thickened skin.

callow (kăl'ō) [A.-S. *calu*, bald], *a.* Unfledged, downy; inexperienced.

calm (kam) [F. *calme*], *a.* Quiet, serene; tranquil. *n.* The state of being calm; absence of wind. *v.i.* To still, to soothe. *v.i.* To become calm. calmative, *a.* Tending to calm. *n.* (*Med.*) A sedative. calmly, *adv.* **calmness,** *n.*

calomel (kăl'ō-mel) [F.], *n.* Mercurous chloride, an active purgative.

caloric (kå-lor'ĭk) [L. *calor*, heat], *n.* The supposed cause of heat, heat. calorie (kăl'ō-ri) [F.], *n.* The unit of heat (*i.e.* the amount that will raise the temperature of 1 kilogramme of water 1° C.). calorif'ic, *a.* Producing heat; thermal.

calumniate (kå-lŭm'nĭ-āt) [L. *calumniātus*, falsely accused], *v.t.* To slander; to charge falsely. *v.i.* To utter calumnies. calumnia'tion, *n.* The act of calumniating. **calumniator,** *n.* **calumnious,** *a.* **calumny** (kăl'ŭm-ni), *n.* A malicious misrepresentation; slander.

calve (kav) [A.-S. *cealfian*], *v.i.* To bring forth a calf.

Calvinism (kăl'vin-izm), *n.* The tenets of John *Calvin* (1509–64), esp. on predestination and election. Calvinist, *n.* Calvinis'tic, *a.*

calypso (kå-lĭp'sō), *n.* A kind of extemporaneous singing in syncopated rhythm, with a continual narrative or ruminating theme.

calyx (kā'lĭks) [Gr. *kalux*, cup], *n.* (*pl.* calyces) The whorl of leaves or sepals forming the outer integument of a flower.

cam (kăm), *n.* A device on a wheel, etc., conveying eccentric or alternating motion.

camber (kăm'bĕr) [F. *cambre*], *n.* The condition of being slightly convex above; a piece of timber so bent.

Cambrian (kăm'brĭ-án) [L. *Cambria*, Wales], *a.* Pertaining to Wales.

cambric (kām'brĭk) [*Cambray*], *n.* A very fine white linen.

camel (kăm'ĕl) [Heb. *gāmāl*], *n.* A large, hornless, humpbacked ruminant used in Africa and the East as a beast of burden.

camellia (kå-mē'lĭ-å) [G. J. *Kamel*, Jesuit botanist traveller], *n.* A genus of evergreen shrubs with beautiful flowers.

camelopard (kăm'el-ō-pard) [Gr. *kamēlopardis*], *n.* The giraffe.

cameo (kăm'ĕ-ō) [It. *cammēo*], *n.* A precious stone (or shell) with two layers of colours, carved in relief.

camera (kăm'ĕr-å) [L., vault, chamber], *n.* A private chamber, esp. of a judge; a dark box used in photography; an instrument for taking photographs.

camisole (kăm'ĭ-sōl) [F.], *n.* A loose under-bodice worn by women.

camomile (kăm'ō-mīl) [Gr. *chamaimēlon*, earth-apple], *n.* A bitter aromatic creeping plant.

camouflage (ka-moo-flazh') [F. *camoufler*, to disguise], *n.* Disguise, esp. concealment of guns, camps, vehicles, etc., by means of deceptive painting, etc.

camp (kămp) [L. *campus*, a field], *n.* The place where an army is lodged in tents; a station for training troops; temporary quarters of travellers, etc.; a body of adherents. camp-follower, *n.* A civilian who follows an army; a hanger-on. camp meeting, *n.* A religious revivalist meeting held in the open air. camp-stool, *n.* A folding stool.

campaign (kăm-pān') [L. *campania*, a plain], *n.* The operations of an army in the field; analogous operations; a course of political propaganda. *v.i.* To serve on a campaign. campaigner, *n.*

campanile (kăm'på-nē'li) [It.], *n.* A bell-tower, esp. a detached one.

campanology (kăm-på-nol'ō-ji) [L. *campāna*, a bell], *n.* The principles of bell-ringing, founding, etc.

campanula (kăm-păn'ū-là), *n.* A genus of plants with bell-shaped flowers.

camphor (kăm'fŏr) [F. *camphre*], *n.* A whitish, translucent, volatile, crystalline gum with a peculiar odour, obtained from certain trees.

campion (kăm'pĭ-ŏn) [?], *n.* English flowering plants of the genus *Lychnis*.

campus (kăm'pŭs) [L.], *n.* (*Am.*) The fields or grounds of a university.

can (1) (kăn) [A.-S. *canne*], *n.* A metal vessel for holding liquid, and for preserving meat, fruit, fish, etc.

can (2) (kăn) [A.-S. *cunnan*, to know], *aux. v.* (*negative* cannot, *past* could, A.-S. *cūthe*, M.E. *coude*) To be able to; to be allowed to; to be possible to.

canal (kå-năl') [L. *canālis*], *n.* An artificial watercourse; (*Physiol.*) a duct.

canard (kå-nard') [F.], *n.* A hoax, false report.

Canary (kå-nâr'i) [the islands off the west coast of Africa], *n.* A light sweet wine made there; a yellow-feathered songbird. *a.* Bright yellow.

cancel (kăn'sĕl) [L. *cancellāre*, *cancelli*, cross-bars], *v.t.* To obliterate, annul, revoke, neutralize. cancella'tion, *n.*

cancer (kăn'sĕr) [L. *cancer*, a crab], *n.* The 4th of the 12 signs of the zodiac; a malignant spreading growth; (*fig.*) a vice of a spreading kind. cancerous, *a.*

candelabrum (kăn-dĕ-lā'brŭm), *n.* An ornamental branched candlestick.

candid (kăn'did) [L. *candidus*, white], *a.* Frank, sincere, open. candid camera, *n.* (*Phot.*) A small camera with a large lens and high-speed shutter for taking unposed snapshots.

candidate (kăn'di-dāt) [L. *candidātus*, white-robed], *n.* One who seeks or is proposed for some office or appointment.

candle (kăndl) [A.-S. *candel* (L. *candēre*, to glow)], *n.* A cylindrical body of tallow, wax, etc., with a wick, used as an illuminant. candle-power *n.* The unit for measuring light. **candlestick**, *n.* A utensil for holding a candle.

candour (kăn'dŏr) [L. *candor*, whiteness], *n.* Candidness, openness; freedom from bias.

candy (kăn'di) [Arab. and Pers. *qand*, sugar], *n.* Crystallized sugar. *v.t.* To preserve or coat with sugar; to crystallize. *v.i.* To become candied. **candied**, *a.*

candytuft (kăn'di-tŭft) [*Candia*], *n.* A common herbaceous plant.

cane (kān) [L. *canna*], *n.* A slender, hollow, jointed stem of the bamboo or other reed; the stem of a raspberry and other plants. *v.t.* To beat with a cane. **cane sugar**, *n.* The sugar made from canes as opposed to that made from beet.

canine (kăn'in) [L. *canis*, dog], *a.* Pertaining to dogs; dog-like. *n.* One of the pointed teeth in each jaw between the incisors and the molars.

canister (kăn'is-tĕr) [Gr. *kanastron*, a basket], *n.* A metal case for holding § tea, coffee, etc.

canker (kăng'kĕr), *n.* A corroding ulcer; a fungous excrescence in a horse's foot; a fungus injuring fruit trees; anything which corrupts. *v.t.* To infect or rot with canker; to eat into like a canker. *v.i.* To become cankered, infected, or corrupt. **cankerous**, *a.*

cannibal (kăn'i-băl) [Sp.], *n.* A human being or animal that feeds on its own kind. *a.* Pertaining to cannibalism; ravenous, bloodthirsty. **cannibalism**, *n.* Feeding on one's own kind.

cannon (1) (kăn'ŏn) [F.], *n.* A heavy mounted gun. **cannon-ball**, *n.* A solid shot fired from a cannon. **cannonade**, *n.* A continued attack with artillery. *v.t.* To batter with cannon. **cannoneer**, *n.* A gunner, an artilleryman.

cannon (2) (kăn'ŏn) [Sp. *carambola*], *n.* (*Billiards*) A strike by which two balls are hit successively. *v.i.* To make a cannon; come into violent contact with.

canny (kăn'i), *a.* Knowing, artful; cautious. **to ca' canny**: To go gently; not to work too well.

canoe (ká-noo') [Haytian], *n.* A light boat propelled by paddles.

canon (kăn'ŏn) [A.-S., Gr. *kanōn*], *n.* A rule, general law or principle; a decree of the Church; the ring suspending a bell; a list of the books of Scriptures received as inspired; a resident member of a cathedral chapter. **canon law**, *n.* Ecclesiastical law. **canonical** (ká-non'-ikál), *a.* Pertaining to canon law; included in the canon of Scripture; authoritative; belonging or pertaining to a cathedral chapter. **canonicals**, *n.pl.* The full robes of an officiating priest. **canonic'ity**, *n.* **canonize**, *v.t.* To enrol in the list of saints. **canoniza'tion**, *n.* **canonry**, *n.* The dignity, position, or benefice of a canon.

canopy (kăn'ŏ-pi) [F. *canapé*], *n.* A rich covering suspended over an altar, throne, bed, etc. *v.t.* To cover with or as with a canopy.

cant (1) (kănt) [L. *cantāre*, to sing], *n.* The jargon of beggars, gipsies, etc.; slang; phraseology peculiar to any sect or party; hypocritical talk. *v.i.* To speak whiningly or insincerely; to talk cant. **canting**, *a.* Whining, hypocritical.

cant (2) (kănt) [med. L. *cantus*, corner], *n.* A slant. *v.t.* To tilt; to give a bevel to. *v.i.* To slant over.

cantankerous (kăn-tăng'kĕr-ŭs), *a.* Disagreeable, quarrelsome, crotchety.

canteen (kăn-tēn') [F. *cantine*], *n.* A place in which drink, provisions, etc., are sold to soldiers; a vessel used by soldiers for carrying water; a chest for cutlery.

canter (kăn'tĕr) [short for Canterbury], *n.* An easy gallop. *v.i.* To ride at a canter.

canticle (kăn'tikl) [L. *canticulum*], *n.* A chant, esp. a portion of Scripture appointed to be said or sung in churches; (*pl.*) the Song of Solomon.

cantilever (kăn'ti-lē-vĕr) [?], *n.* a projecting beam for supporting a balcony, etc.

cantle (kăntl), *n.* A fragment; the projection at the rear of a saddle.

canto (kăn'tŏ) [It.], *n.* (*pl.* -os) A principal division of a poem.

canton (kăn'tŏn) [O.F., a corner], *n.* A division of a country, esp. of Switzerland; (*Her.*) a small division in the corner of a shield. *v.t.* To divide into parts; (kăn-toon') to billet, provide with quarters. **cantonment** (kăn-toon'mĕnt), *n.* A quarter assigned for lodging to troops; a permanent military station.

canvas (kăn'văs) [O.North.F. *canevas*, Gr. *kannabis*, hemp], *n.* Coarse cloth made of hemp or flax, used for sails, tents, paintings, etc.; sails; a picture.

canvass (kăn'văs) [orig. to sift through canvas], *n.* Scrutiny; the act of soliciting votes. *v.t.* To examine thoroughly; to solicit votes, orders, etc. **canvasser**, *n.*

canyon (kăn'yŏn) [Sp. *cañon*, a tube], *n.* A deep ravine with precipitous sides.

cap (kăp) [A.-S. *cæppe*], *n.* A brimless head-covering; a covering resembling this in form or function; the top part of anything; a percussion cap. *v.t.* To cover with a cap; to put a cap on; to confer a degree upon; to be on the top of; to complete. *v.i.* To take one's cap off (to). **cap-stone**, *n.* The top stone; a coping.

capable (kā'pábl) [L. *capābilis*], *a.* Competent, able, skilful. **capably**, *adv.* **capabil'ity**, *n.*

capacious (ká-pā'shŭs) [L. *capax -ācis*], *a.* Wide, extensive; comprehensive. **capaciously**, *adv.* **capaciousness**, *n.*

capacitate (ká-păs'i-tāt) [as prec.], *v.t.* To qualify; to render competent. **capacity**, *n.* Power of receiving; room, cubic extent; capability; scope; (*Elec.*) the output of a piece of electrical machinery.

caparison (ká-păr'i-zŏn) [F. *caparaçon*], *n.* Horse ornament. *v.t.* To outfit, to deck out.

cape (1) (kāp) [F.], *n.* A covering for the shoulders.

cape (2) (kāp) [F. *cap*, L. *caput*, head], *n.* A headland projecting into the sea.

caper (1) (kā'pĕr) [short for *capriole*], *n.* A frolicsome leap; eccentric behaviour.

caper (2) (kā'pĕr) [Gr. *kapparis*], *n.* A prickly shrub; (*pl.*) its flower-buds, used for pickling.

capercailzie (kăp-ẽr-kā'lyi) [Gael.], *n.* The wood-grouse.

capillary (kà-pïl'á-ri) [L. *capíllus*, hair], *a.* Resembling a hair in tenuity; having a minute bore. *n.* A minute blood-vessel. **capillar'ity,** *n.*

capital (kăp'ĭ-tăl) [L. *capitālis*, relating to the head], *a.* Chief, most important; first-rate; punishable by death; initial, of larger size and distinguishing shape (of letters). *n.* A capital letter; a head city, metropolis; a principal or fund employed in earning interest or profits; the head of a pillar. **capit'alism,** *n.* The economic system of employing capital to produce wealth. **capit'alist,** *n.* One who employs capital. **capit'alize,** *v.t.* To convert into or use as capital. **capitaliza'tion,** *n.* **capitally,** *adv.* In a capital manner; involving life.

capitation (kăp-i-tā'shŭn) [F., from L. *caput*, head], *n.* A tax, fee, or grant per head.

capitulate (kà-pĭt'ū-lāt) [med. L. *capitulāre*, to divide into chapters, to propose terms], *v.t.* To surrender on stipulated terms. **capitula'tion,** *n.*

capon (kā'pŏn) [A.-S.], *n.* A castrated cock.

caprice (kà-prēs') [F.], *n.* A sudden impulsive change of opinion or humour; a whim. **capricious** (-prish'ŭs), *a.*

capricorn (kăp'ri-kŏrn) [L. *caper*, goat, *cornu*, a horn], *n.* The zodiacal constella-tion of the Goat.

capsize (kăp-sīz') [?], *v.t.* To upset, to overturn. *n.* An overturn.

capstan (kăp'stán) [Prov. and F. *cabestan*], *n.* A vertical drum worked by horizontal levers, to wind up cables, etc.

capsule (kăp'sūl) [L. *capsula*, a small case], *n.* A dry seed-vessel that opens when ripe; a wrapper of gelatine for medicine. **capsular,** *a.*

captain (kăp'tán) [O.F. *capitain*, chief], *n.* A leader; the commander of a company, troop, man-of-war, or merchant ship; the head of a team. *v.t.* To act as captain to. **captaincy,** *n.*

caption (kăp'shŭn) [L. *captio*], *n.* Arrest; the descriptive preamble of a legal document; (*Print.*) the wording under an illustration.

captious (kăp'shŭs) [L. *captiōsus*], *a.* Quibbling, carping. **captiousness,** *n.*

captivate (kăp'ti-vāt) [L. *captīvātus*, made captive], *v.t.* To fascinate, charm. **capti-va'tion,** *n.* The act of fascinating.

captive (kăp'tiv) [L. *captīvus*, taken], *n.* One taken prisoner, or fascinated. *a.* Held in bondage; pertaining to captivity; fascinated. **captiv'ity,** *n.* **captor,** *n.* **capture,** *n.* The act of seizing; the person or thing so taken. *v.t.* To seize as a prize.

Capuchin (kăp'u-shin) [It. *cappuccino*, a little cowl], *n.* A Franciscan; a hooded cloak, worn by women.

car (kar) [O.F. *carre*], *n.* A wheeled vehicle; a railway or balloon carriage; a motor-car, tram-car.

carafe (kà-raf') [Arab. *gharafa*, to draw water], *n.* A glass water-bottle.

caramel (kăr'á-mel) [Sp. *caramello*], *n.* A sweetmeat.

carapace (kăr'á-pās) [Sp. *carapacho*], *n.* The upper shell of the tortoise, etc.

carat (kăr'ăt) [Arab. *qirāt*], *n.* A weight (about 3¼ grains) used for diamonds; a proportional measure of one 24th part, used to describe the fineness of gold.

caravan (kăr'á-văn) [Pers. *karwān*], *n.* A company travelling together for security; a vehicle for living in.

caravanserai (kăr-á-văn'sẽr-ī) [Pers.], *n.* An Oriental inn with a large courtyard for caravans.

caraway (kăr'á-wā) [Arab. *karawiyū*], *n.* A European umbelliferous plant whose seeds are used for flavouring.

carb-, carbo-, *comb. forms.* (*Chem.*) Of, with, containing, or pertaining to carbon; *e.g.* **carbide** (kar'bïd),*n.* A compound of carbon with a metal.

carbine (kar'bĭn) [F.], *n.* A short rifle used by cavalry. **carbineer', carabinier',** *n.* A soldier armed with this.

carbo-hydrate, *n.* (*Chem.*) A compound of carbon and hydrogen and oxygen in-cluding sugars and starches.

carbolic (kar-bol'ik), *a.* Derived from coal or coal-tar. *n.* An antiseptic and disinfectant acid.

carbon (kar'bŏn) [L. *carbo -ōnem*, a coal], *n.* A non-metallic element found in nearly all organic substances, and un-combined in diamond, graphite, and charcoal. **carbon paper,** *n.* Paper for taking impressions of writing, etc. **carbona'ceous,** *a.* Pertaining to or containing coal or charcoal. **car'bonate,** *n.* A salt of carbonic acid. *v.t.* (kar'bŏ-nāt) to impregnate or aerate with car-bonic acid. **carbon'ic,** *a.* Pertaining to or obtained from carbon. **carbonif'erous,** *a.* Producing coal. **car'bonize,** *v.t.* To convert into carbon. **carboniza'tion,** *n.*

carboy (kar'boi) [Pers. *qarābah*], *n.* A large bottle protected with wickerwork used for holding corrosive liquids.

carbuncle (kar'bŭnkl) [L. *carbunculus*, a small coal, a gem], *n.* A precious stone of a fiery red colour; a hard, painful boil.

carbureted, *a.* Combined with carbon.

carburettor, *n.* An apparatus designed to vaporize a liquid and to mix it with air, in proportions to ensure ignition and combustion.

carcass, carcase (kar'kás) [A.-F. *carcois*], *n.* A dead body, esp. the trunk of a slaughtered beast.

card (1) (kard) [F. *carte*, L. *charta*], *n.* A piece of pasteboard, esp. one marked with pips and pictures, used in games, or a visiting-card giving one's name and address; (*pl.*) a game with cards; card-playing; (*slang*) a character, an eccentric.

card (2) (kard) [F. *carde*, a teazel], *n.* A toothed instrument for combing wool, etc. *v.t.* To comb with a card; to raise a nap.

cardiac (kar'di-ăk) [Gr. *kardia*, the heart], *a.* Pertaining to the heart; heart-shaped.

cardigan (kar'di-gàn) [7th Earl of *Car-digan*], *n.* A sleeved and knitted over-waistcoat.

cardinal (kar'di-năl) [L. *cardo -inis*, a hinge], *a.* Fundamental, chief, principal; deep scarlet. *n.* A high dignitary of the

R. C. Church; a short cloak for women. **cardinalate, cardinalship,** n. The office or dignity of a cardinal. **cardinal numbers,** n.pl. The simple numbers 1, 2, 3, etc., as distinguished from 1st, 2nd, 3rd, etc. **cardinal points,** n.pl. North, south, east, and west.

care (kâr) [A.-S. *caru*], n. Solicitude, anxiety, concern; a cause of these; caution, heed; oversight; object of solicitude. v.i. To be solicitous or concerned about; to provide (for), attend (upon); to be willing or inclined (to). **care-taker,** n. One in charge of premises.

careen (kà-rēn') [L. *carīna*, a keel], v.t. (*Naut.*) To turn (a ship) on one side for cleaning, etc.

career (kà-rēr') [F. *carrière*], n. A running; course through life; progress and development; business, profession, etc. v.i. To move in a swift, headlong course.

careful (kâr'fŭl), a. Cautious, circumspect; painstaking. **carefulness,** n.

careless (kâr'lĕs), a. Heedless, thoughtless, inattentive; free from care. **carelessly,** adv. **carelessness,** n.

caress (kà-res') [F. *caresse*], n. An act of endearment. v.t. To fondle, stroke affectionately. **caressing,** a. **caressingly,** adv.

caret (kâr'ĕt) [L., is wanting], n. A mark (∧) showing that something has been left out.

cargo (kar'gō) [Sp., a load], n. The freight of a ship; a ship-load.

caricature (kăr-i-kà-tūr') [It.], n. Ludicrously exaggerated representation; a burlesque, parody. v.t. To represent in this way; to burlesque. **caricatur'ist,** n.

carillon (kà-ril'yŏn) [F.], n. A chime of bells; an air played on them.

Carmelite (kar'mé-līt) [Mount *Carmel*], n. One of an order of friars (*White Friars*).

carminative (kar'min-à-tiv) [L.], a. Expelling flatulence. n. A medicine that does this.

carmine (kar'min) [Arab. *qirmazī*], n. A bright red pigment obtained from cochineal.

carnage (kar'nàj) [L. *caro carnis*, flesh], n. Butchery, slaughter, esp. of men.

carnal (kar'nàl), a. Fleshly, sensual; unregenerate (opp. to spiritual).

carnation (kar-nā'shŭn) [F., from L. *carnātio*], n. A light rose pink; the cultivated clove-pink. a. Of this colour.

carnival (kar'ni-vàl) [It. *carnevale*, L. *carnem*, flesh, *levāre*, to remove], n. The season immediately before Lent; revelry.

carnivora (kar-niv'ŏ-rà), n.pl. A large order of mammals subsisting on flesh. **carnivorous,** a.

carol (kar'ŏl) [O.F. *carole*], n. A joyous hymn, esp. in honour of the Nativity. v.i. To sing carols; to warble.

carotid (kà-rot'id) [G. *karōtides*], a. Related to the arteries (one on each side of the neck) supplying blood to the head.

carouse (kà-rouz') [G.], n. A drinking bout. v.i. To drink freely. **carousal,** n.

carp (1) (karp) [Icel. *karpa*, to boast], v.i. To talk querulously; find fault.

carp (2) (karp) [O.F. *carpe*], n. A freshwater fish.

carpenter (kar'pén-tér) [O.North.F. *car-*

pentier], n. One who prepares and fixes woodwork, makes wooden articles, etc. **carpentry,** n. The work of a carpenter.

carpet (kar'pĕt) [O.F. *carpite*], n. A thick fabric for covering floors and stairs. v.t. To cover with a carpet; (*colloq.*) to reprimand. **carpet-bag,** n. A travelling-bag made of carpet material. **carpet-bagger,** n. (*Am.*) A political adventurer.

carriage (kar'àj) [O.North.F. *cariage*], n. Carrying, transporting, esp. of merchandise; the cost or manner of carrying; bearing, behaviour; management; a wheeled vehicle, or that which carries.

carrier (kar'i-ér), n. One who or that which carries; applied to various parts of machines or instruments which act as transmitters or bearers. **carrier pigeon,** n. Breed of pigeons trained to carry communications.

carrion (kar'i-ón) [M.E. and O.F. *caroigne*], n. Putrefying flesh; garbage. a. Feeding on carrion; putrid; loathsome.

carrot (kar'ŏt) [F. *carotte*], n. A plant with an edible tapering root. **carroty,** a. Of the colour of a carrot; red-haired.

carry (kar'i) [O.North.F. *carier*], v.t. To bear, to transport with oneself; to transfer, bring, effect, accomplish; to imply; to take by assault. v.i. To act as bearer; to propel.

cart (kart) [Icel. *kartr*], n. A vehicle for heavy goods, etc.; a light, two-wheeled vehicle. v.t. To convey in a cart. **cartage** (kar'tàj), n. The act of carting, or the price paid. **carter,** n.

carte (kart), n. A bill of fare. **carte-blanche,** n. (*fig.*) Unlimited power to act.

cartilage (kar'ti-làj) [L. *cartilāgo*], n. Gristle, an elastic, pearly-white animal tissue. **cartilag'inous,** a.

cartography (kar-tog'rà-fi) [F. *carte*], n. Map- and chart-making. **cartog'rapher,** n.

carton (kar'ton) [F., cardboard], n. A cardboard box.

cartoon (kar-toon') [F. *CARTE*], n. A design for tapestry, mosaic, etc.; a topical (usu. political) sketch. **cartoonist,** n.

cartridge (kar'trij) [corr. of *cartouche*], n. A case of pasteboard, metal, etc., holding the charge for a gun. **cartridge-paper,** n. A stout, rough-surfaced paper for drawing, making strong envelopes, etc.

carve (karv) [A.-S. *ceorfan*], v.t. (*p.p.* -ed or -en) To cut into slices; to make, shape, or adorn by cutting. v.i. To exercise the profession of a sculptor or carver; to carve meat. **carver,** n. One who carves; a large knife for carving.

caryatid (kar-i-àt'id) [Gr. *Karuatis* -*idos*, a priestess of Artemis], n. A draped sculptured female figure supporting an entablature.

cascade (kàs-kād') [It. *cascata*, fallen], n. A small waterfall; a wavy fall of lace, etc.

case (1) (kàs) [O.North.F. *casse*, L. *capsa* (*capere*, to hold)], n. That which encloses or holds something else. v.t. To cover with or put into a case. **case-harden,** v.t. To harden the outside surface, esp. of iron. **case-shot,** n. Small projectiles discharged from cannon in cases. **casing,** n. Something that encases; an outside covering.

case (2) (kās) [L. *cāsus*, fallen], *n.* That which befalls; an event, position, state; an instance; (*Gram.*) change in termination to express relation, a suit in court; a statement for submission to a court; the evidence and arguments considered collectively; a cause that has been decided; the condition of a sick person.

casein (kā'sē-in) [L. *caseus*, cheese], *n.* The albuminoid or proteid in milk, forming the basis of cheese. **case'ic**, **case'ous**, *a.* A material for shawls.

casement (kāz'mênt) [It. *casamento*], *n.* A hinged window.

cash (kāsh) [F. *casse*, box], *n.* Coin, money. *v.t.* To turn into or exchange for cash.

cashier (1) (kà-shēr') [F. *caissier*], *n.* One who has charge of money transactions.

cashier (2) (kà-shēr') [Dut. *casseren*, L. *quassāre*, to shatter], *v.t.* To dismiss from the service.

cashmere (kāsh'mēr) [*Kashmir*, India], *n.* A material for shawls.

casino (kà-sē'nō) [It.], *n.* A public dancing-room; a building for gambling, dancing, etc.

cask (kask) [?], *n.* A barrel.

casket (kās'kĕt) [?], *n.* A small case for jewels, etc.

cassation (kās-ā'shŭn) [L. *cassare*, to make void], *n.* (*Law*) Reversal of a judicial sentence.

casserole (kās'ĕ-rōl) [F.], *n.* A stew-pan.

cassock (kās'ŏk) [F. *casaque*], *n.* A long, close garment worn by clerics.

cast (kast) [Icel. *kasta*, to throw], *v.t.* To throw, cause to fall, to emit; to shed; to assign (parts in a play); to reject; to add up, calculate; to mould. *v.i.* To throw a fishing-line; to reckon accounts; to take shape (in a mould). *n.* The act of throwing; a throw; the thing or the distance thrown; the allotment of parts in a play, the actors; ejectments from the stomach of a bird of prey; the end portion of a fishing-line; a computation; a squint; characteristic quality; a mould; the thing moulded, the shape. *a.* Thrown; (*Law*) condemned; made by founding or casting. **cast-iron**, *n.* Iron melted and run in moulds. *a.* Rigid, unyielding. **cast-off**, *a.* Laid aside, rejected. **cast-steel**, *n.* Steel melted and run into moulds.

castanet (kās-tà-net') [Sp.], *n.* A small instrument of ivory or hard wood rattled in pairs as an accompaniment to music.

castaway (kast'à-wā), *n.* An outcast; a shipwrecked person.

caste (kast) [L. *castus*, pure, unmixed], *n.* An hereditary, exclusive class, esp. in India.

castellated (kās'tĕ-lā-tĕd) [med. L. *castellātus*], *a.* Having turrets and battlements.

caster (kas'tĕr), *n.* One who or that which casts; a small vessel for holding condiments at table; a cruet-stand; a small swivelled wheel attached to the leg of a chair, etc. (in last three senses also spelt castor). **caster-sugar**, *n.* White powdered sugar for table use.

castigate (kās'tĭ-gāt) [L. *castigātus*, chastened], *v.t.* To chastise, to punish. **castiga'tion**, *n.* **cas'tigator**, *n.*

castle (kasl) [O.North.F. *castel*, L. *castel-*

lum, a small fort], *n.* A fortified building or a mansion that was formerly a fortress; a piece at chess, a rook. *v.i.* (*Chess*) To interchange the positions of king and castle according to rule. **castled**, *a.* Having a castle.

castor, *n.* An oily compound secreted by the beaver, formerly used in medicine.

castor-oil, *n.* An oil from the seeds of Palma Christi, used as a cathartic.

castrate (kās'trāt) [L. *castrātus*], *v.t.* To geld, deprive of generative power, excise the testicles. **castra'tion**, *n.*

casual (kāzh'ŭ-àl) [F. *casuel*], *a.* Happening by chance; occasional, unmethodical. **casually**, *adv.* **cas'ualty**, *n.* An accident attended with injury or loss of life; (*pl.*) the killed or wounded in war.

casuist (kāzh'ŭ-ist) [F. *casuiste*], *n.* One who studies doubtful questions of conduct; a sophist, hair-splitter. **casuis'tic**, **-al**, *a.* **casuistry** (kāz'ū-is-tri), *n.*

cat (kāt) [A.-S.], *n.* One of the genus *Felis* (lion, tiger, leopard, etc.), esp. the domestic cat; a strong tackle used to hoist the anchor; the game of tip-cat, the stick used in it; a cat-o'-nine-tails. *v.t.* To draw the anchor to the cat-head. **cat burglar**, *n.* A thief who enters a house by climbing up the outside. **cat-gut**, *n.* String made from the intestines of animals. **cat-o'-nine-tails**, *n.* A scourge with a number of lashes. **cat's paw**, *n.* A dupe used as a tool; a breeze which just ripples the surface of the water. **cat's whisker**, *n.* (*Rad.*) A component part of a crystal receiving set.

cat-, **cata-**, **cath-** [Gr. *kata*, down, downwards], *pref.* Down; against; away; wrongly; entirely, thoroughly; according to.

cataclysm (kāt'à-klizm) [Gr. *kluzein*, to wash], *n.* A deluge; a catastrophe.

catacomb (kāt'à-kōm) [late L. *Catacumbas* (prob. a place-name)], *n.* A subterranean burying-place.

catafalque (kāt'à-fālk) [It. *catafalco*], *n.* A temporary stage for a coffin during the funeral service.

catalepsy (kāt'à-lep-si) [Gr. *lambanein*, to seize], *n.* A sudden trance or suspension of sensation. **catalep'tic**, *a.*

catalogue (kāt'à-log) [Gr. *legein*, to choose], *n.* A methodical list. *v.t.* To enter in a list, make a complete list of.

catamaran (kāt-à-mà-rān') [Tamil], *n.* A surf-boat in the East and West Indies.

cataplasm (kāt'à-plāzm) [Gr. *kataplassein*, to spread over], *n.* A poultice, a plaster.

catapult (kāt'à-pŭlt) [Gr. *pallein*, to hurl], *n.* An ancient military engine for hurling; a toy for propelling stones.

cataract (kāt'à-rākt) [Gr. *katarassein*, to dash down], *n.* A large, rushing waterfall; a violent rush of water; a disease of the eye.

catarrh (kà-tar') [Gr. *rheein*, to flow], *n.* A running from the mucous membrane of the nose; a cold in the head.

catastrophe (kà-tās'trō-fē) [Gr. *strephein*, to turn], *n.* A great misfortune; violent convulsion; change which brings about the conclusion of a drama. **catastroph'ic**, *a.*

catch (kàch) [O.North.F. *cachier*], *v.t.*

(*past* and *p.p.* caught) To seize, esp. in pursuit; to entrap or take by angling; to intercept (as a ball) when falling; to surprise, detect; to take hold of (as fire); to receive by infection or contagion; to be in time for; to comprehend; to fascinate. *v.i.* To ignite; to spread epidemically; to lay hold; to become entangled. *n.* The act of grasping; anything that seizes, takes hold, or checks; the fish caught; a part-song. **catchment**, *n.* A surface on which water may be caught and collected. **catchpenny**, *a.* Worthless, made only to sell. **catchword**, *n.* A popular cry; an actor's cue; a word specially printed to attract attention. **catching**, *a.* Infectious; taking, attractive. **catchy**, *a.* Easy to catch (as a tune).

catechism (kăt'ĕkizm) [Gr. *ēchein*, to sound],*n.* A form of instruction by means of question and answer. **cat'echist**,*n.* One who teaches by catechizing. **catechize** (kăt'ĕ-kiz), *v.t.* To instruct by means of questions and answers; to question closely. **catechizer**,*n.* **catechumen** (kăt-ĕ-kū'mĕn), *n.* One who is under Christian instruction preparatory to baptism.

category (kăt'ĕ-gŏr-i) [Gr. *agora*, the assembly], *n.* An order, division; one of the ten classes of Aristotle to which all objects of thought or knowledge can be reduced. **categor'ical**, *a.* Unconditional; explicit.

catenary (kă-tē'năr-i) [L. *catēna*, a chain], *n.* A curve formed by a chain or rope hanging from two points. **cat'enate**, *v.t.* To link together.

cater (kā'tēr) [O.F. *acateor* (*acat, achat*, a purchasing)], *v.i.* To supply food, amusement, etc. (for). **caterer**, *n.*

caterpillar (kăt'ĕr-pil-ăr) [?], *n.* The larva of a moth or butterfly; (*reg. trade name*) a device for motor vehicles consisting of articulated belts in lieu of wheels.

caterwaul (kăt'ĕr-wawl), *v.i.* To make a noise as cats.

cathartic (kăthar'tik) [Gr. *katharos*, clean], *a.* Cleansing the bowels; purgative. *n.* A purgative medicine.

cathedral (kă-thē'drăl) [Gr. *hedra*, a seat], *n.* The principal church in a diocese, containing the bishop's throne.

catholic (kăth'ŏ-lik) [Gr. *katholikos*, *kath'-holou*, on the whole, universally], *a.* Universal, comprehensive; liberal, tolerant; pertaining to the whole Church; pertaining to the Roman Church. *n.* A member of the Universal Church; a Roman Catholic. **cathol'ically**, *adv.* **cathol'icism**, *n.* **catholic'ity**, *n.* The quality of being catholic. **cathol'icize**, *v.* To make or become Catholic.

catkin (kăt'kin) [?], *n.* The pendulous uni-sexual flowers of the willow, birch, poplar, etc.

cattle (kătl) [O.North.F. *catel*], *n.* Domesticated oxen and cows; (*slang*) horses.

caucus (kaw'kŭs) [?], *n.* (*Am.*) A preparatory meeting of a political party to decide a policy; a committee controlling electoral organization.

caudal (kaw'dăl) [L. *cauda*, tail], *a.* Pertaining to the tail.

caudle (kawdl) [O.North.F. *caudel* (L. *calidus*, warm)], *n.* A warm drink for invalids or a woman in childbed.

caul (kawl) [O.F. *cale*], *n.* A net for the hair; the membrane sometimes enclosing the head of a child when born.

cauldron (kawl'drŏn) [O.North.F. *caudron*], *n.* A deep, bowl-shaped vessel for boiling.

cauliflower (kol'i-flou-ĕr) [earlier *cole-*, *colie-florie*, from O. North. F. *col*, L. *caulis*, stem], *n.* A cabbage with an edible flowering head.

caulk (kawk) [O.F. *cauquer*], *v.t.* To stuff the seams (of a ship) with oakum. **caulker**, *n.* **caulking**, *n.*

causal (kaw'zăl), *a.* Relating to, expressing or due to, a cause or causes. **causal'ity**, *n.* The operation of a cause; relation of cause and effect. **causa'tion**, *n.* The act of causing; connexion between cause and effect. **can'sative**, *a.* That causes; effective as a cause; (*Gram.*) expressing cause.

cause (kawz) [L. *causa*]. *n.* That which produces or contributes to an effect; reason, motive; a movement, agitation, propaganda; the grounds for an action; a suit, an action. *v.t.* To act as an agent in producing; to effect.

causeless, *a.* Having no cause; without just reason. **causelessly**, *adv.*

causeway (kawz'wā) [O.North.F. *cauciĕ* (F. *chaussée*)], *n.* A raised road or footway.

caustic (kaw'stik) [Gr. *kaustikos*], *a.* Burning, corrosive; sarcastic. *n.* A substance that burns or corrodes organic matter.

cauterize (kaw'tĕr-iz), *v.t.* To burn or sear (some morbid part) with a hot iron or caustic. **cauteriza'tion**, *n.* **cau'tery**, *n.* Burning with a hot iron, electricity, or a caustic.

caution (kaw'shŭn) [L. *cautio -ōnem*], *n.* Wariness, prudence, a warning, *v.t.* To warn. **cautionary**, *a.* Given as security; containing a caution. **cautious**, *a.* Heedful, careful, wary. **cautiousness**, *n.*

cavalcade (kăv-ăl-kād') [L. *caballus*, a horse], *n.* A company on horseback.

cavalier (kăvă-lēr') [F.], *n.* A horseman; a gallant, lady's man. *a.* Off-hand, haughty, supercilious. *v.i.* To act as cavalier to a lady. **cavalierly**, *adv.* In a haughty manner.

cavalry (kăv'ăl-ri), *n.* Horse soldiers who act as a body.

cave (kāv) [F., L. *cavus*, hollow], *n.* A hollow place in the earth; a den.

caveat (kā'vĕ-ăt) [L., let him beware], *n.* A process to stop proceedings.

cavern (kăv'ĕrn), *n.* A large cave. **cavernous**, *a.* Hollow or huge, like a cavern; full of caverns.

caviar, caviare (kăv-i-ar') [?], *n.* The roe of the sturgeon, dried and salted.

cavil (kăv'il) [O.F. *caviller*], *n.* A frivolous objection. *v.i.* To argue or object to frivolously. **caviller**, *n.* **cavilling**, *a.*

cavity (kăv'i-ti) [F. *cavité*], *n.* A hollow place.

cavy (kā'vi) [F. Guiana, *cabiai*], *n.* A South American rodent; the guinea-pig.

caw (kaw) [imit.], *v.i.* To cry like a rook.

cay, kay (kā) [Sp. *cayo*], *n.* (*Geog.*) A reef, shoal.

cayenne (kā-en') [Braz. *kyỹnha*], *n.* The powdered fruit of capsicum, used as a condiment.

cease (sēs) [L. *cessāre*, to go, yield], *v.i.* To leave off; to desist (from). *v.t.* To put a stop to. **ceaseless,** *a.* Incessant.

cedar (sē'dàr) [Gr. *kedros*], *n.* An evergreen coniferous tree. *a.* Made of cedar-wood.

cede (sēd) [L. *cēdere*, to yield], *v.t.* To give up, surrender; to yield, grant.

cedilla (sē-dil'á) [Sp.], *n.* A mark (ç) placed under *c* to show that it has the sound of *s*.

ceil (sēl) [L. *cœlum*, heaven], *v.t.* To line the roof of a room. **ceiling,** *n.* The inner, upper surface of a room; the plaster on it; the maximum height to which an aeroplane can rise; a maximum height, price, etc.

celandine (sel'án-dīn) [Gr. *chelidonion*, swallow-wort], *n.* Two plants with yellow flowers, the *greater*, related to the poppy, and the *lesser* to the buttercup.

celebrate (sel'ē-brāt) [L. *celebrātus*], *v.t.* To praise; to commemorate; to perform (as Mass), to administer (as Communion). *v.i.* To officiate at the Eucharist. **celebrated,** *a.* Famous, renowned. **celebra'tion,** *n.* **celebrant,** *n.* The priest who officiates in any solemn office. **celeb'rity,** *n.* Renown; a celebrated personage.

celerity (sē-ler'i-ti) [L. *celeritas* (*celer*, swift)], *n.* Speed, swiftness, promptness

celery (sel'ér-i) [F. *céleri*], *n.* A plant, the blanched stems of which are eaten.

celestial (sē-les'ti-ál) [L. *cœlestis*; -AL], *a.* Pertaining to heaven or the heavens; divine. *n.* An inhabitant of heaven; a native of China, the "Celestial Empire".

celibate (sel'i-bàt) [L. *cœlebs*, unmarried], *n.* An unmarried person; one vowed to a single life. *a.* Unmarried. **celibacy,** *n.*

cell (sel) [L. *cēlāre*, to hide], *n.* A small room; a small cavity; a compartment in a bees' comb; the unit-mass of living matter; a division of an electric battery; a subsidiary unit of a political organization.

cellar (sel'àr) [L. *cellārium*], *n.* An under vault, esp. for wine; a stock of wine; a salt-cellar. **cellarage** (sel'àr-àj), *n.* Cellars collectively, charge for storage in cellars. **cellarer,** *n.* One in charge of stores. **cellaret',** *n.* A case with compartments for holding bottles.

cellophane (sel'ō-fān), *n.* Protected trade name of a transparent packing material.

cellule (sel'ūl) [L. *cellula*], *n.* A little cell. **cellular,** *a.* Pertaining to, composed of, or resembling a cell.

celluloid (sel'ū-loid), *n.* A compound of cellulose used as a substitute for ivory, etc. **cellulose,** *n.* The basis of vegetable tissues.

Celt (1) (kelt) [L. *Celtœ*], *n.* One of a race comprising the Welsh, Cornish, Manx, Irish, Gaels, and Bretons. **Celtic,** *a.*

celt (2) (selt) [late Lat. *celtis*, a chisel], *n.* A prehistoric cutting implement.

cement (sē-ment') [L. *cœmentum*], *n.* An adhesive substance used for sticking things together. *v.t.* To unite with or as with cement; to unite firmly and closely.

cemetery (sem'é-tèr-i) [L. *cœmētērium*], *n.* A burial-ground other than a churchyard.

cenotaph (sen'ō-tàf) [Gr. *kenos*, empty, *taphos*, tomb], *n.* A sepulchral monument raised to a person buried elsewhere. **The Cenotaph,** *n.* Monument in Whitehall, London, commemorating the fallen in the World Wars.

censer (sen'sèr), *n.* A vessel for burning incense; a thurible.

censor (sen'sór) [L. *censēre*, to tax], *n.* An official who examines books, plays, etc., before they are published; one who censures. *a.* **censor'ious,** *a.* Expressing or addicted to criticism. **censorship,** *n.*

censure (sen'shùr) [L. *censūra*], *n.* Disapproval, condemnation, blame. *v.t.* To blame, find fault with. **censurable,** *a.*

census (sen'sùs), *n.* An official enumeration of inhabitants; the result.

cent (sent) [L. *centum*], *n.* A 100th part of a dollar. **per cent.:** By the hundred.

centaur (sen'tawr) [Gr. *kentauros;* etym. doubtful], *n.* A mythical figure, half man, half horse.

centenarian (sen-tē-nâr'i-án) [L. *centēndrius*, from *centēni*, a hundred each], *n.* A person one hundred years old. *a.* Relating to a hundred. **centenary** (sen-tē'nā-ri), *n.* A hundredth anniversary, or its celebration. **centennial** (sén-ten'i-ál), *a.* Pertaining to a hundredth anniversary.

centi- [L. *centum*, a hundred], *comb. form.*

centigrade (sen'ti-grād) [L. *gradus*, step], *n.* The thermometer of Celsius (freezing-point 0°, boiling-point 100°).

centime (san-tēm) [F.], *n.* A French coin worth the 100th of a franc.

centimetre (sen'ti-mē-tèr), *n.* The hundredth of a metre, ·394 inch.

centipede (sen'ti-pēd) [L. *pes pedis*, foot], *n.* A small creature with many feet.

central (sen'tràl) [L. *centrālis*], *a.* Relating to or situated in the centre; of chief importance. **cen'tralize,** *v.t.* To bring to a centre; to concentrate. *v.i.* To come to a centre. **centraliza'tion,** *n.* The system or policy of concentrating organization in a centre.

centre (sen'tèr) [F. *centre*, L. *centrum*], *n.* The middle point, the pivot, nucleus; **centering.** *v.i.* To be fixed on a centre, collected at one point. **centre-board,** *n.* A sliding-keel.

centrifugal (sen-trif'ū-gàl) [L. *fugere*, to fly from], *a.* Tending to fly from the centre.

centripetal (sen-trip'é-tàl) [L. *petere*, to seek], *a.* Tending to approach the centre.

centurion (sen-tū'ri-òn) [L.], *n.* A Roman officer commanding a hundred men.

century (sen'tūri), *n.* An aggregate of a hundred things; a period of a hundred years.

cephal- (sef'ál) [Gr. *kephalē*, the head], *comb. forms.* Pertaining to the head. **cephal'ic,** *a.* Pertaining to the head, *n.* A remedy for pains in the head. **ceph'alous,** *a.* Having a head.

ceramic (sē-răm'ik) [Gr. *keramos*, pottery], *a.* Pertaining to pottery. **ceramics,** *n.pl.* The art of pottery.

cerecloth (sēr'kloth), *n.* A cloth dipped in melted wax, used to wrap embalmed bodies in. **cere'ment** (F. *cirement*], *n.* A cerecloth; (*pl.*) grave-clothes.

cereal (sēr'-āl) [L. *Ceres*, goddess of corn], *a.* Pertaining to grain. *n.* Any edible grain.

cerebellum (ser-ē-bel'ŭm) [L. *cerebrum*, brain], *n.* The part of the brain beneath the posterior lobes of the cerebrum. **cer'ebrum**, *n.* The chief portion of the brain. **cerebral**, *a.* Pertaining to the brain. **cerebra'tion**, *n.* The action of the brain, whether conscious or unconscious.

ceremony (ser'ē-mō-ni) [O.F. *ceremonie*], *n.* A rite, formality; a usage of politeness. **ceremo'nial**, *a.* Relating to or performed with ceremonies or rites. *n.* The prescribed order for a function. **ceremonious**, *a.* Punctilious; observant of ceremony.

cerise (sē-rēz') [F., cherry], *n.* Cherry colour.

certain (sēr'tān) [O.F. *certein*, L. *certus*], *a.* Sure, convinced; established beyond a doubt; absolutely, regular; inevitable; reliable, unerring; indefinite, unspecified. **certainly**, *adv.* Assuredly; beyond doubt; without fail; admittedly. **certainty**, *n.* That which is certain; absolute assurance.

certify (sēr'tĭ-fī), *v.t.* To testify to in writing; to give certain information. **certifiable**, *a.* certifier, *n.* certif'icate, *n.* A written testimony, esp. of character or ability. **cer'titude**, *n.* Certainty.

cerulean (sē-roo'lē-ăn) [L. *cœruleus*], *a.* Sky-blue; sky-coloured.

cervical (sēr'vi-kăl) [L. *cervix*, the neck], *a.* (*Anat.*) Pertaining to the neck.

cessation (sē-sā'shŭn), *n.* The act of ceasing; pause, rest.

cession (sech'ŏn), *n.* Ceding; a yielding, surrender, esp. of territory.

cesspool (ses'pool) [?], *n.* A hole for sewage to drain into.

cetacean (se-ta'shiăn) [L. *cetus*, a whale], *a.* Pertaining to the whales, etc.

chafe (chāf) [O.F. *chaufer*], *v.t.* To make warm, fret, or make sore by rubbing; to gall, irritate. *v.i.* To be worn by rubbing; to fret. *n.* A sore caused thus.

chaff (chaf) [A.-S. *ceaf*], *n.* The husks of grain; hay or straw cut fine for fodder; anything worthless; banter. *v.* To banter or indulge in banter.

chaffer (chăf'ēr) [A.-S. *cēap*, bargain, *faru*, a journey], *v.i.* To haggle, to bargain.

chaffinch (chăf'inch), *n.* A small British bird.

chagrin (shà-grēn') [F.], *n.* Vexation.

chain (chān) [O.F. *chaêne*, L. *catēna*], *n.* A series of connected links for binding, hauling, ornamenting, etc.; a measure of 100 links (66 ft.); bonds, fetters; a connected series. *v.t.* To fasten or bind with a chain. **chain-stitch**, *n.* A loop-stitch made by a sewing-machine.

chair (châr) [O.F. *chaêre*], *n.* A backed movable seat for one; a seat of authority or office; a professorship or chairmanship; (*Railway*) an iron socket to secure the rails. *v.t.* To carry publicly in a chair in triumph; to install as president. **chairman**, *n.* The president of a meeting, committee, etc.; a man who draws a Bath chair. **chairmanship**, *n.*

chaise (shāz) [F.], *n.* A light carriage.

chalcedony (kăl-sed'ō-ni) [Gr. *chalkēdōn*], *n.* (*Min.*) A crypto-crystalline variety of quartz.

chaldron (chawl'drŏn) [O.F. *chauderon*], *n.* A measure (36 bushels) for coals.

chalet (shăl'ā) [F. Swiss.], *n.* A villa.

chalice (chăl'is) [O.F.], *n.* A cup, esp. that used in Communion.

chalk (chawk) [A.-S. *cealc*, L. *calx*, lime], *n.* Soft white limestone or massive carbonate of lime, chiefly composed of marine shells. *v.t.* To rub, mark, or write with chalk. **chalky**, *a.*

challenge (chăl'enj) [O.F. *chalenge*], *n.* A summons to fight; a calling in question; the call of a sentry. *v.t.* To invite or defy to a duel or contest; to call on to answer; to object to, dispute. **challenger**, *n.*

chalybeate (kà-lib'-ē-át) [Gr. *chalups -ubos*, steel], *a.* Impregnated with iron or steel. *n.* A mineral water so impregnated.

chamber (chām'bēr) [L. *camera*], *n.* A room; the place where a legislative assembly meets; a hall of justice; an association of persons for some common object; chamber-maid, *n.* A woman in charge of bedrooms at a hotel. **chamber music**, *n.* Music adapted to performance in a room.

chamberlain (chām'bēr-lăn) [O.F.], *n.* An officer in charge of the household of a sovereign or nobleman.

chameleon (kà-mē'lē-ŏn) [Gr. *chamai*, dwarf, *leōn*, a lion], *n.* A lizard able to assume varying shades; a changeable person.

chamfer (chăm'fēr) [O.F. *chanfrein*], *n.* An angle slightly pared off; a bevel, fluting. *v.t.* To groove; to bevel off.

chamois (shăm'wa) [F.], *n.* A goat-like European antelope, *rupicapra*.

champ (champ) [imit.], *v.t.* and *i.* To bite with a grinding action; to crunch.

champagne (shăm-pān'), *n.* A light brisk wine made in Champagne, France.

champaign (chăm'pān) [O.F.], *n.* Flat, open country.

champion (chăm'pi-ŏn) [O.F.], *n.* One who engages in combat or argument on behalf of another; the person, animal, or exhibit that defeats all competitors. *v.t.* To defend as a champion; to support a cause. **championship**, *n.*

chance (chans) [O.F.], *n.* Fortune, course of events; issue, result, esp. undesigned; possibility, opportunity (*usu. pl.*); likelihood. *v.i.* To happen, to come to pass. *a.* Fortuitous, unforeseen.

chancel (chan'sĕl) [O.F.], *n.* The east end of a church, formerly cut off by a screen.

chancellery (chan'sĕl-ēr-i), *n.* A chancellor's official establishment; a chancellor's office; an embassy or consulate.

chancellor (chan'sē-lŏr) [O.F. *chancelier*, late L. *cancellārius*], *n.* The president of a court, public department, or university; a bishop's law-officer. **chancellorship**, *n.*

chancery (chan'sēr-i), *n.* The court of the Lord Chancellor, before 1873; a division of the High Court of Justice.

chandelier (shăn-dē-lēr') [O.F.], *n.* A

hanging branched frame for a number of lights.

chandler (chand'lèr) [O.F. *chandelier*, L. *candēla*, candle], *n.* One who makes or sells candles; a dealer in groceries, etc. **chandlery**, *n.* Articles sold by a chandler.

change (chānj) [O.F. *changer*], *v.t.* To make different, to alter; to substitute or take for something else; to exchange. *v.i.* To become different in appearance, state, etc. *n.* Alteration, variation; transition; substitution of one thing for another; small coin or foreign money given in return for other coins; novelty, variety. **change-over**, *n.* (*Elec.*) Changing of circuit from one system to another. **changeable**, *a.* Liable to change; inconstant. **changeability** (-bil'i-ti), *n.* changeableness, *n.* changeful, *a.* Changeable. **changeless**, *a.* Unchanging. **changeling**, *n.* A child substituted for another, an elf-child.

channel (chăn'èl) [O.F. *chanel*], *n.* The bed of a watercourse; the fairway of an estuary; a narrow piece of water joining two seas; a duct; means of passing, conveying, or transmitting. **The Channel**, *n.* The English Channel.

chant (chant) [F. *chanter*, L. *cantāre*], *v.t.* To celebrate in song; to intone. *v.i.* To sing in an intoning fashion. *n.* Song, melody; a psalm, or other piece intoned; a monotonous song. **chanter**, *n.* The drone of a bagpipe.

chantey (shan'ti), *n.* A song sung by sailors whilst heaving or hauling.

chanticleer (chăn'ti-klēr), *n.* A cock.

chantry (chan'tri) [F. *chanterie*], *n.* The chapel used for saying mass for the dead.

chaos (kā'os) Gr.], *n.* Confusion; the confusion of matter said to have existed at the Creation; the primeval void; confusion. **chaot'ic**, *a.* **chaot'ically**, *adv.*

chap (1) (chăp) [M.E. *chappen*], *v.i.* To crack or open in long slits. *n.* (*usu. in pl.*) A longitudinal crack, cleft, or seam on the surface of the skin. (*pl.*) The jaws, the mouth and cheeks. **chap-fallen**, *a.* Downcast, dejected, dispirited.

chap (2) [CHAPMAN], *n.* A man, a fellow.

chap-book (chăp'buk) [on anal. of CHAP-MAN], *n.* A small book of wonderful tales, formerly hawked by chapmen.

chapel (chăp'èl) [O.F. *chapele*], *n.* A place or worship; a part containing an altar in a church; an association of printers, etc., for the settlement of working conditions, etc.

chaperon (shăp'èr-òn) [F.], *n.* A married woman who attends a young woman in public places.

chapiter (chăp'i-tèr) [O.F.], *n.* The upper part of the capital of a column.

chaplain (chap'lăn) [O.F. *chapelain*], *n.* A clergyman who officiates at court, or in a regiment, ship, mansion, or public institution. **chaplaincy**, *n.*

chaplet (chăp'lèt) [O.F. *chapelet*], *n.* A garland for the head.

chapman (chăp'măn) [A.-S. *cēap*, CHEAP, MAN], *n.* An itinerant merchant.

chaps (chăps) [Sp. *chaparajos*], *n.pl.* Leather leggings with hair outside worn by cowboys.

chapter (chăp'tèr), *n.* A division of a book, or of Acts of Parliament in chronological order; an episode; the general meeting of certain orders; the clergy attached to a cathedral.

char (1) (char) [?], *n.* A small fish.

char (2), **chare** (chār) [A.-S. *cierr*], *n.* A turn of work, an odd job. *v.i.* To work by the day. **charwoman**, *n.* A woman who does housework by the hour or day.

char (3), *v.t.* To burn slightly.

char-à-banc (shär-á-băng) [F., carriage with benches], *n.* A long car (horse or motor) with transverse seats.

character (kăr'ăk-tèr) [Gr. *charactēr* (*charassein*, to furrow, engrave)], *n.* A mark made by engraving, writing, etc.; a letter, sign; distinctive qualities or traits; the sum of one's mental and moral qualities; reputation, standing; certificate of capacity, etc.; a personality created by a writer; an eccentric person. **characteris'tic**, *a.* **char'acterize**, *v.t.* To give character to, to distinguish. **characteriza'tion**, *n.*

charade (shá-rad') [F.], *n.* A kind of riddle in which description or action represents each syllable of a word.

charcoal (char'kōl) [?], *n.* Wood partially burnt.

charge (charj) [F. *charger*], *v.t.* To fill; to put the proper load, etc., into (apparatus), as to load (a gun), to accumulate electricity in (a battery), etc.; to rush on and attack; to enjoin, command, accuse; to ask a price for; to give directions to (esp. of a judge or a bishop). *v.i.* To make an attack or onset. *n.* A burden; an office, duty, or obligation; care, custody; the thing under one's care; price demanded, cost; accusation; attack, onset; the quantity with which any apparatus, esp. a fire-arm, is loaded; instructions, directions. **chargeable**, *a.* Liable to be accused; liable to a monetary demand. **charger**, *n.* A war-horse.

chargé d'affaires (shar'zhā-dá-fâr') [F., charged with affairs], *n.* A deputy to an ambassador; an ambassador to a minor court.

chariot (chăr'i-òt) [O.F.], *n.* (*poet. and rhet.*) A stately vehicle; a carriage anciently used in war, etc. **charioteer'**, *n.* A chariot-driver.

charity (chăr'i-ti) [O.F. *charité*], *n.* Love of one's fellows; almsgiving; alms; kindness; leniency. **charity-boy, -girl**, *n.* One brought up in a charity school. **charity school**, *n.* An endowed school for the education of the poor. **charitable**, *a.* Full of charity; liberal to the poor; benevolent, kind, large-hearted; **charitableness**, *n.*

charlatan (shar'lá-tăn) [It. *ciarlare*, to prattle], *n.* A pretender, quack, impostor. **char'latanism**, *n.*

charlock (char'lok) [A.-S. *cerlic*], *n.* The wild mustard.

charm (charm) [O.F. *charme*], *n.* A spell, enchantment; an article worn to avert evil or ensure good luck; a power of pleasing or exciting love or desire. *v.t.* To enchant, fascinate, bewitch. **charmer**, *n.* **charming**, *a.*

charnel-house (char'nĕl) [O.F. *charnel*, a cemetery], *n.* A place where the bones of the dead are deposited.

chart (chart) [Gr. *chartē*, a sheet of papyrus], *n.* A map, esp. of some part of the sea or coast; a statement in tabular form or as a graphic curve.

charter (char'tẽr) [O.F. *chartre*], *n.* A deed incorporating a borough, company, or institution, or conferring certain rights and privileges. *v.t.* To establish or license by charter; to hire. **chartered,** *a.* Invested with privileges.

Chartism (char'tizm), *n.* The principles of the Chartists, an English democratic party (1838-48) whose objects were embodied in the People's Charter. **Chartist,** *n.*

chary (char'ĭ) [A.-S. *cearig*], *a.* Wary, cautious, frugal. **chariness,** *n.*

chase (1) (chās) [O.F. *chacier*], *v.t.* To hunt, drive away, put to flight. *n.* Earnest pursuit; the hunting of wild animals; that which is hunted; a preserve for game.

chase (2) [F. *enchâsser*], *v.t.* To engrave; to cut the worm of (a screw). **chasing,** *n.* The art of engraving metals; the pattern engraved or embossed.

chasm (kăzm) [Gr. *chasma*], *n.* A cleft, a fissure, yawning gulf.

chassis (shăs'ē) [F.], *n.* (*pl. unaltered*) The under-framework and gear of a motor-car, motor-bus, etc.

chaste (chāst) [O.F., L. *castus*, pure], *a.* Pure from unlawful sexual commerce or desires; free from obscenity; pure in style; simple, unadorned.

chasten (chāsn) [O.F. *chastier*], *v.t.* To punish with a view to reformation.

chastise (chăs-tīz'), *v.t.* To punish, esp. with bodily pain, to correct an offence or wrong. **chastisement** (chăs'tiz-mĕnt), *n.*

chastity (chăs'ti-ti), *n.* The state of being chaste; purity of body, conduct, or taste.

chasuble (chăz'ūbl) [F.], *n.* A vestment worn by a priest.

chat (chăt), *v.i.* To talk easily and familiarly; to gossip. *n.* Easy, familiar talk; gossip. **chatty,** *a.*

chatelaine (shăt'ē-lān) [F.], *n.* An ornament worn by a lady at her waist, having short chains for keys, trinkets, etc; mistress of a country house, etc.

chattel (chăt'ĕl) [O.F.], *n.* (*usu. in pl.*) Movable property; (*Law*) any property except freehold.

chatter (chăt'ẽr) [onomat.], *v.i.* To make a noise like rattling the teeth together; to jabber, prattle. *n.* Idle talk. **chatterbox,** *n.* An incessant talker.

chauffeur (shō-fẽr') [F.], *n.* A paid motor-car driver.

chauvinism (shō'vin-izm) [F., from Nicolas *Chauvin*, an old soldier blindly attached to Napoleon], *n.* Exaggerated patriotism; jingoism. **chauvinist,** *n.* and *a.*

cheap (chēp) [A.-S. *ceap*, price, barter], *a.* Low in or worth more than its price; of small value or esteem. **cheapen,** *v.t.* To beat down the price of; to depreciate. *v.i.* To become cheap, depreciate. **cheapish,** *a.* **cheap-jack,** *n.* A travelling hawker. **cheaply,** *adv.* **cheapness,** *n.*

cheat (chēt), *n.* A fraud, imposition, swindle; a trickster, swindler. *v.t.* To defraud, deceive, impose upon. *v.i.* To act as a cheat. **cheater,** *n.*

check (1) (chek) [O.F. *eschec*, Pers. *shāh*, a king], *n.* A sudden stoppage; a reverse, a repulse; a pause; restraint, repression; a mark serving for identification; a term in chess when one player obliges the other to move or guard his king; the situation of such a king. *v.t.* To arrest; to cause to stop; to repress, curb; to test the accuracy of by comparison; (*Chess*) to put an opponent's king in check. *v.i.* To pause, to halt.

check (2) (chek), *n.* A chequered or cross-lined pattern.

checkmate (chek'māt') [O.F. *eschec mat*, Pers. *shāh mat*, the king is dead], *n.* (*Chess*) The winning movement when one king is in check and cannot escape. *v.t.* To give checkmate to; to defeat.

cheek (chēk) [A.-S. *cēace*], *n.* The side of the face below the eye; (*colloq.*) impudence, effrontery, assurance. *v.t.* To be impudent to. *v.i.* To be saucy. **cheeky,** *a.* Impudent, saucy.

cheep (chēp), *v.i.* To chirp feebly. *n.* The cry of a young bird.

cheer (chēr) [M.E. and O.F. *chere*, the face, look], *n.* Disposition, esp. as shown by the face; entertainment, good fare, a state of joy; a shout of joy or applause. *v.t.* To make glad; to applaud, encourage. *v.i.* To grow cheerful; to utter cheers. **cheerful,** *a.* **cheerfulness,** *n.* **cheering,** *a.* **cheerless,** *a.* Dull, gloomy, dispiriting. **cheery,** *a.* Lively, sprightly, genial.

cheese (chēz) [A.-S. *cēse*], *n.* The curd of milk pressed into a solid mass and ripened by keeping.

cheetah (chē'tā) [Hind. *chītā*, spotted], *n.* The hunting leopard.

chef (shef) [F.], *n.* A head or professional cook. **chef-d'œuvre** (shā-dẽvr') [F. *œuvre*, work], *n.* (*pl. chefs-*) A masterpiece.

chemical (kem'ĭk-ăl), *a.* Pertaining to chemistry, its laws, or phenomena. *n.* A substance produced by chemical processes.

chemise (shē-mēz') [F.], *n.* An under body-garment of linen or cotton worn by women.

chemist (kem'ĭst) [ALCHEMIST], *n.* One versed in chemistry; a dealer in drugs.

chemistry (kem'is-tri), *n.* The science which investigates the elements and the compounds that they compose; the practical application of this science.

chemurgy (kem'ẽr'ji) [Gr. *ergos*, working], *n.* The branch of chemistry devoted to the utilization of raw material.

cheque (chek), *n.* A draft on a banker for money.

chequer, checker (chek'ẽr) [O.F. *eschekier*, chess-board], *n.* A pattern made of squares in alternating colours, like a chess-board; (*pl., Am.*) the game of draughts.

cherish (cher'ish) [O.F. *cherir*], *v.t.* To hold dear, treat with affection; to foster.

cheroot (shē-root') [Tamil *shuruttu*], *n.* A cigar with both ends cut off square.

cherry (cher'i) [M.E. *chery*, O.F. *cerise*], *n.* A small fruit of the plum family; the tree on which it grows; the wood of this.

cherub (cher'ŭb) [Heb.], *n.* (*pl.* -**s**, -**im**, -**ims**) A celestial spirit next in order to the seraphim; a beautiful child. **cherubic** (chē-rū'bik), *a.* Pertaining to cherubs; ruddy, full-cheeked.

chess (ches), *n.* A game played by two with sixteen pieces each on a board divided into sixty-four squares.

chest (chest) [A.-S. *cest*], *n.* A large box or case; the treasury or funds of an institution; the fore part of the body from neck to belly.

chestnut (chest'nŭt) [O.F. *chastaigne*], *n.* A tree of the genus *Castanea*, esp. the Spanish or sweet chestnut, or its fruit; a reddish-brown colour; a horse of this colour; a stale joke.

chevalier (shev-à-lēr') [F. *cheval*, horse], *n.* A knight, a gallant.

cheviot (chev'i-ot) [Cheviot Hills], *n.* Sheep bred on these hills; rough cloth made from wool of these sheep.

chevron (shev'rŏn) [F., rafter], *n.* (*Her.*) A device representing two rafters meeting at the top; the mark on sleeves of non-commissioned officers.

chevy (chev'i), **chivy** (chiv'i) [*Chevy* Chase], *v.t.* To chase about, hunt.

chew (choo) [A.-S. *cēowan*], *v.t.* To masticate, grind with the teeth; to digest mentally. *v.i.* To masticate food, tobacco, or gum. *n.* A quid of tobacco.

chic (shik) [F.], *n.* Smartness, style; the best fashion or taste. *a.* Stylish.

chicane (shi-kān') [F.], *n.* The use of mean petty subterfuge; artifice; (*Bridge*) a hand containing no trumps. **chicanery**, *n.*

chick, chicken (chik'ĕn) [A.-S. *cicen*], *n.* The young of various birds, esp. the domestic fowl; (*fig.*) a child. **chicken-hearted**, *a.* Timid, cowardly. **chicken-pox**, *n.* A pustulous, contagious disease, usually occurring in childhood.

chicory (chik'ō-ri) [Gr. *kichōrē*, succory], *n.* The succory, a blue-flowered plant, or its root, which is used to adulterate coffee.

chide (chīd) [A.-S. *cīdan*], *v.t.* To find fault with, blame. *v.i.* To scold.

chief (chēf) [F. *chef*], *a.* Principal, first; leading, main. *n.* A leader or commander, esp. of a tribe or clan; the head of a department; the principal thing. **chiefdom**, *n.* **chiefly**, *adv.* Principally, especially; for the most part.

chieftain (chēf'tàn), *n.* A leader.

chiffon (shif'on) [F. *chiffe*, a rag], *n.* A gauzy fabric used as a trimming.

chiffonier (shif-ò-nēr') [F. *chiffonnier*, a rag-gatherer], *n.* A movable sideboard.

chilblain (chil'blān), *n.* An inflamed sore caused by cold.

child (chīld) [A.-S. *cild*], *n.* (*pl.* **children**, chil'drĕn) A descendant in the first degree, a son or daughter; an infant, young person; (*pl.*) disciples, followers. **childe**, *n.* A scion of a noble family. **childhood**, *n.* The state of being a child. **childish**, *a.* Of or befitting a child; puerile. **childishness**, *n.* **childless**, *a.* Without offspring. **childlike**, *a.* Resembling a child; simple, innocent.

chill (chil) [A.-S. *ciele*], *n.* A cold, shivering sensation preceding fever or ague. *a.* Cold; causing coolness. *v.t.* To make cold; to cool suddenly; to depress, dispirit. **chilling**, *a.* **chilly**, *a.* Making cold; distant in manner. **chilliness**, *n.*

chilli (chil'i) [Mex.], *n.* (*pl.* -**ies**) The dried ripe pod of red pepper, *capsicum*.

chime (chīm) [O.F. *chimble*, Gr. *kumbalon*], *n.* Harmonic or consonant musical sounds; a number of bells tuned in harmonious succession; harmony, accord. *v.i.* To sound in harmony or accord; to ring, strike the hour, etc.; to accord, agree. *v.t.* To ring a series of bells.

chimera (kī-mēr'à) [Gr. *chimaira*, she-goat], *n.* A fabulous fire-eating monster, with a lion's head, a serpent's tail, and the body of a goat; (*fig.*) an idle fancy, a bugbear. **chimer'ical**, *a.* Purely imaginary.

chimney (chim'ni) [O.F. *cheminée*], *n.* The passage through which smoke escapes from a fire into the open air; a glass tube for a lamp; a vertical fissure in rock. **chimney-piece**, *n.* The ornamental frame round a fireplace. **chimney stack**, *n.* The part of a chimney carried above the roof. **chimney stalk**, *n.* A tall factory chimney.

chimpanzee (chim-păn-zē') [native name], *n.* A large African anthropoid ape.

chin (chin) [A.-S. *cin*], *n.* The front part of the lower jaw.

china (chī'nà), *n.* Porcelain, first brought from China.

chine (chīn) [O.F. *eschine*], *n.* The backbone or spine.

Chinese (chī-nēz'), *a.* Of or belonging to China. *n.* A native or the language of China.

chink (1) (chingk) [?], *n.* A narrow cleft.

chink (2) (chingk), *n.* A jingling sound as of coin; money.

chintz (chints) [Hind. *chint*, variegated], *n.* Cotton cloth, printed in colours with floral devices, etc.

chip (chip), *n.* A small piece of wood, stone, etc., chopped off; a thin slice of potato; wood or fibre in thin strips for making hats. *v.t.* To cut into chips. *v.i.* To break off in chips.

Chippendale (chip'ĕn-dāl), *a.* Applied to furniture of the light style introduced by T. Chippendale in the 18th cent.

chir-, chiro- [Gr. *cheir*, hand], *comb. form.* Manual; having hands or hand-like organs.

chiromancy (kī'rò-măn-si), *n.* Divination by means of the hand; palmistry.

chiropodist (shi-rop'ō-dist, kī-rop'ò-dist) [Gr. *pous podos*, foot], *n.* One skilled in the care of the feet. **chiropody**, *n.*

chirp (chĕrp), *v.i.* To make a quick, sharp sound (as birds); to talk cheerfully. *n.* A sharp, quick sound of a bird, or one like it. **chirpy**, *a.* Cheerful; vivacious.

chisel (chiz'ĕl) [O.F. *cisel*], *n.* An edged tool for cutting wood, iron, or stone. *v.t.* To cut, pare, or grave with a chisel; (*slang*) to cheat. **chiselled**, *a.*

chit (1) (chit), *n.* A child; young girl.

chit (2) [Hind.], *n.* A letter or note.

chivalry (shiv'àl-ri) [O.F. *chevalerie*], *n.* The knightly system of the Middle Ages;

c

nobleness and gallantry of spirit, courtesy, respect for and defence of the weak; knights collectively. **chivalrous, -ric** (shiv'ål-rŭs, -rĭk), *a.* Pertaining to chivalry; high-spirited, gallant, noble.

chive (chīv) [F. *cive*], *n.* A small onion-like herb.

chlor-, chloro- [Gr. *chlōros*, green], *comb. form.* Greenish; pertaining to chlorine.

chloral (klōr'ål), *n.* (*Chem.*) A narcotic obtained by the action of chlorine on alcohol.

chlorine (klōr'īn), *n.* A yellow-green gas obtained from common salt, used as a disinfectant and for bleaching.

chloroform (klōr'ō-fôrm), *n.* A volatile fluid used to produce anæsthesia.

chlorophyll (klōr'ō-fĭl) [Gr. *phullon*, a leaf], *n.* Green colouring-matter of plants.

chock (chŏk) [?], *n.* A wood block, wedge-shaped. *adv.* As close as possible; tightly, fully. **chock-full,** *adv.* Quite full.

chocolate (chŏk'ō-lāt) [*Mex. choco,* cacao, *latl,* water], *n.* The paste, cake, or beverage made from the roasted kernels of the cacao-tree.

choice (chois) [O.F. *chois*], *n.* The power or act of choosing; the thing chosen; selection; the best part. *a.* Selected; of great value; careful, fastidious.

choir (kwīr) [M.E. *queir*], *n.* A band of singers, esp. in a church; the part of the church allotted to the singers.

choke (chōk) [A.-S. *ā-cēocian*], *v.t.* To block or compress the windpipe so as to prevent breathing; to smother, to stifle. *v.i.* To have the windpipe stopped; to be blocked up. *n.* The action of choking; (*Rad.*) an inductance coil to prevent high-frequency currents from passing. **choker,** *n.* A high stiff collar.

choler (kol'ĕr) [O.F. *colere*], *n.* Anger; tendency to anger. **choleric,** *a.*

cholera (kol'ĕr-å) [Gr. *chole,* bile], *n.* (*Med.*) A disease characterized by violent vomiting and purging, tending to run a rapidly fatal course.

choose (chooz) [A.-S. *cēosan*], *v.t.* (*past chose, p.p.* chosen) To take by preference, to select; to feel inclined. *v.i.* To make one's choice.

chop (1) (chop), *v.t.* To cut off suddenly; to cut short or into parts. *n.* The act of chopping; a stroke; a piece chopped off; a piece of mutton or pork on a rib; (*pl.*) broken waves. **chopper,** *n.* A butcher's cleaver.

chop (2) [?], *v.t.* To exchange, barter. *v.i.* To shift suddenly, as the wind.

chopsticks (chop'stĭks) [Chinese *k'wāi-tsze,* quick ones], *n.pl.* Two small sticks used by the Chinese to eat with.

choral (kōr'ål), *a.* Sung by a choir; chanted or sung. **chorally,** *adv.*

chord (kôrd) [Gr. *chordē*], *n.* The string of a musical instrument; the simultaneous and harmonious union of sounds; (*Geom.*) a straight line joining two points in a curve.

choreographic (kŏr-ĕ-ō-grăf'ĭk) [Gr. *choros,* a dance; GRAPHIC], *n.* Relating to ballet.

chorister (kor'ĭs-tĕr), *n.* A singer in a choir.

chorus (kōr'ŭs) [Gr. *choros*], *n.* A band of

persons singing in concert; the refrain of a song.

chough (chŭf) [imit.], *n.* A bird of the crow family.

chrism (krĭzm) [A.-S. *crisma,* Gr. *chriein,* to anoint], *n.* Consecrated oil.

Christ (krīst) [Gr. *Christos*], *n.* The Anointed One; the Saviour, Messiah. **Christlike,** *a.*

christen (krĭsn) [A.-S *cristnian*], *v.t.* To baptize; to name.

Christendom (krĭsn'dŏm), *n.* Christians collectively; the parts inhabited by them.

Christian (krĭs'tyån), *n.* One who believes in or professes the religion of Christ, a civilized person as distinguished from a savage. *a.* Pertaining to Christ or Christianity. **Christianity,** *n.* The doctrines and precepts taught by Christ; faith in Christ and His teaching. **christianize,** *v.t.* To convert to Christianity.

Christmas (krĭs'mas) [A.-S. *cristes mæsse*], *n.* The festival of the Nativity, Dec. 25; Christmas-tide. *a.* Pertaining or appropriate to Christmas or its festivities. **Christmas-box,** *n.* A Christmas present. **Christmas-tide,** *n.* The season of Christmas.

chromatic (krō-măt'ĭk) [Gr. *chrōma -atos,* colour], *a.* Relating to colour; (*Mus.*) including notes not belonging to the regular scale. **chromatic scale,** *n.* (*Mus.*) A succession of semi-tones.

chrome [as prec.], *n.* Chromium; a yellow pigment. **chromium,** *n.* A steel-grey metal, one of the elements, with shining burnish. **chromosome** (krō'mō-sōm), *n.* (*Biol.*) One of the carriers of hereditary characters.

chronic (kron'ĭk) [Gr. *chronos,* time], *a.* Applied to diseases of long duration.

chronicle (kron'ĭkl), *n.* A register of events in order of time; a history. *v.t.* To record in a chronicle.

chrono- [Gr. *chronos,* time], *comb. form.* Pertaining to time or dates.

chronology (krō-nol'ō-ji), *n.* The science of computing time; a tabular list of dates. **chronologist,** *n.* **chronolog'ical,** *a.*

chronometer (krō-nom'ē-tĕr). *n.* An instrument that measures time with great exactness.

chrysalis (kris'å-lis) [Gr. *chrusallis*], *n.* (*pl.* -ises, -ides). The last stage through which a caterpillar passes before becoming perfect; the pupa.

chrysanthemum (kris-ån'thē-mŭm) [Gr. *chrusanthemon,* marigold], *n.* A genus of composite plants.

chub (chŭb) [?], *n.* A coarse river-fish. **chubby.** *a.* Fat, plump (esp. in the face). **chubbiness,** *n.*

chuck (chŭk) [?], *n.* A slight tap or blow under the chin; a toss or throw. *v.t.* To tap under the chin; to fling, throw.

chuckle (chŭkl), *v.i.* To utter a half-suppressed laugh; to exult to oneself. *n.* A short half-laugh.

chum (chŭm) [?], *n.* A comrade and close companion. **chummy,** *a.*

chunk (chŭngk) [?], *n.* A short, thick lump of anything. **chunky,** *a.*

church (chĕrch) [A.-S. *circe*], *n*. A building consecrated for Christian worship; a body of Christian believers worshipping in one place; Christians collectively; the organization of a religious body; the clergy. *v.t.* To say the thanksgiving service for a woman after child-birth. *a*. Of or pertaining to church; ecclesiastical. **churchman,** *n*. A cleric, ecclesiastic. **churchwarden,** *n*. A lay officer of a church who acts as its legal representative; a long clay pipe. **churchyard,** *n*. The ground adjoining the church consecrated for the burial of the dead.

churl (chĕrl) [A.-S. *ceorl*], *n*. A serf; a peasant, boor; a surly, clownish fellow. **churlish,** *a*.

churn (chĕrn) [A.-S. *cyrin*], *n*. A vessel in which milk or cream is agitated in order to produce butter; a large can for transporting milk. *v.t.* To agitate in a churn.

chute (shoot) [F.], *n*. An inclined trough for conveying water, timber, grain, etc. to a lower level; a toboggan-slide.

chutney (chŭt′ni) [Hind. *chatnī*], *n*. A hot East Indian condiment.

chyle (kīl) [Gr. *chulos*], *n*. The milky fluid separated from the chyme in the intestines and assimilated with the blood.

chyme (kīm) [Gr. *chumos*], *n*. The pulpy mass of digested food before the chyle is separated from it.

cicada (si-kā′dà) [L.], *n*. (*Zool*.) A genus of insects with stridulating organs, like a cricket.

cicatrix (sik′à-triks) [L.], *n*. (*pl*. -trices) The scar left after a wound has healed. **cic′atrize,** *v.i.* To skin over.

cicerone (chich-ĕr-ō′ni) [It.], *n*. (*pl.*-oni) A guide.

cider (sī′dĕr) [O.F. *sidre*, Gr. *sikera*, Heb. *shēkār*, strong drink], *n*. The juice of apples fermented.

cigar (si-gar′) [Sp. *cigarro*], *n*. A roll of tobacco leaf for smoking. **cigarette** (sig-à-ret′) [dim. of prec.], *n*. Cut tobacco rolled in thin paper for smoking.

Cimmerian (si-mēr′i-àn), *a*. Pertaining to the Cimmerii or their country, which was fabled to be in a state of perpetual darkness; profoundly dark.

cinch (sinch) [Sp. *cincha*], *n*. A broad saddle-girth; a firm grip; a certainty.

cinchona (sin-kō′nà) [*Chinchon*, Peruvian Viceroy in 17th cent.], *n*. A tree yielding Peruvian bark, the source of quinine.

cincture (sink′tūr) [L. *cinctūra*], *n*. A belt, girdle.

cinder (sin′dĕr) [A.-S. *sinder*], *n*. A partly-burnt coal; light slag.

cinematograph (sin-ē-mǎt′ò-grǎf) [Gr. *kinema*, *-matos*, movement], *n*. An apparatus for throwing a series of photographs on to a screen at high speed so as to give the effect of continuous motion. **cinematography,** *n*. **cinema** (sin′e-mà), *n*. The theatre where such pictures are shown.

cinerary (sin′ĕr-àr-i) [L. *cinis*, ashes], *a*. Pertaining to ashes. **cinerary-urn,** *n*. An urn for the ashes of the dead.

Cingalese (sing′gà-lēz′) [Sansk. *sinhalam*, Ceylon], *n*. A native or the language of Ceylon. *a*. Pertaining to Ceylon, its people, or language.

cinnamon (sin′à-mòn) [Gr. *kinamōmon*, Heb. *qinnāmōn*], *n*. The aromatic bark of an East Indian tree used as a spice.

cinque (singk) [F.], *n*. Five, esp. at cards or dice. **cinquefoil,** *n*. Plants of the genus *Potentilla*; an ornamental foliation used in tracery, etc. **Cinque Ports,** *n.pl.* Five English Channel ports, Dover, Sandwich, Hastings, Hythe, Romney (later Rye, Winchelsea).

cipher (sī′fer) [Arab. *ṣifr*, empty], *n*. The symbol 0, naught; a monogram, device; a code used for secret correspondence; a coded message; a person or thing of no importance. *v.i.* To do arithmetic.

circle (sĕrkl) [L. *circulus*, a small ring], *n*. A plane figure bounded by a curved line (the circumference) which is equidistant at every point from a point within the figure called the centre; a ring, a round figure or enclosure; a complete series; any series ending as it begins, and perpetually repeated; a period, cycle; a number of persons or things bound together by some bond. *v.t.* To move round; to surround. **circled,** *a*. **circlet,** *n*. **great circle,** *n*. (*Geom.*) A circle dividing a sphere into two equal parts.

circuit (sĕr′kit), *n*. The act of moving round, a revolution; the line enclosing a space, the distance round about; the periodical visitation of judges, the district visited; a continuous electrical communication between the poles of a battery; a series of conductors through which a current passes. **circu′itous** (sĕr-kū′it-ùs), *a*. Indirect, roundabout.

circular (sĕr′kū-lår), *a*. In the shape of or pertaining to a circle; addressed in identical terms to a number of persons. *n*. A letter, etc., of which a copy is sent to many persons. **circularize,** *v.t.* To send circulars to.

circulate (sĕr′kū-lāt), *v.i.* To move round; to pass from point to point or hand to hand (as money); to be diffused. *v.t.* To cause to pass from point to point or hand to hand; to spread. **circulating,** *a*. That circulates; current; (*Math.*) recurring. **circula′tion,** *n*. The act of circulating; the state of being circulated; the motion of the blood, by which it is propelled by the heart through the arteries and returned through the veins; distribution.

circum- (sĕr′kùm) [L.], *pref.* Round, round about; indirectly.

circumambient (sĕr-kùm-ăm′bi-ènt) [L. *ambiens -entem*], *a*. Going round about; surrounding.

circumcise (sĕr′kùm-sīz) [L. *cædere*, to cut], *v.t.* To cut off the foreskin. **circumcis′ion,** *n*.

circumference (sĕr-kùm′fĕr-èns) [L. *ferre*, to bear], *n*. The line that bounds a circle; a periphery, circuit.

circumflex (sĕr′kùm-fleks) [L. *flexus*, bent], *n*. A mark (∧) used to indicate accent quality, or contraction.

circumjacent (sĕr-kùm-jā′sènt) [L. *jacēre*, to lie], *a*. Bordering.

circumlocution (sĕr-kùm-lô-kū′shùn), *n*.

The use of roundabout or evasive language, or of many words where few would suffice. circumlocutory, *a.*

circumnavigate (sĕr-kŭm-năv'ĭ-gāt), *v.t.* To sail completely round.

circumscribe (sĕr'kŭm-skrīb) [L. *scrībere,* to write], *v.t.* To limit, define by bounds, restrict; (*Geom.*) to surround with a figure that touches at every point.

circumspect (sĕr'kŭm-spekt) [L. *specere,* to look], *a.* Looking on all sides; cautious, wary. circumspec'tion, *n.*

circumstance (sĕr'kŭm-stăns) [L. *stāre,* to stand], *n.* Something attending or relative to a fact or case; an incident, event; (*pl.*) the facts, relations, influences, etc., that affect an act, an event, or one's living. circumstan'tial, *a.* Depending on circumstances; incidental, not essential. circumstantial evidence, *n.* (*Law*) Evidence inferred from circumstances which usually attend facts of a particular nature.

circumvent (sĕr'kŭm-vent) [L. *venīre,* to come], *v.t.* To outwit, to get the best of. circumven'tion, *n.*

circus (sĕr'kŭs) [L., a ring], *n.* A place where horsemanship and acrobatic feats are exhibited; a circle of buildings at the intersection of streets.

cist (sist) [Gr. *kistē,* chest], *n.* A prehistoric tomb consisting of a row of stones with a flat stone for cover.

cistern (sis'tĕrn) [O.F. *cisterne*], *n.* A storage place for water, etc.; a reservoir.

citadel (sit'ă-dĕl) [F. *citadelle*], *n.* A fort in a city; a stronghold; a final retreat.

cite (sīt) [F. *citer*], *v.t.* To quote, allege as an authority; to summon to appear in court. ci'table, *a.* cita'tion, *n.* Summons; mention in despatches, recorded qualifications for a medal, etc.

citizen (sit'ĭ-zĕn) [M.E., *citesein*], *n.* A member of a state in the enjoyment of political rights; a burgess; a dweller in a town. citizenship, *n.*

citron (sit'rŏn) [L. *citrus*], *n.* A tree bearing large lemon-like fruit. citrate, *n.* A salt of citric acid. citric, *a.* Derived from the citron, esp. of the acid found in lemons, citrons, limes, oranges, etc.

city (sit'ĭ) [O.F. *cité,* L. *civitas*], *n.* A town incorporated by a charter; a cathedral town; the inhabitants of a city.

civet (siv'ĕt) [Arab. *zabād*], *n.* A resinous musky substance obtained from the civet-cat and used as a perfume. civet-cat, *n.* A carnivorous quadruped from Asia.

civic (siv'ik) [L. *civicus*], *a.* Pertaining to a city or citizens; urban, municipal.

civil (siv'il) [L. *civilis*], *a.* Relating to the community; pertaining to citizens or to social, commercial, and administrative affairs; not military or naval; municipal, legislative; civilized, polite, courteous. civil law, *n.* The law dealing with private rights, not criminal matters. civil list, *n.* The yearly sum granted to royalty from the public treasury.

civilian (si-vil'yăn), *n.* A person not belonging to the armed forces of a state. civility, *n.* The quality of being civil; politeness, courtesy. civilly, *adv.*

civilize (siv'il-īz), *v.t.* To instruct in the arts and refinements of civilized society. civiliza'tion, *n.* The act or process of civilizing; the state of being civilized; civilized society.

clack (klăk), *v.i.* To make a sharp, sudden noise; to chatter noisily.

claim (klām) [L. *clāmāre,* to call out], *v.t.* To demand as a right; to assert that one has or is (something) or has done (something). *n.* A real or supposed right; a piece of land allotted to one or marked out with the intention of acquiring it. claimable, *a.* claimant, *n.* One who makes a claim.

clairvoyance (klâr-voi'ăns) [F. *clair,* clear, *voir,* to see], *n.* The power of perceiving objects not present to the senses. clairvoyant, *n.* One who has this power.

clam (klăm) [A.-S. *clamm,* fetter], *n.* A clamp or vice; an edible bivalve.

clamber (klăm'bĕr), *v.i.* To climb up with difficulty. *n.* A climb.

clammy (klăm'ĭ), *a.* Damp; sticky, adhesive. clamminess, *n.*

clamour (klăm'ĕr) [L. *clāmor*], *n.* An outcry; loud and continuous shouting, expressions of complaint, demand, or appeal. *v.i.* To cry out loudly and earnestly; to demand or complain importunately. clamorous, *a.*

clamp (klămp) [?], *n.* Anything rigid which strengthens, fastens, or binds; a heap of turf, potatoes, etc. *v.t.* To unite with a clamp.

clan (klăn) [Gael. *clann*], *n.* A tribe or number of families of the same name, united under a chieftain representing a common ancestor; (*fig.*) a clique, set. clannish, *a.* United closely together. clansman, *n.* A member of a clan.

clandestine (klăn-des'tin) [F.], *a.* Secret, surreptitious, underhand.

clang (klăng) [L. *clangere*], *v.t.* To strike together, so as to cause a sharp, ringing sound. clangor, *n.* A sharp, ringing sound. clangorous, *a.*

clank (klăngk) [onomat.], *v.t.* To strike together so as to make a heavy rattling sound. *n.* A sound as of solid metallic bodies struck together.

clap (klăp) [M.E. *clappen*], *v.t.* To strike together noisily; to shut, put, or place suddenly or hastily; to applaud by striking the hands together. *v.i.* To shut (as a door) with a bang; to strike the hands together in applause. *n.* The noise made by the collision of flat surfaces; a sudden loud noise; a peal of thunder. clapper, *n.* The tongue of a bell.

claptrap (klăp'trăp), *n.* Showy words or deeds designed to win applause or public favour.

claret (klăr'ĕt) [O.F. *clairet,* dim. of *clair,* clear], *n.* A light red Bordeaux wine.

clarify (klăr'ĭ-fī) [L. *clārus,* clear, *facere,* to make], *v.t.* To clear from impurities; to make transparent. *v.i.* To become transparent. clarifica'tion, *n.*

clarinet (clă'ri-net), *n.* (*Mus.*) A woodwind instrument with a single reed.

clarion (klăr'ĭ-ŏn) [O.F. *claron*], *n.* A kind of trumpet, with a narrow tube, and loud and clear note. *a.* Loud and clear.

clarity (klăr'i-ti) [O.F. *clarté*], *n.* Clearness.

clash (klăsh), *v.i.* To make a loud noise by striking against something; to come into collision; to disagree. *v.t.* To cause one thing to strike against another so as to produce a noise. *n.* The noise produced by the violent collision of two bodies; opposition, conflict.

clasp (klasp) [M.E. *claspen*, A.-S. *clyppan*], *n.* A catch, hook, etc., for fastening; a close embrace, a grasp; a commemorating bar attached to a medal-ribbon. *v.t.* To fasten or shut with a clasp or buckle; to fasten (a clasp); to embrace, grasp. *v.i.* To cling (to).

class (klas) [L. *classis*], *n.* A number of persons or things ranked together; social rank; a number of students taught together; a division of animals or plants next above an order. *v.t.* To arrange in a class or classes. class warfare, *n.* Overt antagonism between the social classes in a community.

classic (klăs'ik) [L. *classicus*], *n.* An author (esp. Greek or Latin) of the first rank; a recognized masterpiece; one versed in Greek and Latin literature; a follower of classic models as opposed to romantic; (*pl.*) ancient Greek and Latin literature; the study of these. *a.* Pertaining to this literature; of the first rank in literature or art; pure, restrained; of standard authority; clear-cut, regular (of the features). classic races, *n.pl.* The five principal horse-races in England, being the 2000 Guineas, the 1000 Guineas, Derby, Oaks, and St. Leger. classical, *a.* classicalism, *n.* clas'sicism, *n.* A classic style or idiom; devotion to or imitation of the classics; classical scholarship.

classify (klăs'i-fī), *v.t.* To assign to a class. classifiable, *a.* classifica'tion, *n.* classifier, *n.*

clatter (klăt'ér) [A.-S. *clatrian*], *v.i.* To make a sharp rattling noise. *v.t.* To cause to rattle. *n.* A continuous rattling.

clause (klawz) [O.F., L. *clausa*, closed], *n.* A distinct part of a composition; a short sentence; a subdivision of a compound sentence.

claustrophobia (klaw-strŏ-fō'bi-ā) [L. *claustra*, a bolt; Gr. *phobia*, fear], *n.* (*Path.*) A morbid dread of being in a confined space.

clavicle (klăv'ikl) [L. *clavicula*, a small key], *n.* The collar-bone.

claw (klaw) [A.-S. *clawu*], *n.* The sharp hooked nail of a bird or beast; the pincers of a crab, lobster, etc. *v.t.* To use the claws for tearing.

clay (klā) [A.-S. *clæg*], *n.* Tenacious, plastic earth; (*fig.*) the grosser part of human nature, the body; a clay-pipe.

claymore (klā'môr) [Gael. *claidheamh mor*, great sword], *n.* A two-edged sword used by Highlanders.

clean (klēn) [A.-S. *clæne*], *a.* Free from dirt, stain, blemish, imperfection, disease, defilement; pure, holy; smart, dexterous, unerring; complete. *adv.* Quite, completely; cleverly. *v.t.* To cleanse, to purify. cleanable, *a.* cleaner, *n.* cleanly (1) (klēn'li), *adv.* In a clean manner. cleanness, *n.*

cleanly (2) (klen'li), *a.* Clean; clean in person and habits. cleanlily, *adv.* cleanliness, *n.*

cleanse (klenz), *v.t.* To make clean, purify; (*Bibl.*) to cure.

clear (klēr) [L. *clārus*], *a.* Free from darkness, dullness, or opacity; luminous, transparent, serene, unclouded; brightly intelligent; lucid, evident; easily apprehended; net. *adv.* Completely; quite; apart, free from risk of contact. *v.t.* To make clear; to free from dimness, ambiguity, imputation, etc.; to exonerate; to pay off all charges; to realize as profit; to pass over without touching. *v.i.* To become clear, bright, or serene. clearance, *n.* The act of clearing; the state of being cleared; clear profit; passing through the Clearing House; a certificate that a ship has been cleared at the Custom-house. clearing, *n.* A tract of land cleared for cultivation. clearing-house, *n.* A house or office where the operation of clearing cheques and drafts is performed, esp. that in London for banks. clearness, *n.* The state of being clear; perspicuity.

cleat (klēt) [M.E. *clete*, a wedge], *n.* A piece of wood or iron for fastening ropes upon.

cleave (1) (klēv) [A.-S. *clifian*], *v.i.* (*past* cleaved, *clave). To stick, to adhere.

cleave (2) [A.-S. *cléofan*], *v.t.* (*past* clove, cleft, *p.p.* cloven, cleft). To split asunder with violence; to divide forcibly; to make one's way through. *v.i.* To split, to crack. cleavage (klē'văj), *n.* The act of cleaving. cleaver, *n.* A butcher's axe.

cleek (klēk) [M.E. *cleche*], *n.* An iron-headed golf-club.

clef (klef) [F.], *n.* (*Mus.*) A character at the beginning of a stave denoting the pitch.

cleft (kleft) [cleave (2)], *n.* A split, crack.

clematis (klem'ā-tis) [Gr. *klēmatis*], *n.* A ranunculaceous plant, traveller's joy.

clement (klem'ent) [L. *clēmens*], *a.* Mild, gentle; forgiving, merciful. clemency, *n.*

clench (klench) [A.-S. *be-clencan*], *v.t.* To rivet; to grasp firmly; to close or fix firmly (as the hands or teeth).

clerestory (klēr'stôr-i), *n.* The upper part of the nave, choir, etc., of a church containing windows above the roofs of the aisles.

clergy (klēr'ji) [O.F. *clergie*, Gr. *klērikos*], *n.* The body of men ordained for the service of the Christian Church. clergyman, *n.* An ordained Christian minister.

cleric (kler'ik), *n.* A clergyman, ecclesiastic.

clerical (kler'ik-ăl), *a.* Relating to the clergy or to the work of clerks, etc. clericalism, *n.* Undue influence of the clergy.

clerk (klark) [A.-S. *clerc*], *n.* A cleric, clergyman; the lay officer of a parish church; one employed to assist in correspondence, book-keeping, etc.; one who has charge of an office or department, subject to a higher authority. clerk in Holy Orders, *n.* An ordained clergyman. clerk of works, *n.* A surveyor who watches over the performance of a building contract.

clever (klev'ér) [?], *a.* Dexterous, skilful; expert, ingenious. **cleverness**, *n.*

clew (kloo) [A.-S. *cliwen*], *n.* The corner of a **sail**; the cords by which a hammock is suspended; a clue. *v.t.* To truss up to the yard.

cliché (klē'shā) [F., stereotyped], *n.* A stereotype; (*Phot.*) a negative; (*fig.*) a hackneyed phrase.

click (klik), *v.i.* To make a slight, sharp noise; (*Slang*) to have luck, to succeed, to meet with approval. *n.* A slight, sharp sound; a latch.

client (kli'ént) [L. *cliens*], *n.* One who employs a lawyer; one who entrusts any business to a professional man, a customer. **clientele** (klē-an-tāl],; *n.* Clients collectively.

cliff (klif) [A.-S. *clif*], *n.* A steep rock; a precipice.

climacteric (kli-mǎk'tér-ik), *n.* A critical period in human life, when some great change is supposed to take place.

climate (kli'mát) [Gr. *klima-atos*, a slope, region], *n.* The meteorological conditions of a place or country.

climax (kli'mǎks) [Gr. *klimax*, a ladder], *n.* The highest point.

climb (klim) [A.-S. *climban*], *v.t.* To ascend (esp. by hands and feet), tendrils, etc.; to rise; to slope upwards. *n.* An ascent; the act of ascending. **climbable** (kli'mábl), *a.* **climber** (kli'mér), *n.*

clime (klim), *n.* A region; a climate.

clinch (klinch), *v.t.* To clench, rivet; to drive home or establish; to make a rope-end fast. *n.* The act of clinching; a grip; a pun. **clincher**, *n.* A conclusive argument or statement.

cling (kling) [A.-S. *clingan*], *v.i.* (*past and p.p.* clung). To adhere closely and tenaciously; to be faithful to.

clinic (klin'ik) [Gr. *klinē*, a bed], *n.* One confined to bed by sickness; bedside instruction in hospitals; a place where medical attention is given. **clinical**, *a.*

clink (klingk), *n.* A sharp, tinkling, metallic sound. *v.* To cause to clink.

clinker (kling'kér) [M. Dut. *klinckaert*], *n.* Vitrified slag; bricks run together in a mass by heat; fused cinders.

clip (1) (klip) [prob. Icel. *klippa*], *v.t.* To cut with shears; to trim; to cut away. *v.i.* To run or go swiftly. *n.* A shearing; the whole wool of a season; a blow. **clipper**, *n.* A fast-sailing vessel. **clipping**, *n.* A piece clipped off.

clip (2) [A.-S. *clyppan*], *v.t.* To clasp, to embrace. *n.* An appliance for gripping.

clique (klēk) [F.], *n.* A small number of associated persons; an exclusive set.

cloak (klōk) [M.E. and O.F. *cloke*], *n.* A loose, wide, outer garment; a disguise, pretext. *v.t.* To cover with a cloak; to disguise; to hide. **cloak-room**, *n.* A public place where small parcels, etc., can be deposited; a lavatory.

cloche (klosh) [F., a bell], *n.* A bell-shaped glass put over young or tender plants to protect them from frost.

clock (1) (klok) [O.F. *cloque*, a bell], *n.* An instrument for measuring time. **clockwise**, *adv.* In the way of the hands of a clock, from left to right. **clockwork**, *n.*

The train of wheels, springs, etc., producing motion in a clock.

clock (2) [?], *n.* Ornamental work on a stocking.

clod (klod), *n.* A lump of earth or clay; any concreted mass; mere lifeless matter.

clog (klog) [?], *n.* Anything that impedes motion or freedom; a shoe with a wooden sole, a sabot. *v.t.* To hamper with a weight; to hinder; to choke up.

cloister (klois'tér) [O.F. *cloistre*], *n.* A place of religious seclusion; an arcade along the sides of a quadrangle, etc. **cloistered**, *a.* Furnished with cloisters; shut away from the world.

close (1) (klōz) [O.F. *clos*, shut], *v.t.* To shut to; to fill (up) an opening; to bring together; to conclude. *v.i.* To shut; to coalesce; to cease; to come to terms; to grapple. *n.* The act of closing; an end.

close (2) (klōs), *a.* Closed, confined, shut in; solid, compact; near together in time or space; intimate; nearly alike; attentive; apt, accurate; oppressive, stifling; limited; secret, reticent; parsimonious. *adv.* Near, close to; closely. *n.* An enclosure; the precincts of a cathedral, etc.; a blind alley. **close-up**, *n.* (*Cinema*) A view taken with the camera at very close range. **closed shop**, *n.* A factory, etc., where none but trade unionists are employed. **closely**, *adv.* **closeness**, *n.*

closet (kloz'ét), *n.* A small room for retirement; a privy.

closure (klō'zhér) [O.F.], *n.* The act of shutting; the power of terminating debate in a legislative assembly. *v.t.* To apply this power.

clot (klot) [A.-S. *clott*], *n.* A clod, lump, ball; a small coagulated mass, esp. of blood.

cloth (kloth) [A.-S. *clāth*], *n.* A woven fabric of wool, flax, cotton, etc.

clothe (klōth) [A.-S. *clāthian*], *v.t.* (*past* clothed, clad). To furnish or cover with clothes. **clothing**, *n.* Clothes.

clothes (klōthz), *n.pl.* Garments, dress.

clothier (klō'thi-ér), *n.* A manufacturer or seller of cloth or clothing.

cloud (kloud) [A.-S. *clūd*], *n.* A mass of visible vapour floating in the upper regions of the atmosphere; a volume of smoke, etc., resembling a cloud; a veil which obscures or darkens; a temporary depression; a great number, a multitude. *v.t.* To overspread with clouds, to darken; to mark with cloud-like spots. *v.i.* To grow cloudy. **cloud-burst**, *n.* A sudden and heavy fall of rain. **cloudless**, *a.* **cloudy**, *a.* Consisting of or overspread with clouds; marked with veins or spots; obscure, confused; dull, gloomy.

clout (klout) [A.-S. *clūt*], *n.* A piece of rag, etc.; a rap, a blow.

clove (1) (klōv) [F. *clou*], *n.* A dried, unexpanded flower-bud of the clove-tree, used as a spice.

clove (2) [A.-S. *clufu*], *n.* A small bulb forming part of a compound bulb, as in garlic.

cloven (klō'vén), *a.* Divided into two parts; cleft.

clover (klō'vér) [A.-S. *clāfre*], *n.* A trefoil used for fodder.

clown (kloun) [?], *n.* A rustic, a clumsy, awkward lout; a buffoon in a circus or pantomime. **clownery,** *n.* **clownish,** *a.*

cloy (kloi) [?], *v.t.* To satiate, to glut.

club (klŭb) [M.E. *clubbe*], *n.* A wooden weapon with one end heavier than the other; a bent stick for driving a ball; a suit at cards (denoted by a trefoil); an association of persons governed by self-imposed regulations; the place in which such an association meets. *v.t.* To beat with a club; to gather into a clump; to contribute for a common object. *v.i.* To join for a common object. **club-foot,** *n.* A short, deformed foot. **club-house,** *n.* The house occupied by a club. **club-law,** *n.* Government by force.

cluck (klŭk), *n.* The call of a hen or similar sound. *v.i.* To utter the cry of a hen to her chickens.

clue (kloo), *n.* A ball of thread, esp. serving as a guide; anything that serves as a hint for the solution of a problem or mystery. **clueless,** *n.*

clumber (klŭm'bẽr) [Duke of Newcastle's seat, Notts.], *n.* A variety of spaniel.

clump (klump), *n.* A thick cluster of shrubs, flowers, etc.

clumsy (klŭm'zi) [M.E. *clumsed*, be-numbed], *a.* Awkward, ill-constructed; tactless. **clumsily,** *adv.* **clumsiness,** *n.*

cluster (klŭs'tẽr) [A.-S. *clyster*], *n.* A number of persons or things of the same kind gathered or growing together; a bunch; a group. *v.i.* To come or to grow into clusters.

clutch (1) (klŭch) [A.-S. *clyccan*, to clench], *n.* A snatch, grasp; the paw of a rapacious animal; a coupling for shafting; a contrivance for connecting and disconnecting machinery. *v.t.* To seize or grip.

clutch (2) [obs. *cleck*, to hatch], *n.* A sitting (of eggs); a brood (of chickens).

co- [L.], *pref.* CUM-, with, together, jointly, mutual; as in *coalesce, coeternal, coefficient, coheir.*

coach (kōch) [F. *coche*], *n.* A large, close, four-wheeled vehicle; a railway carriage; a tutor, trainer. *v.t.* To prepare for an examination; to train. *v.i.* To travel in a coach; to read with a tutor. **coach-house,** *n.* **coachman,** *n.*

coadjutor (kō-ăd-joo'tẽr) [L.], *n.* An assistant, colleague. **coadjutrix,** *n.* A female coadjutor.

coagulate (kō-ăg'ū-lāt) [L. *coāgulātus*, impelled together], *v.t.* To cause to curdle. *v.i.* To become curdled; to congeal.

coal (kōl) [A.-S. *col*], *n.* A black solid carbonaceous fossil of vegetable origin used for fuel. *v.t.* To supply a ship with coals. *v.i.* To take in a supply of coals. **coal-field,** *n.* (*Geol.*) A district where coal abounds. **coal-gas,** *n.* Impure carburetted hydrogen obtained from coal and used for lighting and heating. **coal-heaver,** *n.* One employed in carrying, loading, or discharging coals. **coal-hole,** *n.* A small cellar for keeping coals. **coal-measures,** *n.pl.* The upper division of the carboniferous system. **coal-scuttle,** *n.* A utensil for holding coals for present use. **coal-tar,** *n.* Tar

produced in the destructive distillation of bituminous coal.

coalesce (kō-á-les') [L. *alescere*, to nourish], *v.i.* To unite into groups spontaneously; to combine, form a coalition. **coalescence,** *n.* Concretion. **coalescent,** *a.* **coali'tion,** *n.* A combination of persons or parties having different interests. **coalitionist,** *n.*

coamings (kō'mingz) [?], *n.pl.* (*Naut.*) The raised borders round hatches, etc., to keep water from pouring into the hold.

coarse (kôrs) [?], *a.* Common, inferior; large in size or texture; rude, rough, unpolished, indelicate. **coarseness,** *n.*

coast (kōst) [O.F. *coste*], *n.* That part of a country by the sea; the shore. *v.i.* To sail near the shore or from port to port on the same coast; to descend a hill on a cycle, etc., without applying motive power. **coastal,** *a.* Pertaining to coast-line. **coaster,** *n.* A vessel that coasts. **coast-guard,** *n.* A body of officials who watch to prevent smuggling.

coat (kōt) [O.F. *cote*], *n.* An upper outer garment with sleeves; the fur or natural external covering of an animal; a layer covering and protecting another. *v.t.* To cover; to overspread with a layer. **coat of arms,** *n.* A herald's tabard; an escutcheon; armorial bearings.

coax (kōks) [*cokes*, a fool], *v.t.* To wheedle, to cajole. *v.i.* To practise cajolery in order to persuade. **coaxer,** *n.*

cob (kob) [?], *n.* A lump or ball; a spider; a short stout horse for riding; a hazel-nut; the spike of Indian corn.

cobalt (kō'bawlt) [G. *kobold*, a mine-demon], *n.* A greyish, brittle, close-grained metallic element.

cobble (kobl) [?], *n.* A rounded stone used for paving; a roundish lump of coal. *v.t.* To pave with cobbles; to mend or patch clumsily. **cobbler,** *n.* One who mends shoes; a patcher, a clumsy workman.

coble (kōbl) [W. *ceubal*], *n.* A flat, square-sterned fishing-boat.

cobra (kō'brá) [Port.], *n.* An Indian viperine snake, which distends the neck into a kind of hood when excited.

cobweb (kob'web), *n.* The net spun by a spider to catch its prey.

coca (kō'ká) [Peruv. *cuca*], *n.* The dried leaf of a Peruvian plant chewed as a narcotic; the plant itself.

cocaine (kō'kān), *n.* An alkaloid contained in coca leaves, used as a local anæsthetic.

cochineal (koch'i-nēl) [L. *coccineus*], *n.* A scarlet dye made from the S. American insect, *Coccus cacti.*

cock (1) (kok) [A.-S. *cocc*], *n.* The male of birds, esp. domestic fowls; a weather-cock; a short spout, a tap; the hammer of a gun or pistol; the act of sticking anything upward; the turn so given, as of a hat, the eye, etc. *v.t.* To set erect; to set (the hat) jauntily on one side; to turn up (the nose), to turn (the eye) in a knowing fashion; to raise the hammer of. *v.i.* To stick up, project; to strut, swagger, bluster. **cock-a-hoop:** Strutting like a cock; exultant. **cock-and-bull:** Applied to silly, exaggerated stories. **cock-crow,** *n.* Early dawn. **cock-pit,** *n.* A pit where game-cocks fight; part of the lower deck of a man-of-war, used as a hospital in action; (*Av.*) the part of an aeroplane where the pilot is accommodated. **cock-shy,** *n.* A rough-and-ready target; a throw at a mark; a butt.

cock (2) [Icel. *kokkr*, a lump, a ball], *n.* A small conical pile of hay.

cockade (kŏ-kād′) [F. *coquarde*, saucy], *n.* A knot, tuft, rosette, etc., worn in the hat as a badge.

cockatoo (kok-a-too′) [Malay *kakatūa*], *n.* A large crested parrot.

cockatrice (kok′ā-tris) [O.F. *cocatrice*], *n.* The basilisk.

cockchafer (kok′chā-fèr), *n.* A large brown beetle, the May-bug.

cocker (kok′ér) [?], *v.t.* To pamper, fondle. *n.* A small spaniel.

cockerel (kok′ér-él), *n.* A young cock.

cockle (1) (kokl) [A.-S. *coccel*], *n.* The darnel; a weed that chokes corn.

cockle (2) [F. *coquille*, a shell], *n.* An edible bivalve mollusc; a shallow skiff. **cockles of the heart:** The feelings.

cockle (3) [F. *coquiller*, to blister], *v.i.* To pucker up.

cockney (kok′ni) [M.E. *cokeney*, a cock's egg (applied to a foolish or effeminate person)], *n.* A native of London, formerly one born within sound of Bow bells, Cheapside. **cockneydom,** *n.*

cockroach (kok′rōch) [Sp. *cucaracha*], *n.* An insect, the black beetle.

cocktail (kok′tāl), *n.* A horse with tail docked very short; a kind of beetle; a short drink taken before a meal as an appetizer.

coco (kō′kō) [Port. and Sp. *coco*, a bug-bear], *n.* A tropical palm tree, *Cocos, nucifera.* **coco-nut,** *n.* The fruit of this, a large nut with a white edible lining and a sweet liquid (coco-nut milk).

cocoa (kō′kō) [corr. of *cacao*], *n.* A preparation from the seeds of *Theobroma cacao*. **cocoa-bean,** *n.* The cacao seed.

cocoon (kō-koon′) [F. *cocon*], *n.* A silky covering spun by the larvæ of certain insects in the chrysalis state.

cod (1) (kod) [?], *n.* A large deep-sea food-fish.

cod (2) [A.-S.], *n.* A husk or pod.

coddle (kodl), *v.t.* To pamper.

code (kŏd) [L. *codex*, a tablet, book], *n.* A collection of statutes; a body of regulations systematically arranged, a system of signals; characters and words used for brevity or secrecy; the principles accepted in any sphere of art, taste, conduct, etc. **codify,** *v.t.* To reduce to a systematic body. **codifica′tion,** *n.*

codex (kō′deks) [L.], *n.* (*pl.* codices) A manuscript, esp. of the Bible or classical texts.

codicil (kod′is-il), *n.* An appendix to a will.

codling (1) (kod′ling), *n.* A young cod.

codling (2) -lin [M.E. *querdling*], *n.* A tapering kind of apple; a baked apple.

co-education, *n.* Education of the two sexes together.

coefficient (kō-é-fish′ént), *n.* Anything co-operating; (*Math.*) a factor (in *4ab*, 4 is the *numerical* and *ab* the *literal* coefficient).

coerce (kō-ērs′) [L. *arcēre*, to enclose], *v.t.*

To restrain by force; to compel to obey. **coercible,** *a.* **coercion,** *n.* Compulsion of a free agent; government by force. **coercionist,** *n.* **coercive,** *a.*

coeternal (kō-ē-tēr′nál), *a.* Equally eternal with another.

coeval (kō-ē′vál) [L. *ævum*, an age], *a.* Of the same age; existing at the same period. *n.* A contemporary.

coexecutor (kō-ég-zek′û-tòr), *n.* A joint executor. **coexecutrix,** *n.*

coexist (kō-ég-zist′), *v.i.* To exist at the same time with. **coexistent,** *a.*

coffee (kof′i) [Arab. *qahweh*], *n.* A tropical Asiatic and African shrub; its seeds; a beverage made from these roasted and ground. **coffee-room,** *n.* The public dining-room of an hotel.

coffer (kof′ér) [O.F. *cofre*, Gr. *kophinos*], *n.* A chest or box for holding valuables. **coffer-dam,** *n.* A water-tight enclosure used in laying foundations under water.

coffin (kof′in) [O.F. *cofin*, as prec.], *n.* The chest in which a corpse is buried. *v.t.* To put into a coffin.

cog (kog) [Scand.], *n.* A tooth in a wheel or other gear for transmitting motion. *v.t.* To furnish with cogs. **cog-wheel,** *n.* A wheel furnished with cogs.

cogent (kō′jént) [L. *cōgentem*, compelling], *a.* Powerful, convincing. **cogency,** *n.*

cogitate (koj′i-tāt) [L. *cōgitātus*], *v.i.* To think, reflect. *v.t.* To meditate, devise. **cogita′tion,** *n.* **cog′itative,** *a.*

cognac (kō′nyăk), *n.* French brandy of fine quality.

cognate (kog′nāt) [co-, L. *gnātus*, born], *a.* Akin, of common origin.

cognition (kog-nish′ûn) [L. *cognoscere*, to learn], *n.* The faculty of perceiving and knowing, as distinguished from the feelings and the will; a perception, intuition. *a.* **cog′nitive.**

cognizance (kog′ni-zàns, kon′i-zans), *n.* Knowledge, recognition; judicial notice; jurisdiction.

cognizant (kog′ni-zànt), *a.* Having cognizance (of); (*Law*) competent to take notice of.

cognomen (kog-nō′men) [L. *nōmen*, name], *n.* A surname; a nickname.

cohabit (kō-hăb′it) [L. *habitāre*, to dwell], *v.i.* To live together as husband and wife. **cohabita′tion,** *n.*

coheir (kō-âr′), *n.* A joint heir.

cohere (kō-hēr′) [L. *hærēre*, to stick], *v. i.* To stick or hold together; to be logically consistent. **coherence,** *n.* **coherent,** *a.*

cohesion (kō-hē′zhûn), *n.* State of cohering; consistency. **cohesive,** *a.*

cohort (kō′hòrt) [L. *cohors*], *n.* The tenth part of a Roman legion; a body of soldiers.

coif (koif) [O.F. *coife*], *n.* A close-fitting cap. *v.t.* To cover with a coif.

coiffure (kwa′fūr′) [F.], *n.* A head-dress, method of dressing the hair.

coil (koil) [O.F. *coillir*], *v.t.* To wind into rings (as a rope); to twist, curl. *v.i.* To wind itself, as a snake or creeping plant. *n.* A series of rings into which anything is coiled up; (*Elec.*) a wire wound round a bobbin as a resistance coil, etc.; turmoil, confusion, a fuss.

coin (koin) [O.F., a wedge], *n.* A piece of metal stamped as money; coined money. *v.t.* To mint or stamp, as money; to invent, fabricate. *v.i.* To make counterfeit money. **coiner,** *n.* One who makes counterfeit coin.

coinage (koi'náj), *n.* The act of coining; the pieces coined; the monetary system in use; fabrication.

coincide (kō-in-sīd') [F. *coincider*], *v.i.* To correspond in time, place, etc.; to happen at the same time; to agree, concur. **coin'cidence,** *n.* The act, fact, or condition of coinciding; a fortuitous concurrence.

coke (kōk) [?], *n.* Coal from which gas has been extracted.

colander (kŭl'ĕn-dėr) [L. *cōlāre*, to strain], *n.* A kitchen strainer.

cold (kōld) [A.-S. *ceald*], *a.* Low in temperature, lacking heat or warmth; without ardour, indifferent; calm, chaste; bluish in tone, as opposed to warm tones such as red. *n.* Absence of warmth; the sensation produced by this; inflammation resulting from chills. **cold storage,** *n.* Keeping foodstuffs fresh in an artificially icy atmosphere. **cold war,** *n.* The state of tension between two countries not actually at war when aggressive and irritating acts take place. **coldish,** *a.* **coldness,** *n.*

cole (kōl) [L. *caulis*, a cabbage], *n.* A kind of cabbage. **cole-seed,** *n.* Rape-seed.

colic (kol'ik) [Gr. *kolikos*], *n.* Acute pains in the bowels; stomach-ache.

collaborate (kó-lăb'ó-rāt) [L. *labōrāre*, to labour], *v.i.* To work with another, esp. in literary and scientific pursuit. **collabora'tion,** *n.* **collaborationist,** *n.,* A traitor who aids an enemy in occupation of his country. **collab'orator,** *n.*

collapse (kó-lăps') [L. *lābī*, to glide down, to lapse], *v.i.* To fall in; to break down; to come to nothing. *n.* A falling in; complete failure; general prostration. **collapsed,** *a.* **collapsible,** *a.* Liable to collapse; made so as to fall together easily (for ease in packing).

collar (kol'ăr) [L. *cōlāre* (*collum*, neck)], *n.* Something worn round the neck, either separate or as part of a garment; a leather loop for the neck of a horse, dog, etc. *v.t.* To seize by the collar; to put a collar on; to capture. **collar-bone,** *n.* The clavicle. **collared,** *a.* Wearing a collar; pickled and rolled (as meat); seized.

collate (kó-lāt') [L. *collātus*, brought together], *v.t.* To bring together in order to compare; to examine critically; to place in order; (*Church*) to present to a benefice (used of a bishop). **collation,** *n.* The act of collating; a light repast.

collateral (kó-lăt'ėr-ăl) [L. *latus -eris,* side], *a.* Being by the side; concurrent, subordinate; having the same common ancestor but not lineally related. *n.* A collateral relation; collateral security.

colleague (kol'ēg) [L. *legere*, to choose], *n.* One associated with another in office or employment.

collect (kol'ĕkt) [L. *collecta*, a summing-up], *n.* A brief comprehensive form of prayer, adapted for a particular occasion. *v.t.* (kó-lekt') To gather together; to gather (taxes, curiosities, etc.) from a number of sources; to concentrate, bring under control. *v.i.* To come or meet together. **collected,** *a.* Cool, self-possessed, composed. **collectedness,** *n.*

collection (kó-lek'shŭn), *n.* The act of collecting; that which is collected; an accumulation.

collective (kó-lek'tiv), *a.* Tending to collect; collected, aggregated; pertaining to many persons.

collectivism (kó-lek'tiv-izm), *n.* The theory that industry should be carried on with a collective capital (opp. to individualism).

collector (kó-lek'tór), *n.* One who collects; a gatherer of rarities, etc.

college (kol'ĕj) [L. *collēgium*], *n.* A corporation of scholars, teachers, and fellows forming one of the constituent bodies of a University; an institution for higher education; a large and important secondary school. **collegiate** (kó-lē'ji-āt), *a.*

collide (kó-līd') [L. *collidere*], *v.i.* To come into collision or conflict.

collie (kol'i) [?], *n.* A Scotch sheep-dog.

collier (kol'yėr), *n.* One who works in a coal-mine or on a collier; a coal-carrying ship. **colliery,** *n.*

collision (kó-lizh'ŭn), *n.* The act of striking violently together; the state of being dashed together; antagonism, conflict; clashing.

collocate (kol'ó-kāt), *v.t.* To place together, to dispose; to station in a particular place. **colloca'tion,** *n.*

collop (kol'óp) [?], *n.* A slice of meat; *pl.* meat chopped up.

colloquial (kó-lō'kwi-ăl), *a.* Pertaining to familiar conversation. **colloquialism,** *n.* **colloquially,** *adv.*

colloquy (kol'ó-kwi) [L. *colloquium*], *n.* A conference, conversation.

collusion (kó-loo'zhŭn) [L. *collūsio*], *n.* Secret agreement for a fraudulent purpose. **collusive,** *a.* **collusively,** *adv.*

colon (kō'lón) [Gr. *kōlon*, a member, clause], *n.* A grammatical point (:); the largest division of the intestinal canal.

colonel (kėr'nĕl) [F.], *n.* The chief officer of a regiment. **colonelcy, -ship,** *n.*

colonial (kó-lō'ni-ăl), *a.* Pertaining to a colony. *n.* An inhabitant of a colony.

colonist (kol'ó-nist), *n.* A settler in or inhabitant of a colony.

colonize (kol'ó-nīz) [L. *colōnus*, a farmer], *v.t.* To found a colony in; to people with colonists, settle in. **colonizer,** *n.* **coloniza'tion,** *n.*

colonnade (kol-ó-nād') [F.], *n.* A series of columns at regular intervals.

colony (kol'ó-ni) [L. *colōnia*], *n.* A settlement founded by emigrants, and remaining subject to the parent state; a group of people of the same nationality in a foreign town.

colophon (kol'ó-fón) [Gr. *kolophōn*, a summit], *n.* A device at the beginning or end of a book.

colossal (kó-los'ăl), *a.* Pertaining to a colossus; gigantic.

colossus (kólos'ŭs) [Gr. *kolossos*], *n.* A

statue of gigantic size; a man of great power or genius.

colour (kŭl'ẽr) [O.F. and L. *color*], *n.* A variety of light; any one of the hues into which light can be decomposed, a tint or a shade; a pigment, paint; the complexion, ruddiness; (*pl.*) a flag, standard; ribbons worn as a badge of party, membership, etc.; (*fig.*) semblance, appearance, pretence, pretext; quality of tone; general character. *v.t.* To give colour to; to tinge, paint, dye; to misrepresent or disguise. **man of colour:** A Negro. **colour-blindness,** *n.* Inability to distinguish colours. **colour-sergeant,** *n.* A non-commissioned officer in the infantry ranking above a sergeant. **colourable,** *a.* Specious, plausible. **colouring,** *n.* The act of giving a colour to; the colour applied; a false appearance. **colourist,** *n.* A painter distinguished for his management of colour. **colourless,** *a.*

colporteur (kol'por-tẽr) [F. *col*, neck, *porter*, to carry], *n.* An itinerant retailer of religious books, etc.

colt (kōlt) [A.-S.], *n.* A young horse, esp. a male under four; a young, inexperienced fellow. **coltish,** *a.* **colt's foot,** *n.* A coarse-leaved, yellow-flowered weed.

columbine (kol'ŭm-bīn) [O.F. *colombin,* L. *columba,* a dove], *a.* Pertaining to doves or pigeons. *n.* A plant with five-spurred flowers; the female dancer in a pantomime, wife of Harlequin.

column (kol'ŭm) [L. *columna*], *n.* A pillar or solid body of considerably greater length than thickness; a vertical mass of smoke, a perpendicular line of figures, etc.; (*Mil.*) a body of troops in deep files. **colum'nar,** *a.* **columnist** (kol'ŭmnist), *n.* Writer on general subjects in a newspaper.

colza (kol'zä) [F.], *n.* Cole-seed. **colzaoil,** *n.* Oil expressed from this.

com- [L., *cum-*], *pref.* With, together, etc.

coma (kō'mä) [Gr. *kōma,* sleep], *n.* A state of deep torpor; a trance. **comatose,** *a.*

comb (kōm) [A.-S. *camb*], *n.* A toothed instrument for dressing or ornamenting the hair, for cleaning wool or flax, for collecting electricity, etc.; the fleshy tuft on the head of a fowl, esp. the cock; the cells in which bees deposit their honey. *v.t.* To dress, etc., with a comb. **comb-out,** *n.* (*colloq.*) A clearing out of offices, etc., of men of military age; police search of a neighbourhood.

combat (kŭm'băt) [O.F. *combatre*], *v.i.* To fight, to struggle. *v.t.* To oppose, to contend against. *n.* A fight, battle. **combatant** (kŭm'bä-tänt), *a.* Engaged in combat; antagonistic. *n.* One who fights.

combative (kŭm'bä-tiv), *a.* Pugnacious. **combativeness,** *n.*

combination (kom'bi-nā'shŭn), *n.* The act or process of combining; the state of being combined; a union, association; combined action; (*pl.*) underclothing for body and legs in one piece.

combine (kŏm-bīn') [L. *combināre* (*bini,*

two by two)], *v.t.* To cause to coalesce; to settle by agreement; to bring together. *v.i.* To unite, to coalesce; to be joined in friendship or plans. *n.* (kom'bīn) A combination of persons or firms to further their own commercial interests; a reaping and threshing machine.

combustible (kŏm-bŭs-tibl) [F., L. *combustibilis*], *a.* Capable of being set on fire; irascible, hot-tempered. *n.* Inflammable material or thing.

combustion (kŏm-bŭs-tyŏn), *n.* The act of burning, the state of being destroyed by fire.

come (kŭm) [A.-S. *cuman*], *v.i.* (*past* came, *p.p.* come) To move nearer, approach, move towards (opp. to GO); to arrive; to appear; to happen, befall; to result, arise; to become, to get to be, *int.* Used to excite attention or rouse to action, etc.

comedian (kŏ-mē'di-ăn), *n.* An actor or writer of comedy. **comedienne'** [F.], *n.* A comedy actress.

comedy (kom'ẽ-di) [Gr. *kōmōidos,* a comic actor], *n.* A drama of a light and entertaining character.

comely (kŭm'li) [A.-S. *cymlic*], *a.* Pleasing, becoming, decent. **comeliness,** *n.*

comestible (kŏ-mes'tibl) [F.], *n.* An eatable.

comet (kom'ĕt) [Gr. *komētēs* (*komē,* the hair)] *n.* A luminous heavenly body with a tail, revolving round the sun in a very eccentric orbit.

comfit (kŭm'fit) [O.F. *confit*], *n.* A dry sweetmeat; a seed coated with sugar.

comfort (kŭm'fŏrt) [O.F. *conforter*], *v.t.* To cheer, encourage, console. *n.* Support in time of weakness; consolation, encouragement or that which affords these; ease, general well-being; (*pl.*) the things that contribute to bodily satisfaction. **com'fortless,** *a.*

comfortable (kŭm'fŏr-tăbl), *a.* At ease, in good circumstances. **comfortableness,** *n.*

comforter (kŭm'fŏr-tẽr), *n.* One who or that which comforts; a long woollen scarf; (*Theol.*) the Holy Ghost.

comfrey (kŭm'fri) [O.F. *confirie*], *n.* A tall wild plant with yellowish flowers.

comic (kom'ik) [Gr. *kōmikos* (*kōmos,* a revel)], *a.* Pertaining to comedy, laughable, provoking mirth; facetious, burlesque. *n.* A comic paper. **comic strip,** *n.* A row of drawings in a newspaper presenting in sequence some humorous incident. **com'ical,** *a.* **comical'ity,** *n.*

coming (kŭm'ing), *a.* Approaching; future, to come. *n.* The act of approaching or arriving.

comity (kom'i-ti) [L. *cōmitās* (*cōmis,* courteous)], *n.* Affability, courtesy, civility.

comma (kom'ä) [Gr. *komma,* a clause], *n.* A punctuation mark (,), denoting the shortest pause in reading.

command (kŏ-mand') [O.F. *comander*], *v.t.* To order; to govern, exercise authority over; to dominate, control, have at one's disposal. *v.i.* To give orders; to exercise supreme authority. *n.* An order; power, authority; control, mastery, the power of dominating; a self-contained naval or military force. **commandant'** [F.], *n.* The governor of a place. **commandeer'** [Dut. *kommanderen*], *v.t.* To seize for military purposes. **comman'der,** *n.* One who commands; (*Nav.*) an officer next above a lieutenant. **comman'dery,** *n.* In military orders of knighthood, a district which was administered by a commander. **commanding,** *a.* Giving commands; fitted to command; impressive, dominating. **commandment,** *n.* An order, a precept; a law, esp. of the decalogue.

commando (kŏ-man'dō) [Port.], *n.* (*pl.* -os) A body of men called out for military service; a body of men trained to undertake hazardous work; a man thus trained.

commemorate (kŏ-mem'ō-rāt) [L. *memorare*, to mention], *v.t.* To keep in remembrance or celebrate by some solemn act; to be a memorial of. **commemora'tion,** *n.* **commemorative,** *a.*

commence (kŏ-mens') [O.F. *comencer*], *v.i.* To start, begin. *v.t.* To enter upon; to perform the first act of. **commencement,** *n.* Beginning, origin, rise.

commend (kŏ-mend') [L. *mandāre*, to entrust], *v.t.* To commit to the charge of; to recommend as worthy of notice, regard, etc.; to praise, to approve. **commendable,** *a.* Worthy of commendation. **commendably,** *adv.* **commen'dam,** *n.* Holding a benefice in the absence of the regular incumbent. **commenda'tion,** *n.*

commensurable (kŏ-men'shĕr-ábl), *a.* Measurable by a common unit, proportionate (to).

commensurate (kŏ-men'shĕr-át) [L. *mensūrātus*, measured], *a.* Having the same measure or extent; proportional.

comment (kom'ént) [O.F. *comment*], *n.* A remark, an interpretative or illustrative note. *v.i.* (kŏ-ment') To make explanatory or critical remarks or notes, usu. unfavourably. *v.t.* To expound; to annotate. **com'mentary,** *n.* A series of explanatory notes. **com'mentator,** *n.* One who comments; a radio reporter.

commerce (kom'ĕrs) [L. *merx -cis*, wares, merchandise], *n.* Trade, the interchange of commodities; intercourse. **commer'cial,** *a.* **commercialism,** *n.* A trading spirit; commercial practices.

commination (kom-i-nā'shŭn) [L. *minārī*, to threaten], *n.* A threat, a denunciation; a service denouncing God's judgments on sinners. **comminatory,** *a.*

commingle (kŏ-mingl'), *v.t.* and *i.* To mingle or mix together.

commiserate (kŏ-miz'ĕr-āt) [L. *miserārī*, to pity], *v.t.* To pity, to express compassion for. **commisera'tion,** *n.*

commissar (kom'i-sar) [*Rus.*], *n.* Head of a government department in the U.S.S.R. **commissariat** (kom-i-sâr'i-át), *n.* The department of an army supplying provisions and stores.

commissary (kom'i-sâr-i) [L. *mittere*, to send], *n.* A delegate.

commission (kŏ-mish'ŭn), *n.* Trust, delegation of authority; the document conferring authority, esp. that of military and naval officers; a body of commissioners; an allowance made to an agent. *v.t.* To authorize, empower, appoint, or send by commission; to order (the writing of a book, etc.). **commissioned,** *a.* Holding a commission (esp. from the Crown). **commissionaire',** *n.* One enrolled to carry messages, act as caretaker, timekeeper, etc. **commissioner,** *n.* One empowered to act by a commission; a member of a commission.

commit (kŏ-mit') [L. *mittere*, to send], *v.t.* To entrust, to consign; to perpetrate; to refer to a committee; to send for trial or to prison. **committable,** *a.* **committal, committment,** *n.*

committee (kŏ-mit'i), *n.* A board which considers and reports on business referred to it.

commode (kŏ-mōd') [L. *modus*, measure], *n.* A bureau; a night-stool.

commodious (kŏ-mō'di-ús), *a.* Roomy; suited to its purpose. **commodiously,** *adv.* **commodiousness,** *n.*

commodity (kŏ-mod'i-ti) [F. *commodité*], *n.* An article of commerce; anything useful.

commodore (kom'ō-dôr), *n.* (*Naut.*) An officer ranking below rear-admiral; the president of a yacht-club.

common (kom'ŏn) [O.F. *comun*, L. *communis*], *a.* Belonging to more than one; open or free to all; often met with, ordinary, usual; of low position, or birth; inferior, mean. *n.* A tract of ground, the common property of the community. **common law:** The unwritten law, based on immemorial usage. **common sense:** Sound practical judgment; the general feeling of mankind. *a.* Marked by common sense. **commonly,** *adv.* Usually, frequently; meanly, cheaply; in an ordinary manner. **commonweal,** *n.* The welfare of the community.

commonable (kom'ŏn-ábl), *a.* Held in common; that may be pastured on common land. **commonage,** *n.* The right of using anything in common.

commonalty (kom'ŏn-ál-ti) [L. *communālis*], *n.* The common people.

commoner (kom'ŏ-nĕr), *n.* One below the rank of a peer; a member of the House of Commons.

commonplace (kom'ŏn-plās), *a.* Trivial, trite, unoriginal. *n.* A general idea; a trite remark. **commonplaceness,** *n.*

commons (kom'ŏnz), *n.pl.* The common people; the House of Commons; food provided at a common table. **House of Commons:** The lower House of Parliament, the third estate of the realm.

commonwealth (kom'ŏn-welth), *n.* The whole body of citizens; a republic.

commotion (kŏ-mō'shŭn) [L. *motio*, from *movēre*, to move], *n.* Violent motion; excitement; a popular tumult.

commune (1) (kom'ūn) [F.], *n.* A small territorial district in France and Belgium; the inhabitants or the council of this; the communistic body who took possession of Paris in 1871 after its evacuation by the Germans. **com'munal,** *a.*

commune (2) (kŏ-mūn') [O.F. *comunier*, as foll.], *v.i.* To converse together familiarly, to hold converse with one's heart.

communicate (kŏ-mū'nĭ-kāt) [L. *communi-cāre*], *v.t.* To impart, transmit; to reveal; to give Holy Communion to. *v.i.* To hold intercourse, confer; to be connected, to open into; to partake of the Holy Communion. commu'nicable, *a.* Capable of being communicated or imparted. communicant, *a.* Communicating. *n.* One who partakes of Holy Communion. communica'tion, *n.* The act or means of communicating; that which is communicated; news. commu'nicative, *a.* Inclined to communicate; not reserved. communicativeness, *n.*

communion (kŏ-mū'nyŏn) [F.], *n.* The act of communicating or communing; sharing, fellowship, intercourse; the act of partaking of the Eucharist; a religious body.

Communism (kŏm'ū-nĭzm), *n.* (*Polit.*) A theory of government based on the belief that true Socialism can be attained only through the violent overthrow of Capitalism and the establishment of dictatorship by the proletariat. Communist, *n.* An active believer in this.

community (kŏ-mū'nĭ-tĭ) [O.F. *communeté*], *n.* A body of people having common rights, interests, occupation, religion, nationality, etc.

commute (kŏ-mūt') [L. *mūtāre*, to change], *v.t.* To put one for the other; to exchange. *v.i.* (*Am.*) To travel with a season ticket. commu'table, *a.* commutabil'ity, *n.* commuta'tion, *n.* The act of, or payment made in, commuting; exchange; the substitution of a less penalty for a greater. commutator, *n.* (*Elec.*) An instrument which reverses an electric current without changing the arrangement of the conductors.

compact (kom'păkt) [L. *compactus*], *n.* An agreement, covenant. *a.* (kŏm-păkt') Closely packed or joined together. *v.t.* To consolidate; to join closely together; to compose. *n.* A small box for face-powder, puff, etc. compactly, *adv.* compactness, *n.*

companion (1) (kŏm-păn'yŏn) [O.F. *compaignon*], *n.* One who keeps company with another; a comrade; a member of the lowest grade in orders of knighthood. *a.* Accompanying; matching something. *v.t.* To accompany. *v.i.* To go or consort (with). companionable, *a.* Fit to be a companion; sociable. companionably, *adv.* companionship, *n.* Fellowship, association.

companion (2) [L. *compānāticum*, provisions], *n.* The raised window-frame on the quarter-deck of a ship. companion-hatch, *n.* A porch over the entrance to the cabin. companion-ladder, -stairs, -way, *n.* The steps leading from the cabin to the quarter-deck.

company (kŭm'pȧ-nĭ) [O.F. *compaignie*], *n.* Society, fellowship; a number of persons associated; guests, visitors; a body of actors at a theatre; a division of a regiment under a captain.

compare (kŏm-pâr') [L. *par*, equal], *v.t.* To show how one thing agrees with another; to liken one thing to another;

(*Gram.*) to inflect according to degrees of comparison. *v.i.* To bear comparison. com'parable, *a.* Capable or worthy of being compared. compar'ative, *a.* Estimated by comparison; expressing a higher or lower degree of a quality.

comparison (kŏm-păr'ĭ-sŏn), *n.* The act of comparing.

compartment (kŏm-part'mĕnt) [F. *compartiment*], *n.* A division; a separate portion of a railway carriage, etc.

compass (kŭm'păs) [F. *compas*], *n.* A circle, area; a roundabout course; reach, capacity; the range of the voice or a musical instrument; an instrument indicating the magnetic meridian, used to ascertain direction; (*pl.*) an instrument with two connected legs for describing circles, etc. *v.t.* To go round; to besiege, comprehend, accomplish, plot.

compassion (kŏm-păsh'ŏn) [L. *patī*, to suffer], *n.* Pity, sympathy for the sufferings of others; an act of pity or mercy. compass'ionate, *a.* Merciful, sympathetic. *v.t.* To feel compassion for.

compatible (kŏm-păt'ĭbl), *a.* That may co-exist; consistent, harmonious. compatibly *adv.* compatibil'ity, *n.*

compatriot (kŏm-păt'rĭ-ŏt), *n.* A fellow-countryman.

compel (kŏm-pel') [L. *pellere*, to drive], *v.t.* To force, to oblige; to cause by or drive with force. compellable, *a.*

compendium (kŏm-pen'dĭ-ŭm) [L. *pendere*, to weigh], *n.* (*pl.* -diums, -dia) A brief compilation; an epitome, summary. compen'dious, *a.* Abridged; succinct.

compensate (kŏm'pĕn-sāt) [L. *pensatus*, weighed], *v.t.* To make amends for; to recompense; to furnish with an equivalent. *v.i.* To supply an equivalent. compensa'tion, *n.*

compete (kŏm-pēt') [L. *petere*, to aim at], *v.i.* To contend as a rival; to strive in emulation.

competent (kom'pĕ-tĕnt), *a.* Qualified; suitable, adequate. competence, -tency, *n.*

competition (kŏm-pĕ-tish'ŭn) [L. *competitio*] *n.* Emulous striving for the same object; rivalry. compet'itive, *a.* compet'itor, *n.*

compile (kŏm-pīl') [L. *compilāre*, to plunder], *v.t.* To compose out of materials from various authors. compiler, *n.* compila'tion, *n.*

complacent (kŏm-plā'sĕnt) [L. *placēre*, to please], *a.* Satisfied, gratified, self-satisfied. complacently, *adv.* complacence, -ency, *n.* A feeling of inward satisfaction; its manifestation by courtesy.

complain (kŏm-plān') [L. *plangere*, to bewail], *v.i.* To express dissatisfaction; to state a grievance or charge; to find fault. complainant, *n.* One who makes complaint; a prosecutor, plaintiff. complaining, *a.* Querulous. complaint, *n.* An expression of grief or pain, resentment or censure; the subject or ground of such expression; a formal charge.

complement (kŏm'plĕ-mĕnt) [L. *plēre*, to fill], *n.* That which is necessary to make complete. *v.t.* To supply a deficiency; to complete. complemen'tary, *a.*

complete (kòm-plēt') [L. *complētus*, filled], *a.* Fulfilled, finished; free from deficiency. *v.t.* To bring to a state of perfection; to finish. **completely,** *adv.* **completeness,** *n.* **completion,** *n.*

complex (kom'pleks) [L. *complexus*, twined together], *a.* Composed of several parts; complicated.

complexion (kòm-plek'shùn), *n.* The colour and appearance of the face; character, aspect.

compliance (kòm-plī'àns), *n.* The act of complying; consent. **compliant,** *a.* Yielding.

complicate (kom'pli-kāt) [L. *plicatus*, folded], *v.t.* To make complex; to involve. **complicated,** *a.* **complica'tion,** *n.*

complicity (kòm-plis'i-ti) [F. *complicité*], *n.* Participation, esp. in wrong-doing.

compliment (kom'pli-mènt)[F.], *n.* An act of courtesy, respect, or regard; delicate flattery; (*pl.*) courtesies, respects. *v.t.* (kom-pli-ment')To pay compliments to; to congratulate, flatter. **complimentary,** *a.*

comply (kòm-plī') [It. *complire*, to complete], *v.i.* To assent, agree.

component (kòm-pō'nènt) [L. *compōnens*, putting], *a.* Serving to make up a compound. *n.* A constituent part.

comport (kòm-pôrt') [L. *portāre*, to carry], *v.t.* To conduct, behave (oneself). *v.i.* To suit, accord.

compose (kòm-pōz') [F. *composer*], *v.t.* To make a whole by putting together parts; to constitute; to write (a literary or musical work); to soothe, adjust; to arrange in order (as type for printing). **composed,** *a.* Calm, tranquil, settled. **composer,** *n.* One who composes, esp. music.

composite (kom'pō-zit) [L. *compositus*, put], *a.* Made up of distinct parts.

composition (kom-pò-zish'ùn), *n.* The act of composing; the thing composed; orderly arrangement, style; an agreement to terms; a compound; settlement by compromise; the amount so accepted; the process of setting type; a piece written as practice in literary expression. **compos'itor,** *n.* One who sets type.

compost (kom'post) [O.F. *composte*], *n.* (*Agric.*) Fertilizing mixture of decayed vegetable matter.

composure (kòm-pō'zhèr), *n.* Calmness, tranquillity, a calm frame of mind.

compound (1) (kòm-pound')[L. *pōnere*, to put], *v.t.* To make into one mass; to mix, combine; to settle amicably, to compromise; to come to terms. *a.* (kom'-pound) Composed of two or more ingredients, elements or parts; composite. *n.* A combination, mixture. **compoundable,** *a.*

compound (2) (kom'pound) [Malay *kampong*], *n.* The yard round a dwelling in India, etc.

comprehend (kom-prè-hend') [L. *prae*, beforehand, *hendere*, to seize], *v.t.* To understand; to comprise, include. **comprehensible,** *a.* That may be comprehended; clear, intelligible.

comprehension(kom-prè-hen'shùn),*n.*The act or power of comprehending; the faculty by which ideas are comprehended; inclusion. **comprehensive,** *a.*

compress (kòm-pres') [L. *compressāre*], *v.t.* To squeeze or press together, bring into narrow limits, condense. *n* (kom'-pres). A soft pad; a wet cloth for reducing inflammation. **compressible,** *a.* **compressibil'ity,** *n.* **compress'ion,** *n.* The act of compressing.

comprise (kòm-prīz'), *v.t.* To contain, to include; to bring (within certain limits).

compromise (kom'prò-mīz) [L. *prōmittere*, PROMISE], *n.* A settlement by mutual concession or partial surrender; a medium between conflicting courses of action. *v.t.* To settle by mutual concession; to place in a difficult position, expose to risk of disgrace. *v.i.* To make a compromise.

compulsion (kòm-pŭl'shùn), *n.* The act of compelling; constraint of the will. **compulsory,** *a.* Enforced.

compunction(kòm-pŭnk'shùn)[L.*pungere*, to prick], *n.* Reproach of conscience.

compute (kòm-pūt') [L. *putāre*, to think], *v.t.* To determine by calculation. **computer,** *n.* An electronic calculating machine.

comrade (kom'rād) [F. *camarade*, a chamber-mate], *n.* A mate, companion; a fellow-socialist. **comradeship,** *n.*

con (kon), *v.t.* To study over, to learn; to know; to direct the steering of a ship. **conning-tower,** *n.* The armoured shelter in a warship or submarine from which the vessel is steered.

concatenate (kòn-kăt'ê-nāt) [L. *catēna*, a chain], *v.t.* To link together in a successive series. **concatena'tion,** *n.*

concave (kon'kāv) [L. *cavus*, hollow], *a.* Having a hollowed surface. *n.* A hollow curve or surface; an arch. **concavity** (-kăv'i-ti), *n.*

conceal (kòn-sēl') [L. *cēlāre*, to hide], *v.t.* To hide or cover; to keep secret. **concealment,** *n.*

concede (kòn-sēd') [L. *cēdere*, to yield], *v.t.* To yield, give up, surrender; to grant. *v.i.* To make concessions.

conceit (kòn-sēt'), *n.* Overweening self-esteem; a whim, a fanciful idea. **conceited,** *a.* Full of conceit.

conceive (kòn-sēv') [L. *capere*, to take], *v.t.* To form in the womb; to imagine or suppose as possible; to formulate clearly in mind. *v.i.* To become pregnant; to form an idea or concept in the mind. **conceivable,** *a.*

concentrate (kon'sèn-trāt), *v.t.* To bring to a common focus; to bring all one's energies to bear; to condense. **concentration',** *n.* **concen'trative,** *a.*

concentric (kòn-sen'trik), *a.* Having a common centre.

concept (kon'sept) [L. *conceptum*, *concipere*, to CONCEIVE], *n.* A general notion or idea comprising all the attributes common to a class. **conception** (kòn-sep'shùn), *n.* The act of conceiving.

concern(kòn-sèrn')[L.*cernere*, to separate, sift], *v.t.* To relate to; to affect, be of importance to; to interest; to render uneasy. *n.* That which affects a person;

interest, anxiety, solicitude; a firm, an establishment; (*pl.*) affairs. **concerned,** *a.* Interested, anxious, solicitous. **concerning,** *prep.* With respect to.

concert (kŏn-sĕrt') [L. *certāre*, to vie], *v.t.* To plan together, contrive. *n.* (kon'-sĕrt). Harmony, accordance of ideas; a public musical entertainment. **concerted,** *a.* Mutually planned.

concertina (kon-sĕr-tē'nä), *n.* A portable musical instrument with keyboard at each end and bellows between.

concerto (kon-chĕr'to) [It.], *n.* (*Mus.*) A composition for a solo instrument with orchestral accompaniment.

concession (kŏn-sesh'ŭn), *n.* The act of conceding; the thing conceded. **concessionnaire',** *n.* One who holds a concession from the government.

conch (kongk) [L. *concha*], *n.* A spiral marine shell. **conchol'ogy,** *n.* The branch of zoology dealing with shells and molluscs.

concierge (kon-sē-ârzh') [F.], *n.* A door-keeper, hall porter.

conciliate (kŏn-sil'i-āt) [L. *conciliātus*], *v.t.* To gain over, win; to reconcile conflicting views. **concilia'tion,** *n.* The act of conciliating. **conciliatory,** *a.*

concise (kŏn-sīs') [L. *concīsus*], *a.* Condensed, brief, terse. **conciseness,** *n.*

conclave (kon'klāv) [L. *clāvis*, key], *n.* The assembly of cardinals that elects a pope; a close or secret assembly.

conclude (kŏn-klood') [L. *claudere*, to shut], *v.t.* To bring to an end, to finish; to infer. *v.i.* To make an end; to draw an inference. **conclu'sion,** *n.* **conclusive,** *a.*

concoct (kŏn-kokt') [L. *coquere*, to cook], *v.t.* To plot, devise. **concoction,** *n.* The act or result of mixing together.

concomitant (kŏn-kom'i-tănt) [L. *comitāri*, to accompany], *a.* Existing in conjunction with. *n.* That which accompanies.

concord (kong'kôrd) [L. *cor cordis*, heart], *n.* Union in opinions, sentiments, or interests; the agreement of one word with another; an harmonious combination of notes. **concor'dance,** *n.* The state of being concordant; a list of the words in a book, with references to their occurrence. **concordant,** *a.* In harmony or accord; agreeing.

concourse (kon'kôrs), *n.* A confluence, gathering together.

concrete (kon'krēt) [L. *concrētus*, grown together], *a.* Formed by the union of many particles; existing, real, not abstract; made of concrete. *n.* Lime, coarse gravel, and sand mixed with mortar. **concretion** (kŏn-krē'shŭn), *n.*

concubine (kon'kū-bīn) [L. *concubīna*], *n.* A woman who cohabits with a man without being married to him; **concu'binage,** *n.*

concupiscence (kŏn-kū'pi-sĕns) [L. *concupiscentia*, desire], *n.* Unlawful or excessive lust. **concupiscent,** *a.*

concur (kŏn-kĕr') [L. *currere*, to run], *v.i.* To coincide; to agree; to act in conjunction with. **concurrence,** *n.* **concurrent,** *a.* Happening or existing at the same time; acting in union.

concussion (kŏn-kŭsh'ŭn) [L. *concussus*,

shaken together], *n.* Shaking by sudden impact; a shock.

condemn (kŏn-dem') [L. *damnāre*, to condemn], *v.t.* To pronounce guilty, incurable, or unfit to use; to pass sentence on. **condemna'tion,** *n.*

condense (kŏn-dens') [L. *densāre*, to thicken], *v.t.* To compress, concentrate; to reduce into denser form (as a gas into a liquid). *v.i.* To become dense or compact. **condensa'tion,** *n.* The act or result of condensing; the state of being condensed; conciseness. **condenser,** *n.* (*Elec.*) A device for holding or storing an electric charge; (*Eng.*) an apparatus for reducing steam to a liquid form.

condescend (kŏn-dĕ-send') [L. *dēscendere*, to DESCEND], *v.i.* To stoop or lower oneself; to deign. **condescending,** *a.* Patronizing. **condescension,** *n.*

condign (kŏn-dīn') [L. *dignus*, worthy], *a.* Well-deserved, merited.

condiment (kon'di-mĕnt) [L. *condīre*, to pickle], *n.* Anything used to give a relish to food.

condition (kŏn-dish'ŭn) [L. *dīcere*, to speak], *n.* A stipulation, a term of a contract; that on which anything depends; state or mode of existence; high social position; a good state of health. **conditional,** *a.* Implying, or depending on certain conditions; (*Gram.*) expressing condition. **conditioned,** *a.* Limited by certain conditions.

condole (kŏn-dōl') [L. *dolēre*, to grieve], *v.i.* To lament; to sympathize (with). **condolence,** *n.*

condominium (kon-dō-min'i-ŭm) [L., with dominion], *n.* (*Pol.*) Joint sovereignty over a state.

condone (kŏn-dōn') [L. *dōnāre*, to give], *v.t.* To forgive, remit.

condor (kon'dôr) [Peruv. *cuntur*], *n.* A large S. American vulture.

conduce (kŏn-dūs') [L. *dūcere*, to lead], *v.i.* To contribute; to tend (to). **conducive,** *a.*

conduct (kon'dŭkt) [L. *conductus*, lead with], *n.* Behaviour; management, direction, control. *v.t.* (kŏn-dŭkt'). To lead, guide, to manage, direct; to transmit (as heat, electricity, etc.); (*refl.*) to behave. *v.i.* To act as a conductor. **conductor,** *n.* A leader, manager; the director of an orchestra; the man in charge of a bus or tramcar; a body capable of transmitting heat, electricity, etc.

conduit (kon'dĭt), *n.* A channel, pipe, etc., to convey water.

cone (kōn) [Gr. *kōnos*], *n.* A solid pointed figure with straight sides and circular base; the fruit of the pines, firs, etc.

confabulate (kŏn-făb'ū-lāt) [L. *fābulāri*, to converse], *v.i.* To chat, to gossip. **confabula'tion,** *n.*

confection (kŏn-fek'shŭn) [L. *facere*, to make], *n.* A compound, esp. a sweet delicacy or a drug made palatable by sweetening. **confectioner,** *n.* One who makes or sells sweetmeats, etc.; a pastry-cook. **confectionery,** *n.* Sweetmeats or preserves.

confederacy (kŏn-fed'ĕr-à-si), *n.* A league or confederation; conspiracy.

confederate (kòn-fed'èr-àt) [L. *fœdus*, a league], *a.* United in a league. **confedera'tion**, *n.* An alliance.

confer (kòn-fèr') [L. *ferre*, to bring], *v.t.* To bestow, grant. *v.i.* To consult together; to compare views. **conference** (kon'fèr-èns), *n.* A meeting for consultation to adjust differences.

confess (kòn-fes') [L. *confessus*, acknowledged], *v.t.* To own, acknowledge, admit; to declare one's belief in; to hear the confession of. *v.i.* To make confession, esp. to a priest. **confessedly**, *adv.* Admittedly, avowedly. **confession**, *n.* The act of confessing; acknowledgment of sins to a priest in order to receive absolution. **confessional**, *n.* The place where a priest sits to hear confessions. **confessor**, *n.* One who confesses; a saint who is neither an apostle nor martyr; (kon'fes-òr) a priest who hears confessions.

confetti (kòn-fet'ï) [It.], *n.pl.* Bits of coloured paper thrown at weddings.

confidant (fem. -dante) (kon-fi-dant') [F.], *n.* A bosom friend.

confide (kòn-fïd') [L. *fïdere*, to trust], *v.i.* To have trust or confidence (in). *v.t.* To entrust (to). **confidence** (kon'fï-dèns), *n.* Trust, belief; self-reliance; revelation of private matters to a friend; the matter revealed. **con'fident**, *a.* Full of confidence; self-reliant. **confiden'tial**, *a.* Trustworthy; told or done in confidence. **confiden'tially**, *adv.*

configuration (kòn-fig-û-rā'shùn) [L. *figura*, form], *n.* Form; structural arrangement.

confine (kon'fïn) [L. *confines* (*pl.* a.), bordering upon], *n.* (*usu. in pl.*) Limits, frontier. *v.t.* (kòn-fïn'). To imprison, to keep within bounds; to limit. **to be confined**: To be in child-bed or delivered of a child. **confinement**, *n.*

confirm (kòn-fèrm') [L. *firmāre*, to make firm], *v.t.* To establish, ratify, make firm or valid; to bear witness to; to administer confirmation to. **confirma'tion**, *n.* Corroborative testimony; the rite of admitting into full communion with an episcopal church by the laying on of hands. **confir'mative**, *a.* confirmatory, *a.* **confirmed**, *a.* Established, settled; having received confirmation.

confiscate (kon'fis-kāt) [L. *fiscus*, the treasury], *v.t.* To seize as forfeited to the public treasury. **confisca'tion**, *n.*

conflagration (kon'flå-grā'shùn) [L. *flagrāre*, to burn], *n.* A great fire.

conflict (kon'flïkt) [L. *conflictus*, struck together], *n.* A fight, struggle, contest; opposition of interest, etc. *v.i.* (kòn-flïkt'). To come into collision; to strive, differ, disagree; to be discrepant. **conflic'ting**, *a.* Contradictory.

confluent (kon'flü-ènt) [L. *fluere*, to flow], *a.* Flowing or running together; uniting. *n.* A stream which unites with another. **confluence**, *n.*

conform (kòn-fôrm') [L. *formāre*, to fashion], *v.t.* To make like in form; to adapt. *v.i.* To comply, to assent; to be in harmony or agreement. **conformable**, *a.* Having the same form; corresponding, similar; compliant. **conforma'tion**, *n.* Shape, structure; adaptation.

conformity, *n.* Resemblance, agreement, compliance.

confound (kòn-found') [L. *fundere*, to pour], *v.t.* To throw into confusion, perplex; to put to shame; to defeat, overthrow; to mix up, confuse. **confoundedly**, *adv.* Exceedingly.

confront (kòn-frùnt') [L. *frons -ntis*, forehead], *v.t.* To face; to bring face to face; to oppose, to meet in hostility; to compare (with). **confronta'tion**, *n.*

confuse (kòn-fûz') *v.t.* To mix or mingle indistinguishably; to jumble up; to disconcert. **confusion**, *n.*

confute (kòn-fût') [L. *confūtāre*], *v.t.* To overcome in argument; to prove to be false. **confuta'tion**, *n.* Refutation.

congeal (kòn-jēl') [L. *gelu*, frost], *v.t.* To convert from liquid to solid by cold; to coagulate. *v.i.* To become hard with cold; to coagulate. **congela'tion**, *n.*

congenial (kòn-jē'ni-àl), *a.* Partaking of the same characteristics; sympathetic; suitable. **congenial'ity**, *n.*

congenital (kòn-jen'i-tàl) [L. *genitus*, produced], *a.* Existing from birth; constitutional. **congenitally**, *adv.*

conger (kong'gèr) [Gr. *gongros*], *n.* A genus of marine eels.

congest (kon-jest') [L. *gerere*, to bring], *v.i.* To become congested. **congested**, *a.* Closely crowded; unduly distended with blood. **conges'tion**, *n.*

conglomerate (kòn-glom'èr-àt) [L. *glomus -eris*, a ball], *a.* Gathered into a round body. *n.* A rock composed of pieces of stone naturally cemented together; pudding-stone. *v.t.* and *i.* To gather into a ball, collect into a mass. **conglomera'tion**, *n.*

congratulate (kòn-grăt'û-lāt) [L. *grātulārī*, to wish joy], *v.t.* To express pleasure or joy at some event; to compliment upon, felicitate. **congratula'tion**, *n.* **congratula'tory**, *a.*

congregate (kong'grè-gāt) [L. *gregāre*, to collect], *v.t.* To gather or collect together into a crowd. *v.i.* To come together, assemble. **congrega'tion**, *n.* The act of gathering together; an assembly of persons, esp. for religious worship. **congregational**, *a.* Pertaining to a congregation, or to Congregationalism. **Congregationalism**, *n.* That form of church government in which each church is self-governed. **Congregationalist**, *a.* and *n.*

congress (kong'gres) [L. *congressus*, met together], *n.* A conference; a meeting of envoys for settlement of international affairs; the legislature of the U.S.A.

congruent (kong'grü-ènt) [L. *congruere*, to agree], *a.* Agreeing, suitable, correspondent. **congruence**, **-ency**, *n.* **congruous**, *a.* Suitable, conformable, appropriate, fitting. **congru'ity**, *n.*

conic (kon'ik) [Gr. *kōnikos*], *a.* Pertaining to a cone; (*pl.*) the branch of mathematics dealing with conic sections, *i.e.* curves formed by the intersection of a cone and a plane. **conical**, *a.*

conifer (kō'ni-fèr), *n.* A cone-bearing plant or tree.

conjecture (kòn-jek'tūr) [L. *conjectūra*], *n.*

A guess, surmise, or doubtful inference; opinion based on this. *v.t.* and *i.* To guess, surmise. **conjecturable,** *a.* That may be conjectured. **conjecturably,** *adv.* **conjectural,** *a.* Depending on conjecture.

conjugal (kon'jū-gǎl) [L. *conjugālis*], *a.* Of or pertaining to matrimony or to married life. **conjugally,** *adv.*

conjugate (kon'jū-gāt) [L. *conjugātus*], *v.t.* To inflect (a verb) by going through the voices, moods, tenses, etc.; (*Biol.*) to become united. *a.* (-gǎt) Joined in pairs. *n.* A word agreeing in derivation with another word. **conjuga'tion,** *n.* The act or process of conjugating; a class of verbs conjugated alike.

conjunct (kon-jŭnkt') [L. *jungere*, to join], *a.* Conjoined; in union. **conjunctly,** *adv.* **conjunction,** *n.* Union, association, combination; a word connecting sentences, clauses, or words. **conjunctive,** *a.* Serving to unite; connective, copulative. *n.* A conjunctive word or mood. **conjuncture,** *n.* A combination of circumstances; a crisis.

conjure (1) (kon-joor') [L. *jūrāre*, to swear], *v.t.* To appeal to solemnly; to bind by an oath. **conjura'tion,** *n.* The act of invoking; a magic spell, a charm.

conjure (2) (kŭn'jẽr), *v.t.* To raise up by or as by magic. *v.i.* To practise as a conjurer. **conjurer** (kŭn'jẽr-ẽr), *n.* A juggler.

connect (kŏ-nekt') [L. *nectere*, to bind], *v.t.* To link or fasten together; to unite, correlate, associate. *v.i.* To join, to cohere. **connected,** *a.* **connective,** *a.* Having the power of connecting; that connects. *n.* (*Gram.*) A connecting word or thing. **connexion,** *n.* The act of connecting; the state of being connected; relationship or one related; a connecting part; a religious body; a body of customers or clients.

connive (kŏ-nīv') [L. *connīvēre*], *v.i.* To wink (at); to omit or neglect to see or prevent any wrong. **connivance,** *n.* Passive co-operation in a fault or crime.

connoisseur (kon-à-sẽr') [F.], *n.* One skilled in judging of the fine arts.

connote (kŏ-nōt') [L. *notāre*, to mark], *v.t.* To imply, signify, mean, involve. **connota'tion,** *n.*

connubial (kŏ-nū'bi-ǎl) [L. *nūbere*, to marry], *a.* Relating to marriage or the marriage state.

conquer (kong'kẽr) [L. *conquīrere*], *v.t.* To win or gain by conquest; to overcome, to surmount. *v.i.* To be victorious. **conquerable,** *a.* **conqueror,** *n.* **The Conqueror,** *n.* William I of England.

conquest (kong'kwest) [O.F. *conquest*], *n.* The act of conquering; that which is conquered; victory.

conscience (kon'shĕns) [L. *scīre*, to know], *n.* Moral sense; the sense of right and wrong. **conscientious** (kon-shi-en'shŭs), *a.* Actuated by strict regard to the dictates of conscience; scrupulous. **conscientious objector,** *n.* One who refuses to take part on principle in war or the activities connected with it.

conscious (kon'shŭs) [L. *aware*], *a.* Aware of one's own existence; self-conscious; cognizant, aware. **consciously,** *adv.*

consciousness, *n.* The state of being conscious; immediate knowledge, sense, perception; the intellectual faculties.

conscript (kon'skript) [L. *conscriptus*, p.p. of *conscrībere*], *v.t.* To enlist compulsorily. *n.* One compelled to serve, esp. as a soldier. **conscrip'tion,** *n.*

consecrate (kon'sĕ-krāt) [L. *consecrāre*, to consecrate], *v.t.* To set apart as sacred; to dedicate, hallow. **consecra'tion,** *n.* The act of consecrating; the state of being consecrated; dedication.

consecutive (kŏn-sek'ū-tiv) [L. *sequi*, to follow], *a.* Following without break. **consensus** (kŏn-sen'sŭs) [L., p.p. of *consentīre*, as foll.], *n.* A general agreement.

consent (kŏn-sent') [L. *consentīre*], *v.i.* To concur, assent, yield. *n.* Acquiescence, permission; agreement, concurrence.

consequent (kon'sĕ-kwĕnt) [L. *sequi*, to follow], *a.* Following as a natural or logical result; consistent. **consequence,** *n.* A result or effect; inference; importance. **consequen'tial,** *a.* Following as a result or a necessary deduction; self-important, pompous. **consequently,** *adv.* As a consequence; accordingly.

conservancy (kŏn-sẽr'vàn-si), *n.* Official preservation of forests, fisheries, etc.; a commission or court charged with this.

conservation (kon-sẽr-vā'shùn), *n.* The act of conserving; preservation. **conser'vative,** *a.* Tending to conserve what is established or to maintain existing institutions. *n.* A person inclined to preserve established things. **Conservative Party,** *n.* (*Polit.*) A party that upholds the Capitalist system and opposes any form of constitutional change. **conservatism,** *n.*

conservatory (kŏn-sẽr'và-tŏ-ri), *n.* A glass-house for plants.

conserve (kŏn-sẽrv') [L. *conservāre*], *v.t.* To preserve from injury, decay, or loss.

consider (kŏn-sid'ẽr) [L. *considerāre*], *v.t.* To think on, contemplate, ponder; to look upon as of importance; to estimate. *v.i.* To reflect, deliberate. **considerable,** *a.* Worth consideration; important. **consid'erate,** *a.* Characterized by consideration for others, **considera'tion,** *n.* Reflection, thought; regard for others; motive for action; an equivalent. **considering,** *prep.* In view of.

consign (kŏn-sīn') [L. *signāre*, to mark], *v.t.* To commit to the care of another. **consignee** (kon-sī-nē'), *n.* One to whom goods are consigned. **consignor',** *n.* One who consigns goods to another. **consign'ment,** *n.*

consist (kŏn-sist') [L. *sistere*, to make to stand], *v.i.* To be composed (of); to be founded (in); to be compatible (with). **consistence, -ency,** *n.* Degree of density; cohesion; solidity; accord, compatibility. **consistent,** *a.*

consistory (kŏn-sis'tŏ-ri), *n.* The court of a bishop for dealing with ecclesiastical causes; the college of cardinals at Rome. **consistor'ial,** *a.*

console (kŏn-sōl') [L. *sōlārī*, to solace], *v.t.* To comfort in trouble or distress. **consolable,** *a.* **consola'tion,** *n.* That which cheers or comforts; alleviation of distress. **consolatory** (kŏn-sŏl'à-tori), *a.*

consolidate (kŏn-sŏl'i-dāt) [L. *solidāre*, to make solid], *v.t.* To form into a solid mass; to strengthen, bring into close union; to combine. **consolida'tion**, *n.*

consols (kon-solz') [Consolidated Funds], *n.* (*Fin.*) British Government stock.

consonant (kon'sŏ-nànt) [L. *sonāre*, to sound], *a.* Agreeing or according, esp. in sound; congruous, in harmony. *n.* A letter which cannot be sounded by itself, as *b* or *p.* **consonance,** *n.* Accord or agreement, esp. of sound.

consort (kon'sôrt) [CON-], *n.* A companion, mate, partner; a husband, a wife. *v.i.* (kŏn-sôrt'). To associate, keep company with; to agree.

conspicuous (kŏn-spĭk'ū-ús) [L. *specere,* to look], *a.* Obvious; striking.

conspiracy (kŏn-spĭr'à-si), *n.* The act of conspiring; a secret agreement between persons to commit an unlawful act.

conspire (kŏn-spĭr') [L. *spīrāre,* to breathe], *v.i.* To combine secretly to do any unlawful act. *v.t.* To plot, concert. **conspir'ator,** *n.*

constable (kŭn'stàbl) [O.F. *conestable,* L. *comes stabulī,* count of the stable], *n.* A policeman; an officer charged with the preservation of the peace. **constab'ulary,** *n.* A body of police under one authority. *a.* Pertaining to the police.

constant (kon'stànt) [L. *stāre,* to stand], *a.* Firm, unshaken; steadfast; continuous, unceasing; unvarying. *n.* A fixed quantity, one which is assumed not to vary throughout a series of calculations. **constancy,** *n.* **constantly,** *adv.* Continually, always.

constellation (kon-stè-lā'shŭn) [L. *stellātus,* set with stars], *n.* A number of fixed stars grouped within the outlines of an imaginary figure in the sky.

consternate (kon'stèr-nāt) [L. *consternātus,* affrighted], *v.t.* To affright, dismay. **consterna'tion,** *n.*

constipate (kon'sti-pāt) [L. *stīpāre,* to cram], *v.t.* To make costive. **constipa'tion,** *n.*

constituent (kŏn-stĭt'ū-ènt), *a.* Constituting, composing. *n.* One who or that which constitutes; a component part; one of a body which elects a representative; one who appoints another as his agent, a client. **constituency,** *n.* A body of electors; the place or persons represented by a member of Parliament.

constitute (kon'stĭ-tūt) [L. *statuere,* to place], *v.t.* To establish; to give legal form or a definite nature or character to.

constitution (kon-stĭ-tū'shŭn) [F.], *n.* The nature, form, or structure of a system or body; natural strength of the body; the established form of government in a state. **constitutional,** *a.* Inherent in the constitution; pertaining to established form of government; legal. *n.* A walk or other exercise for the benefit of one's health. **constitutionalism,** *n.* Government based on a constitution; adherence to such a government. **constitutionalist,** *n.* An upholder of or writer or authority on this.

constrain (kŏn-strān) [L. *stringere,* to draw tight], *v.t.* To compel, oblige; to keep down by force; to confine, repress. **constrained,** *a.* **constraint,** *n.*

constrict (kŏn-strĭkt') [L. *constrictus,* as prec.], *v.t.* To draw together, cause to contract. **constriction,** *n.*

construct (kŏn-strŭkt') [L. *constructus,* piled together], *v.t.* To build up, put together in proper order; to form mentally. **construction,** *n.* The act or art of constructing; the thing constructed or its style or form; the syntactical arrangement of words in a sentence; interpretation (of words, conduct, etc.). **constructional,** *a.* Pertaining to construction; structural. **constructive,** *a.* Having ability or power to construct; tending to construct; inferential, virtual.

construe (kon'stroo), *v.t.* To explain, interpret. *v.i.* To apply the rules of syntax; to translate.

consul (kon'sŭl) [L.], *n.* (*Hist.*) One of the two supreme magistrates of ancient Rome; an officer appointed by a state to reside in a foreign country to promote its mercantile interests, protect its subjects. **consular,** *a.* **consulate,** *n.* The official residence, term of office, of a consul.

consult (kŏn-sŭlt') [L. *consultāre*], *v.i.* To take counsel together; to deliberate. *v.t.* To ask advice or counsel from; to refer to (a book) for information. **consulta'tion,** *n.* The act of consulting; a meeting of experts to consider a case. **consulting,** *a.* Giving advice; called in or used for consultation.

consume (kŏn-sūm') [L. *sūmere,* to take], *v.t.* To destroy by fire, decomposition, etc.; to use up, to squander. *v.i.* To waste away, to be burned. **consumedly** (-sū'mèd-li), *adv.* Unrestrainedly, excessively. **consumer,** *n.*

consummate (kŏn-sŭm'àt) [L. *summa,* a sum], *a.* Complete, perfect; of the highest quality. *v.t.* (kon'sŭ-māt) To bring to completion, to perfect, to finish. **consumma'tion,** *n.* The end of something begun; perfect development.

consumption (kŏn-sŭmp'shŭn) [L. *consumptio*], *n.* The act of consuming; state or process of being consumed; a wasting disease, phthisis. **consumptive,** *a.* Consuming; disposed to or affected with consumption. *n.* A person suffering from consumption.

contact (kon'tàkt) [L. *tactus,* touched], *n.* Touch, meeting, the relation of touching. *v.t.* To get in touch with (a person).

contagion (kŏn-tā'jŭn) [L. *contāgio,* as prec.], *n.* Communication of disease by contact; contagious disease; deleterious influence. **contagious,** *a.*

contain (kŏn-tān') [L. *tenēre,* to hold], *v.t.* To hold within fixed limits; to comprise, to include; to enclose; (*Arith.*) to be exactly divisible by; (*Mil.*) to hem in. **containable,** *a.* **container,** *n.*

contaminate (kŏn-tăm'i-nāt) [L. *contāminātus*], *v.t.* To defile, pollute, corrupt. **contamina'tion,** *n.*

contango (kŏn-tăng'gō) [L. *continēre*], *n.* The commission paid by a buyer for the postponement of transactions on the Stock Exchange.

contemn (kŏn-tem') [L. *temnere*, to despise], *v.t.* To scorn; to slight, neglect.

contemplate (kon'tĕm-plāt) [L. *contemplāre*, to observe], *v.t.* To look at, study; to meditate and reflect on; to purpose, intend; to regard as possible. *v.i.* To meditate. **contempla'tion**, *n.* **contem'plative**, *a.* Thoughtful, studious.

contemporaneous (kŏn-tem-pó-rā'né-ŭs) [L. *tempus*, time], *a.* Existing or happening at the same time or period.

contemporary (kŏn-tem'pó-rà-ri), *a.* Living at the same time; of the same age or period. *n.* A contemporary person or thing.

contempt (kŏn-tempt'), *n.* Scorn, disdain; shame, disgrace; disobedience to the rules of a sovereign, court, or legislative body. **contemptible**, *a.* Worthy of contempt, despicable. **contemptuous**, *a.* Disdainful, scornful.

contend (kŏn-tend') [L. *tendere*, to stretch], *v.i.* To strive in opposition, or in defence or support of anything; to compete, dispute. *v.t.* To maintain by argument.

content (cón-tent') [L. *contentus*, contained], *a.* Satisfied, pleased, willing. *v.t.* To satisfy, make easy in any situation; to gratify. *n.* Satisfaction, ease of mind; (kon'tent) capacity or power of containing; volume; meaning; (*pl.*) that which a vessel, book, etc. contains; a summary of subject-matter. **contentedly**, *adv.* **contentedness**, *n.* **contentment**, *n.* The state of being contented or satisfied.

contention (kŏn-ten'shŭn), *n.* Quarrel, strife, controversy; a point contended for. **contentious**, *a.*

contest (kŏn-test') [L. *testārī*, to bear witness], *v.t.* To contend for or about; to dispute, call in question, oppose. *v.i.* To strive, contend, vie. *n.* (kon'test) A struggle, dispute, controversy; competition, rivalry. **contestant**, *n.* One who contests. **contesta'tion**, *n.*

context (kon'tekst) [L. *contextus*, woven together], *n.* The parts of a discourse, etc., immediately connected with a passage quoted. **contex'tual**, *a.*

contiguous (kŏn-tig'ū-ŭs) [L. *contiguus*], *a.* Meeting so as to touch; adjoining. **contigu'ity**, *n.*

continent (1) (kon'ti-nĕnt) [L. *continēre*, to contain], *a.* Chaste; temperate. **continence**, **-nency**, *n.* **continently** *adv.*

continent (2) (kon'ti-nĕnt), *n.* A large tract of land not disjoined by a sea; the mainland of Europe; the summary, the sum total. **continen'tal**, *a.*

contingent (kŏn-tin'jĕnt) [L. *contingens*, touching together], *a.* Dependent on an uncertain issue; not essential, conditional. *n.* A fortuitous event; that which falls to one by chance; an armed force furnished by a state for a joint enterprise. **contingency**, *n.*

continual (kŏn-tin'ū-ǎl) [O.F. *continuel*, as CONTINUOUS], *a.* Incessant; without interruption. **continually**, *adv.*

continuance (kŏn-tin'ū-ǎns) [O.F., as above], *n.* Permanence; duration; stay.

continuation (kŏn-tin-ū-ā'shŭn) [L. *continuatus*, continued], *n.* That which continues anything; extension, prolongation.

continue (kŏn-tin'ū) [F. *continuer*], *v.t.* To carry on without interruption; to extend, complete. *v.i.* To remain, stay; to remain in existence; to persevere. **continuable**, *a.*

continuous (kŏn-tin'ū-ŭs) [L. *continuus* (CON-, *tinēre*, to hold)], *a.* Connected without a break; uninterrupted, unceasing. **continu'ity**, *n.*

contort (kŏn-tört') [L. *contortus*, twisted together], *v.t.* To twist with violence, wrench; to distort. **contortion**, *n.* The act of twisting; a writhing movement; partial dislocation. **contortionist**, *n.* An acrobat who bends his body unnaturally.

contour (kon'toor) [F.], *n.* The outline, esp. of a coast or other geographical feature.

contra (kon'trà) [L.], *prep.* Against, opposite. *n.* The opposite (usu. the credit) side of an account.

contraband (kon'trà-bănd) [Sp. *contrabanda*], *a.* Prohibited, unlawful. *n.* Articles forbidden to be exported or imported; smuggled articles.

contract (kŏn-trăkt') [L. *contractus*, drawn together], *v.t.* To draw together; to abbreviate, shorten; to acquire; to become liable for; to agree or to settle by covenant. *v.i.* To shrink; to agree (to do or supply something for a price). *n.* (kon'trăkt) An agreement, compact; a formal betrothal; an offer or promise which has been formally accepted. **contracted**, *a.* Drawn together; betrothed; mean, narrow. **contractible**, *a.* Capable of contraction. **contraction**, *n.* An abbreviation, shortening; the act of contracting. **contractor**, *n.* One who undertakes a contract; an employer who contracts to perform building, engineering, or other undertakings.

contradict (kon-trà-dĭkt') [L. *dicere*, to speak], *v.t.* To deny the truth of; to assert the opposite of. **contradiction**, *n.* **contradictor**, *n.* **contradictory**, *a.* Affirming the contrary; logically incompatible; disputatious.

contralto (kŏn-trăl'tō) [It.], *n.* The lowest female voice; a singer with this voice.

contrary (kon'trà-ri) [L. *contrārius*], *a.* Opposite; diametrically different; repugnant; wayward, perverse. *n.* The opposite; a thing that contradicts. *adv.* Adversely; in an opposite manner or direction. **contrari'ety**, *n.* The state of being contrary; opposition. **contrarily**, *adv.* In a contrary manner. **contrariwise** (kon'trà-ri-, kŏn-trör'i-wiz), *adv.* On the other hand, conversely; perversely.

contrast (kŏn-trast') [O.F. *contraster*], *v.t.* To set in opposition, so as to show the difference between. *v.i.* To stand in contrast or opposition. *n.* (kon'trast) Unlikeness of things or qualities; the presentation of opposites with a view to comparison.

contravene (kon-trà-vēn') [L. *venīre*, to come], *v.t.* To violate, to transgress. **contraven'tion**, *n.* Violation.

contretemps (kon'trĕ-ton) [F.], *n.* An

unexpected event, throwing everything into confusion.

contribute (kŏn-trĭb'ūt) [L. *tribuere*, to pay], *v.t.* To give for a common purpose; to pay as one's share. *v.i.* To give a part; to have a share in. **contribu'tion**, *n.* **contrib'utive**, *a.* Assisting, promoting. **contributor**, *n.* One who contributes; one who supplies articles to a newspaper, etc. **contributory**, *a.* Contributing to the same result, etc.

contrite (kŏn'trīt) [L. *terere*, to rub, to grind], *a.* Deeply sorry for sin; thoroughly penitent. **contrition** (kŏn-trĭsh'ŭn), *n.*

contrive (kŏn-trīv') [O.F. *trover*, to find], *v.t.* To devise, invent; to bring to pass. *v.i.* To form designs, to scheme. **contrivance**, *n.*

control (kŏn-trōl') [O.F. *contre-rolle*, a duplicate register], *n.* Check, restraint; regulating power; authority, command. *v.t.* To exercise power over; to restrain, regulate. **controller**, *n.* A director; an officer who checks the accounts of other officers by means of a duplicate register. **controllership**, *n.*

controversy (kŏn'trō-vĕr-sĭ) [L. *contrōversia*, a quarrel], *n.* Disputation, esp. in writing. **controver'sial**, *a.* Inclined or pertaining to controversy. **controversialist**, *n.* A disputant.

controvert (kŏn'trō-vĕrt) [L. *contrō-*, against, *vertere*, to turn], *v.t.* To call in question; to oppose or refute by argument.

contumacious (kŏn-tū-mā'shŭs) [L. *tumēre*, to swell with pride], *a.* Perverse, obstinate; stubbornly opposing lawful authority. **con'tumacy**, *n.*

contumely (kŏn'tū-mē-lĭ) [O.F. *contumelie*], *n.* Rude scornful abuse or reproach; insolence; ignominy. **contume'lious**, *a.*

contuse (kŏn-tūz') [L. *tūsus*, beaten], *v.t.* To bruise without breaking the skin. **contusion**, *n.* A bruise.

conundrum (kŏ-nŭn'drŭm) [?], *n.* A riddle; a puzzling question.

convalesce (kŏn-vá-lĕs') [L. *valēscere*, to grow strong], *v.i.* To recover health. **convalescence**, *n.* **convalescent**, *a.*

convene (kŏn-vēn') [L. *venīre*, to come], *v.t.* To convoke; to summon to appear. *v.i.* To meet together, assemble.

convenient (kŏn-vē'nĭ-ĕnt), *a.* Suitable; opportune, at hand, close by. **convenience**, **-ency**, *n.* The quality or state of being convenient; accommodation; a cause or source of comfort or accommodation; a thing that is useful; a lavatory.

convent (kŏn'vĕnt) [L. *conventus*, assembled together], *n.* A community of religious persons of either sex; the building occupied by it.

conventicle (kŏn-vĕn'tĭkl), *n.* A clandestine gathering; a dissenters' meeting-place.

convention (kŏn-vĕn'shŭn) [L. *conventio*], *n.* A meeting; the persons assembled; a treaty; an accepted usage. **conventional**, *a.* Agreed on by compact; founded on custom; slavishly observant of society customs or of accepted models. **conventionalism**, *n.* **conventionalist**, *n.* **conventional'ity**, *n.*

converge (kŏn-vĕrj') [L. *vergere*, to turn, incline], *v.i.* To tend towards one point. **convergent**, *a.* Tending to meet in one point.

conversant (kŏn-vĕr'sánt), *a.* Having knowledge of or familiarity with; proficient, versed in.

conversazione (kon-vĕr-sät-sĭ-ō'nĭ) [It.], *n.* A social meeting devoted to literary, artistic, or scientific subjects.

converse (kŏn-vĕrs') [F. *converser*], *v.i.* To discourse easily and familiarly. *n.* (kŏn'vĕrs) Familiarity; conversation; the opposite, counterpart, or complement. *a.* Opposite, reciprocal. **conversa'tion**, *n.* Familiar talk; intimate fellowship or intercourse. **conversational**, *a.*

conversion (kŏn-vĕr'shŭn), *n.* Change or the act of changing to a new mode of life, religion, morals, politics, etc.

convert (kŏn-vĕrt') [L. *vertere*, to turn], *v.t.* To change or cause to change from one state, religion, party, etc., to another; to change one kind of securities into another; (*Log.*) to transpose the terms of. *n.* (kŏn'vĕrt) One who is converted from one religion or party to another. **conver'tible**, *a.* That may be converted or changed; transmutable. **convertibil'ity**, *n.*

convex (kon'veks) [L. *convexus*, arched], *a.* Having a rounded form on the exterior (opp. to concave). **convex'ity**, *n.*

convey (kŏn-vā') [O.F. *conveier*], *v.t.* To transport, transmit; to impart; to transfer (property). **conveyance**, *n.* The act, means, or instrument of conveying; a vehicle; the act of transferring real property; the document by which it is transferred. **conveyancer**, *n.* (*Law*) One who draws up conveyances. **conveyancing**, *n.* (*Law*) The act of drawing up conveyances.

convict (kŏn-vĭkt') [L. *victus*, conquered], *v.t.* To prove or declare to be guilty. *n.* (kŏn'vĭkt) One sentenced to penal servitude. **convic'tion**, *n.*

convince (kŏn-vĭns') [L. *vincere*, to conquer], *v.t.* To satisfy the mind of; to persuade to conviction, overcome by proof.

convivial (kŏn-vĭv'ĭ-ál) [L. *vīvere*, to live], *a.* Festive, social, jovial. **convivial'ity**, *n.* **convivially**, *adv.*

convoke (kŏn-vōk') [L. *vocāre*, to call], *v.t.* To summon together; to convene. **convoca'tion**, *n.* The act of calling together; an assembly, esp. of qualified graduates of Universities or of the clergy of a province. **convocational**, *a.*

convolution (kon-vol-ū'shŏn) [L. *volutus*, rolled], *n.* A fold (esp. of brain matter); a winding motion. **convol'vulus**, *n.* A genus of climbing plants.

convoy (kŏn-voi'), *v.t.* To accompany on the way, as protection or escort. *n.* (kon'voi) The act of convoying; a protecting force; an escort, guard; that which is convoyed.

convulse (kŏn-vŭls') [L. *vulsus*, plucked], *v.t.* To agitate violently; to affect with convulsions; to excite spasms of laughter in. **convulsion**, *n.* (*usu. in pl.*) Violent involuntary contractions and relaxations of the muscles; a violent agitation or commotion. **convulsionary**, *a.* convulsive, *a.* Producing or attended with convulsions; spasmodic.

cony (kō'ni) [O.F. *conil*], *n.* A rabbit, a simpleton.

coo (koo) [imit.], *v.i.* To make a sound like a dove; to make love.

cook (kuk) [A.-S. *cōc*, L. *coquus*], *n.* One who prepares food for the table. *v.t.* To prepare food by boiling, roasting, etc.; (*fig.*) to garble, falsify, concoct. *v.i.* To undergo the process of cooking. **cookery**, *n.* The act or art of cooking.

cool (kool) [A.-S. *cōl*], *a.* Moderately cold; not retaining or causing heat; apathetic; calm, dispassionate; deliberate; impudent, audacious. *n.* Moderate temperature; a cool place. *v.t.* To make cool; to calm, allay. *v.i.* To become cool. **cooler**, *n.* coolish, *a.* **coolness**, *n.*

coolie (koo'li) [Hind. *qūlī*], *n.* A labourer in or from India or the East.

coop (koop) [M.E. *cupe*, a basket], *n.* A barred or wired box for fowls, etc. *v.t.* To confine in or as in a coop.

cooper (koo'pẽr) [L. *cupa*, a cask], *n.* One who makes barrels, tubs, etc.; a mixture of stout and porter. **cooperage**, *n.* The trade or workshop of a cooper.

co-operate (kō-op'ẽr-āt) [L. *operāri*, to work], *v.i.* To work or act with others for a common end; to contribute to an effect. **co-operation**, *n.* **co-op'erative**, *a.* co-operative society, *n.* Association for the production and distribution of goods without the services of a middle man.

co-opt (kō-opt') [L. *optāre*, to choose], *v.t.* To elect into a body by the votes of the members.

co-ordinate (kō-ôrd'in-āt) [L. *ordinātus*, arranged], *a.* Of the same order, rank, etc. *n.pl.* (*Math.*) Lines used as elements of reference to determine the position of any point. *v.t.* To correlate, bring into orderly relation. **co-ordina'tion**, *n.*

coot (koot) [Dut. *koet*], *n.* A small black wading-bird; a stupid fellow.

cop (kop), *v.t.* (*slang*) To seize, to arrest; to get, catch. *n.* A policeman.

coparcener (kō-par'sē-nẽr), *n.* A coheir or coheiress.

cope (1) (kōp) [late L. *cāpa*], *n.* An ecclesiastical sleeveless vestment; (*fig.*) the sky; (*Foundry*) the outer covering of a mould. *v.t.* To cover with or as with a cope or coping. **coping**, *n.* The course projecting horizontally on the top of a wall.

cope (2), (kōp), *v.i.* To encounter, to contend successfully (with).

Copernican (kō-pẽr'nik-ăn), *a.* Pertaining to the astronomical system of Copernicus (d. 1543) which has the sun as its centre.

copious (kō'pi-ŭs) [L. *cōpia*, plenty], *a.* Plentiful, abundant; profuse.

copper (kop'ẽr) [A.-S. *copor*, L. *cuprum*], *n.* A red malleable, ductile, tenacious metal; a vessel, coin, etc., made (or formerly made) of copper; (*slang*) a policeman. *a.* Made of or resembling copper. *v.t.* To sheath with copper; to deposit a coating of copper on. **copperplate**, *n.* A polished

plate of copper on which is an engraving; an impression from this; neat, elegant writing.

coppice (kop'is) [O.F. *copeiz*, cut wood], *n.* A small wood of small trees and underwood.

copra (kop'rà) [Malay *koppara*, coco-nut], *n.* The dried kernel of the coco-nut.

copse (kops), *n.* A coppice.

copula (kop'ū-là), *n.* (*pl.* -læ) That which couples; a word which links subject and predicate together.

copulate (kop'ū-lāt) [L. *copulātus*, fastened together], *v.t.* To couple together. *v.i.* To have sexual intercourse. *a.* Joined, connected. **copula'tion**, *n.* **cop'ulative**, *a.* Serving to unite.

copy (kop'i) [F. *copie*], *n.* A transcript or imitation of an original; an original, pattern; matter to be set up in type; a writing exercise; a single example of a book, etc. *v.t.* To transcribe, imitate, make a copy of; to follow as pattern or model. **copyhold**, *n.* A tenure for which the tenant has nothing to show but the copy of the rolls made by the steward of his lord's court; property held by such tenure. **copyholder**, *n.* **copier**, *n.* One who copies or transcribes; an imitator, plagiarist. **copying**, *a.* Pertaining to or used for copying. **copyist**, *n.* **copyright**, *n.* The exclusive right of an author, etc., to his literary or artistic productions.

coquet (kō-ket') [F.], *v.i.* To flirt (with); to trifle in making love. **co'quetry**, *n.* The practices of a coquette; flirtation. **coquette**, *n.* A female flirt; a jilt.

coracle (kor'ăkl) [W. *curwgl*], *n.* A boat made of wickerwork covered with leather or oiled cloth.

coral (kor'ăl) [Gr. *korallion*], *n.* The calcareous structure secreted by Polyps or zoophytes growing in colonies in the sea; the calcareous structure secreted and built up by them; an infant's toy made of coral; the unimpregnated eggs of a lobster (from their colour). *a.* Made of or resembling coral; red, pink. **corallif'erous**, *a.* Producing or containing coral. **cor'alline**, *a.* Of the nature, containing, or resembling coral.

corbel (kor'bĕl) [O.F.], *n.* A bracket projecting from a wall as a support.

cord (kôrd) [Gr. *chordē*, the string of a musical instrument], *n.* Thick string or thin rope; corduroy; a measure for cut wood, 128 cub. ft. *v.t.* To bind with a cord. **corded**, *a.* Bound or made with cords; ribbed or twilled (like corduroy). **cordage**, *n.* A quantity or store of ropes.

Cordelier (kôr-dē-lēr') [F.], *n.* A Franciscan friar, from the knotted rope worn round the waist.

cordial (kôr'di-ăl) [F.], *a.* Proceeding from the heart; sincere, hearty; cheering or comforting the heart. *n.* A sweetened spirit used as a beverage; a medicine to increase the circulation or to raise the spirits. **cordial'ity**, *n.* **cordially**, *adv.*

cordite (kôr'dīt), *n.* A smokeless explosive, prepared in string-like grains.

cordon (kôr'dòn) [F.], *n.* A ribbon or cord worn as a mark of rank, the badge of an order, etc.; a line of men, posts, or ships guarding or blockading a place. **sanitary cordon,** *n.* A line of military posts to cut off communication to a particular area.

corduroy (kôr-dù-roi') [prob. F. *corde du roi,* king's cord], *n.* A stout, ribbed cotton fustian; *(pl.)* corduroy trousers.

cordwain (kôrd'wān) [O.F. *cordoan,* from *Cordoa,* Cordova], *n.* A kind of leather orig. from Cordova, Spain. **cordwainer,** *n.* A shoemaker.

core (kôr) [?], *n.* The heart or inner part of anything, as of an apple, pear, etc.; the pith, gist, essence.

co-respondent (kō-rė-spon'dėnt), *n.* A joint respondent, esp. in a divorce suit.

coriander (kor-i-ăn'dėr) [Gr. *koriannon*], *n.* An umbelliferous plant with aromatic and carminative seeds.

Corinthian (kó-rin'thi-ản), *a.* Of or pertaining to Corinth, Greece, or to the most elaborate and ornate of the three Grecian orders of architecture; licentious, dissipated. *n.* A native of Corinth; a debauchee; a fast man.

cork (kôrk) [?], *n.* The outer layer of bark of the cork-tree, a species of oak; a stopper for a bottle, cask, etc., made of this. *a.* Made of cork. *v.t.* To stop with a cork; to blacken with burnt cork. **corkscrew,** *n.* A screw for drawing corks. *v.t.* To direct or push forward in a wriggling fashion. **corked,** *a.* Stopped with cork; blackened with burnt cork; tasting of the cork.

cormorant (kôr'mó-rảnt) [O.F. *cormerant*], *n.* A voracious sea-bird; *(fig.)* a glutton.

corn (1) (kôrn) [A.-S.], *n.* Grain; the seed of cereals. *v.t.* To preserve and season with salt; to granulate. **corn-chandler,** *n.* A retail dealer in corn, etc. **corn-crake,** *n.* The landrail. **corn-flour,** *n.* The meal of Indian corn ground very fine. **corn-flower,** *n.* A popular name for several plants that grow amongst corn.

corn (2) (kôrn) [L. *cornū,* horn], *n.* A horny excrescence on a toe, etc.

cornea (kôr'nė-á) [L., horny], *n.* The transparent fore-part of the external coat of the eye, through which rays of light pass.

cornelian (kôr-nĕ'li-ản) [F. *cornaline*], *n.* A variety of semi-transparent chalcedony.

corner (kôr'nėr) [L. *cornū,* horn], *n.* An angle; a place enclosed by converging lines or surfaces; a nook; a position of difficulty or embarrassment; a ring, or combination to buy up the supply of a commodity, in order to raise the price; *(Football)* a free kick from a corner. *v.t.* To drive into a corner, or into a position of difficulty; to buy up) a commodity) so as to raise the price. **corner man,** *n.* (*Theat.*) Performer in a nigger-minstrel troupe. **corner-stone,** *n.* The stone uniting two walls; the principal stone.

cornet (kôr'nĕt) [L. *cornū*], *n.* A wind instrument; formerly the lowest commissioned officer in a cavalry regiment; a conical paper bag.

cornice (kôr'nis) [F.], *n.* A moulded horizontal projection crowning a wall, pillar, etc.

cornucopia (kôr-nū-kō'pi-á) [L. *cornu copiæ*], *n.* The horn of plenty; a goat's horn wreathed and filled to overflowing with flowers, fruit, corn, etc., the symbol of plenty and peace.

corny (kôr'ni), *a.* (*Slang*) Crude, unsophisticated; trite, stale.

corolla (kó-rol'á) [L., dim. of *corōna,* a crown], *n.* (*Bot.*) The inner whorl, or petals, of flowers.

corollary (kó-rol'á-ri) [L. *corollārium*], *n.* An additional inference from a proposition; a natural consequence.

corona (kó-rō'ná) [L., a crown], *n.* A disk or halo round the sun or the moon; the zone of radiance round the moon in a total eclipse of the sun.

coronation (kor-ó-nā'shủn), *n.* The act or ceremony of crowning a sovereign.

coroner (kor'ó-nėr) [A.-F. *coruner*], *n.* An officer of the Crown who inquires into cases of sudden or suspicious death.

coronet (kor'ó-nĕt) [O.F.], *n.* A little crown.

corporal (1) (kôr'pó-rảl), *n.* An infantry non-commissioned officer of the lowest grade.

corporal (2) (kôr'pó-rảl) [L. *corporālis* (*corpus,* the body)], *a.* Relating to the body; material, corporeal. **corporal punishment,** *n.* Punishment inflicted on the human body.

corporate (kôr'pó-rảt) [L. *corporātus*], *a.* United in a body and acting as an individual; pertaining to a corporation.

corporation (kôr-pó-rā'shủn), *n.* A corporate body empowered to act as an individual; a commercial company or association; a prominent stomach.

corporeal (kôr-pôr'ê-ảl) [L. *corporeus*], *a.* Having a body; pertaining to the body; material, physical.

corps (kôr), *n.* A body of troops; a division of an army. **corps de ballet,** *n.* A body of dancers in a ballet.

corpse (kôrps) [O.F. *cors,* L. *corpus,* the body], *n.* A dead body, esp. of a human being.

corpulent (kôr'pū-lėnt) [L. *corpulentus* (*corpus,* body)], *a.* Excessively fat or fleshy. **corpulence, -lency,** *n.*

corpuscle (kôr'pủsl) [L. *corpusculum,* dim. of *corpus,* body], *n.* A minute particle of matter; a minute body forming part of an organism; *(pl.)* those which exist free in the blood. **corpus'cular,** *a.*

corral (kó-răl') [Sp.], *n.* An enclosure for cattle or defence, or an enclosure for capturing elephants, etc. *v.t.* To pen up; to form into a corral.

correct (kó-rekt') [L. *rectus,* ruled, ordered], *v.t.* To set right; to remove faults from; to mark errors for rectification; to admonish, punish. *a.* Right, proper, decorous; true, exact, accurate. **correction,** *n.* The act of correcting; that which is substituted for what is wrong; punishment, chastisement; criticism. **correctional,** *a* **corrective,** *a.* Having power or tending to correct. *n.* That which tends to correct or counteract; an antidote. **correctly,** *adv.* **correctness,** *n.* **corrector,** *n.*

correlate (kor'ė-lāt), *v.i.* To be reciprocally

related. *v.t.* To bring into mutual relation. *n.* A correlative. **correla'tion,** *n.* Reciprocal relation; interdependence of forces and phenomena; the mutual relation of structure, functions, etc., in an organism. **correl'ative,** *a.*

correspond (kor-ê-spond') [L. *respondēre*], *v.i.* To be congruous; to fit, suit; to communicate by letters. **correspondence,** *n.* Mutual adaptation; congruity; intercourse by means of letters; the letters which pass. **correspondent,** *a.* Congruous with; answering. *n.* One with whom intercourse is kept up by letters; one who sends news to a journal. **corresponding,** *a.* Suiting; communicating by correspondence.

corridor (kor'i-dôr) [It. *corridore*], *n.* A communicating passage; a covered way.

corrigendum (kor-i-jen'dùm) [L.], *n.* (*pl.* -da) An error needing correction, esp. in a book.

corroborate (kŏ-rob'ô-rāt) [L. *rŏborātus,* strengthened], *v.t.* To strengthen, confirm; to bear additional witness to. **corroborant,** *a.* **corrobora'tion,** *n.* **corrob'orative,** *a.* **corroboratory,** *a.*

corroboree (ko-rob'o-rē) [native name], *n.* Dance of the Australian aborigines.

corrode (kŏ-rōd') [L. *rōdere,* to gnaw], *v.t.* To wear away or consume gradually. *v.i.* To waste away gradually. **corro'sion,** *n.* **corrosive,** *a.*

corrugate (kor'ù-gāt) [L. *rugatus,* wrinkled], *v.t.* To become wrinkled. **corrugated,** *a.* Wrinkled; marked with more or less acute parallel angles; pressed into folds and galvanized (of sheet iron).

corrupt (kŏ-rŭpt') [L. *ruptus,* broken], *a.* Putrid, tainted; unsound; (*fig.*) depraved; perverted by bribery; not genuine. *v.t.* To infect, make impure or unwholesome; (*fig.*) to vitiate; to debauch, seduce; to bribe. *v.i.* To become corrupt. **corrupter,** *n.* **corruptibil'ity,** *n.* **corruptible,** *a.* Liable to corruption. **corruption,** *n.* The act of corrupting or state of being corrupt; decomposition, putrefaction; putrid matter; (*fig.*) moral deterioration; bribery; a corrupt reading or version. **corruptive,** *a.* **corruptly.** *adv.* **corruptness,** *n.*

corsage (kôr'sáj) [O.F.], *n.* A bodice.

corsair (kôr'sâr) [F.], *n.* A pirate.

corset (kôr'sèt) [F.], *n.* A close-fitting, stiffened garment, worn by women to give shape to the body; stays.

corslet (kôrs'lèt) [F.], *n.* Body armour; a light cuirass.

cortège (kôr'tāzh) [F.], *n.* A train of attendants.

coruscate (kor'ús-kāt) [L. *coruscātus*], *v.i.* To glitter in flashes. **corusca'tion,** *n.*

corvette (kôr-vet') [F.], *n.* A flush-decked, full-rigged ship of war; (*Navy*) a small, fast escort vessel armed with anti-submarine devices.

cosmetic (kŏz-met'ik) [F. *cosmetique,* Gr. *kosmein,* to adorn], *a.* Beautifying. *n.* A preparation for improving the skin.

cosmic (koz'mik), *a.* Pertaining to the universe; derived from some part of the solar system other than the earth;

of inconceivably long duration. **cosmical,** *a.* Rising or setting with the sun.

cosmo- [Gr. *kosmos,* the universe], *comb. form.* Pertaining to the universe.

cosmogony (kŏz-mog'ô-ni), *n.* A theory or investigation respecting the origin of the world. **cosmog'onist,** *n.*

cosmography (kŏz-mog'rà-fi), *n.* A description or delineation of the features of the universe.

cosmology (kŏz-mol'ô-ji), *n.* The science which investigates the laws of the universe as an ordered whole; the branch of metaphysics dealing with the relation of the universe to the mind.

cosmonaut (koz -mō-nawt), *n.* An astronaut.

cosmopolitan (koz-mô-pol'i-tàn) [Gr. *politēs,* a citizen], *a.* Common to all the world; at home in any part of the world; free from national prejudices. *n.* A cosmopolite. **cosmopolitanism,** *n.* **cosmopolite** (kŏz-mop'ô-līt), *n.* One who is at home in any part of the world.

cosmos (koz'mos) [Gr.], *n.* The universe regarded as an ordered system; an ordered system of knowledge.

cosset (kos'ét) [?], *v.t.* To pet, pamper.

cost (kost) [O.F. *coster,* L. *constāre*], *v.i.* To require as the price; to cause the expenditure of; to result in the loss of or the infliction of. *n.* The price paid for a thing; expense; penalty, loss; pain, trouble; (*pl.*) expenses of a lawsuit. **costly,** *a.* Of high price. **costliness,** *n.*

costal (kŏ'stàl) [L.], *a.* Pertaining to the ribs.

costard (kos'tàrd) [?], *n.* A large apple.

coster, costermonger (kos'tèr-mùng'gèr), *n.* A seller of fruit, vegetables, etc., from a barrow.

costive (kos'tiv) [O.F. *costivé*], *a.* With confined bowels, failing motion of the bowels.

costume (kŏs-tūm') [F.], *n.* Dress; the customary mode of dressing at a particular time or in a country; fancy dress. **costumier** (kos-tū'mi-ér), *n.* A maker or dealer in costumes.

cosy (kŏ'zi) [?], *a.* Comfortable; snug. *n.* A padded covering for a teapot put on it to retain the heat. **cosiness,** *n.*

cot (1) (kot) [A.-S.], *n.* A small house, hut; a shelter for beasts.

cot (2) (kot) [Hind. *khāt*], *n.* A light bedstead; a crib; a child's bedstead; a swing bed for invalids, etc.

cote (kōt), *n.* A sheepfold; a shelter.

coterie (kŏ'tèr-i) [F.], *n.* An exclusive circle of people; a clique.

cotillion (kŏ-til'yón) [F., a petticoat], *n.* A dance for four or eight persons.

cottage (kot'áj), *n.* A small house, a cot; a small country or suburban residence. **cottage piano,** *n.* A small upright piano. **cottager,** *n.* One who lives in a cottage.

cottar (kot'àr), *n.* A peasant who pays rent for his cottage by his labour.

cotter (kot'ér) *n.* (*Eng.*) A key wedge or bolt for holding part of a machine in place.

cotton (kotn) [Arab. *qutun*], *n.* A downy substance, resembling wool, growing in the fruit of the cotton-plant, used for making thread, cloth, etc.; thread or cloth made from this. *v.i.* To agree well (with), become attached (to). **cotton-wool,** *n.* Cotton in its raw state, used as wadding, etc.

couch (kouch) [F. *coucher*], *v.t.* To cause to lie, to lay (oneself) down; to express in words, to imply; to set (a spear) in rest; to operate upon for cataract. *v.i.* To lie down, to rest. *n.* A place of rest; a lounge or sofa. **couch-grass,** *n.* A grass with long, creeping roots.

cougar (koo´gàr) [Guarani], *n.* The puma.

cough (kawf) [A.-S. *cohhetan*], *n.* A convulsive effort, attended with noise, to expel irritating matter from the lungs. *v.t.* To drive from the lungs by a cough. *v.i.* To expel air from the lungs in a convulsive and noisy manner.

coulter (kōl´tér) [A.-S. *culter*], *n.* The iron blade fixed in front of the share in a plough.

council (koun´sil) [F. *concile*, L. *concilium*], *n.* Persons met together for deliberation or advice or as advisers to a sovereign, etc.; the governing body of a University. **council-board,** *n.* The table round which a council deliberates; a council, esp. when in session. **councillor,** *n.* A member of a council. **councillorship,** *n.*

counsel (koun´sél) [O.F. *conseil*], *n.* A consultation; advice; opinion given after deliberation; a barrister. *v.t.* To give advice to; to advise. **counsellor,** *n.*

count (1) (kount) [O.F. *conter*], *v.t.* To reckon up in numbers, compute, enumerate; to esteem. *v.i.* To possess a certain value; to depend or rely (upon). *n.* A reckoning or numbering; the sum (of); a statement of plaintiff's case; one of several charges in an indictment. **countable,** *a.* **counting-house,** *n.* An office appropriated to the business of keeping accounts, etc. **countless,** *a.* Innumerable; beyond calculation.

count (2) (kount) [O.F. *conte*, L. *comes*, companion], *n.* A foreign title of rank corresponding to earl. **countship,** *n.*

countenance (koun´té-náns) [O.F. *contenance*], *n.* The face; air, look, or expression; favour, support; estimation. *v.t.* To sanction, permit; to abet, encourage.

counter (1) (koun´tér) [A.-F. *counteour*], *n.* One who or that which counts; a calculator; a piece of metal, ivory, etc., used for reckoning, as in games; a bench on which money is counted, or across which goods are sold.

counter (2) (kounter) [F. *contre*, L. *contra*, against], *n.* The opposite, the contrary; the curved part of a ship's stern. *a.* Contrary, opposed; opposing; duplicate. *adv.* In the opposite direction; wrongly; contrarily. *v.* To oppose, to return a blow by dealing another one.

counteract (koun-tér-ăkt´), *v.t.* To act in opposition to; to neutralize.

counterbalance (koun-tér-băl´ans), *v.t.* To weigh against or oppose with equal effect. *n.* An equal weight or force acting in opposition.

counterblast (koun´tér-blast), *n.* An argument or statement in opposition.

countercharge (koun´tér-charj), *n.* A

charge in opposition to another; a counter-claim.

counterfeit (koun´tér-fēt) [O.F. *contrefait*], *v.t.* To imitate, mimic, to copy and pass off as genuine; to coin, to imitate in base metal; to simulate. *a.* Made in imitation with intent to be passed off as genuine; forged. *n.* An impostor; a counterfeit thing. **counterfeiter,** *n.*

counterfoil (koun´tér-foil), *n.* The counterpart of a cheque, receipt, or other document, retained by the giver.

countermand (koun-tér-mand´) [CONTRA, L. *mandāre*, to command], *v.t.* To revoke, annul; to recall. *n.* An order contrary to or revoking a previous order.

countermarch (koun´tér-march), *v.* To march or cause to march in an opposite direction.

countermine (koun´tér-mīn), *n.* A gallery or mine to intercept or frustrate one made by the enemy; a stratagem to frustrate any project. *v.* To oppose by countermine.

counterpane (koun´tér-pān) [earlier *counterpoint*, O.F. *contrepointe*, stitched quilt], *n.* A coverlet, a quilt.

counterpart (koun´tér-part), *n.* A corresponding part; a duplicate; one who is exactly like another.

counterplot (koun´tér-plot), *v.t.* To frustrate by another plot. *n.* A plot to defeat another plot.

counterpoint (koun´tér-point) [F. *contrepoint*], *n.* A melodious part or combination of parts written to accompany a melody; the art of constructing harmonious parts, or of harmonious composition.

counterpoise (koun´tér-poiz), *n.* A weight in opposition and equal to another; a counterbalancing force; equilibrium. *v.t.* To oppose with an equal weight, force, power, or influence.

countersign (koun´tér-sīn), *v.t.* To attest by an additional signature; to ratify. *n.* A secret word or sign by which one may pass a sentry, or by which the members of an association may recognize each other.

countersink (koun´tér-sink), *v.t.* To chamfer a hole for a screw or bolt head; to sink (the head of a screw, etc.) into such a hole.

counter-tenor, *n.* (*Mus.*) A man's voice higher than tenor.

countervail (koun-tér-văl´) [O.F. *contrevail*], *v.t.* To act against with equal effect or power; to counterbalance. *v.i.* To be of equal weight, power, or influence on the opposite side.

countess (koun´tes), *n.* The wife of a count or of an earl; a lady holding this rank in her own right.

countrified (kŭn-tri-fīd) [p.p.], *a.* Rustic in manners or appearance.

country (kŭn´tri) [O.F. *cuntrée*, late L. *contrāta*, a region over against, *contrā*, against], *n.* A region or state, or its inhabitants; one's native land; the rural part as distinct from towns; the rest of a land as distinguished from the capital. *a.* Pertaining to the country; rural. **country-dance,** *n.* A dance in which partners are ranged in lines opposite to each other. **countryman**, *n.* One who lives in a rural district; an inhabitant of any particular region; a native of the same country as another. **countrywoman**, *n.* **countryside**, *n.* A rural district; the inhabitants of this.

county (koun'ti) [L. *comitātus*], *n.* A shire; a division of land for administrative, judical, and political purposes. *a.* Pertaining to a county. **county council**, *n.* Board administering the civil affairs of a county. **county court**, *n.* A local court for the recovery of small debts. **county town**, *n.* The chief town of any county.

coup (koo) [F.], *n.* A telling or decisive blow; a victory, a successful move. **coup d'état** (-dā-ta'), *n.* A sudden and violent change of government, esp. of a revolutionary nature. **coup de grâce** (-dĕ-gras'), *n.* The finishing stroke.

coupé (koo'pā) [F.], *n.* A four-wheeled close carriage; a railway compartment with a seat on one side only; (*Motor*) a two-seater car with an enclosed body.

couple (kŭpl) [O.F. *cople*], *n.* Two of the same kind considered together; a leash; a pair; a betrothed or married pair. *v.t.* To connect or fasten together; to unite in marriage. **couplet**, *n.* Two lines of running verse. **coupling**, *n.* The action of the verb; a device for connecting railway carriages, etc., together.

coupon (koo'pon) [F., a piece cut off], *n.* A detachable certificate for the payment of interest on bonds; a detachable ticket or certificate of various kinds.

courage (kŭr'áj) [O.F. *corage*], *n.* Bravery, intrepidity. **courageous** (kŭ-rā'jŭs), *a.*

courier (kur'i-ér) [M.E. *corour*, O.F. *coreor*, from L. *currere*, to run], *n.* An express messenger; a travelling servant who makes all arrangements beforehand.

course (kôrs) [O.F. *cours*, as prec.], *n.* A race; passage from one place to another; the track passed over; the direction of a stream; the ground on which a race is run; a chase after a hare; career; a series; one of a series of dishes served at a meal; mode of procedure; a row of laid bricks. *v.t.* To run after, pursue; to traverse. *v.i.* To chase hares with greyhounds; to run or move quickly; to circulate (as the blood). **of course:** By consequence, naturally. **courser**, *n.* A swift horse, a war-horse; one who practises coursing; a dog used in coursing. **coursing**, *n.* The sport of hunting hares with greyhounds.

court (kôrt) [O.F. *cort*, L. *cohors*, an enclosure], *n.* A place enclosed by buildings; a narrow street; a quadrangle; an enclosed or marked out piece of ground used for games; the residence or retinue of a sovereign; the sovereign and advisers regarded as the ruling power; a state reception; a body having jurisdiction; the chamber in which justice is administered; the judges or persons assembled to hear any cause; deferential attention paid to secure favour or regard. *v.t.* To seek the favour of; to pay court to; to seek the affections of, to woo. *v.i.* To make love. **courtcard**, *n.* The king, queen, or knave

in any suit in a pack of cards. **courthouse**, *n.* A building containing rooms used by any court. **court-martial**, *n.* A court for the trial of naval or military offenders. *v.t.* To try by court-martial. **courtyard**, *n.* An area round or within a large building.

courteous (kĕr'tĕ-ŭs) [O.F. *cortois*], *a.* Having court-like manners, polite, affable, considerate. *adv.* **courteously**, *n.*

courtesan, **-zan** (kôr-tĕ-zăn') [F. *courtisane*], *n.* A prostitute.

courtesy (kĕr'tĕ-si) [O.F. *cortesie*], *n.* Courteousness, politeness; favour, as opposed to right; an act of civility.

courtier (kôr'ti-ér) [O.F. *cortoier*], *n.* One who is a frequenter at the court of a prince.

courtly (kôrt'li), *a.* Of or pertaining to a court; elegant, polite; obsequious.

courtship (kôrt'ship), *n.* The act of soliciting in marriage.

cousin (kŭzn) [F.], *n.* The child of an uncle or aunt; a kinsman.

cove (1) (kōv) [A.-S. *cofa*, a chamber], *n.* A small creek or bay; a sheltered recess.

cove (2) (kōv), *n.* A man, a fellow, a chap.

covenant (kŭv'é-nánt) [O.F.], *n.* An agreement on certain terms; a compact; a document containing this. *v.i.* To enter into a covenant. **covenanted**, *a.* Secured by or held under a covenant; bound by a covenant. **covenanter**, *n.* One who enters into a covenant; an adherent of the Scottish National Covenant of 1638 or the Solemn League and Covenant of 1643.

cover (kŭv'ér) [O.F. *cuvrir*], *v.t.* To overlay; to overspread with something; to protect, conceal, cloak, screen; to include; to be enough to defray; to extend over; to hold under aim with a fire-arm. *n.* Anything which covers or hides; a lid; the outside of a book; an envelope; pretence, pretext; shelter, protection; the articles for one person at table; a thicket, woods which conceal game; sufficient funds to meet a liability, etc. **covering**, *n.*

coverlet (kŭv'ér-lĕt), *n.* A bed covering; counterpane.

covert (kŭv'ert), *a.* Covered; disguised; private; under protection. *n.* A shelter; a cover for game. **covertly**, *adv.* **coverture**, *n.* A hiding-place; secrecy; the state of a married woman, as under the authority of her husband.

covet (kŭv'et) [A.-F. and O.F. *coveiter*], *v.t.* To desire (something unlawful) inordinately; to long for. *v.i.* To have an inordinate desire. **covetous**, *a.* **covetously**, *adv.* **covetousness**, *n.*

covey (kŭv'i) [F., hatched], *n.* A brood or small flock of birds, esp. partridges.

cow (1) (kou) [A.-S. *cu*], *n.* (*pl.* **cows**, *kine) The female of any bovine species, esp. of the domesticated bull; a female elephant or cetacean. **cowboy**, *n.* One who tends cattle, esp. on a ranch. **cowherd**, *n.* One who tends cattle. **cowpuncher**, *n.* (*Am.*) A cowboy.

cow (2) (kou) [?], *v.t.* To intimidate, deprive of spirit or courage; to daunt. **cowed**, *a.*

coward (kou'ård) [O.F. *coart*], *n.* A poltroon; one without courage. *a.* Timid, pusillanimous. **cowardice,** *n.* cowardliness, *n.*

cower (kou'ér) [?], *v.i.* To stoop, bend, crouch; to shrink or quail through fear.

cowl (koul) [A.-S. *cugele*, L. *cucullus*, a hood], *n.* A hooded garment, esp. one worn by a monk; a chimney-top which moves with the wind.

cowry (kou'ri) [Hind. *kawri*], *n.* A small shell used as money in parts of S. Asia and Africa.

cowslip (kou'slip) [A.-S. *cū-slyppe*, cowdung], *n.* A species of primrose with fragrant flowers, growing in pastures.

coxcomb (koks'kōm), *n.* A conceited person, a fop, dandy. coxcombry, *n.*

coxswain (koksn, kok'swān), *n.* One who steers, esp. in a race; the petty officer in charge of a boat.

coy (koi) [F.], *a.* Shrinking from familiarity; shy, reserved; coquettish. coyly, *adv.* coyness, *n.*

coypu (koi-poo'), *n.* An aquatic rodent valued for its fur, the nutria.

cozen (kŭzn) [?], *v.i.* To deceive, cheat.

crab (krăb) [A.-S. *crabba*], *n.* A marine crustacean; the zodiacal constellation Cancer; a sour, wild apple, crab-apple; a peevish, morose person. *v.i.* To claw, scratch; to criticize savagely, pull to pieces. crabbed (krăb'ĕd), *a.* Peevish, morose; cramped, undecipherable.

crack (krăk) [A.-S. *cracian*], *v.i.* To break without entire separation; to cause to give a sharp, sudden noise; to say smartly or sententiously. *v.i.* To break partially asunder; to utter a loud sharp sound; to boast, brag; to change (of voices at puberty); to chat. *n.* A sudden and partial separation of parts; a chink, fissure, or opening; a sharp sudden sound; a smart blow; a chat. *a.* Having qualities to be boasted of; superior. **crack-brained,** *a.* Crazy. cracked, *a.* Half-witted; insane. cracker, *n.* One who or that which cracks: a firework; a thin biscuit; a bonbon that gives a report on being torn open.

crackle (krăkl), *v.i.* To make short sharp cracking noises. *n.* A rapid succession of slight, sharp noises like cracks. crackling, *a.* Making short, sharp, frequent cracks. *n.* The browned scored skin of roast pork.

cracknel (krăk'nĕl) [F. *craquelin*], *n.* A hard, brittle biscuit.

-cracy [Gr. *-kratia*, from *kratos*, power], *suf.* Rule of; influential or dominant by means of; as in *aristocracy*, *democracy*.

cradle (krădl) [A.-S. *cradol*], *n.* A baby's cot, usu. rocking or swinging; (*fig.*) place of early nurture; a frame to protect a wounded limb in bed, to support a vessel out of water, etc.; (*Mining*) a gold-washing machine; the frame-work for an arch, etc. *v.i.* To lay or rock in a cradle.

craft (kraft) [A.-S. *cræft*], *n.* Skill; cunning, deceit; a handicraft, occupation, trade, or its members; a vessel (*pl. unchanged*). craftsman, *n.* A skilled artisan. craftsmanship, *n.* crafty, *a.* Artful, sly, wily. craftiness, *n.*

crag (krăg) [Gael. *creag*], *n.* A rugged or precipitous rock; shelly deposits.

cram (krăm) [A.-S. *crammian*], *v.i.* To stuff or press in so as to fill to overflowing; to coach hurriedly for examination. *v.i.* To eat greedily, to stuff oneself; to get up a subject hastily and superficially.

crambo (krăm'bō) [L. *crambē* (*repetita*), cabbage (served up again)], *n.* A game in which one selects a word to which another finds a rhyme.

cramp (krămp) [O.F. *crampe*], *n.* A spasmodic contraction of a limb or muscle; a cramp-iron, clamp. *v.i.* To affect with cramp; to confine closely; to hinder, restrain; to fasten with a cramp-iron. *a.* Cramped, contracted. cramp-iron, *n.* An iron with bent ends binding two stones together in a course.

cranberry (krăn'bĕr-i) [L.G. *kraanbere*], *n.* The bitter marsh whortleberry.

crane (krān) [A.-S. *cran*], *n.* A migratory wading bird with long neck and legs; a machine for hoisting heavy weights; a siphon for drawing liquors from a cask, for supplying a locomotive with water, etc. *v.i.* To stretch out the neck like a crane.

cranio- [Gr. *kranion*, the skull], *comb. form.* Pertaining to the skull. craniol'ogy, *n.* The scientific study of crania.

cranium (krā'ni-ŭm), *n.* (*pl. -ia*) The skull, esp. the part enclosing the brain.

crank (krăngk) [A.-S. *cranc*, past of *crincan*, to be bent up], *n.* An apparatus for converting rotary into reciprocating motion, or the converse; an elbow-shaped brace; a caprice, whim; a crotchety person, an eccentric; a crook, a turn. *a.* (*Naut.*) Liable to upset; shaky, liable to break down.

cranky (krăng'ki), *a.* Irritable, whimsical; full of twists; shaky, sickly; (*Naut.*) liable to upset.

cranny (krăn'i) [?], *n.* A crevice, chink; a corner, hole, crannied, *a.*

crape (krāp) [F., *crêpe*], *n.* A gauzy fabric with a crisped, frizzly surface, usually dyed black, used for mourning.

crapulent (krăp'ū-lĕnt) [L. *crāpulentus*, drunken], *a.* Surfeited, drunken. crapulence, *n.* crapulous, *a.*

crash (krăsh), *v.i.* To break to pieces or dash together violently. *v.i.* To make a loud smashing noise; (*Av.*) to fall suddenly to the ground; (*slang*) to go to a party uninvited. *n.* A violent smash or the noise of this; a sudden collapse, bankruptcy; a coarse linen cloth.

crass (krăs) [L. *crassus*], *a.* Thick, coarse, gross, stupid, obtuse. crassness, *n.*

crate (krāt) [L. *crātes*], *n.* A large wicker case for packing crockery; an open framework of wood for packing.

crater (krā'tér) [Gr. *kratēr*, a bowl], *n.* The mouth of a volcano; a funnel-shaped cavity; a cavity formed by a mine or shell exploding.

cravat (krā-văt') [F. *cravate*], *n.* A neckcloth for men; a tie.

crave (krāv) [A.-S. *crafian*], *v.i.* To ask for earnestly and submissively; to long for.

craven (krā'vĕn) [M.E. *crauant*], *n.* A coward, recreant, a dastard. *a.* Cowardly, faint-hearted. **cravenly**, *adv.*

crawl (krawl) [Scand.], *v.i.* To move slowly along the ground; to creep; to assume an abject manner; to get on by meanness and servility. *n.* The act of crawling. **crawler**, *n.*

crayfish (krā'fish) [M.E. *crevice*], *n.* The freshwater lobster; the marine spiny lobster.

crayon (krā'ŏn) [F.], *n.* A pencil of coloured chalk or similar material; a drawing made with crayons.

craze (krāz) [Scand.], *v.t.* To derange the intellect; to make flaws in (china, etc.). *n.* A mania, an extravagant enthusiasm, a rage. **crazed**, *a.* Deranged in intellect. **crazy**, *a.* Broken down, unsound, shaky; broken-witted, deranged. **crazy paving**, *n.* A pavement of irregularly-shaped paving stones. **crazily**, *adv.*

creak (krēk) *v.i.* To make a continued grating noise.

cream (krēm) [F. *crème*], *n.* The rich, oily part of milk which rises and collects on the surface; something prepared from this; the best part of anything.

crease (krēs) [?], *n.* A line or mark made by folding or doubling; (*Cricket*) a line marking the position of bowler and batsman. *v.t.* To make a crease or mark in. *v.i.* To become creased or wrinkled.

create (krē-āt') [L. *creātus*], *v.t.* To cause to exist; to produce, originate; to invest with an office or dignity; (*colloq.*) to make a scene; to scream. **creative**, *a.*

creation (krē-ā'shŭn) [L. *creātio*], *n.* The act of creating, esp. creating the world; the universe, all created things; the act of investing with a new character or position; a production of art, craft, or intellect. **creator**, *n.* One who or that which creates; the Maker of the Universe.

creature (krē'chĕr), *n.* That which is created; a living being; one who owes his rise or fortune to another; a mere tool. *a.* Of or pertaining to the body.

crèche (krāsh) [F.], *n.* A public nursery in which the children are left while their parents are at work.

credence (krē'dĕns) [L. *crēdere*, to believe], *n.* Credit, reliance, confidence; that which gives a claim to confidence. **creden'tial**, *n.* Anything which gives a title to confidence; (*pl.*) documents accrediting a person. **credible**, *a.* **credibil'ity**, *n.*

credit (kred'it) [F. *crédit*, as prec.], *n.* Belief, trust, faith; a reputation inspiring confidence, esp. a reputation for solvency; anything due to any person; time given for payment; the side of an account in which payment is entered; an entry on this side. *v.t.* To believe; to set to the credit of or give credit for; to ascribe to. **creditable**, *a.* Bringing credit or honour. **creditably**, *adv.* **creditor**, *n.* One to whom a debt is due.

credulous (kred'ū-lŭs) [L. *crēdulus*], *a.* Disposed to believe, esp. without sufficient evidence. **credu'lity**, *n.*

creed (krēd) [L. *crēdo*, I believe], *n.* A summary of the articles of religious belief; a system of religious belief.

creek (krēk) [?], *n.* A small inlet on the coast; a backwater or arm of a river.

creel (krēl) [?], *n.* An osier basket.

creep (krēp) [A.-S. *créopan*], *v.i.* To crawl along as a serpent; to grow along, as a creeping plant; to move slowly, stealthily, or with timidity; to behave with servility; to have a sensation of shivering or shrinking. *n.* Creeping; a low arch or passage for animals; (*pl.*) a feeling of shrinking horror. **creeper**, *n.* One who or that which creeps or crawls; a plant with a creeping stem; a grapnel used in dragging. **creepy**, *a.* Having or causing the sensation of creeping of the flesh.

cremate (krĕ-māt') [L. *cremātus*, burnt], *v.t.* To dispose of a corpse by burning. **cremation**, *n.* **cremator'ium**, *n.* A place where bodies are cremated.

creole (krē'ōl) [Sp. *criollo*], *n.* One born of European parentage in the West Indies or Spanish America.

creosote (krē'ŏ-sōt) [Gr. *kreas*, flesh, *sōtēr*, saviour], *n.* An oily, colourless liquid with strong antiseptic properties.

crepuscular (krĕ-pŭs'kū-lár) [L. *crepusculum*, twilight], *a.* Pertaining to or connected with twilight; indistinct, obscure.

crescendo (krĕ-shen'dō) [It., growing], *n.* (*Mus.*) A gradual increase in the force of sound. *adv.* With increasing volume.

crescent (kre'sĕnt) [L. *crēscens -ntem*, growing], *a.* Shaped like the young moon. *n.* The increasing moon in her first quarter; a figure like the new moon, esp. as the badge of Turkey; Mohammedanism; a row of buildings in this form.

cress (kres) [A.-S. *cærse*], *n.* Various plants with a pungent taste.

cresset (kres'ĕt) [O.F.], *n.* An iron frame to contain a fire for a beacon.

crest (krest) [O.F. *criste*, L. *cresta*], *n.* A plume or tuft on the head of an animal, esp. a bird; a tuft of feathers, esp. on a helmet; a family or personal device placed above the shield in a coat-of-arms; the summit of a mountain, ridge, or a wave. **crestfallen**, *a.* Dispirited, abashed.

cretin (krē'tin) [F.], *n.* A person of defective mental development or arrested growth due to unhealthy thyroid gland. **cretinism**, *n.*

cretonne (kret'ŏn) [F.], *n.* A cotton fabric with pictorial patterns.

crevasse (krĕ-văs') [F.], *n.* A deep fissure in a glacier.

crevice (krev'is) [L. *crepāre*, to crackle, burst], *n.* A crack, cleft, fissure.

crew (kroo) [O.F. *creue*], *n.* The seamen manning a ship or boat; a number of associated persons; a gang, mob.

crewel (kroo'ĕl) [?], *n.* Fine two-threaded worsted.

crib (krib) [A.-S.], *n.* A child's cot; a manger; a stall for cattle; a hovel; a wicker salmon-trap; cribbage; a plagiarism; a key to a foreign literary work; a situation, berth. *v.t.* To confine; to steal, appropriate; to use a translation.

cribbage (krib′áj), *n.* A game at cards for two, three, or four players.

crick (krik) [?], *n.* A spasmodic affection from stiffness, esp. of the neck or back.

cricket (1) (krik′ét) [O.F. *criquer*, to creak], *n.* An insect making a chirping noise.

cricket (2) (krik′ét) [?], *n.* An open-air game played by two sides of eleven each, with bats, a ball, and wickets. *v.i.* To play cricket. **cricketer,** *n.* **not cricket:** not fair, not straightforward.

crier (kri′ér), *n.* One who cries or proclaims, esp. an official who publicly proclaims sales, lost articles, etc.

crime (krīm) [L. *crimen*], *n.* An act contrary to law, human or divine; any act of wickedness; wrong-doing, sin. **criminal** (krim′i-nál), *a.* Of the nature of a crime; contrary to law; guilty of or tainted with crime. *n.* One guilty of a crime; a convict. **criminal′ity,** *n.* **criminally,** *adv.* **criminate,** *v.t.* To accuse or prove guilty of a crime. **crimina′tion,** *n.* Accusation. **crim′inative,** *a.* **criminatory,** *a.* **criminol′ogy,** *n.* The science of crime.

crimp (krimp) [?], *v.t.* To curl; to frill, corrugate, crease; to cause to become crisp and firm; to shape or mould; to decoy into the military or naval service. *n.* One who decoys men into the army or navy; a disreputable agent.

crimson (crim′zón) [Arab. *qirmazī*], *n.* A deep red colour. *a.* Of this colour.

cringe (krinj) [M.E. *cringan,* to sink], *v.i.* To bend humbly; to crouch, fawn, pay servile court. *n.* An obsequious action.

cringle (kring′gel) [L.G. *kringel,* a little ring], *n.* An iron ring on the bolt-rope of a sail.

crinkle (kringk′él) [A.-S. *crinkan*], *n.* A wrinkle, short bend or turn. **crinkly,** *a.*

crinoline (krin′ò-lin) [F., L. *crinis,* hair, *linum,* flax], *n.* A stiff fabric of horse-hair; a stiff petticoat, esp. of this material.

cripple (kripl) [A.-S. *crypel* (*crēopan,* to creep)], *n.* A lame person. *v.t.* To make lame; to deprive of the power of action.

crisis (kri′sis) [G. *krisis,* a decision], *n.* (*pl.* -ses) The turning-point, esp. of a disease; a momentous juncture.

crisp (krisp) [A.-S., L. *crispus,* curled], *a.* Firm but brittle; fresh-looking, brisk; curt. *v.t.* To curl, wrinkle, ripple. *v.i.* To become curly or wrinkly.

criterion (kri-tēr′i-ón), *n.* (*pl.* -ia) A standard by which a thing is or can be judged.

critic (krit′ik) [Gr. *kritikos*], *n.* One skilled in judging of literary or artistic merit; a reviewer; a censurer, caviller. **critical,** *a.* criticism (krit′is-izm), The act of judging, esp. literary or artistic works; a critical essay or opinion; the work of criticizing. **criticize,** *v.t.* To examine critically and deliver an opinion upon; to censure; *v.i.* To play the critic. **critique** (kri-tēk′), *n.* A critical essay or judgment.

croak (krōk), *v.i.* To make a hoarse low sound in the throat, as a frog or raven; to grumble, forbode evil. *v.t.* To utter in a low hoarse voice. *n.* The sound made by a frog or raven. **croaker,** *n.*

crochet (krō′shā) [F., a small hook], *n.* A kind of knitting performed with a hooked needle. *v.* To knit or make in crochet.

crock (krok) [A.-S. *crocca*], *n.* An earthenware pot, pitcher, jar, etc.; soot from combustion on pots or kettles, etc.; a broken-down horse or machine; an invalid **crockery,** *n.* Earthenware vessels.

crocodile (krok′ò-dīl) [Gr. *krokodeilos*], *n.* A large amphibian scaly-backed reptile. **crocodile tears:** Hypocritical tears.

crocus (krō′kŭs) [Gr. *krokos*], *n.* A genus of bulbous plants.

croft (kroft) [A.-S.], *n.* A piece of enclosed ground adjoining a house; a small farm. **crofter,** *n.* One who farms a croft.

cromlech (krom′lek) [W., *crom,* bent, *llech,* stone], *n.* A prehistoric structure in which a large flat stone rests horizontally on upright ones.

crone (krōn) [O.F. *carogne,* an old woman], *n.* An old ewe; an old woman.

crony (krō′ni) [?], *n.* An intimate friend.

crook (kruk) [O. Teut.], *n.* A bent or curved instrument; a shepherd's or bishop's staff; a curve, meander; a swindler. *v.t.* To make crooked or curved; to pervert. *v.i.* To be bent or crooked. **crooked** (kruk′éd), *a.* Bent, curved; twisting; deformed; not straight-forward.

croon (kroon) [imit.], *v.i.* To sing in a low voice.

crop (krop) [A.-S.], *n.* The stomach of a fowl; the highest part; a whipstock with loop instead of lash; that which is cut or gathered; the harvest yield; an entire hide; various cuts of meat; the outcrop of a lode, a seam, or a stratum of rock. *v.t.* To cut off the ends of; to mow, reap; to gather; to cultivate.

croquet (krō′kā) [O.F. *croket*], *n.* A game played on a lawn with balls and mallets.

crosier (krō′zhyér) [O.F. *crossier*], *n.* The pastoral staff of a bishop or abbot.

cross (1) (kraws, kros) [L. *crux crucis*], *n.* An ancient instrument of torture made of two pieces of timber set transversely; a monument, staff, sign, mark, etc., in this form; the Christian religion, Christianity; the mixture of two distinct stocks, and the animal resulting from such mixture; anything that thwarts or obstructs; trouble, affliction; a preconcerted fraud. *a.* Transverse, oblique, lateral; intersecting; adverse, contrary; peevish; ill-gotten. **cross-bench,** *n.* (*Pol.*) One of the benches in Parliament for members independent of party. **crossbow,** *n.* An ancient weapon for shooting. **cross-breed,** *n.* A breed produced by a male and female of different strains or varieties; a hybrid. **cross-examine,** *v.t.* To examine systematically for the purpose of eliciting facts not brought out in direct examination or for confirming or contradicting the direct evidence. **cross-grained,** *a.* Having the grain or fibres running across or irregular; perverse, peevish; intractable. **cross-patch,** *n.* A cross, ill-tempered person. **cross-purpose,** *n.* A contrary purpose; contradiction, misunderstanding. **cross-**

road, *n.* A road that crosses another or connects two others; a by-way. **cross-stitch,** *n.* A kind of stitch crossing others in series. **cross-trees,** *n.pl.* Timbers on the top of masts to support the rigging of the mast above.

cross (2), *v.t.* To draw a line across; to cancel by cross lines; to make the sign of the cross; to pass across, traverse; to intersect; to pass in front of; to meet and pass; to bestride; to cause to inter-breed; to thwart, counteract; to be inconsistent with. *v.i.* To lie, pass, or be across or over something; to be incon-sistent; to interbreed. **crossing,** *n.* The action of the verb; a place of crossing; contradiction, opposition. **crossly,** *adv.* In an ill-humoured manner. **crossness,** *n.*

crotch (kroch) [?], *n.* A forking.

crotchet (kroch'ét) [F. *crochet,* a little hook], *n.* A peculiar turn of mind; a whimsical fancy; (*Mus.*) a note, the double of a quaver. **crotchety,** *a.* Irritable.

crouch (krouch) [?], *v.i.* To bend low; to lie close to the ground; to cringe, fawn.

croup (1) (kroop) [F. *croupe*], *n.* The rump, buttocks (esp. of a horse); the part behind the saddle.

croup (2) (kroop), *n.* A disease of the throat characterized by hoarse coughing and difficulty of breathing, common in infancy.

croupier (kroo'pér) [F.], *n.* One who superintends at a gaming-table.

crow (krō) [A.-S. *cráwe, crawan,* to crow], *n.* A large black bird, the hooded crow, the carrion crow; the cry of a cock; the cry of delight of an infant. *v.i.* (*past* crew, crowed) To make a loud cry like a cock; to make a cry of delight like an infant; to exult; to brag, boast. *v.t.* To proclaim by crowing. **crowbar,** *n.* A bar of iron bent at one end (like a crow's beak) and used as a lever. **crow's nest,** *n.* (*Naut.*) Station for the look-out man on the mast.

crowd (kroud) [A.-S. *crúdan*], *v.t.* To press or squeeze closely together; to throng or press upon. *v.i.* To throng, swarm; to collect in crowds. *n.* A number of per-sons or things collected closely and con-fusedly together; the mob, the populace.

crown (kroun) [A.-F. *coroune,* L. *coróna*], *n.* A garland of honour worn on the head; the ornamental circlet worn on the head by emperors, kings, etc., as a badge of sovereignty; royal power; the sovereign; a five-shilling piece; a foreign coin of various values; the top of the head, a hat, a mountain, arch, cornice, road, bridge, etc.; the portion of a tooth above the gum; the culmination, glory; reward, distinction. *v.t.* To invest with a crown, or regal or imperial dignity; to form a crown or top to; to dignify to adorn, to consummate. **Crown prince,** *n.* The name given in some countries to the heir apparent. **crowned,** *a.*

crucial (kroo'shi-ál), *a.* Decisive; searching; in the form of a cross.

crucible (kroo'sibl) [late L. *crucibulum*], *n.* A melting-pot adapted to withstand high temperatures.

crucifix (kroo'si-fiks) [L. *cruci- fixus,* fixed to a cross], *n.* A cross bearing a figure of Christ. **crucifix'ion,** *n.* The act of cruci-fying; the death of Christ on the cross. **cru'ciform,** *a.* Cross-shaped; arranged in the form of a cross. **cru'cify,** *v.t.* To punish or kill by affixing to a cross.

crude (krood) [L. *crúdus,* raw], *a.* Raw; in a natural state; unripe; inexperienced; rude; coarse, rough. **crudely,** *adv.* **crudeness,** *n.* **crudity,** *n.*

cruel (kroo'él) [L. *crúdélis*], *a.* Inhuman, unfeeling, hard-hearted; causing pain. **cruelly,** *adv.* **cruelty,** *n.*

cruet (kroo'ét) [A.-F.], *n.* A small bottle or set of bottles for vinegar, oil, etc.

cruise (krooz) [Dut. *kruisen*], *v.i.* To sail to and fro. *n.* Such a voyage. **cruiser,** *n.* A person or ship that cruises, esp. a swift warship.

crumb (krŭm) [A.-S. *crúma*], *n.* A small piece, esp. of bread; the soft inner part of bread; a tiny portion. *v.t.* To break into or cover with crumbs.

crumble (krŭmbl), *v.* To break or fall into small particles; to fall into ruin.

crumpet (krŭm'pét) [?], *n.* A thin spongy tea-cake.

crumple (krŭmpl), *v.t.* To wrinkle.

crunch (krŭnch), *v.t.* To crush noisily with the teeth or foot.

crupper (krŭp'ér), *n.* A strap to keep a saddle from slipping forward; the hind-quarters of a horse.

crusade (krŭ-sād') [F. *croisade*], *n.* A mediæval expedition under the banner of the Cross to take possession of the Holy Land; any hostile enterprise conducted in a fanatical spirit. **crusader** (krŭ-sā'dér).

cruse (krooz) [Icel. *krús*], *n.* A small pot or bottle.

crush (krŭsh) [O.F. *cruisir*], *v.t.* To squeeze together so as to break or bruise; to crumple; to overwhelm, oppress, ruin. *n.* The act of crushing; a crowd.

crust (krŭst) [L. *crusta*], *n.* The hard outer part of bread; any hard rind or coating; a hard piece of bread; a deposit from wine; the solid outer portion of the earth. **crusted,** *a.* Having a crust; hoary, vener-able. **crusty,** *a.* Harsh, peevish, morose.

crustacea (krŭs-tā'shi-á), *n.pl.* A class containing lobsters, crabs, shrimps, etc., named from their shelly covering. **crustacean,** *a.* and *n.*

crutch (krŭch) [A.-S. *cryce*], *n.* A staff with a cross-piece used by the lame; a support.

cry (krī) [F. *crier*], *v.i.* To call loudly or importunately; to lament loudly, weep; to make proclamation; to exclaim; to call (of animals), yelp. *v.t.* To utter loudly; to proclaim, declare publicly. *n.* A loud utterance, expressive of joy, pain, suffering, astonishment, etc.; an importunate call; proclamation; a catch-word; a bitter complaint of injustice or oppression; weeping, lamentation; yelping. **crying,** *a.* That cries; calling for notice or vengeance, flagrant.

crypt (kript) [Gr. *kruptos,* hidden], *n.* A vault, esp. one beneath a church. **cryptic,** *a.* Hidden, secret, occult.

crystal (kris'tál) [Gr. *krustallos,* ice, rock-crystal]. *n.* Transparent quartz or rock crystal; (*Chem.* and *Min.*) an aggregation of molecules which have assumed a definite geometrical form with the form of a certain number of smooth plane surfaces; (*fig.*) anything clear as crystal; a very pellucid kind of glass. *a.* Clear, transparent, or bright as crystal; made of crystal. **crys'talline,** *a.* Clear, pellucid; applied to the lens behind the iris of the eye. **crys'tallize,** *v.t.* To cause to form crystals; *v.i.* To assume a crystalline form. **crystalliza'tion,** *n.*

cub (kŭb) [?], *n.* The young of certain animals, a whelp; an uncouth youth; a junior boy-scout.

cube (kūb) [Gr. *kubos*], *n.* A solid figure contained by six equal squares; the third power of a number (as 8 is the cube of 2). *v.t.* To raise to the third power. **cubic,** **-bical,** *a.* Having the properties or form of a cube. **cubist,** *n.* (*Art*) A school of artists that represents everything in geometrical figures.

cubicle (kū'bĭkl) [L. *cubiculum*], *n.* A compartment for one bed in a dormitory.

cubit (kū'bĭt) [L. *cubitus*, elbow], *n.* A measure of length, from the elbow to the tip of the middle finger, 18 to 22 in.

cuckoo (kuk'oo) [F. *coucou*], *n.* A migratory bird which lays its eggs in the nests of other birds; (*fig.*) a foolish fellow.

cucumber (kū'kŭm-bẽr) [L. *cucumis*], *n.* A trailing plant; its elongated fruit, used as a salad and pickle.

cud (kŭd) [A.-S. *cudu*], *n.* Food deposited by ruminating animals in the first stomach, thence drawn and chewed over again.

cuddle (kŭdl) [?], *v.i.* To lie close or snug together. *v.t.* To embrace, hug, fondle. *n.* A hug.

cuddy (kŭd'ĭ) [?], *n.* A small cabin in the stern of a ship where meals are taken.

cudgel (kŭjl) [A.-S. *cycgel*], *n.* A short club, a bludgeon. *v.t.* To beat with or as with a cudgel.

cue (kū) [O.F. *cue* (F. *queue*), L. *cauda*, a tail], *n.* The last words of a speech, which the player who follows waits for as an intimation to begin; a hint; the right course of action; a long straight rod used by billiard-players.

cuff (1) (kŭf) [Swed. *kuffa*, to thrust], *v.t.* To strike with the open hand. *n.* A blow of this kind.

cuff (2) (kŭf) [?], *n.* A fold or band worn round the wrist.

cuirass (kwi-răs') [F. *cuirasse*], *n.* A breastplate and back-plate, body armour. **cuirassier,** *n.* A soldier wearing a cuirass.

cuisine (kwi-zēn') [F.], *n.* The kitchen; style of cooking; cookery.

cul-de-sac (kul-dé-săk) [F., bottom of a bag], *n.* A street or lane open only at one end.

-cule, *dim. suf.*, as in *animalcule, corpuscule.*

culinary (kū'lĭn-ăr-ĭ) [L. *culina*, a kitchen], *a.* Relating to or used in the kitchen or cooking.

cull (kŭl) [O.F. *cuillir*], *v.t.* To pick, choose.

culminate (kŭl'mĭ-nāt) [late L. *culmīnātus*], *v.i.* To reach the highest point. **culmina'tion,** *n.*

culpable (kŭl'pȧbl) [L. *culpa* a fault], *a.* Blameable; guilty. **culpabil'ity,** *n.*

culprit (kŭl'prĭt), *n.* One who is in fault; one who is arraigned before a judge.

cult (kŭlt) [L. *cultus*], *n.* A system of religious belief, or its rites and ceremonies.

cultivate (kŭl'tĭ-vāt) [L. *cultīvātus*], *v.t.* To prepare for crops; to raise or develop by tilling, etc.; to improve, to civilize; to foster. **cultiva'tion,** *n.* The art or practice of cultivating; a state of refinement or culture. **cultivator,** *n.*

culture (kŭl'tyūr) [F., as CULT], *n.* Husbandry, farming; a state of refinement or intellectual and artistic development; a set of microscopic organisms produced by artificial development. **cultured,** *a.* In a state of intellectual development; having taste.

culvert (kŭl'vẽrt) [?], *n.* An arched drain or waterway under a road, etc.

cumber (kŭm'bẽr) [O.F. *combrer*, to hinder], *v.t.* To hamper, clog, to impede; to perplex, embarrass. **cumbersome,** *a.* Unwieldy; burdensome. **cumbrous,** *a.*

cumulate (kū'mū-lāt) [L. *cumulus*, a heap], *a.* Heaped up, accumulated. **cumulative,** *a.* Increasing by additions; tending to accumulate.

cumulus (kū'mū-lŭs), *n.* (*pl.* **-li**) A series of round masses of cloud. **cumulous, a,**

cuneiform (kū-nē-ĭ-fôrm) [L. *cuneus, a* wedge], *a.* Wedge-shaped; esp. of the arrow-headed characters of Babylonian, Persian and other inscriptions.

cunning (kŭn'ing) [A.-S. *cunnan*, to know], *a.* Knowing, artful, crafty. *n.* Skill, knowledge acquired by experience; artfulness, subtilty.

cup (kŭp) [A.-S. *cuppe*], *n.* A vessel to drink from; the liquor in it; an ornamental vessel, usu. of silver, awarded as a trophy; a cup-shaped object; the chalice used in Holy Communion. *v.t.* To bleed by means of a cupping-glass. **in one's cups:** Intoxicated. **cupful,** *n.*

cupboard (kŭb'ôrd), *n.* An enclosed case with shelves, a sideboard, wardrobe. **cupboard-love,** *n.* Interested love.

cupid (kū'pĭd) [L. *Cupīdo* (*cupere*, to desire)], *n.* The Roman god of Love; a beautiful boy. **cupid'ity,** *n.* An inordinate desire to possess; avarice.

cupola (kūp'ò-lá) [It., a little cask], *n.* A small apartment on the summit of a dome; a small dome; a revolving turret on a warship.

cupreous (kū'prē-ŭs) [L. *cuprum*, copper], *a.* Of, like, or composed of copper.

cur (kẽr) [L.G. *kurren*, to snarl], *n.* A mongrel; an ill-conditioned, surly fellow. **currish,** *a.*

curaçao (kū-rȧ-sō'), *n.* A liqueur flavoured with orange-peel, cinnamon, etc., orig. from Curaçao.

curate (kū'rȧt) [L. *cūra*, a charge, cure], *n.* One with a cure of souls; a clergyman who assists the incumbent. **curacy,** *n.*

curative (kū'rȧ-tĭv), *a.* Tending to cure. *n.* Anything that tends to cure.

curator (kū-rā'tòr) [L. *cūrāre*, to cure], *n.* One in charge of a museum or similar establishment.

curb (kĕrb) [F. *courbe*], *n.* A check, restraint; a chain on a curb-bit; a kerb-stone. *v.t.* To restrain, keep in check, put a curb on. **curb-bit,** *n.* A stiff bit forming a leverage upon the jaws of a horse.

curd (kĕrd) [?], *n.* The coagulated part, esp. of milk. **curdle,** *v.t.* To form into curds; to coagulate, congeal. *v.i.* To become curdled. **curdy,** *a.* Full of curds; curdled, congealed.

cure (kūr) [O.F., from L. *cūra*, care, whence *cūrāre*, to take care of], *n.* Healing or curing; a remedy, restorative; the care or spiritual charge of souls. *v.t.* To heal, restore to health; to preserve or pickle; to correct a habit or practice. *v.i.* To effect a cure. **curer,** *n.* One who cures; one who prepares preserved food.

curfew (kĕr'fū) [O.F. *couvre-feu*, cover fire], *n.* The extinguishment of fires at a stated hour in the Middle Ages; the bell announcing or the hour for this; time after which inhabitants may not be abroad.

curia (kū'ri-a) [L.], *n.* The Papal See in its temporal activity.

curio (kū'ri-ō), *n.* A curious piece of art; a bit of bric-à-brac.

curious (kū'ri-ŭs) [L. *cūriōsus*], *a.* Inquisitive, desirous to know; extraordinary, odd. **curios'ity,** *n.* A desire to know; inquisitiveness; a rarity; a strange personage. **curiously,** *adv.*

curl (kĕrl) [earlier *crul*, Dut. *krul*], *n.* A ringlet of hair; anything coiled, twisted, or spiral; a contemptuous curving of the lip. *v.t.* To twist into curls; to dress with ringlets; to curve up. *v.i.* To twist, curve up; to rise in curves or undulations; to play at curling. **curler,** *n.* A player at curling. **curling,** *n.* The act of dressing in curls; a game on the ice, in which large smooth stones are slid towards a mark. **curly,** *a.*

curlew (kĕr'lū) [O.F., *courlieus*], *n.* A migratory wading bird, named from its cry.

curmudgeon (kŭr-mŭj'ŏn) [?], *n.* A miserly, niggardly person.

currant (kŭr'ǎnt) [F. *raisins de Corinthe*], *n.* The dried fruit of a dwarf seedless grape from Corinth and the Levant.

currency (kŭr'ĕn-si) [L. *currere*, to run], *n.* A continual passing from hand to hand, as of money; the circulating monetary medium of a country; the state of being current.

current (kŭr'ĕnt), *a.* Passing at the present time; belonging to the present; in circulation (esp. of money); generally acknowledged, *n.* A flowing stream (of water, air, etc.); a flow of electricity; general drift or tendency. **currently,** *adv.* Commonly, generally.

curriculum (kŭ-rĭk'ū-lŭm) [L., race-course (*currere*, to run)], *n.* (*pl.* -la) A fixed course of study.

currier (kŭr'i-er) [L. *corium*, hide], *n.* One who dresses leather.

curry (1) (kŭr'i), *v.t.* To dress a horse with a comb; to dress leather; to flatter (in to curry favour). **curry-comb,** *n.* A comb used for grooming horses.

curry (2) (kŭr'i) [Tamil *kari*], *n.* A highly spiced sauce; a stew prepared with this. *v.t.* To season or dress with curry.

curse (kĕrs) [A.-S. *cursian*], *v.t.* To invoke evil upon; to blast, to excommunicate. *v.i.* To swear, utter imprecations. *n.* A solemn invocation of divine vengeance (upon); an oath, imprecation; anything which causes trouble or great vexation; a sentence of excommunication. **cursed,** *curst* (kĕr'sĕd, kĕrst), *a.* Execrable, accursed; vexatious, troublesome; shrewish. **cursedly,** *adv.*

cursive (kĕr'siv) [L. *cursīvus*, *currere*, to run], *a.* Written in a running hand.

cursory (kĕr'sō-ri) [L. *cursōrius*, as prec.], *a.* Hasty, superficial, careless.

curt (kĕrt) [L. *curtus*, docked], *a.* Short, concise, rudely terse and abrupt.

curtail (kĕr-tāl'), *v.t.* To shorten, lessen, reduce. **curtailment,** *n.*

curtain (kĕr'tǎn) [L. *cortīna*], *n.* A hanging cloth at a window, door, etc., which can be drawn aside; a cover, protection; a screen, esp. that in a theatre separating stage and spectators. *v.t.* To enclose, furnish, or decorate with curtains. **curtain raiser** *n.* (*Theat.*) A short piece given before a regular play.

curtsy (kĕrt'si), *n.* A bow; a woman's act of respect or salutation.

curvate (kĕr'vāt) [L. *curvātus*, bent], *a.* Curved, bent. **curvature,** *n.*

curve (kĕrv) [L. *curvus*, bent], *n.* A bending without angles; that which is bent. *v.* To bend or cause to bend without angles.

curvet (kĕr-vet') [It. *corvetta*], *n.* A leap given by a horse with all four feet off the ground at once.

cushion (kush'ŏn) [F. *coussin*], *n.* A kind of pillow for sitting, kneeling, or leaning on; anything resembling or acting as a cushion; the lining at the sides of a billiard-table.

cusp (kŭsp) [L. *cuspis*, a point], *n.* A point, apex; a projecting point formed by the meeting of curves; a projection on a molar tooth.

custard (kŭs'tǎrd) [O.F. *croustade*], *n.* A composition of milk and eggs, sweetened and flavoured.

custody (kŭs'tō-di) [L. *custōdia*], *n.* Guardianship, security; imprisonment, confinement. **custodian,** *n.* One who has the custody or guardianship of anything.

custom (kŭs'tŏm) [O.F. *costume*, L. consuētūdinem, custom (CON-, *suescere*, to be accustomed)], *n.* Habit, established usage; buying of goods, business; a frequenting a shop to purchase; (*pl.*) custom-duties on imports, etc. **customary,** *a.* Habitual, usual, wonted. **customer,** *n.* One who deals regularly at a particular shop. **custom-house,** *n.* The office where vessels enter and clear, and where custom-duties are paid.

cut (kŭt) [?], *v.t.* To penetrate, wound, divide, or separate with a sharp instrument; to hew, fell, mow; to carve, to trim or clip; to form, reduce, or mutilate by cutting; to intersect, to cross; to divide (as a pack of cards); to renounce the acquaintance of. *v.i.* To make a wound or incision; to have a good edge; to come through the gums; to divide a pack of cards; to run away quickly. *a.* Severed; shaped by cutting; castrated. *n.* The action of cutting; a stroke with a sharp-edged instrument or a whip; an opening, gash, or wound; anything that hurts the feelings; a slit, groove, trench; a part cut off or out; the shape in which a thing is cut, style; the act of ignoring a former acquaintance. **cut-out,** *n.* (*Motor.*) A device for disconnecting the exhaust from the silencer; (*Elec.*) a device which automatically breaks the circuit of an electric current. **cut-throat,** *n.* A murderer, an assassin; *a.* Murderous, barbarous. **cutter,** *n.* One who or that which cuts; one who cuts out clothes; a man-of-war's boat with four to eight oars; a one-masted vessel with fore-and-aft sails. **cutting,** *a.*

cutaneous (kū-tā'nē-ŭs) [L. *cutis,* skin], *a.* Belonging to or affecting the skin.

cute (kūt), *a.* Cunning, sharp.

cuticle (kū'tikl), *n.* The epidermis or outer skin.

cutlass (kŭt'lăs) [F. *coutelas*], *n.* A broad curved sword, used esp. by sailors.

cutler (kŭt'lẽr) [O.F. *coutelier*], *n.* One who makes or deals in cutting instruments. **cutlery,** *n.* The business of a cutler; edged instruments or tools.

cutlet (kŭt'lĕt) [F. *côtelette,* dim. of *côte,* L. *costa,* rib], *n.* A small slice of meat, from the loin or neck, for cooking.

cuttle (kŭtl) [A.-S. *cudele*], *n.* A cuttlefish. **cuttle-fish,** *n.* The octopus.

cutwater (kŭt'waw-tẽr), *n.* The fore part of a ship's prow which cuts the water.

-cy, *suf.* Forming nouns of quality from adjectives, and nouns of office (cp. SHIP) from nouns.

cyan-, cyano- [Gr. *kuanos,* a dark-blue mineral], *comb. form.* Of a blue colour; pertaining to cyanogen. **cyanic** (sī-ăn'ik), *a.* Derived from cyanogen. **cy'anide,** *n.* A compound of cyanogen with a metallic element. **cyanogen,** *n.* Gas compounded of carbon and nitrogen.

cycle (sīkl) [Gr. *kuklos,* a circle], *n.* A series of events, etc., recurring in the same order; a series that repeats itself; the period in which a series of events is completed; a long period; a body of legend connected with some myth; a bicycle or tricycle. *v.i.* To revolve in a circle; to ride a bicycle or tricycle. **cyclic, -al,** *a.* Pertaining to, or moving or recurring in, a cycle; (*Bot.*) arranged in whorls. **cyclist,** *n.* One who rides a bicycle or tricycle.

cyclone (sī'klōn), *n.* A violent hurricane caused by a system of winds blowing spirally towards a central region of low barometric pressure. **cyclon'ic,** *a.*

cyclopean (sī-klō-pē'án), *a.* Of or pertaining to the Cyclops, a race of one-eyed giants in Greek myth; immense, gigantic.

cygnet (sig'nĕt) [L. *cygnus,* a swan], *n.* A young swan.

cylinder (sil'in-dẽr) [Gr. *kulindros*], *n.* A straight roller-shaped body of uniform circumference; a cylindrical member of

various machines, as the chamber in a steam-engine in which the piston works, the roller used in machine-printing, etc. **cylin'drical,** *a.*

cymbal (sim'băl) [Gr. *kumbalon*], *n.* One of a pair of metal disks clashed together to produce a sharp sound. **cymbalist,** *n.*

Cymric (kim'rik) [W. *Cymru,* Wales], *a.* Pertaining to the Welsh. *n.* The Welsh language.

cynic (sin'ik) [Gr. *kunikos kuŏn,* a dog], *n.* An ancient Greek philosopher (follower of Diogenes) who scorned all luxury, the arts, etc.; a morose, sarcastic, sneering person. **cynical,** *a.* **cynicism,** *n.*

cynosure (sin'ō-sūr) [Gr. *kunosoura,* the dog's tail], *n.* The constellation of the Lesser Bear, containing the north star; a centre of interest or attraction.

cypress (sī'prĕs) [Gr. *kupressos*], *n.* A coniferous tree with very durable wood; a branch of this as emblem of mourning.

cyst (sist) [Gr. *kustis,* a bladder], *n.* A bladder, vesicle, or hollow organ; a sac containing morbid matter.

Czech (chek), *n.* Bohemian; the Bohemian language. *a.* Pertaining to the Czechs. **Czechoslovak,** *n.* A member of a nation comprising the Czechs and the Slovaks, whose independence was acknowledged in 1918. *a.* Of or pertaining to this nation.

D

dab (dăb) [?], *v.t.* To strike gently with something moist or soft; to pat. *n.* A gentle blow; a light stroke or wipe with a soft substance; a lump; an adept, expert; a small flat-fish.

dabble (dăbl), *v.t.* To keep on dabbing; to besprinkle, splash. *v.i.* To play or splash about in water; to do anything in a superficial manner; to dip into a subject. **dabbler,** *n.* One who dabbles with any subject.

dabchick (dăb'chik), *n.* The little grebe.

dace (dās) [O.F. *darz*], *n.* A small river fish.

dachshund (daks'hund) [G., badger-hound], *n.* A short-legged breed of dog.

dacoit (dä-koit') (Hind, *dākā,* robbery by a gang], *n.* One of an Indian band of armed robbers. **dacoity,** *n.*

dactyl (dăk'til) [Gr. a finger], *n.* A metrical foot consisting of one long followed by two short syllables. **dactyl'ic,** *a.*

dado (dā'dō) [It., a cube], *n.* A wainscoting or decoration round the lower part of walls.

dæmon [DEMON].

daffodil (dăf'ō-dil) [Gr. *asphodelos*], *n.* The Lent lily or other varieties of narcissus.

daft (daft) [A.-S. *gedæfte,* gentle], *a.* Weakminded, imbecile; silly.

dagger (dăg'ẽr) [F. *dague*], *n.* A short two-edged stabbing weapon.

dago (dā'gō) [Sp. *Diego*], *n.* (*slang*) A contemptuous name for a Southern European.

daguerreotype (dä-ger'rō-tīp) [L. J. M. *Daguerre* (1787-1851), the inventor], *n.* A photograph on a polished metal plate.

dahlia (dä´li-à) [*Dahl*, a pupil of Linnæus], *n.* A genus of composite plants.

daily (dāl´i), *a.* Happening, done, recurring, or necessary for every day. *adv.* Day by day. *n.* A newspaper published every week-day.

dainty (dān´ti) [O.F. *dainté*, L. *dignus*, worthy], *n.* A delicacy; a choice morsel. *a.* Pleasing to the taste, choice; pretty, delicate; fastidious, over-nice.

dairy (dâr´i) [A.-S. *dæge*, a maid-servant], *n.* The place where milk is kept and converted into butter or cheese, or where milk, cream, and butter are sold. *a.* Belonging to a dairy or its business. **dairy-farm**, *n.* **dairying**, *n.* **Dairy-farming**. **dairymaid**, *n.*

dais (dā´is) [A.-F. *déis*], *n.* The raised floor at the upper end of a dining-hall; the principal table or seat at it; a platform.

daisy (dā´zi) [A.-S. *dæges éage*, day's eye], *n.* A small composite flower.

dale (dāl) [A.-S. *dœl*, a valley], *n.* A valley. **dalesman**, *n.* A dweller in a dale.

dally (dăl´i) [O.F. *dalier*, to chat], *v.i.* To exchange caresses; to idle, delay, waste time. **dalliance**, *n.*

dam (1) (dăm), *n.* A mother (of beasts).

dam (2) (dăm) [Teut.], *n.* A bank to keep back water; a causeway. *v.t.* To keep back or confine by a dam; to obstruct, hinder.

damage (dăm-ȧj) [L. *damnum*, cost, loss], *n.* Hurt, injury, detriment; loss or harm incurred; (*pl.*) value of or reparation for injury done. *v.t.* To cause damage to. **damageable**, *a.* Susceptible of damage.

damascene (dăm-à-sēn´) [Gr. *Damaskēnos*, of Damascus], *v.t.* To ornament steel, etc., by inlaying with another metal.

damask (dăm´ásk), *n.* A silk or linen fabric with raised figures woven in the pattern; pink, the colour of the damask rose. *a.* Made of damask; like the damask rose. *v.t.* To work or imprint flowers on; to damascene. **damask rose**, *n.* An old-fashioned pink rose.

dame (dām) [O.F., L. *domina*], *n.* A lady; a female title of honour.

damn (dăm) [L. *damnum*, loss, fine], *v.t.* To condemn; to call down curses on. *v.i.* To swear profanely. *n.* A profane oath; a negligible amount. **damnable**, (dăm´nábl) *a.* Deserving damnation; execrable. **damnably**, *adv.* **damna´tion**, *n.* Eternal punishment or condemnation to it; the damning of a play, etc.; a profane oath. **dam´natory**, *a.* Causing or implying condemnation. **damned**, *a.* Condemned; execrable, damnable. **damning**, *a.* Involving damnation; damnable.

damp (dămp) [Teut.], *a.* Moist, humid; clammy. *n.* Humidity, moisture; chill, discouragement; depression. *v.t.* To moisten; to depress, discourage. **dampen**, *v.t.* To make damp; to dull, deject. *v.i.* To become damp. **damper**, *n.* One who or that which damps or deadens; a valve in a flue for regulating a fire; (*Austral.*) a hastily baked unfermented cake.

damsel (dăm zĕl) [O.F. *damoisele*], *n.* A young unmarried woman.

damson (dăm´zón) [L. *Damascēnum*, of

Damascus], *n.* A small black plum; the tree that bears it.

dance (dans) [O.F. *danser*], *v.i.* To move or trip, usu. to music with rhythmical steps; to skip, frolic. *v.t.* To express or accomplish by dancing; to toss up and down, dandle, cause to dance. *n.* A rhythmical stepping with motions of the body, usu. to music; the tune by which such movements are regulated; a figure or set of figures in dancing; a ball. **dancer**, *n.*

dandelion (dăn´dé-lïón) [F. *dent de lion*, lion's tooth], *n.* A well-known composite plant with yellow flower.

dandle (dăndl) [It. *dandola*, doll], *v.t.* To dance up and down or toss in the arms (as a child); to pet.

dandruff (dăn´drŭf) [?], *n.* Scurf on the head.

dandy (dăn´di) [?], *n.* One extravagantly fond of dress; a fop, a coxcomb.

danger (dān´jèr) [O.F. *dangier*], *n.* Risk, hazard; exposure to injury or loss; anything that causes peril. **dangerous**, *a.*

dangle (dăng´gĕl) [?], *v.i.* To hang loosely; to swing or wave about, hang about, hover, *v.t.* To cause to dangle; to hold out (as a bait, etc.).

dank (dăngk) [Scand.], *a.* Damp, chilly, or soaked with moisture.

danseuse (dan-serz´) [F.], *n.* A female professional dancer.

dapper (dăp´ér) [Teut.], *a.* Spruce, smart, active. **dapperness**, *n.*

dapple (dăpl) [Icel. *depill*, a spot], *n.* A spot; a mottled marking.

dare (dâr) [A.-S. *durran*], *v.i.* (*past and conditional* durst, dared) To venture; to have the courage or impudence; to be bold or adventurous. *v.t.* To attempt, to venture on; to defy. **dare-devil**, *n.* A fearless, reckless fellow. **daring**, *a.*

dark (dark) [A.-S. *deorc*], *a.* Destitute of light; shaded; brown-complexioned; gloomy, sombre; obscure, ambiguous. *n.* Darkness; absence of light; night; shadow, the dark part of a picture; lack of knowledge. **darken**, *v.i.* To become dark or darker; obscure, gloomy, or displeased. *v.t.* To make dark or darker; to render gloomy or obscure. **darkish**, *a.* **darkling**, *adv.* In the dark. **darkly**, *adv.* **darkness**, *n.* The state or quality of being dark; obscurity; ignorance; the powers of hell.

darling (dar´ling) [A.-S. *dēorling*], *n.* One who is dearly beloved; a pet. *a.* Dearly beloved.

darn (darn) [A.-S. *gedyrnan*, to stop up a hole], *v.t.* To mend cloth, etc., by imitating the texture. *n.* A place mended by darning; (*inter.*) (Euphemism for) Damn!

dart (dart) [O.F. *dart*], *n.* A pointed missile thrown by the hand; the act of throwing; a sudden or rapid movement. *v.t.* To shoot or send forth suddenly. *v.i.* To run or move swiftly.

dash (dăsh) [Scand.], *v.t.* To strike, knock, etc., with violence; to cause to collide; to throw violently or suddenly; to bespatter; to dilute by throwing in some other substance; to sketch hastily; to confound, abash, daunt. *v.i.* To rush, fall, or throw oneself with violence; to strike against something and break; to go smartly or spiritedly. *n.* A sharp collision; the sound of this, the sound of water in commotion; a rapid movement, a rush, onset; a slight admixture; activity, daring; brilliancy, display; a mark (—) denoting a break in a parenthesis, omission, etc.; a hasty stroke with a pen, etc. **dashboard,** *n.* (*Motor.*) The indicator board in front of the driver. **dashing,** *a.* Daring, spirited; showy.

dastard (dăs′tărd), *n.* A coward, poltroon. *a.* Cowardly.

date (1) (dāt) [L. *data*, given], *n.* A fixed point of time; the specification of this in a book, document, etc.; period, age; (*colloq.*) an appointment. *v.t.* To affix a date to. *v.i.* To reckon; to begin, be dated. **date-line,** *n.* The meridional line in the Pacific Ocean on either side of which the date differs, theoretically 180° from Greenwich.

date (2) (dāt) [O.F., Gr. *daktulos*, a finger, a date], *n.* The fruit of the date-palm. **date-palm,** **-tree,** *n.* The palm-tree of Scripture, common in N. Africa and Asia Minor.

dative (dā′tiv) [L. *dativus*, pertaining to giving], *a.* Denoting the grammatical case used to represent the remoter object.

datum (dā′tŭm) [L., given], *n.* (*pl.* **data**) A quantity, fact, or other premise, given or admitted, from which results may be found.

daub (dawb) [O.F. *dauber*, to plaster], *v.t.* To smear with a soft adhesive substance; to paint coarsely; to stain, soil. *v.i.* To paint in a crude style.

daughter (daw′tér) [A.-S. *dohtor*], *n.* A female child; a female in a child-like relation, as a penitent to her confessor. **daughter-in-law,** *n.* A son's wife. **daughterly,** *a.*

daunt (dawnt) [O.F. *danter*], *v.t.* To intimidate, to check by frightening. **dauntless,** *a.* Fearless, intrepid.

dauphin (daw′fin) [O.F. *dauphin*], *n.* The title of the heir-apparent to the French kings.

davit (dăv′it) [?], *n.* A beam projecting over a ship's side, with tackle to hoist or lower a boat.

daw (daw) [Teut.], *n.* A jackdaw.

dawdle (dawdl) [?], *v.i.* To trifle, idle about, waste time.

dawn (dawn) [Scand.], *v.i.* To grow light, to break (as day); to begin to open or appear. *n.* The break of day; the first rise or appearance.

day (dā) [A.-S. *dæg*], *n.* The time the sun is above the horizon; daylight; the space of twenty-four hours, commencing at midnight, roughly the time in which the earth revolves on its axis; day-time; the day for receiving visitors; (*often in pl.*) life, lifetime, period of vigour or prosperity. **day-break,** *n.* The first appearance of daylight. **day-dream,** *n.* A reverie, a castle in the air. **daylight,** *n.* The light of day; dawn; (*fig.*) openness, publicity. **day-spring,** *n.* The dawn;

daybreak. **daylight saving,** *n.* Summer time.

daze (dāz) [M.E. *dasen*], *v.t.* To stupefy, dazzle, overpower with light. *n.* The state of being dazed.

dazzle (dăzl), *v.t.* To overpower with a glare of light; to daze with rapidity of motion, brilliant display, etc. *v.i.* To be dazzled, to be excessively bright. **dazzling,** *a.*

de-, *pref.* From; down; away; out; (*intens.*) completely, thoroughly; (*priv.*) UN- (expressing undoing, deprivation; reversal, or separation).

deacon (dē′kŏn) [Gr. *diakonos*, a servant], *n.* A cleric next below a priest; an official among the Presbyterians and dissenters. **deaconess,** *n.* A female deacon.

dead (ded) [A.-S.], *a.* Having ceased to live; lifeless; temporarily deprived of the power of action; unconscious or unappreciative; cooled, obsolete, effete, useless; lustreless, motionless, soundless; flat, vapid, dull; certain, unerring. **dead-eye,** *n.* A flat round block by which rigging is set up. **dead letter,** *n.* A letter which for any reason cannot be delivered. **dead-lights,** *n.pl.* (*Naut.*) Shutters for port-holes or cabin windows in rough weather. **deadlock,** *n.* A complete standstill, a position whence there is no exit. **dead reckoning,** *n.* The calculation of a ship's position from the log and compass, when observations cannot be taken.

deaden (dedn), *v.t.* To diminish the brightness, force, or power of; to make insensible, to dull.

deadly (ded′li), *a.* Causing death; fatal; like death; implacable, irreconcilable; very, excessive. *adv.* As if dead; extremely; to death, mortally.

deaf (def) [A.-S.], *a.* Incapable or dull of hearing; disregarding, refusing to listen or to comply. **deafly,** *adv.* **deafness,** *n.* **deaf-mute,** *n.* One who is deaf and dumb. **deaf-mutism,** *n.*

deafen (defn), *v.t.* To make deaf; to stun with noise.

deal (1) (dēl) [A.-S. *dǽl*, a share], *n.* An indefinite quantity; the distribution of playing-cards; a part, portion; a piece of business. *v.t.* (*past and p.p.* **dealt** (delt)) To distribute; to award as one's proper share; to distribute. *v.i.* To have business or traffic (with); to associate or occupy oneself (with); to distribute cards to players. **dealer,** *n.* A trader; one who deals the cards. **dealing,** *n.*

deal (2) (dēl) [A.-S. *thille*], *n.* Fir or pine wood; a plank of this.

dean (dēn) [L. *decānus*, one set over ten], *n.* A dignitary presiding over the chapter of a cathedral or collegiate church; a clergyman having jurisdiction over a part of an archdeaconry (as the head of a faculty or a resident fellow at a University). **deanery,** *n.* The office, district, or residence of a dean.

dear (dēr) [A.-S. *déore*], *a.* Beloved, cherished; costly; of a high price; characterized by high prices. *n.* A darling, a loved one. *adv.* Dearly, at a high price. **dearly,** *adv.* **dearness,** *n.*

D

dearth (derth), *n.* Scarcity.

death (deth) [A.-S. *déadh*], *n.* Extinction of life; the act of dying; decay, destruction. **death-bed,** *n.* The bed on which a person dies; a last illness. **deathless,** *a.* Immortal, imperishable. **deathlike,** *a.* Resembling death. **deathly,** *a.* Like death; deadly; pertaining to death. **death's-head,** *n.* A human skull, or a representation of one, as an emblem of mortality. **death-warrant,** *n.* An order for the execution of a criminal; an act or measure putting an end to something. **death-watch,** *n.* A wood-boring beetle that makes a clicking sound, formerly supposed to presage a death.

debacle (dė-bakl´) [F.], *n.* A rout, a complete overthrow.

debar (dė-bar´), *v.t.* To hinder or exclude; to prohibit, forbid.

debase (dė-bās´), *v.t.* To lower in condition, value, etc.; to adulterate, degrade. **debasingly,** *adv.*

debate (dė-bāt´) [O.F. *debatre*], *v.t.* To contend about by words or arguments; to discuss, consider, *v.i.* To engage in argument; to fight. *n.* A discussion, argumentative contest; contention, strife. **debatable,** *a.* **debater,** *n.*

debauch (dė-bawch´) [F. *débaucher*], *v.t.* To corrupt, pervert. *n.* An act of debauchery; a carouse. **debauchee** (deb-aw-shē´), *n.* A profligate. **debauchery,** *n.* Vicious indulgence of the sensual appetites; seduction from duty.

debenture (dė-ben´chŭr) [L. *débenter*, they are due], *n.* A deed issued as security for a loan of money on which interest is payable till it is redeemed.

debilitate (dė-bil´i-tāt) [L. *débilitātus*, weakened], *v.t.* To weaken, enervate. **debility,** *n.* Weakness, feebleness.

debit (deb´it) [L. *débitum*, debt], *n.* An amount set down as a debt; the left-hand side of an account. *v.t.* To charge to as a debt; to enter on the debit side.

debonair (deb-ó-nâr´) [O.F. *debonaire*, of good disposition], *a.* Courteous, pleasing.

debouch (dė-boosh´) [F. *déboucher*], *v.i.* To march out from a confined place.

debris (deb´ri) [F. *débris*, fragments], *n.* Broken rubbish, fragments.

debt (det) [L. *debitum*], *n.* That which is owing from one person to another; obligation, liability. **debtor,** *n.* One who is indebted to another; the left-hand or debit side of an account.

debunk (dē-bŭngk´), *v.t.* (*colloq.*) To destroy sentimental legends.

debut (dė-bu´) [F.], *n.* A first appearance in public; a first attempt. **debutant,** *n.* **fem. debutante,** *n.*

deca-, dec- [Gr. *deka*], *comb. form.* Ten; consisting of ten parts.

decade (dek´ād) [Gr. *dekas -ados*], *n.* A group of ten; a period of ten years.

decadence (dė-kā´dèns, dek´-) [F.], *n.* Decay, deterioration. **decadent,** *a.*

decagon (dek´á-gón) [Gr. *gōnos*, angled], *n.* A plane figure with ten sides and ten angles.

decahedron (dek-á-hē´dròn) [Gr. *hedra*, a base], *n.* A solid figure with ten sides.

decalogue (dek´á-log) [Gr. *logos*, word], *n.* The ten commandments.

decamp (dė-kămp´), *v.i.* To depart quickly; to take oneself off.

decant (dė-kănt´) [F. *décanter*], *v.t.* To pour from one vessel into another without disturbing the sediment. **decanter,** *n.* An ornamental bottle for holding wine or spirit.

decapitate (dė-kăp´i-tāt) [L. *caput*, head], *v.t.* To behead. **decapita´tion,** *n.*

decarbonize (dē-kar´bòn-īz), *v.t.* (*Motor.*) To remove carbon deposits in the combustion chamber or on piston heads.

decay (dė-kā´) [L. *cadere*, to fall], *v.i.* To fall away, deteriorate; to waste away. *v.t.* To impair, cause to fall away. *n.* Gradual failure or decline; a state of ruin; gradual dissolution; decomposition.

decease (dė-sēs´) [L. *cedère*, to go], *n.* Death. **deceased,** *a.*

deceit (dė-sēt´) [O.F. *deceite*], *n.* The act of deceiving; trickery, duplicity; delusive appearance. **deceitful,** *a.*

deceive (dė-sēv´) [O.F. *deceveir*], *v.t.* To mislead, impose upon; to cheat, delude. *v.i.* To act deceitfully. **deceiver,** *n.*

December (dė-sem´bèr) [L.], *n.* The twelfth and last month of the year (originally the tenth).

decency (dē´sėn-si) [L. *decentia*], *n.* Propriety; decorum.

decennial (dė-sen´i-ál) [L. *decem*, ten, *annus*, year], *a.* Lasting ten years; occurring every ten years.

decent (dē´sènt) [L. *decens -ntem*, becoming], *a.* Becoming, seemly; modest; decorous; passable. **decently,** *adv.*

decentralize (dē-sen´trá-līz), *v.t.* To distribute; to organize on the principle of local management. **decentraliza´tion,** *n.*

deception (dė-sep´shŭn) [F. *déception*], *n.* The act of deceiving; the state of being deceived; a deceit, fraud. **deceptive,** *a.*

decide (dė-sīd´) [L. *cædere*, to cut], *v.t.* To determine; to adjudge, settle by adjudging. *v.i.* To come to a decision. **decided,** *a.* Settled; evident, unmistakable; resolute, unwavering.

deciduous (dė-sid´ū-ŭs) [L. *dēciduus*], *a.* Falling off, not permanent.

decimal (des´i-mál) [L. *decimus*, tenth], *a.* Of or pertaining to ten or tenths; counting by tens. *n.* A decimal fraction, *i.e.,* one having some power of 10 for its denominator.

decimate (des´i-māt), *v.t.* To take the tenth part of; to slay every tenth man or a large proportion. **decima´tion,** *n.*

decipher (dė-sī´fėr), *v.t.* To turn from cipher into ordinary language; to detect; to read bad or indistinct writing.

decision (dė-sizh´ŭn) [F.], *n.* The act or result of deciding; resolution, firmness of character. **deci´sive,** *a.* Having the power of deciding; conclusive; characterized by decision.

deck (dek) [Teut.], *v.t.* To adorn, beautify; to put a deck to. *n.* The flooring of a ship; a pack of cards. **deck-chair,** *n.* A collapsible chair.

declaim (dė-klām´) [L. *clāmāre*, to cry out], *v.t.* To utter rhetorically. *v.t.* To deliver an oration in public; to inveigh, harangue. **declama´tion,** *n.* **declamatory** (dėklăm´á-tó-ri), *a.*

declare (dė-klâr') [L. *clārus*, clear], *v.t.* To make known; to announce publicly; to assert or affirm positively. *v.t.* To make a declaration, to make an affirmation in lieu of oath; (*Cards*) to name the trump suit; (*Cricket*) to announce an innings as closed. **declara'tion**, *n.* The act of declaring; that which is declared or proclaimed, the document by which this is done; a manifesto; an affirmation in lieu of oath.

declension (dė-klen'shŭn), *n.* Declining, falling-off; the case-inflection of nouns, adjectives, and pronouns; a class of nouns declined in the same way.

declination (dek-li-nā'shŭn) [O.F.], *n.* Bending or moving downwards.

decline (dė-klīn') [F. *decliner*, L. *dēclīnāre* (DE-, *clīnāre*, to lean)], *v.i.* To slop downwards; to droop. *v.t.* To lower; to direct to one side; to refuse, reject; to inflect (as a noun); to recite the cases of a noun in order. *n.* A falling-off; deterioration, diminution; consumption. **declinable**, *a.*

declivity (dė-kliv'i-ti) [L. *clīvus*, a slope], *n.* A gradual slope.

decoct (dė-kokt') [L. *coctus*, cooked], *v.t.* To boil down or extract the virtue of by boiling. **decoction**, *n.*

decode (dė-kōd'), *v.t.* To translate (a telegraphic message) from code into plain language.

decollate (dė-kol'āt) [L. *collum*, the neck], *v.t.* To behead. **decolla'tion**, *n.*

décolleté (de-kol'e-tā) [F.], *a.* Low-necked, wearing a low-necked dress.

decompose (dē-kŏm-pōz'), *v.t.* To resolve into constituent elements; to analyse; to cause to rot. *v.i.* To become decomposed; to putrefy. **decomposable**, *a.* **decomposit'ion**, *n.*

decontaminate (dē-kon-tăm'in-āt), *v.t.* To clear of poison gas or fluid.

decor (dā'kôr) [F.], *n.* (*Theat.*) The setting and decoration of a scene.

decorate (dek'ó-rāt) [L. *decorātus*, ornamented], *v.t.* To adorn, beautify; to confer an honour on. **decora'tion**, *n.* The act of decorating; ornamentation; a badge of honour. **deco'rative**, *a.* **dec'orator**, *n.*

decorous (dė-kôr'ŭs) [L. *decōrus*, seemly], *a.* Becoming, seemly; decent. **decorously**, *adv.* **decor'um**, *n.*

decoy (dė-koi'), *v.t.* To lure into a snare; to entrap. *n.* A place for entrapping wild-fowl; a bait, attraction.

decrease (dė-krēs') [L. *crēscere*, to grow], *v.t.* To become less, to wane, fail. *v.t.* To make less; to reduce in size gradually. *n.* Lessening, diminution; the waning of the moon. **decreasingly**, *adv.*

decree (dė-krē') [L. *crētus*, sifted], *n.* An edict, law, or ordinance; the predetermined purpose of God; the award of an umpire. *v.t.* To command by a decree, to decide by law or authoritatively. *v.i.* To make an edict; to resolve, determine.

decrepit (dė-krep'it) [*dēcrepitus* (L. *crepitus*, crackled)], *a.* Broken down by age and infirmities; decayed. **decrepitude**, *n.*

decretal (dė-krē'tăl), *a.* Pertaining to a decree. *n.* A decree, esp. of the Pope.

decry (dė-krī'), *v.t.* To cry down; to clamour against; to depreciate.

dedicate (ded'i-kāt) [L. *dicatus*, devoted], *v.t.* To apply wholly to some purpose or person; to inscribe or address (as a literary work to a patron); to consecrate solemnly to God. **dedica'tion**, *n.* **dedicatory**, *a.*

deduce (dė-dūs') [L. *dūcere*, to lead], *v.t.* To draw a conclusion, to infer; to trace the descent (from). **deducible**, *a.*

deduct (dė-dŭkt'), *v.t.* To take away, subtract. **deduction**, *n.* **deductive**, *a.* Deduced from premises.

deed (dēd) [A.-S. *dæd*], *n.* A thing done with intention; an achievement; reality; a document comprehending the terms of a contract, and the evidence of its execution. **deed-poll**, *n.* A deed made by one person only.

deem (dēm) [A.-S. *dēman*], *v.t.* To suppose, think; to judge. *v.i.* To come to a decision; to estimate. **deemster**, *n.* One of two judges in the Isle of Man.

deep (dēp) [A.-S. *dēop*], *a.* Extending far down; having a thickness down; dark-coloured; profound, abstruse; heartfelt; intense, heinous; low in pitch, sonorous; well-versed; artful, scheming. *adv.* Deeply, far down; far on; intensely. *n.* The sea; a deep place, abyss, cavity; the bottom of the heart. **deepen**, *v.* To make or become deeper.

deer (dēr) [A.-S. *dēor*], *n.* A ruminant quadruped, stag, roebuck, fallow deer, reindeer, etc.; (*Shak.*) small, insignificant animals.

deface (dė-fās'), *v.t.* To disfigure; to spoil the appearance of; to erase. **deface-ment**, *n.*

defalcate (dė'făl-kāt) [L. *falcātus*, cut with a sickle], *v.t.* To take away fraudulently, to embezzle. **defalca'tion**, *n.* Embezzlement. **defalcator**, *n.*

defame (dė-fām') [O.F. *defamer*], *v.t.* To slander, asperse the character of. **defamation** (def-à-mā'shŭn), *n.* **defam'atory**, *a.*

default (dė-fawlt') [O.F. *defaute*], *n.* Omission or failure to do any act; neglect; failure to appear in court on the day assigned, or to meet liabilities. *v.i.* To fail in duty, etc. **defaulter**, *n.*

defeat (dė-fēt) [O.F. *defait*], *v.t.* To overthrow; to frustrate; to baffle. *n.* Overthrow, discomfiture; a rendering null.

defecate (def'e-kāt) [L. *fæx*, dregs], *v.t.* To clear from impurities. *v.i.* To void excrement.

defect (dė-fekt') [L. *dēfectus*, a want], *n.* Absence of something essential; blemish; moral imperfection. **defection**, *n.* A falling away from allegiance. **defective**, *a.* Imperfect, faulty.

defence (dė-fens') [L. *dēfensa*, forbidden], *n.* The state or act of defending; that which defends; justification; defendant's reply to plaintiff. **defenceless**, *a.* **defencelessness**, *n.*

defend (dė-fend') [L. *fendere*, to strike], *v.t.* To protect, guard; to keep safe against attack; to maintain by argument, to vindicate; to plead in justification of. *v.i.* To plead on behalf of the defendant;

to contest a suit. **defendable,** *a.* **defendant,** *n.* One who has to answer some charge. **defender,** *n.* One who defends, supports, or vindicates. **defensible,** *a.* Capable of being defended. **defensive,** *a.* Serving to defend; done in self-defence. *n.* An attitude or condition of defence.

defer (dĕ-fẽr') [O.F. *différer,* F. *déférer*], *v.t.* To put off; to postpone. *v.i.* To delay; to procrastinate; to yield to the opinion of another. **def'erence,** *n.* Submission to the opinions of another; compliance; courteous submissiveness. **deferen'tial,** *a.* With deference.

defiance (dĕ-fī'áns), *n.* Challenge to any contest; opposition; open disobedience. **defiant,** *a.*

deficiency (dĕ-fish'ĕn-si) [L. *dēficiens*], *n.* Deficit, lack, want. **deficient,** *a.* deficit (def'l-sit), *n.* A falling short (of estimated receipts); a deficiency.

defile (1) (dĕ-fīl') [O.F. *defouler,* to trample on], *v.t.* To make foul; to soil, stain; to violate the chastity of; to pollute. **defilement,** *n.*

defile (2) (dĕ-fīl') [F. *défiler*], *v.i.* To march in a file. *n.* A narrow pass between hills, etc., along which men can march only in file.

define (dĕ-fīn') [L. *fīnīre,* to set a bound], *v.t.* To limit; to mark out; to describe a thing by its qualities and circumstances. *v.i.* To give a definition. **definable,** *a.*

definite (def'l-nit) [L. *dēfīnītus,* bounded], *a.* Limited; exact, distinct; positive. **definitely,** *adv.* **definiteness,** *n.*

definition (def-i-nish'ŭn), *n.* The act of defining; an exact description of a thing by its qualities, etc.; distinctness.

definitive (dĕ-fin'l-tiv), *a.* Decisive, positive; conclusive. *n.* A word used to limit the application of a noun.

deflate (dĕ-flāt') [L. *flātus,* blown], *v.t.* To let down by allowing the air to escape. **deflation,** *n.*

deflect (dĕ-flekt') [L. *flectere,* to bend], *v.i.* To turn to one side, to deviate. *v.t.* To cause to turn or bend.

deflower (dĕ-flou'ẽr), *v.t.* To deprive of virginity, to ravish.

deform (dĕ-fõrm') [L. *forma,* beauty, form], *v.t.* To disfigure, distort; to mar. **deforma'tion,** *n.* A disfigurement, distortion. **deformed,** *a.* **deformity,** *n.*

defraud (dĕ-frawd'), *v.t.* To deprive by deception; to cheat.

defray (dĕ-frā') [F. *frais,* cost], *v.t.* To bear the charge of; to settle.

deft (deft) [A.-S. *gedæfte*], *a.* Neat in handling; dexterous, clever. **deftly,** *adv.* **deftness,** *n.*

defunct (dĕ-fŭnkt') [L. *functus,* performed], *a.* Dead, deceased. *n.* A dead person.

defy (dĕ-fī') [DIS-, L. *fīdus,* faithful], *v.t.* To challenge; to dare, brave; to disregard openly.

degauss (dĕ-gous) [DE-, name of inventor], *v.t.* (*Elec.*) To neutralize the magnetization of a ship.

degenerate (dĕ-jen'ẽr-āt) [L. *genus -eris,* race], *a.* Fallen from a better to a worse state; declined in natural or moral growth; mean, corrupt. *n.* One that

has sunk below the normal type. *v.i.* (-āt). To fall off in quality; to deteriorate. **degeneracy,** *n.* **degeneration,** *n.* The act or process of degenerating; the state of being degenerated.

degrade (dĕ-grād') [L. *gradus,* a step], *v.t.* To reduce in rank; to strip of rank, office, or dignity; to debase, bring into contempt. **degrada'tion,** *n.* **degraded,** *a.* Reduced in rank, estimation, etc.; *w,* mean. **degrading,** *a.* Lowering the level or character.

degree (dĕ-grē'), *n.* A stage in progression, elevation, quality, rank, etc.; relative position, condition, quantity, intensity, etc.; a grade of academic proficiency conferred by Universities; the 360th part of the circumference of a circle or of the earth; the unit of measurement of temperature; a grade of comparison of adjectives and adverbs.

dehydrate (dĕ-hī'drāt), *v.t.* To liberate or remove water from.

deify (dĕ'i-fī) [L. *deus,* god, *facere,* to make], *v.t.* To make a god of; to adore as a god. **deifica'tion,** *n.*

deign (dān) [O.F. *degnier*], *v.i.* To condescend, to vouchsafe.

deism (dē'izm) [L. *deus,* god], *n.* The belief in the being of a god without accepting divine revelation. **deist,** *n.* **deistic, -ical,** *a.*

deity (dē'i-ti) [L. *deitās,* from *deus,* god], *n.* Divine nature; the Supreme Being.

deject (dĕ-jekt') [L. *jectus,* thrown], *v.t.* To depress in spirit; to dishearten. **dejectedly,** *adv.* **dejection,** *n.*

déjeuner (dā'zhu-nā) [F.], *n.* Breakfast, luncheon.

delay (dĕ-lā') [O.F. *delaier*], *v.t.* To postpone; to hinder, retard. *v.i.* To put off action; to linger. *n.* A stopping; postponement, retardation; hindrance.

delectable (dĕ-lek'tábl) [L. *dēlectāre,* to delight], *a.* Delightful, highly pleasing. **delecta'tion,** *n.* Delight, enjoyment.

delegate (del'ĕ-gāt) [L. *lēgātus,* deputed], *n.* A representative, deputy, agent. *v.t.* (-gāt). To depute as delegate with authority to transact business. **delega'tion,** *n.* The act of delegating; a body of delegates.

delete (dĕ-lēt') [L. *dēlētus,* erased], *v.t.* To strike out, to erase. **deletion,** *n.*

deleterious (del-ĕ-tēr'i-ŭs) [Gr. *dēlētērios, dēlētēr,* a destroyer], *a.* Noxious; injurious to health or mind.

deliberate (dĕ-lib'ẽr-āt) [L. *līberātus,* weighed], *a.* Circumspect, cautious; leisurely, not hasty. *v.i.* (-āt) To weigh matters in the mind, to ponder; to discuss, take counsel. *v.t.* To weigh in the mind. **deliberately,** *adv.* **deliberateness,** *n.* **delibera'tion,** *n.*

delicacy (del'i-ká-si), *n.* The quality of being delicate; a luxury, a dainty; fineness of texture, workmanship, etc.; fragility, susceptibility to injury; nicety of perception; sensitiveness.

delicate (del'i-kát) [L. *dēlicātus*], *a.* Highly pleasing to the taste; dainty, palatable; fine, smooth; fastidious, effeminate; sensitive, subtle in colour, form, or style; easily injured, fragile; weak or feeble;

critical, ticklish; refined, gentle, considerate.

delicious (dē-lish'ŭs) [L. *deliciæ*, delight], *a.* Yielding great pleasure to the senses or taste. deliciously, *adv.*

delight (dē-līt') [L. *dēlectāre*], *v.t.* To please greatly, to charm. *v.i.* To be highly pleased. *n.* A state or source of great pleasure and satisfaction. delightedly, *adv.* delightful, *a.*

delineate (dē-lin'ē-āt) [L. *lineātus*, marked out], *v.t.* To sketch out; to describe, depict. delinea'tion, *n.*

delinquent (dē-ling'kwĕnt) [L. *dēlinquens*], *a.* Failing, neglecting. *n.* One who fails in his duty; an offender; a culprit. delinquency, *n.*

delirious (dē-lir'i-ŭs), *a.* Wandering in mind; raving, madly excited.

delirium (dē-lir'i-ŭm) [L.], *n.* A wandering of the mind; frantic excitement or enthusiasm, rapture, ecstasy.

deliver (dē-liv'ĕr) [L. *līberāre*, to set free], *v.t.* To free from danger or restraint, to rescue; to disburden of a child; to send forth; to utter, esp. formally or officially; to surrender, to give over, to hand over or on. deliverance, *n.* The act of delivering; the state of being delivered; acquittal; the decision of a judge. deliverer, *n.*

delivery (dē-liv'ĕr-i), *n.* The act of delivering; rescue, surrender; a distribution from the post; utterance or style or manner of speaking; child-birth; discharge of a blow or missile.

dell (del) [A.-S.], *n.* A hollow, or a small wooded valley.

delta (del'tà) [Gr.], *n.* The fourth letter of the Greek alphabet (Δ); the delta-shaped alluvial deposit at the mouth of a river. deltoid, *a.* Shaped like a delta.

delude (dē-lūd') [L. *lūdere*, to play], *v.t.* To deceive, to impose upon. deluder, *n.*

deluge (del'ūj) [F. *déluge*], *n.* A general flood, esp. that of Noah; (*fig.*) a heavy downpour of rain. *v.t.* To flood.

delusion (dē-lū'zhŭn), *n.* The act of deluding; the state of being deluded; an imposition, error, fallacy; a persistent illusion. delusive, *a.* Deceptive, unreal.

delve (delv) [A.-S. *delfan*], *v.* To dig; to fathom, get to the bottom of; to carry on laborious research; to descend suddenly.

demagnetize (dē-măg'nē-tīz), *v.t.* To deprive of magnetism.

demagogue (dem'à-gog) [Gr. *dēmagōgus*], *n.* A leader of the people; an agitator.

demand (dē-mand') [L. *mandāre*, to order], *n.* An authoritative claim or request; the thing demanded, esp. price; a peremptory question; desire to purchase or possess. *v.t.* To ask or claim with authority or as a right; to question or ask, esp. in a peremptory or insistent manner; to need, require. demandable, *a.*

demean (dē-mēn') [O.F. *demener*], *v.t.* To conduct (oneself), to behave; to debase, lower. demeanour, *n.* Conduct, behaviour, deportment.

demented (dē-men'tĕd) [L. *mens mentis*, mind], *a.* Deprived of reason; insane. dementia, *n.* Infatuation; loss or feebleness of the mental faculties.

demerit (dē-mer'it) [L. *merēre*, to deserve], *n.* Fault, vice.

demesne (dē-mān) [O.F.], *n.* The manor-house and adjoining lands which a lord retains; a region, territory.

demi- [F., half], *pref.* Half, partially. demigod, *n.* An inferior deity; the offspring of a god and a human; a deified man. demijohn, *n.* A glass vessel with a large body and small neck, enclosed in wickerwork.

demise (dē-mīz') [O.F., laid down], *n.* Decease, esp. of a sovereign or nobleman; a transfer or conveyance for a term of years or in fee simple. *v.t.* To bequeath; to transfer or convey by lease or will.

demobilize (dē-mō'bi-līz), *v.t.* To disband, to dismiss (as troops) from a war footing. demobiliza'tion, *n.*

democracy (dē-mok'rà-si) [Gr. *demos*, -CRACY], *n.* Government by the people directly or indirectly; a democratic State; the people at large. demo'crat, *n.* One in favour of democracy. democrat'ic, *a.*

demolish (dē-mol'ish) [L. *mōlīrī*, to construct], *v.t.* To throw down; to ruin, destroy. dem'olition, *n.* Ruin.

demon (dē'mŏn) [Gr. *daimōn*, a deity], *n.* A spirit, esp. an evil spirit able to take possession of human beings; a fallen angel, a devil; a very cruel or malignant person. demoniac (dē-mō'ni-ăk), *a.* Pertaining to demons; possessed by a demon; devilish, *n.* One possessed by a demon.

demonstrate (dem'ŏn-strāt) [L. *monstrātus*, shown], *v.t.* To prove beyond the possibility of doubt; to exhibit, describe, and prove; to indicate. demon'strable, *a.* That may be proved beyond doubt. demonstrably, *adv.* demonstra'tion, *n.* The act of demonstrating; indubitable proof; a manifestation of feeling, public exhibition or declaration of principles, exhibition and description of objects for teaching, etc.; a movement of troops as if to attack. demon'strative, *a.* Pertaining to proof; serving to make clear; manifesting the feelings strongly and openly. dem'onstrator, *n.* One who teaches by means of exhibition and experiment; one who takes part in a public demonstration.

demoralize (dē-mor'à-līz), *v.t.* To subvert and corrupt the principles, discipline, or moral of. demoraliza'tion, *n.*

demur (dē-mĕr') [O.F. *demeurer*], *v.i.* To hesitate; to have or express scruples; to take exception. *n.* The act of demurring; scruple, objection. demurrage (dē-mŭr'àj), *n.* Compensation for delay in loading or unloading a vessel, railway truck, etc.; the period of such delay; a discount paid in exchanging notes or coin for bullion. demurrer (dē-mŭr'ĕr), *n.* An objection, esp. one made on a point of law.

demure (dē-mūr') [M.E. *mure*], *a.* Sober, staid; grave; prudish. demurely, *adv.* demureness, *n.*

demy (de-mī') [DEMI-], *n.* A particular size of paper; a scholar of Magdalen College, Oxford.

den (den) [A.-S. *denn*], *n.* A lair, retreat, lurking-place.

deniable (dē-nī'abl), *a.* That may be denied. **denial**, *n.* The act of contradicting, or refusing; a negation.

denim (den'ĭm) [F. *serge de Nîmes*], *n.* (*Am.*) A coarse twilled cotton fabric.

denizen (den'ĭ-zĕn) [A.-F. *denizein*], *n.* A dweller, resident.

denominate (dē-nom'ĭ-nāt), *v.t.* To give a name, epithet, or title to; to designate. **denomina'tion**, *n.* The act of naming; a designation; a class, kind, esp. of particular units (coins, weights, etc.); a sect. **denominational**, *a.* Sectarian. **denominationalism**, *n.* **denominator**, *n.* One who or that which denominates; the number below the line in a vulgar fraction.

denote (dē-nōt') [L. *notāre*, to mark], *v.t.* To indicate, signify; to mark out. **denotable**, *a.* **denotation** (-tā'shŭn), *n.*

dénouement (dā-noo'man) [F.], *n.* The unravelling of a plot or story; the final solution of a plot, upshot.

denounce (dē-nouns') [L. *nuntiāre*, to announce], *v.t.* To accuse publicly; to inform against; to terminate a treaty or convention. **denouncement**, *n.*

dense (dens) [L. *densus*], *a.* Thick, compact; stupid, obtuse; opaque. **densely**, *adv.* **denseness**, *n.* **density**, *n.*

dent (dent), *n.* A depression such as is caused by a blunt instrument; an indentation. *v.t.* To make a dent in.

dental (den'tăl) [L. *dens dentis*, a tooth], *a.* Pertaining to or formed by the teeth. *n.* A letter or sound formed by placing the tip of the tongue against the upper teeth. **den'tate**, **-ta'ted**, *a.* Toothed; indented. **denta'tion**, *n.*

denti- [as prec.], *comb. form.* Pertaining to the teeth. **dentifrice** [L. *fricāre*, to rub], *n.* Material for cleansing the teeth.

dentist (den'tist), *n.* A dental surgeon. **dentistry**, *n.*

dentition, *n.* Teething; the arrangement of teeth in the head.

denture (den'tūr) [DENTI-], *n.* A set of artificial teeth.

denude (de-nūd') [L. *denudare*, to strip], *v.t.* To make bare.

denunciate (dē-nŭn'sĭ-āt), *v.t.* To denounce. **denuncia'tion**, *n.* **denunciatory**, *a.*

deny (dē-nī') [L. *dēnegāre*], *v.t.* To assert to be untrue or non-existent; to reject, refuse to grant, refuse access to.

deodorize (dē-ō'dŏr-īz), *v.t.* To deprive of odour; to disinfect. **deodorizer**, **deodorant**, *n.*

depart (dē-part') [L. *partīre*, to part], *v.i.* To go away; to diverge, to deviate; to die. **the departed:** The dead.

department (dē-part'mĕnt) [F. *département*], *n.* A branch of a business, an administration, duty, study, science, etc.; an administrative division. **departmen'tal**, *a.*

departure (dē-par'chūr), *n.* The act of departing; leaving; starting; death; a deviation.

depend (dē-pend') [L. *pendēre*, to hang], *v.i.* To hang from; to be contingent on something else; to trust, to reckon (upon); to be pending. **dependable**, *a.*

That may be depended upon. **dependant**, *n.* One depending upon another; a retainer. **dependence**, *n.* The state of being dependent; connection; trust, confidence. **dependency**, *n.* Something dependent, esp. a state subject to another. **dependent**, *a.*

depict (dē-pikt') [L. *pictus*, painted], *v.t.* To portray.

deplete (dē-plēt') [L. *plētus*, filled], *v.t.* To empty, to exhaust. **depletion**, *n.*

deplore (dē-plōr') [L. *plōrāre*, to wail], *v.t.* To lament over; to grieve, regret. **deplorable**, *a.* **deplorably**, *adv.*

deploy (dē-ploi') [F. *déployer*], *v.t.* (*Mil.*) To open out; to extend from column into line. *v.i.* To form a more extended front.

deponent [L. *pōnere*, to put], *n.* One who makes an affidavit to any statement of fact; applied to a Latin verb with a passive form and active meaning.

depopulate (dē-pop'ū-lāt) [L. *dēpopulātus*, laid waste], *v.t.* To clear of inhabitants. **depopula'tion**, *n.*

deport (dē-pōrt') [L. *portāre*, to carry], *v.t.* To transport, send away from one country to another; to demean, behave (oneself, etc.). **deporta'tion**, *n.* The act of transporting to a foreign land; exile. **deportment**, *n.* Demeanour, manners.

depose (dē-pōz') [L. *pausāre*, to pause], *v.t.* To remove from a throne or other high office; to testify on oath. *v.i.* To bear witness. **deposable**, *a.*

deposit (dē-poz'ĭt) [L. *depositum*], *v.t.* To lay down, to place; to lodge for safety or as a pledge; to lay (as eggs); to leave as precipitation. *n.* Anything deposited or laid down; a pledge, a first instalment, security; money lodged in a bank; matter precipitated and left behind. **depositary**, *n.* One with whom anything is deposited for safety; a trustee. **depositor**, *n.* One who makes a deposit, esp. of money. **depository**, *n.* A place where anything is deposited for safety; a repository.

deposition (dē-pō-zish'ŭn), *n.* The act of depositing or deposing; a statement, declaration; the act of bearing witness on oath; the evidence of a witness in writing.

depot (dep'ō) [F. *dépôt*], *n.* A storehouse; the headquarters of a regiment; (*Am.*) a railway station.

deprave (dē-prāv') [L. *prāvus*, crooked], *v.t.* To make bad or corrupt; to vitiate. **depravity** (dē-prăv'ĭ-ti), *n.* Viciousness.

deprecate (dep'rē-kāt) [L. *precātus*, prayed], *v.t.* To try to avert by prayer; to express disapproval of or regret for.

depreciate (dē-prē'shi-āt) [L. *pretiātus*, valued], *v.t.* To lower the value of; to disparage, decry. *v.i.* To fall in value. **deprecia'tion**, *n.*

depredation (dep-rē-dā'shŭn) [L. *prœdāri*, to rob], *n.* Plundering, spoliation. **dep'redator**, *n.* A pillager, a plunderer.

depress (dē-pres') [L. *pressus*, pressed], *v.t.* To press down, lower; to humble, abase; to keep down the energy of, to dispirit. **depressing**, *a.* **depression** (dē-presh'ŭn), *n.* The act of depressing; the state of being depressed; dejection; lowering of energy or activity, slackness of business;

a hollow place on a surface; a low state of the barometer indicative of bad weather; the centre of low pressure in a cyclone.

deprive (dė-prīv') [L. *prīvāre*], *v.t.* To take from, dispossess, to bereave. **depriva'tion,** *n.*

depth (depth), *n.* Deepness; measurement from the surface or front downwards or backwards; an abyss; the innermost part; the middle of a season; abstruseness, profundity; intensity of colour, etc. **depth charge,** *n.* (*Naut.*) A mine exploded under water.

depute (dė-pūt') [L. *putāre*, to consider], *v.t.* To appoint as a substitute or agent; to give as a charge. **deputa'tion,** *n.* The act of deputing; an authority or commission to act; the person or persons sent as representatives. **dep'utize,** *v.i.* To act as deputy. **deputy,** *n.* One who is appointed to act for others.

derail (dė-rāl'), *v.* To throw or run off the rails. **derailment,** *n.*

derange (dė-rānj'), *v.t.* To put out of order; to disorganize, disturb, unsettle. **deranged,** *a.* Slightly insane. **derangement,** *n.*

derelict (der'ė-likt) [L. *relictus*, relinquished], *a.* Forsaken, abandoned. *n.* Anything abandoned, esp. a vessel at sea. **derelic'tion,** *n.* Omission or neglect (as of a duty); forsaking, abandonment.

deride (dė-rīd') [L. *rīdēre*, to laugh], *v.* To laugh at, to mock, ridicule. **derision** (dė-rizh'ŭn), *n.* The act of deriding; the state of being derided; ridicule, contempt. **derisive, -sory,** *a.* Scoffing, deriding.

derive (dė-rīv') [L. *dērīvāre*, to draw off water], *v.t.* To obtain as by logical sequence; to deduce; to draw, as from a source, root or principle; to trace. *v.i.* To come from; to originate. **derivable,** *a.* That may be derived; deducible. **deriva'tion,** *n.* The act of deriving; deduction; the etymology of a word or process of tracing it. **deriv'ative,** *a.* Derived; secondary, not original. *n.* Anything derived from a source, as a word from another. **derivatively,** *adv.*

derogate (der'ō-gāt) [L. *rogātus*, asked], *v.i.* To detract. *v.t.* To lessen the effect of; to detract from, disparage. **deroga'tion,** *n.* **derog'atory,** *a.* Tending to detract; disparaging, depreciatory.

derrick (der'ik) [*Derrick*, a 17th-cent. Tyburn hangman], *n.* A crane for raising heavy weights.

derris (der'is), *n.* (*Chem.*) An extract from the root of the Derris tree used as an insecticide.

dervish (dẽr'vish) [Pers.], *n.* A Mohammedan friar who vows poverty.

descant (des'kȧnt) [DIS-], L. *cantus*, song], *n.* A song, a melody. *v.i.* (des-kȧnt') To comment or discourse at large, to dilate (on).

descend (dė-send') [L. *scandere*, to climb], *v.i.* To come or go down, to sink, to slope downwards; to attack, fall upon suddenly; to be derived; to be handed down; to lower or humble oneself. *v.t.* To walk, move, or pass along downwards.

descendant, *n.* One who descends from an ancestor; offspring.

descent (dė-sent'), *n.* The act of descending; a declivity, way of descending; decline in rank or prosperity; a sudden attack; pedigree, lineage; transmission by succession or inheritance.

describe (dė-skrīb') [L. *scrībere*, to write], *v.t.* To draw, to trace out; to portray in words, to relate. *v.i.* To give a description. **describable,** *a.* **descrip'tion,** *n.* The act of describing; an account of anything; a kind, sort.

descry (dė-skrī') [O.F. *descrire*], *v.t.* To make out, to espy.

desecrate (des'ė-krāt) [L. *dēsecrātus*], *v.t.* To divert from any sacred purpose; to profane. **desecra'tion,** *n.* **des'ecrator,** *n.*

desert (1) (dez'ẽrt) [L. *dēsertus*], *a.* Uninhabited, waste. *n.* A waste, uninhabited, uncultivated place.

desert (2) (dė-zẽrt'), *v.t.* To forsake, to abandon; to quit, fail to help. *v.i.* To abandon a service without leave. **deserter,** *n.* **desertion,** *n.*

desert (3) (dė-zẽrt'), *n.* What one deserves; reward or punishment; merit or demerit; state of deserving; (*pl.*) deserved reward or punishment.

deserve (dė-zẽrv') [L. *servīre*, to serve], *v.t.* To be worthy of, to merit by conduct or qualities. *v.i.* To be worthy or deserving. **deservedly,** *adv.* **deserving,** *a.*

deshabille (des-à-bēl') [F. *déshabillé*, undressed], *n.* Undress, being partly or carelessly attired.

desiccate (des'i-kāt) [L. *siccātus*, dried], *v.t.* To dry, to exhaust of moisture.

desiderate (dė-zid'ẽr-āt) [L. *dēsiderātus*, desired], *v.t.* To feel the loss of; to want, to miss. **desiderative,** *a.* Expressing or having desire. **desidera'tum,** *n.* (*pl.* **-ta**) Anything desired.

design (dė-zīn') [L. *signāre*, to mark], *v.t.* To contrive, project; to draw, plan, sketch out; to purpose, intend. *v.i.* To draw, esp. decorative figures. *n.* A plan, a scheme; a purpose, intention, project; a sketch of something intended to be executed in durable material; the art of designing; artistic structure or invention; plot, construction, general idea. **designedly** (dė-zī-nėd-li), *adv.* Intentionally. **designer,** *n.* One who designs, esp. artistic patterns. **designing,** *a.* Crafty, scheming.

designate (dez'ig-nāt), *v.t.* To point out, to specify by a distinctive mark or name; to indicate, nominate, appoint. **designa'tion,** *n.*

desire (dė-zīr') [O.F. *desirer*], *v.t.* To covet, wish for the attainment or possession of; to request, command. *n.* An eagerness to obtain or enjoy some object; a request, entreaty; the object of desire; sensual appetite. **desirable,** *a.* Worthy of being desired; agreeable. **desirabil'ity,** *n.* **desirous,** *a.* Desiring, wishful.

desist (dė-zist', -sist') [L. *sistere*, to put, stop], *v.i.* To cease, to forbear.

desk (desk) [L. *discus*, a disk], *n.* A table, frame, or case for a writer or reader; a reading-stand, lectern.

desolate (des'ō-lāt) [L. *sōlātus*, made

lonely], *a.* Uninhabited, deserted, forlorn, comfortless. *v.t.* To deprive of inhabitants; to lay waste; to make wretched. **desolating,** *a.* Wasting, ruining, ravaging. **desola'tion,** *n.*

despair (dĕ-spâr') [L. *spērāre*, to hope], *v.i.* To be without or to give up hope. *n.* Hopelessness.

desperado (des-pĕr-ā'dō) [O.Sp.], *n.* A desperate or reckless ruffian.

desperate (des'pĕr-åt) [L. *dēspērāre*, to despair], *a.* Reckless, regardless of danger or consequences; extremely dangerous. **despera'tion,** *n.*

despicable (des'pik-åbl), *a.* Contemptible; vile, mean.

despise (dĕ-spīz') [L. *specere*, to look at], *v.t.* To regard with contempt.

despite (dĕ-spīt'), *n.* Spite, malice; outrage, contumely. *prep.* Notwithstanding; in spite of.

despoil (dĕ-spoil') [L. *spoliāre*, to spoil], *v.t.* To take away from by force.

despond (dĕ-spond') [L. *spondēre*, to promise], *v.i.* To be cast down in spirits. **despondency,** *n.* **despondent,** *a.*

despot (des'pŏt) [O.F.], *n.* An absolute ruler; a tyrant, oppressor. **despot'ic,** *a.* **des'potism,** *n.* Absolute authority; autocracy; tyranny.

dessert (dĕ-zĕrt') [F. *desservir*, to clear the table], *n.* The last course at dinner, fruit, sweetmeats, etc.

destination (des-ti-nā'shŭn) [L. *dēstinātus*, destined], *n.* The act of destining; ultimate purpose; the place to which one is bound, or a thing is sent.

destine (des'tin) [F. *destiner*], *v.t.* To appoint, fix, or determine to a use, etc. **destiny,** *n.* The end to which any person or thing is appointed; fate, fortune; invincible necessity.

destitute (des'ti-tūt) [L. *stitūtus*, placed], *a.* In want of the necessities of life; forlorn.

destroy (dĕ-stroi') [L. *struere*, to build], *v.t.* To pull down, demolish; to lay waste, kill, extirpate; to disprove, to put an end to. **destroyer,** *n.* One who destroys; a fast warship armed with torpedoes. **destructible,** *a.* **destructibil'ity,** *n.* **destruc'tion,** *n.* Demolition; death, slaughter; that which destroys. **destruc'tive,** *a.* Causing destruction.

desultory (des'ŭl-tòr-i) [L. *dēsultōrius*], *a.* Following no regular plan; loose, discursive. **desultorily,** *adv.* **desultoriness,** *n.*

detach (dĕ-tåch') [F. *détacher*], *v.t.* To disconnect, separate, disengage. **detachable,** *a.* **detached,** *a.* Separated; free from prejudice; disinterested. **detachment,** *n.* The act of detaching; state of being detached; a body of troops or a number of ships detached from the main body for special service; freedom from prejudice.

detail (dĕ-tāl') [F. *tailler*, to cut], *v.t.* To relate minutely; (*Mil.*) to appoint for a particular service. *n.* (dē'tāl) An item, a minor matter; a minute account; (*pl.*) a number of particulars; men selected for a special duty. **detailed,** *a.* Related in detail; minute; complete.

detain (dĕ-tān') [L. *tenēre*, to hold], *v.t.* To keep back or from; to withhold; to hinder, restrain, keep in custody.

detect (dĕ-tekt') [L. *tectus*, covered], *v.t.* To discover, find out, bring to light. **detection,** *n.* The act of detecting; the discovery of crime, etc. **detective,** *a.* Employed in or suitable for detecting. *n.* One employed to investigate cases of crime, etc.

detention (dĕ-ten'shŭn), *n.* The act of detaining; state of being detained; arrest; restraint.

deter (dĕ-tĕr') [L. *terrēre*, to frighten], *v.t.* To discourage, hinder, or prevent. **deterrent,** *a.* Tending to deter. *n.* That which deters.

detergent (de-ter'jĕnt) [L. *detergens*], *a.* Cleansing, purging. *n.* Chemical agent for cleansing.

deteriorate (dĕ-tĕr'ĭ-òr-āt) [L. *deterior*, worse], *v.* To make or become worse; to degenerate; to reduce in value. **deteriora'tion,** *n.*

determinate (dĕ-tĕr'mĭ-nåt), *a.* Limited, definite; distinct.

determination (dĕ-tĕr'mĭ-nā'shŭn), *n.* The act of determining; that which is determined on; a fixed intention; resolution, strength of mind; direction to a certain end; settlement by a judicial decision; final conclusion.

determine (dĕ-tĕr'min) [L. *termināre*, to bound], *v.t.* To terminate, conclude; to fix the limits of, define; to decide finally; to direct, shape; to ascertain exactly. *v.i.* To decide, resolve. **determinable,** *a.* **determined,** *a.* Resolute; having a fixed purpose; ended.

detest (dĕ-test') [L. *testāri*, to testify], *v.t.* To hate exceedingly, abhor. **detestable,** *a.* **detesta'tion,** *n.*

dethrone (dĕ-thrōn'), *v.t.* To depose; to drive from power or pre-eminence. **dethronement,** *n.*

detonate (de'tò-nāt) [L. *tonātus*, thundered], *v.t.* To cause to explode with a report. *v.i.* To explode. **detonation,** *n.* An explosion with a loud report.

detour (dĕ-toor') [F. *détour*], *n.* A round-about way; a deviation, digression.

detract (dĕ-träkt') [L. *tractus*, drawn], *v.t.* To take (something) away from. *v.i.* To disparage. **detraction,** *n.* The act of detracting; depreciation, slander.

detrain (dĕ-trān'), *v.* To alight from or cause to alight from a train.

detriment (det'ri-mĕnt) [L. *dētrīmentum*], *n.* Loss; injury, damage. **detrimen'tal,** *a.* Causing detriment.

detritus (det'ri-tŭs) [L., rubbed down], *n.* Accumulated matter produced by the disintegration of rock.

deuce (dūs) [F. *deux*], *n.* A card or die with two spots; (*Tennis*) a score of 40 all; the devil, invoked as a mild oath.

devastate (dev'á-stāt) [L. *vastātus*, wasted], *v.t.* To lay waste, ravage. **devasta'tion,** *n.* **dev'astator,** *n.*

develop (dĕ-vel'ŏp) [F. *développer*], *v.t.* To unfold, to bring to light gradually; to work out, bring to completion; (*Photo.*) to render visible the picture latent in a sensitized film. *v.i.* To expand; to be evolved; to come to light or maturity. **development,** *n.*

deviate (dē'vi-āt) [L. *via*, way], *v.i.* To

turn aside; **to** stray from the path of duty. *v.t.* To cause to stray or err. **devia′tion,** *n.* The act of deviating; error; the deflection of a compass, etc.

device (dē-vīs′) [O.F. *devis*], *n.* A scheme, stratagem, trick; **an** invention; inventive skill; a design, pattern; a motto; (*pl.*) will, inclination.

devil (devl) [A.-S. *dēoful*, L. *diabolus*], *n.* Satan, the tempter; any evil spirit, as one possessing a demoniac; a wicked, malignant, or cruel person; a wretch; energy, dash, unconquerable spirit; a device for tearing rags; one who does literary or legal work for which another takes the credit or fees; a printer's errand-boy. *v.t.* To make devilish; to grill with pepper; to tear up rags with a devil. *v.i.* To act as a literary or legal devil. **devil-may-care,** *a.* Reckless. **dev′ilish,** *a.* **dev′ilment,** *n.* **dev′ilry,** *n.*

devious (dē′vi-ŭs) [L. *via*, way], *a.* Sequestered; wandering out of the way; circuitous; rambling. **deviously,** *adv.*

devise (dē-vīz′) [O.F. *deviser*], *v.t.* To invent, contrive; to scheme, plot; to give or assign by will. *n.* The act of bequeathing landed property by will; a will or clause doing this. **deviser,** *n.* One who devises. **devisor,** *n.* One who bequeaths.

devoid (dē-void′), *a.* Vacant, destitute, empty (of).

devolution (dē-vō-loo′shŭn) [L. *volūtus*, rolled], *n.* Transference or delegation of authority; passage from one to another; descent in natural succession.

devolve (dē-volv′) [L. *volvere*, to roll], *v.t.* To cause to pass to another, to transfer. *v.i.* To be transferred or delegated; to fall by succession.

devote (dē-vōt′) [L. *vōtus*, vowed], *v.t.* To consecrate; to give wholly up (to); to doom, consign (to ruin, etc.). **devoted,** *a.* Dedicated, consecrated; wholly given up, zealous. **devotee′,** *n.* A votary, a person devoted to; a bigot, enthusiast. **devotion,** *n.* The act of devoting; state of being devoted; deep, self-sacrificing attachment, intense loyalty; (*pl.*) prayer, religious worship. **devotional,** *a.*

devour (dē-vour′) [L. *vorāre*, to swallow], *v.t.* To eat up ravenously or swiftly; to swallow up.

devout (dē-vout′), *a.* Pious, filled with or expressing devotion; heartfelt, earnest. **devoutness,** *n.*

dew (dū) [A.-S. *dēaw*], *n.* Moisture condensed from the atmosphere upon cold surfaces after sunset; anything falling cool and light, so as to refresh; tears, sweat. *v.t.* To wet with dew. **dewdrop,** *n.* A drop of dew. **dew pond,** *n.* An artificial pond where water collects at night from condensation. **dewy,** *a.*

dewlap (dū′lăp) [?; A.-S. *læppa*, a skirt], *n.* The flesh that hangs loosely from the throat of oxen.

dexter (deks′tĕr) [L.], *a.* Pertaining to or situated on the right-hand side. **dexterity,** *n.* Skill, expertness; readiness and ease; cleverness, quickness, tact. **dex′terous,** *a.* Expert in any manual employment; quick, skilful, able. **dexterously,** *adv.*

dhow (dou) [?], *n.* An Arab vessel, esp. one used in the slave-trade.

di- (1) [see [DIS], *pref.*

di- (2) [Gr. *di-*, double], *pref.* Twice, double.

di- (3), **dia-** [Gr. *dia*], *pref.* Through; thorough.

diabetes (dī-à-bē′tēz) [Gr. *bainein*, to go], *n.* A disease marked by excessive discharge of urine containing glucose.

diabolic, -ical (dī-à-bol′ik, -àl) [Gr. *diabolos*, devil], *a.* Pertaining to the devil; fiendish, devilish. **diabolically,** *adv.* **diab′olism,** *n.* Devil-worship; belief in the Devil or in devils; black magic.

diaconal (dī-ăk′ō-nàl) [F.], *a.* Pertaining to a deacon. **diac′onate,** *n.* The office, dignity, etc., of a deacon; deacons collectively.

diadem (dī′à-dem) [Gr. *deein*, to bind], *n.* An ornamental head-band as an emblem of sovereignty; a crown, wreath.

diæresis (dī-ēr′ē-sis) [Gr., from *diaireein*, to divide], *n.* (*pl.* **-eses**). The resolution of one syllable into two; a mark (¨) indicating this, as *Laïs*.

diagnosis (dī-àg-nō′sis) [Gr. *gnōsis*, inquiry], *n.* Determination of diseases by their symptoms; a summary of these. **diagnose′,** *v.t.* To ascertain the nature (esp. of a disease) from the symptoms. *v.t.* To make a diagnosis.

diagonal (dī-ăg′ō-nàl) [Gr. *gōnia*, an angle], *a.* Extending from one angle of a figure to a non-adjacent angle; oblique, crossing obliquely. *n.* A right line or plane extending from one angle or edge to a non-adjacent one. **diagonally,** *adv.*

diagram (dī′à-grăm) [L. and Gr. *diagramma*], *n.* A drawing demonstrating some proposition, statement, or definition; a rough outline. **diagrammat′ic,** *a.*

dial (dī′àl) [L. *didis*, daily], *n.* An instrument for showing the time by the sun's shadow; the face of a time-piece; a similar plate on which a pointer marks revolutions, indicates steam-pressure, etc.; (*Wire.*) the device for adjusting the tuning controls. *v.i.* To call by means of a telephone dial.

dialect (dī′à-lekt) [Gr. *dialektos*], *n.* A form of speech peculiar to a limited district or people. **dialec′tal,** *a.*

dialectic (dī-à-lek′tik) [Gr. *dialektikē* (*technē*), the dialectic (art)], *a.* Dialectal; pertaining to logic; argumentative. *n.* (*often in pl.*) The rules and methods of reasoning; hair-splitting; logic of probabilities. **dialectically,** *adv.* In a logical manner; dialectally.

dialogue (dī′à-log) [Gr. *logos*, discourse], *n.* A conversation between two or more persons; a literary composition in conversational form.

diameter (dī-ăm′é-tĕr), *n.* A straight line passing through the centre of a circle and terminating each way in the circumference; the length of such a line; the length of a straight line extending from side to side of anything. **diamet′rical,** *a.* Pertaining to or along a diameter, direct; directly opposed; as far removed as possible. **diametrically,** *adv.*

diamond (dī′à-mŏnd) [Gr. *adamas,*

adamant], *n.* The hardest, most brilliant, and most valuable of the precious stones; a playing-card with figures of this shape; a very small printing type. *a.* Made of, or set with, diamonds. **diamond wedding**, *n.* The sixtieth anniversary of a wedding.

diapason (dī-à-pā'zòn) [Gr.], *n.* An harmonious combination or melodious succession of notes; the foundation stops of an organ; harmony, concord; range, pitch.

diaper (dī'à-pèr) [Gr. *aspros*, white], *n.* A silk or linen cloth woven with geometric patterns; a towel or napkin made of this. *v.t.* To decorate thus.

diaphanous (dī-àf'à-nùs) [Gr. *phainein*, to show], *a.* Transparent; having the power of transmitting light.

diaphragm (dī'à-frăm) [Gr. *diaphragma*], *n.* The muscle separating the thorax from the abdomen; a dividing membrane or partition.

diarrhœa (dī-à-rē'à) [Gr. *rheein*, to flow], *n.* Excessive discharge of fluid evacuations from the intestines.

diary (dī'à-ri) [L. *diārium, diēs*, a day], *n.* An account of daily occurrences; the book in which these are registered; a journal.

diastole (dī-ăs'tò-lē) [Gr. *stellein*, to send], *n.* Dilatation of the heart and arteries alternating with systole.

diatom (dī'à-tòm) [Gr. *temnein*, to cut], *n.* One of the microscopic algæ with siliceous coverings which exist in immense numbers at the bottom of the sea.

diatribe (dī'à-trīb) [Gr. *diatribē*, a wearing away], *n.* An invective discourse.

dibble (dibl) [?], *n.* A pointed instrument used to make a hole to receive seed.

dice (dīs), *n.pl.* See DIE. *v.t.* To gamble (away) at dice; to ornament with squares. **dicer**, *n.*

dichotomy (di-kot'ō-mi) [Gr. *dicho*, asunder], *n.* A separation into two; division into two separate parts.

dicky (dik'i) [?], *n.* A bib; a front separate from the shirt; a seat behind the body of a carriage; a bird. *a.* Doubtful, questionable; queer, unwell.

dictaphone (dik'tà-fōn), *n.* An apparatus for recording and audibly reproducing dictated letters, etc.

dictate (dik-tāt') [L. *dictātus*], *v.t.* To read or recite words to be written or repeated; to prescribe, to lay down with authority, to impose, as terms. *v.i.* To give orders; to utter words to be written or repeated by another. *n.* (dik'tāt). An order, injunction. **dicta'tion**, *n.* **dicta'tor**, *n.* One who dictates; one invested with supreme authority, esp. in a time of civil disorder or after a revolution. **dictator'ial**, *a.* Imperious, overbearing. **dictatorially**, *adv.* **dictatorship**, *n.*

diction (dik'shùn) [L. *dictio*], *n.* The use of words; manner of expression; style.

dictionary (dīk'shùn-àr-i) [L. *dictiōnārium*], *n.* A book containing the words of a language in alphabetical order, with their definitions.

dictum (dik'tùm) [L. *dīcere*, to say], *n.* (*pl.* -ta) A dogmatic assertion.

didactic (di-dăk'tik) [Gr. *didaktikos*], *a.*

Adapted or tending to teach; in the manner of a teacher. *n.pl.* The science of teaching.

die (1) (dī) [M.E. *degen*], *v.i.* To lose life, to expire; to come to an end; to wither, lose vitality, decay; to go out, disappear; to fade away, to languish with affection.

die (2) (dī) [O.F. *de, det*], *n.* A small cube marked on the sides, used in gaming; hazard, chance; (*pl.* dice) the game played with these; (*pl.* dies) a machine for cutting out, shaping, or stamping; a stamp for coining money, or for impressing upon metal, paper, etc. **diesinker**, *n.* One who cuts dies for coins, medals, etc.

diesel engine (dē'zel) [name of inventor], *n.* (*Eng.*) An engine which burns heavy oil.

diet (dī'et) [O.F. *diete*], *n.* A prescribed course of food; a legislative assembly or federal parliament holding its meetings from day to day; a conference or congress. *v.t.* To feed according to rules. *v.i.* To take food as prescribed. **di'etary**, *a.* Pertaining to a rule of diet; *n.* A prescribed course of diet, fixed daily allowance of food. **dietet'ic**, *a.* Pertaining to diet. **dietetics**, *n.pl.* The science or rules of diet.

dif- [DIS-], *pref.*, before *f* in words from Latin.

differ (dif'èr) [L. *ferre*, to bear], *v.i.* To be dissimiliar; to disagree, dissent. **difference**, *n.* The state of being unlike or distinct; that by which one differs from another; the remainder of a quantity after another quantity has been subtracted from it; a distinction, differential mark; a point in dispute, a disagreement in opinion, a controversy. *v.t.* To distinguish between; to make different. **different**, *a.* **differential**, *a.* Consisting of, depending on, or creating a difference; relating to specific differences. **differential gear**, *n.* (*Motor.*) A device which enables the rear (driving) wheels to rotate at different speeds when rounding a corner.

differentiate (dif-èr-en'shi-āt), *v.t.* To make different; to constitute difference between, of, or in, to mark off as different. **differentia'tion**, *n.*

difficult (dif'i-kùlt) [L. *difficultās*], *a.* Hard to do, to please, or to understand; not easily managed; troublesome; perplexing. **difficultly**, *adv.* **difficulty**, *n.* The quality of being difficult; anything difficult; an obstacle; reluctance, scruple; (*pl.*) pecuniary embarrassment.

diffident (dif'i-dènt) [L. *fidens*, trusting], *a.* Distrustful of oneself or of one's powers; shy. **diffidence**, *n.* Distrust of oneself; bashfulness, shyness.

diffract (di-frăkt') [L. *fractus*, broken], *v.t.* To break, esp. as in a prism.

diffuse (1) (di-fūz') [L. *fusus*, poured], *v.t.* To pour forth: to circulate, spread.

diffuse (2) (di-fūs'), *a.* Diffused, spread out; copious, prolix, not concise. **diffusely**, *adv.* Copiously, verbosely. **diffu'sion**, *n.* The act of diffusing; a spreading abroad of news, etc.

dig (dig) [?], *v.t.* To excavate or turn up with a spade, etc.; to obtain or make by digging. *v.i.* To work with a spade; to search, make one's way, pierce, or make a hole by digging. *n.* A thrust, a poke.

digger, *n.* One who digs, esp. a gold-miner; a machine that digs; (*Austral.*) a fellow, a man. digging, *n.*

digest (di-jest') [L. *gestus*, carried], *v.t.* To arrange under proper heads, to classify; to think over; to soften and prepare by heat; to concoct in the stomach in order to assimilate; to assimilate. *v.i.* To be digested; to be prepared by heat. *n.* (dī'jêst). A compendium or summary arranged under proper heads or titles, esp. a collection of Roman laws. digestible, *a.* digestibil'ity, *n.* digestibly, *adv.* diges'tion, *n.* The act or process of assimilating food in the stomach; the power of digesting; mental reduction to order and method. digestive, *a.* and *n.* Any substance which aids digestion.

digit (dij'ĭt) [L. *digitus*], *n.* A finger.

dignify (dig'nĭ-fī) [L. *dignus*, worthy], *v.t.* To invest with dignity; to make illustrious; to exalt. dignified, *a.* Stately; gravely courteous.

dignity (dig'nĭ-ti), *n.* Rank; the importance due to rank or position; elevation of mien or manner, stateliness; a high office. dignitary, *n.* One who holds a high office or rank.

digress (di-gres') [L. *gressus*, stepped], *v.i.* To turn aside from the direct path; to wander from the main topic. digress'ion, *n.* A deviation; a part of a discourse, etc., which wanders from the main subject. digres'sive, *a.*

dike (dīk) [A.-S. *dīc*], *n.* A ditch, a natural or artificial channel; a dam to protect low-lying lands; (*Scots.*) a stone wall (between fields); a vein of volcanic or igneous rock.

dilapidate (di-lăp'ĭ-dāt) [L. *dilapidātus*], *v.t.* To damage, to bring into decay or ruin. *v.i.* To fall into decay or ruin. dilapida'tion, *n.* Decay for want of repair; decay of buildings, etc.; charge for making this good.

dilate (dī-lāt') [L. *lātus*, broad], *v.t.* To expand, widen, enlarge in all directions. *v.i.* To be enlarged; to expand, swell; to expatiate, to speak fully and copiously (upon a subject). dilata'tion, *n.*

dilatory (dĭl'à-tòr-i) [L. *dīlātōr*, a delayer], *a.* Causing delay, marked by procrastination; tardy; wanting in diligence. dilatorily, *adv.* dilatoriness, *n.*

dilemma (di-lem'à) [Gr. *lêmma*, an assumption], *n.* (*Log.*) An argument in which the only two alternatives are equally fatal; a position in which one is forced to choose between such alternatives.

dilettante (dil-è-tăn'ti) [It.], *n.* (*pl.* -ti). An amateur of the fine arts; a would-be connoisseur, a dabbler. *a.* Amateurish.

diligent (dil'ĭ-jênt) [L. *ligens*, chosen], *a.* Assiduous, persevering, industrious, painstaking. diligently, *adv.* diligence, *n.* Steady application or assiduity in business of any kind; a public stage-coach.

dill (dil) [A.-S. *dile*], *n.* An annual umbelli-fer, cultivated for its carminative seeds.

dilute (dī-lūt') [L. *lūtus*, washed], *v.t.* To make thin or weaken by the admixture of water; to reduce the strength. *a.* Weakened, washed out, faded. dilution, *n.*

diluvial (di-lū'vi-ăl), -vian (-vi-àn) [L. *diluvium*, a deluge], *a.* Pertaining to a deluge, esp. that of Noah; produced by or resulting from a flood.

dim (dim) [A.-S.], *a.* Obscure; not clear, not bright; faint, misty; tarnished, dull; not clearly, heard, or understood. *v.t.* To render dim. dimmer, *n.* (*Elect.*) A device for switching a lamp on and off gradually. dimly, *adv.* dimmish, *a.* dimness, *n.*

dimension (di-men'shŭn) [L. *mensus*, measured], *n.* Measurable extent, magnitude, or capacity. (*usu. in pl.*). dimensional, *a.*

diminish (di-min'ish) [L. *diminuere*, to break small], *v.t.* To make smaller or less, to reduce; to degrade; to subtract from. *v.i.* To become less, to decrease; to taper. diminished, *a.* Made less or smaller; reduced in size or quality. diminu'tion, *n.* The act of diminishing; subtraction; amount subtracted; the state of becoming less or smaller. dimin'utive, *a.* Small, tiny. *n.* A word formed from another to express diminution in size or importance.

dimity (dim'i-ti) [Gr. *mitos*, a thread], *n.* A stout figured cotton fabric.

dimple (dimpl) [?], *n.* A little depression or hollow, esp. on the cheek or chin; a ripple.

din (din) [A.-S. *dyn*], *n.* A loud and continued noise; a rattling or clattering.

dine (dīn) [F. *dîner*], *v.i.* To take dinner. *v.t.* To give or provide a dinner for. diner, *n.* One who dines; a railway dining-car.

dinghy (ding'gi) [Hind. *dēngī*], *n.* A small ship's boat; any small boat.

dingle (ding'gèl) [?], *n.* A dell.

dingy (din'ji) [?], *a.* Soiled; of a dusky colour; faded. dinginess, *n.*

dinner (din'èr) [F. *dîner*, to dine], *n.* The principal meal of the day; a feast, banquet

dinosaur (dī'nò-sawr) [Gr. *deinos*, terrible, *sauros*, lizard], *n.* A gigantic extinct reptile.

dint (dint) [A.-S. *dynt*], *n.* A blow; the mark or dent caused by a blow. *v.* To mark with or make a dint. by dint of: By force of, or by means of.

diocese (dī'ò-sēs) [Gr. *oikeein*, to inhabit], *n.* The district under the jurisdiction of a bishop. dioc'esan, *a.*

dioptric (dī-op'trik) [Gr. *dioptra*, an optical instrument], *a.* Refractive; pertaining to dioptrics. *n.* The unit of refractive power; (*pl.*) the science which treats of the refraction of light in passing through different mediums.

dioxide (dī-ok'sīd), *n.* A combination of a metal with oxygen.

dip (dip) [A.-S. *dyppan*], *v.t.* To plunge into a liquid, to immerse; to baptize by immersion; to lower for an instant. *v.i.* To plunge into liquid for a short time; to sink; to slope or extend downwards; to read cursorily, choose by chance. *n.* The act of dipping in a liquid; bathing; a candle; a preparation for washing sheep.

diphtheria (dif-thēr'i-á) [Gr. *diphthera*, leather, skin], *n.* An infectious disease characterized by acute inflammation and the formation of a false membrane on the pharynx, nostrils, etc.

diphthong (dif'thong) [Gr. *phthongos*, voice], *n.* The union of two vowels in one syllable. **diphthong'al**, *a.*

diploma (di-plō'má) [Gr. *diploos*, double, folded], *n.* A document conveying some authority, privilege, or honour; a certificate of a degree, licence, etc.

diplomacy (di-plō'má-si) [F. *diplomatie*], *n.* The art or act of conducting negotiations or negotiating, esp. as between nations; adroitness, tact. **dip'lomat**, *n.* One skilled in or practising diplomacy. **diplomat'ic**, *a.* **diplomatist**, *n.* One skilled or engaged in diplomacy.

dipsomania (dip-sō-mā'ni-á) [Gr. *dipsa*, thirst, -MANIA], *n.* Alcoholism; an irresistible morbid craving for stimulants. **dipsomaniac**, *n.*

dire (dir) [L. *dirus*], *a.* Dreadful, fearful, lamentable, sad. **direfully**, *adv.* **direly**, *adv.*

direct (di-, di-rekt') [L. *directus*], *a.* Straight; in a straight line; nearest; shortest; not circuitous; not collateral in the line of descent; immediate; to the point, straight-forward. *v.t.* To point or turn towards any object; to show the right road to; to address; to prescribe a course to, to advise; to order, command; to manage, control, act as leader of. **direction**, *n.* The act of directing; the course taken; the point towards which one looks; the act of inscribing with an address, or the inscription on a letter, etc.; an order or instruction; a directorate. **directive**, *n.* An instruction giving directions; an order. **directly**, *adv.* In a straight line; in a direct manner; as an immediate step; at once. **directness**, *n.*

director (di-rek'tór), *n.* One who or that which directs, controls, or manages; an instructor, counsellor; one appointed to direct the affairs of a company. **direct'-orate**, *n.* The position of a director; a body or board of directors. **director'ial**, *a.* **directorship**, *n.* **directory**, *a.* Directing, commanding, advising. *n.* A directorate; a book containing the names and addresses of the inhabitants of a district; the executive council of the French Republic, 1795-99.

dirge (dĕrg) [L. *dirige* (first word of antiphon in the office for the dead)], *n.* A funeral hymn; a mournful tune or song.

dirigible (dir'i-jibl) [L. *dirigere*, to direct], *a.* That may be directed or steered. *n.* A balloon or airship that can be steered.

dirk (dĕrk) [?], *n.* A dagger, esp. a Highlander's; the short sword of a midshipman.

dirt (dĕrt) [M.E. *drit*], *n.* Foul or unclean matter, matter that soils; mud, mire; trash, refuse. **dirt track**, *n.* A racing track with soft surface for motor-cycle racing, a speedway. **dirty**, *a.* dirtiness, *n.*

dis- [L.], *pref.* Asunder, apart; between, separating; exceedingly; (*forming nega-*

tive compounds) UN-, not, undoing, depriving.

disability (dis-á-bil'i-ti), *n.* Want of means; incapacity; legal disqualification.

disable (dis-ābl'), *v.t.* To render unable; to deprive of power; to incapacitate; to disqualify legally. **disablement**, *n.*

disabuse (dis-á-būz'), *v.t.* To undeceive.

disadvantage (dis-ád-van'táj), *n.* Injury, detriment; an unfavourable position or condition. *v.t.* To cause disadvantage to. **disadvanta'geous**, *a.* Detrimental.

disaffected (dis-á-fek'tĕd), *a.* Alienated in affection, estranged; disloyal. **disaffection**, *n.* Disloyalty.

disagree (dis-á-grē') [F. *désagréer*], *v.i.* To be different or unlike; to differ in opinion; to quarrel; to be unsuitable or injurious (to health, etc.). **disagreeable**, *a.* Not in agreement; unpleasant, repugnant; ill-tempered. **disagreeably**, *adv.* **disagreement**, *n.* Want of agreement; difference of opinion; a quarrel, falling out.

disallow (dis-á-lou'), *v.t.* To refuse assent to; to reject; to prohibit.

disappear (dis-á-pēr'), *v.i.* To go out of sight; to be lost; to cease to exist. **disappearance**, *n.*

disappoint (dis-á-point') [F. *désappointer*], *v.t.* To defeat of expectation, hope, etc.; to frustrate. **disappointed**, *a.* **disappointing**, *a.* **disappointment**, *n.*

disapprobation (dis-ăp-rō-bā'shŭn), *n.* Disapproval, condemnation.

disapprove (dis-á-proov'), *v.t.* To condemn or censure; to reject, as not approved of. **disapproval**, *n.*

disarm (dis-arm') [F. *désarmer*], *v.t.* To deprive of weapons; to disband, dismantle; to reduce to a peace footing; to subdue, tame. *v.i.* To lay aside arms. **disarmament**, *n.*

disarrange (dis-á-rānj'), *v.t.* To put out of order; to derange. **disarrangement**, *n.*

disaster (di-zas'tér) [F. *désastre*], *n.* A sudden misfortune, calamity; a mishap. **disastrous**, *a.* Ruinous, calamitous.

disavow (dis-á-vou'), *v.t.* To deny the truth of, to disown; to disclaim, repudiate. **disavowal**, *n.*

disband (dis-bänd') [F. *desbander*], *v.t.* To break up (as a body of men in military service). *v.i.* To be disbanded; to separate, to disperse. **disbandment**, *n.*

disbelieve (dis-bē-lēv'), *v.t.* To refuse, refuse to believe in. **disbelief**, *n.*

disburse (dis-bĕrs') [O.F. *desbourser*], *v.t.* To pay out, expend; to defray. **disbursement**, *n.*

discard (dis-kard'), *v.t.* To throw away as useless; to get rid of, reject.

discern (di-zĕrn') [L. *cernere*, to separate], *v.t.* To perceive the difference between, to distinguish (from); to recognize clearly. *v.i.* To make distinction (between); to discriminate. **discernible**, *a.* discerning, *a.* Having power to discern; discriminating, acute. **discerningly**, *adv.* **discernment**, *n.*

discharge (dis-charj') [O.F. *descharger*], *v.t.* To unload; to get rid of; to emit, let fly; to set free from something binding; to fire off; to pay off; to settle. *n.* The act of discharging; unloading, release, emission, firing off; payment, satisfaction; dismissal, acquittal, liberation, a document certifying any of these.

disciple (di-sīpl') [A.-S. *discipul* (L. *discipulus*, a learner)], *n.* A pupil of a philosopher, teacher, etc.; one of the early followers, esp. one of the twelve personal followers of Christ. **discipleship,** *n.*

discipline (dis'ī-plin) [L. *disciplina*, as prec.], *n.* Training, exercise, or practice of the mental, moral, and physical powers; correction, chastisement; systematic obedience, methodical action, the state of being under control; the rules binding on the member of a church, action against a transgressor of these. *v.t.* To bring into a state of discipline; to teach, train, drill, esp. in obedience, orderly habits, and methodical action; to chastise. **disciplinable,** *a.* **disciplinar'ian,** *a.* Pertaining to discipline. *n.* One who rigidly enforces or is skilled in maintaining discipline. **disciplinary** (dis'ī-plin-ár-i), *a.* Pertaining to or promoting discipline; tending to promote efficient mental action.

disclaim (dis-klām') [A.-F. *desclamer*], *v.t.* To repudiate, disown, disavow; to reject; to renounce, relinquish. **disclaimer,** *n.* The act of disclaiming; renunciation.

disclose (dis-klōz') [O.F. *desclore*], *v.t.* To uncover; to lay bare or open; to reveal, divulge. **disclosure** (dis-klō'zhŭr), *n.* The act of disclosing; that which is disclosed.

discography (dis-kog'rà-fi) [DISK], *n.* The study and enumeration of gramophone records.

discolour (dis-kŭl'ĕr) [O.F. *descolorer*], *v.t.* To alter the colour of; to stain. *v.i.* To become stained or tarnished; to fade, become pale. **discolora'tion,** *n.*

discomfit (dis-kŭm'fit) [L. *conficere*, to finish], *v.t.* To defeat, rout; to disconcert, confound. **discomfiture,** *n.*

discomfort (dis-kŭm'fŏrt) [O.F. *desconforter*], *v.t.* To deprive of comfort; to cause pain or uneasiness to. *n.* Deprivation of comfort; disquietude, distress.

discompose (dis-kŏm-pōz'), *v.t.* To disturb; to vex, disquiet. **discomposure,** *n.* Agitation, perturbation, disquiet.

disconcert (dis-kŏn-sĕrt') [M.F. *disconcerter*], *v.t.* To disorder; to baffle, foil.

disconnect (dis-kŏ-nekt'), *v.t.* To disunite, sever. **disconnected,** *a.* Separated; incoherent, ill-connected.

disconsolate (dis-kon'sŏ-làt) [L. *consolātus*, consoled], *a.* Inconsolable, cheerless, forlorn; without hope.

discontent (dis-kŏn-tent'), *n.* Want of content, dissatisfaction; a grievance. *a.* Not content, dissatisfied. **discontented,** *a.* Dissatisfied, disquiet.

discontinue (dis-kŏn-tin'ū), *v.t.* To break off, interrupt; to leave off; to give up. *v.i.* To cease; to lose continuity. **discontinuance,** *n.* A break in succession; cessation, interruption. **discontinuous,** *a.* Not continuous, disconnected; incoherent. **discontinu'ity,** *n.*

discord (dis'kŏrd) [O.F. *descord*], *n.* Want of concord or agreement; contention, strife; a lack of harmony; the sounding together of inharmonious or inconclusive notes; the interval or the chord so sounded.

discount (dis-kount') [O.F. *desconter*], *v.t.* To advance the amount of, deducting a certain rate per cent.; to leave out of the account; to anticipate; to make allowance for, to disregard. *v.i.* To advance money on bills, etc., due at some future date, deducting the interest. *n.* (dis'-kount). A deduction from an account, etc., for early or immediate payment; a deduction at a certain rate from an advance on a bill of exchange not yet due.

discountenance (dis-koun'tĕ-nàns) [M.F. *descontenancer*], *v.t.* To set one's face against; to express disapprobation of.

discourage (dis-kŭr'àj) [O.F. *descoragier*], *v.t.* To dishearten, dispirit; to dissuade or deter (from). **discouragement,** *n.* **discouraging,** *a.*

discourse (dis-kŏrs') [F. *discours*, as DISCURSIVE], *n.* Conversation; a dissertation, a lecture or sermon; a formal treatise. *v.i.* To converse; to talk formally, hold forth (upon).

discourteous (dis-kĕr'tĕ-ûs), *a.* Uncivil, rude.

discover (dis-kŭv'ĕr) [O.F. *descovrir*], *v.t.* To disclose, reveal, make known; to gain the first sight of, find by exploration; to realize suddenly; to detect. **discoverable,** *a.* **discoverer,** *n.* **discovery,** *n.*

discredit (dis-kred'it), *n.* Want of credit; disrepute; the cause of disrepute or disgrace; disbelief. *v.t.* To disbelieve; to bring into disrepute. **discreditable,** *a.* Disreputable, disgraceful.

discreet (dis-krēt') [L. *discrētus*, discerned], *a.* Prudent, circumspect; careful in choosing the best means of action.

discrepant (dis-krep'ànt) [DIS-, L. *crepans*, sounding], *a.* Disagreeing, inconsistent.

discrete (dis'crēt), *a.* Separate, distinct.

discretion (dis-kresh'ŭn) [O.F. *discrecion*, as DISCREET], *n.* The faculty of distinguishing things, or discriminating between what is right and wrong, useful and injurious; judgment, circumspection; freedom of action or choice. **discretionary,** *a.*

discriminate (dis-krim'ī-nāt) [L. *discriminātus*, separated], *v.t.* To distinguish; to mark the difference or distinction between; to differentiate. *v.i.* To make a distinction. *a.* Distinctive; having the difference clearly marked. **discrimina'tion,** *n.* Discernment, penetration, judgment; the act or power of discriminating; a distinguishing mark.

discursive (dis-kĕr'siv) [L. *cursus*, ran], *a.* Passing from one subject to another; rambling, desultory. **discursively,** *adv.* **discursiveness,** *n.*

discuss (dis-kŭs') [L. *discussus*, shaken asunder], *v.t.* To debate; to examine by argument; to try the flavour of (wine, etc.). **discussible,** *a.* **discussion** (dis-kŭsh'ŭn), *n.*

disdain (dis-dān') [O.F. *desdaigner*, to scorn], *n.* Scorn, a feeling of contempt; haughtiness. *v.t.* To regard as unworthy of notice; to despise and repulse; to scorn, to contemn. *v.i.* To feel or manifest scorn. **disdainful,** *a.*

disease (di-zēz') [O.F. *desaise*], *n.* Any alteration of the normal vital processes through some unnatural or hurtful condition; disorder, morbid condition, illness. **diseased**, *a.* Morbid, unhealthy, deranged.

disembark (dis-ĕm-bark'), *v.t.* To put on shore. *v.i.* To come on shore. **disembarka'tion**, *n.*

disembarrass (dis-ĕm-băr'ås), *v.t.* To free from embarrassment or perplexity. **disembarrassment**, *n.*

disembody (dis-ĕm-bod'i), *v.t.* To divest of body; to disband.

disembogue (dis-ĕm-bōg) [Sp. *disembocar*], *v.t.* To discharge (as a stream).

disenchant (dis-ĕn-chant') [F. *désenchanter*], *v.t.* To free from enchantment or glamour; to disillusion. **disenchantment**, *n.*

disencumber (dis-ĕn-kŭm'bĕr), *v.t.* To free from incumbrance.

disengage (dis-ĕn-gāj'), *v.t.* To loosen, detach, release; to disentangle; to set free from any engagement. **disengaged**, *a.* At leisure, free from any engagement.

disentangle (dis-ĕn-tăngl'), *v.t.* To unravel, free from entanglement.

disestablish (dis-ĕs-tăb'lish), *v.t.* To annul the establishment of, esp. to deprive a Church of its connexion with the State. **disestablishment**, *n.*

disfavour (dis-fā'vŏr), *n.* A feeling of dislike or disapprobation; odium.

disfigure (dis-fig'ĕr), *v.t.* To injure the appearance of; to mar, spoil. **disfigurement**, *n.*

disfranchise (dis-frăn'chīz), *v.t.* To deprive of electoral privileges, or of the rights of citizenship. **disfranchisement**, *n.*

disgorge (dis-gôrj'), *v.t.* To vomit; to empty (as a river); to give up (esp. what has been unjustly acquired).

disgrace (dis-grās') [F. *disgrâce*], *n.* The state of being out of favour; discredit, ignominy, shame; the cause or occasion of discredit or shame. *v.t.* To dismiss from favour; to dishonour, bring disgrace on. **disgraceful**, *a.* **disgracefully**, *adv.*

disgruntled (dis-grŭntld'), *a.* Disgusted, discontented.

disguise (dis-gīz') [O.F. *desguisier*], *v.t.* To alter the appearance of; to hide by a counterfeit appearance; to misrepresent. *n.* A dress, mask, or manner put on to disguise or conceal; a pretence or show.

disgust (dis-gŭst') [M.F. *desgouster*], *v.t.* To excite loathing or aversion in; to offend the taste of. *n.* A strong distaste; aversion, loathing, repulsion. **disgusting**, *a.* Loathsome; exciting disgust; beastly.

dish (dish) [A.-S. *disc*, DISK], *n.* A broad, shallow, open vessel for serving food; the food so served; any particular kind of food.

dishearten (dis-har'tĕn), *v.t.* To discourage, dispirit.

dishevelled (di-shev'ĕld) [O.F. *descheveler*], *a.* Flowing in disorder (of the hair); untidy, unkempt.

dishonest (dis-ŏn'ĕst), *a.* Destitute of honesty, or good faith; deceitful, untrustworthy. **dishonesty**, *n.*

dishonour (dis-on'ŏr), *n.* Lack of honour; disgrace, ignominy; reproach, or its cause, *v.i.* To bring disgrace on; to damage the reputation of; to treat with indignity; to violate the chastity of; to refuse to accept or pay (as a bill or draft). **dishonourable**, *a.*

disillusion (dis-i-loo'zhŭn), *v.t.* To free or deliver from an illusion. *n.* Disenchantment. **disillusionment**, *n.*

disincline (dis-in-klīn'), *v.t.* To make averse or indisposed (to). **disinclina'tion**, *n.* A want of desire; unwillingness.

disinfect (dis-in-fekt'), *v.t.* To free from infection. **disinfectant**, *n.* That which removes infection by destroying its causes.

disinherit (dis-in-her'it), *v.t.* To deprive of an inheritance.

disintegrate (dis-in'tĕ-grāt), *v.t.* To separate into component parts; to reduce to fragments. *v.i.* To fall to pieces, to crumble, *n.* **disintegra'tion**, *n.* The separation of a solid body into its component parts.

disinter (dis-in-tĕr'), *v.t.* To dig up from a grave; to unearth. **disinterment**, *n.*

disinterested (dis-in'tĕr-ĕst-ĕd), *a.* Without personal interest; unbiased.

disjoint (dis-joint'), *v.t.* To put out of joint, dislocate, separate at the joints; to break the connexion of. **disjointed**, *a.* Out of joint; incoherent.

disk (disk) [Gr. *diskos*], *n.* A thin, flat, circular plate or surface; a gramophone record; the face of a celestial body.

dislike (dis-līk'), *v.t.* To regard with repugnance or aversion. *n.* A feeling of repugnance; aversion.

dislocate (dis'lō-kāt) [L. *locātus*, placed], *v.t.* To put out of joint; to disturb, derange. **disloca'tion**, *n.*

dislodge (dis-loj'), *v.t.* To eject from a place of rest or defence; to drive out, expel.

disloyal (dis-loi'ăl), *a.* Not true to allegiance; disaffected towards the sovereign or the Government. **disloyalty**, *n.*

dismal (diz'măl) [O.F. *dis mal*, L. *diĕs mali*, unlucky days], *a.* Cheerless, depressing.

dismantle (dis-măntl'), *v.t.* To strip of covering, equipment, or means of defence; to unrig (as a ship).

dismast (dis-mast'), *v.t.* To deprive a ship of a mast or masts.

dismay (dis-mā) [Teut.], *v.t.* To deprive of courage; to terrify, daunt. *n.* Utter loss of courage or resolution; a state of terror or affright.

dismember (dis-mem'bĕr), *v.t.* To separate limb from limb; to distribute, partition. **dismemberment**, *n.*

dismiss (dis-mis') [L. *dīmittere*], *v.t.* To send away; to dissolve, disband; to discharge. **dismissal**, *n.*

dismount (dis-mount'), *v.i.* To alight from a horse. *v.t.* To throw down from a support (as cannon); to unhorse; to take to pieces.

disobedience (dis-ŏ-bē'di-ĕns), *n.* Refusal to obey; wilful neglect or violation of duty. **disobedient**, *a.*

disobey (dis-ŏ-bā'), *v.t.* To neglect or refuse to obey.

disoblige (dis-ŏ-blīj'), *v.t.* To act contrary to the wishes of; to inconvenience, to incommode. **disobliging,** *a.* Not obliging, not disposed to gratify; churlish, ungracious. **disobligingly,** *adv.*

disorder (dis-ôr'dèr), *n.* Want of order; confusion; tumult, commotion; disease, illness. *v.t.* To throw into confusion; to derange the natural functions of. **disorderly,** *a.* Confused, disarranged; unlawful; turbulent.

disorganize (dis-ôr'gà-nīz), *v.t.* To throw into confusion; to destroy the systematic arrangement of. **disorganiza'tion,** *n.*

disown (dis-ōn'), *v.t.* To refuse to own; to disclaim, repudiate.

disparage (dis-pàr'àj) [O.F. *desparagier, parage,* lineage], *v.t.* To undervalue; to treat or speak of slightingly; to depreciate. **disparagement,** *n.* The act of disparaging; depreciation, detraction.

disparate (dis'pà-ràt) [L. *disparatus*], *a.* Dissimilar, having nothing in common. **disparity,** *n,* Inequality, unlikeness.

dispassionate (dis-pàsh'ô-nàt), *a.* Free from passion; calm, temperate.

dispatch (dis-pàch') [L. *pactum,* an agreement], *v.t.* To send off, esp. with haste; to transact quickly; to settle; to put to death; *v.i.* To go quickly; to hasten, *n.* The act of dispatching or being dispatched; prompt execution; an official communication on State affairs, etc.; a putting to death.

dispel (dis-pel') [L. *pellere,* to drive], *v.t.* To dissipate, disperse; to drive away.

dispensable (dis-pen'sàbl), *a.* That may be dispensed with, inessential; that for which a dispensation may be granted.

dispensary (dis-pen'sàr-i), *n.* A place where medicines are dispensed.

dispensation (dis-pèn-sā'shùn), *n.* The act of dispensing or dispensing with; distribution; scheme, plan, the government of the universe; God's dealings with man; (*R.-C. Ch.*) a licence to omit or commit something enjoined or forbidden by canon law.

dispense (dis-pens') [L. *dispensāre,* to distribute, manage], *v.t.* To deal out, distribute; to prepare and give out medicine; to grant a dispensation to or exemption from. *v.i.* To dispense medicines. **to dispense with:** To forgo, to do without; to render unnecessary. **dispenser,** *n.* One who dispenses, esp. medicines.

disperse (dis-pèrs') [L. *dispersus,* scattered], *v.t.* To scatter; to send, throw, etc., in different directions; to dissipate, diffuse, disseminate. *v.i.* To break up, vanish; to become spread abroad. **dispersal,** *n.*

dispersion (dis-pèr'shùn), *n.* The act of dispersing; state of being dispersed.

dispirit (dis-pir'it), *v.t.* To deprive of spirit or courage; to dishearten, deject.

displace (dis-plās'), *v.t.* To remove from the usual place, from a position or dignity, etc.; to dismiss; to supersede. **displaced persons,** *n.* (*Pol.*) Refugees who cannot be repatriated. **displacement,** *n.* The act of displacing; state of being displaced; supersession; the water displaced by a floating body.

display (dis-plā') [L. *plicāre,* to fold], *v.t.* To exhibit, expose, parade; to make

known, unfold, reveal. *n.* Show, exhibition; ostentatious parade.

displease (dis-plēz'), *v.t.* To dissatisfy; to vex, annoy; to be disagreeable to. *v.i.* To cause displeasure or offence.

displeasure (dis-plezh'úr), *n.* A feeling of annoyance, vexation, or anger.

disport (dis-pôrt') [O.F. *desporter* (*porter,* to carry)], *v.* To amuse, to divert (oneself); to sport; to gambol.

dispose (dis-pōz') [O.F. *poser,* to cease], *v.t.* To set in order; to place; to adjust, incline; to regulate, fix.

disposition (dis-pô-zish'ún), *n.* The act of disposing, arranging, etc.; disposal; fitness, aptitude; inclination, temperament, propensity.

dispossess (dis-pô-zes'), *v.t.* To oust from possession, to eject, dislodge.

dispraise (dis-prāz'), *v.t.* To censure, to express disapprobation of. *n.* Blame, disparagement.

disproportion (dis-prô-pôr'shùn), *n.* Want of proportion; disparity; lack of symmetry. **disproportionate,** *a.*

disprove (dis-proov'), *v.t.* To prove to be erroneous or unfounded; to refute.

dispute (dis-pūt') [L. *disputāre*], *v.i.* To contend in argument; to argue; to quarrel, wrangle; to strive against another, compete. *v.t.* To argue about; to oppose, question, challenge or deny the truth of; to contest. *n.* Contention or strife in argument; debate, difference of opinion; a falling out; contest, strife. **dis'putable,** *a.* Open to dispute, controvertible; questionable. **dis'putant,** *n.* **disputa'tion,** *n.* **disputatious,** *a.* Given to dispute; cavilling, contentious.

disqualify (dis-kwol'i-fī), *v.t.* To disable, debar. **disqualifica'tion,** *n.* The act of disqualifying; that which disqualifies.

disquiet (dis-kwī'ét), *v.t.* To disturb, to make uneasy. *a.* Uneasy, restless. *n.* Want of quiet or peace; anxiety.

disquisition (dis-kwi-zish'ún) [L. *quisitus,* sought], *n.* A systematic inquiry into, an investigation; a formal discourse or treatise.

disregard (dis-rè-gard'), *n.* Slight, neglect. *v.t.* To take no notice of; to neglect. **disregardful,** *a.* Negligent, careless, heedless.

disrepair (dis-rè-pâr'), *n.* A state of being out of repair; dilapidation.

disreputable (dis-rep'ū-tabl), *a.* Of bad repute, not respectable; discreditable. **disrepute',** *n.*

disrespect (dis-rè-spekt'), *n.* Want of respect or reverence; incivility; an act of rudeness. **disrespectful,** *a.*

disrobe (dis-rōb'), *v.* To undress.

disrupt (dis-rúpt') [L. *ruptus,* broken], *v.t.* To tear asunder, break in pieces.

dissatisfy (di-sàt'is-fī), *v.t.* To fall short of the expectations of; to make discontented. **dissatisfac'tion,** *n.*

dissect (di-sekt') [L. *sectus,* cut], *v.t.* To cut in pieces; to cut up an organism so as to examine the parts, etc., in detail; to criticize; to analyse; to apportion items (in book-keeping). **dissection,** *n.* **dissector,** *n.*

dissemble (di-sembl') [L. *simulāre,* to

simulate], *v.t.* To hide under a false appearance; to simulate. *v.i.* To cloak, conceal; to hide one's feelings, etc., play the hypocrite. **dissembler,** *n.*

disseminate (di-sem'ināt) [L. *sēminātus,* sown], *v.t.* To scatter abroad, as seed; to diffuse.

dissension (di-sen'shŭn), *n.* Disagreement of opinion; discord, strife.

dissent (di-sent') [L. *sentīre,* to feel], *v.t.* To differ in opinion; to hold opposite views; to withhold assent or approval. *n.* Difference or disagreement of opinion; refusal or assent; the principles of dissenters from the established Church. **Dissenter,** *n.* One who dissents from an established Church, esp. a member of a sect that has separated from the Church of England.

dissentient (di-sen'shi-ĕnt), *a.* Disagreeing or differing in opinion. *n.* One who holds or expresses contrary views.

dissertation (dis-ĕr-tā'shŭn) [L. *sertus,* joined], *n.* A formal discourse; a disquisition, treatise, essay.

disservice (dis-sĕr'vis), *n.* An injury, detriment.

dissident (dis'i-dĕnt) [L. *sidens,* sitting], *a.* Disagreeing, dissenting. *n.* One who dissents from any motion.

dissimilar (di-sim'i-lăr), *a.* Not similar; unlike; discordant.

dissimulate (di-sim'ū-lāt) [L. *dissimulātus*], *v.t.* To dissemble, conceal, disguise. **dissimula'tion,** *n.*

dissipate (dis'i-pāt) [L. *dissipātus*], *v.t.* To scatter, disperse; to squander, waste, fritter away. *v.i.* To be dispersed, vanish; to indulge in dissolute enjoyment. **dissipated,** *a.* Scattered; given to dissipation, dissolute. **dissipa'tion,** *n.*

dissociate (di-sō'shi-āt) [L. *sociātus,* associated], *v.t.* To separate, to disconnect. **dissocia'tion,** *n.*

dissoluble (dis'ŏl-ūbl), *a.* That can be dissolved or decomposed.

dissolute (dis'ŏ-lūt), *a.* Loose in conduct; licentious, debauched.

dissolution (dis-ŏ-lū'shŭn), *n.* The act or process of dissolving, disintegrating, etc.; liquefaction; death; separation of a meeting, assembly, or Parliament.

dissolve (di-zolv') [L. *solvere,* to loosen], *v.t.* To liquefy, melt; to decompose; to break up; to put an end to (as a meeting, etc.); to annul. *v.i.* To become liquefied; to disintegrate; to break up, separate; to fade away.

dissonant (dis'ŏ-nănt) [L. *dissonans,* being unlike in sound], *a.* Discordant, inharmonious; harsh. **dissonance,** *n.*

dissuade (di-swād') [L. *suādēre,* to persuade], *v.t.* To seek to persuade not to do some act; to advise against. **dissuasion,** *n.* **dissuasive,** *a.* Tending to dissuade. *n.* A dissuasive argument.

distaff (dis'taf) [A.-S. *distæf*], *n.* A cleft stick, on which wool or carded cotton can be wound for spinning.

distance (dis'tăns), *n.* The extent of separation between two objects; remoteness in space or time; a set interval; reserve, coolness; separation in rank or relationship; the remoter parts of a view,

background of a picture. *v.t.* To leave behind in a race; to outstrip, outdo.

distant (dis'tănt) [L. *distans, pres. p.* of *distāre* (DIS-, *stāre,* to stand)], *a.* Separated by intervening space; remote in space, time, succession, consanguinity, resemblance, kind, or nature; not plain or obvious; reserved, cool.

distaste (dis-tāst'), *n.* Disrelish, dislike, disinclination (for). **distasteful,** *a.* Offensive, displeasing. **distastefulness,** *n.*

distemper (1) (dis-tem'pĕr) [L. *temperāre,* to temper, mix in due proportions], *n.* A derangement of the health or mind; a catarrhal disorder in young dogs; discontent; political disturbance. **distempered,** *a.* Disordered in mind or body; intemperate, immoderate.

distemper (2) (dis-tem'pĕr) [as prec.], *v.t.* To paint or colour with distemper. *n.* A method of painting with colours diluted with size instead of oil; the coloured preparation.

distend (dis-tend') [L. *tendere,* to stretch], *v.t.* To spread out; to inflate; to cause to open. *v.i.* To swell out. **distension,** *n.*

distich (dis'tik) [Gr. *stichos,* a row], *n.* Two lines of poetry making complete sense.

distil (dis-til') [L. *stilla,* a drop], *v.i.* To fall in drops; to trickle; to undergo the process of distillation. *v.t.* To extract by means of vaporization and condensation; to make, obtain, or purify by this process; to let fall in drops. **distilla'tion,** *n.* **distiller,** *n.* A manufacturer of spirits by distillation. **distillery,** *n.* A building where spirits are produced by distillation.

distinct (dis-tinkt'), *a.* Different, separate; unmistakable, clear, plain, definite. **distinction,** *n.* A mark or note of difference; a distinguishing quality; discrimination, that which differentiates; title, rank; superiority. **distinctive,** *a.* **distinctness,** *n.*

distinguish (dis-ting'gwish) [L. *distinguere,* to mark with a prick], *v.t.* To discriminate, differentiate; to indicate difference by some external mark; to perceive, recognize; to make eminent, prominent, or well known. *v.i.* To differentiate; to draw distinctions. **distinguishable,** *a.* **distinguished,** *a.* Marked by some distinctive sign or property; eminent, remarkable. **distinguishing,** *a.*

distort (dis-tôrt') [L. *tortus,* twisted], *v.t.* To twist the natural shape or direction; to pervert from the true meaning. **distortion,** *n.*

distract (dis-trăkt') [L. *tractus,* drawn], *v.t.* To divert the mind or attention (from); to draw in different directions, to confuse, bewilder, perplex; to drive mad, to craze. **distracted,** *a.* Disturbed mentally, crazed; harassed, perplexed. **distraction,** *n.*

distrain (dis-trān') [L. *stringere,* to strain, compress], *v.t.* To seize (person or goods) for debt. *v.i.* To levy a distress. **distraint,** *n.*

distraught (dis-trawt'), *a.* Bewildered, agitated, distracted.

distress (dis-tres') [L. *districtus,* as DIS-TRAIN], *n.* Extreme anguish of mind or body; misery, poverty, destitution; calamity, misfortune; the act of distraining; goods taken in distraint. *v.t.* To afflict with anxiety, unhappiness, or anguish; to vex; to distrain. **distressful**, *a.* Painful, afflictive; attended by distress. **distressing**, *a.* Afflicting; awakening pity or compassion.

distribute (dis-trib'ūt) [L. *distribūtus*], *v.t.* To divide or deal out, to disperse, to give in charity; to classify. **distributable**, *a.* **distribu'tion**, *n.*

distributive (dis-trib'ū-tiv), *a.* Distributing or allotting the proper share to each; pertaining to distribution. *n.* A word that expresses distribution, *e.g.* each, *every, either, neither.* **distributively**, *adv.*

district (dis'trikt) [L. *districtus*, *p.p.* of *distringere*, to DISTRAIN], *n.* A limited portion of territory for judicial, administrative, fiscal, or other purposes; a region, tract of country.

distrust (dis-trŭst'), *v.t.* To have no confidence in, to question the reality, truth, or sincerity of. *n.* Want of confidence or faith (in); suspicion. **distrustful**, *a.* Suspicious, without confidence.

disturb (dis-tĕrb') [L. *turbāre*, to trouble], *v.t.* To agitate, disquiet, discompose, unsettle; to hinder, interrupt, interfere with. **disturbance**, *n.*

disunion (dis-ū'nyŏn), *n.* Disagreement.

disuse (dis-ūs'), *n.* A cessation of use, practice, or exercise.

disyllable (di-sil'ábl), *n.* A word or metrical foot of two syllables. **disyllab'ic**, *a.*

ditch (dich) [A.-S. *dīc*], *n.* A trench forming a boundary, drain, or protection to a fortress. *v.i.* To dig or repair ditches.

dithyramb (dith'i-rămb) [L. *dithyrambus*], *n.* A wild poem or song.

ditto (dit'ō) [It.], *n.* (*pl.* -os). That which has been said before; the same thing, a similar thing (often written do.).

ditty (dit'ī) [L. *dictātum*, a thing dictated], *n.* A little song, an air. **ditty bag**, *n.* A sailor's bag for needles, thread, etc.

diurnal (dīēr'-nál) [L. *diurnus*, daily], *a.* Pertaining to day-time; performed in a day; daily.

diva (dē'vá) [It.], *n.* (*Theat.*) A prima donna.

divagation (dī-va-gā'shŭn) [L. *vagātus*, wandered], *n.* A rambling, digression.

divan (di-văn') [Turk.], *n.* A court of justice, the highest council of state in the East; a thickly-cushioned seat against the wall of a room.

dive (dīv) [A.-S. *dūfan*], *v.i.* To plunge head first under water; to descend quickly; to thrust one's hand rapidly into something; to enter deeply into anything. *n.* A sudden plunge head foremost into water; a sudden dart; an (underground) smoking-room; a disreputable resort. **diver**, *n.* **dive-bombing**, *n.* (*Av.*) Diving suddenly on a target to release bombs.

diverge (di-vĕrj') [L. *vergere*, to bend], *v.i.* To tend in different directions, to branch off; to vary from a normal form; to deviate. **divergence**, **-ency**, *n.* divergent, *a.*

divers (dī'vêrz) [O.F., from L. *diversus*, various], *a.* Several, sundry.

diverse (di-vĕrs'), *a.* Different, varying, multiform. **diversely**, *adv.* **diverseness**, *n.* **diversify**, *v.t.* To make different from others; to give variety to.

diversion (di-vêr-shŭn), *n.* The act of diverting; that which serves to divert the mind, business, etc.; a relaxation, distraction, amusement. **diversity**, *n.* Difference, unlikeness; variety.

divert (di-vĕrt') [L. *vertere*, to turn], *v.t.* To turn aside, to deflect; to turn in another direction, to avert; to distract, entertain, amuse. **diverting**, *a.*

divest (di-vest') [L. *vestis*, a garment], *v.t.* To strip of clothing; to deprive, rid (of).

divide (di-vīd') [L. *dīvidere*], *v.t.* To part asunder; to sever, separate, break into parts; to distribute, deal out; to make a passage through; to form the boundary between, to sunder, to classify; to take a portion of with others; to destroy unity amongst; to perform the operation of division. *v.i.* To be separated; to share; to diverge; to express decision by separating into two parts; to be disunited in feelings, opinions, etc. **divider**, *n.*

dividend (div'i-dend) [L. *dividendum*], *n.* Share of a bankrupt's assets, the profits of a company, etc.

divine (1) (di-vīn') [L. *dīvināre*], *v.t.* To find out by inspiration, magic, or intuition; to foresee; to guess, feel a presentiment of. *v.i.* To practise divination. **diviner**, *n.* **divina'tion**, *n.* **divining-rod**, *n.* A forked twig used by dowsers to discover water.

divine (2) (di-vīn') [L. *dīvīnus*, cogn. with *dīvus, deus*, god], *a.* Pertaining to, of the nature of God or a god; godlike, celestial; pertaining to theology. *n.* A clergyman, ecclesiastic, theologian. **divinely**, *adv.* **divinity**, *n.* The quality of being divine, deity, godhead; God; a deity; the science of divine things; theology.

divisible (di-viz'ibl) [L. *dīvisibilis*], *a.* Capable of division. esp, into equal parts by a divisor without a remainder. **divisibil'ity**, *n.* **division** (di-vizh'ŭn), *n.* The act of dividing; the state of being divided; separation; distribution; a boundary, partition, distinct part; an administrative unit; a separate body of men, esp. soldiers under the command of a general officer; a number of vessels under one command; disunion, disagreement; (*Parl.*) the separation of members for the purpose of voting; (*Math.*) the process of dividing. **divisional**, *a.* **divisor** (di-vī'zŏr), *n.* That number by which a dividend is divided; one that divides another without a remainder.

divorce (di-vôrs') [L. *dīvortium*], *n.* Legal dissolution of the marriage tie; a separation of things closely connected. *v.t.* To dissolve by legal process the bonds of marriage between; to obtain a divorce from; to disunite things closely connected.

divulge (di-vŭlj') [L. *vulgāre*, to publish]. *v.t.* To make known; to reveal, disclose, **divulgence**, *n.*

dixie (dick'si) [Hind. *degshi*, a pot], *n.* A pot for cooking over a fire.

dizzy (diz'i) [A.-S. *dysig*, foolish], *a.* Giddy dazed; causing dizziness, confusing. **dizzily,** *adv.* **dizziness,** *n.*

do (doo) [A.-S. *dōn*] (*past,* **did,** **didst;** *p.p.* **done** (dŭn)), *v.t.* and *aux.* To execute, perform, effect, transact, carry out; to produce, make; to complete, accomplish; to cause, to render (good, evil, honour, etc., to); to cook; to play the part of; to cheat, swindle; to fatigue, exhaust. *v.i.* To act, behave; to perform deeds; to finish, cease; to fare; to get on; to suffice, to answer the purpose, *n.* A swindle.

docile (dō'sil) [L. *docilis*], *a.* Willing or ready to learn; tractable. **docil'ity,** *n.*

dock (1) (dok) [A.-S. *docce*], *n.* A common weed.

dock (2) (dok) [Teut.], *n.* The solid part of an animal's tail; the tail after being cut short. *v.t.* To cut the tail off; to abridge.

dock (3) (dok) [cp. M. Dut. *dock dockke* (mod. Dut. *dok*), also prov. Eng. *doke,* a hollow], *n.* An artificial basin in which ships are built or repaired, or where they load and unload; an enclosure between platforms where railway lines terminate. *v.t.* To bring into or place in dock. **docker,** *n.* A labourer at the docks. **dockyard,** *n.* A large enclosed area where vessels are built or repaired.

dock (4) (dok) [Fl. *dok,* a hutch, a pen], *n.* The enclosure for prisoners in a criminal court.

docket (dok'ét) [?], *n.* A summary; a register of judgments; a list of cases for trial, summary of business to be dealt with; a label with address.

doctor (dok'tŏr) [L., from *docēre,* to teach], *n.* A qualified practitioner of medicine or surgery; one who has taken the highest degree at a University; a learned man. *v.t.* To administer medicines to; to treat medically; to patch up; to adulterate; to falsify. **doctorate,** *n.* The degree, rank, or title of a doctor.

doctrinaire (dok-tri-nâr'), *n.* One who theorizes, esp. in politics. *a.* Visionary, impractical.

doctrine (dok'trin) [L. *doctrīna*], *n.* That which is taught; the principles, tenets, or dogmas of any church, sect, school, etc. **doctri'nal,** *a.*

document (dok'ū-mént) [L. *documentum,* from *docēre,* to teach], *n.* A paper containing information for the establishment of facts; written evidence or proof. *v.t.* To furnish with or prove by means of documents. **documen'tary,** *a. n.* (*Cinema.*) A film of real life.

dodec-, **dodeca-** (Gr. *dōdeka*], *pref.* Twelve. **dodec'agon,** *n.* A plane figure of 12 equal angles and sides. **dodecahe'dron,** *n.* A solid figure of 12 equal sides, each of which is a regular pentagon.

dodge (doj) [?], *v.i.* To start aside suddenly, esp. so as to elude pursuit, etc.; to act trickily, to quibble. *v.t.* To escape from by starting aside; to evade by craft; to cheat. *n.* A sudden start or movement to one side; a trick, artifice, evasion; a skilful expedient. **dodger,** *n.*

dodo (dō'dō) [Port. *doudo,* foolish], *n.* A large bird with rudimentary wings, formerly found in Mauritius.

doe (dō) [A.-S. *dā*], *n.* The female of the fallow deer; also of the rabbit, hare, and some other animals.

doff (dof), *v.t.* To take off (as clothes); to discard.

dog (dog) [A.-S. *docga*], *n.* A wild or domesticated quadruped of numerous breeds; the male of the wolf, fox, and other animals; a surly or a contemptible person; a gay young fellow; various mechanical contrivances acting as holdfasts; an andiron, hammer of a fire-arm. *v.t.* To follow like a dog; to track. **dogcart,** *n.* A light, two-wheeled, double-seated, one-horse vehicle. **dog-days,** *n.pl.* The period (July and Aug.) when the dog-star rises and sets with the sun, a conjunction formerly supposed to bring great heat. **dog-fish,** *n.* A species of small sharks which follow their prey in packs, whence the name. **dog-rose,** *n.* The wild brier. **dog's-ear,** *n.* A corner of a leaf turned down like a dog's ear. **dog-watch,** *n.* (*Naut.*) One of two watches of two hours each between 4 and 8 p.m.

doge (dōj) [It.], *n.* The chief magistrate of the old republics of Venice and Genoa.

dogged (dog'éd), *a.* Stubborn, persistent, tenacious. **doggedly** *adv.*

doggerel (dog'ér-él) [?], *a.* and *n.* Loose, irregular verses.

dogma (dog'mà) [Gr., from *dokein,* to seem, to think], *n.* A principle, tenet, or system of doctrines established on authority, as opposed to one deduced from experience or reasoning; a positive or arrogant expression of opinion. **dogma'tic,** *a.* Pertaining to dogma, doctrinal; based on theory; positive, authoritative; arrogant, dictatorial. **dog'matism,** *n.* **dog'matize,** *v.i.* To make dogmatic assertions.

doily (doi'li) [name of maker], *n..* A small ornamental mat for bottles, glasses, etc.

doings (doo'ingz), *n.pl.* Things done; events, affairs, goings-on; objects.

doldrums (dol'drŭmz) [?], *n.pl.* Low spirits, the dumps; that part of the ocean near the equator where calms and variable winds prevail.

dole (1) (dōl) [O.F. *doel,* L. *dolor*], *n.* Sorrow, lamentation; a cause of grief. **doleful,** *a.* Sad; afflicted, dismal, gloomy. **dolefulness,** *n.*

dole (2) (dōl) [A.-S. *dāl,* DEAL (1)], *n.* A share, portion; free distribution of alms, money, or food. *v.t.* To distribute.

doll (dol) [*Dorothy*], *n.* A child's toy-baby; a pretty but vacuous woman. **dollish,** *a.*

dollar (dol'ár) [G. *thaler*], *n.* A silver coin of the U.S.; (*slang*) five shillings.

dolly (dol'i), *n.* A pet name for a doll; a stick to stir round clothes in a wash-tub.

dolman (dol'mán) [Turk. *dōlāmān*], *n.* A woman's loose mantle with hanging sleeves; a hussar's jacket.

dolmen (dol'mén) [Corn.], *n.* A cromlech.

dolour (dol'ŏr) [O.F., from L. *dolor,* grief], *n.* Pain, suffering, sorrow, lamentation. **dolorous** (dol'ŏr-ŭs), *a.*

dolphin (dol'fin) [L. *delphīnus,* see DAU-

PHIN-], _n._ A cetacean resembling the porpoise.

dolt (dōlt) [?], _n._ A stupid fellow; a numskull. **doltish,** _a._

domain (dō-mān'), _n._ District over which control is or may be exercised; one's landed property, estate.

dome (dōm) [It. _duomo,_ L. _domus,_ a house], _n._ A rounded roof, the base of which is a circle, ellipse, or polygon; a stately building; any dome-shaped object.

domestic (dŏmes'tik) [F. _domestique,_ L. _domesticus,_ from _domus,_ home], _a._ Pertaining to the home or household; fond of home; tame, not wild; relating to the internal affairs of a nation; not foreign. _n._ A household servant. **domesticate,** _v.t._ To accustom to domestic life and household management; to tame.

domicile (dom'i-sil) [L. _domicilium_], _n._ A place of abode, esp. of permanent residence. _v.t._ To establish in a residence.

dominant (dom'i-nant) [L. _dominans,_ ruling], _a._ Governing; overshadowing; supereminent. _n._ (_Mus._) The fifth note of the scale of any key.

dominate (dom'i-nāt) [L. _dominātus,_ ruled], _v.t._ To predominate over; to be the chief; to overlook (as a hill). _v.i._ To prevail. **domina'tion,** _n._ Rule control.

domineer (dom-i-nēr'), _v.i._ To exercise authority arrogantly.

dominical (dō-min'ik-ăl) [L. _dominus,_ lord], _a._ Pertaining to the Lord or the Lord's Day.

Dominican (dō-min'ik-an), _n._ One of an order of preaching friars, founded in 1216 by St. Dominic; a black friar.

dominie (dom'i-ni), _n._ A pedagogue, schoolmaster.

dominion (dō-min'yŏn) [L. _dominium_], _n._ Sovereign authority; control, rule; a district, region, etc., under one government.

domino (dom'i-nō) [Sp. or F.], _n._ A masquerade dress, a loose cloak with a small mask; a half mask; a person wearing this; (_pl._) a game played with twenty-eight oblong dotted pieces of ivory.

don (1) (don) [Sp., from L. _dominus,_ lord], _n._ A Spanish title (like Eng. "Mr."); a Spaniard; a fellow or tutor of a college; a person of distinction.

don (2) (don), _v.t._ To put on, assume.

donation (dō-nā'shŭn) [L. _dōnum,_ a gift], _n._ A gift, presentation, contribution. **donative,** _n._ A gift, gratuity.

done (dŭn), _p.p._ Performed, executed; cooked; (_colloq._) cheated, baffled.

donkey (dong'ki) [?], _n._ An ass; (_fig._) a stupid person.

donor (dō'nŏr) [L. _dōnāre,_ to give], _n._ A giver.

doodle, _v.i._ To draw or scribble unconsciously.

doom (doom) [A.-S. _dōm_], _n._ Judgment; judicial decision; condemnation; destiny; ruin, perdition. _v.t._ To condemn to punishment; to consign to ruin. **dooms-day,** _n._ The Day of Judgment; the end of the world.

door (dŏr) [A.-S. _dor_], _n._ A hinged frame of boards, etc., closing an entrance; entrance, exit, access, means of approach.

door-keeper, _n._ A porter, janitor. **door-step,** _n._ A step leading up to an outer door. **door-way,** _n._ An opening in a wall fitted with a door.

dope (dōp) [Dut. _doop,_ sauce], _n._ A lubricant; a varnish; any stupefying drink or drug. _v.t._ To stupefy with drink, to drug. _v.i._ To indulge in harmful drugs.

dor (dŏr) [A.-S. _dora_], _n._ Name of several insects that make a loud humming in flying.

Dorian (dôr'i-ăn), _a._ Of or relating to Doris, in ancient Greece, or its inhabitants. **Doric** (dor'ik), _a._ Dorian; applied to a broad rustic dialect, and to the earliest, strongest, and most simple of the three Grecian orders of architecture.

dormant (dôr'mănt) [F., sleeping], _a._ Torpid, inactive; inoperative, in abeyance. **dormancy,** _n._

dormer (dôr'mėr) [O.F. _dormeor_], _n._ A window in a sloping roof, having a vertical frame and a gable.

dormitory (dôr'mi-tôr-i) [L. _dormitōrium_], _n._ A sleeping-chamber for a number of occupants, esp. in a school, etc.

dormouse (dôr'mous) [F. _dormir,_ to sleep, MOUSE], _n._ A small hibernating rodent.

dorsal (dôr'săl) [L. _dorsum,_ the back], _a._ Pertaining to the back; ridge-shaped.

dory (1) (dôr'i) [F. _dorée,_ gilded], _n._ A golden-yellow sea-fish, the John Dory.

dory (2), _n._ A small, flat-bottomed boat.

dose (dōs) [Gr. _dosis,_ a giving], _n._ The quantity of medicine taken at one time; anything unpleasant which one has to take. _v.t._ To administer doses.

doss (dos) [F. _dos,_ the back], _n._ (_slang_) A bed, sleeping-place, _v.i._

dossier (dos'yā) [F.], _n._ A collection of papers relating to person or thing.

dot (dot) [A.-S. _dott_], _n._ A little spot made with a pen, etc.; a period mark, a point over _i_ or _j_; a tiny thing or child. _v.i._ To make dots or spots. _v.t._ To mark with dots.

dote (dōt) [Teut.], _v.i._ To have the intellect impaired, esp. by age; to be infatuated; **dotage,** _n._ **dotard,** _n._

dotterel (dot'ėr-ĕl), _n._ A small migratory plover; a dupe, a dotard.

double (dŭbl) [O.F., from L. _duplus,_ twofold], _a._ Composed of two; forming a pair, twofold; folded; twice as much, as great, or as many; of two kinds; ambiguous; hypocritical, deceitful. _adv._ Twice; in two ways; in twice the number, quantity, amount, strength, etc.; two together. _n._ Twice as much or as many, a double quantity; a bend or twist (in a road, etc.); a wraith; an understudy; (_Mil._) running, the pace for charging; a turn in running; a game between two pairs. _v.t._ To increase by an equal quantity, amount, number, value, etc.; to multiply by two; to fold, to bend, turn upon itself; to be twice as much as; to play two (parts) in the same play; to sail round or by; to make a duplicate of. _v.i._ To become twice as much or as great; to enlarge a wager to twice the previous amount; to turn or wind to escape pursuit. **double-bass,** _n._ The largest and lowest-toned of the

stringed instruments. **double-dealing,** *a.*
Deceitful, tricky. *n.* Such conduct,
duplicity. **double-Dutch,** *n.* Gibberish,
jargon; a language not understood by
the hearer. **double-dyed,** *a.* Stained or
tainted with infamy; doubly infamous.
double entendre, double entente
(doobl on tondr, on tont) [F.], *n.* A
double meaning, esp. indelicate. **double-
faced,** *a.* Double-dealing; insincere.
doubly, *adv.*

doublet (dŭb'lĕt), *n.* One of a pair; one
of two words from the same root, but
differing in meaning; a close-fitting
garment from the neck to a little below
the waist.

doubloon (dŭb-loon') [Sp.], *n.* A Spanish
gold coin, worth about a guinea.

doubt (dout) [L. *dubitāre*], *v.i.* To be in
uncertainty about anything; to hesitate,
waver. *v.t.* To think questionable; to
hesitate to believe or assent to; to distrust or suspect. *n.* Uncertainty upon
any point, action, or statement; an
unsettled state of opinion; indecision,
hesitation; distrust, inclination to disbelieve; a question, problem; suspicion.
doubter, *n.* **doubtful,** *a.* Uncertain,
admitting of doubt; ambiguous; undecided, hesitating; suspicious. **doubt-
fully,** *adv.* **doubtingly,** *adv.* **doubtless,**
adv. Assuredly, admittedly.

douche (doosh) [F.], *n.* A jet of water
directed upon some part of the body; an
instrument for applying this. *v.i.* To
apply or take a douche.

dough (dō) [A.-S. *dāh*], *n.* The paste of
bread, etc., yet unbaked; (*slang*) money.
doughy, *a.*

doughty (dou'ti) [A.-S. *dohtig*], *a.* Brave,
valiant, redoubtable. **doughtily,** *adv.*

dour (door) [L. *dūrus*, hard], *a.* Stern,
severe, sullen, pertinacious.

douse (dous) [?], *v.t.* To plunge into
water, to drench; to extinguish.

dove (dŭv) [A.-S. *dūfe*], *n.* One of several
kinds of pigeon; an emblem of innocence;
the symbol of the Holy Ghost; a term of
endearment. **dove-cot,** *n.* A small house
for domestic pigeons.

dovetail (dŭv'tāl), *n.* A mode of fastening
boards together by fitting tenons (shaped
like a dove's tail spread out), into
corresponding cavities; a joint of this
kind. *v.t.* To fit together; to fit exactly.

dowager (dou'á-jẽr) [O.F. *douagere*, as
DOWER], *n.* A widow in possession of
a dower; a title given to a widow to
distinguish her from the wife of her
husband's heir.

dowdy (dou'di) [M.E. *dowd*, a shabby
person], *n.* A shabby, badly or vulgarly
dressed woman. *a.* Awkward, shabby,
unfashionable. **dowdily,** *adv.*

dowel (dou'el) [?], *n.* A pin or peg for
connecting two stones or pieces of wood.

dower (dou'ẽr) [O.F. *doaire*, L. *dōtārium*,
from *dōtāre*, to endow], *n.* The property
which a wife brings to her husband in
marriage; that part of the husband's
property which his widow enjoys during
her life; dowry. *v.t.* To endow.

down (1) (doun) [A.-S. *dūn*], *n.* A tract
of upland, esp. the chalk uplands of S.

England. **The Downs:** roadstead off
East Kent.

down (2) (doun) [Icel. *dūnn*], *n.* The fine
soft plumage of young birds or that
found under the feathers; a soft covering
of fluffy hair. **downy,** *a.*

down (3) (doun) [A.-S. *of-dūne,* ADOWN],
adv. From a higher to a lower position;
on the ground; below the horizon; from
former to later times; from north to
south; away from the capital, etc.;
with a stream or current; into less bulk;
to finer consistency; at a low level,
prostrate; downstairs out of bed. *prep.*
Along, in a descending direction; from
the upper to a lower part of; at a
lower part of; towards the mouth of. *a.*
Moving or directed towards a lower
position; downcast.

downfall (doun'fawl), *n.* A fall of rain,
snow, etc.; a sudden loss of prosperity,
reputation, etc., ruin, overthrow.

downhill (doun'hil), *a.* Descending, sloping
downwards. *adv.* (doun-hil'). On a
descending slope; towards ruin or
disgrace.

downpour (doun'pōr), *n.* A heavy persistent fall of rain.

downright (doun'rit, doun-rit'), *a.* Directed
straight downwards; directly to the
point; unequivocal; outspoken, blunt.
adv. Straight downwards; thoroughly.

downstairs (doun-stârz'), *adv.* Down the
stairs; on or to a lower floor. *n.* The
lower part of a building.

downtrodden (doun'trodn), *a.* Trodden
under foot; oppressed; tyrannized over.

downward, -s (doun'wârd, -z), *adv.* From
a higher to a lower position, condition,
etc.; from earlier to later; from superior
to inferior, etc. *a.* Moving or tending
from higher, superior, or earlier to lower,
inferior, or later.

dowry (dou'ri) [A.-F. *dowarie*], *n.* The
property which a wife brings to her
husband.

dowse (douz) [?], *v.i.* To find subterranean
water by means of a divining-rod.

doxology (dok-sol'ŏ-ji) [Gr. *doxa,* glory,
-LOGY], *n.* A brief formula or hymn of
praise to God.

doyen (dwa-yen) [F. from L. *decānus,* a
dean], *n.* The senior member of a body
of persons.

doze (dōz) [Scand.], *v.i.* To be half asleep,
to sleep lightly. *v.t.* To spend in drowsy
inaction. *n.* A light sleep.

dozen (dŭzn) [O.F. *dozaine*) *n.* An aggregate of twelve things.

drab (1) (drăb) [Gael. *drabach*], *n.* A
prostitute; a slut.

drab (2) (drăb) [F. *drap,* cloth], *a.* Of a
dull brown or dun colour; commonplace,
monotonous. *n.* Drab colour.

draconian, draconic (drá-kŏ'ni-án, -kon'-
ik) [*Draco,* an extremely severe Athenian
legislator], *a.* Inflexible, severe, cruel.

draft (draft), *n.* The first outline of a
document; a rough sketch of work to be
executed; an order for the payment of
money; a number of men selected for
some special purpose, a contingent. *v.t.*
To draw up an outline of; to draw off (a
portion of a larger body) for some special

purpose. **draftsman**, *n.* One who draws up documents; a draughtsman.

drag (drag) [? a var. of DRAW], *v.t.* To pull along the ground by main force; to haul; to draw along with difficulty; to search (a river, etc.) with a grapnel; to put a drag on (a wheel). *v.i.* To trail along the ground; to search a river, etc., with a grapnel. *n.* Anything which retards movement; a skid to check the speed of a vehicle; an open four-horse coach; a dredge, grapnel, drag-net; an artificial scent.

dragoman (drăg'ō-màn) [O.Arab. *targumān*, interpreter], *n.* (*pl.* -mans) A guide, interpreter, and agent for travellers in the East.

dragon (drăg'ŏn) [Gr. *drakōn*, serpent], *n.* A fabulous winged serpent with formidable claws, etc.; a violent, spiteful person; a duenna. **dragon-fly**, *n.* An insect with a long, brilliant body and two pairs of large wings.

dragoon (drà-goon') [F. *dragon*, a kind of musket], *n.* A heavy-cavalry soldier. *v.t.* To subdue by force.

drain (drān) [A.-S. *dreahnian*], *v.t.* To draw off gradually; to exhaust; to drink up; to deprive (of vitality, resources, etc.). *v.i.* To flow off gradually; to be emptied of moisture. *n.* The act of draining; a strain, exhaustion; a channel for conveying water, sewage, etc. **drainage**, *n.* **drainer**, *n.* One who or that which drains; one who constructs drains; a vessel in which things are put to drain; pumping-engine for removing water from mines, etc.

drake (drāk) [?], *n.* The male of the duck.

dram (drăm), *n.* The eighth part of an ounce (apoth. wt.); the sixteenth part of an ounce (avoirdupois); a small drink of spirits.

drama (drä'mà) [Gr.], *n.* A composition representing life and action, usually intended for performance on the stage; a series of related and interesting events; dramatic art or literature. **dramat'ic**, **-ical**, *a.* **dram'atist**, *n.* **dramatize**, *v.t.* To set forth as drama; to convert (story, novel, etc.) into a play. **dramatis personæ** (drăm'ā-tis pĕr-sō'nē), *n.* (*Theat.*) The set of characters in a play.

drape (drāp) [F. *drap*, cloth], *v.t.* To cover with cloth, etc. **draper**, *n.* One who deals in cloth and other fabrics.

drastic (drăs'tik) [Gr. *drastikos*], *a.* Acting vigorously; effective, efficacious.

draught (draft), *n.* The act of drawing; the quantity of fish taken in one sweep of a net, or of liquor drunk at once; a dose; a current of air; the depth to which a ship sinks in water; a draft, a preliminary design or plan; (*pl.*) a game for two played on a chess-board with draughtsmen.

draughtsman (drafts'màn), *n.* One who draws, designs, or plans; a piece used in the game of draughts. **draughtsmanship**, *n.*

draughty (draf'ti), *a.* Full of currents of air. **draughtiness**, *n.*

draw (draw) [A.-S. *dragan*], *v.t.* (*p.p.* drawn). To pull or haul along, towards,

out, or up from; to cause to come forth, to elicit; to take; to infer, deduce; to inhale; to draft, picture; to stretch, protract; to disembowel; to unsheathe (as a sword); to attract; to search for game; to write (cheque, draft, order) on a banker, etc.; to require a specified depth of water to float; to leave undecided (in a match). *v.i.* To pull; to attract; to allow free current, etc. (as a chimney, pipe); to practise the art of delineation; to write out a draft for payment. *n.* The act or power of drawing; a pull, attraction, lure; the act of drawing lots, or a covert; a lot or chance drawn; a drawn contest.

drawback (draw'băk), *n.* Money paid back, esp. excise or import duty; a deduction, rebate; a disadvantage, inconvenience, obstacle.

drawbridge (draw'brij), *n.* A bridge that may be raised on hinges.

drawer (draw'ĕr), *n.* One who draws; one who draws a bill or order for the payment of money; a tapster, a barman; (draw) a sliding receptacle in a table, etc.; (*pl.*, drawz) an undergarment for the lower limbs. **drawing**, *n.* The action of the verb; the art of representing objects by means of lines drawn with a pencil, crayon, etc.; a delineation of this kind; the distribution of prizes in a lottery; (*pl.*) takings, receipts.

drawing-room (draw'ing room) [formerly *withdrawing*], *n.* A room for the reception of company; formal reception by a sovereign.

drawl (drawl), *v.t.* To utter in a slow, lengthened tone. *v.i.* To speak thus. *n.* This manner of speaking.

dray (drā), *n.* A low cart of strong and heavy construction.

dread (dred) [A.-S. *drǣden*], *v.* To fear greatly; to anticipate with terror. *n.* Great fear; apprehension of evil; awe; the person or thing dreaded. *a.* Exciting great fear or terror, frightful; awe-inspiring. **dreadful**, *a.* Inspiring dread; terrible.

dreadnought (dred'nawt), *n.* A large and powerful battleship.

dream (drēm) [A.-S. *drēam*], *n.* A vision; thoughts and images that pass through the mind of a sleeping person; a fancy, reverie; a chimerical scheme. *v.i.* (*past* dreamt or dreamed). To have visions; to think, to imagine as in a dream. *v.t.* To see, hear, feel, etc., in a dream; to imagine or conceive in a visionary fashion or in imagination. **dreamland**, *n.* The region of fancy or imagination. **dreamer**, *n.*

dreary (drēr'i), **drear** (drēr) [A.-S. *drēorig*], *a.* Dismal, gloomy. **drearily**, *adv.* **dreariness**, *n.*

dredge (1) (drej), *n.* A drag-net for taking oysters; an apparatus for dragging up objects from the bottom of the sea, etc. *v.t.* To gather, bring up, remove, or clear away with a dredge. **dredger** (1), *n.* One who or that which dredges; a ballast-lighter.

dredge (2) (drej) [M.E. *dragie*, O.F. *dragee*, late L. and Gr. *tragēmata*, condiments], *v.t.* To sprinkle with flour, etc. **dredger**

(2), *n.* A box with perforated lid for sprinkling.

dregs (dregz) [Scand.], *n.* The sediment or lees of liquor; worthless refuse.

drench (drench) [A.-S. *drencan*], *v.t.* To wet thoroughly; to soak, saturate; to purge violently. *n.* A liquid medicine for horses or cattle; a soaking; a large medicinal draught.

dress (dres) [O.F. *dresser*], *v.t.* To make straight; to order, arrange; to clothe, attire; to decorate with flags, etc.; to furnish with costumes; to cleanse, trim; to curry or rub down (as a horse); to prepare for use, to cook; to manure; to square and give a smooth surface to. *v.i.* To clothe oneself; to put on evening clothes; to pay great attention to dress; (*Mil.*) to arrange oneself in proper position in a line. *n.* Garments, apparel; a lady's gown. **dressy,** *a.* Fond of showy dress; stylish, smart.

dresser (1) (dres'ẽr), *n.* One who dresses another, esp. an actor for the stage; a surgeon's assistant who dresses wounds, etc.

dresser (2) (dres'ẽr) [O.F. *dresseur*], *n.* A kitchen sideboard; formerly a bench on which meat was dressed for use.

dressing (dres'ing), *n.* The action of the verb; gum, starch, etc., used in sizing or stiffening fabrics; sauce; manure; ointment, bandages, etc., applied to a wound. **dressing-down:** A severe reproof. **dressing-gown,** *n.* A light, loose gown worn during the toilet or in deshabille.

dribble (dribl) [?], *v.i.* To drip quickly, to trickle; to slaver.

drift (drift), *n.* That which is driven along by a wind or current; a current, a driving or compelling force; the course of drifting; tendency, aim, tenor; that which is driven together; a loose accumulation of sand and debris deposited by water or ice. *v.i.* To be driven into heaps; to float or be carried along by a current, or by circumstances. *v.t.* To drive along or into heaps. **drifter,** *n.* (*Naut.*) A type of trawler or fishing boat.

drill (1) (dril) [Dut. *drillen*, to bore, to turn round, to exercise], *v.t.* To bore with a pointed tool, to perforate; to train by repeated exercise, esp. in the use of arms. *v.i.* To go through a course of military exercise. *n.* A tool for boring holes in hard material; constant practice or exercise; the act of drilling soldiers or sailors, the series of exercises by which they are rendered efficient; rigorous training or discipline.

drill (2) (dril) [obs. *drill*, a rill]. A small furrow for seeds or plants; a row of plants.

drill (3) (dril) [corr. of L. *trilix* (*tri-*, three, *licium*, a thread)], *n.* A heavy cotton twilled cloth.

drink (dringk) [A.-S. *drincan*], *v.t.* (past **drank,** *p.p.* **drunk**). To swallow (a liquid); to absorb, suck in; to pledge, toast. *v.i.* To swallow a liquid; to take intoxicating liquors to excess. *n.* Something to be drunk; a draught; intoxicating liquor; excessive indulgence in this, intemperance; (*slang*) the sea.

drip (drip) [A.-S. *dryppan*], *v.i.* To fall in drops; to throw off moisture in drops. *v.t.* To let fall in drops. *n.* The act of dripping; that which falls in drops; the projecting edge of a moulding, eaves. **dripping,** *n.* The act of falling in drops; the fat which falls from roasting meat.

drive (drīv) [A.-S. *drīfan*], *v.t.* (*past* **drove,** *p.p.* **driven**) To push or urge by force, esp. in a particular direction; to guide, direct (as a horse, engine, motor); to convey in a carriage; to compel; to carry on; to frighten into an enclosure or towards guns; to force (a nail, etc.) with blows; to bore (a tunnel, etc.). *v.i.* To be urged forward by violence; to dash, hasten; to drift; to travel in a carriage, esp. under one's own control; to control a vehicle, engine, etc.; (*Cricket*) to hit strongly down the pitch; (*Golf*) to play from the tee or with a driver; (*Tennis*) to return forcibly underarm. *n.* A ride in or on a vehicle; the distance one is driven; a carriageway to a house; a forward stroke at cricket, etc.; a driving of game, cattle, or an enemy; an organized tournament for whist, etc.; energy of character, forcefulness. **driver,** *n.*

drizzle (drizl) [A.-S. *drēosan*, to fall in drops], *v.i.* To fall, as rain, in fine drops; to rain slightly. *n.* Fine small rain. **drizzly,** *a.*

droll (drōl) [F. *drôle*], *a.* Odd, facetious, ludicrous, comical, queer. **drollery,** *n.*

dromedary (drom'-, drüm'ė-dár-i) [Gr. *dromas -ada*, running, runner], *n.* The one-humped camel of Arabia.

drone (drōn) [A.-S. *drān*, *drǣn*, a bee], *n.* The male of the bee, a non-worker; an idler, one who lives on the industry of others; a deep humming sound; one of the three lower pipes of the bagpipe.

droop (droop), *v.i.* To hang or bend down; to fail, flag, languish; to despond, lose heart. *v.t.* To let (the head, eyes, face) fall or hang down.

drop (drop) [A.-S. *dropa*], *n.* A globule of liquid; a minute quantity, an infinitesimal particle; anything resembling a drop, as an ear-ring; the act of dropping; a fall, collapse; a thing that drops or is dropped; part of a gallows; the distance a person falls when hanged; an abrupt fall in a surface, the amount of this. *v.t.* To allow or cause to fall in drops; to cause to fall; to let down; to let go. *v.i.* To fall in drops; to fall; to collapse suddenly; to fall gently asleep; to be uttered; to cease, lapse, come to an end.

dropsy (drop'si) [Gr. *hudrōps* (*hudōr*, water)], *n.* An accumulation of watery fluid in the tissues or cavities of the body. **dropsical,** *a.* **dropsied,** *a.*

dross (dros) [A.-S. *drōs*], *n.* The scum left from the melting of metals; anything utterly useless. **drossy,** *a.*

drought (drout) [A.-S. *drūgath*, from *drūgian*, to dry], *n.* Dryness; dry weather long continued; thirst. **droughty,** *a.*

drove (drōv) [A.-S. *drāf*], *n.* A collection of animals driven in a body; a crowd, a mass of people, esp. as moving together. *v.i.* To drive cattle in droves.

drover, *n.* One who drives cattle or sheep to market; a cattle-dealer.

drown (droun) [A.-S. *druncnian*], *v.i.* To be suffocated in water or other liquid. *v.t.* To suffocate by submersion; to submerge, drench, overwhelm with water; to make imperceptible.

drowse (drouz) [A.-S. *drūsian*], *v.i.* To be sleepy or half asleep. *v.t.* To make drowsy. *n.* The state of being half asleep; a doze; heaviness. **drowsy,** *a.* Sleepy; disposing to sleep; sluggish, stupid. **drowsiness,** *n.* **drowsily,** *adv.*

drub (drŭb) [?], *v.t.* To cudgel; to beat thoroughly in a contest. **drubbing,** *n.*

drudge (drŭj) [?], *v.i.* To perform menial work; to work hard with little reward. *n.* One employed in menial work, or in ill-paid uncongenial work; a hack. **drudgery,** *n.*

drug (drŭg) [F. *drogue*], *n.* Any substance used as an ingredient in medical preparations; anything for which there is only a slow sale. *v.t.* To mix drugs with; to administer drugs to, esp. narcotics; to render insensible with drugs; to surfeit, cloy. **druggist,** *n.* One who deals in drugs.

drugget (drŭg'ĕt) [F. *droguet*], *n.* A coarse woollen fabric, felted or woven.

druid (droo'id) [O. Celt. *druidh*, a magician], *n.* A priest or teacher of the early Gauls and Britons; an officer of the Welsh Gorsedd. **druid'ic, -ical,** *a.* **dru'idism,** *n.*

drum (drŭm) [Teut.], *n.* A musical instrument made by stretching parchment over the head of a hollow cylinder or hemisphere; the tympanum or hollow part of the middle-ear; a revolving cylinder over which a belt or band passes. *v.i.* To beat or play on a drum; to beat rapidly, as on a table. **drum-head,** *n.* The parchment stretched at the top of a drum.

drunk (drŭngk), *pred.a.* Intoxicated, stupefied or overcome with alcoholic liquors. **drunkard,** *n.* One addicted to the excessive use of alcoholic liquors. **drunken,** *p.p.* and *a.* Intoxicated. **drunkenly,** *adv.* **drunkenness,** *n.*

dry (drī) [A.-S. *dryge*], *a.* Devoid of moisture; arid; without sap or juice; thirsty; not giving milk; not under water (of land); not sweet (of wines, etc.); lacking interest, dull; sarcastic. *v.t.* To free from or deprive of water, moisture, juice, sap, etc.; to drain, to wipe; to exhaust. *v.i.* To lose or be deprived of moisture. **dry-goods,** *n. pl.* Cloths, silks, drapery, haberdashery, etc. **dry-rot,** *n.* Decay in timber caused by fungi which reduce it to a dry brittle mass. **drysalter,** *n.* A dealer in dried and salted meat, pickles, etc. **dryshod,** *a.* and *adv.* Without wetting the feet. **drily, dryly,** *adv.* **dryness,** *n.*

dryad (drī'ăd) [Gr. *druas -ades* (*drūs,* a tree)], *n.* (*pl.* **-ades**) A nymph of the woods.

dual (dū'ăl) [L. *duo,* two], *a.* Consisting of two; twofold: expressing two; a pronoun, or noun, which, in certain languages expresses two persons or things, as distinct from the plural which expresses more than two. *n.* (*Gram.*) The dual number.

dub (dŭb) [late A.-S. *dubbian*], *v.t.* To confer knighthood upon by a tap of a sword; to give a nickname to; to trim, smear with grease. **dubbing,** *n.* Grease for preserving and softening leather.

dubious (dū'bi-ŭs) [L. *dubiōsus*], *a.* Undetermined; wavering; of uncertain result; obscure, vague; open to suspicion. **dubi'ety,** *n.* **dubiously,** *adv.*

ducal (dū'kăl), *a.* Of or pertaining to a duke. **ducally,** *adv.*

ducat (dŭk'ăt) [It. *ducato*], *n.* A coin formerly current in several European countries.

duchess (dŭch'es) [F. *duchesse*], *n.* The wife or widow of a duke; a lady who holds a duchy in her own right. **duchy** (dŭch'i), *n.* The territory, jurisdiction, or dominions of a duke.

duck (1) (dŭk) [Teut.], *n.* An untwilled linen or cotton fabric.

duck (2) (dŭk) [A.-S. *dūce*], *n.* A web-footed bird, esp. the female (male being a drake); (*colloq.*) darling; (*Cricket*) a score of nothing. **duckling,** *n.* A young duck.

duck (3) (dŭk) [M.E. *duken*], *v.i.* To dip under water; to bob the head; to bow, cringe. *v.t.* To throw into water; to wet thoroughly. *n.* A quick plunge or dip under water; a sudden lowering of the head. **ducking,** *n.*

duct (dŭkt) [L. *ductus,* a leading], *n.* A passage by which fluid is conveyed.

ductile (dŭk'til) [L. *ductilis*], *a.* That may be drawn out into threads or wire; malleable, plastic; tractable, yielding to persuasion or advice. **ductility** (-til'i-ti), *n.*

dude (dūd) [G.], *n.* A fop, affected person.

dudgeon (dŭj'ón) [?], *n.* Anger, resentment, indignation.

due (dū) [O.F. *deü,* owed], *a.* Owing, that ought to be paid, rendered, or done; suitable, appropriate; expected to arrive, calculated to happen; ascribable. *adv.* Exactly, directly. *n.* That which is owing to one, or one owes; an obligation, fee, or legal exaction.

duel (dū'ĕl) [It. *duello* (L. *duo,* two)], *n.* A combat between two (esp. with deadly weapons) to decide a quarrel. *v.i.* To fight in a duel; to contest. **duellist,** *n.*

duenna (dū-en'á) [Sp. *dueña*], *n.* An elderly lady in charge of young ones; a chaperon.

duet (dū-et') [It. *duetto*], *n.* A composition for two performers, vocal or instrumental.

duffer (dŭf'ér) [?], *n.* A stupid person.

dug (dŭg) [?], *n.* A teat, nipple (of beasts).

duke (dūk) [L. *dux, ducis,* a leader], *n.* A noble holding the highest hereditary rank below royal; the sovereign prince of a duchy. **dukedom,** *n.* The territory or quality, etc., of a duke.

dulcet (dŭl'sĕt) [L. *dulcis,* sweet], *a.* Sweet to the ear or senses.

dulcimer (dŭl'si-mér) [O.F. *doulcemer*], *n.* A musical instrument with wires which are struck with rods.

dull (dŭl) [A.-S. *dol,* stupid], *a.* Slow of understanding; stupid; blunt; wanting keenness in any of the senses. *v.t.* To make stupid; to blunt, to render less sensitive, interesting, or effective. **dullard,** *n.* A blockhead; a dunce. **dullish,** *a.* **dullness,** *n.*

duly (dū'li), *adv.* Properly; becomingly; regularly; punctually.

dumb (dŭm) [A.-S.], *a.* Unable to utter articulate sounds or to speak; mute, speechless, taciturn; stupid, dull. **dumbbells,** *n.pl.* Pairs of weights connected by short bars, used for exercise. **dumbshow,** *n.* Gestures without speech; pantomime. **dumbness,** *n.*

dumbfound (dŭm'found), *v.t.* To strike dumb; to confound.

dummy (dŭm'i), *n.* One who is dumb; any sham article; a lay-figure; a rubber teat for a baby to suck; the exposed hand at bridge, etc.

dump (dŭmp) [Scand.], *v.t.* To unload (as dirt) from wagons; to send surplus produce to a foreign market for sale at a low price. *n.* A pile of refuse.

dumpling (dŭmp'ling) [?], *n.* A mass of dough, boiled or baked.

dumpy (dŭm'pi) [?], *a.* Short and thick.

dun (1) (dŭn) [A.-S. *dunn*], *a.* Dull brown.

dun (2) (dŭn) [? var. of DIN], *v.t.* To demand payment from with persistence; to pester. *n.* A creditor who presses persistently.

dunce (dŭns) [in ridicule of the schoolman, John *Duns* Scotus (d. 1308)], *n.* A dullard; one slow in learning.

dunderhead (dŭn'dėr-hed) [?], *n.* A blockhead, numskull, dolt, dunce.

dune (dūn) [A.-S. *dūn*], *n.* A sand-hill on the sea-shore.

dung (dŭng) [A.-S.], *n.* The excrement of animals; manure. **dunghill,** *n.* A heap of dung and farmyard refuse.

dungarees (dŭng'gà-rēz) [Hind. *dungri*], *n.pl.* Overalls.

dungeon (dŭn'jŏn) [F. *donjon*], *n.* A mediæval keep; a place of confinement.

dunnage (dŭn'åj) [?], *n.* Faggots, boughs, etc., laid in the hold of a ship to pack or support the cargo.

duo- [L., two], *pref.* Two.

duodecimal (dū-ō-des'i-mál) [DUO-, L. *decem*, ten], *a.* Proceeding in computation by twelves. **duodecimo,** *n.* A book consisting of sheets of twelve leaves or twenty-four pages.

duodenum (dū-ō-dē'num) [L.], *n.* (*Anat.*) The first portion of the small intestine. **duodenal,** *a.*

duologue (dū'ō-log), *n.* A dialogue or dramatic composition for two.

dupe (dūp) [F.], *n.* A credulous person; one easily deceived. *v.t.* To trick, cheat.

duplex (dū'pleks), *a.* Double, twofold; compounded of two.

duplicate (dū'pli-kát) [L. *duo*, two, *plicātus*, folded], *a.* Twofold, existing in two parts exactly corresponding. *n.* One of two things exactly similar; a replica, copy. *v.t.* To make a reproduction or copy of; to double. **duplication,** *n.*

duplicity (dū-plis'i-ti), *n.* Double-dealing, dissimulation.

durable (dūr'ábl) [L. *dūrābilis*], *a.* Having the quality of endurance; firm, stable. **durabil'ity,** *n.* **durably,** *adv.*

durance (dūr'áns) [F.], *n.* Imprisonment.

duration (dū-rā'shŭn) [L. *dūrāre*, to last], *n.* Continuance in time; power of continuance.

durbar (dėr'bar) [Hind. *darbār*], *n.* An Indian ruler's court; a state-reception in India.

duress (dū-res') [O.F. *duresce*], *n.* Constraint, compulsion, imprisonment.

during (dū'ring) [pres. p. of obs. *dure*, to last], *prep.* In or within the time of.

dusk (dŭsk) [A.-S. *dox*], *a.* Tending to darkness or blackness; dim, obscure. *n.* A tendency to darkness; shade, gloom; twilight. **dusky,** *a.*

dust (dŭst) [A.-S. *dūst*], *n.* Dry earth, etc., reduced to such small particles as to be easily blown about; pollen; mortal remains; the grave. *v.t.* To remove dust from; to sprinkle with dust; to make dusty. **duster,** *n.* A cloth or brush used to remove dust. **dustman,** *n.* One who removes refuse from dustbins. **dustpan,** *n.* A domestic utensil into which dust is swept. **dusty,** *a.*

Dutch (dŭch) [M. Dut. *Dutsch*, Hollandish], *a.* Pertaining to Holland, its people, or language, Hollandish. *n.* The language of Holland; Low German; the Hollanders. **Dutchman,** *n.* A native of Holland.

duty (dū'ti) [A.-F. *dueté*], *n.* That which is bound or ought to be paid, done, or performed; moral or legal obligation; an act of reverence, deference, etc.; impost or custom charged upon the importation or exportation of goods; office, occupation. **du'teous,** *a.* Obedient, obsequious, dutiful. **dutiable,** *a.* Liable to a duty or custom. **dutiful,** *a.* Careful in performing duties; reverential, deferential.

dwarf (dwawf) [A.-S. *dweorh*], *n.* A person, animal, or plant much below the normal size. *a.* Below the ordinary or natural size; stunted. *v.t.* To stunt, check the development of; to cause to look small by comparison. **dwarfish,** *a.*

dwell (dwel) [A.-S. *dwellan*, to tarry], *v.i.* (*past* and *p.p.* **dwelt**) To reside, to abide (in a place); to linger, tarry. **dweller,** *n.* **dwelling,** *n.*

dwindle (dwindl) [A.-S. *dwīnan*], *v.i.* To shrink, become smaller; to waste away.

dye (dī) [A.-S. *dēag*, a dye], *v.t.* To stain, impregnate with colouring-matter. *v.i.* To follow the business of a dyer; to take a colour (of material). *n.* A fluid used for dyeing, colouring-matter; tinge produced by dyeing. **dyer,** *n.*

dying (dī'ing), *a.* About to die; mortal; done, uttered, etc., just before death; associated with death; perishing.

dynamic (dī-năm'ik) [Gr. *dunamikos*, powerful], *a.* Pertaining to forces in motion; motive, active, as opp. to potential; involving or dependent upon mechanical activity; (*Med.*) functional. *n.* The motive force of any action. **dynamics,** *n.* The science which treats of the action of force, divided into statics and kinetics; the forces producing or governing activity of any kind or in any sphere.

dynamite (dī'nà-mīt) [Gr. *dunamis*, power], *n.* A powerful explosive consisting of nitro-glycerine mixed with an absorbent. **dynamiter, -ard, -ist,** *n.* A revolutionary or criminal employing dynamite.

dynamo-, *comb. form.* Pertaining to force or power.

dynamo (dī'nả-mō), n. (pl. -os) A machine for converting mechanical energy into electric by means of electro-magnetic induction.

dynast (dĭn'ăst) [Gr. dunastēs, a lord], n. A ruler, monarch. **dynastic** (di-năs'tĭk), a. **dynasty** (dĭn'ă-sti), n. A line of sovereigns of the same family.

dyne (dīn) [F. from Gr. dunamis, power], n. The unit for measuring force.

dys- [Gr. dus-, badly, with difficulty], pref. Bad; difficult, working badly, painful.

dysentery (dĭs'ĕn-tĕr-i) [Gr. hentera, bowels], n. An infectious disease of the large intestines, accompanied by mucous and bloody evacuations.

dyspepsia, dyspepsy (dĭs-pep'si-ả, -si) [Gr. peptein, to cook], n. Indigestion arising from functional derangement of the stomach. **dyspeptic**, a.

E

each (ēch) [A.-S. ælc], a and pron. Every one (of a number) considered separately.

eager (ē'gėr) [A.-F. egre], a. Excited by ardent desire; keen, vehement, impatient. **eagerly**, adv. **eagerness**, n.

eagle (ēgl) [A.-F. egle], n. A large bird of prey, esp. the golden eagle; a lectern in the form of an eagle with expanded wings; a military ensign bearing such a device. **eaglet**, n. A young eagle.

ear (1) (ēr) [A.-S. ēare], n. The organ of hearing, esp. the external part; the sense of hearing; perception of differences of sounds, judgment of harmony; attention, favourable consideration; an ear-like projection; judgment, opinion, taste. **earache**, n. A pain in the drum of the ear. **ear-drum**, n. The tympanum, or its membrane. **ear-mark**, n. A mark on the ear by which a sheep can be identified; any distinctive mark. v.t. To set a distinctive mark upon; to allocate (funds, etc.) for a particular purpose. **ear-phone**, n. (Wire.) A headphone. **ear-piercing** a. Shrill. **ear-ring**, n. A pendant worn in the lobe of the ear. **ear-shot**, n Hearing distance.

ear (2) (ēr) [A.-S. ēar], n. A spike or head of corn. v.i. To form ears, as corn.

earl (ērl) [A.-S. eorl, a warrior], n. A nobleman ranking next below a marquess and above a viscount [cp. COUNT]. **earldom**, n. The rank, title, or position of an earl.

early (ēr'li) [A.-S. ǣrlīce], adv. (earlier, earliest) In good time; betimes; near the beginning. a. Soon; in advance as compared with something; coming before the usual time; situated in or near the beginning. **Early English**, n. and a. (Arch.) An early type of Gothic style.

earn (ērn) [A.-S. earnian], v.t. To gain by labour; to merit, deserve, or become entitled to as the result of action or conduct. **earnings**, n.pl. That which is earned; wages, reward.

earnest (1) (ēr'nĕst) [A.-S. eornost], n. Seriousness; reality. a. Serious, important, grave; ardent, eager, or zealous in the performance of any act or the pursuit of any object; heartfelt, sincere. **earnestly**, adv. **earnestness**, n.

earnest (2) (ĕr'nĕst) [M.E. ernes], n. A pledge, an assurance of something to come.

earth (ērth) [A.-S. eorthe], n. The ground, the visible surface of the planet on which we live; this world, as opposed to other scenes of existence; soil, mould, dry land; the hole of a fox, etc.; (Elec.) the ground connexion of an electric current. v.t. To cover with earth; to drive (fox, etc.) to his earth; (Elect.) to connect to earth. **earthquake**, n. A movement of a portion of the earth's crust produced by volcanic forces. **earth satellite**, n. A man-made projectile circling the earth, a sputnik. **earthwork**, n. (Fort.) Mounds, ramparts, etc., raised for defensive purposes; embankments, cuttings.

earthen (ēr'thĕn), a. Made of earth, baked clay, or similar substance. **earthenware**, n. Ware made of baked clay; pottery.

earthly (ērth'li), a. Of or pertaining to this world or life; mortal, human; carnal, corporeal.

earwig (ēr'wig) [A.-S. ēar-wicga, ear-runner], n. An insect having curved forceps at its tail.

ease (ēz) [O.F. aise], n. Freedom from labour, trouble, pain, constraint, formality, etc.; quiet, tranquillity; readiness; absence of effort. v.t. To free from pain, anxiety, labour, or trouble; to relieve from a burden; to make easier; to mitigate; to render less difficult; to relax, adjust. v.i. To relax one's efforts or exertions.

easel (ē'zĕl) [Dut. ezel, a little ass], n. A frame used to support a picture.

easement (ēz'mĕnt), n. The liberty or privilege, without profit, which one proprietor has through the estate of another, as a right of way, etc.

east (ēst) [A.-S. ēast, adv.], a. Situated towards the sunrise; coming from this direction. n. The point of the compass where the sun rises at the equinox; the countries east of Europe; the east wind. adv. Towards, at, or near the quarter of the rising sun. **eastward**, a. and n.

Easter (ēs'tėr) [Ēostre (Teutonic dawn-goddess)], n. The festival in commemoration of the resurrection of Christ, taking place in March or April.

easterly (ēs'tėr-li), a. Situated, in the direction of, or coming from, the east; looking towards the east. adv. In the direction of the east; in or from the east.

eastern (ēs'tėrn) [A.-S. ēasterne], a. pertaining to the east. n. An inhabitant of the East.

easy (ē'zi) [O.F. aisié, eased], a. At ease; free from pain, care, discomfort, embarrassment, constraint, affectation, etc.; well-to-do; not strict; smooth, flowing; not difficult, not requiring great labour or effort; complaint; indulgent; fitting loosely. adv. In an easy manner.

eat (ēt) [A.-S. etan], v.t. (past **ate** (et), p.p. **eaten** (ētn)). To masticate and swallow as food; to devour, destroy by eating; to corrode, to consume, wear away. *v.i* To take food; to taste, relish. **eatable**, *a.* Fit to be eaten; proper for food. *n.* Anything fit or proper for food.

eau de vie (ō'dè-vē) [F.], *n.* Brandy.

eaves (ēvz) [A.-S. *efes*], *n.pl.* The lower edge of the roof projecting beyond the wall. **eavesdrop**, *v.i* To listen so as to surprise confidences. **eavesdropper**, *n.*

ebb (eb) [A.-S. *ebba*], *n.* The reflux of the tide; decay, failure. *v.i.* To flow back; to recede, decay. **ebb-tide**, *n.* The retiring tide.

ebony (eb'ò-ni) [Gr. *ebenos*], *n.* A very solid and black wood, capable of a high polish.

ebriety (e-bri'é-ti) [L. *ēbrius*, drunk], *n.* Drunkenness, intoxication.

ebullient (e-bŭl'yènt)[L. *ēbulliens*, boiling], *a.* Boiling over; overflowing with high spirits, etc.

eccentric (ek-sen'trik)[Gr. *ek*, out, *kentron*, CENTRE], *a.* Deviating from the centre; not having the same centre; departing from the usual practice; erratic; peculiar or odd. *n.* A person of odd or peculiar habits; a mechanical contrivance for converting circular into reciprocating rectilinear motion. **eccentrically**, *adv.* **eccentric'ity**, *n.* The state of not being concentric; deviation from the centre; departure from what is usual or established.

ecclesiastic (è-klē-zi-ăs'tik) [Gr. *ekklesia*, an assembly of citizens, a Church], *a.* Ecclesiastical. *n.* A person in holy orders, a clergyman. **ecclesiastical**, *a.* Pertaining to the Church or clergy.

echelon (esh'è-lòn) [F., from *échelle*, a ladder], *n.* The arrangement of troops as in the form of steps.

echo (ek'ō) [Gr. *ēchō*, *ēchē*, sound], *n.* The repetition of a sound caused by reflection; close imitation in words or sentiment; a hearty response. *v.i.* To give an echo; to resound.

éclat (è-kla') [F., from *éclater*, to split, burst], *n.* Brilliant success; striking effect.

eclectic (ek-lek'tik)[Gr. *eklektikos* (*eklegein*, to pick out)], *a.* Selecting, picking out from the doctrines, etc., of others; containing or consisting of selections. *n.* One who borrows doctrines, opinions, tastes, or practical methods from various schools or sources. **eclecticism**, *n.*

eclipse (è-klips') [Gr. *ek*, out of, *leipein*, to leave], *n.* Obscuration of light from a heavenly body by the passage of another between it and the eye or between it and the source of its light, a temporary failure; loss of brightness, honour, reputation, etc. *v.t.* To cause an eclipse of, to intercept the light of, to obscure; to outshine.

ecliptic (ek-lip'tik) [Gr. *ekleiptikos*, as prec.], *n.* The apparent path of the sun round the earth.

econometrics (ē-kon-ò-met'riks), *n.* The statistical study of economics.

economic (ē-kò-nom'ik), *a.* Relating to economy or economics; economical. **economical**, *a.* Careful, frugal, thrifty. **economics**, *n.* The science of the production and distribution of wealth, political

economy. **econ'omist**, *n.* One skilled in the science of economics. **econ'omize**, *v.i.* To manage with economy. *v.t.* To use, administer, or expend with economy, to use sparingly.

economy (è-kon'ò-mi)[Gr. *oikonomia*, from *oikonomein*, to manage a household], *n.* The management, regulation, and government of household affairs; frugal and judicious expenditure of money, or time; carefulness; cheapness of operation; the operations of nature; the administration of the internal affairs of a State, etc.; organization, system.

ecstasy (ek'stà-si) [Gr. *ek*, out, *stasis*, a standing], *n.* Excessive emotion, as rapture, delight, distress, pain; frenzy; a trance; a morbid state in which the mind is completely absorbed by one idea. **ecstat'ic**, *a.*

ecto- [Gr. *ektos*, outside], *comb. form* (*Biol.* and *Zool.*) **ectoplasm**, *n.* The outer layer of protoplasm; (*Spiritualism*) the supposed emanation from the body of a medium.

eczema (ek'zè-mà) [Gr., a pustule], *n.* An inflammatory disease of the skin.

-ed, *suf.* Forming the past tense and p.p. of regular verbs; and adjectives, as *cultured*, *moneyed*.

eddy (ed'i) [?], *n.* A small whirlpool; a whirling current of air, fog, etc.

edelweiss (ädl'vis) [G. *edel*, noble, *weiss*, white], *n.* A small Alpine plant growing in rocky places.

Eden (ēdn) [Heb. *'ēden*, pleasure, delight], *n.* The first abode of Adam and Eve; a region of perfect bliss.

edentate (e-den'tāt) [L. *edenture*, to render toothless], *a.* (*Zool.*) Having no incisor teeth.

edge (ej) [A.-S. *ecg*], *n.* The cutting part of an instrument, or its sharpness; the line where two surfaces of a solid meet; a border, margin, or extremity; keenness of mind or appetite. *v.t.* To sharpen; to make an edge or border to; to egg, instigate; to move by little and little. *v.i.* To move forward or away by little and little. **edging**, *n.* That which forms the border or edge of anything.

edible (ed'ibl) [late L. *edibilis*, *edere*, to eat], *a.* Fit for food, eatable, *n.* Anything fit for food. **edibil'ity**, *n.*

edict (ē'dikt) [L. *ēdictum*, proclaimed], *n.* A decree issued by authority.

edifice (ed'i-fis) [L. *ædes*, a building, *facere*, to make], *n.* A building, esp. one of some size and pretension.

edify (ed'i-fi), *v.t.* To build up morally or spiritually; to improve, instruct, enlighten. **edifica'tion**, *n.*

edit (ed'it) [L. *ēditus*, given out, put forth], *v.t.* To prepare for publication; to conduct or manage, as a periodical, by selecting and revising the literary matter. **edition** (è-dish'ùn), *n.* The form in which a literary work is published; the whole number of copies published at one time. **editor**, *n.* One who prepares the work of others for publication, or who conducts or manages a periodical. **editor'ial**, *a.* Pertaining to an editor, *n.* A leading article. **editorship**, *n.*

educate (ed'ū-kāt) [L. *ēducātus*, p.p. of *ēducāre*, to bring up], *v.t.* To teach; to train and develop the intellectual and moral powers of an organ or faculty. **educa'tion**, *n.* educational, *a.* educationalist, educationist, *n.* An advocate of education; a student of educational methods.

educe (ė-dūs') [L. *ēdūcere*, to lead out], *v.t.* To bring out, evolve, deduce, infer; to extract. educible, *a.* education, *n.*

Edwardian (ed-wôrd'i-àn), *a.* Referring usu. to the period of Edward VII (1901–10).

eel (ēl) [A.-S. *cel*], *n.* A snake-like fish.

eerie (er'i) [M.E. *eri*], *a.* Superstitiously frightened; causing fear; weird. **eerily**, *adv.* eeriness, *n.*

efface (ė-fās') [F. *effacer*], *v.t.* To wipe out, obliterate; to render negligible. **effaceable**, *a.* effacement, *n.*

effect (ė-fekt') [L. *effectus*], *n.* The result or product of a cause, etc., consequence; efficacy, fulfilment; aim, purpose; a combination of colours, forms, sounds, etc., calculated to produce an impression, the impression produced; (*pl.*) goods, personal estate. *v.t.* To produce as a result; to bring about, accomplish. **effective**, *a.* Producing its proper effect or a striking impression; fit for service; real, actual. effectiveness, *n.* effectual, *a.* Adequate.

effeminate (ė-fem'i-nàt) [L. *effēminātus*], *a.* Womanish, unmanly, weak. **effeminacy**, *n.* effeminately, *adv.*

effervesce (ef-ėr-ves') [L. *fervescere*, to begin boiling], *v.i.* To bubble up with the escape of gas, as fermenting liquors; to escape in bubbles; to boil over with excitement. **effervescence**, *n.* effervescent, *a.*

effete (ė-fēt') [L. *effētus*, weakened by breeding], *a.* Worn out.

efficacious (ef-i-kā'shùs), *a.* Producing the effect intended. ef'ficacy, *n.*

efficient (ė-fish'ènt) [L *efficiens*, effecting], *a.* Producing effects or results; competent, capable. efficiency, *n.*

effigy (ef'i-ji) [F. *fingere*, to fashion], *n.* The likeness of a person, as on coins, etc.

effluent (ef'lù-ènt) [L. *effluens*, flowing out], *a.* Flowing or issuing out; emanating. *n.* A stream which flows out of another or out of a lake; the discharge from a sewage tank. **effluence**, *n.* The act or state of flowing out; that which flows out.

effluvium (ė-floo'vi-ùm), *n.* (*pl.* **-via**) An odorous emanation, esp. a noxious exhalation.

effort (ef'ôrt) [L. *fortis*, strong], *n.* An exertion of physical or mental power, a strenuous attempt, an endeavour. effortless, *a.*

effrontery (ė-frŭn'tėr-i) [F. *effronterie*], *n.* Impudence, shamelessness.

effulgence (ė-fŭl'jèns) [L. *fulgēre*, to shine], *n.* Radiance; a flood of light, effulgent, *a.* Shining brightly.

effuse (ė-fūz') [L. *effūsus*, poured out], *v.t.* To pour out, emit, shed abroad. **effusion**, *n.* The act of pouring out; that which is poured out; an outpouring of genius or emotion; frank expression of feeling.

effusive, *a.* Gushing, exuberant, demonstrative. effusively, *adv.* effusiveness, *n.*

eft (eft) [A.-S. *efete*], *n.* The common newt.

egg (1) (eg) [A.-S. *œg*], *n.* The ovum of birds, reptiles, fishes, and many of the invertebrates, containing the embryo of a new individual; the early stage of anything; the germ, origin. **egg-shell**, *n.* The calcareous envelope in which an egg is enclosed. **egg-shell china**; Very thin porcelain.

egg (2) (eg) [Icel.], *v.t.* To incite, to urge (on).

eglantine (eg'làn-tīn) [F.], *n.* The sweet brier.

ego (eg'ō) [L., I], *n.* Individuality; the self-conscious subject, as opp. to object. **egoism**, *n.* The theory that man's chief good, and the true basis of morality, is the complete development and happiness of self; the doctrine that man can be certain of nothing but his own existence and the operations of his own mind; egotism. **egoist**, *n.* egois'tic, -ical, *a.* **egotism** (eg'ō-tizm) [as prec.], *n.* The habit of frequently using *I* in writing or speaking; self-glorification, self-conceit. **egotist**, *n.* egotis'tic, -ical, *a.*

egregious (ė-grē'jyùs) (L. *ēgregius*], *a.* Extraordinary, out of the common; notable, notorious. egregiously, *adv.*

egress (ē'gres) [L. *ēgressus*, gone out], *n.* A means of exit.

egret (ē'grėt) [O.F. *egrette*], *n.* The lesser white heron.

Egyptian (ė-jip'shàn), *a.* Pertaining to Egypt or the Egyptians. *n.* A native of Egypt; a gipsy. **Egyptol'ogy**, *n.* The study of the antiquities, etc., of ancient Egypt.

eh (ā) [A.-S. *ēa*], *int.* Expressive of doubt, inquiry, surprise, etc.

eider (ī'dėr) [Icel. *œthr*], *n.* A large Arctic sea-duck. **eider-down**, *n.* The soft, elastic down from the breast of this bird; a quilt filled with this.

eight (āt) [A.-S. *eahta*], *n.* The sum of one and seven; the figure 8 or viii, representing this; a crew of eight in a boat. *a.* Consisting of one more than seven. **eightfold**, *a.* **eighth** (ātth), *a.* Coming next in order to the seventh. *n.* One of eight equal parts; (*Mus.*) the interval of an octave. **eighthly**, *adv.*

eighteen (ā-tēn') [A.-S. *eahtatȳne*], *a.* and *n.* The sum of eight and ten.

eighty (ā'ti) [A.S. *eahtatig*], *a.* and *n.* Eight times ten; the numeral representing this. 80 or lxxx. **eightieth**, *a.*

eisteddfod (ī-steth'vod) [W., a sitting], *n.* A congress held annually in Wales to encourage native poetry and music.

either (ī-, ē'thėr) [A.-S. *œgther*], *a.* and *pron.* One or the other of two; each of two. *a.*, *adv.*, or *conj.* In one or the other case (as a disjunctive correlative); (*colloq.*) any more than the other (with neg. or interrog., as *If you don't I don't either*).

ejaculate (ė-jăk'ū-lāt) [L. *ējaculātus*, cast forth]. *v.t.* To utter suddenly and briefly; to emit with a jerk. **ejacula'tion**, *n.*

eject (ė-jekt') [L. *ējectus*, thrown out], *v.t.* To discharge, emit, to expel; to dispossess,

ejection, *n.* **ejectment,** *n.* The act of casting out or expelling; dispossession; an action to recover possession.

eke (ēk) [A.-S. *īecan*], *v.t.* To supply deficiencies in (with *out*); to protract, lengthen. *adv.* Also, likewise.

elaborate (ė-lăb'ō-rāt) [L. *ēlabōrātus*, worked out], *a.* Carefully wrought; highly finished. *v.t.* (-rāt) To develop in detail. **elaborateness,** *n.* **elabora'tion,** *n.*

eland (ē'lǎnd) [Dut., an elk], *n.* A large ox-like antelope from S. Africa.

elapse (ė-lǎps') [L. *ēlapsus*, glided out], *v.i.* To glide or pass away.

elastic (ė-lǎs'tǐk) [Gr. *elastikos*, propulsive], *a.* Springy; flexible, adaptable; readily recovering from depression, etc., buoyant. *n.* A strip or string of elastic substance. **elastic'ity,** *n.*

elate (ė-lāt') [L. *ēlātus*, borne up], *v.t.* To raise the spirits of, to make exultant. *a.* In high spirits, exultant. **ela'tion,** *n.*

elbow (el'bō) [A.-S. *eln*, ell, *boga*, bow], *n.* The joint uniting the forearm and upper arm; an elbow-shaped angle, or bend.

elder (1) (el'dėr) [A.-S. *ieldra*], *a.* Older; senior in position. *n.* A senior; one whose age entitles him to respect; an officer in the Presbyterian and other Churches. **elderly,** *a.* Bordering on old age. **eldest,** *a.* Oldest; first born of those surviving.

elder (2) (el'dėr) [A.-S. *ellen, ellern*], *n.* A small tree bearing white flowers and dark purple berries.

elect (ė-lekt') [L. *ēlectus*, chosen, selected], *a.* Chosen, picked out; designated to an office, but not yet in possession of it. *v.t.* To choose for any office, etc., esp. by vote; to determine on a course of action.

election (ė-lek'shŭn), *n.* The act of choosing, esp. by vote; the process of electing; (*Theol.*) the selection of certain individuals to be eternally saved (a doctrine of Calvinism). **electioneer',** *v.i.* To work at an election in the interests of a candidate. **elective,** *a.* **elector,** *n.* One entitled to vote; a German prince formerly entitled to vote in the election of the Emperor. **electoral,** *a.* **electorate,** *n.* The whole body of electors; the dignity or territory of a German Elector. **electress,** *n.* The wife of a German elector.

electric (ė-lek'trǐk) [Gr. *elektron*, amber], *a.* Containing, generating, or operated by electricity; (*fig.*) magnetic, spirited. **electrical,** *a.* **electrician** (el-ėk-trǐsh'ǎn), *n.* One skilled in the science and application of electricity.

electricity (el-ėk-trǐs'ĭ-tǐ), *n.* A powerful physical agent which makes its existence manifest by attractions and repulsions, by producing light and heat, chemical decomposition, and other phenomena; the science of the laws and phenomena of this.

electrify (ė-lek'trǐ-fī), *v.t.* To charge with electricity; to make suitable for operating by electrical power. (*fig.*) to thrill with joy or exciting emotion. **electrification,** *n.*

electro- [Gr. *elektron*, amber], *comb. form.* Having electricity for its motive power; resulting from, or pertaining to, electricity. **electro-biology,** *n.* The science

of the electric phenomena of living organisms. **electrolysis** (ė-lek-trol'ǐ-sǐs), *n.* (*Phys.*) The decomposition of chemical compounds by passage of an electric current. **electroplats,** *v.t.* To cover with a coating of silver, etc., by exposure in a solution of a metallic salt, which is decomposed by electricity. *n.* Articles so produced. **electrotype,** *n.* The process of producing copies of medals, woodcuts, type, etc., by the electric deposition of copper upon a mould; the facsimile so produced. *v.t.* To copy by this process.

electrocution (ė-lek-trō-kū'shŭn), *n.* Capital punishment, or death, by electricity.

electron (ė-lek'trŏn) [Gr.], *n.* (*Phys.*) The basic unit of negative electricity which associates with a positively charged nucleus to form the atom, being probably the cause of all electrical phenomena.

eleemosynary (el-ė-ē-mos'ǐn-ár-ǐ) [Gr. *eleēmosunē*, alms], *a.* By way of alms; supported by charity.

elegant (el'ė-gǎnt) [L. *ēlegans*], *a.* Pleasing to good taste; graceful, refined. **elegance,** *n.* **elegantly,** *adv.*

elegiac (el-ė-jī'ǎk), *a.* Pertaining to or of the nature of elegies; mournful. *n.pl.* Alternate hexameters and pentameters.

elegy (el'ė-jǐ) [Gr. *elegeia* (*elegos*, a lament)], *n.* A poem of lamentation.

element (el'ė-mėnt) [L. *elementum*], *n.* A fundamental part; (*Chem.*) a substance which cannot be resolved by analysis; (*pl.*) earth, air, fire, and water; natural habitat (as water of fish), the natural sphere of any person or thing; the rudiments of any science or art; the bread and wine used in the eucharist. **elemen'tal,** *a.* Pertaining to first principles, or to the primitive forces of nature; ultimate, simple, uncompounded. **elementary** (el-ė-men'tār-ǐ), *a.* Primary, uncompounded; rudimentary.

elephant (el'ė-fǎnt) [Gr. *elephas*], *n.* A large pachydermatous quadruped, with flexible proboscis and long curved tusks.

elevate (el'ė-vāt) [L. *ēlevātus*, lifted up], *v.t.* To lift up; to raise; to exalt in position or dignity; to make louder; to refine, improve; to exhilarate. **eleva'tion,** *n.* Act of elevating; state of being elevated; an elevated position or ground; height above sea-level; view of a building, etc., drawn to scale but not in perspective; the angular altitude of a heavenly body above the horizon; angle of the line of fire. **el'evator,** *n.* One who or that which elevates; a lift.

eleven (ė-lev'én) [A.-S. *endlufon*], *a.* and *n.* Ten with one added; the symbol representing this, 11 or xi; (*Cricket, Assoc. Football*) the eleven men on one side.

elf (elf) [A.-S. *ælf*], *n.* (*pl.* **elves**) A tiny supernatural being, a fairy; a mischievous person, an imp. **elf-arrow,** *n.* A stone arrow-head. **elfin,** *a.* Elfish. *n.* A little elf; an urchin. **elfish, elvish,** *a.*

elicit (ė-lis'ǐt) [L. *ēlicitus*], *v.t.* To draw out, evoke.

elide (ė-līd') [L. *ēlīdere*], *v.t.* To strike out, omit. **elision,** *n.*

eligible (el'i-jibl) [L. *ēligibilis*], *a.* Fit to be chosen; desirable, suitable. **eligibil'ity,** *n.* **el'igibly,** *adv.*

eliminate (è-lim'i-nāt) [L. *ēliminātus*], *v.t.* To cast out, expel, get rid of; to exclude. **elimina'tion,** *n.* Act of eliminating.

elision (è-lizh'ón), *n.* (*Gram.*) The suppression of a letter.

élite (ā-lēt') [F.], *n.* The pick, the flower.

elixir (è-lik'sèr) [Arab. *al-iksīr*], *n.* The alchemists' liquor for transmuting metals into gold; a potion for prolonging life; a cordial.

Elizabethan (è-liz-à-bē'thàn), *a.* Pertaining to Queen Elizabeth I (1558–1603) or her time.

elk (elk) [A.-S. *elch*], *n.* The largest member of the deer family; the moose.

ell (el) [A.-S. *eln*], *n.* A measure for cloth; the (obsolete) English ell is 45 in.

ellipse (è-lips') [Gr. *elleipsis*], *n.* A regular oval; a conic section formed by a plane intersecting a cone obliquely. **ellip'tic, -al,** *a.* Pertaining to an ellipse, or to ellipsis. **elliptically,** *adv.*

ellipsis (è-lip'sis), *n.* (*pl.* -ses) Omission of one or more necessary words from a sentence.

elm (elm) [A.-S.], *n.* A common English tree.

elocution (el-ò-kū'shùn) [L. *loquī*, to speak], *n.* The art or manner of speaking, etc.; effective oral delivery.

elongate (ē'long-gāt) [L. *elongatus*, removed], *v.t.* To extend, to make longer.

elope (è-lōp') [A.-F. *aloper*], *v.i.* To run away with a lover, or clandestinely; to abscond. **elopement,** *n.*

eloquence (el'ò-kwèns), *n.* Fluent, powerful, and appropriate verbal expression, esp. of emotional ideas. **eloquent,** *a.*

else (els) [A.-S. *elles*], *adv.* Besides, in addition; otherwise, in the other case, if not. **elsewhere,** *adv.* In or to some other place.

elucidate (è-loo'si-dāt) [late L. *ēlūcidātus,* p.p. of *ēlūcidāre* (**E**-(**EX**-), *lūcidus,* bright)], *v.t.* To make clear, throw light on; to explain. **elucida'tion,** *n.* **elucidative,** *a.*

elude (è-lood') [L. *lūdere*, to play], *v.t.* To escape from by artifice or dexterity; to evade; to baffle. **elusion,** *n.* **elusive,** *a.* **elusory,** *a.*

elvish (el'vish), *a.* Pertaining to elves; elfish; mischievous.

elysium (è-liz'i-ùm) [Gr. *Elusion* (*pedion*), the plain of the blessed], *n.* A place or state of perfect happiness. **elysian,** *a.*

em-, *pref.* As in *embank, empower.*

emaciate (è-mā'shi-āt) [L. *macer*, lean], *v.t.* To cause to lose flesh; to reduce to leanness. **emacia'tion,** *n.*

emanate (em'à-nāt) [L. *ēmānātus*, flowed out], *v.i.* To issue from, to originate; to proceed from. **emana'tion,** *n.*

emancipate (è-măn'si-pāt) [L. *mancipāre*, to transfer property], *v.t.* To release from bondage, etc., or legal, social, or moral restraint; to liberate. **emancipa'tion,** *n.* The releasing from slavery, legal disabilities, etc.; the state of being freed. **emancipator,** *n.*

emasculate (è-măs'kū-lāt) [L. *masculus*, male], *v.t.* To castrate; to deprive of virility; to effeminate, weaken; to deprive of force or energy; to expurgate a literary work. *a.* (-làt) Castrated; effeminate, weak. **emascula'tion,** *n.*

embalm (em-bam') [F. *baume,* balm], *v.t.* To preserve (as a body) from putrefaction with spices and aromatics; to preserve from oblivion. **embalmer,** *n.*

embankment, *n.* An artificial bank for confining a river; a raised mound for carrying a road, etc.

embargo (em-bar'gō) [Sp., from *embargar,* to hinder], *n.* An official prohibition against vessels leaving port; a suspension of foreign trade; a hindrance.

embark (em-bark') [F. *embarquer*], *v.t.* To put on board ship; to invest in a business. *v.i.* To go on board ship; enter upon any undertaking. **embarka'tion,** *n.*

embarrass (em-băr'ás) [F. *embarrasser*], *v.t.* To hamper, entangle, hinder; to disconcert; to involve in pecuniary or other difficulties. **embarrassing,** *a.* Causing embarrassment. **embarrassment,** *n.* Perplexity of mind, discomposure, uneasiness; pecuniary difficulties.

embassy (em'bà-si) [O.F. *ambassée*], *n.* The function, office, or mission of an ambassador; himself and suite; his official residence.

embed (em-bed'), *v.t.* To lay as in a bed; to set firmly in surrounding matter.

embellish (em-bel'ish) [O.F. *embellir*], *v.t.* To beautify, adorn; to add incidents so as to heighten a narrative. **embellishment,** *n.*

ember (1) (em'bèr) [A.-S. *æmerge*], *n.* A live coal; (*pl.*) smouldering remnants of a fire.

ember (2) (em-bèr) [A.-S. *ymbren*], *a.* Applied to successive Wednesdays, Fridays, and Saturdays on four occasions during the year, which are set apart by the Church for prayer and fasting.

embezzle (èm-bezl') [O.F. *besillier,* to maltreat], *v.t.* To appropriate fraudulently what is committed to one's care. **embezzlement,** *n.* **embezzler,** *n.*

embitter (em-bit'èr), *v.t.* To make bitter, or more bitter; to aggravate; to exasperate. **embitterment,** *n.*

emblem (em'blèm) [L. and Gr. *emblēma*], *n.* A symbolical figure, picture, object, representation, etc.; a symbol, type, a personification. **emblemat'ic, -ical,** *a.*

embody (em-bod'ì), *v.t.* To invest with a body, to express in concrete form; to incorporate, include. **embodiment,** *n.*

embolden (em-bōl'dèn), *v.t.* To give boldness to; to encourage.

embolism (em'bò-lizm) [L. *embolismus*], *n.* (*Path.*) Blocking up of a blood vessel by a clot of blood.

embonpoint (an-bon-pwan) [F., in good condition], *n.* Plumpness.

emboss (em-bos') [O.F. *embosser*], *v.t.* To engrave or mould in relief; to cause to stand out in relief. **embossment,** *n.*

embrace (em-brās') [L. *bracchia,* the arms], *v.t.* To clasp and hold fondly in the arms; to encircle; to include, comprise; to accept eagerly. *v.i.* To join in an embrace. *n.* A clasping in the arms.

embrasure (em-brā'zhŭr) [M.F. *embraser,*

to splay or chamfer], *n.* An opening in a parapet or wall to fire guns through; the inward splaying of the sides of a window or door.

embrocate (em'brō-kāt) [Gr. *embrochē*, lotion], *v.t.* To moisten, bathe, or foment (as a diseased part). **embroca'tion**, *n.* The act of fomenting; the liquid used.

embroider (em-broi'dèr) [F. *bord*, edge], *v.t.* To ornament with needlework designs; to diversify; to embellish with additions, esp. with exaggerations. **embroidery**, *n.*

embroil (em-broil') [F. *brouiller*], *v.t.* To entangle, confuse; to involve (some one) in a quarrel or contention (with another). **embroilment**, *n.*

embryo (em'bri-ō) [Gr. *bruon*, pres. p. of *bruein*, to be full of a thing], *n.* (*pl.* -os) The unborn offspring; the rudimentary plant in the seed; the germ; the beginning or first stage of anything. *a.* Undeveloped; rudimentary.

emend (é-mend') [L. *menda*, a fault], *v.t.* To correct, remove faults; to improve. **emenda'tion**, *n.* **e'mendator**, *n.*

emerald (em'èr-áld) [O.F. *esmeralde*, Gr. *smaragdos*], *n.* A green variety of beryl; the colour of this.

emerge (é-mèrj') [L. *mergere*, to dip], *v.i.* To raise up out of a fluid, etc., in which it has been immersed; to appear in sight; to come out (as facts on enquiry); to issue from a state of depression, obscurity, etc. **emergence**, *n.* **emergent**, *a.* Emerging.

emergency (é-mèr'jèn-si), *n.* A situation demanding immediate action, a crisis.

emery (em'èr-i) [F. *émeri*, Gr. *smēris*], *n.* A coarse mineral of extreme hardness.

emetic (é-met'ik) [Gr. *emetikos, emeein*, to vomit], *a.* Inducing vomiting. *n.* A preparation for causing vomiting.

emigrate (em'i-grāt) [L. *migrāre*, to migrate], *v.i.* To leave one's country and settle in another. **emigrant**, *a.* Emigrating; pertaining to emigration. *n.* One who emigrates. **emigra'tion**, *n.*

émigré (em'i-grā) [F.], *n.* An emigrant, esp. one who fled from France in the Revolution.

eminent (em'i-nènt) [L. *ēminens*, standing out], *a.* Rising above others; distinguished; remarkable. **eminence**, **-nency**, *n.* Height; a part rising above the rest; high rank; distinction; a title given to cardinals. **eminently**, *adv.*

emir (é-mēr') [Arab.], *n.* A Mohammedan prince, governor, or commander.

emissary (em'i-sâr-i), *n.* A messenger, a secret agent.

emission (é-mish'ùn) [L.], *n.* Act or process of emitting or being emitted; the thing given off or out. **emissive**, **emissory**, *a.*

emit (é-mit') [L. *ēmittere*, to send], *v.t.* To give out, send forth; to issue, discharge.

emmet (em'èt) [A.-S. *ǣmete*], *n.* An ant.

emollient (é-mol'i-ènt) [L. *ēmolliens*, softening], *a.* Softening, relaxing.

emolument (é-mol'ū-mènt) [L. *ēmolumentum*, profit], *n.* Profit arising from employment; remuneration.

emotion (é-mō'shùn), *n.* Agitation of the mind; a state of excited feeling; excitement. **emotional**, *a.*

empanel (em-păn'èl), *v.t.* To enter on the list of jurors; to enrol as a jury.

emperor (em'pèr-ór) [L. *imperātor*], *n.* The sovereign of an empire; the highest dignity, superior to a king.

emphasis (em'fá-sis) [Gr. *phainein*, to show], *n.* Stress laid upon a word or words to indicate special significance; force of expression; accent, prominence, sharp definition. **emphasize**, *v.t.* To pronounce with emphasis; to lay stress on; to make more distinct or impressive. **emphat'ic**, *a.* Bearing special stress; accentuated, forcible; earnest.

empire (em'pīr) [L. *imperium*], *n.* Supreme and extensive dominion or power; the region over which an emperor rules.

empiric (em-pir'ik) [Gr. *empeirikos*, experienced], *a.* Founded on experience or observation, not theory. *n.* One who relies solely on experience or observation, esp. an untrained medical practitioner; a quack. **empirical**, *a.* **empiricism**, *n.*

employ (em-ploi') [O.F. *employer*], *v.t.* To use; to keep in one's service; to spend or pass (time, oneself, etc.) in occupation. *n.* Occupation, business. **employee**, *n.* One who is employed for salary or wages. **employer**, *n.* **employment**, *n.*

emporium (em-pôr'i-ùm) [Gr. *emporion*, commercial], *n.* (*pl.* -ia) A commercial centre; a mart.

empower (em-pou'èr), *v.t.* To authorize.

empress (em'pres), *n.* The consort of an emperor; a female ruler of an empire.

empty (emp'ti) [A.-S. *ǣmtig*], *a.* Containing nothing; devoid (of); vacant, unoccupied; meaningless, inane; without intelligence; unsatisfied. *v.t.* To remove the contents from, to make vacant; to pour out, discharge. *v.i.* To become empty; to discharge (as a river). **emptiness**, *n.*

empyrean (em-pi-rē'án) [Gr. *empuros*, fiery], *n.* The highest and purest region of heaven; the upper sky.

emu (ē'mū) [Port.], *n.* A large Australian cursorial bird resembling the cassowary.

emulate (em'ū-lāt) [L. *œmulātus*], *v.t.* To try to equal or excel; to rival. **emula'tion**, *n.* The act of emulating; rivalry.

emulous (em'ū-lùs), *a.* Desirous of equalling or excelling others, or of fame or honour; engaged in competition; envious, contentious.

emulsion (e-mŭlsh'ón) [L. *mulgēre*, to drink], *n.* A milky substance, the union of oil and water through the use of an alkali; (*Phot.*) a mixture of silver salts suspended in collodion, used for coating photographic plates.

en-, *pref.* In, on, into, upon; as *encamp, engulf, energy.*

-en (1), *suf.* Diminutive; as *chicken, maiden.* (2) Noting the feminine; as *vixen.* (3) Pertaining to, made of, of the nature of; as *earthen, flaxen, golden, woollen.* (4) Forming pl.; as *oxen.* (5) Forming verbs from adjectives; as *deepen, moisten.* (6) Forming p.p. of strong verbs; as *bounden, spoken, sworn.*

enable (en-ābl'), *v.t.* To make able; to authorize, empower (to).

enact (en-ăkt'), *v.t.* To decree; to pass into a law; to act, play. **enactive**, *a.* **enactment**, *n.* enactory, *a.*

enamel (en-ăm'ĕl) [M.E. *enamayl*, O.F. *esmail*, med. L. *smaltum*, from Teut. (cp. O.H.G. *smalzjan*, Dut. *smelten*, to SMELT)], *n.* A glass-like material used for coating metal, porcelain, etc., by fusion; any smooth, hard, glossy coating as lacquer, or varnish; the surface covering of teeth. *v.t.* To coat with paint, encrust, or inlay with enamel; to form a smooth glossy surface upon; to decorate with various colours. *v.i.* To practise the art of enamelling. **enameller, enamelist,** *n.*

enamour (ĕ-năm'ŏr) [O.F. *enamorer*], *v.t.* To captivate, charm; to inflame with love.

encamp (en-kămp'), *v.i.* To form an encampment; to settle down temporarily in tents. *v.t.* To lodge (troops) in tents. **encampment,** *n.* A camp.

encase (en-kās'), *v.t.* To put into or protect with a case.

enceinte (ong-sănt') [F.], *a.* Pregnant.

enchain (en-chān'), *v.t.* To bind with chains; to hold fast, to rivet (attention, etc.).

enchant (en-chant') [F. *enchanter*], *v.t.* To influence by magic, to bewitch, fascinate, charm. **enchanter,** *n.* A magician; one who delights or fascinates. **enchantingly,** *adv.* **enchantment,** *n.* **enchantress,** *n.*

encircle (en-sĕrkl'), *v.t.* To enclose or surround (with).

enclasp (en-klasp'), *v.t.* To enfold in or fasten with a clasp; to embrace.

enclave (en-klāv') [L. *clāvis*, key], *n.* A territory completely surrounded by that of another power.

enclitic (en-klĭt'ĭk) [Gr. *enklitikos*, inclining], *a.* (*Gr. Gram.*) Applied to a word which cannot, as it were, stand by itself, but is pronounced as part of the preceding word, on which it throws its accent. *n.* An enclitic word or particle.

enclose (en-klōz'), *v.t.* To shut in; to surround on all sides; to put one thing inside another for transmission; to contain. **enclosure** (-klō'zhŭr), *n.*

encomium (en-kō'mi-ŭm) [Gr. *enkōmios*, laudatory], *n.* (*pl.* -ums) A formal eulogy; high commendation.

encompass (en-kŭm'pás), *v.t.* To surround, invest; to include, contain.

encore (on-kŏr') [F., again], *adv.* Again, once more; a call for a repetition at a concert, theatre, etc. *n.* A demand for this; the repetition itself. *v.* To call for a repetition of.

encounter (en-koun'tĕr) [O.F. *encontrer*], *v.t.* To meet face to face; to confront hostilely or resolutely. *n.* A meeting face to face; a hostile or undesigned meeting.

encourage (en-kŭr'áj) [O.F. *encoragier*], *v.t.* To give courage or confidence to; to urge, to incite (to do); to stimulate, to foster (trade, opinion, etc.). **encouragement,** *n.* **encourager,** *n.*

encroach (en-krōch') [O.F. *encrochier*], *v.i.* To intrude; to infringe (upon); to get possession of anything gradually or by stealth. **encroachment,** *n.*

encumber (en-kŭm'ber) [O.F. *encombrer*, see CUMBER], *v.t.* To hamper, impede, or embarrass by a burden or difficulty; to weigh down with debt. **encumbrance,** *n.*

-ency, *suf.* Forming nouns of state or quality.

encyclopædia (en-sī-klò-pē'di-à) [late L. from Gr., *enkuklios paideia*, general instruction], *n.* A book containing information on all branches of knowledge, or on a particular branch, usually arranged alphabetically. **encyclopædic,** *a.*

end (end) [A.-S. *ende*], *n.* The extreme point of anything that has length; the termination, last portion; the conclusion of a state or action; a ceasing to exist; death; a result, natural consequence; a purpose, object; a final cause. *v.i.* To come to an end; to result (in). *v.t.* To bring or put to an end; to destroy. **odds and ends:** Odd remnants. **ending,** *n.* A conclusion, termination.

endanger (en-dān'jĕr), *v.t.* To expose to danger, to put in hazard.

endear (en-dēr'), *v.t.* To make dear (to); to cause to be loved. **endearing,** *a.* **endearment,** *n.*

endeavour (en-dev'ŏr) [F. *devoir*, to owe], *v.i.* To strive (after) a certain end; to try. *n.* An effort, attempt; exertion.

endemic (en-dem'ĭk) [Gr. *dēmos*, people], *a.* Peculiar to a particular locality or people, esp. of a disease. *n.* An endemic disease. **endemically,** *adv.*

endive (en'dĭv) [F.], *n.* A kind of chicory used in salads.

endless (end'les), *a.* Having no end; infinite, unlimited, perpetual.

endorse (en-dôrs') [L. *dorsum*, the back], *v.t.* To write (one's name, a note of contents, etc.) on the back of (a document); to ratify, confirm, approve. **endorsement,** *n.*

endow (en-dou') [F. *douer*, to dower], *v.t.* To invest with goods, privileges, qualities, etc.; to bestow a permanent income upon; to give a dowry to. **endowment,** *n.*

endue (en-dū') [L. *dūcere*, to lead], *v.t.* To put on, clothe, invest (with).

endure (en-dūr') [L. *dūrus*, hard], *v.t.* To bear, sustain; to undergo, suffer; to submit to. *v.i.* To last, esp. in the same state; to bear suffering with patience and fortitude. **enduring,** *a.* Bearing; durable, permanent. **endurabil'ity,** *n.* **endur'able,** *a.* **endurance,** *n.* Act or state of enduring or suffering; capacity of suffering with patience; continuance, duration.

-ene, *suf.* (*Chem.*) Denoting a hydrocarbon, such as *benzene, naphthalene.*

enemy (en'ĕ-mi) [L. *inimīcus*], *n.* One hostile to another; an adversary, one opposed to any subject or cause; a hostile army, ship, etc.

energy (enĕr-ji) [Gr. *ergon*, work], *n.* Internal or inherent power; force, vigour; capability of action; active operation; emphasis. **energet'ic,** *a.*

enervate (en'ĕr-vāt) [L. *ēnervātus*], *v.t.* To

deprive of force or strength; to weaken; to render effeminate. **enerva'tion**, *n.*

enfeeble (en-fē'bl) [O.F. *enfeblir*], *v.t.* To make feeble or weak. **enfeeblement**, *n.*

enfilade (en-fi-lād') [F., from *enfiler*, to thread], *v.t.* To rake with shot from end to end.

enfold (en-fōld'), *v.t.* To wrap up, enclose; to clasp, embrace.

enforce (en-fōrs') [L. *fortis*, strong], *v.t.* To compel obedience to; to give force to; to press or urge forcibly. **enforceable**, *a.* **enforced**, *a.* Forced, not voluntary.

enfranchise (en-frăn'chiz) [O.F. *enfranchir*], *v.t.* To set free; to give full municipal or parliamentary rights and privileges; to give the right to vote. **enfranchisement**, *n.*

engage (en-gāj') [F. *gage*, a pledge], *v.t.* To bind by a promise or contract; to order, bespeak; to occupy the time or attention of; to come into conflict with. *v.i.* To pledge oneself (to do something); to undertake; to embark (in); to enter into conflict (with); to interlock (with). **engaged**, *a.* Pledged, promised in marriage. **engagement**, *n.* The act of engaging; an obligation, contract; a mutual promise of marriage; occupation of time or attention; an appointment; a contract to employ; the state of being hired; an action or battle. **engaging**, *a.*

engender (en-jen'dér) [L. *genus*, a race, brood], *v.t.* To beget; to be the cause of, to bring about.

engine (en'jin) [O.F. *engin*], *n.* A machine consisting of a complication of parts for applying mechanical power, esp. one that converts mechanical energy into motion; an instrument, tool.

engineer (en-ji-nēr'), *n.* One who designs or carries out the construction of works of public or military utility; one who constructs or attends to engines. *v.t.* To carry out as an engineer the formation or execution of (as railways, canals, etc.); to manage by tact or ingenuity.

English (ing'glish) [A.-S. *Englisc*, from *Engle*, the Angles], *a.* Pertaining to England, its inhabitants, or language; characteristic of or becoming an Englishman. *n.* The language or the people of England. *v.t.* To translate into the English language.

engraft (en-graft'), *v.t.* To graft upon, to insert (a scion of one tree) upon or into another; to incorporate; to instil.

engrain (en-grān'), *v.t.* To implant (qualities, esp. vices) ineradicably.

engrave (en-grāv'), *v.t.* To cut figures, letters, etc., on, with a chisel or graver; to represent by carving; to imprint; to impress deeply. *v.i.* To practise the art of engraving. **engraver**, *n.* **engraving**, *n.* The act, process, or art of cutting figures, letters, etc., on wood, stone, or metal; that which is engraved; an impression from an engraved plate, a print.

engross (en-grōs') [late L. *grossa*, large writing], *v.t.* To write in large letters, or in legal form.

enhance (en-hans') [A.-F. *enhauncer*], *v.t.* To raise in importance, degree, etc.; to augment, heighten (in price); to ex-

aggerate. *v.i.* To be raised; to increase. **enhancement**, *n.* **enhancive**, *a.*

enigma (ē-nig'mả) [Gr. *ainigma*], *n.* A dark saying, a riddle; any inexplicable proceeding. **enigmat'ic, -al**, *a.*

enjoin (en-join'), *v.t.* To prescribe, impose (an act or conduct); to instruct (that).

enjoy (en-joi') [EN-, F. *joie*, joy], *v.t.* To take pleasure or delight in; to have the use or benefit of. **enjoyable**, *a.* **enjoyment**, *n.*

enkindle (en-kindl'), *v.t.* To kindle, to set on fire; to rouse into passion, etc.

enlarge (en-larj'), *v.t.* To make greater, expand, widen; to set free. *v.i.* To become bigger; to expatiate (upon). **enlargement**, *n.*

enlighten (en-lī'tèn), *v.t.* To give mental or spiritual light to, to instruct. **enlightenment**, *n.*

enlist (en-list'), *v.t.* To enrol; to engage for military service; to gain the interest or support of. *v.i.* To engage oneself for military service. **enlistment**, *n.*

enliven (en-lī'vèn), *v.t.* To give spirit or animation to; to stimulate; to brighten.

enmity (en'mi-ti) [A.-F. *enemité*, as ENEMY], *n.* Hostility.

ennoble (ė-nōbl') [O.F. *ennoblir*], *v.t.* To make noble; to dignify, make famous or illustrious. **ennoblement**, *n.*

ennui (on'nwē) [F.], *n.* Listlessness; want of interest; boredom.

enormous (ė-nôr'mùs) [E-(EX-), L. *norma*, pattern], *a.* Very great in size, number, or quantity; huge, immense; outrageously wicked, atrocious. **enormity**, *n.* The state or quality of being enormous, inordinate, outrageous; a monstrous crime, an atrocity. **enormously**, *adv.*

enough (ė-nŭf') [A.-S. *genōh*], *a.* Sufficient for or adequate to need or demand. *n.* A sufficiency. *int.* Denoting sufficiency or satisfaction. *adv.* Sufficiently, tolerably, passably.

enrage (en-rāj'), *v.t.* To put in a rage.

enrapture (en-răp'tūr), *v.t.* To fill with rapture; to transport with delight.

enrich (en-rich'), *v.t.* To make rich or richer. **enrichment**, *n.*

enrol (en-rōl') [O.F. *enroller*], *v.t.* To enter in a roll; to record, register; to include as a member. **enrolment**, *n.*

ensconce (en-skons'), *v.t.* To hide; to settle (oneself) comfortably or securely.

ensemble (ong-sombl) [F.], *n.* All the parts of anything taken together; (*Mus.*) concerted singing and playing.

enshrine (en-shrīn'), *v.t.* To place in or as in a shrine; to cherish.

ensign (en'sīn) [O.F. *enseigne*, L. *insignis*, remarkable], *n.* A banner, the flag of a regiment or a ship; a badge of rank or office; formerly, the lowest rank of commissioned officers in an infantry regiment. **ensigncy, ensignship**, *n.*

ensilage (en'si-lảj) [F.], *n.* A method of preserving forage crops by storing them whilst moist in pits; fodder so preserved.

enslave (en-slāv'), *v.t.* To make a slave of, to bring under some influence, habit, vice, etc. **enslavement**, *n.* Servitude.

ensnare (en-snār'), *v.t.* To entrap.

ensue (en-sū') [F. *ensuivre*], *v.i.* To follow

in course of time, to succeed; to result (from).

ensure (en-shoor') [O.F. *seur*], *v.t.* To make certain (that).

entablature (en-tăb'lá-tūr) [late L. *intabulāre*, to form a flooring], *n.* That part of a structure that rests on the capitals of columns (architrave, frieze, and cornice).

entail (en-tāl') [F. *taille*], *v.t.* To bestow or settle a possession inalienably on a certain person and his heirs, or a particular class of heirs; to impose (duties, expenses, etc., upon one); to involve, necessitate, *n.* An estate in fee limited in descent to a particular heir or heirs; the limitation of inheritance in this way.

entangle (en-tăng'gĕl), *v.t.* To twist so that unravelling is difficult; to ensnare, involve in difficulties, contradictions, etc. **entanglement**, *n.*

entente (on-tont) [F.], *n.* (*Polit.*) A friendly understanding.

enter (en'tĕr) [F. *entrer*], *v.t.* To go or come into; to set down in a writing, list, book, etc. *v.i.* To go or come in; to become a competitor.

enteric (en-ter'ik) [Gr. *enteron*, intestine], *a.* Pertaining to the intestines. **enteric fever**, *n.* Typhoid fever.

enterprise (en'tĕr-priz) [O.F. *enterprise*, undertaken], *n.* An undertaking, esp. a bold or difficult one; spirit of adventure, boldness. *v.t.* To undertake, venture on. **enterprising**, *a.* Adventurous; full of enterprise. **enterprisingly**, *adv.*

entertain (en-tĕr-tān') [F. *entretenir*], *v.t.* To receive and treat as a guest; to divert, amuse; to hold in mind, cherish. *v.i.* To exercise hospitality; to receive company. **entertainer**, *n.* One who entertains, esp. one paid to do so. **entertaining**, *a.* Amusing. **entertainment**, *n.*

enthral (en-thrawl'), *v.t.* To enslave, captivate.

enthrone (en-thrōn'), *v.t.* To place on a throne; to invest with sovereign power; to induct (as a bishop) into the powers or privileges of a see. **enthronement**, *n.*

enthusiasm (en-thū'zi-ăzm) [Gr. *enthousiasmos*, inspired, from *entheos*, possessed by a god], *n.* Intense and passionate zeal; ardent admiration. **enthusiast**, *n.* One filled with enthusiasm; one completely possessed by any subject; a visionary. **enthusiastic**, *a.*

entice (en-tis') [O.F. *enticer*], *v.t.* To allure, especially into evil; to tempt. **enticement**, *n.* **enticer**, *n.* **enticing**, *a.* Alluring, seductive.

entire (en-tir') [O.F. *entier*], *a.* Whole, complete; not castrated; unmixed; unqualified; unfeigned. *n.* A kind of porter, or stout. **entirely**, *adv.* Wholly, fully, exclusively. **entirety** (en-tir'ti), *n.* Completeness.

entitle (en-titl'), *v.t.* To give a name or title to, to designate; to give a right, title, or claim to anything.

entity (en'ti-ti) [L. *entitās*], *n.* Essence, existence, as distinguished from qualities or relations, a being; that which constitutes its being. **entitative**, *a.*

entomb (en-toom'), *v.t.* To place in a tomb, to bury. **entombment**, *n.*

entomo- [Gr. *entomon*, an insect], *comb. form.* Pertaining to insects. **entomology** (en-tó-mol'ó-ji), *n.* The science which treats of insects. **entomol'ogist**, *n.* A student of this.

entourage (ong-too'razh) [F.], *n.* Surroundings, environment.

entrails (en'trālz) [O.F. *entraile*], *n.pl.* The internal parts of animals; the intestines; bowels.

entrain (en-trān'), *v.t.* To put into a railway train. *v.i.* To get into a train.

entrance (1) (en'tráns), *n.* The act or the power, right, or liberty of entering; the passage or doorway by which a place is entered.

entrance (2) (en-trans'), *v.t.* To throw into a state of ecstasy; to transport, enrapture. **entrancement**, *n.*

entrap (en-trăp'), *v.t.* To catch in a trap.

entreat (en-trēt') [F. *traiter*, to treat], *v.t.* To beseech; to treat, to act towards. *v.i.* To make entreaties. **entreatingly**, *adv.* **entreaty**, *n.* An urgent solicitation; importunity.

entrée (on'trā, an-trā) [F., entry], *n.* Freedom or right of entrance; a made dish.

entrench (en-trench'), *v.t.* To surround or defend with trenches; to encroach (upon). **entrenchment**, *n.*

entrust (en-trŭst'), *v.t.* To commit or confide to a person's care; to charge with (a duty, care, etc.).

entry (en'tri) [F. *entrée*], *n.* The act of entering, esp. ceremonially; the passage, etc., by which anything is entered; the act of inscribing in a book, etc.; an item so entered.

entwine (en-twin'), *v.t.* To twine or twist together; to embrace, enfold.

enumerate (e-nū'mér-āt) [L. *numerātus*, numbered], *v.t.* To reckon up one by one; to specify the items of. **enumera'tion**, *n.* **enu'merative**, *a.* **enu'merator**, *n.*

enunciate (e-nŭn'si-āt) [L. *nuntiātus*, announced], *v.t.* To pronounce distinctly; to express definitely, state with formal precision. **enuncia'tion**, *n.*

envelop (en-vel'óp) [O.F. *enveloper*], *v.t.* To enwrap, surround so as to hide; to surround with troops or offensive works. **envelopment**, *n.*

envelope (en'vė-lōp) [F. *enveloppe*, as prec.], *n.* A wrapper, covering, esp. a paper case to contain a letter.

envenom (en-ven'óm) [O.F. *venim*, venom], *v.t.* To poison or make poisonous; to make bitter or spiteful.

environ (en-vi'rón) [F. *virer*, to veer, turn], *v.t.* To surround, to extend round, encompass, to beset. **environment**, *n.* The act of environing; that which encompasses surrounding objects, scenery, circumstances, etc.; the sum of external influences affecting an organism. **environs**, *n.pl.* The parts or districts round any place.

envisage (en-viz'áj), *v.t.* To look into the face of or directly at.

envoy (en'voi) [O.F. *envoié*, a message], *n.* A diplomatic agent, next below an ambassador; a messenger, representative; a concluding stanza to a poem.

envy (en'vi) [O.F. *envie*, L. *invidia* (IN-,

E

vidēre, to see)], *n.* Ill-will at the superiority, success, or good fortune of others; the object of this feeling. *v.t.* To regard with envy; to feel jealous of; to covet. *v.i.* To have envious feelings. **enviable**, *a.* Capable of exciting envy; of a nature to be envied. **envious**, *a.* Infected with or instigated by envy.

ep-, epi- [Gr. *upon*, besides], *pref.*, as *epigram, episode.*

epact (ĕ′păkt) [Gr. *agein*, to bring], *n.* The moon's age at the beginning of the year; the excess of the solar above the lunar year.

epaulet (ep′ŏ-let) [F. *épaulette* (*épaule*, shoulder)], *n.* An ornament worn on the shoulder in certain uniforms.

epergne (ĕ-părn′, -pĕrn′) [?], *n.* An ornamental stand for the centre of a table, etc.

ephemera (ĕ-fem′ĕr-à) [Gr. *ephēmeros*], *n.* (*pl. -ræ*). A short-lived insect, esp. the May-fly; a fever of only one day's continuance. **ephemeral**, *a.* Beginning and ending in a day; transient.

epic (ep′ĭk) [Gr. *epikos, epos*, a word], *a.* Narrating some heroic event in a lofty style. *n.* A poem narrating some notable action or series of actions, accomplished by a hero or heroes. **epical**, *a.*

epicene (ep′ĭ-sēn) [L. *epicœnus*], *a.* Pertaining to both sexes.

epicure (ep′ĭ-kūr), *n.* One devoted to sensual pleasures, esp. those of the table. **epicurism**, *n.* **Epicure′an**, *n.* A follower of Epicurus, who taught that pleasure is the supreme good and the basis of morality, a person devoted to pleasure; a gourmand. *a.* Pertaining to the philosophy of Epicurus. **epicureanism**, *n.*

epicycle (ep′ĭ-sīkl) [Gr. *kuklos*, circle], *n.* A small circle the centre of which is carried round upon another circle.

epidemic (ep-i-dem′ĭk) [Gr. *dēmos*, people], *a.* Affecting at once a large number in a community. *n.* A disease attacking many persons at the same time, and spreading with great rapidity. **epidemical**, *a.*

epidermis (ep-i-dĕr′mis) [Gr. *derma*, skin], *n.* The external skin in animals.

epigram (ep′ĭ-grăm) [L. and Gr.], *n.* A short poem or composition of a pointed or antithetical character. **epigrammat′ic**, *a.*

epigraph (ep′ĭ-grăf) [Gr. *graphein*; to write], *n.* A motto; an inscription placed on buildings, statues, tombs, etc.

epilepsy (ep′ĭ-lep-si) [Gr. *lambanein*, to take], *n.* A nervous disease involving convulsions and loss of consciousness; falling sickness. **epilep′tic**. *a. n.*

epilogue (ep′ĭ-log) [Gr. *logos*, speech], *n.* A short speech or poem following a play; the concluding part of a book, etc.

Epiphany (ĕ-pif′à-ni) [Gr. *phainein*, to show], *n.* The festival held on January 6 to commemorate the manifestation of Christ to the Magi at Bethlehem.

episcopacy (ĕ-pis′kŏ-pà-si) [L. *episcopus*, bishop], *n.* Government of a Church by bishops; bishops collectively. **episcopal**, *a.* Appertaining to a bishop; constituted on this form of government. **episcopa′lian**, *n.* A member of an episcopal Church. *a.* Episcopal. **episcopalianism**, *n.* **epis′copate**, *n.* The office or see of a bishop,

the term during which he holds office; bishops collectively.

episode (ep′ĭ-sōd) [Gr. *epeisodion*, adventitious], *n.* An incident or series of events in a story, separable though arising out of it. **episodic, -al** (-sod′ĭk, -ăl), *a.*

epistle (ĕ-pisl′) [Gr. *stellein*, to send], *n.* A written communication, a letter; a literary work in the form of a letter. **epis′tolary**, *a.* Pertaining to or suitable for letters; carried on by means of letters.

epitaph (ep′ĭ-tăf) [Gr. *taphos*, tomb], *n.* An inscription on or for a tomb or monument.

epithet (ep′ĭ-thet) [Gr. *epitithenai*, to place upon], *n.* A word or phrase denoting any quality or attribute.

epitome (ĕ-pit′ŏ-mi) [Gr. *temnein*, to cut], *n.* A brief summary; a condensation, abridgment. **epitomize**, *v.t.* To make an abstract or abridgment of.

epoch (ē′pok) [Gr. *epochē*, a check, pause], *n.* A fixed point from which succeeding years are numbered; a period, an era.

eponym (ep′ŏ-nim) [Gr. *onoma*, name], *n.* A name given to a people, place, etc., after some person; the name of a mythical person made to account for the name of a country or people. **epon′ymous**, *a.*

equable (ek′-, ĕk-wàbl) [L. *œquābilis*], *a.* Smooth, level, even; not varying, not irregular. **equabil′ity**, *n.* **equably**, *adv.*

equal (ē′kwàl) [L. *œquālis*], *a.* The same in magnitude, number, quality, degree, etc.; even, uniform; impartial, fair; having adequate power or means (to). *n.* One not inferior or superior to another; a match. *v.t.* To be equal (to). **equality** (ē-kwol′ĭ-ti), *n.* The state of being equal. **e′qualize**, *v.t.* To make equal (to, with). **equaliza′tion**, *n.*

equanimity (ē-kwä-nim′ĭ-ti) [L. *œquus*, equal, *animus*, mind], *n.* Evenness of temper, composure of mind; resignation.

equation (ĕ-kwā′shŭn) [L.], *n.* The act of making equal; two algebraic expressions equal to one another and connected by the sign =.

equator (ĕ-kwā′tòr), *n.* A great circle on the earth's surface, equidistant from the poles; a great circle of the heavens, constituted by the production of the plane of the earth's equator. **equator′ial**, *a.* Pertaining to the equator.

equerry (ek′wĕr-i) [F. *écurie*, a stable], *n.* An officer having the care of horses and stables; an officer of a royal household.

equestrian (ĕ-kwes′tri-àn) [L. *equestris*, from *equus*, horse], *a.* Pertaining to horses or horsemanship; on horseback. *n.* A horseman.

equi- [L. *equus*, equal], *comb. form.* **equi-ang′ular**, *a.* Having or consisting of equal angles. **equidis′tant**, *a.* Equally distant from some point.

equilateral (ē-kwi-lăt′ĕr-àl), *a.* Having all the sides equal. **equilaterally**, *adv.*

equilibrium (ē-kwi-lib′ri-ŭm) [L. *librāre*, to balance], *n.* A state of equal balance, equipoise.

equine (ek′wīn) [L. *equus*, a horse], *a.* Pertaining to or resembling a horse.

equinox (ē′kwi-noks) [EQUI-, L. *nox*, night], *n.* The moment at which the sun crosses the equator and renders day and night equal (vernal equinox, 21st Mar., autumnal, 23rd Sept.). **equinoctial** (-nok'shǎl), *a*.

equip (ê-kwip') [F. *équiper*], *v.t.* To furnish, esp. to supply with arms; to qualify. **equipage** (ek'wi-pǎj), *n.* That with which one is equipped; arms and military outfit; a carriage with horses and attendants. **equip'ment**, *n.*

equipoise (e'kwi-poiz), *n.* A state of equality of weight or force, equilibrium; that which counterbalances.

equipollent (ê-kwi-pol'ênt) [L. *pollĕre*, to be strong], *a.* Having equal force, significance, etc.

equitable (ek'wi-tǎbl), *a.* Acting or done with equity; fair, just.

equity (ek'wi-ti) [L. *æquitǎs*, from *æquus*, fair], *n.* Justice, fairness; the application of principles of justice to correct the deficiencies of law.

equivalent (ê-kwiv'ǎ-lênt) [L. *valēre*, to be worth], *a.* Of equal value, force, or weight; alike in significance or effect; interchangeable. *n.* Anything which is equal to something else in amount, force, etc. **equivalence, -lency**, *n.*

equivocal (ê-kwiv'ô-kǎl) [L. *vocāre*, to call], *a.* Ambiguous, capable of a twofold interpretation.

equivocate (ê-kwiv'ô-kǎt), *v.i.* To speak ambiguously so as to deceive; to prevaricate. **equivoca'tion**, *n.*

-er, *suf.* (1) Denoting an agent or doer, as *hatter, player, poulterer*; denoting residence, etc., as *Berliner, Londoner*; (2) denoting a person or thing connected with, as *butler, officer, sampler*; (3) denoting comparison, as *richer, taller*; (4) denoting an action, as *disclaimer, user*; (5) frequentative, as *chatter, slumber*.

era (ēr'ǎ) [late L. *æra*, a number], *n.* A system of chronology running from a fixed point of time.

eradicate (ê-rǎd'i-kāt) [E-(EX-), L. *rādix*, root], *v.t.* To root up, extirpate. **eradicable**, *a.* **eradica'tion**, *n.*

erase (e-rāz') [L. *rādere*, to scrape], *v.t.* To rub out; to obliterate, expunge.

Erastian (ê-rǎs'ti-ǎn), *n.* One holding that the State has supreme authority over the Church, the opinion attributed to Erastus, a German physician (1524–83). **Erastianism**, *n.*

ere (âr) [A.-S. *ær*], *prep.* and *conj.* Before, sooner than.

erect (ê-rekt') [L. *ērectus*, set up], *a.* Upright; not bending; vertical; undismayed, firm, alert. *v.t.* To raise; to construct, build; to exalt; to set up. **erectile** (ê-rek'til), *a.* Susceptible of erection. **erection**, *n.*

erg, ergon [Gr., work], *n.* The unit of work.

ergo (ēr'gō) [L.], *adv.* Therefore.

ergot (ēr'gŏt) [O.F. *argot*, a cock's spur, spurred rye], *n.* A disease in rye, etc., caused by a fungus; a preparation from this used in medicine.

ermine (ēr'min) [O.F.], *n.* An animal of the weasel tribe; its fur, which becomes snowy white in winter except the tip of the tail, which is black. **ermined**, *a.* Clothed with or wearing ermine, as judges.

erode (ê-rōd') [L. *rōdere*, to gnaw], *v.t.* To eat into; to corrode, wear away. **erosion** (ê-rō'zhŭn), *n.*

erotic (ê-rot'ik) [Gr. *erōtikos*, from *erōs*, love], *a.* Pertaining to or caused by love; amatory.

err (ēr) [L. *errāre*, to stray, wander], *v.i.* To blunder, to miss the truth, etc.; to be incorrect; to deviate from duty.

errand (er'ǎnd) [A.-S. *ærende*], *n.* A short journey to carry a message, etc.; the object of such a journey.

errant (er'ǎnt) [O.F., wandering, as ERR], *a.* Wandering, roving.

erratic (ê-rǎt'ik) [L. *errāticus*], *a.* Irregular in movement, eccentric.

erratum (ê-rā'tǔm) [L.], *n.* (*pl.* -ta). An error or mistake in printing or writing; (*pl.*) a list of corrections.

erroneous (ê-rō'nê-ŭs) [L. *errōneus*, as ERR], *a.* Mistaken, incorrect.

error (er'ŏr) [L. *error*, a wandering, as ERR], *n.* A mistake; deviation from truth or accuracy; wrong opinion; a sin of a venial kind.

ersatz (ēr'sǎts) [G.], *n.* A poor substitute for something genuine.

Erse (ērs) [Sc. var. of *Irish*], *n.* The Gaelic dialect of the Scottish Highlands. *a.* Gaelic.

erst (ērst) [A.-S. *ærest*, superl. of *ær*, soon], *adv.* Formerly, of yore.

eructation (ê-rŭk-tā'shŭn) [L. *ructāre*, to belch], *n.* The act of belching.

erudite (er'ū-dīt) [L. *ērudītus*], *a.* Learned; well-read, well informed. **erudition** (-dish'ŭn), *n.* Learning, extensive knowledge gained by study.

erupt (ê-rŭpt') [L. *ēruptus*, broken forth], *v.t.* To emit violently, as a volcano, etc. *v.i.* To burst out; to break through. **eruption**, *n.* The act of bursting forth; an outburst of lava, etc., from a volcano. **-ery, -ry**, *suf.* Forming abstract or collective nouns, meaning a business, cultivation, etc., conduct, things connected with or of the nature of, etc.; *e.g. foolery, grocery, rockery, witchery.*

erysipelas (er-i-sip'ê-lǎs) [Gr. *eruthros*, red, *pella*, skin], *n.* A deep red inflammation of the skin, with diffused swelling.

escalade (es-kǎ-lād') [Sp. *escalada*], *n.* An attack in which scaling-ladders are used to mount ramparts, etc. *v.t.* To storm by means of scaling-ladders.

escalator (es'kǎ-lā-tör), *n.* A moving stairway.

escapade (es-kǎ-pād'), *n.* A wild freak or prank; an escape from restraint.

escape (es-kāp') [O.F. *eschaper*, prob. from L. EX-, *cappa*, cloak], *v.t.* To get safely away from; to evade; to avoid (a thing or act); to slip away from, elude attention. *v.i.* To get safely away; to find an issue, to leak; to evade capture, danger, etc. *n.* Act or means of escaping; state of having escaped; flight, deliverance; a leakage. **escape'ment**, *n.* A checking and regulating device in a clock or watch. **escapism**, *n.* (Psych.). The attempt at escape from reality. **escapist**, *n.*

escarpment, *n.* The precipitous face of a ridge, fortifications, etc.

-esce, *suf.* Forming inceptive verbs, as

acquiesce, coalesce, effervesce. **-escent,
suf.** Forming adjectives from these, as
acquiescent, coalescent. **-escence** [-ENCE],
suf. Forming abstract nouns from the
same, as acquiescence, coalescence.

eschatology (es-kà-tol'ò-ji) [Gr. eschatos,
last], n. The doctrine of the last things,
death, the last judgment, the future
state.

escheat (es-chēt') [O.F. eschete], n. The
reverting of property to the lord of the
fee, the Crown, or the State, on the death
of the owner intestate without heirs.

eschew (es-choo') [O.F. eschiver, cogn. with
A.-S. sceoh, shy], v.t. To avoid, shun.

escort (es'kôrt) [F. escorte], n. An armed
guard attending baggage, munitions,
etc., en route; a guard of honour. v.t.
(es-kôrt'). To act as escort to; to attend
upon.

escritoire (es-kri-twar') [F. écritoire, L.
scriptōrium (scribere, to write)], n. A
writing-desk, with drawers, etc., a
bureau.

esculent (es'kū-lènt) [L. esca, food], a.
Good for food; edible. n. An edible.

escutcheon (es-kŭch'ŏn) [A.-F. escuchon, L.
scūtum, a shield], n. A shield.

esoteric (es-ò-ter'ik) [Gr. esōteros, inner],
a. Meant for or intelligible only to the
initiated; secret, confidential; initiated.

espalier (es-păl'i-ĕr) [F.], n. Lattice-
work on which to train fruit trees, etc.;
a tree so trained.

esparto (es-par'tō) [Sp.], n. A coarse grass
or rush.

Esperanto (es-pe-răn'tō) [Esp., hopeful],
n. An artificial language based on the
chief European languages.

especial (es-pesh'ál) [L. speciālis, special],
a. Distinguished in a certain class or
kind; exceptional; pertaining to a
particular case, not general or indefinite.
especially, adv.

espionage (es-pi-ò-nazh') [F. from espion,
spy], n. The practice of spying; the
employment of spies.

esplanade (es-plà-nād') [M.F., from es-
planer, to level], n. A level space, esp.
a walk or drive by the seaside, etc.

espouse (es-pouz') [O.F. espouser], v.t. To
marry; to give in marriage (to); to
support (a cause, etc.). espousal, n.
(usu. in pl.). Betrothal, marriage.

espy (es-pī') [O.F. espier, to spy], v.t. To
catch sight of; to detect.

-esque, suf. Like, in the manner or style
of; as arabesque, Dantesque, picturesque.

esquire (es-kwīr') [O.F. escuyer, L. scū-
tārius, from scūtum, shield], n. The
armour-bearer or attendant on a knight,
a squire; a title next below a knight's.

-ess, suf. Noting the feminine; as empress.

essay (es'ā) [O.F. essai], n. An attempt;
an informal literary composition. v.t.
(é-sā'). To try, to attempt; to test.
v.i. To make an endeavour. **essayist**
(es'ā-ist), n. A writer of essays.

essence (es'ĕns) [L. essentia, from essens,
being], n. That which constitutes the
nature of a thing, or makes it what it is;
being, existence; a solution or extract
obtained by distillation.

essential (é-sen'shál), a. Pertaining to or

containing the essence of a thing; necessary to the existence of, indispensable
(to); real, actual, not accidental. n.
That which is fundamental, characteristic or indispensable.

-est, suf. Forming the superlative degree,
as richest, tallest, wiseliest.

establish (es-tăb'lish) [L. stabilīre (stabilis,
firm)], v.t. To set upon a firm foundation; to found, institute; to verify, put
beyond dispute; to ordain officially and
settle on a permanent basis (as a Church).
establishment, n. Act of establishing;
state of being established; a permanent
organization such as the army, navy,
civil service, a staff, etc.

estate (es-tāt') [O.F. estat], n. Property,
esp. a landed property; a person's assets
and liabilities taken collectively; state,
condition, standing, rank; a class or
order invested with political rights, one
of the Three Estates, viz., the Lords
Spiritual, the Lords Temporal, and the
Commons.

esteem (es-tēm'), v.t. To hold in high
estimation, regard with respect; to prize;
to reckon. n. Opinion or judgment as
to merit or demerit; respect, regard.
es'timable, a.

estimate (es'ti-māt) [L. æstimātus, valued],
v.t. To appraise; to form an opinion
about. n. An approximate calculation
of the value, number, extent, etc., of
anything; a judgment respecting character, circumstances, etc.; (pl.) statement
of probable expenditure submitted to
Parliament or other authoritative body.
estima'tion, n. The act of estimating;
opinion or judgment; esteem.

estoppel (es-top'el) [A.-F. estopper], n. An
act or statement that cannot legally be
denied.

estrange (es-trānj'), v.t. To alienate, to
make (oneself) a stranger to. estrange-
ment, n.

estreat (es-trēt') [L. extrahere, to extract],
v.t. (Law) To extract a copy from
court records; to levy a fine.

estuary (es'tū-à-ri) [L. æstuāre, to surge],
n. The mouth of a river, etc., in which
the tide meets the current.

esurient (é-sū'ri-ènt) [L. ēsuriens, desiring
to eat], a. Hungry; needy.

-et, suf. Diminutive, as circlet, coronet.

etch (ech) [O. Teut. atjan, to make eat], v.t.
To produce designs on metallic plates by
biting with an acid through the lines
previously drawn on a coated surface.
v.i. To practise this art. etcher, n.
etching, n. Art of etching; an impression
taken from an etched plate.

eternal (ē-tĕr'nàl) [L. æternus], a. Without
beginning or end; everlasting, perpetual.
eternity, n. Eternal duration; endless
past or future time.

ethane (eth-ān'), n. (Chem.) A gaseous
compound of the paraffin series.

ether (ē'thĕr) [L. æther], n. A hypothetical
fluid of extreme subtlety and elasticity
assumed to permeate space and all substances, and to form the medium of transmission of light and heat; the higher regions of the sky; volatile fluid, produced
by the distillation of alcohol with an acid,

used as an anæsthetic. ether'eal, a. Airy, tenuous, impalpable, spiritual.

ethic, ethical (eth'ik, -ăl) [Gr. *ethos*, character, disposition], a. Treating of or relating to morals; dealing with moral questions or theory. ethic, n. (*usu. in pl.*) The science of or a treatise on morals; a system of principles and rules of conduct. ethically, adv.

ethnic (eth'nik) [Gr. *ethnos*, nation], a. Pertaining to or characteristic of a race or people; racial; not Jewish or Christian.

ethnol'ogy, n. The science which treats of the varieties of the human race, and attempts to trace them to their origin. ethnol'ogist, n.

ethyl (eth'il), n. (*Chem.*) The base of alcohol, ether, etc.

etiquette (et'i-ket) [F. *étiquette*, a ticket], n. The conventional rules of behaviour in polite society; the rules of ceremonial in a court, or a professional or other body.

-ette, *suf.* Diminutive, as *cigarette, novelette*; sham, as *leatherette*; facetious fem., as *suffragette*.

etui (ĕ-twē') [F.], n. A pocket-case for pins, needles, etc.

etymology (et-i-mol'ŏ-ji) [Gr. *etumos*, real, -LOGY], n. The science that treats of the origin and history of words; the history of a particular word; derivation. etymologist, n. etymolog'ic, -al, a.

eu- [Gr.], *comb. form.* Good, well, pleasant, as in *eulogy, euphony.*

eucalyptus (ū-kà-lip'tús) [EU-, Gr. *kaluptos*, covered], n. An Australian gum-tree.

eucharist (ū'kà-rist) [*eucharistos*, grateful], n. The sacrament of the Lord's Supper.

euchre (ū'kėr) [?], n. A card game for two to four persons.

eugenic (ū-jen'ik) [Gr. *eugenēs*, well-born], a. Pertaining to the development and improvement of offspring. n.pl. The science relating to this.

eulogy (ū-lŏ-ji), n. Praise, panegyric; a writing or speech in praise of a person. eulogist, n. eulogis'tic, -al, a. eu'logize, v.t. To speak or write of in praise.

eunuch (ū'nŭk) [Gr. *eunouchos*], n. A castrated man.

euphemism (ū'fė-mizm) [Gr. *phēmē*, speaking, fame], n. The use of a pleasing term for one that is harsh or offensive; a softened expression. euphemis'tic, a.

euphony (ū'fŏ-ni) [Gr. *phōnē*, voice], n. Smoothness or agreeableness of sound; pleasing pronunciation. euphonic (ū-fon'ik), euphonious (ū-fō'ni-ús), a.

euphuism (ū-fū-izm) [Gr. *euphuēs*, well-endowed], n. A pedantic affectation of high-flown language (from Lyly's *Euphues* (1578), which popularized the style). euphuist, n. euphuistic, a.

Eurasian (ū-rā'shán), a. Of mixed European and Asiatic blood. n. One born of a European father and an Asiatic mother.

European (ū-rŏ-pē'án), a. Pertaining to Europe. n. A native of Europe.

euthanasia (ū-thà-nā'zhá) [Gr. *thanatos*, death], n. Painless death; a method of producing this.

evacuate (ė-văk'ū-āt) [L. *vacuatus*, emptied], v.t. To make empty; to withdraw from (esp. of troops). evacua'tion, n.

evade (ė-vād') [L. *vādere*, to go], v.t. To avoid or elude by artifice, sophistry, etc.; to shirk; to defeat, baffle.

evanesce (ev-à-nes') [L. *vānescere*], v.i. To disappear; to vanish. evanescence, n. evanescent, a.

evangelical (ė-văn-jel'ik-ál) [Gr. *euangelikos* (EU-, *angellein*, to announce)], a. Pertaining to or according to the Gospel; proclaiming or maintaining the truth taught in the Gospel; accepting for gospel only what Protestants consider to be so. n. A member of the Low-Church Party of the Church of England.

evangelist (ė-văn'jė-list), n. One of the four writers of the gospels; a missionary, lay preacher. evangelis'tic, a.

evaporate (ėvăp'ŏ-rāt) [L. *vaporatus*, steamed, heated], v.t. To convert into vapour; to expel the moisture by heating or drying. v.i. To become or pass away in vapour; to exhale moisture. evapora'tion, n.

evasion (ė-vā'zhún), n. The act of evading (esp. a question, argument, or charge); a subterfuge, equivocation. evasive (ė-vā'siv), a. evasiveness, n.

eve (ēv) [A.-S. *ēfen*], n. The evening before a festival, etc.

even (1) (ē'vėn), n. Evening. evensong, n. A form of worship for the evening; the time for evening prayer. eventide, n. Evening.

even (2) [A.-S. *efen, efn*], a. Level, smooth, uniform; capable of being divided by 2 without any remainder; equal; balanced, unvarying, equable. v.t. To make smooth or level; to place on a level; to equalize, satisfy. adv. To a like degree, as much as, so much as; exactly, just, neither more nor less than. evenhanded, a. Impartial. evenness, n.

evening (ēv'ning), n. The close of the day.

event (ė-vent') [E-(EX-), L. *ventus*, came], n. Anything that happens, an occurrence, esp. one of importance; the possibility of an occurrence; consequence, issue, conclusion; an item in a programme of games, etc. eventful, a. Full of events; attended by important changes.

eventual (ė-ven'tū-ál), a. Happening as a consequence; finally resulting, ultimate, final. eventual'ity, n. eventuate, v.i. To happen, come to pass.

ever (ev'ėr) [A.-S. *æfre*], adv. At all times; always; at any time; in any degree. evermore, adv. Always, eternally.

evergreen (ev'ėr-grēn), a. Always green; always young or fresh. n. A plant which retains its verdure through the year.

everlasting (ev-ėr-las'ting), a. Lasting for ever, eternal.

every (ev'ri), a. Each of a number, all separately; each. every one: Each one. everyone, n. Everybody. every other: Every alternate (day, week, etc.). everybody, n. Every person. everyday, n. Met with or happening daily; used on ordinary occasions; common, usual. everything, n. All things; all of the things making up a whole. everywhere, adv. In every place.

evict (ė-vikt') [L. *victus*, conquered], v.t. To dispossess or eject by legal process. eviction, n.

evidence (ev'i-dĕns) [L. *ēvidentia*], *n.* Anything that makes clear or obvious; indication, testimony; such statements, proofs, etc., as are legally admissible as testimony.

evident (ev'i-dĕnt), *a.* Open or plain to the sight; obvious. **eviden'tial,** *a.* Affording evidence; proving conclusively.

evil (ē'vil) [A.-S. *yfel*], *a.* Bad, injurious worthless, wicked; calamitous, sorrowful; malicious. *adv.* In an evil manner; maliciously, abusively; unfortunately, cruelly. *n.* That which injures or displeases, calamity, harm; sin, depravity.

evince (ê-vins') [L. *vincere*, to conquer], *v.t.* To show clearly; to demonstrate.

eviscerate (ê-vis'ĕr-āt) [L. *viscera*, bowels], *v.t.* To disembowel; to empty of all that is vital. **eviscera'tion,** *n.*

evoke (ê-vōk') [L. *vocāre*, to call], *v.t.* To call up, summon forth. **evoca'tion,** *n.* **evoc'ative,** *a.*

evolution (ē-vô-loo'shŭn) [L. *ēvolūtus,* evolved], *n.* The act of unfolding or developing; development, as of an argument, design, political, social, or natural system, etc.; the process by which a germ develops into a complex organism; the derivation of all forms of life from simpler forms or from a single rudimentary form; the theory based on this principle; (*pl.*) movements, changes of position, etc., in military or naval manœuvres, dancing, etc. **evolutional, -tionary,** *a.*

evolve (ê-volv') [L. *volvere*, to roll], *v.t.* To unfold, expand; to develop, to bring to maturity; to set forth (an argument, etc.) in an orderly manner. *v.i.* To open, develop.

ewe (ū) [A.-S. *eowu*], *n.* A female sheep.

ewer (ū'ĕr) [O.F. *aiguier*, from L. *aqua*, water], *n.* A large jug for water.

ex-, *pref.* Out of; thoroughly; without; formerly; as *exceed, exit, exacerbate, exonerate, expatriate; ex-president.*

exacerbate (ek-săs'ĕr-bāt) [L. *acerbus,* bitter], *v.t.* To irritate, embitter.

exact (eg-zăkt') [L. *exactus*], *a.* Precisely agreeing in amount, number, etc.; accurate, strictly correct; precise. *v.t.* To compel; to demand as of right, to insist upon, to require authoritatively. **exacting,** *a.* Severe or excessive in demanding; urgently requiring (of circumstances, etc.). **exaction,** *n.* **exactitude,** *n.* Exactness, precision. **exactly,** *adv.* In an exact manner; quite so, precisely.

exaggerate (eg-zăj'ĕr-āt) [L. *exaggerātus*], *v.t.* To heighten, overstate, represent as greater than truth warrants; to intensify, aggravate. **exaggera'tion,** *n.*

exalt (eg-zawlt') [L. *altus,* high], *v.t.* To raise in dignity, position, etc.; to elevate in character, spirits, or diction, to ennoble, dignify; to praise, extol; to intensify. **exalta'tion,** *n.*

examination (eg-zăm-i-nā'shŭn), *n.* The act of examining; careful scrutiny; the process of testing the qualifications of a candidate.

examine (eg-zăm'in) [F. *examiner*, L. *exāmināre*, conn. with *exigere*, to weigh out], *v.t.* To inquire into, investigate, scrutinize; to consider critically; to test

the capabilities, qualifications, knowledge of, etc. *v.i.* To make inquiry or research. **exam'iner,** *n.*

example (eg-zam'pl) [L. *exemplum*], *n.* A sample, specimen, model, pattern, person or fact illustrating a general rule.

exasperate (eg-zas'pĕr-āt) [L. *asperātus,* roughened], *v.t.* To aggravate, embitter. **exaspera'tion,** *n.*

excavate (eks'kă-vāt) [L. *excavātus,* hollowed out], *v.t.* To remove or uncover by digging. **excava'tion,** *n.* **ex'cavator,** *n.*

exceed (ek-sēd') [L. *cēdere*], *v.t.* To go beyond; to be more or greater than; to surpass, outdo, excel. *v.i.* To go beyond bounds; to be greater; to excel. **exceeding,** *a.* Very great in amount, duration, extent, etc. **exceedingly,** *adv.*

excel (ek-sel') [L. *excellere*], *v.t.* To surpass, exceed, outdo. *v.i.* To be superior, distinguished, or pre-eminent (in or at). **ex'cellence,** *n.* State of excelling; superiority; surpassing merit, etc. **ex'cellency,** *n.* Excellence; a title of honour given to a governor, ambassador, and certain other officers. **excellent,** *a.* Surpassing others in some good quality; of great virtue, worth, etc.

except (ek-sept') [L. *exceptāre*], *v.t.* To leave out, omit, exclude. *v.i.* To make objection (to or against). *prep.* Exclusive of, omitting, but. **excepting,** prep. Omitting, with the exception of. **exception,** *n.* Act of excepting; that which is excepted; an objection, disapproval. **exceptionable,** *a.* Liable to objection; unusual. **exceptional,** *a.*

excerpt (ek'-, ek-sĕrpt') [L. *excerptus,* selected], *n.* (*pl.* -ta.) An extract from a writing or book.

excess (ek-ses') [L. *excessus,* a going out], *n.* That which exceeds; the quality or fact of exceeding the ordinary measure, proportion, or limit; the amount by which one exceeds another; intemperance, extravagance. **excessive,** *a.*

exchange (eks-chānj'), *v.t.* To give or receive in return for something else; to interchange. *v.i.* To be given or received in exchange; to pass from one regiment to another by taking the place of another officer. *n.* The act of exchanging, or of resigning one state for another; interchange; that which is given or received in exchange; exchanging of coin for its value in other or foreign coins; the place where merchants, brokers, etc., meet to transact business. **exchangeable,** *a.*

exchequer (eks-chek'ĕr) [med. L. *scaccārium*, a chess-board], *n.* The State treasury; the Government department dealing with public revenue; finances or pecuniary resources.

excise (1) (ek-sīz') [L. *accensāre*, to tax], *n.* A tax on articles produced and consumed in a country. *v.t.* To impose an excise duty on. **excisable,** *a.* Subject to excise duty. **exciseman,** *n.* An officer who collects the excise duties, and prevents evasion of the excise laws.

excise (2) (ek-sīz') [L. *excīsus,* cut out], *v.t.* To cut out (a part). **excision** (ek-sizh'ŭn), *n.*

excite (ek-sīt') [L. *excitāre*], *v.t.* To rouse, stir into action or agitation; to stimulate, inflame the spirits of; to provoke. **excitable**, *a.* Susceptible of excitement; characterized by excitability. **excitabil'ity**, *n.* **excitement**, *n.* Stimulation, agitation; state or course of being excited. **exciting**, *a.* Stimulating; producing excitement.

exclaim (eks-klām') [L. *clāmāre*, to cry aloud], *v.i.* To cry out abruptly or passionately. *v.t.* To utter loudly or in an abrupt manner. **exclama'tion**, *n.*

exclude (eks-klood') [L. *exclūdere*, to shut out], *v.t.* To shut out, prevent from coming in or participating; to debar; to reject, except. **exclusion**, *n.*

exclusive (eks-kloo'siv), *a.* Shutting out, tending, or desiring to shut out; fastidious. **exclusiveness**, *n.*

excogitate (eks-koj'i-tāt), *v.t.* To think out; to devise by thinking.

excommunicate (eks-kō-mū'ni-kāt) [L. *communis*, common], *v.t.* To exclude from the communion and privileges of the Church. **excommunica'tion**, *n.*

excoriate (eks-kōr'i-āt) [L. *corium*, skin], *v.t.* To strip the skin from.

excrement (eks'krē-mėnt), *n.* Refuse matter discharged from the body after digestion.

excrescence (eks-kres'éns) [L. *crescere*, to grow], *n.* An unnatural or disfiguring outgrowth. **excrescent**, *a.*

excrete (eks-krēt') [L. *excrētus*, sifted out], *v.t.* To separate and discharge superfluous matter from the organism. **excretion**, *n.* **excretory**, *a.* Pertaining to excretion.

excruciate (eks-kroo'shi-āt) [L. *excruciātus*, tortured], *v.t.* To torture, to inflict severe pain or mental agony upon.

exculpate (eks'kul-pāt) [L. *culpa*, fault], *v.t.* To clear from a charge; to free from blame. **exculpa'tion**, *n.*

excursion (eks-kėr'shùn) [L. *excursio*], *n.* A journey for health or pleasure; a short tour, a trip; a wandering from the subject, a digression. **excursionist**, *n.* **excursive**, *a.* Rambling, deviating, exploring. **excursiveness**, *n.*

excuse (eks-kūz') [L. *excūsāre*], *v.t.* To free from blame; to pardon, acquit; to ask pardon for; to justify; to exempt from an obligation or duty; to remit; to dispense with. *n.* (eks-kūs'). An apology, justification; a pretended reason; an exculpation. **excusable**, *a.*

execrate (ek'sē-krāt) [L. *execrātus*, accursed], *v.t.* To curse; to detest. **execrable**, *a.* Detestable, accursed; abominable. **execra'tion**, *n.*

execute (ek'sē-kūt) [L. *execūtus*], *v.t.* To carry into effect, put in force; to perform, accomplish, complete, esp. by signing and sealing; to inflict capital punishment on.

execution (ek-sē-kū'shùn), *n.* The act of executing; performance, accomplishment; the infliction of capital punishment; destruction, slaughter; the mode of performing a work of art, skill, dexterity; the act of giving validity to a legal instrument, as by signing. **executioner**, *n.* One who inflicts capital punishment.

executive (eg-zek'ū-tiv), *a.* Having the function or power of executing; pertaining to performance; carrying laws, decrees, etc., into effect. *n.* The person or persons carrying laws, sentences, etc., into effect; the administrative branch of a government.

executor (eg-zek'ū-tór), *n.* One who executes, esp. a person appointed by a testator to carry out the provisions of his will. **executorship**, *n.* **executrix**, *n.* (*pl.* -trices) A female executor.

exegesis (ek-sē-jē'sis) [Gr. *hēgeisthai*, to lead], *n.* Exposition, interpretation, esp. of the Scriptures. **exegetic** (-jet'ik), *a.* Pertaining to exegesis, expository. *n.pl.* Scientific interpretation, esp. of Scripture. **exeget'ical**, *a.*

exemplar (eg-zem'plàr), *n.* A pattern, model; a noted example; an instance. **exemplary**, *a.*

exemplify (eg-zem'pli-fī) [L. *exemplum*, example], *v.t.* To illustrate by example; to prove by an attested copy.

exempt (eg-zempt') [L. *emere*, to take], *a.* Free (from); not liable or subject to. *v.t.* To free or allow to be free; to grant immunity (from). **exemption**, *n.*

exequies (ek'sē-kwiz) [L. *exequiæ*], *n.pl.* Funeral rites; obsequies.

exercise (ek'sėr-sīz) [L. *exercēre*, to keep at work], *n.* The act of using, employing, or exerting; practice; an act of public or private worship; exertion of the body or the mind for health or training; a task set for this purpose; (*pl.*) drill, athletics. *v.t.* To employ, exert, put in practice or operation; to perform the duties of; to train; to keep employed or busy.

exert (eg-zėrt') [L. *exertus*, put forth], *v.t.* To put forth (as strength, power, or ability), to put in action or operation. **exertion**, *n.*

exhale (eks-hāl') [L. *hālāre*, to breathe], *v.t.* To breathe forth; to emit, or cause to be emitted, in vapour. *v.i.* To be given off as vapour. **exhala'tion**, *n.*

exhaust (eg-zawst') [L. *exhaustus*, drawn out], *v.t.* To empty by drawing out the contents; to use up the whole of; to wear out by exertion; to drain of resources, strength, etc.; to treat the whole of a subject. *n.* The discharge or escape of steam, gas, etc., after it has performed its work; apparatus for this. **exhaustible**, *a.* **exhausting**, *a.* Tending to tire out completely. **exhaus'tion**, *n.* **exhaustive**, *a.* Tending to exhaust; comprehensive.

exhibit (ég-zib'it) [L. *exhibitus*, displayed], *v.t.* To show, display, manifest. *n.* Anything offered to public view; a document, etc., produced in court as evidence. **exhibitor**, *n.*

exhibition (ek-si-bish'ùn), *n.* The act of exhibiting; a display; production of documents, etc., in proof of facts; an allowance to a student, pecuniary assistance. **exhibitioner**, *n.* One who obtains an exhibition at a college, etc. **exhibitionism**, *n.* (*Psych.*) A tendency to show off, to attract attention to oneself; a tendency to indecent exposure in public.

exhilarate (eg-zil′à-rāt) [L. *hilaris*, glad], *v.t.* To gladden, enliven. **exhilara′tion**, *n.* **exhil′arative**, *a.*

exhort (eg-zŏrt′) [L. *hortārī*, to urge], *v.t.* To incite by words; to urge, admonish. **exhorta′tion**, *n.* **exhor′tatory**, *a.*

exhume (eks-hūm′) [EX-, L. *humus*, the ground], *v.t.* To disinter. **exhuma′tion**, *n.*

exigence, **-gency** (eks′i-jēns, -si) [L. *exigentia*], *n.* Urgent necessity; a state of affairs demanding immediate action, an emergency. **exigent**, *a.*

exiguous (eg-zig′ū-ùs) [L. *exiguus*], *a.* Small, slender, scanty. **exigu′ity**, *n.*

exile (ek′sīl) [L. *salīre*, to leap], *n.* Expatriation; long absence from one's native country; one who is banished, or has been long absent. *v.t.* To banish from one's native country.

exist (eg-zist′) [L. *sistere*, to cause to stand], *v.i.* To be; to live; to continue to be. **existence**, *n.* **existent**, *a.* **existentialism**, *n.* (*Phil.*) A theory based on the consideration of self as finiteness.

exit (ek′sit) [L. *exitus*, a going out], *n.* The departure of an actor from the stage; death; a way out. *v.i.* (*Stage direction*) Goes off the stage.

exo- [Gr., without, outside], *comb. form.*

exodus (ek′sŏ-dùs) [Gr. *hodos*, a way], *n.* A departure, esp. of a large body of persons; the second book of the Old Testament.

exonerate (eg-zon′èr-āt) [L. *onus oneris*, a burden], *v.t.* To free from a charge; to exculpate; to relieve from an obligation or liability. **exon′erative**, *a.*

exorbitant (eg-zŏr′bi-tȧnt) [EX-, L. *orbita*, a track], *a.* Out of all bounds, grossly excessive. **exorbitance**, *n.*

exorcize (ek′sŏr-sīz) [EX-, Gr. *horkos*, oath], *v.t.* To expel (as an evil spirit) by adjurations, prayers, etc. **exorcism**, *n.* **exorcist**, *n.* One who exorcizes.

exordium (eg-zŏr′di-ùm) [L. *ordīrī*, to begin], *n.* The introductory part of a literary work or discourse.

exoteric, **-al** (ek-sŏ-ter′ik, -ál) [Gr. *exōterikos*], *a.* Fit to be imparted to outsiders; comprehensible to the vulgar, public, opposed to esoteric.

exotic (ek-sot′ik) [Gr. *exōtikos*], *a.* Foreign; introduced from a foreign country. *n.* Anything introduced from a foreign country, as a plant.

expand (ek-spănd′) [L. *pandere*, to spread], *v.t.* To open or spread out; to distend, extend, enlarge. *v.i.* To become opened or distended. **expansible**, **expansile**, *a.* Capable of expanding.

expanse (ek-spăns′), *n.* A wide, open extent or area.

expansion (ek-spăn′shŭn), *n.* Act of expanding; state of being expanded; enlargement, extension.

expansive (ek-spăn′siv), *a.* Having the power of expanding; tending to expand; extending widely; frank.

expatiate (ek-spā-shi-āt) [L. *spatiārī*, to roam], *v.i.* To dilate; to speak or write copiously on a subject.

expatriate (ek-spā′tri-āt) [L. *patria*, one's native land], *v.t.* To exile, drive into banishment. **expatria′tion**, *n.*

expect (ek-spekt′) [L. *expectāre*], *v.t.* To look forward to; to regard as certain or likely to happen; to suppose. **expectancy**, **-ance**, *n.* Act or state of expecting, expectation; state of being expected; that which is expected. **expectant**, *a.* **expecta′tion**, *n.* Act or state of expecting, anticipation; the ground for this; the probability of a future event; (*pl.*) prospects.

expectorate (ek-spek′tŏ-rāt) [L. *pectus*, the breast], *v.t.* To discharge by coughing, hawking, or spitting. **expectora′tion**, *n.*

expedient (ek-spē′di-ènt) [L. *expediens*], *a.* Promoting the object in view; advantageous; politic as opposed to just. *n.* That which promotes an object; an advantageous way or means; a makeshift. **expedience**, **-ency**, *n.*

expedite (ek′spē-dīt) [L. *expedītus*], *v.t.* To facilitate, to accelerate the progress of; to dispatch. **expedi′tion**, *n.* Speed, promptness, dispatch; any journey by an organized body for some definite object; the persons engaged in this. **expeditionary**, *a.* **expeditious**, *a.* Speedy, active.

expel (ek-spel′) [L. *pellere*, to drive], *v.t.* To drive or force out; to eject.

expend (ek-spend′) [L. *pendere*, to weigh], *v.t.* To spend, lay out; to consume. **expenditure**, *n.*

expense (ĕk-spens′), *n.* A laying out; cost, outlay, price paid. **expensive**, *a.* Costly, requiring a large expenditure.

experience (ek-spēr′i-èns) [L. *experientia*], *n.* Practical acquaintance with any matter; knowledge gained by observation or trial; something undergone. *v.t.* To gain knowledge of by trial or observation; to undergo, feel, meet with. **experienced**, *a.* Taught by experience.

experiment (ek-sper′i-mènt) [*experimentum*], *n.* A trial, proof, or test of anything; an operation, etc., designed to discover some unknown truth, principle, or effect, or to test an hypothesis. *v.i.* To make an experiment; to investigate by this means. **experimen′tal**, *a.*

expert (ek-spĕrt′) [L. *expertus*, experienced], *a.* Experienced, dexterous; practised, skilful. *n.* (ek′spĕrt) One who has special skill or knowledge. **expertise**, *n.* Expert knowledge. **expertly**, *adv.*

expiate (ek′spi-āt) [L. *piātus*, propitiated], *v.t.* To atone for; to make amends for. **expia′tion**, *n.*

expire (ek-spīr′) L. *spīrāre*, to breathe], *v.t.* To breathe out, send forth, emit, exhale. *v.i.* To breathe out; to die. **expira′tion**, *n.* The act of breathing out; cessation, termination.

explain (ek-splān′) [L. *plānāre*, to flatten], *v.t.* To make clear or plain; to expound and illustrate the meaning of; to account for. *v.i.* To give explanations. **explana′tion**, *n.* **explan′atory**, *a.*

expletive (ĕk-splē′tiv) [L. *explētivus*, from *explētus*, filled out], *a.* Serving to fill out or complete. *n.* A word not necessary to the sense introduced to fill up; an interjection; a profane exclamation.

explicate (eks'pli-kāt) [L. *plicātus*, folded], *v.t.* To display the meaning of; to free from obscurity, explain. **explicable**, *a.* That can be explained. **explica'tion**, *n.*

explicit (ek-splis'it) [F. *explicite*, as prec.], *a.* Plainly stated; outspoken.

explode (ek-splōd') [L. *plaudere*, to clap], *v.t.* To cause to burst with a loud report; to refute, expose. *v.i.* To burst with a loud report.

exploit (ek'sploit) [O.F. *esploit*, profit], *n.* A feat, a great or noble achievement. *v.t.* (ek-sploit'). To turn to account. **exploita'tion**, *n.*

explore (ek-splōr') [L. *explōrāre*, to search out], *v.t.* To investigate, examine; to travel over in order to examine. **exploration**, *n*, explorer, *n.*

explosion (ek-splō'zhŭn), *n.* A bursting with a loud report; a sudden and violent noise; an outbreak, as of physical forces, anger, etc. **explo'sive**, *a.* Bursting forth with great force and noise; liable to explode; produced by a sudden expulsion of breath, as *p, b, t, d, k, g. n.* An explosive substance, as gunpowder, dynamite, etc.; one of the above consonants.

exponent (ek-spō'nènt) [L. *pōnere*, to put], *a.* Setting forth or explaining; exemplifying. *n.* One who does this.

export (ek-spōrt') [L. *portāre*, to carry], *v.t.* To carry or send (goods) to foreign countries. *n.* (ek'spōrt). Act of exporting, exportation; a commodity sent to a foreign country; (*pl.*) the quantity or value of goods exported. **export'able**, *a.* **exporta'tion**, *n.* **exporter**, *n.*

expose (ek-spōz') L. *pausāre*, to lay down], *v.t.* To lay bare or open, disclose, reveal; to leave unprotected; to abandon (as a child), to display, esp. for sale; to unmask. **exposé** (ek-spō' zā), *n.* A formal declaration; a disclosure, exposure. **exposition** (-zish'ŭn), *n.* The act of exposing; an explanation, a commentary.

expostulate (ek-spos'tū-lāt) [L. *postulātus*, demanded], *v.i.* To reason earnestly (with a person), to remonstrate. **expostula'tion**, *n.* **expostulatory**, *a.*

exposure (ek-spō'zhŭr), *n.* Act of exposing; state of being exposed; abandonment (of a child, etc.); display, esp. of goods for sale; a revelation; (*Phot.*) the act of allowing light from an object to fall upon a sensitized plate.

expound (ek-spound'), *v.t.* To explain, interpret. **expounder**, *n.*

express (ek-spres) [L. *pressus*, pressed], *a.* Set forth distinctly; direct, explicit; intended, done, made, etc., for a special purpose. *adv.* With speed; by express messenger. *n.* An express train, messenger, or rifle. *v.t.* To set forth, make clear, put into words; to send by express post.

expression (ek-spresh'ŭn), *n.* Act of expressing; that which is expressed, a saying, statement, word, phrase. **expressionless**, *a.*

expressive (ek-spres'iv), *a.* Serving to express; significant. **expressively**, *adv.* **expres'iveness**, *n.*

expropriate (eks-prō'pri-āt) [L. *proprium,*

property], *v.t.* To take from an owner for public use; to dispossess. **expropria'tion**, *n.*

expulsion (ek-spŭl'shŭn), *n.* Act of expelling; state of being expelled; ejection. **expulsive**, *a.*

expunge (ek-spŭnj') [L. *pungere*, to prick], *v.t.* To efface, to erase.

expurgate (ek-spŭr-gāt) [L. *purgātus*, cleansed], *v.t.* To free from anything offensive, obscene, or noxious.

exquisite (ek'skwi-zit) [L. *quisitus*, sought] *a.* Fine, dainty; delicately beautiful; keenly sensitive, nice, fastidious.

extant (ek-stănt') [L. *extans*, standing forth], *a.* Still in existence; surviving.

extempore (ek-stem'pō-ri) [L. *ex tempore*, from the time], *adv.* and *a.* Without premeditation or preparation: unstudied. **extempora'neous, extemporary**, *a.* extemporize, *v.t.*

extend (ek'stend') [L. *tendere*, to stretch], *v.t.* To stretch out, prolong; to make larger in space, time, or scope; to expand; to hold out, offer. *v.i.* To stretch, to reach (in space, time, or scope). **extensible**, *a.* **extension** (ēk-sten'shŭn), *n.*

extensive (ēk-sten'siv), *a.* Widely spread; large; comprehensive.

extent (ēk-stent'), *n.* Size, scope, comprehension, distribution; a large space.

extenuate (ēk-sten'ū-āt) [L. *extenuātus*, lessened], *v.t.* To diminish the gravity of, to palliate; to offer excuses for. **extenua'tion**, *n.*

exterior (ēk-stēr'i-ŏr)]L. comp. of *exter*, outer], *a.* External, on the outside. *n.* The outer surface; the external features.

exterminate (ēk-stēr'mi-nāt) [L. *exterminātus*, driven forth], *v.t.* To extirpate, destroy utterly. **extermina'tion**, *n.*

external (ēk-stēr'nál), *a.* Situated on, or pertaining to the outside, superficial; objective; foreign, extraneous, extrinsic. *n.* An exterior or outer part; (*pl.*) outward features, rites, etc.; non-essentials. **externally**, *adv.*

exterritorial (ek-ster-i-tōr'i-ál), *a.* Beyond the jurisdiction of the country in which one resides. **exterritorial'ity**, *n.* Immunity from the laws of a country (as that of ambassadors).

extinct (ek-stingkt'), *a.* Extinguished; that has died out. **extinction** (ek-stingk'-shŭn), *n.*

extinguish (ēk-sting'gwish) [L. *stinguere*, to quench], *v.t.* To put out, quench (as a light, hope, life, etc.); to eclipse, to obscure, throw into the shade; to annihilate; to pay off (a debt, mortgage, etc.). **extinguishable**, *a.* **extinguisher**, *n.*

extirpate (ek'stir-pāt) [L. *extirpātus*, rooted out] *v.t.* To root out, destroy utterly, exterminate. **extirpa'tion**, *n.*

extol (ēk-stol') [L. *tollere*, to raise], *v.t.* To praise in the highest terms.

extort (ēk-stōrt') [L. *extortus*, wrenched away], *v.t.* To wrest or wring (from) by force, threats, etc. **extortion**, *n.* **extortionate**, *a.* **extortioner**, *n.*

extra (ek'strä) [L. *extrā*, beyond, from outside], *a.* Beyond what is necessary; larger or better than is usual: additional.

adv. Over and above what is usual. *n.* Something beyond what is absolutely necessary or usual.

extra- [L., on the outside, without], *comb. form.* **extramundane,** *a.* Existing in or pertaining to a region outside our world or outside the universe.

extract (ĕk-străkt′) [L. *extractus*, drawn out], *v.t.* To draw or pull out; to draw out by chemical means; to select from, to copy out or quote; to deduce (from); to find the root of a number. *n.* (ek′străkt) That which is extracted by distillation, solution, etc.; a passage quoted from a book, etc.; a preparation containing the essence of a substance. **extraction,** *n.* Act of extracting; descent, family, derivation.

extradition (ek-strȧ-dish′ŭn), *n.* The surrender of fugitives from justice by a government to that of the country where the crime was committed. **ex′tradite,** *v.t.*

extrajudicial (ek-strȧ-jū-dish′ȧl), *a.* Taking place outside the court, not legally authorized; outside the ordinary course of law or justice. **extrajudicially,** *adv.*

extraneous (ĕk-strā′nē-ŭs) [L. *extrāneus*], *a.* Foreign, not belonging to a subject, etc.; external, not essential. **extraneously,** *adv.* **extrane′ity,** *n.*

extraordinary (ĕk-strôr′-, ĕk-strȧ-ôr′di-nȧr-i) [L. *extrā ordinem*, outside the usual order], *a.* Out of the ordinary course, unusual; remarkable, exceptional, surprising; appointed for a special purpose or occasion. **extraordinarily,** *adv.*

extravagant (ĕk-străv′ȧ-gȧnt) [L. *vagans*, wandering], *a.* Exceeding due bounds, immoderate; visionary, fantastic; prodigal in expenditure; (of prices, etc.) exorbitant. **extravagance,** *n.* State or quality of being extravagant.

extreme (ek-strēm′) [L. *extrēmus*, superl. of *exterus*, outward], *a.* Outermost, farthest; at the utmost limit; last, final; most intense; going to great lengths, immoderate. *n.* The utmost or furthest point, the extremity; the utmost or highest degree; (*pl.*) things or qualities as different or as far removed from each other as possible. **extremely,** *adv.* **extremist,** *n.* One ready to go to extremes; holder of extreme opinions. **extremity** (ĕks-trem′i-ti), *n.* The utmost point, side, or limit.

extricate (ek′stri-kāt) [L. *extrīcātus*], *v.t.* To disentangle, set free from any perplexity, embarrassment, etc. **extricable,** *a.* **extrica′tion,** *n.*

extrinsic (ek-strin′sik) [L. *extrinsecus*, from without], *a.* Being external; not inherent or contained in a body; not essential.

extrude (ĕk-strood′) [L. *trūdere*, to thrust], *v.t.* To thrust or push out or away; to expel. **extrusion,** *n.*

exuberant (eg-zū′bér-ȧnt) [L. *exūberans*], *a.* Luxuriant in growth; overflowing, copious, superabundant. **exuberance,** *n.*

exude (ĕk-sūd′) [L. *sūdāre*, to sweat], *v.t.* To emit or discharge through pores; to give out slowly. *v.i.* To ooze out through pores, etc. **exuda′tion,** *n.*

exult (ĕg-zŭlt′) [L. *esaultāre*, to leap up],

v.i. To rejoice exceedingly; to triumph (over). exultant, *a.* **exulta′tion,** *n.*

exuviæ (eg-zū′vi-ē) [L.], *n.pl.* The cast or shed skin, shells, teeth, etc., of animals; fragmentary fossil remains of animals.

eye (ī) [A.-S. *ēage*], *n.* The organ of vision; the part containing it; sight, the power of seeing, acuteness of vision; careful observation, care, attention; look, expression; anything eye-shaped; a spot on some feathers, as those of the peacock; a bull's-eye; the thread-hole of a needle; the loop in which a hook is fastened. *v.t.* To watch, to observe, esp. fixedly, suspiciously, jealously, etc. **eyeball,** *n.* The pupil, apple, or globe of the eye. **eye-bolt,** *n.* A bolt having a loop at one end for the reception of a hook, etc. **eyebrow,** *n.* The fringe of hair above the orbit of the eyes. **eyeglass,** *n.* A lens to aid the sight; (*pl.*) a pair of these; the lens nearest the eye in an optical instrument; a glass for applying lotion to the eyes. **eyelash,** *n.* The row of hairs edging the eyelids; a single hair from the eyelid. **eyelid,** *n.* One of the movable folds of skin for covering the eye. **eyepiece,** *n.* The lens or combination of lenses at the end nearest the eye in an optical instrument. **eyeservice,** *n.* Service performed only while under supervision. **eyesight,** *n.* Vision; view, observation. **eyesore,** *n.* Anything offensive to the sight. **eyeteeth,** *n.pl.* The upper canine teeth of man. **eyewitness,** *n.* One who sees a transaction with his own eyes.

eyelet (ī′lĕt), *n.* A small hole or opening; a loophole; a small eye.

eyre (âr) [O.F. *eire*], *n.* (*Law*) A journey, circuit.

F

Fabian (fā′bi-ȧn) [L. *Fabianus*], *a.* Gaining ends by a policy of caution and wearing down.

fable (fābl) [L. *fābula*], *n.* A story, esp. one in which lower animals speak and convey some moral lesson; a myth; the plot of a drama or epic; a falsehood. *v.i.* To write fables; to romance; to tell falsehoods. *v.t.* To feign, invent. **fabled,** *a.*

fabric (făb′rik) [L. *fabrica*], *n.* Something put together; a building, frame, or structure; woven, felted, or knitted material. **fabricate,** *v.t.* To form by art, to manufacture; to invent, trump up. **fabrica′tion,** *n.* **fabricator,** *n.*

fabulist (făb′ū-list), *n.* A writer or inventor of fables. **fabulous,** *a.* Feigned, fictitious; mythical.

façade (fȧ-sad′) [F.], *n.* The front of a building.

face (fās) [L. *facies*], *n.* The front part of the head, the visage, countenance; expression, appearance, aspect; the visible state of things; that part of anything which presents itself to the view; effrontery. *v.t.* To turn the face towards; to meet in front; to confront boldly; to stand opposite to; to put a coating, covering, or facings on. *v.i.* To look or be situated in a certain direction. **face-value,** *n.* The nominal value shown on coin, bank-notes, etc. **to lose face:** To be humiliated, to suffer loss of personal prestige.

facet [făs'ĕt] [F. *facette*], *n.* A small plane forming the side of a crystal, diamond, etc.

facetiæ (fȧ-sē'shi-ē) [L.], *n.pl.* Humorous or witty sayings; comic or indecent books.

facetious (fȧ-sē'shŭs) [F.], *a.* Given to pleasantry; waggish, jocular.

facial (fā'shȧl) [L. *faciális*], *a.* Of or pertaining to the face.

facile (făs'īl) [L. *facilis*], *a.* Easy to be done; easily led, pliant; dexterous, fluent; easy-tempered. **facilitate** (fȧ-sĭl'ĭ-tāt), *v.t.* To make easy; to further, help forward. **facil'ity,** *n.* Easiness in performing or in being performed; opportunity or advantage for the performance or attainment of anything; readiness, fluency; quickness, dexterity, pliability.

facing (fā'sing), *n.* The action of the verb; a covering in front for ornament, defence, etc.; (*pl.*) trimmings on uniforms.

facsimile (făk-sim'ĭ-li) [L.], *n.* An exact copy of writing, printing, a picture, etc.

fact (făkt) [L. *factum*, a thing done], *n.* An act or deed; something that has occurred or been done; something true or existing as distinct from an inference or conjecture; reality, actuality.

faction (făk'shŭn) [L. *factio*, a way of making a party], *n.* A united body of persons, esp. a party within a party; party spirit, dissension. **factious,** *a.* Given to faction; seditious, turbulent.

factitious (făk-tish'ŭs) [L. *facticius*], *a.* Artificial; conventional, affected.

factor (făk'tŏr) [L.], *n.* An agent, deputy; (*Sc.*) a steward or estate agent; one of the quantities that multiplied together make a given number or expression; any circumstance, fact, or influence which contributes to a result.

factory (făk'tŏr-i) [L. *factus*, made], *n.* A trading station established in a foreign place by a company of merchants; a building in which any manufacture is carried on.

factotum (făk-tō'tŭm) [L. *fac*, imper. of *facere*, to do, *totum*, all], *n.* A man of all work, a handy-man.

faculty (făk'ŭl-ti) [L. *facultās*], *n.* Power or ability of any special kind; capacity for any natural action, as seeing, feeling, speaking; the members of a learned profession, esp. medicine; one of the departments of instruction in a University; an authorization to perform certain functions, esp. ecclesiastical.

fad (făd) [?], *n.* A whim, passing fancy; a hobby; a favourite theory. **faddish,** *a.* **faddist,** *n.* **faddy,** *a.*

fade (fād) [O.F. *fader*, from *fade*, dull], *v.i.* To wither, to lose freshness, vigour, or beauty; to grow indistinct. **fadeless,** *a.* Unfading.

faeces (fē'siz) [L.], *n.pl.* Excrement from the bowels; sediment, dregs.

fag (făg) [?], *v.i.* To toil wearily; to work

till one is weary; to act as a fag. *v.t.* To tire, weary out; to use as a drudge. *n.* Laborious drudgery; fatigue; a tiresome task; a junior at a public school who performs certain duties for some senior boy; (*slang*) a cigarette.

faggot (făg'ŏt) [F. *fagot*], *n.* A bundle of sticks or small branches.

Fahrenheit (fa'rĕn-hīt) [G. D. *Fahrenheit* (1686–1736), inventor], *a.* Pertaining to the thermometer with the freezing-point at 32° and boiling-point at 212°.

faience (fa-yåns) [It. town *Faenza*], *n.* A fine kind of pottery with painted designs.

fail (fāl) [O.F. *faillir*, to miss, L. *fallere*, to deceive], *v.i.* To be or become deficient or wanting; to run short; not to succeed (in); to lose strength, sink; to die away; to become bankrupt. *v.t.* To be wanting to; to be insufficient for; to come short of. *n.* Failure, default. **failing,** *n.* A weakness, foible. *prep.* In default of. **failure,** *n.* A coming short; an omission, non-performance; bankruptcy; an unsuccessful person or thing.

fain (fān) [A.-S. *fægen*], *a.* Glad, well-pleased; contented. *adv.* Readily.

faint (fānt) [O.F. *feint*, feigned], *a.* Weak, languid; giddy, inclined to swoon; dim, indistinct, slight. *v.i.* To swoon. *n.* A swoon, a fainting fit.

fair (1) (fâr) [A.-S. *fæger*], *a.* Beautiful, pleasing to the eye; satisfactory, specious; just, equitable, above-board; passably good, of moderate quality; clear, pure; legible, plain; of light complexion. *adv.* Courteously, plausibly; openly, justly; on equal terms; according to the rules. *n.* A beautiful woman. **fairway,** *n.* The navigable part of a river, etc.; an open drive on a golf-course. **fairish,** *a.* Pretty fair. **fairly,** *adv.* In a fair manner; completely, utterly; passably. **fairness,** *n.*

fair (2) (fâr) [O.F. *feire*, L. *fēriæ*, holiday], *n.* A market or gathering for trade in a particular town or place (usu. annually), with shows and entertainments. **fairing,** *n.* A present bought at a fair.

fairy (fâr'i) [O.F. *faerie*, enchantment], *n.* An imaginary being having magical powers and human form supposed to meddle in the affairs of men. *a.* Pertaining to fairies; fairy-like.

faith (fāth) [O.F. *fei*, L. *fides*], *n.* Mental assent to what is stated or put forward without having absolute proof; firm and earnest belief; conviction, complete reliance; belief in the doctrines and moral principles of a religion; system of belief or of doctrines; fidelity, loyalty, a pledge, engagement; reliability, trustworthiness. **faithful,** *a.* **faithfulness,** *n.* **faithless,** *a.* Unbelieving; disloyal, not true to promises or duty, unreliable; treacherous.

fake (fāk), *v.t.* To cheat; to cover up defects and faults, to make something appear right. *n.* A thing thus prepared for deception; a swindle, a dodge.

fakir (fȧ-kēr') [Arab. *faqīr*], *n.* A Mohammedan religious mendicant.

falcon (fawl'-, faw'kŏn) [O.F. *faucon*,], *n.* A small bird of prey, esp. one trained to hawk game. falconer, n. One who keeps and trains hawks, or who hunts with hawks. falconry, n.

fall (fawl) [A.-S. *feallan*], v.i. (past fell, p.p. fallen). To descend by the force of gravity; to descend suddenly, to drop; to sink, to flow or be poured down, to become lower; to come down, to be killed; to decline; to decrease in power, value, weight, etc.; to subside, abate, languish, die away; to fail, be disgraced; to sink into sin; to turn out, result, happen; to be uttered (as by chance); to droop. n. The act of falling; a bout at wrestling, a throw; a waterfall; degree of inclination, the slope; amount of descent, distance through which anything falls; autumn, the fall of the leaf; amount of rain, snow, etc., in a district; downfall, declension from greatness or prosperity, ruin, overthrow; a lapse from virtue; a veil; that part of the rope in hoisting-tackle to which the power is applied; a cadence.

fallacy (făl'ȧ-si) [L. *fallācia*, from *fallere*, to deceive], n. An unsound or misleading argument, anything that misleads or deceives; a sophism; sophistry, unsoundness of reasoning or of belief. falla'cious, a.

fallible (făl'ibl) [late L. *fallibilis*, as prec.], a. Liable to err or be mistaken. fallibil'ity, n.

fallow (1) (făl'ō) [A.-S. *fealu*], a. Pale brownish or reddish-yellow.

fallow (2) [A.-S. *fœlging*, rel. to *fealga*, harrows], n. Land ploughed and harrowed but left unsown. a. Ploughed and tilled but not sown; unused.

false (fawls) [A.-S. *fals*, L. *falsus*, deceived], a. Not true; deceptive, misleading; erroneous, wrong; lying, deceiving; deceitful, faithless; sham, spurious. falsehood, n. Untruthfulness; a lie, an untruth, lying; deceitfulness, unfaithfulness; a counterfeit. falseness, n. falsity, n.

falsetto (fawl-set'ō) [It.], n. A pitch of voice higher than the natural register. a. Pertaining to such voice.

falsify (fawl'si-fī), v.t. To give a false or spurious appearance to (a document, statement, etc.); to misrepresent; to counterfeit; to disappoint (expectations). falsifica'tion, n.

falter (fawl'tẽr) [?], v.i. To stumble, waver, be unsteady; to stutter; to hesitate. falteringly, adv.

fame (fām) [L. *fāma*]; n. Public report or rumour; reputation, renown, celebrity. famed, a. Much talked of; celebrated.

familiar (fȧ-mil'yȧr) [as next], a. Well-known, intimate; usual, ordinary, not novel; easily understood; unconstrained, free, unceremonious. n. A close friend; a spirit supposed to attend at call. familiarity (-ȧr'i-ti), n. Use, habitude; close friendship, intimacy; unceremoniousness, esp. towards superiors or inferiors; an unwarranted liberty. familiarize, v.t. To make familiar; to habituate, accustom.

family (făm'i-li) [L. *familia*, from *famulus*, a servant], n. Those that live in the same house, including servants; father and mother and children; those with

other relations; children, as dist. from their parents; those descended from a common ancestor; a race, a group of peoples from a common stock.

famine (făm'in) [L. *famēs*, hunger], n. Great scarcity; hunger, starvation.

famish (făm'ish), v.i. To suffer extreme hunger; to die of hunger.

famous (fā'mŭs) [L. *fama*, fame], a. Renowned, celebrated; first-rate.

fan (1) (făn) [A.-S. *fann*], n. An instrument opening out in a wedge-shape for agitating the air and cooling the face; a winnowing implement or machine; the blade of a propeller; a bird's tail; a rotatory ventilating apparatus. v.t. To agitate the air with a fan; to cool with a fan; to stimulate; to winnow. fan-light, n. A window shaped like an open fan, esp. over a doorway. fantail, n. A variety of domestic pigeon.

fan (2) (făn) [FANATIC], n. An enthusiastic admirer, a devotee. fan mail, n. Letters sent to cinema stars, etc., usu. by enthusiastic adolescents.

fanatic (fȧ-năt'ik) [L. *fānăticus*, from *fānum*, a temple], a. Extravagant in opinions (esp. religious); enthusiastic in the extreme; bigoted. n. A person affected with fanaticism. fanatical, a. fanaticism, n.

fancy (făn'si), n. The faculty or act of forming images, esp. those of a playful or capricious kind; inventive (not creative) imagination; a mental image; a delusion, a baseless impression, a caprice, whim; a personal liking; a fad, hobby. v.t. To picture to oneself; to suppose; to imagine or believe erroneously; to like, take a fancy to; to breed as a hobby or sport. a. Adapted to please the fancy rather than for use; ornamental. fancy dress, n. Masquerade costume. fancy work, n. Ornamental knitting, embroidery, crocheting, etc. fancier, n. One who breeds or sells birds, dogs, rabbits, etc. fanciful, a. Dictated by or arising in the fancy; unreal, imaginary; whimsical.

fandango (făn-dăng'gō) [Sp.], n. A lively Spanish dance for two persons.

fane (fān) [L. *fānum*], n. A temple.

fanfare (făn'fār) [F.], n. A flourish of trumpets.

fang (făng) [A.-S., a seizing], n. A tusk or long pointed tooth.

fantasia (făn-tȧ-zē'ȧ, făn-tȧ'zi-ȧ) [It.], n. (Mus.) A composition in which form is subservient to fancy.

fantasy (făn'tȧ-si) [Gr. *phantazein*, to make visible], n. An extravagant or whimsical fancy or design; the faculty of forming fanciful images; a visionary idea. fantas'tic, a. Fanciful, whimsical, odd, grotesque.

far (fär) [A.-S. *feor*], a. (farther, -est, further, -est) Distant, a long way off; reaching a long way; remote from. adv. At or to a great distance in space, time, or proportion, by a great deal; by a great interval, widely. far-fetched, a. Unnatural, fanciful. Far West, n. That part of the U.S.A. lying to the west of the Mississippi.

farce (fars) [F. *farcer*, L. *farcīre*, to stuff], *n.* A play in which the action is trivial and mirth the sole purpose; an absurd proceeding; pretence, mockery. *v.t.* To stuff, to fill, to puff out; to season. **farcical**, *a.* Droll, comical.

fare (fâr) [A.-S. *faran*], *v.i.* To go, to travel; to get on, to be in any state, to turn out (well or ill); to be entertained, to live as regards food and drink. *n.* The sum paid for conveyance, passage-money; the person or persons conveyed; food provided. **farewell**, *int.* Adieu, good-bye. *n.* A good-bye, an adieu. *a.* valedictory.

farina (fâ-rī'-, -rē'nà) [L. *far*, corn], *n.* Flour or meal; any powder; pollen; starch. **farina'ceous**, *a.*

farm (farm) [A.-F. and O.F. *ferme* (*à ferme*, on lease)], *n.* A tract of land cultivated under one management; a farm-house; a place where children are farmed. *v.t.* To till, cultivate, take (land) on lease for cultivating; to let out (as taxes, offices, etc.) at a fixed sum or rate per cent.; to contract for (as one who engages to feed or lodge children) at so much per head. *v.i.* To be a farmer. **farmstead**, *n.* A farm with the buildings on it. **farmyard**, *n.* The enclosure attached to farm buildings. **farmer**, *n.* **farming**, *n.* The business of cultivating land.

farrago (fâ-rā'gŏ) [L.], *n.* A mixture.

farrier (fâr'i-ér) [L. *ferrārius* (*ferrum*, iron)], *n.* One who shoes horses; a shoeing smith and horse-doctor. **farriery**, *n.*

farrow (fâr'ō) [A.-S. *fearh*, a pig], *n.* A litter of pigs. *v.* To bring forth pigs.

farther (far'thèr), *a.* More distant or remote; additional. *adv.* At or to a greater distance, extent, or degree; in addition, besides. **farthest**, *a.* The most distant. *n.* The greatest distance, the latest, the most. *adv.* At or to the greatest distance.

farthing (far'thing) [A.-S. *fēorthing*], *n.* The fourth part of a penny.

farthingale (far'thing-gāl) [Sp. *verdugado* (*verdugo*, a rod)], *n.* A hooped skirt used to extend the wide gown of the 16th cent.

fascinate (fâs'i-nāt) [L. *fascināre*, to cast a spell], *v.t.* To exercise an irresistible influence over; to captivate, enchant, charm. **fascinating**, *a.* Charming, bewitching. **fascina'tion**, *n.*

fashion (fāsh'ŏn) [L. *factiōnem*, nom. *-tio*, a making], *n.* The make, style, or appearance of anything; mode, manner; prevailing style of dress; custom, usage; the conventional usages of society; genteel society. *v.t.* To give shape and form to; to fit, adapt. **fashionable**, *a.*

fast (1) (fast) [A.-S. *fæst*], *a.* Firmly fixed, tight; faithful, steady; durable, unfading, not washing out; swift, moving quickly; dissipated, rakish. *adv.* Firmly, securely; quickly, in rapid succession; in a dissipated manner.

fast (2) [A.-S. *fæstan*], *v.i.* To abstain from food; to mortify the body thus. *n.* Total or partial abstinence from or deprivation of food, esp. from religious motives; a time set apart for fasting; any holy time or season.

fasten (fasn) [A.-S. *fæstnian*], *v.t.* To fix firmly; to make fast, to secure, as by a bolt, knot, etc. *v.i.* To become fast; to seize, to lay hold (upon). **fastener**, *n.* One who or that which fastens. **fastening**, *n.* The act of making secure; that which makes fast or secure, as a bolt, bar.

fastidious (fâs-tid'i-ùs) [L. *fastidium*, loathing], *a.* Difficult to please; squeamish.

fastness (fast'nes), *n.* Quality or state of being fast or secure; a fortress.

fat (fât) [A.-S. *fǣt*], *a.* Plump, corpulent, full-fed; (of animals) fed up for killing; fertile, fruitful. *n.* An animal substance of a more or less oily character. **fatling**, *n.* A fattened animal. **fatness** *n.* **fatten**, *v.t.* To make fat, to feed for the table; to fertilize. *v.i.* To become fat, to gain flesh. **fattish**, *a.* Somewhat fat. **fatty**, *a.*

fatal (fā'tàl) [L. *fatālis*], *a.* Proceeding from or decreed by fate; inevitable; fraught with heavy consequences, decisive; causing death (to); deadly, mortal. **fatalism**, *n.* The doctrine that all events are ordered by inevitable necessity; submission to all that happens as the work of fate. **fatalist**, *n.* One who believes this. **fatal'ity**, *n.* A fixed and unalterable course of things; supremacy of fate; a fatal occurrence; calamity.

fate (fāt) [L. *fātum*], *n.* The power predetermining the course of events; destiny, lot; one's ultimate condition; what is destined; death, destruction; (*pl.*) the three Greek goddesses supposed to preside over the birth, life, and fortunes of men. **fated**, *a.* Decreed by fate; doomed. **fateful**, *a.* Fraught with fate.

father (fa'thèr) [A.-S. *fæder*], *n.* A male parent; a male ancestor; an originator, an early leader, esp. of the primitive Church; one who exercises paternal care; the senior member of any profession or body; the First Person of the Trinity; a priest, a confessor, religious teacher, etc.; (*pl.*) elders, senators, the leading men (of a city, etc.). *v.t.* To beget; to be or act as father of; to originate; to adopt or assume as one's own; to accept responsibility for; to ascribe to anyone as his. **father-in-law**, *n.* The father of one's husband or wife. **fatherhood**, *n.* The state of being a father; the character or authority of a father. **fatherland**, *n.* One's native country. **fatherless**, *a.* Destitute of a living father; without any known author. **fatherly**, *a.* Like a father; kind, tender.

fathom (fāth'ŏm) [A.-S. *fæthm*], *n.* A measure of length, 6 ft. *v.t.* To ascertain the depth of; to get to the bottom of, to comprehend. **fathomless**, *a.* Not to be fathomed.

fatigue (fâ-tēg') [L. *fatigāre*], *n.* Weariness, exhaustion from bodily or mental exertion; toil; labour not of a military nature performed by soldiers. *v.t.* To tire; to exhaust the bodily or mental strength of; to harass, importune.

fatuous (fǎt'ū-ùs) [L. *fatuus*], *a.* Stupid, foolish; meaningless, silly. **fatu'ity**, *n.*

faucet (faw'sĕt) [F. *fausset*], *n.* A tap, esp. for barrels.

fault (fawlt) [M.E. and O.F. *faute*], *n.* Defect, blemish; an error, failing, blunder. **faultless,** *a.* faulty, *a.* **faultily,** *adv.*

fauna (faw'na) [L., a Roman goddess], *n.* The animals peculiar to a certain region or epoch.

fauteuil (fō-tu-i) [F.], *n.* An upholstered arm-chair; a stall in a theatre.

favour (fā'vòr) [L. *favēre*, to show goodwill], *n.* Kindness, goodwill; approval; partiality, preference; a kind or indulgent act; aid, support, facility; leave, consent; a token of love or affection; a knot of ribbons. *v.t.* To behave towards with kindness; to support, facilitate, promote; to oblige (with); to be fortunate for; to approve, show partiality to; to resemble in features. **favourable,** *a.* Friendly, well-disposed; propitious; approving, commending, tending to promote or encourage; advantageous. **favourably,** *adv.*

favourite (fā-vòr-ĭt), *n.* A person or thing regarded with special affection or partiality; one unduly favoured; a competitor considered to have the best chance. *a.* Regarded with special favour. **favouritism,** *n.*

fawn (1) (fawn) [O.F. *fan*, *faon*], *n.* A young deer; a buck or doe in its first year; the colour of a young deer. *a.* Yellowish-brown. *v.* To bring forth a fawn.

fawn (2) (fawn) [A.-S. *fahnian*, as FAIN], *v.i.* To show affection by cringing (of dogs, etc.); to court in a servile manner.

fay (fā) [L. *fata*], *n.* A fairy.

fealty (fē'ăl-ti), *n.* Fidelity to a superior; loyalty, allegiance.

fear (fēr) [A.-S. *fǣr*, danger], *n.* A painful apprehension of danger or evil; a state of alarm; anxiety, solicitude; awe, reverence. *v.t.* To be afraid of, to dread; to shrink from; to reverence, venerate; to suspect. *v.i.* To be afraid; to feel anxiety; to mistrust. **fearful,** *a.* Timid, apprehensive, afraid (lest); terrible, awful; unusual, annoying. **fearfully,** *adv.* **fearless,** *a.* Free from fear; courageous, undaunted. **fearlessly,** *adv.* **fearlessness,** *n.* **fearsome,** *a.* Fearful, terrible, alarming.

feasible (fē'zibl) [O.F. *faisable*, L. *facere*, to do], *a.* That may or can be done; practicable; plausible. **feasibil'ity,** *n.*

feast (fēst) [L. *festus*, joyful], *n.* A sumptuous meal or entertainment, esp. a public banquet; a celebration of some great event or personage, esp. a religious anniversary; anything giving great enjoyment. *v.t.* To entertain sumptuously; to please greatly, as with something delicious. *v.i.* To feed sumptuously.

feat (fēt) [O.F. *fait*], *n.* A notable act; an exploit, achievement.

feather (feth'ér) [A.-S. *fether*], *n.* A plume or quill, a number of which form the covering of a bird; a hairy fringe on a dog's tail or legs; a tongue on the edge of a board fitting into a groove; (*Rowing*) the act of feathering. *v.t.* To dress, cover, or adorn with feathers. *v.i.* (*Rowing*) To turn the oar and carry through the air

edgeways; (of hounds) to make a quivering movement with the tail when hunting.

feature (fē'chúr) [O.F. *faiture*], *n.* A part of the face, esp. such as gives individual expression (*usu. in pl.*); a distinctive part of anything, a salient point, striking incident. *v.t.* (*colloq.*) To portray; to present on a cinematograph film. **featured,** *a.* Having a certain cast of face; presented in a newspaper, on a film, etc.

febrifuge (feb'ri-fūj) [L. *febris*, fever, *fugāre*, to drive away], *n.* A medicine that dispels or mitigates fever.

febrile (fē'bril), *a.* Pertaining to fever.

February (feb'rū-à-ri) [L. *februa*, a purification festival], *n.* The second month of the year.

feckless (fek'lĕs) [?], *a.* Puny, futile.

feculent (fek'ū-lĕnt) [L. *fæculentus*], *a.* Full of dregs or sediment.

fecund (fē'kŭnd) [L. *fēcundus*], *a.* Fruitful, prolific. **fe'cundate,** *v.t.* To make fruitful; to impregnate. **fecunda'tion,** *n.* **fecun'dity,** *n.*

federal (fed'ér-ăl) [F. *fédéral*, L. *fœdus -eris*, a treaty], *a.* Pertaining to a treaty, league, or contract; relating to a polity formed by the union of several states, or to such a Government as dist. from the separate states. **federalism,** *n.*

federate (fed'ér-āt), *v.t.* To organize as a federal group of states; to bring together for a common object. *v.i.* To combine and form a federal group; to league together for a common object. *a.* United under a federal government; leagued together. **federa'tion,** *n.*

fee (fē) [A.-F. O.F. *fé*], *n.* Remuneration for the execution of official functions or performance of professional service. *v.t.* To pay a fee to; to engage for a fee. **fee-simple,** *n.* An estate held in one's own right, without limitation to any particular class of heirs.

feeble (fēbl) [O.F. *foible*], *a.* Weak, infirm, debilitated; lacking in force, vigour, or power; pointless, insipid; faint.

feed (fēd) [A.-S. *fēdan*], *v.t.* To give food to; to supply with material, or with that which is necessary to existence, continuance, or development; to serve as nourishment for; to fatten; to gratify. *v.i.* To take food; to eat; to subsist (on or upon). *n.* Fodder, pasturage; the act of feeding or giving food; amount of provender given to cattle, etc., at a time; a feast. **feeder,** *n.* One who fattens cattle; one who eats, esp. in a certain manner; a child's bib; a tributary stream; canal, etc.

feel (fēl) [A.-S. *fēlan*], *v.t.* To perceive by the touch; to have the sense of touch; to have a sensation of, or be conscious of; to experience, undergo, be affected by; to touch, try, or find out by handling or groping. *v.i.* To have perception by the touch; to be conscious of (as cold, wet, hungry, tiredness). *n.* The sense of touch; characteristic sensation of something; perception, esp. of an emotional kind. **feeler,** *n.* Any device to ascertain the designs, wishes, or opinions of others; an organ of touch in invertebrates. **feel-**

ing, a. Perceiving by the touch; easily affected, sensitive, of great sensibility. n. The sense of touch; the sensation produced by touching; a mental impression, consciousness; emotion, sensitiveness; (pl.) susceptibilities, sympathies. feelingly, adv.

feign (fān) [O.F. feindre, L. fingere], v.t. To invent; to pretend, simulate. v.i. To dissimulate. feignedly, adv.

feint (fānt) [F. feinte, as prec.], n. A pretence of aiming at one point while another is the real object; a pretence. v.i. To make a feint or pretended attack.

feldspar (feld´spar) [G. feld, field, spath, spar], n. (Min.) A crystalline mineral.

felicitate (fē-lis´i-tāt) [L. fēlicitāre], v.t. To congratulate. felicita´tion, n. Congratulation. felicitous, a. Happy, prosperous; apt, well-expressed; charming in manner, etc. felicity, n. Happiness; appropriateness; a happy expression.

feline (fē-līn) [L. fēles, a cat], a. Pertaining to cats, or the cat tribe; catlike; sly.

fell (1) (fel) [A.-S. fiellan], v.t. To knock down, bring to the ground.

fell (2) [A.-S. fel, skin], n. The hide of an animal, esp. if covered with hair; a fleece.

fell (3) [Icel. fjall], n. A rocky hill.

fell (4) (O.F. fel), a. Cruel, savage; terrible, dire.

fellah (fel´à) [Arab. fellāh], n. (pl. fallaheen) An Egyptian agricultural labourer.

felloe (fel´i, -ō) [A.-S. felg], n. One of the curved segments forming the rim of a wheel; the whole rim.

fellow (fel´ō) [Icel. fēlagi], n. An associate, partner; one of the same kind or species; an equal, a peer, compeer; one of a pair; a member of an incorporated society; the holder of a fellowship; a man, a boy; a person of little estimation; (in comb.) one associated with oneself. v.t. To match, pair with, suit. fellowship, n. Companionship, close intercourse, cordiality of feeling, community of interest; a brotherhood, a corporation; the dignity of fellow in a college or learned society; an endowment for maintaining one engaged in research. fellow traveller, n. (Pol.) One who sympathizes with a political party but refrains from joining it.

felo-de-se (fel´ō-dē-sē) [A.-L., felon upon himself], n. (pl. felos) A suicide.

felon (fel´ón) [late L. fellōnem], n. One who has committed a felony. a. Cruel, malicious; wicked, murderous. felo´nious, a. felony, n. An offence of a heinous character.

felt (felt) [A.-S.], n. A kind of cloth made of wool, etc., rolled, beaten and pressed, with lees or size; a piece of this.

female (fē´māl) [L. fēmella, dim. of fēmina, woman], a. Denoting the sex which brings forth young or lays eggs; pertaining to or characteristic of woman. n. A woman or girl; a she-animal.

feminine (fem´i-nin), a. Pertaining to, or characteristic of the female sex; womanly; effeminate; (Gram.) belonging to the gender denoting females. femin´ity, femin´ity, n. The qualities or manners becoming a woman. fem´in-

ism, n. Advocacy of the claims of women, esp. to equality with men.

femur (fē´mûr) [L. femur, the thigh], n. (pl. femora) The thigh-bone. femoral (fem´ór-àl), a. Pertaining to the thigh.

fen (fen) [A.-S. fenn], n. Low, flat, and marshy land; a marsh, bog.

fence (fens), n. A structure enclosing a piece of ground, or to keep cattle from straying, as a wall, hedge, paling, etc.; a guardplate, etc., in machinery; the art of fencing or sword-play; skill in debate; a purchaser or receiver of stolen goods. v.t. To defend, shield, or protect; to enclose with a fence; to parry. v.i. To practise the art of sword-play; to defend oneself or repel attack skilfully; to argue adroitly, to equivocate; to deal in stolen goods. to sit on the fence: To remain neutral in respect to opposing policies. fenced, a. fencer, n. fencing, n. Fences, a railing or railings; materials for fences; the act or art of using a sword; a protection round machinery; equivocation, parrying of argument.

fencible (fen´sibl), n. A soldier enlisted only for home defence.

fend (fend), v.t. To keep off, ward off. v.i. To provide or to get a living (for).

fender (fen´dèr), n. A fitting round a hearth to confine the ashes; a rope or timber buffer to protect the side of a vessel from injury by collision.

Fenian (fē´ni-àn) [O.Ir. Fēne, a name of the ancient Irish], n. A member of an Irish secret society (formed 1858), whose object was to establish an independent republic in Ireland. a. Pertaining to this society.

fennel (fen´èl) [A.-S. finol], n. A fragrant umbelliferous plant with yellow flowers.

feoff (fef) [O.F. feoffer, from fief, FEE], v.t. (Law) To grant possession. n. A fief.

feral (fēr´àl) [L.], a. Wild, savage.

ferment (fēr´mènt) [L. fermentum, fervēre, to boil], n. Any substance which causes fermentation; leaven; internal motion of the constituent parts of a fluid; tumult, agitation. v.t. (fēr-ment´) To excite fermentation in; to rouse, agitate, excite. v.i. To be in a state of fermentation; to be agitated, as by violent emotions. fermenta´tion, n. A process excited in certain substances by living organisms or chemical agents, with evolution of heat, effervescence, and chemical decomposition; commotion, agitation, excitement.

fern (fērn) [A.-S. fearn], n. A plant with fronds, or leaves, which are often divided in a graceful, feathery form. fernery, n. A place where ferns are cultivated. ferny, a.

ferocious (fē-rō´shûs) [L. ferox, ferus, wild], a. Fierce, cruel, barbarous. ferociously, adv. ferocity (fē-ros´i-ti), n. State or quality of being ferocious.

-ferous, suf. Bearing, producing, as auriferous, fossiliferous.

ferret (fer´èt) [O.F. furet, L. fûr, robber], n. A partially-tamed variety of polecat used for ratting and rabbiting. v.t. To drive out of a hole, clear (ground), hunt, or take with ferrets. v.i. To hunt rabbits, etc., with a ferret; to search or rummage about (for).

ferri- [L. *ferrum*, iron], *comb. form.* Denoting a compound of iron. **ferrif'erous,** *a.* Yielding iron.

ferro- [as prec.], *comb. form.* Denoting a substance containing iron; denoting a compound of iron. **ferro-concrete,** *n.* Concrete strengthened by incorporating bars, etc., of iron.

fer'rous, *a.* Pertaining to iron.

ferrule (fer'ŭl) [L. *viriola,* dim. of *viriæ,* bracelets], *n.* A metallic ring or cap on a walking-stick, etc.

ferry (fer'i) [A.-S. *ferian*], *v.t.* To transport over a river or other narrow water, in a boat, etc. *n.* The passage where a ferry-boat plies; the provision of such transport; the right of ferrying; a boat used at a ferry. **ferryman,** *n.*

fertile (fĕr'til, -til) [L. *fertilis*], *a.* Productive, fruitful; having abundant resources; quick, ready. **fertil'ity,** *n.* **fer'tilize,** *v.t.* To make fertile or productive; to make rich (as soil). **fertilizer,** *n.* A manure.

ferule (fer'ŭl) [L. *ferula*, a rod], *n.* A rod or cane used to punish children in school.

fervent (fĕr'vĕnt) [L. *fervens*, boiling], *a.* Glowing; ardent, zealous, vehement. **fervently,** *adv.* **fervency,** *n.*

fervid (fĕr'vid), *a.* Burning, fervent; impassioned. **fer'vour,** *n.* Heat; ardour, intensity of feeling; zeal.

festal (fes'tal), *a.* Pertaining to a feast or holiday; festive, joyous.

fester (fes'tĕr) [O.F. *festre*], *v.t.* To suppurate; to form purulent matter; to rankle; to become corrupted or rotten. *v.t.* To cause to fester or rankle.

festival (fes'ti-val), *a.* Pertaining to a feast; festal. *n.* A festal day or time, a joyous celebration.

festive (fes'tiv) [L. *festivus*], *a.* Of or befitting a feast or festival; joyous, mirthful. **festiv'ity,** *n.* A festival, a joyous celebration or entertainment; gaiety, mirth; *(pl.)* merry-making.

festoon (fĕs-toon') [It. *festone*], *n.* A suspended chain of flowers, foliage, etc., forming a curve or curves.

fetch (fech) [A.-S. *feccan*], *v.t.* To go for and bring; to cause to come; to draw forth, to heave (as a sigh.); to sell for (a price); to bring to any state, etc.; to reach, arrive at, accomplish; to delight, charm; to strike. *n.* A stratagem, a trick, a dodge; a deep sigh. **fetching,** *a.* Fascinating, charming, taking.

fête (fāt) [F.], *n.* A festival.

fetid (fē'tid, fet'id) [L. *fētēre*, to stink], *a.* Having an offensive smell; stinking.

fetish (fē'tish) [Port. *feitico,* sorcery, L. *factitius,* artificial], *n.* Any material object supposed to be the vehicle or instrument of a supernatural being, the possession of which gives power over that being; *(fig.)* an object of devotion, an idol.

fetlock (fet'lok) [?], *n.* A tuft of hair behind the pastern joint of a horse; the joint.

fetter (fet'ĕr) [A.-S. *fetor*], *n.* A chain for the feet, a shackle; anything which restrains or confines. *v.t.* To put fetters upon; to restrain, hamper, impede.

fettle (fetl) [?], *v.t.* To clean or put right; to work with zeal. *v.i.* To fuss about.
n. Condition, order, trim.

feu (fū) [var. of FEE], *n.* In Scotland, a perpetual lease at a fixed rent; the land, houses, etc., so held.

feud (1) (fūd) [O.H.G. *fēhida*], *n.* Hostility between two tribes or families as revenge; enmity, animosity.

feud (2), *n.* A fief; lands, etc., held in fee. **feudal** (fū'dal), *a.* Pertaining to a feud or fief; according to or resembling the feudal system of the Middle Ages, by which the ownership of land inhered in the lord, possession or tenancy being granted to the vassal in return for military service. **feudalism,** *n.*

feuilleton (fu-yĕ-ton) [F.], *n.* A light article or serial story in a newspaper.

fever (fē'vĕr) [A.-S. *fēfor*], *n.* A disease characterized by high temperature, quickened pulse, nervous and muscular prostration, and destruction of tissues; a state of nervous excitement; agitation. **feverish,** *a.*

few (fū) [A.-S. *fēawe*], *a.* Not many; small or restricted in number. *n.* A small number (of). **fewness,** *n.*

fez (fez) [town in Morocco], *n.* A close-fitting, brimless red cap with a tassel.

fiancé (fē-an-sā) [F., betrothed], *n.* (*fem.* **-cée**) One who is betrothed.

fiasco (fi-ás'kō) [It., a flask], *n.* (*pl.* **-os**) A failure; an ignominious sequel.

fiat (fī'át) [L., let it be done], *n.* An order, esp. by a judge; a command, decree.

fib (fib) [?], *n.* A harmless or venial lie. *v.i.* To tell fibs.

fibre (fī'bĕr) [F.], *n.* A slender filament; a thread or filament of which the tissues of animals and plants are constituted; forming the raw material in textile manufactures. **fibrous,** *a.*

fibula (fib'ŭ-lá) [L., a brooch], *n.* The outer and smaller bone of the leg.

fichu (fish'u) [F. *ficher,* to put on], *n.* A light covering worn by women on the neck and shoulders.

fickle (fikl) [A.-S. *ficol*], *a.* Changeable, inconstant. **fickleness,** *n.*

fiction (fik'shŭn) [L. *fictio*], *n.* That which is feigned, imagined, or invented; a story, romance, novel. **fictional,** *a.* **fictionist,** *n.* A novelist. **fictitious,** (-tish'ús), *a.* Feigned, counterfeit, false.

fid (fid) [?], *n.* A bar of wood or iron to support a top-mast; a wooden pin, etc.

fiddle (fidl) [A.-S. *fithele*], *n.* A violin (*in contempt or familiarly*); a frame to keep things from rolling off the table in bad weather at sea. *v.i.* To play upon a fiddle; to trifle; to fidget the hands about. *v.t.* To play on a fiddle; to worry, to fritter away; to swindle. **fiddlededee,** *int.* and *n.* Nonsense. **fiddle-faddle,** *n.* Trifling talk; nonsense. **fiddle-head,** *n.* Ornamental carving at the bows of a ship. **fiddle-stick,** *n.* A fiddle-bow; *(pl. fig.)* rubbish, something absurd. *int.* (*pl.*) Fiddlededee. **fiddler,** *n.* One who plays the fiddle; one who fusses about trifles.

fidelity (fi-del'i-ti) [L. *fidēlitās*], *n.* Loyal observance of duty; loyalty, faithfulness; veracity, reliability.

fidget (fĭj'ĕt) [?], *n.* A state of nervous restlessness; one who worries or makes others uncomfortable. *v.i.* To move about restlessly; to worry, be uneasy. **fidgety**, *a.*

fiduciary (fĭ-dū'shár-ĭ) [L. *fīdūciālis*], *a.* Pertaining to or of the nature of a trust or a trusteeship; held in trust. *n.* A trustee.

fie (fī) [M.E. and O.F. *fi*, L. *fī*], *int.* Indicating contempt, disgust, or impatience.

fief (fēf) [O.F.], *n.* An estate held of a superior under feudal tenure.

field (fēld) [A.-S. *feld*], *n.* A piece of land, esp. one enclosed for tillage or pasture; a region yielding some natural product abundantly (as an oil- or coal-field); the place where a battle is fought; the battle itself; cricket or football players taken collectively; all the competitors in a race, or all except the favourite, the participants in a hunt; a wide expanse, as of sea or sky; the space visible in an optical instrument at one view; (*Her.*) the surface of a shield. *v.t.* (*Cricket, etc.*) To stop and return the ball; to act as fielder; to back the field against the favourite. **field-day**, *n.* A day on which troops are exercised in field evolutions; a day of unusual importance. **field-glass**, *n.* A binocular telescope in compact form. **field-marshal**, *n.* A military officer of the highest rank. **field-officer**, *n.* An officer above a captain, but below a general. **field-piece**, *n.* A light piece of artillery for service in the field. **field-work**, *n.* The outdoor operations necessary in surveying, etc., (*pl.*) temporary fortifications. **fielder**, **fieldsman**, *n.* One who fields at cricket, etc.

fieldfare (fēld'fār) [A.-S. *feldefare*], *n.* A species of thrush.

fiend (fēnd) [A.-S. *fēond*, from *fēogan*, to hate], *n.* A devil, an infernal being; a person of diabolical wickedness or cruelty. **fiendish**, *a.* **fiendishly**, *adv.*

fierce (fērs) [O.F. *fers*, L. *ferus*, wild], *a.* Savage, furiously combative; ardent, eager, raging, impetuous. **fierceness**, *n.*

fiery (fīr'ĭ), *a.* Consisting of fire or flaming with fire; like fire; ardent, eager, inflamed; hot-tempered, irascible, untamed. **fierily**, *adv.*

fife (fīf) [F. *fifre* or G. *pfeife*, pipe], *n.* A small flute-like pipe. **fifer**, *n.*

fifteen (fif'tēn, tēn') [A.-S. *fīftyne*], *a.* One more than fourteen. *n.* The symbol 15 or **xv.**; a set of fifteen players, a Rugby football team.

fifth (fifth) [A.-S. *fīfta*], *a.* Next in order to the fourth. *n.* One of five equal parts; a diatonic interval of five notes, equal to three tones and a semitone. **fifth column**, *n.* Traitors in a country who give aid to the enemy. **fifthly**, *adv.* In the fifth place.

fifty (fif'ti) [A.-S. *fīftig*], *a.* Five times ten; (*colloq.*) a great many. *n.* The symbol representing this, viz. 50, **l.**, or **L**. **fifty-fifty**, equal shares.

fig (1) (fig) [L. *ficus*], *n.* A fleshy fruit; the tree bearing this.

fig (2) [G. *fegen*], *v.t.* To dress, rig (up or out). *n.* Dress, outfit.

fight (fīt) [A.-S. *feohtan*], *v.i.* To contend in battle or in single combat; to strive for victory; to oppose, offer resistance. *v.t.* To contend with, struggle against; to carry on or wage (a contest, battle, etc.). *n.* A struggle between individuals or armies. **fighter**, *n.*

figment (fig'mént) [L. *figmentum*], *n.* A fiction, something existing only in the imagination.

figurative (fig'ûr-à-tiv), *a.* Representation by figure or type; emblematic, symbolic; full of figures of speech; flowery; pictorial. **figuratively**, *adv.*

figure (fig'ûr, -ûr) [F., from L. *figūra*, from *fig-*, stem of *fingere*, as FEIGN], *n.* External form or shape; bodily shape; the representation of any form, as by carving, modelling, painting, etc.; a statue, image; a diagram; an emblem, type, simile; an idea; a personage, character; the impression that a person makes; a symbol representing a number, esp. an Arabic numeral; a movement or division in a set dance; words deflected from their literal or ordinary sense, metaphor, ellipsis, hyperbole. *v.t.* To form an image or likeness of; to represent, picture, imagine; to symbolize; to cover, or ornament with figures; to work out in figures; to mark with numbers or prices; to express by a metaphor. *v.i.* To cipher; to appear, be conspicuous. **figure-head**, *n.* The ornamental carving on the prow of a ship; a nominal leader, one without real authority. **figured**, *a.*

filament (fĭl'á-mént) [L. *fīlāre*, to spin], *n.* A slender, thread-like process, esp. in animal and vegetable tissues; the thread in an incandescent electric lamp.

filbert (fĭl'bèrt) [F. *noix de filbert*, from St. *Philibert*], *n.* The nut of the cultivated hazel.

filch (filch) [?], *v.t.* To steal, pilfer.

file (1) (fīl) [L. *fīlum*, a thread], *n.* A device on or in which documents, etc., are kept in order; the collection so arranged; a row of soldiers, persons, or things ranged one behind the other; (*Chess*) a line of squares from player to player. *v.t.* To place in or on a file; to place on the records. *v.i.* To march in a file or line, as soldiers. **rank and file**: The general body as distinguished from the leaders; privates and corporals who take their places in the ranks.

file (2) [A.-S. *fēol*], *n.* A steel instrument with ridged surface, used for cutting and smoothing metals, etc. *v.t.* To smooth or polish; to cut (the surface) away with a file.

filial (fĭl'ĭ-ál) [L. *filius*, son], *a.* Pertaining to a son or daughter; befitting a child in relation to parents.

filibuster (fĭl'ĭ-bŭs-tèr) [Dut. *vrijbuiter*, a freebooter], *n.* An adventurer in quest of plunder, a freebooter.

filigree (fĭl'ĭ-grē) [F. *filigrane*, L. *fīlum*, a thread, *grānum*, grain], *n.* Ornamental tracery or open-work in fine gold or silver wire; anything delicate and fantastic.

filings (fī'lĭngz), *n.pl.* The fine particles cut or rubbed off with a file.

fill (fil) [A.-S. *fyllan*], *v.t.* To make full;

to occupy the whole of, to pervade; to appoint one to discharge the duties of; to discharge the duties of; to distend (as sails). *v.i.* To become or grow full; to be distended; to be satisfied. *n.* As much as will satisfy; a full supply. **filler,** *n.*

filling, *a.* Satisfying. *n.* Anything serving to fill up; substances used to fill holes, cavities, or defects.

fillet (fil'ĕt) [M.E. and O.F. *filet,* dim. of *fil,* L. *filum,* a thread], *n.* A band (metal, string, or ribbon) for binding the hair or worn on the head; a bandage; a fleshy portion of meat, esp. of the thigh of veal; meat or fish removed from the bone; a raised rim or moulding; (*pl.*) the loins of a horse. *v.t.* To bind or adorn with a fillet; to cut meat or fish into fillets.

fillip (fil'ip), *v.t.* To strike with the nail of the finger by a sudden jerk from under the thumb; to incite, encourage. *n.* A sharp blow with the finger sprung from under the thumb; an incentive; a trifle.

filly (fil'i), *n.* A female foal; a young, lively girl.

film (film) [A.-S. *filmen,* membrane], *n.* A thin skin or coating; a thin strip of celluloid, etc., covered with a sensitized material for photography; a complete cinematograph picture. *v.t.* To cover with a film; to record on a cinematographic film. **filminess,** *n.*

filter (fil'tĕr) [O.F. *filtre*], *n.* An apparatus for straining or purifying liquids; the porous material through which liquids are passed. *v.t.* To strain, purify, by passing through a filter. *v.i.* To pass through a filter; to percolate.

filth (filth) [A.-S. *fylth*], *n.* Foulness, corruption, pollution; anything that defiles morally; obscenity. **filthy,** *a.* **filthiness,** *n.*

filtrate (fil'trāt), *v.t.* and *i.* To filter. **filtra'tion,** *n.*

fin (fin) [A.-S. *finn*], *n.* The organ by which fishes and cetaceans propel and steer themselves; the flipper of a seal, whale, etc. **finny,** *a.*

final (fī'nál) [L. *finis,* the end], *a.* Pertaining to the end; last; conclusive, decisive. *n.* The deciding heat of an athletic contest; the last of a series of examinations. **final'ity,** *n.* State or quality of being final; the end of everything. **finally,** *adv.*

finale (fi-na'li), *n.* The last part, etc., the close.

finance (fi-nåns') [late L. *financia,* from *finäre,* to pay a fine], *n.* The science or system of management of revenue and expenditure, esp. public; (*pl.*) monetary affairs, the income of a state, firm, or individual. *v.t.* To provide with capital. *v.i.* To manage financial operations. **financial,** *a.* **financier,** *n.*

finch (finch) [A.-S. *finc*], *n.* A name for various small birds.

find (find) [A.-S. *findan*], *v.t.* (*past and p.p.* found) To chance on, meet with, come across; to discover by search, study, experience, etc.; to perceive, recognize; to supply, provide, support; (*Law*) to decide, determine. *n.* The discovery of anything valuable; the thing so found; the finding of a fox. **findable,** *a.* **finder,**

n. One who finds; an inventor; a small telescope fixed to and parallel to the axis of a larger one, for finding objects; a similar contrivance attached to a microscope or camera. **finding,** *n.*

fine (1) (fin) [L. *finis,* end], *n.* A money penalty for an offence; a fee paid by an incoming tenant. *v.t.* To impose a pecuniary penalty upon; to punish by fine. **in fine:** In conclusion, in short, finally; to sum up. **finable,** *a.* Deserving or liable to a fine.

fine (2) (fin) [late L. *finus*], *a.* Excellent in quality or appearance; refined, pure; delicate, nice, dainty (of taste, etc., also of differences, etc.); in small grains or particles; slender, tenuous; keen, sharp; of delicate texture; finished, accomplished, beautiful, showy, smart; free from clouds or rain, sunshiny; euphemistic. *v.t.* To refine, purify; to make finer, to sharpen, taper. *v.i.* To become clarified; to taper, dwindle (away). **fineness,** *n.* **finery,** *n.* Fine clothes, showy decorations.

finesse (fi-nes'), *n.* Artifice, stratagem; a subtle contrivance to gain an end. *v.i.* To use artifice to gain an end.

finger (fing'gĕr) [A.-S.], *n.* One of the five members of the hand; one of the four longer digits as dist. from the thumb; anything resembling or serving the purpose of a finger; an index, catch, guide. *v.t.* To touch with or turn about in the fingers; to meddle with. **finger-board,** *n.* The board at the neck of a stringed instrument; a key-board. **finger-bowl,** *n.* A bowl in which to rinse the fingers after dessert. **finger-post,** *n.* A sign-post. **finger-print,** *n.* An impression of the whorls of lines on fingers, used for identifying criminals. **finger-stall,** *n.* A cover for protecting a finger. **fingered,** *a.* Having fingers, or a certain kind of fingers (as *light-fingered*). **fingering,** *n.* Act of touching with the fingers; (*Mus.*) the management of the fingers in playing an instrument; marks to indicate this.

finial (fin'i-ál) [FINAL], *n.* A terminal ornament surmounting the apex of a gable, etc.

finical (fin'i-kál) [?], *a.* Affecting great precision, or delicacy; over-nice, fastidious. **finicking, finicky,** *a.* Finical.

finis (fī'nis) [L.], *n.* The end, finish.

finish (fin'ish) [L. *finire,* to end], *v.t.* To bring to an end; to complete; to arrive at the end of. *v.i.* To come to the end, cease, expire. *n.* The act of finishing; the final stage, the end of a race; the last touches; the final stage of any work. **finisher,** *n.* Workman or machine that performs the final operation in manufacture.

finite (fī'nit) [L. *finitus,* finished], *a.* Having limits or bounds, not infinite; (*Gram.*) limited by number and person, not infinitive as the indicative, subjunctive, imperative.

Finn (fin) [A.-S. *Finnas,* pl.], *n.* A native of Finland. **Finnish,** *a.*

fiord (fyôrd) [Norw.], *n.* A long, narrow inlet of the sea, bounded by high cliffs.

fir (fĕr) [M.E. *firre,* prob. from Scand.], *n.*

A coniferous timber tree; its wood. **fir-cone,** *n.* The cone-shaped fruit of the fir. **fir-needle,** *n.* The spine-like leaf of the fir.

fire (1) (fīr) [A.-S. *fȳr*], *n.* The production of heat and light by combustion; combustion, flame, incandescence; fuel burning, as in a grate, etc.; a conflagration; the discharge of fire-arms; ardent emotion, liveliness of imagination, poetic inspiration. **fire-alarm,** *n.* An apparatus for communicating warning of a fire. **fire-arm,** *n.* A weapon that projects a missile by explosive force, esp. a rifle or pistol. **fire-box,** *n.* The chamber in which the fuel is burned in a locomotive, etc. **fire-brand,** *n.* A piece of wood kindled or on fire; (*fig.*) an incendiary. **fire-brick,** *n.* A brick capable of withstanding intense heat. **fire-brigade,** *n.* An organized body of men for the extinction of fires. **fire-clay,** *n.* A kind of clay capable of standing intense heat. **fire-damp,** *n.* The explosive carburetted hydrogen which accumulates in coal-mines. **fire-engine,** *n.* A machine for throwing water to extinguish fires. **fire-escape,** *n.* An apparatus for enabling persons to escape from buildings that are on fire. **fire-fly,** *n.* A small luminous winged insect. **fire-irons,** *n.pl.* The implements for tending a fire—poker, tongs, and shovel. **fireman,** *n.* One employed to extinguish or tend fires; a member of a fire-brigade; a stoker. **fire-place,** *n.* A grate; a hearth. **fire-plug,** *n.* A hydrant for connecting a fire-hose with a water-main. **fire-proof,** *a.* Proof against fire; incombustible. **fire-ship,** *n.* A vessel freighted with combustibles and explosives, sent among an enemy's ships in order to set them on fire. **fireside,** *n.* The space around a fire-place, the hearth; home life. *a.* Home, domestic. **firewood,** *n.* Wood for burning; fuel. **firework,** *n.* A preparation of combustibles and explosives for producing a brilliant display, signalling, incendiary purposes, or in war.

fire (2) (fīr), *v.t.* To set on fire, kindle, ignite. *v.i.* To take fire; to discharge fire-arms; to shoot (at) with fire-arms. **firing,** *n.* The act of discharging fire-arms, or of cauterizing; the application of a cautery to a horse; fuel. **firing-line,** *n.* A line of troops engaging the enemy with fire-arms. **firing-party,** *n.* A detachment told off to fire over a grave, or to shoot a condemned man.

firkin (fĕr′kin), *n.* A fourth of a barrel, or nine gallons; a small cask used for butter, etc.

firm (1) (fĕrm) [O.F. *ferme*, L. *firmus*], *a.* Fixed, stable; solid, unyielding. **firmness,** *n.*

firm (2) (fĕrm) [L. *firmāre*, to confirm], *n.* A partnership or association for carrying on a business.

firmament (fĕr′mȧ-mĕnt) [L. *firmāmentum*], *n.* The sky regarded as a solid expanse. **firmamental** (-men′tȧl), *a.*

first (fĕrst) [A.-S. *fyrst*], *a.* Foremost in order, time, place, rank, etc.; earliest in occurrence. *adv.* Before all others in order, etc.; before some time, act, or event; rather, in preference, for the first time. *n.* That which or the person who comes first; the beginning; (*pl.*) the best quality of a commodity (such as flour); (*Mus.*) the upper part in a duet, etc. **first-born,** *a.* Eldest. *n.* The first in order of birth. **first-class,** *a.* First-rate; of the highest quality or degree. *n.* The highest division in an examination list; the best class of railway carriage or other accommodation. **first-hand,** *a.* Obtained directly from the source; direct. **first-rate,** *a.* Of the highest class or quality. *adv.* Excellently, very well. **firstling,** *n.* The first-born, the first-born in a season. **firstly,** *adv.*

firth (fĕrth) [Sc.], *n.* An estuary.

fiscal (fis′kȧl) [L. *fiscus*, a basket, purse], *a.* Pertaining to the public revenue or exchequer, financial. *n.* A public functionary with legal or financial duties.

fish (fish) [A.-S. *fisc*, L. *piscis*], *n.* (*pl.* **fish, -es**). An aquatic, oviparous, cold-blooded vertebrate, having permanent gills, usually covered with scales, and progressing by means of fins; the flesh of fish used as food. *v.i.* To try to catch fish; to seek to learn or obtain anything by indirect means. *v.t.* To attempt to catch fish in; to drag up from under water; to search (water, etc.) by sweeping, dragging, etc. **fish-glue,** *n.* Isinglass. **fish-hook,** *n.* A barbed hook for catching fish. **fishmonger,** *n.* A retailer of fish. **fish-plate,** *n.* (*Rail.*) A plate used to fasten rails together. **fish-wife,** *n.* A woman that sells fish. **fisher,** *n.* One who is employed in fishing; an animal that fishes; a fishing-boat. **fisherman,** *n.* **fishing,** *n.* The action of the verb; the sport of angling; a place where angling is carried on. **fishing-rod,** *n.* A long, slender, tapering rod, usu. in sections, for angling. **fishing-tackle,** *n.* Apparatus required by a fisherman. **fishy,** *a.* Like, consisting of, pertaining to, or suggestive of fish; of a doubtful character.

fissile (fis′il) [L. *fissilis*, from *findere*, to cleave], *a.* That may be cleft or split.

fissure (fish′ūr), *n.* A cleft made by the splitting or parting of any substance.

fist (fist) [A.-S. *fyst*], *n.* The clenched hand, esp. in readiness to strike; the hand; handwriting. *v.t.* To strike with the fist. **fisticuffs,** *n.pl.* A fight with fists.

fistula (fis′tū-lȧ) [L., a pipe], *n.* A kind of ulcer in form like a pipe.

fit (1) (fit) [A.-S. *fitt*], *n.* A violent seizure or paroxysm; a sudden transitory attack of illness, or of epilepsy or other disease characterized by convulsions, swooning, and hysteria; a transient state of impulsive action, a caprice. **fitful,** *a.* Spasmodic, capricious.

fit (2) (fit) [M.E. *fyt*], *a.* Adapted, suitable, becoming, meet; qualified, prepared, in a suitable condition (to do or for); in good bodily condition. *v.t.* To adapt to any shape, size, etc.; to accommodate; to try on a garment; to equip; to qualify, prepare; to be adapted or proper for;

to correspond to exactly. *v.i.* To be adjusted or adapted to the right shape, etc.; to be suitable, becoming, etc. *n.* Exact adjustment, as of a dress to the body; the manner in which anything fits. **fitly,** *adv.* **fitments,** *n.* Fittings. **fitness,** *n.* **fitted,** *a.* Adapted, suitable (for). **fitter,** *n.* One who or that which fits; one who puts machinery together. **fitting,** *a.* Suitable, appropriate, right, proper. *n.* The act of making fit; (*pl.*) fixtures, furniture in a house, shop, etc.

five (fīv) [A.-S. *fíf*], *a.* and *n.* Amounting to one more than four; a symbol representing this, 5 or v; a set of five things; a card, counter, etc., with five pips. **five-fold,** *a.* and *adv.* Five times as much or as great.

fives (fīvz), *n.* A game in which a ball is struck against a wall by the open hand or a small bat. **fives-court,** *n.* A walled court where the game is played.

fix (fĭks) [L. *fixus,* fixed], *v.t.* To make fast or firm; to fasten, secure firmly; to establish; to make permanent or stable (as colours, a photograph, etc.); to arrest (as attention, etc.); to settle, determine, decide (on); to adjust, arrange properly, set to rights. *v.i.* To become fixed; to settle down permanently. *n.* An awkward predicament, a dilemma. **fixa'tion,** *n.* (*Psych.*) An emotional arrest of development of the personality. **fix'ative,** *a.* Serving to fix. *n.* A substance used to make colours permanent. **fixed,** *a.* Fast, firm; established, settled, unalterable. **fix'ture,** *n.* Any thing or person fixed in a permanent position; (*pl.*) furniture or fittings permanently fastened to the structure of a building; a sporting event, or the date for it.

fizz (fĭz), *v.i.* To make a hissing or sputtering sound. *n.* That sound; champagne, ginger-beer, lemonade.

fizzle (fĭzl), *v.i.* To fizz feebly. *n.* The sound or action of this; a lame ending, a fiasco.

flabby (flăb'ĭ), *a.* Hanging loosely, limp; lacking in fibre or nerve. **flabbily,** *adv.* **flabbiness,** *n.*

flaccid (flăk'sĭd) [L. *flaccidus,* from *flaccus,* flabby], *a.* Lacking firmness or vigour.

flag (1) (flăg) [O.F. *flaquir,* to become flaccid], *v.i.* To droop; to become limp, spiritless, or dejected; to lose interest.

flag (2) (flăg) [Teut.], *n.* A piece of bunting or other cloth, usu. square or oblong, plain or bearing a device, attached by one edge to a halyard and hoisted on a pole or mast as a banner, ensign, or signal; a flagship. *v.t.* To put a flag over; to decorate with or mark out with flags; to signal by means of flags. **flag captain,** *n.* Commanding officer of a flag-ship. **flag-lieutenant,** *n.* An officer in immediate attendance upon an admiral. **flag-officer,** *n.* A commander of a squadron; an admiral, vice-admiral, or rear-admiral. **flagship,** *n.* The ship which carries the admiral, and on which his flag is displayed. **flagstaff,** *n.* The pole or staff on which a flag is displayed.

flag (3) (flăg) [prob. as prec., from its waving], *n.* An herbaceous plant with long blade-like leaves growing in moist places.

flag (4) (flăg) **flagstone,** *n.* A broad flat stone used for paving.

flagellate (flăj'ĕ-lāt) [L. *flagellātus,* scourged], *v.t.* To whip, scourge. *a.* (*Zool., Bot., etc.*) Having whip-like processes. **flagellant** (flăj'ĕ-lănt), *n.* One who thrashes (himself or others), esp. as a religious discipline. *a.* Given to scourging. **flagella'tion,** *n.* A scourging.

flageolet (flăj-ŏ-lĕt') [O.F. *flageol*], *n.* A small wind-instrument.

flagitious (flá-jĭsh'ŭs) [L. *flāgitium,* a disgraceful act], *a.* Heinous, villainous.

flagon (flăg'ŏn) [O.F. *flacon*], *n.* A vessel with a narrow mouth for holding liquors.

flagrant (flā'grănt) [L. *flāgrans,* blazing], *a.* Glaring, notorious, scandalous.

flail (flāl) [A.-S. *flígel*], *n.* A wooden staff hinged to a longer staff, used for threshing grain.

flair (flâr) [F.], *n.* Keen perception.

flake (flāk) [?], *n.* A thin scale-like fragment, a chip; a loosely cohering mass, a fleecy particle (as of snow); a gleam of light. *v.t.* To form into flakes or loose particles; to chip in flakes; to fleck.

flambeau (flăm'bō) [F.], *n.* A torch.

flamboyant (flăm-boi'ănt) [F.], *a.* Applied to decorated French Gothic architecture, from its flame-like tracery; florid, highly decorated; wavy or flame-like (as hair).

flame (flām) [L. *flamma*], *n.* Burning gas or vapour; a blaze, fire, glow, a bright light, a blaze of colour; ardour, passion; a sweetheart. *v.i.* To burn with or send out flame, to blaze; to blaze up in passion; to glow. **flaming,** *a.* **flamy,** *a.*

flamingo (flá-ming'gō) [Port. *flamengo*], *n.* A long-necked bird, with small body and very long legs, and rose-coloured feathers.

flange (flănj) [?], *n.* A projecting rib on a wheel, pipe, etc., for strength, guide, or attachment to something else.

flank (flăngk) [F. *flanc*], *n.* The side, between the hips and the ribs; either side of a building, mountain, army, etc. *v.t.* To stand or be at the flank or side of, to border; to attack, turn, threaten, secure, or guard the flank of. *v.i.* To border; to be posted on the flank.

flannel (flăn'ĕl) [from W. *gwlanen*], *n.* A soft woollen stuff of open texture, with a light nap; (*pl.*) garments made of this. **flannelled,** *a.* Covered with or wrapped up in flannel. **flannelette',** *n.* A cotton fabric made to imitate flannel.

flap (flăp), *v.t.* To beat with anything broad and flexible; to move rapidly up and down or to and fro (as wings). *v.i.* To move the wings rapidly; to flutter, swing about, or oscillate; to hang down, as the brim of a hat; to strike a loose blow. *n.* Anything broad and flexible, hanging loosely; the hinged leaf of a table, etc.; the motion of flapping; a light stroke with something broad and loose; an implement for driving flies away. **flapper,** *n.* A wild-duck not yet able to fly; a flap; a young girl.

flare (flâr) [?], *v.i.* To blaze, to flame up, esp. unsteadily; (*fig.*) to be gaudy, too showy in dress. *n.* A large unsteady light, a glare. **flaring,** *a.*

flash (flăsh) [?], *v.i.* To appear with or

send out a sudden and transient gleam; to glitter, burst forth, appear, or occur suddenly. *v.t.* To emit or send forth in flashes, to cause to gleam, to transmit instantaneously (as by telegraph); to send swiftly along. *n.* A sudden and transitory blaze or gleam; an instant; a sudden outburst, as of anger, merriment, etc.; show, ostentation; (*Mil.*) a badge; thieves' jargon, slang. *a.* Gaudy; counterfeit, forged; slang. **flash-light,** *n.* A brilliant light used in night or indoor photography. **flashy,** *a.* Showy but empty; gaudy, tawdry.

flask (flask) [F. *flasque* or It. *fiasco*], *n.* A small bottle, esp. for the pocket.

flat (1) (flăt) [Icel. *flatr*], *a.* Having a level and even surface; horizontal, smooth, having few or no elevations or depressions; prostrate, overthrown, ruined; depressed; monotonous, dull, pointless, spiritless; absolute, downright; without variety of tint or shading; below the true pitch. *adv.* Flatly, positively; prostrate. *n.* A plain surface; a level plain or low tract of land; a flat part of anything; a note a semitone lower than the one from which it is named; one easily duped; a duffer. **flat-iron,** *n.* An instrument for smoothing clothes, etc. **flat-race,** *n.* A race on level ground without obstacles. **flatten,** *v.t.* To make flat, to level; to make dull or insipid; to dispirit. **flattish,** *a.* **flatly,** *adv.* **flatness,** *n.*

flat (2) (flăt) [A.-S. *flet,* a floor], *n.* A story of a house; a self-contained suite of rooms on one floor.

flatter (flăt'ér) [?], *v.t.* To cajole or gratify by compliment, etc.; to praise falsely or unduly; to raise false hopes in; to represent too favourably. *v.i.* To use flattery. **flatterer,** *n.* **flattery,** *n.*

flatulent (flăt'ū-lĕnt) [L. *flātulens*], *a.* Troubled by gases generated in the alimentary canal or the stomach; (*fig.*) inflated, pretentious. **flatulence,** *n.*

flaunt (flawnt) [?], *v.i.* To make an ostentatious show; to behave pertly. *v.t.* To display ostentatiously or impudently; to parade, show off.

flautist (flaw'tist) [FLUTE] *n.* A flute-player.

flavour (flā'vór) [O.F. *flaur*, smell], *n.* That quality in a substance which affects the taste or smell. *v.t.* To impart a flavour to; to season. **flavoured,** *a.* **flavouring,** *n.* Something that flavours.

flaw (flaw) [Scand.], *n.* A crack, a defect, an imperfection; a sudden gust of wind, a squall. *v.t.* To break, crack; to render invalid. *v.i.* To crack. **flawless,** *a.*

flax (flăks) [A.-S. *fleax*], *n.* A plant the fibre of which is made into yarn and spun into linen cloth. **flax-dresser,** *n.* One who prepares flax for the spinner. **flaxen,** *a.* Made of flax; like flax; light yellow or straw-coloured. **flaxy,** *a.*

flay (flā) [A.-S. *flēan*], *v.t.* To strip the skin from; (*fig.*) to criticize savagely.

flea (flē) [A.-S. *flēah*], *n.* An insect belonging to the genus *Pulex*, esp. *P. irritans,* which is parasitic on man, and remarkable for its leaping powers. **flea-bite,** *n.* The bite of a flea; a tiny amount.

fleck (flek) [Scand.], *n.* A spot, freckle, stain; a patch of colour or light.

fledge (flej) [A.-S. *flycge*], *v.t.* To furnish with feathers or plumage. *v.i.* To acquire feathers or plumage for flight. **fledged,** *a.* Feathered; able to fly. **fledgeling,** *n.* A young bird just fledged; an inexperienced person.

flee (flē) [A.-S. *flēon*], *v.i.* (*past and p.p.* fled) To run away, as from danger; to vanish. *v.t.* To run away from; to shun.

fleece (flēs) [A.-S. *flēos*], *n.* The woolly covering of a sheep or similar animal; the wool shorn from a sheep at one time; a web of carded fibres of cotton, etc. *v.t.* To shear the wool from; to furnish with a fleece; (*fig.*) to plunder, strip. **fleecy,** *a.* Woolly, wool-bearing.

fleet (flēt) [A.-S. *flēot,* a ship], *n.* A number of ships in company, esp. a body of warships under one command; the entire body of warships belonging to one government, a navy. *v.i.* To move swiftly; (*fig.*) to glide away, to vanish. **fleet, fleet-footed,** *a.* Able to run with great speed. **fleeting,** *a.* Passing quickly, transient. **fleetingly,** *adv.* and *a.* Swift of pace, nimble, rapid, speedy. **fleetly,** *adv.* **fleetness,** *n.*

Fleming (flem'ing) [M.Dut. *Vlāming*], *n.* A native of Flanders. **Flemish,** *a.*

flench (flench), **flense** (flens) [Dan.], *v.t.* To strip the blubber or the skin from (a whale or seal).

flesh (flesh) [A.-S. *flæsc*], *n.* The soft part of an animal body covered by the skin; animal (as apart from fish) tissue used as food; the body, as distinguished from the soul; the human race. *v.t.* To encourage by giving flesh to, to make eager (of hawks, dogs, etc.), hence to initiate, to exercise or use for the first time. **flesher,** *n.* A butcher. **fleshly,** *a.* Pertaining to the flesh, corporeal, sensual; human, as distinct from spiritual. **fleshy,** *a.* Fat, plump; pulpy (as fruit).

fleur-de-lis (flĕr-dė-lē) [F., lily flower], *n.* (*pl.* **fleurs-**) Various species of iris; the heraldic charge borne in the French royal arms.

flex (fleks) [L. *flexus*, bent], *v.t.* To bend or cause to bend. *n.* (*Elec.*) A piece of flexible insulated wire. **flexible,** *a.* Pliant, easily bent; easily persuaded, manageable, versatile. **flexibil'ity,** *n.* **flexile,** *a.* Easily bent; pliant, tractable; supple, versatile.

flick (flik), *n.* A smart, light blow as with a whip. *n.pl.* (*colloq.*) A cinematograph entertainment, the pictures. *v.t.* To strike with a whip.

flicker (flik'ér), *v.i.* To flutter, flap the wings; to burn unsteadily, waver. *n.* An unsteady light.

flight (1) (flīt) [A.-S. *flyht,* from O.Teut. *fleugan,* to FLY (2)], *n.* Act or power of flying; swift movement or passage, as of a projectile, or of time; a soaring, a sally, a sustained effort; the distance to which anything can fly; a number of birds or insects moving together; a volley (of arrows, etc.); a series of steps; (*Aero.*) A R.A.F. unit usu. consisting of three aircraft. **flighty,** *a.* Capricious, volatile. **flightiness,** *n.*

flight (2) (flit) [M.E. *fliht, fluhte*, from O.Teut. *thliuhan*, to FLEE], *n.* The act of fleeing or running away; a hasty departure, retreat, or evasion.

flimsy (flĭm'zĭ) [?], *a.* Thin, slight, unsubstantial; easily torn; ineffective, frivolous, paltry. **flimsily,** *adv.*

flinch (flĭnch) [?], *v.i.* To shrink from; to wince, give way, fail.

fling (fling) [Scand.], *v.i.* To rush violently, to flounce; (*of horses*) to kick, struggle; to flout, throw aspersions (at). *v.t.* To cast or throw with sudden force; to hurl, send forth, emit; to throw to the ground. *n.* A cast or throw from the hand; a gibe, a sneer; a lively Highland dance; a plunge, flounce.

flint (flint) [A.-S.], *n.* A variety of quartz easily chipped into a sharp cutting edge, which strikes fire with steel; a piece of this shaped for use in a gun, etc., or as an implement used by prehistoric man; anything extremely hard. **flint-glass,** *n.* A very pure and lustrous kind of glass. **flint-lock,** *n.* A lock for fire-arms, in which the cock holds a piece of flint for striking fire. **flinty,** *a.*

flip (flĭp) [?], *v.* To fillip or jerk; to strike lightly; to flap or flick (at). *n.* A quick light blow or stroke. **flipper,** *n.* The broad fin of a fish; the limb of a turtle, penguin, etc.

flippant (flĭp'ănt) [?], *a.* Pert, trifling, lacking in seriousness. **flippancy,** *n.*

flirt (flĕrt) [?], *v.t.* To jerk or fillip (away); to wave rapidly (as a fan). *v.i.* To play at love-making, to coquet; to move with jerks. *n.* A flirting motion, a jerk, a fling; a person, esp. woman, who plays at courtship. **flirta'tion,** *n.* Coquetry.

flit (flit), *v.i.* To pass from place to place; to fly about rapidly; to depart.

flitch (flĭch) [A.-S. *flicce*], *n.* The side of a pig salted and cured.

float (1) (flōt) [A.-S. *flotian*], *v.i.* To be supported, or to drift, on the surface of a fluid; to hover in the air. *v.t.* To support on a fluid; to convey on water; to set afloat; to put into circulation. **floating,** *a.* Resting on the surface of a fluid; circulating, not fixed or invested; fluctuating.

float (2) (flōt) [A.-S. *flota*, a ship], *n.* Anything buoyed up on the surface of a liquid; the cork or quill on a fishing-line or net; a fish's bladder; a timber-raft; a dray for heavy goods; (*pl.*) (*Theat.*) footlights; a plastering trowel.

flocculent (flŏk'ū-lĕnt) [L. *floccus*, a tuft], *a.* In small flakes, woolly, tufted.

flock (1) (flŏk) [A.-S. *flocc*], *n.* A company of animals, esp. sheep, goats, or birds; a crowd; a congregation in relation to their minister. *v.i.* To come together in a flock; to assemble. *v.t.* To crowd.

flock (2) (flŏk) [L. *floccus*, a tuft], *n.* A lock or tuft of wool, cotton, hair, etc.; wool-dust; torn rags used to stuff mattresses, etc.

floe (flō) [Scand.], *n.* A large sheet of floating ice.

flog (flŏg) [?], *v.t.* To thrash, esp. with a birch rod; to whip, lash; to urge or drive by beating; (*slang*) to sell. **flogging,** *n.*

flood (flŭd) [A.-S. *flōd*], *n.* An abundant flow of water, esp. one that overflows land not usually covered, an inundation; the inflow of the tide; a downpour; a river, the sea; (*fig.*) an overflowing, abundance. *v.t.* To overflow, deluge; to supply copiously (with). *v.i.* To be at the flood (of the sea); to rise and overflow. **flood-gate,** *n.* A gate in a waterway opening when the water attains a certain height, a sluice; the lower gate of a lock. **flood-lighting,** *n.* Artificial lighting by projectors of the outside of buildings. **flood-tide,** *n.* The rising tide.

floor (flōr) [A.-S. *flōr*], *n.* The bottom surface of a room, etc.; the material of which this is made; a story in a building; the part of the house assigned to members of a legislative assembly; the bottom of a coal seam, etc. *v.t.* To furnish with a floor; to knock down; to get the better of, to defeat. **flooring,** *n.* Material for floors.

flop (flŏp), *v.i.* To fall loosely and heavily; to sway about heavily, to flap (as wings); to fail completely. *n.* A failure.

flora (flō'rá) [Roman goddess of flowers], *n.* The whole vegetation of a country or geological period. **floral,** *a.* Pertaining to flowers.

florescence (flō-res'ĕns) [L. *florescens*, beginning to flourish], *n.* The flowering of a plant; the season when a plant flowers.

floriculture (flor'ĭ-kŭl-tūr) [L. *flos, floris*, flower, CULTURE], *n.* The cultivation of flowering plants. **floriculturist,** *n.*

florid (flor'id) [L. *floridus*], *a.* Covered with or abounding in flowers; bright in colour; ruddy; elaborately ornate.

florin (flor'in) [It. *fiorino*], *n.* An English silver coin, worth 2s.; a foreign coin of various values (orig. Florentine, stamped with a lily).

florist (flor'ist) [L. *flōs flōris*, flower], *n.* A cultivator of or dealer in flowers.

floss (flos) [?], *n.* The exterior soft envelope of a silk-worm's cocoon; the downy substance on the husks of certain plants, as the bean. **floss-silk,** *n.* Untwisted filaments of the finest silk.

flotation (flō-tā'shŭn), *n.* Act or state of floating; the floating of a company.

flotilla (flō-til'á) [Sp., dim. of *flota*, a fleet], *n.* A small fleet; a fleet of small vessels.

flotsam (flot'săm) [A.-F. *floteson*], *n.* Goods lost in shipwreck and found floating.

flounce (1) (flouns) [Scand.], *v.i.* To throw oneself about; to make agitated movements of the limbs.

flounce (2) (flouns) [O.F. *froncer*, to wrinkle, L. *frons*, forehead], *n.* A gathered or plaited strip of cloth sewed to a petticoat, dress, etc.

flounder (floun'dẽr) [Scand.], *n.* A flatfish resembling the plaice. *v.i.* To struggle or stumble about, as when stuck in mire; to blunder along, do things badly.

flour (flour) [var. of FLOWER], *n.* The finer part of meal, esp. wheat-meal; fine soft powder of any substance. *v.t.* To sprinkle flour upon. **floury,** *a.*

flourish (flŭr'ish) [L. *florere*], *v.i.* To grow luxuriantly; to prosper, increase in wealth, etc.; to be alive (about a certain date); to use florid language; to make fanciful strokes in writing; to sound a fanfare. *v.t.* To brandish, fling, or wave about; to flaunt. *n.* A figure formed by strokes fancifully drawn; rhetorical display; a brandishing or waving of a weapon, etc. **flourishing,** *a.* Thriving, prosperous; making a show.

flout (flout) [?], *v.t.* To insult; to treat with contempt. *n.* A word or act of contempt; a sneer, insult.

flow (flō) [A.-S. *flōwan*], *v.i.* To move or spread as a fluid; to circulate, as blood; to rise, as the tide; to issue, gush out; to glide or float, to move easily or freely; to abound, to come or go in abundance. *n.* Act, state, or motion of flowing; the quantity that flows; a stream; abundance, a plentiful supply; the rise of the tide; undulation (of drapery, etc.). **flowing,** *a.*

flower (flou'ér) [L. *flōrem*, nom. *flōs*], *n.* The blossom of a plant; the growth comprising its organs of reproduction; a flowering plant; (*fig.*) the finest or choicest individual, part, period, etc.; an embellishment; the period of youthful vigour; (*Chem., pl.*) substances of a powdery consistence. *v.i.* To bloom, to blossom; to be in the prime. **flowerpot,** *n.* A pot to hold plants. **flowered,** *a.* Embellished with flowers or figures of flowers. **flowering,** *a.* That flowers; flowery. **flowery,** *a.* Abounding in flowers or blossoms; highly figurative, florid.

fluctuate (flŭk'tū-āt) [L. *fluctuātus*, waved], *v.i.* To rise and fall like waves; to vary, be unsettled; to waver. **fluctuating,** *a.* **fluctua'tion,** *n.*

flue (floo) [?], *n.* A passage or tube by which smoke can escape or hot air be conveyed; light down or fluff.

fluent (floo'ént) [L. *fluens*, flowing], *a.* Fluid, mobile, changeable; graceful; ready with words. **fluency,** *n.*

fluff (flŭf) [?], *n.* Light down or fur; flocculent matter; nap. **fluffy,** *a.*

fluid (floo'id) [L. *fluidus* (*fluere*, to flow)], *a.* Composed of particles that move freely in relation to each other; capable of flowing, liquid, gaseous; readily accessible. *n.* A liquid, not a solid; a substance whose particles readily change their relative positions. **fluid'ity,** *n.*

fluke (1) (flook) [A.-S. *flōc*], *n.* A flounder or other flat-fish; a parasitic worm found in the livers of sheep; the broad holding portion of an anchor; a barb of a harpoon.

fluke (2) (flook) [?], *n.* An accidentally successful stroke, esp. in billiards; any lucky chance. *v.* To score, hit, or obtain by luck.

flume (floom) [O.F. *flum*, L. *flumen*, a river, from *fluere*, to flow], *n.* An artificial channel for conveying water to a mill, etc.

flummery (flŭm'ér-i) [W. *llymry*], *n.* A food made of meal boiled to a jelly; humbug; empty compliment.

flunkey (flŭng'ki) [?], *n.* A servant in livery; a toady. **flunkeydom,** *n.*

fluor (floo'ôr) [L. *fluere*, to flow], *n.* A metal with many shades of colour. **fluorescence,** *n.* The quality in certain substances of throwing out light of a different colour from their own. **fluorescent lamp,** *n.* A glass bulb or tube with a metallic coating inside which exhibits fluorescence when an electric current is passed through it.

flurry (flŭr'i) [onomat.], *n.* Agitation, bustle; a sudden and violent shower; the death struggle of a whale. *v.t.* To agitate, fluster.

flush (1) (flŭsh) [?], *v.i.* To start up suddenly (of game-birds). *v.t.* To cause to take wing; to put up.

flush (2) (flŭsh) [?], *v.i.* To flow swiftly; to rush; to become suffused; to colour as with a rush of blood, to redden up, blush. *v.t.* To cleanse by a rush of water; to flood; to redden; to level (up); to fill in (a joint) so as to make even with the surface. *n.* A sudden flow of water or rush of blood to the face causing a redness; the race from a mill-wheel; the cleansing of a drain with a rush of water; a sudden access of emotion, elation, excitement; a hot fit in fever; vigour; bloom; (*Cards*) a hand of cards all of one suit. *a.* Full to overflowing; plentifully supplied, esp. with money.

fluster (flŭs'tér) [Scand.], *v.t.* To flurry, to make nervous; to befuddle with drink. *v.i.* To be in an agitated or confused state. *n.* Flurry, agitation.

flute (floot) [O.F. *fleute*], *n.* A tubular wind-instrument with blow-hole near the end and holes stopped by the fingers or with keys; a long vertical groove in the shaft of a column, etc. *v.i.* To play a flute; to whistle or sing with a flute-like sound. *v.t.* To play, sing, or utter with flute-like tones; to form flutes or grooves in. **fluted,** *a.* Channelled, furrowed. **fluting,** *n.* A groove, channel; fluted work in pillars, etc. **flutist,** *n.*

flutter (flŭt'ér) [A.-S. *flotorian*], *v.i.* To flap the wings rapidly; to flit or move about with quick, irregular motions; to quiver, vibrate; to be agitated or uncertain. *v.t.* To cause to vibrate, or to quiver or flap about rapidly; to agitate. *n.* The act of fluttering; a state of excitement; a gamble, a speculation.

fluvial, fluviatile (floo'vi-ál, -å-til) [L., from *fluvium*, river], *a.* Of or belonging to a river; caused by a river.

flux (flŭks) [L. *fluxus* (*fluere*, to flow)], *n.* Act or state of flowing; motion of a fluid; state of continual change; an issue or flowing out, a discharge; the flow of the tide; an abnormal fluid discharge from the body; rate or quantity of flow of water, heat, electricity, etc.

fluxion (flŭk'shŭn), *n.* Act or state of flowing; that which flows; fusion of metals; continuous variation.

fly (1) (flī) [as foll.], *n.* (*pl.* **flies**) A two-winged insect, esp. the house-fly; a disease in turnips, etc., caused by flies;

an artificial fly for fishing. **fly-blow**, v.t. To deposit eggs in, as the blow-fly in meat; to taint. n. The egg of a blow-fly.

fly (2) (fli) [A.-S. *flēogan*], v.i. (*past* flew, *p.p.* flown) To move or ride through the air with or as with wings; to flutter or wave in the air; to pass through the air with great speed; to ride in an aircraft; to navigate an aeroplane, etc.; to flee, try to escape, depart (*with p.p.* fled); to burst (in pieces); to start, spring, hasten, burst (as to arms or into a rage). v.t. To cause to fly or float in the air; to flee from.

fly (3) (fli) [from prec.], n. Act or state of flying; distance something flies; (*pl.* flys) a one-horse carriage; a fly-wheel; a flap covering button-holes, the entrance to a tent, etc.; (*pl.*) a gallery where the curtains or scenes in a theatre are controlled. **fly-leaf**, n. A blank leaf at the beginning or end of a book. **fly-wheel**, n. A heavy-rimmed wheel attached to a machine for regulating the speed.

flying (fli'ing), a. Moving with or as with wings; adapted to move swiftly; brief, hurried. **flying saucers**, n.pl. Unaccounted for moving objects said to have been seen in the sky, usu. in U.S.A.

foal (fōl) [A.-S. *fola*], n. The young of the horse or ass; a colt, a filly. v. To bring forth young (as a mare or she-ass).

foam (fōm) [A.-S. *fām*], n. Froth, spume; bubbles produced in liquids by violent agitation or fermentation. v.i. To produce, or emit foam; to be filled with or pass (away) in foam; to rage.

fob (fob) [?], n. A watch-pocket in the waistband of breeches. v.t. To put into one's pocket; to cheat, to impose upon.

focus (fō'kŭs) [L., hearth], n. (*pl.* -ci (-sī), -cuses) A point at which rays of light, heat, etc., meet after reflection or refraction; the point from which any activity originates, point of concentration. v.t. To bring (rays) to a point; to adjust (eye or instrument) so as to be at the right focus; to bring into focus. **focal**, a. Pertaining to, or situated at a focus.

fodder (fod'ẽr) [A.-S. *fōdor*, as FOOD], n. Food served to cattle, as hay, etc. v.t. To supply with fodder.

foe (fō) [A.-S. *fāh*, hostile], n. A personal enemy; an enemy in war; an ill-wisher. **foeman**, n. An enemy in war.

foetus (fē'tŭs) [L. *fētus*, offspring], n. The young of viviparous animals in the womb, and of oviparous vertebrates in the egg. **foetal**, a. Pertaining to a foetus.

fog (fog) [?], n. Coarse, rank grass, aftermath; a dense watery vapour suspended near the surface of land or sea; (*Phot.*) a cloudiness on a negative; (*fig.*) a state of confusion or perplexity. v.t. To becloud, perplex, bewilder; (*Phot.*) to make (a negative) cloudy. v.i. To become foggy. **fog-bank**, n. A dense mass of fog at sea resembling land at a distance. **fog-horn**, n. An instrument to give warning to ships, etc., in a fog. **fog-signal**, n. A detonator placed on a railway for the guidance of engine-drivers. **foggy**, a.

fogy (fō'gi) [?], n. An old-fashioned, eccentric person.

foible (foible) [F.], n. A weak point in one's character.

foil (1) (foil) [O.F. *foil* (F. *feuille*), L. *folium*, a leaf (cp. Gr. *phullion*)], n. An amalgam of quicksilver and tin at the back of a mirror; a thin leaf of metal put under gems; that which serves to set off something to advantage.

foil (2) (foil) [O.F. *fouler*, to full (cloth)], v.t. To baffle, frustrate, throw off the scent; to defeat, parry.

foil (3) (foil) [?], n. A straight thin sword, blunted by a button, used in fencing.

foist (foist) [?], v.t. To introduce surreptitiously or wrongfully; to palm off (on or upon) as genuine.

fold (1) (fōld) [A.-S. *fald*], n. A pen for sheep; a flock of sheep.

fold (2) (fōld) [A.-S. *fealdan*], v.t. To double or lay one part over another; to clasp, embrace. v.i. To become doubled; to shut in folds. n. A part doubled or laid on another; a bend, a plait. **folder**, n.

-fold, suf. Forming adjectives and adverbs denoting multiplication, as *fourfold*, *manifold*.

foliaceous (fō-li-ā'shŭs) [L. *folium*, leaf], a. Having the texture, structure, etc., of leaves; leaf-shaped.

foliage (fō'li-aj), n. Leaves in the aggregate.

folio (fō'li-ō), n. A sheet of paper folded once; a book of the largest size, with sheets folded once; a leaf of paper or page of manuscript, or of an account book; the number of a page; 72 (or 90) words of manuscript.

folk (fōk) [A.-S. *folc*), n. People collectively; a particular class, as old folk; a people or race. **folk dance**, n. A traditional dance of countryfolk. **folk-lore**, n. Popular superstitions, tales, traditions, or legends; the systematic study of these. **folk-lorist**, n. One versed in this. **folk-song**, n. A song or ballad that has been handed down by tradition. **folk-tale**, n. A popular myth.

follicle (fol'ikl) [L. *folliculus*, a little bag], n. A small cavity, sac, or gland.

follow (fol'ō) [A.-S. *folgian*], v.t. To go or come after; to pursue; to accompany, attend upon, side with, espouse the cause of; to pattern oneself upon; to go along (a road, etc.); to engage in, practise as a profession; to act upon (a rule, etc.); to happen after in time, order, or importance; to watch the course of; to grasp the meaning of; to result; to seek after. v.i. To come or go after another person or thing; to pursue; to ensue; to be the logical consequence. **follower**, n. One who follows, a disciple, adherent. **following**, a. Coming next after, succeeding. n. A body of adherents.

folly (fol'i) [O.F. *folie*, fol], n. Foolishness, want of judgment; a foolish act, idea, or conduct.

foment (fō-ment') [L. *fōmentāre*], v.t. To apply lotions to; to warm, poultice; (*fig.*) to foster, promote. **fomenta'tion**, n.

fond (fond) [M.E. *fonned*], a. Foolish, tender, or loving; doting. **fondly**, adv.

fondle (fondl), *v.t.* To caress. *v.i.* To indulge in caresses (with).

font (font) [L. *fons*, a fount], *n.* The vessel to contain water for baptism.

food (food) [A.-S. *fōda*], *n.* Any substance which is capable of nourishing the living being.

fool (1) (fool) [O.F. *fol*], *n.* A person without common sense or judgment; a silly person; a dupe; a jester. *v.t.* To make a fool of; to dupe, cheat, play tricks upon; to disappoint; to waste (time). **foolhardy**, *a.* Daring without sense or judgment; rash, reckless. **foolhardiness**, *n.* **foolscap**, *n.* A pointed cap with bells, worn by jesters; a size of paper about 17 × 13½ in. (from its water-mark, a fool's cap and bells). **foolery**, *n.* Act of playing the fool; folly; absurdity. **fooling**, *n.* **foolish**, *a.* **foolishness**, *n.*

fool (2) (fool) [?], *n.* A dish made of fruit.

foot (fut) [A.-S. *fōt*], *n.* (*pl.* **feet**) The part of the leg which touches the ground in standing; the part below the ankle; the locomotive organ of invertebrates; that part of dress which receives the foot; a measure containing 12 in.; the lowest part, the base; foot-soldiers, infantry; a set of syllables forming the rhythmical unit in verse. *v.i.* To walk, dance; to go on foot. *v.t.* To travel over by walking; to add a new foot to (as stockings); to pay (a bill). **football**, *n.* An inflated bladder encased in leather used in the game; a game played by two parties, fifteen (*Rugby*) or eleven (*Association*) on each side. **foot-board**, *n.* A step for getting into or out of a vehicle; a footplate. **foot-fall**, *n.* The sound of a footstep. **foothold**, *n.* Support at or to the foot; a position of stability or security. **footing**, *n.* Place for standing; foothold; a firm or secure position; entrance into a new sphere, society, trade, etc.; (*Arch.*) a course at the base or foundation of a wall. **footlights**, *n. pl.* A screened row of lights in front of the stage of a theatre. **foot-loose**, *a.* Free, unbound by ties. **footman**, *n.* A male domestic servant in livery. **footnote**, *n.* A note at the bottom of a page. **footpad**, *n.* A highwayman who robs on foot. **foot-bath**, *n.* A vessel for washing feet. **foot-path**, *n.* A narrow path for foot-passengers. **footplate**, *n.* The platform for the driver and fireman on a locomotive. **foot-pound**, *n.* The unit of energy, the amount that will raise one pound avoirdupois one foot. **foot-soldier**, *n.* An infantry soldier. **footsore**, *a.* Having the feet sore or tender. **footstep**, *n.* Tread; a footprint; the sound of the step of a foot; trace of a course pursued or of action done.

fop (fop) [M.E. *foppe*], *n.* A coxcomb. **foppery**, *n.* **foppish**, *a.*

for (fôr, fŏr) [A.-S.], *prep.* In place of; in exchange against; as the price of; in consideration of; because of, in favour of; in order to; appropriate to; toward, conducive to; on behalf of, in relation to; as regards; so far as; as, as being; to the amount of; notwithstanding; during. *conj.* Since, because; seeing that.

for-, *pref.* Away, off, as in *forget, forgive*; negative, or privative, as in *forbear, forbid, forsake*; intensive, as in *forlorn*.

forage (for'áj) [O.F. *fourrage*], *n.* Food for horses and cattle; the act of foraging. *v.i.* To collect forage; to hunt for supplies. *v.t.* To obtain or supply with forage.

forasmuch (for-áz-mŭch'), *conj.* (*foll. by as*). Seeing that; in consideration that.

foray (for'ā), *n.* A predatory expedition, raid.

forbear (1) (fôr'bâr), *n.* (*usu. pl.*) A forefather, ancestor.

forbear (2) (fôr-bâr'), *v.t.* (*past -bore, p.p.* -borne) To refrain from; to bear with, treat with patience. *v.i.* To be patient, to refrain from resentment. **forbearance**, *n.*

forbid (fôr-bid'), *v.t.* (*past -bad, -bade, p.p.* -bidden) To prohibit; to exclude, oppose. **forbidden**, *a.* Prohibited, interdicted. **forbidding**, *a.* Repulsive, disagreeable.

force (1) (fôrs) [L. *fortis*, strong], *n.* Strength, energy, active power; military or naval strength; an army; (*pl.*) troops; violence, coercion; efficacy, validity; significance, import; persuasive power; animation, vividness; (*Phys.*) that which causes, stops, or alters motion in a body. *v.t.* To compel, to constrain by force; to use violence to, to ravish; to strain, distort; to impose or impress (upon) with force; to make a way by force; to stimulate, cause to grow, etc., artificially; to cause to ripen prematurely; (*Cards*) to compel (a player) to play in a certain way. **forced**, *a.* Constrained, affected; unnatural. **forcedly**, *adv.* **forceful**, *a.* Full of, possessing, or impelled with force; violent, impetuous, forcible. **forcing-house**, *n.* A hothouse. **force-meat**, *n.* Meat chopped fine and seasoned.

force (2) (fôrs) [Scand.], *n.* A waterfall.

forceps (fôr'seps) [L.], *n.* A pair of tongs, pincers, or pliers.

forcible (fôr'sibl), *a.* Done by force; having force, powerful, efficacious. **forcibly**, *adv.*

ford (fôrd) [A.-S.], *n.* A shallow part of a river where it may be crossed by wading. *v.t.* To cross (as water) by wading. **fordable**, *a.*

fore (fôr) [A.-S.], *prep.* Before. *adv.* In the front; in or towards the bows of a ship. *a.* Being in front or the front part; anterior, prior, first. *n.* The front part; (*Naut.*) the bow. **fore-and-aft**: At, along, or over the whole length of a ship from stem to stern.

fore-, *pref.* Before, in front, beforehand, as *foreordain, forerunner*; in the front or front part of; of or near the bow or fore-mast; as *forecourt, forecastle, forepeak*.

forearm (fôr-arm'), *v.t.* To prepare beforehand for attack or defence.

fore-arm (fôr'arm), *n.* The part of the arm between the wrist and elbow.

forebode (fôr-bōd'), *v.t.* To foretell, predict, portend; to feel a presentiment of. *v.i.* To prognosticate, esp. evil. **foreboding**, *n.* Presage, esp. of evil.

forecast (fôr-kast'), *v.t.* (*past and p.p.*

forecast) To foresee, predict. *v.i.* To form a scheme beforehand. *n.* (fôr'kast) Provision against the future; calculation of probable events.

forecastle, fo'c'sle (fôr'kasl, fōksl), *n.* The forward part of the upper deck; in merchant-ships, a forward space below deck where the crew lives.

foreclose (fôr-klōz') [O.F. *forclos*, L. *foris*, outside, CLOSE], *v.t.* To exclude or bar; to preclude; to settle beforehand. *v.i.* To deprive a mortgager of his equity of redemption on failure to pay money due. **foreclosure,** *n.* The act of foreclosing.

forefather (fôr'fa-thêr), *n.* An ancestor.

forefinger (fôr'fing-gêr), *n.* The finger next to the thumb, the first or index finger.

fore-foot (fôr'fut), *n.* A front foot of a quadruped.

forefront (fôr'frŭnt), *n.* The foremost part or position.

forego (fôr-gō'), *v.t.* and *i.* (*past* -went, *p.p.* -gone) To go before, to precede in time, order, or place. **fore'going,** *a.* Preceding, previously mentioned. **foregone'**, *a.* Past; preceding; determined before.

foreground (fôr'ground), *n.* The nearest part of a view; the part of a picture showing this.

forehead (fôr'ĕd) [A.-S. *forhēafod*], *n.* The face from the eyebrows to the hair.

foreign (fôr'in) [O.F. *forain*, L. *forās*, out of doors], *a.* Belonging to another country or nation; alien, strange, extraneous; irrelevant. **foreigner,** *n.*

forejudge (fôr-jŭj'), *v.t.* To judge or decide before trial.

foreknow (fôr-nō'), *v.t.* (*past* -knew, *p.p.* -known) To know beforehand. **foreknowl'edge,** *n.*

foreland (fôr'land), *n.* A promontory.

foreleg (fôr'-leg), *n.* A front leg of an animal, chair, etc.

forelock (fôr'lok), *n.* A lock of hair growing over the forehead.

foreman (fôr'man), *u.* The chief man of a jury, the spokesman; a workman supervising others.

foremast (fôr'mast) *n.* The mast nearest the bow of a vessel.

foremost (fôr'mōst) [A.-S., double superl. from *forma*, first], *a.* First in time, place, order, rank, or importance; chief. *adv.* In the first place; before anything else.

forenoon (fôr'noon), *n.* The part of the day from morning to noon.

forensic (fô-ren'sik) [L. *forensis*, pertaining to the forum], *a.* Pertaining to courts of judicature, or to public debate.

foreordain (fôr-ôr-dān'), *v.t.* To ordain beforehand, to predestinate.

fore-part (fôr'part), *n.* The first, most advanced, or earlier part.

forerunner (fôr-rŭn'êr), *n.* A messenger sent before; a precursor.

foresail (fôrsl, fôr'sāl), *n.* The principal sail on the foremast.

foresee (fôr-sē'), *v.t.* (*past* -saw, *p.p.* -seen) To see or know beforehand, to have prescience of. **foreseeing,** *a.*

foreshore (fôr'shôr), *n.* The part of the shore lying between high- and low-water marks; ground between sea and land.

foreshorten (fôr-shôr'tĕn), *v.t.* In drawing, etc., to represent (figures or parts) so as to give a correct impression of form and proportions.

foreshow (fôr-shō') [A.-S. *fore-scēawian*], *v.t.* (*p.p.* -shown) To predict.

foresight (fôr'sit), *n.* Forethought, prudence; the muzzle-sight of a gun.

forest (fôr'ĕst) [O.F., from L. *foris*, outside], *n.* An extensive wood or tract of wooded country; a wild uncultivated tract; a large tract of country set apart for hunting. *a.* Relating or pertaining to a forest; sylvan. **forester,** *n.* One who has charge of or lives in a forest. **forestry,** *n.* Act or art of cultivating forests.

forestall (fôr-stawl') [A.-S. *forsteall*, interception], *v.t.* To hinder by preoccupation; to anticipate, be beforehand with.

foretaste (fôr'tāst), *n.* Experience or enjoyment (of) beforehand; anticipation.

foretell (fôr-tel'), *v.t.* (*past and p.p.* -told) To predict, prophesy; to foreshadow.

forethought (fôr'thawt), *n.* Consideration beforehand; premeditation.

foretop (fôr'top), *n.* The top or platform at the head of the foremast.

forever (fôr-ev'ĕr), *adv.* For ever. *n.* Eternity.

forewarn (fôr-wôrn'), *v.t.* To warn or give notice to beforehand.

forewoman (fôr'wum-ăn), *n.* A workwoman who supervises others.

foreword (fôr'wĕrd), *n.* A preface.

forfeit (fôr'fit) [O.F. *forfait*], *n.* That which is lost through fault, neglect, etc.; a penalty, a fine, a stipulated sum to be paid for breach of contract; (*pl.*) a parlour-game. *a.* Lost or alienated through fault or crime. *v.t.* To lose the right to or possession of by fault, crime, omission, or neglect; to confiscate. **forfeiture,** *n.* The act of forfeiting.

forfend (fôr-fend'), *v.t.* To avert, ward off.

forgather (fôr-găth'êr), *v.i.* To meet or associate (with); to assemble.

forge (1) (fôrj) [O.F., ult. from L. *fabrica*, FABRIC], *n.* The workshop of a smith; the open hearth where iron is heated or wrought. *v.t.* To form or fabricate by heating and hammering; to make or construct; to make or imitate fraudulently, to counterfeit; to alter a signature or document with intent to defraud. *v.i.* To commit forgery. **forgeable,** *a.* **forger,** *n.* One who commits forgery. **forgery,** *n.* The act of forging, counterfeiting, or falsifying; a fraudulent imitation. **forging,** *n.* That which is forged; a piece of forged metal work.

forge (2) (fôrj) [?], *v.i.* To move (forward or ahead) slowly or with difficulty.

forget (fôr-get') [A.-S. *forgitan*], *v.t.* (*past* -got, *p.p.* -gotten, *poet.* -got) To lose remembrance of; to put out of mind, to fail to remember, neglect (to do something). **forget-me-not,** *n.* A small plant with bright blue flowers. **forgettable,** *a.* **forgetful,** *a.*

forgive (fôr-giv') [A.-S. *forgifan*], *v.t.* (*past* -gave, *p.p.* -given) To pardon or remit, as an offence or debt; not to exact the penalty for. *v.i.* To show forgiveness.

forgivable, *a.* **forgiveness,** *n.* **forgiving,** *a.*

forgo (fôr-gō') [A.-S. *forgān* (FOR-, GO)], *v.t.* (*past* -**went,** *p.p.* -**gone**) To give up, deny oneself, renounce; to quit.

fork (fôrk) [A.-S. *forc*], *n.* An instrument with two or more prongs, used for digging, lifting, carrying, etc., or in cooking and at table; a diverging branch, a point where a road divides into two. *v.t.* To raise, pitch, dig or break up, etc., with a fork. *v.i.* To divide into two; to send out branches. **forked,** *a.*

forlorn (fôr-lôrn') [A.-S. *forloren*], *a.* Deserted; wretched, hopeless. **forlorn hope** [Dut. *verloren hoop*, lit. lost troop], *n.* A detachment of men selected for some service of uncommon danger; a bold, desperate enterprise. **forlornness,** *n.*

form (fôrm) [O.F. *forme*, L. *forma*], *n.* Shape, configuration; figure, esp. the human; particular arrangement, organization, or constitution; a rule of procedure, ceremony, or ritual; the mode in which anything is perceptible; kind, species, variety; a mould or model upon which a thing is fashioned; a formula, a fixed order of words, a document with blanks to be filled in; behaviour according to accepted rules; fitness, a good state of health or training; a long seat without a back; a class at school; the seat or bed of a hare; a body of type ready for printing. *v.t.* To shape; to arrange; to make, construct, mould to a pattern; to conceive, devise; to articulate; to become; to be the material for. **-form,** *suf.* Like, having the shape of, as *cruciform;* having a certain number of forms, as *multiform, uniform.*

formal (fôr'mál) [L. *formālis*], *a.* In a set form; orderly, according to established forms; ceremonious, punctilious, precise; perfunctory; of or pertaining to the outward form as opposed to reality. **formalism,** *n.* **formalist,** *n.* **formal'ity,** *n.* The condition or quality of being formal; conformity to custom, etc.; conventionality; an established order or method. **formally,** *adv.*

formation (fôr-mā'shùn) [L. *formātio*], *n.* Act or process of forming or creating; state of being formed; manner in which anything is formed; conformation, arrangement; a thing formed. **for'mative,** *a.* Having the power of giving form.

former (fôr'mêr), *a.* Preceding in time; the first-mentioned (of two); ancient, bygone. **formerly,** *adv.* In former times; of the past.

formic (fôr'mik) [L. *formica*, ant], *a.* Pertaining to or produced by ants.

formidable (fôr'mi-dàbl) [L. *formīdāre*, to dread], *a.* Tending to excite fear; dangerous to encounter; difficult to resist, overcome, or accomplish.

formless (fôrm'lès), *a.* Without form, shapeless.

formula (fôr'mū-là) [L., dim of *forma*], *n.* (*pl.* -**læ,** -**las**) A prescribed form of words; a formal enunciation of faith, etc.; a conventional usage; a prescription. **formulate,** *v.t.* To express in formula.

fornicate (fôr'ni-kāt) [L. *fornicārī*], *v.i.* To commit fornication. **fornica'tion,** *n.* Sexual intercourse of persons not married to one another. **fornicator,** *n.*

forsake (fôr-sāk') [A.-S. *forsacan*], *v.t.* (*past* -**sook,** *p.p.* -**saken**) To leave, abandon, withdraw from; to cast off.

forsooth (fôr-sooth'), *adv.* (*ironically*) In truth, certainly, doubtless.

forswear (fôr-swâr') [A.-S. *forswerian*], *v.t.* (*past* -**swore,** *p.p.* -**sworn**) To abjure; to renounce upon oath or with protestations. *v.i.* To swear falsely, perjure oneself.

fort (fôrt) [L. *fortis* (*domus*), strong (house)], *n.* A fortified place.

forte (1) (fôrt) [F.], *n.* A person's strong point; that in which one excels.

forte (2) (fôr'tā) [It., strong], *adv.* (*Mus.*) With loudness or force.

forth (fôrth) [A.-S.], *adv.* Out; out from home; out of doors; forward in place, time, or order. **forthcom'ing,** *a.* Coming forth, ready to appear. *n.* A coming forth. **forthwith,** (fôrth-with'), *adv.* Immediately; without delay.

fortify (fôr'ti-fī) [O.F. *fortifier*], *v.t.* To make strong; to invigorate; to add strength to; to confirm, corroborate; to strengthen by forts, ramparts, etc.; to make defensible. **fortifica'tion,** *n.*

fortissimo (fôr-tis'i-mō) [It., superl. of FORTE (2)], *adv.* (*Mus.*) Very loud.

fortitude (fôr'ti-tūd) [L. *fortitūdo*], *n.* Strength, esp. strength of mind which enables one to meet danger or endure pain.

fortnight (fôrt'nit) [A.-S. *fēowertȳne niht*, fourteen nights], *n.* A period of two weeks. **fortnightly,** *a.* Happening once a fortnight. *adv.* Once a fortnight.

fortress (fôr'tres) [O.F. *forteresse*], *n.* A fortified place.

fortuitous (fôr-tū'i-tùs) [L. *fortuitus*, from *fors*, chance], *a.* Happening by chance; casual, accidental.

fortunate (fôr'chù-nát) [L. *fortūnātus*], *a.* Happening by good luck; bringing or presaging good fortune; lucky.

fortune (fôr'chùn) [L. *fortūna*], *n.* Chance, luck; that which brings good or ill hap; one's future lot; prosperity; wealth; a large property. *v.i.* To happen, to chance.

forty (fôr'ti) [A.-S. *fēowertig*], *a.* Four times ten. *n.* The sum of four times ten; a symbol expressing this, 40 or xl; (*pl.*) the years of one's life between 39 and 50, the corresponding period in a century. **fortieth,** *a.* the **Forty-five,** *n.* (*Hist.*) The Jacobite rebellion of 1745.

forum (fôr'ùm) [L.], *n.* The public place in Rome in which were the law courts, etc., and where orations were delivered; a tribunal; a place or means of public discussion.

forward (1) (fôr'wàrd) [A.-S. *foreweard*], *a.* At, near, or towards the front; onward; advancing, well advanced, early, premature; eager, prompt; pert. *n.* A player at football, etc., stationed at the front of his side. *v.t.* To help onward, promote; to send on or to a further destination. **forwardly,** *adv.* **forward-**

ness, *n.* The quality or state of being forward; assurance; pertness.

forward (2), **-s,** *adv.* Towards the front or the fore-part; onward in place or time.

fosse (fos) [L. *fossa*], *n.* A ditch.

fossil (fos'il) [L. *fossilis*, from *fossus*, p.p. of *fodere*, to dig], *a.* Preserved in the strata of the earth's crust, esp. if mineralized; (*fig.*) antiquated. *n.* An organic body preserved in the strata of the earth's crust; an antiquated person. **fossilif'erous,** *a.* Containing fossils.

foster (fos'tẽr) [A.-S. *fōstrian*, from *fōstor*, nourishment], *v.t.* To nourish, rear, promote the growth of; to nurse, cherish; to harbour (as an ill feeling). **foster-brother, -sister, -child,** etc., *n.* One by nursing or upbringing, but not by birth. **foster-father, -mother, -parent,** *n.* One who takes the place of a parent in rearing a child.

foul (foul) [A.-S. *fūl*], *a.* Dirty, filthy, loathsome, offensive; covered or filled with noxious matter, clogged, choked; obscene, polluted; unfair, against the rules; cloudy, rainy; full of printer's errors, inaccurate (of a proof). *n.* A wilful collision, an interference, any breach of the rules of a game or contest. *v.t.* To defile, soil, pollute; to dishonour; to come into collision with, to impede, block, or entangle. *v.i.* To become foul, clogged, or entangled; to come into collision. **foully,** *adv.* **foulness,** *n.*

found (1) (found) [L. *fundere*, to pour], *v.t.* To cast by melting (metal) or fusing (material for glass) and pouring it into a mould; to make of molten metal or glass. **founder** (1), *n.* One who casts metal. **foundry,** *n.* A place where metals are cast; the act or art of casting metals.

found (2) (found) [L. *fundāre*, from *fundus*, bottom], *v.t.* To lay the foundation or basis of; to fix firmly; to establish, endow, originate; to conduct or base (upon) *v.i.* To rest (upon) as a foundation. **founder** (2), *n.* One who originates anything, esp. one who endows an institution.

foundation (foun-dā'shŭn), *n.* The act of establishing; that on which anything is established or by which it is sustained; permanent basis; the endowment of an institution; the basis of a structure. **foundationer,** *n.* One supported by the endowment of a college or school.

founder (3) (foun'dẽr) [O.F. *fondrer*, to sink in], *v.i.* To fill with water and sink (as a ship); to fall lame (of a horse).

foundling (found'ling), *n.* A deserted child of unknown parents.

fount (1) (fount) [L. *fons fontem*], *n.* A spring, a fountain, a well.

fount (2) (fount) [F. *fonte*, from *fondre*], *n.* A set of type of one face and size.

fountain (foun'tăn) [O.F. *fontaine*, L. *fons fontis*], *n.* A spring of water; the source of a river; a jet of water driven into the air by pressure; the structure for producing this; a public erection with a drinking-supply; a reservoir to contain a liquid, as in a pen, etc.; a source, a first principle.

four (fôr) [A.-S. *fēower*], *a.* Consisting of one more than three, or twice two. *n.* The sum of one and three; a symbol expressing this, 4, iiii, or iv; a set of four, a team of four horses, a four-oared boat or its crew, etc. **on all fours:** On the hands and knees; agreeing precisely with. **four-in-hand,** *a.* Drawn by four horses. *n.* A vehicle so drawn. **four-poster,** *n.* A large bedstead with four high posts at the corners. **fourscore,** *a.* and *n.* Four times twenty, eighty; eighty years old. **four-square,** *a.* Square-shaped; firmly established, immovable. **four-wheeler,** *n.* A vehicle having four wheels, esp. a cab. **fourfold,** *a.* Four times as many or as much, quadruple. *adv.* In fourfold measure. **foursome,** *n.* (*Golf*) A game between two pairs, the partners playing alternately. **fourteen,** *a.* Amounting to four and ten. *n.* The number amounting to four and ten; a symbol denoting this, 14 or xiv. **fourteenth,** *a.* and *n.* **fourth,** *a.* and *n.* **fourthly,** *adv.*

fowl (foul) [A.-S. *fugol*], *n.* A bird, esp. of the domestic or poultry kind; birds collectively; their flesh as food. *v.i.* To hunt, catch, or kill birds for sport. **fowler,** *n.* One who pursues wild-fowl for sport. **fowling-piece,** *n.* A light smooth-bore gun for shooting wild-fowl.

fox (foks) [A.-S.], *n.* A small quadruped, notorious for its cunning, hunted in England for sport; a sly, cunning fellow. *v.i.* To become sour; to turn reddish (of paper, etc.). **fox-brush,** *n.* The tail of a fox. **foxglove,** *n.* A plant with purple flowers resembling the fingers of a glove. **fox-hole,** *n.* (*Mil.*) A hole hastily dug to obtain shelter from gunfire. **fox-hound,** *n.* A hound trained to hunt foxes. **fox-terrier,** *n.* A short-haired dog, orig. employed to unearth foxes. **fox-trot,** *n.* A kind of dance. **foxed,** *a.* Stained with spots, as a book or print. **foxy,** *a.*

foyer (fwa'yā) [F.], *n.* A large public room in a theatre.

fracas (fra-ka) [F.], *n.* A disturbance, a row; an uproar; a noisy quarrel.

fraction (frăk'shŭn) [L. *fractus*, broken], *n.* A fragment, a small piece; (*Math.*) the expression of one or more parts of a unit. **fractional,** *a.*

fractious (frăk'shŭs), *a.* Apt to quarrel; snappish, fretful. **fractiousness,** *n.*

fracture (frăk'chŭr), *n.* Breaking by violence; a break; breakage, esp. of a bone. *v.t.* To break across. *v.i.* To break or crack.

fragile (frăj'īl) [F., from L. *frangere*, to break], *a.* Brittle, easily broken; frail. **fragil'ity,** *n.*

fragment (frăg'mẽnt) [L. *fragmentum*], *n.* A piece broken off; an incomplete portion. **frag'mentary,** *a.*

fragrant (frā'grănt) [L. *frāgrans*, emitting a perfume], *a.* Sweet-smelling, odorous. **fragrance,** *n.* **fragrantly,** *adv.*

frail (frāl) [O.F. *fraile*, as **FRAGILE**], *a.* Fragile, delicate; in weak health; liable to be led astray. **frailty,** *n.*

frame (frām) [A.-S. *framian*, to avail, to further], *v.t.* To construct by fitting parts together; to fit, adjust, contrive; to devise, compose, express; to plan, to form in the mind, conceive, imagine; to surround with a frame, to serve as a frame to. *n.* Anything composed of parts fitted together; a structure, skeleton of a structure; the build of anything; disposition of mind; a case to enclose or surround a picture, pane of glass, etc. **frame-up,** *n.* Evidence concocted for incriminating. **framework,** *n.* The frame of a structure; the fabric for enclosing or supporting anything, or forming a substructure, structure, arrangement (of society, etc.).

franc (frăngk) [F.], *n.* The French unit of value.

franchise (frăn′chiz) [O.F., from *franchir,* to free oneself], *n.* A right, privilege, etc., granted to an individual or a body; the district to which a certain privilege extended; citizenship; the right of voting for a member of Parliament.

Franciscan (frăn-sis′kăn) [L. *Franciscus*], *a.* Of or pertaining to St. Francis of Assisi. *n.* A member of the Franciscan Order, a grey friar.

frangible (frăn′jibl) [L. *frangere,* to break], *a.* That may be easily broken. **frangibil′ity,** *n.*

Frank (1) (frăngk) [L. *Francus*], *n.* A member of the ancient German peoples who conquered France in the 6th cent.; a name given by Orientals to a European.

frank (frăngk) [L. *francus,* free, from prec.], *a.* Ingenuous, sincere, candid; generous, unrestrained. *v.t.* To send under an official privilege, so as to pass free; to secure the free passage of (a person or thing). *n.* A signature authorizing a letter to go through the post free of charge. **frankly,** *adv.* **frankness,** *n.*

frankincense (frăngk′in-sens) [O.F. *franc encens*], *n.* A resin burning with a fragrant smell.

franklin (frăngk′lin) [A.-F. *fraunclein*], *n.* Formerly, an English freeholder, not liable to feudal service.

frantic (frăn′tik) [Gr. *phrenitis,* inflammation of the brain], *a.* Raving, outrageously excited; suffering from frenzy. **frantically, -ticly,** *adv.*

fraternal (fră-tĕr′năl) [L. *frāter,* brother], *a.* Brotherly; pertaining to or becoming brethren. **fraternity,** *n.* The state of a brother; brotherliness; a brotherhood, a body of men associated for a common interest or by similarity of rank, profession, etc. **frat′ernize,** *v.i.* To associate with others of like occupation or tastes.

fratricide (frăt′ri-sīd), *n.* The murder or murderer of a brother. **fratricidal,** *a.*

fraud (frawd) [O.F. *fraude*], *n.* An act or course of deliberate deception, esp. directed to the detriment of another; a trick, trickery; a deceptive person, a humbug. **fraudulent, -ticly,** *a.* **fraudulence,** *n.*

fraught (frawt) [obs. n., cargo, cp. FREIGHT], *a.* Freighted, laden, stored (with).

fray (1) (frā), *n.* A noisy quarrel, brawl, riot; a combat, contest.

fray (2) (frā) [L. *fricāre,* to rub], *v.t.* To

wear away by rubbing; to chafe. *v.i.* To become rubbed or worn.

freak (frēk [?], *n.* A sudden wanton whim or caprice; a vagary; a monstrosity, a living curiosity. **freakish,** *a.*

freckle (frekl) [Scand.], *n.* A light-brown spot on the skin.

free (frē) [A.-S. *frēo*], *a.* At liberty; not under restraint; under a government based on the consent of the governed; not under foreign domination; released from authority or control; independent, unattached; exempt (from); not bound or limited (by rules, etc.), not literal (of a translation); unceremonious, reckless; impudent; indelicate; unreserved, ingenuous; admitted to certain privileges (of); liberal, generous; spontaneous. *adv.* Freely. *v.t.* To set at liberty, to emancipate; to rid or relieve (of or from); to clear, disentangle. **free-board,** *n.* The space between the water-line on a vessel and the upper side of the deck, or the uppermost full deck. **freedman,** *n.* A manumitted slave. **free-hand,** *a.* (*Drawing*) Executed by the hand without the aid of instruments. **free-handed,** *n.* Open-handed, liberal. **freehold,** *n.* An estate held in fee-simple or fee-tail. **freeholder,** *n.* **free-lance,** *n.* A member of one of the free companies of mercenaries in the Middle Ages; one who works independently of party; an unattached journalist. **freeman, -woman,** *n.* One not a slave; one who holds the franchise of a citizen, the freedom of a city, company, etc. **freespoken,** *n.* Speaking without reserve; blunt, candid, frank. **freestone,** *n.* A stone which can be cut in any direction. **free-thinker,** *n.* A rationalist, sceptic, or agnostic; one who rejects authority in religious belief. **free-thinking,** *n.* and *a.* **free-thought,** *n.* **free-wheel,** *n.* A driving wheel on a cycle that can revolve when disconnected from the driving gear; a cycle with such a wheel. *v.i.* To run (on a cycle or motor-car) without employing motive power.

freebooter (frē′boo-tĕr) [Duc. *vrijbuiter*], *n.* A pirate, a plundering adventurer.

freedom (frē-dŏm), *n.* State of being free, liberty, exemption from constraint.

Freemason (frē′mā-sŏn), *n.* A member of the "Free and Accepted Masons", a secret association. **Freemasonry,** *n.*

freesia (frē′ziǎ) [etym. unknown], *n.* A genus of bulbous flowering plants allied to the iris.

freeze (frēz) [A.-S. *frēosan*], *v.i.* (*past* froze, *p.p.* frozen) To be turned from fluid to solid by cold; (*impers.*) to be at that degree of cold at which water turns to ice; to feel cold, to lose animation through cold; to be chilled (by fear). *v.t.* To congeal by cold; to form ice upon or convert into ice; to chill, to paralyse. **freezing,** *a.* (*fig.*) Very cold; distant, chilling. **freezing-point,** *n.* The point at which water freezes (32° Fahrenheit, 0° Centigrade).

freight (frāt) [O.F. *fret*], *n.* Charge for transportation of goods, esp. by water; a cargo, *v.t.* To load (a ship); to hire or charter for carrying. **freightage,** *n.*

French (french) [A.-S. *Frencisc*], *a.* Pertaining to France or its inhabitants; belonging to or native of France. *n.* The language spoken by the people of France; the people of France.

frenzy (fren'zĭ), *n.* Delirium, madness; temporary mental derangement. **frenzied,** *a.*

frequent (fré'kwĕnt) [L. *frequens*], *a.* Occurring often; occurring near together. *v.t.* (fré-kwent') To resort to often or habitually. **frequence, -quency,** *n.* The quality of occurring frequently; repetition at short intervals; rate of occurrence or recurrence; (*Elect.*) speed of variations of alternating currents, electro-motive forces, and magnetic waves. **frequen'tative,** *a.* Expressing frequent repetition of an action. *n.* A verb doing this. **frequen'ter,** *n.* One who frequents. **fre'quently,** *adv.*

fresco (fres'kō) [It., fresh], *n.* (*pl.* -coes) Water-colour painting on fresh plaster.

fresh (fresh) [A.-S. *fersc*], *a.* New; not known or used previously; different; newly produced, not decayed or tainted; pure, not salt, drinkable; not preserved; just arrived (from); looking healthy; clearly remembered; frisky (of a horse); brisk, active; refreshing (of a breeze), etc. **freshen,** *v.t.* To make fresh; to enliven, revive. *v.i.* To become fresh; to lose saltness. **freshet,** *n.* A sudden flood caused by heavy rains, etc. **freshly,** *adv.* **freshman,** *n.* A beginner, esp. a student in his first term at a university. **freshness,** *n.* **freshwater,** *a.* Pertaining to fresh water, as dist. from the sea.

fret (1) (fret) [A.-S. *fretan*], *v.t.* To eat away, corrode, wear away, chafe; to vex, annoy; to disturb (as water). *v.i.* To be worn or eaten away; to be irritated or troubled, to chafe. *n.* Act or process of fretting or rubbing away; a state of chafing or vexation. **fretful,** *a.* Peevish, irritable; captious. **fretfulness,** *n.*

fret (2) (fret) [O.F. *freten*], *v.t.* To ornament (esp. a ceiling) with carved work; to variegate. **fretsaw,** *n.* A small ribbon-saw used in cutting fretwork. **fretwork,** *n.* Carved or open woodwork in ornamental patterns.

fret (3) (fret) [?], *n.* A cross-bar on the finger-board of certain stringed instruments.

Freudian (froi'dĭ-ăn) [S. *Freud* (1856–1939)], *a.* (*Psychol.*) Pertaining to the system of psychological theories of Freud.

friable (frī'ăbl) [L. *friāre*, to crumble], *a.* Easily reducible to powder.

friar (frī'ár) [L. *frāter*, brother], *n.* A member of a male monastic order, esp. the Augustinians, Franciscans, Dominicans, or Carmelites. **friary,** *n.* A monastery.

fricassee (frik-á-sē') [F.], *n.* A dish of birds, rabbits, etc., cut into pieces, fried or stewed, and served with sauce. *v.t.* To cook thus.

friction (frik'shŭn) [L. *fricāre*, to rub], *n.* Act of rubbing; resistance which a body meets with in moving over another; conflict, disagreement. **frictional,** *a.*

Friday (frī'dā, -dĭ) [A.-S. *frige-dæg*], *n.* The sixth day of the week. **Good Friday:** The Friday before Easter, kept sacred by the Christian Church in memory of the Crucifixion.

friend (frend) [A.-S. *frēond*], *n.* One attached to another by affection, as dist. from family relationship; an acquaintance, adherent, sympathizer, colleague; a Quaker; anything that helps one in an emergency. **friendless,** *a.* **friendly,** *a.* Good-natured; acting as a friend; characteristic of friends; favourable. **friendliness,** *n.* **friendship,** *n.*

frieze (1) (frēz) [F. *frise*], *n.* The middle division of an entablature; the band of sculpture occupying this.

frieze (2) (frēz) [Dut. *Vries*, a Frieslander], *n.* A coarse woollen cloth.

frigate (frig'át) [It. *fregata*], *n.* An obsolete war-ship, next smaller to a line-of-battle ship; a convoy escort vessel, in size between a destroyer and a corvette. **frigate-bird,** *n.* A large tropical raptorial sea-bird.

fright (frīt) [A.-S. *fyrhto*], *n.* Sudden and violent fear; a state of terror; one of ridiculous appearance in person or dress. **frighten,** *v.t.* To alarm, terrify, scare. **frightful,** *a.* Dreadful, horrible, hideous; causing fright; extraordinary. **frightfully,** *adv.* **frightfulness,** *n.*

frigid (frij'ĭd) [L. *frigus*, cold], *a.* Cold; lacking warmth of feeling or ardour; stiff, formal; dull, flat. **frigid'ity,** *n.*

frill (fril) [?], *n.* A pleated or fluted edging, on a shirt, etc. **frilling,** *n.*

fringe (frinj) [O.F. *frenge*, L. *fimbria*], *n.* An ornamental border of loose threads or tassels; an edging; the front hair cut short and straight. *v.t.* To border with a fringe.

frippery (frip'ẽr-ĭ) [O.F. *freperie*], *n.* Worthless, needless, or trumpery finery.

frisk (frisk) [O.F. *frisque*, lively], *v.i.* To gambol about; to frolic. *v.t.* To search the person for concealed arms. *n.* A gambol, a frolic. **frisky,** *a.* **friskily,** *adv.*

fritillary (frit'ĭ-lăr-ĭ) [L. *fritillus*, a dice-box], *n.* A liliaceous genus with flowers speckled dull purple; a butterfly with wings similarly marked.

fritter (1) (frit'ẽr) [L. *frictus*, fried], *n.* A light batter containing slices of fruit.

fritter (2) (frit'ẽr) [?], *n.* (*pl.*) Fragments, shreds. *v.t.* To break into small pieces; to trifle away (time, money, etc.).

frivolous (friv'ó-lŭs) [L. *frivolus*], *a.* Trumpery; inclined to unbecoming levity, silly. **frivol'ity,** *n.*

frizz (friz), *v.t.* To crisp; to form into a curly, crinkled mass (of hair); to raise a nap on (cloth). *n.* Frizzed hair. **frizzy,** *a.*

frizzle (1) (frizl), *v.t.* To curl; to crisp. *n.* Frizzed hair.

frizzle (2) (frizl) [?], *v.t.* To fry (bacon, etc.) with a hissing noise. *v.i.* To hiss while being fried.

fro (frō), *adv.* Away, backward, from.

frock (frok) [F. *froc*], *n.* The long upper garment worn by monks; a gown or dress worn by women or children; a frock-coat; a smock-frock. **frock-coat,** *n.* A close-fitting body-coat, with broad skirts of the same length before and behind.

frog (1) (frog) [A.-S. *frogga*], *n.* An amphibious animal of the genus *Rana*.

frog (2) (frog) [Port. *froco*], *n.* A spindle-shaped button used for fastening military cloaks, ladies' mantles, etc.; the loop of a scabbard.

frog (3) (frog) [?], *n.* A tender horny substance in the middle of a horse's sole.

frolic (frol'ik) [?], *a.* Gay, sportive; full of pranks. *n.* A prank; an outburst of gaiety. *v.i.* To play pranks; to indulge in merry-making. **frolicsome**, *a.*

from (from) [A.-S. *from, fram* (cp. Icel. *frā*, fro)], *prep.* Away, out of; beginning with, after; because of.

frond (frond) [L. *frons*, a leaf], *n.* (*Bot.*) A leaf-like expansion, esp. of the ferns and allied plants.

front (frŭnt) [L. *frons*, the forehead], *n.* The fore-part of anything; the most conspicuous part; a position directly before one; the forehead; the principal face of a building; (*Mil.*) the line of battle, the ground on which fighting is going on. *a.* Relating to or situated in or at the front. *v.t.* To face, to look (to or towards); to confront, to meet face to face; to furnish with a front. *v.i.* To face, look, be situated with the front (towards). **frontage**, *n.* The front part of a building; land facing a road or water. **frontal**, *a.*

frontier (frun'tēr) [O.F., as prec.], *n.* That part of a country which borders upon another. *a.* Pertaining to or situated on the frontier.

frontispiece (frŭn'tis-pēs) [L. *frons*, forehead, *specere*, to look], *n.* A picture fronting the title-page of a book.

frost (frost) [A.-S. *forst*], *n.* Act or state of freezing, congelation of fluids by cold; temperature below freezing-point; frosty weather; rime; (*fig.*) frigidity. *v.t.* To injure by frost; to cover with or as with rime; to furnish with frost-nails. **frost-bite**, *n.* Inflammation, usu. of the extremities, caused by extreme cold. **frost-nail**, *n.* Projecting nail in a horse's shoe to prevent slipping on ice. **frosted**, *a.* frosting. *n.* A mixture used to cover cakes; a rough surface on glass, metal, etc., in imitation of frost. **frosty**, *a.*

froth (frawth) [Scand., A.-S. *āfrēothan*], *n.* Foam, bubbles caused in liquors by agitation or fermentation; scum; empty display of wit or rhetoric. *v.t.* To cause to foam. *v.i.* To form or emit froth. **frothy**, *a.*

froward (frō'wàrd), *a.* Refractory, perverse, mutinous. **frowardly**, *adv.* **frowardness**, *n.*

frown (froun) [O.F.*frong nier*], *v.i.* To express displeasure or seriousness by contracting the brows; to look gloomy, threatening, or with disfavour; to scowl. *n.* A knitting of the brows in displeasure or mental absorption.

frowzy (frou'zi) [?], *a.* Musty, fusty.

fructify (frŭk'ti-fī) [L. *fructificāre*], *v.t.* To make fruitful; to fertilize. *v.i.* To bear fruit. **fructuate**, *v.i.* To bear or come to fruit. **fructuation**, *n.* **fructif'erous**, *a.* Bearing fruit. **fructifica'tion**, *n.*

frugal (froo'gàl) [L. *frūgālis*], *a.* Thrifty, sparing; economical. **frugal'ity**, *n.* Economy, thrift. **frugally**, *adv.*

fruit (froot) [L. *frux*], *n.* The edible succulent product of a plant in which the seeds are enclosed; (*Bot.*) the matured ovary with parts adhering thereto, the spores of ferns, etc.; (*pl.*) vegetable products serving for food; (*fig.*) product, result; benefit, profit. *v.i.* To bear fruit. **fruitage**, *n.* **fruitar'ian**, *n.* One that feeds on fruit. **fruiterer**, *n.* One who deals in fruits. **fruitful**, *a.* Producing fruit in abundance; fertile; prolific. **fruitfully**, *adv.* **fruitfulness**, *n.* **fruity**, *a.* Like fruit; (of wine) tasting of the grape; rich, full-flavoured.

fruition (froo-ish'ŭn), *n.* Attainment, fulfilment.

frumenty (froo'mĕn-ti) [L. *frumentum*, corn], *n.* A dish of wheat boiled in milk and spiced.

frump (frŭmp) [?], *n.* An old-fashioned, prim, or dowdy woman.

frustrate (frŭs-trāt') [L. *frustrā*, in vain], *v.t.* To thwart, to balk; to nullify, disappoint. *a.* (frŭs'-) Vain; of no effect. **frustra'tion**, *n.*

fry (1) (frī) [L. *frīgere*], *v.t.* To cook with fat in a pan over the fire. *v.i.* To be cooked thus. *n.* A dish of anything fried; the offal of pigs, sheep, oxen, etc.

fry (2) (frī) [Scand.], *n.* Very young fish; yearling salmon; a swarm of children.

fuchsia (fū'shà) [L. *Fuchs* (1501–66), German botanist], *n.* A genus of plants with pendulous funnel-shaped flowers.

fuddle (fŭdl) [Teut.], *v.t.* To make stupid, esp. with drink. *v.i.* To tipple, get drunk.

fuel (fū'él) [A.-F. *fewaile*], *n.* Wood, coal, peat, etc., for fires; anything serving to feed or increase excitement, etc.

fugitive (fū'ji-tiv) [L. *fugere*, to flee], *a.* Fleeing, runaway; transient, volatile, easily carried away; evanescent, ephemeral. *n.* One who flees from danger, pursuit, justice, etc.; a deserter, a refugee.

fugleman (fūgl-màn) [G. *flügel*, wing, *mann*, man], *n.* A soldier who took up position as a guide to the others in drill.

fugue (fūg) [F.], *n.* A polyphonic composition on one short theme, which is harmonized in counterpoint and reintroduced from time to time with variations.

fulcrum (fŭl'krŭm) [L., a support], *n.* (*pl.* -cra) The fixed point on which a lever rests or about which it turns.

fulfil (ful-fil') [A.-S. *fullfyllan*], *v.t.* To carry out, execute, satisfy; to perform, correspond to, comply with; to complete (a term of office, etc.). **fulfilment**, *n.* **fulfilling**, *n.*

fulgent (fŭl'jĕnt) [L. *fulgens*, shining], *a.* Dazzling, exceedingly bright.

full (1) (ful) [A.-S.], *a.* Containing as much as it can; well supplied, having abundance (of); satisfied with; charged or overflowing (with feeling, etc.); plentiful; perfect; wholly visible; swelling, plump; sonorous; pregnant; high (as the tide). *adv.* Quite, equally; completely, exactly; very. *n.* Complete measure; the fullest extent, highest state or point. *v.t.* To give fullness to, to make full. *v.i.* To become full. **full-**

blooded, *a.* Vigorous; of pure blood. **full-blown,** *a.* Fully expanded (as a flower); mature. **full-swing,** *adv.* At full speed.

full (2) (ful) [L. *fullo,* a fuller], *v.t.* To cleanse and thicken (as cloth). **fuller** (ful'ėr), *n.* One who fulls cloth. **fuller's earth,** *n.* An earth which absorbs grease, used in fulling cloth.

fullness (ful'nės), *n.* State or quality of being full; satiety; largeness, volume.

fulmar (ful'már) [Scand.], *n.* An Arctic sea-bird allied to the petrels.

fulminate (ful'mi-nāt) [L. *fulmen,* lightning], *v.i.* To lighten or thunder; to explode with a loud noise; to thunder out denunciations. *v.t.* To cause to explode; to utter (threats, etc.). **fulmina'tion,** *n.* **ful'minator,** *n.*

fulsome (ful'sům), *a.* Disgusting by excess, coarse, satiating (esp. of flattery, etc.).

fumble (fůmbl) [?], *v.i.* To grope about in an aimless or awkward manner. *v.i.* To handle or manage awkwardly.

fume (fūm) [L. *fūmus,* smoke], *n.* A vaporous exhalation; a narcotic vapour (*usu. in pl.*); mental agitation, esp. anger; anything unsubstantial. *v.i.* To emit or pass off in smoke or vapour; to show irritation, to fret, chafe. **fumy,** *a.*

fumigate (fū'mi-gāt), *v.t.* To disinfect by smoke or vapour; to perfume. **fumiga'tion,** *n.* **fu'migator,** *n.*

fun (fůn) [?], *n.* Sport, amusement, frolic, drollery.

function (fůngk'shůn) [L. *functio,* from *fungi,* to perform], *n.* The specific activity, operation, or power belonging to an agent or organ; occupation, office; a public or official ceremony; a social entertainment of some importance; (*Math.*) a quantity dependent for its value on another or others so that a change in one affects the first. *v.i.* To perform a function or duty; to operate. **functional,** *a.* **functionary,** *n.* One who holds an office or trust; an official. *a.* Pertaining to functions; official.

fund (fůnd) [L. *fundus,* bottom], *n.* A sum of money or a stock available; assets, capital; (*pl.*) money constituting a national debt; this regarded as an investment; pecuniary resources. *v.t.* To convert into a single fund or debt; to collect, store; to place in a fund. **funded,** *a.* Invested in public funds; forming part of a national debt.

fundament (fůn'dá-mėnt) [L. *fundāmentum*], *n.* The lower part of the body, the buttocks.

fundamental (fůn-dá-men'tál), *a.* Pertaining to or serving as a foundation or base; essential, primary, indispensable. *n.* A principle, rule, etc., forming the basis or ground-work.

funeral (fū'nér-ál) [L. *fūnus,* a funeral procession], *a.* Pertaining to burial. *n.* The solemn and ceremonial burying of the dead; interment, obsequies. **funer'eal,** *a.* Suitable for a funeral; dismal, sad, mournful.

fungus (fůng'gůs) [L.], *n.* A mushroom, toadstool, or other similar plant. **fungous,** *a.* Like or of the nature of a fungus; ephemeral; spongy.

funicular (fū-nik'ū-lár) [L. *fūniculus,* a little rope, -AR], *a.* Pertaining to, consisting of, or depending on a rope or cable.

funk (fůngk) [?], *n.* A state of fear or panic; a coward. *v.i.* To flinch, to shrink in fear or cowardice. *v.t.* To be afraid of; to shirk.

funnel (fůn'ėl) [M.E. *fonel,* prob. through O.F. from L. *fundere,* to pour], *n.* A conical vessel for conducting liquids into vessels with a small opening; a tube or shaft for ventilation, etc.; the chimney of a steamship, etc.

funny (fůn'i), *a.* Droll, laughable; causing mirth; strange, queer, puzzling.

fur (fėr) [O.F. *forrer,* to line, from Teut.], *n.* The soft fine hair growing thick upon certain animals; (*pl.*) the skins, esp. dressed skins of such animals; a crust deposited by a liquid, esp. on the interior of kettles by hard water; a deposit from wine; morbid matter on the tongue. *v.t.* To line or trim with fur. **furred,** *a.* **furrier** (fůr'i-ėr), *n.* A dealer in furs; one who prepares furs. **furry,** *a.*

furbelow (fėr'bė-lō) [?], *n.* A piece of puckered stuff used as trimming, a flounce.

furbish (fėr'bish) [O.H.G. *furban*], *v.t.* To polish up; to renovate.

furcate (fėr'kāt, -kát) [L. *furcātus*], *a.* Forked, dividing like a fork.

furious (fū'ri-ůs), *a.* Raging, violent, frantic; tempestuous; vehement, eager. **furiously,** *adv.*

furl (fėrl) [?], *v.t.* To roll up (a sail) and wrap about a yard, etc.

furlong (fėr'long) [A.-S. *furh,* FURROW, *lang,* LONG], *n.* The eighth of a mile, 220 yards.

furlough (fėr'lō) [Dut. *verlof*], *n.* Leave of absence, esp. to a soldier. *v.t.* To grant this to.

furnace (fėr'nás) [L. *fornācem,* oven], *n.* A chamber in which fuel is burned for the production of intense heat.

furnish (fėr'nish) [F. *fournir*], *v.t.* To provide or supply (with); to equip, fit up. **furnisher,** *n.* **furnishings,** *n.pl.*

furniture (fėr'ni-chůr) [F. *fourniture*], *n.* Equipment, outfit; movable articles with which a room is furnished.

furore (fū-rōr'ā) [It.]. Great excitement or enthusiasm; a craze, a rage.

furrow (fůr'ō) [A.-S. *furh*], *n.* A trench made by a plough; a narrow groove; a rut; the track of a ship; a wrinkle. *v.t.* To plough, to make grooves, furrows, or wrinkles in. **furrowy,** *a.*

further (fėr'thėr) [A.-S. *furthra*], *a.* More remote; more advanced; beyond that already existing or stated, additional. *adv.* To a greater distance, degree, or extent; moreover, also. *v.t.* To help forward, advance, promote. **furtherance,** *n.* Promotion, help. **furtherer,** *n.* **furthermore,** *adv.* Moreover, besides. **furthermost,** *a.* Furthest, most remote. **furthest,** *a.* Most remote. *adv.* At or to the greatest distance or extent.

furtive (fėr'tiv) [L. *furtīvus,* theft], *a.* Stealthy, sly; designed to escape attention; obtained by or as by theft. **furtively,** *adv.*

fury (fū'ri) [L. *furere*, to rage], *n.* Vehement, uncontrollable anger, rage; impetuosity.

furze (fĕrz) [A.-S. *fyrs*], *n.* Gorse or whin, a spinous evergreen shrub with bright yellow flowers.

fuse (1) (fūz) [L. *fūsus*, poured], *v.t.* To melt; to unite by or as by melting together. *v.i.* To melt, become fluid, or united by melting together. *n.* (*Elec.*) A device for protecting against a short circuit; the melting of wire caused by a short circuit. fusible, *a.*

fuse (2) (fūz) [L. *fūsus*, a spindle], *n.* A cord, etc., saturated with combustible material, used for igniting an explosive.

fusee (fū-zē') [as prec.], *n.* The cone round which the chain is wound in a clock or watch; a large-headed match.

fuselage (fū'zĕ-lāj), *n.* The light framework of the body of an aeroplane.

fusel oil (fū'zĕl oil) [G. *fusel*, inferior spirit], *n.* A poisonous alcoholic oil formed during the manufacture of corn, potato, or grape spirits.

fusil (fū'zil) [F. *fusil*, a fire-steel], *n.* An obsolete firelock, lighter than a musket. fusilier', *n.* Orig. a soldier armed with this; now a member of certain line regiments.

fusillade (fū-zi-lād') [F. *fusiller*, to shoot, as prec.], *n.* A continuous discharge of firearms.

fusion (fū'zhŭn) [L. *fūsio*], *n.* Act of melting or rendering liquid by heat; state of being so melted or liquefied; union by melting together, blending.

fuss (fŭs) [?], *n.* Excessive activity or trouble; bustle, commotion, too much ado. *v.i.* To make much ado about nothing; to worry. fussy, *a.*

fustian (fŭs'ti-ăn) [O.F. *fustaigne*, Arab. *Fustāt*, a suburb of Cairo], *n.* A coarse twilled cotton cloth, with velvety pile; velveteen, corduroy; (*fig.*) bombast.

futile (fū'til) [L. *fūtilis*, leaky], *a.* Useless; trifling, worthless. futil'ity, *n.*

future (fū'chŭr) [L. *futurus*, fut. p. of *esse*, to be], *a.* That will be; that is to come or happen. *n.* Time to come, that which will be; prospective condition, state, etc.; the future tense; (*pl.*) stocks, etc., bought or sold for future delivery. Futurism, *n.* (*Art*) A movement aiming at visualizing the movement and development of objects instead of the picture they present at a given moment. Futurist, *a.*; futurity (fū-tūr'i-ti), *n.* The state of being future; future time, esp. eternity.

G

gab (găb) [?], *n.* (*vulg.*) Idle talk, chatter.

gabble (găbl) [?], *v.i.* To utter inarticulate sounds; to talk rapidly and incoherently. *v.t.* To utter noisily or inarticulately. *n.* Rapid, incoherent talk.

gaberdine (găb'ér-dēn) [Sp. *gabardina*], *n.* A long rough cloak, esp. as worn in the Middle Ages by Jews, almsmen, etc.

gaberlunzie (găb-er-lŭn'zi, -yi) [Sc.], *n.* A strolling beggar.

gable (găbl) [O.F.], *n.* The triangular portion of the end of a building under the roof; a wall with upper part shaped like this. gabled, *a.*

gaby (gā'bi) [?], *n.* A fool, a simpleton.

gad (1) (găd) [Scand.], *n.* A pointed metal tool; an iron punch with a wooden handle; a sharp wedge for splitting stone.

gad (2) (găd) [?], *v.i.* To rove or wander idly (about); to straggle (as a plant).

gadfly (găd'flī), *n.* An insect which bites cattle, etc.; a horse-fly; something or someone that irritates.

gadget (găj'ét) [?], *n.* (*colloq.*) An appliance, a tool, a contrivance for doing a job; a trick of the trade.

Gael (gāl) [Gael. *Gaidheal*], *n.* A Scottish Celt. Gaelic (gāl'ik), *a.* Pertaining to the Gaels. *n.* Their language.

gaff (găf) [O.F. *gaffe*], *n.* A stick with a metal hook, used to land heavy fish; the spar extending the upper edge of fore-and-aft sails not set on stays. *v.t.* To seize or land with a gaff.

gaffer (găf'ér), *n.* An old fellow, esp. an aged rustic; grandfather; a foreman.

gag (găg) [?], *v.t.* To stop the mouth (of a person) by thrusting something into it; to deprive of freedom of speech; (*Theat. slang*) to put interpolations into. *n.* Something thrust into the mouth to prevent one from speaking.

gage (gāj), *n.* A pledge, a security to be forfeited in case of non-performance of some act; a glove or other symbol thrown as a challenge; a challenge. *v.t.* To deposit as pledge.

gaiety (gā'ė-ti) [O.F. *gayeté*], *n.* State of being gay; mirth, festivity.

gain (gān) [O.F., from *gaigner*], *n.* Anything obtained as an advantage or in return for labour; increase, growth; (*pl.*) profits, emoluments. *v.t.* To obtain; to earn, win, acquire; to progress, to advance, reach, attain to; to win (over). *v.i.* To advance; to gain ground, to encroach (upon); to get the advantage (on or upon). gainer, *n.* gainings, *n.pl.* Profits, gains.

gainsay (gān'sā) [Scand.], *v.t.* To contradict, deny; to dispute. gainsayer, *n.*

gait (gāt) [Icel. *gata*], *n.* Manner of walking or going, carriage.

gaiter (gā'tér) [F. *guêtre*], *n.* A covering for the leg from knee to ankle.

gala (gā'lä) [It.], *n.* A festivity, fête.

galactic (gȧ-lăk'tik) [Gr. *galaktikos*, milky], *a.* Pertaining to milk; (*Astron.*) to the galaxy.

galantine (găl'ăn-tēn) [F.], *n.* A dish of white meat, freed from bone, spiced, jellied, and served cold.

galaxy (găl'ak-si) [O.F. *galaxie*], *n.* The Milky Way, a luminous band, consisting of innumerable small stars, stretching across the sky; (*fig.*) a brilliant assemblage.

gale (1) (gāl) [Scand.], *n.* A strong wind, one less violent than a tempest.

gale (2) (gāl), *n.* A periodic payment of rent.

F

gall (1) (gawl) [A.-S. *gealla*], *n.* A bitter, yellowish fluid secreted by the liver, bile; rancour, malignity, bitterness of mind.

gall (2) (gawl) (L. *galla*], *n.* A morbid excrescence on plants, esp. the oak, caused by an insect.

gall (3) (gawl) [A.-S. *gealla*], *n.* A sore or blister, esp. one produced on a horse by chafing. *v.t.* To chafe, to injure by rubbing or friction; to annoy, harass, vex. **galling**, *a.*

gallant (găl'ănt) [O.F., pres. p. of *galer*, to make merry], *a.* Gay, showy; fine, stately, high-spirited, courageous, chivalrous; (gă-lănt') specially attentive to women. *n.* A man of fashion, a beau; (gă-lănt') a man attentive and polite to women. *v.t.* (gă-lănt') To attend as a cavalier, to escort; to pay court to; to flirt with. *v.i.* To play the gallant. **gal'lantry**, *n.*

galleon (găl'ě-ŏn) [Sp. *galeon*], *n.* A large ship, used in 15th–17th cents.

gallery (găl'ěr-i) [O.F. *galerie*], *n.* An elevated floor or platform projecting from the wall of a church, theatre, etc.; (*Theat.*) the highest and cheapest seats; the persons occupying these; a corridor, passage, a long and narrow room; a balcony.

galley (găl'i) [O.F. *galie*, late L. *galea*, a galley], *n.* A low, flat vessel, with one deck, with sails and oars; a large rowboat used by the captain of a man-of-war; a state barge; the cook-house on board ship; (*Print.*) a tray on which type is placed as it is set.

Gallic [L. *Gallicus*], *a.* Of or pertaining to ancient Gaul. **Gallicism**, *n.* A French expression or idiom.

gallimaufry (găl-i-maw'fri) [F. *gallimafrée*], *n.* A hodge-podge; a ridiculous medley.

gallinaceous (găl-i-nā'shŭs) [L. *gallīna*, a hen], *a.* Of or pertaining to the group of birds containing pheasants, partridges, grouse, turkeys, domestic fowls, etc.

gallipot (găl'i-pot) [?], *n.* A small glazed earthenware pot for ointments, etc.

gallivant (găl-i-vănt') [?], *v.i.* To gad about.

gallon (găl'ŏn) [O.F. *galon*], *n.* A dry measure of capacity, one-eighth of a bushel; a measure for liquids, containing 277¼ cubic inches, 8 pints or 4 quarts.

galloon (gă-loon') [F. *galon*], *n.* A narrow braid interwoven with gold or silver thread.

gallop (găl'ŏp) [O.F. *galoper*], *v.i.* To run in a series of springs, as a horse; to ride at a gallop; to go or do anything at a very rapid pace. *v.t.* To make (a horse) gallop. *n.* The motion of a horse at its fastest speed, with all the feet off the ground at one point in the motion; the act of riding or a ride at this pace. **galloper**, *n.* An aide-de-camp.

gallows (găl'ōz) [A.-S. *galga*], *n.* A framework on which murderers are hanged.

Gallup Poll (găl'ŭp) [G. *Gallup*, the inventor], *n.* Trade name of a method of ascertaining the trend of public opinion by interrogating a cross-section of the population.

galop (găl'ŏp), *n.* A lively dance in 2–4 time; music for this.

galore (gă-lôr') [Ir. *go*, to, *leor*, sufficient], *n.* Plenty, abundance. *adv.* In plenty.

galoshes (gă-losh'iz) [F. *galoche*], *n. pl.* Over-shoes for use in wet weather.

galvanism (găl'vă-nizm) [L. *Galvani*, Ital. physician (1737–98)], *n.* Electricity produced by chemical action; the science dealing with this; its application for medical purposes. **galvan'ic**, *a.* **gal'vanist**, *n.* **gal'vanize**, *v.t.* To stimulate muscular action or to plate with metal by galvanism; to rouse into life or activity as by a galvanic shock. **galvanized iron**, *n.* Iron coated with zinc (orig. by galvanic deposition).

gambit (găm'bit) [It. *gambetto*, a tripping up], *n.* An opening in chess, in which a pawn is sacrificed.

gamble (gămbl), *v.i.* To play, esp. a game of chance, for money. *n.* A gambling venture. **gambler**, *n.*

gamboge (găm-bōj') [*Cambodia*], *n.* A gum-resin, from Cambodia, Ceylon, etc., used as a yellow pigment, and in medicine.

gambol (găm'bŏl) [O.F. *gambade*, It. *gambata* (*gamba*, leg)], *v.i.* To frisk or skip about, frolic. *n.* A frolic; a skipping or playing about.

game (1) (găm) [A.-S. *gamen*], *n.* Sport, diversion; jest, as opp. to earnest; an exercise for diversion, usu. with others, a contest played according to rules; (*pl.*) athletic contests, esp. those held at set dates, like the Olympic Games, etc.; (*colloq.*, *pl.*) tricks, dodges, subterfuges; wild animals or birds pursued in the chase, as hares, grouse, etc.; the flesh of these; an object of pursuit. *a.* Pertaining to game; plucky, spirited; ready, willing (to do, etc.). *v.i.* To play at games of chance; to gamble. **gamecock**, *n.* A cock bred for fighting. **gamekeeper**, *n.* One employed to look after game, coverts, etc., and to prevent poaching. **gamesome**, *a.* Inclined to play; merry, gay. **gamester**, *n.* One addicted to gaming, a gambler.

game (2) (găm) [?], *a.* Lame, crippled; crooked (of the arm or leg).

gamin (găm'in) [F.], *n.* A street arab.

gammer (găm'ĕr), *n.* Grandmother; an old woman.

gammon (1) (găm'ŏn) [O.F. *gambon* (*gambe*, a leg)], *n.* The buttock or thigh of a hog salted and dried; a cured ham. *v.t.* To salt and dry in smoke.

gammon (2) (găm'ŏn), *n.* Nonsense, humbug; a fraud, hoax. *v.t.* To hoax, to impose upon. *v.i.* To chaff.

gammy (găm'my), *a.* Spurious; crooked, crippled, lame.

gamp (gămp) [Mrs. *Gamp*, in Dickens's 'Martin Chuzzlewit'], *n.* (*facet.*) A large and clumsy umbrella.

gamut (găm'ŭt) [med. L. *gamma ut* (*gamma*, third letter of Greek alphabet, used to mark the lowest note in the mediæval music scale, *ut*, first word in mnemonic stanza containing the names of the hexachord *Ut re mi fa sol la*)], *n.* The major diatonic scale; the whole series of notes recognized by musicians; (*fig.*) the whole range, compass, or extent.

gander (găn'dẽr) [A.-S. *gandra*], *n.* The male of the goose; a simpleton.

gang (găng) [A.-S.], *n.* A number of persons associated, often for a bad purpose; a number of workmen under a foreman, or of slaves or convicts. **ganger,** *n.* An overseer or foreman.

ganglion (găng'gli-ŏn) [Gr.], *n.* (*pl.* -glia). An enlargement in the course of a nerve forming a local centre for nervous action.

gangrene (găng'grēn) [Gr. *gangraina*], *n.* Cessation of vitality, the first stage of mortification. *v.t.* To cause this in; (*fig.*) to corrupt. *v.i.* To mortify.

gangway (găng'wā) [A.-S. *gangweg*], *n.* A passage, as between rows of seats; a temporary bridge from a ship to the shore; an opening for this.

gannet (găn'ĕt) [A.-S. *ganot*], *n.* A seabird, the solan goose.

gantry (găn'tri) [?], *n.* A wooden stand for barrels; a framework for a travelling crane.

gaol [JAIL]

gap (găp), *n.* An opening, breach; a chasm; a blank.

gape (gāp) [Icel. *gapa*], *v.i.* To yawn; to stare with open mouth in wonder, etc.; to open in a fissure, to split open. *n.* Act of gaping; (*pl.*) a disease in young fowls, characterized by much gaping; a fit of yawning.

garage (găr'aj) [F.], *n.* A building for housing or repairing motor-cars.

garb (garb) [It. *garbo*, elegance], *n.* Costume; distinctive style of dress; outward appearance. *v.t.* To dress.

garbage (gar'báj) [?], *n.* Animal refuse, offal.

garble (garbl) [?], *v.t.* To pervert, falsify.

garden (gardn) [A.-F. *gardin* (F. *jardin*)], *n.* An enclosed piece of ground for fruit, flowers, or vegetables; a particularly fertile region. *a.* Pertaining to a garden; cultivated, not wild. *v.i.* To cultivate a garden. **gardener,** *n.* **gardening,** *n.* Horticulture; work in a garden.

gardenia (gar-dē'ni-à) [Dr. A. *Garden*, Am. botanist (1730–91)], *n.* A tropical shrub cultivated for its large fragrant flowers.

gargantuan (gar-găn'tū-ăn) [*Gargantua*, the giant described by Rabelais], *a.* Immense, enormous, grossly big.

gargle (gargl) [F. *gargouiller*], *v.t.* To rinse (the mouth or throat) with medicated liquid. *n.* A liquid used for this.

gargoyle (gar'goil) [F. *gargouille*, weasand], *n.* A grotesque spout to throw rainwater clear of the wall.

garish (găr'ish) [obs. *gauren*, to stare], *a.* Gaudy flashy; excessively decorated.

garland (gar'land) [O.F. *garlande*], *n.* A wreath or festoon of flowers, etc.

garlic (gar'lik) [A.-S. *gārlēac*], *n.* A bulbous-rooted plant with a strong odour and pungent taste. **garlicky,** *a.*

garment (gar'mĕnt) [F. *garnir*], *n.* An article of clothing, apparel.

garner (gar'nẽr), *n.* A granary; a store, repository. *v.t.* To store, to gather (up).

garnet (gar'nĕt) [L. (*mālum*) *grānātum*,

POMEGRANATE, from resemblance to its seeds], *n.* A red vitreous mineral. prized as a gem.

garnish (gar'nish) [O.F. *garniss-*, stem of *garnir*, to defend, fortify], *v.t.* To adorn; to embellish (as a dish) with something laid round; (*Law*) to warn, to give notice to. *n.* A decoration, esp. things put round a dish, **garnishee,** *n.* (*Law*) One who received notice not to pay any money he owes to a third person who is indebted to the one giving notice. **garniture,** *n.* Appurtenances; trimmings, ornament.

garret (găr'ĕt) [O.F. *garite*], *n.* A room or story immediately under the roof.

garrison (găr'i-sŏn) [F. *garison*, defence], *n.* A body of troops stationed in a fort; a fortified place manned with soldiers, guns, etc. *v.t.* To furnish (a fortress) with soldiers; to occupy as a garrison.

garrotte (gà-rot') [Sp. *garrote*, a stick], *n.* Strangulation, esp. as a means of execution; robbery by means of strangling. *v.t.* To execute by this means; to render insensible in order to rob. **garrotter,** *n.*

garrulous (găr'ù-lùs) [L. *garrulus*], *a.* Talkative; chattering. **garru'lity,** *n.*

garter (gar'tẽr) [O.F. *gartier*, from *garet* (F. *jarret*), the leg], *n.* A band for holding the stocking up. *v.t.* To fasten with a garter; to put a garter upon.

garth (garth) [Icel. *garthr*], *n.* A garden, croft, or yard.

gas (găs) [Gr. *chaos*], *n.* An air-like substance of perfect fluid elasticity; such a fluid used for lighting and heating, esp. that obtained from coal; (*Coalmining*) an explosive mixture of firedamp and air; (*Am.*) petrol; a gas-jet; empty talk, brag. *v.i.* To indulge in empty talk; to boast. *v.t.* To subject to the action of gas; to attack or kill by poison-gas. **gas-burner,** *n.* The tube or jet at which the gas issues and is lighted. **gaseous** (gā'sé-ùs), *a.* In the form of gas; like gas. **gas-fitter,** *n.* A workman who lays the pipes and puts up fixtures for gas. **gasify,** *v.t.* To convert into gas. **gas-jet,** *n.* A gas-burner; a jet of flame from it. **gas-meter,** *n.* A machine for measuring and recording the quantity of gas consumed.

Gascon (găs'kŏn) [F.], *n.* A native of Gascony; a boaster. **gasconade',** *n.* Boasting, bravado.

gash (găsh) [O.F. *garser*], *v.t.* To make a long gaping cut in. *n.* A deep, open cut, especially in flesh; a cleft.

gasket (găs'kĕt) [?], *n.* A cord by which furled sails are bound to the yards.

gasolene (găs'ó-lēn), *n.* (*Am.*) Petrol.

gasometer (gà-som'e-tẽr), *n.* A reservoir for the storage of gas at gas-works.

gasp (gasp) [Scand.], *v.i.* To breathe in a convulsive manner. *v.t.* To emit or utter with gasps. *n.* A short painful catching of the breath.

gastric (găs'trik), *a.* Pertaining to the stomach. **gastri'tis,** *n.* Inflammation of the stomach.

gastro- [Gr. *gastēr*, the stomach], *comb. form.* Pertaining to the stomach.

gastronomy (găs-tron'ó-mi) [Gr. *gastro-*

nomia], *n.* The art or science of good eating, epicurism. **gastronom'ic**, *a.*

gate (gāt) [A.-S. *geat*], *n.* A movable frame of open wood or iron bars, etc., swinging or sliding, to close a passage or opening; an opening in a wall or fence as entrance to an enclosure; an opening, an opportunity; a strait, a mountain pass, etc.; a sluice in a lock or dock; the number of people attending a sporting event, the money taken at the gates. *v.t.* (*Oxf. and Camb. Univ.*) To confine to college. **gate-crash**, *v.i.* To join a party, etc., uninvited. **gateway**, *n.* An opening or passage that may be closed by a gate.

gather (găth'ĕr) [A.-S. *gœdrian*, from *geador*, together], *v.t.* To bring together, collect, accumulate, acquire; to cull, pluck; to get in, as harvest; to deduce, infer; to draw together, pucker, draw into folds or plaits; to sum (up). *v.i.* To come together, assemble, unite; to grow by addition; to concentrate, to generate pus or matter. *n.* A plait or fold of cloth, drawn together. **gathering**, *n.* Act of collecting or assembling; an assembly, a party; a boil.

gaucherie (gō'shĕ-rē) [F.], *n.* A social mistake; awkward manners.

gaud (gawd) [L. *gaudĕre*, to rejoice], *n.* A showy trinket, finery; (*pl.*) pomps and shows. **gaudery**, *n.* Finery, showy ornament, show. **gaudy**, *a.* Tastelessly ornate, flashy. *n.* A festival, esp. at college. **gaudiness**, *n.*

gauge (gāj) [*Naut.*] **gage** (O.F. *gauger*], *v.t.* To ascertain the dimensions, content, etc.; to test the capacity of (casks, etc.) for excise; to estimate (abilities, character, etc.). *n.* A standard of measurement; a measuring rod; a graduated instrument showing the quantity of rainfall, force of steam-pressure in a boiler, etc.; the depth to which a vessel sinks in the water; (*Railway*) the width between the rails. **gaugeable**, *a.* **gauger**, *n.* One who gauges; an excise-officer.

Gaul, (gawl) [L. *Gallus*], *n.* A native of ancient Gaul. **Gaulish**, *a.*

gaunt (gawnt) [?], *a.* Thin, haggard.

gauntlet (1) (gawnt'lĕt) [O.F. *gantelet*, a small glove], *n.* A long metal-covered glove, worn with armour; a long stout glove covering the wrists.

gauntlet (2) (gawnt'lĕt) [Swed. *gatlopp*], *n.* A punishment, in which the culprit runs between two rows of men armed with knotted cords or the like, with which they strike him.

gauze (gawz) [F. *gaze*], *n.* A light, transparent stuff; perforated or other material resembling this. **gauzy**, *a.* **gauziness**, *n.*

gavel (1) (găvl) [A.-S. *gafol*, tribute], *n.* Partition of land among a whole tribe at the holder's death. **gavelkind** (găvl'kĭnd), *n.* A custom whereby the lands of one dying intestate descend to all the sons in equal shares; holding land by this tenure.

gavel (2) (găvl) [?], *n.* A mason's setting-maul; a chairman's mallet.

gavotte (gă-vot') [F.], *n.* A dance resembling the minuet; music for this.

gawk (gawk) [?], *n.* A simpleton, booby. **gawky**, *a.* Awkward, clownish.

gay (gā) [O.F. *gai*], *a.* Full of mirth; light-hearted, merry; given to pleasure; showy, finely dressed. **gaily**, *adv.*

gaze (gāz) [?], *v.i.* To fix the eye intently on. *n.* A fixed look; a look of curiosity.

gazelle (gă-zel') [Arab. *ghazāl*], *n.* A swift and very graceful antelope.

gazette (gă-zet') [It. *gazzetta*], *n.* A newspaper; an official journal (one of these published in London, Edinburgh, and Belfast respectively) containing lists of appointments, bankrupts, legal notices, etc. *v.t.* To publish in a gazette; to announce the bankruptcy of (*usu. in p.p.*). **gazetteer'**, *n.* A geographical dictionary.

gear (gēr) [M.E. *gere*], *n.* Apparatus, tools, mechanical appliances, harness, tackle, equipment, dress; (*Mech.*) combinations of cog-wheels, links, levers, etc.; the state of being connected up or in working order; (*Sc.*) property, wealth. *v.t.* To harness; to put into gear; to furnish with gearing. **gearing**, *n.* Gear, working parts.

gee (jē), **gee-up**, *int.* Go on, move faster (to a horse). **gee-gee**, *n.* (*childish and colloq.*) A horse.

gelatine (jel'ă-tēn) [L. *gelata*, jelly], *n.* A transparent substance, forming a jelly in water, obtained from connective animal tissue. **gelat'inous**, *a.* Of the nature or consisting of gelatine, jelly-like.

geld (geld) [Scand.], *v.t.* To castrate (esp. a horse), to emasculate. **gelding**, *n.* Act of castrating; a castrated animal, esp. a castrated horse.

gelid (jel'id) [L. *gelu*, frost], *a.* Extremely cold; icy.

gem (jem) [L. *gemma*, a bud, jewel], *n.* A precious stone, esp. when cut and polished; an object of great rarity or beauty; a treasure. *v.t.* To adorn with or as with gems. **gemmy**, *a.* Full of or set with gems; bright, glittering.

gemel (jem'ĕl) [L. *gemellus*, dim of *geminus*, twin], *n.* A kind of finger-ring formed of two (or more) rings, also called a gemel-ring.

-gen [Gr., from root of *gignesthai*, to be born], *suf.* Producing; produced; growth; as in *hydrogen*, *nitrogen*.

gen (jen), *n.* [General Information], *n.* (*colloq.*) Full particulars of, information about.

gendarme (zhan-darm) [F.], *n.* A policeman in France and some other Continental countries.

gender (jen'dĕr) [O.F. *genre*], *n.* (*Gram.*) One of the classes into which words are divided according to the sex of the things they represent.

genealogy (jē-nē-ăl'ô-ji) [Gr. *genea*, race], *n.* The history of the descent of families; a record of such a descent; pedigree, lineage. **genealog'ical**, *a.* Pertaining to genealogy. **genealogist**, *n.*

general (jen'ĕr-ăl) [O.F., from L. *generālis*], *a.* Relating to a whole genus or class; not special; common, usual, universal; indefinite, vague; not specialized or restricted. *n.* An officer ranking next below a field-marshal; the commander of an army; (*R.-C. Ch.*) the chief of a religious order; a general servant, a maid-of-all-work. **generally,** *adv.* In general; in most cases; commonly, usually; without specifying.

generalissimo (jen-ẽr-à-lis'i-mō) [It.], *n.* The chief commander of a combined military and naval force or one furnished by several powers.

generality (jen-ẽr-ăl'i-ti), *n.* The state of being general, as opposed to specific; a general principle; a vague statement; the majority.

generalize (jen'ẽr-à-līz), *v.t.* To deal with as a class, not an individual; to apply generally, to make of universal application; to deduce or infer (as a general principle) from many particulars. *v.i.* To form general ideas; to reason inductively; to employ generalities. **generaliza'tion,** *n.*

generalship (jen'ẽr-ál-ship), *n.* Office or rank of a general; skill in the conduct of war, strategy.

generate (jen'ẽr-āt) [L. *generātus,* begotten], *v.t.* To produce or bring into existence; to originate, beget, procreate. **genera'tion,** *n.* Act of generating; propagation; bringing into existence; a single step in natural descent; a period between one succession and another; those of the same period; offspring, a race. **gen'erative,** *a.* **gen'erator,** *n.* One who or that which begets or generates; an apparatus for the production of gas; (*Elec.*) a dynamo.

generic, -al (jé-ner'ik, -ăl), *a.* Pertaining to a genus, opp. to specific; comprehensive.

generous (jen'ẽr-ús) [L. *generōsus,* as prec.], *a.* Liberal, open-handed; abundant. **generos'ity,** *n.*

genesis (jen'ē-sis) [Gr., from *gen-,* root of *gignesthai,* to be born], *n.* (*pl.* -ses) The act of giving origin to; creation, mode of production or formation. **Genesis,** *n.* The first book of the Old Testament.

genetic (jé-net'ik), *a.* Relating to the origin, or creation of a thing.

geneva (jē-nē'và) [Dut. *genever,* L. *juniperus,* juniper], *n.* A spirit distilled from grain flavoured with juniper-berries.

genial (jē'ni-ál) [L. *geniālis*], *a.* Kindly, cordial, sympathetic; conducive to life and growth. **genial'ity,** *n.*

genista (jē-nis'tà [L.], *n.* A genus of leguminous shrubs, with yellow flowers.

genital (jen'i-tál) [L. *genitālis*], *a.* Pertaining to procreation. *n.pl.* The external organs of generation.

genitive (jen'i-tiv) [L. *genetīvus,* of generation], *a.* and *n.* (*Gram.*) Indicating origin, possession, or the like (applied to a case corresponding to the Eng. possessive).

genius (jē'nyús) [L., from *gen-,* root of *gignere,* to beget], *n.* (*pl.* genii) A tutelary deity or spirit; one who exercises a powerful influence over another for good or ill; (*pl.* geniuses) natural bent or inclination of the mind; the dominant spirit or sentiment (of); a large endowment of intellectual, imaginative, or inventive faculty, etc.; a person so endowed.

-genous, *suf.* Born; bearing, producing; as *indigenous.*

genocide (jen'ō-sīd) [Gr. *genos,* born], *n.* (*Polit.*) The systematic destruction of a racial, ethical, or religious group.

genre (zhanr) [F.], *n.* Sort, class; manner; a painting of some scene in every-day life; this style of painting.

genteel (jen-tēl') [O.F. *gentil*], *a.* (*now vulg. or iron.*) Suitable or pertaining to the upper class; well-bred, refined.

gentian (jen'shàn) [L. *gentiāna*], *n.* A genus of bitter herbs, used in medicine as a tonic.

gentile (jen'til) [L. *gentīlis,* from *gens gentis,* a clan], *a.* Not a Jew; heathen. *n.* One who is not a Jew; a heathen, a pagan.

gentility (jen-til'i-ti), *n.* Manners and habits distinctive of good society.

gentle (jentl) [O.F. *gentil*], *a.* Mild, tender, not rough, violent, or stern; not severe, not steep; of honourable birth, belonging to the gentry. *n.* The larva of the flesh-fly. **gentlefolk,** *n.* People of good position or gentle birth. **gentleness,** *n.* **gently,** *adv.*

gentleman (jentl'màn), *n.* A man belonging to the gentry, not the nobility, one entitled to bear arms; a man of good breeding, kindly feelings, and high principles, a man of honour or good social position. **gentlemanlike,** *a.* **gentlemanly,** *a.* **gentlemanliness,** *n.*

gentlewoman (jentl'wu-màn), *n.* A woman of gentle birth or breeding; a woman who waits upon another of high rank.

gentry (jen'tri), *n.* The class below the nobility and above the common people.

genuflect (jen'ū-flekt) [L. *genu,* knee, *flectere,* to bend], *v.i.* To bend the knee, esp. in worship. **genuflexion** (-flek'shùn), *n.*

genuine (jen'ū-in) [L. *genuīnus*], *a.* Belonging to the true stock; real, not counterfeit or adulterated; true to type. **genuinely,** *adv.* **genuineness,** *n.*

genus (jē'nús), *n.* (*pl.* genera) A group or class, esp. of animals or plants, differentiated from all others by common characteristics; kind, order, family.

geo- [Gr., from *gē,* earth], *comb. form.* Pertaining to the earth. **geocentric** (jē-ō-sen'trik), *a.* As viewed from or having relation to the earth as centre; referring to the centre of the earth.

geodesy (jē-od'ē-si) [Gr. *-daisia,* division], *n.* Science or art of measuring large portions of the earth's surface. **geode'sic, geodet'ic,** *a.*

geography (jē-og'rà-fi), *n.* The science of the surface of the earth, its physical features, natural productions, inhabitants, political divisions, commerce, etc.; a book dealing with this. **geographer,** *n.* **geograph'ic, -al,** *a.*

geology (jē-ol'ō-ji), *n.* The science of the earth's crust, its composition, structure, and history of its development; a treatise on this. **geolog'ical,** *a.* **geol'ogist,** *n.*

geomancy (jē-ō-măn'si), *n.* Divination by means of lines, etc., on the earth or on paper.

geometry (jē-om'ē-tri), *n.* The science of

magnitudes, whether linear, superficial, or solid, with their properties and relations in space. geomet'ric, -al, a. geometric'ian, n.

geopolitics, n.pl. The study of how the political views and aims of a nation are affected by its geographical position.

georgic (jôr'jik) [Gr. geōrgos, a husbandman], n. A poem on husbandry or rural affairs.

geranium (jĕ-rā'ni-ùm) [Gr. geranos, a crane], n. A genus of hardy herbaceous plants.

gerfalcon (jĕr'faw-kòn) [M.H.G. girvalke (cp. G. geier, vulture)], n. A large and powerful falcon.

geriatrics (jer-i-ăt'riks) [Gr. geras, old age], n. The science dealing with the phenomena of old age.

germ (jĕrm) [L. germen -inis], n. The portion of living matter from which an organism develops; an embryo; a partially-developed organism; (Path.) a micro-organism, esp. as disease-carrier, a microbe; origin, source, elementary principle. **germ warfare** [BACTERIOLOGY]. **germicide**, a. Destroying germs, esp. disease-germs. n. A substance for this purpose. **germinal**, a. Of the nature of a germ; germinative; in the earliest stage.

german (1) (jĕr'mán) [L. germānus, having the same parents], a. Sprung from the same parents, relevant, pertinent.

German (2) (jĕr'mán) [L. Germānus], a. Pertaining to Germany. n. A native of or the language of Germany. **German'ic**, a.

germinate (jĕr'mi-nāt) [L. germinātus], v.i. To sprout, bud; to develop. v.t. To cause to sprout or bud; to put forth; **germina'tion**, n. **germinative**, a.

gerrymander (ger-, jer-i-măn'dér) [Elbridge Gerry, Governor of Massachusetts, salamander, which the map of one district was supposed to resemble], v.t. To tamper with (an electoral district or constituency) so as to secure unfair advantages; to garble so as to arrive at unfair conclusions.

gerund (jer'ùnd) [L. gerundium, from gerere, to do], n. (Lat. Gram.) A part of the verb used as a noun instead of the infinitive in cases other than the nominative; (Eng. Gram.) a verbal noun ending in -ing, when used as a part of the verb. **gerundial** (jĕ-rün'di-ál), a.

gestation (jes-tā'shùn) [L. gestātio, from gestāre, to carry], n. The act of carrying or process of being carried in the uterus from the time of conception; the period of this.

gesticulate (jes-tik'ū-lāt) [L. gesticulārī, from gestus, gesture], v.i. To make expressive gestures or motions. v.t. To express or represent by gestures. **gesticula'tion**, n.

gesture (jes'chùr), n. A motion expressive of emotion or illustrating or enforcing something said.

get (get) [Scand.], v.t. (past and p.p. got) To procure, obtain, gain possession of, acquire; to receive as one's portion or penalty; to beget; to persuade (to); to betake (oneself). v.i. To arrive at any place, condition, or posture; to depart; to be a gainer, to profit. **get-at-able**, a. **gettable**, a. **getting**, n. (pl.) Gains, profits.

gewgaw (gū'gaw) [?], n. A showy trifle.

geyser (gā'zēr) [Icel. geysir, gusher], n. A hot spring throwing up a column of water at intervals; an apparatus for rapidly heating bath-water.

ghastly (gast'li) [A.-S. gæstan, to terrify], a. Haggard, deathlike; frightful, shocking. **ghastliness**, n.

gherkin (gĕr'kin) [Dut. agurkken], n. A small variety of cucumber, used for pickling.

ghetto (get'ō) [It.], n. The quarter of a town to which Jews used to be strictly confined.

ghost (gōst) [A.-S. gāst], n. The visible spirit of a deceased person, an apparition; the soul of a dead person in the other world; soul, spirit, vital principle. **ghostly**, a. Pertaining to the soul, spiritual; pertaining to religious matters; pertaining to ghosts; dismal, gloomy.

ghoul (gool) [Arab. ghūl], n. An evil spirit supposed, in Eastern tales, to devour the dead.

giant (ji'ánt) [O.F. geant, Gr. gigas-antos], n. A mythical being of human form but superhuman size; any person, animal, plant, etc., of abnormal size; a person of extraordinary powers, ability, etc. a. Gigantic. **giantess**, n.

giaour (jour) [Pers. gāwr], n. A Turkish name for disbelievers in Mohammed.

gibber (jib'ér) [imit.], v.i. To jabber, to talk rapidly and inarticulately. n. Talk of this kind. **gibberish** (gib'ér-ish), n. Inarticulate sounds; unmeaning language.

gibbet (jib'ét) [O.F. gibet, dim. of gibe, a staff], n. A gallows; death by hanging. v.t. To execute by hanging.

gibbon (gib'ón) [F.], n. A long-armed anthropoid ape.

gibbous (gib'ús) [L. gibbus, a hump], a. Humped, crook-backed; protuberant, convex, esp. of the moon when the illuminated portion exceeds a semicircle but falls short of a circle. **gibbos'ity**, n.

gibe (jib) [?], v.i. To sneer or taunt; to rail, flout, scoff (at). v.t. To use sneering or taunting expressions towards; to mock, sneer at. n. A sneer, scoff, taunt.

giblets (jib'lĕts) [O.F. gibelet], n.pl. The heart, liver, gizzard, etc., of a fowl.

giddy (gid'i) [A.-S. gydig], a. Having a swimming or dizziness in the head; reeling, tending to stagger; changeable, fickle; elated, rash. **giddily**, adv. **giddiness**, n.

gift (gift), n. Act, right, or power of giving; that which is given; a natural quality, talent, or endowment. v.t. To bestow or confer; to endow with gifts. **gifted**, a. Largely endowed with intellect, talented.

gig (gig) [Scand.], n. A light two-wheeled vehicle drawn by one horse; a lightly built row-boat.

gigantic (ji-găn'tik), a. Huge, enormous, giant-like. **gigante'an**, **gigantesque** (-tesk'), a.

giggle (gigl), *v.i.* To laugh in a silly manner, to titter; to laugh nervously. *n.* A laugh of such a kind.

gigolo (jig′ō-lō) [F., slang], *n.* A professional dance partner; a creature who battens on vain women.

Gilbertian (gil-bĕr′ti-ån) [Sir W. S. *Gilbert* (1836–1911), *a.* Absurdly topsy-turvy.

gild (gild) [A.-S. *begyldan*], *v.t.* (*p.p.* gilded, *part.a.* gilt) To coat or wash thinly with gold; to impart a golden appearance to; to give a specious or agreeable appearance to, to gloss over. **gilder,** *n.* One whose occupation is to coat articles with gold. **gilding,** *n.*

gill (1) (gil) [?], *n.* (*usu. in pl.*) The organs of respiration of fishes and some amphibia; respiratory processes projecting from some aquatic insects; the flesh about the jaws and chin.

gill (2) (jil) [short for *Gillian*, L. *Juliana*], *n.* A lass; a sweetheart.

gill (3) (jil) [O.F. *gille*], *n.* One-fourth of a pint.

gillie (gil′i) [Gael. *gille*], *n.* A Highland manservant, esp. one who attends a sportsman.

gillyflower (jil′i-flou-ẽr) [O.F. *girofle*, Gr. *karuon*, nut, *phullon*, leaf], *n.* The clove-pink; the white stock; the wallflower.

gilt (gilt), *a.* Gilded; adorned with or as with gold. *n.* Gold laid over the surface of a thing, gilding.

gimbal (jim′bål), *n.* (*usu. in pl.*) A form of universal joint for suspending anything so that it may always retain a horizontal or other required position.

gimcrack (jim′krăk) [?], *n.* A pretty but useless article, a gewgaw. *a.* Showy but flimsy and worthless.

gimlet (gim′lĕt) [O.F. *guimbelet*], *n.* A small screwed boring-tool for wood.

gimmick (gim′ik), *n.* A special device; a trick of manner, speech, dress etc. by which a person's identity is emphasised.

gimp (gimp) [?], *n.* Silk or other twist interlaced with wire or coarse cord; a fishing-line whipped with thin wire.

gin (1) (jin) [short for GENEVA], *n.* An ardent spirit flavoured with juniper.

gin (2) (jin) [contr. of O.F. *engin*], *n.* A trap, a snare; a machine for separating cotton-fibre from the seeds.

gin (3) (jin) [Austral.], *n.* An Australian aboriginal woman.

ginger (jin′jẽr) [A.-S. *gingifere*, Gr. *zingiberis*], *n.* A plant, with a pungent, spicy root-stock; the root-stock used in cookery, as a sweetmeat, or in medicine; (*slang*) mettle, dash, go. *v.t.* To flavour or treat with ginger; (*fig.*) to spirit (up). **gingery,** *a.* Spiced with ginger; (*slang*) red-haired, carroty.

gingerly (jin′jẽr-li) [?], *adv.* Fastidiously, cautiously.

gingham (ging′åm) [Malay *ginggang*, striped], *n.* A fabric woven of dyed yarn, usu. in stripes or checks.

gipsy (jip′si) [O.F. *Egyptian*, L. *Ægyptius*, an Egyptian], *n.* One of a nomad race (calling themselves Romany), prob. of Hindu extraction, dark in complexion and hair, and speaking a corrupt Sanskrit dialect, who live largely by horse-dealing, fortune-telling, etc.; one resembling a gipsy; a mischievous or erratic person.

giraffe (ji-raf′) [Arab. *zarāfah*], *n.* An African ruminant with an extremely long neck; the camelopard.

gird (1) (gẽrd) [A.-S. *gyrdan*], *v.t.* (*past and p.p.* girded, girt) To bind round with a flexible band, esp. to secure the clothes; to fasten (a sword on or to) with a girdle; to invest or equip (with); to surround or encircle with or as with a girdle, to encompass, to besiege.

gird (2) (gẽrd) [?], *v.i.* To sneer, mock (at). *n.* A sarcasm, a sneer.

girder (gẽr′dẽr), *n.* A principal beam supporting joints, walls, roof, roadway, or other weight.

girdle (1) (gẽrdl) [A.-S. *gyrdel*], *n.* A belt, cord, etc., for securing a loose garment or encircling the waist; anything that encircles as a belt or zone; bones by which limbs are united to the trunk. *v.t.* To surround with or as with a girdle, to environ.

girdle (2) (gẽrdl), *n.* A round flat plate of iron for baking cakes.

girl (gẽrl) [M.E. *gerle*, a young person], *n.* A female child, a young unmarried woman; a maidservant. **girlhood,** *n.* **girlish,** *a.*

girt (gẽrt) [*p.p.* of GIRD (1)], *a.* Girded, bound.

girth (gẽrth) [Icel. *gjŏrth*, a girdle], *n.* The band by which a saddle or burden is kept secure on a horse's back; a circular bandage, anything that girds; measure round anything, waist-measure.

gist (jist) [O.F. (F. *gît*, it lies],[1] *n.* The essence or main point of a question.

give (giv) [A.-S. *giefan*], *v.t.* (*past gave, p.p.* given) To transfer possession of or right to without compensation; to bestow, confer, present; to grant, concede, put in one's power; to hand over, commit, consign, put in one's keeping; to transfer in exchange, to pay, sell; to render as due; to surrender, to yield up; to yield as product; to impart. *v.i.* To part with freely; to yield as to pressure, to collapse; to recede; to make way or room; to open (upon). *n.* The state of yielding or giving way; elasticity.

gizzard (giz′ård) [M.E. and O.F. *giser*, L. *gigeria*, cooked entrails of poultry], *n.* The second stomach in birds.

glacial (glås′i-ål) [L. *glaciālis*], *a.* Pertaining to ice; like ice, icy; (*Geol.*) due to or characterized by glaciers or floating ice.

glacier (glås′i-ẽr), *n.* A stream-like mass of ice slowly descending from high altitudes.

glad (glăd) [A.-S. *glœd*], *a.* Pleased, gratified; indicating satisfaction; affording pleasure, joy, etc.; bright, gay. **gladden,** *v.t.* To make glad; to cheer. **gladly,** *a.* and *adv.* **gladness,** *n.* **gladsome,** *a.*

glade (glåd) [Scand.], *n.* An open space in a forest.

gladiator (glăd′i-å-tòr) [L., from *gladius*, a sword], *n.* A man employed to fight in the Roman amphitheatre; (*fig.*) a controversialist. **gladiator′ial,** *a.*

gladiolus (glăd-i-ō′-lŭs), *n.* (*pl.* -li) A genus of plants with a fleshy bulb, sword-shaped leaves, and bright flowers.

gladstone (glăd′stŏn) [W. E. *Gladstone* (1809–98), Eng. statesman], *n.* A light, narrow portmanteau.

glamour (glăm′ŏr), *n.* The influence of some charm causing things to seem different from what they are; magic, enchantment.

glance (glans) [?], *v.i.* To give a quick look (at); to glide off or from (as a blow); (*fig.*) to allude, to hint (at); to dart a gleam of light or brightness. *v.t.* To shoot or dart swiftly or suddenly; to direct (a look) rapidly or cursorily. *n.* A quick or transient look, a hurried glimpse (at).

gland (glănd) [L. *glans -ndis*, acorn], *n.* An organ secreting certain constituents of the blood; a cellular organ in plants. **glandular,** *a.* Characterized by glands.

glanders (glăn′dĕrz) [O.F. *glandre*, as prec.], *n.pl.* A dangerous and contagious disease in horses. **glandered,** *a.*

glare (glâr) [?], *v.i.* To shine with a dazzling light; to look with piercing eyes, to stare. *n.* A fierce overpowering light, disagreeable brightness; an intense, fierce look or stare. **glaring,** *a.*

glass (glas) [A.-S. *glæs*], *n.* A hard, brittle, transparent substance; a mirror, looking-glass; a drinking-vessel of glass; the quantity which this will hold; a lens; an optical instrument, an eye-glass, telescope; an hour-glass; a barometer; a window; (*pl.*) a pair of spectacles. *v.t.* To case in or cover with or as with glass, to glaze; to make (the eye) glassy. **glass-blower,** *n.* One who fashions glass vessels by blowing. **glass-furnace,** *n.* A furnace in which the materials of glass are fused. **glass-house,** *n.* A house or building where glass is made; a conservatory; a military prison. **glass-snake,** *n.* An American limbless lizard. **glass-ware,** *n.* Articles made of glass. **glassy,** *a.* Like glass, vitreous; smooth, mirror-like (of water); dull, lacking fire (of the eye).

glaucous (glaw′kŭs) [Gr. *glaukos*, sea-green], *a.* Sea-green, pale greyish-blue.

glaze (glāz), *v.t.* To furnish with glass, or with windows; to overlay (pottery) with a vitreous substance; to cover (a surface) with a thin glossy coating. *v.i.* To become glassy (as the eyes). *n.* A smooth, lustrous coating on earthenware, pictures, paper, confectionery, etc. **glazer,** *n.* A workman who glazes earthenware: a wheel for grinding or polishing cutlery or for smoothing calico. **glazier** (glā′zi-ĕr), *n.* One who sets glass in windows, etc. **glazing,** *n.*

gleam (glēm) [A.-S. *glæm*], *n.* A flash, beam, ray, esp. when transient. *v.i.* To send out quick and transient rays.

glean (glēn) [O.F. *glener*], *v.t.* To gather (ears of corn which have been passed over on the cornfield); (*fig.*) to collect bit by bit, pick up here and there. *v.i.* To gather the ears of corn left on the ground. **gleaner,** *n.* **gleaning,** *n.*

glebe (glēb) [L. *glēba*, the soil], *n.* Land furnishing part of the revenue of a benefice.

glee (glē) [A.-S. *glēo*], *n.* Joy, mirth, gladness; a composition for several voices in harmony, usually without instrumental accompaniment. **gleeful,** *a.* Merry, gay, joyous. **gleeman,** *n.* A minstrel.

glen (glen) [Gael. *gleann*], *n.* A narrow valley, a dale.

glengarry (glen-găr′i) [place in Inverness], *n.* A woollen Scottish cap.

glib (glib) [?], *a.* Smooth, slippery; voluble, fluent, not very weighty or sincere. **glibly,** *adv.* **glibness,** *n.*

glide (glīd) [A.-S. *glīdan*], *v.t.* To move smoothly and gently; to slip along rapidly, smoothly, and easily. *n.* Act of gliding. **glider,** *n.* One who or that which glides; an aeroplane which glides through the air without an engine.

glimmer (glim′ĕr) [?], *v.i.* To emit a feeble light. *n.* A faint, uncertain, or unsteady light; an uncertain sign (as of intelligence, etc.). **glimmering,** *n.*

glimpse (glimps) [M.E. *glimsen*], *n.* A momentary look, an imperfect view (of); a faint and transient appearance. *v.t.* To see for an instant.

glint (glint) [?], *v.i.* To gleam, glitter, sparkle. *n.* A gleam, a flash, a sparkle.

glisten (glisn) [A.-S. *glisian*, to shine], *v.i.* To gleam, to sparkle, usu. by reflection.

glitter (glit′ĕr) [Icel. *glitra*, Teut. *glit*, to shine], *v.i.* To sparkle; to shine with a succession of brilliant gleams or flashes; to be brilliant or showy. *n.* A bright sparkling light; brilliancy; speciousness.

gloaming (glō′ming) [A.-S. *glōmung*], *n.* Evening twilight.

gloat (glōt) [Teut.], *v.i.* To look or dwell (on or over) with feelings of malignity, lust, or avarice.

global (glō′băl), *a.* World-wide.

globe (glōb) [L. *globatus*], *n.* A ball, a sphere; the earth; a sphere on which are represented the heavenly bodies, or a map of the world; an orb as emblem of sovereignty; a spherical aquarium, lamp-shade, etc. *v.t.* To form into a globe.

globule (glob′ŭl) [L. *globulus*, a little globe], *n.* A particle of matter in the form of a small globe; a blood-corpuscle. **globular,** *a.* Shaped like a small globe.

gloom (gloom) [M.E. *gloumen*, to lour], *v.i.* To appear dimly; to look dismal or frowning; to lour, to be cloudy or dark. *n.* Obscurity, partial darkness; depression, melancholy; circumstances that occasion this. **gloomy,** *a.* **gloominess,** *n.*

glorify (glŏr′i-fī) [L. *glōria*, glory, *facere*, to make], *v.t.* To magnify, make glorious, pay honour to in worship, to praise; to beautify. **glorifica′tion,** *n.*

glory (glŏr′i) [O.F. *glorie*, L. *glōria*], *n.* High honour, distinction; fame; an occasion of praise, subject for pride or boasting; magnificence, grandeur; brilliance, splendour; a state of exaltation; adoration in worship; the felicity of heaven; a halo. *v.i.* To boast, feel pride, exult. **glorious** (glŏr′i-ŭs), *a.*

gloss (1) (glos) [L. and Gr. *glōssa*, the tongue], *n.* An explanatory note in a book; a comment, interpretation; a glossary, translation, or commentary. *v.t.* To explain, annotate; to comment upon.

gloss (2) (glos) [prob. Scand.], *n.* Lustre from a polished surface; sheen; (*fig.*) a deceptive outward appearance. *v.t.* To make glossy or lustrous; to render plausible. **glossy,** *a.* **glossiness,** *n.*

glossary (glos'á-ri) [L. *glōssārium,* as GLOSS (1)], *n.* A list or vocabulary of explanations of obsolete or strange words or forms. **glossarial** (glŏ-sâr'i-ál), *a.*

glottis (glot'is) [Gr. *glōttis,* var. of *glōssa,* GLOSS (1)], *n.* (*Anat.*) The mouth of the windpipe contributing, by its dilatation and contraction, to the modulation of the voice. **glottal,** *a.*

glove (glŭv) [A.-S. *glōf*], *n.* A covering for the hand, usu. with a separate division for each finger; a padded glove for boxing. *v.t.* To cover with a glove. **glover,** *n.* One who makes or sells gloves.

glow (glō) [A.-S. *glōwan*], *v.i.* To radiate light and heat, esp. without flame; to show a warm colour; to feel great bodily heat; to be warm, flushed, or ardent. *n.* Incandescence, red or white heat; warmth of colour; ardour; heat produced by exercise. **glow-worm,** *n.* A beetle, the female of which is phosphorescent.

glower (glou'ẽr) [?], *v.i.* To scowl, stare fiercely or angrily. *n.* A savage stare.

gloze (glōz) [F. *gloser*], *v.t.* To palliate, extenuate. *v.i.* To comment. *n.* Flattery, wheedling; specious show. **to gloze over:** To palliate speciously or explain away.

glucose (gloo'kōs) [Gr. *glukus,* sweet], *n.* A fermentable sugar obtained from dried grapes, starch, etc.

glue (gloo) [O.F. *glu*], *n.* An impure gelatine made from hides, horns, and hoofs, boiled to a jelly, and used hot as a cement; an adhesive substance. *v.t.* To join or fasten with glue; to attach firmly. **gluey,** *a.* **gluing,** *pres.p.*

glum (glŭm) [?], *a.* Sullen, moody, dissatisfied.

glut (glŭt) [O.F. *gloutir,* L. *glūtīre,* to swallow], *v.t.* To fill to excess, to gorge, sate; to over-supply (as a market). *n.* A surfeit; an over-supply of a market.

gluten (gloo'tĕn) [L. *glūten*], *n.* A yellowish-grey, elastic albuminous substance in wheat-flour, etc. **glutin,** *n.* Vegetable gelatine. **glutinize,** *v.t.* To render viscous or gluey. **glutinous,** *a.* Gluey, tenacious; covered with a sticky exudation. **glutinos'ity,** *n.*

glutton (glŭtn) *n.* One who eats to excess; one who indulges to excess, as in reading, working, etc.; a carnivorous animal of the weasel tribe, the wolverine. **gluttonous,** *a.* **gluttony,** *n.*

glycerine (glis'ẽr-in) [F. *glycérine,* Gr. *glukus,* sweet], *n.* A sweet, colourless, viscid liquid obtained from fats and oils.

gnarl (narl) [Teut.], *v.t.* To twist or contort (*usu. in p.p.*). *n.* A protuberance, twisted growth, or knot, in a tree.

gnash (năsh) [Icel. *gnastan*], *v.t.* To strike or grind (the teeth) together; to champ. *v.i.* To grind the teeth as in rage.

gnat (năt) [A.-S. *gnæt*], *n.* A small two-winged fly, the female of which bites.

gnathic (năth'ik) [Gr. *gnathos,* jaw], *a.* Of or pertaining to the jaw.

gnaw (naw) [A.-S. *gnagan*], *v.t.* (*p.p.* gnawed, gnawn) To bite or eat away by degrees; to bite persistently, or in agony, rage, or despair; to corrode. *v.i.* To use the teeth in biting thus; to cause corrosion or wearing away.

gneiss (nīs) [O.H.G. *gneistan,* to sparkle], *n.* A rock consisting of feldspar, quartz, and mica.

gnome (1) (nōm) [F.], *n.* A misshapen sprite formerly supposed to inhabit the interior of the earth, and to guard mines, quarries, etc.

gnome (2) (nōm) [Gr. *gnōmē,* from *gignōskein,* to know], *n.* A maxim, a saw. **gnomic,** *a.*

gnomon (nō'mŏn), *n.* The rod or plate showing the time by its shadow on a sundial; a vertical pillar used for determining the altitude of the sun; the figure remaining when a parallelogram has been removed from the corner of a larger one of the same form.

gnostic (nos'tik) [Gr. *gnōstos*], *a.* Relating to knowledge, intellectual; having esoteric knowledge; of the Gnostics. *n.* An adherent of Gnosticism. **Gnosticism,** *n.* An early system of religious philosophy that combined ideas from Greek and Oriental philosophy with Christianity.

gnu (nū) [Hottentot], *n.* An oxlike antelope.

go (gō) [A.-S. *gān*], *v.i.* (*past* went, *p.p.* gone (gawn, gon), 2*nd sing.* goest, 3*rd sing.* goes (gōz), goeth) To move (from one place, condition, or station to another); to depart, pass away; to be moving, acting, operating, working; to travel; to proceed; to come out, succeed, turn out (well or ill); to take a certain course (for or against); to be habitually (as hungry, naked); to be used, said, etc., habitually, to be circulated or current; to extend, point in a certain direction; to tend; to have a certain tenor; to fit, to suit (with); to be harmonious (with a tune, etc.); to be abandoned, abolished, or lost; to give way, break down; (*usu. in p.p.*) to die; to become (as wild, mad); (*aux.*) to be about (to do), to intend, purpose. **go-ahead,** *a.* Characterized by energy and enterprise. **go-as-you-please,** *a.* Unceremonious, untroubled by rules. **go-between,** *n.* An intermediary between two parties. **go-by,** *n.* The act of passing without notice; intentional failure to notice; evasion. **go-off,** *n.* The start. *n.* (*pl.* goes) Spirit, animation; push, enterprise; a scrape, an awkward turn of affairs; a bout (of doing something); one's turn in a game; fashion, the mode; a drink, especially of spirits.

goad (gōd) [A.-S. *gād*], *n.* A pointed instrument to urge oxen to move faster; anything that spurs or incites. *v.t.* To urge on with a goad; to stimulate, incite.

goal (gōl) [?], *n.* A winning-post; (*Football*) the posts between which the ball is to be driven; the act of kicking the ball here; the end of one's ambition; purpose.

goat (gōt) [A.-S. *gāt*], *n.* A hairy, horned, and bearded domesticated ruminant. **goatherd,** *n.* One who tends goats. **goatee,** *n.* A small beard on the point of the chin. **goatish,** *a.* Resembling a goat; of a rank smell; lecherous.

gobbet (gob'ĕt) [O.F. *gobet*], *n.* A mouthful, a lump, a piece, esp. of meat.

gobble (gobl) [O.F. *gobe*, mouthful], *v.t.* To swallow down hastily and noisily. *v.i.* To swallow food in this manner; to make a noise in the throat as a turkey-cock. *n.* A noise like this. **gobbler,** *n.* A glutton; a turkey-cock.

goblet (gob'lĕt) [O.F. *gobelet*], *n.* A drinking-vessel with a stem and no handle.

goblin (gob'lin) [F. *gobeline*], *n.* A mischievous spirit, a gnome.

god (god) [A.-S.], *n.* (*Monotheism,* **God**) The Supreme Being, the self-existent and eternal Creator and Ruler of the universe, a deity, a divinity; an image worshipped as an embodiment or symbol of supernatural power, an idol; a person or thing greatly idolized; (*pl.*) the occupants of the upper gallery in a theatre. **godchild, goddaughter, godson,** *n.* One for whom a person stands sponsor at baptism. **godfather, -mother, -parent,** *n.* One who is sponsor for a child at baptism. *v.t.* To act as sponsor to; to give one's name to, be responsible for. **godsend,** *n.* An unlooked-for acquisition. **goddess,** *n.* A female deity; a woman of pre-eminent beauty, goodness, or charm. **Godhead,** *n.* Divine nature or essence; a deity. **godless,** *a.* **godlike,** *a.* **godly,** *a.* God-fearing, pious, devout. **godliness,** *n.*

goer (gō'ér), *n.* One who or that which goes (as *a fast goer*, a fast horse).

goffer (gof'er, gō'fer) [F. *gauffrer*], *v.t.* To plait, to crimp edges, etc., with a heated iron.

goggle (gogl) [?], *v.i.* To strain the eyes; to squint, stare; to project (of the eyes). *v.t.* To roll (the eyes) about or turn (the eyes) sideways. *a.* Prominent, staring; rolling from side to side. *n.* A strained or staring rolling of the eyes; a leer; (*pl.*) spectacles. **goggle-eyed,** *a.*

going (gō'ing), *n.* The act of moving; departure; condition of ground, roads, racecourse, etc. *a.* Working, in actual operation. **goings-on,** *n.pl.* Questionable behaviour, conduct.

goitre (goi'ter) [F. *goître*, from L. *guttur,* throat], *n.* A morbid enlargement of the thyroid gland, causing an unsightly deformity of the neck. **goitrous,** *a.*

gold (gōld) [A.-S.], *n.* A precious metal of a bright yellow colour, used for coins, jewellery, etc.; money, wealth, riches; anything very precious or pure; gilding; the colour of gold. *a.* Made or consisting of gold; coloured like gold. **gold-beater,** *n.* One who beats out gold for gilding. **gold-digger,** *n.* A woman who gets round men for their money. **gold-field,** *n.* A district where gold is found. **goldfinch,** *n.* A yellow-marked singing bird. **goldfish,** *n.* A golden-red carp. **gold-foil,** *n.* A thick kind of gold-leaf. **gold-mine,** *n.* A place where gold is mined. **gold-plate,**

n. Vessels, dishes, etc., of gold. **goldsmith,** *n.* A worker in gold; a dealer in gold-plate.

golden (gōl'dĕn), *a.* Made or consisting of gold; of the colour or lustre of gold; excellent, precious, most valuable. **golden number:** The number denoting the year's place in a Metonic lunar cycle of 19 years, used in calculating Easter.

golf (golf) [?], *n.* A game played with club-headed sticks and small hard balls, over commons or links, consisting in driving the balls into small holes in as few strokes as possible. *v.i.* To play golf. **golfer,** *n.*

-gon [Gr. *-gōnos*, angled], *suf.* Angled, as in *hexagon, octagon, pentagon.*

gondola (gon'dō-lá) [It.], *n.* A long, narrow Venetian rowing boat with peaked ends. **gondolier,** *n.* A man that rows a gondola.

gone (gawn, gon), [*p.p.* of **GO**], *a.* Ruined, undone; lost, beyond hope; past, bygone.

gong (gong) [Malay], *n.* A tambourine-shaped metal instrument emitting a sonorous note when struck with a padded stick.

good (gud) [A.-S. *gōd*], *a.* (*comp.* **better,** *superl.* **best**) Having such qualities as are useful and satisfactory; fit, proper, expedient; conducive to the end desired, profitable, serviceable; adequate; beneficial; genuine, sound; perfect, complete, thorough; safe, sure; possessed of moral excellence, virtuous; kind, friendly, amiable; pleasant, acceptable, palatable. *n.* That which contributes to happiness, advantage, etc.; that which is right, useful, etc.; welfare; prosperity; goodness, virtuous and charitable deeds; (*pl.*) movable property, effects; wares, merchandise. **for good:** Entirely, finally. **good day, good morning, good eve.,** *n.* and *int.* Forms of salutation at meeting or parting. **good-fellowship:** Sociability; pleasant company; conviviality. **good-for-nothing,** *a.* Of no value, worthless. *n.* An idle fellow, a vagabond. **goodwill,** *n.* Kindly feeling or disposition, benevolence; ready consent; the established custom of a business sold with the business itself.

good-bye (gud-bī') [corr. of *God be with you!*], *int.* and *n.* Farewell.

goodly (gud'li), *a.* Handsome, comely; kind; large, considerable. **goodliness,** *n.*

goodness (gud'nĕs), *n.* The quality or state of being good; moral excellence, virtue; kindness, good nature; the virtue or essence of anything.

goody (gud'i), *n.* A rustic term for an old woman; (*pl.*) sweetmeats.

googly (goo'gli) [?], *n.* (*Cricket*) A ball bowled so as to break a different way from the way it swerves.

goose (goos) [A.-S. *gōs*, *n.* (*pl.* **geese,** (gēs)) A web-footed bird larger than the duck, esp. the domesticated variety; the female of this, dist. from gander; (*fig.*) a simpleton; (*pl.* **gooses**) a tailor's smoothing iron. **goose-flesh,** *n.* A peculiar roughness of the human skin produced by cold, fear, etc. **gooseherd,** *n.* One who tends geese.

gooseberry (guz'bér-l), *n.* The fruit of a

thorny shrub; a chaperon to a pair of lovers.

gore (1) (gōr) [A.-S. *gor*, dirt], *n.* Blood from a wound. **gory**, *a.* **goriness**, *n.*

gore (2) (gōr) [A.-S. *gāra*, as foll.], *n.* A triangular piece sewed into a dress, a sail, etc., to widen it out.

gore (3) (gōr) [A.-S. *gār*, a spear], *v.t.* To pierce, esp. with a horn or horn-like point.

gorge (gōrj) [O.F.], *n.* The throat; the gullet; a heavy meal, a surfeit; a narrow pass between cliffs, hills, bastions, etc. *v.t.* To devour greedily. *v.i.* To feed greedily.

gorgeous (gōr'jŭs) [O.F. *gorgias*], *a.* Splendid, richly decorated, magnificent.

gorget (gōr'jĕt) [O.F. *gorgete*], *n.* A piece of armour for the throat or neck.

gorgon (gōr'gon) [Gr. mythology], *n.* A terrible, hideous creature, esp. a repulsive woman.

gorilla (gŏ-ril'à) [Gr.], *n.* A powerful and ferocious African anthropoid ape.

gormandize (gōr'măn-dīz), *n.* Appreciation of table delicacies. *v.i.* To eat food greedily or in excess. **gormandizer**, *n.*

gorse (gōrs) [A.-S. *gorst*], *n.* A prickly shrub with yellow flowers, furze. **gorsy**, *a.*

goshawk (gos'hawk) [A.-S. *gos-hafuc*], *n.* A large hawk.

gosling (goz'ling), *n.* A young goose.

gospel (gos'pĕl) [A.-S. *godspell*, good tidings], *n.* The revelation of the grace of God through Jesus Christ; the doctrine preached by Christ and the Apostles; the four canonical books ascribed respectively to Matthew, Mark, Luke, and John; a selection from these read in the Church service; anything accepted as infallibly true; the creed of a party, etc.

gossamer (gos'á-mėr) [M.E. *gossomer*], *n.* Cobweb-like threads floating in the air in calm weather, produced by small spiders; anything filmsy or unsubstantial.

gossip (gos'ip) [A.-S. *godsibb*, related in God, a sponsor], *n.* Formerly a sponsor; an acquaintance; a news-spreader, tattler; idle talk, tittle-tattle; rumour. *v.i.* To tattle, to chat; to talk or write in an informal easy-going way. **gossiper**, *n.* **gossipy**, *a.*

Goth (goth) [late L. *Gothī*, Gr. *Gothoi*], *n.* One of an ancient tribe of Teutons which swept down upon southern Europe in the 3rd–5th cents.; a barbarian, a rude, ignorant person. **Gothic**, *a.* Pertaining to the Goths or their language; in the style of architecture characterized by pointed arches, clustered columns, etc.; *(fig.)* rude, barbarous.

gouge (gouj, gooj) [F.], *n.* A concave chisel used to cut holes or grooves. *v.t.* To scoop (out) with a gouge.

gourd (goord) [F. *gourde*], *n.* A large fleshy fruit of climbing or trailing plants, the outer coat of which serves for water vessels; a bottle, cup, etc., made of its hard rind.

gourmand (goor'mănd) [F.], *n.* One who loves delicate fare, a gourmet; a glutton.

gourmet (goor-mā) [F., orig. a winetaster], *n.* A connoisseur in wines and meats; an epicure.

gout (gout) [O.F. *goute*, L. *gutta*, a drop], *n.* A disease affecting the joints, pain and irritability being the leading symptoms; a drop, a clot. **gouty**, *a.*

govern (gŭv'ėrn) [O.F. *governer*, L. *gubernāre*, to steer], *v.t.* To direct and control; to administer the affairs of a State; to regulate, sway, influence; to conduct (oneself) in a specific way; to restrain; *(Gram.)* to require a particular case in the word following it, to have a noun or case dependent upon it (of a verb or preposition). *v.i.* To exercise authority; to administer the law; to have the control (over). **governable**, *a.* **governance**, *n.*

governess (gŭv'ėr-nės), *n.* A woman who instructs young children, esp. in a family.

government (gŭv'ėrn-mėnt) [O.F. *governement*], *n.* Control, regulation, exercise of authority, esp. in public affairs; the form or system of such administration; the body of persons in charge of the government of a State, an administration, ministry; self-control; the power of controlling; the form of policy in a State; the right of governing; the executive power; territory under a governor; *(Gram.)* the influence of a word in determining the case or mood of another. **governmen'tal**, *a.*

governor (gŭv'ėr-nŏr) [O.F. *governeur*], *n.* One who governs, esp. one executing the laws and administering the affairs of a State, province, etc.; the Crown representative in a colony, etc.; the commander in a fortress; *(slang)* one's father, one's employer. **governorship**, *n.*

gowan (gou'ăn) [Sc.], *n.* The daisy.

gown (goun) [O.F. *gaune*, late L. *gunna*, a fur garment], *n.* A woman's loose outer garment, a dress, a frock; a long, loose robe worn by clergymen, judges, lawyers, university men, etc. **gownsman**, *n.* A member of a university; a lawyer.

grab (grăb) [?], *v.t.* To seize, snatch, take violently or lawlessly. *n.* A sudden snatch, grasping, or seizing (at); an implement for clutching, a grip; rapacious acquisition. **grabber**, *n.*

grace (grās) [L. *grātia*, from *grātus*, pleasing], *n.* That quality which makes form, expression, etc., elegant, harmonious, refined; a natural endowment or acquired accomplishment; a courteous demeanour; *(Mus.)* a note or passage as an embellishment; mercy; a boon; the free, unmerited favour of God; a divine, regenerating, and invigorating influence; the state of being reconciled to God; a short prayer before or after a meal; extension of time legally allowed after a payment falls due; *(Univ.)* a licence to take a degree, a dispensation from statutes, etc. **graceful**, *a.* Full of grace, elegance, or beauty. **gracefulness**, *n.* **graceless**, *a.* Lacking in propriety, mannerless; abandoned.

gracile (grăs'il) [L. *gracilis*], *a.* Slender.

gracious (grā'shŭs) [L. *grātiōsus*, as **GRACE**], *a.* Exhibiting grace, favour, or kindness; courteous, affable; proceeding from divine grace; merciful. **graciously**, *adv.* **graciousness**, *n.*

gradation (grȧ-dā'shŭn) [L. *gradus*, a step], *n.* Orderly arrangement or progression step by step; a stage or degree in rank, merit, etc. **gra'datory,** *a.*

grade (grād), *n.* A degree or step in rank, quality, value, order, etc.; a class of people of similar rank, etc.; gradient, degree of slope. *v.t.* To arrange in grades; to adjust the rate of slope in, as a road.

gradient (grā'di-ĕnt) [L. *gradiens*, walking], *n.* Rate of ascent or descent in a railway or road.

gradual (grăd'ū-ăl), *a.* Proceeding by degrees; regular and slow.

graduate (grăd'ū-āt), *v.t.* To mark with degrees; to divide into or arrange by gradations; to apportion (a tax, etc.) according to a scale; to modify by degrees; to confer a degree upon. *v.i.* To alter by degrees; to take a degree in a university. *n.* (grăd'ū-ăt) One who has received a degree in a university. **gradua'tion,** *n.*

graft (1) (graft) [O.F. *grafe*], *n.* A small shoot inserted into a tree of different stock which supplies the sap to nourish it; living tissue transplanted to another animal. *v.t.* To insert as a graft.

graft (2), *n.* A swindle; bribery; manipulation of funds to secure illicit profit.

grail (grāl) [O.F. *graal*, *greal*], *n.* A dish or cup said to have been used by Christ at the Last Supper, and employed by Joseph of Arimathea to collect His blood while on the Cross.

grain (grān) [L. *grānum*], *n.* A single seed, particularly of those kinds used for food; corn in general; (*pl.*) refuse of malt after brewing or of any grain after distillation; a small, hard particle; the unit of weight in the English system (7000 in 1) $\frac{1}{7000}$ lb. av., 5760 in 1 lb. troy; texture, esp. the arrangement of the fibres of wood; the lines of fibre in wood or, in stone, of cleavage planes; a red dye made from cochineal; any fast dye; temper, natural tendency. *v.t.* To form into grains, to granulate; to bring out, or give the appearance of, the natural grain. *v.i.* To become granulated. **graining,** *n.* The act of producing a grain; a process in tanning; painting in imitation of the grain of wood.

-gram [Gr. *gramma*, a letter, from *graphein*, to write], *suf.* Forming compounds with prepositional prefixes, numerals, etc., as in *epigram, monogram, telegram.*

gramineous (grà-min'ĕ-ŭs) [L. *grāmen*, grass], *a.* Pertaining to grass, or the tribe of grasses. **graminiv'orous,** *a.* Subsisting on vegetable food.

grammar (grăm-ăr) [O.F. *gramaire*], *n.* The principles or science of the correct use of language; dealing with phonology, etymology, accidence, and syntax; a system of principles and rules for speaking and writing a language; a book containing these; the elements of an art or science. **grammarian** (grà-mâr'-ĭ-ăn), *n.* One versed in grammar; one who teaches grammar. **grammat'ical,** *a.* Pertaining to grammar; according to the rules of grammar.

gramme (grăm) [Gr. *gramma*, a small weight], *n.* The standard unit of weight

in the metric system, equalling 15·432 grains troy.

gramophone (grăm'ō-fōn) [Gr. *gramma*, a letter, *phonē*, sound], *n.* An instrument for recording and reproducing sounds.

grampus (grăm'pŭs) [A.-F. *grampais*, L. *crassum piscem*, fat fish], *n.* A large voracious cetacean.

granary (grăn'ăr-ĭ) [L. *grānārium*, as GRAIN], *n.* A storehouse for grain.

grand (grănd) [L. *grandis*, great], *a.* Great or imposing in size, character, or appearance; magnificent, fine, dignified, noble; morally impressive, inspiring; fashionable, or aristocratic (society); excellent; pre-eminent in rank, etc., chief; (*Law*) principal, as opp. to petty, common, etc. **grandchild,** *n.* The child of a son or daughter. **granddaughter,** *n.* The daughter of a son or daughter. **grandfather,** *n.* The father of a parent. **grandfather clock;** A clock worked by weights, in a tall wooden case. **grandmother,** *n.* The mother of a parent. **grandmotherly,** *a.* **Grand National,** *n.* (*Racing*) An annual steeple-chase run at Aintree. **grandparent,** *n.* A grandfather or grandmother. **grand piano,** *n.* (*Mus.*) A large pianoforte with horizontal framing. **grandsire,** *n.* A grandfather; a male ancestor. **grandson,** *n.* The son of one's son or daughter. **grandly,** *adv.* **grandness,** *n.*

grandee (grăn-dē'), *n.* A Spanish or Portuguese nobleman of the highest rank; a powerful or important person.

grandeur (grăn'djŭr), *n.* Greatness, nobility, sublimity, majesty; splendour.

grandiloquent (grăn-dil'ŏ-kwent), *a.* Using lofty or pompous language; bombastic. **grandiloquence,** *n.*

grandiose (grăn'di-ōz) [It. *grandioso*], *a.* Producing or intended to produce the effect of grandeur, affecting impressiveness, pompous.

grange (grānj) [L. *grānea*], *n.* A farmhouse with the outbuildings, etc.

grangerize (grăn'jĕr-īz) [James *Granger* (1716–76)], *v.t.* To extra-illustrate (a book, etc.) with portraits, etc.

granite (grăn'it) [It. *granito*, speckled], *n.* A granular, igneous rock consisting of feldspar, quartz, and mica, confusedly crystallized. **granit'ic,** *a.*

granny (grăn'ĭ), *n.* A grandmother; a badly-made reef knot.

grant (grant) [O.F. *graunter*], *v.t.* To bestow, give, esp. in answer to request; (*Law*) to transfer the title to, to confer or bestow (a privilege, charter, etc.); to admit as true, to concede. *n.* The act of granting; the thing granted; an assignment; a sum bestowed or allowed; a concession or admission of something as true; (*Law*) a conveyance in writing; the thing conveyed. **grantee',** *n.* (*Law*) The person to whom a grant or conveyance is made. **granter,** *n.* One who grants. **grantor,** *n.* (*Law*) One who makes a conveyance.

granule (grăn'ūl) [late L. *grānulum*], *n.* A little grain; a small particle. **gran'ular,** *a.* Composed of or resembling granules. **gran'ulate,** *v.t.* To form into granules;

to make rough on the surface. *v.i.* To collect or be formed into grains. **granula'tion**, *n.*

grape (grāp) [O.F.], *n.* The fruit of the vine; (*Mil.*) grape-shot; (*pl.*) a mangy tumour on the legs of horses. **grapefruit**, *n.* A large citrus. **grape-shot**, *n.* Shot arranged between plates, so as to scatter when fired. **grapevine telegraph**, *n.* (*fig.*) News conveyed by underground sources of intelligence.

graph (grăf), *n.* A diagram representing mathematical or chemical relationship. **-graph** (Gr. *graphein*, to write], *suf.* -written, -writing, -writer, as in *autograph, lithograph, telegraph.*

graphic, -al (grăf'ĭk, -ăl), *a.* Pertaining to the art of writing, delineating, engraving, etc.; forcibly descriptive; having the faculty of vivid description; indicating by means of diagrams instead of statistics, etc. **graphically**, *adv.*

graphite (grăf'īt) *n.* Blacklead.

grapnel (grăp'nĕl) [O.F. *grapin*, from *grape*, a hook], *n.* A grappling-iron; an anchor.

grapple (grăpl) [M.F. *grappil*, a ship's grapnel], *n.* A close hold or grip in wrestling, etc.; a close struggle; a grapnel. *v.t.* To lay fast hold of, to seize, clutch; to come to close quarters with. *v.i.* To contend or struggle (with or together) in close fight or at close quarters. **grappling-iron**, *n.* An iron instrument with claws or hooks for seizing and holding fast.

grasp (grasp) [M.E. *grapsen*], *v.t.* To seize and hold fast; to lay hold of and keep with eagerness or greed; to comprehend. *v.i.* To clutch (at). *n.* A fast grip, clutch, or hold; ability to seize and hold; intellectual comprehension.

grass (gras) [A.-S. *gærs, græs*], *n.* The green-bladed herbage on which cattle, sheep, etc., feed; pasture, grazing. *v.t.* To cover with grass or turf. **grasshopper**, *n.* An insect with hind-legs formed for leaping. **grass-snake**, *n.* The common, harmless ringed snake. **grass widow**, *n.* (*colloq.*) A woman temporarily separated from her husband; a divorced woman.

grate (1) (grāt) [L. *crātes*, hurdle], *n.* A frame of parallel or cross bars, a grating; a frame of iron bars for holding fuel for a fire.

grate (2) (grāt) [O.F. *grater*, from Teut.], *v.t.* To rub against a rough surface so as to reduce to particles; to rub against something, so as to cause a harsh sound, to grind down; to irritate, vex, offend (one's nerves). *v.i.* To rub (upon) so as to emit a harsh, discordant noise, to have an irritating effect (upon). **grater**, *n.* **grating** (1), *a.* Harsh, discordant, irritating.

grateful (grāt'fŭl) [L. *grātus*, pleasing], *a.* Pleasing, agreeable, acceptable; marked by or indicative of gratitude. **gratefully**, *adv.* **gratefulness**, *n.*

gratify (grăt'i-fī), *v.t.* To please, to delight; to satisfy the desire of; to give free rein to, to reward. **gratifying**, *a.* **gratifica'tion**, *n.*

grating (2) (grā'tĭng), *n.* A lattice of metal bars or wooden slats.

gratis (grā'tĭs) [L.], *adv.* and *a.* For nothing; without charge, free.

gratitude (grăt'i-tūd) [F., from L. *grātus*, pleasing], *n.* Grateful feeling, thankfulness.

gratuitous (grá-tū'i-tŭs) [L. *grātuītus*, freely given], *a.* Granted without claim or charge; voluntary; without cause; uncalled for, unnecessary.

gratuity (grá-tū'i-ti), *n.* A gift, a tip; a bounty paid to soldiers on retirement, discharge, etc.

gratulatory (grătū-lā'-tŏr-ĭ) [L. *grātulārī*], *a.* Congratulatory, expressing joy.

gravamen (grá-vā'mĕn) [L., from *gravāre*, to load], *n.* (*pl.* -mina) The substantial cause of an action; the burden of a complaint.

grave (1) (grāv) [?], *v.t.* To clean by scraping, etc., and cover with pitch and tallow (as a ship's bottom). **graving-dock**, *n.* A dry dock.

grave (2) (grāv) [A.-S. *grafan*], *v.t.* To shape by cutting into a surface, to engrave; to carve, sculpture. *n.* A hole in the earth for burying a dead body in; a tomb; mortality, death. **gravestone**, *n.* A stone, usu. inscribed, set over or at a grave. **graveyard**, *n.* A burial ground.

grave (3) (grāv) [L. *gravis*, heavy], *a.* Important, momentous; solemn, dignified; sombre, plain. **gravely**, *adv.*

gravel (grăvl) [O.F. *gravele*, dim of *grave*, strand, gravel, cp. GRAVE (1)], *n.* Small pebbles intermixed with sand, etc.

gravid (gră'vĭd), *a.* Pregnant.

gravitate (grăv'i-tāt), *v.i.* To be acted on by gravity; to be attracted to; tend downwards, to sink. **gravita'tion**, *n.*

gravity (grăv'i-ti), *n.* Heaviness; importance, enormity; solemnity, sedateness, grave demeanour; the force causing bodies to tend towards the centre of the earth.

gravy (grā'vĭ) [?], *n.* The fat and juice from meat during and after cooking.

gray [GREY]

grayling (grā'lĭng), *n.* A freshwater fish of the salmon family.

graze (1) (grāz) [A.-S. *grasian*, from *græs*, GRASS], *v.i.* To eat growing grass; to feed, browse. *v.t.* To feed (cattle, etc.) on growing grass; to supply with pasturage; to pasture; to eat. **grazer**, *n.* An animal that grazes. **grazier** (grā'zĭ-ĕr), *n.* One who rears and fattens cattle for market. **grazing**, *n.* The act of feeding on grass; a pasture.

graze (2) (grāz) [?], *v.t.* To touch or brush slightly in passing; to scrape in rubbing past. *v.i.* To touch some person or thing lightly in passing. *n.* A slight touch in passing; a slight abrasion.

grease (grēs) [O.F. *graisse*, L. *crassus*, adj., fat], *n.* Animal fat in a soft state; oily or fatty matter. *v.t.* (grēs, grēz) To smear or lubricate with grease; to cause to go smoothly, hence to bribe. **greasy** (grē'zĭ, -sĭ), *a.* **greasily**, *adv.* **greasiness**, *n.*

great (grāt) [A.-S. *grēat*], *a.* Large in bulk, amount, extent, etc.; big, vast;

important, momentous; pre-eminent. the chief; of exceptional ability, possessing genius; grand, majestic; gravid; grievous, burdensome; notorious; denoting a step in relationship (as great-**grandfather**, the father of a grandfather; **great-grandson**, the son of a grandson). *n.* (*collect.*) Important, highly-placed people. **great-coat**, *n.* An overcoat. **great toe**: The big toe. **greatly**, *adv.* In a great degree, much, exceedingly; nobly. **greatness**, *n.* **greats**, *n.pl.* The final examination at Oxford for B.A.

grebe (grēb) [F. *grèbe*], *n.* A diving-bird.

Grecian (grē'shǎn), *a.* Pertaining to Greece. *n.* A Greek; one well versed in Greek.

greed (grēd), *n.* Avarice, insatiable desire or covetousness. **greedy** [A.-S. *grǣdig*], *a.* **greedily**, *adv.* **greediness**, *n.*

Greek (grēk) [Gr. *Graikos*, ancient name for the Hellenes], *n.* A native of Greece; the language of Greece.

green (grēn) [A.-S. *grēne* (cp. Dit. *groen*, G. *grün*) cogn. with *grōwan*, to GROW], *a.* Having a colour like growing herbage; unripe, immature; easily imposed on; fresh, not withered, not dried, seasoned, cured, or tanned; (of a wound) not healed. *n.* The colour of growing herbage; a colour composed of blue and yellow; a grassy plot; (*pl.*) young leaves and stems of cabbages, etc., used for food; (*fig.*) vigour, youth, prime. **green-back**, *n.* A United States bank-note. **greenfinch**, *n.* A common British singing bird. **green-fly**, *n.* An aphis or plant-louse. **greengage**, *n.* A green, fine-flavoured variety of plum. **greengrocer**, *n.* A retailer of vegetables. **greenhorn**, *n.* A simpleton, a raw person. **green-house**, *n.* A glass-house for cultivating and preserving tender plants. **green-room**, *n.* A room in which actors and actresses wait during intervals. **green-sward**, *n.* Turf covered with grass. **greenwood**, *n.* A wood in summer. *a.* Pertaining to a greenwood. **greenery**, *n.* **greenish**, *a.* **greenness**, *n.*

greet (grēt) [A.-S. *grētan*], *v.t.* To salute at meeting; to accost; to receive at meeting or on arrival (with speech, gesture, etc.). *v.i.* To exchange greetings. **greeting**, *n.*

gregarious (grē-gâr'ï-ŭs) [L. *grex gregis*, herd], *a.* Living in flocks or herds; tending to associate. **gregariously**, *adv.* **gregariousness**, *n.*

gremlin (grem'lin) [*Aer. slang*], *n.* An airman's sprite.

grenade (grē-nād') [Sp. *granada*, pome-granate], *n.* A small explosive shell thrown by hand.

grenadier (gren-à-dēr'), *n.* One of a British regiment of Guards; formerly a foot-soldier armed with grenades.

grey (grā) [A.-S. *grǣg*], *a.* Ash-coloured; between white and black, dull, clouded, dismal, depressing, aged, pertaining to old age. *n.* A grey colour; twilight, cold, sunless light; a grey horse. **grey-beard**, *n.* An old man; a large earthen jar for spirit. **Grey Friar**: A Franciscan friar. **grey-haired**, **-headed**, *a.* **grey-hound**, *n.* A swift, slender, and keen-

sighted dog used for coursing. **greyish**, *a.* **greyly**, *adv.* **greyness**, *n.*

grid (grid) [as GRIDIRON], *n.* A grating of parallel bars; a gridiron; (*Elec.*) a system of main transmission supply lines.

griddle (gridl) [A.-F. *gridil*, O.F. *greil*], *n.* A circular iron plate for baking cakes.

gridiron (grid'īrn) [M.E. *gredire*], *n.* A grated iron utensil for broiling on; a framework of parallel beams for supporting a ship in dry dock.

grief (grēf), *n.* Deep sorrow or mental distress due to loss, disappointment, etc.; regret, sadness.

grievance (grē'vǎns) [O.F. *grevance*, as foll.], *n.* That which causes grief; a wrong, a ground for complaint.

grieve (grēv) [O.F. *grever*, L. *gravāre*], *v.t.* To cause pain or sorrow to; to lament, sorrow over. *v.i.* To feel grief, to sorrow. **grievous**, *a.* Causing grief; hard to be borne, distressing.

griffin -on (grif'in, -ŏn) [Gr. *grupos*, hook-beaked], *n.* A fabulous creature, with the body and legs of a lion, the head and wings of an eagle; (*fig.*) a watchful guardian, a duenna; (-on) a vulture; a dog like a terrier, with short, coarse hair.

grig (grig) [?], *n.* A young eel; a cricket or grasshopper; a merry person.

grill (gril) [F. *griller*], *v.t.* To broil on a gridiron; to torture as by fire. *n.* Meat, etc., broiled; a gridiron. **griller**, *n.*

grille (gril), *n.* A screen of lattice-work, to enclose a place, to fill an opening in a door, etc.

grilse (grils) [?] *n.* A young salmon when it first returns from the sea, usu. in its second year.

grim (grim) [A.-S.], *a.* Stern, relentless; cruel; hideous, ghastly. **grimly**, *adv.*

grimace (grim-mās') [F.], *n.* A distortion of the face, expressing disgust, contempt, affectation, etc. *v.i.* To make grimaces.

grimalkin (gri-mǎl'kin) [GREY, *Malkin*, dim. of *Matilda*], *n.* An old cat, esp. a she-cat.

grime (grim) [Scand.], *n.* Dirt, smut; dirt deeply engrained. *v.t.* To dirty. **grimy**, *a.* **grimily**, *adv.* **griminess**, *n.*

grin (grin) [A.-S. *grennian*], *v.i.* To show the teeth as in laughter; to smile in a malicious, sickly, or affected manner. *n.* A smile with the teeth showing.

grind (grīnd) [A.-S. *grindan*], *v.t.* To reduce to fine particles by crushing and friction; to sharpen, smooth, or polish by friction; to oppress, to harass, esp. with exactions; to work (a mill, handle, etc.); to study laboriously. *v.i.* To perform the act of grinding; to be ground; to rub gratingly; to drudge; to study laboriously. *n.* Act or process of grinding; hard and monotonous work; a turn at the handle of a machine or instrument. **grinder**, *n.* One who or that which grinds; a grinding-machine; a molar tooth; one who studies hard. **grind-stone**, *n.* A flat circular stone, rotated for grinding tools.

grip (grip) [A.-S. *gripe*, a clutch], *n.* The act of holding firmly; a firm grasp; power of grasping; the part of a weapon, etc., that is held in the hand. *v.t.* To seize hold of; to grasp or hold tightly. *v.i.* To take firm hold. *n.* A traveller's hand-bag.

gripe (grīp) [A.-S. *grīpan*], *v.t.* To grip, clutch, to pinch; to oppress; to affect the bowels with colic pains. *v.i.* To lay fast hold of anything; to get money by extortion. *n.* A grasp; a pinch, squeeze; (*pl.*) pains in the abdomen. **griping**, *a.*

grisly (griz'li) [A.-S. *grislic*], *a.* Horrible, fearful, grim.

grist (grist) [A.-S. *grist*], *n.* Corn to be ground or which has been ground; malt for a brewing.

gristle (grisl) [A.-S.], *n.* Cartilage.

grit (grit) [A.-S. *grēot*], *n.* Coarse rough particles such as sand; (*colloq.*) firmness, pluck. **gritty**, *a.* **grittiness**, *n.*

grizzle (1) (grizl) [O.F. *grisel*, from *gris*, grey], *a.* Grey. *n.* A grey colour; grey hair; a kind of wig. **grizzled**, *a.* Grey, grey-haired. **grizzly**, *a.* Grey, greyish. *n.* A grizzly bear, a North American bear of great size and strength.

grizzle (2) (grizl) [?], *v.i.* To worry, fret.

groan (grōn) [A.-S. *grānian*], *v.i.* To utter a deep moaning sound, as in pain or grief; (*fig.*) to grieve. *n.* A low moaning sound, as of one in pain or sorrow.

groat (grōt) [M.E. and L.G. *grote*], *n.* A silver fourpenny-piece.

groats (grōts) [cp. A.-S. *grūt*, cp. GRIT], *n.pl.* Husked oats or wheat.

grocer (grō'sẽr) [O.F. *grossier*, one who sells in the gross], *n.* A dealer in tea, sugar, coffee, spices, etc. **grocery**, *n.* Grocers' wares.

grog (grog) [from nickname of Admiral Vernon, "Old Grog"], *n.* A mixture of rum and water.

grogram (grog'răm) [F. *gros grain*, coarse grain], *n.* A coarse stuff of silk and mohair or silk and wool.

groin (groin) [?], *n.* The hollow in the human body where the thigh and the trunk unite; (*Arch.*) the edge formed by an intersection of vaults; a groyne. **groined**, *a.* **groining**, *n.* (*Arch.*)

groom (groom, grum) [?], *n.* A servant who has charge of horses; one of several officers in the royal household; a bridegroom. *v.t.* To tend or care for, as a groom does a horse. **groomsman**, *n.* An unmarried friend who attends on the bridegroom.

groove (groov) [A.-S. *grafan*], *n.* A channel or long hollow for something to fit into or work in; natural course of events of one's life, a rut. *v.t.* To cut or form a groove in.

grope (grōp) [A.-S. *grāpian*], *v.i.* To feel about with the hands as in the dark; to feel one's way; to seek blindly.

gross (grōs) [O.F. *gros*, thick], *a.* Fat, bloated, overfed; coarse, uncleanly; dense, thick; (*fig.*) dull, unrefined; indelicate; flagrant; total, not net; general, not specific. *n.* Twelve dozen; the mass; the sum total. **grossness**, *n.*

grotesque (grō-tesk') [It. *grottesca*, antique work], *a.* Extravagant or fantastic; ludicrous through these qualities, bizarre.

grotto (grot'ō) [It. *grotta*], *n.* A small cave.

ground (1) (ground) [A.-S. *grund*], *n.* The surface of the earth; a floor or other supporting surface; land, landed estates; (*pl.*) private land attached to a house; the solid earth; the base or foundation; the background, the surface on which a picture, etc., is laid, the prevailing colour or tone; (*fig.*) the reason, motive, origin, cause; (*pl.*) pretext, the first or fundamental principles; dregs, esp. of coffee. *v.t.* To set on or in the ground; to base or establish (on); to instruct thoroughly (in) the elementary principles of; to run (a ship) aground. **ground-bait**, *n.* Bait thrown into the water to attract fish. **ground floor:** The rooms level with the exterior ground. **ground-landlord**, *n.* The owner of land let on a building lease. **groundless**, *a.* Without foundation or reason, baseless. **groundling**, *n.* A spectator who stood on the floor of a theatre; one of the vulgar. **ground-plan**, *n.* A horizontal plan of a building at the ground level; an outline of anything. **ground-rent**, *n.* Rent paid to a ground-landlord for a building-site. **ground-swell**, *n.* A long, deep swell or rolling of the sea, occasioned by a past or distant storm, etc. **ground-work**, *n.* That which forms the foundation or basis; fundamental principle; parts of any object not covered by decoration, etc. **grounding**, *n.* Instruction in the elements of a subject. **groundsman**, *n.* The man who looks after a cricket pitch.

ground (2) (ground) [*p.p.* of GRIND], *a.* **ground glass:** Glass with the surface ground to make it obscure.

groundsel (ground'sĕl) [A.-S. *gundswylige*], *n.* A weed with small yellow flowers used for feeding cage-birds.

group (groop) [F. *groupe*], *n.* The combination of several things to form a single mass; a cluster, an assemblage; a number of persons or things classed together; a grade in classification; (*Aer.*) in the R.A.F. the highest subdivision of a command. *v.t.* To form into or place in a group, to bring together so as to produce a harmonious whole or effect.

grouse (1) (grous) [?], *n.* (*pl. unchanged*). A game-bird.

grouse (2) *v.i.* To grumble. *n.* A grievance. **grouser**, *n.*

grout (grout) [A.-S. *grūt*], *n.* Coarse meal; (*pl.*) dregs; mortar to run into the joints of masonry, etc.

grove (grōv) [A.-S. *grāf*], *n.* A small wood, esp. one sacred to a divinity.

grovel (grovl) [obs. adv. *grovelling*], *v.i.* To lie or move with the body prostrate on the earth; (*fig.*) to prostrate oneself, to be abject. **groveller**, *n.*

grow (grō) [A.-S. *grōwan*], *v.i.* (*past grew*, *p.p.* grown) To increase by the assimilation of new matter; to develop; to increase in number, power, etc.; to spring up, be produced, arise; to pass into a certain state; to adhere. *v.t.* To cultivate; to produce.

growl (groul) [imit.], *v.i.* To make a deep guttural sound as of anger; to grumble; to speak gruffly; to rumble. *v.t.* To express by a growl. *n.* A deep guttural sound like that made by an angry dog; a complaint. **growler,** *n.* One who growls; a four-wheeled cab.

growth (grōth), *n.* Act or process of growing; increase, development in number, bulk, etc.; that which grows or is grown; a morbid formation.

groyne (groin) [?], *n.* A small breakwater on a foreshore, causing shingle, etc., to be retained.

grub (grŭb) [?], *v.i.* To scratch or tear up the ground superficially; to rummage; to drudge, toil; (*slang*) to take one's food. *v.t.* To dig (up or out); to clear (ground) of roots, etc.; to find by searching. *n.* The larva of an insect, a caterpillar, maggot; (*slang*) food.

grudge (grŭj) [O.F. *groucier*], *v.i.* To be envious, to cherish ill-will. *v.t.* To feel envy at; to give or take unwillingly or reluctantly. *n.* Ill-will, a feeling of malice; unwillingness, reluctance. **grudgingly,** *adv.*

gruel (groo'ĕl) [O.F.], *n.* Semi-liquid food made by boiling meal in water or milk.

gruesome (groo'sŭm), *a.* Frightful, horrible, repulsive. **gruesomely,** *adv.* **gruesomeness,** *n.*

gruff (grŭf) [Teut.], *a.* Of a rough, surly, or harsh aspect; sour, hoarse-voiced.

grumble (grŭmbl) [?], *v.i.* To murmur with discontent; to complain surlily, to growl, mutter. *v.t.* To express in a complaining manner. *n.* Act of grumbling; a complaint. **grumbler,** *n.*

grumpy (grŭm'pi) [obs. n. *grump,* offence], *a.* Surly, peevish, ill-tempered.

grunt (grŭnt) [A.-S. *grunnettan*], *v.i.* To make a noise like a pig; to grumble, growl. *v.t.* To express or utter in a grunting manner. *n.* A deep guttural sound, as of a hog. **grunter,** *n.* A hog.

guano (gwa'nō) [Sp., from Quichua *huanu,* dung], *n.* The excrement of sea-fowl from South America and the Pacific used as manure.

guarantee (găr-ăn-tē'), *n.* An engagement on the part of a third person to see an agreement, etc., fulfilled; act of guaranteeing; security, warranty, or surety given; the person to whom the guarantee is given. *v.t.* To become guarantor for; to undertake responsibility for the fulfilment of a contract; to pledge oneself; to assure the continuance of; to undertake to secure (to another). **guarantor,** *n.* One who guarantees.

guaranty (găr'ăn-ti) [A.-F. *guarantie,* O.F. *garantir,* to warrant], *n.* Act of guaranteeing, esp. an undertaking to be responsible for a debt of another person; that on which a guarantee or security is based.

guard (gard) [Teut.], *v.t.* To secure the safety of; to watch over, protect, defend, to prevent the escape of. *v.i.* To be cautious or take precautions (against). *n.* Defence, protection, a state of vigilance; a protector; men on guard; a sentry, escort; one in charge of a railway train, etc.; a watch-chain; a screen for a fire-place, window, etc.; (*pl.*) the British household troops. **guard-house,**

-room, *n.* A house or room for those on guard or for prisoners. **guardship,** *n.* A vessel stationed in a harbour for defence. **guardsman,** *n.* An officer or private in the Guards. **guardedly,** *adv.*

guardian (gar'di-ăn), *n.* One who has the charge or custody of any person or thing; a member of a board elected to administer the former Poor Laws; the superior of a Franciscan convent. *a.* Guarding; acting as a guardian or protector. **guardianship,** *n.*

gudgeon (1) (gŭj'ŏn) [F. *goujon*], *n.* A small freshwater fish, easily caught; (*fig.*) one easily taken in.

gudgeon (2) (gŭj'ŏn), *n.* (*Eng.*) The bearing of a shaft; the eye in which a rudder turns.

guelder rose (gel'dĕr-rōz) [*Guelders,* town], *n.* A shrubby plant bearing ball-shaped bunches of white flowers.

guerdon (gĕr'dŏn) [O.H.G. *widar,* against, *lōn,* loan], *n.* A reward, recompense.

guerrilla (gĕ-ril'ă) [Sp. dim. of *guerra,* war], *n.* Irregular warfare; an irregular, petty war; one engaged in such.

guess (ges) [M.E. *gessen,* as GET], *v.t.* To judge on imperfect grounds, to conjecture; to imagine, suppose, divine (one to be) *v.i.* To form a conjecture, to judge at random. *n.* A conjecture; an opinion, estimate, etc., based on imperfect grounds. **guess-work,** *n.* Calculation based on guess; procedure by this means.

guest (gest) [A.-S. *gæst*], *n.* One entertained in the house or at the table of another; one residing at a boarding-house or hotel. **guest-house,** *n.* A boarding-house.

guffaw (gŭ-faw') [imit.], *n.* A burst of coarse laughter. *v.i.* To laugh loudly or coarsely.

guide (gīd) [O.F. *guider*], *v.t.* To direct, lead, or conduct; to rule, regulate. *n.* One who leads another or points the way; a person who conducts a party of tourists, etc.; an adviser; anything adopted as a sign of direction or criterion of accuracy; a mechanical device acting as indicator or regulating motion; a guide-book describing places of interest, means of transit, etc.

guild (gild) [A.-S. *gild,* a payment], *n.* A society of craftsmen or others of the same class or pursuit, combined for mutual aid and protection. **guild-hall,** *n.* A hall where a guild or corporation meets; a town-hall.

guile (gīl) [O.F.], *n.* Deceit, craft, cunning. **guileful,** *a.* **guileless,** *a.*

guillemot (gil'ĕ-mot) [F., dim. of *Guillaume,* William], *n.* A diving sea-bird.

guillotine (gil'ō-tēn) [F., J. I. *Guillotin* (1738–1814), who introduced it (1792)], *n.* An apparatus for beheading persons at a stroke; a machine for cutting many thicknesses of paper; (*Parl.*) the curtailment of debate by previous arrangement. *v.t.* To execute by or cut with a guillotine.

guilt (gilt) [A.-S. *gylt*], *n.* The state of having committed an offence; criminality, culpability. **guiltless,** *a.* Innocent. **guilty,** *a.*

guinea (gĭn'ĭ) [*Guinea*, on W. coast of Africa], *n.* A former British gold coin. value 21s.; a sum of money equivalent to this. **guinea-fowl**, *n.* A gallinaceous bird something like the turkey, originally from Africa. **guinea-pig**, *n.* A small domesticated cavy from Brazil; (*fig.*) a person used to experiment upon in medicine, etc.

guise (gīz) [O.F.], *n.* External appearance; semblance; manner, way; dress.

guitar (gi-tar') [Sp. *guitarra*, Gr. *kithara*], *n.* A stringed musical instrument.

gulch (gŭlch) [?], *n.* A deep ravine.

gules (gŭlz) [O.F. *goules*], *n.* (*Her.*) A red colour, represented in engraving by vertical lines.

gulf (gŭlf) [F. *golfe*, Gr. *kolpos*], *n.* An inlet of the sea; a deep hollow, chasm, or abyss; a whirlpool, anything that engulfs; an impassable chasm, difference.

gull (gŭl) [prob. Corn. *gullan*], *n.* A long-winged, web-footed marine bird; (*fig.*) a simpleton, a dupe. *v.t.* To fool, impose upon. **gullible**, *a.* **gullibil'ity**, *n.*

gullet (gŭl'ĕt) [O.F., dim. of *gole*, L. *gula*, the throat], *n.* The throat.

gully (gŭl'ĭ), *n.* A channel or ravine worn by water; a ditch, gutter.

gulp (gŭlp) [imit.], *v.t.* To swallow (down) eagerly or in large draughts. *v.i.* To make a noise in swallowing, to gasp or choke. *n.* The act of gulping; a large mouthful; a catching or choking in the throat.

gum (1) (gŭm) [A.-S. *gōma*], *n.* The flesh round the necks of the teeth. **gumboil**, *n.* A small abscess on the gums.

gum (2) (gŭm) [M.E. and O.F. *gomme*], *n.* A viscid substance which exudes from trees, used for sticking things together; a gum-tree; chewing-gum. *v.t.* To cover, stiffen, or fasten with gum.

gumption (gŭmp'shŭn) [Sc. ?], *n.* Common sense.

gun (gŭn) [Icel. *gunn*, war], *n.* A tube from which projectiles are shot by explosive force, a cannon, rifle, etc., a member of a shooting party. **gunboat**, *n.* A small warship carrying heavy guns. **gun-carriage**, *n.* The frame upon which a cannon is mounted. **gun-cotton**, *n.* A highly explosive substance made by soaking cotton in nitric and sulphuric acids, and then drying. **gun-fire**, *n.* The hour at which the morning or evening gun is fired; discharge of guns. **gunman**, *n.* One who uses a gun, esp. illicitly. **gun-metal**, *n.* An alloy of copper and tin or zinc from which cannon were formerly cast. **gunner**, *n.* (*Nav.*) A warrant-officer in charge of ordnance or ordnance stores; (*Mil.*) an artilleryman. **gunnery**, *n.* The art of managing heavy guns; the science of artillery; practice with heavy guns. **gunpowder**, *n.* A mixture of saltpetre, carbon, and sulphur used as an explosive. **gun-room**, *n.* A room on one of the lower decks of a war vessel for junior officers. **gun-runner**, *n.* A smuggler of firearms. **gunshot**, *n.* The range of a gun. **gunsmith**, *n.* One who makes or repairs small fire-arms.

gunwale, gunnel (gŭnl), *n.* The upper edge of a ship's side next the bulwarks.

gurgle (gĕrgl) [?], *v.i.* To make a bubbling sound, as water poured from a bottle; to run or flow with such a sound.

gurnard, -net (gĕr'nård, -nĕt) [?], *n.* A sea-fish having a large angular head, covered with bony plates.

gush (gŭsh) [Teut.], *v.i.* To flow out copiously or with violence; to be filled with water, tears, etc.; to be effusive or affectedly sentimental. *n.* A violent and copious issue of a fluid; the fluid thus emitted; an outburst; extravagant affectation of sentiment.

gusset (gŭs'ĕt) [O.F. *gousset*, dim. of *gousse*, nut-shell], *n.* A small triangular piece of cloth inserted in a dress.

gust (1) (gŭst) [Icel. *gustr*], *n.* A short but violent rush of wind; a squall; an outburst of passion. **gusty**, *a.*

gust (2) (gŭst) [L. *gustus*, taste], *n.* The sense or pleasure of tasting; relish. **gus'tatory**, *a.* Of or pertaining to taste. **gusto**, *n.* Zest, enjoyment; flavour, relish.

gut (gŭt) [A.-S. *gutt*], *n.* The intestinal canal; an intestine; catgut, esp. as strings of musical instruments; a narrow passage, esp. a sound or strait; (*pl.*) stamina. endurance. *v.t.* To draw the entrails out of; (*fig.*) to remove or destroy the contents of (as by fire).

gutta-percha (gŭt'á-pĕr'chá) [Malay *gatah*, gum, *percha*, name of tree], *n.* The inspissated juice of a Malayan tree.

gutter (gŭt'ĕr) [O.F. *gutiere*], *n.* A channel or trough for carrying away water. *v.i.* To become channelled, as a burning candle. **gutter-snipe**, *n.* A street arab.

guttural (gŭt'ŭr-ăl) [L. *guttur*, throat], *a.* Pertaining to the throat; formed in the throat. *n.* A sound or letter produced in the throat. **gutturally**, *adv.*

guy (1) (gī) [O.F. *guie*, see **GUIDE**], *n.* A rope, etc., to steady a load in hoisting. *v.t.* To guide or steady by means of guys.

guy (2) (gī) [*Guy Fawkes*], *n.* An effigy, burnt on 5th Nov. in memory of the Gunpowder Plot; a fantastic figure. (*Amer.*) a fellow. *v.t.* To display in effigy; to ridicule.

gybe (jīb) [Dut. *gijben*], *v.i.* To swing from one side of the mast to the other (of a fore-and-aft sail). *v.t.* To shift (a sail) in this way; to make (a vessel) take the wind on the opposite quarter. *n.* Act or process of gybing.

gymkhana (jĭm-ka'ná) [Hind.], *n.* A meeting for athletic sports and games.

gymnasium (jĭm-nā'zi-ŭm) [Gr. *gumnazein*, to exercise naked (*gumnos*, naked)], *n.* A place for athletic exercises; a place of instruction for the higher branches of literature and science.

gymnast (jĭm'năst), *n.* An expert in gymnastic exercises. **gymnas'tic**, *a.*

gynæco- [Gr. *gunē gunaikos*, woman], *comb. form.* Pertaining to women. **gynæcol'ogy**, *n.* The science dealing with the functions and diseases peculiar to women. **gynæcol'ogist**, *n.*

-gynous [Gr. *-gunos*, from *gunē*, woman], *suf.* Pertaining to women; (*Bot.*) having female organs or pistils; as *androgynous*.

gypsum (jip'sùm) [Gr. *gupsos*, chalk], *n.* Hydrous sulphate of lime.

gyrate (jir'āt) [L. *gyrātus*], *a.* Circular, convoluted. *v.i.* (ji-rāt') To rotate, revolve, whirl, in a circle or spiral. **gyra'tion**, *n.* **gyr'atory**, *a.*

gyro- [Gr. *guros*, circle], *comb. form.* Round, curved; relating to revolutions. **gyro-compass**, *n.* (*Naut.*) A navigating compass worked by a gyroscope. **gyroplane**, *n.* A helicopter. **gyroscope**, *n.* A heavy fly-wheel rotated at a high speed preventing any alteration in the axis of rotation.

H

ha (ha) [onomat.], *int.* An exclamation denoting surprise, etc., or, when repeated, laughter.

habeas corpus (hā'bē-ås kôr'pus) [L., thou must have the body], *n.* (*Law*) A writ to produce a prisoner before a court.

haberdasher (hăb'ĕr-dăsh-ĕr) [A.-F. *hapertas*], *n.* A seller of ribbons, laces, silks, etc. **haberdashery**, *n.*

habiliment (há-bil'i-mènt) [O.F. *habiller*, to get ready], *n.* (*pl.*) Dress, garb.

habilitate (há-bil'-i tāt) [L. *habilitare*, to make fit], *v.t.* To furnish with means; to become qualified for; to equip.

habit (hăb'it) [L. *habēre*, to have, refl. to be constituted, to be], *n.* A settled inclination, disposition, or trend of mind; manner, use, or custom, acquired by frequent repetition; dress, costume, esp. one of a distinctive kind, as of a religious order, or a riding-dress for women. *v.t.* To dress, to clothe.

habitable (hăb'it-ábl), *a.* That may be dwelt in or inhabited. **habitably**, *adv.* **habitant**, *n.* (a-bē-tan) An inhabitant of Lower Canada of French origin. **habitat**, *n.* The natural abode of an animal or plant. **habita'tion**, *n.* State of being inhabited; place of abode; natural locality. **habited**, *a.* Wearing a habit.

habitual (há-bit'ū-ál), *a.* Formed by, acquired by, or according to habit, usual; constant; rendered permanent by use. **habituate**, *v.t.* To accustom; to make familiar by frequent repetition. **hab'itude**, *n.* **habitué** (há-bit'ū-ā), *n.* One who frequents a place, esp. of amusement.

hack (1) (hăk) [A.-S. *-haccian*], *v.t.* To cut irregularly or unskilfully; to chop, notch; to kick (a player's shins) at football. *v.i.* To chop away at anything; to emit a short dry cough. *n.* An irregular cut, gash, notch; a kick (on the shins, etc.); a miner's pick. **hacking**, *a.* Slashing, mangling; short, dry, and intermittent (of a cough).

hack (2) (hăk) [HACKNEY], *n.* A horse for hire, or for general purposes as dist. from a hunter, racer, etc.; a drudge, esp. a literary drudge. **hack-work**, *n.* Work done by a literary drudge.

hackle (hăkl) [M.E. *hachele*], *n.* A sharp steel comb for dressing flax, etc.; fibrous substance unspun, as raw silk; a long shining feather on a cock's neck; a fly for angling. *v.t.* To dress or comb (flax etc.) with a hackle.

hackney (hăk'ni) [prob. *Hackney*, Middlesex], *n.* A horse (or a cab or carriage) kept for hire. **hackneyed**, *a.* Stale, trite.

haddock (hăd-ŏk) [?], *n.* A sea-fish allied to the cod.

Hades (hā'dēz) [Gr., the god of the lower world], *n.* The abode of the spirits of the dead.

hæma-, hæmat-, hæmato- [Gr. *-haima haimatos*, blood], *comb. form.* Consisting or containing blood; pertaining to or resembling blood.

hæmophilia (hē-mō-fil'1-a) [Gr. *philia*, affection], *n.* (*Path.*) A constitutional tendency to hæmorrhage.

hæmorrhage (hem'ŏr-áj) [Gr. *haimorrhagia*, a breaking forth of blood], *n.* Discharge of blood from the heart, arteries, veins, or capillaries.

hæmorrhoids (hem'ŏ-roidz) [Gr. *hæmorrhoïdēs*, discharging blood], *n.pl.* Piles.

haft (haft) [A.-S. *hæft*], *n.* A handle of a dagger, knife, tool, etc.

hag (hăg) [?], *n.* A witch; an ugly old woman; an eel-like fish, parasitic within other fishes; the turfy hillocks of firmer ground in a bog.

haggard (hăg'ard) [F. *hagard*], *a.* Wild-looking; careworn, or gaunt from fatigue, etc. *n.* A wild or untrained hawk.

haggis (hăg'is) [Sc.], *n.* A Scottish dish of liver, lights, heart, etc., minced with onions, suet, oatmeal, etc., boiled in a sheep's stomach.

haggle (hăgl) [?], *v.i.* To chaffer, to wrangle (over or about a bargain). *n.* A wrangle about terms. **haggler**, *n.*

hagio- (hăg'i-ō) [Gr. *hagios*, holy], *comb. form.* Pertaining to saints or to holy things. **hagiol'atry**, *n.* The worship of saints. **hagiol'ogy**, *n.* Literature relating to the lives and legends of saints; a work on the lives of saints.

ha-ha (ha'ha) [F., a sudden obstacle that laughs at one], *n.* A fence or wall concealed in a ditch.

hail (1) (hāl) [A.-S. *hagol*], *n.* Frozen rain falling in showers. *v.i.* (*impers.*) To pour down hail; to come down with swiftness or violence. *v.t.* To pour down or out, as hail. **hailstone**, *n.* A single pellet of hail. **hailstorm**, *n.*

hail (2) (hāl) [Icel. *heill*], *v.t.* To call to (as one at a distance); to greet or designate (as); to welcome. *v.i.* To come (as a ship). *int.* An address of welcome or salutation.

hair (hâr) [Teut., A.-S. *hær*], *n.* A filament growing from the skin of an animal; the mass of such filaments forming a covering; hair-like cellular processes on the surface of plants; (*fig.*) something very small or fine, a hair's breadth. **hair-breadth, hair's breadth**, *n.* A very minute distance. **haircloth**, *n.* Cloth made wholly or in part of hair. **hair-compasses**, *n.pl.* Compasses that can be finely adjusted. **hairdresser**, *n.* One who dresses and cuts hair. **hair-line**, *n.* The up-stroke of a letter; a fishing-line of horse-hair. **hair-pencil**, *n.* A fine brush made of hair for painting. **hairpin**, *n.*

A pin for fastening the hair. **hair-shirt,** *n.* A shirt made of horse-hair, worn as a penance. **hair-splitting,** *n.* The practice of making minute distinctions. *a.* Quibbling. **hair-spring,** *n.* The fine steel spring regulating the balance-wheel in a watch. **hairy,** *a.*

hake (hāk) [?], *n.* A fish allied to the cod.

halation (hā-lā′shŭn) [HALO], *n.* (*Phot.*) A blurring in a negative caused by reflection.

halberd (hăl′bĕrd) [O.F. *halebarde*], *n.* A combination of spear and battle-axe, mounted on a long pole. **halberdier′,** *n.* One armed with a halberd.

halcyon (hăl′si-ŏn) [Gr. *alkuōn*, kingfisher], *n.* The kingfisher, fabled by the ancients to have the power of calming the sea while it was breeding. *a.* (*fig.*) Peaceful, happy, pleasant.

hale (1) (hāl) [A.-S. *hāl*, whole], *a.* Sound and vigorous, robust.

hale (2) (hāl) [O.F. *haler*], *v.t.* To drag, to draw violently.

half (haf) [A.-S. *healf*], *n.* (*pl.* **halves**) One of two equal parts into which a thing is or may be divided; a half-year, a school term. *a.* Consisting of or forming a half. *adv.* To the extent or degree of a half, or thereabouts; partially, imperfectly. **half-blood,** *n.* Relationship between two persons having but one parent in common; a half-breed. **half-boot,** *n.* A boot reaching high up the ankle. **half-bred,** *a.* Wanting in refinement; of mixed breed, mongrel. **half-breed,** *n.* An offspring of parents of different races. **half-brother,** *n.* A brother by one parent, but not by both. **half-caste,** *n.* A half-breed. **half-cock,** *n.* The position of the cock of a fire-arm when it cannot be moved by the trigger. **half-crown,** *n.* A silver English coin, value 2s. 6d. **half-dozen,** *n.* and *a.* Six. **half-hearted,** *a.* Lukewarm, indifferent; poor-spirited. **half-length,** *n.* A portrait showing only the upper half of the body. **half-mast:** Half-way up the mast, the position of a flag denoting respect for a dead person. **half-pay,** *n.* A reduced allowance to an officer not in active service. *a.* Entitled to or on half-pay. **halfpenny** (hā′pĕn-ĭ), *n.* An English copper coin, half the value of a penny. *a.* Of the value of a halfpenny; trumpery, almost worthless. **halfpennyworth** (hā′pŏrth), *n.* As much as can be bought for a halfpenny. **half-seas-over,** *a.* Half drunk. **half-starved,** *a.* Poorly fed, not having sufficient food. **half-time,** *n.* Half the time allotted. **half-tone,** *a.* (*Photo-engraving*) Pertaining to a process of reproducing and printing illustrations by photographing through a finely ruled screen. **half-truth,** *n.* A statement omitting or suppressing part of the truth. **half-witted,** *a.* Weak in intellect, imbecile.

halibut (hăl′ĭ-bŭt) [M.E. *hali*, holy, and *butte*, a flounder], *n.* A large flat-fish.

hall (hawl) [A.-S. *heall*], *n.* A large room, esp. one for public meetings, etc.; a large building for public business; the building occupied by a guild, etc.; a room in which scholars dine in common,

the dinner itself; a manor-house **or** mansion; (*Am.*) a passage; a room **or** passage at the entrance of a house; (*Univ.*) a building for undergraduates; a small college. **hall-mark,** *n.* An official stamp on gold and silver articles to guarantee the standard; any mark of genuineness. *v.t.* To stamp with this.

Hallelujah (hăl-ĕ-loo′yä) [Heb., **praise** Jehovah], *n.* Praise to God.

hallo (hă-lō) [imit.], *int.* An exclamation of surprise; a call for attention; a call to dogs. *n.* This cry. *v.i.* To cry 'hallo'; to cheer dogs on with cries. *v.t.* To shout loudly to; to urge on.

hallow (hăl′ō) [A.-S. *hālgian*], *v.t.* To make sacred, to revere; to consecrate, sanctify. **All-Hallows: All Saints' Day. Hallowe'en,** *n.* The eve of All-Hallows, 31st Oct.

hallucination (hă-loo-si-nā′-shŏn) [L. *hallūcinātus*, mentally fogged], *n.* An apparent perception of an external object arising from mental disorder, an illusion.

halo (hā′lō) [Gr. *halōs*, a round threshing-floor], *n.* (*pl.* -oes) A luminous circle round the sun or moon caused by refraction of light through mist; a bright disk surrounding the heads of saints in art.

halt (1) (hawlt) [A.-S. *healt*], *a.* Limping, lame. *v.i.* To limp, to be lame; to doubt, hesitate; (*fig.*) to come short, to be faulty. *n.* Lame persons generally.

halt (2) (hawlt) [G. *halt*, a stoppage], *n.* The act of stopping on a march. *v.i.* To come to a stand.

halter (hawl′tĕr) [A.-S. *hælfter*], *n.* A head-stall and rope by which an animal is fastened; a rope to hang malefactors; death by hanging. *v.t.* To put a halter upon; to tie up with a halter.

halve (hav), *v.t.* To divide into two equal parts; to share equally; to reduce to half.

halyard (hăl′yärd) [M.E. *halier*], *n.* Tackle for hoisting or lowering yards, sails, or flags.

ham (hăm) [A.-S. *hamm*], *n.* The hind part of the thigh; the thigh of a hog, salted and cured; (*Theat. slang*) an inexperienced or amateur actor.

hamadryad (hăm′à-drī-ăd) [Gr. *hama*, with, *drus*, tree], *n.* (Gr. *Myth.*) A nymph who died with the tree in which she lived; an Indian venomous snake.

hamlet (hăm′lĕt) [O.F. *hamelet*, from Teut.], *n.* A small village.

hammer (hăm′ĕr) [A.-S. *hamor*], *n.* A tool for driving nails, beating metals, etc.; the part of a gun-lock for exploding the charge, the striker of a bell, etc.; an auctioneer's mallet. *v.t.* To strike, beat, drive, forge, or form with a hammer; (*fig.*) to work (out) laboriously in the mind; (*Stock Exch.*) to declare a defaulter. *v.i.* To work with or as with a hammer; to make a noise like a hammer. **hammer-toe,** *n.* (*Med.*) A malformation of the foot.

hammock (hăm′ŏk) [Sp. *hamaca*], *n.* A bed of canvas or network hung from a ceiling, tree, etc.

hamper (1) (hăm′pĕr) [O.F. *hanapier*], *n.* A large wicker-work basket, with a cover.

hamper (2) (hăm′pĕr) [?], *v.t.* To impede

the free action of; to obstruct (movement, etc.); to hinder, fetter. *n.* Anything which encumbers, or impedes free action; (*Naut.*) rigging and other heavy gear.

hamstring (hăm'string), *n.* One of the tendons of the thigh. *v.t.* To lame by severing this.

hand (hănd) [A.-S. *hand*, *hond*], *n.* The palm and fingers at the extremity of the human arm serving as organ of prehension; a similar member in monkeys and other animals, when serving as a prehensile organ; (*fig.*) skill, performance, handiwork; a pledge of marriage; authority, power (*often in pl.*); (*pl.*) labourers, crew, persons engaged in a game, etc.; a turn, an innings; a game at cards; the cards held by a player; style of workmanship, writing, etc.; signature; a measure of four inches; the pointer or index finger of a watch, etc.; a shoulder (of pork); side direction (right or left). *v.t.* To give or transmit with the hand; to assist or conduct with the hand (into, out of, etc.); (*Naut.*) to furl. to hand down: To give in succession; to pass on. hand-bag, *n.* A small bag for carrying things by hand. handbill, *n.* A small printed sheet for circulating information. handbook, *n.* A small treatise on any subject, a manual. handbreadth, hand's breadth, *n.* A measurement equal to the breadth of the hand. hand-cart, *n.* A two-wheeled vehicle for goods pushed or drawn by hand. handcuff, *n.* (*usu. pl.*) A manacle for the wrists, *v.t.* To secure with handcuffs. handful, *n.* As much as can be held in the hand; a small number or quantity; (*colloq.*) a troublesome person or task. hand-made, *a.* Produced by hand, not by machinery. handmaid, -maiden, *n.* A female servant. handmill, *n.* A small mill worked by hand. handrail, *n.* A rail protecting stairs, landings, etc. handshake, *n.* A shake of another's hand as a greeting. hand-spike, *n.* A lever for lifting, heaving, etc. handwriting, *n.* Writing done by hand; style of writing peculiar to a person. handless, *a.*

handicap (hăn'di-kăp) [*hand i(n) cap*, from drawing lots out of a cap], *n.* A race or contest in which an allowance is made to the inferior competitors; the conditions imposed on a superior competitor. *v.t.* To impose heavier weight or other disadvantageous conditions.

handicraft (hăn'di-kraft) [A.-S. *handcræft*], *n.* Skill in working with the hands; manual occupation. *a.* Pertaining to manual labour. handicraftsman, *n.*

handiwork (hăn'di-wĕrk) [A.-S. *handgeweorc*], *n.* Work done by the hands; the product of one's labour.

handkerchief (hăng'kĕr-chif), *n.* A piece of cloth (silk, linen, etc.) for wiping the nose, face, etc.

handle (hăndl) [A.-S. *handlian*], *v.t.* To touch, to feel with, to wield or use with the hands; to manage, to treat of; to deal in. *v.i.* To work with the hands; to be handled. *n.* That part of anything by which it is grasped; (*fig.*) an instru-

ment or means by which anything is done. handling, *n.* The action of touching, feeling, etc.

handsel (hăn-sel) [Scand.], *n.* A gift for luck, esp. at the New Year; earnest money; the first sale, use, etc. *v.t.* To give a handsel to; to use for the first time.

handsome (hăn'sŭm), *a.* Finely-featured, good-looking; noble; liberal, ample, large. handsomeness, *n.*

handy (hăn'di), *a.* Convenient to the hand; close at hand; dexterous, skilful with the hands. handy-man, *n.* A man of all work. handily, *adv.*

hang (hăng) [A.-S.], *v.t.* (*past and p.p.* hung; for put to death and as imprecation hanged) To suspend; to fasten so as to leave movable (as a bell, gate, body of a coach, etc.); to suspend by the neck till dead; to cause to droop; to cover or decorate with anything suspended; to attach, fasten. *v.i.* To be suspended; to dangle, swing; to cling; to be executed by hanging; to droop, to bend forwards; to project (over), to impend; to be in suspense. *n.* A slope, a declivity; mode of hanging; (*fig.*) general tendency, drift, or bent. hangdog, *n.* A low, base fellow. *a.* Base, sullen. hangman, *n.* A public executioner.

hangar (hăng'gar) [F.], *n.* A large shed, esp. for air-ships or aeroplanes.

hanger (hăng'ĕr), *n.* That on which a thing is suspended; a pot-hook; a short, curved cutlass. hanger-on, *n.* A dependant, a parasite.

hanging (hăng'ing), *n.* The act of suspending; an execution by the gallows; (*pl.*) fabrics hung up to furnish walls, etc. *a.* Suspended, dangling; steep; punishable with hanging.

hank (hăngk) [Scand.], *n.* A coil; two or more skeins of yarn, silk, wool, etc., tied together.

hanker (hăng'kĕr) [?], *v.i.* To have an importunate desire (after).

hansom (hăn'sŏm) [J. A. *Hansom*, patentee, 1834], *n.* A two-wheeled cab in which the driver's seat is behind the body.

hap (1) (hăp) [Scand.], *n.* Chance, luck; that which happens or chances. *v.i.* To befall, to happen by chance. haphazard, (hăp-hăz'ård) *n.* Mere chance, accident. hapless, *a.* Unhappy, unfortunate. haply, *adv.* By hap; perhaps.

hap (2) (hăp), *v.t.* To cover over, to wrap up.

happen (hăpn), *v.i.* To fall out; to chance (to); to light (upon). happening, *n.* (*usu. pl.*) Something that happens, a chance event.

happy (hăp'i), *a.* Contented, satisfied; enjoying pleasure from the fruition or expectation of good; apt, felicitous; prosperous, successful; favourable; dexterous, skilful. happily, *adv.* happiness, *n.*

harangue (há-răng') [M.F.], *n.* A declamatory address; a noisy and vehement speech, a tirade. *v.i.* To make an harangue. *v.t.* To address in an harangue.

harass (hăr'ás) [M.F. *harasser*], *v.t.* To

torment by importunity; to tire out with care or worry.

harbinger (har'bin-jėr) [O.F. *herbergere*, from O.H.G. *heriberga* (*hari*, army, *bergan*, to shelter)], *n.* One who went before to secure lodgings; a precursor.

harbour (har'bŏr) [M.E. *hereberge*], *n.* A refuge, esp. for ships; a port, haven. *v.t.* To shelter, to entertain, cherish.

hard (hard) [A.-S. *heard*], *a.* Firm, solid; not yielding to pressure; difficult of accomplishment, comprehension, or explanation; fatiguing; perplexing; severe, inflexible, cruel, unfeeling; sordid, miserly; oppressive, unjust; rough and harsh to the palate, touch, etc.; containing mineral salts (of water); (*Phon.*) sounded gutturally, aspirated. *adv.* Forcibly, strenuously, severely; with effort or difficulty; close, near. **hardbake**, *n.* Toffee in which blanched almonds are mixed. **hard-bitten**, *a.* Tough, resolute. **hardness**, *n.* **hard-up**, *a.* In great want, esp. of money; very poor. **hard-ware**, *n.* Articles of metal, ironmongery.

harden (hardn), *v.t.* To make hard or harder; to temper (tools); to confirm (in effrontery, etc.); to make unfeeling or callous. *v.i.* To become hard or harder; to become inured, or confirmed (in vice).

hardly (hard'li), *adv.* With difficulty; harshly, rigorously; unfavourably; scarcely, not quite.

hardship (hard'ship), *n.* That which is hard to bear; privation, suffering, toil, fatigue, injury, injustice.

hardy (har-di) [F. *hardi*], *a.* Over confident, audacious; robust; (of plants) capable of bearing exposure in winter. **hardihood**, *n.* **hardiness**, *n.*

hare (hår) [A.-S. *hara*], *n.* A long-eared, short-tailed rodent with cleft upper lip. **harebell**, *n.* The blue bell of Scotland, the round-leaved bell-flower. **harebrained**, *a.* Rash, giddy, flighty. **harelip**, *n.* A congenital fissure of the upper lip.

harem (hâr'ém) [Arab. *haram*], *n.* The apartments reserved for women in a Mohammedan household; the occupants of these.

haricot (hăr'i-kō) [F.], *n.* A stew of meat with beans and other vegetables; the kidney or French bean.

hark (hark) [M.E. *herkien*], *v.i.* To listen. **to hark back**: To return to some point from which a digression has been made.

harlequin (har'lé-kwin) [It. *arlecchino*], *n.* The leading character in a pantomime or harlequinade, dressed in a mask and spangled clothes; a buffoon. **harlequinade** (-nād'), *n.* That part of a pantomime in which the harlequin and clown play the principal parts; a piece of fantastic conduct.

harlot (har'lŏt) [O.F., orig. masc., rogue], *n.* A prostitute.

harm (harm) [A.-S. *hearm*], *n.* Hurt, injury, evil. *v.t.* To hurt or damage. **harmful**, *a.* **harmless**, *a.*

harmonic (har-mon'ik) [L. *harmonicus*], *a.* Pertaining to harmony or music; con-

cordant, harmonious. *n.* An harmonic tone. **harmonical**, *a.* **harmonically**, *adv.* **harmon'ica, -con,** *n.* The musical glasses, a mouth-organ, a series of metal plates played on with a mallet, etc.

harmonious (har-mŏ'-ni-ùs), *a.* Concordant; having parts proportioned to each other, symmetrical; without discord or dissension; tuneful.

harmonist (har'mŏ-nist), *n.* One skilled in harmony.

harmonium (har-mŏ'ni-ùm), *n.* A keyed musical wind-instrument.

harmonize (har'mŏ-nīz), *v.t.* To make harmonious; to arrange in musical concord, to add the proper accompaniment to. *v.i.* To agree in sound or effect; to live in peace and concord; to be congruous (with).

harmony (har'mŏ-ni) [F. *harmonie*, L. and Gr. *harmonia* (*harmos*, a fitting or joining)], *n.* Adaptation of parts so as to form a complete, symmetrical, or pleasing whole; the agreeable combination of sounds, music; an arrangement of musical parts; the science dealing with musical combination of sounds; concord in views, sentiments, etc.

harness (har'nės) [M.G. and O.F. *harneis*], *n.* The gear of a horse or other draught-animal; the accoutrement of a man-at-arms, arms and armour; working apparatus or equipment. *v.t.* To put harness on (a horse, etc.).

harp (harp) [A.-S. *hearpe*], *n.* A musical instrument of triangular shape, with strings which are plucked by the fingers. *v.i.* To play upon a harp.

harpoon (har-poon') [F. *harpon*, from *harpe*, a claw], *n.* A barbed missile weapon with a line attached, used for striking whales, etc. *v.t.* To strike, catch, or kill with a harpoon. **harpooner** (har-poo'nėr), *n.*

harpsichord (harp'si-kôrd) [O.F. *harpe*, harp, *chorde*, chord], *n.* A musical instrument, similar in form to the pianoforte, in which the strings are plucked.

harpy (har'pi) [Gr. *harpuiai*], *n.* A fabulous monster with the face of a woman, the body of a vulture, and fingers armed with sharp claws; (*fig.*) an extortioner, a rapacious person or animal.

harridan (hăr'i-dàn) [?], *n.* An old vixen; a trollop.

harrier (1) (hăr'-lėr), *n.* A dog smaller than the foxhound, used for hare hunting.

harrier (2) (hăr'-lėr), *n.* One who harries or plunders; a falconoid bird.

harrow (hăr'ō) [M.G. *harwe*], *n.* A large rake or frame with teeth, drawn over ground to level it, destroy weeds, cover seed, etc. *v.t.* To draw a harrow over; to torment, to lacerate (feelings, etc.). **harrowing**, *a.* Causing anguish.

harry (hăr'i) [A.-S. *hergian*], *v.t.* To plunder, pillage, lay waste. *v.i.* To make plundering excursions.

harsh (harsh) [Scand.], *a.* Rough to the touch or other senses; discordant, irritating; austere, rigorous, unfeeling. **harshly**, *adv.* **harshness**, *n.*

hart (hart) [A.-S. *heort*], *n.* A male red

deer, from its fifth year onwards. **hart's-tongue**, *n.* A fern with tongue-shaped leaves.

hartshorn (harts'hŏrn), *n.* Solution of ammonia in water, smelling-salts.

harvest (har'vest) [A.-S. *hœrfest*], *n.* The season of reaping and gathering crops, esp. corn; ripe corn, etc., gathered and stored; the product or result of any labour or conduct. *v.t.* To reap and gather in; to garner, lay up. **harvester**, *n.* A reaper; a reaping and binding machine.

hash (hăsh) [O.F. *hacher*, to hack, mince], *n.* Meat cut small, mixed with vegetables, and stewed; (*fig.*) a second preparation of old matter; a mess, muddle. *v.t.* To cut or chop up in small pieces; to mince.

hasp (hasp) [A.-S. *hœpse*], *n.* A hinged clamp passing over a staple and secured by a pin, key, or padlock.

hassock (hăs'ŏk) [A.-S. *hassuc*], *n.* A small stuffed cushion for kneeling on; a matted tuft of rank grass.

haste (hāst) [O.F. *haste*], *n.* Hurry, celerity of movement, urgency, precipitance. *v.i.* To be quick; to be in a hurry. **hasten** (hāsn), *v.t.* To cause to hurry; to press on, expedite. *v.i.* To move with speed. **hasty**, *a.* Hurried.

hat (hăt) [A.-S. *hœt*], *n.* A covering for the head, usu. with a crown and a continuous brim; (*fig.*) the dignity of a cardinal. **hat trick:** (*Cricket*) The feat of taking three wickets with consecutive balls. **hatter**, *n.* One who makes or sells hats.

hatch (1) (hăch) [A.-S. *hœce*], *n.* A half-door, a wicket; a door in a roof; a grated opening in a weir; a hatchway, a trap-door or shutter to cover this. **hatchway**, *n.* A large opening in the deck of a ship.

hatch (2) (hăch) [Scand.], *v.t.* To produce from eggs; (*fig.*) to evolve, contrive. *v.i.* To come out of the egg; to be developed from ova, cells of a brood-comb, etc.

hatch (3) (hăch) [F. *hacher*], *v.t.* To mark with fine lines, parallel or crossing each other.

hatchet (hăch'ĕt) [F. *hachette*, dim. of *hache*, a sickle], *n.* A small axe with a short handle for use with one hand.

hate (hāt) [A.-S. *hete*], *n.* Extreme dislike or aversion; detestation. *v.t.* To dislike exceedingly; to abhor, detest. **hateful**, *a.* Causing hate; odious; feeling hatred. **hater**, *n.* hatred, *n.* Exceeding dislike or aversion; active malevolence, enmity.

haughty (haw'ti) [F. *haut*, L. *altus*, high], *a.* Proud, arrogant, supercilious; proceeding from or expressing disdainful pride.

haul (hawl), *v.t.* To pull or drag with force; to move by dragging. *v.i.* To pull or drag (at or upon) with force. *n.* A pull; the drawing of a net; the amount taken at once, acquisition.

haulm (hawm) [A.-S. *healm*], *n.* A stem, the stem of corn, peas, potatoes, etc.

haunch (hawnch) [O.F. *hanche*], *n.* The body between the ribs and the thigh; the basal joint.

haunt (hawnt) [O.F. *hanter*], *v.t.* To frequent, to resort to often; to recur to the mind of frequently in an irritating way; to frequent as a ghost or spirit. *v.i.* To stay or be frequently (about, in, etc.). *n.* A place to which one often or customarily resorts; a feeding-place for animals, etc.; habit of frequenting a place.

hautboy (hō'boi) [F. *hautbois*], *n.* An oboe.

hauteur (hō-tŏr') [F.], *n.* Haughtiness, lofty manners or demeanour.

have (hăv) [A.-S. *habban*], *v.t.* (*2nd sing.* hast, *3rd sing.* has, hath; *past* had, *2nd sing.* *hadst*, *p.p.* had) To possess; to enjoy, suffer, experience; to receive, get; to require, claim; to hold mentally, retain; to entertain; to maintain; to comprise; to understand, to be engaged in; to vanquish; to circumvent, cheat; to bring forth, bear. *v.i.* (*usu. in imper.*) To go, to betake oneself, to get (at, after, with, etc.). **aux.** Used with past participles to denote the completed action of verbs. *n.* (*slang*) A take-in, a sell.

haven (hāvn) [A.-S. *hœfene*], *n.* A port, a harbour; a refuge for ships; (*fig.*) an asylum.

haversack (hăv'ĕr-săk) [G. *haber*, oats, *sack*, sack], *n.* A canvas bag to hold rations, etc., on march.

havoc (hăv'ŏk) [A.-F. *havok*, O.F. *havot*, plunder], *n.* Widespread destruction.

haw (haw) [A.-S. *haga*], *n.* The berry or fruit of the hawthorn; a hedge, an enclosed field or yard.

hawk (1) (hawk) [A.-S. *hafoc*], *n.* A raptorial bird allied to the falcons; a bird of prey used in falconry; (*fig.*) a rapacious person, a sharper. *v.i.* To hunt birds, etc., by means of trained hawks; to attack on the wing, to soar (at). *v.t.* To pursue or attack on the wing. **hawk-eyed**, *a.* Having sharp sight. **hawking**, *n.* Falconry.

hawk (2) (hawk) [imit.], *v.i.* To clear the throat in a noisy manner. *v.t.* To force (up) phlegm from the throat.

hawk (3) (hawk), *v.t.* To carry about for sale, to cry for sale; (*fig.*) to spread about. **hawker** (haw'kĕr) [prob. conn. with G. *höker*], *n.* One who hawks goods for sale; a pedlar.

hawse (hawz) [Scand.], *n.* (*Naut.*) That part of the bow in which are the hawse-holes. **hawse-hole**, *n.* A hole in each bow for a cable or hawser.

hawser (haw'ser) [O.F. *haucier*, late L. *altiāre*, to raise], *n.* A small cable, used in warping and mooring.

hawthorn (haw'thŏrn) [A.-S. *hœgthorn*], *n.* The white-thorn, often called may.

hay (hā) [A.-S. *hieg*], *n.* Grass cut and dried for fodder. *v.t.* To make (grass, etc.) into hay; to supply with hay. **hay-box**, *n.* An airtight, non-conducting box with a thick layer of hay, used for keeping food hot. **haycock**, *n.* A conical heap of hay. **hay-fever**, *n.* A severe catarrh with asthmatic symptoms, frequent in summer. **haymaker**, *n.* One employed in making hay; a machine for tossing hay. **hayrick, -stack**, *n.* A pile of hay in the open air, thatched to keep it dry.

hazard (hăz'ărd) [O.F. *hasard*], *n.* A game at dice; risk; chance, casualty; the stake in gaming; bunkers, etc., on a golf-course;

(*Billiards*) a stroke putting a ball into a pocket. *v.t.* To risk; to expose to danger; to run the risk of; to venture (a statement, etc.). *v.i.* To run a risk, to venture. **hazardous**, *a.* Full of danger or risk.

haze (hāz) [?], *n.* A very thin mist or vapour, usu. due to heat; obscurity, indistinctness of perception. *v.t.* (*colloq.*) To play jokes on. **hazy**, *a.*

hazel (hāzl) [A.-S. *hæsel*], *n.* A nut-bearing shrub; a reddish-brown colour. *a.* Light-brown.

he (hē) [A.-S. *hē*], *pron.* (*obj.* him, *poss.* his; *pl.* they, *obj.* them, *poss.* their) The male person or animal referred to. *n.* A male person. **he-cat**, **-goat**, etc. *n.* A male cat, goat, etc.

head (hed) [A.-S. *hēafod*], *n.* The foremost part of the body of an animal, the uppermost in man, consisting of the skull, with the brain and sense-organs; any part of an analogous kind; the top; the upper end of a valley, gulf, etc.; the front part of a ship, procession, etc.; a promontory; the part of a bed where the head rests; the more honourable end of a table, etc.; the knobbed end of a nail, etc.; the striking part of a tool; the flowers or leaves at the top of a stem; the most honourable place, the forefront, the place of command; a chief, principal, leader; a single one (as of cattle); a main division, a category; culmination, crisis; the ripened part of a boil; froth on liquor; pressure of steam or water available; licence, freedom from restraint; the intellect. *v.t.* To lead, to direct; to be or form a head to; to provide with a head; to put or to be a heading to a chapter, etc.; to lop (as trees). *v.i.* To go or tend in a direction; to form a head. **headache**, *n.* A neuralgic or persistent pain in the head. **headband**, *n.* A fillet for the head or hair; a band at the top and bottom inside the back of a book. **head-dress**, *n.* Covering and ornaments for the head, esp. of a woman. **head-first**, *adv.* With the head in front (of a plunge); precipitately. **heading** (hed′ing), *n.* The action of the verb; an inscription at the head of an article, chapter, etc.; a running title. **headland**, *n.* A point of land projecting into the sea; the border of a field where the plough turns. **head-light**, *n.* The lamp carried at the front of a motor-car, etc. **head-line**, *n.* The line at the head of a page or paragraph giving the title, etc. **headlong**, *adv.* Head-foremost; hastily, rashly. *a.* Steep, precipitous; (*fig.*) violent, rash, thoughtless. **head-man**, *n.* A chief, a leader. **headmost**, *a.* Most forward, most advanced. **headquarters**, *n.pl.* The official quarters of the commander-in-chief of an army, the place whence orders are issued. **headship**, *n.* Chief place; the office of a head or leader. **headsman** (hedz′măn), *n.* An executioner. **headstall**, *n.* The bridle without the bit and reins. **headstone**, *n.* A stone at the head of a grave. **headstrong**, *a.* Ungovernable, obstinate, intractable, obstinately self-willed. **headway**, *n.*

Motion ahead; rate of progress. **head-wind**, *n.* A contrary wind. **head-work**, *n.* Brain-work. **heady**, *a.* Headstrong, precipitate; violent, impetuous, intoxicating. **-head**, **-hood** (A.-S. *-hād*], *suf.* Denoting state or quality, as in *godhead*, *childhood*, *manhood*.

heal (hēl) [A.-S. *hælan*], *v.t.* To make whole, restore to health; to cause to cicatrize; to free from guilt, purify. *v.i.* To grow or become sound or whole. **healer**, *n.* healing, *a.* Tending to heal; soothing, mollifying.

health (helth) [A.-S. *hælth*, from *hāl*, WHOLE], *n.* A state of soundness, freedom from bodily or mental disease or decay; physical condition; a toast wishing health, happiness, etc. **healthful**, *a.* **healthy**, *a.* **healthily**, *adv.* **healthiness**, *n.*

heap (hēp) [A.-S. *hēap*], *n.* A pile or accumulation of many things on one another; a lot, a crowd, a good many times, a good deal. *v.t.* To throw (together) or pile (up) in a heap.

hear (hēr) [A.-S. *hieran*], *v.t.* (*past and p.p.* heard (hĕrd)) To perceive by the ear; to be a hearer of; to listen to, attend to; to understand by listening; to heed, obey; to be informed of by report. *v.i.* To have the sense of hearing; to be told. **hearer**, *n.* One who hears; one of an audience. **hearing**, *n.* Act of perceiving sound; the sense by which sound is perceived; a judicial trial or investigation. **hearsay**, *n.* Common talk, gossip. *a.* Told or given at second-hand.

hearken (här′kĕn), *v.i.* To listen attentively (to); to hark (to).

hearse (hērs) [O.F. *herce*, L. *hirpex*, a harrow], *n.* A carriage in which the dead are taken to the place of burial; a bier.

heart (härt) [A.-S. *heorte*], *n.* The central organ of circulation, which it keeps going by its contraction and dilatation; the mind, the soul; the emotions, the passion of love; courage, spirit, ardour; the central part of anything, the vital or most essential part; a term of endearment; anything heart-shaped; (*pl.*) a suit of cards marked with figures like hearts. *v.i.* To grow into a compact head as a plant. **heartache**, *n.* Anguish of mind. **heart-breaking**, *a.* **heart-broken**, *a.* **heartburn**, *n.* A burning pain in the stomach arising from indigestion. **heart-burning**, *a.* Distressing the heart. *n.* Secret enmity, envy. **heart-felt**, *a.* Deeply felt, sincere. **heart-rending**, *a.* Heart-breaking, intensely afflictive. **heartsease**, *n.* The wild pansy. **heart-strings**, *n.pl.* (*fig.*) The sensibilities; pity, compassion; one's deepest affections. **heart-whole**, *a.* Having the affections free, not in love.

hearten (här′tĕn), *v.t.* To encourage, inspirit, stir up.

hearth (härth) [A.-S. *heorth*], *n.* The floor of a fire-place, or of a reverberatory furnace, or a blast furnace; the fireside, the domestic circle, home. **hearthstone**, *n.* The stone forming the hearth.

heartless (härt′lĕs), *a.* Destitute of feeling or affection; pitiless, cruel; spiritless. **heartlessly**, *adv.*

hearty (har′ti), *a.* Sincere; cordial, kindly; healthy; of keen appetite; full, satisfying. **heartily,** *adv.* **heartiness,** *n.*

heat (hēt) [A.-S. *hœtu*], *n.* A form of energy capable of melting and decomposing matter, transmissible by radiation or conduction; hotness; the sensation produced by this; hot weather; flush, high colour; pungency of flavour; violence vehemence, anger; intense excitement; warmth of temperament; animation; sexual excitement (in a female animal); a single course in a race, etc. *v.t.* To make hot; to inflame, cause to ferment; to excite. *v.i.* To become hot, inflamed, or excited. **heat-wave,** *n.* A wave of high temperature affecting the weather. **heatedly,** *adv.* **heater,** *n.* One who or that which heats; a heating-apparatus. **heating,** *a.* Promoting warmth or heat; exciting; stimulating.

heath (hēth) [A.-S. *hœth*], *n.* An open space of country, esp. with shrubs and coarse herbage; a narrow-leaved evergreen shrub.

heathen (hē′thĕn) [A.-S. *hœthen*], *n.* One who is not Christian, Jew, or Mohammedan, an idolater; an unenlightened or barbarous person. *a.* Gentile; pagan; barbarous. **heathendom,** *n.* The portion of the world in which heathenism is dominant; heathens collectively. **heathenish,** *a.*

heather (heth′ẽr) [?], *n.* Heath, ling.

heave (hēv) [A.-S. *hebban*], *v.t.* (*past and p.p.* heaved, **hove*) To raise with effort; to utter or force from the breast; to cast (something heavy); to hoist (the anchor), to haul. *v.i.* To rise; to rise and fall alternately; to retch, to vomit. *n.* An upward motion or swelling; act of heaving.

heaven (hevn) [A.-S. *heofon*], *n.* The sky, the firmament (*often in pl.*); the abode of God and the blessed; the place of supreme felicity; God; providence. **heavenly,** *a.*

heavy (hev′i) [A.-S. *hefig*], *a.* Weighty, ponderous (of a large and ponderous kind (as artillery, etc.); of great specific gravity, dense; not properly raised (as bread); not easily borne; oppressive, grievous; burdensome, difficult; drowsy, dull, sluggish; tedious; depressing, depressed; louring. **heavy water,** *n.* (*Phys.*) A liquid similar to water with density about 10 per cent. greater.

hebdomadal (heb-dom′ȧ-dȧl) [Gr. *hebdomos*, seventh], *a.* Consisting of seven days; meeting or occurring weekly.

Hebraic (hē-brā′ik), *a.* Pertaining to the Hebrews, or their language. **He′braism,** *n.* The thought or religion of the Hebrews; a Hebrew characteristic, idiom, or expression.

Hebrew (hē′broo) [Gr. *Hebraios*, Heb. *'ibri*], *n.* A Jew, an Israelite: the language of the ancient Jews. *a.* Pertaining to the Jews.

hecatomb (hek′ȧ-tom) [Gr. *hekaton*, a hundred, *bous*, ox], *n.* The sacrifice of a hundred oxen; any great sacrifice.

heckle (hekl), *v.t.* To hackle; to worry (a candidate) by inconvenient questions. **heckler,** *n.*

hectare (hek′tȧr) [F.], *n.* A French measure, containing 100 ares or 2·471 acres.

hectic (hek′tik) [Gr. *hexis*, habit of body], *a.* Habitual, continual (of fever); consumptive; feverish, flushed; (*colloq.*) very exciting or excitable.

hecto- [Gr. *hekaton*, a hundred], *comb. form.* A hundred times. **hec′togram,** *n.* A French weight of 100 grams or 3·52 oz. av. **hec′tolitre,** *n.* A liquid measure, containing 100 litres or 3·531 cubic ft. **hec′tometre,** *n.* 100 metres or 109·3633 yds.

hector (hek′tŏr) [Gr. *Hectōr*, Trojan warrior], *n.* A bully, blusterer. *v.t.* To bully; to treat with insolence.

hedge (hej) [A.-S. *hecg*], *n.* A fence of bushes or small trees; (*fig.*) a barrier. *v.t.* To surround or enclose with a hedge; to secure oneself against loss by transactions tending to indemnify one. *v.i.* To plant or repair hedges; (*fig.*) to act in a shifty way, to avoid making a decisive statement. **hedge-bill,** *n.* A bill-hook for trimming hedges. **hedge-row,** *n.* a row of shrubs planted as a hedge.

hedgehog (hej′hog), *n.* A small insectivorous mammal covered with spines, and able to roll itself into a ball.

he′donism (hē′dŏn-izm) [Gr. *hēdonē*, pleasure], *n.* The doctrine that pleasure is the chief good. **hedonist,** *n.* **hedonis′tic,** *a.*

heed (hēd) [A.-S. *hēdan*], *v.t.* To regard, to take notice of. *n.* Care, atten′tion; careful consideration. **heedful,** *a.* **heedless,** *a.*

heel (1) (hēl) [A.-S. *hēla*], *n.* The hinder part of the foot, or of a shoe, stocking, etc., covering this; (*pl.*) the feet, esp. the hind feet of animals; a block to raise the hinder part of a boot or shoe from the ground; a heel-like knob, part, etc.; the latter part, the fag end of anything; (*Am. slang*) a disreputable fellow. *v.t.* To add a heel to.

heel (2) (hēl) [A.-S. *hyldan*], *v.i.* (*Naut.*) To incline or cant over to one side. *v.t.* To make (a vessel) do this. *n.* An inclination to one side (of a ship).

hefty (hef′ti) [from HEAVE], *a.* (*colloq.*) Strong, muscular; big.

hegemony (hē-gem′ó-ni) [Gr. *hēgemōn*, leader], *n.* Leadership, predominance.

heifer (hef′ẽr) [A.-S. *hēahfore*], *n.* A young cow that has not yet calved.

height (hīt) [A.-S. *hīehtho*], *n.* Quality or state of being high; distance of the top of an object above its foot; altitude; an elevated position; stature; elevation in rank, etc. **heighten,** *v.t.* To make high or higher; to enhance, intensify, emphasize; to exaggerate.

heinous (hā′nŭs) [O.F. *haïnos*, from *haïne*, hate], *a.* Abominable, atrocious; wicked in the highest degree. **heinously,** *adv.*

heir (âr) [O.F., from L. *hērēs*], *n.* One who is entitled to succeed another in the possession of property or rank; (*fig.*) one who succeeds to any gift, quality, etc. **heirdom,** *n.* **heiress,** *n.* A female heir. **heirloom,** *n.* A chattel which descends with an estate to the heir. **heirship,** *n.*

heli-, helio- [Gr. *hēlios*, the sun], *comb. form.* Pertaining to the sun; produced by the sun's rays.

heliacal (hē-lī'á-kál), *a.* Closely connected with the sun; rising just before the sun.

helicopter (hel'í-kop-tér) [Gr. *helix*, spiral; *pteron*, a wing], *n.* (*Av.*) A form of aircraft that rises from the horizontal plane.

heliograph (hē'li-ō-gráf), *n.* An apparatus for signalling by reflecting flashes of sunlight. *v.i.* To signal with this.

heliotrope (hē'li-ō-trōp) [Gr. *trop-*, stem of *trepein*, to turn], *n.* A genus of plants of the borage family, whose flowers turn with the sun; a purple tint; a red-spotted variety of quartz, blood-stone.

helium (hē'li-ŭm), *n.* An element found in the sun's atmosphere and in certain minerals.

hell (hel) [A.-S. *hel*], *n.* The place of punishment for the wicked after death; a place of extreme misery, or suffering; torment, torture; a gambling-house. **hell-cat, n.** A witch, a hag. **hell-fire, n.** The torments of hell. **hellish, a.**

hellebore (hel'é-bōr) [Gr. *helleboros*], *n.* A plant, the Christmas rose; a plant supposed by the ancients to be a cure for insanity.

Hellene (hé-lēn') [Gr. *Hellēn*], *n.* An ancient Greek; a citizen of modern Greece. **Hellenic** (hé-lĕ'nĭk), *a.*

helm (helm) [A.-S. *helma*], *n.* The apparatus by which a vessel is steered; the rudder and tiller or wheel; the tiller; a position of management. **helmsman, n.** The man who steers.

helmet (hel'mĕt), *n.* A piece of defensive armour for the head; a hat of cork, pith, etc., worn as a protection against the sun. **helmeted, a.**

helminth (hel'mĭnth) [Gr. *helmins*, a worm], *n.* A worm, esp. a parasitic intestinal worm.

helot (hel'ŏt) [Gr. *Heilōtes*, inhabitants of *Helos*, a Laconian town enslaved by the Spartans], *n.* A serf, bondsman.

help (help) [A.-S. *helpan*], *v.t.* To assist, further; to supply succour or relief to; to remedy, prevent; to serve (with food). *v.i.* To lend assistance; to avail. *n.* Aid; succour, relief; remedy; a helper; a helping (of food, etc.). **helper, n. helpful, a.** Furnishing help, useful. **helpfully, adv. helpfulness, n.** helping, *n.* A portion of food given at table. **helpless, a.** Wanting power to help oneself; affording no help. **helplessly, adv. helplessness, n.** helpmate, *n.* A partner or helpful companion, a spouse.

helter-skelter (hel'tér-skel'tér) [imit.], *adv.* In great hurry and confusion. *a.* Confused. *n.* Hurry.

helve (helv) [A.-S. *hielf*], *n.* The handle of an axe or tool. *v.t.* To fit a helve to.

Helvetian (hel-vē'shán) [L. *Helvetius*], *a.* Swiss. *n.* A Swiss; one of the ancient Helvetii. **Helvetic** (-vet'ĭk), *a.*

hem (1) (hem) [A.-S. *hemm, hem*], *n.* The edge of a garment or piece of cloth, doubled and sewn. *v.t.* To double over and sew in the border of; to enclose or shut in. **hem-stitch, n.** An ornamental stitch. *v.t.* To hem with this.

hem (2) (hem) [imit.], *int.* and *n.* A short cough, uttered by way of warning, encouragement, etc. *v.i.* To cry 'hem'; to hesitate.

hemi- [Gr. *hēmi-*], *pref.* Half, halved; affecting one half.

hemisphere (hem'i-sfēr), *n.* The half of a sphere or globe, esp. of the terrestrial or celestial sphere; a map or projection of either of these. **hemispher'ic, -al, a.**

hemistich (hem'i-stĭk) [Gr. *stichos*, a row], *n.* Half a verse, usu. as divided by the cæsura; an imperfect verse.

hemlock (hem'lok) [A.-S. *hemlic, hymlic*], *n.* A poisonous umbelliferous genus of plants; the poison obtained from them.

hemp (hemp) [A.-S. *henep*], *n.* An Indian herbaceous plant; its fibre, used for making ropes, etc.; hashish; the hangman's rope. **hempen, a.**

hen (hen) [A.-S. *henn*], *n.* The female of any bird, esp. the domestic fowl. **hen-bane, n.** A plant; a poisonous drug obtained from it. **hen-harrier, n.** The blue hawk. **hen-house, n.** A fowl-house. **hen-peck, v.t.** To rule (of a wife who has the upper hand of her husband). *n.* A wife who nags at her husband. **hen-roost, n.** A place for fowls to roost in. **hen-wife, n.** A woman who has the charge of fowls.

hence (hens) [A.-S. *heonan*], *adv.* From this place, time, source, or origin; in consequence of this, therefore. *int.* Away, begone, depart. **henceforth, henceforward, adv.** From this time forward.

henchman (hench'mán) [A.-S.], *n.* A male servant or attendant; a faithful follower.

hendecagon (hen-dek'á-gŏn) [Gr. *hendeka*, eleven, *gōnia*, angle], *n.* A plane rectilinear figure of eleven sides or angles.

henna (hen'á) [Arab. *hinnā*], *n.* The Egyptian privet; a dye from this used by Oriental women.

henry (hen'ri) [J. *Henry*], *n.* (*Elec.*) Unit of inductance.

hepatic (hē-păt'ĭk) [Gr. *hēpar hēpatos*, the liver], *a.* Of or resembling the liver.

hepta- [Gr. *hepta*, seven], *comb. form.* Consisting of seven.

heptagon (hep'tá-gŏn) [Gr. *gōnia*, angle], *n.* A plane rectilinear figure having seven sides and seven angles. **heptag'-onal, a.**

heptangular (hep-tăng'gū-lár), *a.* Having seven angles.

heptarchy (hep'tár-ki) [Gr. *-archia*, government], *n.* A government by seven rulers; the seven kingdoms flourishing in Britain from the 5th to the 8th century.

her (hĕr) [A.-S. *hire*], *pron.* Possessive, dative, or accusative case of personal pronoun SHE.

herald (her'áld) [O.F. *heralt*], *n.* An officer who proclaimed peace or war, challenged to battle, and carried messages between sovereigns and princes; an officer super-intending State ceremonies, granting, recording, and blazoning arms, tracing genealogies, etc.; (*fig.*) a messenger, a precursor. *v.t.* To act as herald to; to proclaim, announce, usher in. **heraldic**

(hĕ-răl′dĭk), *a.* heraldry (her′ăl-dri), *n.* The art or office of a herald; pomp, ceremony; heraldic bearings.

herb (hĕrb) [L. *herba*, grass], *n.* A plant producing shoots only of annual duration, one having medicinal, culinary, or aromatic properties; grass, green food for cattle. **herbaceous** (-bă′shŭs), *a.* Pertaining to or of the nature of herbs. **herbage,** *n.* Herbs collectively; grass, pasture; right of pasture. **herbal,** *n.* A book containing the names of plants, with descriptions of their properties, etc. **herbalist,** *n.* One skilled in the uses of herbs; a dealer in medicinal herbs. **herbarium** (-băr′i-ŭm), *n.* (*pl.* **-ia**). A systematic collection of dried plants.

Herculean (hĕr-kū′lē-ăn), *a.* Pertaining to Hercules, a Greek hero, celebrated for his prodigious bodily strength; exceedingly strong or powerful.

herd (1) (hĕrd) [A.-S. *heord*], *n.* A number of beasts feeding or driven together; (*fig.*) a crowd of people, a rabble. *v.i.* To go in herds; to associate; to act as a herd or shepherd. *v.t.* To form or bring into a herd. **herdsman,** *n.* One who tends cattle.

herd (2) (hĕrd) [A.-S. *hierde*], *n.* A keeper of a herd (usu. in comb., as *shepherd, swineherd*).

here (hĕr) [A.-S. *hēr*], *adv.* In or to this place; hither, in this direction; in the present life or state; at this point; on this occasion; hence. *n.* This place, point, or time. **hereabouts,** *adv.* About or near this place. **hereaf′ter,** *adv.* For the future; in a future state. *n.* A future state. **hereby′,** *adv.* By this, by means of this; close by. **herein′,** *adv.* In this; here. **hereinaf′ter,** *adv.* Later in this (book, document, etc.). **hereto′,** *adv.* Up to this place, point, or time. **heretofore′,** *adv.* Up to or before this time; formerly. **hereunto′,** *adv.* Up to this; hereto. **hereupon′,** *adv.* Upon, after, or at this, in consequence of this. **herewith′,** *adv.* With this.

hereditable (hĕ-red′i-tăbl) [L. *hērēditāre*], *a.* That may be inherited.

hereditament (her-ĕ-dĭt′à-mĕnt), *n.* Property that may be inherited; real property.

hereditary (hĕ-red′i-tăr-ĭ), *a.* Descending by inheritance; transmitted from generation to generation; holding by inheritance. **hereditarily,** *adv.*

heredity (hĕ-red′i-tĭ), *n.* The tendency to transmit characters to one's offspring; the tendency to resemble the parent.

heresy (her′ĕ-sĭ) [Gr. *hairesis*, from *haireisthai*, to choose], *n.* Departure from what is held to be true doctrine. **her′esiarch,** *n.* A leader of a sect of heretics.

heretic (her′ĕ-tĭk), *n.* One who holds unorthodox opinions, esp. in religious matters. **heret′ical,** *a.* **heretically,** *adv.*

heritable (her′i-tăbl), *a.* Capable of being inherited.

heritage (her′i-tăj), *n.* Property that passes to an heir; share, portion, an inherited quality. **her′itor,** *n.*

hermaphrodite (hĕr-măf′rō-dīt) [Gr. *Hermaphroditos*, son of Hermes and Aphrodite], *n.* A person or animal in which male and female characters or organs are combined.

hermeneutic (hĕr-mē-nū′tĭk) [Gr. *hermēneutikos*], *a.* Interpreting, explanatory. *n.pl.* The art or science of interpretation.

hermetic (hĕr-met′ĭk), *a.* Of or belonging to alchemy, fabled to have originated with Hermes Trismegistus; fitting so as to be air-tight. **hermetically,** *adv.* Sealed and air-tight by fusion.

hermit (hĕr′mĭt) [F. *hermite*, Gr. *erēmos*, deserted], *n.* One who lives in solitary contemplation or devotion, an anchorite. **hermitage,** *n.* The cell of a hermit.

hernia (hĕr′ni-à) [L.], *n.* Rupture; protrusion of an organ from its natural place.

hero (hĕr′ō) [Gr. *hērōs*], *n.* (*pl.*-**roes** (-rōz)) A person of extraordinary valour; the principal male character in a novel, play, etc.

heroic (hĕ-rō′ĭk), *a.* Pertaining to a hero; having the attributes of a hero; describing the deeds of heroes; bold, vigorous. *n.pl.* Heroic verses (in Lat. and Gr. the hexameter, in Eng. the five-foot iambic); high-flown language or sentiments. **heroical,** *a.* **heroine** (her′ō-in), *n.* An heroic woman; the principal female character in a literary work or actual occurrence. **heroism,** *n.*

heroin (hĕr′-ō-ĭn) [?] *n.* A morphine derivative used by drug-addicts.

heron (her′ŏn) [O.F. *hairon*], *n.* A long-legged, long-necked wading bird. **heronry,** *n.* A place where herons breed.

herring (her′ing) [A.-S. *hæring*], *n.* A common marine fish of the North Atlantic moving in shoals and spawning near the coast. **herring-bone,** *a.* Like the spine and bones of a herring; denoting masonry in which the stones are set obliquely in alternate rows; a kind of cross-stitch. *v.t.* To sew with herring-bone stitch. **Herring Pond,** *n.* (*colloq.*) The Atlantic Ocean.

herself (hĕr-self′), *pron.* The emphatic and reflexive form of SHE.

hesitate (hez′i-tāt) [L. *hæsitāre*, freq. of *hærēre*, to stick, cling], *v.i.* To pause in action; to be undecided; to be reluctant (to). **hesitant,** *a.* Dubious, vacillating, undecided. **hesitance, -tancy,** *n.* hesitatingly, *adv.* **hesita′tion,** *n.*

Hesperian (hes-pēr′i-àn) [Gr. *Hesperos*, the evening star], *a.* (*poet.*) Situated in the west, western.

heter-, hetero- [Gr. *heteros*, other], *comb. form.* Different, abnormal; erroneous. **het′eroclite** [Gr. *heteroklitos* (*klinein*, to be inflected)], *a.* Anomalous, irregular. *n.* A word that deviates from the ordinary forms of inflexion. **het′erodyne,** *n.* (*Wire.*) A beat frequency in a radio receiver caused by the interplay of two alternating currents of similar frequencies.

heterodox (het′ĕr-ō-doks) [Gr. *doxa*, opinion], *a.* Contrary to received or established doctrines, principles, or standards; heretical; not orthodox. **heterodoxy,** *n.*

heterogeneous (het-ĕr-ō-jē′nē-ŭs) [Gr. *genos*, kind], *a.* Diverse in character or composition.

hew (hū) [A.-S. *héawan*], *v.t.* To cut (down, etc.) with an axe; to hack, chop. **hewer,** *n.* One who hews, esp. a miner.

hexa- [Gr. *hex*, six], *comb. form.*

hexagon (hek'så-gòn) [Gr. *gōnia*, angle], *n.* A plane figure having six sides and six angles. **hexag'onal,** *a.*

hexahedron (hek-så-hē'dròn) [Gr. *hedra*, seat, base], *n.* A solid body of six sides, esp. a regular cube. **hexahedral,** *a.*

hexameter (hek-săm'é-tér), *n.* Verse consisting of lines of six feet, of which the first five are dactyls or spondees, and the sixth a spondee or trochee.

hey-day (hā'dā), *n.* The prime, the time of unexhausted prosperity, etc.

hiatus (hī-ā'tús) [L., from *hiāre*, to yawn], *n.* A gap, break, a lacuna in a manuscript, etc.; the coming together of two vowels.

hibernate (hī'bér-nāt) [L. *hiberna*, winter quarters, *hibernus*, wintry], *v.i.* To pass the winter in sleep or torpor, as some animals.

Hibernian (hī-bér'ni-án) [L. *Hibernia,* Ireland], *a.* Pertaining to Ireland. *n.* A native of Ireland.

hiccup, hiccough (hik'úp), *n.* An audible catching of the breath due to spasmodic contraction of the diaphragm and glottis. *v.* To have hiccups; to utter with a hiccup.

hickory (hik'ô-ri) [N. Am. Ind.], *n.* A North American tree allied to the walnut.

hidalgo (hi-dăl'gō) [Sp.], *n.* A Spanish nobleman of the lowest class, a gentleman by birth.

hide (1) (hīd) [A.-S. *hȳdan*], *v.t.* (*past* hid (hīd), *p.p.* **hidden** (hīdn), **hid**). To conceal; to put out of sight; to keep secret; to suppress. *v.i.* To lie concealed, to conceal oneself. **hiding** (1), *n.* Concealing, lying in concealment.

hide (2) (hīd) [A.-S. *hȳd*], *n.* A skin, raw or dressed. *v.t.* (*colloq.*) To flog. **hidebound,** *a.* Having the skin very tight; having the bark so tight as to impede growth (of trees); narrow-minded, bigoted. **hiding** (2), *n.* (*colloq.*) A thrashing.

hideous (hid'é-ús) [M.E. *hidous*], *a.* Horrible, frightful, or shocking to the eye or ear; ghastly. **hideousness,** *n.*

hie (hī) [A.-S. *hīgian*], *v.i.* (*pres.p.* hying) To hasten, hurry.

hierarch (hī'ér-ark) [Gr. *hieros,* sacred, *archein,* to govern], *n.* One who has authority in sacred things, a chief priest, archbishop. **hierar'chic, -al,** *a.*

hierarchy (hī'ér-ar-ki), *n.* A rank or order of sacred persons; one of the orders of angels; priestly or ecclesiastical government; organization of a priesthood in grades or orders.

hieratic (hī-ér-ăt'ik) [Gr. *hierātikos,* from *hierasthai,* to be a priest], *a.* Pertaining to the priesthood, priestly; applied to ancient Egyptian characters and to early styles in Egyptian and Greek art.

hiero- [Gr. *hieros,* holy], *comb. form.* Sacred; pertaining to sacred things.

hieroglyph (hī'ér-ô-glif) [Gr. *gluphē*, carving], *n.* The figure of an animate or inanimate object used to represent a word, a kind of writing among the ancient Egyptians, Aztecs, etc.; a symbol employed to convey a secret meaning. **hieroglyph'ic,** *a.*

hierophant (hī'ér-ô-fănt) [Gr. *phainein,* to show], *n.* One who explains the mysteries of religion.

higgle (higl) [?], *v.i.* To chaffer; to make a fuss about trifles as in striking a bargain.

high (hī) [A.-S. *héah*], *a.* Lofty, elevated; rising or extending upwards for or to a specified extent; upper, inland; exalted in rank, position, office, or character; proud, lofty in tone or temper; great, extreme, intense; full, consummate; far advanced (of time); costly (in price); lively, boisterous, violent; (*Mus.*) sharp, acute in pitch; tainted, strong-smelling (of meat, etc.). *adv.* To a great altitude, aloft; in or to a high degree; eminently, powerfully; at a high price; at or to a high pitch. **high-brow,** *a.* Intellectual, superior. *n.* A highly superior person; one who takes an academic line. **high day:** A feast, a festival; broad daylight, noon. **highfalutin,** *a.* Bombastic, affected. *n.* Bombast, fustian. **high-flown,** *a.* Proud, turgid, bombastic. **high-flyer,** *n.* One who is extravagant in opinions or pretensions. **high-flying,** *a.* Extravagant in opinions, claims, etc. **high-handed,** *a.* Overbearing, domineering, arbitrary. **high-jinks,** *n.pl.* High festivities or revelry; great sport. **highlands,** *n.pl.* A mountainous region, esp. of Scotland. **Highland,** *a.* Pertaining to the Highlands of Scotland. **Highlander,** *n.* An inhabitant of these. **high-lows,** *n.pl.* Laced boots reaching to the ankle. **highly,** *adv.* In a high degree, extremely, intensely; honourably, favourably. **high-minded,** *a.* Magnanimous; having honourable pride. **highness,** *n.* Quality or state of being high; a title of honour given to princes. **high-pitched,** *a.* Aspiring, haughty; steeply sloping (of roofs); (*Mus.*) tuned high. **high priest,** *n.* A chief priest, esp. the head of the Jewish hierarchy. **high road:** A main road, highway. **high seas:** The open sea or ocean. **high-sounding,** *a.* Pompous, ostentatious. **high - stomached,** *a.* Haughty. **high-strung,** *a.* Extremely sensitive, of acute nervous temperament. **high-toned,** *a.* High in pitch; strong in sound; high-principled. **highway,** *n.* A public road open to all. **highwayman,** *n.* One who robs on the highway.

hight (hīt) [A.-S. *hātan,* to call], *v.i.* (3*rd sing. past*). To be named or called.

hike (hīk) [?], *v.t.* To go for a tramp. **hitch-hike,** *v.t.* To make a journey by obtaining lifts.

hilarious (hi-lâr'i-ús) [Gr. *hilaros*], *a.* Cheerful, mirthful, merry. **hilarity,** *n.*

hill (hil) [A.-S. *hyll*], *n.* A natural elevation on the earth, a small mountain, a mound. **hillock,** *n.* A little hill or mound.

hilt (hilt) [A.-S.], *n.* The handle of a sword or dagger. **hilted,** *a.*

him (him), *pron.* The objective or accusative case of HE. **himself** (him-self'), *pron.* An emphatic or reflexive form of HE or HIM.

hind (1) (hīnd) [A.-S.], *n.* The female of the red deer.

hind (2) (hīnd) [A.-S. *hīna*, domestics], *n.* A farm-servant; a peasant, rustic.

hind (3) (hīnd), **hinder** (1) (hin'dĕr) [A.-S. *hindan*], *a.* Pertaining to or situated at the back. **hind-foremost, hind-first,** *a.* and *adv.* **hindmost,** *a.* The last; that is or comes last of all.

hinder (2) (hin'dĕr) [A.-S. *hindrian*], *v.t.* To obstruct, impede; to prevent from proceeding. *v.i.* To cause a hindrance; to interpose impediments. **hindrance,** *n.*

Hindu (hin-doo') [Pers., *hind*, India], *n.* A native of India, not of Parsee, Mussulman, or Christian descent. *a.* Pertaining to the Hindus.

hinge (hinj) [M.E. *heng*, cogn. with HANG], *n.* The joint on which a door or lid turns; the point on which anything depends or turns. *v.i.* To turn on or as on a hinge; to depend (upon).

hinny (hin'ī) [Gr. *hinnos*], *n.* The offspring of a stallion and a she-ass.

hint (hint) [?], *n.* A distant allusion; an indirect mention or suggestion. *v.t.* To mention indirectly, suggest. *v.i.* To make remote allusion.

hinterland (hin'tĕr-lănd) [G.], *n.* The region situated behind that on the coast or along a river, etc.

hip (1) (hip) [A.-S. *hype*], *n.* The projecting fleshy part covering the hip-joint; the haunch; the external angle formed by the sides of a roof.

hip (2) (hip) [A.-S. *hēope*], *n.* The fruit of the dog-rose.

hippo-, hipp- [Gr. *hippos*, a horse], *comb. form.* Pertaining to or resembling a horse.

hippodrome (hip'ō-drōm) [Gr. *dromos*, a course], *n.* A circus, anciently for equestrian games and chariot races; a place of entertainment.

hippopotamus (hip-ō-pot'à-mŭs) [Gr. *potamos*, river], *n.* A large African pachydermatous amphibious quadruped.

hire (hīr) [A.-S. *hȳr*], *n.* The price paid for services or the use of things; the engagement for such a price; (*fig.*) a bribe. *v.t.* To procure at a price for temporary use; to employ (a person) for a stipulated payment; to grant the use of for a stipulated price; to bribe. **hireling,** *n.* One who serves for hire; a mercenary. **hirer,** *n.* One who hires or lets on hire.

hirsute (hĕr'sūt) [L. *hirsūtus*], *a.* Hairy, shaggy, unshorn.

hirundine (hi-rŭn'dīn) [L. *hirundo*, a swallow], *a.* Like a swallow.

his (hiz) [A.-S.], *pron.* and *a.* Of or belonging to him.

hiss (his) [imit.], *v.i.* To make a sound like that of the letter *s*, to make a sibilant sound; to express disapprobation thus. *v.t.* To utter with a hissing sound; to condemn or drive (away, etc.) thus. *n.* A hissing sound.

histo-, *comb. form.* Pertaining to organic tissues. **histology,** *n.* The science of organic tissues.

historian (his-tôr'i-ăn), *n.* A writer of history; one versed in history.

historic (his-tor'ik), *a.* Celebrated in history, associated with historical events. **historical,** *a.*

historiographer (his-tôr-i-og'rà-fĕr), *n.* A writer of history, esp. an official historian.

history (his'tŏr-i) [L. and Gr. *historia*, from *histōr*, knowing], *n.* A systematic record of past events; a study of or a book dealing with the past of any country, people, science, art, etc.; past events; an eventful past, an interesting career.

histrionic (his-tri-on'ik) [L. *histrio*, an actor], *a.* Pertaining to actors or acting; theatrical; affected, unreal. *n.pl.* Art of theatrical representation; (*fig.*) humbug.

hit (hit) [Scand.], *v.t.* To strike, esp. after taking aim; (*fig.*) to guess, to affect, to wound. *v.i.* To strike (at, against, etc.); (*fig.*) to agree, suit, fall in with. *n.* A blow, a stroke; (*fig.*) a lucky chance; a felicitous expression; a successful effort.

hitch (hich) [?], *v.t.* To fasten loosely; to hook; to pull up with a jerk. *v.i.* To move with jerks; to become entangled. *n.* A stoppage; an impediment, a temporary difficulty; the act of catching, as on a hook; a pull or jerk up; (*Naut.*) various kinds of knots.

hither (hith'ĕr) [A.-S. *hider*], *adv.* To this place, end, or point; in this direction. *a.* Situated on this side; the nearer (of two objects). **hitherto,** *adv.* Up to this limit or time.

hive (hīv) [A.-S. *hȳf*], *n.* An artificial house for bees; bees inhabiting a hive; (*fig.*) a place swarming with busy occupants. *v.t.* To secure in a hive; (*fig.*) to house as in a hive; to store up for future use. *v.i.* To enter or live in a hive; to take shelter or swarm together, as bees.

hoar (hōr) [A.-S. *hār*], *a.* Greyish-white; grey with age; ancient; white with foam. *n.* Antiquity; hoar-frost, rime. **hoar-frost,** *n.* Frozen dew, white frost.

hoard (hôrd) [A.-S. *hord*], *n.* A store, money laid by; an accumulated stock of anything. *v.t.* To collect and lay by; to store up. *v.i.* To amass and store up things. **hoarder,** *n.*

hoarding (hôr'ding) [O.F. *hourd*, scaffold], *n.* A screen of boards round a building being built or repaired; a screen for posting bills on.

hoarse (hôrs) [A.-S. *hās*], *a.* Rough (of the voice); grating, discordant; having such a voice, as from a cold.

hoary (hôr'ī), *a.* Whitish-grey as with age; of great antiquity; venerable. **hoariness,** *n.*

hoax (hōks) [?], *n.* A practical joke, or sportive deception. *v.t.* To play a practical joke upon, to delude in sport.

hob (hob) [?], *n.* The part of a grate on which things are placed to be kept warm.

hobble (hobl) [Dut. *hobbelen*, to rock about], *v.i.* To walk lamely or awkwardly; to move in a halting way. *v.t.* To shackle the legs of (horses, etc.). *n.* An awkward, uneven, or limping gait; a clog, etc.

hobbledehoy (hobl-dē-hoi') [?], *n.* A raw, awkward young fellow.

hobby (1) (hob'ī) [O.F. *hobet*], *n.* A small British falcon.

hobby (2) (hob'ī) [O.F. *hobin*], *n.* An easy

ambling horse; a hobby-horse; one's favourite recreation or pursuit. **hobby-horse**, *n.* A figure rudely imitating a horse used in morris-dances, etc.; a child's rocking-horse; a hobby.

hobgoblin (hob'gob-lin) [obs. *hob*, an elf, GOBLIN], *n.* A kind of goblin, esp. one of a frightful appearance.

hobnail (hob'nāl), *n.* A short thick nail with a large head, used for heavy boots.

hob-nob (hob'nob) [A.-S. *habban*, to have, *nabban*, not to have], *v.i.* To associate familiarly (with).

hock (hok) [G. *Hochheimer*], *n.* A light wine, still or sparkling.

hockey (hok'i) [F. *hoquet*, a crook], *n.* A game of ball played with a club having a curved end.

hocus (hō'kŭs) [mock L.], *v.t.* To take in, to impose upon; to stupefy with drugs; to put a drug into (liquor). *n.* A cheat, an impostor; drugged liquor. **hocus-pocus**: A juggler's trick, a fraud, a hoax.

hod (hod) [?], *n.* A wooden holder on a long handle for carrying mortar or bricks on the shoulder. **hodman**, *n.* A labourer who carries a hod for bricklayers, etc.

hoe (hō) [F. *houe*], *n.* A tool used to scrape or stir up earth, root out weeds, etc. *v.t.* To scrape or loosen (ground), cut (weeds), or dig with a hoe. *v.i.* To use a hoe.

hog (hog) [?], *n.* A swine, esp. a castrated boar meant for killing; (*prov.*) a sheep or bullock a year old; (*fig.*) a dirty, gluttonous, or low fellow. *v.t.* To cut short like the bristles of a hog; to grab greedily. *v.i.* To droop at both ends. **hogget**, *n.* A yearling sheep; a colt of a year old. **hoggish**, *a.* **hog-mane**, *n.* A horse's mane cut so as to stand erect. **hog-wash**, *n.* Refuse used for feeding hogs. **hog's back**, *n.* A long ridged hill.

hogmanay (hog'má-nā) [?], *n.* In Scotland, the last day of the year.

hogshead (hogz'hed), *n.* A measure containing 52½ imperial gal.; a large cask; a butt.

hoist (hoist) [?], *v.t.* To raise or heave up; to lift with tackle; to run up (a sail or flag). *n.* Act of lifting or hoisting up; an apparatus for raising; a lift.

hold (1) (hōld) [A.-S. *healdan*], *v.t.* (*past* and *p.p.* held, *†p.p.* holden) To grasp and retain; to keep in, confine, enclose, contain; to be able to contain; to keep back, restrain; to retain possession or control of; to possess; to regard; to maintain or assert (that); to celebrate. *v.i.* To maintain a grasp or attachment; to continue firm, not to break; to be valid or true, to stand; to be consistent; (*usu. in imper.*) to stop, refrain. **hold-all**, *n.* A hand-bag or case for carrying clothes, etc. **holder**, *n.* A tenant, an owner. **hold forth**, *v.i.* To harangue. **holdfast**, *n.* A means by which something is clamped to another; a support. **holding**, *n.* A grasp; tenure or occupation, esp. land, property, stocks, etc., held.

hold (2) (hōld), *n.* Act of grasping in the hands; a grasp, clutch; a support, anything to hold by; (*fig.*) moral influence; possession; a fortified place.

hold (3) (hōld), *n.* The cavity of a ship, in which cargo is stowed.

hole (hōl) [A.-S. *hol*], *n.* A hollow place or cavity; an aperture, orifice, perforation; a wild animal's burrow; (*Golf*) a point made by the player who drives his ball from one hole to another with the fewest strokes, the distance between two consecutive holes; (*fig.*) a difficulty, a fix. **hole-and-corner**, *a.* Secret, clandestine.

holiday (hol'i-dā) [A.-S. *hǽligdæg*, holy day], *n.* A day of exemption from work; any period devoted to pleasure or amusement; a vacation.

holland (hol'ánd) [name of country], *n.* Coarse unbleached linen with a glazed surface. **hollands**, *n.* A kind of gin.

hollow (hol'ō) [M.E. *holwe*, A.-S. *holge*], *a.* Containing a cavity; not solid; sunken, concave; empty; deep (of sounds); (*fig.*) insincere, not genuine. *n.* A depression or unoccupied space; a cavity, hole. *v.t.* To make hollow, to excavate.

holly (hol'i) [A.-S. *holen*], *n.* A shrub or tree with glossy, prickly leaves.

hollyhock (hol'i-hok) [M.E. *holi*, HOLY, *hoc*, mallow], *n.* A tall garden plant with red, yellow, and other coloured flowers.

holm (1) (hōm) [Icel. *hólmr*], *n.* Flat ground along the side of a river; an island in a river.

holm (2) (hōm) [A.-S. *holen*, HOLLY], *n.* The ilex or evergreen oak, the holm-oak.

holo- [Gr. *holos*, whole], *comb. form.* Entire, complete; completely.

holocaust (hol'ō-kawst) [Gr. *kausō*, will burn], *n.* A sacrifice entirely consumed by fire; (*fig.*) a general destruction, esp. by fire.

holograph (hol'ō-gräf) [Gr. *graphein*, to write], *a.* Wholly in the handwriting of the author or signatory. *n.* A document, etc., so written.

holster (hōl'stèr) [Dut.], *n.* A leather case to hold a pistol.

holt (hōlt) [A.-S.], *n.* A wood, a copse.

holy (hō'li) [A.-S. *hālig*], *a.* Sacred; set apart for sacred use; morally pure; free from sin. **holily**, *adv.* **holiness**, *n.* The state of being holy; moral purity or integrity; the state of being consecrated to God or His worship; that which is so consecrated. **his Holiness**: A title of the Pope. **holystone**, *n.* A soft sandstone used for scrubbing decks. *v.t.* To scrub with this. **holy writ**: Sacred Scriptures, the Bible.

homage (hom'áj) [L. *homo*, man], *n.* The service paid and fealty professed to a superior; deference, obeisance, worship.

home (hōm) [A.-S. *hām*], *n.* One's own abode, or that of one's family; one's own country; the place where anything is indigenous; a place of rest or comfort; a charitable institution for orphans, the destitute, or the afflicted; the goal in various games. *a.* Connected with home or one's native country; domestic, opposed to foreign; (*fig.*) personal, touching the heart or conscience. *adv.* To one's home or country; to the point, closely, intimately. *v.i.* To fly home (of pigeons); (*fig.*) to go home. *v.t.* To send (pigeons) home; to provide with a home.

home-born, *a.* Native, domestic, natural. home-coming, *n.* and *a.* homeless, *a.* homely, *a.* Plain, not handsome; simple; without affectation, unpretending; unadorned. homeliness, *n.* homeward, *adv.* Towards home. *a.* Being or going in the direction of home. homekeeping, *a.* Staying at home, untravelled. homesick, *a.* home-sickness, *n.* A vehement desire to return home, causing depression of spirits. homespun, *a.* Spun at home; home-made; (*fig.*) plain, unaffected, rude. *n.* Cloth spun at home. homestead, *n.* A house, esp. a farmhouse, with the buildings attached.

homicide (hom'i-sīd) [L. *homicīdium*], *n.* The act of killing a human being; one who kills another. homici'dal, *a.*

homily (hom'i-li) [L. *homīlia*], *n.* A religious discourse; a tedious moral exhortation.

hominy (hom'i-ni) [N. Am. Ind.], *n.* Maize hulled and coarsely ground, boiled for food.

homo-, hom- [Gr. *homos*, same], *comb. form.* Noting likeness or sameness.

homœo- [Gr. *homoios*, of the same kind, similar], *comb. form.*

homœopathy (hō-mi-op'à-thi), *n.* The system of administering in small doses medicines which would produce in healthy persons symptoms similar to those they are designed to remove. homœopath'ic, *a.*

homogeneous (hom-ō-jē-ni-ūs) [Gr. *genos*, kind], *a.* Composed of similar parts or elements; of the same kind or nature throughout. homogene'ity, *n.*

homologous (hō-mol'ō-gūs) [Gr. *logos*, ratio], *a.* Having the same relative position, proportion, value, structure.

homonym (hom'ō-nim) [Gr. *onuma*, name], *n.* A word having the same sound and perhaps the same spelling as another, but differing in meaning.

homosexual, *a.* and *n.* Sexually attracted by one of the same sex.

homunculus, -uncle (hō-mŭng-kū'lŭs, -mŭnkl) [L., dim. of *homo*, man], *n.* A little man; a dwarf.

hone (hōn) [A.-S. *hān*], *n.* A stone for giving an edge to a cutting tool. *v.t.* To sharpen on this.

honest (on'ĕst) [L. *honestus*], *a.* Upright, fair, trustworthy; just, equitable; open, sincere, honourable; chaste, virtuous; unimpeached; respectable; worthy. honesty, *n.*

honey (hŭn'i) [A.-S. *hunig*], *n.* A sweet viscid product collected from plants by bees, and used as food; (*fig.*) sweetness; a term of endearment. honeycomb, *n.* A waxy substance formed in hexagonal cells by bees for the reception of honey and for the eggs and larvæ. *v.t.* To fill with holes or cavities. honeymoon, *n.* A period immediately after marriage, often spent in travel or pleasure-making. *v.i.* To spend the honeymoon (in, at, etc.). honeysuckle, *n.* The woodbine, a wild climbing plant with sweet-scented flowers.

honorarium (on-ō-râr'i-ŭm), *n.* Payment to a professional man for his services.

honorary (on'ōr-àr-i), *a.* Conferred, etc., as a mark of honour; holding an office without payment or without undertaking the duties, not enforceable by law (of duties or obligations).

honour (on'ōr) [L. *honōrem*, nom. *honos*], *n.* Respect, esteem, reverence; reputation, glory, distinction, high rank; nobleness of mind; conformity to the accepted code of social conduct; chastity; (*pl.*) courteous attentions; (*Univ., pl.*) distinction awarded for high proficiency; a title of address given to county court judges, etc.; (*pl.*) the four highest trump cards. *v.t.* To treat with reverence or respect; to bestow honour upon; to dignify, exalt; to acknowledge; to accept and pay when due (as a bill). honourable, *a.* Worthy of honour; illustrious, noble; conferring honour; actuated by principles of honour; proceeding from a laudable cause; not base; a title of respect or distinction borne by the children of peers below the rank of marquess, maids of honour, Justices of the High Court, etc. honourably, *adv.*

hood (hud) [A.-S. *hōd*], *n.* A loose covering for the head and neck; an appendage to an academic gown marking a degree; anything resembling a hood, a carriage-top. *v.t.* To dress in a hood; to blind, cover. hooded, *a.* hoodwink, *v.t.* To blindfold; (*fig.*) to deceive, take in.

hoodoo (hoo'doo) [Negro], *n.* Bad luck, the cause of bad luck.

hoof (hoof) [A.-S. *hōf*], *n.* (*pl.* hoofs, hooves) The horny covering of the feet of horses, oxen, etc.

hook (huk) [A.-S. *hōc*], *n.* A curved piece of metal for catching or suspending; a barbed and pointed wire for catching fish; a sickle; a sharp bend. *v.t.* To catch or hold with a hook; to fasten with hooks. *v.i.* To fit or fasten (on) with or as with hooks. hook-nosed, *a.* Having an aquiline nose. hooked (hukt), *a.* Bent; furnished with hooks.

hookah (huk'à) [Arab. *huqqah*], *n.* A tobacco-pipe in which the smoke passes through water.

hooligan (hoo'li-gàn) [pers. Irish name], *n.* A street rough given to violent attacks on persons. hooliganism, *n.*

hoop (hoop) [A.-S. *hōp*], *n.* A large ring of wood or metal; a child's toy to trundle; a croquet arch; a strip of wood or metal bent into a ring to hold the staves of casks, etc., together. *v.t.* To bind with hoops; to encircle. hooping-cough [WHOOP].

hoot (hoot) [M.E. *houten*], *v.i.* To shout in derision or contempt; to cry as an owl. *v.t.* To shout (down, out, away, etc.) in contempt or derision. *n.* A cry like that of an owl; a shout in contempt, etc. hooter, *n.* One who or that which hoots; a steam-whistle or siren.

hop (1) (hop) [A.-S. *hoppian*], *v.i.* To spring on one foot; to skip with both feet (as birds) or with all four feet (as quadrupeds); to limp. *v.t.* To jump lightly over. *n.* A jump, spring, or light leap on one foot; (*colloq.*) a dance. **hopper** (1), *n.* One who hops; a hopping insect; a funnel-shaped vessel for feeding material to a machine, a mill, into cars, etc.; a barge for receiving mud, etc., from a dredging-machine.

hop (2) (hop) [M.Dut. *hoppe*], *n.* A perennial climbing plant, the mature cones of which are used in brewing. *v.i.* To pick hops. **hopper** (2), *n.* A hop-picker. **hop-picker**, *n.* One who gathers hops; a machine for this purpose. **hop-yard, -garden**, *n.* A field where hops are grown.

hope (hōp) [A.-S. *hopa*], *n.* An expectant desire; confidence in a future event; a ground for expectation or confidence; the object of one's desires. *v.i.* To trust with confidence; to look (for) with desire or expectation. *v.t.* To expect with desire; to look forward to with trust. **hopeful**, *a.* **hopefulness**, *n.* **hopeless**, *a.*

horde (hôrd) [Turk. *ordū*, camp], *n.* A nomadic tribe; a gang, a multitude (usu. in contempt). *v.i.* To live in hordes; to gather together in gangs.

horizon (hò-rī'zòn) [Gr. *horizein*, to bound], *n.* The circular line where the sky and the earth seem to meet; (*fig.*) the boundary of one's mental vision, experience, etc.

horizontal (hor-i-zon'tàl), *a.* Pertaining to the horizon.

horn (hôrn) [A.-S.], *n.* A projecting bony growth on the heads of certain animals; the substance of which such are composed; anything made of or like a horn in shape, as a powder-flask or drinking-vessel; the feeler of a snail, etc.; an extremity of the moon when on the wane or waxing; a metal wind instrument; (*fig.*) one of the alternatives of a dilemma. *v.t.* To gore. **hornbeam**, *n.* A small tree yielding a tough timber. **hornbill**, *n.* An Indian bird with bone-crested bill. **horned**, *a.* **hornpipe**, *n.* An old wind instrument; a lively dance; the music for this. **horny**, *a.*

hornblende (hôrn'blend) [G.], *n.* A dark-coloured mineral consisting of silica, magnesia, lime, and iron.

hornet (hôr'nèt) [A.-S. *hyrnet*], *n.* A large social wasp with a formidable sting.

horo- [Gr. *hōra*, a season, hour], *comb. form.* Pertaining to times or seasons, or to the measurement of time.

horoscope (hor'ò-skōp) [Gr. *skopos*, observer], *n.* (*Astrol.*) An observation of the planets, etc., at the moment of one's birth, in order to foretell one's future.

horrible (hor'ibl) [L. *horribilis*, from *horrēre*, to bristle, shudder], *a.* Causing horror; dreadful, shocking, harrowing.

horrid (hor'id), *a.* Causing horror; shocking; extremely unpleasant, frightful. **horridly**, *adv.*

horrify (hor'i-fī), *v.t.* To strike with horror; (*colloq.*) to scandalize.

horror (hor'òr), *n.* Dread or terror, mingled with detestation or abhorrence; that which excites terror or repulsion.

horse (hôrs) [A.-S. *hors*], *n.* A solid-hoofed quadruped, domesticated and employed as beast of draught and burden; the adult male; (*collect.*) cavalry; a frame or other device used as a support, etc.; a vaulting-

block; appliances used in various trades. *v.t.* To provide with a horse or horses; (*fig.*) to carry on the back; to put astride of anyone for flogging. **horseback**, *n.* The back of a horse. **horseblock**, *n.* A block to assist a person in mounting on horseback. **horse-box**, *n.* A closed van for taking horses by rail; a compartment for horses on ship-board or in a stable, a box for slinging horses on board. **horse-chestnut**, *n.* A large variety of chestnut with coarse, bitter fruit. **horsehair**, *n.* The long hair of the mane and tail of horses. *a.* Made of this. **horse-latitudes**, *n.pl.* The region of calms on the northern edge of the north-east trade winds. **horse-leech**, *n.* A farrier; a large kind of leech which is often drawn in by horses and cattle when drinking; (*fig.*) a rapacious person (Prov. xxx. 15). **horseman**, *n.* One skilled in the management of horses, **horsemanship**, *n.* **horse-play**, *n.* Rough, boisterous play. **horse-power**, *n.* A unit of measurement of mechanical work, equivalent to 33,000 foot-pounds per minute; mechanical power expressed in such units. **horse-radish**, *n.* A plant with a pungent, acrid root, used as a condiment. **horse-sense**, *n.* Rough, practical common sense. **horseshoe**, *n.* A shoe for horses; anything resembling this in shape. *a.* Shaped like this. **horsewhip**, *n.* A whip for driving horses. *v.t.* To flog with a horsewhip; to thrash. **horsewoman**, *n.* A woman skilled in riding or managing horses. **horsy**, *a.* Pertaining to or fond of horses or horse-racing. **horsiness**, *n.*

hortative (hôr'tà-tiv) [L. *hortāri*, to exhort], **hortatory** (hôr'tà-tòr-i), *a.* Giving or containing advice or encouragement.

horticulture (hôr'ti-kŭl-chùr) [L. *hortus*, garden, CULTURE], *n.* The art of cultivating or managing gardens. **horticul'tural**, *a.*

hosanna (hò-zăn'à) [Heb., save, we pray], *n.* A prayer for blessing; a shout of adoration.

hose (hōz) [A.-S. *hosa*], *n.* (*collect.*) Orig., close-fitting breeches; stockings; (*as sing. with pl.* hoses) flexible tubing as for fire-engine service. **half-hose**, *n.* Socks. **hosier** (hō'zhèr), *n.* One who deals in hosiery. **hosiery**, *n.* Stockings and other underclothing.

hospice (hos'pis) [L. *hospitium*, from *hospes*, guest], *n.* A place for the reception of travellers as among the Alps; a home for the needy or afflicted.

hospitable (hos'pi-tàbl), *a.* Entertaining or disposed to entertain strangers or guests with kindness. **hospitably**, *adv.* **hospital'ity**, *n.* Liberal entertainment of strangers or guests.

hospital (hos'pi-tàl), *n.* An institution for the reception and treatment of the sick or injured; applied to some charitable foundations. **hospitalize** (hos'pi-tà-līz), *v.t.* To remove to a hospital for care. **hos'pitaller**, *n.* One of a religious brotherhood which relieved the poor, strangers, and the sick.

host (1) (hōst) [O.F. *hoste*, L. *hospes*, *hos-*

pitem], *n.* One who entertains another; the landlord of an inn. **hostess,** *n.*

host (2) (hŏst) [O.F., from L. *hostis*, stranger, enemy], *n.* An army; a multitude.

host (3) (hŏst) [M.E. *oste*, L. *hostia*, sacrificial victim], *n.* The consecrated bread or wafer used in the eucharist.

hostage (hos'tăj) [O.F.], *n.* One given in pledge for the performance of certain conditions or for the safety of others.

hostel (hos'tĕl), *n.* An inn; a house or hall for the residence of students. **hostelry,** *n.* An inn.

hostile (hos'tĭl) [L. *hostilis*, as HOST (2)], *a.* Pertaining to an enemy; unfriendly; inimical. **hostil'ity,** *n.*

hot (hot) [A.-S. *hât*], *a.* Having a high temperature; having much sensible heat; burning, acrid, pungent; ardent, impetuous; passionate, excited, trying; strong (of scent); recent (of news). *adv.* Hotly, ardently, angrily. **hotbed,** *n.* A bed of earth heated by means of fermenting manure, used for raising early and tender plants; (*fig.*) any place which favours rapid growth (of disease, vice, etc.). **hot-blooded,** *a.* Excitable, irritable. **hot dog,** *n.* A sausage in a roll. **hot-headed,** *a.* Fiery, impetuous, passionate. **hot-house,** *n.* A plant-house where a relatively high artificial temperature is maintained to facilitate growth. **hot music,** *n.* A form of swing or jazz music. **hot-pot,** *n.* Meat cooked with potatoes in a closed pot.

hotchpot (hoch'pot) (F. *hochepot*], *n.* A general commixture of property to secure equal division (among heirs of an intestate person, etc.).

hotchpotch (hoch'poch) [corr. of prec.], *n.* A confused mixture; a dish of various ingredients.

hotel (hō-tel'), *n.* A superior inn for the entertainment of strangers and travellers; in France, a town mansion.

Hottentot (hot'ĕn-tot) [Dut.], *n.* A member of an aboriginal S. African race.

hough (hok) [A.-S. *hôh*], *n.* The joint between the knee and the fetlock in the hind-leg of quadrupeds. *v.t.* To hamstring.

hound (hound) [A.-S. *hund*], *n.* A dog used in hunting; one of those who chase the hares in hare and hounds; (*fig.*) a mean, contemptible fellow. *v.t.* To hunt with or as with hounds; to set on the chase; to urge on.

hour (our) [L. and Gr. *hôra*, season, hour], *n.* The twenty-fourth part of a natural day, sixty minutes; a particular time; (*Astron.*) fifteen degrees of longitude; (*pl.*) times appointed for work, etc.; (*R.-C. Ch.*) certain prayers to be said at fixed times. **hour-glass,** *n.* A glass having two bulbs and a connecting opening through which the sand runs, used for measuring small periods of time.

house (1) (hous) [A.-S. *hûs*], *n.* A building for shelter or residence; a dwelling, place of abode, place used for a specified purpose (as *bake-house, hen-house, warehouse*); the abode of a fraternity, the fraternity itself; a household; a family;

esp. noble; one of the legislative assemblies of a country; a quorum of this; a theatre; an audience; a commercial establishment or firm; (*Astrol.*) the station of a planet in the heavens; a twelfth part of the heavens. **house-agent,** *n.* One who sells and lets houses, collects rents, etc. **house-boat,** *n.* A boat or barge for living in. **house-breaker,** *n.* One who breaks into houses, a burglar; a workman who pulls down houses. **household,** *n.* Those who live together under the same roof; a domestic establishment. *a.* Pertaining to the family, domestic. **householder,** *n.* The head of a household, the occupier of a house. **housekeeper,** *n.* An upper female servant who manages the affairs of a household; a person in charge of a place of business, etc. **housekeeping,** *n.* The care of a household; domestic economy. **houseleek,** *n.* A plant with thick fleshy leaves, growing on walls. **houseless,** *a.* **housemaid,** *n.* A female servant employed to keep a house clean, etc. **house-party,** *n.* A party of guests at a country house. **house-surgeon, -physician,** *n.* A resident surgeon or physician in a hospital. **house-warming,** *n.* A merry-making on going into a new house. **housewife** (hous'wif), *n.* The mistress of a family; a female domestic manager; (hŭz'if) a case for holding pins, needles, and the like. **housewifery** (hous'wif-ri), *n.*

house (2) (houz) [A.-S. *hûsian*, as prec.], *v.t.* To place or store in a house; to shelter. *v.i.* To have a lodging, to dwell.

hovel (hovl) [?], *n.* A shed open at the sides; a miserable dwelling-house.

hover (hov'ĕr) [?], *v.i.* To hang or remain (over or about) fluttering or on the wing; (*fig.*) to be irresolute, to waver.

hovercraft, *n.* Trade name of an aircraft supported above land or water on a cushion of air generated by itself.

how (hou) [A.-S. *hû*], *adv.* In what way or manner; by what means; to what extent, degree, etc.; in what condition; by what name; at what price. **howbe'it,** *adv.* Nevertheless, however it may be. **however,** *adv.* In whatever manner or degree; nevertheless, notwithstanding. **howsoev'er,** *adv.* In whatsoever manner.

howdah (hou'dă) [Arab. *haudaj*], *n.* A seat carried on an elephant's back.

howitzer (hou'it-zĕr) [G. *haubitze*], *n.* A short piece of ordnance for throwing shells at low velocity.

howl (houl) [imit.], *v.i.* To cry as a dog or wolf; to wail; to make a wailing sound like the wind. *v.t.* To utter in wailing or mournful tones. *n.* A protracted, hollow cry, as of a dog, etc., esp. one of anguish, distress, or derision. **howling,** *a.* (*fig.*) Wild and dreary (of a desert, etc.); extreme, glaring.

hoyden (hoi'dĕn) [?], *n.* A rude, bold girl; a romp. *a.* Rude, rough, bold. *v.i.* To romp roughly. **hoydenish,** *a.*

hub (hŭb) [?], *n.* The central part of a wheel from which the spokes radiate, the nave, a place of central importance.

huckaback (hŭk'á-băk) [?]. *n.* A coarse linen or cotton cloth, used for towels.

huckle (hŭkl) [?], *n.* The hip, the haunch. **huckle-bone**, *n.* The hip-bone.

huckster (hŭk'stêr) [?], *n.* A retailer of small goods, a pedlar; a mean, mercenary fellow. *v.i.* To deal in petty goods; to higgle.

huddle (hŭdl) [Teut.], *v.t.* To throw or crowd (together) promiscuously; to do hastily and carelessly; to coil (oneself up) anyhow. *v.i.* To gather or crowd (up or together) promiscuously. *n.* A confused crowd; disorder.

hue (1) (hū) [A.-S. *hīw*], *n.* Colour, tint. **hued**, *a.* Having a particular hue (as *light-hued*).

hue (2) (hū) [O.F. *hu* (*huer*, to shout)], *n.* A loud shout, a clamour. **hue and cry:** A general summons to pursue a felon.

huff (hŭf) [imit.], *v.t.* To bully, hector; (*Draughts*) to remove (one's opponent's piece) from the board when he omits to capture with it.

hug (hŭg) [?], *v.t.* To embrace closely; to squeeze tightly; to hold fast or cling to, to cherish; to keep close to (the shore). *n.* A close embrace, a particular grip in wrestling.

huge (hūj) [O.F. *ahuge*], *a.* Very large; immense. **hugely**, *adv.* In a huge manner; (*colloq.*) exceedingly, extremely.

hugger-mugger (hŭg'êr-mŭg'êr) [?], *n.* Secrecy; disorder, confusion. *a.* Clandestine; confused, slovenly. *adv.* Secretly.

Huguenot (hū'gĕ-not) [F.], *n.* A name applied to the Protestants of France.

hulk (hŭlk) [A.-S. *hulc*], *n.* The hull or body of a ship, esp. an unseaworthy one; an old ship used as a store, a prison, or for other purposes; any unwieldy object or person. **hulking**, *a.*

hull (1) (hŭl) [A.-S. *hulu*], *n.* An outer covering, esp. of a nut or seed; the pod, shell, husk. *v.t.* To strip the husk off.

hull (2) (hŭl) [?], *n.* The body of a ship. *v.t.* To pierce the hull of with a cannon-ball.

hum (hŭm) [imit.], *v.i.* To make a prolonged murmuring sound like a bee; to sing with the lips closed; to make an inarticulate sound.

human (hū'măn) [L. *hūmānus*], *a.* Pertaining to man or mankind; having the nature, characteristics, etc., of man. *n.* A human being. **humankind**, *n.* Mankind.

humane (hū-mān'), *a.* Having the feelings proper to man; tender, compassionate; elevating, refining; relieving distress. **humanely**, *adv.*

humanitarian (hū-măn-i-târ'i-ăn), *a.* Humane. *n.* One who believes that Christ was a mere man; one who believes in the perfectibility of humanity; a philanthropist.

humanity (hū-măn'i-ti), *n.* Human nature; (*collect.*) mankind; kindness, humaneness. **the humanities:** Polite learning, the study of philology, rhetoric, poetry, and the classics.

humble (hŭmbl) [O.F., L. *humilis*], *a.* Having a sense of lowliness, modest; of lowly condition, kind, etc.; deferential. *v.t.* To bring to a state of subjection.

humble-bee (hŭmbl'bē) [HUM BEE], *n.* A bumble-bee.

humbug (hŭm'bŭg) [?], *n.* A hoax; an imposition; trickery; an impostor. *int.* Nonsense. *v.t.* To impose upon.

humdrum (hŭm'drŭm) [redupl. of HUM], *a.* Dull, commonplace.

humerus (hū'mêr-ŭs) [L., shoulder], *n.* The long bone of the upper arm.

humid (hū'mid) [L. *hūmēre*, to be moist], *a.* Damp; rather wet. **humidity**, *n.*

humiliate (hū-mil'i-āt) [L. *humiliātus*], *v.t.* To mortify; to humble, to lower in condition. **humiliating**, *a.* **humilia'tion**, *n.*

humility (hū-mil'i-ti), *n.* The state of being humble; modesty.

humming (hŭm'ing), *a.* That hums; strong (applied to ale). **humming-bird**, *n.* A tropical bird of brilliant plumage and very rapid flight.

hummock (hŭm'ŏk) [?], *n.* A mound or hillock.

humorist (hū'mŏr-ist), *n.* One who displays humour; a facetious person, a wag.

humorous (hū'mŏr-ŭs), *a.* Full of humour; tending to excite laughter; whimsical, capricious. **humorously**, *adv.*

humour (hū'mŏr) [L. *hūmōrem*, moisture], *n.* Mental disposition, mood; bias, caprice; drollery; the capacity of perceiving the ludicrous; playful yet sympathetic imagination or mode of regarding things, delighting in the absurdity of incongruities. *v.t.* To indulge, give way to. **humoursome**, *a.*

hump (hŭmp) [Scand.], *n.* A swelling or protuberance, esp. on the back; a rounded hillock; ill-temper, the blues. *v.t.* To make the back hump-shaped. **humpback**, *n.* A crooked back; a person having this; an American whale.

hunch (hŭnch) [?], *n.* A hump; a thick piece; a push with the elbow; (*slang*) a premonition. *v.t.* To crook (esp. the back); to bend into a hump; to push, to shove. **hunchback**, *n.* A person with a humped back.

hundred (hŭn'dred) [A.-S.], *n.* Ten times ten; (*colloq.*) a hundred pounds (money); an administrative division of a county. **hundredweight**, *n.* A weight of a 112 lb. *av.* **hundredfold**, *n.* **hundredth**, *n.* The ordinal of a hundred. *n.* One of a hundred equal parts.

Hungarian (hŭng-gâr'i-ăn), *a.* Pertaining to Hungary. *n.* A native of Hungary; the Hungarian language.

hunger (hŭng'gêr) [A.-S. *hungor*], *n.* A craving for food; pain caused by lack of food; any strong desire. *v.i.* To feel the pain of hunger; to crave for food; to desire eagerly. **hunger-strike**, *n.* Voluntary abstinence from food as a protest. **hungry**, *a.* Feeling a sensation of hunger.

hunt (hŭnt) [A.-S. *huntian*], *v.t.* To chase (as wild animals) for the purpose of catching and killing; to employ (dogs, etc.) in hunting; to search for, seek after. *v.i.* To follow the chase; to pursue game, etc.; to search (after or for). *n.* Hunting, the chase; a pack of hounds, an association of hunting men; a district hunted. **hunter**, *n.* hunting, *a.* **huntress**, *n.* A female hunter. **huntsman**, *n.* One who hunts, or who manages the hounds.

hurdle (hêrdl) [A.-S. *hyrdel*], *n.* A movable framework of split timber, etc., serving for gates; a barrier of hurdles. *v.t.* To enclose or barricade with hurdles.

hurdy-gurdy (hĕr'di-gĕr'di) [?], *n.* A stringed instrument; a barrel-organ.

hurl (hĕrl) [imit.], *v.t.* To throw with violence; to fling with great force; to utter with vehemence. *n.* The act of throwing with violence. **hurler,** *n.*

hurly-burly (hĕr'li-bĕr'li) [?], *n.* A tumult, commotion, uproar.

hurricane (hŭr'i-kán) [Sp. *huracan,* from Carib.], *n.* A storm with violent wind.

hurry (hŭr'i) [imit.], *v.t.* To impel to greater speed, to push forward; to cause to act carelessly or precipitately. *v.i.* To hasten. *n.* The act of hurrying; urgency, bustle; eagerness (to do, etc.). **hurried,** *a.*

hurst (hĕrst) [A.-S. *hyrst*], *n.* A wood, a thicket; a knoll.

hurt (hĕrt) [?], *v.t.* To cause pain, loss, or detriment to; to damage; to distress (as the feelings). *n.* A wound; an injury; anything that causes pain, injury, or detriment. **hurtful,** *a.* Causing hurt; noxious. **hurtfully,** *adv.*

hurtle (hĕrtl) [?], *v.t.* To dash against with violence; to move or whirl with great force.

husband (hŭz'bánd) [A.-S. *hūsbonda*], *n.* A man joined to a woman in marriage. *v.t.* To manage with frugality, to economize. **husbandman,** *n.* A farmer, a tiller of the soil. **husbandry,** *n.* Agriculture; the products of farming; economy.

hush (hŭsh) [imit.], *v.t.* To make silent; to repress the noise of. *v.i.* To be still or silent. *n.* Silence, stillness. *int.* Silence! **hush-money,** *n.* A bribe to secure silence.

husk (hŭsk) [?], *n.* The integument of certain fruits or seeds; (*fig.*) a worthless part. *v.t.* To strip the husk from. **husky** (1), *a.* Abounding in husks; dry, hoarse, rough and harsh in sound; strong, robust.

husky (2) (hŭs'ki) [perh. ESKIMO], *n.* A sledge-dog; an Eskimo.

hussar (hu-zar') [Hung.], *n.* A light horseman; a soldier of a light cavalry regiment.

hussy (hŭz'i), *n.* A pert, forward girl; a worthless woman.

hustings (hŭs'tingz) [A.-S.], *n.* A platform from which candidates addressed electors; proceedings at an election.

hustle (hŭsl) [Dut. *hutselen*], *v.t.* To jostle, push violently; to hurry. *v.i.* To press roughly; to act with rough energy, to push one's way unceremoniously. *n.* Hustling. **hustler,** *n.*

hut (hŭt) [F. *hutte*], *n.* A mean dwelling; a cabin, hovel; a small temporary camp-shelter. *v.t.* To place (troops) in huts. *v.i.* To lodge in huts. **hutment,** *n.* An encampment of huts; lodging in huts.

hutch (hŭch) [O.F. *huche*], *n.* A coop or pen for small animals; a chest, bin; a kneading-trough.

huzza (hu-za') [imit.], *int.* A cry of joy, applause, etc.

hyacinth (hi'á-sinth) [Gr. *huakinthos,* prob. iris or larkspur], *n.* A beautiful bulbous-rooted flowering plant; a flower fabled by the ancients to have sprung from the blood of the youth Hyacinth, beloved of Apollo. **hyacin'thine,** *a.*

hyalo- [Gr. *hualos,* glass], *comb. form.* Colourless, transparence.

hybrid (hi'brid) [L. *hybrida,* mongrel], *a.* Produced by the union of two distinct species, etc.; mongrel, cross-bred. *n.* A mongrel; an animal or plant produced by the union of two distinct species, varieties, etc.; a word compounded from different languages; anything composed of heterogeneous parts.

hydr-, hydro- [Gr. *hudŏr hudros,* water], *comb. form.* Pertaining to or connected with water. **hydrocarbon,** *n.* A compound of carbon and hydrogen.

hydrangea (hi-drăn'jé-á) [Gr. *angeion,* vessel], *n.* A flowering shrub of the saxifrage family.

hydrant (hi'dránt), *n.* A spout connected with a water-main, for drawing water.

hydrate (hi'drăt), *v.t.* To combine with water.

hydraulic (hi-draw'lik) [Gr. *aulos,* pipe], *a.* Pertaining to fluids in motion, or to water-power. *n.pl.* The science treating of liquids in motion, esp. the conveyance of water through pipes, etc.

hydro (hi'drŏ), *n.* A hydropathic establishment.

hydrogen (hi'drŏ-jén) [F. *hydrogène*], *n.* An invisible, inflammable, gaseous element, the lightest of known bodies, which in combination with oxygen produces water. **hydrogen bomb,** *n.* Bomb in which overwhelming release of energy is achieved by converting hydrogen nuclei into helium nuclei. Also known as H-bomb. **hydrogenous** (hi-droj'é-nŭs), *a.*

hydropathy (hi-drop'á-thi), *n.* The treatment of disease by the application of water. **hydropathic,** *a.*

hydrophobia (hi-drŏ-fō'bi-á), *n.* An unnatural dread of water, a symptom of rabies; rabies.

hydrophone (hi'drŏ-fōn) [Gr. *phōnē,* sound], *n.* An instrument for detecting sound by water.

hydroplane (hi'drŏ-plān), *n.* A light motor-boat; a flat fin for governing the vertical direction of a submarine; a plane for lifting a boat partially from the water.

hydrostatic, -al (hi-drŏ-stăt'ik, -ál), *a.* Pertaining to hydrostatics. **hydrostatics,** *n.* The science which treats of the pressure and equilibrium of liquids at rest.

hyena (hi-ē'ná) [Gr. *huaina,* sow-like], *n.* A carnivorous scavenging quadruped.

hygiene (hi'jēn) [Gr. *hugienē technē,* the art of health], *n.* The science of the prevention of disease as preservation of health, esp. of the community at large; sanitary science. **hygienic** (hi-ji-en'ik), *a.*

hygro- [Gr. *hugros,* wet], *comb. form.* Moist, pertaining to the presence of moisture.

hylo- [Gr. *hute,* matter], *comb. form.* Pertaining to wood; materialistic.

Hymen (hi'mĕn), *n.* The Greek god of marriage. **hymen,** *n.* A membrane partially closing the virginal vagina. **hymeneal** (hi-mē-nē'ál), *a.* Pertaining to marriage. *n.* A marriage song.

hymeno- [Gr. *humen*, membrane], *comb. form.* Membranous.

hymenoptera (hī-mè-nop'tèr-à) [Gr. *humen*, a membrane, *pteron*, wing], *n.pl.* An order of insects having four membranous wings as the bee, wasp, ant, etc. **hymenopterous,** *a.*

hymn (him) [Gr. *humnos*], *n.* A song in praise or adoration of God; a sacred or solemn song or ode. *v.t.* To praise or worship in hymns. *v.i.* To sing hymns. **hymnal** (him'nàl), *n.* A collection of hymns, esp. for public worship. **hymnol'ogy,** *n.* The composition or study of hymns; hymns collectively.

hyper- [Gr. *huper*], *comb. form.* Beyond; excessive, beyond measure.

hyperbola (hī-pèr'bò-là), *n.* A plane curve formed by cutting a cone when the intersecting plane makes a greater angle with the base than the side of the cone makes. **hyperbolic** (-bol'ik), *a.* Pertaining to or like an hyperbola.

hyperbole (hī-pèr'bò-lē) [Gr. *ballein*, to throw], *n.* A figure of speech expressing much more than the truth; exaggeration. **hyperbolical** (-bol'i-kàl), *a.*

hyperborean (hī-pèr-bôr'ē-àn) [Gr. *Boreas*, the north wind], *a.* Belonging to the extreme north. *n.* One living in the extreme north. **hyperboreanism,** *n.*

hypercritical (hī-pèr-krit'ik-àl), *a.* Unreasonably critical; captiously censorious, over-nice.

hypersensitive (hī-pèr-sen'si-tiv), *a.* Excessively sensitive.

hyphen (hī'fèn) [Gr. *huphen*], *n.* A short stroke (-) joining two words or parts of words. *v.t.* To join by a hyphen. **hyphenate** (hī'fè-nāt), *v.t.*

hypno- [Gr. *kupnos*, sleep], *comb. form.* **hypnosis** (hip-nō'sis), *n.* A morbid state of sleep; the hypnotic state. **hypnotic** (hip-not'ik), *a.* Causing sleep; pertaining to or inducing hypnotism. *n.* A medicine which produces sleep. **hypnotism** (hip'-nō-tizm), *n.* An artificial method of inducing sleep or an analogous state; sleep artificially induced. **hyp'notist,** *n.*

hypo- [Gr. *hupo*, under], *comb. form.* Below; less than.

hypochondria (hī-pò-kon'dri-à) [Gr. *chondros*, cartilage], *n.* A morbid condition characterized by excessive anxiety with regard to the health, and attended by depression of spirits. **hypochon'driac,** *a.*

hypocrisy (hi-pok'ri-si) [Gr. *hupokrisis*, acting of a part], *n.* Dissimulation; a feigning to be what one is not; a pretence to virtue or goodness. **hypocrite** (hip'ò-krit), *n.* One who practises hypocrisy; a dissembler.

hypodermic (hī-pò-dèr'mik) [Gr. *derma*, skin], *a.* Pertaining to parts underlying the skin. *n.* A drug introduced by injection under the skin.

hypotenuse (hī-pot'è-nūz) [Gr. *teinein*, to stretch], *n.* The side of a right-angled triangle opposite to the right angle.

hypothecate (hī-poth'è-kāt) [Gr. *thēkē*, from *tithenai*, to place], *v.t.* To pledge as security for some liability.

hypothesis (hī-poth'è-sis), *n.* (*pl.* -ses) A proposition assumed for the purpose of argument; a theory assumed to account for something not understood; a mere supposition. **hypothet'ic,** *a.* Conjectural.

hyssop (his'òp) [Gr. *hussōpos*], *n.* A plant with blue flowers.

hysteria (his-tēr'i-à) [Gr. *hustera*, the womb], *n.* A nervous disorder. **hysteric** (his-ter'k), *a.* hysterical, *a.* Moved by temporary excitement.

I

I (ī) [A.-S. *ic*], *nom. sing. 1st pers. pron.* (*obj.* me, *poss.* my; *pl. nom.* we, *obj.* us, *poss.* our) In speaking or writing denotes oneself.

-ia [L. and Gr.], *suf.* Forming abstract nouns, as *mania, militia*; names of countries, etc., as *Australia, Bulgaria*; names of diseases, as *malaria, neuralgia*; name of alkaloids, as *morphia*; (*pl.* of L. *-ium*, Gr. *-ion*) *bacteria, regalia*.

iamb, iambus (ī- ăm'bùs) [Gr. *iambos*], *n.* (*pl.* -buses) A poetic foot of one short and one long, or one unaccented and one accented syllable. **iambic,** *a.* An iambic foot or verse.

-iasis [from Gr. *iästhai*, to heal], *comb. form.* Noting a disease, as *elephantiasis*.

ibex (ī'beks) [L.], *n.* A species of wild goat.

ibidem (ī'bi'dem) [L.], *adv.* In the same place (in a book, page, etc.)

ibis (ī'bis) [prob. Egypt.], *n.* A heron-like wading bird, esp. the sacred ibis of the ancient Egyptians.

ice (is) [A.-S. *is*], *n.* Water congealed by cold; a frozen confection, ice-cream; sugar, etc., used for coating cakes. *v.t.* To cover or cool with ice, to convert into ice; to coat with concreted sugar. **iceberg** (is'bèrg), *n.* A large mass of floating ice, usu. formed by detachment from a glacier. **iceblink,** *n.* A luminous reflection over the horizon from snow- or ice-fields. **ice-cream,** *n.* Cream or custard flavoured and artificially frozen. **ice-field,** *n.* A large expanse of ice, esp. in the Polar regions. **ice-floe, -pack,** *n.* A sheet of floating ice. **icing,** *n.* A coating of concreted sugar. **icy,** *a.*

ichneumon (ik-nū'mòn) [Gr. from *ich-neuein*, to track], *n.* A small carnivorous animal related to the mungoose, found in Egypt where it was formerly held sacred because it devours crocodiles' eggs.

ichor (ī'kòr) [Gr.], *n.* (*Gr. Myth.*) The ethereal fluid which took the place of blood in the veins of the gods.

ichthy-, ichthyo- [Gr. *ichthus*, a fish], *comb. form.* Pertaining to fish; fish-like.

ichthyology (ik-thi-ol'-ò-ji), *n.* The branch of zoology concerned with fishes, the natural history of fishes. **ichthyol'ogist,** *n.*

ichthyosaurus (ik-thi-ò-saw'rùs) [Gr. *sauros*, lizard], *n.* A gigantic fossil marine reptile.

icicle (ī'sikl) [A.-S. *ises piecel*], *n.* A hanging point of ice, formed by the freezing of dripping water.

icon (ī'kòn) [Gr. *eikon*, image], *n.* (*Eastern Ch.*) A sacred image, or figure of a holy personage.

icono- [as prec.], *comb. form.* Pertaining to images or idols. **iconoclasm** (ī-kŏn'-ŏ-klăzm) [Gr. *klasma*, from *klaein*, to break], *n.* The breaking of idols; (*fig.*) attack on or disregard of established usages, opinions, etc. **iconoclast**, *n.* A breaker of images; an assailant of established usages, etc. **iconoclas'tic**, *a.*

id (id) [Gr. *idios*, peculiar to oneself], *n.* (*Psych.*) The instinctive impulses of the individual.

-ide, *suf.* Indicating chemical compounds of an element with another element or a radical, as *chloride*, *oxide*.

idea (ī-dē'ā) [Gr. *idein*, to see], *n.* A mental image, a notion, conception, supposition; a more or less vague opinion; a plan, intention. **ideal** (ī-dē'ăl), *a.* Consisting of, existing in, or pertaining to ideas; visionary, fanciful; reaching one's standard of perfection. *n.* An imaginary standard of perfection; an actual thing realizing this. **idealism**, *n.* The practice of forming or seeking ideals; the representation of things in conformity with an ideal standard. **idealist**, *n.* **idealis'tic**, *a.* **ide'alize**, *v.t.* To make ideal; to portray in conformity with an ideal. **ideally**, *adv.*

idem (ī'dem) [L.], *n.* The same (word, author, book, etc.).

identical (ī-dĕn'ti-kăl), *a.* Absolutely the same; uniform in quality, appearance, etc. **identic**, *a.*

identify (ī-dĕn'ti-fī), *v.t.* To consider or represent as precisely the same (with), to prove the identity of; to prove to be the same (with). **identifica'tion**, *n.*

identity (ī-dĕn'ti-ti) [late L. *identitas*, from L. **idem**, the same], *n.* The state of being identical; absolute sameness; one's individuality.

ideo- [IDEA], *comb. form.* Pertaining to or expressing ideas. **ideograph**, **-gram** (ī-dē-ō-grăf, -grăm), *n.* A symbol, figure, etc., suggesting or conveying the idea of an object, without expressing its name.

Ides (īdz) [L. *idūs*], *n.pl.* In the ancient Roman calendar, the 15th of March, May, July, October, and 13th of the other months.

idio- [Gr. *idios*, peculiar to oneself], *comb. form.*

idiom (ĭd'ĭ-ôm), *n.* A mode of expression peculiar to a language; a peculiarity of phraseology. **idiomat'ic**, *a.*

idiosyncrasy (ĭd-ĭ-ō-sĭn'krā-si) [SYN-, Gr. *krāsia*, mixing], *n.* Individual attitude of mind; a characteristic peculiar to an individual. **idiosyncrat'ic**, *a.*

idiot (ĭd'ĭ-ŏt) [Gr. *idiōtēs*, a private person, hence one who is ignorant], *n.* A person of defective understanding; one destitute of reason; a stupid, silly person. **idiocy**, *n.* **idiot'ic**, *a.*

idle (īdl) [A.-S. *idel*, empty, vain], *a.* Doing nothing; disengaged, not occupied, free; averse to work, lazy; vain, ineffectual. *v.i.* (*pres. p.* idling) To spend time in idleness. **idleness**, *n.* **idler**, *n.*

idol (ī'dŏl) [Gr. *eidōlon*, from *eidos*, form], *n.* An image, esp. one worshipped as a god; a person or thing loved or honoured excessively. **idol'ater**, *n.* One who worships idols; a pagan; an extravagant admirer. **idolatrous**, *a.* **idolatrously**, *adv.* **idolatry**, *n.* **idolize**, *v.t.* To worship as an idol; to make an idol of.

idyll (ī'dil) [Gr. *eidullion*, dim. of *eidos*, form], *n.* A short pastoral poem; a brief and picturesque narrative or description of rustic life. **idyl'lic**, *a.*

if (if) [A.-S. *gif*], *conj.* On the supposition that, in case that; allowing that; whenever; whether; also used in an exclamatory sense (as *if you were only here!*)

igneous (ig'nē-ŭs) [L. *ignis*, fire], *a.* Containing or of the nature of fire.

ignis fatuus (ig'nis-făt'ū-ŭs) [L., foolish fire], *n.* (*pl.* **ignes fatui**) A flame-like meteor floating above marshes, etc.; will-o'-the wisp; (*fig.*) a delusive aim.

ignite (ig-nīt'), *v.t.* To set on fire; to render luminous with heat. *v.i.* To take fire; to become red with heat. **ignitible**, *a.* **ignition** (ig-nish'ŭn), *n.* Act of igniting; state of being ignited.

ignoble (ig-nōbl') [L. *ignōbilis*], *a.* Of humble birth; mean, base, dishonourable.

ignominy (ig'nō-mi-ni) [L. *ignōminia*], *n.* Public disgrace or shame; dishonour, infamy. **ignomin'ious**, *a.*

ignoramus (ig-nō-rā'mŭs) [L., we do not know], *n.* (*pl.* **-muses**) An ignorant fellow; a blockhead.

ignorance (ig'nō-răns) [L. *ignōrans*, ignorant], *n.* The state of being ignorant; want of knowledge (of). **ignorant**, *a.* Destitute of knowledge, unconscious (of); illiterate, uneducated.

ignore (ig-nōr') [L. *ignōrāre*], *v.t.* To pass over without notice, to disregard.

iguana (ig-wa'nà) [Sp., from Carib.], *n.* A genus of large American lizards. **iguanodon**, *n.* A genus of extinct gigantic lizard.

ilex (ī'leks) [L.], *n.* (*pl.* **-exes**) The holm-oak; a genus of trees including the holly.

iliac (il'ĭ-ăk) [L. *ilia*], *a.* Belonging to the smaller intestines; pertaining to the *ilium* or hip-bone.

ilk (ilk) [A.-S. *ilca*], *a.* The same. **of that ilk:** Of the same name (used when the surname of a person is the same as that of his estate).

ill (il) [Icel. *illr*], *a.* Unwell, sick, diseased; bad morally, evil; mischievous, harmful, unfavourable, unlucky; not right, faulty; improper; awkward. *adv.* Not well, badly; imperfectly, scarcely; unfavourably, in bad part. *n.* Evil; injury; wickedness; (*pl.*) misfortunes. **ill-advised**, *a.* Imprudent; injudicious. **ill blood:** Resentment, enmity. **ill-bred**, *a.* Brought up badly. **ill-conditioned**, *a.* Having a bad disposition; in a bad physical condition. **ill-disposed**, *a.* Unfavourably inclined (towards). **ill-fated**, *a.* Unfortunate, unlucky. **ill-favoured**, *a.* Ugly, forbidding, repulsive. **ill-got**, **ill-gotten**, *a.* Obtained in an improper way. **ill-omened**, *a.* Unlucky, of evil augury. **ill-timed**, *a.* Done, etc., at an unsuitable time. **ill-treat**, *v.t.* To treat badly. **ill will:** Malevolence, enmity.

illation (i-lā'shŭn) [F.], *n.* Deduction; an inference. **il'lative**, *a.*

illegal (i-lē'găl), *a.* Not according to law; unlawful. **illegal'ity**, *n.*

illegible (i-lej′ibl), *a.* That cannot be read or deciphered. **illegibil′ity,** *n.* **illeg′ibly,** *adv.*

illegitimate (il-è-jit′i-màt), *a.* Not lawfully begotten; born out of wedlock; contrary to law; irregular. **illegit′imacy,** *n.*

illiberal (i-lib′ér-àl), *a.* Not generous, sordid; narrow-minded, not catholic; rude, vulgar.

illicit (i-lis′it), *a.* Not permitted; unlawful.

illimitable (i-lim′it-àbl), *a.* Boundless, limitless.

illiterate (i-lit′ér-àt), *a.* Unlearned, unable to read or write; rude, uncultivated. *n.* An uneducated person. **illiteracy,** **illiterateness,** *n.*

illness (il′nès), *n.* The state of being ill, sickness, physical indisposition.

illogical (i-loj′i-kàl), *a.* Ignorant or careless of the rules of logic; contrary to the rules of logic.

illude (i-lood′) [L. *lūdere,* to play], *v.t.* To deceive, to cheat; to mock.

illuminate (i-lū′mi-nāt), *v.t.* To throw light upon; to light up; to adorn with festal lamps; to adorn (a manuscript) with coloured pictures, letters, etc.; to enlighten mentally or spiritually. *v.i.* To adorn manuscripts, etc., with coloured pictures, etc. **illuminant,** *a.* **illumina′tion,** *n.*

illumine (i-lū′min) [F. *illuminer*], *v.t.* To illuminate; to enlighten.

illusion (i-lū-zhŭn) [F., from L. *illūdere,* to illude], *n.* Act of deceiving; that which deceives; a false show, a delusion; a deceptive sensuous impression; (*Psych.*) a wrong interpretation of what is perceived through the senses. **illusionist,** *n.* One who produces illusions; a conjurer; a visionary. **illu′sory,** *a.* Delusive, deceptive.

illustrate (il′ŭs-trāt), *v.t.* To make clear, to explain by means of examples, etc.; to ornament by pictures, etc. **illustra′tion,** *n.* **illus′trative,** *a.* **il′lustrator,** *n.*

illustrious (i-lŭs′tri-ŭs) [L. *-lustris,* from stem of *lux,* light], *a.* Distinguished, famous; conferring renown or glory.

image (im′àj) [L. *imāgo*], *n.* A representation or similitude of a person or thing; an effigy, a statue, esp. one intended for worship, an idol; an idea, conception; an expanded metaphor or simile; the figure of an object formed (through the medium of a mirror, lens, etc.) by rays of light. *v.t.* To make an image of; to mirror; to represent mentally; to typify, symbolize. **imagery,** *n.* (*collect.*) Images, statues; figures evoked by the fancy; rhetorical figures, figurative description.

imagine (i-màj′in) [L. *imāginārī*], *v.t.* To form an image of in the mind, to form an idea of; to suppose, think; to guess; to plot, devise. **imaginable,** *a.* **imaginary,** *a.* Existing only in imagination or fancy; not real. **imagina′tion,** *n.* Act or process of imagining; power of imagining; the mental faculty that forms ideal images from impressions; fancy; the constructive or creative faculty of the mind; a fanciful opinion. **imag′inative,** *a.* Endowed with imagination.

imbecile (im′bè-sil) [L. *imbecillus*], *a.*

Half-witted; stupid, fatuous. *n.* One mentally weak. **imbecil′ity,** *n.*

imbibe (im-bīb), *v.t.* To drink in; to absorb.

imbroglio (im-brō-li-ō), *n.* (*pl.* **-os**) A perplexing or confused state of affairs; a misunderstanding.

imbrue (im-broo′) [O.F. *embruer*], *v.t.* To steep; to moisten (with blood, carnage, etc.); to stain.

imbue (im-bū′), *v.t.* To saturate (with); to dye (with); to tinge strongly (with); (*fig.*) to inspire.

imitate (im′i-tāt) [L. *imitātus*], *v.t.* To produce a likeness of; to follow the example of; to mimic, ape. **imitable,** *a.* **imita′tion,** *n.* **im′itative,** *a.*

immaculate (i-măk′ū-làt) [L. *macula,* spot], *a.* Spotless, pure; free from blemish. **Immaculate Conception,** *n.* (*R. C. theol.*) The doctrine that the Virgin Mary was conceived free from original sin.

immanent (im′à-nènt) [L. *manens,* dwelling], *a.* Inherent, not transient; indwelling; (*Theol.*) present throughout the universe as an essential sustaining spirit. **immanence,** *n.*

immaterial (im-à-tēr′i-àl), *a.* Not consisting of matter; spiritual; unimportant.

immature (im′à-tūr), *a.* Not mature, imperfect. **immatur′ity,** *n.*

immeasurable (i-mezh′ūr-àbl), *a.* That cannot be measured; immense. **immeasurably,** *adv.*

immediate (i-mē′di-àt), *a.* Situated in the closest relation; not separated; direct; next, present; done or occurring at once, without delay. **immediately,** *adv.*

immemorial (im-è-mór′i-àl), *a.* Beyond memory or record; beyond the reach of record or tradition.

immense (i-mens′) [L. *mensus,* measured], *a.* Huge, vast, immeasurable; (*slang*) very good, excellent.

immerse (i-mèrs′) [L. *immersus,* plunged], *v.t.* To plunge; to dip (into water, etc.); to baptize in this manner; (*fig.*) to involve deeply (in difficulty, thought, etc.). **immersion,** *n.* Act of immersing.

immigrate (im′i-grāt), *v.i.* To come into a foreign country for settlement. **immigrant,** *n.*

imminent (im′i-nént), *a.* Impending; close at hand. **imminence,** *n.*

immobile (i-mō′bil), *a.* Immovable; impassable. **immobil′ity,** *n.*

immoderate (i-mod′ér-àt), *a.* Excessive; unreasonable.

immodest (i-mod′èst), *a.* Not modest, forward; indelicate, indecent. **immodestly,** *adv.* **immodesty,** *n.*

immolate (im′ō-lāt) [L. *molatus,* sprinkled with meal, sacrificed], *v.t.* To kill in sacrifice, to sacrifice (to). **immola′tion,** *n.* **im′molator,** *n.*

immoral (i-mor′àl), *a.* Not moral; inconsistent with or contrary to morality; licentious. **immoral′ity,** *n.*

immortal (i-mór′tal), *a.* Not subject to death; imperishable; relating to immortality; (*colloq.*) not changing. *n.* One who is immortal; (*pl.*) the forty members of the French Academy. **immortal′ity,** *n.* State of being immortal; exemption from annihilation or oblivion. **immor-**

talize, *v.t.* To perpetuate the memory of. immor'tally, *adv.*

immortelle (im-ôr-tel') [F.], *n.* A plant with flowers that keep their shape and colour after being gathered.

immovable (i-moo'vàbl), *a.* That cannot be moved; firmly fixed; steadfast; unchanging, unfeeling.

immune (i-mūn') [L. *mūnis*, serving], *a.* Free or exempt (from infection, etc.). immunity, *n.* Freedom or exemption from any obligation, duty, etc., or from liability to infection.

immure (i-mūr') [L. *mūrus*, wall], *v.t.* To shut in or up; to confine.

immutable (i-mū'tàbl), *a.* Unchangeable, not susceptible to variation. immutabil'ity, *n.*

imp (imp) [A.-S. *impa*, shoot, graft], *n.* A young or little devil; a mischievous child.

impact (im'pàkt) [L. *impactus*, driven], *n.* A forcible striking (upon or against), a collision.

impair (im-pâr') [L. *pejor*, worse], *v.t.* To diminish in excellence, value, strength, etc., to injure.

impale (im-pāl') [L. *pālus*, a stake], *v.t.* To transfix, esp. to put to death by trans-fixing with a sharp stake; (*Her.*) to arrange two coats of arms on one shield.

impalpable (im-pàl'pàbl), *a.* Not perceptible to the touch; not to be readily apprehended, intangible.

impart (im-part') [L. *partīre*, to PART], *v.t.* To grant a share of, to communicate the knowledge of; to bestow.

impartial (im-par'shàl), *a.* Not favouring one party or side more than another; equitable, disinterested. impartial'ity, *n.*

impassable (im-pas'àbl), *a.* That cannot be passed.

impasse (ăn-pas', im-pas') [F.], *n.* An insurmountable obstacle.

impassible (im-pàs'ibl), *a.* Insensible to pain; incapable of being injured; not subject to passion. impassibil'ity, impassibleness, *n.*

impassion (im-pàsh'ŏn), *v.t.* To rouse the deepest feelings of.

impassive (im-pàs'iv), *a.* Not affected by pain, feeling, or passion; apathetic; unmoved. impassively, *adv.*

impatient (im-pā'shènt), *a.* Fretful; not patient or tolerant (of); eager (for or to). impatience, *n.*

impeach (im-pēch') [late L. *impedicāre*], *v.t.* To charge with a crime or misdemeanour; to bring a charge of maladministration or treason against; to call in question; to bring discredit upon. impeachment, *n.*

impeccable (im-pek'àbl), *a.* Not liable to fall into sin; faultless. impeccabil'ity, *n.*

impecunious (im-pē-kū'ni-ùs) [L. *pecunia*, money], *a.* Destitute of money. impecunios'ity, *n.*

impede (im-pēd') [L. *impedīre*, to entangle the feet], *v.t.* To hinder, obstruct. impediment (-ped'i-mènt), *n.*

impel (im-pel') [L. *pellere*, to drive], *v.t.* To drive forward; to urge (to an action).

impend (im-pend') [L. *pendēre*, to hang], *v.i.* To hang (over), to be suspended (over); to be imminent.

impenetrable (im-pen'ē-tràbl), *a.* That cannot be penetrated; inscrutable; not penetrable to ideas, etc., dull. impenetrabil'ity, *n.*

impenitent (im-pen'i-tènt), *a.* Not penitent. *n.* A hardened sinner. impenitence, *n.*

imperative (im-per'à-tiv) [L. *parāre*, to make ready], *a.* Expressive of command; authoritative, peremptory; urgent. *n.* That mood of a verb which expresses command, entreaty, or exhortation. imperatively, *adv.*

imperceptible (im-pér-sep'tibl), *a.* Not perceptible; indistinguishable; insignificant.

imperfect (im-pér'fèkt), *a.* Defective; not fully made, done, etc.; lacking some part or member; (*Gram.*) expressing action as continuous and not completed. *n.* The imperfect tense. imperfec'tible, *a.* Incapable of being perfected. imperfec'tion, *n.* A moral or physical fault; a defect.

imperial (im-pēr'i-àl) [L. *imperiālis*, from *imperium*, command], *a.* Pertaining to an empire or an emperor, esp. British Empire, as dist. from any particular kingdom, dominion, colony, etc.; sovereign, supreme; majestic. *n.* A size of paper about 22 × 32 in.; a tuft of hair on a man's chin (made fashionable by Emperor Napoleon III). imperialism, *n.* Government by an emperor; imperial spirit, etc.; the policy of extending the authority of a nation by means of colonies or dependencies. imperialist, *n.*

imperil (im-per'il), *v.t.* To endanger.

imperious (im-pēr'i-ùs) [L. *imperiōsus*], *a.* Arbitrary, dictatorial.

imperishable (im-per'ish-àbl), *a.* Enduring permanently; not subject to decay. imperishably, *adv.*

impermeable (im-pér'mē-àbl), *a.* Not allowing passage, esp. of a fluid, impervious.

impersonal (im-pér'sŏ-nàl), *a.* Without personality; not relating to any particular person or thing; (*Gram.*) applied to verbs used only in the third person singular. impersonally, *adv.* impersonate, *v.t.* To invest with personality; to personify; to represent in character. impersona'tion, *n.*

impertinent (im-pér'ti-nènt), *a.* Not pertaining to the matter in hand; frivolous; impudent, insolent, esp. to a superior. impertinence, *n.*

imperturbable (im-pér-tér'bàbl), *a.* That cannot be easily excited; unmoved, calm. imperturbabil'ity, *n.* impertur'bably, *adv.*

impervious (im-pér'vi-ùs), *a.* Not admitting of passage or entrance; (*fig.*) impenetrable (to feeling, argument, etc.).

impetration (im-pē-trā'shŭn) [L. *impetrare*, to bring to pass], *n.* The act of obtaining by petition.

impetuous (im-pet'ū-ùs) [as foll.], *a.* Moving with great speed; acting violently or suddenly; hasty, impulsive. impetuos'ity, *n.*

impetus (im'pē-tùs) [L. *petere*, to seek], *n.* The force with which a body moves or is impelled; impulse.

impiety (im-pī'ē-ti), *n.* Quality of being impious; an impious act.

impinge (im-pinj') [L. *pangere*, to drive, fasten], *v.i.* To come into collision, to strike (on, against, etc.).

impious (im'pi-ùs), *a.* Wanting in piety or reverence towards God; irreverent, profane.

impish (im'pish), *a.* Having the characteristics of an imp.

implacable (im-plă-kăbl), *a.* Not to be appeased; unrelenting. implacabil'ity, *n.*

implant (im-plant'), *v.t.* To plant for the purpose of growth; (*fig.*) to inculcate, to instil.

implement (im'plĕ-mĕnt) [L. *plēre*, to fill], *n.* A tool, a utensil; (*fig.*) an instrument, an agent; (*pl.*) things that serve for equipment, etc. *v.t.* To fulfil; to complete, supplement.

implicate (im'pli-kāt) [L. *plicāre*, to fold], *v.t.* To entangle, entwine; to involve, bring into connexion with. implica'tion, *n.* Act of implicating; state of being implicated; an inference.

implicit (im-plis'it) [L. *implicitus*, as prec.], *a.* Implied; understood or inferable; depending upon complete belief or trust in another, unquestioning, unreserved.

implore (im-plōr') [L. *plorāre*, to weep], *v.t.* To call upon or ask for earnestly. *v.i.* To entreat, supplicate.

imply (im-plī') [L., as IMPLICATE], *v.t.* To involve or contain by implication; to mean indirectly, to hint. implied, *a.* Contained in substance though not actually expressed. impli'edly, *adv.*

impolite (im-pó-līt'), *a.* Not polite, ill-mannered.

impolitic (im-pol'i-tik), *a.* Not politic; injudicious, inexpedient.

imponderable (im-pon'dér-ăbl), *a.* Not having sensible weight; very light. imponderabil'ity, *n.*

import (im-pōrt') [L. *portāre*, to bring], *v.t.* To bring (goods) from a foreign country (into); to introduce; to imply, to signify; to concern. *v.i.* To be important, to matter. *n.* (im'pōrt) That which is imported from abroad; that which is signified or implied; importance, consequence. importance, *n.* The quality of being important; authority, consequence; self-esteem, pretentiousness. important, *a.* Of great moment or consequence; of great personal consequence, pretentious. importa'tion, *n.* Act or practice of importing; that which is imported. impor'ter, *n.* One who imports goods.

importunate (im-pôr'tū-nàt) [L. *importūnus*, unsuitable]. *a.* Unreasonably and pertinaciously solicitous; troublesome.

importune (im'pôr-tūn, im-pôr'tūn], *a.* Untimely; importunate; irksome. *v.t.* To solicit pertinaciously or urgently; to signify.

impose (im-pōz') [L. *impōnere* (cp. COM-POSE], *v.i.* To lay (as a burden, tax, etc.) upon; to force (views, etc.) upon; to palm off (upon); (*Print.*) to arrange (pages of type) for printing. *v.i.* To impress oneself (upon); to practise deception (upon). imposing, *a.* Commanding; impressive, majestic. imposition (-zish'-ùn), *n.* The act of imposing.

impossible (im-pos'ĭbl), *a.* Not possible;

impracticable; that cannot be done, thought, etc. impossibil'ity, *n.* impos'sibly, *adv.*

impost (im'post) [as IMPOSE], *n.* That which is imposed as a tax, a duty (esp. on imports).

impostor (im-pos'tòr) [as IMPOSE], *n.* One who falsely assumes a character; a deceiver. imposture, *n.* Deception by the assumption of a false character; a swindle.

impotent (im'pó-tént), *a.* Wanting in physical, intellectual, or moral power. impotence, *n.*

impound (im-pound'), *v.t.* To confine; to confiscate.

impoverish (im-pov'ér-ish) [O.F. *empoverir*], *v.t.* To make poor; to exhaust the fertility, or resources of. impoverishment, *n.*

impracticable (im-prăk'ti-kăbl), *a.* Not feasible; intractable, stubborn. impracticabil'ity, *n.*

imprecate (im'prĕ-kāt) [L. *precārī*, to pray], *v.t.* To invoke, as an evil or curse (on). impreca'tion, *n.*

impregnable (im-preg'năbl) [L. *prehendere*, to seize], *a.* That cannot be taken by assault; able to resist all attacks, invincible. impregnabil'ity, *n.*

impregnate (im-preg'năt) [L. *prægnāre*], *v.t.* To make pregnant; to fertilize, render fruitful; to saturate (with); to imbue. impregna'tion, *n.*

impresario (im-prĕ-za'ri-ō) [It.], *n.* One who organizes a concert, or manages an opera company, etc.

impress (1) (im-pres') [L. *premere*, to press], *v.t.* To stamp (a mark, etc., on); to produce (a mark) by pressure; to affect strongly. *n.* (im'pres) A mark or stamp made by pressure; an impression.

impress (2) (im-pres'), *v.t.* To compel (seamen) to enter the public service; to seize (property, etc.) for the public service, *n.* impressible, *a.* Capable of being impressed; yielding to pressure; susceptible. impression (-presh'ùn), *n.* Act of impressing; the mark made; a copy from type, an engraved plate, etc.; copies constituting a single issue of a book, engraving, etc.; effect produced, an indistinct notion, a slight recollection. impressionable, *a.* Easily impressed. impressionist, *n.* One of a school of artists who aim at a broad general effect. *a.* Pertaining to such school. impressive, *a.* Adapted to make an impression on the mind. impressively, *adv.* impressiveness, *n.*

imprest (im'-prest), *n.* Earnest money; money advanced.

imprimatur (im-pri-mā'tùr) [L., let it be printed], *n.* A licence to print a book granted by a censor.

imprimis (im-pri'mis) [L.], *adv.* First in order.

imprint (im-print'), *v.t.* To impress, to print. *n.* (im'print) A mark, impression, esp. the name of the printer or publisher of a book, etc., with the place, the date of publication, etc.

imprison (im-priz'ôn), *v.t.* To put into prison; to confine, hold in captivity. imprisonment, *n.*

improbable (im-prob′ábl), *a*. Not likely to be true, or to happen. **improbabil′ity**, *n*. **improbably**, *adv*.

impromptu (im-promp′tū) [L. *in promptū*, in readiness], *adv*. Off-hand, without previous study. *a*. Done off-hand, extempore. *n*. An extemporaneous performance, act, etc.

improper (im-prop′ér), *a*. Not proper; unsuitable; unbecoming, indecent; erroneous. **improperly**, *adv*.

impropriate (im-prō′pri-āt) [L. *propriāre*, to appropriate], *v.t*. To convert (esp. ecclesiastical property) to one's own or to private use. **impropria′tion**, *n*.

impropriety (im-prò-prī′é-ti), *n*. Quality of being improper; an unbecoming act, expression, etc.

improve (im-proov′) [A.-F. *emprouver*, from O.F. *prou*, profit], *v.t*. To make better; to turn to profitable account; to take advantage of. *v.i*. To grow or become better; to recover from illness; to increase in value. **improvable**, *a*. **improvement**, *n*. Act of improving; advancement in value, knowledge, etc.; profitable use; that which is added or done to improve a thing. **improver**, *n*.

improvident (im-prov′i-dént), *a*. Not provident; thriftless; careless, heedless. **improvidence**, *n*.

improvise (im′prò-vīz) [L. *prōvīsus*, provided], *v.t*. To compose and perform off-hand; to extemporize; to do on the spur of the moment. **improvisa′tion** (-zā′shùn), *n*.

imprudent (im-proo′dént), *a*. Wanting in foresight; rash, indiscreet. **imprudence**, *n*.

impudent (im′pū-dént) [L. *pudens*, feeling shame], *a*. Wanting in modesty; impertinent, insolent. **impudence**, *n*.

impugn (im-pūn′) [L. *pugnāre*, to fight], *v.t*. To call in question, contradict. **impugnable** (im-pū′nábl), *a*.

impulse (im′pūls) [L. *impulsus*, impelled], *n*. Application or effect of an impelling force; influence acting suddenly on the mind tending to produce action; a sudden tendency to action. **impulsion** (-pūl′shùn), *n*. Act of impelling; state of being impelled; impetus; instigation. **impulsive**, *a*. Communicating impulse; actuated by impulse rather than by reflection. **impulsively**, *adv*. **impulsiveness**, *n*.

impunity (im-pū′ni-ti) [L. *pœna*, penalty], *n*. Exemption from punishment, penalty, or loss.

impure (im-pūr′), *a*. Not pure; adulterated; unclean. **impurity**, *n*.

impute (im-pūt′) [L. *putāre*, to reckon], *v.t*. To ascribe; to set to the account or charge of. **imputable**, *a*. **imputation** (-tā′shùn), *n*. Act of imputing; reproach, censure.

in (in) [A.-S., L. *in*, Gr. *en*], *prep*. Within. inside of; denoting presence or situation within the limits of time, place, circumstance, reason, etc. *adv*. Inside some place; indoors; in office; over and above.

in- (1), *pref*. In; into; within; on; against; towards; as in *indicate*, *induce*; (2) [L., not], *pref*. Un-, not, without, as in *incomprehensible*.

inability (in-á-bil′i-ti), *n*. Want of ability; lack of power or means.

inaccessible (in-ák-ses′ibl), *a*. Not accessible; that cannot be reached; not affable. **inaccessibil′ity**, *n*.

inaccurate (in-ák′ū-rát), *a*. Not accurate. **inaccuracy**, *n*.

inaction (in-ák-shùn), *n*. Idleness, sloth. **inactive**, *a*. **inactiv′ity**, *n*.

inadequate (in-ád′é-kwát), *a*. Insufficient, unequal. **inadequately**, *adv*. **inadequacy**, *n*.

inadmissible (in-ád-mis′ibl), *a*. That cannot be admitted, allowed, or received. **inadmissibil′ity**, *n*.

inadvertent (in-ád-vér′tént), *a*. Not paying attention; careless, negligent. **inadvertence**, *n*.

inalienable (in-ā′li-é-nábl), *a*. That cannot be alienated or transferred.

inalterable (in-awl′tér-ábl), *a*. Incapable of alteration.

inamorato -a (in-ăm-ôr-a′tô, -a) [It.], *n*. A lover.

inane (i-nān′) [L. *inānis*, empty], *a*. Empty, void; senseless; silly. *n*. Infinite void space. **inanity** (i-năn′i-ti), *n*.

inanimate (i-năn i-mát), *a*. Not living; dull, lifeless.

inanition (in-á-nish′ùn) [L., as **INANE**], *n*. Emptiness; exhaustion from want of nourishment.

inapplicable (in-ăp′li-kábl), *a*. Not applicable; irrelevant.

inappreciable (in-á-prē′shábl), *a*. Not perceptible; too insignificant to be considered. **inappreciably**, *adv*. **inappre′ciative**, *a*.

inapproachable (in-á-prō′chábl), *a*. Inaccessible; unrivalled.

inappropriate (in-á-prō′pri-át), *a*. Unsuitable. **inappropriateness**, *n*.

inapt (in-ăpt′), *a*. Not apt; unsuitable. **inaptitude**, **inaptness**, *n*.

inarticulate (in-ar-tik′ūlát), *a*. Not articulated, not jointed; not uttered distinctly; dumb; incapable of fluent expression.

inartistic (in-ar-tis′tik), *a*. Not done, etc., according to the principles of art; not having artistic taste.

inasmuch (in-áz-mùch′), *adv*. Seeing that; since (followed by *as*).

inattention (in-á-ten′shùn), *n*. Heedlessness, negligence; disregard of courtesy. **inattentive**, *a*.

inaudible (in-aw′dibl), *a*. So low as not to be heard. **inaudibly**, *adv*.

inaugurate (in-aw′gū-rāt) [L. *augurāre*, to take omens], *v.t*. To install or induct into an office; to celebrate the opening of with formality, pomp, or dignity.

inauspicious (in-aw-spish′ùs), *a*. Unlucky, ill-omened, unfavourable.

inboard (in′bôrd), *adv*. (*Naut*.) Within the sides of a ship.

inborn (in′bôrn), *a*. Innate.

inbred (in′bred), *v.t*. To breed from parents nearly related. **in′bred**, *a*. Innate, inborn; bred from nearly related parents.

incalculable (in-kăl′kū-lábl), *a*. Not to be reckoned or estimated in advance; uncertain.

incandesce (in-kán-des′) [L. *candescere*, to

become white], v. To glow or cause to glow with heat. **incandescence**, n. **incandescent**, a.

incantation (in-kăn-tā'shŭn) [L. *incantāre*, as **ENCHANT**], n. A formula supposed to add force to magical ceremonies, a charm.

incapable (in-kā'păbl), a. Not capable (of); not susceptible (of); legally incapacitated.

incapacitate (in-kȧ-păs'ĭ-tāt), v.t. To disable; to render unfit, to disqualify.

incapacity (in-kȧ-păs'ĭ-ti), n. Want of capacity; legal disqualification.

incarcerate (in-kar'sẽr-āt) [L. *carcer*, prison], v.t. To imprison. **incarcera'tion**, n.

incarnate (in-kar'nāt) [L. *caro carnis*, flesh], a. Clothed with flesh, in human form; flesh-coloured. v.t. (in'kar-nāt) To clothe with or embody in flesh; to embody (an idea) in a living form. **incarna'tion**, n. Embodiment in human form; Christ's assumption of human nature.

incautious (in-kaw'shŭs), a. Wanting in caution; rash.

incendiary (in-sen'di-ȧr-i) [L. *incendium*, a conflagration], a. Pertaining to the malicious burning of property; (*fig.*) inflammatory. n. One who maliciously sets fire to a building, etc. **incendiarism**, n.

incense (1) (in'sens) [L. *incensum*, that which is burnt], n. Fragrant gums, spices, etc., producing perfumes when burnt, used in religious rites. v.t. To perfume with incense; to offer incense to; (2) (in-sens') to inflame, exasperate, enrage.

incentive (in-sen'tiv) [L. *incentīvus*, setting a tune], a. Inciting, urging. n. That which acts as a motive or incitement.

inception (in-sep'shŭn) [L. *inceptus*, begun], n. A commencement; the first stage. **inceptive**, a. (*Gram.*) Denoting the beginning of an action.

incertitude (in-sẽr'ti-tūd) [late L. *certitūdo*], n. Uncertainty.

incessant (in-ses'ȧnt) [L. *cessans*, ceasing], a. Unceasing, unintermittent.

incest (in'sest) [L. *castus*, chaste], n. Sexual intercourse between persons nearly related. **inces'tuous**, a.

inch (inch) [A.-S. *ynce*, L. *uncia*], n. A twelfth of a linear foot; (*fig.*) the least quantity or degree; (*pl.*) stature.

inchoate (in'kō-āt) [L. *incohātus*, begun], a. Only begun, existing only in elements, undeveloped. **inchoately**, adv.

incidence (in'si-dĕns) [as foll.], n. Act or state of falling on; the direction in which a body, a ray of light, heat, etc., falls upon a surface; (*fig.*) scope, range.

incident (in'si-dĕnt) [L. *cadere*, to fall], a. Falling or striking (on or upon); likely to happen; appertaining (to); fortuitous. n. That which falls out or happens; a subsidiary event; an occurrence, esp. of a striking nature; a privilege, burden, etc., legally attaching to property, etc. **inciden'tal**, a. Casual, contingent; fortuitous, not essential; naturally connected with. n. Something that is incidental; (*pl.*) expenses. **incidentally**, adv.

incinerate (in-sin'ẽr-āt) [L. *cinis*, ashes], v.t. To reduce to ashes. **incinera'tion**, n. **incin'erator**, n.

incipient (in-sip'ĭ-ĕnt) [as **INCEPTION**], a. Beginning, in the first stages.

incise (in-sīz') [L. *incisus*, cut into], v.t. To engrave, to carve (inscription, pattern, etc.). **incision** (in-sizh'ŭn), n. The art of incising; a cut, gash. **incisive** (in-sī'siv), a. Having the quality of cutting into; sharp, penetrating; trenchant. **incisor** (in-sī'zŏr), n. A tooth adapted for cutting food, one between the canines.

incite (in-sīt'), v.t. To urge; to stimulate, prompt, encourage (to action). **incitement**, n. An incentive, motive.

incivil (in-siv'il), a. Rude, unpolished. **incivil'ity**, n. Impoliteness.

inclement (in-klem'ĕnt), a. Merciless; rough, severe; stormy. **inclemently**, adv. **inclemency**, n.

incline (in-klīn') [L. *clināre*, to bend], v.i. To deviate from a normal direction; to lean; to be disposed; to have a propensity or inclination. v.t. To cause to deviate; to give a leaning to; to bow or stoop; (*fig.*) to dispose, turn. n. (in'klīn) An inclination; a slope, gradient. **inclina'tion**, n. Act of inclining or bending; a deviation; bent of the mind or will; disposition, propensity (to or for); liking (for).

include (in-klood') [L. *claudere*, to shut], v.t. To contain, to hold, to comprise, to comprehend. **inclusion** (in-kloo'zhŭn), n. **inclusive** (-siv), a.

incognito (in-kog'ni-tō) [L. *cognitus*, learned], a. Living or going under an assumed name or character. n. (fem. -ta)

incoherent (in-kō-hēr'ĕnt), a. Wanting cohesion of parts; disconnected, inconsistent; loose, rambling. **incoherence**, -ency, **incohesion** (-hē'zhŭn).

incombustible (in-kŏm-bŭs'tibl), a. Incapable of being burnt. n. An incombustible substance, etc. **incombustibil'ity**, n.

income (in'kŭm), n. Amount of money (usu. annual) accruing as payment, interest, etc., from labour, business, or property. **income-tax**: A tax levied on incomes above a certain amount.

incommensurable (in-kō-men'shŭr-ȧbl), a. Having no common measure (with another number or quantity); not fit or worthy to be measured (with). **incommensurabil'ity**, n.

incommode (in-kō-mōd') [L. *commodus*, convenient], v.t. To cause inconvenience to; to embarrass, hinder. **incommo'dious**, a. Not commodious; inconvenient. **incommod'ity**, n.

incommunicable (in-kō-mū'ni-kȧbl), a. That cannot be communicated to or shared with another.

incomparable (in-kom'pȧr-ȧbl), a. Not to be compared (to or with); unequalled.

incompatible (in-kŏm-păt'ibl), a. Inconsistent with something else; incongruous. **incompatibil'ity**, n.

incompetent (in-kom'pĕ-tĕnt), a. Lacking adequate power, means, etc. (to do); wanting legal fitness or qualification. **incompetence**, n.

incomplete (in-kóm-plēt'), *a.* Not complete, not perfect.

incomprehensible (in-kom-prė-hen'sibl), *a.* That cannot be comprehended or understood, inconceivable. **incomprehensibil'ity,** *n.*

incompressible (in-kóm-pres'ibl), *a.* Not compressible; resisting compression. **incompressibil'ity,** *n.*

inconceivable (in-kón-sē'vábl), *a.* Not conceivable; incredible, most extraordinary.

inconclusive (in-kón-kloo'siv), *a.* Not conclusive; not decisive (of evidence). **inconclusively,** *adv.*

incongruous (in-kong'groo-ús), *a.* Not agreeing or harmonizing; inconsistent; out of place. **incongruity** (-groo'i-ti), *n.* **incongruously,** *adv.*

inconsequent (in-kon'sė-kwėnt), *a.* Irrelevant; illogical; disconnected. **inconsequence,** *n.* **inconsequential,** *a.*

inconsiderable (in-kón-sid'ér-ábl), *a.* Not deserving consideration; insignificant, trivial.

inconsiderate (in-kón-sid'ér-át), *a.* Hasty, incautious; having no consideration for others.

inconsistent (in-kón-sis'tént), *a.* Incongruous; incompatible (with); self-contradictory, not uniform, changeable. **inconsistency,** *n.*

inconsolable (in-kón-sō'lábl), *a.* Not to be consoled (of a person, grief, etc.). **inconsolably,** *adv.*

inconspicuous (in-kón-spik'ū-ús), *a.* Not readily discernible by the sight; small, obscure.

inconstant (in-kon'stánt), *a.* Changeable, fickle; variable, irregular. **inconstancy,** *n.*

incontestable (in-kón-tes'tábl), *a.* Indisputable, undeniable. **incontestably,** *adv.*

incontinent (in-kon'ti-nént), *a.* Not restraining the passions or appetites; licentious; (*Med.*) unable to restrain natural evacuations.

incontrollable (in-kón-trō'lábl), *a.* Not controllable.

incontrovertible (in-kon-tró-vėr'tibl), *a.* Incontestable, indisputable. **incontrovertibil'ity,** *n.*

inconvenient (in-kón-vē-ni-ént), *a.* Not convenient, incommodious; causing or tending to cause trouble, uneasiness, etc.; inopportune. **inconvenience,** *n.*

inconvertible (in-kón-vėr'tibl), *a.* Incapable of being converted into or exchanged for something else, esp. money. **inconvertibly,** *adv.*

incorporate (in-kór'pó-rát) [L. *corpus,* body], *a.* Combined into one body or corporation, closely united; made into a corporation. *v.t.* (-rát) To unite or combine into one mass or body (with); to form into a legal corporation; to embody. *v.i.* To become united or incorporated (with another) so as to form one body. **incorpora'tion,** *n.*

incorporeal (in-kór-pór'é-ál), *a.* Not corporeal; immaterial.

incorrect (in-kó-rekt'), *a.* Not in accordance with truth, propriety, etc.; inaccurate; unbecoming.

incorrigible (in-kor'i-jibl), *a.* Incapable

of being improved; beyond hope of amendment.

incorrupt (in-kó-rúpt'), *a.* Not decayed, marred, or impaired; untainted; above bribery. **incorruptible,** *a.* Incapable of corruption or decay; eternal; not to be bribed. **incorruptibil'ity,** *n.* **incorruption** (-rúp'shún), *n.* Freedom from corruption.

increase (in-krēs') [L. *crescere,* to grow], *v.i.* To become greater in bulk, quantity, value, degree, etc.; to multiply by the production of young. *v.t.* To make greater in number, bulk, etc.; to add to, to extend, intensify. *n.* (in'-) Act, state, or process of increasing; growth; that which is added; increment.

incredible (in-kred'ibl), *a.* Passing belief; astounding. **incredibil'ity,** *n.* **incredibly,** *adv.*

incredulous (in-kred'ū-lús), *a.* Sceptical (of); unbelieving. **incredu'lity,** *n.* **incredulously,** *adv.*

increment (in-krė-mėnt) [L. *incrēmentum,* as INCREASE], *n.* Act or process of increasing; an addition, increase; amount of increase. **incremen'tal,** *a.*

incriminate (in-krim'i-nát), *v.t.* To charge with a crime; to involve (a person) in a charge.

incrustation (in-krós-tā'shún), *n.* Act or process of encrusting; a hard coating on a surface.

incubate (in'kū-bāt) [L. *cubāre,* to lie], *v.t.* To sit on (eggs) in order to hatch; to hatch by natural or artificial means; *v.i.* To brood. **incuba'tion,** *n.* **in'cubator,** *n.* An apparatus for hatching eggs artificially.

incubus (in'kū-bús) [as prec.], *n.* (*pl.* -bi) A nightmare; (*fig.*) any person or influence that oppresses, harasses, or restrains.

inculcate (in'kúl-kāt) [L. *calcāre,* to tread], *v.t.* To impress (upon the mind); to enforce, instil. **inculca'tion,** *n.*

inculpate (in'-kúl-pāt) [L. *culpa,* fault], *v.t.* To charge with participation in a crime. **inculpa'tion,** *n.*

incumbent (in-kúm'bėnt) [L. *cumbens,* lying], *a.* Lying, pressing, or weighing (upon); imposed (upon) as a duty or obligation. *n.* One in possession of an office, esp. a clergyman holding a benefice.

incunabula (in-kū-náb'ū-lá) [L., swaddling clothes], *n.pl.* (*sing.* -**lum**) Books printed before A.D. 1500.

incur (in-kėr') [L. *currere,* to run], *v.t.* To render oneself liable to (injury, punishment, etc.).

incurable (in-kūr'ábl), *a.* That cannot be cured or healed; hopeless, irreparable. *n.* One suffering from an incurable disease.

incurious (in-kūr'i-ús), *a.* Not curious or inquisitive; indifferent.

incursion (in-kėr'shún) [as INCUR], *n.* A sudden inroad, a raid. **incur'sive,** *a.*

indebted (in-det'éd) [O.F. *endetté*], *a.* Being under an obligation (to or for), owing money (to). **indebtedness,** *n.*

indecent (in-dē'sént), *a.* Unseemly; immodest, grossly indelicate, obscene. **indecency,** *n.*

indecipherable (in-dē-sī'fér-ábl), *a.* Illegible.

indecision (in-dĕ-sizh'ŭn), *n.* Want of decision; irresolution. **indecisive** (-sī'siv), *a.* Not decisive or conclusive; hesitating. **indecisively,** *adv.* **indecisiveness,** *n.*

indeclinable (in-dĕ-klī'nàbl), *a.* (*Gram.*) Not varied by inflexions.

indecorous (in-dĕ-kōr'ŭs, -dek'ō-rŭs), *a.* Violating decorum or good manners **indecorum** (in-dĕ-kōr'ŭm), *n.*

indeed (in-dēd'), *adv.* In reality, of a truth (expressing emphasis, interrogation, etc.). *int.* Expressing surprise, irony, interrogation, etc.

indefatigable (in-dĕ-făt'ĭ-gàbl) [L. *dēfatigāre,* to wear out], *a.* Not yielding to fatigue; unwearied.

indefeasible (in-dĕ-fē'zibl), *a.* Incapable of being annulled or forfeited. **indefeasibil'ity,** *n.*

indefensible (in-dĕ-fen'sibl), *a.* Incapable of being defended.

indefinable (in-dĕ-fī'nàbl), *a.* That cannot be defined.

indefinite (in-def'i-nit), *a.* Not limited or defined, not determinate; vague, uncertain; without limit; (*Gram.*) not defining or determining the things, etc., to which they apply; applied to tenses by which an action is expressed but not when it is continuous or complete. **indefinitely,** *adv.*

indelible (in-del'ibl) [L. *dēlēbilis,* as DELETE], *a.* That cannot be effaced.

indelicate (in-del'i-kàt), *a.* Wanting in delicacy; unrefined; offensive to propriety. **indelicacy,** *n.*

indemnify (in-dem'ni-fī) [L. *damnum,* loss, -FY], *v.t.* To secure from or compensate for damage, loss, etc. **indemnifica'tion,** *n.* **indem'nity,** *n.* Security against or compensation for damage, loss, or penalties; a sum paid as such compensation.

indemonstrable (in-dĕ-mon'stràbl), *a.* That cannot be demonstrated; axiomatic.

indent (in-dent') [L. *dens dentis,* tooth], *v.t.* To notch or cut into as with teeth; (*Print.*) to set in farther from the margin than the rest of the paragraph; to order by an indent. *n.* A notch in the margin of anything; an official order for stores from the commissariat; an order for goods. **inden'ture,** *n.* An agreement binding an apprentice to a master; an official voucher, certificate, register, etc.

independent (in-dĕ-pen'dènt), *a.* Not subject to the control, power, or authority of another, not subordinate; free to manage one's own affairs; affording the means of independence; self-reliant; free from bias. *n.* One who is independent; a Congregationalist. **independently,** *adv.* **independence,** *n.*

indescribable (in-dĕ-skrī'bàbl), *a.* Too fine or too bad for description.

indestructible (in-dĕ-strŭk'tibl), *a.* Incapable of being destroyed.

indeterminable (in-dĕ-tĕr'mi-nàbl), *a.* That cannot be determined or defined; that cannot be terminated.

indeterminate (in-dĕ-tĕr'mi-nàt), *a.* Indefinite, undefined, not precise.

index (in'deks) [L. *index,* a forefinger, an informer], *n.* (*pl.* **indexes,** *Math.* **indices**) That which serves to point out; the forefinger; a hand (of a watch, etc.), a pointer to anything; the contents of a book in alphabetical order with page-references; (*Alg.*) the exponent of a power. *v.t.* To provide with an index; to enter in an index.

India (in'di-à) [the *Indus,* Sansk. *sindhu,* river], *n.* A great peninsula in the south of Asia. **Indiaman,** *n.* A large ship employed in the Indian trade. **India paper:** A fine, absorbent paper, imported from China, used by engravers for taking proofs; a very thin, tough, and opaque paper. **india-rubber,** *n.* A soft, elastic substance obtained from the coagulated juice of certain tropical plants. **Indian,** *a.* Belonging to the East or West Indies, to the natives of India, or to the aborigines of America. *n.* A native of India; one of the aborigines of America or the West Indies. **Indian ink,** *n.* A dead black pigment compounded of lamp-black and glue.

indicate (in'di-kāt) [L. *dicāre,* to point out], *v.t.* To show, point out; to be a sign or token of. **indica'tion,** *n.* **indic'ative,** *a.* (*Gram.*) Applied to that mood of a verb which affirms, denies, or asks questions; denoting something not visible or obvious. *n.* The indicative mood. **in'dicator,** *n.* One who or that which indicates.

indict (in-dīt') [as INDITE], *v.t.* To charge with a crime, esp. by an indictment. **indictable,** *a.* Liable to be indicted; forming a ground of indictment.

indictment (in-dīt'mènt), *n.* The act of indicting; a formal accusation; the document embodying this.

indifferent (in-dif'ér-ènt), *a.* Impartial, neutral; unconcerned, apathetic; neither good nor bad; of little moment (to); of a barely passable quality. **indifference,** *n.*

indigenous (in-dij'é-nŭs) [L. *indigenus*], *a.* Native, not exotic; innate (to).

indigent (in'di-jènt) [L. *indigens*], *a.* In want, necessitous; in need (of), destitute (of). **indigence,** *n.*

indigested (in-di-jes'tèd) [L. *dīgestus,* digested], *a.* Not digested; not reduced to order; crude; shapeless. **indiges'tion,** *n.* Dyspepsia.

indignant (in-dig'nànt) [L. *dignus,* worthy], *a.* Inflamed with or expressive of wrath and disdain. **indignantly,** *adv.* **indigna'tion,** *n.* The feeling excited by that which is unworthy, mean, base, or unjust; anger, disdain. **indig'nity,** *n.* Undeserved contemptuous conduct; an act of incivility, an insult.

indigo (in'di-gō) [Gr. *indikon,* Indian], *n.* A blue dye obtained from the indigo-plant; a deep-blue colour.

indirect (in-di-rekt'), *a.* Deviating; not straight or rectilinear; not resulting directly or immediately from a cause; (of taxes) not paid directly, but in the form of increased prices, etc.; not fair, not open or straightforward.

indiscipline (in-dis'i-plin), *n.* Want of discipline.

indiscreet (in-dis-krēt'), *a.* Wanting in discretion; incautious. **indiscretion**

(-kresh'ŭn), *n.* Want of discretion; imprudence; indiscreet act or conduct.

indiscrete (in-dis'krēt), *a.* Not discrete, homogeneous.

indiscriminate (in-dis-krim'i-nàt), *a.* Wanting in discrimination; making no distinction; confused. **indiscriminating, indiscriminative,** *a.* **indiscrimina'tion,** *n.*

indispensable (in-dis-pen'sàbl), *a.* That cannot be dispensed with; absolutely necessary.

indispose (in-dis-pōz'), *v.t.* To make disinclined or unfavourable; to make slightly ill. **indisposed,** *a.* **indisposition** (-pŏ-zish'ŭn), *n.* Disinclination; a slight illness.

indisputable (in-dis'pŭ-tàbl), *a.* Too clear to admit of question. **indisputabil'ity,** *n.*

indissoluble (in-dis'ŏ-lūbl), *a.* Not to be dissolved or disintegrated; stable, binding.

indistinct (in-dis-tingkt'), *a.* Obscure; not readily distinguishable; faint. **indistinctive.** *a.* Not distinctive.

indistinguishable (in-dis-ting'gwish-àbl), *a.* Not distinguishable.

indite (in-dīt') [L. *indictare,* to dictate], *v.t.* To put in words, to set down in writing.

individual (in-di-vid'ū-àl) [med. L. *individuālis* (IN- (2), *dīvīdere,* to divide)], *a.* Subsisting as a single indivisible entity; particular as opp. to general; distinctive. *n.* A single person, animal, or thing; (*vulg.*) a person. **individ'ualism,** *n.* Egoism, self-interest, selfishness; idiosyncrasy, personal peculiarity; a system in which each individual works for his own ends; independent action as opp. to co-operation. **individualis'tic,** *a.* **individual'ity,** *n.*

indivisible (in-di-viz'ibl), *a.* Not divisible; that cannot be exactly divided. **indivisibly,** *adv.*

Indo- [INDIA], *comb. form.* Belonging to, or connected with India. **Indo-Germanic, Indo-European,** *a.* Pertaining to the family of languages spoken over most of Europe and over Asia as far as N. India.

indolent (in'dŏ-lènt) [late L. *indolens*], *a.* Habitually idle or lazy. **indolence,** *n.*

indomitable (in-dom'i-tàbl) [L. *domitāre,* to tame], *a.* Untameable, unconquerable. **indomitably,** *adv.*

Indonesian (in-dŏ-nē'-shiàn), *a.* Of or pertaining to the E. Indian Islands, esp. to the Malay Archipelago.

indoor (in'dòr), *a.* Being or done within doors. **indoors,** *adv.* Within a house or building.

indubitable (in-dū'bi-tàbl), *a.* Not doubtful, unquestionable.

induce (in-dūs') [L. *dūcere,* to lead], *v.t.* To lead by persuasion or reasoning, to prevail on; to bring about; (*Log.*) to derive as a deduction. **inducement,** *n.* Act of inducing; a motive, reason, incitement.

induct (in-dŭkt') [as prec.], *v.t.* To put in actual possession of an ecclesiastical benefice.

induction (in-dŭk'shŭn) [as prec.], *n.* The process of adducing facts to prove a general statement; (*Log.*) the process of inferring a law from particular

instances, dist. from deduction; (*Phys.*) the production of an electric or magnetic state by the proximity or movement of an electric body. **induc'tive,** *a.*

indulge (in-dŭlj') [L. *indulgēre*], *v.t.* To yield to the desires, humours, or wishes of; to gratify (one's weakness, etc.); to harbour, foster. *v.i.* To yield to one's desires (in). **indulgence,** *n.* Act or practice of indulging, complying to desires, etc.; a favour or privilege granted; liberality, tolerance; (*R.-C. Ch.*) a remission of the punishment still due to sin after sacramental absolution.

indurate (in'dū-rāt) [L. *durāre,* to make hard], *v.t.* To harden; to render obdurate or unfeeling. *v.i.* To become hard; to become fixed. **indura'tion,** *n.*

industrial (in-dŭs'tri-àl), *a.* Pertaining to industry.

industrious (in-dŭs'tri-ŭs) [as foll.], *a.* Characterized by industry; assiduous in business or study. **industriously,** *adv.*

industry (in'dŭs-tri) [L. *industria*], *n.* Diligence, assiduity, steady application to any business or pursuit; useful work, esp. mechanical and manufacturing pursuits as dist. from **agriculture** and commerce.

-ine, *suf.* Pertaining to, of the nature of; forming adjectives, as *crystalline, divine, marine;* forming feminine nouns, as *heroine;* abstract nouns, as *discipline, medicine;* names of alkaloids and basic substances, as *cocaine, morphine.*

inebriate (in-ē'bri-āt) [L. *ebrius,* drunk], *v.t.* To make drunk. *a.* (-àt) Intoxicated. *n.* An habitual drunkard. **inebriant,** *a.* **inebriety** (in-ē-brī'ē-ti), *n.*

ineffable (in-ef'àbl) [L. *effāri,* ɪʜ-, *fāri,* to speak], *a.* Unutterable, beyond expression. **ineffably,** *adv.*

ineffaceable (in-ē-fā'sàbl), *a.* That cannot be rubbed out.

ineffective (in-ē-fek'tiv), *a.* Not producing any or the desired effect; inefficient. **ineffectively,** *adv.*

ineffectual (in-ē-fek'tū-àl), *a.* Not producing any effect; powerless.

inefficacious (in-ef-i-kā'shŭs), *a.* Not efficacious; producing no result. **inef'ficacy,** *n.*

inefficient (in-ē-fish'ènt), *a.* Wanting in ability or capacity. **inefficiency,** *n.*

inelegant (in-el'ē-gànt), *a.* Wanting in grace, polish, refinement, etc.

ineligible (in-el'i-jibl), *a.* Not eligible, not capable of being selected. **ineligibil'ity,** *n.*

inept (in-ept') [L. *aptus,* apt], *a.* Not fit or suitable; silly, absurd. **ineptitude, ineptness,** *n.* **ineptly,** *adv.*

inequality (in-ē-kwol'i-ti), *n.* Want of equality; diversity, irregularity, variability, disparity; unfairness, partiality.

inequitable (in-ek'wi-tàbl), *a.* Not fair or just.

ineradicable (in-ē-rǎd'i-kàbl), *a.* That cannot be eradicated.

inert (in-ĕrt') [L. *ars,* art], *a.* Destitute of inherent power; motionless, sluggish; indisposed to move or act; destitute of active chemical powers. **inertia** (in-ĕr'shà), *n.* That property of a body by which it persists in an existing state of rest or of uniform motion, unless an external force changes that state.

inestimable (in-es'ti-mȧbl), *a.* That cannot be estimated; too valuable to be rated.

inevitable (in-ev'i-tȧbl) [L. *ēvītāre*, to avoid], *a.* That cannot be avoided or prevented. **inevitableness**, *n.*

inexact (in-ĕg-zȧkt'), *a.* Not precisely accurate. **inexactitude**, *n.*

inexcusable (in-ĕks-kū'zȧbl), *a.* Not to be excused or justified. **inexcusably**, *adv.*

inexhaustible (in-ĕg-zaws'tibl), *a.* That cannot be exhausted; unfailing.

inexorable (in-ek'sŏr-ȧbl) [L. *ōrāre*, to pray], *a.* Incapable of being persuaded; unbending, relentless.

inexpedient (in-ĕk-spē'di-ĕnt), *a.* Not expedient; unadvisable. **inexpedience, -diency**, *n.*

inexpensive (in-ĕk-spen'siv), *a.* Not expensive; cheap.

inexperienced (in-ĕk-spēr'i-ĕnst), *n.* Not having knowledge gained by experience.

inexpert (in-ĕk-spĕrt'), *a.* Not expert, unskilful. **inexpertly**, *adv.*

inexpiable (in-ek'spi-ȧbl), *a.* That cannot be atoned for.

inexplicable (in-ek'spli-kȧbl), *a.* Not capable of being made plain or intelligible; not to be explained.

inexpressible (in-ĕk-spres'ibl), *a.* Incapable of being expressed or described; unutterable, unspeakable. **inexpressive**, *a.*

inextinguishable (in-ĕk-sting'gwish-ȧbl), *a.* Incapable of being extinguished.

inextricable (in-ek'stri-kȧbl), *a.* That cannot be disentangled.

infallible (in-fȧl'ibl), *a.* Exempt from liability to error or failure. **infallibil'ity**, *n.* **infallibly**, *adv.*

infamous (in'fȧ-mŭs) [L. *infāmis*], *a.* Having an ill reputation; notoriously vile; branded with infamy by conviction for a crime. **infamously**, *adv.* **infamy**, *n.* Total loss of reputation; public reproach.

infant (in'fȧnt) [O.F. *enfant*, L. *infans* (IN- (2), *fans*, speaking)], *n.* A child during its earliest years; (*Law*) a person under twenty-one, a minor. *a.* Young, tender, pertaining to infants. **infancy**, *n.*

infanticide (in-fȧn'ti-sīd), *n.* Murder of a new-born infant; the murderer of an infant.

infantile (in'fȧn-tīl), *a.* Pertaining to infants or infancy, childish.

infantry (in'fȧn-tri) [It. *infanteria*, from *infante*, a youth], *n.* (*collect.*) Footsoldiers. **infantryman**, *n.* A soldier in an infantry regiment.

infatuate (in-fȧt'ū-āt) [L. *infatuātus*], *v.t.* To deprive of judgment, to affect with folly; to inspire with an extravagant passion. **infatua'tion**, *n.*

infect (in-fekt') [L. *infectus*, tainted], *v.t.* To act upon by contagion or infection; to taint with disease; to corrupt; to affect (with depravity, noxious opinions, etc.). **infection**, *n.* **infectious**, *a.*

infer (in-fĕr') [L. *ferre*, to bear, bring], *v.t.* To deduce as a fact, consequence, or result; to conclude; to imply. *v.i.* To draw inferences. **inferable**, *a.* **in'ference**, *n.*

inferior (in-fēr'i-ŏr) [L., comp. of *inferus*,

low], *a.* Lower in place, rank, quality, etc.; subordinate. *n.* One who is inferior to another; a subordinate. **inferior'ity**, *n.* inferiority complex, *n.* (*Psych.*) A suppressed sense of inferiority which compensates itself by assertiveness, etc.

infernal (in-fĕr'nȧl) [L. *infernālis*, as prec.], *a.* Pertaining to hell or the lower regions; hellish, diabolical, confounded.

infertile (in-fĕr'til), *a.* Not fertile, unfruitful. **infertil'ity**, *n.*

infest (in-fest') [L. *infestus*, hostile], *v.t.* To overrun, to haunt, so as to harass.

infidel (in'fi-dĕl) [L. *fidēlis*, faith], *a.* Disbelieving in the faith of the person using the epithet; rejecting the Christian religion; agnostic, sceptical; also non-Jewish or non-Mohammedan. *n.* One who disbelieves in a given form of faith. **infidelity** (-del'i-ti), *n.* Disbelief in Christianity; breach of trust, disloyalty.

infinite (in'fi-nit), *a.* Having no limits, endless; indefinitely great or numerous. *n.* Infinite space, infinity; (*fig.*) a vast or infinite amount; the infinite Being, God. **infinitesimal** (-tes'i-mȧl), *a.* Infinitely small; insignificant, less than any assignable quantity. **infin'itude**, *n.* **infin'ity**, *n.*

infinitive (in-fin'i-tiv), *a.* (*Gram.*) Unlimited, applied to that mood of a verb which expresses the action without regard to any person, etc. *n.* The infinitive mood.

infirm (in-fĕrm'), *a.* Lacking health through age or disease; weak-minded, irresolute. **infirmary**, *n.* A place in which the sick or injured are lodged and nursed. **infirmity**, *n.*

inflame (in-flām'), *v.t.* To kindle; to cause inflammation in, to render morbidly hot; to excite, stir up passion, etc.; to intensify, aggravate. *v.i.* To burst into a blaze; to become inflamed or excited. **inflammable** (-flām'ȧbl), *a.* That may be easily set on fire; readily enkindled.

inflate (in-flāt') [L. *flātus*, blown], *v.t.* To distend with air; to puff out; to expand or raise (prices, reputation, etc.) artificially. **inflated**, *a.* Distended with air; bombastic, turgid; expanded or raised artificially. **infla'tion**, *n.*

inflect (in-flekt') [L. *flectere*, to bend], *v.t.* To bend; to turn from a straight course; to modulate (as the voice); to change the terminations of (words), to decline, conjugate. **inflective**, *a.* Capable of bending; (*Gram.*) inflexional. **inflexed** (-flekst'), *a.* Bent, curved. **inflexible, a** Incapable of being bent; that will not yield to entreaties; firm of will or purpose. **inflexibil'ity**, *n.* **inflexibly**, *adv.* **inflexion** (in-flek'shŭn), *n.* Act of inflecting; state of being inflected; modulation of the voice; variation of the termination of words in declension and conjugation. **inflexional**, *a.*

inflict (in-flikt') [L. *inflictus*, p.p. of *infligere* (IN- (1), L. *flictus*, dashed)], *v.t.* To impose upon as a penalty or punishment; to cause to suffer (something). **infliction** (-flik'shŭn), *n.* The act of inflicting; a punishment inflicted; an annoyance.

inflorescence (in-flôr-es'ens) [L. *inflorescere*], *n.* (*Bot.*) The act of flowering; the arrangement of flowers upon a stem.

influence (in'flŭ-ĕns) [L. *fluere*, to flow], *n.* Power to move, direct, or control, ascendency (over); energy affecting other bodies, as electric and magnetic induction; a person, thing, etc., exercising moral power (over). *v.t.* To exercise influence upon; to modify (motives, etc.) to any end; to bias, sway. **influential** (-en'shăl), *a.*

influenza (in-flŭ-ĕn'ză) [It., as INFLUENCE], *n.* A severe and epidemic catarrh, contagious and infective.

influx (in'flŭks) [as INFLUENCE], *n.* A flowing (into).

inform (in-frôm') [L. *formāre*, to form], *v.t.* To imbue (with feeling, vitality, etc.); to communicate knowledge to, to give form to. *v.i.* To take form or shape; to disclose facts, to bring a charge (against). **informant**, *n.* **informa'tion**, *n.* The act of communicating knowledge; intelligence communicated; notice; a complaint presented as a preliminary to criminal proceedings. **informer**, *n.* One who informs, esp. one who lays an information respecting a breach of the law.

informal (in-fôr'măl), *a.* Not in accordance with proper or customary forms; without formality. **informal'ity**, *n.*

infra- [L., below], *pref.* Below, beneath. **infra-red rays**, *n.pl.* (*Phys.*) Invisible radiations beyond the limit of the visible spectrum at the red end.

infrangible (in-frăn'jibl), *a.* That cannot be broken.

infrequent (in-frē'kwĕnt), *a.* Rare, unusual.

infringe (in-frinj') [L. *frangere*, to break], *v.t.* To break (a law, contract, etc.); to violate, neglect to obey. *v.i.* To intrude (upon). **infringement**, *n.*

infuriate (in-fū'ri-āt) [L. *furia*, FURY], *v.t.* To provoke to fury.

infuse (in-fūz') [L. *fūsus*, poured], *v.t.* To pour (into); to inculcate, implant; to obtain an extract by steeping. **infu'sion**, *n.* Act of infusing; inculcation.

-ing, *suf.* Forming verbal nouns, as *cleansing, hunting*; denoting occupations, as *bricklaying, soldiering*; denoting the results, material used, etc., as *painting, scaffolding, washing*; used as a gerund, as *my having written*; as participial adjectives, as *charming, fleeting*; forming diminutives, as *farthing, lording.*

ingathering (in-găth'ĕr-ing), *n.* The act of gathering.

ingenious (in-jē'ni-ŭs) [L. *ingeniōsus*, as GENIUS], *a.* Possessed of natural capacity; skilful, clever in contriving, etc.; curious in design or contrivance. **ingenu'ity**, *n.*

ingenuous (in-jen'ū-ŭs) [L. *ingenuus*, frank], *a.* Open, candid. **ingenuousness**, *n.*

ingest (in-jest') [L. *gerere*, to carry], *v.t.* To take food into the stomach.

ingle (ing'gĕl) [?], *n.* A fire on the hearth. **ingle-nook**, *n.* A chimney-corner.

inglorious (in-glôr'i-ŭs), *a.* Not glorious; shameful.

ingoing (in'gō-ing), *a.* Going in, entering. *n.* Entrance.

ingot (ing'gŏt) [?], *n.* A mass of cast metal from the crucible.

ingrate (in-grāt') [L. *grātus*, pleasing], *n.* An ungrateful person.

ingratiate (in-grā'shi-āt) [L. *in grātiam*, into favour], *v.t.* To insinuate oneself into goodwill with another.

ingratitude (in-grăt'i-tūd), *n.* Want of gratitude.

ingredient (in-grē'di-ĕnt) [L. *ingrediens*, walking in (IN- (1), *gradī*, to walk)], *n.* That which enters into a compound as an element, a component part.

ingress (in'gres) [as prec.], *n.* The act of entering, entrance; power or liberty of entrance.

inguinal (ing'gwi-năl) [L. *inguen*, the groin], *n.* Pertaining to the groin.

ingurgitate (in-gĕr'ji-tāt) [L. *gurges*, a whirlpool], *v.t.* To swallow down greedily; to engulf. *v.i.* To gorge.

inhabit (in-hăb'it) [L. *habitāre*, to dwell], *v.t.* To dwell in; to occupy as a place of settled residence. **inhabitable**, *a.* Fit for habitation. **inhabitant**, *n.*

inhale (in-hāl') [L. *hālāre*, to breathe], *v.t.* To breathe in, draw into the lungs. **inhala'tion**, *n.* **inhaler**, *n.* One who inhales; a respirator.

inharmonious (in-har-mō'ni-ŭs), *a.* Not harmonious; unmusical.

inhere (in-hēr') [L. *hærēre*, to stick], *v.i.* To belong or exist (in) as an attribute; to be an essential or necessary part (in). **inherence, -ency**, *n.* inherent, *a.* Permanently belonging (in or to); inseparable; innate. **inherently**, *adv.*

inherit (in-her'it) [O.F. *enheriter*], *v.t.* To receive by legal succession; to derive from one's ancestors as part of one's nature. *v.i.* To take or come into possession as an heir. **inheritance**, *n.* **inheritor, inheritress, -trix**, *n.*

inhibit (in-hib'it) [L. *habēre*, to have, hold], *v.t.* To restrain, hinder, put a stop to (an action, nervous process, etc.); to forbid, interdict; to prohibit (a priest) from exercising his office. **inhibi'tion**, *n.* Act of inhibiting; (*Psych.*) habitual shrinking from some action which is instinctively thought of as a thing forbidden.

inhospitable (in-hos'pi-tăbl), *a.* Not inclined to show hospitality; affording no shelter, desolate.

inhuman (in-hū'măn), *a.* Destitute of kindness towards one's fellow-creatures; brutal, unfeeling. **inhuman'ity**, *n.*

inimical (i-nim'i-kăl) [L. *amicus*, friend], *a.* Having the disposition of an enemy; adverse.

inimitable (i-nim'i-tăbl), *a.* That cannot be imitated.

iniquity (i-nik'wi-ti) [L. *æquus*, just], *n.* Want of equity, gross injustice; wickedness, crime. **iniquitous**, *a.*

initial (i-nish'ăl) [L. *initiālis*], *a.* Beginning; placed at or pertaining to the beginning. *n.* The first letter of a word; (*pl.*) the first letters of a Christian name and surname. *v.t.* To mark with one's initials. **initially**, *adv.* At the beginning.

initiate (i-nish'i-āt), *v.t.* To begin, originate; to instruct in the rudiments;

to admit (into a society, etc.). *n.* One who is newly initiated. **initia'tion**, *n.* **initiatory**, *a.* **initiative**, *n.* The first move; ability or right to take the lead.

inject (in-jekt') [L. *jectus*, thrown], *v.t.* To throw or force (into); to introduce (as a liquid) by mechanical means. **injec'tion**, *n.* Act of injecting; that which is injected.

injudicious (in-jū-dish'ūs),*a.* Not judicious; rash, hasty; done without judgment. **injudicial**, *a.* Not judicial.

injunction (in-jŭngk'shŭn) [as ENJOIN], *n.* Act of enjoining; that which is enjoined; a writ whereby a party is required to do or refrain from doing certain acts.

injure (in'jŭr) [from next], *v.t.* To do wrong or harm to; to damage; to slander; to impair. **injur'ious,** *a.*

injury (in'jū-ri) [L. *jūs jūris*, justice], *n.* A wrong; that which occasions loss, detriment, etc.; hurt, harm.

injustice (in-jŭs'tis), *n.* Quality of being unjust, lack of right, unfairness; violation of justice, a wrong.

ink (ingk) [O.F. *enque*, Gr. *enkaustikos*, burnt in], *n.* A coloured (usu. black) liquid or viscous material used in writing or printing; the dark fluid exuded by cuttle-fish. *v.t.* To cover with ink (as type, etc.); to mark (in or over) with ink. **inkhorn**, *n.* A small vessel to hold ink. *a.* Pedantic, high-sounding. **inkstand**, *n.* A stand for one or more inkpots, usu. with a place for pens. **inky**, *a.*

inkling (ingk'ling) [?], *n.* A hint, whisper, intimation; a mere suspicion (of).

inland (in'lånd), *a.* Remote from the sea; carried on within a country, not foreign. *adv.* In or towards the interior of a country. *n.* The interior of a country.

inlay (in-lā'), *v.t.* (*past and p.p.* -laid). To decorate by inserting different materials into a ground-work; to fasten a print, etc., evenly (into a page or sheet). *n.* (in'lā). Material inlaid or prepared for inlaying. **inlayer**, *n.* **inlaying**, *n.* Inlaid work.

inlet (in'lĕt), *n.* A means of entrance, admission; a small arm of the sea. *a.* Let in.

inly (in'li), *adv.* Inwardly, internally; closely, deeply.

inmate (in'māt), *n.* One who dwells with another; an occupant (of).

inmost (in'mōst), *a.* Remotest from the surface; most inward.

inn (in) [A.-S.], *n.* A public house with lodging and entertainment for travellers. **innkeeper**, *n.* **Inns of Court:** Four corporate societies in London (*Inner Temple, Middle Temple, Lincoln's Inn, Gray's Inn*) which have the exclusive right of admitting persons to practise at the English bar.

innate (i-nāt') [L. *nātus*, born], *a.* Inborn, natural; not acquired.

inner (in'ér) [A.-S.], *a.* Farther in or nearer the centre; internal; spiritual; hidden, esoteric. *n.* That part of a target immediately outside the bull's eye; a shot striking this. **innermost**, *a.*

innervate (i-nĕr'vāt), *v.t.* To give a nerve

impulse to; to supply with nerves. **innerva'tion**, *n.*

innings (in'ingz), *n.* (*Cricket*) The turn for batting of a player or a side.

innocent (in'ó-sènt) [L. *nocens*, hurting], *a.* Guiltless (of); sinless; pure, unspotted, guileless; (*colloq.*) without. *n.* A child; an idiot. **innocence**, *n.*

innocuous (in-ok'ū-ūs) [L. *nocuus*, hurtful], *a.* Having no injurious qualities, harmless. **innocuously**, *adv.*

innominate (in-nom'i-nāt) [L. *innominatus*], *a.* Not named, nameless.

innovate (in'ō-vāt) [L. *novātus*, made new], *v.i.* To introduce alterations (in anything); to put forward novelties. *v.t.* To alter or change, by new introductions. **innova'tion**, *n.* **in'novator**, *n.*

innuendo (in-ū-en'dō) [L. *innuendō*, by way of intimation], *n.* (*pl.* -oes) An indirect hint; an insinuation.

innumerable (i-nū'mér-ábl), *a.* Countless; indefinitely numerous **innumerably**, *adv.*

inobservant (in-ŏb-zĕr'vánt), *a.* Not observant; heedless. **inobservance**, *n.* Want of observance (of a law, etc.).

inoculate (in-ok'ū-lāt) [L. *inoculātus*, engrafted], *v.t.* To communicate a disease by introduction of infectious matter, in order to induce a mild form of the disease and render the subject immune against further attack; (*fig.*) to imbue (with). **inocula'tion**, *n.*

inodorous (in-ō'dòr-ūs), *a.* Odourless.

inoffensive (in-ō-fen'siv), *a.* Giving no offence; unobjectionable, harmless. **inoffensively**, *adv.* **inoffensiveness**, *n.*

inoperative (in-op'ér-à-tiv), *a.* Producing no result.

inopportune (in-op'ór-tūn), *a.* Not opportune; unseasonable.

inordinate (in-ôr'di-nåt) [L. *ordinātus*, ordered], *a.* Irregular, disorderly; passing all bounds.

inorganic (in-ôr-gàn'ik), *a.* Not having the organs of life; not having organic structure.

input (in'put), *n.* The amount of material or energy put into a machine.

inquest (in'kwest) [O.F. *enqueste*, as INQUIRE], *n.* A judicial inquiry into a matter, usu. before a jury, esp. a coroner's inquiry into a death.

inquietude (in-kwī'è-tūd), *n.* Restlessness, uneasiness.

inquire (in-kwīr') [L. *quærere*, to seek], *v.i.* To ask questions (of); to seek information by asking questions; to investigate (into). *v.t.* To ask information about; to search out, to find out. **inquirer**, *n.* **inquiring**, *a.* Given to inquiry; inquisitive. **inquiry**, *n.* Act of inquiring; a question, interrogation; a searching for truth, information, or knowledge; a judicial investigation.

inquisition (in-kwi-zish'ŭn) [L. *inquisītio*, as INQUIRE], *n.* Investigation; a judicial inquiry, an inquest; a tribunal in the R.-C. Church for inquiring into offences against the canon law, the Holy Office. **inquisi'tional**, *a.* **inquis'itive**, *a.* Unduly given to asking questions; prying, curious. **inquisitor**, *n.* One who makes inquisition officially; a functionary of the Inquisition. inquisitor'ial, a.

inroad (in'rōd), n. A hostile incursion; a desultory invasion; (fig.) an encroachment.

inrush (in'rŭsh), n. An irruption.

insalubrious (in-sal-ū'bri-ŭs), a. Not salubrious, unhealthy. insalubrity, n.

insane (in-sān'), a. Deranged in mind, mad; exceedingly rash. insanely, adv. insanity (in-săn'i-ti), n.

insanitary (in-săn'i-tăr-i), a. Not sanitary.

insatiable (in-sā'shábl), a. That cannot be satisfied; immoderately greedy (of). insatiabil'ity, n. insatiate, a. Never satisfied.

inscribe (in-skrīb') [L. scrībere, to write], v.t. To write, carve, or engrave (on stone, paper, etc.); to dedicate (as a book to a friend); to enter on a list, etc., to register names of shareholders; (Geom.) to delineate (a figure) within another so that it touches the boundaries of the latter. inscrip'tion, n.

inscrutable (in-skroo'tábl) [L. scrūtāri, to search], a. Incapable of being understood; unfathomable.

insect (in'sekt) [L. secāre, to cut], n. One of a class of articulate, usually winged, animals, with three pairs of legs, and divided into three distinct segments, head, thorax, and abdomen, as flies. insect-powder, n. A powder for destroying fleas, bugs, etc.

insecure (in-sē-kūr'), a. Not safe: not effectually guarded; apprehensive of danger. insecurity, n.

insemination (in-sem-i-nā'shŭn) [L. semināre, to sow], n. Sowing, planting. artificial insemination, n. Artificial impregnation with selected semen.

insensate (in-sen'sát) [L. sensus, sense], a. Destitute of sense, unconscious; wanting in sensibility, unfeeling; foolish, mad.

insensible (in-sen'sibl), a. That cannot be perceived; destitute of the power of feeling or perceiving, unconscious; indifferent, heedless (of, how, etc.); callous, apathetic. insensibil'ity, n. Lack of feeling, emotion, or passion; insusceptibility or indifference (to). insensibly, adv. Imperceptibly, gradually. insensitive, a.

inseparable (in-sep'ăr-ábl), a. Incapable of being separated. n. (usu. pl.) Things which cannot be separated; persons who are constantly together. inseparably, adv.

insert (in-sĕrt') [L. sertus, joined], v.t. To set or place (in, amongst, etc.); to introduce (into). inser'tion, n. Act of inserting; that which is inserted; lace, embroidery, etc., inserted in fancy work.

inset (in-set'), v.t. To set or fix (in). n. (in'set) That which is set or fixed in; an insertion.

inshore (in-shôr'), a. or adv. On, near, or towards the shore.

inside (in'sīd), a. Situated within; interior. adv. (in-sīd') In or into the interior, within. prep. (in-sīd') Within, on the inner side of, into. n. (in'sīd) The interior part; the inner side, surface, etc. (of); (in-sīd') the contents.

insidious (in-sīd'i-ŭs) [L. insidiōsus], a.

Treacherous, sly; working secretly; intended to deceive or betray.

insight (in'sīt), n. Power of observation; discernment; penetration.

insignia (in-sig'ni-á) [L.], n.pl. Badges of office or honour; distinguishing marks.

insignificant (in-sig-nif'i-kánt), a. Trivial; contemptible; without meaning. insignificance, n.

insincere (in-sin-sēr'), a. Not sincere; dissembling; hypocritical. insincer'ity, n.

insinuate (in-sin'ū-āt) [L. sinuāre, to wind], v.t. To introduce (into favour, etc.) by gradual and artful means; to indicate indirectly or obliquely, to hint or suggest. v.i. To make way (into) by indirect means; to make an insinuation; to wheedle. insinua'tion, n.

insipid (in-sip'id) [L. sapidus, well-tasting], a. Tasteless; wanting in animation, dull. insipid'ity, n.

insist (in-sist') [L. sistere, to set], v.i. To dilate (on); to be emphatic, positive, or persistent (on). insistence, -ency, n. insistent, a.

insobriety (in-sō-brī'é-ti), n. Want of sobriety; intemperance (usu. in drinking).

insolent (in'sō-lént) [L. solens, being wont], a. Showing overbearing contempt; insulting. insolence, n.

insoluble (in-sol'ŭbl), a. That cannot be dissolved, or solved; inexplicable. insolubil'ity, n.

insolvable (in-sol'vábl), a. That cannot be solved or explained.

insolvent (in-sol'vént), a. Not able to discharge all debts. n. One unable to pay his debts. insolvency, n.

insomnia (in-som'ni-á) [L. somnis, sleep], n. Sleeplessness.

insomuch (in-sō-mŭch'), adv. So, to such a degree, in such wise (that).

insouciant (in-soo'si-ong) [F.], a. Careless, unconcerned.

inspect (in-spekt') [L. inspectāre], v.t. To look closely into; to examine officially. inspec'tion, n. inspector, n.

inspire (in-spīr') [L. spirāre, to breathe], v.t. To breathe or take into the lungs, to breathe into; to instil (ideas, etc.) into, esp. by supernatural agency; to imbue or animate (with). v.i. To take air into the lungs. inspiration (-spi-rā'shŭn), n. Act of drawing air into the lungs; act of infusing feelings, ideas, etc.; supernatural influence, esp. that exerted by the Holy Spirit on certain teachers so as to impart a divine element to their utterances; the feelings, ideas, or other influences imparted by divine agency; an inspiring idea. inspir'atory, a. inspired, a. Inhaled, infused; imparted, actuated or produced by or as by supernatural agency.

inspirit (in-spir'it), v.t. To infuse spirit or animation into.

inspissate (in-spis'āt) [L. spissus, thick], v.t. To thicken, to bring to a greater consistence by boiling or evaporation. a. (-sát) Thickened.

instability (in-stá-bil'i-ti), n. Want of stability or firmness; inconstancy.

install (in-stawl') [L. stallum, stall], v.t. To induct by placing (in an office, dignity, etc.) with customary ceremonies; to establish in an office, etc.; to put (apparatus, etc.) in position. **installa′-tion,** *n.* Act of installing; a complete plant or set of apparatus, machinery, etc.

instalment (in-stawl′mĕnt) [obs. verb *install,* to arrange or fix, as a payment], *n.* A part of a sum due paid at successive periods; a part (of anything) supplied at different times.

instance (in′stăns) [as foll.], *n.* An example, precedent; (*Law*) a process or suit. *v.t.* To bring forward as an instance or example. **at the instance of:** At the suggestion or desire of. **in the first instance:** In the first place.

instant (in′stănt) [L. *stāre,* to stand], *a.* Pressing, urgent, immediate; present, still going on; of the current month. *n.* A particular point of time; a moment. **instantaneous** (-tă′nĕ-ŭs), *a.* Happening in an instant; relating to a particular instant. **instantly,** *adv.* Immediately.

instead (in-sted′), *adv.* In the place or stead of; as a substitute.

instep (in′step), *n.* The arched upper side of the foot, near the ankle.

instigate (in′sti-gāt) [L. *instigātus, -gāre*], *v.t.* To incite, to urge on; to provoke or bring about (an evil action). **instiga′tion,** *n.* **in′stigator,** *n.*

instil (in-stil′) [L. *stillāre,* to drop], *v.t.* To pour by drops (into); to insinuate gradually (into the mind of a person).

instinct (in′stingkt) [L. *instinctus*], *n.* A natural impulse, esp. in the lower animals; an innate or intuitive tendency or aptitude; intuition, unreasoning perception. *a.* (in-stingkt′) Impelled from within; imbued (with). **instinc′tive,** *a.*

institute (in′sti-tūt) [L. *statuere,* to place], *v.t.* To set up, establish, originate; to appoint (to), esp. to a benefice. *n.* A society established for the furtherance of some object (usu. literary or scientific); the building in which this meets; an established law or principle; (*pl.*) a book of elements or principles, esp. of jurisprudence or medicine. **institu′tion,** *n.*

instruct (in-strŭkt′) [L. *instructus*], *v.t.* To teach, to educate (in a subject); to inform; to furnish with orders. **instruc′-tion,** *n.* Act of instructing: teaching. education; (*pl.*) directions, orders, injunctions. **instructive,** *a.* Conveying instruction. **instructively,** *adv.* **in-structor, -tress,** *n.*

instrument (in′strŭ-mĕnt) [L. *instrū-mentum*], *n.* That by means of which work is done or an object effected; a tool; a mechanical contrivance for producing music; a document giving formal expression to an act; (*fig.*) an agent. **instrumen′tal,** *a.* Serving as means (to an end or in some act); pertaining to the instrument used; (*Gram.*) denoting the means, as certain cases in Sanskrit, etc. **instrumentalist,** *n.* (*Mus.*) One who plays an instrument. **instru-mental′ity,** *n.* **instrumentally,** *adv.*

insubordinate (in-sŭ-bŏr′di-năt), *a.* Not submissive; disobedient, disorderly. **in-subordina′tion,** *n.*

insufferable (in-sŭf′ĕr-àbl), *a.* Not to be endured; intolerable.

insufficient (in-sŭ-fish′ĕnt), *a.* Not sufficient; deficient, inadequate. **insufficiency,** *n.*

insufflate (in′sŭ-flāt) [L. *insufflare,* to blow in], *v.t.* To blow air, etc., into an opening, the lungs, etc.

insular (in-sū-làr) [L. *insula,* island], *a.* Pertaining to or of the nature of an island; narrow, contracted (in outlook), like the inhabitants of an island. **insular′ity,** *n.*

insulate (in′sū-lāt) [L. *insulātus,* made like an island], *v.t.* To make into an island; to isolate; to separate by a non-conductor, so as to prevent the passage of electricity or heat. **insula′tion,** *n.* **in′sulator,** *n.*

insulin (in′sū-lin) [L. *insula,* an island], *n.* (*Med.*) An extract from animal pancreas used in the treatment of diabetes.

insult (in-sŭlt′) [L. *insultāre*], *v.t.* To treat with gross indignity or insolence; to affront. *n.* (in′-) An affront, an indignity; an insolent act or speech. **insultingly,** *adv.*

insuperable (in-sū′pĕr-àbl), *a.* Insurmountable.

insupportable (in-sŭ-pōr′tàbl), *a.* Intolerable.

insure (in-shoor′) [var. of ENSURE], *v.t.* To contract for the payment of (a specified sum) in the event of loss, injury, etc. (of property, life, etc.); to ensure. *v.i.* To take out an insurance policy. **insur-able,** *a.* **insurance,** *n.* The act of insuring against damage or loss.

insurgent (in-sĕr′jĕnt) [L. *surgens,* rising], *a.* Rising up against the government, rebellious; (of waves) surging in. *n.* One who rises up against established authority; a rebel.

insurmountable (in-sŭr-moun′tàbl), *a.* That cannot be passed over or overcome.

insurrection (in-sŭ-rek′shŭn) [L. *insur-rectio*], *n.* The act of rebelling; rebellion in the initial stage. **insurrectional, -tionary,** *a.*

insusceptible (in-sŭ-sep′tibl), *a.* Incapable of being moved by any feeling or impression. **insusceptibil′ity,** *n.*

intact (in-tăkt′) [L. *tactus,* touched], *a.* Untouched; unimpaired; entire.

intaglio (in-ta′lyō [It.], *n.* (*pl.* -lios) A gem with a figure cut or engraved into it.

intangible (in-tăn′jibl), *a.* Imperceptible to the touch, impalpable; not to be grasped mentally; unfounded. **intangi-bil′ity,** *n.*

integer (in′tĕ-jĕr) [L.], *n.* A whole, esp. a whole number as dist. from a fraction. **integral,** *a.* Whole, complete; an essential part of a whole; (*Math.*) pertaining to an integer or to integration. *n.* A whole, a total, an integer.

integrity (in-teg′ri-ti) [L. *integritātas,* wholeness], *n.* Entireness; soundness; genuine, unadulterated state; probity.

integument (in-teg′ū-mĕnt) [L. *tegere,* to cover], *n.* A natural covering; the skin; a husk, rind, etc.

intellect (in′tĕ-lekt) [L. *intellectus,* as INTELLIGENT], *n.* The faculty by which the mind receives and comprehends; the understanding; the philosophic mind; intellectual people collectively. **intel-lec′tual**, *a.* Possessing intellect in a high degree; pertaining to, appealing to, or perceived by the intellect. *n.* An intellectual person; (*pl.*) the most en-lightened people (in a country, etc.).

intelligence (in-tel′i-jĕns), *n.* Exercise of the understanding; intellectual power; capacity for the higher functions of the intellect; quickness of intellect; news, information; an incorporeal being re-garded as pure intellect.

intelligent (in-tel′i-jĕnt) [L. *intelligens*, understanding (INTER-, *legere*, to choose)], *a.* Endowed with understanding; saga-cious, clever, quick.

intelligentsia (in-tel-i-jen′si-à), *n.* (*iron.*) People who claim or assume special culture or enlightenment.

intelligible (in-tel′i-jibl), *a.* Capable of being understood; plain, clear.

intemperate (in-tem′pĕr-àt), *a.* Not exercising due moderation or self-restraint; addicted to excessive indul-gence in alcohol; exceeding proper bounds; inclement. **intemperance**, *n.* Want of self-restraint.

intend (in-tend′) [L. *tendere*, to stretch], *v.t.* To design, purpose; to signify, mean; to destine (for); to have a certain intention. **intendant**, *n.* A superinten-dent or manager. **intendancy**, *n.* **intended**, *n.* (*colloq.*) An affianced lover.

intense (in-tens′) [as prec.], *a.* Strained, forced; extreme in degree; severe, immoderate, ardent, eager; strongly emotional. **intensely**, *adv.* **intensify**, *v.t.* To render more intense; (*Phot.*) to increase the density of (a negative). *v.i.* To become more intense. **intensity**, *n.* **intensive**, *a.* Concentrated, thorough (opp. to extensive); conducive to high productiveness within a narrow area.

intent (in-tent′), *a.* Having the mind bent on an object; sedulously applied (on); resolved, earnest. *n.* Design, purpose, intention; meaning, drift. **intention**, *n.* Determination to act in some particular manner; purpose; ultimate aim or object; (*pl., colloq.*) designs with regard to marriage. **intentional**, *a.* **intently**, *adv.*

inter (in-tĕr′) [L. *terra*, earth], *v.t.* (*past* and *p.p.* **interred**) To bury; (*fig.*) to put out of sight. **interment**, *n.*

inter- [L.], *pref.* Between, among; with, into, or upon each other; as *intercede*, *international*, *interwoven*. **interact** (in′tĕr-ăkt), *n.* The interval between two acts of a play; an interlude. (in-ter-akt′) *v.i.* To act reciprocally.

intercalary (in-tĕr′kà-làr-i) [L. *calāre*, to proclaim], *a.* Inserted between others, as a day in the calendar to make this correspond with the solar year; con-taining such an addition (of a year); interpolated. **intercalate**, *v.t.* To insert amongst others; to interpolate.

intercede (in-tĕr-sēd′) [L. *cēdere*, to go], *v.i.* To plead (with someone) in favour of another; to mediate. **interceder**, *n.*

intercept (in-tĕr-sept′) [L. *interceptus*], *v.t.* To stop, take, or seize by the way; to obstruct, shut off. **intercep′tion**, *n.*

intercession (in-tĕr-sesh′ùn) [as INTER-CEDE], *n.* The act of interceding; a prayer for others. **intercessor**, *n.* A mediator; one who administers a bishop-ric during a vacancy. **interces′sory**, *a.*

interchange (in-tĕr-chānj′), *v.t.* To ex-change with each other; to put each in the place of the other. *v.i.* To alternate. *n.* Reciprocal exchange; alternation. **interchangeable**, *a.* **interchangeably**, *adv.*

intercostal (in-tĕr-kos′tàl), *a.* Situated between the ribs.

intercourse (in′tĕr-kôrs), *n.* Reciprocal dealings, association, communication, etc., between persons, nations, etc.; coition.

interdenominational (in-tĕr-dè-nom-i-nā′-shŏnàl), *a.* Existing or carried on be-tween different denominations.

interdict (in′tĕr-dikt) [L. *dictus*, said], *n.* A prohibitory decree; (*R.-C. Ch.*) a sentence debarring places or persons from ecclesiastical functions and privi-leges. *v.t.* (-dikt′) To forbid, prohibit; (*R.-C. Ch.*) to lay under an interdict. **interdiction**. *n.* **interdictory**, *a.*

interest (in′-ter-ĕst) [L. *interesse*, to con-cern], *n.* Personal concern, sympathy; participation in benefits, profits, etc.; advantage, behoof; proprietary right, a share, a portion or stake (in); (*collect.*) those having a concern in a particular business, etc.; influence over others; payment for the use of borrowed money or on a debt. *v.t.* To arouse or hold the attention or curiosity of; to concern; to cause to take a share (in). **interested** (in′tĕr-ès-tĕd), *a.* Having the interest excited; concerned (in); having a share in; liable to be biased, not disinterested. **interesting**, *a.* Arousing interest.

interfere (in-tĕr-fēr′) [L. *ferire*, to strike], *v.i.* To come into collision, to clash (with); to interpose. **interference**, *n.* **interfering**, *a.*

interfuse (in-tĕr-fūz′) [L. *fūsus*, poured out], *v.t.* To cause to flow into each other.

interim (in′tĕr-im) [L.], *n.* The meantime; the intervening time or period. *a.* Temporary, provisional.

interior (in-tĕr′i-ôr) [L., compar. of *inter*, see INTER-], *a.* Internal, inner; inland; domestic, as dist. from foreign. *n.* The internal part of anything, the inside; the central part of a country; a picture, etc., of the inside of a building or room.

interjacent (in-tĕr-jā′sĕnt) [L. *jacēre*, to lie], *a.* Lying between or among.

interject (in-tĕr-jekt′) [L. *jectus*, thrown], *v.t.* To throw or cast between (as a remark); to interpose. **interjec′tion**, *n.* The act of interjecting; an exclamation, a word thrown in to express feeling.

interlace (in-tĕr-lās′), *v.t.* To lace together.

interlard (in-tĕr-lard′) [F. *entrelarder*], *v.t.* To diversify a conversation, passage in a book, etc., with phrases, etc.

interleave (in-tĕr-lēv′), *v.t.* To insert (blank leaves) between the leaves of.

interline (in-tĕr-līn′), *v.t.* To insert between lines; to write or print in alternate lines. **interlin′ear**, *a.*

interlock (in-tĕr-lok′), *v.t.* To connect firmly together by reciprocal engagement of parts; to link together. *v.i.* To engage with each other thus.

interlocution (in-tẽr-lō-kū'shŭn) [L. *loquī*, to speak], *n.* Conversation, discussion. **interloc'utor**, *n.* One who takes part in a conversation. **interlocutory**, *a.* (*Law*) Not final.

interloper (in'tẽr-lō-per) [obs. *lope*, to swing along with strides], *n.* One who thrusts himself into a place, affairs, etc., without a right; an intruder.

interlude (in'tẽr-lood) [L. *lūdus*, play], *n.* A short entertainment between the acts of a play, or between two plays; music played between the acts of a drama, the verses of a hymn, etc.; (*fig.*) an incident, esp. an amusing one, coming between graver events.

interlunar (in-tẽr-loo'når), *a.* Pertaining to the time when the moon is invisible.

intermarriage (in-tẽr-mãr'åj), *n.* Marriage between persons of different families, tribes, nations, etc.

intermeddle (in-tẽr-medl'), *v.i.* To interfere improperly or officiously (with).

intermediary (in-tẽr-mē'di-år-i) [L. *medius*, middle], *a.* Intermediate; mediatory. *n.* An intermediate agent, a go-between. **intermediate**, *a.* Coming or being between; interposing. *n.* An intermediate thing.

intermezzo (in-tẽr-med'zō) [It.], *n.* An interlude; a short movement connecting the main divisions of a large musical composition.

interminable (in-tẽr'mi-nåbl), *a.* Endless; tediously protracted. **interminably**, *adv.*

intermingle (in-tẽr-mingl'), *v.t.* To mingle together. *v.i.* To be mingled (with).

intermit (in-tẽr-mit') [L. *mittere*, to send], *v.t.* To cause to cease for a time; to suspend. *v.i.* To cease or relax at intervals (as a fever, etc.) **intermission** (-mish'ŭn), *n.* **intermittent**, *a.*

intermix (in-tẽr-miks'), *v.t.* To mix together. *v.i.* To intermingle. *v.i.* To be intermingled. **intermixture**, *n.*

intern (in-tẽrn') [as next], *v.t.* To send to or confine in the interior of a country; to keep under restraint. **internment**, *n.*

internal (in-tẽr'nål) [med. L. *internālis*, from *internus*, inward (*in*, IN)], *a.* Situated in or pertaining to the inside, inherent, intrinsic; domestic as opp. to foreign. *n.pl.* The internal organs, the entrails.

international (in-tẽr-nǎsh'ō-nål), *a.* Pertaining to, subsisting or carried on between, or mutually affecting different nations. **internationalism**, *n.* The promotion of community of interests between nations. **interna'tionalize**, *v.t.* To bring under the joint protection or control of different nations.

internecine (in-tẽr-nē'sīn) [L. *necāre*, to kill], *a.* Deadly; mutually destructive.

interpellate (in-tẽr'-pel-āt) [L. *pellātus*, driven], *v.t.* To interrogate.

interplay (in'tẽr-plā), *n.* Reciprocal action between parts or things.

interpolate (in-tẽr'pō-lāt) [L. *polātus*, furbished up], *v.t.* To add a spurious word or passage to; to insert or intercalate; to corrupt. **interpolator**, *n.* **interpola'tion**, *n.*

interpose (in-tẽr-pōz'), *v.t.* To place between; to put forward (an objection, etc.) by way of intervention or interference. *v.i.* To intervene, to intercede, to interrupt. **interposal**, *n.*

interpret (in-tẽr'prĕt) [F. *interpréter*], *v.t.* To explain the meaning of; to translate from one language into another; to construe or understand (in a particular way). *v.i.* To act as an interpreter. **interpretable**, *a.* **interpreta'tion**, *n.* **inter'pretative**, *a.* **interpreter**, *n.* One who interprets.

interregnum (in-tẽr-reg'nŭm) [L. *regnum*, REIGN], *n.* The period between two reigns or governments; a suspension of normal authority, succession, etc.

interrelation (in-tẽr-rē-lā'shŭn), *n.* Mutual relation.

interrogate (in-tẽr'ō-gāt) [L. *rogāre*, to ask], *v.t.* To put questions to; to examine in a formal manner. *v.i.* To ask questions. **interroga'tion**, *n.* **interrog'ative**, *a.* Denoting a question; expressed in the form of a question. *n.* A word used in asking questions. **inter'rogator**, *n.* **interrog'atory**, *a.* Interrogative. *n.* A question; an inquiry.

interrupt (in-tẽr-rŭpt') [L. *ruptus*, broken], *v.t.* To break in upon; to break the continuity of; to cause a gap in; to obstruct; to disturb. *v.i.* To make interruption. **interrup'tion**, *n.*

intersect (in-tẽr-sekt') [L. *sectus*, cut], *v.t.* To pass across; to divide by cutting or passing across. *v.i.* To cross each other. **intersec'tion**, *n.*

intersperse (in-tẽr-spẽrs') [L. *spersus*, scattered], *v.t.* To scatter here and there among other things.

interstellar, **-lary** (in-tẽr-stel'år, -år-i), *a.* Situated between or passing through the regions between the stars.

interstice (in-tẽr'stis) [L. *sistere*, to place], *n.* A small space, opening, crevice, etc. **interstitial** (-stish'ål), *a.*

intertwine (in-tẽr-twīn'), *v.t.* To entwine or twist together. *v.i.* To be twisted together.

interval (in'tẽr-vål) [L. *vallum*, rampart], *n.* Intermediate space, distance, or time; extent of difference between two things, persons, etc.

intervene (in-tẽr-vēn') [L. *venīre*, to come], *v.i.* To come in as an extraneous feature; to be situated (between); to occur between points of time or events; to interfere, interpose. **intervener**, *n.* One who intervenes, esp. in a law-suit. **interven'tion**, *n.*

interview (in'tẽr-vū) [O.F. *entrevue*], *n.* A conference; a formal meeting between persons, esp. between some person and one employed to obtain information or opinions for publication; the article recording the result. *v.t.* To have an interview with, esp. for publication. **interviewer**, *n.*

interweave (in'tẽr-wēv), *v.t.* To blend closely together.

intestate (in-tes'tāt) [L. *testātus*, witnessed], *a.* Dying without having made a will; not disposed of by will. *n.* An intestate person. **intestacy**, *n.*

intestine (in-tes'tin) [L. *intestinus*], *a.*
Internal, domestic, not foreign. *n.* (*usu.
pl.*) The tube from the stomach to the
anus; the bowels, guts. **intestinal,** *a.*

intimate (in'ti-māt) [late L. *intimātus*], *v.t.*
To make known; to signify, hint. *a.*
(-māt) Close in friendship; confidential;
pertaining to one's inner being. **intimacy,** *n.* The state of being intimate, close
familiarity; illicit sexual intercourse.
intima'tion, *n.*

intimidate (in-tim'i-dāt) [L. *timidus*, timid],
v.t. To frighten, to cow; to deter (from
an action). **intimida'tion,** *n.*

into (in'tu) [A.-S. *in to*], *prep.* Expressing
motion or direction towards the interior,
or change from one state to another; **in**
and **to.**

intolerable (in-tol'ér-ábl), *a.* Not tolerable,
unendurable.

intolerant (in-tol'ér-ánt), *a.* Not tolerant
(of); not enduring difference of opinion,
teaching, or worship, bigoted. **intoler-
ance, intolera'tion,** *n.*

intone (in-tōn') [L. *in tonum*, in tone], *v.i.*
To chant prayers, etc., in a monotone; to
give a musical tone to one's delivery.
v.t. To recite or chant in a monotone.
intona'tion, *n.* Modulation of the voice,
accent; intoning.

intoxicate (in-tok'si-kāt) [med. L. *intoxi-
cātus*, p.p. of *intoxicāre*, to smear with
poison ([N- (1), *toxicātus*, poisoned)], *v.t.*
To make drunk; to excite to enthusiasm;
(*Med.*) to poison. **intoxicant,** *a.* and *n.*
intoxicating, *a.* Tending to intoxicate.
intoxica'tion, *n.*

intra- [L.], *pref.* Within, on the inside.

intractable (in-trák'tábl), *a.* Unmanageable, indocile, refractory. **intracta-
bil'ity,** *n.*

intramural (in-trà-mū'rál), *a.* Situated or
happening within the walls or boundaries.

intransigent (in-trăn'si-jént) [F. *intran-
sigeant*], *n.* Irreconcilable, uncompromising. *n.* An uncompromising
adherent of any creed.

intransitive (in-trăn'si-tiv), *a.* Not passing
on or over; (*Gram.*) denoting action
confined to the agent.

intrepid (in-trep'id) [L. *intrepidus*], *a.*
Fearless, bold. **intrepid'ity,** *n.*

intricate (in'tri-kát) [L. *tricæ*, wiles], *a.*
Entangled, complicated; obscure. **intricacy,** *n.* **intricately,** *adv.*

intrigue (in-trēg') [F. *intriguer*], *v.i.* To
scheme to effect some object by underhand means; to carry on illicit love. *v.t.*
To perplex; to interest much. *n.* Act
of intriguing; a plot to effect some object;
a liaison. **intriguer,** *n.* **intriguingly,** *adv.*

intrinsic (in-trin'sik) [L. *secus*, following],
a. Inherent; belonging to the nature
of a thing; essential; real.

intro- [L. *intrō*, to the inside], *pref.* In, into;
inward.

introduce (in-trō-dūs') [L. *dūcere*, to lead],
v.t. To usher in; to insert; to bring
(to a person's notice); to make known,
esp. (a person) in a formal way (to
another); to bring out into society,
before the public, Parliament, etc.
introduction (-duk'shŭn), *n.* The act of
introducing; formal presentation of a

person to another; a preface; an elementary treatise. **introductory,** *a.*

introit (in-trō'it) [L. *introitus*, from *intrŏire*,
to enter], *n.* A psalm or antiphon sung
or recited as the priest approaches the
altar to begin the Mass.

intromit (in-trō-mit') [L. *mittere*, to send],
v.t. To send in; to admit; to insert. **intro-
mission** (-mish'ŭn), *n.* **intromittent** *a.*

introspection (in-trō-spek'shŭn) [L. *specere*,
to look], *n.* Examination of one's own
mind or feelings. **introspective,** *a.*
introspectively, *adv.*

introvert (in'trō-vĕrt') [L. *vertere*, to turn],
v.t. To turn inward or upon itself.
n. (in'trō-vĕrt) (*Psych.*) A person interested chiefly in his own mental processes
and his standing with other people, this
making him unsociable. **introversible,** *a.*
introversion, *n.*

intrude (in-trood') [*intrŭdere* (IN- (1), L.
trŭdere, to thrust)], *v.t.* To thrust or
force (into). *v.i.* To thrust oneself or
force one's way (into); to force oneself
(upon others); to enter without invita-
tion. **intruder,** *n.* **intru'sion,** *n.* **intrusive.** *a.* Tending to intrude; entering
without invitation.

intuition (in-tū-ish'ŭn) [L. *tuĕri*, to look],
n. Immediate perception by the mind
without reasoning; a truth so perceived.
intu'itive, *a.*

inundate (in'ŭn-dāt) [L. *unda*, a wave],
v.t. To overflow, to flood; to submerge.
inund'ation, *n.*

inure (i-nūr') [O.F. *eure*, work], *v.t.* To
use habitually; to habituate.

invade (in-vād') [L. *vādere*, to go], *v.t.* To
enter (a country) as an enemy; to
encroach on, to violate. *v.i.* To make
an invasion. **invader,** *n.*

invalid (in-văl'id), *a.* Of no force, weight,
or cogency; null; (in'vá-lēd) infirm or
disabled through ill-health or injury. *n.*
An infirm or disabled person. *v.t.*
(in-vá-lēd') To disable by illness or
injury; to register as unfit for duty on
this account. *v.i.* To be enrolled as an
invalid. **inval'idate,** *v.t.* To weaken or
destroy the validity of, to render not
valid. **invalida'tion, invalid'ity,** *n.*

invaluable (in-văl'ū-ábl), *a.* Precious above
estimation; priceless.

invariable (in-vār'i-ábl), *a.* Uniform; not
liable to change; constant. *n.* A constant
quantity. **invariabil'ity,** *n.* **invariably,**
adv.

invasion (in-vā'zhŭn) [as INVADE], *n.* Act
of invading; a hostile attack upon or
entrance into the territory of others;
violation. **invasive** (-siv), *a.*

invective (in-vek'tiv) [L. *invectus*, p.p. of
invehere, see foll.], *n.* A violent expression of censure or abuse; vituperation.

inveigh (in-vā') [L. *invehere, vehere*, to
carry], *v.t.* To use invectives; to
declaim abusively (against).

inveigle (in-vēgl') [F. *aveugler*, to blind],
v.t. To seduce, wheedle, entrap (into).
inveiglement, *n.*

invent (in-vent') [L. *inventus*, found,
invented], *v.t.* To devise or contrive (a
new means, instrument, etc.); to concoct, fabricate. **inven'tion, *n.*** Act of

inventing; production of something new; faculty or power of inventing, inventiveness; that which is invented, a contrivance; a fiction, a scheme. **inventive,** *a.* Quick at contrivance; ready at expedients, ingenious; imaginative. **inventiveness,** *n.* inventor, *n.*

inventory (in'věn-tŏr-i) [as prec.], *n.* A detailed catalogue of goods and chattels; the articles enumerated. *v.t.* To enter in an inventory; to make a list, catalogue, or schedule of.

Inverness (in-vĕr-nes') [town in Scotland], *n.* A kind of sleeveless cloak with a cape.

inverse (in-vĕrs') [as INVERT], *a.* Opposite in order or relation; contrary, inverted. *n.* That which is inverted; the direct opposite of. **inversely,** *adv.* **inver'sion,** *n.* Act of inverting; reversal of order, etc., as of words in a sentence.

invert (in-vĕrt') [L. *vertere,* to turn], *v.t.* To turn upside down; to place in a contrary order; to reverse.

invertebrate (in-vĕr'tĕ-brăt), *a.* Destitute of a backbone; (*fig.*) lacking strength or firmness. *n.* An invertebrate animal.

invest (in-vest') [L. *vestīre,* to clothe], *v.t.* To cover (with or as with a garment); to clothe or endue (with office, authority, dignity, etc.); to besiege; to employ (money in remunerative business, stocks, etc.). *v.i.* To make an investment. **investment** (invest'měnt), *n.* **investor,** *n.* One who invests.

investigate (in-ves'ti-gāt) [L. *vestīgāre,* to track], *v.t.* To search or trace out; to inquire into closely. **investiga'tion,** *n.* **investigator,** *n.*

investiture (in-ves'ti-tūr) [as INVEST], *n.* Act or ceremonial of investing (with office, rank, etc.); state of being invested; that with which one is invested.

inveterate (in-vet'ér-ăt) [L. *vetus veteris,* old], *a.* Long and firmly established; deeply-rooted, obstinate, confirmed by long use. **inveteracy,** *n.*

invidious (in-vid'i-ŭs) [L. *invidia*], *a.* Tending to incur envy or ill-will. **invidiousness,** *n.*

invigorate (in-vig'ŏ-rāt), *v.t.* To give vigour to; to animate, encourage. **invigora'tion,** *n.*

invincible (in-vin'sibl), *a.* Not to be conquered. **invincibil'ity,** *n.*

inviolable (in-vī'ŏ-lăbl), *a.* Not to be violated, profaned, or dishonoured; not to be disturbed. **inviolabil'ity,** *n.* **invi'olate,** *a.* Not violated or profaned unbroken.

invisible (in-viz'ibl), *a.* Imperceptible to the eye; (*colloq.*) not in sight, not at home. **invisibil'ity,** *n.*

invite (in-vīt') [L. *invītāre,* to bid], *v.t.* To solicit the company of; to request courteously (to do something); to allure, attract; to draw upon one, esp. unintentionally. *v.i.* To allure, tempt. **invita'tion,** *n.* **inviting,** *a.*

invocation (in-vŏ-kā'shŭn) [as INVOKE], *n.* Act of invoking; a supplication, esp. to God; a petition for help or inspiration.

invoice (in'vois) [?], *n.* A list of goods dispatched, with particulars of quantity and price, sent to a consignee. *v.t.* To enter (goods) in an invoice.

invoke (in-vōk') [L. *vocāre,* to call], *v.t.* To address in prayer; to solicit earnestly for assistance or protection; to appeal to as an authority or as a witness.

involuntary (in-vol'ŭn-tăr-i), *a.* Done unintentionally; independent of will or volition. **involuntarily,** *adv.*

involute (in'vŏ-lūt) [as INVOLVE], *a.* Rolled up, folded, esp. of certain leaves, petals, etc.; complicated, involved. **involu'tion,** *n.* Act of involving; state of being involved; complication, intricacy; a curling of parts.

involve (in-volv') [L. *volvere,* to roll], *v.t.* To enwrap, envelop (in); to entangle, implicate, or include (in); to comprise as a logical or necessary consequence; to imply; to make intricate.

invulnerable (in-vŭl'nér-ăbl), *a.* Incapable of being wounded or injured. **invulnerabil'ity,** *n.*

inward (in'wård) [A.-S. *innan-weard*], *a.* Internal; situated within; towards the interior, connected with the mind or soul. *adv.* (*also* inwards) Towards the interior; in the mind or soul. *n.pl.* The viscera. **inwardly,** *adv.* Internally; towards the centre; mentally, secretly. **inwardness,** *n.* The essence (of); the quality of being inward; mental and spiritual nature.

inwrought (in'rawt, in-rawt'), *a.* Worked in among other things (of a pattern, etc.); adorned with work or figures (of a fabric).

iodine (ī'ŏ-dĕn, ī'ŏ-dīn) [Gr. *iodes,* a violet], *n.* (*Chem.*) An element yielding violet fumes when heated; used in photography and medicine.

ion (ī'on) [Gr. *ienai,* go], *n.* (*Phys.*) An electrically charged atom formed by the loss or gain of electrons.

Ionian (ī-ō'ni-ăn), *a.* Pertaining to Ionia or its inhabitants. *n.* A member of the division of the Hellenic race which settled in Attica and the N. coast of the Peloponnesus, etc., and Euxine and esp. in Asia Minor. **Ionic** (ī-on'ik), *a.* Denoting one of the five orders of architecture, which is distinguished by the volute on both sides of the capital.

-ior [compar. suf. of adjectives, and var. of -IOUR], *suf.* As in *junior, superior, warrior.*

iota (ī-ō'tà) [Gr.], *n.* The Greek letter ι; a jot, a tittle, a very small quantity.

I.O.U. (ī-ō-ū) [I, OWE, YOU], *n.* A formal acknowledgment of debt, bearing these letters, the sum involved, and the debtor's signature.

-ious, *suf.* Characterized by, full of; forming adjectives, as *ambitious, cautious, suspicious.*

ipecacuanha (ip-ĕ-kăk-ū-ăn'à) [Guarani *ipe-kaa-guaña*], *n.* The dried root of a plant from Brazil, used as an emetic and purgative.

ir- [IN- (1) and IN- (2)], *pref.* (*before* r) As in *irradiate, irrelevant, irreligion.*

Iranian (ī-rā'ni-ăn) [Pers. *īrān,* Persia], *a.* Pertaining to Persia or to the Asiatic family of languages comprising Zend, Old Persian, and those derived from them. *n.* A Persian; a native of Iran.

irascible (i-răs'ibl) [L. *irascī,* to be angry], *a.* Easily excited to anger. **irascibly,**

adv. **irascibil'ity,** *n.* **irate** (ī-rāt'), *a.* Angry, enraged.

Ire (īr) [L. *īra*], *n.* Anger, passion.

iridescent (ir-i-des'ént) [IRIS, -ESCENT], *a.* Exhibiting changing colours like those of the rainbow. **iridescence,** *n.*

iridium (i-rid'i-ùm) [Gr. *iris,* an iris], *n.* A white metallic element of the platinum group.

iris (ī-'ris) [Gr. *iris iridos*], *n.* (*pl.* -ses) The rainbow; an appearance resembling the rainbow, an iridescence; the circular coloured membrane surrounding the pupil of the eye; (*Bot.*) a genus of plants with tuberous roots, sword-shaped leaves, and large variously-coloured flowers, the flag, the fleur-de-lis.

Irish (ī'rish) [A.-S. *Iras,* pl.], *a.* Pertaining to Ireland or its inhabitants; like an Irishman. *n.* The Irish language.

irk (ĕrk) [?], *v.t.* To bore; to annoy, disgust. *v.i.* To become tired or worried. **irksome,** *a.* Wearisome, tedious. **irksomely,** *adv.* **irksomeness,** *n.*

iron (ī'érn) [A.-S. *īren*], *n.* The commonest and most useful of all the metals; an article, tool, etc., made of iron; an iron implement for smoothing; a golf-club used for lofting; (*pl.*) fetters. *a.* Made of iron; like iron, robust, inflexible, merciless. *v.t.* To cover with iron; to fetter with irons; to smooth with an iron. **iron-bound,** *a.* Bound with iron; surrounded with rocks (of a coast); (*fig.*) unyielding. **ironclad,** *n.* A war-vessel having the parts above water plated with iron. **iron curtain,** *n.* (*Polit.*) Term used to describe the Communist barrier between the civilization of the West and the Soviet way of life. **iron-master,** *n.* A manufacturer of iron. **ironmonger,** *n.* One who deals in ironware or hardware. **ironmongery,** *n.* **iron-mould,** *n.* A spot on cloth, etc., caused by ink or rust. **ironware,** *n.* Goods made of iron, hardware. **ironwork,** *n.* Anything made of iron; (*pl., usu. as sing.*) an establishment where iron is manufactured or wrought.

irony (ī'rŏ-ni) [Gr. *eirōn,* a dissembler], *n.* Language or an expression intended to convey the opposite to the literal meaning. **ironic, -al** (ī-ron'ik, -ál), *a.* ironically, *adv.*

irradiate (i-rā'di-āt), *v.t.* To shed light upon; to make bright or brilliant; (*fig.*) to light or brighten up.

irrational (i-răsh'ŏ-nál), *a.* Not rational; illogical, contrary to reason, absurd; (*Math.*) not expressible by a whole number or common fraction. *n.* A surd.

irreclaimable (ir-ê-klā'mábl), *a.* Incapable of being reclaimed; obstinate.

irreconcilable (i-rek-ón-sī'lábl), *a.* Incapable of being reconciled; inconsistent, incongruous. *n.* One who cannot be appeased or satisfied, an intransigent. **irreconcilably,** *adv.*

irrecoverable (ir-ê-kŭv'ér-ábl), *a.* That cannot be recovered; irreparable. **irrecoverably,** *adv.*

irreducible (ir-ê-dū'sibl), *a.* Not to be lessened; not to be brought to a required condition, etc.

irrefragable (i-ref'rá-gábl) [late L. *irrefrāgābilis*], *a.* Incapable of being refuted.

irrefutable (ir-ê-fū'tábl), *a.* Incapable of being refuted.

irregular (i-reg'ū-lár), *a.* Not regular, not according to established principles or custom; departing from rules, lawless, disorderly; abnormal; not direct, not uniform; (*Gram.*) deviating from the common form in inflexion; (*Mil.*) not belonging to the regular army. *n.pl.* Irregular troops. **irregular'ity,** *n.*

irrelevant (i-rel'ê-vánt), *a.* Not applicable, not to the point. **irrelevance, -vancy,** *n.* **irrelevantly,** *adv.*

irreligion (ir-ê-lij'ón), *n.* Indifference or hostility to religion. **irreligious,** *a.* **irreligiously,** *adv.*

irremediable (ir-ê-mē'di-ábl), *a.* Incurable; incapable of being remedied.

irremovable (ir-ê-moo'vábl), *a.* That cannot be removed; permanent, immovable.

irreparable (i-rep'á-rábl), *a.* Incapable of being repaired or remedied. **irreparably,** *adv.*

irreplaceable (ir-ê-plā'sábl), *a.* Not to be made good in case of loss.

irrepressible (ir-ê-pres'ibl), *a.* Not to be repressed.

irreproachable (ir-ê-prō'chábl), *a.* Blameless, faultless.

irresistible (ir-ê-zis'tibl), *a.* That cannot be resisted.

irresolute (i-rez'ô-lūt), *a.* Not resolute; undecided, hesitating. **irresolution** (lū'shun), *n.*

irrespective (ir-ê-spek'tiv), *a.* Regardless of, without reference to.

irresponsible (ir-ê-spon'sibl), *a.* Not responsible or trustworthy; without a proper sense of responsibility.

irresponsive (ir-ê-spon'siv), *a.* Not responsive (to). **irresponsiveness,** *n.*

irretrievable (ir-ê-trē'vábl), *a.* Not to be retrieved; irreparable.

irreverent (i-rev'ér-ént), *a.* Lacking in reverence; disrespectful. **irreverence,** *n.* **irreverently,** *adv.*

irrevocable (i-rev'ô-kábl), *a.* Incapable of being revoked, unalterable. **irrevocably,** *adv.*

irrigate (ir'-i-gāt) [L. *irrigātus,* p.p. of *irrigāre,* -IR, L. *rigātus,* moistened], *v.t.* To water (land) by causing a stream to flow over it; (*Med.*) to moisten (a wound, etc.) with a continuous stream. **irrigable,** *a.* **irriga'tion,** *n.*

irritate (ir'i-tāt) [L. *irritāre*], *v.t.* To fret, annoy, exasperate; to cause an uneasy sensation in (the skin, an organ, etc.). **irritable,** *a.* Easily provoked, fretful; highly sensitive. **irritabil'ity,** *n.* **irritant,** *a.* and *n.* **irrita'tion,** *n.*

irruption (i-rŭp'shŭn) [IR-, L. *ruptus,* broken], *n.* A bursting in; a sudden invasion or incursion. **irruptive,** *a.*

-ise, *suf.* Forming abstract nouns, as *franchise, merchandise* (see also -IZE).

-ish (1), *suf.* Of the nature of, pertaining to; rather, somewhat; as in *childish, English, outlandish, reddish*; (2) forming verbs, as *cherish, finish, punish.*

isinglass (ī'zing-glas) [prob. M.Dut. *huyzenblas,* sturgeon's bladder], *n.* A gelatinous substance prepared from the swimming-bladders of certain fish, used for making jellies, glue, etc.

Islam (iz-lam′) [Arab., submission], *n.* Mohammedanism; (*collect.*) believers in Mohammedanism, peoples under Mohammedan rule. **Islam′ic**, *a.* **Is′lamism**, *n.*

island (i′lånd) [A.-S. *igland*], *n.* A piece of land surrounded by water; anything isolated. **islander**, *n.*

isle (il) [M.E. *ile*, L. *insula*], *n.* A small island. **islet**, *n.* A little isle.

-ism, *suf.* Forming abstract nouns denoting doctrine, theory, system, etc., as *altruism*, *Socialism*, *spiritualism.*

iso- [Gr. *isos*], *comb. form.* Equal; having the same number of parts.

isolate (i′só-lāt) [as INSULATE], *v.t.* To place in a detached situation; to subject to quarantine; to insulate. **isola′tion**, *n.*

-ison, *suf.* As in *comparison, orison.*

isosceles (i-sos′é-lēz) [Gr. *isoskelēs*, equal-legged (ISO-, *skelos*, leg)], *a.* Having two sides equal (of a triangle).

issue (ish′ū) [O.F., L. *ire*, to go], *n.* Act of passing or flowing out; outgoing, outflow; way or means of exit; the mouth of a river; offspring; profits from land or other property; consequence; the point in debate or between contending parties; act of sending or giving out; publication; that which is published at a particular time; the whole quantity or number sent out at one time. *v.i.* To pass or flow out; to be published; to emerge (from); to proceed, to be derived (from); to end or result (in). *v.t.* To send out; to put into circulation. **issuable**, *a.*

-ist, *suf.* Denoting an agent, adherent, follower, etc., as *Baptist, botanist, fatalist.*

-ister, *suf.* Denoting an agent, etc., as *chorister, sophister.*

isthmus (is′mùs) [Gr. *isthmos*], *n.* A neck of land connecting two larger portions; (*Anat., etc.*) a narrow passage or part between two larger cavities or parts.

it (it) [A.-S. *hit*], *3rd pers. neut. pron.* (*poss.* its, *pl.* they, *poss.* their, *obj.* them). The thing spoken about; the grammatical subject of an impersonal verb; the indefinite object (as *to rough it, to fight it out*).

Italian (i-tăl′yàn), *a.* Pertaining to Italy. *n.* A native of Italy; the Italian language.

italic (i-tăl′ik) [Gr. *Italikos*, as prec.], *a.* Applied to a sloping type (*thus*); pertaining to ancient Italy or the Italian races, esp. as distinguished from Roman. *n.pl.* Italic letters or type. **italicize** (-siz), *v.t.* To print in italics; (*fig.*) to emphasize.

itch (ich) [A.-S. *giccan*], *v.i.* To have a sensation of uneasiness in the skin exciting a desire to scratch the part; to feel a constant desire (for). *n.* A sensation of uneasiness in the skin; an uneasy desire or craving (for, etc.); a contagious skin-disease; scabies. **itchy**, *a.*

-ite, *suf.* Belonging to, a follower of, as *Jacobite, Moabite*; denoting fossils, minerals, chemical substances, explosives, etc., as *ammonite, chrysolite, dolomite, dynamite.*

item (i′tèm) [L., in like manner], *n.* A

separate article in an enumeration; an individual entry; a detail of news in a newspaper. *adv.* Likewise, also.

iterate (it′ér-āt) [L. *iterum*, again], *v.t.* To say, make, or do over and over again. **iterant**, *a.* Repeating. **itera′tion**, *n.* **iterative**, *a.*

itinerant (i-tin′er-ànt) [L. *iter*, a journey], *a.* Passing from place to place; travelling on a circuit. *n.* One who journeys from place to place; a travelling preacher, player, etc. **itinerary**, *n.* An account of places and their distances on a road, a guide-book; a route; an account of travels.

-itious, *suf.* As in *adventitious, factitious, ambitious, nutritious.*

-itis, *suf.* Denoting inflammation, as *gastritis, peritonitis.*

itself (it-self′) [IT, SELF], *pron.* Used emphatically (*usu. in apposition*) and reflexively.

-ium, *suf.* Used chiefly to form names of metals, as *aluminium, sodium.*

ivory (i′vór-i) [A.-F. *ivorie*, L. *ebur*, ivory], *n.* The hard white substance composing the tusks of the elephant, etc. *a.* Consisting, made of, or resembling ivory.

ivy (i′vi) [A.-S. *ifig*], *n.* An evergreen climbing plant, usu. having five-angled leaves, and adhering by aerial rootlets. **ivied**, *a.* Overgrown with ivy.

-ize, *suf.* Forming verbs denoting to speak or act as; to follow or practise; to come into such a state; (*transitively*) to cause to follow or resemble; as *Anglicize, Christianize, galvanize, naturalize, terrorize.*

J

jab (jăb) [?], *v.t.* To poke violently; to stab. *n.* A sharp poke, stab, thrust.

jabber (jăb′ér) [?], *v.i.* To talk volubly and incoherently; to chatter. *v.t.* To utter rapidly and indistinctly. *n.* Rapid or nonsensical talk; gabble. **jabberer**, *n.*

jacinth (jăs′inth) [O.F. *jacinthe*, HYACINTH], *n.* A translucent gem.

jack (jăk) [?], *n.* A fellow, a common person; a sailor; a pike, esp. a young one; the knave of cards; contrivances for turning a spit, lifting heavy weights, raising a carriage-wheel, etc.; a lever or other part in various machines; a small flag (UNION-JACK); a coat of mail; a leather flagon. *v.t.* To lift, hoist, or move with a jack; (*slang*) to resign, give up. **jackass**, *n.* A male ass; a stupid, ignorant fellow. **jack-boot**, *n.* A large boot reaching to the thigh. **jackdaw**, *n.* The smallest of the British crows. **Jack-in-office**, *n.* One who assumes authority on account of holding a petty office. **jack-knife**, *n.* A large clasp-knife. **jack-plane**, *n.* The coarsest of the joiner's bench-planes.

jackal (jăk′awl) [Pers. *shaghâl*], *n.* A gregarious animal closely allied to the dog; one who does dirty work for another.

jackanapes (jăk′á-nāps) [nickname], *n.* A pert fellow; a coxcomb.

jackaroo (jăk-à-roo') [*Austral slang*], *n.* A new-comer, a novice.

jacket (jăk'ĕt) [O.F. *jaquette*], *n.* A short coat for men or women; the skin of a potato; a wrapper.

Jacobean (jăk-ô-bē'ăn) [*L. Jacobus*, whence *James*], *a.* Belonging to the reign of James I.

Jacobin (jăk'ô-bĭn), *n.* An extreme revolutionist during the French Revolution. **Jac'obinism**, *n.*

Jacobite (jăk'ô-bĭt), *n.* A partisan of James II after his abdication, or of his descendants. **Jacobitism**, *n.*

jactation (jăk-tā'shŭn) [L. *jactāre*, to throw], *n.* Agitation of the body in exercise, as in riding; jactitation. **jactita'tion**, *n.* Restlessness, a tossing or twitching of the limbs; a false pretension to marriage.

jade (1) (jād) [?], *n.* A broken-down, worthless horse; an old or an untrustworthy woman, a wench. *v.t.* To tire out (*usu. in. p.p.*). **jadedly**, *adv.*

jade (2) [Sp. (*piedra di*) *ijada*], *n.* A green silicate of lime and magnesia, an ornamental stone.

jag (jăg) [?], *n.* A notch; a stab, prick. *v.t.* To cut or tear raggedly. **jagged**, *a.*

jaguar (jăg'ûâr) [native *yagouara*], *n.* A S. American animal resembling the leopard.

jail, gaol (jāl) [A.-F. *gaole*, O.F. *jaiole*], *n.* A prison. **jail-bird**, *n.* One who has been to prison. **jailer, gaoler**, *n.* The keeper of a prison.

jalap (jăl'ăp) [Aztec *Xalapan*, place in Mexico], *n.* The dried tubercles of a Mexican plant, used as a purgative.

jalousie (zhăl'oo-zē) [F.], *n.* A Venetian shutter, louvre blind.

jam (jăm) [?], *v.t.* To wedge or squeeze (in); to compress, to squeeze together; to block up by crowding into; to make (a machine, etc.) unworkable by forcible handling; (*Wireless Teleg.*) to block (another station) with equal wave-impulses. *v.i.* To become immovable or unworkable by rough handling (of a machine, etc.). *n.* A crush, a squeeze; a stoppage in a machine due to jamming; a crowd, a press; a conserve of fruit made by boiling with sugar.

jamb (jăm) [F. *jambe*, leg], *n.* One of the upright sides of a doorway, window, etc.

jangle (jăng'-gĕl) [?], *v.i.* To sound harshly to wrangle, bicker. *v.t.* To cause to sound discordantly; to utter harshly. *n.* Wrangling, bickering; discordant sound.

janitor (jăn'ĭ-tŏr) [L.], *n.* A door-keeper.

janizary (jăn'ĭ-zăr-ĭ) [Turk. *yeni-tsheri, tsheri*, soldiery], *n.* (*Hist.*) A soldier of the Sultan's bodyguard.

January (jăn'û-âr-ĭ) [L., from *Janus*, a Roman deity], *n.* The first month of the year.

Japan (jà-păn') [island empire east of China], *n.* An intensely hard varnish; work varnished and figured in the Japanese style. *v.t.* To cover with or as with japan. **Japanese'**, *a.* and *n.*

jape (jāp) [?], *v.i.* To jest, to play tricks. *n.* A jest, a trick, a joke.

jar (1) (jar) [?], *v.i.* To emit a harsh sound; to vibrate harshly; to be discordant or disagreeable; to clash, be inconsistent (with). *v.t.* To cause to tremble, to give a shock to. *n.* A harsh vibration; a discordant sound; a shock; a conflict of opinions or interests.

jar (2) [Arab. *jarrah*], *n.* A vessel of glass or earthenware, used for various domestic purposes.

jargon (jar'gŏn) [O.F.], *n.* Unintelligible talk, debased or illiterate speech or language, any specialized language.

jargonelle (jar-gŏ-nel') [F.], *n.* A kind of pear.

jasmine (jăs'mĭn) [Arab. *yāsmīn*], *n.* A climbing plant with sweet-scented white or yellow flowers.

jasper (jăs'pĕr) [Gr. *iaspis*, Oriental in origin], *n.* An impure, coloured variety of quartz; a greenish marble with small red spots.

jaundice (jawn'dĭs) [M.E. *jaunys*, from F. *jaune*, yellow], *n.* A disease characterized by yellowness of the skin, diarrhœa, and general debility; (*fig.*) a mental attitude or condition which warps the vision. *v.t.* To affect with or as with jaundice; (*fig.*) to poison the mind with jealousy, prejudice, etc.

jaunt (jawnt) [?], *v.i.* To rove about; to take a short excursion. *n.* A ramble, a short journey, a trip. **jaunting-car**, *n.* An Irish vehicle with two seats, back to back, over the wheels, and one for the driver in front.

jaunty (jawn'tĭ) [F. *gentil*], *a.* Sprightly, airy, self-satisfied. *n.* (*Nav.*) Master-at-arms, *also* **jonty**. **jauntily**, *adv.*

javelin (jăv'ĕ-lĭn) [F. *javeline*, prob. from Celt], *n.* A light spear thrown by the hand.

jaw (jaw) [?], *n.* The bony structure in which the teeth are fixed, forming the framework of the mouth; (*pl.*) the mouth; the narrow opening of a gorge, valley, etc.; one of two opposing members of a vice, etc.; the forked end of a boom or gaff.

jay (jā) [O.F.], *n.* A chattering bird of brilliant plumage; a foolish dupe.

jazz (jăz) [Am. Negro], *n.* Syncopated music of Negro origin; the form of dancing that goes with this.

jealous (jel'ŭs) [M.E. and O.F. *gelos*], *a.* Suspicious or apprehensive of being supplanted in the love or favour (of wife, husband, friend); anxiously watchful (of one's honour, rights, etc.); envious; (*Bibl.*) requiring exclusive devotion (of God). **jealously**, *adv.* **jealousy**, *n.*

jean (jēn) [M.E. *Gene*, Genoa], *n.* A twilled undressed cloth with cotton warp; *n.pl.* trousers or overalls made of this.

jeep (jēp) [G.P. initials of General Purposes], *n.* (*Am.*) A type of fast light car or van.

jeer (jĕr) [?], *v.* To scoff (at), to make a mock of, to deride. *n.* A gibe, a taunt.

Jehovah (jê-hō'và) [Heb. *Yahovāh*], *n.* The most sacred name given in the Old Testament to God.

jejune (jê-joon') [L. *jējūnus*, fasting], *a.* Meagre, scanty; wanting in substance; (*fig.*) devoid of interest or life.

jelly (jel'i) [F. *gelée*, frost], *n.* Any gelatinous substance, esp. from animal matter; a conserve made of thickened fruit-juice boiled with sugar. *v.i.* To turn into jelly. **jelly-fish,** *n.* The marine medusae and other allied species. **jellify,** *v.t.* and *i.*

jemmy (jem'i) [dim. of *James*], *n.* A short, stout crowbar, used by burglars.

jennet (jen'ĕt) [Sp. *ginete*], *n.* A small Spanish horse.

jeopardy (jep'ar-di) [O.F. *jeu parti*, even game], *n.* Exposure to danger, loss, or injury, risk, peril. **jeopardize,** *v.t.* To risk.

jerboa (jĕr-bō'à) [Arab. *yarbū*], *n.* A small mouse-like rodent with long hind legs adapted for leaping.

jeremiad (jer-ê-mī'ăd) [*Jeremiah*], *n.* A lamentation, esp. over modern degeneracy, in the style of the prophet Jeremiah.

jerk (1) (jĕrk) [?], *v.t.* To pull, push, or thrust sharply; to throw with a sharp, suddenly arrested action. *v.i.* To move with jerks. *n.* A sharp, sudden push or tug; a twitch. **jerky,** *a.*

jerk (2) [Am. Sp. *charquear*], *v.t.* To cut (beef) into long pieces and dry in the sun.

jerkin (jĕr'kin) [?], *n.* A short jacket, formerly often made of leather.

jerry (jer'i) [prob. *Jeremiah*], *a.* Cheaply and badly built, flimsy. **jerry-builder,** *n.* A speculative builder of inferior houses. **jerry-built,** *a.*

jersey (jĕr'zi) [the island], *n.* A close-fitting knitted tunic with long sleeves.

jest (jest) [O.F. *geste*], *n.* A joke, something to provoke mirth; a laughing-stock; a frolic. *v.i.* To joke; to jeer (at). **jester,** *n.* A buffoon, esp. one formerly retained by persons of high rank.

Jesuit (jez'ū-it) [Sp. *Jesuita* (*Jesus,* -ITE)], *n.* A member of the Society of Jesus, a R.-C. order founded in 1534 by St. Ignatius Loyola.

jet (1) (jet) [Gr. *gagatēs* (*Gagai*, in Lycia)], *n.* A variety of black stones susceptible of a brilliant polish.

jet (2) [O.F. *jetter*, L. *jactāre*, to throw], *v.i.* To spurt out, to come out in a jet. *v.t.* To send out in a jet or jets. *n.* A sudden spurt or shooting out of water or flame, esp. from a small orifice; a nozzle for the discharge of water, etc. **jet propulsion,** *n.* (*Mech.*) A method of powering aircraft by the reaction of heated, compressed gases forced out against the air.

jetsam (jet'sàm) [as foll.], *n.* Goods, etc. thrown overboard to lighten a ship and subsequently washed ashore.

jettison (jet'i-sŏn) [O.F. *getaison*, from L. *jactāre*, to throw], *n.* The casting of goods overboard to lighten a vessel in distress. *v.t.* To throw goods overboard.

jetty (jet'i) [O.F. *getee*, as JET (2)], *n.* A solid structure projecting into water and serving as a mole, pier, or wharf.

Jew (joo) [A.-F. *Jeu*, L. *Iūdæus*], *n.* A Hebrew. **Jewess,** *n.* **Jewish,** *a.*

jewel (joo'ĕl) [A.-F. *juel*], *n.* A precious stone; a personal ornament containing a precious stone or stones; a person or thing of very great value or excellence. *v.t.* To adorn or fit with jewels. **jeweller,**

n. A maker of or dealer in jewels. **jewellery, jewelry,** *n.* Jewels in general; the art or trade of a jeweller.

Jewry (joo'ri) [JEW, -ERY], *n.* The Jews or the land where they dwell or dwelt; the Jews' quarter in a town or country.

jib (1) (jib) [?], *n.* A triangular foremost sail; the extended arm of a crane. **jib-boom,** *n.* A movable spar running out beyond the bowsprit.

jib (2) [?], *v.i.* To move restively sideways or backwards, as a horse; to make difficulties (at some task, etc.). **jibber,** *n.* A horse that jibs.

jiffy (jif'i) [?], *n.* An instant, an extremely short time.

jig (jig) [?], *n.* A lively dance, and the music for it; (*Mech.*) a tool for holding an object and guiding a cutting tool. **jig-saw,** *n.* A vertical saw used for cutting scrolls, fretwork, etc. **jig-saw puzzle,** *n.* Puzzle to put together irregular pieces to form a picture.

jilt (jilt) [?], *n.* A woman who gives her lover encouragement and then throws him over. *v.t.* To throw over (one's lover).

jingle (jing'-gĕl) [imit.], *v.i.* To make a tinkling sound like that of small bells, etc.; to correspond in rhyme, etc.; to rhyme (in a depreciative sense). *v.t.* To cause to make a clinking or tinkling sound. *n.* A tinkling metallic sound; a correspondence or repetition of sounds in words, esp. of a catchy, inartistic kind; doggerel.

Jingo (jing'gō) [?], *n.* (*pl.* -goes) A mild oath; one who advocates a spirited or bellicose foreign policy. **Jingoism,** *n.*

jinricksha (jin-rik'sha) [Jap. *jin*, man, *riki*, strength, *sha*, vehicle], *n.* A light two-wheeled Japanese carriage, drawn by one or two men.

jiu-jitsu (joo'jit-soo') [Jap.], *n.* The Japanese art of wrestling.

jive (jïv) [?], *v.i.* To dance to swing or hot music.

job (1) (job) [?], *n.* A piece of work, esp. one done for a stated price; business (esp. public) yielding unfair profit or advantage; (*colloq.*) a situation, a berth. *a.* Applied to collections of things sold together; let on hire. *v.t.* To let out by the job, or for hire; to buy up in miscellaneous lots and retail; to deal in (stocks); to deal with in an underhand way for private benefit. *v.i.* To buy and sell as a broker; to do job-work; to let or hire by the job; to profit corruptly at the public expense. **jobmaster,** *n.* One who lets out carriages or horses. **jobber,** *n.* One who deals in stocks and shares, esp. a middleman.

Job (2) (jōb) [the Patriarch, subject of the *Book of Job* in the O.T.], *n.* (*fig.*) An uncomplaining sufferer or victim.

jobbery (job'ê-ri) [JOB (1), -ERY], *n.* Underhand business.

jockey (jok'i) [*Jackey*, dim. of JACK], *n.* A professional rider in horse-races. *v.t.* To employ sharp practices against; to outwit, out-manœuvre, etc.; (*Horse-racing*) to jostle by riding against.

jocose (jȯ-kōs') [as JOKE], *a.* Humorous,

facetious; **given** to jesting. **jocosely,** *adv.* **jocoseness, jocosity** (-kos'it-i), *n.*

jocular (jok'ū-lär), *a.* Addicted to jesting; facetious, amusing; embodying a joke. **jocular'ity,** *n.* **joc'ularly,** *adv.*

jocund (jok'ŭnd) [L. *jūcundus*], *a.* Sportive, gay; inspiring mirth.

jog (jog) [?], *v.t.* To push or jerk lightly, to nudge, esp. to excite attention; to stimulate (one's memory). *v.i.* To move with a leisurely pace. *n.* A slight push or nudge; a leisurely trotting motion. **jog-trot,** *n.* A slow, monotonous trot. *a.* Monotonous, humdrum progress; slow routine.

join (join) [O.F. *joindre*, L. *jungere*], *v.t.* To connect, fasten together; to couple, associate; to engage in (battle). *v.i.* To be contiguous or in contact; to become associated (with); to become a member of a society, etc.). *n.* A joint; a mark of junction. **joiner,** *n.* One who joins; a carpenter who makes furniture, finishes woodwork, etc. **joinery,** *n.*

joint (joint) [O.F., as prec.], *n.* A junction or mode of joining parts together; the union of two bones; one of the pieces into which a carcass is cut up; (*Am. slang*) a low resort. *a.* Belonging to, produced by, etc., different persons in conjunction; sharing (with others). *v.t.* To form with joints or connect by joints. **joint stock:** Capital divided into shares and held jointly by several persons. **joint-stool,** *n.* A stool made with parts jointed together. **jointed,** *a.* **jointly,** *adv.* In conjuction with others. **jointure,** *n.* An estate settled upon a woman in consideration of marriage, which she is to enjoy after her husband's decease.

joist (joist) [O.F. *giste*, a bed], *n.* One of the timbers to which floor boards or the laths of a ceiling are nailed.

joke (jōk) [L. *jocus*], *n.* Something said or done to excite merriment; a jest; a ridiculous incident, circumstance, etc. *v.i.* To make jokes, to jest. **joker,** *n.* One who jokes; (*Cards*) an extra card used with various values.

jolly (jol'i) [O.F. *jolif*, gay, fine], *a.* Merry, gay, jovial; inspiring or expressing mirth; pleasant, agreeable, remarkable. **jollify,** *v.i.* To make merry; to tipple **jollifica'tion,** *n.* **jollity,** *n.*

jolly-boat (jol'i-bōt) [Scand.], *n.* A small boat for the general work of a ship.

jolt (jōlt) [?], *v.t.* To shake with sharp, sudden jerks. *v.i.* To move thus. *n.* A sudden shock or jerk.

jonquil (jong'kwil) [F. *jonquille* (L. *juncus*, rush)], *n.* The rush-leaved narcissus or daffodil.

jorum (jôr'ŭm) [?], *n.* A large drinking vessel; its contents.

jostle (josl) [as JOUST], *v.* To push against, to hustle. *n.* A hustling; a collision.

jot (jot) [Gr. *iōta*, the letter *i*], *n.* A tittle, an iota. *v.t.* To write (a brief memorandum). **jotting,** *n.* A note or memorandum.

joule (jool) [J. P. *Joule* (1818–89) physicist], *n.* (*Elec.*) The unit of electrical energy.

journal (jer'nàl) [L. *diurnālis*, diurnal], *n.* An account of daily transactions; the book from which daily entries are posted up in the ledger; a diary; a newspaper or periodical published at regular intervals. **journalist,** *n.* One who keeps a diary; a literary worker on a newspaper or periodical. **journalism,** *n.* **journalis'tic,** *a.*

journey (jer'ni) [L. *diurnāta*, a day's work], *n.* Travel from one place to another, esp. by land; the distance travelled in a given time. *v.i.* To travel; to make a journey. **journeyman,** *n.* A mechanic or artisan who has served his apprenticeship and works for an employer.

joust (joost) [O.F. *jouster*, low L. *juxtāre*, to approach], *v.i.* To tilt, to encounter on horseback with lances. *n.* A tilting-match; a combat on horseback.

jovial (jō'vi-ál) [L. *joviālis*, of Jupiter], *a.* Mirthful, joyous. **jovial'ity,** *n.*

jowl (joul) [A.-S. *cēafl*, jaw], *n.* The jaw; the cheek; the head and shoulders of a fish.

joy (joi) [O.F. *joie*], *n.* The emotion produced by gratified desire, success, happy fortune, etc.; gladness, delight; a cause of happiness. *v.i.* To rejoice. *v.t.* To gladden. **joyful,** *a.* **joyless,** *a.* **joyous,** *a.* **joy-ride,** *n.* (*colloq.*) A ride in a motor-car for pleasure, esp. if unauthorized. **joystick,** *n.* (*Av.*) The control lever of an aeroplane.

jubilate (joo'bi-lāt) [L. *jūbilāre*], *v.i.* To exult; to express intense joy. **jubila'tion** (shŭn), *n.* **jubilant,** *a.*

jubilee (joo'bi-lē) [as prec.], *n.* An important festival among the Jews, celebrated every 50th year to commemorate the exodus from Egypt; a 50th anniversary; a season of great public rejoicing; (*R.-C. Ch.*) a year of special indulgence or remission of the consequences of sin. **diamond jubilee:** A sixtieth anniversary.

Judaic, -al (joo-dā'ik, -ál) [L. *Judāicus*], *a.* Pertaining to the Jews, Jewish. **Ju'daism,** *n.* The religious doctrines and rites of the Jews; conformity to these.

judge (jŭj) [M.E. and O.F. *juge*, L. *jūdex*], *n.* A civil officer who hears and determines causes in a court of justice; one authorized to decide a dispute or contest; a connoisseur. *v.t.* To decide (a question); to hear or try (a cause); to pass sentence upon; to criticize. *v.i.* To hear and determine a case; to give sentence; to come to a conclusion; to criticize, be censorious. **judgeship,** *n.* **judgment,** *n.* Act of judging; a judicial decision, a sentence of a court of justice; discernment, discrimination, good sense; the critical faculty; opinion; (*fig.*) a misfortune regarded as a punishment for sin.

judicature (joo'di-kà-tūr) [L. *judicāre*, to judge], *n.* The administration of justice by trial and judgment; the authority of a judge; a court of justice, and its jurisdiction.

judicial (joo-dish'ál) [L. *jūdiciālis*, as prec.], *a.* Pertaining or proper to courts of law or the administration of justice; showing judgment; discriminating. **judicially,** *adv.* **judiciary,** *n.* The judicature.

judicious (joo-dish'ŭs) [as prec.], *a.* Sagacious, discerning; prudent; done with reason. **judiciousness,** *n.*

Judo (joo'dō) [Jap.] *n.* A variety of jiu-jitsu.

jug (jŭg) [?], *n.* A vessel with a handle for holding liquors; (*slang*) a prison. *v.t.* (*usu. in p.p.*) To stew (a hare).

juggernaut (jŭg'ér-nawt) [Hindi, *Jagganāth*, lord of the world], *n.* A belief, institution, etc., to which one is ruthlessly sacrificed or by which one is destroyed.

juggle (jŭgl) [L. *joculātor*, a juggler, a JOKE], *v.i.* To play tricks by sleight of hand; to practise artifice or imposture (with). *v.t.* To deceive by trickery. **juggler,** *n.* **jugglery,** *n.*

jugular (jŭg'ū-lár) [L. *jugŭlum,* the collarbone], *a.* Belonging to the neck or throat.

juice (joos) [L. *jūs,* soup], *n.* The watery part of vegetable or the fluid part of animal bodies; (*fig.*) the essence of anything; (*Slang*) electric current, petrol, or other source of power. **juicy,** *a.* Abounding in juice, succulent.

Jujitsu [Jiu-jitsu]

jujube (joo'joob) [Gr. *zizuphon*], *n.* The berry-like fruit of spiny shrubs of the *Rhamnus* family, dried as a sweetmeat; a lozenge flavoured with or imitating this.

juke-box (jūk'boks), *n.* A mechanical musical box operated by the insertion of a coin.

julep (joo'lĕp) [Arab. *julāb*], *n.* A sweet drink.

julienne (zhu-li-en') [F.], *n.* A clear soup; a variety of pear.

July (ju-lī') [after *Jūlius* Cæsar], *n.* The seventh month of the year.

jumble (jŭmbl) [?], *v.t.* To mix confusedly; to throw together without order. *n.* A muddle, disorder, confusion. **jumblesale,** *n.* A sale of miscellaneous articles at a bazaar.

jumbo (jŭm'bō) [name of an elephant], *n.* An elephant; anything big.

jump (jŭmp) [?], *v.i.* To spring, leap, bound; to move suddenly with springs or bounds; to start up abruptly. *v.t.* To cross by leaping; to skip (a chapter, etc.); (*colloq.*) to seize by surprise. *n.* The act of jumping; a leap, a bound. **jumpable,** *a.* **jumper,** *n.* One who or that which jumps; a loose, coarse outer jacket worn by sailors, labourers, etc.; a knitted or other garment of a similar shape. **jumpy,** *a.* Nervous, inclined to start.

junction (jŭngk'shŭn) [L. *junctio,* as JOIN], *n.* Act of joining, the state of being joined; a joint, a point or place of union, esp. where lines of railway meet.

juncture (jŭngk'chúr) [as prec.], *n.* The place at which two things are joined, a joint; a point of time marked by the concurrence of critical circumstances.

June (joon) [L. *Jūnius*], *n.* The sixth month of the year.

jungle (jŭng'gĕl) [Hind. *jangal*], *n.* Land covered with forest trees or dense vegetation, esp. in India. **jungly,** *a.*

junior (joo'nyór) [L., comp. of *juvenis,* young], *a.* Younger; lower in standing. *n.* One younger or of lower standing than another. **junior'ity,** *n.*

juniper (joo'ni-pér) [L. *jūniperus*], *n.* A genus of prickly evergreen shrubs, the berries of which are used to flavour gin.

junk (1) (jŭngk) [Jav. *jong*], *n.* A flat-bottomed vessel used in the China seas.

junk (2) (jŭngk) [?], *n.* Pieces of old cable; worthless odds and ends; salt beef. **junk shop,** *n.* Shop where second-hand odds and ends are sold.

junket (jŭng'kĕt) [M.F. *juncade*], *n.* A dish of curds sweetened and flavoured, and served with cream. *v.* To make good cheer.

junta (jŭn'tá) [Sp., as JOIN], *n.* A legislative or administrative council, esp. in Spain, Italy, and S. America.

junto (jŭn'tō) [from prec.], *n.* A secret political or other council.

juridical (joo-rid'i-kál) [L. *jūridicus*], *a.* Pertaining to the administration of justice, or to jurisprudence.

jurisconsult (joo-ris-kón-sŭlt') [as prec., CONSULT], *n.* One learned in law, esp. civil or international; a jurist.

jurisdiction (joo-ris-dik'shŭn) [L. *jūrisdictiō*], *n.* The legal power or right of administering justice, making and enforcing laws; the district within which such power may be exercised.

jurisprudence (joo-ris-proo'dĕns) [L. *jūrisprudentia*], *n.* The philosophy of law; the science of the laws, constitutions, and rights of men; the legal system of a particular country.

jurist (joo'rist) [L. *jūs jūris,* law], *n.* One learned in the law.

juror (joor'ór) [L. *jūrāre,* to swear], *n.* One who serves on a jury.

jury (joor'i) [O.F. *furée,* an oath, as prec.], *n.* A body of men sworn to try and give a true verdict upon questions put before them. **juryman,** *n.*

jury-mast (joor'i-mast) [?], *n.* A temporary mast erected in place of one carried away.

just (jŭst) [L. *justus,* from *jūs,* right], *a.* Acting according to what is right; fair, impartial, honest; accurate, precise; fit, proper; deserved; righteous. *adv.* Exactly; barely, with nothing to spare; a very little time ago; perfectly, quite. **justly,** *adv.* **justness,** *n.*

justice (jŭs'tis) [L. *justitia,* as prec.], *n.* The quality of being just; fairness in dealing with others; uprightness, honesty; just requital of deserts; authoritative administration or maintenance of law and right; one who holds courts, hears causes, and administers justice between individuals; a magistrate. **justiceship,** *n.* **justiciary,** *n.* An administrator of justice. *a.* Pertaining to the administration of justice.

justify (jŭs'ti-fī), *v.t.* To prove to be just; to vindicate, make good, show grounds for; to declare free from the penalty of sin; to adjust. **justif'able,** *a.* **justifica'tion,** *n.*

jut (jŭt), *v.i.* To project, protrude; to stick (out). *n.* A protruding point.

jute (joot) [Bengali, *jhōto*], *n.* Fibre from the inner bark of certain plants, from which paper, cordage, etc., are prepared.

juvenile (joo'vĕ-nīl) [L. *juventīis* from

juvenis, young], *a.* Young; befitting or characteristic of youth.

juxtapose (jŭk-stá-pōz´) [L. *juxtā,* next, F. *poser,* to put], *v.t.* To place (a thing) next to or (things) side by side. **juxtaposi´tion,** *n.*

K

Kafir (kăf´ir) [Arab., infidel], *n.* One of a S. African Bantu race (nowadays used as a strongly pejorative term); their language. *a.* Of or pertaining to the Kafirs.

Kaiser (kī´zĕr) [G., from L. *Cæsar*], *n.* An emperor; the title of the former Emperors of Germany.

kale (kāl) [COLE], *n.* Cabbage, esp. with crinkled leaves. **kale-yard,** kail-yard, *n.* A kitchen garden.

kaleidoscope (ká-lī´dó-skōp) [Gr. *kalos,* beautiful, *eidos,* appearance, -SCOPE], *n.* An instrument showing an endless variety of symmetrical forms.

kali (kăl´ī, kā´lī) [Arab. *qalī*], *n.* The salt-wort, from which soda-ash was obtained

Kalmuck (kăl´mŭk) [Rus. *Kalmuikŭ*], *n.* One of a race of Mongols living between W. China and the Volga; a coarse shaggy cloth or coloured cotton.

Kanaka (ká-năk´á, kăn´á-ká) [Hawaiian], *n.* A South Sea islander.

kangaroo (kăng-gá-roo´) [native], *n.* A marsupial quadruped peculiar to Australasia, distinguished by large hind limbs and short fore limbs.

kayak (kī´ăk) [Eskimo], *n.* A canoe of sealskins stretched on a light framework.

kedge (kej) [?], *n.* A small portable anchor used in warping.

kedgeree (kej´ĕr-ē) [Hind. *khichri*], *n.* A dish of fish, rice, egg, etc.

keel (kēl) [prob. from Icel. *kjölr*], *n.* The principal timber of a ship, extending from bow to stern; a corresponding part in an iron vessel. **keelhaul,** *v.t.* To drag under water on one side of the ship and up again on the other.

keen (1) (kēn) [A.-S. *cēne*], *a.* Having a sharp edge or point; sensitive, acute; biting, piercing (of cold); acrimonious; eager, ardent (on). **keenness,** *n.*

keen (2) [Ir. *caoinim,* to weep], *n.* Lamentation over a deceased person. *v.t.* To mourn; to utter with keening.

keep (kēp) [A.-S. *cēpan*], *v.t.* (*past* and *p.p.* **kept**) To have in charge; to guard, preserve, protect; to maintain; to pay proper regard to; to celebrate; to remain in; to have regularly on sale; to restrain (from); to detain (in custody, etc.); to reserve (for). *v.i.* To continue or retain one's place; to continue to be (in a specified condition); to restrict oneself (to). *n.* Subsistence, maintenance; food required for subsistence; the main tower of a mediæval castle. **keeper,** *n.* **keeping,** *n.* **keepsake,** *n.* Anything kept for the sake of the giver.

keg (keg) [Scand.], *n.* A small cask or barrel.

kelp (kelp) [?], *n.* The calcined ashes of seaweed, from which carbonate of soda

was obtained, now used for obtaining iodine; the large, coarse seaweed from which kelp is produced.

kelson (kel´són), *n.* A longitudinal piece placed along the floor-timbers of a ship binding them to the keel.

ken (ken) [?], *v.t.* (*chiefly Sc.*) To understand; to know. *n.* View, sight; range of sight or knowledge.

kennel (1) (ken´ĕl) [O.F. *chenil,* L. *canis,* dog], *n.* A shelter for a dog or hounds; a hovel; a pack of hounds. *v.i.* To lodge in or as in a kennel.

kennel (2) [O.F. *canel*], *n.* A gutter, a puddle.

Kentish (ken´tish), *a.* Pertaining to the county of Kent. **Kentish Man;** A native of Kent born west of the Medway; **Man of Kent;** one born east of that river.

kerb (kĕrb) [CURB], *n.* A row of stones set as edging to a pavement, etc. **kerb-stone,** *n.*

kerchief (kĕr´chif) [O.F. (*covrir,* to cover, *chief,* head)], *n.* A cloth to cover the head, a napkin.

kernel (kĕr´nĕl) [A.-S. *cyrnel*], *n.* The substance contained in a nut or a fruit-stone; (*fig.*) the core, gist or essence.

kerosene (ker´ó-sēn) [Gr. *kēros,* wax], *n.* A lamp-oil distilled from petroleum, coal, etc.

kersey (kĕr´zi) [place in Suffolk], *n.* A coarse woollen cloth, usu. ribbed.

kestrel (kes´trĕl) [?], *n.* A small hawk.

ketch (kech) [formerly CATCH], *n.* A fore-and-aft rigged two-masted vessel.

ketchup (kech´ŭp) [Malay *kēchap*], *n.* A sauce made from mushrooms, tomatoes, etc.

kettle (ketl) [A.-S. *cetel*], *n.* A metal vessel for heating water, etc. **kettledrum,** *n.* A drum made of a hemispherical copper shell with a parchment head,

key (1) (kē) [A.-S. *cæg*], *n.* An instrument for working the bolt of a lock to and fro; that which gives access to or opportunity for something; that which explains anything difficult; a translation; (*Mus.*) one of several systems of notes having definite tonic relations among themselves and to the keynote; (*fig.*) the general tone or style (of a picture, speech, etc.). *v.t.* (*fig.*) To stir (up) to an action, etc. **keyboard,** *n.* The range of keys on a piano, organ, etc. **keyhole,** *n.* The hole in a lock, door, etc., by which a key is inserted. **key industry,** *n.* An industry upon which other industries and the economic welfare of a country depend. **key-note,** *n.* (*Mus.*) The fundamental note of a key; (*fig.*) the general tone or spirit (of a picture, poem, etc.). **keystone,** *n.* The central stone of an arch locking the others together; (*fig.*) the fundamental element, principle, etc. **keyed,** *a.* **keyless,** *a.* Not having a key; wound without a key.

key (2) [Sp. *cayo*], *n.* A low island, esp. of coral, on the coast of Florida.

khaki (ka´ki) [Hind., dusty], *a.* Dust-coloured, dull-yellow. *n.* Material of this colour, used for army uniforms.

kick (kik) [M.E. *kiken*], *v.t.* To strike with the foot; to push, move, or drive, by kicking; to strike in recoil. *v.i.* To strike out with the foot or feet; to recoil (as a gun); (*fig.*) to show opposition (at, etc.); (*colloq.*) a stimulating reaction (as to alcohol). *n.* The act of kicking; a blow with the foot; a recoil (of a gun).

kid (1) (kid) [Scand.], *n.* The young of the goat; leather from its skin; (*pl.*) gloves of this leather; (*slang*) a child. *v.i.* To bring forth a kid or kids.

kid (2) [?] *v.t.* (*Slang*) To humbug, deceive. *n.*

kidnap (kid'năp), *v.t.* To steal (a child); to abduct. **kidnapper,** *n.*

kidney (kid'ni) [?], *n.* One of the two glands in the lumbar region which secrete urine and remove nitrogenous matter from the blood; (*fig.*) temperament, kind, fashion.

kill (kil) [?], *v.t.* To deprive of life, to slay; to put an end to, to quell; to still (pain, etc.); to neutralize (effects of colour, etc.); to pass (time) idly. *v.i.* To slaughter, esp. in sport; (*slang*) to fascinate, to do execution. *n.* The act of killing; an animal or number of animals killed.

kiln (kiln, kil) [A.-S. *cyln*], *n.* A furnace for calcining, drying, etc.

kilo- [Gr. *chilioi*, a thousand], *comb. form.* **kilogramme** (kil'ŏ-grăm), *n.* A French measure of weight, 1,000 grammes or 2·2046 lb. av. **kilolitre** (kil'ŏ-lē-tėr), *n.* 1,000 litres, or 220 gallons. **kilometre** (kil'ŏ-mē-tėr), *n.* A measure of distance, 1,000 metres or ·621 mile.

kilt (kilt) [Scand.], *v.t.* To tuck up (the skirts of a dress); to gather together (material) into vertical pleats. *n.* A kind of short petticoat worn by the Highlanders of Scotland.

kimono (ki-mō'nō) [Jap.], *n.* A loose robe fastened with a sash, a Japanese outer garment.

kin (kin) [A.-S. *cynn*], *n.* Stock, family; kindred. *a.* Of the same family, nature, or kind; akin.

kind (kīnd) [A.-S. *cynd*], *n.* Race, natural group; sort, class; manner, fashion, way. *a.* Disposed to do good to others; sympathetic, tender; proceeding from or characterized by goodness of heart. **kindness,** *n.*

kindergarten (kin'dėr-gar-tėn) [G., children's garden], *n.* A school for infants.

kindle (kindl) [Scand.], *v.t.* To set fire to; to light; to inspire (the passions, etc.); to excite, to stir up (to action, etc.); to light up or illumine. *v.i.* To take fire; (fig.) to become inflamed or excited, to become illumined.

kindly (kīnd'li), *a.* Kind, good-natured, genial; favourable, auspicious. **kindliness,** *n.*

kindred (kin'drĕd), *n.* Relationship by blood or marriage; (*fig.*) likeness of character; (*collect.*) relatives, kin. *a.* Related by blood; (*fig.*) congenial, sympathetic.

kinematic (ki-nė-măt'ik) [Gr. *kinēma* -*matos*, movement, from *kinein*, to move], *a.* Pertaining to movement or to kinematics. *n.pl.* The science of pure

motion, admitting conceptions of time and velocity but excluding that of force.

kinetic (ki-net'ik) [as prec.], *a.* Of, producing, or depending upon motion. *n.pl.* That branch of dynamics which treats of forces imparting motion to bodies.

king (king) [A.-S. *cyning*], *n.* The male sovereign of a nation; (*fig.*) one who is pre-eminent in any sphere; (*Cards*) a card ranking next to the ace and before the queen; (*Chess*) a piece which has to be protected from checkmate; (*Draughts*) a piece which is entitled to move in any direction. **king-cup,** *n.* The bulbous buttercup, the marsh marigold, and allied species. **kingfisher,** *n.* A small British bird with brilliant blue and green plumage, subsisting on fish. **king'dom,** *n.* The territory under a king; the position or attributes of a king; sovereign power; the highest of the divisions into which natural objects are arranged.

kink (kingk) [Scand.], *n.* A twist or abrupt bend in a rope, wire, etc.; a prejudice, a crotchet.

kinsfolk (kinz'fŏk), *n.* Family relations, kindred. **kinsman, -woman,** *n.*

kiosk (kee-osk') [Turk. *kiushk*], *n.* A summer-house; a light structure for the sale of newspapers; a band-stand.

kipper (kip'ėr) [?], *n.* A herring split open, salted, and smoke-dried. *v.t.* To cure and preserve (salmon, herrings, etc.).

kirk (kėrk) [Sc.], *n.* A church.

kirtle (kėrtl) [A.-S. *cyrtel*], *n.* A woman's gown or petticoat; a man's short jacket.

kismet (kis'mét) [Arab. *qisma(t*), from *qasama*, to divide], *n.* Fate, destiny.

kiss (kis) [A.-S. *coss*], *n.* A caress or salute with the lips; (*Billiards*) a mere touch of the moving balls. *v.t.* To salute or caress by pressing or touching with the lips. *v.i.* To join lips in affection or respect.

kit (kit) [M.Dut. *kitte*], *n.* An outfit, esp. of a soldier.

kitchen (kich'ėn) [A.-S. *cycene*], *n.* A room where food is cooked. **kitchen-garden,** *n.* A garden in which vegetables, etc., are cultivated for the table. **kitchen-range,** *n.* A grate with oven, boiler, etc., for cooking.

kite (kīt) [A.-S. *cýta*], *n.* A medium-sized bird of prey; (*fig.*) a greedy or rapacious person, a sharper; a light device of wood and paper constructed for flying in the air.

kith (kith) [A.-S. *cythth*, native country], *n.* Kindred.

kitten (kitn) [M.E. *kitoun*], *n.* The young of the cat; a playful girl. *v.i.* To bring forth kittens.

kittiwake (kit'i-wāk) [imit. cry], *n.* A sea-gull, common on the British coasts.

kleptomania (klep-tŏ-mā'ni-ă) [Gr. *kleptēs*, thief, -MANIA], *n.* An irresistible propensity to steal. **kleptomaniac,** *n.*

knack (năk) [?], *n.* An adroit way of doing a thing; dexterity.

knacker (năk'ėr) [?], *n.* A dealer in worn-out horses; a horse-slaughterer.

knap (năp) [imit.], *v.t.* To break into pieces, esp. with a snap; to flake or chip flint.

knapsack (năp'săk) [Dut.], *n.* A case for clothes, etc., carried on the back.

knave (nāv) [A.-S. *cnafa*, a boy], *n.* A tricky fellow, a rogue; (*Cards*) a court-card below the queen and above the ten, the jack. **knavery,** *n.* **knavish,** *a.*

knead (nĕd) [A.-S. *cnedan*], *v.t.* To work up (flour, etc.) with the hands; to work into dough; to shape, or mingle by this method; to work thus on (the muscles) in massage. **kneading-trough,** *n.* A trough in which dough is worked up.

knee (nē) [A.-S. *cnēo*], *n.* The joint of the thigh with the leg; part of a garment covering this; a piece of timber or metal with a similar angle to connect beams, etc. **knee-breeches,** *n.pl.* Breeches reaching just below the knee. **knee-cap,** *n.* The bone in front of the knee-joint. **knee-pan,** *n.* The knee-cap or socket of the knee.

kneel (nēl) [A.-S. *cnēowlian*], *v.i.* (*past* and *p.p.* knelt). To bend or fall on the knees.

knell (nel) [A.-S. *cnyllan*], *v.i.* To toll as a funeral bell; to sound in a mournful or ominous manner. *n.* The sound of a bell, esp. at a death or funeral.

knickerbockers (nik'ĕr-bok-ĕrz) [imag. author of Washington Irving's "History of New York"], *n.* Loose breeches gathered in below the knee. **knickers,** *n.* A woman's undergarment covering the upper part of the legs up to the waist, drawers.

knick-knack (nik'năk) *n.* A showy trifle; a trinket.

knife (nīf) [A.-S. *cnīf*], *n.* A blade with one edge sharpened, set in a handle; a cutting part of a machine.

knight (nīt) [A.-S. *cniht*, a boy, servant], *n.* Formerly, one of gentle birth, admitted to an honourable degree of military rank; one who holds a non-hereditary dignity entitling him to the title "Sir"; (*Chess*) a piece shaped like a horse's head. *v.t.* To create or dub (a person) a knight. **knight-errant,** *n.* A mediæval knight who wandered about in quest of adventures. **knight-errantry,** *n.* **knight of the shire:** Formerly, a parliamentary representative of a county. **knightly,** *a.* and *adv.*

knit (nit) [A.-S. *cnyttan*, rel. to KNOT], *v.t.* To form into a fabric or a garment by looping a continuous yarn; (*fig.*) to join closely together, to unite; to contract into wrinkles. *v.i.* To make a textile fabric by interweaving yarn or thread; (*fig.*) to become closely united. **knitting,** *n.* **knitting-needle, -pin,** *n.* A long eyeless needle with blunt ends, used in knitting.

knob (nob) [cogn. with KNAP], *n.* A rounded protuberance, as a handle of a door, lock, drawer, etc.

knock (nok) [A.-S. *cnocian*], *v.t.* To give a hard blow to; to force by striking; to cause to strike together. *v.i.* To strike hard or smartly (at, against, together, etc.). *n.* A blow; a rap, esp. on a door for admission. **knock-kneed,** *a.* Having knees bent inwards in walking. **knock-out,** *a.* Disabling (of a blow). **knocker,** *n.* A hammer-like attachment to a door for knocking for admittance.

knoll (nōl) [A.-S. *cnoll*], *n.* A rounded hill; a mound, a hillock.

knot (not) [A.-S. *cnotta*], *n.* The interlacement of a rope or ropes, etc., so as to fasten to itself or to another object; an ornamental bow on a dress; a shoulder-pad used by market-porters for carrying burdens; (*fig.*) a difficulty, perplexity, problem; an irregular portion in a tree caused by branches, buds, etc.; the rate of a nautical mile per hour. *v.t.* To tie in or fasten with a knot; to intertwine; to join together closely or intricately; to entangle, perplex. *v.i.* To form knots (of plants); to make knots for fringe. **knotted,** *a.* **knotty,** *a.*

knout (nout) [Rus. *knutu*], *n.* A scourge used in Russia for punishment.

know (nō) [A.-S. *cnāwan*], *v.t.* (*past* knew, (nū), *p.p.* known) To have a clear perception of; to identify; to be convinced of the truth or reality of; to be acquainted with, have personal experience of, or be on intimate terms with; to be aware of; to understand from learning or study. *v.i.* To have knowledge; to be assured (of). *n.* Knowledge of. **in the know:** having inside knowledge. **knowing,** *a.* Intelligent; experienced; sharp, cunning.

knowledge (nol'ĕj), *n.* The result of knowing; that which is known; familiarity gained by experience; learning; erudition, science.

knuckle (nŭkl) [M.E. *knokil*], *n.* A joint of a finger, esp. at the base; the middle or tarsal joint of a quadruped. *v.i.* To submit, to yield (with *down* or *under*). **knuckle-duster,** *n.* An iron instrument to add force to a blow.

kohlrabi (kōl-ra'bi) [G.], *n.* The turnip-stemmed cabbage.

Koran (kō-ran') [Arab. *qurān*, from *qara'a*, to read], *n.* The Mohammedan scriptures.

kosher (kō'shĕr) [Heb. *kāshēr*, right], *a.* Permitted (of food fulfilling requirements of Jewish law).

kraal (kral) [S. Afr. Dut.], *n.* A S. African village or group of huts enclosed by a palisade; a hut.

kudos (kū'dos) [Gr.], *n.* Fame, credit.

kummel (kim'ĕl) [G.], *n.* A liqueur flavoured with caraway-seeds.

L

laager (la'gĕr) [S. Afr. Dut.], *n.* A defensive encampment, esp. formed with wagons, etc. *v.i.* To encamp.

label (lā'bĕl) [O.F., a ribbon], *n.* A narrow strip of paper, etc., attached to an object to indicate contents, destination, ownership, etc. *v.t.* To affix a label to; (*fig.*) to describe, to set down (as).

labial (lā'bi-ăl) [L. *labium*, lip], *a.* Pertaining to the lips or lip-like organs; (*Phon.*) formed or modified in sound by the lips. *n.* A sound or letter representing a sound formed with the lips.

laboratory (lăb'ŏr-á-tŏr-i) [L. *labŏrāre*, to labour], *n.* A place in which scientific experiments are conducted; a manufactory of chemical articles, etc.

laborious (là-bôr'i-ùs) [as foll.], *a.* Working hard or perseveringly; industrious; betraying marks of labour, laboured; hard, fatiguing. laboriously, *adv.*

labour (lā'bòr) [L. *labor*, whence *labōrāre*, F. *labourer*, to labour], *n.* Physical or mental exertion, esp. in obtaining the means of subsistence; a task, esp. one requiring great effort; travail, the pains of childbirth; (*Polit. Econ.*) the element contributed by toil to production, esp. in opp. to capital; the Labour Party, *v.i.* To toil, to exert oneself; to proceed with difficulty; to be burdened with difficulties; (*Naut.*) to move heavily and slowly, to pitch or roll; to be in travail or the pains of childbirth. Labour Exchange, *n.* State office for the registration of unemployed and for placing them in work. Labour Party, *n.* (*Polit.*) British political party professing Socialism. labourer, *n.* One who performs work requiring manual labour but little skill.

laburnum (là-bĕr'nùm) [L.], *n.* A tree with yellow flowers.

labyrinth (lăb'i-rinth) [Gr. *laburinthos*], *n.* A maze. labyrinthine, *a.*

lace (lās) [O.F. *las*], *n.* A cord used to bind or fasten, esp. by interweaving; ornamental network of threads forming a fabric of open texture; ornamental braid for uniforms, etc. *v.t.* To fasten with a lace through eyelet-holes. lace-pillow, *n.* A cushion on which various kinds of lace are made. lacing, *n.* A fastening by a cord passing through holes, etc.

lacerate (lăs'ėr-āt) [L. *lacerātus*, torn], *v.t.* To tear, to mangle; (*fig.*) to rend, harrow. *a.* Torn. lacera'tion, *n.*

lachrymal (lăk'ri-mál) [L. *lacryma*, tear], *a.* Pertaining to tears; secreting or conveying tears (of glands, ducts, etc.). lach'rymatory, *a.* lachrymose, *a.* Shedding or ready to shed tears.

lack (lăk) [Teut.], *n.* Deficiency, want, need (of); that which is needed. *v.t.* To be in need of, to be without; to feel the want of. *v.i.* To be deficient (in); to be wanting.

lackadaisical (lăk-à-dā'zi-kàl), *a.* Affectedly pensive, languishing, sentimental.

lackey (lăk'i) [F. *laquais*], *n.* A footman; (*fig.*) a servile follower.

laconic (là-kon'ik) [Gr. *Lakōnikos*, Spartan], *a.* Pertaining to Laconia or Sparta, or its inhabitants; hence brief, sententious, pithy. laconism, *n.*

lacquer (lăk'ėr) [as LAC], *n.* A shellac varnish coloured with gold, gamboge, etc.; woodwork coated with such a varnish, usu. decorated with inlaid figures. *v.t.* To cover with lacquer.

lacrosse (la-kros') [F.], *n.* A ball-game resembling hockey, played with a crosse or stringed bat.

lacteal (lăk'tê-ál) [L. *lac*, milk], *a.* Pertaining to milk; milky; conveying chyle. *n.pl.* The vessels which convey chyle from the alimentary canal. lacteous, *a.* Milky. lactation, *n.* Giving suck to an infant. lactic, *a.* Pertaining to milk; contained in or derived from sour milk.

lacuna (là-kū'nà) [L.], *n.* (*pl.* -næ) A gap, a hiatus; a small pit or depression.

lad (lăd) [M.E. *ladde*], *n.* A boy, a stripling; (*colloq.*) a fellow. laddie, *n.*

ladder (lăd-ėr) [A.-S. *hlæder*], *n.* A device of wood, iron, rope, etc., consisting of two long uprights, connected by crosspieces forming steps by which one may ascend. *v.i.* (Of stockings and knitted fabrics) to form a rent through the snapping of a longitudinal thread.

lade (lād) [A.-S. *hladan*], *v.t.* (*p.p.* laden) To put a load or burden on; to put a cargo on board; to ship (goods) as cargo.

ladle (lādl) [A.-S. *hlœdel*, as LADE], *n.* A large spoon with which liquids are lifted. *v.t.* To serve out with a ladle.

lady (lā'di) [A.-S. *hlæfdīge*], *n.* A woman of good breeding or social standing; the mistress of a house; a title given to the wife of a knight or any superior to him in rank, and the daughter (or the wife of a son) of an earl, marquess, or duke. Our Lady: The Virgin Mary. lady-bird, *n.* A small red coleopterous insect with black spots. ladylike, *a.* ladyship, *n.*

lag (lăg) [?], *a.* Last; sluggish, tardy. *v.i.* To loiter, to fall behind. *n.* Retardation of movement; one who lags behind or comes last; (*colloq.*) a convict. laggard, *a.* Slow, sluggish, backward; wanting in energy. *n.* A slow, sluggish fellow; a loiterer.

lagoon (là-goon') [F. *lagune*, L. *lacuna*], *n.* A shallow lake near a river or the sea; the water enclosed by a coral island.

laic (lā'ik) [LAY], *a.* Lay, secular.

lair (lâr) [A.-S. *leger*, a bed], *n.* The den of a wild beast.

laird (lârd) [Sc., LORD], *n.* The owner of a landed estate; a landlord, squire.

laissez-faire (lā-sā-fâr') [F., let them do], *n.* (*Polit.*) Policy of non-interference.

laity (lā'i-ti) [A.-F. *laité*], *n.* The people as distinct from the clergy, laymen.

lake (1) (lāk) [O.F. *lac*, L. *lacus*], *n.* A large sheet of water entirely surrounded by land.

lake (2) [LAC], *n.* A crimson pigment.

lama (la'mà) [Tibetan], *n.* A Tibetan or Mongolian Buddhist priest.

lamb (lăm) [A.-S.], *n.* The young of the sheep; its flesh as food; (*fig.*) one as innocent and gentle as a lamb, a member of a flock. *v.i.* To bring forth lambs.

lambent (lăm'bènt) [L. *lambens*, licking], *a.* Touching slightly without burning (as flame); softly radiant; playing about.

lame (lām) [A.-S. *lama*], *a.* Disabled in a limb, esp. the foot or leg; limping, halting; unsatisfactory; imperfect. *v.t.* To make lame, to cripple. lameness, *n.*

lament (là-ment') [L. *lāmentāri*], *v.i.* To mourn, wail; to feel or express sorrow. *v.t.* To bewail, to mourn over; to deplore. *n.* Sorrow audibly expressed; an elegy, a dirge; a mournful song. lam'entable, *a.* To be lamented; mournful, unfortunate, deplorable. lamentation, *n.* lamen'ted, *a.* Mourned for; deceased.

lamina (lăm'i-nà) [L.], *n.* (*pl.* -næ) A thin plate, layer, flake, stratum, etc.

Lammas (làm'às) [S.-S. *hlāfmœsse*], *n.* The

1st August. **latter Lammas:** A day that will never arrive.

lamp (lămp) [Gr. *lampein*, to shine], *n.* A contrivance for the production of artificial light, esp. a vessel containing oil for combustion with a wick; (*fig.*) any source of light or of spiritual light. **lamppost,** *n.* A pillar supporting a street lamp.

lampoon (lăm-poon') [F.], *n.* A sarcastic personal satire. *v.t.* To write lampoons upon; to abuse with personal satire.

lamprey (lăm'pri) [L. *lambere*, to lick, *petra*, rock], *n.* An eel-like fish with a mouth used as a sucker.

lance (lans) [L. *lancea*], *n.* A long shaft with a sharp point, formerly the peculiar weapon of knights, later used by some regiments of cavalry; a similar weapon used for spearing fish, etc. *v.t.* To pierce with a lance; (*Surg.*) to open with a lancet. **lance corporal, sergeant,** *n.* (*Mil.*) A private or corporal doing the duties of a corporal or sergeant. **lancer,** *n.* A cavalry soldier armed with a lance; (*pl.*) a square dance.

lanceolate (lan'sē-ô-lăt) [dim. L. of *lancea*, LANCE], *a.* Tapering to a point at each end.

lancet (lan'sĕt), *n.* A surgical instrument used in bleeding, cutting of abscesses, tumours, etc.

land (lănd) [A.-S.], *n.* The solid portion of the earth, as dist. from the sea; the ground, soil, a tract of country; a country, a region; a nation; landed property, real estate. *v.t.* To set or place on shore; to bring to shore; to set down from a vehicle; to deal (a blow); to bring (fish) to land. *v.i.* To disembark; to find oneself in a certain position; to alight. **land-breeze,** *n.* A wind blowing seawards off the land. **landlady,** *n.* A woman who keeps an inn or lodging-house; a woman who lets houses, etc. **landlocked.** *p.p.* Enclosed with land. **landlord,** *n.* One who has tenants holding under him; the master of an inn or of a lodging-house. **land-lubber,** *n.* A landsman, one unused to the sea or ships. **landmark,** *n.* Anything set up to mark the boundaries of land; an object on land serving as a guide for sailors, etc. **landrail,** *n.* The corn-crake. **landslide,** *n.* A landslip; a political debacle. **landslip,** *n.* The sliding down of a considerable portion of ground to a lower level; the ground thus slipping. **landsman,** *n.* One who lives on land; one unused to the sea and its ways. **land-steward,** *n.* One who manages a landed estate. **land-surveyor,** *n.* One who measures and draws plans of estates, etc. **land-swell,** *n.* The roll of the sea inshore. **landed,** *a.* Having an estate in land; consisting of real estate. **landing,** *n.* The act of going or setting on land, esp. from a vessel; a pier, wharf; a level space at the top of a flight of stairs. **landing-net,** *n.* A net used to take fish when hooked. **landward,** *a.* and *adv.*

landau (lăn'dō) [German town], *n.* A four-wheeled carriage with a folding top.

landscape (lănd'skāp) [Dut. *landschap*], *n.* A picture representing country scenery; a view of country scenery.

lane (lān) [A.-S.], *n.* A narrow road, esp. between hedges; a narrow street.

language (lăng'gwáj) [F. *langage*, L. *lingua*, tongue], *n.* Human speech; the communication of ideas by words; the vocabulary peculiar to a nation, etc., or appropriate to a science, profession, etc.; the phrases, etc., peculiar to an individual; literary style; phraseology, wording.

languid (lăng'gwid) [as foll.], *a.* Faint, lacking energy; spiritless, listless, dull; sluggish, slow. **languidly,** *adv.*

languish (lăng'gwish) [L. *languēre*, rel. to *laxus*, LAX], *v.i.* To become feeble or sluggish; to lose energy or animation; to fade, grow slack; to droop, to pine (for); to put on a languid expression, to affect a tender, wistful, or sentimental air. **languishment,** *n.*

langour (lăng'gòr), *n.* Languidness, lassitude, faintness, inertness; debility, nervous prostration; tenderness of mood or expression; oppressive stillness (of the air, etc.). **languorous,** *a.*

lank (lăngk) [A.-S. *hlanc*], *a.* Lean, long and straight (of the hair). **lanky,** *a.*

lanolin ((lăn'ô-lin) [L. *lāna*, wool], *n.* An unctuous substance extracted from wool.

lantern (lăn'tèrn) [L. *lanterna*], *n.* A case with transparent panes for holding and protecting a light; a glazed structure on the top of a dome or roof for the admission of light and air; the lighthouse chamber containing the light. **lantern-jawed,** *a.* Having a long, thin face.

lanyard (lăn'yàrd) [F. *lanière*], *n.* (*Naut.*) A short line for seizing or lashing.

lap (1) (lăp) [A.-S. *læppa*], *n.* A loose hanging part of a garment, esp. that part which hangs over the knees when a person sits down; the part of the person from the waist to the knees in sitting.

lap (2) [?], *v.t.* To wrap, to roll (round, about, etc.); to fold, bend over; to enwrap, surround, involve; to cause to overlap; to bind. *n.* That part of anything that extends over something else; one round of a race-course.

lap (3) (lăp) [A.-S. *lapian*], *v.i.* To drink by lifting with the tongue; (*fig.*) to beat (as waves on the shore) with a sound as of lapping. *v.t.* To lick or take up with the tongue; to drink or consume by lapping. *n.* The act of lapping; a lick.

lapel (lăp'él), *n.* That part of a garment made to lap over, esp. the fold on the front of a coat below the collar.

lapidary (lăp'ĭ-dăr-ĭ) [L. *lapidārius*], *n.* One who cuts, polishes, engraves, or deals in gems; a connoisseur of gems. *a.* Pertaining to cutting stones; suitable for inscription; terse, uninspired.

lapis lazuli (lăp'ĭs-lăz'ū-lĭ) [L. *lapis*, stone, *lazulum*, azure], *n.* A rich blue silicate containing lime, and soda.

lapse (lăps) [L. *lapsāre*, freq. of *lābĭ*, to glide], *v.i.* To pass insensibly or by degrees; to fall into disuse; to make a slip, to fall in duty; to pass from one proprietor to another by omission, negligence, etc.; to become void. *n.* The act of lapsing, gliding, slipping, or gradually falling (away, from, etc.); the imperceptible passage of time; a slip, an error, a fault, deviation from what is right; a falling into disuse, neglect, decay, or ruin.

lapwing [A.-S. *hléapewince*], *n.* A bird of the plover family, the peewit.

larboard (lar'bôrd, -bórd) [M.E. *ladeborde*], *n.* The left side of a vessel to a person facing the bow; port.

larceny (lar'sĕ-ni) [A.-F. *larcin*, L. *latrōcinium* (*latro*, a robber)], *n.* The unlawful taking away of another's personal goods, theft.

larch (larch) [L. *larix*], *n.* A coniferous tree having deciduous bright-green foliage, and tough, durable timber.

lard (lard) [L. *lardum*], *n.* The fat of hogs melted and separated from the flesh. *v.t.* To fatten; to smear with lard; to insert strips of bacon in before roasting; (*fig.*) to intermix (writing, talk), with foreign phrases, flowers of speech, etc.

larder (lar'dĕr) [as prec.], *n.* A room where meat and other provisions are kept.

large (larj) [L. *largus*], *a.* Great in size, number, quantity, extent, or capacity; big, bulky; extensive; ample, copious; liberal, lavish; wide in range, comprehensive. **at large**: At liberty, free; freely; with ample detail. **large-hearted**, *a.* Having a liberal heart or disposition. **largely**, *adv.* To a large extent.

largess (lar'jes) [F. *largesse*, as prec.], *n.* A present, a generous bounty; liberality.

largo (lar'gō) [It.], *adv.* (*Mus.*) Slowly, broadly, in an ample, dignified style.

lariat (lăr'i-ăt) [Sp. *la reata*, the rope], *n.* A rope for picketing horses in camp.

lark (1) (lark) [A.-S. *laferce*], *n.* A small British song-bird, the skylark. **larkspur**, *n.* A plant with spur-shaped calyx.

lark (2) [?], *n.* A prank, a frolic. *v.i.* To sport, to frolic. **larky**, *a.*

larrikin (lăr'i-kin) [Austral.], *n.* A rowdy young hooligan.

larva (lar'vă) [L., a ghost, mask], *n.* (*pl.* -væ) The first condition of an insect on its issuing from the egg, a caterpillar, maggot. **larval**, *a.*

larynx (lăr'ingks) [Gr. *larunx*], *n.* (*pl.* -ynges) The vocal organ, consisting of the upper part of the windpipe, containing the vocal cords. **laryn'geal**, **laryn'gic**, *a.* Pertaining to the larynx. **laryngitis** (-ji'tis), *n.* Inflammation of the larynx.

lascivious (lă-siv'i-ŭs) [L. *lascīvus*, lustful], *a.* Lewd, wanton, lustful; exciting lust.

lash (lăsh) [?], *n.* The flexible part of a whip; a scourge; a stroke with a whip; flogging; an eyelash; sarcasm, satire, vituperation. *v.t.* To flog with anything pliant and tough; to whip; to drive with a whip; to dash against; to bind with a rope or cord; to assail fiercely with satire. *v.i.* To use a whip; to strike, fling, or kick violently (at, out, etc.); to fling out sarcasm. **lashing**, *n.* A rope by which anything is secured; a flogging.

lass (lăs) [M.E. *lasce*], *n.* A young woman, a girl; a sweetheart. **lassie**, *n.*

lassitude (lăs'i-tūd) [L. *lassus*, weary], *n.* Weariness, lack of energy; languor.

lasso (lăs'ō, lăs-oo') [O.Sp. *laso*], *n.* A leather rope with a running noose, used for catching cattle, etc. *v.t.* To catch with a lasso.

last (1) (last) [A.-S. *latost*, *lætest*, superl. of *læt*, LATE], *a.* Coming after all others or at the end; closing, final; pertaining to the end; conclusive, definitive; utmost, lowest, meanest; only remaining; next before the present, most recent. *n.* The end; the last moment, hour, day, etc.; death; (*ellipt.*) the last thing done, mentioned, etc. *adv.* On or for the last time or occasion; after all others. *v.i.* To continue in existence; to hold out, to continue unexhausted or unimpaired, to endure. **lasting**, *a.* Continuing; enduring; permanent, durable. **lastly**, *adv.* At last; finally.

last (2) [A.-S. *lást*, foot-track], *n.* A shaped block on which boots and shoes are fashioned.

latch (lăch) [A.-S. *læccan*, to catch], *n.* A fastening for a door, gate, etc. *v.t.* To fasten with a latch.

latchet (lăch'ĕt) [LACE], *n.* A string for a shoe or sandal.

late (lāt) [A.-S. *læt*], *a.* Coming after the usual time; slow, backward, long delayed; far on towards the close; far on in any period or in development; far advanced; existing previously but not now; deceased; lately or recently alive, in office, etc.; recent in date. *adv.* After the proper or usual time; at or till a late hour, season.

lateen (lă-tēn') [F. *latine*, LATIN], *n.* A triangular sail used in the Mediterranean.

latent (lā'tĕnt) [L. *latens*], *a.* Lying hid or concealed; not apparent; dormant, not active, potential. **latency**, *n.*

lateral (lăt'ĕr-ăl) [L. *latus*, side], *a.* Pertaining to, at, from, or towards the side.

latex (lā'teks) [L., liquid, fluid], *n.* (*Bot.*) The juice of milky plants.

lath (lath) [A.-S. *læth*], *n.* A thin strip of wood, such as is nailed to rafters to support tiles, or plastering. *v.t.* To cover or line with laths. **lathing**, *n.*

lathe (lāth) [?], *n.* A machine for turning and polishing wood, ivory, metal, etc.

lather (lăth'ĕr) [A.-S. *léathor*], *n.* Froth or foam made by soap moistened with water, or caused by profuse sweating. *v.i.* To form a lather, to become covered with lather (of a horse). *v.t.* To cover with lather.

Latin (lăt'in) [L. *Latīnus*, from *Latium*], *a.* Pertaining to ancient Latium or ancient Rome, the inhabitants, or their language, or to any of the derived languages. *n.* The Latin language. **Latinism**, *n.* **Latinist**, *n.* **latin'ity**, *n.* Quality of Latin style, idiom, or scholarship.

latitude (lăt'i-tūd) [L. *lătitūdo*, from *lătus*, broad], *n.* Breadth; extent, comprehensiveness; looseness of application or meaning; laxity, freedom from rule or restraint; extent of deviation from a standard; angular distance on a meridian, angular distance of a place north or south of the equator; (*pl.*) regions, climates. **latitudinar'ian**, *n.* One who does not attach great importance to dogmas. *a.* Wide in range or scope; free from prejudice, attaching little importance to

H

speculative opinions; lax. **latitudinar-ianism**, *n.*

latrine (là-trēn') [L. *latrina*, from *lavare*, to wash], *n.* A privy, water-closet.

-latry [Gr. *-latreia*, worship (*-later*, Gr. *-latrēs*, worshipper)], *comb. form.* As in *bibliolatry, idolatry.*

latter (lăt'ér) [A.-S. *lœtra*, compar. of *lœt*, LATE], *a.* Coming or happening after something else; last-mentioned; modern, present; lately done; second-mentioned; pertaining to the end of a period, life, the world, etc. **latter-day:** Modern.

lattice (lăt'is) [O.F. *lattis*, from *latte*, lath], *n.* A structure of laths or strips of metal crossing and forming open work. **lattice-window**, *n.* A window consisting of small (usu. diamond-shaped) panes set in strips of lead.

laud (lawd) [L. *laudāre*, to praise], *v.t.* To praise, celebrate, extol. *n.* Praise; thankful adoration; a song of praise; (*pl.*) the psalms immediately following matins. **laudable**, *a.* Praiseworthy, commendable. **lauda'tion**, *n.* Praise.

laudanum (law'dà-nŭm) [?], *n.* Opium prepared in alcohol, tincture of opium.

laugh (laf) [A.-S. *hlehhan*], *v.i.* To express amusement, scorn, or exultation by inarticulate sounds and convulsive movements of the face, etc.; to deride, scoff (at); to be or appear gay or sportive. *v.t.* To express by laughing; to utter with laughter; to move or affect by laughter. *n.* The action or manner of laughing; an explosion of laughter. **laughable**, *a.* Exciting laughter; comical, ridiculous. **laughing gas**, *n.* Nitrous oxide, used as an anæsthetic. **laughing-stock**, *n.* An object of ridicule; a butt. **laughter**, *n.*

launch (1) (lawnch, lanch) [O.F. *lancier*, to lance], *v.t.* To throw, to hurl; to cause (a vessel) to glide into the water; to start or set (a person, etc.) going; to fulminate. *v.i.* To be launched (of a ship); to put to sea; to enter on a new sphere; to expatiate. *n.* The act of launching.

launch (2) (lawnch, lanch) [Sp. and Port. *lancha*], *n.* The largest boat belonging to a man-of-war; a pleasure-boat.

laundress (lawn'drès) [L. *lavanda*, things to be washed], *n.* A washerwoman; a woman who looks after chambers in the Inns of Court. **launder**, *v.t.* To wash and get up (linen). **laundry** (lawn'dri), *n.* A place where clothes are washed.

laureate (law-rē-àt) [L. *laurea*, a laurel-wreath], *a.* Crowned with laurel; eminent, distinguished, esp. as a poet; a Poet Laureate. **laureateship**, *n.*

laurel (lor'él) [F. *laurier*, L. *laurus*], *n.* A glossy-leaved evergreen shrub; its foliage. **laurelled**, *a.* Crowned with laurel.

lava (la'và) [It.], *n.* Molten matter flowing in streams from volcanic vents, or solidified by cooling.

lavatory (lăv'à-tŏr-i) [L. *lavātōrium*], *n.* A place for washing; a water-closet.

lave (lāv) [A.-S. *lafian*, F. *laver*, L. *lavāre*], *v.t.* To wash or flow against.

lavender (lăv'én-dér) [A.-F. *lavendre*], *n.* A sweet-scented flowering shrub, cultivated for its oil which is used in perfumery; the colour of the flowers, a pale lilac.

laver (lā'vér), *n.* A brazen vessel for the Jewish priests to wash in when they offered sacrifices.

lavish (lăv'ish) [O.F. *lavache*, a deluge of words], *a.* Spending or giving with profusion; prodigal, unrestrained; existing or produced in profusion. *v.t.* To expend or bestow profusely.

law (law) [A.-S. *lagu*], *n.* A rule imposed by authority or accepted as binding; a system of such rules, its controlling influence, the condition of order and stability it secures; the practical application of these rules, esp. by litigation, judicial process, etc.; jurisprudence; legal knowledge; the legal profession; rules governing a profession, art, association, sport, etc.; a start or time allowance in a hunt or race. **lawgiver**, *n.* One who makes or enacts laws, a legislator. **lawlord**, *n.* A member of the House of Lords qualified to deal with the judicial business of the House. **lawsuit**, *n.* An action in a court of law. **lawful**, *a.* Conformable to or allowed by law; legitimate. **lawfulness**, *n.* **lawless**, *a.* Regardless of or unrestrained by the law, unbridled, illegal. **lawlessness**, *n.*

lawn (1) (lawn) [O.F. *launde*, from Celt.], *n.* A grassy space kept smooth and closely mown. **lawn-tennis**, *n.* A game resembling tennis, played on a lawn or hard court.

lawn (2) [*Laon*, a French town], *n.* A cotton or linen fabric, finer than cambric.

lawyer (law'yér), *n.* One who practises law, esp. a solicitor.

lax (lăks) [L. *laxus*], *a.* Loose, not tight, firm, or compact; not exact, not strict; negligent, careless; vague; relaxed in the bowels. **lax'ative**, *a.* Opening or loosening the bowels. *n.* A medicine to assist this. **laxity**, *n.*

lay (1) (lā) [A.-S. *lecgan*], *v.t.* (*past and p.p.* laid) To place in a prostrate or recumbent position; to drop (as eggs); to put down, to deposit; to wager; to dispose regularly, put in proper position; to spread; to prostrate; to overthrow; to cause to settle (as dust); to cause to be still, to calm; to exorcize; to bring into a certain state or position; to present; to impose, enjoin, inflict; to bring down (blows, etc., on); to plan, prepare; (*Mil.*) to point (a gun); (*Lit.*) to locate (a story, etc.). *v.i.* To deposit eggs; to wager. *n.* The direction or position in which something is situated; the direction the strands of a rope are twisted; (*slang*) occupation, job. **laying**, *n.*

lay (2) [Gr. *laikos*, from *laos*, the people], *a.* Pertaining to the people as distinct from the clergy; non-professional, esp. with reference to lawyers and doctors. **lay brother or sister:** A monk or nun engaged in manual labour and exempt from other duties. **layman**, *n.* One of the people, as distinguished from the clergy.

lay (3) [O.F. *lai*], *n.* A lyric; a short narrative poem for singing or recitation.

lay (4) [LEA]

layer (lā'ér), *n.* One who or that which lays; a thickness of anything spread out (usu. o ne of several), a stratum; a shoot laid partly beneath the surface so that it may take root.

layette (lā-et´) [F.], *n.* The outfit for a new-born baby.

lay figure (lā´fig´ūr) [*lay*, from Dut. *leeman*, joint-man (*lid*, joint)], *n.* A jointed figure of the human body used by artists for hanging drapery on, etc.

lazy (lā´zĭ) [?], *a.* Idle, disinclined for work or exertion; disposing to sloth. **lazy-bones**, *n.* A lazy fellow, an idler. **laziness**, *n.*

-le, *suf.* Forming diminutives of nouns, as *bramble, kittle*; frequentatives or diminutives of verbs, as *crumple, dwindle, nestle, nibble, waddle*; nouns denoting an instrument or agent, as *beadle, girdle, needle*; adjectives, as *brittle, idle.*

lea (lē) [A.-S.], *n.* A meadow; grassland; land left untilled, fallow land.

leach (lēch) [A.-S.], *v.t.* To wash by letting water percolate through, to strain liquid.

lead (1) (led) [A.-S. *lēad*], *n.* A soft malleable and ductile, bluish-grey, heavy metal; a thin plate of type-metal used to separate lines in printing; blacklead used in lead-pencils; (*pl.*) strips of lead used for covering a roof; a roof covered with lead; a plummet for sounding depths of the sea. *v.t.* To cover, fasten, weight, frame, or fit with lead; (*Print.*) to space out by inserting leads. **lead-pencil**, *n.* A pencil consisting of a slip of graphite enclosed in wood. **leaden**, *a.* Made of lead; slow, indisposed to action.

lead (2) (lēd) [A.-S. *lǣdan*], *v.t.* (*past and p.p.* led) To conduct; to guide; to direct the movements of; to be in command of; to take the first place among; to indicate, esp. by going in advance; to pass or spend (time, etc.); to begin a round at cards with. *v.i.* To act as conductor or guide; to go in advance; to be the commander or head in any undertaking; (*Cards*) to be the first player, to play in a specified way; to go towards, to extend; to tend (to) as a result. *n.* Guidance, direction, esp. by going in front; the first place, command, leadership; an example; a mill-race; a cord, strap, or chain for leading a dog; (*Cards*) the first play or the right to this. **leader**, *n.* One who or that which leads; a guide, conductor; a commander; a chief editorial article in a newspaper. **leadership**, *n.* **leading**, *a.* **leading-strings**, *n.pl.* Strings by which children were formerly supported when learning to walk; unnecessary or unwanted control.

leaf (lēf) [A.-S. *lēaf*], *n.* (*pl.* **leaves**) One of the expanded (usually lateral) organs of plants; anything resembling this; a sheet of paper comprising two pages; a thin sheet of metal; a hinged member of a table, door, shutter, etc. **leaf-mould**, *n.* Decayed leaves reduced to mould and used as compost. **leafless**, *a.* **leaflet**, *n.* A one-page handbill, circular, etc.

league (1) (lēg) [L. *ligāre*, to tie], *n.* A union for mutual help, protection, or pursuit of common interests; a treaty of alliance. *v.i.* To join in a league, to confederate.

league (2) [?], *n.* A measure of length (in Eng. 3 miles).

leak (lēk) [Teut.], *v.i.* To let water, etc. in or out through a hole; to ooze through a hole or fissure. *n.* A hole which admits water, etc.; the oozing of water or other fluid through a crevice. **leakage**, *n.* A leak; the quantity that escapes through a leak; the divulgence of confidential information.

leal (lēl) [A.-F.], *a.* Loyal, true.

lean (1) (lēn) [A.-S. *hlinian*], *v.i.* (*past and p.p.* leaned or leant (lent)) To incline, slope, slant; to incline one's body so as to rest (against or upon); (*fig.*) to depend (upon) as for support; to have a tendency (towards). *v.t.* To cause to incline; to support, to rest (upon or against). **leaning**, *n.* Inclination, partiality, propensity (towards or to).

lean (2) [A.-S. *hlǣne*], *a.* Thin, lank; consisting o muscular tissue (of meat); (*fig.*) meagre, poor, sterile; unprofitable. *n.* Meat that consists of muscular tissue without fat. **leanly**, *adv.* **leanness**, *n.*

leap (lēp) [A.-S. *hlēapan*], *v.i.* (*past and p.p.* leapt (lept), leaped) To jump, to spring; to rush, to dart; to pass over an interval. *v.t.* To jump or spring over or across; to cause to jump. *n.* Act of leaping; a jump, a bound; the space passed over by leaping; a sudden transition. **leap-frog**, *n.* A game in which one stoops down and another vaults over him. **leap year**: An intercalary year of 366 days, adding one day to February (every year the number of which is a multiple of four, except those divisible by 100 and not by 400).

learn (lĕrn) [A.-S. *leornian*], *v.t.* (*past and p.p.* learnt, learned (1) (lĕrnd)) To acquire knowledge of or skill in by study, etc.; to fix in the memory; to ascertain. *v.i.* To acquire knowledge; to receive instruction. **learned** (2) (lĕr´ned), *a.* Having acquired learning; skilful (in); erudite; scholarly. **learnedly**, *adv.* **learner**, *n.* **learning**, *n.* Act of learning; knowledge (esp. of literature, philology, and history); erudition.

lease (lēs) [A.-F. *lesser*], *v.t.* To grant or to hold (land or tenements) on lease, *n.* A letting of lands, etc., for a specified period; the contract for or the term of such letting. **leasehold**, *n.* Tenure by lease; property held by lease. *a.* Held thus. **leaseholder**, *n.*

leash (lēsh) [O.F. *lesse*], *n.* A thong for a hound or hawk; (*Sport*) a brace and a half, three.

least (lēst) [A.-S. *lǣst*, superl. of *lǣs*, LESS], *a.* Smallest (in size, amount, degree, quantity, value, importance, etc.). *adv.* In the smallest or slightest degree. *n.* The smallest amount, degree, etc.

leather (leth´ēr) [A.-S. *lether*], *n.* The tanned skin of an animal; dressed hides collectively; an article made of leather. **leathern**, *a.* **leathery**, *a.*

leave (1) (lēv) [A.-S. *lēaf*], *n.* Liberty; permission to be absent; the period of this; act of departing, a farewell, an adieu. **leave-taking**, *n.* A parting; a farewell.

leave (2) [A.-S. *lǽfan*], *v.t.* (*past and p.p.* left) To allow to remain; to bequeath; to refrain from removing, consuming, etc.; to depart from, to quit; to forsake, abandon; to desist from, to cease; to commit, refer for consideration, approval, etc. *v.i.* To depart; to discontinue. **leaving**, *n.* Act of departing; (*pl.*) residue, refuse.

leaven (levn) [F. *levain*], *n.* Fermenting dough; any substance used to cause fermentation. (*fig.*) an influence tending to cause a general change. *v.t.* To raise and make light with leaven; (*fig.*) to imbue, to taint.

lecher (lech'ẽr) [O.F. *lecheor*], *n.* One addicted to lewdness. **lecherous**, *a.* **lechery**, *n.*

lectern (lek'tẽrn) [O.F. *letrun*, from L. *lect-*, p.p. stem of *legere*, to read], *n.* A reading-desk, esp. in churches.

lecture (lek'chũr), *n.* A formal discourse on a subject before an audience or class; a reproof. *v.i.* To deliver a lecture or give instruction by means of lectures. *v.t.* To instruct by lectures; to reprimand. **lecturer**, *n.* **lectureship**, *n.*

ledge (lej) [?], *n.* A shelf; a shelf-like ridge; (*Mining*) a metal-bearing stratum.

ledger (lej'ẽr) [?], *n.* The principal book in a set of account-books, showing all the debits and credits.

lee (lē) [A.-S. *hlēo*, shelter], *n.* The quarter opposite to that against which the wind blows; the sheltered side; shelter. *a.* Pertaining to the side away from the wind. **lee-way**, *n.* The drift of a vessel to leeward of her course; (*fig.*) arrears; lost time.

leech (lēch) [A.-S. *lǽce*, rel. to *lācnian*, to heal], *n.* An aquatic invertebrate animal, largely employed for the local extraction of blood; (*obs.*) a physician.

leek (lēk) [A.-S. *lēac*], *n.* A culinary vegetable allied to the onion.

leer (lēr) [A.-S. *hlēor*, the cheek], *n.* A sly or arch look; a look expressive of malice, amorousness, or triumph. *v.i.* To look with a leer.

lees (lēz) [O.F. *lie*], *n.pl.* Dregs.

leeward (loo'árd), *a.* Pertaining to the part away from that against which the wind blows. *adv.* Towards the lee side. *n.* The lee side or direction.

left (left) [A.-S. *left*, *lyft*, weak, worthless], *a.* Pertaining to the side that is east when one faces south, opp. to right. *adv.* On or towards the left. *n.* The side opposite to the right; the opposition (sitting on the left of the president in a legislative assembly), the advanced or radical party. **left-handed**, *a.* Using the left hand more readily than the right; delivered with the left hand (of a blow); (*fig.*) awkward, clumsy; insincere; equivocal; morganatic (of marriages).

leg (leg) [Icel. *leggr*], *n.* A limb to walk with, esp. the part from the knee to the ankle; the part of a garment that covers the leg; anything resembling or used as a leg, as a support to a table, bedstead, chair, etc., a limb of a pair of dividers, etc. **leg-bail**, *n.* Escape from custody.

legacy (leg'ȧ-si) [O.F. *legacie*], *n.* A bequest; anything handed on by a predecessor.

legal (lē'gȧl) [F. *legal*, L. *lex legis*, law], *a.* Pertaining or according to law; lawful; appointed by or concerned with the law. **legalist**, *n.* **legal'ity**, *n.* **legalize**, *v.t.*

legate (leg'át) [O.F. *legat*, L. *lēgātus*, appointed], *n.* An ambassador from the Pope.

legatee (leg-à-tē'), *n.* One to whom a legacy is bequeathed.

legation (lē-gā'shŭn), *n.* A diplomatic representative and his suite; his official residence.

legato (lē-ga'tō) [It., bound], *adv.* (*Mus.*) In an even gliding manner without a break.

legend (lej'ẽnd) [L. *legenda*, that which is to be read], *n.* A traditional story, esp. popularly accepted as true; a myth, a fable; non-historical story-telling or literature; an inscription on a coat of arms, coin, etc. **legendary**, *a.*

legerdemain (lej-ẽr-dē-mān') [F. light of hand], *n.* Sleight of hand.

legging (leg'ing), *n.* A covering of leather, canvas, etc., for the leg.

legible (lej'ibl) [L. *legibilis* (*legere*, to read)], *a.* That may be read; easily decipherable. **legibil'ity**, *n.* **legibly**, *adv.*

legion (lē'jŏn) [L. *legio*], *n.* A division of the ancient Roman army (3,000 to 6,000 men); a military force; (*fig.*) a host, multitude. **legionary**, *a.*

legislate (lej'is-lāt) [L. *lex legis*, law], *v.i.* To enact a law or laws. **legisla'tion**, *n.* The act of making laws. **leg'islative**, *a.* Enacting laws; having power to legislate; pertaining to legislation. *n.* The legislative power or function. **leg'islator**, *n.* **legislature**, *n.* The body of men in a State in which is invested the power or right to enact, alter, repeal or suspend laws.

legitimate (lē-jit'i-mȧt), *a.* Lawful; properly authorized; born in wedlock, legally descended; regular, natural; conformable to accepted usage; following by logical sequence. *v.t.* (-māt) To make lawful; to render legitimate; to justify, to serve as justification for. **legitimacy**, *n.* **legitimately**, *adv.* **legitimatize**, **legitimize**, *v.t.* To render legitimate.

leguminous (lē-gū'min-ŭs), *a.* Pertaining to the order of peas, beans, pulse, etc.

leisure (lezh'ũr) [O.F. *leisir*, L. *licēre*, to be allowed], *n.* Freedom from business, etc.; time at one's disposal; opportunity, convenience. *a.* Unoccupied, free. **leisured**, *a.* **leisurely**, *a.* and *adv.*

lemming (lem'ing) [Norw.], *n.* A small migratory rodent allied to the rat.

lemon (lem'ŏn) [F. *limon*, Oriental in orig.], *n.* An acid orange-like fruit; the tree bearing this.

lemur (lē'mŭr, lem'ŭr) [L., a ghost], *n.* A genus of nocturnal animals allied to the monkeys.

lend (lend) [A.-S. *lǣnan*], *v.t.* (*past and p. p.* lent) To grant for temporary use; to let out (money) at interest. **lender**, *n.*

length (length) [A.-S. *lengthu*], *n.* Measure from end to end, as dist. from breadth or thickness; a definite portion of the linear extent of anything; state of being long; extent of time, duration; the distance anything extends; the quantity of a vowel or syllable. **lengthen,** *v.t.* To make long or longer; to extend; to protract. *v.i.* To grow longer. **lengthways,** *adv.* **lengthwise,** *adv.* and *a.* **lengthy,** *a.* Long and tedious; prolix.

lenient (lē'ni-ėnt) [L. *lēniens,* soothing], *a.* Mild, gentle; clement. **leniency,** *n.*

lens (lenz) [L. seed of lentil], *n.* (*pl.* **lenses**) A piece of a transparent substance (or combination of such), so curved as to diminish or increase the apparent size of objects viewed through it; the crystalline body through which rays are focused on the retina.

Lent (lent) [A.-S. *lencten,* spring], *n.* A fast of forty days, from Ash Wednesday to Easter Eve; a season of penitence and fasting. **lenten,** *a.* Pertaining to Lent; sparing, meagre.

lentil (len'til) [as **LENS**], *n.* A small branching leguminous plant; (*pl.*) the seeds of this plant used for food.

lento (len'tō) [It.], *adv.* (*Mus.*) Slowly.

leonine (lē'ō-nīn) [L. *leo.*], *a.* Pertaining to or like a lion.

leopard (lep'ård) [Gr. *leopardos*], *n.* A large, fierce mammal of the cat tribe, with a spotted coat.

leper (lep'ėr) [Gr. *lepis,* scale], *n.* One affected with leprosy.

lepido- [Gr. *lepis lepidos,* a scale], *comb. form.* Having scales.

leprosy (lep'rō-si), *n.* A chronic disease, usually characterized by shining tubercles, thickening of the skin, loss of feeling, and ulceration and decay of parts. **leprous,** *a.*

lepto- [Gr. *leptos*], *comb. form.* Fine, small, narrow, slender.

lese-majesty (lēz-măj'e-sti) [F.], *n.* An offence against the sovereign power, high treason.

lesion (lē'zhŭn) [F. *lésion,* from L. *lædere,* to injure], *n.* A hurt, injury; morbid change in a tissue, etc.

less (les) [A.-S.], *a.* Smaller (in size, extent, number, amount, degree, importance, rank, etc.). *prep.* Minus, with deduction of. *adv.* In a smaller or lower degree; not so much. *n.* A smaller quantity, etc.; the smaller, the junior, etc., of things compared. *conj.* Unless.

-less [A.-S. *lēas,* loose, free from], *suf.* Devoid of, free from; as in *fearless, godless, tireless.*

lessee (le-sē') [A.-F., **LEASE**], *n.* One to whom a lease is granted. **lesseeship,** *n.*

lessen (les'ėn), *v.t.* To make less or diminish in size, number, etc.; to reduce, depreciate, degrade. *v.i.* To become less in size, extent, degree, etc.; to decrease, shrink. **lesser,** *a.* Less, smaller; inferior.

lesson (les'ŏn) [O.F. *lecon*], *n.* An exercise done, or portion learnt, read or recited by a pupil to a teacher; instruction given to a pupil at one time; (*pl.*) a course of instruction; a portion of Scripture read during divine service. *v.t.* To teach; to discipline; to admonish.

lessor (les'ór), *n.* One who grants a lease.

lest (lest) [A.-S. *lǣs*], *conj.* For fear that; in order that not.

let (1) (let) [A.-S. *lǣtan*], *v.t.* To permit, to allow; to give leave to; to lease; to give out on contract. *v.i.* To be let or leased. *n.* A letting.

let (2) [A.-S. *lettan*], *v.t.* To hinder, impede, prevent. *n.* A hindrance, obstacle; (*Rackets, etc.*) a stoppage requiring the ball to be served again.

-let, *suf.* Diminutive, as in *bracelet, cutlet.*

lethal (lē'thål) [L. *lēthālis,* from *lētum,* death], *a.* Deadly, fatal.

lethargy (leth'år-ji) [Gr. *lēthargos,* forgetting], *n.* Morbid drowsiness; a state of torpor, apathy, or inactivity. **lethar'-gic, -al,** *a.*

letter (let'ėr) [L. *littera*], *n.* A mark representing a sound in speech; one of the characters in the alphabet; a written message; the precise meaning of a term, etc., dist. from the spirit; (*pl.*) literature, literary culture; learning. *v.t.* To impress or stamp with letters. **letter-book,** *n.* A book in which copies of letters are kept. **letter-card,** *n.* A folded card with gummed edges for sending by post as a letter. **letter-perfect,** *a.* Having learnt one's part thoroughly (of actors). **letterpress,** *n.* Printed matter other than illustrations. **lettered,** *a.* Marked with letters; learned; pertaining to or suited for literature or learning. **lettering,** *n.*

lettuce (let'is) [M.E. *letuce*], *n.* A crisp-leaved garden plant used in salads.

leuc- [Gr. *leukos*], *comb. form.* White, pale.

Levant (lê-vănt') [F., from It. *levante,* L. *levantem,* nom. *-vans,* pres. p. of *levāre,* to raise], *n.* The eastern coasts of the Mediterranean. *v.i.* To abscond, to run away, esp. with gambling liabilities undischarged. **Levantine,** *a.*

levee (lev'i) [F. *levé* or *lever,* rising], *n.* A morning reception held by a sovereign or prince, or his representative.

level (levl) [L. *libella,* dim. of *libra,* a level], *n.* A horizontal line or plane; an instrument for determining whether a surface, etc., is horizontal; the altitude of a point cr surface; level country; (*fig.*) the standard in a community as regards morality, culture, etc.; (*Mining*) a horizontal passage. *a.* Horizontal, even, flat; equal in rank or degree; (*fig.*) equable, well-balanced. *v.t.* To make horizontal; to bring to the same level; to make smooth or even; to point (a gun) in taking aim; to aim, to direct (an attack, satire, etc.); to raze, make level (with the ground), to knock down; to bring to an equality. **level-headed,** *a.* Sensible, shrewd, common-sense. **leveller,** *n.* One who or that which levels; one who wishes to destroy all social distinctions.

lever (lē'vėr) [O.F. *leveor* (*lever,* to raise)], *n.* A rigid bar having a fixed point (fulcrum), used to overcome resistance (or weight) at some part of the bar by means of a force (or power) applied at another part; a part of a machine acting on the same principle; a watch in which two levers connect the pallet and balance; (*fig.*) anything that brings power or influence to bear. *v.t.* To move or lift with or as with a lever. **leverage,** *n.*

leveret (lev'ėr-ėt) [O.F. *levrete*], *n.* A hare in its first year.

leviathan (lě-vī'á-thǎn) [Heb. *livyāthān*], *n.* A huge aquatic monster; a huge ship.

levitation (lev-i-tā'shŭn) [L. *levis*, light], *n.* Rising in the air against the effects of gravity.

Levite (lě'vīt) [Heb. *Lēvī*, son of Jacob], *n.* One of the tribe of Levi, esp. as assistants to the priests; (*fig.*) a priest. **Levit'ical,** *a.* Pertaining to the Levites or to the book of Leviticus.

levity (lev'i-ti) [L. *levis*, light], *n.* Lightness of disposition, conduct, or manner; want of seriousness, frivolity.

levy (lev'i) [F. *levée,* L. *levāre,* to raise], *n.* Act of raising or collecting for public service; that which is so raised; troops called out for military service. *v.t.* To raise, to collect together (as an army); to impose and collect (as a tax). **leviable,** *n.*

lewd (lūd) [A.-S. *lǣwede,* belonging to the laity], *a.* Unchaste, indecent; depraved.

lexicon (lek'si-kŏn) [Gr. *lexikos,* pertaining to words], *n.* A dictionary.

liable (lī'ábl) [?], *a.* Bound in law or equity; responsible (for); subject (to); exposed (to); tending, apt, or likely (to). **liabil'ity,** *n.* State of being liable; that for which one is liable; (*pl.*) debts.

liaison (li-ā'zŏn) [F.], *n.* An illicit intimacy between a man and woman; (*Mil.*) touch with other troops; (*Phon.*) the carrying on of the sound of a final consonant to a succeeding word beginning with a vowel or *h* mute. **liaison-officer,** *n.* One who correlates the movements of troops under different commands.

liar (lī'ár), *n.* One who knowingly utters falsehoods; one addicted to lying.

libation (li-bā'shŭn) [L. *lībāre,* to pour out], *n.* A sacrifice, by a drink-offering or by pouring oil or wine on the ground.

libel (lī'běl) [L. *libellus,* a little book], *n.* A defamatory publication containing malicious statements tending to bring any person into ridicule or disrepute; a lampoon, satire. *v.t.* To publish a libel upon; to defame or lampoon. **libellous,** *a.*

liberal (lib'ěr-ál) [L. *līber,* free], *a.* Generous, open-handed; ample, abundant; open, candid; not too strict, narrow, or literal; broad-minded; favourable to freedom and democratic government; not technical, tending to free mental development (of education). *n.* One who advocates progress and reform. **liberalism,** *n.* **liberal'ity,** *n.* The quality of being liberal; bounty, munificence; largeness of views, catholicity; freedom from prejudice. **liberally,** *adv.*

liberate (lib'ěr-āt) [L. *līberāre,* as prec.], *v.t.* To set at liberty. **libera'tion,** *n.* **liberator,** *n.*

libertine (lib'ěr-tin) [L. *libertīnus,* a freedman], *n.* A freethinker in religious matters; a debauchee, a profligate.

liberty (lib'ěr-ti) [L. *libertas,* from *līber,* free], *n.* Quality or state of being free; right of self-government, to act as one pleases, or to do a particular thing; permission granted to do any act; (*pl.*) rights or privileges enjoyed by grant or prescription; a place where certain privileges or immunities are enjoyed; a slight of decorum or courtesy.

libidinous (li-bid'i-nŭs) [L. *libido,* lust], *a.* Characterized by lewdness, lustful. **libido** (lib'i-dō), *n.* (*Psych.*) The will to live; urge of sex.

librarian (li-brār'i-an), *n.* One who has charge of a library.

library (lī'brár-i) [L. *librārius,* pertaining to books, from *liber,* book], *n.* A collection of books, esp. classified and catalogued; a room or series of rooms containing such a collection.

libretto (li-bret'ō) [It., dim. of *libro,* book], *n.* (*pl.* -ti) The words of an opera, etc.; a book containing such words. **librettist,** *n.* A libretto-writer.

licence (lī'sěns) [L. *licentia,* from *licēre,* to be allowed], *n.* Leave, permission, esp. consent granted by a constituted authority (as to marry, publish a book, produce a play, carry on a business, etc.); a document containing such permission; a certificate of competence issued by an examining body; unrestrained liberty of action, disregard of law or propriety; abuse of freedom; deviation from the ordinary rules. **license,** *v.t.* To authorize by granting a licence; to allow, permit, to allow entire freedom. **licensee',** *n.* One who holds a licence. **licenser,** *n.* **licen'tiate,** *n.* One holding a certificate of competence in some profession.

licentious (li-sen'shŭs), *a.* Dissolute, profligate; unrestrained by rule. **licentiousness,** *n.*

lich (lich) [A.-S. *lic*], *n.* A corpse. **lichgate,** *n.* A churchyard gate with a roof under which a coffin may be placed.

lichen (lī'kěn) [Gr. *leichēn*], *n.* A parasitic fungus covering rocks, tree-trunks, etc., with coloured crusts.

lick (lik) [A.-S. *liccian*], *v.t.* To pass the tongue over; to take in with the tongue; to pass lightly over (of flame, etc.); (*slang*) to flog, beat, surpass. *v.i.* To make a licking motion (of flames). *n.* The act of licking; a slight smear (as of paint).

lid (lid) [A.-S. *hlid*], *n.* A hinged or detachable cover for shutting a vessel, box, or aperture; an eyelid.

lie (1) (lī) [A.-S. *lēogan*], *v.i.* To say or write anything intending to deceive; to deceive. *n.* An intentional violation of the truth; a false statement deliberately made; (*fig.*) a deception, imposture.

lie (2) [A.-S. *licgan*], *v.i.* (*pres. p.* lying, *past* lay, *p.p.* lain). To place oneself in a reclining posture; to be situated in a specified direction; to sleep, lodge, encamp (at a specified place); to rest, to remain; to be, to reside, in a specified state, position, etc.; (*Law*) to be sustainable (of an action, etc.). *n.* Position, direction, manner of lying; lair.

lief (lēf) [A.-S. *lēof,* cogn. with LOVE], *adv.* Willingly, gladly, freely.

liege (lēj) [O.F. *lige*], *n.* A lord, a sovereign.

lien (lē'ěn) [L. *ligāmen,* a band], *n.* (*Law*) A right to detain the goods of another until some claim has been satisfied.

lieu (lū) [F.], *n.* Place, stead, room.

lieutenant (lěf-ten'ánt) [F.], *n.* An officer

acting as deputy to a superior; (*Mil.*) an officer next below a captain; (*Nav.*) below a lieutenant-commander. **lieutenancy**, *n.*

life (lif) [A.-S. *lif*], *n.* (*pl.* **lives**) The state or condition of being alive; animate existence; the period of this, a specified portion of a person's existence; the living form; (*collect.*) living things; manner or course of living; animating principle, the essential idea (of a movement, etc.); animation, vivacity, spirit; that which imparts animation; human affairs; a narrative of one's existence, a biography. **life-annuity**, *n.* A sum paid yearly to a person from a specified age to death. **life-belt**, *n.* A belt for supporting a person in the water. **life-boat**, *n.* A boat specially constructed for saving life in storms. **life-guard**, *n.* A guard appointed to protect the person of some one, esp. a sovereign. **life-interest**, *n.* An interest or estate terminating with the life of a person. **life-line**, *n.* A rope used for saving life, or as an additional safeguard. **livelong**, *a* Lasting throughout life. **life-preserver**, *n.* A loaded stick for defending one's life. **lifetime**, *n.* The duration of one's life. **lifeless**, *a.* **lifelike**, *a.* Like a living being; like the original (of a portrait).

lift (lift) [Icel.], *v.t.* To raise to a higher position; to hold or support on high; to pick up; to remove (anxiety, etc.); to exalt, elate. *v.i.* To rise (as a ship on the waves) to rise and disperse (as a mist) *n.* Act of lifting; degree of elevation; a rise; a hoisting-machine, an elevator; a helping hand.

ligament (lig'â-mĕnt) [L. *ligāmentum*], *n.* Anything which binds; a tie; a band of fibrous tissue by which bones are bound together. **lig'ature**, *n.* That which binds, esp. a thread to tie arteries, etc.; a bond; (*Print.*) two or more letters cast on one shank, as *ff*, *ffi*; (*Mus.*) a tie connecting notes.

light (1) (lit) [A.-S. *lēoht*], *n.* The natural agent by which objects are rendered visible; the sensation produced by the stimulation of the sight; the state in which things are visible, opp. to darkness; (*fig.*) one's fair opportunities, one's chances; a source of light; daylight; a window, or division of a window; (*fig.*) exposure, general knowledge; elucidation, enlightenment; a model, example; (*pl.*) one's intellectual powers. *a.* Having light; clear, not dark; pale-coloured, fair. *v.t.* (*past and p.p.* lit, lighted) To kindle, set fire to; to give light to; to conduct with a light. *v.i.* To take fire; to be illuminated; to brighten (up). **lighthouse**, *n.* A tower supporting a powerful light for the guidance of mariners. **lightship**, *n.* A moored vessel carrying a light to give warning or guidance. **light year**, *n.* (*Astron.*) The distance travelled by light in one year, 6,000,000,000,000 miles.

light (2) (lit) [A.-S. *lēoht*], *a.* Of small weight; easy to be lifted, moved, etc.; lightly armed (of troops); active, quick; of low specific gravity; below the standard weight; unimportant, trivial; flighty, volatile, fickle; wanton, cheerful, gay. **light-fingered**, *a.* Dexterous in stealing; given to thieving. **light-headed**, *a.* Delirious; thoughtless. **light-heeled**, *a.* Nimble, quick-moving, light-footed. **light-minded**, *a.* Fickle, unsteady, volatile. **light-weight**, *n.* a horse or man below the average weight; a boxer of 135 lb. or under. **lightness**, *n.*

light (3) (lit) [*lihtan*], *v.i.* To descend as from flight; to chance (upon).

lighten (1) (li'tĕn) [A.-S. *lēohtan*], *v.i.* To become light, to brighten; to emit lightning; to shine out. *v.t.* To illuminate, enlighten.

lighten (2) (li'tĕn), *v.t.* To reduce in weight; to relieve, mitigate, alleviate.

lighter (li'tĕr) [?], *n.* A large, open boat, used in loading and unloading ships; a heavy barge.

lightning (lit'ning), *n.* The flash caused by the discharge of electricity between clouds. **lightning-rod**, *n.* A wire for carrying the electrical discharge to earth, thus protecting a building, etc.

lights (lits), *n.pl.* The lungs of animals, esp. as food for cats, etc.

lightsome (lit'sŏm), *a.* Light-hearted, gay; airy, nimble.

ligneous (lig'nĕ-ŭs) [L. *lignum*, wood], *a.* Made or consisting of wood; resembling wood; woody.

like (1) (lik) [A.-S. *lic*], *a* Resembling; such as; equal or nearly equal in quantity, quality, etc.; characteristic of; inclined to. *adv.* As, in the manner of, to the same extent or degree as. *n.* A counterpart.

like (2) (lik) [A.-S. *lician*, as prec.], *v.t.* To be pleased with; to be attracted by; to enjoy. *v.i.* To be pleased; to choose. *n.* A longing desire; predilection (*usu. in pl.*). **likeable**, *a.*

-like, *suf.* Forming adjectives; as in *childlike*; adverbs, as in *childlike she replied*.

likely (lik'li), *a.* (-lier, -liest) Probable, plausible; to be expected (to); suitable, well-adapted. *adv.* Probably. **likelihood**, *n.*

liken (li'kĕn), *v.t.* To compare, to represent as similar (to).

likeness (lik'nĕs), *n.* Similarity, resemblance; a representation of a person or thing; form, guise.

likewise (lik'wiz), *adv.* or *conj.* In like manner; also, moreover, too.

liking (li'king), *n.* State of being pleased; fondness, fancy.

lilac (li'lăk) [Arab. *lilāk*], *n.* A shrub with fragrant pale violet, purple, or white flowers. *a.* Of the colour of lilac.

Lilliputian (lil-i-pū'shăn) [*Lilliput* in Swift's "Gulliver's Travels"], *a.* Pigmy, diminutive. *n.* A pigmy.

lilt (lilt) [M.E. *lulte*], *v.* To sing in cheerful, lively style. *n.* A lively tune; the melody or rhythm of a song.

lily (lil'i) [A.-S. *lilie*, L. *lilium*], *n.* A plant producing white or coloured flowers of great beauty. *a.* Pure white; unsullied.

limb (lim) [A.-S. *lim*], *n.* An arm, leg, or wing; a main branch of a tree; a member, a branch; an impish child.

limber (1) (lim'bẽr) [F. *limonière*], *n.* The wheels, ammunition-box, axle, and pole of a gun-carriage. *v.* To attach the limber to the gun (usu. with *up*).

limber (2) [?], *a.* Flexible, lithe.

limbo (lim'bō) [L., abl. of *limbus*, as LIMB], *n.* The edge of hell, the abode of souls who, through no fault of their own, cannot be redeemed; prison.

lime (1) (līm) [A.-S. *līm*], *n.* A calcareous earth used for making mortar, for manure, etc.; bird-lime. *v.t.* To smear with bird-lime; to ensnare; to spread lime over (land); to dress (hides) in lime and water. **lime-kiln**, *n.* A kiln in which limestone is calcined and reduced to lime. **limelight**, *n.* A light produced by projecting a jet of ignited hydrogen and oxygen upon a ball of lime; (*fig.*) the glare of publicity. **limestone**, *n.* Any rock the basis of which is carbonate of lime.

lime (2) [as LINDEN], *n.* The linden-tree.

lime (3) [Arab. *līmah* (cp. LEMON)], *n.* The fruit of a West Indian tree, smaller and more acid than the lemon.

limit (lim'it) [L. *limes*, *-mitis*], *n.* A boundary or edge marking utmost extent; a restraint, check; that which has bounds. *v.t.* To set a bound to; to confine within certain bounds; to serve as boundary or restriction to. **limita'tion**, *n.*

limn (lim) [O.F. *luminer*, to illumine], *v.t.* To paint, depict, portray.

limousine (lim-oo-zēn'), *n.* A closed motor-car with roof projecting over the driver's seat.

limp (limp) [?], *v.i.* To walk lamely; to be irregular (of verse, logic, etc.). *n.* Act of limping; a limping step or walk. *a.* Wanting in stiffness, flaccid, pliable.

limpet (lim'pẽt) [A.-S. *lempedu*], *n.* A shellfish having an open conical shell, adhering firmly to rocks.

limpid (lim'pid) [L. *limpidus*], *a.* Clear, transparent; perspicuous. **limpid'ity**, *n.*

linch-pin (linch'pin) [A.-S. *lynis*, an axle-tree, PIN], *n.* A pin holding a wheel on the axle.

linden (lin'dẽn) [A.-S. *lind*], *n.* The lime-tree.

line (1) (līn) [L. *linea* (from *līnum*, flax), through A.-S. *līne*], *n.* A thread; string; (*Naut.*) rope; a cable for telegraph or telephone or the route traversed; (*fig.*) a rule or direction; (*pl.*) one's lot in life; a thread-like mark; a streak, seam, furrow, etc.; the equator; (*fig.*) a scheme, design; a limit, boundary; a row of letters, words, men, or other objects; (*colloq.*) a short letter; a single verse of poetry; (*pl.*) a schoolboy's imposition; (*pl.*) a certificate of marriage; a series of trenches, etc.; row of men ranged as in order of battle; infantry regiments apart from the Guards, Engineers, supply corps, etc.; persons related in direct descent, family, lineage; ships, etc. plying between certain places or under one management; a railway track; a railway system; a certain branch of business, a certain class of goods; (*fig.*) field of activity; the twelfth part of an inch. *v.t.* To draw lines upon; to mark (in, off, etc.) with lines; to spread out or post (troops) in line. *v.i.* To come or extend into line; to form a line beside or along (of troops).

line (2) (līn), *v.t.* To put a covering of different material on the inside of; to serve as such a covering; to fill. **lining**, *n.* The covering of the inside of anything.

lineage (lin'ē-āj) [O.F. *lignage*], *n.* Descendants from a common progenitor; pedigree.

lineal (lin'ē-ăl) [F. *linéal*], *a.* Ascending or descending in the direct line of ancestry. **lineally**, *adv.*

lineament (lin'ē-à-mẽnt) [F. *linéament*], *n.* (*usu. in pl.*) Characteristic lines or features; contour.

linear (lin'ē-ăr) [L. *lineāris*], *a.* Composed of or like lines; having a lengthwise direction; involving magnitudes of one degree or dimension only.

linen (lin'ẽn) [A.-S.], *n.* A cloth made of flax; (*collect.*) articles chiefly made of linen. *a.* Made of flax.

liner (lī'nẽr), *n.* A vessel belonging to a regular line of passenger ships.

ling (1) (ling) [Icel. *langa*, cogn. with LONG], *n.* A long slender food-fish of northern seas.

ling (2) [Icel. LYNG], *n.* Heather or heath. **-ling**, *suf.* Forming nouns (now only diminutive), as *darling*, *gosling*, *lordling*; forming adverbs, as *darkling*.

linger (ling'gẽr) [A.-S. *lengan*, to protract], *v.i.* To delay going, to tarry, loiter; to be long in going or coming, to hesitate. **lingerer**, *n.* **lingeringly**, *adv.*

lingerie (lan-zhri) [F.], *n.* Linen articles.

lingo (ling'gō) [as LINGUAL], *n.* A foreign language, peculiar dialect.

lingual (ling'gwăl) [L. *lingua*, tongue], *a.* Pertaining to the tongue; (*Phon.*) formed by the tongue. *n.* A letter or sound produced by the tongue, as *t, d, n, l, r.* **linguist**, *n.* One skilled in languages.

liniment (lin'i-mẽnt) [L. *linīre*, to anoint], *n.* A liquid preparation for rubbing on bruised or inflamed parts; embrocation.

link (1) (lingk) [Icel. *hlekkr*, A.-S. *hlence*], *n.* A loop of a chain; a connecting part in machinery, or in a series, argument, etc.; a measure of 7·92 inches. *v.t.* To connect or attach (to, etc.) by links. *v.i.* To be connected.

link (2) [?], *n.* A torch made of tow and pitch. **link-boy**, *n.* A boy carrying a link.

links (lingks) [Sc.], *n.pl.* Undulating sandy ground near the shore; ground on which golf is played.

linnet (lin'ẽt) [O.F. *linette*, from *lin*, flax, on which it feeds], *n.* A common song-bird.

linoleum (li-nō'lē-ùm) [L. *līnum*, flax, *oleum*, oil], *n.* A preparation of linseed-oil and ground cork on canvas, used for floor-cloth.

linotype (lī'nō-tīp), *n.* A machine for producing stereotyped lines of words.

linseed (lin'sēd) [A.-S. *lin*], *n.* Flax-seed. **linseed-oil**, *n.* The oil expressed from linseed.

linsey-woolsey (lin'zi-wul'zi), *n.* A coarse fabric of linen or cotton warp with wool filling.

lint (lint), *n.* The down of scraped linen used for dressing wounds.

lintel (lin′těl) [O.F.], *n.* The horizontal beam over a door or window.

lion (lī′ŏn) [L. *leo, leōnis*], *n.* A large and powerful carnivorous quadruped of the cat tribe; (*fig., pl.*) sights to be seen by visitors; eminent celebrities, objects of general attention.

lip (lip) [A.-S. *lippa*], *n.* One of the two fleshy parts enclosing the opening of the mouth; the edge of an orifice, chasm, etc.; (*slang*) impudence, cheek.

liquefy (lik′wě-fī) [L. *liquāre*, to become fluid], *v.t.* To melt, to dissolve; to convert to a liquid form. *v.i.* To become liquid. **liquefa′cient,** *n.* That which liquefies. *a.* Serving to liquefy. **liquefac′tion,** *n.* **liques′cent,** *a.*

liqueur (li-kūr′) [F.], *n.* An alcoholic cordial flavoured with aromatic substance.

liquid (lik′wid) [L. *liquidus*], *a.* Fluid; flowing or capable of flowing; (*fig.*) limpid, clear; (of vowels) not guttural, easily pronounced; (of assets) readily convertible into cash; (of principles, etc.) unstable. *n.* A substance whose particles are incompressible and inelastic and move freely among themselves, as water in a fluid state; a letter pronounced with a slight contact of the organs of articulation, as *l, r.* **liquidate,** *v.t.* To pay off (a debt, etc.); to wind up (a bankrupt estate, etc.); to kill. *v.i.* To have its debts, etc., liquidated (of a company). **liquida′tion,** *n.* **liq′uidator,** *n.*

liquor (lik′ŏr) [A.-F. *licur,* L. *liquor*], *n.* A liquid or fluid substance, the liquid part of anything; an alcoholic (esp. spirituous) beverage.

liquorice (lik′or-is) [Gr. *glukus*, sweet, *rhiza*, root], *n.* The root of a plant; a sweetmeat or drug prepared from this.

lisp (lisp) [A.-S. *wlisp*, lisping], *v.i.* To pronounce *s* and *z* with the sound of *th* or *dh*; to speak affectedly or imperfectly. *v.t.* To pronounce with a lisp. *n.* The act or habit of lisping.

lissom (lis′ŏm), *a.* Lithe, nimble.

list (1) (list) [A.-S. *liste*], *n.* The border or selvedge of cloth; a strip of this; a boundary, limit; (*pl.*) palisades enclosing ground for a tournament, the ground so enclosed, a scene of contest; a roll, a catalogue or schedule of persons or things. *v.t.* To enter in a list.

list (2) [A.-S. *lystan*, as LUST], *v.t.* To please, to be pleasing to; to careen or heel (a ship) over. *v.i.* To lean over, to careen. *n.* A leaning over.

listen (lis′ěn) [A.-S. *hlosnian*], *v.i.* To give ear (to), to hearken; to heed, obey. **listen in,** *v.t.* To listen to radio; to tap a telephone line. **listener,** *n.*

listless (list′lěs), *a.* Careless, heedless, indifferent; languid.

litany (lit′á-ni) [Gr. *litaneia*, from *litanos*, a suppliant], *n.* A solemn form of supplicatory prayer, esp. a series of short prayers with responses.

-lite [Gr. *lithos*, stone], *suf.* Forming names of minerals, as *aerolite.*

literal (lit′ěr-ăl) [L. *litterālis*], *a.* According to the verbal meaning; not figurative; pertaining to letters. *n.* (*Print.*) A misprint.

literary (lit′ěr-ár-i) [L. *litterārius*], *a.* Pertaining to literature or polite learning; versed in or engaged in literature; consisting of written compositions. **litera′tim** [L.], *adv.* Letter for letter, literally.

literature (lit′ěr-a-tūr, -chŭr) [L. *litterātūra*], *n.* The written productions of a country or period or pertaining to a particular subject; printed matter; writings distinguished for beauty of form or expression, as dist. from works dealing with positive knowledge.

lith-, litho- [Gr. *lithos*, a stone], *comb. form.* Pertaining to stone. **-lith,** *suf.*, as in *monolith.*

lithe (lĭth) [A.-S.], *a.* Flexible, supple.

lithograph (lith′ŏ-gräf), *v.t.* To engrave on stone and transfer to paper, etc.; to print by lithography. *n.* An impression from a drawing on stone. **litho′grapher,** *n.* **lithog′raphy,** *n.*

litigate (lit′i-gāt) [L. *lītigāre*, to go to law], *v.t.* To contest in a court of law. *v.i.* To go to law; to carry on a lawsuit. **litigant,** *a.* and *n.* **litiga′tion,** *n.*

litigious (li-tij′ŭs) [*Lītigiōsus*], *a.* Fond of litigation; quarrelsome, contentious; pertaining to legal dispute.

litmus (lit′mŭs) [M. Dut. *leecmos*], *n.* A blue dye obtained from lichens, turned red by acids or restored to its original colour by alkalis.

litre (lē′těr) [F., Gr. *lītra*, a pound], *n.* The metric unit of capacity, about 1¾ pints.

litter (lit′ěr) [O.F. *litiere,* L. *lectus,* bed], *n.* A stretcher supporting a couch in which a person may be carried; straw, hay, etc., used as a bed for animals, or covering for plants; odds and ends scattered about; a state of untidiness; the young brought forth by a sow, bitch, cat, etc., at a birth.

littérateur (lit-ěr-à-tur′) [F.], *n.* A literary man.

little (litl) [A.-S. *lȳtel*], *a.* (*comp.* **less, lesser,** *superl.* **least**) Small, not big, in size, extent, amount, or quantity; short in duration or distance; of small importance; petty; mean, contemptible; young, weak. *adv.* In a small degree; not at all. *n.* A small amount, space, time, etc.; only a trifle. **littleness,** *n.*

littoral (lit′ŏr-ăl) [L. *litus -toris*, shore], *a.* Pertaining to the shore, esp. between high- and low-water marks. *n.* A coastal region.

liturgy (lit′ŭr-ji) [Gr. *leitourgia,* a public service], *n.* A ritual for public worship, the formal set of words in which this is set forth. **litur′gic,** *a.* **lit′urgist,** *n.*

live (1) (liv), *a.* Alive, living; ignited; ready for use; charged with electricity; moving or transmitting motion; full of energy, of present interest, etc. **live stock:** Animals kept for farming or domestic purposes.

live (2) (liv) [A.-S. *lifian*], *v.i.* To have life; to be alive; to exist as animal or vegetable (*fig.*) to remain in operation; to reside, dwell (at, in, etc.); to subsist (upon); to gain a livelihood (by); to pass one's life in a particular condition, etc.; to live strenuously or intensely. *v.t.* To spend (a specified kind of life); to survive.

livelihood (liv'li-hud) [A.-S. *liflād*], *n.* Means of subsistence.

livelong (liv'long), *a.* Long-lasting; the whole length of.

lively (liv'li) [A.-S. *liflic*], *a.* Life-like, vivid; full of life, active; animated, gay, bright. **liveliness,** *n.*

liven (li'ven), *v.t.* To make lively, to enliven (up).

liver (1) (liv'er), *n.* One who lives, esp. in a specified way (as a *good liver*).

liver (2) [A.-S. *lifer*], *n.* The glandular organ in vertebrates which secretes bile; (*colloq.*) a disordered liver.

livery (liv'er-i) [O.F. *livrée*, L. *liberāre* to give], *n.* A distinctive dress worn by male servants or the members of a city company; the privileges of a city company; formerly, the allowance for keeping and feeding a horse. **liveryman,** *n.* A freeman of the City of London, who is entitled to wear the livery of the company to which he belongs. **livery-stable,** *n.* A stable where horses are kept at livery or let out on hire.

livid (liv'id) [L. *lividus*], *a.* Of a leaden colour.

living (liv'ing), *a.* Having life; in a state of combustion; quickening; active, efficient; contemporary; true to life (of a portrait). *n.* State of being alive; livelihood, power of continuing life; the benefice of a clergyman; manner of life.

lizard (liz'ard) [L. *lacertus*], *n.* A reptile having a scaly body and four limbs.

llama (lä'må) [Peruv.], *n.* A domesticated Peruvian wool-bearing animal, *Auchenia lama*, resembling a small humpless camel; material made from its wool.

loach (lōch) [?], *n.* A small river-fish.

load (lōd) [A.-S. *lād*, way], *n.* A burden, esp. for conveyance; as much as can be carried at a time; that which is borne with difficulty. *v.t.* To put a load on or in; to make heavy, to weigh down, to oppress; to charge (a gun); to fill to overflowing; to overwhelm (with abuse, honours, etc.). *v.i.* To take in a load or cargo (usu. with *up*); to charge a firearm. **loadstone,** *n.* Magnetic oxide of iron, a natural magnet.

loaf (1) (lōf) [A.-S. *hlāf*], *n.* (*pl.* **loaves**) A shaped mass of bread; a conical mass of refined sugar.

loaf (2) [?], *v.i.* To lounge or idle about. *v.t.* To spend or pass (time away) idly. *n.* A saunter, an idle time. **loafer,** *n.*

loam (lōm) [A.-S. *lām*], *n.* A rich loose soil consisting chiefly of sand and clay.

loan (lōn) [A.-S. *lān*], *n.* Act of lending; that which is lent, esp. money lent at interest. *v.t.* To grant the loan of.

loath (lōth) [A.-S. *lāth*], *a.* Unwilling, reluctant.

loathe (lōth) [A.-S. *lāthian*], *v.* To feel disgust at; to abhor, detest. **loathing,** *a.* Abhorring. *n.* Disgust, aversion, abhorrence. **loathsome,** *a.* Causing loathing or disgust; odious.

lob (lob) [?], *n.* A dull, stupid fellow; (*Cricket*) a slow underhand ball; (*Lawn-tennis*) a ball pitched high in the air. *v.t.* To bowl or pitch a lob.

lobby (lob'i) [low L. *lobia*, lodge], *n.* A vestibule opening into several apartments; a small hall; the hall of a legislative assembly open to the public, also one of two corridors in which members vote. *v.i.* To solicit the votes of members. **lobbyist,** *n.* One who does this.

lobe (lōb) [Gr. *lobos*], *n.* A rounded and projecting or hanging part; the soft lower part of the ear; a rounded division of a leaf.

lobster (lob'ster) [A.-S. *loppestre*], *n.* A large marine long-tailed and stalk-eyed ten-legged crustacean.

lobworm (lob'werm), *n.* A large earthworm, used as bait by anglers.

local (lō-kál) [F., from L. *localis*, from *locus*, place], *a.* Pertaining to a place or particular place or places; pertaining to a part only (as a disease, etc.). *n.* An inhabitant of a particular place; a suburban train; an examination held in a provincial centre; an item of local news; (*colloq.*) a public-house. **locale** (lō-kal'). The scene or locality of an event, etc. **local'ity,** *n.* Particular place, site, geographical position; limitation to a place. **lo'calize,** *v.t.* To make local; to ascertain or indicate the exact place of; to identify with or restrict to a particular place. **locate** (lō-kāt'), *v.t.* To set in a particular locality; (*in p.p.*) to situate; to discover the site of. **loca'tion,** *n.* Situation or position. **loc'ative,** *n.* (*Gram.*) A case denoting place.

loch (loch) [Gael.], *n.* A lake or narrow or land-locked arm of the sea in Scotland.

lock (1) (lok) [A.-S. *loc*], *n.* A device for fastening doors, etc., usu. worked by a key; a device for preventing movement of a wheel; the firing-apparatus of a gun; a gated enclosure in a canal for raising and lowering vessels by the alteration of water-level; an air-tight antechamber to a caisson; a block, a jam. *v.t.* To fasten with a lock; to shut up thus; to fasten by means of parts that engage together; (*in p.p.*) to embrace, to tangle together. *v.i.* To become fastened by or as by a lock; to intertwine. **lock-jaw,** *n.* A variety of tetanus in which the muscles of the jaw are violently contracted. **lock-out,** *n.* Temporary discharge of workmen to bring them to terms. *v.t.* To coerce by closing a factory against them. **locksmith,** *n.* A maker and repairer of locks. **lock-stitch,** *n.* A sewing-machine stitch which locks two threads together. **lock-up,** *n.* A place of temporary confinement; time for locking up; investing of capital so that it cannot be realized. *a.* That may be locked.

lock (2) [A.-S. *locc*], *n.* A tuft, esp. of hair; a tress, ringlet.

locker (lok'er), *n.* A chest or other close receptacle, with lock and key.

locket (lok'et) [F. *loquet*, dim. of O.F. *loc*, latch], *n.* A small ornamental case for wearing, adapted to contain hair, a miniature, etc.

locomotion (lō-kò-mō'shŭn) [L. *locus*, place], *n.* Act or power of moving from place to place. **locomo'tive,** *a.* Pertaining to locomotion; moving from place to place; having the power of or causing locomotion. *n.* A railway-engine.

locum-tenens (lō'kŭm-tē'nèns) [L., holding place], *n.* (*pl.* **-tenentes**) One acting in the place of another, esp. a doctor or clergyman.

locust (lō'kŭst) [L. *locusta*], *n.* A migratory winged insect allied to the grasshopper, very destructive to vegetation; a locust-tree or its fruit. **locust-tree,** *n.* The carob, and various West Indian trees.

locution (lō-kū'shŭn) [L. *locūtio*], *n.* Style of speech, mode of delivery.

lode (lōd) [A.-S. *lād*], *n.* An open ditch; a reach of water in a canal; a vein bearing metal. **lodestar,** *n.* A guiding star, the pole-star; one's guiding principle.

lodge (loj) [O.F. *loge*], *n.* A temporary residence; a small house in a park; a gate-keeper's or gardener's cottage; quarters for a porter in a college, chambers, etc.; (*Freemasonry, etc.*) a local branch. *v.t.* To supply with temporary accommodation; to deposit, leave for security. *v.i.* To reside temporarily, esp. to have sleeping quarters, etc., at a fixed charge; to stay or become fixed (in). **lodger,** *n.* **lodging,** *n.*

loft (loft) [Icel. *lopt*], *n.* The space under a roof; a gallery in a church, etc.; a room over a barn or stable; a pigeon-house, a flock of pigeons. **lofty,** *a.* Towering, of imposing height; elevated in character, sentiment, style, etc.; high-flown; haughty.

log (log) [M.E. *logge*], *n.* A bulky piece of unhewn timber; an apparatus for ascertaining the rate of a ship's motion; a log-book. **log-book,** *n.* A book in which a diary of events occurring in a ship's voyage is kept, with a record of observations with the log. **log-cabin,** *n.* One built of logs.

loganberry (lō'gàn-bèr-ĭ) [*Logan*, pers. name], *n.* A fruit obtained by crossing the raspberry and blackberry.

logarithm (log'à-rithm) [Gr. *log-os*, word, ratio, *arithmos*, number], *n.* The exponent of the power to which a fixed number, called the base, must be raised to produce a given number. **logarith'mic,** *a.*

loggerhead (log'èr-hed) [LOG, HEAD], *n.* A stupid fellow, a dolt. **at loggerheads:** Disagreeing, quarrelling.

loggia (loj'ĭ-à) [It.], *n.* An open corridor, arcade; an open balcony.

logic (loj'ĭk) [Gr. *logikē*, reasoning], *n.* The science of reasoning, correct thinking, proving and deducing; force of argument; (*fig.*) force of circumstances, situation, etc. **logical,** *a.* **logician** (lò-jish'án), *n.* One skilled in logic.

logistics (lō-jis'tĭks) [F. *loger*, to lodge], *n.pl.* (*Mil.*) The mathematics of transportation, quartering troops and supplies.

logo- [Gr. *logos*, word, reasoning], *comb. form.* **Pertaining** to words; wordy.

-logy, *suf.* Forming names of sciences and departments of knowledge, and nouns denoting modes of speaking; as *astrology, eulogy, tautology.*

loin (loin) [O.F. *loigne*], *n.* The part between the false ribs and the hip-joint; a joint of meat.

loiter (loi'tèr) [? Dut.], *v.i.* To dawdle; to move with frequent halts.

loll (lol) [prob. imit.], *v.i.* To hang from the mouth (of the tongue); to lounge. *v.t.* To allow to hang out or about.

lone (lōn), *a.* Solitary, uninhabited, deserted; without company.

lonely (lōn'lĭ), *a.* Solitary, unfrequented, sequestered; lone; addicted to seclusion. **loneliness,** *n.* **lonesome,** *a.* Unfrequented.

long (1) (long) [A.-S. *lang*], *a.* Of relatively great extent in dimension or in time; of a specified linear extent or duration in time; protracted in sound; dilatory; far-reaching; lengthy, verbose, tedious. *adv.* To a great extent in distance or time; for or by a long time; throughout a specified period. *n.* Anything that is long. **long-boat,** *n.* The largest boat of a sailing-ship. **longbow,** *n.* A powerful bow drawn by hand, formerly the national English weapon. **long-hand,** *n.* Ordinary writing, opp. to shorthand. **long-headed,** *a.* Shrewd, sensible. **long-suffering,** *a.* Forbearing, patient. *n.* Forbearance to punish. **long-winded,** *a.* Wearisome from prolixity. **longish,** *a.*

long (2) (long) [A.-S. *longian*], *v.i.* To have an earnest desire (for); to yearn (to or for). **longing,** *a.* **longingly,** *adv.*

-long, *suf.* Forming adverbs, as *sidelong.*

longeval (lòn-jē'vàl) [L. *longus, ævum,* age], *a.* Long-lived. **longev'ity,** *n.*

longitude (lon'ji-tūd) [L. *longitūdo*], *n.* Angular distance of a place east or west of a given meridian; distance in degrees on the ecliptic from the vernal equinox to the foot of a perpendicular from, or circle of latitude of, a heavenly body. **longitudinal,** *a.* Pertaining to longitude.

loofah (loo'fà) [Arab. *lūfa*, plant], *n.* The fibre of the sponge-gourd.

look (luk) [A.-S. *lōcian* (cp. G. dial. *lugen*)], *v.i.* To direct the eye (towards) in order to see; to gaze, stare; to give consideration; to face, have a particular direction (towards, etc.); to seem, appear; to take care. *v.t.* To express or show by the looks; to inspect, examine. *n.* Act of looking or seeing, a glance; (*pl.*) appearance, aspect, mien. **looker-on,** *n.* A mere spectator. **looking-glass,** *n.* A mirror.

loom (1) (loom) [A.-S. *gelōma*, a tool], *n.* A machine in which yarn or thread is woven into a fabric.

loom (2) [Teut.], *v.i.* To appear faintly in the distance; to appear as in a mist.

loon (loon) [?], *n.* A scamp, a worthless person; the great northern diver (bird).

loop (loop) [prob. Celt.], *n.* A doubling of a string, etc., across itself to form a curve or eye; a noose; a stitch in crochet or knitting; a loop-line. *v.t.* To form into or to fasten with loops. *v.i.* To make a loop. **loop-line,** *n.* A railway, telegraph-line, etc., diverging from the main line and joining it again.

loophole (loop'hōl) [Dut. *lūpen*, to watch], *n.* An aperture in a wall for shooting, for looking through, or for light; (*fig.*) a means of escape.

loose (loos) [Icel. *lauss*], *a.* Not tied, or confined; unfastened, detachable, hanging partly free; not crowded together, not compact; slack; careless, slovenly; not strict; vague, incorrect; dissolute. *v.t.* To undo, untie, unfasten; to release; to dissolve; to relax; to free from burden; to discharge. **loosen**, *v.* looseness, *n.*

loot (loot) [Hind. *lut*], *n.* Booty, plunder, esp. from a conquered city; (*fig.*) illicit gains. *v.t.* To plunder, to pillage.

lop (lop) [?], *v.t.* To cut off the extremities of; to trim (trees, shrubs, etc.). **lop-eared**, *a.* Having hanging ears. **lop-sided**, *a.* Heavier on one side than the other; ill-balanced.

lope (lōp), *v.i.* To swing or move (along) with long strides.

loquacious (lō-kwā'shŭs) [L. *loqui*, to talk], *a.* Talkative, chattering; apt to disclose secrets. **loquacity** (lō-kwăs'ĭ-tĭ), *n.*

lord (lôrd) [A.-S. *hlāford*], *n.* One possessing supreme power, a sovereign; the Supreme Being; a feudal superior; an owner; a peer of the realm; a courtesy-title given to sons of certain peers and certain official personages as Lord Chief Justice, Lord Mayor, etc.; (*pl.*) the members of the House of Lords. *v.i.* To play the lord (over). **Lord-Lieutenant**, *n.* The chief executive authority and head of the magistracy in a county. **lordly**, *a.* Befitting a lord; grand, haughty. *adv.* Imperiously; arrogantly. **lordship**, *n.*

lore (lôr) [A.-S. *lār*], *n.* (*collect.*) The traditions and facts relating to a given subject.

lorgnette (lôr-nyet') [F., from *lorgner*, to squint], *n.* A pair of eye-glasses with a long handle.

lorn (lôrn) [A.-S. *loren*, lost], *a.* Lost, abandoned, forlorn.

lorry (lor'ĭ) [?], *n.* A motor wagon for heavy loads; a low, flat, four-wheeled wagon without sides.

lory (lôr'ĭ) [Malay *luri*], *n.* A brilliantly coloured parrot-like bird found in S.E. Asia and Australia.

lose (looz) [A.-S. *losian*, to escape (from)], *v.t.* (*past and p.p.* lost) To part with accidentally or as a forfeit, penalty, etc.; to be freed from; to miss, be unable to find; to fail to gain, hear, obtain, etc.; to fail to keep possession of; to waste; (*in. p.p.*) to cause to disappear or perish. *v.i.* To fail to be successful; to suffer loss. **losable**, *a.* loser, *n.*

loss (los) [A.-S. *los*], *n.* Act or state of losing or being lost; failure to gain; that which is lost; disadvantage.

lot (lot) [A.-S. *hlot*], *n.* A die, paper, or other object used in determining chances; decision by chance; the chance, share, or fortune falling to one; a separate thing or collection of things offered for sale at auction; a parcel of land; a number of things or persons; a great deal (*often pl.*). *v.t.* To divide into lots; to apportion.

lotion (lō'shŭn) [L. *lōtio*], *n.* A liquid application for a wound, etc.; a cosmetic.

lottery (lot'ĕr-ĭ) [It. *lotteria*], *n.* A method of allotting valuable prizes by lot; the drawing of lots; a mere hazard.

lotto (lot'-ō), *n.* A game of chance played with disks placed on numbered cards.

lotus (lō'tŭs) [Gr. *lōtos*], *n.* A plant the fruit of which was said to induce a dreamy languor. **lotus-eater**, *n.* One who gives himself up to dreamy ease.

loud (loud) [A.-S. *hlūd*], *a.* Powerful in sound; noisy, clamorous; (*fig.*) ostentatious, flashy. *adv.* Loudly. **loudish**, *a.* **loudly**, *adv.* loudness, *n.*

lough (loch) [Ir. *loch*], *n.* A lake, an arm of the sea.

lounge (lounj) [?], *v.i.* To idle about, to saunter; to loll. *n.* Act of lounging; a saunter; a place for lounging; a sitting-room; a sofa. **lounger**, *n.*

lour, lower (lour) [M.E. *louren*], *v.i.* To appear gloomy; to scowl; to look threatening (of weather). **louring**, *a.*

louse (lous) [A.-S. *lūs*], *n.* (*pl.* lice (lĭs)) An insect parasitic on man; applied to various parasites infesting animals, fish, and plants. **lousy** (lou'zĭ), *a.* Infested with lice; (*colloq.*) bad, mean.

lout (lout) [A.-S. *lūtan*], *n.* An awkward fellow; a clown, a bumpkin. **loutish**, *a.*

louver (loo'vĕr) [M.E. and O.F. *lover*], *n.* An opening for the escape of smoke.

lovable (lŭv'ábl), *a.* Worthy of love; amiable. **lovableness**, *n.*

love (lŭv) [A.-S. *lufu*], *n.* A feeling of deep regard, fondness, and devotion (for, towards, etc.); deep affection between persons of the opposite sex; a personification of this, Cupid; a beloved one, a sweetheart (as a term of endearment); (*Games*) no points scored. *v.t.* To have strong affection for, to be in love with; to delight in. *v.i.* To be in love. **love all**; (*In games*) Nothing scored on either side. **love-bird**, *n.* A short-tailed African or American parrot. **love-god**, *n.* Cupid. **love-in-a-mist**, *n.* The fennel-flower. **love-in-idleness**, *n.* The pansy or heartsease. **love-knot**, *n.* An intricate bow (a token of love). **love-lock**, *n.* A tress hanging at the ear or on the forehead. **love-lorn**, *a.* Forsaken by one's love; pining away for love. **love-sick**, *a.* Languishing with love; expressive of languishing love. **loveless**, *a.* **lovely**, *a.* and *adv.* loveliness, *n.* **lover**, *n.* **loving-cup**, *n.* A large two- or three-handled drinking-vessel passed round with wine.

low (1) (lō) [late A.-S. *lāh*], *a.* (*comp.* lower, *superl.* lowest) Not reaching or situated far up; below the normal height; below or little above a given level; near the horizon (of the sun, moon, etc.); near the equator; below the standard in rank, quality, character, etc.; humble, mean; base, dishonourable; vulgar; not advanced in civilization; not high in organization; weak, feeble; badly nourished; (of sounds) deep, produced by slow vibrations, soft; scanty, nearly exhausted; moderate, cheap; (*Ch. of Eng.*), not favouring sacerdotalism. *adv.* In or to a low position; deeply; at a low price; in a humble rank; softly, quietly; on a poor diet. **lowland**, *n.* Low-lying or level country. *a.* Pertaining to a lowland or the Lowlands of Scotland.

lowermost, *a.* lowly, *a.* Humble, modest; low in size, rank, or condition; mean, inferior. *adv.* Humbly, modestly. **lowness,** *n.*

low (2) (A.-S. *hlōwan*), *v.i.* To utter the moo of a cow. *v.t.* To utter with such a sound. *n.* The moo of a cow. **lowing,** *n.*

lower (lō'ẽr), *v.t.* To bring down in height, force, intensity, amount, price, estimation, etc.; to reduce the condition of. *v.i.* To become lower or less, to sink, to fall.

loyal (loi'ál) [F., from L. *lēgālis*, legal], *a.* Faithful, constant in a trust or obligation (to); faithful to one's sovereign, country, etc. loyalism, *n.* **loyalist,** *n.* loyally, *adv.* loyalty, *n.*

lozenge (loz'ĕnj) [O.F. *losenge*, Prov. *lauza*, tombstone]. *n.* An oblique-angled parallelogram; (*Her.*) a diamond-shaped bearing; a sweetmeat, etc., in a rhomb-shaped tablet.

lubber (lŭb'ẽr) [?], *n.* A lazy clumsy fellow; a bad seaman. lubberly, *a.*

lubricate (lū'bri-kāt) [L. *lūbricus*, slippery], *v.t.* To make slippery with grease, oil, etc., in order to reduce friction. lubricant, *a.* and *n.* lubrica'tion, *n.*

lucent (lū'sĕnt) [L. *lūcens*, shining], *a.* Shining, bright, luminous, resplendent. **lucerne** (lū-sẽrn') [F. *luzerne*], *n.* A fodder-plant.

lucid (lū'sid) [L. *lūcidus*], *a.* Bright, radiant; easily understood. lucid'ity, *n.*

Lucifer (loo'si-fẽr) [L. light-bringing], *n.* The morning-star; Satan; a match ignited by friction.

luck (lŭk) [Dut. *luk*], *n.* Chance as bringer of fortune, whether good or bad; what happens to one, hap. luckless, *a.* Unfortunate. lucklessly, *adv.* lucky, *a.*

lucrative (lū'krà-tiv) [L. *lucrārī*, to gain], *a.* Producing gain, profitable.

lucre (lū'kẽr) [L. *lucrum*], *n.* Pecuniary gain, usu. as an object of greed.

lucubrate (lū'kū-brāt) [L. *lūcubrāre*, from *lux lūcis*, light], *v.i.* To study by lamp-light. *v.t.* To compose or elaborate, as by night study. lucubra'tion, *n.* Night study; that which is composed at night; composition of a too elaborate and pedantic character.

ludicrous (lū'di-krŭs) [L. *lūdicrus*, as *lūdus*, play], *a.* Adapted to excite laughter or derision; comical.

luff (lŭf) [?], *n.* The weather-edge of a fore-and-aft sail. *v.* To bring a ship's head nearer the wind.

lug (1) (lŭg) [?], *n.* A projecting part; the lobe of the ear; a large marine worm.

lug (2) (lŭg) [prob. Scand.], *v.t.* To drag, esp. roughly or with exertion; to tug, haul; to insert unnecessarily. *v.i.* To move heavily or slowly.

luggage (lŭg'áj), *n.* Anything heavy and cumbersome to be carried; the baggage of a traveller, etc.

lugger (lŭg'ẽr) [?], *n.* A vessel with two or three masts, and lug-sails.

lug-sail (lŭgsl) [?], *n.* A four-cornered sail bent to a yard hoisted to the mast.

lugubrious (lū-gū'bri-ŭs) [L. *lūgēre*, to mourn], *a.* Mournful, dismal, funereal.

lukewarm (look'wôrm) [M.E. *luke*, tepid], *a.* Moderately warm; (*fig.*) indifferent.

lull (lŭl) [imit.], *v.t.* To soothe to sleep, to calm. *v.i.* To subside, to become quiet. *n.* A temporary calm. lul'laby, *n.* A refrain for lulling a child to sleep.

lumbago (lŭm-bā'gō) [L. from *lumbus*], *n.* Rheumatism round the loins. lum'bar, *a.* Pertaining to the loins.

lumber (1) (lŭm'bẽr) [?], *v.i.* To move heavily or clumsily; to make a heavy rumbling noise. lumbering, *a.*

lumber (2) (lŭm'bẽr) [perh. the room where the *Lombard* bankers stored their pledges], *n.* Discarded articles of furniture, etc., taking up room; useless things; rubbish, refuse.

lumber (3) (lŭm'bẽr), *n.* (*Am.*) Sawn timber. lumberman, *n.* One who cuts trees for lumber. lumber-jack, *n.* One who cuts or handles lumber.

luminary (lū'mi-nàr-i) [L. *lūmen -inis*, light], *n.* A body yielding light, esp. a heavenly body; (*fig.*) one who enlightens mankind. luminant, *a.* and *n.* luminous (lū'mi-nŭs), *a.* luminos'ity, *n.*

lump (lŭmp) [prob. Scand.], *n.* A small mass of matter of no definite shape; a heap, a lot; a swelling. *v.t.* To put together in a lump, to form into a mass; to treat as all alike. lumping, *a.* Large, heavy; bulky. lumpish, *a.* lumpy, *a.* Full of lumps; (*Naut.*) running in short waves that do not break.

lunacy (loo'nà-si), *n.* Insanity, formerly supposed to be caused by the moon; senseless conduct.

lunar (loo'nàr) [L. *lūna*, the moon], *a.* Pertaining to the moon; resembling the moon.

lunatic (loo'nà-tik) [F. *lunatique*], *a.* Insane; mad, crazy, extremely foolish. *n.* An insane person.

lunch (lŭnch) [?], *n.* A light repast between breakfast and dinner. *v.i.* To take this. **luncheon** (lŭn'chŏn), *n.* Lunch (in formal usage).

lung (lŭng) [A.-S. *lungen*], *n.* One of the two organs of respiration in air-breathing animals.

lunge (lŭnj) [earlier *allonge*], *n.* A sudden thrust with a sword, etc.; a plunge. *v.i.* To make a lunge; to strike out from the shoulder.

lupine (1) (loo'pin) [L. *lupīnus*], *n.* A leguminous plant with spikes of white or coloured flowers, and for fodder.

lupine (2) (l-oopīn) [L. *lupus*, wolf], *a.* Pertaining to wolves; like a wolf.

lupus (loo'pŭs) [L., wolf], *n.* A spreading tuberculous or ulcerous inflammation of the skin, esp. of the face.

lurch (lẽrch) [?], *v.i.* To roll suddenly to one side (of a ship); to stagger. *n.* A sudden roll sideways.

lurcher (lẽrch'ẽr), *n.* A dog supposed to be a cross between a collie and a greyhound.

lure (lūr) [O.F. *leurre*], *n.* An object resembling a fowl, used to recall a hawk; an enticement, an allurement. *v.t.* To attract by a lure; to entice.

lurid (lū'rid) [L. *lūridus*], *a.* Of a pale colour, wan; ghastly, unearthly; (*fig.*) sensational (of a story, etc.).

lurk (lĕrk) [?], v.i. To lie hid; to lie in wait; to exist unperceived.

luscious (lŭsh'ŭs) [?], a. Very sweet, delicious; cloying, over-rich in imagery.

lush (lŭsh) [O.F. lasche], a. Luxuriant in growth; succulent, juicy.

lust (lŭst) [A.-S.], n. Animal desire or indulgence, lasciviousness; sensual appetite. v.i. To have powerful desire (for or after). lustful, a.

lustre (lŭs'tĕr) [L. lūstrāre, to lighten], n. Brightness, luminousness, gloss, sheen; a chandelier with pendants of cut glass; a fabric with a glossy surface; a glossy enamel on pottery, etc. lustrous, a.

lusty (lŭs'ti), a. Full of health and vigour. lustily, adv.

lute (lūt) [Arab. al-'ūd], n. A stringed instrument somewhat resembling the guitar. v.t. To play on or as on the lute.

luxuriant (lŭg-zūr'i-ànt) [L. luxuria, sumptuousness], a. Abundant in growth; plentiful, exuberant; fertile, prolific, rank; (fig.) ornate, florid, extravagant. luxuriance, n. luxurious, a. luxuriously, adv. luxury (lŭk'sū-ri), n. Habitual indulgence in expensive pleasures; luxurious living; that which is delightful, esp. to the appetite.

-ly [A.-S. *-līc, a., like], suf. Forming adjectives, as ghastly, manly, or adverbs, as badly, heavily.

lyceum (lī-sē'ŭm) [Gr. Lukeion, nom. -os, pertaining to Apollo], n. The garden at Athens in which Aristotle taught; the Aristotelean philosophy or philosophic school; an institution for literary instruction.

Lydian (lid'i-àn), a. Pertaining to Lydia, in Asia Minor, whose inhabitants were noted for voluptuousness; hence, effeminate, soft.

lye (lī) [A.-S. lēag], n. An alkaline solution strained from vegetable ashes; a cleansing material.

lying (1) (lī'ing), n. Act or habit of telling lies. a. False, deceitful. lyingly, adv.

lying (2), n. Act or state of being recumbent. lying-in, n. Child-bed; lying in child-birth.

lymph (limf) [L. lympha], n. (poet.) Water or any clear fluid; (Physiol.) a colourless, alkaline fluid in the body resembling blood without the red corpuscles; matter containing the virus of a disease used in vaccination. lymphat'ic, a. Pertaining to lymph; phlegmatic.

lynch (lĭnch) [Charles Lynch (1736-96), a Virginian farmer], v.t. To judge and punish, esp. by death, by lynch law. lynch law: Summary punishment without regular trial.

lynx (lĭngks) [Gr. lunx], n. An animal of the cat tribe, with tufted ear-tips, short tail, and extremely sharp sight. lynx-eyed, n. Having sharp sight.

lyre (līr) [Gr. lura], n. A stringed musical instrument of the harp kind; the constellation Lyra. lyre-bird, n. An Australian bird having the tail in the form of a lyre.

lyric (lir'ik), a. Intended to be sung to the lyre; (of a poem) expressing the individual emotions of the poet. n. A lyric poem; (pl.) verses in lyric poetry. lyrical, a. lyricism, n.

M

ma (ma) [childish shortening of MAMMA], n. Mother.

ma'am (măm, mam, m'm) [MADAM].

macabre (mà-ka-br') [F.], a. Gruesome

macadam (mà-kăd'ăm) [J. L. McAdam (1756-1836), road-engineer], n. Broken stone for macadamizing. macadamize, v.t. To make (a road) with macadam.

macaroni (măk-à-rō'ni) [It.], n. A paste of fine wheaten flour formed into long slender tubes; a fop, a dandy. macaronic (-ron'ik), a. Consisting of a jumble of words of different languages in burlesque poetry. n. (pl.) Macaronic verse.

macaroon (măk-à-roon') [It.], n. A small sweet cake flavoured with almonds.

macaw (mà-kaw') [Port.], n. A large S. American parrot with beautiful plumage.

mace (1) (mās) [O.F.], n. A club with a heavy metal head, usu. spiked; a staff of office; a flat-headed stick used in bagatelle.

mace (2) (mās) [F. macis], n. A spice made from the dried covering of the nutmeg.

macerate (măs'ĕr-āt) [L. măcerātus], v.t. To soften by steeping; to separate by a digestive process; to cause to waste away. macera'tion, n.

Machiavel'lian (măk'i-à-vel-i-àn) [N. Machiavelli (1469-1527), Florentine statesman], a. and n. Intriguing and unscrupulous.

machinate (măk'i-nāt) [L. măchinātus, contrived], v.i. To contrive, plot, intrigue. machina'tion, n.

machine (mà-shēn') [Gr. měchanē, from měchos, means, contrivance], n. An apparatus by which motive power is applied; any mechanism for applying or directing force; (fig.) a person who acts without intelligence; a bicycle or tricycle; (Gr. Ant.) a contrivance for effecting change of scenery or introducing a supernatural being; hence, supernatural agency in a poem, etc. v.t. To effect by means of machinery. machine-gun, n. A light piece of ordnance loaded and fired automatically. machine-shop, n. A large workshop where machines are made or repaired. machinery, n. machinist, n. One who constructs, works, or tends a machine.

mackerel (măk'ĕr-ĕl) [O.F. makerel (F. maquereau)], n. A well-known, edible sea-fish. mackerel-sky, n. A sky with small roundish masses of cirro-cumulus.

mackintosh (măk'in-tosh) [Charles Macintosh (1766-1843), inventor], n. A waterproof material of rubber and cloth; a coat made of this.

macro- [Gr. makros, long], comb. form. Great, large (as opp. to small). macrocephalic (măk-rô-sĕ-făl'ik), a. Large-headed. macrocosm (măk'rō-kozm), n.

The great world, the universe, opp. to microcosm.

mad (măd) [A.-S. *gemǽdd*], *a.* Disordered in mind, insane, crazy; furious, wildly excited; infatuated, wild; exceedingly foolish. *v.t.* To make mad. **madcap**, *a.* Eccentric. *n.* A person of wild and eccentric habits. **madhouse**, *n.* A lunatic-asylum. **madly**, *adv.* madman, -woman, *n.* **madness**, *n.* **madden**, *v.* To make or become mad.

madam (măd´ăm) [O.F. *ma dame*, my lady], *n.* A title usu. given to married or elderly women.

madder (măd´ĕr) [A.-S. *mœdere*], *n.* A shrubby climbing plant the root of which is used in dyeing; the dye obtained thence.

made (mād) [p.p. of MAKE], *a.* made up: Artificial (of complexion, etc.); invented, coined (as a story).

Madeira (mȧ-dēr´ȧ), *n.* A white wine made in Madeira.

mademoiselle (măd-ê-mô-zel´) [F.], *n.* (*pl.* mesdemoiselles) A title given to an unmarried woman, Miss.

Madonna (mȧ-don´ȧ) [It.], *n.* The Virgin Mary; a picture or statue of the Virgin Mary.

madrigal (măd´ri-găl) [It. *madrigale*], *n.* An unaccompanied vocal composition in parts; a glee.

maelstrom (māl´strom) [Dut. *malen*, to whirl, *stroom*, stream], *n.* A dangerous whirlpool of Norway; (*fig.*) a turmoil, an overwhelming situation.

maestro (ma-es´trō) [It.], *n.* (*pl.* -tri (-trē)) A master in any art, esp. in music.

magazine (măg-ȧ-zēn´) [Arab. *makhāzin*, storehouses], *n.* A depot, warehouse, esp. for military stores and ammunition; a storeroom for gunpowder, etc., aboard ship; the cartridge-chamber in a magazine-gun; a periodical publication containing articles by different writers. **magazine-gun**, *n.* A rifle or other gun fed with cartridges from a magazine.

magenta (mȧ-jen´tȧ) [Ital. city where a bloody battle was fought just before this was discovered (1859)], *n.* A brilliant crimson aniline dye.

maggot (măg´ŏt) [?], *n.* A grub, the larva of a fly; (*fig.*) a whim, a crotchet. **maggoty**, *a.*

magic (măj´ik) [Gr. *magikos*], *n.* The pretended art of employing supernatural power; sorcery, witchcraft; (*fig.*) any agency that has astonishing results. *a.* Pertaining to, used in, or using magic; exercising supernatural powers. **magical**, *a.* **magician** (mȧ-jish´ȧn), *n.* An enchanter; a wizard.

magisterial (măj-is-tēr´i-ȧl) [L. *magister*, master], *a.* Pertaining to or befitting a magistrate; authoritative, commanding; domineering; oracular.

magistrate (măj´is-trāt) [L. *magistrātus*], *n.* A public officer, commissioned to administer the Law, a Justice of the Peace. **magistracy**, *n.*

magnanimous (măg-năn´i-mŭs) [L. *magnus*, great, *animus*, soul], *a.* Great-minded, elevated in sentiment; brave, generous. **magnanim´ity**, *n.*

magnate (măg´nāt) [L. *magnus*, great], *n.* A person of rank or distinction.

magnesia (măg-nē´shȧ) [pertaining to Magnesia, Thessaly], *n.* Oxide of magnesium, a white alkaline antacid earth; hydrated carbonate of magnesia, used as a laxative. **magnesium**, *n.* A diatomic metallic element, the base of magnesia.

magnet (măg´nĕt) [Gr. *Magnēs -nētos*, (stone) of Magnesia], *n.* The loadstone; a body to which the properties of attracting iron and pointing to the poles have been imparted; (*fig.*) a thing or person exercising powerful attraction. **magnet´ic**, *a.* Pertaining to or having the properties of a magnet; (*fig.*) attractive; mesmeric; (*pl.*) the science or principles of magnetism. **magnetic needle**: A slender poised bar of magnetized steel, as in the mariner's compass, pointing north and south. **magnetic north, south, pole**, *n.* The point north or south where the magnetic needle dips vertically. **mag´netism**, *n.* The property whereby certain bodies, esp. iron and its compounds, attract or repel each other according to certain laws; the science treating of this property, its conditions or laws; the attractive power itself; (*fig.*) personal attractiveness, charm. **magnetize**, *v.t.* To communicate magnetic properties to; to attract as with a magnet; to mesmerize. *v.i.* To become magnetic. **magnetiza´tion**, *n.* **mag´netizer**, *n.* **magneto** (măg-nē´tŏ), *n.* A magneto-electric machine used for igniting the explosive mixture in the cylinder of an internal-combustion engine.

magnificent (măg-nif´i-sĕnt) [L. *magnificentior*, compar. of *magnificus* (*magnus*, great)], *a.* Grand in appearance, majestic; characterized by sumptuousness, splendour, or generous profusion; excellent. **magni´ficence**, *n.*

magnify (măg´ni-fī) [L. *magnus*, great], *v.t.* To increase the apparent size of (an object); to make greater, to increase; to extol, glorify; to exaggerate. **magnifica´tion**, *n.* **mag´nifier**, *n.*

magniloquent (măg-nil´ô-kwĕnt) [L. *magnus*, great, *loqui*, to speak], *a.* Using high-flown, pompous language. **magniloquence**, *n.*

magnitude (măg´ni-tūd) [L. *magnus*, great], *n.* Size, extent, amount.

magnum (măg´nŭm) [L., great], *n.* A bottle containing two quarts; two quarts.

magpie (măg´pī) [*Mag*, short for *Margaret*], *n.* A chattering bird with black and white plumage; (*fig.*) a chatterer; (*shooting*) a hit on the outermost division but one of the target.

Magus (mā´gŭs) [L., from Gr. *magos*], *n.* (*pl.* -gi (-jī)) A priest among the Medes and Persians; a magician. **the Magi**: The three Wise Men of the East who brought presents to the infant Saviour.

Magyar (măg´yar, mȧ-jar´), *n.* One of the Mongoloid race dominant in Hungary; their language.

Maharajah (ma-ha-ra´jȧ) [Sansk. *mahā*, great, RAJAH], *n.* The title of some Indian princes.

Mahatma (má-hăt'má) [Sansk. *mahā*, great, *ātman*, soul], *n.* An adept of the highest order.

mahogany (má-hog'á-ni) [prob. native Amer.], *n.* The hard, fine-grained wood of a tree of tropical America; the tree itself; the colour yellowish-brown.

maid (mād), *n.* A girl, a young unmarried woman, a virgin; a female servant.

maiden (mādn) [A.-S. *mœgden*, dim. of *mœgth*], *n.* A girl; a spinster; an early form of guillotine; (*Cricket*) an over in which no runs are made. *a.* Pertaining to a maid; unmarried; new, unused, untried; never captured (of a fortress); never having won a prize (of a horse); open to such horses (of a race). **maiden-hair**, *n.* A fern with delicate fronds.

mail (1) (māl) [O.F. *maille* L. *macula*], *n.* Defensive armour for the body, formed of rings, chains, or scales; (*fig.*) any defensive covering.

mail (2) (māl) [O.F. *male* (F. *malle*)], *n.* A bag for the conveyance of letters, etc.; the letters, etc., conveyed by the post; the system of conveying these; the post, esp. for abroad; a mail-train or ship. *v.t.* To send by mail, to post.

maim (mām) [M.E. *mahaym*, O.F. *mahaignier*], *n.* A disabling mutilation or injury. *v.t.* To deprive of the use of a limb; to cripple, mutilate.

main (1) (mān) [Icel. *megn*, strong, or foll.], *a.* Concentrated or fully exerted (of force); principal, most important. **main-brace**, *n.* (*Naut.*) A brace attached to the mainyard. **mainland**, *n.* The principal body of land, as opposed to islands, etc. **mainmast**, *n.* The principal mast of a ship. **mainsail** (mān'sāl, mānsl), *n.* A sail bent to the main-yard of a square-rigged ship; the sail set on the after part of the mainmast of a fore-and-aft rigged vessel. **mainspring**, *n.* The chief spring of a watch, etc. **mainstay**, *n.* (*Naut.*) The stay from the main-top to the foot of the foremast; (*fig.*) the chief support. **main-top**, *n.* (*Naut.*) A platform above the head of the lower mainmast. **main-yard**, *n.* (*Naut.*) The yard on which the mainsail is extended. **mainly**, *adv.* Principally, chiefly; in the main; greatly, strongly.

main (2) [A.-S. *mœgen*], *n.* Strength, force, violent effort; the main or high sea, the ocean; a chief sewer, conduit, conductor, etc.

maintain (mán-tān') [F. *maintenir*, L. *manū*, with the hand, *tenēre*, to hold], *v.t.* To hold, preserve, or carry on in any state; to keep up; to provide with the means of living; to keep in proper repair; to affirm, to support by reasoning, argument, etc. **maintainable**, *a.* **maintenance**, *n.* Act of maintaining; sustenance; (*Law*) officious intermeddling in a suit in which the person has no interest.

maize (māz) [Cuban, *mahiz*], *n.* Indian corn.

majesty (măj'ĕ-sti) [L. *majestas*], *n.* The quality of inspiring awe; impressive dignity, stateliness; sovereign power; a title of kings, queens, and emperors. **majestic**, *a.*

majolica (má-jol'-, -yol'i-ká) [It.], *n.* A fine enamelled Italian pottery.

major (mā'jŏr) [L., comp. of *magnus*, great], *a.* Greater in number, quantity, or extent; more important; (*Mus.*) standard, applied to a third consisting of four semitones. *n.* A person of full age; (*Mil.*) an officer next above captain and below lieutenant-colonel. **major-domo**, *n.* The chief officer of a household, a steward. **major-general**, *n.* An officer ranking next below lieutenant-general. **majority** (má-jor'i-ti), *n.* The greater number; more than half; amount of difference between the greater and the less number; full age; rank or office of a major; the great majority; the dead.

make (māk) [A.-S. *macian*], *v.t.* (*past and p.p.* made) To frame, produce, give rise to, effect, bring about; to execute, accomplish (with nouns expressing action); to compose (as verses, etc.); to prepare for use; to enact; to raise to a rank; to constitute, form, turn out to be; to gain, acquire; to move (towards, etc.); to compel (to do); to represent to be; to calculate or decide to be; to reach the end of; to serve for; to fetch, as a price; (*Naut.*) to come near or in sight of; to arrive at. *v.i.* To move, tend, or lie (in a specified direction); to contribute, to have effect (for or to); to flow (of the tide); to act in a specified way (as *make bold*). *n.* Form, shape; style; disposition, mental or moral constitution. **make-believe**, *n.* A pretence, a sham. *a.* Unreal; counterfeit. **makeshift**, *n.* A temporary expedient. *a.* Used as a makeshift. **make-up**, *n.* The arrangement of type into columns or pages; the manner in which an actor is dressed, etc., for a character; the materials used for this; face cosmetics. **make-weight**, *n.* That which is thrown into a scale to make weight; a stop-gap. **maker**, *n.* **making**, *n.* **making-up**, *n.* Balancing of accounts.

mal-, **male-** [L. *male*, badly], *pref.* Bad, badly, as in *malodorous*, *maltreat*.

malachite (măl'á-kit) [Gr. *malache*, mallow], *n.* A bright green carbonate of copper.

maladministra'tion (măl-ád-min-is-trā'-shŏn), *n.* Defective or vicious management, esp. of public affairs.

maladroit (măl-á-droit') [F.], *a.* Awkward, clumsy.

malady (măl'á-di) [F. *maladie*], *n.* A disease, ailment; a moral defect or disorder.

malaise (má-lāz') [F.], *n.* A feeling of uneasiness.

malapropism (măl'á-prop-izm) [Mrs. *Malaprop* in Sheridan's "Rivals"], *n.* Grotesque misapplication of words; a word misapplied.

malapropos (măl-a-prŏ-pō') [F. *mal à propos*], *adv.* Unseasonably, unsuitably, out of place. *a.* Unseasonable, etc. *n.* An inopportune thing, remark, event, etc.

malaria (má-lār'i-á) [It. *mal'aria*], *n.* Noxious exhalations of marshy districts, formerly believed to produce fevers, etc.; various intermittent and remittent fevers due to germs introduced by mosquitoes. **malarial, -ian, -ious,** *a.*

malcontent (măl'kŏn-tent) [O.F.], *a.* Discontented.

male (māl) [O.F., from L. *masculus*], *a.* Pertaining to the sex that begets young; having stamens but no pistil (of flowers); (*fig.*) masculine, virile. *n.* One of the male sex; a plant or part that bears the fecundating organs.

malediction (măl-ē-dĭk'shŭn) [L. *maledictio*], *n.* A curse, imprecation. **maledictory,** *a.*

malefactor (măl'ē-făk-tŏr) [L.], *n.* An evil-doer, a criminal. **maleficent** (mă-lef'-i-sĕnt), *a.* Hurtful, mischievous.

malevolent (mă-lev'ŏ-lĕnt), *a.* Wishing evil or injury to others; ill-disposed, malicious. **malevolence,** *n.*

malformation (măl-fŏr-mā'shŭn), *n.* Faulty formation; a faulty structure.

malice (măl'is) [L. *malus*, bad], *n.* A disposition to injure others; a premeditated design to do evil. **malicious** (mă-lish'ŭs), *a.*

malign (mă-līn'), *a.* Pernicious, hurtful. *v.t.* To speak evil of, to slander. **malignant** (mă-lig'nănt), *a.* **malignancy,** *n.* **malignity,** *n.*

malinger (mă-ling'gĕr) [F. *malingre*, sickly], *v.i.* To pretend illness in order to shirk duty. **malingerer,** *n.*

mall (mawl), *n.* A public walk, orig. a place where pall-mall was played.

mallard (măl'ărd) [O.F. *malart*], *n.* A wild duck.

malleable (măl'ē-ăbl) [O.F.], *a.* Capable of being shaped by hammering; pliant.

mallet (măl'ĕt) [F. *maillet*], *n.* A light hammer, usu. of wood.

mallow (măl'ō) [A.-S. *mealwe*], *n.* A plant with pink or mauve flowers and hairy stems and foliage.

malt (mawlt) [A.-S. *mealt*], *n.* Grain, usu. barley, steeped in water and fermented, dried on a kiln, and used for brewing and distilling; malt-liquor. *v.t.* To convert into or treat with malt. *v.i.* To be converted into malt. **malt-liquor,** *n.* Liquor made from malt by fermentation, beer, stout, etc. **maltster,** *n.* A malt-maker.

Maltese (mawl-tēz') [*Malta*, Mediterranean isl.], *a.* Pertaining to Malta or its inhabitants. *n.* A native or natives of Malta; the Maltese language; a small spaniel with long silky hair.

maltreat (măl-trēt'), *v.t.* To ill-treat; to abuse. **maltreatment,** *n.*

malversation (măl-vĕr-sā'shŭn), *n.* Fraudulent conduct, esp. corrupt administration of public funds.

mamma (mă-ma') [instinctive sound by infants], *n.* Mother.

mammal (măm'ăl) [L. *mamma*, the milk-secreting organs], *n.* One of the Mammalia. **Mamma'lia,** *n.pl.* Animals having milk-secreting organs for suckling their young, the highest division of vertebrates. **mammalian,** *a.*

mammon (măm'ŏn) [Aram. *māmōnā*, riches], *n.* Riches personified as an evil.

mammoth (măm'ŏth) [Russ. *mammat*], *n.* An extinct species of elephant. *a.* Gigantic, huge.

man (măn) [A.-S. *mann*], *n.* (*pl.* **men**) A human being, esp. an adult male; (*collect.*) mankind, the human race; an individual; manhood; a manservant, a workman; (*pl.*) soldiers, esp. privates; pieces used in playing chess, etc. *v.t.* To furnish with men, esp. for military service; (*fig.*) to fortify the courage of (esp. oneself). **man-hole,** *n.* A hole in a floor, parts of machinery, etc., to allow entrance for cleansing and repairs. **man-of-war,** *n.* A warship belonging to a navy. **manservant,** *n.* **manslaughter,** *n.* The killing of a human being, without malice. **manful,** *a.* Brave, courageous; resolute, manly. **manhood,** *n.* State of being a man; manliness, courage, resolution. **mankind',** *n.* The human species; (măn'kīnd) men as dist. from humanity. **manly,** *a.* Having the finer qualities characteristic of a man, courageous, magnanimous; befitting a man; mannish. **mannish,** *a.* Masculine, characteristic of a man, unwomanly.

manacle (măn'ăkl) [L. *manicula*, dim. of *manus*, hand], *n.* A handcuff, fetter. *v.t.* To put manacles on; to fetter.

manage (măn'ăj) [It. *maneggiare*], *v.t.* To conduct, carry on, control; to conduct the affairs of; to handle; to lead or guide by flattery, etc.; to train (as a horse); to deal with, make use of. *v.i.* To direct affairs; to get on (with or without); to succeed (with). **manageable,** *a.* **management,** *n.* Act of managing; administration; board of directors, etc.; skilful employment of means. **manager,** *n.* One who manages a business, institution, etc.; one skilled in management (*usu. with* good, bad, *etc.*). **manageress,** *n.* **managerial** (-jĕr'i-ăl), *a.* **managing,** *a.* Having the management of a business, department, etc.; careful, economical; officious.

manatee (măn-à-tē') [Carib. *manattoui*], *n.* The sea-cow, a large herbivorous mammal.

-mancy [Gr. *manteia*, divination], *suf.* Divination by, as in *necromancy, pyromancy.*

mandamus (măn-dā'mŭs) [L., we command], *n.* A writ requiring a person, corporation, or inferior court to do some particular thing.

mandarin (măn'dă-rin) [Port. *mandarim*, Hindi *mantrī*], *n.* A Chinese official.

mandate (măn'dāt) [L. *mandātum*, commanded], *n.* An authoritative charge or order; a judicial command to an officer or subordinate court; an agreement by a mandatary to perform gratuitously a duty regarding property committed to him; a rescript of the Pope; a direction to a representative to undertake certain legislation, etc. **mandatary** (măn'dă-tăr-i), *n.* **mandatory,** *a.* and *n.*

mandible (măn'dibl) [L. *mandibula*], *n.* The jaw.

mandolin (măn'dŏ-lin) [It. *mandolino*], *n.* A stringed, guitar-like musical instrument.

mandrake (măn'drāk) [Gr. *mandragoras*],

I

n. (*Bot.*) A genus of fleshy plants yielding a narcotic poison.

mandrill (măn′dril), *n.* A ferocious W. African baboon.

mane (mān) [A.-S. *manu*], *n.* The long hair on the neck of the horse, lion, etc.

manganese (măng′gà-nēz), *n.* A greyish-white metallic element.

mange (mānj) [O.F. *manjue*], *n.* A skin disease of cattle, dogs, etc. **mangy**, *a.*

mangel-wurzel (măng′gel-wĕrzl) [G. *mangold*, beet, *wurzel*, root], *n.* A large-rooted variety of beet.

manger (mān′jér) [O.F. *mangeure*], *n.* A trough for horses or cattle to eat out of.

mangle (1) (mang′gĕl) [O.F. *mahaigner*, to maim], *v.t.* To mutilate; to disfigure by hacking; (*fig.*) to mar, destroy the symmetry or completeness of.

mangle (2) [Dut. *mangel*], *n.* A rolling-machine for pressing and smoothing damp linen. *v.t.* To press and smooth with a mangle; to calender.

mango (măng′gō) [Tamil *mānkāy*], *n.* (*pl.* -goes) An East Indian tree.

mangrove (măng′grōv) [?], *n.* A tropical tree growing in muddy places by the coast.

mania (mā′ni-á) [Gr. cogn. with *mainesthai*, to be mad], *n.* A form of mental derangement characterized by hallucination, emotional excitement, and violence; (*fig.*) a craze. **maniac**, *n.* **mani′acal**, *a.*

-mania [as prec.], *suf.* Denoting special kinds of derangement, excessive enthusiasm, etc., as *kleptomania*, *megalomania*, *monomania*. **-maniac**, *pers. suf.*

manicure (măn′i-kūr) [L. *manus*, hand, *cura*, care], *v.t.* To trim the finger-nails, etc. **manicurist**, *n.* One who manicures.

manifest (măn′i-fest) [L. *manifestus* (prob. *mani-*, *manu*, *manus*, hand, *festus*, struck], *a.* Not concealed; plainly apparent, clear, obvious; detected. *v.t.* To make manifest, to show clearly; to display, to exhibit, to evince; to be evidence of; to reveal or exhibit (itself); to record in a ship's manifest. *v.i.* To make a public demonstration of opinion; (*Spiritualism*) to reveal its presence (of a spirit). *n.* A list of a ship's cargo for the use of the custom-house officers; a manifesto. **manifesta′tion** (-tā′shŭn), *n.*

manifesto (măn-i-fes′tō) [It.], *n.* (*pl.* -tos) A public declaration, esp. by a government, sovereign, or other authoritative body, of opinions, motives, or intentions.

manifold (măn′i-fōld) [A.-S. *manigfeald*], *a.* Of various forms or kinds; many and various, abundant; shown, applied, or acting in various ways.

manikin (măn′i-kin) [Dut. *manneken*, dim. of *man*], *n.* A little man, a dwarf.

Manila (mà-nil′á) [capital of Philippine Is.], *n.* A kind of cheroot made at Manila; applied to a tough hemp and a strong brown paper made from this.

manipulate (mà-nip′ū-lāt) [L. *manipulus*], *v.t.* To handle, to treat with the hands, esp. skilfully; to manage, influence, or tamper with. **manipula′tion**, *n.* **manip′-ulative**, *a.* **manipulator**, *n.*

manna (măn′á) [Heb.], *n.* The food miraculously supplied to the Israelites in the wilderness.

mannequin (măn′e-kin) [F.], *n.* A woman employed to wear and display clothes.

manner (măn′ér) [L. *manuărius*, pertaining to the hand], *n.* The mode in which anything is done; method, style; use, custom; bearing, address; sort, kind; (*pl.*). behaviour, deportment, habits showing good breeding; social conditions. **mannered**, *a.* Having manners (as *ill-mannered*); affected. **mannerism**, *n.* Peculiarity of style. **mannerless**, *a.*

manœuvre (mà-noo′vér) [F., from L. *manū operārī*, to work with the hand], *n.* A tactical movement by troops or warships; (*pl.*) tactical exercises in imitation of war; (*fig.*) artful management, a stratagem. *v.i.* To perform manœuvres; to manage with skill. *v.t.* To cause (troops) to perform manœuvres to effect by means of strategy; to manipulate.

manor (măn′ór) [O.F. *manoir*, L. *manēre*, to dwell], *n.* A landed estate consisting of a demesne and certain rights over lands held by freehold tenants. **manor-house**, *n.* manor′ial, *a.*

manse (măns) [med. L. *mansa*, a house], *n.* The residence of a Presbyterian minister.

mansion (măn′shŭn) [O.F., from L. *mansio*], *n.* A superior residence of considerable size; (*pl.*) a large building divided into residential flats; an abode. **mansion-house**, *n.* A manor-house; the official residence of a Lord Mayor.

mantel (măntl) [as MANTLE], *n.* The ornamental facing around a fire-place with the shelf above it. **mantelpiece**, *n.* A mantel, esp. the shelf.

mantilla (măn-til′á) [Sp.], *n.* A woman's light cloak, a hood or veil.

mantle (măntl) [O.F. *mantel*, L. *mantellum*], *n.* A loose outer garment; (*fig.*) a covering; coated network placed round a gas-jet to give an incandescent light. *v.t.* To clothe in a mantle; to cover, envelop; to suffuse. *v.i.* To be overspread (as with a blush); to suffuse the cheeks (of a blush); to become coated (of liquids).

manual (măn′ū-ál) [L. *manus*, hand], *a.* Pertaining to or performed with the hands. *n.* A handbook; a service book; an organ keyboard.

manufacture (măn-ū-făk′chŭr) [L. *manū*, by hand, *factūra*, from *facere*, to make], *n.* The making of articles by means of labour or machinery; (*pl.*) the products of industry or any particular industry. *v.t.* To make or work up for use, to produce or fashion by labour or machinery, esp. on a large scale; to fabricate, invent (a story, evidence, etc.). **manufac′tory**, *n.* **manufacturer**, *n.*

manumit (măn-ū-mit′) [L. *manū*, by hand, *mittere*, to send], *v.t.* To release from slavery. **manumission**, *n.*

manure (mà-nūr′) [corr. of MANŒUVRE], *v.t.* To enrich (soil) with fertilizers. *n.* Any substance, as dung or chemical preparations, used to fertilize land.

manuscript (măn′ū-skript) [L. *manū*, by hand, *scriptus*, written], *a.* Written by hand. *n.* A written (as opp. to printed) document.

Manx (măngks) [Icel. *manskr*], *a.* Pertaining to the Isle of Man or its inhabitants. *n.* The people of the Isle of Man; the Celtic language spoken by these.

many (men'i) [A.-S. *manig*], *a.* Numerous; comprising a great number.

Maori (mou'ri) [native], *n.* One of the brown race of New Zealand; their language.

map (măp) [L. *mappa*, napkin], *n.* A representation of a portion of the earth's surface, or the heavens, upon a plane. *v.t.* To represent in a map; to plan (out) in exact detail.

maple (māpl) [A.-S.], *n.* A tree allied to the sycamore; the wood of this.

maquis (măk'ē) [F.], *n.* Scrub or brush in Corsica; those surreptitiously resisting the German invaders of France, 1940–45.

mar (mar) [A.-S. *merran*], *v.t.* To spoil, ruin; to disfigure.

maraschino (măr-ă-skē'nō) [It.], *n.* A liqueur distilled from bitter black cherries.

maraud (mă-rawd') [F. *maraud*, rogue], *v.i.* To rove in quest of plunder; to make a raid (on). *v.t.* To plunder. **marauder**, *n.*

marble (marbl) [O.F. *marbre*, L. *marmor*], *n.* A crystalline limestone taking a fine polish; a piece of sculpture in this (*usu. in pl.*), a small hard ball used as a toy.

march (1) (march) [F. *marche*], *n.* The boundary of a territory; a borderland between two countries. *v.i.* To border (upon) or have a common frontier (with).

march (2) [F. *marcher*], *v.i.* To move with regular steps; to walk in a grave deliberate manner. *v.t.* To cause to move in military order. *n.* Act of marching; a deliberate or measured movement, esp. of soldiers; the distance marched in a day; (*Mus.*) a composition for accompanying a march.

March (3) [A.-F. *marche*, L. *Martius*, pertaining to Mars], *n.* The third month of the year.

marchioness (mar'shŏ-nĕs) [low L. *marchiŏnissa*], *n.* The wife or widow of a marquess, or a woman holding this rank in her own right.

marconigram (mar-kō'ni-grăm) [Guglielmo *Marconi* (1874–1937), inventor, -GRAM], *n.* A radio message.

mare (mār) [A.-S. *mere*], *n.* The female of the horse. **mare's-nest**, *n.* A discovery that turns out a delusion.

margarine (mar'jả-rēn, mar'gả-rēn) [F. *margarin*, Gr. *margaritēs*, pearl], *n.* An artificial butter.

margin (mar'jin) [L. *margo -ginis*], *n.* An edge, a border, a brink; the space round the printed matter on a page; the space within which a thing is just possible; an allowance for contingencies, growth, etc.; the difference between cost and selling price. **marginal**, *a.* **margina'lia**, *n.pl.* Marginal notes.

marguerite (mar'gĕr-ēt) [F.], *n.* The ox-eye daisy and other varieties of chrysanthemum.

marigold (măr'i-gōld) [the Virgin *Mary*, GOLD], *n.* A plant bearing a bright yellow flower.

marine (mả-rēn') [L. *mare*, the sea], *a.*

Pertaining to the sea; used in navigation, nautical, naval. *n.* The shipping or navy of a country; (*pl.*) troops for service on warships. **mar'iner**, *n.* A seaman, a sailor.

marionette (măr-i-ŏ-net') [dim. of *Marion*, dim. of *Mary*], *n.* A puppet moved by strings on a mimic stage.

marital (măr'i-tăl) [L. *maritus*, husband], *a.* Pertaining to a husband or to wedded life.

maritime (măr'i-tim) [L. *maritimus*], *a.* Pertaining to or bordering on the sea; having a navy or commerce by sea (of countries, cities, etc.).

marjoram (mar'jŏ-răm) [O.F. *marjorane*], *n.* A herb of the mint family.

mark (1) (mark) [A.-S. *mearc*], *n.* A visible sign, a stroke, cut, dot, etc.; a symbol, character, token; an object to aim at; a limit, a standard; a distinguishing feature, a symptom; a boundary, frontier, or limit. *v.t.* To make a mark on; to distinguish by a mark or marks; to single out; to pay heed to; to be a feature of; to express or produce by marks; to record (points in games); to award (merit in examination). *v.i.* To observe critically, to take note. **markedly**, *adv.* **markedness**, *n.* **marker**, *n.* One who marks; a counter used in card-playing; one who notes the score at billiards, etc.

mark (2) (mark) [A.-S. *marc*], *n.* A German silver coin, the standard of monetary value; (*Hist.*) English money of account valued at 13*s.* 4*d.*

market (mar'kĕt) [late A.-S. and O. North. F.], *n.* A meeting for buying and selling; the place for this; a locality regarded as a place for buying and selling commodities in general or a particular form of merchandise; demand for a commodity, value as determined by this. *v.i.* To deal in a market. *v.t.* To sell in a market. **market-garden**, *n.* A garden in which vegetables and fruit are raised for market. **market town**, *n.* A town holding a public market. **marketable**, *a.*

marking (mar'king), *a.* Producing a mark. *n.* Marks or colouring, esp. on natural objects.

marksman (marks'măn), *n.* One skilled in aiming at a mark; one who shoots well. **marksmanship**, *n.*

marl (marl) [O.F. *marle*], *n.* Clay containing calcareous matter, used as a fertilizer. *v.t.* To manure with marl.

marline (mar'lin) [Dut. *marlijn*], *n.* (*Naut.*) A small two-stranded line, used for lashing, etc. **marline-spike**, *n.* A pin for opening the strands of rope.

marmalade (mar'mả-lăd) [Port. *marmelada* (*marmelo*, quince)], *n.* A preserve prepared from oranges or lemons.

marmoreal (mar-mŏr'ē-ăl) [L. *marmor*, marble], *a.* Like marble, cold, smooth.

marmoset (mar'mŏ'zet) [O.F., a grotesque image], *n.* A small monkey.

marmot (mar'mŏt) [F. *marmotte*], *n.* A squirrel-like rodent about the size of a rabbit.

maroon (1) (mả-roon') [F. *marron*, chestnut], *a.* and *n.* A brownish-crimson colour.

maroon (2) (mà-roon') [Sp. *cimarron*, savage], *n.* Fugitive slaves in the West Indies and their descendants; one who has been marooned. *v.t.* To put ashore and abandon on a desolate island.

marquee (mar-kē') [F. *Marquise*], *n.* A large field-tent.

marquess, marquis (mar'kwès) [O.F. *marchis*, warden of the marches], *n.* A title of nobility next below a duke and above an earl. **marquisate**, *n.*

marquetry (mar'kèt-ri) [F. *marqueter*, to inlay], *n.* Work inlaid with fine wood, ivory, metal, plates, etc.

marriage (mär'áj) [F. *mariage*], *n.* The legal union of a man and woman, wedlock; a wedding. **marriageable**, *a.* Fit or of age for marriage.

married (mär'id), *a.* United in marriage; pertaining to married persons, conjugal.

marrow (mär'ō) [A.-S. *mearg*], *n.* A fatty substance in the cavities of bones; (*fig.*) the essence, the pith; a vegetable marrow. **marrowbone**, *n.* A bone containing marrow. **marrowfat**, *n.* A large variety of pea.

marry (mär'i) [L. *maritāre*], *v.t.* To unite as man and wife; to give in marriage; to take for one's husband or wife. *v.i.* To enter into wedlock.

marsh (marsh) [A.-S. *mersc*], *n.* Land covered wholly or partially with water; a swamp. **marshy**, *a.*

marshal (mar'shàl) [O.H.G. *marah*, horse, *scalh*, servant], *n.* An officer regulating ceremonies and directing processions; an officer of state; a military and Air-Force officer of high rank; a field-marshal. *v.t.* To arrange in order; to conduct in a ceremonious manner. *v.i.* To assemble, to take up a position (of armies, processions, etc.). **marshaller**, *n.*

marsupial (mar-sū'pi-àl) [Gr. *marsipos*, bag], *a.* Belonging to the *Marsupialia*, carrying the young in a pouch, as the kangaroos and opossums. *n.* Any individual of the *Marsupialia*.

mart (mart), *n.* A market or market-place; an auction-room.

marten (mar-tèn) [O.Teut., *marthuz*], *n.* A small carnivorous mammal allied to the weasel, with a valuable fur.

martial (mar'shàl) [L. *Martiālis*, from MARS], *a.* Pertaining to war; courageous.

martin (mar'tin) [St. *Martin* of Tours (4th cent.)], *n.* A bird allied to the swallow.

martinet (mar-ti-net') [Gen. *Martinet*, officer under Louis XIV], *n.* A strict disciplinarian.

martingale (mar'ting-gāl) [F.], *n.* A strap fastened to a horse's girth to keep the head down.

Martinmas (mar'tin-màs), *n.* The feast of St. Martin, 11th Nov.

martyr (mar'tèr) [Gr. *martur*, a witness], *n.* One who suffers death or persecution in defence of his faith or principles. *v.t.* To put to death for adherence to one's belief etc.; to persecute. **martyrdom**, *n.* **martyrol'ogy**, *n.* A list or history of martyrs.

marvel (mar'vèl) [O.F. *merveille*], *n.* A wonderful or astonishing thing; a prodigy. *v.i.* To be astonished (at or that); to wonder. **marvellous**, *a.*

mascot (mäs'kòt) [F.], *n.* An object or person that brings luck.

masculine (mäs'kū-lin) [L. *masculīnus*], *a.* Belonging to or having the qualities of the male sex; robust, vigorous; manly; denoting the male gender. **masculin'ity**, *n.*

mash (mäsh) [A.-S.], *n.* Ingredients crushed and mixed into a pulp. *v.t.* To crush into a pulpy mass.

mask (mask) [F. *masque*], *n.* A covering for the face, for protection or disguise; an impression of a face in plastic material; a pretence, a subterfuge; a masque. *v.t.* To cover or disguise with a mask; (*Mil.*) to hide (a battery, etc.) behind cover. *v.i.* To go in disguise.

masochism (mäz'ō-kizm) [von *Masoch* (1836–95), Austrian novelist], *n.* A form of sexual perversion requiring the acceptance of cruelty by another.

mason (mä'sòn) [O.F. *maçon*], *n.* A mechanic who works in stone; a free-mason. **mason'ic**, *a.* **ma'sonry**, *n.*

masque (mask) [F.], *n.* A play formerly presented in noblemen's houses, the performers wearing masks, orig. in dumb show. **masquer**, *n.*

masquerade (mäs-kèr-ād') [Sp. *mascarada*, Arab. *maskhara*, a buffoon], *n.* A ball at which people wear masks; disguise, pretence. *v.i.* To pass oneself off in a false guise. **masquerader**, *n.*

mass (1) (mäs) [A.-S. *mæsse*], *n.* The R.-C. celebration of the Eucharist; the office for this; a setting of certain portions of this to music.

mass (2) (mäs) [F. *masse*], *n.* A body of matter collected into a whole of indefinite shape; a compact aggregation of things; a great quantity; the principal part, the majority (of); volume, bulk. *v.t.* To form into a mass; to concentrate (as troops). *v.i.* To gather into a mass. **massive**, *a.* Heavy, ponderous; bulky. **massy**, *a.*

massacre (mäs'á-kèr) [F.], *n.* Indiscriminate slaughter; carnage. *v.t.* To kill indiscriminately.

massage (mä-sazh') [F.], *n.* Treatment by kneading the muscles and body with the hands. *v.t.* To subject to this treatment. **masseur** (mä-sèr') (*fem.* **masseuse** (-sèrz')), *n.* One who gives massage.

mast (1) (mast) [A.-S. *mæst*], *n.* A long pole placed upright in a ship to support the yards, sails, etc. **masted**, *a.*

mast (2) [A.-S. *mæst*], *n.* The fruit of the beech or other forest trees.

master (mas'tèr) [A.-S. *mægester*, L. *magister*], *n.* A man who has authority over others; an employer; the head of a household; the owner of a slave, dog, etc.; one skilled in an art, craft, etc.; a great artist; a schoolmaster; the highest degree in arts and surgery; a title of certain judicial officers; (*Sc.*) the courtesy title of a viscount or baron's eldest son; the captain of a merchant vessel. *a.* Having control or authority. *v.t.* To become the master of; to subdue, bring under control. **Old Masters;** The great painters of the 13th–17th centuries; their pictures. **master-hand,** *n.* An expert. **master-key,** *n.* A key which opens all the locks of a set. **master-mind,** *n.* The ruling mind or intellect. **masterpiece,** *n.* A performance superior to anything of the same kind. **masterful,** *a.* Expressing mastery; domineering. **masterless,** *a.* **masterly,** *a.* With the skill of a master.

mastic (măs′tik) [Gr. *mastichē*], *n.* A resin from a Mediterranean evergreen tree, used for varnish.

masticate (măs′ti-kāt) [L. *masticātus*], *v.t.* To grind and crush with the teeth. **mastica′tion,** *n.* **mas′ticatory,** *a.*

mastiff (măs′tif) [A.-F. and O.F. *mastin*], *n.* A large dog of great strength and courage.

mastodon (măs′tō-dŏn) [Gr. *mastos*, breast, *odous odontos*, tooth], *n.* An extinct mammal allied to the elephant.

mat (1) (măt) [A.-S. *meatte*], *n.* A coarse fabric of rushes, hemp, etc., used to wipe shoes on, for packing, etc.; a tangled mass of anything. *v.i.* To become twisted into a mat (of hair, etc.).

mat (2) [F.], *a.* Dull, lustreless, not glossy.

matador (măt′ȧ-dôr) [Sp.], *n.* The man who has to kill the bull in bull-fights.

match (1) (măch) [A.-S. *mœcca*], *n.* A person or thing like or corresponding to another; one able to cope with another; a contest of skill, strength, etc.; an alliance by marriage; one eligible for marrying. *v.t.* To compare as equal; to oppose as equal; to correspond. *v.i.* To agree, to be equal, to tally. **matchboard,** *n.* A board having a tongue along one edge and a corresponding groove on the other for fitting into similar boards.

match (2) [O.F. *mesche*, wick], *n.* A small strip of wood or taper tipped with combustible material; a fuse for firing charges.

mate (1) (māt), *v.t.* To checkmate; to confound, paralyse. *n.* A checkmate.

mate (2) (māt) [Teut.], *n.* A comrade, a fellow-worker; an equal; a suitable partner, esp. in marriage; an officer in a merchant ship ranking below the captain; an assistant to a ship's surgeon, cook, etc. *v.t.* To match, to join together in marriage; to pair (birds).

material (mȧ-tēr′i-ȧl) [O.F. *materiel*], *a.* Pertaining to or consisting of matter; substantial; unspiritual, pertaining to the essence of a thing, not to the form; important, momentous. *n.* The substance from which anything is made; stuff, fabric; component parts (of). **materialism,** *n.* The theory that there is nothing in the universe but matter; regard for secular to the neglect of spiritual interests. **materialist,** *n.* **materialis′tic,** *a.* **mater′ialize,** *v.t.* To make material, to invest with matter. *v.i.* To appear (of a spirit); to become actual fact. **materializa′tion,** *n.*

materiel (mȧ-tār-i-el′) [F.], *n.* Material, supplies, machinery, etc., as distinguished from personnel.

maternal (mȧ-tēr′nȧl) [F. *maternel*, L. *māter*, mother], *a.* Motherly; pertaining to maternity; related on the mother's side. **maternity,** *n.* Motherhood.

mathematical (măth-ē-măt′i-kȧl) [Gr. *mathēmatikos*, from *manthanein*, to learn], *a.* Pertaining to mathematics; rigidly accurate. **mathematician** (-mȧ-tish′ȧn), *n.* **mathematics** (-măt′iks), *n.* The science of quantity as expressed by numbers.

matin (măt′in) [L. *mātūtinus*, of the morning], *n.* (*in pl.*) One of the canonical hours of the breviary; the daily office of morning prayer. **matinee** (măt′i-nā), *n.* An afternoon performance.

matriarch (mā′tri-ark) [L. *matri-* from *mater*, mother; -ARCH], *n.* A woman who rules a tribe; mother of a clan.

matricide (mā′tri-sīd) [L. *mātricīda*], *n.* One who murders his mother; the murder of a mother.

matriculate (mȧ-trik′ū-lāt) [L. *mātricula*, register], *v.t.* To admit to membership of a college or university. *v.i.* To be so admitted. **matricula′tion,** *n.*

matrimony (măt′ri-mō-ni) [L. *mātrimōnium*, from *māter*, mother], *n.* The state of being married, marriage, wedlock. **matrimo′nial,** *a.*

matrix (mā′triks), *n.* The womb; a place where anything is developed; a mould in which type, a die, etc., is cast; that in which a mineral or fossil is embedded.

matron (mā′trŏn), *n.* A married woman; the female superintendent of an institution. **matronly,** *a.* and *adv.*

matter (măt′ėr) [M.E. and O.F. *matere*, F. *matière*, L. *mātēria*, stuff, esp. for building], *n.* Substance as dist. from thought, mind, spirit, etc.; that which has weight, occupies space, and is perceptible by the senses; meaning, sense (of a book, discourse, etc.); (*Log.*) content as opposed to form; an affair, a business; cause or occasion for difficulty, regret, etc.; importance. *v.i.* To be of moment, to signify. **matter-of-fact,** *a.* Treating of facts or realities; not fanciful or imaginary; commonplace, prosaic.

matting (măt′ing), *n.* Mat-work; mats; material for mats; coarse fabric for packing and covering.

mattock (măt′ŏk) [A.-S. *mattuc*], *n.* A pick with one broad end.

mattress (măt′rĕs) [O.F. *materas*], *n.* A case stuffed with hair, wool, etc., used as a bed; a similar appliance of woven wire or springs.

mature (mȧ-tūr′) [L. *mātūrus*, ripe], *a.* Ripe, completely developed; fully considered, etc.; become payable (as a bill). *v.t.* To bring to a state of ripeness. *v.i.* To become fully developed; to become payable (of a bill). **maturity,** *n.*

matutinal (măt-ū-tī′nȧl) [L. (as MATIN)], *a.* Pertaining to the morning; early.

maudlin (mawd′lin) [MAGDALEN], *a.* Muddled with drink; sentimental.

maugre (maw′gėr) [O.F. *maugré*], *prep.* In spite of.

maul (mawl) [L. *malleus*, hammer], *n.* A heavy wooden hammer. *v.t.* To beat, bruise; to handle roughly.

maulstick (mawl′stik) [Dut. *maalstok*], *n.* A light stick with a round pad at the end used as a rest for the right hand by painters.

maunder (mawn'dẽr) [?], *v.i.* To grumble, mutter; to talk incoherently.

maundy (mawn'di) [O.F. *mandé*, L. *mandātum*], *n.* The ceremony of washing the feet of the poor on Holy Thursday; a distribution of alms following this.

mausoleum (maw-sȯ-lẽ'ŭm) [L. from Gr.], *n.* The stately tomb of Mausolus, king of Caria, one of the seven wonders of the world; an elaborate sepulchral monument.

mauve (mōv) [L. *malva*, mallow], *n.* A lilac-coloured aniline dye; the colour.

maverick (mǎv'ẽr-ik) [Sam *Maverick*, a Texan rancher], *n.* (*Am.*) An unbranded beast; (*fig.*) an irresponsible person.

mavis (mā'vis) [F. *mauvis*], *n.* The song-thrush.

maw (maw) [A.-S. *maga*], *n.* The fourth stomach of ruminants; the crop of birds.

mawkish (maw'kish) [Icel. *mathkr*], *a.* Apt to cause satiety; sickly, insipid.

maxilla (mǎk-sil'ȧ) [L.], *n.* (*pl.* -læ (-lē)) One of the jaw-bones, esp. the upper.

maxim (1) (mǎk'sim) [L. *maximus*, greatest], *n.* A general principle of a practical kind.

Maxim (2) [Sir Hiram S. *Maxim* (1840–1916), inventor], *n.* An automatic single-barrelled quick-firing machine-gun.

maximum (mǎk'si-mŭm), *n.* (*pl.* -ma) The greatest quantity or degree attainable. *a.* Greatest; at the greatest or highest degree.

may (1) (mā) [A.-S. *mœg*, 1st sing. of *mugan*, to be able], *aux.v.* (*2nd sing.* mayest, *past* might) Expressing possibility, permission, desire, obligation, or uncertainty. **maybe,** *adv.* Perhaps, possibly. **mayhap,** *conj.* Peradventure.

May (2) [F. *mai*, L. *Māius*], *n.* The fifth month of the year; the springtime of life, youth; hawthorn-blossom.

mayonnaise (mā'ȯ-nāz) [F.], *n.* A sauce made of egg-yolk, oil, vinegar, etc.

mayor (mâr) [F. *maire*], *n.* The chief officer of a city. **mayoral,** *a.* **mayoralty,** *n.* **mayoress,** *n.*

maze (māz) [?], *n.* A labyrinth, a confusing network of passages; a state of uncertainty, perplexity. *v.t.* To bewilder, to confuse. **mazy,** *a.* Involved, perplexing, intricate; giddy.

mazurka (má-zẽr'kȧ) [Pol., woman of the prov. Mazovia], *n.* A lively Polish dance.

me (mē, mē) [A.-S.], *pers. pron.* The dative and objective of the first personal pronoun.

mead (1) (mēd) [A.-S. *medu*], *n.* A fermented liquor made from honey.

mead (2) [A.-S. *mǣd*], *n.* (*poet.*) A meadow.

meadow (med'ō) [A.-S. *mǣdwe*], *n.* A tract of land under grass; rich, moist ground, esp. near a river. **meadow-sweet,** *n.* A plant with white flowers.

meagre (mē'gẽr) [O.F. *megre*, n *aigre*], *a.* Lean, wanting flesh; destitute of richness; (*fig.*) scanty. **meagreness,** *n.*

meal (1) (mēl) [A.-S. *mǣl*], *n.* Food taken at a customary time, a repast.

meal (2) [A.-S. *melu*], *n.* The edible portion of grain ground into flour. **mealy,** *a.*

mealie (mē'li) [S. Afric. Dut. *milje*, Port. *milho*], *n.* (*usu. pl.*) Maize.

mean (1) (mēn) [A.-S. *mǣnan*], *v.t.* (*past and p.p.* meant (ment)) To have in the mind; to intend; to denote, signify. *v.i.* To have a specified intention or disposition. **meaning,** *n.* That which is meant, significance, import. *a.* Significant. **meaningless,** *a.*

mean (2) (mēn) [O.F. *meien* (F. *moyen*)], *a.* Occupying a middle position; moderate, not excessive; average. *n.* The middle point, course, quality, etc., between two extremes; an average; (*pl.*) that by which a result is attained; income, wealth. **meantime, -while,** *adv.* In the intervening time. *n.* The interval between two given times.

mean (3) (mēn) [A.-S. *mǣne*], *a.* Low in quality, value, rank, etc.; inferior, poor; petty, stingy; ignoble, despicable. **meanly,** *adv.* **meanness,** *n.*

meander (mē-ǎn'dẽr) [L. *Mæander*, winding river in Phrygia], *v.i.* To wander, wind, or flow in a tortuous course.

measles (mēzls) [M.E. *maseles*], *n.pl.* An infectious disease usu. attacking children. **measly,** *a.*

measure (mezh'ŭr) [O.F. *mesure*], *n.* The extent or dimensions of a thing; measurements; standard of measurement; a definite unit of capacity or extent; an instrument for measuring, a system of measuring, act of measuring; prescribed extent, quantity, etc.; limit, just degree or amount; metre, poetical rhythm; means to an end; a law, a statute; (*Geol.*) (*pl.*) a series of beds, strata; (*Mus.*) pace, the contents of a bar; dance. *v.t.* To determine the extent or quantity of; to take the dimensions of; to weigh, value, or estimate by comparison with a standard; to serve as the measure of; to allot or apportion by measure; (*fig.*) to travel over, to survey. **measurable,** *a.* **measured,** *a.* Of definite measure; deliberate and uniform; rhythmical; well-considered. **measureless,** *a.* **measurement,** *n.*

meat (mēt) [A.-S. *mete*], *n.* The flesh of animals, usu. excluding fish and fowl, used as food. **meaty,** *a.* **meatiness,** *n.*

mechanic (mē-kǎn'ik) [Gr. *mēchanikos*], *n.* A handicraftsman, an artisan; one employed or skilled in any craft or mechanical occupation; (*pl.*) the branch of physics treating of the motion and equilibrium of material bodies. *a.* Mechanical; industrial. **mechanical,** *a.* Pertaining to mechanics, mechanism, or machinery; in accordance with physical laws; produced by or working with machinery; machine-like, done from force of habit; unoriginal. **mechanical powers:** The simple machines, the wedge, the inclined plane, the screw, the lever, the wheel and axle, and the pulley. **mechanician** (-nish'ȧn), *n.* One skilled in mechanics or in machine-making. **mech'anism,** *n.* The structure or correlation of parts of a machine; machinery; a system of correlated parts working together; (*Art*) mechanical execution as dist. from style.

medal (med′ăl) [F. *médaille*], *n.* A piece of metal, usu. coin-shaped, stamped with a figure and inscription to commemorate some event or person.

meddle (medl) [A.-F. *medler*], *v.i.* To interfere (in) officiously; to concern or busy oneself (with) unnecessarily. **meddler**, *n.* **meddlesome**, *a.*

mediæval (med-i-ē′văl) [L. *medius*, middle, *ævum*, age], *a.* Pertaining to or characteristic of the Middle Ages. **mediæval-ism**, *n.* **mediævalist**, *n.*

medial (mē′di-ăl) [L. *mediālis*, as prec.], *a.* Pertaining to or situated in the middle; mean, average.

mediate (mē′di-ăt), *a.* Situated between two extremes; intervening, indirect; acting as or effected by indirect means. *v.i.* (āt′) To interpose (between) in order to reconcile parties, etc.; to serve as connecting link (between). **media′tion**, *n.* **me′diator**, *n.*

medical (med′i-kăl) [L. *medicus*, a physician], *a.* Pertaining to or employed in medicine; healing, medicinal. **medic′-ament**, *n.* A healing substance.

medicine (med′i-sin) [O.F. *medecine*], *n.* A substance for alleviating or removing disease; the science of preserving health and curing disease, esp. as dist. from surgery; applied by the N. Am. Indians to anything supposed to possess supernatural powers, a charm, fetish. **medicine-ball**, *n.* A heavy ball tossed for exercise. **medicine man**, *n.* A witch-doctor among savages. **medic′inal**, *a.*

mediocre (mē′di-ō-kėr) [F. *médiocre*, L. *medius*, middle], *a.* Of middling quality; average, commonplace. **medioc′rity**, *n.*

meditate (med′i-tāt) [L. *meditātus*, mused over], *v.i.* To ponder, to engage in thought (upon); to cogitate. *v.t.* To dwell upon mentally; to design, intend. **medita′tion**, *n.* **med′itative**, *a.*

medium (mē′di-ŭm) [L., neut. of *medius*, middle], *n.* Anything serving as an intermediary; instrumentality, agency; an instrument of exchange, as money; a middle or intermediate object, quality, degree, etc.; a person claiming to receive and transmit communications from the spirit world. *a.* Intermediate in quality, etc.; average, middling, mediocre.

medlar (med′lăr) [A.-F. *medler*, L. *mespila*], *n.* A rosaceous tree, the fruit of which is eaten when beginning to decay.

medley (med′li) [A.-F. *medlee*], *n.* A confused mass of incongruous objects, persons, etc.

medulla (mē-dŭl′ă) [L.], *n.* Marrow, esp. of the spine; the spinal cord.

medusa (mē-dū′să) [Gr. *Medousa*, one of the Gorgons of myth], *n.* (*pl.* -sæ) A jelly-fish.

meed (mēd) [A.-S. *mēd*], *n.* Reward, recompense.

meek (mēk) [M.G. *meoc*], *a.* Mild, submissive, gentle, forbearing. **meekness**, *n.*

meerschaum (mēr′shawm, -shŭm) [G., sea-foam], *n.* A white clay used for tobacco-pipes; a pipe made of this.

meet (1) (mēt) [A.-S. *gemœte*, fitting well], *a.* Fit, proper, suitable. **meetly**, *adv.*

meet (2) [A.-S. *mētan*], *v.t.* To come face

to face with; to reach and unite with (of a road, railway, etc.); to encounter, confront, oppose; to answer, satisfy, discharge. *v.i.* To come together, to assemble; to be united. *n.* A meeting for hunting, or of cyclists, etc.; the persons assembled or the place of assembly. **meeting**, *n.* A coming together, an assembly; the persons assembled. **meeting-house**, *n.* A dissenters' place of worship.

mega-, **megalo-** [Gr. *megas*, fem. *megalē*, great], *comb. form.* Great, large. **meg′a-phone**, *n.* An apparatus for enabling the voice to travel a long distance.

megrim (mē′grim) [F. *migraine*], *n.* A severe headache; (*pl.*) low spirits.

melancholia (mel-ăn-kō′li-ă), *n.* A mental disorder characterized by lowness of spirits.

melancholy (mel′ăn-kŏl-i) [Gr. *melancholia* (*melas*, black, *cholos*, bile)], *n.* A gloomy, dejected state of mind; depression, despondency; melancholia. *a.* Sad, gloomy, mournful; pensive. **melancho′lic**, *a.*

mêlée (mel′ā) [F., medley], *n.* A confused hand-to-hand fight, an affray.

meliorate (mē′li-ō-rāt) [L. *melior*, better], *v.t.* To make or grow better. **meliora′tion**, *n.*

mellifluous (mē-lif′lu-ŭs) [L. *mel*, honey, *fluere*, to flow], *a.* Flowing smoothly and sweetly. **mellifluence**, *n.*

mellow (mel′ō) [?], *a.* Fully ripe; soft and rich (of tones and colours); kindly; half tipsy. *v.t.* To ripen, mature, soften. *v.i.* To become ripe, etc.

melodeon (mē-lō′dē-ŏn), *n.* A wind-instrument with a row of reeds and a keyboard, an early type of American organ.

melodrama (mel′ō-dra-mă) [Gr. *melos*, song, DRAMA], *n.* A sensational play with startling situations; a novel of a similar kind. **melodramat′ic**, *a.*

melody (mel′ō-di), *n.* An agreeable succession of sounds, an air or tune; the chief part in harmonic music. **melodic** (mē-lod′ik), **melodious** (mē-lō′di-ŭs), *a.*

melon (mel′ŏn) [Gr. *mēlon*, apple, fruit], *n.* A gourd, esp. the musk-melon and the water-melon.

melt (melt) [A.-S. *meltan*], *v.i.* (*p.p.* **melted**, **molten**). To pass from solid to liquid by heat; to dissolve; (*fig.*) to disappear; to give way, to dissolve in tears. *v.t.* To make liquid by heat; to dissolve; to soften to tenderness; to dissipate.

member (mem′bėr) [L. *membrum*], *n.* A limb or organ of the body; a component part of a complex whole; one belonging to a society or body. **membership**, *n.*

membrane (mem′brān) [L. *membrāna*], *n.* A thin lining or covering to parts of an organism. **mem′branous**, *a.*

memento (mē-men′tō) [L., remember], *n.* (*pl.* -oes) A memorial, a reminder.

memoir (mem′war), *n.* (*usu. pl.*) An account of events, etc., in which the narrator took part; a biography.

memorable (mem′ŏr-ăbl) [L. *memorābilis*], *a.* Worthy to be remembered; notable, remarkable.

memorandum (mem-ō-răn′dŭm) [L.], *n.* (*pl.* -da) A note to help the memory;

a short informal letter; a summary or draft of an agreement, etc.

memorial (mê-môr'i-ȧl), *a.* Preservative of memory; commemorative; preserved in memory. *n.* That which preserves the memory of something; a monument; a written petition, remonstrance, etc.; a chronicle. **memorialist**, *n.* One who signs a memorial.

memorize (mem'ô-rīz), *v.t.* To commemorate; to learn by heart.

memory (mem'ô-ri) [O.F. *memoire*, L. *memoria*, from *memor*, mindful], *n.* The mental faculty that retains and recalls impressions, etc.; remembrance, recollection; the state of being remembered.

menace (men'ȧs) [L. *minax -ācis*, threatening], *n.* A threat. *v.t.* To threaten.

ménage (mê-nazh') [F.], *n.* A household; housekeeping, household management.

menagerie (mê-nǎj'ér-i) [F. *ménagerie*], *n.* A collection of wild animals; a place where wild animals are kept.

mend (mend), *v.t.* To repair, restore, make good; to correct, to amend. *v.i.* To grow better, to improve; to recover health.

mendacious (men-dā'shŭs) [L. *mendax -dācis*, lying], *a.* Given to lying, untruthful. **mendacity** (-dǎs'i-ti), *n.*

mendicant (men'di-kȧnt) [L. *mendīcans*, begging], *a.* Begging. *n.* A beggar; a member of a monastic order subsisting on alms. **men'dicancy**, *n.* **mendic'ity**, *n.*

menhir (men'hēr) [Bret., long stone], *n.* A prehistoric monument consisting of a tall upright stone.

menial (mê'ni-ȧl) [O.F. *meyné*, a household], *a.* Pertaining to servants; servile, mean. *n.* A domestic servant; one doing servile work.

menstruation (men-stroo-ā'shŭn) [L. *mensis*, month], *n.* The periodical discharge of blood from the uterus.

mensurable (men'shoor-ȧbl) [L. *mensūra*, measure], *a.* Measurable.

mensuration (men-sū-rā'shŭn), *n.* Act or practice of measuring.

-ment, *suf.* Forming nouns denoting result, state, action, etc., as in *agreement, impediment, ornament.*

mental (men'tȧl) [L. *mens mentis*, mind], *a.* Pertaining to the mind, intellectual; due to or done by the mind. **mental'-ity**, *n.*

menthol (men'thŏl) [L. *mentha*, mint], *n.* A waxy crystalline substance obtained from oil of peppermint.

mention (men'shŭn) [L. *mentio*], *n.* A concise notice, allusion to (or of); a naming. *v.t.* To refer or allude to; to indicate by naming. **mentionable**, *a.*

mentor (men'tôr) [Gr. *Mentōr*, counsellor to Telemachus], *n.* A wise counsellor.

menu (men'ū) [F.], *n.* A bill of fare.

mercantile (mêr'kȧn-til), *a.* Pertaining to buying and selling.

mercenary (mêr'sê-nȧr-i) [L. *mercēnārius*], *a.* Serving for money; done from motives of gain; venal. *n.* One who is hired, esp. a soldier in foreign service.

mercer (mêr'sêr) [F. *mercier*, L. *merx mercis*, merchandise], *n.* One who deals in silk, cotton, woollen, and linen goods. **mercery**, *n.*

merchandise (mêr'chȧn-diz), *n.* Articles of commerce; commodities for purchase.

merchant (mêr'chȧnt) [O.F. *marchand*, L. *mercans*, trading], *n.* One who trades on a large scale, esp. with foreign countries. *a.* Mercantile, commercial. **merchantman**, *n.* A merchant ship. **merchant service:** The mercantile marine.

Mercury (mêr'kū-ri) [L. *Mercurius*], *n.* The messenger of the gods (*Rom. Myth.*); the planet nearest the sun; quicksilver. **mercurial** (-kūr'i-ȧl), *a.* Flighty, volatile, fickle; pertaining to or caused by mercury.

mercy (mêr'si) [F. *merci*, L. *merces*, reward], *n.* Forbearance, compassion; an act of clemency or pity; forgiveness; something to be thankful for. **merciful**, *a.* **merciless**, *a.*

mere (1) (mēr) [A.-S.], *n.* A lake, a pool.

mere (2) [L. *merus*, pure], *a.* Such and no more; absolute, unqualified. **merely**, *adv.* Only, solely.

meretricious (mer-ê-trish'ŭs) [L. *meretrix*, harlot], *a.* Alluring by empty show; unreal, tawdry.

merge (mêrj) [L. *mergere*, to dip], *v.t.* To cause to be absorbed, to sink (in a larger estate, title, etc.) *v.i.* To be absorbed or swallowed up; to lose identity (in).

meridian (mê-rid'i-ȧn) [L. *merīdiēs*, midday], *a.* Pertaining to midday, to a geographical or astronomical meridian, or to the period of highest splendour or vigour. *n.* (*Astron.*) A great circle drawn through the poles and the zenith of any given place on the earth's surface; (*Geog.*) the line in which the plane of this circle intersects the earth's surface; the time when the sun crosses this; noon; (*fig.*) zenith point of highest splendour, etc. **meridional**, *a.* Pertaining to a meridian; culminating; pertaining to the south, esp. of Europe; running north and south (as a mountain range).

meringue (mê-rǎng') [F.], *n.* A cake or confection of white of eggs, sugar, etc.

merino (mê-rē'nŏ) [Sp.], *n.* A Spanish breed of sheep valuable for their fine wool.

merit (mer'it) [L. *meritus*, earned], *n.* Desert; excellence deserving reward; worth, worthiness; (*pl.*) the essential rights and wrongs of a case. *v.t.* To deserve; to have a just title to. **meritori'ous**, *a.* Praiseworthy.

merle (mêrl) [L. *merula*], *n.* The blackbird.

merlin (mêr'lin) [A.-F. *merilun*, O.F. *esmerillon*], *n.* The smallest of the European falcons.

mermaid (mêr'mād), *n.* A fabulous marine creature, its upper half like a woman and the lower like a fish.

merriment (me'ri-mênt) [MERRY], *n.* Gaiety with noise and laughter; mirth; hilarity.

merry (mer'i) [A.-S. *myrige*], *a.* Joyous, gay, mirthful; causing merriment; (*colloq.*) slightly tipsy. **merry-andrew**, *n.* A buffoon, esp. one assisting a quack. **merry-go-round**, *n.* A revolving frame with seats or wooden horses on which persons ride at fairs, etc. **merry-making**, *a.* Making merry, jovial. *n.* Merriment; a festivity. **merrythought**, *n.* The forked bone in the breast of a bird.

meseems (mē-sēmz'), *v.impers.* It seems to me.

mesh (mesh) [?], *n.* The space between the threads of a net; (*pl.*) network; (*fig.*) a trap, a snare; interlacing structure. *v.t.* To catch in a net, to ensnare. **meshy,** *a.*

mesmerism (mez'mĕr-izm) [F. A. *Mesmer* (1733–1815), Ger. physician], *n.* The art or power of inducing an abnormal state of the nervous system, in which the will of the patient is controlled; the hypnotic state so induced. **mesmer'ic,** *a.* **mes'-merist,** *n.* **mes'merize,** *v.t.*

meso- (Gr. *mesos*, middle], *comb. form.* Intermediate, in the middle.

mess (mes) [O.F. *mes*], *n.* A portion of food at table; semi-liquid food, esp. for animals; a number of persons who sit at table together (esp. of soldiers, sailors and airmen); a meal taken thus; a state of disorder; a muddle, a difficulty. *v.i.* To take meals in company, esp. of soldiers, etc.; (*fig.*) to muddle or potter (about). *v.t.* To muddle, to jumble; to soil.

message (mes'āj) [F., L. *missāticum*, from *mittere*, to send], *n.* A communication from one person to another. **messenger,** *n.* One who carries a message or goes an errand.

Messiah (mē-sī'á) [Heb. *māshiah*, from *māshah*, to annoint], *n.* The Anointed One, Christ; an expected saviour or deliverer. **messian'ic,** *a.*

messieurs (mes'yĕrz), *n.pl.* Sirs; gentlemen (pl. of Mr., usu. abbr. to Messrs.).

messuage (mes'wâj) [A.-F.], *n.* (*Law*) A dwelling-house with the adjacent buildings.

meta-, met-, meth- [Gr., on, with, among, after (implying change)], *comb. form.*

metabolism (mē-tab'ò-lizm) [Gr. *ballein*, to throw], *n.* The continuous chemical change going on in living matter. **metabol'ic.** *a.*

metal (met'ál) [L. *metallum*, Gr. *metallon*, mine, mineral], *n.* An elementary substance, usu. lustrous, malleable, and ductile, as the six known to the ancients, viz., gold, silver, copper, iron, lead, and tin; an alloy; broken stone for road-making; (*pl.*) rails of a railway. **metal'lic,** *a.* **metallif'erous,** *a.* **met'alline,** *a.*

metamorphic (met-à-môr'fik) [Gr. *morphē*, form], *a.* Causing or showing the results of metamorphosis; transforming or transformed.

metamorphose (met-à-môr'fōz) [Gr. *metamorphosis*, transformation, as prec.], *v.t.* To change into a different form; to transmute. **metamorpho'sis,** *n.*

metaphor (met'à-fòr) [Gr. *pherein*, to bear], *n.* A figure of speech by which a word is transferred from one object to another, so as to imply comparison. **metaphor'ic, -al,** *a.*

metaphysics (met-à-fiz'iks) [Gr. *meta ta phusika* (coming next) after (the study of) natural science], *n.* The philosophy of being and knowing; the theoretical principles forming the basis of any particular science; the philosophy of mind. **metaphysical,** *a.* Pertaining to metaphysics; transcendental, dealing with abstractions; abstruse, over-subtle. **metaphysician** (-zish'án), *n.*

metathesis (met-a-thē sis) [Gr. *tithenai*, to put], *n.* The transposition of sounds or letters in a word.

mete (mēt) [A.-S. *metan*], *v.t.* To measure; to allot; to appraise.

metempsychosis (mē-temp-si-kō'sis) [Gr. *en*, in, *psuchē*, soul], *n.* The passage of the soul after death from one animal body to another.

meteor (mē'tè-ór) [Gr. *meteōron* (*eōra*, to raise)], *n.* A luminous body appearing in the sky and then disappearing, a shooting-star. **meteor'ic,** *a.* **me'teorite,** *n.* A fallen meteor. **meteorolite,** *n.* A meteoric stone. **meteorology** (-ol-ò-ji), *n.* The science of the atmosphere and its phenomena.

meter (1) (mē'tèr), *n.* A measurer, esp. an instrument for registering the quantity of gas, water, electric energy, etc., supplied; metre.

-meter (2) [Gr. *metron*, measure], *suf.* A measuring instrument; as *barometer, thermometer.*

methinks (mē-thinks'), *v.impers.* (*past* -thought) It seems to me; I think.

method (meth'ód) [Gr. *hodos*, way], *n.* Mode of procedure; an orderly, systematic arrangement; orderliness, system. **method'ic, -al,** *a.*

Methodism (meth'ò-dizm), *n.* The doctrines, etc., of the Methodists. **Methodist,** *n.* A member of any of the religious bodies proceeding from the evangelical movement begun in the middle of the 18th cent. by the Wesleys and George Whitefield. **methodis'tic, -al,** *a.*

methodize (meth'ò-dīz), *v.t.* To reduce to order; to arrange systematically.

methyl (meth'il) [Gr. *methu*, wine, *hulē*, wood], *n.* The hypothetical radical of wood spirit and other organic compounds. **meth'ylate,** *v.t.* To mix or saturate with methyl alcohol. **methylated,** *a.*

meticulous (mē-tik'ū-lùs) [L. *metus*, fear], *a.* Over-scrupulous about trivial details, finical.

metonic (mē-ton'ik), *a.* Pertaining to Meton, Athenian astronomer; applied to the cycle of 19 Julian years at the end of which the new and full moons recur on the same dates.

metonymy (mē-ton'i-mi) [Gr. *onoma*, name], *n.* A figure in which one word is used for another (as "the bottle" for "drink").

metre (1) (mē'tèr) [Gr. *metron*, measure], *n.* The rhythmical arrangement of syllables in verse; verse; rhythm. **metric** (1). **metrical,** *a.* Pertaining to metre, or to measurement.

metre (2) (mē'tèr) [F. *mètre*, as prec.], *n.* The French standard measure of length, 39·37 in. **metric** (2), *a.*

metro- [Gr. *metron*, measure], *comb. form.* **metronome** (met'rò-nōm) [Gr. *nomos*, law], *n.* An instrument for marking time in music by means of a pendulum.

metropolis (mē-trop'ò-lis) [Gr. *mētēr -tros*, mother, *polis*, city], *n.* The capital of a country; the see of a metropolitan bishop. **metropol'itan,** *a.* Pertaining to a capital or an archbishopric. *n.* A bishop or archbishop having authority over other bishops.

-metry [Gr., as -METER], *suf.* Science of measuring; as *geometry, trigonometry.*

mettle (metl), *n.* Quality of temperament; spirit, courage. **mettled, mettlesome,** *a.* High-spirited, fiery.

mew (1) (mū) [A.-S.], *n.* A kind of sea-gull.

mew (2) (mū) [imit.], *v.* and *n.* The cry of the cat.

mew (3) (mū) [O.F. *mue*], *n.* A cage for hawks; a place of confinement; (*pl.*) stables for carriage-horses, etc. *v.t.* To shut up, to confine.

mezzanine (mez'a-nēn, -nīn) [It. *mezzanino*], *n.* A low story between two higher ones.

mezzo (med'zō) [It.], *a.* Half or medium.

mezzotint (med'zō-tint) [It. *tinto*, tint], *n.* Copper-plate engraving in which lights and half-lights are produced by scraping away the burr.

mho (mō) [OHM reversed], *n.* (*Elec.*) Unit of conductivity.

miasma (mī-ăz'mā) [Gr.], *n.* Poisonous or infectious exhalation, malaria. **mias'mal, miasmat'ic,** *a.*

mica (mī'kà) [L.], *n.* A silicate cleaving into thin, tough, and shining plates, formerly used instead of glass. **mica'ceous,** *a.*

Michaelmas (mik'ĕl-màs), *n.* The feast of St. Michael, 29 Sept.; autumn.

mickle (mikl) [A.-S. *micel*], *a.* (*now chiefly Sc.*). Much, great. *n.* A large amount.

micr-, micro- [Gr. *mikros*, small], *comb. form.* Noting smallness.

microbe (mī'krōb) [Gr. *bios*, life], *n.* A minute organism, esp. a bacterium causing disease or fermentation.

microcosm (mī'krō-kozm), *n.* The universe on a small scale; man as an epitome of the universe.

microfilm (mī'krō-film), *n.* A strip of cinematograph film on which successive pages of a document or book are photographed for purposes of record.

microscope (mī'krō-skōp), *n.* An optical instrument for magnifying details invisible to the naked eye. **microscop'ic,** *a.* Pertaining to the microscope; too small to be visible except through a microscope.

mid (mid) [A.-S.], *a.* (*superl.* midmost) Middle (*usu. in comb.*, as in **midday,** noon, **midstream, midwinter,** in the middle of the stream, of winter, etc.). *prep.* Amid.

midden (midn) [Scand.], *n.* A dunghill.

middle (midl) [A.-S. *middel*], *a.* Equally distant from the extremes; intermediate; (*Gram.*) between active and passive, reflexive. *n.* The point equally distant from the extremes; the midst, the centre. **Middle Ages,** *n.pl.* The period from the 5th to the 15th centuries. **middleman,** *n.* An agent, an intermediary, esp. between the producer and the consumer. **middling,** *a.* Of middle size, quality, or condition; mediocre; second-rate. *adv.* Moderately, tolerably.

midge (mij) [A.-S. *mycg*], *n.* A gnat or other minute fly. **midget,** *n.* A very small person.

midland (mid'lànd), *a.* Situated in the interior of a country. *n.* (*pl.*) The midland counties of England.

midnight (mid'nīt), *n.* The middle of the night, twelve o'clock; intense darkness. *a.* Pertaining to midnight; very dark.

midriff (mid'rif) [A.-S.], *n.* The diaphragm.

midship (mid'ship), *n.* The middle part of a ship. *a.* Situated in or belonging to this. **midshipman,** *n.* A naval officer ranking between a cadet and a sub-lieutenant. **midships** [AMIDSHIPS].

midst (midst) [A.-S. *middes,* gen. of [MID], *n.* The middle. *prep.* In the middle of.

midsummer (mid'sŭm-ĕr), *n.* The middle of summer, esp. near the summer solstice, about 21 June. **midsummer day:** 24 June.

midway (mid'wā), *a.* Situated in the middle of the way. *adv.* Half-way.

midwife (mid'wīf) [A.-S. *mid,* with WIFE], *n.* A woman who assists at childbirth. **midwifery** (-wif-ri), *n.*

mien (mēn) [F. *mine*], *n.* Air or manner; appearance, demeanour, bearing.

might (mīt) [A.-S. *miht*], *n.* Strength, force; power to enforce authority. **mighty,** *a.* Strong, powerful; very great.

mignonette (min-yŏ-net') [F.], *n.* An annual plant with fragrant greenish flowers.

migrate (mī-grāt') [L. *migrāre*, to wander], *v.i.* To remove from one country, etc. to another; to pass from one region to another according to the season (of birds, fishes, etc.). **mi'grant,** *a.* and *n.* **migra'-tion,** *n.* **mi'gratory,** *a.*

mikado (mi-ka'dō) [Jap.], *n.* The Emperor of Japan.

milch (milch) [A.-S. *meolc*], *a.* Giving milk.

mild (mīld) [A.-S. *milde*], *a.* Gentle in manners or disposition; tender, bland, pleasant; not harsh, sharp, or strong (of liquor, etc.); moderate, not extreme; operating gently (of medicines). **mildly,** *adv.* **mildness,** *n.*

mildew (mil'dū) [A.-S. *meledēaw*, honey-dew], *n.* A fungoid growth on plants, paper, food, etc., after exposure to damp. *v.* To taint with mildew. **mildewy,** *a.*

mile (mīl) [A.-S. *mīl,* L. *milia,* a thousand (paces)], *n.* A measure of length or distance, 1760 yards. **geographical** or **nautical mile:** One-sixtieth of a degree, 2026⅔ yards. **milestone,** *n.* A stone marking the miles on a road. **mileage,** *n.* A distance stated in miles.

milfoil (mil'foil) [L. *mille,* thousand, *folium,* leaf], *n.* The yarrow.

militant (mil'i-tànt), *a.* Combative, war-like. **militancy,** *n.*

military (mil'i-tàr-i) [L. *mīlitāris,* from *miles,* soldier], *a.* Pertaining to soldiers, arms, or warfare; soldierly, martial; engaged in war. *n.* (*collect.*) Soldiers generally. **mil'itarism,** *n.* Warlike policy; domination by the military, the spirit of aggression. **militarist,** *n.*

militate (mil'i-tāt) [L. *mīlitātus,* soldier], *v.i.* To stand opposed; to have weight or influence, to tell (against).

militia (mi-lish'à), *n.* A military body not permanently enrolled in time of peace.

milk (milk) [A.-S. *meolc*], *n.* The whitish fluid secreted by female mammals for the nourishment of their young, esp. that of the cow; the white juice of certain plants.

v.t. To draw milk from; (*fig.*) to get money out of (a person) in an underhand way. **milkmaid,** *n.* **milkman,** *n.* **milksop,** *n.* An effeminate person. **milksugar,** *n.* Lactose. **milk-tooth,** *n.* One of the temporary teeth in young mammals. **milky,** *a.* **Milky Way:** The galaxy.

mill (mil) [A.-S. *myln*, L. *mola*, a mill], *n.* A machine for grinding corn, etc., to a fine powder; a building with machinery for this purpose, or for any industrial purpose, a factory. *v.t.* To grind (as corn); to produce (flour) by grinding; to serrate the edge of (a coin); to full (cloth). **millboard,** *n.* Thick pasteboard used for book-covers. **mill-race,** *n.* The current of water for driving a mill-wheel. **mill-stone,** *n.* One of a pair of circular stones for grinding corn. **mill-wheel,** *n.* A large wheel moved by water, for driving the machinery in a mill. **milled,** *a.* Passed through a mill; having the edges serrated (of coin); fulled (of cloth). **miller,** *n.*

millennium (mi-len'i-ŭm) [L. *mille*, thousand, *annus*, year], *n.* A period of 1000 years, esp. that when Satan shall be bound and Christ reign on earth (Rev. xx. 1-5). **millenar'ian,** *a.* Consisting of 1000 years; pertaining to the millennium. *n.* One who believes in this. **mil'lenary,** *a.* and *n.* **millen'nial,** *a.* Pertaining to the millennium. *n.* A thousandth anniversary.

millesimal (mi-les'i-mál) [L. *millēsimus*, thousandth], *a.* Consisting of thousandths. *n.* A thousandth.

millet (mil'ét) [L. *milium*], *n.* An East Indian plant or its nutritive seeds.

milliard (mil'i-árd) [F., from L. *mille*, a thousand], *n.* A thousand millions.

milligramme (mil'i-grăm) [L. *mille*, thousand], *n.* The 1000th part of a gramme, ·0154 of an English grain. **millilitre,** *n.* The 1000th part of a litre, ·06103 cubic in. **millimetre,** *n.* The 1000th part of a metre, or ·03937 in.

milliner (mil'i-nér) [a dealer in *Milan* wares], *n.* One who makes and sells hats, etc., for women. **millinery,** *n.*

milling (mil'ing), *n.* Act or process of working a mill; the serrated edging of a coin.

million (mil'yón) [L. *mille*, thousand], *n.* A thousand thousand; (*fig.*) an indefinitely great number. **millionaire',** *n.* A man having a million pounds, or dollars; one immensely rich.

milt (milt) [A.-S. *milte*], *n.* The spleen; the spermatic organ of a male fish; the soft roe of fishes. **milter,** *n.*

mimic (mim'ik) [Gr. *mimos*], *a.* Imitative; imitating, counterfeit. *n.* One who mimics. *v.t.* To imitate, esp. in mockery; to resemble closely (of animals, plants, etc.). **mimicker,** *n.* **mimicry,** *n.*

mimosa (mi-, mi-mō'sá) [L.], *n.* A leguminous shrub.

minaret (min'ár-ét) [Arab. *manărat*], *n.* A lofty slender turret on a mosque.

minatory (min'á-tòr-i) [L. *minări*, to threaten], *a.* Threatening, menacing.

mince (mins) [O.F. *mincier*], *v.t.* To cut into very small pieces; to utter with affected delicacy; to palliate, gloss over.

v.i. To talk with affected elegance; to walk in a prim manner. *n.* Minced meat; mincemeat. **mincemeat,** *n.* Suet, raisins, currants, candied-peel, etc., chopped fine and mixed. **mincing,** *a.* Affectedly elegant.

mind (mind) [A.-S. *gemynd*], *n.* The intellectual powers in man; the understanding; intellectual capacity; memory; one's candid opinion; liking, way of feeling or thinking; purpose; inclination. *v.t.* To heed, regard; to apply oneself to; (*colloq.*) to object to; to look after. *v.i.* To take care, to be on the watch. **minded,** *a.* (*usu. in comb.*, as *evil-minded*). **mindful,** *a.* Attentive, heedful.

mine (1) (mīn) [A.-S. *mīn*], *poss. pron.* Belonging to me.

mine (2) [F. *miner*], *v.t.* To dig into or burrow in; to obtain or make by digging; to undermine, to sap; to set with mines. *v.i.* To dig a mine; (*fig.*) to burrow. *n.* An excavation for obtaining minerals; a rich deposit of minerals; an excavation under an enemy's works for blowing them up; an explosive machine for this purpose or for use against ships at sea; (*fig.*) a rich source of wealth, information, etc. **miner,** *n.*

mineral (min'ér-ál) [F. *mineral*, med. L. *minerālis*], *n.* An inorganic homogeneous body, with a definite chemical composition, found in the earth; (*pl.*) mineral waters. *a.* Pertaining to or consisting of minerals; impregnated with mineral matter. **mineral waters:** Waters impregnated with mineral matter.

mineralogy (min-ér-ăl'ò-ji), *n.* The science of minerals, their nature and properties. **mineralog'ical,** *a.* **mineral'ogist,** *n.*

mingle (ming'gél) [A.-S. *mengan*], *v.t.* To mix up together; to blend (with). *v.i.* To be mixed, blended, or united (with). **minglement,** *n.* **mingler,** *n.*

miniature (min'i-á-tūr) [med. L. *miniatura*, from *minium*, native red lead], *n.* A small-sized painting, esp. a portrait, orig. a small picture in an illuminated manuscript. *a.* Represented on a very small scale. **miniaturist,** *n.*

minim (min'im) [L. *minimus*, very small], *n.* (*Mus.*) A note of the value of two crotchets; an apothecaries' fluid-mixture, one drop, the 60th of a drachm. **minimize,** *v.t.* To depreciate; to reduce to the smallest possible amount. **minimum,** *n.* (*pl.* **-ma**) The smallest amount or degree possible or usual. *a.* Least possible.

minion (min'yón) [F. *mignon*], *n.* A favourite; a servile dependant; (*Print.*) a small size of type.

minister (min'is-tèr) [L. *minister*, from *minus*, less], *n.* One who acts under the authority of another, an instrument; a servant; a person entrusted with the direction of a State department, or representing his Government with another State; the pastor of a church, esp. Nonconformist. *v.i.* To render service or attendance; to contribute, be conducive (to); to serve as minister. **minister'ial,** *a.* **ministerialist,** *n.* **ministrant,** *a.* and *n.* **ministra'tion,** *n.* **ministry,** *n.* The act of ministering; administration; the ministers of State or of religion collectively.

miniver (min'i-vẽr) [A.-F. *menu*, small, *vair*, a kind of fur], *n*. A fur used for ceremonial robes; Siberian squirrel.

mink (mingk) [cp. L.G. *mink*, Swed. *menk*], *n*. A stoat-like animal esteemed for its fur.

minnow (min'ō) [A.-S. *myne*], *n*. A small fish common all over Europe.

minor (mī'nŏr) [L.], *a*. Less, smaller; petty, comparatively unimportant; (*Mus*.) less by a semitone. *n*. A person under age. **minor'ity**, *n*. The smaller number, esp. in an election, on a Bill, etc.; the party getting the fewest votes; the state or period of being under age.

minster (min'stẽr) [A.-S. *mynster*], *n*. The church of a monastery; a cathedral or other large and important church.

minstrel (min'strĕl) [O.F. *menestral*], *n*. One who in the Middle Ages lived by singing and reciting; a travelling gleeman or entertainer. **minstrelsy**, *n*.

mint (1) (mint) [A.-S. *mynet*, L. *monēta*, money], *n*. A place where money is coined; (*fig*.) a great supply or amount. *v.t*. To coin, to stamp (money); (*fig*.) to invent (a phrase, etc.). **mintage**, *n*. That which is coined.

mint (2) [A.-S. *minte*, Gr. *mintha*], *n*. An aromatic plant from which an essential oil is distilled.

minuend (min'ū-end) [L. *minuendus*], *n*. (*Arith*.) The quantity from which another is to be subtracted.

minuet (min-ū-et') [F. *menuet*], *n*. A stately dance in triple measure.

minus (mī'nŭs) [L.], *prep*. or *a*. Less by, with the deduction of; (*colloq*.) lacking. *n*. The sign of subtraction (−).

minute (1) (mī-nūt') [L. *minūtus*, diminished], *a*. Very small; particular, precise. **minute'ly**, *adv*. **minuteness**, *n*.

minute (2) (min'it) [F.], *n*. The 60th part of an hour or of a degree; an instant; an exact point of time; a memorandum; (*pl*.) official records of proceedings. *v.t*. To write minutes of; to take a note of. **minute-book**, *n*. A book in which the minutes of meetings are recorded.

minutia (mi-nū'shi-ă) [L.], *n*. (*usu. in pl*. -iæ) Small and precise or trivial particulars.

minx (mingks) [?], *n*. A pert girl, a jade.

miracle (mir'ăkl) [L. *mīrāculum*, as foll.], *n*. A wonder, a prodigy; a supernatural event or act; an extraordinary occurrence. **miracle play**: A mediæval dramatic representation, usu. with a sacred subject. **mirac'ulous**, *a*.

mirage (mi-razh') [F., from L. *mīrārī*, to wonder at, to gaze], *n*. An optical illusion due to atmospheric conditions by which images of distant objects are seen as if inverted.

mire (mir) [Icel. *myrr*], *n*. Swampy ground, bog; mud, dirt. **miry**, *a*.

mirror (mir'ŏr) [O.F. *mirour*], *n*. A polished surface for reflecting images; a looking-glass; (*fig*.) a pattern, a model. *v.t*. To reflect as in a mirror.

mirth (mẽrth) [A.-S. *myrgth*], *n*. Merriment, jollity, gaiety, hilarity. **mirthful**, *a*. Gay, jolly.

mis-, *pref*. Wrongly, badly, amiss, unfavourably. **misadventure**, *n*. Bad luck; an unlucky chance or accident. **misalli'ance**, *n*. An improper alliance, esp. by marriage.

misanthrope (mis'ăn-thrōp) [Gr. *misein*, to hate, *anthrōpos*, man], *n*. A hater of mankind; one who has a morbid dislike of his fellow-men. **misanthropic** (-throp'-ik), *a*. **misan'thropist**, *n*. **misan'thropy**, *n*.

misapply (mis-ă-plī'), *v.t*. To apply wrongly. **misapplica'tion**, *n*. **misapprehend'**, *v.t*. To misunderstand. **misapprehen'sion**, *n*. **misappro'priate**, *v.t*. To apply to a wrong use or purpose (esp. funds). **misbecome'**, *v.t*. To be improper or unseemly to, to ill become. **misbehave'**, *v.i*. To behave ill or improperly. **misbehaved**, *a*. Ill-mannered. **miscal'culate**, *v.t*. To calculate wrongly. **miscalcula'tion**, *n*. **miscar'ry**, *v.i*. To fail, to be unsuccessful; to be delivered of a child prematurely. **miscarriage**, *n*. **miscarriage of justice**: A mistake or wrong committed by a court of justice.

miscellaneous (mis-ĕ-lā'nĕ-ŭs) [L. *miscellāneus*, from *miscēre*, to mix], *a*. Consisting of several kinds; mixed, diversified; many-sided. **miscellanea**, *n.pl*. **miscellany** (mi-sel'ă-ni), *n*. A mixture, a medley, a number of various compositions in one volume.

mischance (mis-chans') [O.F. *meschance*], *n*. Misfortune, ill-luck.

mischief (mis'chif) [O.F. *meschief*], *n*. Injury, damage; vexatious conduct, a vexatious prank. **mischievous** (mis'-chi-vŭs), *a*.

misconceive' (mis-kŏn-sēv') *v.t*. To have a wrong idea of, to misapprehend. **misconcep'tion**. *n* **miscon'duct**, *n*. Improper conduct; mismanagement. *v.t*. (-kŏn-dŭkt') To mismanage. *v.i*. To misbehave. **misconstrue'**, *v.t*. To mistake the meaning of; to put a wrong interpretation upon. **misconstruc'tion**, *n*. **miscount'**, *v.t*. To count wrongly, estimate, or regard wrongly. *v.i*. To make a false count.

miscreant (mis'krē-ănt) [O.F. *mescreant* (*creant*, L. *crēdentem*, believing)], *n*. A vile wretch, a scoundrel.

misdeal, *v.t*. To deal wrongly (as cards). *v.i*. To make a mistake. *n*. A wrong or false deal. **misdeed'** [DEED], *n*. An evil deed, an crime. **misdemean'our**, *n*. Misbehaviour; an indictable offence of less gravity than a felony. **misdirect'**, *v.t*. To direct wrongly. **misdirec'tion**, *n*.

miser (mī'zẽr) [L., wretched], *n*. One who denies himself comforts for the sake of hoarding; an avaricious person. **miserly**, *a*.

miserable (miz'ẽr-ăbl) [L. *miserārī*, to pity], *a*. Very wretched, distressed; causing misery, distressing; despicable, worthless, very poor or mean.

misère (mi'zâr) [F.], *n*. (*Cards*) A declaration in solo whist by which a player undertakes to lose every trick.

misery (miz'ẽr-i) [L. *miser*, wretched], *n*. Great unhappiness or wretchedness of mind or body.

misfeasance (mis-fē'zăns) [O.F. *mesfaisance*, from *mesfaire* (*faire*, to do)], *n*. A trespass, a wrong, esp. negligent or improper performance of a lawful act.

misfire (mis-fīr'), *n.* Failure to go off or explode (of a gun, etc.). *v.i.* To fail to go off. **misfit'**, *n.* A bad fit; a garment that does not fit. *v.t. and i.* To fail to fit. **misfor'tune**, *n.* Ill luck, calamity; a mishap, a disaster. **misgiv'ing**, *n.* Doubt, distrust; a failure of confidence. **misgovern** (mis-gŭv'ĕrn), *v.t.* To govern ill; to administer unfaithfully. **misgovernment**, *n.* misgoverned, *a.* Badly governed, rude. **misguide'**, *v.t.* To guide wrongly; to lead astray. **misguid'ed**, *a.* Foolish. **mishap** (mis-hăp'), *n.* A mischance; ill-luck.

misinform (mis-in-fôrm'), *v.t.* To give erroneous information to. **misinformer**, *n.* **misinter'pret**, *v.t.* To interpret wrongly; to draw a wrong conclusion from. **misinterpreta'tion**, *n.* **misjudge'**, *v.t.* To judge erroneously; to form an erroneous opinion of. **mislay'**, *v.t.* (*past and p.p.* -laid) To lay in a wrong place or in a place that cannot be remembered; to lose.

mislead (mis-lēd'), *v.t.* (*past and p.p.* -led) To lead astray; to cause to go wrong, esp. in conduct; to delude. **misman'age**, *v.t. and i.* To manage ill. **mismanagement**, *n.*

misnomer (mis-nō'mĕr) [O.F. *mesnommer* (L. *nōmināre*, to name)], *n.* A mistaken or misapplied name; an incorrect term.

misogyny (mi-soj'i-ni) [Gr. *gunē*, woman], *n.* Hatred of women. **misogynist** (-soj'i-nist), *n.*

misplace (mis-plās'), *v.t.* To mislay; to devote to an undeserving object. **misplacement**, *n.* **misprint'**, *v.t.* To print incorrectly. *n.* A mistake in printing.

mispronounce (mis-prō-nouns'), *v.t.* To pronounce wrongly. **mispronun'ciation**, *n.* **misquote'**, *v.t.* To quote erroneously. **misquotation**, *n.* **misread** (mis-rēd'), *v.t.* (*past and p.p.* -read (-red) To read incorrectly; to misinterpret. **misrepresent'**, *v.t.* To represent falsely or incorrectly. **misrepresenta'tion**, *n.* **misrule'**, *n.* Bad government; disorder, confusion, riot.

miss (1) (mis), *n.* (*pl.* misses) A title of address for an unmarried woman; a girl.

miss (2) [A.-S. *missan*], *v.t.* To fail to reach, hit, meet, obtain, etc.; to let slip, overlook, to fail to understand; to dispense with, to feel the want of. *v.i.* To fail to hit the mark; to be unsuccessful. *n.* A failure to hit, reach, obtain, etc. **missing**, *a.* Lost, wanting; absent.

missal (mis'ăl), *n.* The book containing the service of the Mass.

misshape (mis-shāp'), *v.t.* (*p.p.* misshapen) To shape ill; to deform. *n.* Deformity.

missile (mis'il, -īl) [L. *missilis*, from *mittere*, to send], *a.* That may be thrown or discharged. *n.* A weapon thrown from the hand or an engine.

mission (mish'ŏn) [L. *missio*, from *mittere*, to send], *n.* A sending or being sent, the commission or office of a messenger, agent, etc.; a vocation; a body of persons sent on a diplomatic errand; a body of missionaries, their field of work or their station; portion of a parish; a series of

services for rousing spiritual interest. **missionary**, *a.* Pertaining to religious missions, or to the propagation of religion or other moral or social influence. *n.* One sent to carry on such work.

missive (mis-iv), *a.* Sent or for sending. *n.* A message, letter.

misspell (mis-spel'), *v.t.* To spell incorrectly. **misspend'**, *v.t.* (*past and p.p.* -spent) To spend ill; to waste. **misstate'**, *v.t.* To state wrongly. **misstatement**, *n.*

mist (mist) [A.-S.], *n.* Visible watery vapour near the ground; a watery condensation; (*fig.*) anything which dims, obscures, or darkens. **misty**, *a.* **mistiness**, *n.*

mistake (mis-tāk'), *v.t.* (*past* -took, *p.p.* -taken) To understand wrongly; to take in a wrong sense; to take one person or thing for another. *v.i.* To be in error. *n.* An error of judgment or opinion; a misunderstanding, a blunder. **mistakable**, *a.* **mistakenly**, *adv.*

Mister (mis'tĕr) [var. of master], *n.* The common prefix to men's names and to certain official titles (abbrev., MR.).

mistime (mis-tim'), *v.t.* To say or do inappropriately to the time or occasion.

mistle-thrush (misl-thrŭsh) [A.-S. *mistel*], *n.* The largest of the European thrushes.

mistletoe (misl'tō) [A.-S. *misteltān*], *n.* A plant parasitic on the apple and other trees, bearing white glutinous berries.

mistress (mis'trĕs) [M.E. and O.F. *maistresse*], *n.* A woman who has authority or control; the female head of a family, school, etc.; a female teacher; a sweetheart; a concubine; a title of address to a married woman (abbrev., MRS. (mis'is)).

mistrust' *v.t.* To regard with doubt or suspicion. *n.* Distrust, suspicion. **mistrustful**, *a.*

misunderstand (mis-ŭn-dĕr-stănd'), *v.t.* (*past and p.p.* -stood) To misapprehend. to mistake the meaning or sense of, **misunderstanding**, *n.* **misuse** (-ūz'), *v.t.* To use improperly; to apply to a wrong purpose; to ill-treat. *n.* (-ūs) Improper use; abuse.

mite (mīt) [A.-S], *n.* A very small coin, orig. Flemish; (*fig.*) a small contribution; a minute amount, a tiny child; a minute insect, esp. one infesting cheese.

mitigate (mi'ti-gāt) [L. *mitigātus*, from *mitis*, gentle], *v.t.* To make less harsh; to alleviate (pain, etc.); to soften, diminish, moderate. **mitiga'tion**, *n.*

mitre (mi'tĕr) [Gr. *mitra*], *n.* A tall ornamental cap shaped like a cleft cone worn by bishops; (*fig.*) the dignity of a bishop; (*Carp.*) a joint at an angle of 90°, as the corner of a picture-frame.

mitten (mit'ĕn) [O.F. *mitaine*], *n.* A glove with a thumb but no fingers.

mittimus (mit'i-mŭs) [L., we send], *n.* A warrant of commitment to prison.

mix (miks) [L. *mixtus*, mixed], *v.t.* To blend into one mass; to mingle (substances, quantities, groups) so that the particles of each are indiscriminately associated; to compound thus. *v.i.* To become united; to be mingled (with or together); to be associated (with). **mixable**, *a.* **mixed**, *a.* Consisting of various kinds; promiscuous, not select (of company).

mixture (miks'chŭr), *n.* Mixing; anything that is mixed.

mizen (mizn) [F. *misaine*, L. *medius*, middle], *n.* A fore-and-aft sail set on the mizen-mast. **mizen-mast,** *n.* The aftermost mast of a three-masted ship.

mnemonic (nĕ-mon'ik) [Gr. *mnēmonikos*, from *mnēmōn*, mindful], *a.* Pertaining to or aiding the memory. *n.pl.* The art of or a system for aiding memory.

moan (mōn) [A.-S. *mǣnan*], *n.* A low prolonged sound expressing pain or sorrow; (*fig.*) a complaint. *v.i.* To utter a moan or moans. *v.t.* To deplore; to mourn; to utter moaningly.

moat (mōt) [O.F. *mote*, a dike], *n.* A ditch for water round a castle, etc.

mob (mob) [contr. from L. *mōbile* (*vulgus*), the fickle (crowd)], *n.* A disorderly crowd, a rabble; the lower orders. *v.t.* To crowd roughly round and annoy.

mob-cap (mob-kăp) [cp. Dut. *mopmuts*, woman's night-cap], *n.* An indoor cap for women.

mobile (mō'bil) [L. *mōbilis*, from *movēre*, to move], *a.* Movable, free to move; easily changing (as expression). **mobil'ity,** *n.* **mo'bilize,** *v.i.* To put (armed forces) in a state of readiness for active service. **mobiliza'tion,** *n.*

moccasin (mok'ă-sin) [Powhatan], *n.* A shoe of soft leather made in one piece.

mock (mok) [O.F. *mocquer*], *v.t.* To deride, laugh at; to mimic in derision; to defy contemptuously. *v.i.* To express ridicule, derision, etc. *a.* Sham, counterfeit; imitating reality. **mocker,** *n.* **mockery,** *n.* **mock-up,** *n.* A full-scale replica or model.

modal (mō'dǎl), *a.* Pertaining to mode as opp. to substance; (*Gram.*) pertaining to mood or denoting manner.

mode (mōd) [L. *modus*], *n.* Manner, method, way of doing, existing, etc.; prevailing custom; (*Mus.*) one of the systems dividing the octave, the form of the scale.

model (modl) [It. *modello*], *n.* A representation of something to be made on a larger scale or in more durable material; one employed to pose to an artist or to wear clothes to display their effect; a standard, an example regarded as a canon of artistic execution. *a.* Serving as a model, worthy of imitation, perfect. *v.t.* To fashion in clay, etc.; to form after a model. *v.i.* To make models. **modeller,** *n.*

moderate (mod'ĕr-ǎt) [L. *moderātus*], *a.* Temperate, reasonable; not extreme; medium. *n.* One of moderate views. *v.t.* To reduce to a calmer or less violent condition; to restrain from excess; to temper, mitigate. *v.i.* To become less violent; to quiet or settle down; to preside as a moderator. **modera'tion,** *n.* Act of moderating; quality or state of being moderate; temperance; self-restraint. **mod'erator,** *n.* One who presides at a meeting, esp. at a court of the Presbyterian Church.

modern (mod'ĕrn) [F. *moderne*], *a.* Per-

taining to the present or recent time; not ancient or old-fashioned. *n.* A person of modern times. **modernism,** *n.* A modern mode of expression, etc.; a modern term or idiom; a tendency towards the acceptance of the results of modern criticism and research in religious matters. **modernist,** *n.* **moder'nity,** *n.* **mod'ernize,** *v.t.* and *i.*

modest (mod'ĕst) [L. *modestus*], *a.* Humble, unassuming, diffident in regard to one's merits, etc.; bashful, retiring; restrained by a sense of propriety; chaste; moderate, not extreme. **modestly,** *adv.* **modesty,** *n.*

modicum (mod'i-kum) [L., moderate], *n.* A little; a small amount.

modify (mod'i-fī), *v.t.* To alter, to change to a moderate extent; (*Gram.*) to qualify the sense of, to alter (a vowel). **modifica'tion,** *n.*

modish (mō'dish), *a.* Fashionable. **modiste** (mô-dēst') [F.], *n.* A milliner or dressmaker.

modulate (mod'ū-lāt) [L. *modulātus*, measured], *v.t.* To adjust, regulate; to inflect the sound or tone of. **modula'tion,** *n.* Inflection of the voice, etc.

mohair (mō'hâr) [Arab. *mukhayyar*], *n.* The hair of the Angora goat; a fabric made from it; an imitation of this.

Mohammedan (mô-hăm'ĕ-dǎn) [Arab. *Muhammad*], *a.* Pertaining to Mohammed or Mohammedanism. *n.* A follower of Mohammed or Mohammedanism. **Mohammedanism,** *n.* The religion founded by Mohammed (*c.* 570–632).

moidore (moi'dôr) [Port.], *n.* An obsolete Portuguese gold coin worth about £1 7s.

moiety (moi'ĕ-ti) [O.F. *moitié*], *n.* A half; a part or share.

moil (moil) [O.F. *moiller*, to paddle through mud], *v.i.* To toil, to drudge.

moire (mwar) [F.], *n.* Watered silk.

moist (moist) [O.F. *moiste*], *a.* Moderately wet, damp; rainy. **moisten** (moisn), *v.t.* and *i.* **moisture,** *n.*

molar (mō'lâr) [L. *mola*, mill], *a.* Having power to grind. *n.* One of the back teeth.

molasses (mô-lăs'ĕz) [Port.], *n.* The viscid, dark-brown syrup drained from sugar during refining; treacle.

mole (1) (mōl) [A.-S. *māl*], *n.* A permanent raised spot on the human skin.

mole (2) [L. *mōles*, mass], *n.* A pile of masonry, such as a break-water before a port.

mole (3) [Teut.], *n.* A small soft-furred burrowing mammal with very imperfect vision. **mole-hill,** *n.* A hillock thrown up by a mole burrowing underground.

molecule (mol'ĕ-, mō'lĕ-kūl) [dim. from L. *mōles*, mass], *n.* One of the structural units of which matter is built up.

molest (mô-lest') [L. *molestus*, troublesome], *v.t.* To trouble, disturb, to interfere with. **molesta'tion,** *n.*

mollify (mol'i-fī) [L. *mollis*, soft], *v.t.* To soften, assuage, to appease. **mollifica'tion,** *n.* **mollifier,** *n.*

mollusc (mol'ŭsk) [L. *molluscus*, softish], *n.* **Mollusca** (mô-lŭs'kǎ), *n.pl.* (*Zool.*) A division of invertebrates with a soft body, as snails, mussels, cuttlefishes, etc.

molten (mōl'tén) [*p.p.* of **melt**], *a.* Made of melted metal.

moment (mō'mént) [L., for *movimentum* (*movēre*, to move)], *n.* A minute portion of time, importance, consequence; (*Mech.*) the measure of a force by its power to cause rotation. **momentary**, *a.* Lasting only for a moment; transient, ephemeral. **momentarily**, *adv.* **momently**, *adv.* From moment to moment; at any moment. **mo₥en'tous**, *a.* Weighty, important.

momentum (mō-men'tŭm), *n.* (pl. **-ta**) Impetus, power of overcoming resistance to motion.

monad (mon'ăd) [Gr. *monas*, from *monos*, sole], *n.* A simple, indivisible unit; a univalent atom, radical, or element; an elementary, single-celled organism.

monarch (mon'ärk), *n.* An hereditary sovereign, as emperor, empress, king, or queen; the chief of its class; a large red and black butterfly. **monarch'ic, -al, monarch'al**, *a.* **mon'archism**, *n.* **mon'archist**, *n.* **mon'archy**, *n.*

monastery (mon'á-stér-i) [Gr. *monastērion*, from *monazein*, to live alone], *n.* A residence for monks living under vows of seclusion. **monas'tic**, *a.* Pertaining to a monastery or monks. **monas'tical**, *a.*

Monday (mŭn'di) [A.-S. *Mōnandæg*, moon day], *n.* The second day of the week.

monetary (mŭn'é-tár-i), *a.* Pertaining to money or the coinage. **monetize**, *v.t.* To give a standard value to (a metal) as currency.

money (mŭn'i) [L. *monēta*, mint, money], *n.* Coin; the medium of exchange; notes, bills, or other documents representing coin; wealth convertible into coin; (*with pl.* **-eys**) coins of a particular country or denomination; (*pl.*) sums of money. **money of account**: a denomination not actually coined, e.g. a guinea. **money-market**, *n.* The field of operation of dealers in stocks, etc., the financial world. **moneyed**, *a.* Rich.

monger (mŭng'gér) [A.-S. *mangere*], *n.* A trader, dealer (in comb., as *ironmonger*, *scandalmonger*).

Mongol (mong'gŏl) [native name], *n.* An Asiatic race inhabiting Mongolia. *a.* Of or pertaining to the Mongols; (*Path.*) denoting a type of idiot resembling the Mongolians in physiognomy.

mongrel (mŭng'grĕl) [?], *a.* Of mixed breed; of mixed nature or character. *n.* Anything, esp. a dog, of mixed breed.

monition (mō-nish'ŭn) [L. *monēre*, to warn], *n.* A warning; an intimation; a summons or citation; a formal letter warning a clergyman to abstain from certain practices. **mon'itive**, *a.* **monitor**, *n.* One who admonishes; a senior pupil appointed to keep order in a school; a large tropical lizard; (**Radio**) official who listens in to foreign broadcasts. **monitor'ial**, *a.*

monk (mŭngk) [A.-S. *munec*, Gr. *monachos*, from *monos*, alone], *n.* A member of a religious community of men, living apart under vows of poverty, chastity, and obedience.

monkey (mŭng'ki) [Teut.], *n.* A long-tailed quadrumanous mammal; (*colloq*). a rogue, an imp, a mimic. **monkey-jacket**, *n.* A pea-jacket worn by sailors, etc.

mono-, mon- [Gr. *monos*], *comb form.* Alone, single; as in *monograph*, *monosyllable*.

mon'ochrome, *n.* A painting in tints of one colour only. *a.* Executed in one colour. **monocle** (mon'ŏkl) [L. *oculus*, eye], *n.* An eye-glass for one eye.

monody (mon'ō-di), *n.* (*Gr. Tragedy*) An ode, usu. of a mournful character, for a single actor; a mournful or plaintive song or poem.

monogamy (mō-nog'á-mi), *n.* Marriage to one wife or husband only; (*Zool.*) the habit of pairing with a single mate. **monog'amous**, *a.* **monog'amist**, *n.*

mon'ogram, *n.* A character composed of two or more letters interwoven. **mon'ograph**, *n.* A treatise on a single thing or class of things.

monolith (mon'ō-lith), *n.* A monument or other structure formed of a single stone. **monolith'ic**, *a.* **monologue** (mon'ō-log), *n.* A dramatic scene in which a person speaks by himself; a piece for one actor.

monomania (mon-ō-mā'ni-á), *n.* Mental derangement on one subject only. **monomaniac**, *n.* and *a.*

monopoly (mō-nop'ō-li) [Gr. *pōlein*, to sell], *n.* An exclusive trading right in a certain commodity or class of business, usu. conferred by Government; a company, etc., enjoying this; the subject of such a right; exclusive possession, control, or enjoyment (of). **monop'olist**, *n.* **monop'olize**, *v.t.* To obtain or possess a monopoly of; to engross the whole of (attention, conversation, etc.). **monosyl'lable**, *n.* A word of one syllable. **monosyllab'ic**, *a.*

monotheism (mon'-ō-thē-izm) [Gr. *theos*, God], *n.* The doctrine that there is only one God. **monotheist**, *n.*

monotone (mon'ō-tōn), *n.* Continuance of in the same tone; a succession of sounds of the same pitch; intoning of words on a single note; monotony. **monot'onous**, *a.* Wearisome through sameness, tedious. **monot'ony**, *n.* Tediousness, sameness.

Monsieur (mo-syér') [F.], *n.* The French title of address, Mr. or Sir.

monsoon (mon-soon') [Arab. *mausim*, time, season], *n.* A wind in the Indian Ocean, blowing from the south-west from April to October, and from the north-east the rest of the year.

monster (mon'stér) [L. *monstrum*, a portent, from *monēre*, to warn], *n.* Something out of the ordinary course of nature; a deformed creature; a person, animal, or thing of great size.

monstrance (mon'stráns) [L. *monstrāre*, to show], *n.* (*R.-C. Ch.*) A transparent vessel in which the Host is exposed for adoration.

monstrous (mon'strŭs), *a.* Unnatural in form; out of the course of nature; enormous; shocking, atrocious; incredible. **monstros'ity**, *n.*

montbretia (mont-brē'shi-à) [de *Montbret* (1780–1801), Fr. botanist], *n.* An iridaceous bulbous-rooted flowering plant.

montage (mon'tij), *n.* (*Cinema*) Cutting and assembling of shots taken when making a film picture.

Montessori method (mon-tes-ôr'i) [Dr. Maria *Montessori* (1870–)], *n.* A system of teaching the very young.

month (mŭnth) [A.-S. *mōnath*, cogn. with MOON], *n.* One of the twelve parts into which the year is divided. **monthly**, *a.* Done in or continuing for a month; happening or payable once a month. *adv.* Once a month. *n.* A periodical published every month.

monument (mon'ū-mėnt) [L. from *monēre*, to remind], *n.* Anything by which the memory of persons or things is preserved, esp. a building or permanent structure; a memorial, a record; a distinctive mark. **monumen'tal**, *a.* **monumentally**, *adv.*

-mony [L. *-monium, -monia*], *suf.* Forming nouns, as *ceremony, matrimony, parsimony*.

mood (1) (mood), *n.* A verb-form expressing the manner in which the act, event, etc., is conceived, whether as actual, contingent, possible, desirable, etc.; (*Log.*) the form of a syllogism with regard to the quantity and quality of the propositions; (*Mus.*) mode.

mood (2) [A.-S. *mōd*], *n.* Temper of mind, disposition, humour. **moody**, *a.* Indulging in moods or humours; peevish, sullen, out of temper. **moodiness**, *n.*

moon (moon) [A.-S. *mōna*], *n.* The earth's satellite revolving round it monthly, the satellite of any planet; a month; anything crescent-shaped. *v.i.* To wander (about) or stare in a listless manner. **moonlight**, *n.* and *a.* **moon-lighter** *n.* A member of gangs of ruffians who committed violent nocturnal outrages, esp. in Ireland. **moonshine**, *n.* Moonlight; (*fig.*) unreality, nonsense. **moonstone**, *n.* A variety of feldspar with whitish or opalescent reflections. **moonstruck, -stricken**, *a.* Affected by the moon; deranged, lunatic; over-sentimental.

moor (1) (moor) [Teut.], *v.t.* To secure (a ship, boat, etc.) with chains, or anchor, etc. *v.i.* To anchor; to lie at anchor or secured by cables, etc. **moorage**, *n.* A place for mooring. **moorings**, *n.* The place where a ship is moored; anchors, chains, etc.

moor (2) [A.-S. *mōr*], *n.* A tract of wild open land. **moor-cock, -fowl, -hen**, *n.* The red grouse. **moorland**, *n.*

Moor (3) [L. and Gr. *Maurus*], *n.* A member of a Berber and Arab race inhabiting Morocco and the adjoining parts of N. W. Africa. **Moorish**, *a.*

moose (moos) [Algonkin *musu*], *n.* The N. American elk.

moot (moot) [A.-S. *gemōt*, an assembly], *v.t.* To raise for discussion. *v.i.* To argue or plead on a supposed case. *n.* Anciently, an assembly of freemen in a township, etc.; a law students' debate on a supposed case. *a.* Open to argument.

mop (mop) [L. *mappa*, napkin], *n.* A bundle of rags, etc., fastened to a handle, and used for cleaning floors, etc.; a thick mass (as of hair). *v.t.* To clean or dry with a mop.

mope (mōp) [?], *v.i.* To be dull or dispirited. *n.* One who mopes; (*pl.*) ennui, the blues.

moraine (mô-rān') [F.], *n.* The debris of rocks brought down by glaciers.

moral (1) (mor'ál) [L. *mōrālis*, from *mōs*, custom], *a.* Pertaining to character and conduct as regards the distinction between right and wrong; good, virtuous, distinguishing between right and wrong; based on morality; concerned with conduct or morality; conveying a moral; probable. *n.* The moral lesson taught by a story, incident, etc.; (*pl.*) moral habits or conduct; ethics, moral science. **moralist**, *n.* **moral'ity**, *n.* The doctrine, principles, or practice of moral duties; moral science, morals, moral conduct; an early kind of drama in which the characters represented virtues, vices, etc. **mor'alize**, *v.t.* To interpret or apply in a moral sense; to provide with moral lessons. *v.i.* To make moral reflections (on). **morally**, *adv.* According to morality; practically, virtually.

moral (2), **morale** (mô-ral'), *n.* Mental or moral condition; courage and endurance in supporting fatigue and danger, esp. of troops in war.

morass (mô-răs') [Dut. *moeras*, O.F. *maresche*, marsh], *n.* A swamp, a bog.

moratorium (mor-à-tôr'i-ùm) [L., from *morārī*, to delay], *n.* Authorized temporary suspension of the payment of debts; an act authorizing this.

morbid (môr'bid) [L. *morbus*, disease], *a.* Sickly, diseased; pathological. **morbid'ity**, *n.* **morbidness**, *n.*

mordant (môr'dánt) [L. *mordēre*, to bite], *a.* Biting, caustic; causing pain or smarting; serving to fix colours, etc. *n.* A substance for fixing colouring-matter in dyeing; an adhesive substance used in applying gold-leaf; a corrosive used by etchers. **mordacious** (-dā'shŭs), *a.* Biting, acrid; sarcastic. **mordacity** (-dăs'i-ti), **mordancy** (môr'dán-si), *n.*

more (môr) [A.-S. *māra*], *a.* (*superl.* **most**) Greater in quantity, extent, degree, etc.; additional, extra. *adv.* In or to a greater degree, etc. (used to form compar. of many adjectives and adverbs); further, besides, again.

moreover (môr-ō'vér), *adv.* Besides, in addition, further.

moresque (môr-esk'), *a.* Moorish in style.

morganatic (môr-gà-năt'ik) [M.H.G. *morgengâbe*, morning-gift], *a.* Applied to a marriage in which the wife does not acquire the husband's rank and neither she nor children of the marriage inherit his title or possessions.

moribund (mor'i-bŭnd) [L. *moribundus*, from *morī*, to die], *a.* In a dying state.

Mormon (môr'môn) [mythic author of the *Book of Mormon*, containing alleged divine revelations], *n.* A member of an American religious body (the "Latter-day Saints", founded 1830) which formerly practised polygamy; a polygamist. Mormonism, *n*.

morn (môrn) [A.-S. *morgen*], *n*. Morning.

morning (môr'nĭng) [M.E. *morwening*, dawning], *n*. The first part of the day, from 12 at night to 12 noon, or from dawn to midday; (*fig.*) the early part of a period. *a*. Pertaining to the morning.

morocco (mŏ-rok'ō), *n*. A fancy leather tanned in a particular way and dyed (formerly made in Morocco).

morose (mŏ-rōs') [L. *mŏrōsus*], *a*. Peevish, sullen; given to brooding.

morphia, -phine (môr'fĭ-à, -fĭn) [G. *morphin*, from *Morpheus*, the god of dreams], *n*. The alkaloid constituting the narcotic principle of opium.

morris (mor'ĭs), *n*. A rustic dance.

morrow (mor'ō) [M.E. *morwen*], *n*. The day next after the present; (*fig.*) the succeeding period. to-morrow, the morrow; on the morrow.

morse (1) (môrs) [Lapp. *morsa*], *n*. The walrus.

Morse (2) (môrs) [Am. inventor (1791–1872)], *n*. The Morse code. Morse alphabet or code: A system of sending messages by telegraph in combinations of dots and dashes.

morsel (môr'sĕl) [O.F., from L. *morsus*, bite], *n*. A mouthful; a small piece of food; a small quantity.

mortal (môr'tàl) [L. *mortālis*, from *mors mortis*, death], *a*. Causing death, fatal; inveterate; involving spiritual death; pertaining to death; liable to death, hence, human. *n*. A human being. mortal'ity, *n*. The quality of being mortal; human nature; human beings; loss of life, esp. on a large scale; the death-rate.

mortar (môr'tàr) [A.-S. *mortere*, L. *mortārium*], *n*. A vessel in which substances are pounded with a pestle; a short cannon for throwing shells at a high angle; a cement made of lime, sand, and water, for use in building. *v.t.* To join, plaster, or close up with mortar. mortarboard, *n*. A square board for holding mortar; a square-topped college cap.

mortgage (môr'găj) [O.F. (L. *mors mortis*, death, GAGE)], *n*. The grant of an estate, etc., as security for the payment of money. *v.t.* To grant or make over property on mortgage; (*fig.*) to pledge, esp. oneself. mortgagee', *n*. One to whom property is mortgaged. mortgagor', *n*. One who mortgages property.

mortify (môr'ti-fī) [L. *mortificāre*], *v.t.* To subdue (the passions, etc.) by self-discipline; to humiliate, wound. *v.i.* To lose vitality, to decay, to gangrene. mortifica'tion, *n*. mortifyingly, *adv*.

mortise (môr'tĭs) [F. *mortaise*], *n*. A hole cut in timber, etc., to receive a tenon.

mortmain (môrt'mān) [med. L. *mortua manus*, dead hand], *n*. Possession of lands or tenements by an ecclesiastical or other corporation who cannot alienate.

mortuary (môr'tū-àr-ĭ) [L. *mortuārius*], *a*. Pertaining to death or burial. *n*. A building for the temporary reception of the dead.

mosaic (1) (mŏ-zā'ĭk) [Gr. *mousaikos*, pertaining to the Muses], *a*. Applied to inlaid work of small pieces of differently-coloured marble, glass, etc.; tesselated, inlaid. *n*. A pattern, picture, etc., produced in this style.

Mosaic (2) [*Moses*], *a*. Pertaining to Moses or to the law given through him.

moselle (mŏ-zel') [name of river], *n*. A white wine made in the Moselle district.

Moslem (moz'lĕm) [Arab. *muslim*], *n*. A Mohammedan. *a*. Pertaining to the Mohammedans.

mosque (mosk) [Arab. *masgid*], *n*. A Mohammedan place of worship.

mosquito (mos-kē'tō) [Sp.], *n*. An insect with a proboscis for piercing the skin and sucking blood.

moss (mos) [A.-S. *mos*, bog], *n*. A bog, wet, spongy land; a low, tufted, herbaceous plant usually growing on damp soil or on stones, trees, etc. moss-rose, *n*. A rose with moss-like calyx. moss-trooper, *n*. One of the marauders who formerly infested the borders of England and Scotland. mossy, *a*.

most (mōst) [A.-S. *mǣst*], *a*. Greatest in amount, extent, quality, degree, etc. *adv*. In the greatest or highest degree (forming the superl. of many adjectives and adverbs). *n*. The greatest number, quantity, etc.; the best, the worst, etc.; the majority. mostly, *adv*.

-most [A.-S. -*mest*], *suf*. Forming superlatives denoting position, order, etc., as in *hindmost*, *inmost*, *utmost*.

mote (mōt) [A.-S. *mot*], *n*. A particle of dust, a speck; anything proverbially small.

motel (mō-tel'), *n*. A roadside hotel or furnished cabins where motorists may put up for the night.

moth (moth) [A.-S. *moththe*], *n*. One of a group of nocturnal or crepuscular winged insects allied to the butterflies, but not having knotted antennæ. mothy, *a*. Full of moths; moth-eaten.

mother (mŭth'ér) [A.-S. *mōder*, cogn. with L. *māter*, Gr. *mētēr*], *n*. A female parent; the source or origin of anything; a motherly woman; the head of a religious community; a thick slimy substance forming in vinegar during fermentation. *v.t.* To act as mother towards. *a*. Holding the place of a mother; giving origin; native, inborn, vernacular. mother country: One's native country; a country in relation to its colonies. mother-in-law, *n*. (*pl.* mothers-in-law), the mother of one's wife or husband. mother-of-pearl, *n*. The iridescent pearly substance forming the internal layer of many shells. mother tongue: One's native language. mother wit: Natural sagacity, common sense.

motion (mō'shŭn) [L. *mōtiōnem*], *n*. Act, process, or state of moving; passage from place to place; a proposal, esp. in a deliberative assembly; an application to a court for a rule or order; (*fig.*) impulse, instigation. *v.t.* To direct by a gesture. *v.i.* To make significant gestures.

motive (mō-tiv) [O.F. *motif*], *a*. Causing or tending to cause motion; pertaining to movement. *n*. That which incites to action, or determines the will; cause, incentive; (*Art*) the predominant idea,

etc. *v.t.* (*usu. in p.p.*) To furnish with
an adequate motive (as a story, play,
etc.). **motiveless,** *a.* **motiv'ity,** *n.*

motley (mot'li) [?], *a.* Variegated; dressed
in parti-coloured clothes; heterogeneous.
n. The parti-coloured dress of jesters.

motor (mō'tòr) [L. *movēre*, to move], *n.*
That which imparts motive power, esp.
a machine; a motor-car; a muscle for
moving some part; a nerve exciting
muscular action. *a.* Causing or imparting motion. *v.i.* To drive or ride in a
motor-car.

mottle (motl), *v.t.* To variegate with spots
or different colours.

motto (mot'ō) [It., a word], *n.* (*pl. -oes*) A
short pithy sentence expressing a sentiment; a maxim adopted as a rule of
conduct; (*Her.*) a word or sentence used
with a crest or coat of arms.

mouch (mooch) [?], *v.i.* To play truant;
to skulk, sneak about.

mould (1) (mōld) [A.-S. *molde*], *n.* Fine
soft earth, the ground; (*fig.*) the grave.

mould (2) [O. North. F. *molde*, L. *modulus*],
n. A hollow shape into which molten
metal or other substance is poured in a
fluid state to cool into a permanent shape;
a templet for shaping cornices, etc., and
analogous appliances; a tin vessel for
shaping puddings, etc.; (*fig.*) physical
form; character, nature. *v.t.* To form
into a particular shape; to fashion.

mould (3) [M.E. *mould*, become mouldy],
n. A fungoid growth forming a furry
coating on matter left in the damp.
mouldy, *a.* **mouldiness,** *n.*

moulder (mōl'dèr), *v.i.* To turn to dust by
natural decay; to crumble.

moulding (mōl'ding), *n.* Act or process of
shaping anything in a mould; anything
formed in a mould; part of a cornice,
capital, etc.

moult (mōlt) [L. *mūtāre*, to change], *v.* To
cast the feathers, skin, horns, etc. (of
certain birds and animals).

mound (mound) [?], *n.* An elevation
of earth, stones, etc., esp. artificial; a
tumulus.

mount (mount) [A.-S. *munt*, L. *mons
montis*], *n.* A high hill; a mountain;
that upon which anything is mounted;
the margin round a picture; a setting,
a strengthening part; a horse; a means
of mounting on horseback. *v.i.* To
ascend; to soar; to get on horseback;
to rise in amount. *v.t.* To climb; to
ascend upon, to get on; to put a picture)
on a mount; to stage (a play); to put (a
person) on a horse; to furnish with a
horse.

mountain (moun'tàn) [O.F. *montaigne*,
L. *mons montis*], *n.* A natural elevation
of the earth's surface rising high above
the surrounding land; a large heap or
pile; something of great bulk. **mountain
ash:** The rowan, a tree with bright
scarlet berries. **mountain-chain,** *n.* A
range or series of mountains. **moun-
taineer',** *n.* One who dwells among
mountains; one who climbs mountains
for amusement or scientific purposes.
mountaineering, *n.* **mountainous,** *a.*

mountebank (moun'tè-bănk) [It. *mon-*

tambanco (*monta in banco*, to mount on a
bench)], *n.* A quack doctor, a charlatan.

mourn (môrn) [A.-S. *murnan*], *v.i.* To
express or feel sorrow or grief; to wear
mourning. *v.t.* To grieve or sorrow for;
to deplore; to utter mournfully. **mourner,**
n. mournful, *a.* **mournfully,** *adv.*
mourning, *a.* Grieving; expressive of
grief or sorrow. *n.* Grief, sorrow,
lamentation; dress worn by mourners.

mouse (mous) [A.-S. *mūs*, L. and Gr.
mūs], *n.* (*pl.* mice (mīs)) A small rodent
quadruped, esp. the common house
mouse; applied to shrews, voles, etc.
v.i. (mouz) To hunt for or catch mice.

mouser (mou'zèr), *n.* A cat good at
catching mice.

moustache (mùs-tash') [F.], *n.* The hair
on the upper lip of men.

mouth (mouth) [A.-S. *mūth*], *n.* The
opening at which food is taken into the
body with the cavity containing the
organs of speech, etc.; (*fig.*) anything
analogous to a mouth; the opening of a
vessel, cave, or the like; the outfall of a
river. *v.t.* (mouth) To utter in an elaborate or constrained manner, to declaim;
to seize with the mouth; to chew. *v.i.*
To talk pompously; to make grimaces.
mouthpiece, *n.* A tube by which a
cigar or cigarette, etc., is held in the
mouth; that part of a musical instrument put between the lips; (*fig.*) a spokesman for others. **mouthy** (mou'thi), *a.*
Talkative; ranting.

move (moov) [O.F. *movoir*, L. *movēre*],
v.t. To cause to change position or posture; to put in motion, to stir; to incite,
prompt, rouse (to action); to excite
(laughter, etc.); to prevail upon; to
propose, to submit for discussion. *v.i.*
To change place or posture; to go from
one place to another; to progress; to
change one's place of residence; to make
an application, appeal, etc; to take
action. *n.* Act of moving; the right
to move (in chess, etc.); proceeding,
line of conduct; a device to obtain an
object; a change of abode. **movable,** *a.*
Capable of being moved; occurring at
varying times (as a festival). *n.* Anything that can be moved or removed;
(*pl.*) goods, furniture, chattels, etc., personal as opp. to real property. **mov-
abil'ity,** *n.* **movement,** *n.* Act or process
of changing position, place, or posture.
moving, *a.* Causing motion; in motion;
impelling; pathetic, affecting.

mow (1) (mou) [A.-S. *mūga*], *n.* A heap of
hay, corn, or other field produce.

mow (2) (mō) [A.-S. *māwan*], *v.t.* To cut
(grass, corn, etc.) with a scythe, mowing-
machine, etc.; (*fig.*) to destroy indiscriminately; to cut (down) in great
numbers. **mower,** *n.*

much (mŭch) [A.-S. *micel*], *a.* Great in
quantity or amount; long in duration.
adv. In or to a great degree or extent;
almost, about. *n.* A great quantity, a
great deal; something uncommon.

mucilage (mū'si-lāj) [F.], *n.* A gummy
substance from the various plants; gum
prepared for use. **mucilaginous** (-lăj'i-
nŭs), *a.*

muck (mŭk) [Scand.], *n.* Dung or manure; refuse, anything filthy, disgusting or nasty. *v.t.* To make dirty; (*slang*) to make a mess of.

mucus (mū'kŭs) [L.], *n.* The viscid secretion of the mucous membrane; slimy secretions in animals and fishes; gummy matter found in plants, soluble in water but not in alcohol. **mucous** (mū'kŭs), *a.*

mud (mŭd) [Teut.], *n.* Moist, soft earth, mire; (*fig.*) anything that is worthless or defiling. **mudguard,** *n.* A guard over a wheel of a cycle or cycle to catch the mud. **muddy,** *a.*

muddle (mŭdl), *v.t.* To confuse, bewilder, stupefy; to make half drunk; to mix (up); to make a mess of, to bungle. *v.i.* To act or proceed in a confused or bungling way. *n.* A mess; a state of confusion or bewilderment. **muddle-headed,** *a.* **muddler,** *n.*

muff (1) (mŭf), *n.* A covering carried by women in which the hands are placed to keep them warm.

muff (2) [?], *n.* An awkward or stupid fellow; a bungling action.

muffin (mŭf'in) [? O.F. *moufflet,* soft bread], *n.* A plain, spongy, round cake.

muffineer (-nēr', *n.* A castor for sprinkling salt or sugar.

muffle (mŭfl) [O.F. *moufle,* med. L. *muffula,* a mitten], *v.t.* To wrap or cover (up) closely and warmly; to wrap up (oars, bells, etc.) so as to deaden the sound; to dull. *n.* A large mitten; anything employed to deaden sound; a receptacle placed in a furnace to keep pottery from direct contact with flames and smoke. **muffler,** *n.* A scarf for the throat.

mufti (mŭf'ti) [Arab.], *n.* An official interpreter of the Koran and Mohammedan law; civilian dress worn by officers off duty; ordinary dress.

mug (1) (mŭg) [Scand.], *n.* A drinking-cup, usu. cylindrical without a lip; (*Slang*) the face or mouth; a silly person.

mug (2), *v.i.* (*Slang*) To study hard for an exam. *n.*

mugger (mŭg'ẽr) [Hind. *magar*], *n.* An East Indian crocodile with a broad snout.

muggy (mŭg'i) [Scand.], *a.* Damp and close, sultry; moist, mouldy.

mugwump (mŭg'wŭmp) [Algonkin, a chief], *n.* An independent member of the American Republican party; one who declines to be led by party politics; a consequential person.

mulatto (mū-lăt'ō) [Sp. *mulato*], *n.* The offspring of a white and a negro.

mulberry (mŭl'bẽr-i) [?], *n.* A tree bearing a fruit like a large blackberry.

mulch (mŭlch) [?], *n.* A surface layer of manure, etc., to keep the roots of plants moist.

mulct (mŭlkt) [L. *mulcta,* a fine], *n.* A fine, esp. for an offence or misdemeanour. *v.t.* To punish with a fine or forfeiture.

mule (mūl) [A.-S. *mūl,* L. *mūlus*], *n.* The offspring of a male ass and a mare; also a hinny; a hybrid between different animals or plants. (*fig.*) a stupidly obstinate person; an instrument for cotton-spinning. **muleteer',** *n.* A mule-driver. **mulish,** *a.* Like a mule; obstinate, sullen.

mull (1) (mŭl) [?], *v.t.* To warm (wine, beer, etc.), sweeten, and flavour with spices.

mull (2) (mŭl), *n.* A horn snuff-box.

mullein (mŭl'in) [A.-F. *moleyne*], *n.* An herbaceous plant with woolly leaves and tall spikes of yellow flowers, Aaron's rod.

mullet (1) (mŭl'ĕt) [O.F. *mulet,* L. *mullus*], *n.* Two fishes, the *red* and *grey mullet,* living near coasts and ascending rivers.

mullet (2) [O.F. *molette,* rowel], *n.* (*Her.*) The figure of a five-pointed star.

mulligatawny (mŭl-i-gà-taw'ni) [Tamil *milagutannīr,* pepper-water], *n.* An East Indian highly-flavoured curry-soup.

mullion (mŭl'i-ŏn) [?], *n.* A vertical bar dividing up a window.

multi-, mult- [L. *multus,* many, much], *pref.*

multifarious (mŭl-ti-fâr'i-ŭs) [L. *multifārius*], *a.* Having great multiplicity, variety, or diversity. **multifariously,** *adv.* **mul'tifold,** *a.* Manifold; many times doubled. **mul'tiform,** *a.* Having many forms. **multilat'eral,** *a.* Many-sided. **multilin'eal, -ear,** *a.* Having many lines. **multimillionaire',** *n.* One who possesses several millions. **multipartite** (-par-tīt), *a.*

multiple (mŭl'tipl) [late L. *multiplus*], *a.* Manifold; having many parts, components, or relations. *n.* A quantity that contains another a number of times without remainder. **multiple mark:** The sign × indicating multiplication. **mul'tiplex,** *a.* Manifold; multiple. **multiplicity** (-plis'i-ti), *n.* The quality of being many or manifold; many of the same kind.

multiply (mŭl'ti-plī) [L. *multiplicāre*], *v.t.* To add (a multiplicand) to itself a certain number of times, producing a quantity called the product. *v.i.* To increase in number or extent; to increase by propagation. **multiplicand',** *n.* The quantity to be multiplied. **multiplica'-tion,** *n.* Act or process of multiplying; increase by multiplying. **mul'tiplicative,** *a.* multiplier, *n.* One who or that which multiplies or increases; the number by which the multiplicand is multiplied; an instrument for intensifying an electric current.

multitude (mŭl'ti-tūd) [L. *multitūdo*], *n.* The state of being numerous; a great number; a very large crowd or throng; the common people. **multitu'dinous,** *a.* Very numerous.

mum (1) (mŭm), *a.* Silent. *int.* Silence, hush! *v.i.* To act in dumb-show; to play as a mummer.

mum (2) [G. *mumme*], *n.* Strong, sweet beer.

mumble (mŭmbl) [M.E. *momelen,* from MUM (1)], *v.i.* To speak indistinctly; to eat with the lips closed. *v.t.* To mutter indistinctly or inarticulately; to chew gently. *n.* Indistinct utterance. **mumbler,** *n.* **mumblingly,** *adv.*

mummer (mŭm'ẽr) [O.F. *momeur*], *n.* An actor in dumb-show, an itinerant masquer; (*contemp.*) an actor. **mummery**

n. The performance of mumming; (*contemp.*) tomfoolery.

mummy (mŭm'ĭ) [Arab. *mūmiyā*, from *mŭm*, wax used in embalming], *n.* A body preserved from decay by embalming, esp. after the manner of the ancient Egyptians; (*fig.*) a dried-up person or body. *v.t.* To mummify. **mummify**, *v.t.* To make into a mummy, to embalm.

mump (1) (mŭmp) [?], *v.i.* To beg in a whining tone. *v.t.* To obtain by begging. **mumper**, *n.*

mump (2) [?], *v.i.* To sulk; to mumble, to munch. *n.pl.* A contagious disease characterized by swelling and inflammation of the salivary glands.

munch (mŭnch) [?], *v.* To chew audibly or with much movement of the jaws.

mundane (mŭn'dān) [L. *mundānus*, from *mundus*, the world], *a.* Belonging to this world, earthly, worldly.

mungoose (mŭng'goos) [Marathi *mangūs*], *n.* (*pl.* -**gooses**) An E. Indian ichneumon preying on snakes.

municipal (mū-nĭs'ĭ-pǎl) [L. *mūniceps*, a citizen], *a.* Pertaining to the government of a town or city, or to local government. **municipal'ity**, *n.* A town, city, or district having a charter of incorporation or enjoying local self-government.

munificent (mū-nĭf'ĭ-sĕnt) [L. *mūnificus*], *a.* Liberal, bountiful; characterized by splendid liberality. **munificence**, *n.*

muniment (mū'nĭ-mĕnt) [O.F., L. *mūnīre*, to fortify], *n.* A title-deed, charter, or record kept as evidence of title.

munition (mū-nĭsh'ŭn) [L. *mūnitio*, as prec.], *n.* (*usu. in pl.*) Military stores of all kinds, esp. ammunition; anything required for an undertaking. *v.t.* To furnish with munitions.

mural (mūr'ǎl) [F., from L. *mūrus*, a wall], *a.* Pertaining to, on, or like a wall.

murder (mĕr'dĕr) [A.-S. *morthor*], *n.* Homicide with malice aforethought. *v.t.* To kill (a human being) with malice aforethought; to slay barbarously; (*fig.*) to spoil by blundering or clumsiness; to mangle. **murderer**, *n.* **murderess**, *n.* **murderous**, *a.*

murk (mĕrk) [A.-S. *mirce*], *n.* Darkness. **murky**, *a.* Thick, obscure. **murkily**, *adv.*

murmur (mĕr'mŭr) [L.], *n.* A low, continuous sound, as of running water; a half-suppressed complaint, a grumble. *v.i.* To make a low continued noise; to mutter in discontent; to find fault. *v.t.* To utter in a low voice. **murmurer**, *n.*

murrain (mŭr'ǎn) [O.F. *morine*], *n.* An infectious disease among cattle.

muscadel (mŭs-kȧ-del') [It. *moscadello*], *n.* A rich wine made from muscadine grapes; the grapes; a sweet fragrant pear. **mus'cadine**, *n.* A grape with a musky flavour.

muscle (mŭsl) [L. *musculus*, dim of *mus*, mouse], *n.* A band or bundle of contractile fibrous tissue serving to effect movement of some part of the body; muscular strength.

Muscovite (mŭs'kȯ-vīt) [F. *Muscovie*, Moscow], *n.* A native of Russia; common mica.

muscular (mŭs'kū-lȧr), *a.* Pertaining to the

muscles; having well-developed muscles; strong, brawny. **muscular'ity**, *n.*

Muse (1) (mūz) [Gr. *Mousa*], *n.* (*Gr. Myth.*) One of nine goddesses, daughters of Zeus and Mnemosyne, who presided over the liberal arts; the inspiring power of poetry, poetical genius.

muse (2) [F. *muser*], *v.i.* To ponder, meditate (upon); to reflect (upon) in silence; to engage in reverie. *v.t.* To meditate on. *n.* Abstraction of mind; reverie. **musingly**, *adv.*

museum (mū'zē'ŭm) [Gr. *mouseion*, a temple of the Muses], *n.* A place for the preservation and exhibition of objects illustrating antiquities, art, natural science, etc.

mush (mŭsh), *n.* A soft pulp, pulpy mass.

mushroom (mŭsh'rum) [F. *mousseron*], *n.* A quick-growing edible fungus; (*fig.*) an upstart. *a.* Ephemeral, upstart.

music (mū'zĭk) [Gr. *mousikē technē*, the art of the Muses], *n.* The art of combining vocal and instrumental tones in a rhythmic form; such a combination of tones; melody, harmony; a musical score. **music-hall**, *n.* A public building for variety entertainments. **musical**, *a.* **musician** (-zish'ȧn), *n.* **musicology** (mū-zi-kol'ȯ-ji), *n.* The study of all connected with music in every aspect.

musk (mŭsk) [Pers.], *n.* An odoriferous resin obtained from the male musk-deer; the odour of this; a plant with a similar scent. **musk-deer**, *n.* A small hornless deer of Central Asia. **musk-ox**, *n.* An Arctic-American bovine ruminant.

musket (mŭs'kĕt) [F. *mousquet*, orig. a sparrowhawk], *n.* The old fire-arm of the infantry; any old-fashioned smooth-bore gun; the male sparrowhawk. **musketeer'**, *n.* A soldier armed with a musket. **musketry**, *n.* The art of using the musket.

muslin (mŭz'lĭn) [F. *mousseline* (Mosul in Mesopotamia, where formerly made)], *n.* A fine cotton fabric used for dresses, curtains, etc.

musquash (mŭs'kwosh) [Algonkin], *n.* A N. American aquatic rodent yielding a valuable fur and secreting a musky substance.

mussel (mŭs'ĕl) [A.-S. *mūscelle*], *n.* An edible bivalve mollusc.

Mussulman (mŭs'ŭl-mȧn) [Arab. *muslim*], *n.* (*pl.* -**mans**) A Mohammedan, a Moslem.

must (1) (mŭst) [A.-S. from L. *mustus*, fresh], *n.* New wine, grape juice before fermentation; mustiness. *v.* To make or grow mouldy.

must (2) (mŭst) [A.-S. *mōste*], *aux. v.* To be obliged to, to be under a necessity to; to be requisite; to be certain to.

mustang (mŭs'tăng) [Sp. *mestengo*], *n.* The wild horse of the American prairies.

mustard (mŭs'tárd) [O.F. *mostarde*], *n.* A plant of the genus *Sinapis*; the seeds of this ground and used as a condiment.

muster (mŭs'tĕr) [It. *mostra*, a show], *n.* The assembling of troops; a register of forces mustered; a gathering. *v.t.* To collect or assemble for review, checking of rolls, etc.; to bring together; to

summon (up strength, courage, etc.). *v.i.*
To meet in one place. **muster-roll**, *n.* A
register of troops, a ship's company, etc.
musty (mŭs'ti), *a.* Mouldy; sour, stale.
mustiness, *n.*

mutable (mū'tàbl) [L. *mūtāre*, to change],
a. Liable to change; fickle, unstable.
mutabil'ity, *n.* **mutate'**, *v.i.* To change,
to be transmuted. *v.t.* (*Gram.*) To
modify. **muta'tion**, *n.* Act or process
of changing.

mute (mūt) [O.F. *muet*], *a.* Silent, speechless; dumb; not spoken; unpronounced;
produced by complete closure of the
organs of the mouth or interruption of
the breath (as *h, p, d, k*, etc.). *n.* One
who is silent; a dumb person; a hired
attendant at a funeral; a contrivance
for deadening sound (as in a piano);
a letter which is not pronounced; a consonant that stops the sound entirely.

mutilate (mū'ti-lāt) [L. *mutilātus*, maimed],
v.t. To cut off a limb or an essential
part of; to maim, disfigure; to injure
(literary work, etc.) by excision. **mutila'-
tion**, *n.* **mu'tilator**, *n.*

mutineer (mū-ti-nēr') [F. *mutinier*, from
mutin, mutinous], *n.* One who mutinies.
v.t. To mutiny. **mutinous**, *a.* mutin-
ously, *adv.* **mutiny**, *n.* Open resistance
to or revolt against constituted authority,
esp. by sailors or soldiers. *v.i.* To rise
or rebel against authority.

mutter (mŭt'ér) [imit.], *v.i.* To speak in
a low voice; to grumble, to murmur (at
or against). *v.t.* To utter in a low or
indistinct voice; to say in secret. *n.*
A low or indistinct utterance; a murmur,
a grumble. **mutteringly**, *adv.*

mutton (mŭt'òn) [O.F. *moton* (F. *mouton*)],
n. The flesh of sheep used as food.

mutual (mū'tū-ål) [L. *mūtuus*, reciprocal],
a. Reciprocal, possessed, done, felt, etc.,
by each of two persons, parties, etc., to
or towards the other. **mutual'ity**, *n.*

muzzle (mŭzl) [O.F. *musel*], *n.* The projecting mouth and nose of a horse, dog,
etc.; the mouth of a cannon; a guard
to prevent an animal biting. *v.t.* To
put a muzzle on; (*fig.*) to silence.

my (mī, mĭ) [M.E. *mi*], *poss. a* (*absol.*
mine) Belonging to me; used in forms of
address (as *my boy, my dear*).

myelitis (mī-e-li'tis) [Gr. *muelos*, narrow],
n. (*Path.*) Inflammation of the spinal
cord.

myope (mī'ōp) [Gr. *muein*, to shut, *ōps*,
eye], *n.* A short-sighted person. **myo'pia**,
n. **myopic** (-op'ik), *a.*

myosotis (mī-ò-sō'tis) [Gr. *mūs muos*,
mouse, *ous ōtos*, ear], *n.* A genus of hardy
plants comprising the forget-me-not.

myriad (mir'i-åd) [Gr. *mūrios*, countless],
a. Innumerable, countless. *n.* A very
great number.

Myrmidon (mér'mi-dòn) [Gr. *Murmi-
dones*], *n.* One of a warlike people of
Thessaly, ruled over by Achilles; a faithful follower, an unscrupulous underling.

myrrh (mér) [A.-S. *myrre*, Gr. *murra*,
from Semitic], *n.* A gum resin from
Arabian and Abyssinian trees used in
incense, perfumes, etc.

myrtle (mértl) [Gr. *murtos*], *n.* A tall

shrub with glossy evergreen leaves and
sweet-scented flowers.

myself (mī, mi-self'), *pron.* Used in the
nominative after 'I', to express emphasis;
in the objective reflexively.

mystery (1) (mis'tér-i) [Gr. *mustērion*, from
muein, to close the eyes], *n.* Something
beyond human comprehension; a secret;
secrecy, obscurity; a form of mediæval
drama drawn from sacred history, a
miracle-play; a divine truth partially
revealed; esoteric rites. **mysterious**, *a.*
Not plain to the understanding; obscure,
occult.

mystery (2) [M.E. *mistere*], *n.* A handicraft, trade, or occupation.

mystic (mis'tik) [Gr. *mustikos*], *a.* Pertaining to or involving mystery or
mysticism; occult, esoteric; emblematical.
n. One addicted to mysticism. **mystical**,
a. **mysticism** (-sizm), *n.* The doctrine
that man may by self-surrender and
spiritual apprehension attain to direct
communion with God.

mystify (mis'ti-fī), *v.t.* To bewilder, puzzle,
hoax. **mystifica'tion**, *n.*

myth (mith) [Gr. *muthos*, fable], *n.* A
legend or tradition, accepted as historical,
embodying the beliefs of a people on the
creation, the gods, the universe, etc.; an
allegorical story; a fictitious event, person, etc. **mythic, -al**, *a.* **mythol'ogy**, *n.*
A system of myths in which are embodied
the beliefs of a people concerning their
origin, deities, heroes, etc.; the science of
myths, a treatise on myths. **mytho-
log'ic, -al** (-loj'ik, ål), *a.*

myxo- (Gr. *muxo*, slime), *comb. form.* Pertaining to, or living in slime.

N

Naafi (nåf'i) [initials of Navy, Army, Air
Force Institutes], *n.* Organization of
Service canteens.

nab (nåb) [Scand.], *v.t.* To catch, seize.

nabob (nā'bob) [Hind. *nawwāb*], *n.* A
deputy-governor under the Mogul empire
in India; (*fig.*) a man who has amassed
great wealth in India; **a man of** great
wealth and commercial power.

nacre (nā'kér) [Sp. and Port. *nacar*], *n.*
A fish yielding mother-of-pearl; mother-
of-pearl. **nacreous, nacrous**, *a.*

nadir (nā'dir) [Arab.], *n.* The point of the
heavens directly opposite to the zenith or
directly under our feet; (*fig.*) the lowest
point (of decline, degradation, etc.).

nag (1) (någ) [?], *n.* A small horse for
riding; a horse.

nag (2) [Scand.], *v.i.* To be continually
finding fault; to scold (at). *v.t.* To
find fault with, complain, or scold continually. **nagger**, *n.*

naiad (nī'åd) [Gr.], *n.* A water-nymph.

nail (nāl) [A.-S. *nægel*], *n.* The horny
substance at the tip of the fingers and
toes; a claw, a talon; a measure of 2¼
inches; a headed metal spike, for hammering into wood, etc., to fasten things
together, or for use as a peg. *v.t.* To

secure with nails; to stud with nails; to fix; to clinch (a bargain). **nailer,** n.

nainsook (nān'suk) [Hind. *nainsukh*], n. A thick muslin or cotton cloth.

naïve (na-ēv') [F.], a. Artless, ingenuous, unaffected. **naïvely,** adv. **naïveté** (-tā), n.

naked (nā'kĕd) [A.-S. *nacod*], a. Destitute of clothing, nude; without natural covering; not sheathed; exposed, defenceless. **nakedness,** n.

namby-pamby (năm'bi-păm'bi) [from *Ambrose* Philips (1671–1749), a sentimental poet], a. Insipidly sentimental; affectedly pretty.

name (nām) [A.-S. *nama*], n. A word by which a person, animal, place, or thing is known, spoken of, or addressed; a term as dist. from substance; sound as opp. to reality; (*fig.*) reputation, honourable character; authority. v.t. To give a name to, to style; to call by name; to nominate; to mention, to cite. **namesake,** n. A person or thing having the same name as or named after another. **nameable,** a. **nameless,** a. Having no name; anonymous; unknown, inglorious; inexpressible, indefinable; unfit to be named. **namely,** adv. That is to say.

nanism (nā'nizm) [Gr. *nanos*, a dwarf], n. Dwarfishness.

nankeen (năn-kēn') [*Nankin*, China], n. A buff or yellow cotton fabric exported from Nankin.

nap (1) (năp) [A.-S. *hnæppian*], v.i. To sleep lightly, to doze; (*fig.*) to be unprepared. n. A short sleep, a doze in the day-time.

nap (2) [?], n. The surface produced on cloth by cutting and smoothing the pile; a smooth, downy growth on a surface.

nap (3) [*Napoleon*], n. A game in which five cards are dealt to each player.

nape (năp) [?], n. The back of the neck.

napery (nā'pér-i) [O.F. *naperie*], n. Linen, esp. table-linen.

naphtha (năf'thá) [Gr.], n. An inflammable oil produced by dry distillation of bituminous shale or coal.

napkin (năp'kin) [M.E. *nappekyn*], n. A small cloth, esp. one used at table; a small towel.

nappy (năp'i) [?], a. Covered with nap (of cloth, etc.); foaming, heady (of beer). n. Towel used for a small baby.

narcissus (nar-sis'ús) [Gr.], n. A genus of plants containing the daffodils and jonquils. **narcissism,** n. (*Psych.*) A form of neurosis exhibiting excessive admiration of one's own body.

narcotic (nar-kot'ik) [Gr. *narkoun*, to benumb], a. Producing torpor; soporific; (*fig.*) causing sleep or dullness. n. A substance that allays pain by inducing torpor.

nard (nard) [Gr. *nardos*], n. A balsam prepared from spikenard.

narrate (ná-rāt') [L. *narrātus*, p.p. of *narrāre*], v.t. To relate, to give an account of in speech or writing. **narration,** n. **nar'rative,** a. In the form of narration; relating to an event or story. n. A tale, a story; an account. **narra'tor,** n.

narrow (năr'ō) [A.-S. *nearu*], a. Of small

extent from side to side; limited, restricted, of limited scope; illiberal in views; prejudiced; niggardly; impoverished; close, near, with little margin; precise, accurate. v.t. To make narrow or narrower; to contract in views or sentiments; to confine, limit, restrict. v.i. To become narrow or narrower. n. (*usu. pl.*) A strait; a narrow mountain-pass. **narrowly,** adv. **narrowness,** n.

narwhal (nar'wál) [Scand.], n. An Arctic cetacean with a long tusk.

nasal (nā'zál) [L. *nāsus*], a. Pertaining to the nose; sounded with the nasal passage open; pronounced as if through the nose. n. A letter or sound produced with the nasal passage open.

nascent (năs'ént) [L. *nascens*, being born], a. Coming into being; beginning to develop.

nasturtium (ná-stér'shúm) [L.], n. A trailing plant with vivid orange flowers.

nasty (nas'ti) [?], a. Dirty, foul, repulsive; indecent; nauseous; annoying, vexatious. **nastiness,** n.

natal (nā'tál) [L. *nātus*, born], a. Of, from, or pertaining to one's birth.

natant (nā'tánt) [L. *natans*, swimming], a. Swimming; floating. **nata'tion,** n.

nation (nā'shún) [L. *natio*], n. A people under the same government and inhabiting the same country, or belonging to the same ethnological family and speaking the same language. **national** (năsh'ó-nál), a. Pertaining to a nation; general, as opp. to local; attached to one's country. n. A member or subject of a particular nation; one's fellow-countryman. **nationalism,** n. Devotion to the nation; nationalization of industry; the policy of national independence; patriotic effort, sentiment, etc. **national'ity,** n. **nationalize,** v.t. To make the nation the owner of. **nationaliza'tion,** n. Making national; (*Polit.*) the placing of industry under national control. **nationally,** adv.

native (nā'tiv), a. Pertaining to a place or country by birth, indigenous; belonging to a person, animal, etc., by nature; inborn, natural, not acquired; pertaining to the place of one's birth. n. One born in a place; an indigenous plant or animal; an oyster raised in home waters. **nativ'ity,** n. Birth, esp. that of Christ, the Virgin, or St. John the Baptist; a festival in commemoration of this; a horoscope.

N.A.T.O. [initials North Atlantic Treaty Organization], n. (*Polit.*) The 12 parties of the N. Atlantic Treaty (4 April, 1949) of Defence: Belgium, Canada, Denmark, France, Iceland, Italy, Luxemburg, Norway, Portugal, United Kingdom and U.S.A.

natty (năt'i) [?], a. Neat, spruce.

natural (năch'úr-ál), a. Pertaining to, produced, or constituted by nature; innate, not artificial; instinctive; in conformity with nature, normal, not irregular or supernatural; animal, not spiritual; true to life; unaffected; undisguised; ordinary; easy (to); related by nature only, illegitimate; concerned with nature or animal life. n. An idiot; (*Mus.*) a sign cancelling the effect of a preceding sharp or flat. **naturalist,** *n.* One versed in natural history. **naturalis'tic,** *a.* Realistic; pertaining to natural history. **naturalize,** *v.t.* To make natural; to acclimatize; to confer the rights and privileges of a natural-born subject on. **naturaliza'tion,** *n.* **naturally,** *adv.* According to nature; as might be expected, of course.

nature (nā'chùr) [L. *nātūra*], *n.* The essential qualities of anything; natural character or disposition; kind, sort, class; vital or animal force; the whole sum of things, forces, activities, and laws constituting the physical universe; the physical power governing these; the material universe regarded as dist. from the supernatural or from a creator; the condition of man preceding social organization; the undomesticated condition of animals or plants.

naught (nawt) [A.-S. *nâwiht* (*nâ*, no, *wiht*, whit)], *n.* Nothing; a cipher. *a.* Worthless. *adv.* In no degree. **to set at naught:** To disregard.

naughty (naw'ti) [prec., -Y], *a.* Perverse, mischievous; disobedient, ill-behaved. **naughtily,** *adv.* **naughtiness,** *n.*

nausea (naw'si-à) [Gr. *naus*, ship], *n.* A feeling of sickness; loathing; sea-sickness. **nauseate,** *v.t.* **nauseating,** *a.* **nauseous,** *a.*

nautical (naw'ti-kàl) [Gr. *naus*, ship], *a.* Pertaining to ships, navigation, or sailors.

nautilus (naw'ti-lùs), *n.* A shell-fish furnished with a sail-like membrane.

naval (nā'vál) [L. *nâvis*, a ship], *a.* Consisting of or pertaining to ships or a navy.

nave (1) [nāv) [A.-S. *nafu*], *n.* The hub of a wheel, in which the axle and spokes are inserted.

nave (2), *n.* The body of a church, excluding the choir or chancel and the aisles.

navel (nā'vèl) [A.-S. *nafela*], *n.* The cicatrix of the umbilical cord, forming a depression on the surface of the abdomen.

navigate (năv'i-gāt) [L. *nāvigāre*], *v.i.* To pass from place to place by water; to manage a ship. *v.t.* To pass over or up or down, in a ship, etc.; to manage, to conduct (a ship, aircraft, etc.). **navigable,** *a.* **navigabil'ity,** *n.* **naviga'tion,** *n.* The act, art, or science of navigating. **nav'igator,** *n.* One skilled in navigation.

navvy (năv'i) [NAVIGATOR], *n.* Orig. a labourer employed on canals; now one employed in any kind of excavating, as the construction of railways.

navy (nā'vi), *n.* The warships of a nation; their officers, men, dockyards. etc.

nay (nā) [Scand.], *adv.* Expressing negation or refusal; not only so, more than that, and even. *n.* A denial, a refusal.

Nazarene (năz'á-rēn), *n.* A native of Nazareth; Jesus Christ; an early Christian. **Nazarite,** *n.* A Hebrew who had taken vows of abstinence.

neap (nēp) [A.-S. *nēp*], *a.* Low or lowest (applied to tides). *n.* A neap tide.

Neapolitan (nē-á-pol'i-tàn), *a.* Pertaining to or distinctive of Naples or its inhabitants. *n.* An inhabitant of Naples.

near (nēr) [A.-S. *rēar* (compar. of *nēah*, NIGH)], *adv.* At or to a short distance, at hand, nigh, in place, time, or degree; almost; closely; carefully, sparingly. *prep.* Close to in place, time, condition, etc. *a.* Nigh, close at hand; closely related; intimate; literal, not loose (of a likeness, translation, etc.); close, narrow; direct (of roads, etc.); on the left (of horses or vehicles); parsimonious, niggardly. *v.t.* To approach, to draw nigh to. **nearly,** *adv.* Almost; intimately; in a parsimonious manner. **nearness,** *n.*

neat (1) (nēt) [A.-S. *nēat*], *n.* Cattle of the bovine kind; an animal of this kind. **neat-herd,** *n.* A cowherd.

neat (2) (nēt) [L. *nitēre*, to shine], *a.* Tidy, trim; simply ordered; nicely proportioned, well made; dexterous, clever; undiluted. **neatness,** *n.*

nebula (neb'ū-là) [L., mist], *n.* (*pl.* -læ) A cloudy patch of light in the heavens produced by groups of stars or by a mass of gaseous matter. **nebular,** *a.* Pertaining to nebulæ. **neb'ulous,** *a.* Cloudy, hazy, obscure, uncertain.

necessary (nes'é-sàr-i) [L. *necesse*, unavoidable], *a.* Needful, indispensable, requiring to be done; inevitable; existing by necessity; determined by natural laws; not voluntary, compulsory; intuitive, conclusive. *n.* That which is indispensably requisite; (*pl.*) things essentially requisite, esp. to life. **necessarily,** *adv.* Of necessity; inevitably.

necessitate (nè-ses'i-tāt), *v.t.* To make necessary or unavoidable; to entail as an unavoidable condition, etc.

necessity (nè-ses'i-ti), *n.* The quality of being necessary; inevitableness; indispensability; constraint, compulsion; compelling force of circumstances, external conditions that make one act in a certain way; that which is necessary (*often in pl.*); want, poverty. **necessitous,** *a.* Needy, in poverty.

neck (nek) [A.-S. *hnecca*], *n.* The portion of the body connecting the trunk with the head; anything resembling this, as an isthmus, a narrow passage, the slender part of a bottle. **neck-band,** *n.* A part of a garment fitting round the neck. **neckcloth,** *n.* A cravat or neck-tie. **neckerchief,** *n.* A kerchief for the neck. **necklace,** *n.* A string of gems, etc., worn round the neck. **necklet,** *n.* A small fur for the neck; an ornament for the neck. **neck-tie,** *n.* A strip of material encircling or worn as if encircling the collar and tied in front.

necro- [Gr. *nekros*, a dead body], *comb. form.* Pertaining to dead bodies.

necromancy (nek'rò-măn-si) [L. *necromantia*, Gr. *nekros*, a dead body], *n.* The art of revealing future events by communication with the dead; magic. **necromancer,** *n.* **necroman'tic,** *a.*

necropolis (nè-krop'ò-lis), *n.* A cemetery, esp. a large one.

nectar (nèk'tàr) [Gr. *nektar*], *n.* The drink of the gods; (*fig.*) any delicious drink; the honey of plants. **nec'tarine,** *n.* A smooth-skinned variety of peach.

need (nēd) [A.-S. *nied*], *n.* Lack of something; a state requiring relief, urgent want; indigence; emergency; that which is wanted. *v.i.* To be wanting or necessary, to be bound, to be under necessity to; to be in want. *v.t.* To be in want of, to require. **needful**, *a.* **needless**, *a.* Unnecessary, not required; superfluous. **needs**, *adv.* Of necessity, necessarily, indispensably (*usu. with* must). **needy**, *a.* In need; necessitous.

needle (nēdl) [A.-S. *nœdl*], *n.* A small rod-shaped steel instrument with an eye for carrying a thread, used in sewing; analogous instruments for knitting, crocheting, etc.; the indicator in a mariner's compass, telegraphic receiver, etc. **needle-woman**, *n.* A seamstress. **needlework**, *n.*

ne'er (når) [contr.], *adv.* Never. **ne'er-do-well**, *a.* Good for nothing. *n.* A good-for-nothing.

nefarious (nė-fār'i-ùs) [L. *nefārius*], *a.* Wicked, abominable.

negation (nė-gā'shùn) [L. *negāre*, to deny], *n.* Denial; refusal, contradiction.

negative (neg'ȧ-tiv), *a.* Containing or implying negation; denying, prohibiting, refusing; the opposite to positive; (*Phot.*) showing the lights dark and the shadows light. *n.* A proposition, reply, etc., expressing negation; a veto; the side of a question that denies; lack or absence of something; (*Phot.*) a plate bearing an image in which lights and shades are reversed; negative electricity, or the negative plates in a voltaic cell; (*Alg.*) a negative or minus sign (—) or quantity. *v.t.* To veto, to refuse to accept, sanction, or enact; to contradict.

neglect (nėg-lekt') [L. *negligere*], *v.t.* To treat carelessly; slight, disregard; to leave undone. *n.* Disregard (of);omission to do anything that should be done; negligence; state of being neglected. **neglectful**, *a.* **négligé** (neg-li-zhā) [F.], *n.* A state of undress or free and easy attire. **negligent**, *a.* negligence, *n.* Neglect, carelessness; disregard of conventions.

negotiate (nė-gō'shi-āt) [L. *negōtium*, business], *v.i.* To treat (with another) in order to make a bargain, compromise, etc.; to traffic. *v.t.* To arrange by negotiating; to transfer (a bill, note, etc.) for value received; to obtain or give value for; (*colloq.*) to accomplish. **negotiable**, *a.* **negotiabil'ity**, *n.*

Negro (nē'grō) [L. *niger*, black], *n.* (*fem.* **Negress**) A person belonging to, or descended from, one of the black-skinned African races. *a.* Pertaining to these races: dark-skinned. **ne'groid**, *a.*

negus (1) (nē'gùs) [name of inventor], *n.* A beverage of wine, hot water, sugar, and spices.

negus (2) [native], *n.* The sovereign of Abyssinia.

neigh (nā) [A.-S. *hnægan*], *v.i.* To utter the cry of a horse; to whinny. *n.* The cry of a horse.

neighbour (nā'bŏr) [A.-S. *nēahgebūr*], *n.* One who lives near; a person or thing happening to be near another; one having the claims of a fellow-man, etc. *a.* Near, adjoining. *v.t.* To adjoin; to

lie near to. **neighbourhood**, *n.* The state of being neighbours; the vicinity; nearness; those who live near, neighbours. **neighbouring**, *a.* Situated or living near. **neighbourly**, *a.* and *adv.* Like or becoming to a neighbour, friendly, sociable.

neither (nī'-, nē'thėr) [A.-S. *nawther*], *a.* Not either. *pron.* Not the one nor the other. *conj.* Not either, not on the one hand (of two alternatives); not, not yet.

Nemesis (nem'ė-sis), *n.* The Greek goddess of retribution; retributive justice.

neo- [Gr. *neos*], *comb. form.* New, recent, fresh.

neolithic (nē-ȯ-lith'ik) [Gr. *lithos*, stone, -IC], *a.* Pertaining to the later Stone Age characterized by ground and polished implements.

neologism (nē-ol'ȯ-jizm), *n.* The use of a new word or phrase, or of a new sense for an old word.

neon (nē'on), *n.* (*Chem.*) A gaseous element, used in the **neon-lamp**, an electric lamp containing rarefied neon gas.

neophyte (nē'ȯ-fīt) [Gr. *phutos*, grown], *n.* One newly converted or newly baptized; one newly admitted to the priesthood, etc.

nephew (nev'ū) [O.F. *neveu*], *n.* The son of a brother or sister.

nephritis (nė-frī-tis) [Gr. *nephros*, kidney], *n.* Inflammation of the kidneys.

nepotism (nē'pȯ-tizm) [It. *nepotismo*, L. *nepos*, grandson], *n.* Favouritism, as in bestowing patronage, towards one's relations.

Neptune (nep'tūn), *n.* The Roman god of the sea; (*fig.*) the sea; one of the Sun's remoter planets.

nerve (nėrv) [L. *nervus*], *n.* One of the fibres conveying sensations and impulses to and from the brain; (*fig.*) strength, coolness, pluck; one of the ribs in a leaf; (*pl.*) the nervous system; an excited or disordered condition of the nerves, nervousness; (*slang*) impudence. *v.t.* To give strength or firmness to. **nerveless**, *a.* Destitute of strength or vigour; feeble, flabby. **nervous**, *a.* Pertaining to nerves; abounding in nervous energy; having weak nerves, excitable, timid; sinewy, muscular; vigorous in sentiment or style. **nervously**, *adv.* **nervousness**, *n.* The state of being nervous. **nervy**, *a.* Nervous, jumpy, on edge; full of nerve, cool, confident; sinewy, muscular.

nescient (nesh'i-ėnt) [L. *nesciens*], *a.* Ignorant, having no knowledge (of). **nescience**, *n.*

ness (nes) [A.-S. *nœs*], *n.* A promontory, cape.

-ness [A.-S.], *suf.* Forming abstract nouns, as *goodness, holiness.*

nest (nest) [A.-S.], *n.* The shelter constructed by a bird in which to lay its eggs and rear its young; any place used similarly by animals or insects; a snug abode or retreat; a haunt (as of robbers); a series or set, as of drawers or boxes. *v.i.* To build and occupy a nest; to hunt for birds' nests. **nest-egg**, *n.* A real or artificial egg left in a nest to prevent a hen from forsaking it; (*fig.*) something

laid by as a nucleus for saving. **nestling,**
n. A bird too young to fly.
nestle (nesl), *v.i.* To be close or snug; to
press closely (up to).
net (1) (net) [A.-S.], *n.* A fabric of cord,
etc., knotted into meshes, for catching
fish, birds, etc., or for covering, protecting, carrying, etc. *v.t.* To make into
a net or netting; to cover or confine
with a net; to catch in a net; to fish with
or set nets; to ensnare. *v.i.* To make
netting, network, or nets.
net (2), *a.* Free from all deductions; not
subject to discount.
nether (neth'ér) [A.-S.- *neothera*], *a.* Lower;
belonging to the region below the
heavens or the earth. **nethermost,** *a.*
nettle (netl) [A.-S. *netel*], *n.* A common
weed with inconspicuous flowers and
minute stinging hairs. *v.t.* To irritate,
to provoke. **nettle-rash,** *n.* An eruption
on the skin.
neural (nūr'ál), *a.* Pertaining to the nerves
or the nervous system. **neural'gia** [Gr.
algos, pain], *n.* An acute pain in a nerve
or nerves, esp. in the head. **neural'gic,** *a.*
neurasthe'nia [Gr. *asthenes*, weak], *n.*
Weakness of the nervous system, nervous
debility. **neurasthenic** (-then'ik), *a.*
neuritis (nū-rī'tis), *n.* Inflammation of a
nerve.
neuro- [Gr. *neuron*, nerve], *comb. form.*
Relating to the nerves.
neurosis (nū-rō'sis), *n.* Functional disease
of the nerves. **neurot'ic,** *a.* Pertaining
to the nerves; suffering from neurosis.
n. A person of abnormal nervous
excitability.
neuter (nū'tér) [L., neither], *a.* (*Gram.*)
Neither masculine nor feminine; (of
verbs) intransitive; neutral, taking
neither side. *n.* The neuter gender.
neutral (nū'trál), *a.* Taking no part with
either side; indifferent, impartial; having
no distinct character, colour, etc. *n.*
A State or person that stands aloof
from a contest; a subject of a neutral
State. **neutral'ity,** *n.* **neutralize,** *v.t.*
To render neutral.
neutron (nū'tron) *n.* (*Chem.*) A mass
produced by the union of a proton and
an electron.
never (nev'ér) [A.-S. *næfre*]. Not ever, at
no time; on no occasion; none; surely
not. **nevermore,** *adv.* At no future
time; never again. **nevertheless,** *conj.*
But for all that; notwithstanding; all
the same.
new (nū) [A.-S. *niwe*], *a.* Lately made,
invented, or introduced; not before
known; recently begun; never before
used; fresh, unfamiliar, unaccustomed;
(to). *adv.* Newly, recently (as *new-
blown, new-born*); anew, fresh. **new-
fangled,** *a.* New-fashioned, different
from the accepted fashion. **newly,** *adv.*
Recently. **newness,** *n.*
newel (nū'él) [O.F. *nuel*], *n.* The central
column from which the steps of a winding
stair radiate; the well of a winding stair;
a post supporting a hand-rail.
Newfoundland (nū-found'lánd), *n.* A large
breed of dog, orig. from Newfoundland.
news (nūz), *n.pl.* (*usu. as sing.*) Recent
information, tidings. **news-boy, -man,**
n. One who delivers or sells newspapers
in the street. **newspaper,** *n.* A printed
publication, usu. issued daily or weekly,
containing news, advertisements, etc.
newt (nūt) [M.E. *ewte* (*a newt*, from *an
ewt*)], *n.* An eft, a small-tailed amphibian.
next (nekst) [A.-S. *néahst*], *a.* Nearest in
place, time, or degree; immediately
following. *adv.* Nearest or immediately
after. *prep.* Nearest to. *n.* The next
person or thing.
nib (nib) [?], *n.* A pen-point for insertion
in a penholder.
nibble (nibl) [?], *v.t.* To bite little by
little; to bite at cautiously (as a fish
at bait). *n.* Act of nibbling; a little
bite; a bit nibbled off.
niblick (nib'lik) [?], *n.* (*Golf*) A club with
a small cup-shaped iron head.
nice (nīs) [O.F.], *a.* Fastidious, dainty,
scrupulous; discerning, sensitive to
minute differences; delicate, subtle,
minute; (*colloq.*) pleasing, toothsome;
delightful, attractive, friendly, kind.
nicely, *adv.* **niceness,** *n.* **nicety** (nī'sé-ti),
n. Exactness; a minute point, a delicate
distinction.
niche (nich) [It. *nicchia*], *n.* A recess in a
wall for a statue, etc.; (*fig.*) one's proper
place or natural position.
nick (nik) [?], *n.* A small notch, etc., esp.
used as a guide, or a score for keeping
account. *v.t.* To make a nick or nicks
in; to snip, to cut.
nickel (nikl) [Swed.], *n.* A lustrous
silvery-white ductile metal; a U.S. five-
cent piece. *v.t.* To coat with nickel.
nickel-silver, *n.* An alloy like German
silver but containing more nickel.
nick-name (nik'nām) [M.E. *ekename*(eke,
name)], *n.* A name given in derision or
familiarity. *v.t.* To give a nick-name to.
nicotine (nik'ó-tēn) [Jean *Nicot* (1530-
1600), who introduced tobacco into
France], *n.* A poisonous alkaloid contained in tobacco.
niece (nēs) [O.F. *nièce*], *n.* The daughter
of one's brother or sister.
niggard (nig' árd) [?], *n.* A stingy person,
a miser. *a.* Miserly, mean, parsimonious.
niggle (nigl) [?], *v.i.* To busy oneself with
petty details; to trifle. **niggling,** *a.* and *n.*
nigh (nī) [A.-S. *néah*], *adv.* Near; almost.
a. Near; closely related. *prep.* Near,
close to.
night (nīt) [A.-S. *niht*], *n.* The time of
darkness from sunset to sunrise; the
darkness of this period; nightfall; a
period or state of darkness; (*fig.*)
ignorance, intellectual and moral darkness. **night-fall,** *n.* The beginning of
night, the coming of darkness; dusk.
night-glass, *n.* A telescope enabling one
to see objects at night. **night-jar,** *n.*
The goatsucker. **night-light,** *n.* A short
thick candle for keeping alight at night.
nightmare, *n.* A terrifying dream
accompanied with pressure on the chest
and a feeling of powerlessness; (*fig.*)
a haunting sense of dread. **nightshade,**
n. One of several plants, esp. *Atropa
belladonna.* **nightly,** *a.*

nightingale (nī′ting-gāl) [A.-S. *nihtegale*], *n.* A small migratory bird, singing at night as well as by day.

nigrescent (nī-, nī-gres′ĕnt) [L. *nigrescens*, growing black], *adj.* Growing black.

nihilism (nī′hil-izm) [L. *nihil*, nothing], *n.* Any doctrine of a negative kind; (*Phil.*) denial of all existence, or of the knowledge of all existence; (*Polit.*) a form of anarchism aiming at subversion of all existing institutions. ni′hilist, *n.* nihilis′tic, *a.*

nil (nil) [L., contr. of *nihil*], *n.* Nothing.

nimble (nimbl) [A.-S. *numol*], *a.* Light and quick in motion; agile; alert, brisk.

nimbus (nim′bŭs) [L., cloud], *n.* (*pl.* -buses) A halo surrounding the heads of divine or sacred personages in paintings.

niminy-piminy (nim′i-ni-pim′i-ni) [imit.], *a.* Affecting niceness; mincing.

nincompoop (nin′kŏm-poop) [?], *n.* A blockhead.

nine (nīn) [A.-S. *nigon*], *a.* Containing eight and one. *n.* The number composed of eight and one, 9, ix. the Nine: The Muses. ninepins, *n.* A game with nine skittles set up to be bowled at. ninefold, *a.* Nine times repeated. nineteen, *a.* and *n.* One more than eighteen; 19, xix. nineteenth, *a.* ninety, *a.* and *n.* Nine times ten; 90, xc. ninetieth, *a.*

ninny (nin′i) [?], *n.* A fool, a simpleton.

ninth (ninth), *a.* Next after the eighth. *n.* One of nine equal parts.

nip (1) (nip) [?], *v.t.* To pinch, to compress sharply; to cut or pinch off the point of; (*fig.*) to check the growth of; to wither; to benumb. *v.i.* To cause pain; (*slang*) to move quickly (in, out, etc.). *n.* A pinch, a sharp squeeze or compression; a bite; (*fig.*) a check, as by frost; a sarcasm. nipper, *n.* One who or that which nips; a device for seizing and holding; a horse's incisor; the great claw of a crustacean; (*Slang*) a boy; (*pl.*) a pair of pincers. nippy, *a.*

nip (2) [?], *n.* A small drink, esp. of spirits. *v.* To take a nip or nips.

nipple (nipl) [?], *n.* The small prominence in the breast of female mammals by which milk is drawn, a teat.

nit (nit) [A.-S. *hnitu*], *n.* The egg of a louse or other small insect.

nitrate (nī′trăt), *a.* A salt of nitric acid; sodium or potassium nitrate.

nitre (nī′tẽr) [Gr. *nitron*], *n.* Saltpetre, potassium nitrate. nitric, *a.*

nitro-, *comb. form.* nitro-compound, *n.* A compound obtained by treatment with nitric acid. nitro-glycerine, *n.* A highly explosive oil, obtained by adding glycerine to a mixture of nitric and sulphuric acids.

nitrogen (nī′trŏ-jĕn), *n.* A colourless, tasteless, gaseous element forming fourfifths of the atmosphere, the basis of nitre and nitric acid.

nizam (ni-zam′) [Hind.], *n.* The title of the ruler of Hyderabad.

no (nŏ) [A.-S. *nā*], *adv.* A word of denial or refusal, the categorical negative; not; (*with comp.*) not at all. *n.* (*pl.* noes) The word "no"; a negative; (*pl.*) voters against a motion. *a.* Not any; not one;

quite opposite or the reverse; absent, lacking. *adv.* Not (usu. at end of sentence with *or*).

Nobel Prizes (nŏ-bel′) [A. *Nobel*], *n.pl.* Prizes for excellence in various branches of learning and the furtherance of peace.

nobility (nŏ-bil′i-ti), *n.* The quality of being noble; magnanimity, dignity; nobleness of birth; the peerage.

noble (nŏbl) [L. *nŏbilis*], *a.* Lofty in character, worth, or dignity; highminded, morally elevated; of high rank; belonging to the nobility; stately, splendid; fine, admirable. *n.* A nobleman; an obsolete gold coin worth usu. 6s. 8d. nobleman, *n.* A peer. nobly, *adv.*

nobody (nŏ′bŏ-di), *n.* No one, no person; (*fig.*) a person of no importance.

noct-, nocti- [L. *nox noctis*, night], *comb. form.* Nocturnal; by night. noctambulism (nok-tăm′bū-lizm) [L. *ambulāre*, to walk, -ISM], *a.* Night-walking, somnambulism. noctam′bulist, *n.* noctur′nal, *a.* Relating to, occurring, or active by night. nocturnally, *adv.* noc′turne, *n.* A painting, piece of music, etc., in some way expressive of night.

nod (nod) [?], *v.i.* To incline the head in token of assent, salutation, etc.; to let the head fall forward; to be drowsy. *v.t.* To bend or incline (the head, etc.); to signify thus. *n.* A quick bend of the head.

noddle (nodl) [?], *n.* (*contemp.*) The head.

noddy (nod′i), *n.* A simpleton, a fool; a tropical sea-bird.

node (nŏd) [L. *nodus*, a knot], *n.* A knot, knob; the point at which the orbit of a planet intersects the ecliptic, or in which two great circles of the celestial sphere intersect. nod′ule, *n.* A small node or lump.

noggin (nog′in) [?], *n.* A small wooden mug; a measure, usu. a gill; its contents.

noise (noiz) [F.], *n.* A sound of any kind, esp. a loud or disagreeable one; clamour. din. *v.t.* To make public. noiseless, *a.*

noisome (noi′sŏm), *a.* Hurtful, noxious.

nomad (nŏm′ăd) [Gr. *nomas*], *n.* One of a wandering tribe, a wanderer. nomad′ic, *a.* nomadically, *adv.*

nomenclature (nŏ′mĕn-klā-chŭr) [L. *nŏmen*, name, *calāre*, to call], *n.* A system of names for the objects of study in any branch of science; a system of terminology.

nominal (nom′i-nál) [L. *nŏmen -inis*, name], *a.* Existing in name only; pertaining to a name or names, or to a noun; (*fig.*) trivial, inconsiderable. nominalism, *n.* The doctrine that general or abstract concepts have no existence but as names or words. nominalist, *n.* nominalis′tic, *a.* nominally, *adv.* In name only.

nominate (nom′i-năt), *v.t.* To name, to mention by name; to appoint; to propose as a candidate; to denominate. nomina′-tion, *n.* nom′inator, *n.* nominee′, *n.* One who is nominated; one proposed for office, etc.

nominative (nom′i-nă-tiv), *a.* (*Gram.*) Applied to the case of the subject. *n.* The case of the subject; the subject of the verb.

non- [L., not], *pref.* Signifying negation, failure to do or refraining from doing (as *non-attendance*, *non-compliance*); person, etc., that is not the thing mentioned (*non-combatant*, *non-metallic*), something or someone unconnected with (*non-party*, *non-unionist*), etc. **noncombatant**, *a.* Not in the fighting line. *n.* A civilian, esp. a surgeon, chaplain, etc., attached to troops. **non-commissioned**, *a.* Not holding a commission, applied to all military officers below the rank of lieutenant. **non-committal**, *n.* Refusal to pledge oneself; the state of not being committed to either side. *a.* Impartial. **non-conducting**, *a.* Not conducting heat or electricity. **nonconductor**, *n.* **non-juror**, *n.* One who would not swear allegiance to William and Mary in 1689.

nonage (nŏ'nåj, non'åj), *n.* The state of being under age; minority.

nonagenarian (non-å-jė-når'i-ån) [L. *nōnāgēnī*, ninety each], *a.* Ninety years old. *n.* A person between 90 and 100.

nonagon (non'å-gŏn) [L. *nōnus*, ninth], *n.* A figure having 9 sides and 9 angles.

nonce (nons) [*for then once*, read as *for the nonce*], *n.* The present time, occasion, etc.

nonchalant (non'shå-lånt) [L. *calere*, to glow], *a.* Careless, unmoved, indifferent. **nonchalance**, *n.*

Nonconformist (non-kŏn-fôr'mist), *n.* One who does not conform, esp. a member of a Protestant sect dissenting from the Church of England. **nonconformity**, *n.*

nondescript (non'dė-skript) [L. *descriptus*, described], *a.* Not easily classified; neither one thing nor another, hybrid. *n.* Such a person or thing.

none (nŭn) [A.-S. *nān*], *pron.* No one, no person; not any. *a.* No, not any. *adv.* In no respect; by no amount.

nonentity (non-en'ti-ti), *n.* Non-existence; a mere figment, an imaginary or unimportant person or thing.

nonesuch (nŭn'sŭch), *n.* One who or that which is without an equal, a paragon.

nonpareil (non-på-rel') [F. *pareil*, L. *par*, equal], *a.* Having no equal; unique. *n.* A thing of unequalled excellence; a variety of apple; (non'på-rėl) a small size of type.

nonplus (non'plŭs) [L. *nōn plūs*, no more], *n.* A state of perplexity; a quandary. *v.t.* To puzzle, confound, bewilder.

nonsense (non'sėns), *n.* Unmeaning words, ideas, etc.; foolish talk or conduct; absurdity; rubbish.

nonsuit (non'sūt), *n.* Stoppage of a suit during trial through insufficient evidence or non-appearance of plaintiff. *v.t.* To subject to a nonsuit.

noodle (noodl) [?], *n.* A simpleton, fool; *pl.* short strips of flour and water paste.

nook (nuk) [?], *n.* A corner; a cozy place, a secluded retreat.

noon (noon) [L. *nōna* (*hōra*), ninth (hour)], *n.* The middle of the day, twelve o'clock. *a.* Pertaining to noon. **noonday**, *n.* and *a.* **noontide**, *n.*

noose (noos) [?], *n.* A loop with a running knot binding the closer the more it is pulled, a snare.

nor (nôr) [short for A.-S. *nāhwœther*], *conj.* And not (marking a subsequent part of a negative proposition); occasionally used without the correlative.

norm (nôrm) [L. *norma*, carpenter's square], *n.* A standard, pattern, type. **normal**, *a.* According to rule or standard; regular, typical; (*Geom.*) perpendicular. *n.* The usual state, quality, quantity, etc. **normality**, *n.* **normally**, *adv.*

Norman (nôr'mån) [Teut., NORTHMAN], *n.* A native or inhabitant of Normandy; a member of a mixed race of Northmen and Franks established there. *a.* Pertaining to Normandy or the Normans.

Norse (nôrs), *a.* Pertaining to Norway or its inhabitants, Norwegian. *n.* The Norwegian language, or the Scandinavian languages, including early Swedish and Danish. **Norseman**, *n.*

north (nôrth) [A.-S.], *n.* The cardinal point to the right of a person facing the setting sun at the equinox; a region north of any given point; the northern part (of any country); the north wind. *a.* Situated in or towards the north; northern. *adv.* Towards or in the north. *v.* To veer or steer to the north. **north-east, -west**, *n.* The point midway between the north and east, or north and west, a region lying in this quarter. *a.* Pertaining to or proceeding from the north-east, etc. **north-easter**, *n.* A north-east wind. **north-easterly**, *a.* **north-eastern**, *a.* In or towards this. **north-eastward**, *a.* **north-man**, *n.* An inhabitant of the north of Europe, esp. of Scandinavia. **north-star**, *n.* The pole-star. **north-west, -wester**, etc. **northerly** (nôr'thėr-li), *a.* and *adv.* **northern**, *a.* **northern lights:** The aurora borealis. **northerner**, *n.* A native or inhabitant of the north. **northernmost**, *a.* **northing** (nôr'thing), *n.* The distance or progress in a northward direction. **northward**, *a., adv.,* and *n.* **northwardly**, *a.* and *adv.* **nor'-wester**, *n.* A wind from the north-west.

Norwegian (nôr-wē'jån), *a.* Pertaining to Norway or its inhabitants. *n.* A native of Norway; the language.

nose (nōz) [A.-S. *nosu*], *n.* The projecting part of the face containing the nostrils and the organ of smell; the power of smelling; a part resembling a nose, as a nozzle, beak, prow, etc. *v.t.* To perceive or detect by smelling; (*fig.*) to find out; to push (one's way). *v.i.* To smell; (*fig.*) to search, to pry; to push ahead. **nose-bag**, *n.* A bag containing provender for hanging over a horse's head. **nosegay**, *n.* A bunch of flowers, esp. fragrant ones.

nostalgia (nos-tăl'ji-å) [Gr. *nostos*, return, *algos*, pain], *n.* Morbid longing for home; home-sickness.

nostril (nos'tril) [A.-S. *nosthyrl*], *n.* One of the apertures of the nose.

nostrum (nos'trŭm) [L., neut. of *noster*, our], *n.* (*pl.* -ums) A medicine based on a secret formula; a quack remedy.

not (not), *adv.* Expressing negation, denial, prohibition, or refusal.

notable (nō'tåbl), *a.* Worthy of note; remarkable, distinguished; excellent, capable. *n.* A person or thing of note or distinction. notability, *n.*

notary (nō'tár-ĭ) [A.-F. *notarie*], *n.* A public official appointed to attest deeds, contracts, etc., administer oaths, etc., frequently called a notary public. notarial (no-târ'ĭ-ăl), *a.*

notation (nō-tā'shŭn), *n.* Act or process of representing by signs, figures, etc.

notch (noch) [F. *oche*, through *an oche*], *n.* A nick, a cut, a V-shaped indentation. *v.t.* To cut a notch in; to score by notches.

note (nōt) [L. *nota*, a mark (whence *notāre*, to mark)], *n.* A sign, mark, or token; a memorandum, a short letter; a diplomatic communication; a written promise to pay money; an annotation or explanation; a musical sound; (*fig.*) a significant sound or mode of expression; a key in a piano, etc. *v.t.* To observe, take notice of; to make a memorandum of; to annotate. notebook, *n.* note-paper, *n.* noted, *a.* Eminent, remarkable. noteworthy, *a.*

nothing (nŭth'ĭng), *n.* Not anything. .naught. *adv.* In no degree, in no way, not at all.

notice (nō'tĭs) [L. *nōtus* known], *n.* Information, warning; a paper giving information or directions; an account of something in a newspaper, etc., a review; regard, attention; the act of noting. *v.t.* To take notice of, to perceive; to remark upon. noticeable, *a.*

notify (nō'tĭ-fī), *v.t.* To make known, declare, publish; to give notice to, to inform (of or that). notifiable, *a.* To be notified (esp. of disease). notifica'tion, *n.*

·**notion** (nō'shŭn), *n.* An idea; an opinion; a theory, scheme, device; (*colloq.*) an intention or whim. notional, *a.* Pertaining to notions or concepts; abstracts speculative, ideal; given to whims, fanciful.

notorious (nō-tôr'ĭ-ŭs), *a.* Widely or commonly known (now only in a bad sense). notori'ety, *n.*

notwithstanding (not-wĭth-stăn'dĭng), *prep.* In spite of, despite. *adv.* Nevertheless.

nougat (noo'ga) [Sp. *nogado*], *n.* A confection of almonds and sugar.

noumenon (nou'mē-non) [Gr. *nooumenon*, apprehending], *n.* (*pl.* -mena) The substance underlying a phenomenon; an object or the conception of an object as it is in itself, or as it appears to pure thought.

noun (noun) [A.-F., L. *nōmen*, name], *n.* A word used as the name of anything, a substantive.

nourish (nŭr'ĭsh) [L. *nutrīre*], *v.t.* To feed, support; to cherish; to nurse. nourishment, *n.*

nous (nous) [Gr.], *n.* Mind, intellect; sense.

novel (nov'ĕl) [L. *novus*, new], *a.* New, fresh; strange. *n.* A fictitious prose narrative portraying characters and actions from real life; this type of literature. novelette, *n.* A short novel, usu. a love story. novelist, *n.* A writer of novels. novelty, *n.* Newness, freshness; something new.

November (nō-vem'bẽr) [L., from *novem*, nine], *n.* The eleventh month, the ninth of the Roman year.

novice (nov'ĭs) [L. *novus*, new], *n.* One entering a religious house on probation; one who is new to any business, a beginner. noviciate (nō-vish'ĭ-ăt), *n.* A term of probation or apprenticeship.

now (nou) [A.-S. *nu*], *adv.* At the present time; forthwith, immediately; very recently; then (in narrative); in these circumstances; used as an expletive in explaining, threatening, etc. *conj.* Since being the case (that). *n.* The present time. nowadays, *adv.* At the present time; in these days. *n.* The present time.

nowhere (nō'hwâr), *adv.* Not in, at, or to any place or state.

noxious (nok'shŭs) [L. *noxa*, harm], *a.* Hurtful, unwholesome; pernicious.

nozzle (nozl), *n.* A spout, projecting mouthpiece, of pipe or hose.

nuance (nū-ans) [F.], *n.* A delicate gradation in colour or tone; a nice distinction.

nubile (nū'bĭl) [L. *nūbere*, to marry], *a.* Marriageable (usu. of women).

nucleus (nū'klē-ŭs) [L., from *nucula*, dim. of *nux*], *n.* (*pl.* -clei) A central part about which growth goes on; a kernel; (*fig.*) a centre of activity; the head of a comet. nuclear, *a.* nuclear fission, *n.* The breakdown of an atomic nucleus into nuclei of lower atomic number, with conversion of part of its mass into energy. nucleate (nū'klē-āt), *v.* To form into or form a nucleus. *a.* Having a nucleus.

nude (nūd) [L. *nūdus*], *a.* Naked, undraped. *n.* An undraped figure in painting or sculpture. nu'dity, *n.*

nudge (nŭj) [?], *v.t.* To push gently, as with the elbow; to hint with or as with this. *n.* Such a push.

nugatory (nū'gă-tŏr-ĭ) [L. *nugæ*, trifles], *a.* Trifling, insignificant; futile, ineffective.

nugget (nŭg'ĕt) [?], *n.* A lump of native metal, esp. gold.

nuisance (nū'sáns) [O.F., from L. *nocēre*, to injure], *n.* Anything that annoys or irritates; an offensive or disagreeable person, action, experience, etc.

null (nŭl) [L. *nullus*], *a.* Void, having no legal force or validity; (*fig.*) without character or individuality.

nullify (nŭl-ĭ-fī), *v.t.* To make void; to cancel, to invalidate. nullifica'tion, *n.* nul'lity, *n.*

numb (nŭm) [A.-S. *num*], *a.* Deprived of sensation and motion; torpid, stupefied. *v.t.* To benumb, to paralyse.

number (nŭm'bẽr) [L. *numerus*], *n.* A measure of discrete quantity; a name or symbol representing such a numeral; a sum or aggregate of persons, things, etc.; one of a numbered series; a single issue of a periodical, etc.; poetical measure, rhythm (*often in pl.*); plurality, multitude (*usu. in pl.*); (*Gram.*) the distinctive form of a word according as it denotes unity or plurality. *v.t.* To count, to ascertain the number of; to amount to; to assign a number to; to include. numberless, *a.* Innumerable.

numeral (nū'mẽr-ăl), *a.* Pertaining to, consisting of, or denoting number. *n.* A word, symbol or group of symbols denoting number. numerable, *a.* numera'tion, *n.* Act or art of numbering.

nu'merator, n. One who numbers, the part of a vulgar fraction above the line indicating how many parts are taken. numer'ical, a. Pertaining to number; consisting of numbers. nu'merous, a. Many in number.

numismatic (nū-miz-măt'ik) [Gr. nomizein, to have in current use], a. Pertaining to coins or coinage. numismatics, n. The science or study of coins and medals.

numskull (nŭm'skŭl), n. A blockhead.

nun (nŭn) [A.-S. nunne], n. A woman devoted to a religious life and living in a convent under vows. nun's veiling: A soft, thin, woollen dress-stuff. nunnery, n. A religious home for women.

nuncio (nŭn'ku-pā-tiv) [L. nuncius, messenger], n. A papal ambassador at a foreign court.

nuncupative (nŭn'kū-pā-tiv) [L. nuncupāre (nōmen, name, capere, to take)], a. Oral, not written, esp. of a will or legacy.

nuptial (nŭp'shăl) [L. nuptiæ, wedding, from nuptus, married], a. Pertaining to a wedding. n.pl. A wedding.

nurse (nĕrs) [L. nūtricia], n. A woman employed to suckle the child of another (wet-nurse), or to have the care of young children (dry-nurse); one who tends the sick, wounded, or infirm; one who or that which fosters or promotes. v.t. To suckle; to hold or clasp, esp. on one's lap; to rear; to foster, tend, promote growth in; to tend in sickness; to manage with care; to cherish; to economize. nursery, n. A room for young children; a place for rearing plants; a race for two-year-old horses. nursery-maid, n. A girl in charge of young children. nurseryman, n. One who raises plants in a nursery. nursling, n. An infant, esp. in relation to the one who nurses it.

nurture (nĕr'tyūr), n. Act of bringing up, training, fostering; nourishment; education, breeding. v.t. To nourish, to rear, train.

nut (nŭt) [A.-S. hnutu], n. A fruit containing a kernel in a hard shell; a metal block for screwing on a bolt, etc.; various parts of machinery, usu. in which a screw works; (pl.) small lumps of coal. nut-brown, a. Brown as a hazel-nut long kept. nutcracker, n. (usu. pl.) An instrument for cracking nuts; a bird. nut-hatch, n. A small bird allied to the woodpecker. nutshell, n. The hard shell enclosing the kernel of a nut.

nutmeg (nŭt'meg) [med. L. nux muscāta, musk-like nut], n. The hard aromatic seed of a Malayan tree, used for flavouring and in medicine.

nutrient (nū'tri-ĕnt) [L. nūtriens], a. Nourishing; serving as or conveying nourishment. n. A nutritious substance. nutriment, n. nutrimen'tal, a. nutri'tion, n. nutri'tious, a. Efficient as food.

nuzzle (nŭzl), v.t. To rub the nose against; to fondle.

nylon (nī'lon), n. A group of plastics used largely for hosiery, etc.

nymph (nimf) [Gr. numphē, bride], n. (Myth.) One of a class of youthful female divinities inhabiting groves, springs, the sea, etc.; (fig.) a beautiful young woman. nymphe'an, a.

O

O, oh (ō), int. An exclamation of earnest or solemn address, entreaty, invocation, surprise, etc.

oaf (ōf) [Icel. álfr], n. (pl. oafs) A changeling left by fairies; a stupid person, a lout. oafish, a.

oak (ōk) [A.-S. āc], n. A forest tree much valued for its timber; the wood of this; (Univ.) the outer door of a set of rooms. oak-apple, -gall, n. An excrescence produced on oaks by various gall-flies. oaken, a.

oakum (ō'kŭm) [A.-S. ācumba, tow], n. Old rope, untwisted and pulled into loose fibres, used for caulking seams, etc.

oar (ōr) [A.-S. ār], n. A long pole with a flattened blade, for rowing a boat; an oarsman. v.t. To propel by rowing. oarsman, n. A rower.

oasis (ō-ā'sis) [L. and Gr., prob from Egyptian], n. (pl. -ses) A fertile spot in a waste or desert.

oast (ōst) [A.-S. āst], n. A kiln for drying hops.

oat (ōt) [A.-S. āte], n. (usu. in pl.) A cereal plant; (pl.) its grain, used for food. oatcake, n. oatmeal, n. oaten, a.

oath (ōth) [A.-S. āth], n. A solemn appeal to God in witness of the truth of a statement, etc.; an attestation made according to prescribed forms; a profane imprecation or expletive, a curse.

ob- [L., in the way of, against], pref. Toward, to meeting, in facing; against-opposing, hindering, resisting, hostile; reversely, obversely, contrary to the normal; as in object, objurgate, oblique.

obbligato (ob-li-ga'tō) [It., as OBLIGE], n. (Mus.) An instrumental part or accompaniment.

obdurate (ob'dū-răt) [L. dūrāre, to harden], a. Hardened in heart, esp. against moral influence; impenitent. obduracy, n. obdurately, adv.

obedience (ō-bē'di-ĕns) [L. obēdientia], n. Act or practice of obeying; submission to authority; act of being obeyed. obedient, a.

obeisance (ō-bā'săns) [F. obéissance], n. A bow, a gesture signifying deference, submission, or respect; homage.

obelisk (ob'ē-lisk) [Gr. obelos, a spit], n. A quadrangular tapering stone shaft, with a pyramidal apex; (Print.) the dagger (†), a reference mark.

obese (ō-bēs') [L. obēsus (L. edere, to eat)], a. Fat, fleshy, corpulent. obes'ity, n. The state of being fat.

obey (ō-bā') [L. obēdīre], v.t. To perform or carry out (a command, etc.); to be obedient to; to act according to. v.i. To do what one is directed or commanded.

obfuscate (ob-fŭs'kāt) [L. fuscāre, from fuscus, dark], v.t. To darken, to obscure; to bewilder. obfusca'tion, n.

obit (ob'it, ō'bit) [L. obitus], n. Death, decease; a service for the soul of a deceased person on the anniversary of his death; a funeral ceremony. obit'uary, a. Relating to a death. n. An account of a person deceased.

object (ob-jekt') [OB-, L. jacere, to throw],

v.t. To oppose; to allege (a fact) in criticism, disapproval, etc. *v.i.* To make objections; to disapprove. *n.* (ob'jĕkt) Anything presented to the senses or the mind; a material thing; aim, ultimate purpose; (*Gram.*) a noun, or phrase, etc., equivalent to a noun, governed by a transitive verb or preposition; (*Phil.*) the correlative to the subjective, an external as distinct from the ego. **object-lesson,** *n.* A lesson in which the actual object described or a representation of it is used for illustration. **objection,** *n.* Act of objecting; an adverse reason or statement; disapproval, dislike. **objectionable,** *a.* Reprehensible; offensive, unpleasant. **objective,** *a.* Proceeding from the object of knowledge or thought as dist. from the perceiving or thinking subject; external, actual, real; pertaining to outward things as dist. from thoughts or feelings; (*Gram.*) denoting the case of the object of a transitive verb or preposition. *n.* An objective point; a point aimed at; the case governed by a transitive verb or a preposition. **objectiv'ity,** *n.*

objurgate (ob'jŭr-gāt) [L. *jurgāre*, to chide], *v.t.* To chide; to reprove. **objurga'tion,** *n.*

oblate (1) (ob-lāt') [L. *lātus*, carried], *a.* Flattened at the poles, opp. to prolate.

oblate (2), *n.* One not under vows but dedicated to a religious life.

oblation (ob-lā'shŭn), *n.* Act of offering or anything offered in worship or as a sacrifice; a donation to the Church.

obligation (ob-li-gā'shŭn), *n.* The binding power of a promise, contract, etc.; one's duty towards one's fellow-men; indebtedness for some benefit, etc.; one with a penal condition. **ob'ligate,** *v.t.* **ob'ligatory,** *a.*

oblige (ŏ-blīj') [L. *ligāre*, to bind], *v.t.* To bind by legal, moral, or physical force; to be binding on; to place under a debt of gratitude; to do a favour to. *v.i.* To be obliging. **obliging,** *a.* Kind, complaisant, imposing obligation.

oblique (ob-lēk') [L. *oblīquus*], *a.* Slanting; deviating from the direct line, round-about; (*Geom.*) inclined at an angle other than a right angle. **oblique oration:** Statements put into reported form, with the consequent changes of person, tense, etc. **obliq'uity,** *n.* State of being oblique; deviation from moral rectitude.

obliterate (ŏb-lit'ĕr-āt) [L. *litera*, letter], *v.t.* To efface, to erase; to wear out. **oblitera'tion,** *n.*

oblivion (ŏb-liv'i-ŏn) [L. *livisci*, to forget], *n.* Forgetfulness, disregard; state of being forgotten. **obliv'ious,** *a.*

oblong (ob'long), *a.* Longer than broad, esp. if rectangular; elliptical (of leaves). *n.* An oblong figure or thing.

obloquy (ob'lŏ-kwi) [L. *loqui*, to speak], *n.* Abusive or reproachful language; disgrace, infamy.

obnoxious (ob-nok'shŭs) [L. *noxa*, harm], *a.* Offensive, objectionable.

oboe (ō'boi) [It.], *n.* An hautboy, a wind-instrument of wood played through a double reed.

obolus (ob'ŏ-lŭs) [Gr. *obolos*], *n.* (*pl.* -li) A small coin of ancient Greece.

obscene (ŏb-sēn') [L. *obscēnus*], *a.* Vile, loathsome; indecent, unchaste. **obscenity** (ob-sen'i-ti), *n.*

obscurant (ob-skūr'ănt), *n.* An opponent of intellectual progress. **obscurantism,** *n.*

obscure (ŏb-skūr') [L. *obscurus*], *a.* Dim; indefinite, indistinct; abstruse; doubtful; secluded, remote from observation; unknown, lowly. *v.t.* To make dark; to make less intelligible, visible, or legible; to outshine. **obscura'tion,** *n.* **obscurely,** *adv.*

obsequies (ob'sĕ-kwiz) [A.-F. *obsequie*], *n.pl.* Funeral rites.

obsequious (ob-sē'kwi-ŭs) [L. *sequi*, to follow], *a.* Servile, cringing.

observe (ŏb-zerv') [L. *servāre*, to heed], *v.t.* To regard attentively, to note, perceive; to scrutinize; to follow attentively; to perform duly; to celebrate; to remark. *v.i.* To make a remark (upon). **observable,** *a.* **observer,** *n.* **observance,** *n.* Act of observing, complying with, keeping, following, performing, etc.; a customary rite; a rule of practice, esp. in a religious order. **obser'vant,** *a.* Watchful, attentive; quick in observing rules, etc. **observa'tion,** *n.* **obser'vatory,** *n.* A building for observation of astronomical phenomena.

obsess (ob-ses') [L. *obsessus*, besieged], *v.t.* To haunt, to trouble (as an evil spirit); to preoccupy the mind of. **obsession** (-sesh'ŭn), *n.*

obsidian (ob-sid'i-ăn) [L. *obsidianus*], *n.* A black or dark-coloured stone used by primitive peoples for making implements.

obsolescent (ob-sŏ-les'ĕnt) [L. *obsolescens*, beginning to be accustomed], *a.* Becoming obsolete. **obsolescence,** *n.* **obsolete** (ob'sŏ-lĕt), *a.* Passed out of use.

obstacle (ob'stăkl) [L. *obstāculum*], *n.* An impediment, an obstruction.

obstetric, -al (ob-stet'rik, -ăl) [L. *obstetrix*, midwife], *a.* Pertaining to midwifery or childbirth; (*pl.*) midwifery.

obstinate (ob'sti-năt) [L. *obstinātus*], *a.* Pertinaciously adhering to one's opinion or purpose, stubborn; (*Med.*) not yielding easily to remedies. **obstinacy,** *n.*

obstreperous (ob-strep'ĕr-ŭs) [L. *strepere*, to make a noise], *a.* Noisy, clamorous; boisterous, unruly.

obstruct (ob-strŭkt') [L. *struere, structus,* built], *v.t.* To block up; to hinder, impede; to check, retard, stop. *v.i.* To practise obstruction, esp. in Parliament. **obstruction,** *n.* **obstructionist,** *n.* **obstructive,** *a.*

obtain (ŏb-tān') [L. *tenēre*, to hold], *v.t.* To gain, acquire, secure; to get; to reach. *v.i.* To be prevalent or in vogue. **obtainable,** *a.*

obtrude (ŏb-trood') [L. *trūdere*, to thrust], *v.t.* To thrust in or upon. *v.i.* To enter without right. **obtrusion,** *n.* **obtrusive,** *a.* **obtrusively,** *adv.*

obtuse (ob-tūs') [L. *tūsus*, beaten], *a.* Blunt, not acute; denoting an angle larger than a right angle; (*fig.*) dull, stupid.

obverse (ob'vĕrs) [L. *versus*, turned], *a.* Turned towards one (of a coin or medal bearing the head). *n.* The front; the side of a coin, etc., bearing the main device.

obviate (ob'vi-āt) [L. *via*, way], *v.t.* To clear away, overcome, neutralize (as dangers, difficulties, etc.). **obviation,** *n.*

obvious (ob'vi-ŭs) [L. *ob viam*, in the way], *a.* Plain to the eye, immediately evident.

oc- [OB-, before *c*], *pref.*

occasion (ŏ-kā'zhŭn) [L. *occāsio*], *n.* An opportunity, reason, or motive for doing something; motive, ground; an incidental cause; a time or occurrence having special interest. *v.t.* To cause; to be the incidental cause of. **occasional,** *a.* Happening, done, etc., as opportunity arises; not at fixed intervals; incidental, casual.

Occident (ok'si-dĕnt) [L. *occidens*], *n.* The west; the western quarter of the sky as the region of sunset. **Occidental,** *a.* Western.

occiput (ok'si-pŭt) [L. *occiput*], *n.* The back part of the head. **occip'ital,** *a.*

occult (ŏ-kŭlt') [L. *occultus*], *a.* Concealed, esoteric; beyond the range of ordinary knowledge or perception. **occultism,** *n.*

occupy (ok'ū-pī) [L. *capere*, to take], *v.t.* To take or hold in possession, to be the tenant of; to take up, to fill; to give occupation to; to employ (oneself, or in p.p.). **occupant, occupier,** *n.* A tenant as dist. from an owner; one who establishes a claim by taking possession. **occupancy,** *n.* **occupa'tion,** *n.* Act of occupying, or taking possession; occupancy, tenure; the state of being employed or engaged; business, calling. **occupational therapy,** *n.* (*Med.*) The treatment of mental and other diseases by providing instruction in an occupation or hobby.

occur (ŏ-kĕr') [L. *currere*, to run], *v.i.* To happen to take place; to be met with; to present itself to the mind. **occurrence** (ŏ-kŭr'ĕns), *n.* An event.

ocean (ō'shăn) [Gr. *ōkeanos*], *n.* The vast body of water covering about two-thirds of the surface of the globe; any one of its five principal divisions; (*fig.*) an immense quantity. *a.* Pertaining to the ocean. **ocean'ic,** *a.* Pertaining to the ocean.

ocelot (ō'sē-lot) [Mex. *ocelotl*], *n.* A small American feline animal, the tiger-cat.

ochre (ō'kĕr) [Gr. *ōchros*, yellow], *n.* A native earth used as a pigment (applied to many metallic oxides); a yellow colour.

oct-, octa-, octo- [Gr. *oktō*, eight], *comb. form.* Having or consisting of eight. **octagon** (ok'tă-gon) [Gr. *gōnia*, corner], *n.* A plane figure of eight sides and angles; any object of this shape. **octag'onal,** *a.* **octahedron** (-hē'-drŏn) [Gr. *hedra*, base], *n.* (*pl.* **-dra**) A solid figure contained by eight plane faces, usu. by triangles. **octane,** *n.* (*Chem.*) A hydrocarbon of the paraffin series. **octang'ular,** *a.* Having eight angles.

octave (ok'tāv) [L. *octavus*, eighth], *n.* The 8th day after a church festival, the festival itself being counted; (*Mus.*) the interval between any note and that produced by twice or half as many vibra-tions per second; the first eight lines of a sonnet; a stanza of eight lines. **octavo** (ok-tā'vō), *n.* (*pl.* **-vos**) A book in which a sheet is folded into 8 leaves or 16 pages; the size of such book or paper (8vo). *a.* Of this size. **octen'nial** (ok-ten'i-ål) [L. *annus*, year], *a.* Recurring every 8th year; lasting 8 years.

October (ok-tō'bĕr) [L.], *n.* The 10th month of the modern, the 8th of the Roman year.

octogenarian (oktŏ-jĕ-nâr'i-ån), *n.* One who is 80 years old or between 80 and 90. *a.* Pertaining to this age.

octopus (ok'tŏ'-pŭs) [Gr. *pous*, foot], *n.* A marine creature having 8 arms furnished with suckers, a cuttlefish.

octoroon', *n.* The offspring of a quadroon and a white.

octroi (ok'trwa) [F.], *n.* A tax levied at the gates of some French towns on goods brought in.

ocular (ok'ū-lår) [L. *oculus*, eye], *a.* Pertaining to the eye or eyes, visual; known from actual sight. **ocularly,** *adv.* **oculist,** *n.* One who treats diseases of the eye.

cdalisque (od'å-lisk) [Turk. *ōdalíq*, a chambermaid], *n.* An Oriental slave or concubine.

odd (od) [Icel. *odda-*], *a.* Not even; not exactly divisible by two; wanting a match or pair; strange, eccentric; occasional; indefinite; and more (added to a round number as *two hundred odd*). **Odd Fellow:** A member of an extensive friendly society modelled on the Freemasons. **oddish,** *a.* **oddity,** *n.*

ode (ōd) [Gr.], *n.* A lyric of lofty style, of varied and often irregular metre, usu. in the form of an invocation.

-ode [Gr. *-ōdēs* (*eidos*, form)], *suf.* Denoting a thing resembling or of the nature of.

odious (ō'di-ŭs) [L. *odium*, hatred], *a.* Hateful, repulsive. **odiously,** *adv.* **odiousness,** *n.* **odium,** *n.*

odont-, odonto- [Gr. *odous odontos*, tooth], *comb. form.* Having teeth or processes resembling teeth.

odour (ō'dŏr) [L. *odor*], *n.* Any smell; scent, fragrance; (*fig.*) repute; perfumes. **in bad odour:** In bad repute; out of favour. **odorif'erous,** *a.* Diffusing fragrance. **odorous,** *a.* Having a sweet scent, fragrant. **odourless,** *a.*

œcumenical (ē-kū-men'i-kál) [Gr. *oikoumenē*], *a.* Universal, world-wide, catholic (of councils representing the whole of Christendom).

Œdipus complex (ē'di-pŭs kom'pleks) [*Œdipus*, king of Thebes], *n.* (*Psych.*) A complex entailing excessive love for the parent of the opposite sex.

œsophagus (ē-sof'å-gŭs) [Gr. *oisophagos*], *n.* (*pl.* **-gi** (-jī)) The gullet, the canal by which food passes to the stomach.

of (ov, ŏv) [A.-S.], *prep.* Denoting connexion with or relation to, in situation, origin, motive, agency, possession, inclusion, partition, identity, reference, direction, distance, quality, condition, etc.

of- [OB-, before *f*], *pref.* As in *offence.*

off (awf), *adv.* Away, at a distance or to a distance in space or time; utterly, completely; (*Naut.*) away from the wind. *prep.* From (denoting deviation, separation, etc.). *a.* More distant, farther, opp. to near; right, opp. to left; divergent; subsidiary; contingent; not occupied (as *a day off*). *int.* Away, begone. **off and on:** Intermittently, now and again. **well or badly off:** In good or bad circumstances. **off-hand, off-handed**, *a.* Unpremeditated; without taking care; supercilious.

offal (of'ǎl), *n.* Parts (e.g. heart, kidneys) cut off when a carcass is being jointed; carrion; garbage.

offence (ŏ-fens'), [L. *offensa*], *n.* The act of offending; an affront, an insult; umbrage; a transgression, a misdeed.

offend (ŏ-fend'), [L. *fendere*, to strike], *v.t.* To wound the feelings of, to make angry, to cause displeasure or disgust in; to transgress. *v.i.* To violate any human or divine law; to give offence, to scandalize. **offender**, *n.*

offensive (ŏ-fen'siv), *a.* Pertaining to attack, aggressive; causing offence; irritating, annoying; disagreeable, repulsive. *n.* The attitude, method, or act of attacking. **offensiveness**, *n.*

offer (of'ěr) [A.-S. *offrian*, to sacrifice], *v.t.* To present as an act of worship; to tender for acceptance or refusal; to bid (as a price); to evince readiness (to do something); to attempt; to proffer; to show for sale. *v.i.* To present or show itself, to appear, occur; to make an attempt (at). *n.* Act of offering; an expression of readiness (to); a tender or proposal to be accepted or refused; a price or sum bid; an attempt, an essay. **offering**, *n.* **offertory**, *n.* That part of the Church service during which offerings are made; the offering of oblations; the collection.

office (of'is) [-OF. L. *facere*, to do], *n.* Duty, function, service attaching to a particular post; a post of service, etc., esp. under a public body; a prescribed act of worship; (*Eccles.*) the daily service of the Breviary; an act of help or kindness, duty; a place where business is carried on, a counting-house; (*collect.*) the official staff or organization; (*pl.*) kitchens and other rooms in which domestic duties are discharged; a privy. **officer**, *n.* One holding an office, esp. a Government functionary or minister, or one appointed to a post of authority in the armed forces, by warrant, commission, etc. *v.t.* To furnish with officers; to act as commander of. **official** (ŏ-fish'ǎl), *a.* Pertaining to an office or public duty; duly authorized; characteristic of persons in office. *n.* One who holds a public office. **officialdom, -ism**, *n.* **officially**, *adv.* **officiate**, *v.i.* To perform official duties.

officious (ŏ-fish'ŭs) [as OFFICE], *a.* Forward in serving, meddling, intrusive; (*Diplomacy*) friendly without official authority.

offing (of'ing), *n.* That portion of the sea nearer the horizon than the coast.

offish (of'ish), *a.* Inclined to be reserved, or stiff in manner. **offishness**, *n.*

offset (of'set), *n.* A lateral shoot that

takes root, a scion; a counterbalance, equivalent, compensation.

offshoot (of'shoot), *n.* A branch or shoot from a main stem; (*fig.*) a side-issue.

offspring (of'spring) [A.-S.], *n.* Issue; children, descendants; a result of any kind.

oft (awft) [A.-S.], *adv.* Often.

often (awfn), *adv.* Frequently, many times; in many instances.

ogee (ō-jē'), *n.* (*Arch.*) A moulding with an inner and outer curve like an S.

ogham (og'ǎm) [O.Ir.], *n.* A writing of the ancient Irish and other Celts, derived from the runes; an inscription in this.

ogive (ō'jiv) [F., perh. from Arab. *âwf*, the summit], *n.* A diagonal rib of a vault; a pointed or Gothic arch. **ogi'val**, *a.*

ogle (ōgl) [Teut.], *v.* To look at coquettishly or amorously. *n.* Such a glance.

ogre (ō'gěr) [F.], *n.* A fairy-tale giant living on human flesh; (*fig.*) a monster. **ogreish**, *a.* **ogress**, *n.*

ohm (ōm) [Georg S. *Ohm* (1787–1854), Ger. electrician], *n.* The unit of electrical resistance.

-oid [Gr. *-oeidēs* (-*eidēs*, like)], *comb. form.* Denoting resemblance, as in *cycloid, rhomboid.*

oil (oil) [L. *olea*, olive], *n.* An unctuous liquid obtained from various animal and vegetable substances; (*pl.*) oil-colours. *v.t.* To smear, anoint or treat with oil. **oilcake**, *n.* The refuse after oil is pressed from linseed, etc. **oilcloth**, *n.* A fabric coated with white lead ground in oil; floor-cloth. **oil-colour, n.** A paint made by grinding a pigment in oil. **oiler**, *n.* One who or that which oils; an oil-can for lubricating machinery, etc. **oil-field**, *n.* A region where mineral oil is obtained. **oiliness, n.** **oil-painting**, *n.* The art of painting in oil-colours; a painting in oil-colours. **oilskin**, *n.* Cloth rendered waterproof by treatment with oil; (*pl.*) a suit of such garments. **oily**, *a.*

ointment (oint'měnt), *n.* A soft unctuous preparation for dressing injured parts; a cosmetic.

old (ōld) [A.-S. *eald*], *a.* Not young, fresh, or recent; like an old person, experienced, cunning, confirmed (in); dilapidated; stale with keeping; wonted; effete, out-of-date, matured; of any specified duration; early, previous, former. **of old:** In or from ancient times; long ago. **olden**, *a.* Old, ancient, bygone. **old-fashioned**, *a.*

oleaginous (ō-lĕ-ăj'i-nŭs), *a.* Oily, greasy; (*fig.*) fawning, insinuating.

oleander (ō-lĕ-ăn'děr) [med. L., corr. of RHODODENDRON], *n.* A poisonous evergreen shrub with pink or white flowers.

oleo- [L. *oleum*, oil], *comb. form.* **oleograph** (ō'lĕ-ō-gräf), *n.* A lithographic picture printed in oil-colours.

olfactory (ol-făkt'ŏr-i) [L. *olēre*, to smell, *facere*, to make], *a.* Pertaining to smelling. *n.* (*usu. pl.*) An organ of smell.

oligarch (ol'i-gark) [Gr. *oligos*, small, *archein*, to govern], *n.* A member of an oligarchy. **oligar'chic,** *a.* **oli'garchy**, *n.* Government in which supreme power is in the hands of a small exclusive class.

olive (ol'iv) [L. *olíva*], *n.* An evergreen

tree with fruit yielding oil; the fruit, or wood, of this; a dull, yellowish green or brown colour. olive-branch, *n.* A branch of the olive as an emblem of peace.

olivine (ol'i-vīn), *n.* A variety of chrysolite.

olla podrida (ol-ă pŏ-drē'dȧ), *n.* A dish of meat chopped fine, stewed with vegetables; (*fig.*) an incongruous mixture.

Olympian (ō-lim'pi-ȧn) [Gr. *olumpias -ados*, pertaining to *Olumpos*], *a.* Pertaining to Mount Olympus, the home of the gods; lofty, superb. *n.* A dweller in Olympus; one of the Greek gods. Olympic, *a.* Olympic games, *n.pl.* The greatest of the ancient Greek national games, held every 4 years; festival of sport revived in 1900.

omega (ō'mē-gȧ) [Gr., the great *o*], *n.* The last letter of the Greek alphabet; (*fig.*) the end, the last phase.

omelet (om'lĕt) [F. *omelette*], *n.* A kind of pancake made with eggs, flour, milk, etc.

omen (ō'mĕn) [L.], *n.* An incident, appearance, etc., taken as indicating a good or evil fortune.

ominous (om'i-nŭs), *a.* Portending evil; inauspicious.

omit (ō-mit') [L. *mittere*, to send], *v.t.* To leave out; not to insert or mention; to neglect. omission (ō-mish'ŭn), *n.*

omni- [L. *omnis*, all], *comb. form.* Universally, in all ways, of all things.

omnibus (om'ni-bŭs) [L., for all], *n.* A long four-wheeled passenger-vehicle. *a.* Inclusive, embracing several or various items, objects, etc.

omnifarious (om-ni-fâr'i-us), *a.* Of all kinds. omnip'otent [POTENT], *a.* Almighty; having unlimited power. the Omnipotent: The Supreme Being. omnipotence, *n.* omnipres'ent, *a.* Present in every place at the same time. omnipresence, *n.* omniscience (om-nish'ėns), *n.* Infinite knowledge. omniscient, *a.* omniv'orous, *a.* All-devouring; feeding on anything available.

on (on) [A.-S.], *prep.* In contact with, esp. as supported by the upper surface of; in contact with from above; tending toward, against; exactly at, next in order to; about, concerning, in the act of. *adv.* So as to be in contact with and supported by, or adhering to something; forward, in operation, continuance of action or movement.

on-, *pref.* on-coming, *n.* The coming on, advance, or approach (of). onfall, *n.* An attack, an onset. onlooker, *n.* A spectator, one who looks on. onrush, *n.* A rushing on, an attack, an onset.

onager (on'ȧ-jėr) [Gr. *onos*, ass, *agrios*, wild], *n.* The wild ass of Asia.

once (wŭns) [A.-S. *ānes*, gen. of *ān*, ONE], *adv.* One time; at one time, formerly; at any time, ever; at some future time, some time or other. *conj.* As soon as. at once: Immediately; simultaneously. for once: For one time or occasion only.

one (wŭn) [A.-S. *ān*], *a.* Single; being a unit and integral; a or an; single in kind; some, any, a certain. *pron.* A person or thing of the kind implied, some one or something, anyone or anything. *n.* A single unit, unity; the number 1; a single thing or person. at one: In accord or

agreement. one by one: Individually, successively. one-horse, *a.* Drawn by a single horse; (*slang*) of meagre capacity; insignificant. one-man, *a.* Employing, worked by, or consisting of one man. oneself, *pron.* The reflexive form of one. one-sided, *a.* Having or happening on one side only; partial, unfair.

-one [Gr.], *suf.* Denoting certain compounds, esp. hydrocarbons, as in *acetone*, *ozone*.

oneness (wŭn'nĕs), *n.* Singleness; uniqueness; unity, agreement.

onerous (on'ėr-ŭs) [L. *onus*, burden], *a.* Burdensome, troublesome.

onion (ŭn'yŏn) [F. *oignon*], *n.* A plant with an underground bulb of several coats and a pungent smell and flavour.

only (ōn'li) [A.-S. *ānlīc*], *a.* Solitary, single in its or their kind; the sole. *adv.* Solely, merely, exclusively, alone. *conj.* Except that; but.

onomatopœia (ō-nom-ȧ-tō-pē'ȧ) [Gr. *onoma -matos*, name, *poiein*, to make], *n.* The formation of words in imitation of the sounds signified. onomatopœ'ic, onomatopoet'ic, *a.*

onset (on'set), *n.* An attack, an assault, an onslaught. onsetting, *n.*

onslaught (on'slawt) [?], *n.* A furious onset.

onus (ō'nŭs) [L.], *n.* A burden; a duty, obligation.

onward (on'wȧrd), *adv.* Toward a point in advance, forward, on. *a.* Moving or directed forward; progressive. onwards, *adv.*

onyx (on'iks, ō'niks) [Gr. *onux*, a nail, onyx], *n.* A kind of agate, with variously coloured layers.

oolite (ō-ō-līt) [Gr. *ōon*, egg], *n.* A limestone composed of grains of sand like fish-roe. oolitic (-lit'ik), *a.*

ooze (ooz) [A.-S. *wāse*, mud], *n.* Slime; a slimy deposit found on ocean-beds; an exudation. *v.i.* To flow gently; to percolate. *v.t.* To emit or exude. oozy, *a.* Miry, muddy, slimy.

op- [OB-, before *p*], *pref.* As in *oppose*.

opal (ō'pȧl) [Sansk. *upala*], *n.* A vitreous precious stone characterized by a play of iridescent colours. opalescence, *n.* The iridescence of the opal. opalescent, *a.*

opaque (ō-pāk') [L. *opācus*, shady], *a.* Impervious to light; not transparent or translucent. opacity (ō-păs'i-ti), *n.*

ope, *a.* (*Poet.*) Open. *v.* To open.

open (ō'pĕn) [A.-S.], *a.* Not closed or obstructed; affording access, view, etc.; unshut, having any barrier, cover, etc., removed or unfastened; bare, unsheltered; unconcealed, undisguised; not exclusive or limited; ready to admit, be affected, etc.; subject (to); unoccupied, free; (*fig.*) generous; frank; not decided, debatable; (of weather) not frosty; (*Mus.*) produced from an unstopped string, etc.; (*Phon.*) enunciated with a full utterance; (of a vowel or syllable) not ended by a consonant. *n.* Unenclosed space; (*fig.*) public view. *v.t.* To make open; to unclose or unfasten; to remove the covering from; to spread out, expand; to make free of access;

(*fig.*) to make public; to enlarge, develop; to begin; (*Law*) to state a case before calling evidence. *v.i.* To become unclosed or unfastened; to crack, to fissure; to expand; (*fig.*) to develop; to make a start. **open-armed,** *a.* Ready to receive with cordiality. **open-eyed,** *a.* Watchful; astonished, surprised. **open-handed,** *a.* Generous, liberal. **open-hearted,** *a.* Sincere, candid, unsuspicious. **open-minded,** *a.* Accessible to ideas, unprejudiced. **opener,** *n.* **opening,** *a.* That opens; beginning, initial. *n.* Act of making or becoming open; a gap, an aperture. **openly,** *adv.*

opera (op'ér-á) [L.], *n.* A dramatic entertainment in which music forms an essential part; composition comprising words and music for this. **operat'ic,** *a.*

operate (op'ér-āt) [L. *operātus*, p.p. of *operāri*, to work], *v.i.* To produce effect; to exert power, force, influence, etc.; to perform an operation on a body. *v.t.* To work or conduct the working of. **opera'tion,** *n.* Act or process of operating; action, mode of working; activity; effect; a series of military or naval movements; (*Surg.*) an act performed upon the body to remove diseased parts, extract foreign matter, remedy deformities, etc. **op'erative,** *a.* Producing the proper result; efficacious; practical. *n.* A workman, a mechanic. **operatively,** *adv.* **operator,** *n.*

operetta (op-ér-et'á), *n.* A short opera of a light character, usu. in one act.

ophidian (ó-fid'i-án) [Gr. *ophis*, snake], *a.* Snake-like. *n.* A snake. **ophidious,** *a.*

ophthalmia (of-thăl'mi-á) [Gr. *ophthalmos*, eye], *n.* Inflammation of the eye.

opiate (ō'pi-át), *n.* A medicine containing opium; a narcotic.

opine (ó-pīn') [L. *opināri*], *v.* To think, to suppose; to express an opinion.

opinion (ó-pin'yón), *n.* A judgment, conviction, or belief falling short of certainty; the formal statement of a judge, counsel, physician, or other expert; estimation, reputation. **opinionated, opinionative,** *a.* Stiff or obstinate in one's opinions; dogmatic, stubborn.

opium (ō'pi-ám) [Gr. *opion*, dim. of *opos*, sap], *n.* A narcotic prepared from the poppy.

opossum (ó-pos'úm) [N. Am. Ind.], *n.* An American marsupial with a prehensile tail and a thumb on the hind-foot.

opponent (ó-pō'nént) [L. *pōnens*, putting], *a.* Opposing, antagonistic, adverse. *n.* One who opposes, esp. in debate or argument; an antagonist.

opportune (op'ór-tūn) [L. *opportūnus*], *a.* Seasonable, timely, well-timed; fit, suitable. **opportunism,** *n.* Utilizing circumstances to gain one's ends; shaping policy according to the needs of the moment; sacrifice of principle to expediency. **opportunist,** *n.* **opportu'nity,** *n.* A convenient occasion, a chance.

oppose (ó-pōz') [F. *poser*, to pose], *v.t.* To set against, to bring forward as an obstacle, counterpoise, or refutation (to); to act against, to resist, obstruct; to dispute; (*in p.p.*) contrasted. *v.i.* To offer objection. **opposable,** *a.* **opposer,**

n. **opposite** (op'ó-zit), *a.* Situated in front of or contrary in position (to); antagonistic, diametrically different (from). *n.* One who or that which is opposite; an opponent. *adv.* In an opposite place or direction. *prep.* Opposite to. **oppositely,** *adv.* **opposition** (-zish'ún), *n.* Act or state of opposing; resistance, hostility; state of being opposite; antithesis, contrariety; an obstacle; the chief party opposed to the party in office.

oppress (ó-pres') [L. *pressāre*, to press], *v.t.* To overburden; to lie heavily on; to weigh down; to govern cruelly or unjustly. **oppression,** *n.* **oppressive,** *a.* **oppressively,** *adv.* **oppressor,** *n.*

opprobrious (ó-prō'bri-ús) [L. *probrum*, infamous act], *a.* Abusive, vituperative. **opprobrium,** *n.* Disgrace, infamy.

oppugn (ó-pūn') [L. *pugnāre*, to fight], *v.t.* To oppose, call in question.

optative (op'tá-tiv) [L. *optāre*, to choose], *a.* (*Gram.*) Expressing a wish or desire. *n.* The optative mood.

optic (op'tik) [Gr. *optikos*], *a.* Pertaining to vision or the eye. *n.* (*pl. as sing.*) The science of the properties of light and vision. **optical,** *a.* **optician** (-tish'án), *n.* One who makes or deals in optical instruments.

optimism (op'ti-mizm) [L. *optimus*, best], *n.* The view that the existing state of things is the best possible, or that the universe is tending towards a better state and that good must ultimately prevail; disposition to take hopeful views. **optimist,** *n.* **optimis'tic,** *a.*

option (op'shún), *n.* The right or power of choosing; choice; the thing chosen or preferred; the purchased right to deliver or call for the delivery of securities, etc., at a specified rate within a specified time. **optional,** *a.*

opulent (op'ū-lént) [L. *opulentus*], *a.* Rich; abounding (in); abundant. **opulence,** *n.* **opulently,** *adv.*

or (1) (ôr) [A.-S.], *conj.* A disjunctive particle introducing an alternative; used also to connect synonyms, words explaining, correcting, etc. *adv.* Ere, before.

or (2) (ôr) [F., from L. *aurum*], *n.* (*Her.*) Gold.

-or, *suf.* Denoting agency or forming nouns of condition, as in *actor*, *author*, *creator*, *equator*, *favour*, *vigour*.

oracle (or'ákl) [L. *ōrāre*, to pray], *n.* A divine answer to a request for advice or prophecy; the medium giving such responses; the place where these were sought. **orac'ular,** *a.*

oral (ōr'ál) [L. *ōs ōris*, mouth], *a.* Spoken, by word of mouth; of, at, or near the mouth. **orally,** *adv.*

orange (1) (or'ánj) [Arab. *nāranj*], *n.* A large roundish cellular pulpy fruit; the evergreen tree bearing this; its colour, reddish-yellow. *a.* Of the colour of an orange.

Orange (2) [from Wm. III, Prince of Orange], *a.* Pertaining to the Society of Orangemen formed 1795 to uphold the Protestant ascendancy in Ireland. **Orangeism,** *n.* **Orangeman,** *n.*

orang-utan, -outang (ö-răng'ŭ-tàn', -tăng') [Malay, wild man of the woods], *n.* A large, anthropoid ape of Borneo and Sumatra.

oration (ö-rā'shŭn) [L. *ōrāre*, to speak], *n.* A formal speech in elevated language. **orate'**, *v.i.* (*slang*) To hold forth, harangue. **or'ator**, *n.* One who delivers an oration; an eloquent speaker. **orator'ical**, *a.* **or'atory** (1), *n.* The art of public speaking, rhetoric; eloquence.

oratorio (or-à-tòr'i-ō), *n.* A musical composition for voices and instruments, usu. treating a scriptural theme.

oratory (2) (or'à-tòr-i) [L. *ōrāre*, to pray], *n.* A small chapel; a congregation of priests living in community without vows.

orb (òrb) [L. *orbis*, ring], *n.* A sphere; a heavenly body; anything circular; the globe of regalia. **orbic'ular**, *a.*

orbit (òr'bit) [L. *orbita*, a track], *n.* The bony cavity of the eye; the path of a heavenly body; (*fig.*) a sphere of action, a career. **orbital**, *a.*

orchard (òr'chàrd) [A.-S. *orceard*], *n.* An enclosure containing fruit trees, a plantation of these.

orchestra (òr'kës-trà) [L. and Gr. *orchēstra*], *n.* (*Gr. Ant.*) The space between the stage and the spectators occupied by the chorus; the place for the band in modern theatres, etc.; the body of musicians in a theatre or concert-room. **orches'tral**, *a.* **or'chestrate**, *v.t.* To arrange music for an orchestra. **orchestra'tion**, *n.*

orchid (òr'kid) [Gr. *orchis*, testicle (from shape of the tubers)], *n.* A plant with a tuberous root and flowers usu. of fantastic shape and brilliant colours.

ordain (òr-dān'), *v.t.* To set apart for an office or duty, to confer Holy orders on; to destine. **ordainment**, *n.*

ordeal (òr'dē-ál, òr'dēl) [A.-S. *ordēl*], *n.* The practice of referring questions of criminality to [supernatural decision, as by tests through fire, boiling water, battle, etc.; (*fig.*) a severe trial or test.

order (òr'dèr) [L. *ordo*], *n.* Regular disposition or arrangement; sequence, succession; normal condition; a state of efficiency; tidiness; established state of things; regulations governing an assembly, etc.; a rule, regulation; an injunction, an authoritative direction; a document instructing the payment of money or delivery of property; kind, sort, quality; a social class; a body of persons united by some common purpose; a grade of the Christian ministry; (*pl.*) the clerical office; a body usually instituted by a sovereign to which distinguished persons are admitted as an honour; the insignia worn by members of this; a grade of angels and archangels; a distinguishing style of architecture, as the Doric, Ionic, Corinthian, etc.; (*Nat. Hist.*) a division below a class and above a family and genus. *v.t.* To put in order; to regulate; to manage; to ordain; to command; to instruct (a person, firm, etc.) to supply goods or perform work; to direct the doing or making of. *v.i.*

To give orders. **Holy orders:** The different ranks of clergy in an episcopal Church; the clerical office. **ordering**, *n.* Arrangement; ordination of priests, etc. **orderly**, *a.* In order; methodical, regular; free from disorder or confusion; (*Mil.*) pertaining to orders and their execution. *adv.* Duly, regularly. *n.* A soldier who attends on an officer to carry orders, etc. **orderly-room**, *n.* A room in barracks used as the office for company or regimental business. **orderliness**, *n.*

ordinal (òr'di-nàl), *a.* Denoting order or position in a series. *n.* A number denoting this; a book containing forms for ordination.

ordinance (òr'di-nàns) [L. *ordināre*, to ordain], *n.* An order or regulation laid down by a constituted authority; an established rite, ceremony, etc.

ordinary (òr'di-nàr-i), *a.* Usual, customary, normal, not exceptional; commonplace; having immediate or ex officio jurisdiction. *n.* A rule or order, as of the Mass; a meal at a fixed rate for all comers; an eating-house.

ordnance (òrd'nàns), *n.* (*collect.*) Cannon, artillery; the public department dealing with military stores and equipment, except those pertaining to the quartermaster's department. **Ordnance Survey:** The Government survey of Great Britain and Northern Ireland.

ordination (òr-di-nā'shŭn), *n.* The act of ordaining to the priesthood.

ordure (òr'dyŭr) [L. *horridus*, horrid], *n.* Excrement, dung, filth.

ore (òr) [A.-S. *ār*, brass], *n.* A natural substance from which metal may be extracted.

organ (òr'gàn) [Gr. *organon*, rel. to *ergon*, work], *n.* A musical wind-instrument composed of pipes sounded by means of a bellows and played by keys; a medium of communication, etc., as a newspaper; a mental faculty regarded as an instrument; the human voice with regard to its musical quality, power, etc.; a part performing some definite vital function. **organ-grinder**, *n.* A worker of a barrel-organ. **organist**, *n.* One who plays an organ.

organic (òr-găn'ik), *a.* Pertaining to a bodily organ or organs; of the nature of organisms; pertaining to or affecting an organ (of diseases, etc.); (*Chem.*) existing as parts of or derived from organisms; pertaining to an organized system; organized, systematic; structural, fundamental, inherent, not accidental; vital, not mechanical. **organically**, *adv.* **or'ganism**, *n.* An organized body consisting of mutually dependent parts fulfilling functions necessary to the life of the whole; an animal, a plant; organic structure. **or'ganize**, *v.t.* To furnish with organs; to make into an organism; to correlate the parts of and make into an organic whole; to put into proper working order. **organiza'tion**, *n.* **or'ganizer**, *n.*

orgasm (òr'găzm) [Gr. *orgaein*, to swell], *n.* Immoderate excitement; a paroxysm of excitement or passion; the culminating excitement in the sexual act; turgescence of any organ.

orgy (ôr'ji) [Gr. *orgia*, pl.], *n.* (*usu. in pl.* -gies) A wild revel, debauchery.

oriel (ôr'i-ĕl) [O.F. *oriol*], *n.* A projecting polygonal windowed recess supported on corbels or a pier.

orient (ôr'i-ĕnt) [L. *oriens, -ntem*, rising], *n.* The East, the countries east of S. Europe and the Mediterranean; the lustre of a pearl of the finest quality; an orient pearl. *a.* Eastern; bright, shining; lustrous, without a flaw (of pearls). *v.t.* To define the position of in respect to the east; to orientate. **Orien'tal**, *a.* **or'ientate**, *v.t.* To place (a building) so that the chancel points due east; to bury (a body) with feet towards the east; to determine the position of, with reference to the east; (*fig.*) to find or correct one's mental relations and principles. **orienta'tion**, *n.*

orifice (or'i-fis) [L. *ōs ōris*, mouth, *facere*, to make], *n.* An aperture, as of a tube, etc.; a mouth, a vent.

oriflamme (or'i-flăm) [F. *or*, gold, *flamme*, flame], *n.* The ancient royal banner of France; (*fig.*) a symbol of lofty endeavour.

origin (or'i-jin) [L. *origo*], *n.* Beginning or rise (of anything); derivation; source; ancestry; occasion. **orig'inal**, *a.* Pertaining to the origin or first stage; first, primitive; innate; not imitated, not produced by translation; novel; able to devise, act, etc., for oneself; inventive, creative. *n.* The pattern, the archetype; that from which a work is copied or translated; the language in which a work is written; an eccentric person. **original'ity**, *n.* **orig'inate**, *v.t.* To be the origin of; to cause to begin. *v.i.* To rise, to begin; to have origin (in, from, or with).

oriole (ôr'i-ōl) [L. *aureus*, golden], *n.* A bird with bright-yellow and black plumage.

orison (or'i-zŏn) [L. *ōrāre*, to pray], *n.* A prayer, a supplication.

orlop (ôr'lŏp) [Dut. *overloop*, a covering], *n.* The lowest deck of a vessel having three or more decks.

ormolu (ôr'mŏ-loo) [F. *or*, gold, *moulu*, p.p. of *moudre*, to grind], *n.* A gold-coloured alloy of copper, zinc, and tin, used for cheap jewellery, clocks, etc.

ornament (ôr'nà-mĕnt) [L. *ornāre*, to equip], *n.* A thing or part that adorns; a decoration; (*fig.*) one or that which reflects honour or credit; accessories pertaining to a church or worship. *v.t.* To adorn, decorate, embellish. **ornamen'tal**, *a.* **ornamenta'tion**, *n.*

ornate (ôr-nāt'), *a.* Adorned, richly embellished; florid (of literary style, etc.). **ornately**, *adv.* **ornateness**, *n.*

ornith-, ornitho- [Gr. *ornis ornithos*, bird], *comb. form.* **ornithology** (ôr-ni-thol'ŏ-ji) [-LOGY], *n.* The branch of zoology dealing with birds. **ornitholog'ical**, *a.* **ornithol'ogist**, *n.* ornithorhynchus (-ring'-kŭs) [Gr. *rhunchos*, bill], *n.* The duck-billed platypus, an Australian aquatic oviparous mammal.

orphan (ôr'făn) [Gr. *orphanos*, bereaved], *n.* A child bereft of one parent, or of both. *a.* Bereaved thus. **orphanage**, *n.* Orphan condition; an asylum for orphans.

orrery (or'ĕr-i) [4th Earl of *Orrery* (1676-1731)], *n.* A contrivance for illustrating the motions of the planetary system.

orris (or'is), *n.* A kind of iris the root of which is used as a perfume and in medicine.

ort (ôrt) [cogn. with A.-S. *ǣt*, food], *n.* (*usu. in pl.*) Refuse, odds and ends, leavings.

ortho- [Gr. *orthos*, straight], *comb. form.*

orthodox (ôr'thŏ-doks) [Gr. *doxa*, opinion], *a.* Holding the accepted views, esp. in matters of faith; in accordance with sound or accepted doctrine; conventional, not heretical, heterodox, or original. **Orthodox Church**, *n.* The Eastern or Greek Church. **orthodoxy**, *n.*

orthoepy (ôr'tho-ep-i) [Gr. *epos*, word], *n.* The branch of grammar dealing with pronunciation, phonology, correct speech or pronunciation. **orthoep'ic, -al**, *a.* orthoepist (ôr'thŏ-ĕ-pist), *n.*

orthography (ôr-thog'ra-fi), *n.* Correct spelling; that part of grammar which deals with letters and spelling. **orthog'rapher, -phist**, *n.* **orthograph'ic, -al**, *a.*

orthopædy (ôr'thŏ-pē-di) [Gr. *paideia*, rearing of children], *n.* (*Surg.*) The curing of deformities, etc., esp. in children. **orthopædic**, *a.*

ortolan (ôr'tŏ-làn) [It. *ortolano*], *n.* A small bunting esteemed as a delicacy.

-ory, *suf.* (1) Denoting place where or instrument, as in *dormitory, lavatory, refectory*. (2) Forming adjectives, as *amatory, admonitory, illusory*.

oscillate (os'i-lāt) [L. *oscillātus*, swung], *v.i.* To swing, to move like a pendulum; to vacillate, to vary. **oscilla'tion**, *n.*

osculate (os'kū-lāt) [L. *osculāri*, to kiss], *v.* To kiss. **oscula'tion**, *n.* A kiss.

-ose, *suf.* Denoting fulness, abundance, as in *grandiose, jocose, verbose*.

osier (ō'zhi-ĕr, -zēr) [L. *ōsāria*, willow-bed], *n.* A species of willow, the shoots of which are used for basket-making.

-osis, *suf.* Denoting condition, esp. morbid states, as *hypnosis, neurosis*.

-osity, *suf.* Forming nouns from adjectives in -OSE or -OUS, as *grandiosity, luminosity*.

osprey (os'prā) [L. *ossifraga* (*os*, bone, *frangere*, to break)], *n.* A large bird preying on fish, the sea-eagle or sea-hawk.

osseous (os'ĕ-ŭs) [L. *os*, bone], *a.* Of the nature of bone, bony; containing fossil bones. **ossif'erous**, *a.* Yielding bones (of cave deposits, etc.). **ossify** (os'i-fi), *v.* To change into bone, or become like bone. **ossifica'tion**, *n.*

ostensible (os-ten'sibl) [L. *ostendere*, to show], *a.* Put forward for show or to hide the reality; pretended, seeming. **ostensive**, *a.* **ostenta'tion**, *n.* Pretentious display; parade. **ostenta'tious**, *a.*

osteo- [Gr. *osteon*, bone], *comb. form.* **osteology** (os-ti-ol'ŏ-ji) *n.* The branch of anatomy treating of bones, osseous tissue, etc.; the bony structure of an animal. **osteol'ogist**, *n.* **osteopathy** (os-te-op'à-thi), *n.* The treatment of disease by manipulation, esp. of the spinal column. **osteopath**, *n.* A practitioner of osteopathy.

ostler (os'lĕr), *n.* A man who tends horses at an inn.

ostracize (os'trà-sīz) [Gr. *ostrakon*, a tile, oyster-shell], *v.t.* (*Gr. Ant.*) To banish by a popular vote recorded on a potsherd or shell; to exclude from society, to ban. **ostracism**, *n.*

ostrich (os'trich) [O.F. *ostruce*], *n.* A large African and Arabian bird having rudimentary wings, but capable of running with great speed, valued for its feathers.

other (ŭth'ĕr) [A.-S.], *a.* Not the same as one specified or implied; different, alternative, extra; only remaining (of two alternatives); contrary. *n.* and *pron.* An or the other person, thing, example, instance, etc. *adv.* Otherwise. **otherwise**, *adv.* In a different way, in other respects; by or from other causes.

-otic, *suf.* Forming adjectives corresponding to nouns in *-osis*, as *neurotic*.

otiose (ō'shi-ōs) [L. *ōtium*, leisure], *a.* Not wanted, useless, superfluous; futile, sterile.

otter (ot'ĕr) [A.-S.], *n.* A furred, web-footed aquatic mammal feeding on fish.

Ottoman (ot'ô-màn) [Arab. *Othmān*, founder of Turkish Empire], *a.* Pertaining to the Turks. *n.* A Turk; a sofa without back or arms, introduced from Turkey.

oubliette (oo-bli-et') [Fr., from *oublier*, to forget], *n.* An underground dungeon.

ought (awt) [A.-S. *āhte*, past of *āgan*, to possess, to owe], *v. aux.* To be bound in duty or rightness; to be necessary; to behove.

ounce (1) (ouns) [L. *uncia*], *n.* The twelfth part of a pound troy, and sixteenth of a pound avoirdupois.

ounce (2) [O.F. *once* (l'*once*)], *n.* A leopard-like animal; the mountain-panther, the snow leopard.

our (our) [A.-S. *ūre*], *a.* Pertaining to or belonging to us; used instead of 'my' by royalty, editors, etc. **ours**, *pred.a.* Belonging to us. *n.* That or those belonging to us. **of ours**: Belonging to our regiment.

-our [-OR], *suf.* Forming nouns, as *amour*, *ardour*.

ourself (our-self'), *pron.* Myself (used in regal or formal style); (*pl.*) we, not others; (*reflex.*) the persons previously alluded to as we.

-ous, *suf.* Full of, abounding in.

oust (oust) [O.F. *oster* (F. *ôter*, to take away)], *v.t.* To eject, expel; to dispossess.

out (out) [A.-S. *ūt*], *adv.* From the inside; not in, not within; from among; forth or away, at a specified distance from; not employed; on strike; in error, wrong; at a loss; not in agreement; so as to be visible, audible, revealed, published, etc. introduced to society; (*Cricket*) dismissed from the wicket. (*usu. in pl.*) Those out of office, the opposition; (*Print.*) matter omitted. *a.* External; outlying, distant. *int.* Begone! away! *v.t.* To expel; to knock out. **out and out**, *adv.* Completely, thoroughly, *n.*

out-, *pref.* Out, towards the outside, external; from within; separate, detached;

denoting issue or result; expressing excess, exaggeration, superiority, enduring, getting through or beyond. **outbid'**, *v.t.* To bid more than; to outdo by offering more. **outboard**, *a.* (*Naut.*) Situated on the outside of a ship or boat; having an engine outside the boat. **out'break** [BREAK], *n.* A sudden bursting forth, an eruption; a riot of insurrection. **out'-building**, *n.* A detached building, an outhouse. **out'burst**, *n.* An outbreak, an explosion; an outcry. **out'cast**, *a.* Rejected, cast out; exiled. *n.* A vagabond; an exile. **outclass'**, *v.t.* To be of a superior kind or qualifications than; to surpass as a competitor. **out'come**, *n.* Issue, result, consequence. **out'crop**, *n.* The exposure of a stratum at the surface. *v.i.* (out-krop') To crop out at the surface. **out'cry**, *n.* A vehement or loud cry; noise, clamour. **outdo'**, *v.t.* To excel, surpass. **out'door**, *a.* Living, existing, being, happening, etc., out of doors or in the open air. **outdoors'**, *adv.* In the open air, out of the house.

outer (ou'tĕr), *a.* Being on the exterior side, external; farther from the inside; material, not subjective or psychical. *n.* The part of a target outside the rings round the bull's-eye. **outermost**, *a.*

out'fall, *n.* The point of discharge of a river, drain, etc. **out'fit**, *n.* Act of equipping for a journey, etc.; equipment required for a trade, profession, etc. **outfitter**, *n.* **outflank'**, *v.t.* To extend beyond or turn the flank of; (*fig.*) to get the better of. **out'go**, *n.* That which goes out; expenditure, outlay, issue. *v.t.* (out-gō') To surpass, go beyond, excel. **outgoing**, *a.* Leaving. *n.* A going out, termination; outlay, expenditure (*usu. in pl.*). **outgrow'**, *v.t.* To surpass in growth; to grow too great for; to grow out of. **out'house**, *n.* A small building away from the main building. **outing** (out'ing), *n.* An excursion, a pleasure-trip, an airing.

out'lander, *n.* A foreigner, an alien settler. **outlan'dish**, *a.* Foreign-looking, strange, extraordinary; alien. **outlast'**, *v.t.* To last longer than; to surpass in duration, endurance, etc. **out'law**, *n.* One deprived of the protection of the law. *v.t.* To deprive of legal protection. **outlawry**, *n.* **out'lay**, *n.* Expenditure. *v.t.* (out-lā'). To expend, to lay out. **out'let**, *n.* A passage outwards; a vent; a means of egress. **out'line**, *n.* The line or lines defining a figure; the first rough draft or summary; (*pl.*) general features, facts, principles, etc. *v.t.* To draw the outline of; to sketch. **outlive'**, *v.t.* To survive; to outlast. **out'look**, *n.* Prospect, general appearance of things, esp. as regards the future; looking out, vigilance. **out'lying**, *a.* Situate at a distance, or on the exterior frontier.

outnumber (out-nŭm'bĕr), *v.t.* To exceed in number. **out'-patient**, *n.* A patient receiving treatment at a hospital without being an inmate. **out'post**, *n.* A post at a distance from the main body. **out'put**, *n.* The produce of a factory, mine, etc.

outrage (out'rāj) [O.F. *ultrage*], n. Wanton violation of the rights of others; a gross offence against order or decency. *v.t.* To commit an outrage on; to injure or insult in a flagrant manner; to violate; to transgress flagrantly. **outrageous** (out-rā'jŭs), *a.*

outreach (out-rēch'), *v.t.* To surpass; to overreach, to reach out. **out'rider**, *n.* A mounted servant who attends a carriage. **out'rigger**, *n.* A projecting spar, framework, etc., extended from the sides of a ship for various purposes, esp. a bracket carrying a rowlock; a boat with these. **outright'**, *adv.* Completely; once for all; openly. *a.* (out'rīt) Downright, positive; thorough. **outrun'**, *v.t.* To run faster or farther than, to outstrip; to escape by running. **out'set** [SET (1)], *n.* Commencement, start.

outside (out-sīd', out'sīd), *n.* The external part or surface; external or superficial aspect; that which is without; external space, position, etc.; the utmost limit. *a.* Pertaining to, situated on, or near the outside, outer; external; highest or greatest possible, extreme. *adv.* To or on the outside; not within. *prep.* At, on, to, or of the exterior of; without, out from; beyond the limits of. **outsider**, *n.* One who is not a member of a profession, party, etc.; one not acquainted with something that is going on; one not admissible to good society; a competitor not among the favourites.

outskirt, *n.* (*usu. in pl.*) The outer border. **outsoar'**, *v.t.* To soar beyond or higher than. **out'span**, *v.* To unyoke or unharness animals. *n.* The act or the place of this. **out'spoken**, *a.* Open, candid, frank. **outspo'kenness**, *n.* **outspread'**, *v.t.* To spread out. *a.* (out'-spred) Spread out. **outstan'ding**, *a.* Remaining unpaid; projecting outward; prominent. **outstrip'**, *v.t.* To outrun, to leave behind; to escape by running; to surpass in progress. **outvote'**, *v.t.* To outnumber in voting; to cast more votes than.

outward (out'wård) [A.-S. *ūteweard*], *a.* Exterior, outer; tending or directed toward the outside; external, apparent, superficial; material, not spiritual. *adv.* Outwards. *n.* External appearance. **outward bound**, *a.* Going away from home; starting on a voyage.

outweigh', *v.t.* To weigh more than; to be too heavy for; to be of more importance, etc., than. **outwit'**, *v.t.* To defeat by superior ingenuity or cunning, to overreach. **out'work**, *n.* A work included in the defence of a place, but outside the parapet. **outworn'**, *a.* Worn out; obsolete.

ouzel (oo'zĕl) [A.-S. *ōsle*], *n.* A thrush-like bird, the dipper or water-ouzel. **ouzel-cock**, *n.* The blackbird.

oval (ō'văl) [L. *ovum*, egg], *a.* Egg-shaped, roughly elliptical. *n.* An egg-shaped figure or thing.

ovary (ō'vàr-i) [L. *ovum*, egg], *n.* One of the organs in a female animal in which the ova are produced.

ovation (ō-vā'shŭn) [L. *ovāre*, to rejoice], *n.* A Roman minor triumph; an enthusiastic display of popular favour.

oven (ŭvn) [A.-S. *ofn*], *n.* A close chamber in which substances are baked, etc.; a furnace or kiln.

over (ō'vẽr) (*poet.*) **o'er** (ôr) [A.-S. *ofer*], *prep.* Above; superior to in excellence, dignity, or value; more than; in charge of, concerned with; across; through the extent or duration of. *adv.* So as to pass from side to side or across some space, barrier, etc.; in width; on the opposite side; so as to be turned down; so as to traverse a space, etc.; from end to end; at an end; in addition; again. *a.* Upper, outer, covering, excessive. *n.* (*Cricket*) The interval between changes in bowling from one end to the other; the number of balls delivered by one bowler during this.

over-, *pref.* Above; across; outer, upper; as a covering; past, beyond; extra; excessively, too much, too great. **overact** (ō-vẽr-ăkt'), *v.t.* To overdo; to act (a part) in an exaggerated way. *v.i.* To act more than is necessary. **overalls** (ō'vẽr-awlz), *n.pl.* Garments worn over others as a protection; a cavalryman's trousers.

overawe', *v.t.* To control or restrain by awe. **overbal'ance**, *v.t.* To outweigh; to destroy the equilibrium of; to upset. *v.i.* To topple over. *n.* Excess of value or amount; that which exceeds an equivalent. **overbear'**, *v.t.* To bear down, to overpower. **overbear'ing**, *a.* Arrogant, haughty, imperious. **overbid'**, *v.t.* To outbid. **o'verboard**, *adv.* Over the side of a ship; out of a ship. **overbur'den**, *v.t.* To overload, overweigh. **overbuy** (ō-vẽr-bī'), *v.i.* To buy more than is required.

overcast', *v.t.* To darken, to cloud, to render gloomy; to sew (an edge, etc.) with long stitches. *a.* (ō'vẽr-kast) Clouded all over (of the sky); sewn or embroidered by overcasting. **overcharge'**, *v.t.* To charge with more than is properly due; to load (a fire-arm) with an excessive charge; to saturate; to exaggerate. *n.* (ō'vẽr-charj) An excessive charge, load, or burden. **overcloud'**, *v.t.* To cloud over; to depress, to deject. **o'vercoat**, *n.* A great-coat, a top-coat. **overcome'**, *v.t.* To overpower, vanquish. **overdo'**, *v.t.* (*past* -did, *p.p.* -done) To do to excess; to exaggerate; to overact; to cook to excess. **o'verdose**, *n.* An excessive dose. *v.t.* (ō-vẽr-dōs') To give too large a dose to. **overdraw'**, *v.t.* To exaggerate; to draw upon for a larger sum than stands to one's credit. **over-due'**, *a.* Remaining unpaid after the date on which it is due; not arrived at the time due. *n.* A debt or account that is overdue. **overeat'**, *v.i.* To eat to excess. **overflow'**, *v.t.* To flow over, to flood; to cover as with liquid. *v.i.* To run over; to abound; to overflow the banks (of a stream). *n.* (ō'vẽr-flō) A flood; a profusion. **overflowing**, *a.* **o'verground**, *a.* Situated above ground, opp. to underground. **overgrow'**, *v.t.* (*past* -grew, *p.p.* -grown) To cover with vegetation to outgrow (one's strength, etc.). *v.i.* To grow too large. overgrowth, *n.* overhand (ō'vėr-hănd) *a.* Done with the hand raised above the level of the shoulder or elbow. overhang', *v.i.* (*past and p.p.* -hung) To hang over, to jut out. *v.t.* To hang or impend over; to threaten. *n.* The part or thing that overhangs. overhaul', *v.t.* To examine thoroughly; (*Naut.*) to overtake, to gain upon. *n.* (ō'vėr-hawl) Inspection, thorough examination. overhead', *adv.* Above the head, aloft. *a.* Situated overhead; (*Mach.*) working from above downwards; (*fig.*) all-round, general. o'verheads, *n.pl.* (*Comm.*) Expenses of administration, etc. overhear', *v.t.* To hear by accident or stratagem. overjoyed (-joid'), *a.* Transported with joy. o'verland, *a.* Lying, going, made, or performed by land. *adv.* Across the land. overlap', *v.t.* To fold over; to extend so as to lie or rest upon. *n.* An act, case, or the extent of overlapping; the part that overlaps. overlay', *v.t.* (*past and p.p.* -laid) To spread over the surface of; to cover with a layer; to cloud. *n.* (ō'vėr-lā) Something laid over (as a covering, layer, etc.). overleaf', *adv.* On the other side of the leaf (of a book). overlook', *v.t.* To view or be situated so as to command a view of from above; to superintend; to inspect in a cursory way; to disregard; to slight. o'verlord, *n.* A superior lord, one who is lord over other lords. o'vermantel, *n.* Ornamental woodwork over a mantelpiece. o'vermuch, *a.* Too much, more than is sufficient. *adv.* In or to too great a degree. *n.* More than enough. overnight', *a.* Done or happening the night before. *adv.* In the course of the night or evening; in or on the evening before. o'verplus, *n.* Surplus, excess; an amount left over. overpow'er, *v.t.* To be too powerful for; to overcome, conquer; to overwhelm. o'ver-proof, *a.* Containing a larger proportion of alcohol than is contained in proof-spirit. overrate' [RATE (1)], *v.t.* To rate too highly. overreach', *v.t.* To extend beyond; to get the better of, to outwit. override', *v.t.* To ride over; to trample as if underfoot, to disregard, to supersede. overrule', *v.t.* To control by superior power or authority; to set aside; to reject. overrun', *v.t.* To spread over; to grow over; to invade; to outrun. *v.i.* To overflow. oversea', *a.* Beyond the sea, foreign. *adv.* From beyond the sea. overseas, *adv.* oversee', *v.t.* To superintend; to disregard. o'verseer, *n.* A superintendent; a parish officer charged with the care of the poor. o'versight, *n.* Superintendence, care; a mistake, an unintentional error or omission. oversleep', *v.* To sleep too long (*often reflex.*). overspend', *v.t.* To spend too much of (income, etc.). *v.i.* To spend beyond one's means (*often reflex.*). overstate', *v.t.* To state too strongly, to exaggerate. overstatement, *n.* overstay', *v.t.* To stay longer than or beyond the limits of. overstep', *v.t.* To exceed, to transgress. overstrung', *a.* Too highly

strung; with the strings crossed (of pianos).
overt (ō'vėrt) [O.F., opened], *a.* Open, public, apparent. overtly, *adv.*
overtake (ō-vėr-tāk'), *v.t.* To come up with, to catch; to attain to; to take by surprise.
overtask', *v.t.* To burden with too heavy a task. overtax', *v.t.* To tax too heavily; to overburden.
overthrow (ō-vėr-thrō'), *v.t.* To overturn, demolish; to conquer, subvert. *n.* (ō'vėr-thrō) Defeat, discomfiture; ruin, destruction. o'vertime, *n.* Time one works beyond the regular hours.
overture (ō'vėr-tyūr), *n.* A preliminary proposal (*usu. in pl.*); (*Mus.*) an introductory piece for instruments, a prelude.
overturn (ō-vėr-tėrn'), *v.t.* To turn over, to upset. *v.i.* To be upset or turned over. *n.* Act of overturning; state of being overturned. overween'ing, *a.* Arrogant, conceited, presumptuous. *n.* Excessive conceit. overweigh', *v.t.* To exceed in weight; to weigh down. o'verweight, *n.* Excess of weight; preponderance. overwhelm', *v.t.* To submerge; to crush, engulf; to destroy utterly; to bear down, overpower. overwhelmingly, *adv.* overwork', *v.t.* (*past and p.p.* -worked, -wrought) To impose too much work upon; to exhaust with work; to work up into a morbid state of excitement. *v.i.* To work to excess.
ovi- (1), ovo- [L. *ovum*, egg], *comb. form.* oviparous (ō-vip'à-rŭs), *a.* Producing young by means of eggs that are hatched outside the body.
ovi- (2) [L. *ovis*, sheep], *comb. form.* ovine (ō'vin), *a.* Pertaining to or like sheep.
ovum (ō'vŭm), *n.* (*pl.* ova) The female germ in animals, produced within the ovary and capable, after fertilization, of developing into a new individual.
owe (ō) [A.-S. *āgan*], *v.t.* To be indebted to for a specified amount; to be under obligation to pay or repay; to be obliged for; to have to thank for. owing, *a.*
owl (oul) [A.-S. *ūle*], *n.* A nocturnal bird of prey; (*fig.*) a solemn-looking blockhead. owlet, *n.* A young or small owl. owlish, *a.*
own (1) (ōn) [A.-S. *āgen*, owed], *a.* Belonging or proper to, individual, not anyone else's (as an intensive to the poss. pronoun, etc.).
own (2) [A.-S. *āgnian*], *v.t.* To possess; to acknowledge as one's own; to admit, to concede as true or existent. to own up: To confess, to make a clean breast (of). owner, *n.* A lawful proprietor. ownership, *n.*
ox (oks) [A.-S. *oxa*], *n.* (*pl.* oxen) The castrated male of domesticated cattle; any bovine animal. ox-eyed, *a.* Having large, full eyes.
oxalic (ok-săl'ĭk) [Gr. *oxus*, sour], *a.* Belonging to or derived from sorrel. oxalic acid: A sour, highly-poisonous acid found in numerous plants.
oxide (ok'sīd), *n.* A binary compound of oxygen with another element or an organic radical. oxidize, *v.t.* To combine with oxygen; to make rusty. *v.i.* To

enter into chemical combination with oxygen; to rust. **oxidiza'tion,** *n.*

Oxonian (ok-sō'nĭ-ăn), *n.* A member or graduate of Oxford University. *a.* Belonging to Oxford.

oxy- [Gr. *oxus,* sharp, biting, acid], *comb. form.* Sharp, keen; denoting the presence of oxygen. **oxyacetylene,** *a.* Yielding a very hot blow-pipe flame from the combustion of oxygen and acetylene.

oxygen (ok'sĭ-jĕn), *n.* A colourless, tasteless, odourless element existing in the atmosphere, in water, and in most mineral and organic substances.

oxymoron (ok-sĭ-môr'ŏn [Gr. *mōros,* stupid], *n.* A rhetorical figure in which an epithet of a quite contrary signification is added to a word.

oyer (oi'ĕr) [A.-F., in *oyer et terminer,* hear and determine], *n.* (*Law*) A hearing or trial of causes under writ of oyer and terminer. **oyer and terminer:** A commission formerly issued to judges of assize, empowering them to hear and determine specified offences.

oyez (ō-yĕs') [O.F., hear ye], *int.* Thrice repeated as introduction to a proclamation made by an officer of a court of law or public crier.

oyster (oi'stĕr) [Gr. *ostreon*], *n.* An edible bivalve mollusc; an oyster-shaped morsel of meat. **oyster-bed,** *n.* A breeding place for oysters. **oyster-catcher,** *n.* A wading-bird.

ozone (ō-zōn'), *n.* A form of oxygen with three atoms to the molecule, having a stimulating and exhilarating influence on the human system.

P

pabulum (păb'ū-lŭm) [L.], *n.* Food; nourishment of a mental or spiritual kind.

pace (pās) [L. *passus*], *n.* A step, the space between the feet in stepping (about 30 in.); gait, manner of going; rate of speed or progress. *v.i.* To walk with slow or regular steps. *v.t.* To measure by carefully regulated steps; to set the pace for.

pachy- [Gr. *pachus,* thick, large], *comb. form.* Denoting thickness. **pachyderm** (păk'ĭ-dĕrm) [Gr. *dermein,* to flay], *n.* A member of an order of mammals containing hoofed non-ruminant animals with thick skins, as the elephant; (*fig.*) a thick-skinned person. **pachyder'matous,** *a.*

pacific (pá-sĭf'ĭk) [L. *pacificus*], *a.* Inclined to peace, conciliatory; tranquil, peaceful. **the Pacific:** The ocean between America and Asia. **pacifica'tion,** *n.* **paci'ficator,** *n.* **pacifica'tory,** *a.* **pac'ifier,** *n.* **pac'ifist,** *n.* One advocating the reference of international disputes to a permanent tribunal; an opponent of militarism; one anxious to make peace at any price.

pack (păk) [Teut.], *n.* A bundle of things; a parcel, burden; a set, a gang; a set of playing-cards, a number of dogs, wolves, or other beasts going together; a quantity of broken floating ice. *v.t.* To put together in a pack; to stow into a bundle,

box, bag, etc., for keeping, carrying, etc.; to crowd closely together; to cover with some material to prevent leakage, loss of heat, etc., to manipulate (cards) so as to win unfairly; to select (a jury) so as to obtain some unfair advantage; to dismiss without ceremony. *v.i.* To put things in a pack, bag, trunk, etc., for sending away, carrying, or keeping; to crowd together; to depart hurriedly. **packthread,** *n.* Strong thread for sewing or tying up parcels. **package,** *n.* A parcel, a bundle; the packing of goods. **packer,** *n.* **packet,** *n.* A small package; a packet-boat. **packet-boat,** *n.* A vessel conveying mails, goods, and passengers at regular intervals. **pack-horse,** *n.* A horse employed in carrying goods. **packing,** *n.* **packing-needle,** *n.* A long curved needle, used for sewing up bales, etc. **packman,** *n.* A pedlar. **pack-saddle,** *n.* One for supporting packs.

pact (păkt) [L. *pactum*], *n.* An agreement, a compact.

pad (1) (păd) [Dut., path], *n.* A footpad; highway robbery; an easy-paced horse. *v.i.* To travel on foot; to trudge.

pad (2) [?], *n.* A soft cushion; a bundle of this nature; a soft saddle; a number of sheets of paper fastened together at one edge; the cushion-like sole of the foot. *v.t.* To stuff or furnish with padding; to fill out (a sentence, etc.) with unnecessary words. **padding,** *n.*

paddle (pădl) [?], *n.* A broad short oar used without a row-lock; the blade of an oar; a paddle-board; a paddle-wheel; a spell of paddling; an implement used in washing clothes. *v.t.* To propel by means of paddles; to dabble in the water with the hands or feet; to toddle. *v.i.* To ply a paddle; to move along by means of a paddle. **paddle-wheel,** *n.* A wheel with floats or boards projecting from the periphery for pressing against the water and propelling a vessel.

paddock (1) (păd'ŏk) [A.-S. *pearruc*], *n.* A small field; a turfed enclosure attached to a stud-farm, or adjoining a race-course where horses are kept before racing.

paddock (2) [M.E. *padde*], *n.* A frog.

paddy (păd'ĭ) [Malay *padi*], *n.* Rice in the husk.

padlock (păd'lok), *n.* A detachable lock for fastening to a staple, etc. *v.t.* To fasten with this.

padre (pa'drā) [It., father, priest], *n.* A priest; an army or naval chaplain.

pæan (pē'ăn) [Gr. *Paian,* a name of Apollo], *n.* A choral song addressed to a deity; a song of triumph or rejoicing.

pædo- [Gr. *pais paidos,* boy, child], *comb. form.* Relating to children.

pagan (pā'găn) [L. *pāgānus,* countryman], *n.* A heathen; (*fig.*) a barbarous or unenlightened person. *a.* Heathenish; unenlightened. **paganism,** *n.* **paganize,** *v.*

page (1) (pāj) [O.F.], *n.* A young male attendant on persons of rank; a boy in livery.

page (2) [L. *pāgina,* from *pangere,* to fasten], *n.* One side of a leaf of a book; (*fig.*) a record. *v.t.* To put numbers on the pages of (a book). **paginal** (păj'-), *a.* paginate, *v.t.* pagina'tion, *n.* The figures showing the number of a page.

pageant (păj'ĕnt) [?], *n.* A brilliant spectacle, an elaborate parade or procession; a theatrical exhibition representing historical events, etc. pageantry, *n.*

pagoda (pá-gō'dá) [Port. *pagode*], *n.* A sacred temple in India, China, and the East; a building imitating this.

pail (păl) [A.-S. *pœgel*], *n.* An open vessel for carrying liquids; a pailful. pailful, *n.*

pain (pān) [Gr. *poinĕ*, penalty], *n.* Bodily or mental suffering; (*pl.*) labour, trouble. *v.t.* To inflict pain upon. to take pains: To take trouble, to labour hard. painful, *a.* Attended with or causing mental or physical pain; laborious, difficult. painless, *a.* painstaking, *a.* Taking great care, giving close application. *n.* The taking of pains, careful labour.

paint (pānt) [O.F. *peint*], *v.t.* To cover with paint; to give a specified colour to; to portray in colours; to adorn with painting; (*fig.*) to depict vividly in words. *v.i.* To practise painting; to rouge. *n.* A solid colouring-substance, often dissolved in a liquid vehicle, used to give a coloured coating to surfaces; a cosmetic, rouge. painter (1), *n.* One whose occupation is to colour walls, etc., with paint; an artist who paints pictures. painting, *n.* The act, art, or occupation of laying on colours or producing representations in colours; a picture.

painter (2) (pān'tĕr) [?], *n.* A bow-rope for fastening a boat to a ring, etc.

pair (pâr) [L. *par*, equal], *n.* Two things of a kind, similar in form, or applied to the same use; a set of two, a couple; a double implement, as scissors, spectacles; an engaged or married couple; a flight (of stairs); (*Parl.*) two members of opposite views abstaining from voting. *v.t.* To arrange in pairs; to cause to mate. *v.i.* To be arranged in pairs; to mate; (*Parl.*) to make a pair (with).

pal (păl) [Gipsy], *n.* A friend, chum.

palace (păl'ás) [PALATINE], *n.* The official residence of a king, bishop, etc.; a splendid mansion; a large building for entertainments.

paladin (păl'á-din), *n.* One of Charlemagne's twelve Peers; a knight-errant.

palæ-, palæo- [Gr. *palaios*, old, ancient], *comb. form.* Pertaining to or existing in the earliest times. palæog'raphy, *n.* The art or science of deciphering ancient inscriptions or manuscripts; ancient manuscripts collectively.

palæontology (păl-ĕ-on-tol'ō-ji), *n.* The branch of biology or geology dealing with fossil animals and plants.

palankeen, -quin (păl-án-kēn') [Hindi *pálakī*], *n.* A litter borne by men.

palatable (păl'á-tábl), *a.* Pleasing to the taste; agreeable.

palate (păl'át) [L. *palātum*], *n.* The roof of the mouth; (*fig.*) the sense of taste; liking, fancy. palatal, *a.* Pertaining to the palate. *n.* A sound produced with the palate, as *k, g, ch, y, s, n.*

palatial (pá-lā'shál), *a.* Pertaining to or befitting a palace; magnificent, splendid.

palatine (păl'á-tīn) [L. *palātinus*, from

palātium, the palace built by Augustus on the Palatine Hill, Rome], *a.* Pertaining to or connected with a palace (esp. of the Cæsars or the German Emperors); possessing royal privileges (as the counties of Chester, Durham, and Lancaster); pertaining to a count palatine. *n.* One invested with royal privileges.

palaver (pá-la'vĕr) [Port.], *n.* A discussion, parley, esp. between African natives and traders; chatter; flattery. *v.t.* To talk over, to flatter. *v.i.* To confer; to talk idly.

pale (1) (păl) [F. *pal*, L. *pālus*], *n.* A pointed stake; a narrow board used in fencing; boundary; a region, territory, sphere.

pale (2) (păl) [L. *pallĕre*, to be pale], *a.* Whitish, wanting in colour; dim, faint. *v.* To make or turn pale; (*fig.*) to be dim or poor in comparison.

paletot (păl'ĕ-tō) [F.], *n.* A loose overcoat.

palette (păl'ĕt) [F., dim of *pale*, shovel], *n.* A flat board for mixing colours on.

palfrey (pawl'fri) [O.F. *palfrei*], *n.* A small saddle-horse, esp. for a lady.

palimpsest (păl'imp-sest) [Gr. *palin*, again, *psēstos*, scraped], *n.* A manuscript from which the original writing has been erased to make room for another record.

palindrome (păl'in-drōm) [Gr. *palin*, again, *dromein*, to run], *n.* A word or sentence that reads the same backwards or forwards.

paling (pā'ling), *n.* A fence of pales.

palisade (păl-i-sād'), *n.* A fence of stakes, iron railings, etc.

pall (1) (pawl) [A.-S. *pœll*, L. *pallium*, cloak], *n.* A large cloth thrown over a coffin or hearse; a cloak, a mantle. pall-bearer, *n.* One who attends the coffin at a funeral, or who holds up the pall.

pall (2), *v.* To become or make vapid, insipid, or spiritless; to cloy, to dull.

palladium (pá-lā'di-ùm) [Gr. *Pallas -ados*, Greek goddess of wisdom], *n.* A statue of Pallas on the preservation of which the safety of Troy depended; (*fig.*) a defence, a safeguard.

pallet (1) (păl'ĕt), *n.* A palette; a tool used by potters for mixing and shaping clay; a pawl on a machine, for converting reciprocating into rotary motion or vice versa; a valve admitting air to an organ pipe.

pallet (2) [L. *pālea*, straw], *n.* A small rude bed; a straw mattress.

palliasse (păl'i-ăs), *n.* A mattress of straw or other material.

palliate (păl'i-āt) [L. *palliātus*, cloaked], *v.t.* To cover with excuses; to extenuate to mitigate (a disease, etc.).

pallid (păl'ld) [L. *pallidus*], *a.* Pale, wan

pallor (păl'ŏr), *n.* Paleness.

palm (1) (pam) [A.-S., L. *palma*], *n.* A tropical or subtropical tree usu. with a tall branched stem and head of large fan-shaped leaves; a palm-branch or leaf as a symbol of triumph; victory, triumph, the prize. palm-oil, *n.* An oil obtained from palm-fruit; (*slang*) a bribe. palmaceous (-mă'shùs), *a.* palmary, *a.* Worthy of the palm, pre-eminent.

palm (2) [M.E. and F. *paume*, L. *palma*], *n.* The inner part of the hand; a measure of breadth (3–4 in.) or of length (8–8½ in.). *v.t.* To conceal (dice, etc.) in the palm; hence, to pass (off) fraudulently. **palmar** (pǎl′mǎr), *a.* Pertaining to the palm. **palmate,** *a.* Resembling a hand with the fingers spread out; webbed (of the foot of a bird).

palmer (pa′mĕr) [O.F. *palmier*], *n.* A pilgrim who carried a palm-branch for having been to the Holy Land; a devotee, itinerant monk, etc. **palmer-worm,** *n.* A hairy caterpillar.

palmistry (pa′mis-tri), *n.* Fortune-telling by the lines, etc., on the palm of the hand. **palmist,** *n.*

palmy (pa′mi), *a.* Abounding in palms; victorious, flourishing.

palpable (pǎl′pàbl) [L. *palpāre*, to feel], *a.* Perceptible to the touch; easily perceived, obvious. **palpably,** *adv.*

palpitate (pǎl′pi-tāt), *v.i.* To throb; to flutter; to beat rapidly (of the heart). **palpita′tion,** *n.*

palsy (pawl′zi), *n.* Paralysis; inefficiency, helplessness. **palsied,** *a.*

palter (pawl′tĕr) [?], *v.i.* To equivocate, shuffle, act trickily (with).

paltry (pawl′tri) [?], *a.* Mean, petty, despicable. **paltriness,** *n.*

paludal (pǎl′ū-dàl), **-dic** (pà-lū′dik), **-dine** [L. *palus palūdis*, marsh], *a.* Pertaining to fens, marshy; malarial.

pampas (pǎm′pàs) [Sp. *pampa*, Peruv. *bamba*, a plain], *n.pl.* The open treeless plains in South America.

pamper (pǎm′pĕr) [?], *v.t.* To feed luxuriously; to gratify (tastes, etc.) to excess.

pamphlet (pǎm′flet) [O.F. *Pamphilet*, title of a Latin poem of 12th cent.], *n.* A few printed sheets, stitched, but not bound. **pamphleteer′,** *n.* and *v.i.*

pan (1) (pǎn) [A.-S. *panne*], *n.* A broad shallow vessel for domestic and manufacturing uses; a hollow in the ground for evaporating brine in salt-making; the part of a flint-lock that holds the priming. **pancake,** *n.* A thin flat cake of batter fried in a pan.

Pan (2) [Gr.], *n.* The chief rural divinity of the Greeks. **Pan-pipe,** *n.* A musical instrument made of a number of pipes.

pan- [Gr. *pas pantos*, all], *comb. form.* **panacea** (pǎn-à-sē′à) [Gr. *akeomai*, I heal], *n.* A universal remedy.

pancreas (pǎn′krē-às) [Gr. *kreas -atos*, flesh], *n.* A gland near the stomach secreting a digestive fluid, the sweetbread. **pancreat′ic,** *a.*

pandemonium (pǎn-dē-mō′ni-ùm), *n.* The abode of the demons; a place or state of lawlessness, confusion, or uproar.

pander (pǎn′dĕr) [*Pandarus*, character in Chaucer's "Troilus and Criseyde"], *n.* A go-between in an amorous intrigue; (*fig.*) one who ministers to evil passions, prejudices, etc. *v.t.* To minister to the gratification of. *v.i.* To act as an agent (to) for the gratification of desires, etc.

pane (pǎn) [L. *pannus*, piece of cloth], *n.* A sheet of glass in a window, etc.; one square of the pattern in a plaid.

panegyric (pǎn-ē-jir′ik) [Gr. *panēgurikos*], *n.* A eulogy in praise of some person, act, or thing; an elaborate encomium. **panegyrical,** *a.* **panegyrist,** *n.*

panel (pǎn′ĕl) [L. *pannus*], *n.* A rectangular piece of wood or other material inserted in a frame or forming a compartment of a door, wainscot, etc.; a thin board on which a picture is painted; a picture of much greater height than width; a piece of stuff let in lengthwise in a dress; a list of persons summoned as jurors, a jury. *v.t.* To fit, furnish, or decorate with panels.

pang (pǎng) [?], *n.* A sudden paroxysm of pain; a throe, agony.

panic (pǎn′ik) [Gr. *panikos*], *n.* Sudden, overpowering, unreasoning fear; a general alarm. *a.* Sudden, extreme, unreasoning; caused by fear.

pannier (pǎn′i-ĕr) [L. *pānārium*, breadbasket], *n.* A large basket, esp. one of a pair carried by a beast of burden.

pannikin (pǎn′i-kin), *n.* A small drinking-cup of metal; a small saucepan.

panoply (pǎn′ō-pli) [Gr. *hopla*, arms], *n.* A complete suit of armour; (*fig.*) complete defence.

panorama (pǎn-ō-ra′mà) [Gr. *horama*, view], *n.* A continuous picture on a sheet unrolled before the spectator; a complete view in all directions. **panoramic** (-rǎm′ik), *a.*

pansy (pǎn′zi) [F. *pensée*, thought], *n.* A species of viola with large flowers of various colours; the heartsease.

pant (pǎnt) [O.F. *pantaisier* (F. *panteler*)], *v.i.* To breathe quickly; to gasp for breath; (*fig.*) to long for. *v.t.* To utter gaspingly or convulsively. *n.* A gasp; a throb, palpitation.

pant, panto, *comb. form.*

pantaloon (pǎn-tà-loon′) [It. *Pantalone* (character on the Italian stage)], *n.* A character in pantomime, the butt of the clown's jokes; (*pl.*) tight trousers fastened below the shoe; trousers generally.

pantechnicon (pǎn-tek′ni-kòn) [Gr. *technikon* (*technē*, art)], *n.* A storehouse for furniture; a place where all sorts of manufactured articles are exposed for sale; a pantechnicon van. **pantechnicon van:** A large van for removing furniture.

pantheism (pǎn′thē-izm) [Gr. *theos*, god, -IZM], *n.* The doctrine that God and the universe are identical. **pantheist,** *n.* **pantheis′tic, -ical,** *a.*

panther (pǎn′thĕr) [Gr.], *n.* The leopard.

pantile (pǎn′til), *n.* A curved tile.

panto-, [Gr. *pas pantos*, all], *comb. form.*

pantomime (pǎn′tō-mīm) [Gr. *mimos*, mimic], *n.* (*Rom. Ant.*) A performer or performance in dumb show; a theatrical entertainment, produced at Christmastime, consisting mainly of burlesque and spectacle. **pantomimic** (-mim′ik), *a.*

pantry (pǎn′tri) [O.F. *paneterie*, place where bread is made (L. *pānis*, bread)], *n.* A closet in which bread and provisions are kept.

pants (pǎnts) [PANTALOON]. *n.pl.* Drawers for men or boys; (*Am.*) trousers.

pap (pǎp) [?], *n.* Semi-liquid food for infants, etc; weak mental nutriment; a teat, a nipple; a conical hill or small peak. **pappy,** *a.*

papa (pá-pa') [L.], *n.* Father.

papacy (pā'pá-si), *n.* The office, dignity, or tenure of office of the Pope; the papal system; the Popes collectively. **papal,** *a.*

papaverous (pá-pā'vêr-ús) [L. *papáver*, poppy], *a.* Resembling or allied to the poppy.

paper (pā'pêr) [L. *papyrus*], *n.* A thin flexible substance made of rags, wood-fibre, etc., used for writing and printing on, wrapping, etc.; a piece of this; a document; an essay; a newspaper; a set of examination questions; bills of exchange, etc.; paper-money. *a.* Made of paper; like paper; stated only on paper. *v.t.* To cover with or decorate with paper; to wrap up in paper. **to send in one's papers:** To resign. **paper-chase,** *n.* A game in which a person or persons called the hares drop pieces of paper for pursuers called the hounds to track them by. **paper-hangings,** *n.pl.* Paper for covering the walls of rooms, etc. **paper-hanger,** *n.* **paper money:** Bank notes, treasury notes, or bills used as currency, opp. to coin.

papier mâché (păp-yä-mă'shä) [F., chewed paper], *n.* A material made from pulped paper, moulded into trays, boxes, etc., and usu. japanned.

papist (pā'pist), *n.* A Roman Catholic.

papyrus (pá-pī'rús) [Gr. *papuros*, of Egypt], *n.* (*pl.* -ri) A rush-like plant found in Abyssinia, etc.; a writing material made from this by the Egyptians; a manuscript written on this.

par (par) [L., equal, equally], *n.* State of equality, esp. between the selling value and the nominal value of share certificates, etc.; average or normal condition, rate, etc.

para- [Gr. *para*, by the side of], *comb.form.* Denoting closeness of position, correspondence of parts, situation on the other side, alteration, etc.

parable (păr'ábl), *n.* An allegorical narrative from which a moral is drawn; an allegory, esp. of a religious kind.

parabola (pá-răb'ó-lá) [Gr. *ballein*, to throw], *n.* A plane curve formed by the intersection of the surface of a cone with a plane parallel to one of its sides. **parabolic, -al,** *a.*

parachute (păr-á-shoot') [F.], *n.* An umbrella-shaped contrivance by which a descent can be made from an airship, etc. **parachutist,** *n.*

paraclete (păr'á-klēt) [Gr. *paraklētos*], *n.* An advocate, esp. the Holy Ghost, the Comforter.

parade (pá-rād') [L. *parāre*, to get ready], *n.* Ostentatious display; a muster of troops; ground where soldiers are paraded; a public promenade. *v.t.* To make display of; to assemble and marshal (troops). *v.i.* To be marshalled in military order for display or review; to walk about ostentatiously.

paradise (păr'á-dīs) [O.Pers. *paradæza* (*pairi*, peri-, *diz*, to mould)], *n.* The garden of Eden; place or state of bliss; heaven. **paradisaic (-sā'ĭk),** *a.*

paradox (păr'á-doks) [Gr. *doxa*, opinion], *n.* A statement, view, etc., contrary to received opinion; an assertion seemingly absurd but really correct; a self-contradictory statement or phenomenon. **paradoxical,** *a.*

paraffin (păr'á-fĭn) [L. *parum*, little, *affinis*, akin, from its small affinity with other bodies], *n.* A colourless, tasteless, odourless, solid fatty substance produced in the distillation of coal, bituminous shale, etc.; paraffin oil. **paraffin oil:** One of several oils obtained in this way, used for illuminating, as a lubricant, etc.

paragon (păr'á-gŏn) [It. *paragone*], *n.* A pattern of perfection; a model; a person or thing of supreme excellence. *v.t.* To rival, to equal.

paragraph (păr'á-graf), *n.* A distinct portion of a writing marked by a break in the lines; a reference mark (¶) denoting a division in the text; an item in a newspaper. **paragraphist,** *n.*

parakeet (păr'a-kēt) [O.F. *paroquet*], *n.* Any small long-tailed parrot.

parallax (păr'á-lăks) [Gr. *allassein*, to change], *n.* Apparent change in the position of an object due to change in the position of the observer. **parallac'tic,** *a.*

parallel (păr'á-lel) [Gr. *allēlos*, one another], *a.* Having the same direction and everywhere equidistant (of lines, etc.); having the same tendency; corresponding. *n.* A line everywhere equidistant from another; any one of the parallel circles on a map or globe marking degrees of latitude on the earth's surface; direction parallel to that of another line; a comparison; a counterpart; a reference-mark (‖). *v.t.* To be parallel to, to match, to rival; to compare. **parallelism,** *n.* The state of being parallel, correspondence; a comparison.

parallelepiped (păr-á-lel-ep'i-ped), **-pipedon** (-pip'é-dòn) [Gr. *epipedon*, a level], *n.* A regular solid bounded by six parallelograms, the opposite pairs of which are parallel.

parallelogram (păr-á-lel'ŏ-grăm), *n.* A four-sided rectilineal figure whose opposite sides are parallel.

paralyse (păr'á-līz), *v.t.* To affect with paralysis; (*fig.*) to render powerless.

paralysis (pá-răl'ĭ-sis) [Gr. *lusis*, from *luein*, to loosen], *n.* Loss of the power of muscular contraction or of sensation; palsy; (*fig.*) inability to act. **paralytic (-lit'ĭk),** *a.* and *n.*

paramount (păr'á-mount) [O.F. *para mont*, at the top], *a.* Supreme above all others, pre-eminent. *n.* The highest.

paramour (păr'á-moor) [O.F.], *n.* A mistress; a lover.

paranoia (păr-á-noi'yà) [Gr.], *n.* Mental derangement characterized by delusions.

parapet (păr'á-pĕt) [It. *parapetto* (*parare*, to guard, *petto*, breast)], *n.* A breast-high wall at the edge of a roof, bridge, etc.; a rampart.

paraphernalia (păr-á-fêr-nā'lǐ-á) [Gr. *phernē*, a dowry], *n.pl.* (*Law*) Personal property allowed to a wife over and above her dower, as apparel, jewellery, etc.; miscellaneous belongings, ornaments, trappings.

paraphrase (păr'á-frāz) [Gr. *phrazein*, to tell], *n.* A free rendering of a passage; a restatement in different terms; a poetical version of a passage of Scripture. *v.t.* To express or interpret in other words. *v.i.* To make a paraphrase.

parasite (păr'á-sīt) [Gr. *sitos*, food], *n.* A hanger-on, a sponger; an animal or plant subsisting at the expense of another. **parasitic, -al** (-sit'ik, -ál), *a.*

parasol (păr-á-sol) [It. *parasole* (*parare*, to ward off, *sole*, sun)], *n.* A small umbrella used for shelter against the sun.

paratroops (pă'-rá-troops), *n.pl.* Troops transported by aeroplane and landed by parachutes.

paravane (păr'á-vān), *n.* (*Nav.*) A torpedo-shaped appliance towed from a ship to catch submerged mines.

parboil (par'boil) [O.F. *parboillir*, to boil thoroughly], *v.t.* To boil partially (formerly, thoroughly).

parcel (par'sěl), *n.* A number or quantity of things dealt with separately; a distinct portion, as of land; a bundle, a package. *v.t.* To divide into parts or lots; to make into a parcel.

parch (parch) [?], *v.t.* To scorch, to dry up. *v.i.* To become hot or dry.

parchment (parch'měnt) [L. *pergaměna*, pertaining to *Pergamum*, city of Mysia], *n.* The skin of calves, sheep, goats, etc., prepared for writing; a document on this.

pard (pard) [Gr. *pardos*], *n.* A panther, leopard.

pardon (par'dón) [O.F. *perduner* (PER-, L. *dōnāre*, to give)], *v.t.* To forgive, to absolve from; to remit the penalty of; to excuse, make allowance for. *n.* The act of pardoning; remission of the legal consequences of crime; a papal indulgence; a religious festival when this is granted. **pardonable,** *a.* **pardonably,** *adv.* **pardoner,** *n.* One licensed to sell pardons or indulgences.

pare (pâr) [L. *parāre*, to prepare], *v.t.* To cut away or remove (as rind of fruit, etc.); to trim by cutting.

paregoric (păr-ĕ-gor'ik) [Gr. *parēgorikos*, soothing], *a.* Assuaging or soothing pain. *n.* A camphorated tincture of opium.

parent (pâr'ĕnt) [L. *parentem*, nom. *-ens*, from *parēre*, to beget], *n.* A father or mother; a forefather; (*fig.*) a source, cause, occasion. **parentage,** *n.* Birth, lineage, origin. **paren'tal,** *a.*

parenthesis (pá-ren'thě-sis), *n.* (*pl.* *-theses*) A word or sentence inserted in a sentence that is grammatically complete without it; (*pl.*) round brackets ( ) to include such words; (*fig.*) an interval, interlude, etc. **paren'thesize,** *v.t.* To insert or mark as a parenthesis. **parenthe'tic, -al,** *a.*

parget (par'jět) [L. *prŏjectāre*], *v.t.* To plaster over. *n.* Plaster; pargeting. **pargeter,** *n.* **pargeting,** *n.* Plaster-work, esp. decorative.

parhelion (par-hē'li-ŏn) [Gr. *hēlios*, sun], *n.* (*pl.* *-lia*) A mock-sun or bright spot in a solar halo, due to ice-crystals in the atmosphere.

pariah (pa'ri-á) [Tamil *paraiyan*, a

drummer], *n.* One of a people of very low caste in India; (*fig.*) a social outcast.

paring (pâr'ing), *n.* Act of pruning or trimming; that which is pared off.

parish (păr'ish) [Gr. *oikos*, dwelling], *n.* An ecclesiastical district with its own clergyman, a subdivision of a county. *a.* Pertaining to or maintained by a parish. **parish'ioner,** *n.* One who belongs to a parish.

Parisian (pá-riz'i-án), *a.* Pertaining to Paris. *n.* A native or inhabitant of Paris.

parity (păr'i-ti) [L. *par*, equal], *n.* Equality of rank, condition, value, etc.; parallelism, analogy.

park (park) [O.F. *parc*], *n.* A piece of land, usu. for ornament, pleasure, or recreation, adjoining a mansion or enclosed for public recreation; a space occupied by the artillery, stores, etc., in an encampment. *v.t.* To enclose as in a park; to mass (artillery).

parlance (par'lâns), *n.* Way of speaking, idiom.

parley (par'li) [F. *parler*, to speak], *v.i.* To confer with an enemy with pacific intentions; to talk. *n.* A conference for discussing terms.

Parliament (par'lá-měnt) [F. *parlement*], *n.* A deliberative assembly; a legislative body, esp. the British legislature, consisting of the Houses of Lords and Commons, together with the sovereign. **Parliamentarian** (-târ'i-án), *n.* One versed in parliamentary rules, debate, etc.; one who supported the Parliament against Charles I. **parliamen'tary,** *a.* Pertaining to, enacted by, or according to the rules of Parliament.

parlour (par'lôr) [O.F. *parleor*], *n.* The family sitting-room in a private house. **parlour-maid,** *n.* A maid-servant waiting at table.

parlous (par'lus), *a.* Awkward. *adv.* Extremely.

Parnassus (par-năs'ús) [Mt. in Greece, the fabled resort of the Muses], *n.* (*fig.*) Poetry, literature. **Parnassian,** *a.*

parochial (pá-rō'ki-ál) [L. *parochia*, parish], *a.* Relating to a parish; (*fig.*) petty, narrow. **paro'chialism,** *n.*

parody (păr'ŏ-di), *n.* A literary composition imitating an author's work for the purpose of ridicule; a travesty. *v.t.* To burlesque. **par'odist,** *n.* One who writes parodies.

parole (pá-rōl) [F.], *n.* A promise by a prisoner of war that he will not attempt to escape or take up arms against his captors; (*Mil.*) a daily password used by officers.

paronomasia (păr-ŏ-nŏ-mā'zi-á) [Gr. *onomazein*, to name], *n.* A play upon words, a pun.

-parous [L. from *parere*, to bring forth], *suf.* Producing, bringing forth.

paroxysm (păr'ŏk-sizm) [Gr. *oxunein*, to sharpen], *n.* A sudden and violent fit; the exacerbation of a disease at periodic times.

parquet (par'ki) [F., a floor], *n.* A flooring of parquetry. **parquetry** (par'kě-tri), *n.* Inlaid woodwork for floors.

parr (par) [?], *n.* A young salmon.

parricide (păr'i-sīd) [L. *parricīda*], *n.* One who murders or the murder of a parent. **parrici'dal**, *a.*

parrot (păr'ŏt) [?], *n.* One of a group of tropical birds with brilliant plumage, remarkable for their faculty of imitating the human voice; *(fig.)* one who repeats words mechanically; a chatterbox.

parry (păr'i) [F. *parer*], *v.t.* To ward off (a blow, etc.). *n.* A defensive movement in fencing, the warding off of a blow.

parse (parz) [L. *pars*, part], *n.* To classify a word grammatically; to analyse a sentence and describe its component words and their relations.

parsimonious (par-si-mō'ni-ûs) [L. *parcimōnia*, from *parcere*, to spare], *a.* Frugal, niggardly, stingy. **parsimoniously**, *adv.* **par'simony** (-i).

parsley (pars'li) [Gr. *petroselinon*], *n.* An umbelliferous herb used for seasoning and garnishing dishes.

parsnip (par'snip) [L. *pastināca*, from *pastinum*, a fork for digging], *n.* An umbelliferous plant with an edible root.

parson (par'sŏn) [M.E. *persone*, person], *n.* A clergyman holding a benefice. **parsonage**, *n.* The dwelling-house of a parson; the benefice of a parish.

part (part) [A.-S., from L. *pars*, *partis*], *n.* A portion, piece, or amount of a thing or number of things, esp. considered as separate; a member, organ; one of several equal portions into which a thing is divided or of which it is composed; a section of a book, etc., issued at one time; a share, a lot; interest, concern; the words, etc., allotted to an actor; *(pl.)* qualities, accomplishments; region, district. *v.t.* To divide into portions, etc.; to separate. *v.i.* To divide; to separate (from); to resign; to give way (of a cable, etc.). *adv.* Partly.

partake (par-tāk'), *v.t.* To take or have a part or share in common with others. *v.i.* To take or have a share (of or in, with another or others); to have something of the nature (of). **partaker**, *n.*

parterre (par-târ') [F. *par terre*, on the ground], *n.* An ornamental arrangement of flower-beds; the ground-floor of a theatre under the galleries.

parthenogenesis (par-then-ō-jen'e-sis) [Gr. *parthenos*, virgin], *n.* (*Biol.*) Generation without sexual union.

Parthian (par'thi-án), *a.* Pertaining to Parthia; an ancient kingdom in W. Asia. **Parthian arrow or shot:** A look, word, etc., delivered as a parting blow.

partial (par'shǎl) [L. *partiālis*], *a.* Affecting a part only; biased, unfair; having a preference for. **partial'ity**, *n.* **partially**, *adv.* Unfairly, with bias; in part.

participate (par-tis'i-pāt) [L. *participāre* (*capere*, to take)], *v.i.* To partake (in); to have something (of the nature of). *v.t.* To have a part or share in (with). **partic'ipant**, *a.* **participa'tion**, *n.* **partic'-ipator**, *n.*

participle (par'ti-sipl), *n.* A word partaking of the nature of a verb and of an adjective. **particip'ial**, *a.*

particle (par'tikl) [L. *pars*, part], *n.* A minute portion; an atom; a word not inflected or not used except in combination.

parti-coloured (par'ti-kŭl-ôrd), *a.* Partly variegated; in motley.

particular (pár-tik'ū-lár), *a.* Pertaining to a single person or thing; special, peculiar; personal, individual; minute, circumstantial; exact, precise; noteworthy. *n.* An item, detail, instance; *(pl.)* a detailed account. **particular'ity**, *n.* The quality of being particular; circumstantiality. **particularize**, *v.t.* To mention individually; to specify; to give the particulars of. **particularly**, *adv.*

parting (par'ting), *a.* Serving to part; departing; given on departure. *n.* Separation, division; a point of departure; a dividing-line; leave-taking.

partisan (par-ti-zǎn') [It. *partigiano*], *n.* An adherent of a party, cause, etc.; one of a body of irregular troops.

partition (par-tish'ûn) [L. *partītio*, from *partīrī*, to part], *n.* Division into parts, distribution; a separate part; that which separates, as a wall. *v.t.* To separate (off); to divide. **par'titive**, *a.* Denoting a part. *n.* A word denoting partition, as *some*, *any*, etc.

partly (part'li), *adv.* In part; to some extent; not wholly.

partner (part'nêr), *n.* One who shares with another; one associated with others in business; one of two who dance together, play on the same side, etc.; a husband or a wife. **partnership**, *n.*

partridge (par'trij) [Gr. *perdix*], *n.* A gallinaceous bird preserved for game.

parturient (par-tūr'i-ênt) [L. *parturīre*, to be in labour], *a.* About to bring forth young. **parturition** (-rish'ûn), *n.*

party (par'ti) [L. *pars partis*, part], *n.* A number of persons united for a particular purpose; the principle or practice of taking sides on questions; a social entertainment; each of the personages on either side in a legal action, contract, etc.; one concerned in any affair. **party-wall**, *n.* A wall separating two buildings.

parvenu (par've-nū) [F., arrived, attained], *n.* (*fem.* -nue) An upstart.

pas (pa) [F., step], *n.* Precedence. **to have the pas:** To take precedence (of).

paschal (pas'kǎl) [Heb. *pasakh*], *a.* Pertaining to the Passover or to Easter.

pasha (pǎ'shá) [Turk.], *n.* A Turkish title of honour. **pa'shalic**, *n.* The jurisdiction of a pasha or governor.

pasquinade (pǎs-kwi-nād') [*Pasquino*, It. name], *n.* A lampoon, a satire. *v.t.* To satirize.

pass (pas) [L. *passus*, pace], *v.i.* To move from one place to another; to be current; to be changed from one state to another; to change gradually; to be transferred; to disappear; to die; to elapse; to go through without challenge; to be enacted (as a Bill); to be approved by examining; to happen, occur; (*Cards*) to give up one's option of playing. *v.t.* To go by, beyond, over, etc.; spend (time, etc.); to admit, to approve, to enact; to satisfy the requirements of (examiners); to surpass; to allow to go through (as a Bill, candidate, etc.) after examination; to pledge (one's word); to overlook, disregard, reject. *n.* A passage, esp. a difficult way or a narrow passage through mountains; permission to pass; a ticket authorizing one to travel (on a railway, etc.) or to be admitted (to a theatre, etc.) free; a critical condition of things; the act of passing an examination, esp. without honours; a thrust; a passing of hands over anything (as in mesmerism); a juggling trick; passing a ball in various games. **pass-book,** *n.* A book that passes between a tradesman and his customer, in which purchases on credit are entered; a bank-book. **pass-key,** *n.* A master-key. **password,** *n.* A word by which to distinguish friends from strangers. **passable,** *a.* That may be passed; acceptable, fairly good. **passably,** *adv.*

passage (păs'áj), *n.* Act of passing; transit, migration; transition from one state to another; a journey; a way by which one passes, an entrance or exit; a corridor; a separate portion of a book, etc.; the passing of a Bill, etc., into law.

passé (păs-ā) [F.], *a.* (*fem.* -**sée**) Past the prime, faded; behind the times.

passenger (păs'én-jėr) [O.F. *passager*], One who travels on a public conveyance; a wayfarer.

passepartout (pas-par-too') [F., pass everywhere], *n.* A light frame for a picture, photograph, etc.

passerine (păs'ér-īn) [L. *passer*, sparrow], *a.* Pertaining to the order *Passeres* or perchers, which contains the great mass of the smaller birds; like a sparrow. *n.* A passerine bird.

passible (păs'ibl) [L. *passibilis*, from *patī*, to suffer], *a.* Capable of feeling or suffering; susceptible to impressions. **passibil'ity,** *n.*

passim (păs'im) [L.], *adv.* Here and there, throughout (of words, allusions, etc.).

passing (pa'sing), *a.* Going by, occurring; incidental, casual; fleeting; notable. *n.* Passage, transit.

passion (păsh'ón) [L. *passio*, *ōnis*, from *patī*, to suffer], *n.* Intense emotion, overpowering affection of the mind, as grief, anger, hatred, love; ardent enthusiasm (for); the last agonies of Christ. **Passion Sunday:** The fifth Sunday in Lent. **Passion Week:** The week following this. **passionate,** *a.* Easily moved to strong feeling, esp. anger; vehement, intense.

passive (păs'iv) [L. *passīvus*], *a.* Suffering, acted upon, not acting; inert, submissive. *n.* The passive voice, *i.e.,* the form of a transitive verb representing the subject as the object of the action. **passively,** *adv.* **passiv'ity,** *n.*

passover (pas'ō-vėr), *n.* A Jewish feast commemorating the destruction of the first-born of the Egyptians and the "passing over" of the Israelites by the destroying angel (Exod. xii.).

passport (pas'pôrt), *n.* An official document authorizing a person to proceed to and travel in a foreign country; (*fig.*) anything ensuring admission (to society, etc.).

past (past), *a.* Gone by; just elapsed;

(*Gram.*) denoting action or state belonging to the past. Past times; one's past career; a history of this, esp. a disreputable one. *adv.* So as to go by. *prep.* Beyond in time or place; after; beyond the range of. **past-master,** *n.* A thorough master (of a subject, etc.).

paste (pāst) [O.F. *pasta*], *n.* A mixture of flour and water, etc., used for making pastry and adhesive purposes; a relish of pounded fish, etc.; any doughy or plastic mixture; a composition for making imitation gems. *v.t.* To fasten with paste; to stick (up) with paste. **pasteboard,** *n.* A board made of sheets of paper pasted together.

pastel (păs'tĕl) [F.], *n.* A coloured crayon; a picture drawn with these.

pastern (păs'tėrn) [O.F. *pasture*, a shackle], *n.* The part of a horse's leg between the fetlock and the hoof.

pasteurize (pas'ter-īz) [L. *Pasteur* (1822–95)], *v.t.* To prevent or cure diseases by inoculation. **pasteurized milk,** *n.* Milk in which organisms have been destroyed by heat.

pastille (păs-tēl') [F.], *n.* A roll or pellet of aromatic paste for burning as a disinfectant; an aromatic lozenge.

pastime (pas'tīm), *n.* That which serves to make time pass agreeably; a game.

pastor (pas'tòr) [L. *pastor*, from *pascere*, to feed], *n.* A minister having charge of a church and congregation. **pastoral,** *a.* Pertaining to shepherds; treating of country life (of romances, etc.); rural, rustic; relating to the duties of a pastor. *n.* A poem, romance, picture, etc., descriptive of rural life and manners. **pas'torate,** *n.* Office or jurisdiction of a pastor; pastors collectively.

pastry (pās'tri), *n.* Articles of food made with a crust of baked flour-paste.

pasture (pas'tūr), *n.* Ground fit for the grazing of cattle; grass for grazing. *v.t.* To put (cattle, etc.) on land to graze; to feed (on grass-land). *v.i.* To graze. **pasturage,** *n.*

pasty (pās'ti), *a.* Or or like paste. *n.* (pas'ti) A small pie, usu. of meat, baked without a dish.

pat (păt) [?], *n.* A light quick blow with the hand, a tap; a small mass (of butter, etc.) moulded by patting; the sound of a light blow. *v.t.* To strike gently and quickly; to tap. *a.* Exactly suitable; opportune, apposite. *adv.* Aptly.

patch (păch) [?], *n.* A piece put on to mend anything; a piece of court-plaster worn on the face by women in the 17th and 18th cents. as adornment; a differently coloured part of a surface; a plot of ground. *v.t.* To put a patch on; to mend with a patch, to mend clumsily. **patchwork,** *n.* Work composed of pieces of different colours, sizes, etc. **patcher,** *n.* **patchy,** *a.*

pate (pāt) [?], *n.* The top of the head.

patella (pà-tel'à) [L., dim. of *patina*, paten], *n.* The knee-cap.

paten (păt'én) [L. *patina*], *n.* A shallow dish for receiving the eucharistic bread.

patent (păt'ént, pā'tént) [L. *patens*, laying open], *a.* Open to the perusal of all, obvious; protected or conferred by letters patent; spreading. *n.* A grant from the Crown by letters patent of a title of nobility, or of the exclusive right to make or sell a new invention; an invention so protected. *v.t.* To secure by patent. **patent rolls:** The register of patents granted by the Crown since 1617. **letters patent:** An open document from the Crown conferring a title, right, privilege, etc. **patentee′,** *n.* A holder of a patent. **patently,** *adv.*

paterfamilias (pā-tĕr-fâ-mĭl′ĭ-ás) [L. *pater*, father, FATHER], *n.* The head or father of a family or household.

paternal (pá-tĕr′nàl), *a.* Pertaining to a father; fatherly; related through the father. **paternally,** *adv.* **paternity,** *a.* Fatherhood; ancestry on the male side.

paternoster (păt-ĕr-nos′tĕr) [L., our Father], *n.* The Lord's Prayer, esp. in Latin; every eleventh bead of a rosary; hence, a rosary; a fishing-line with a weight at the end and short lines with hooks at intervals.

path (path) [A.-S. *pœth*], *n.* A footway; a track; (*fig.*) course of life, action, etc. **pathway,** *n.*

Pathan (pá-tan′) [native], *n.* An Afghan belonging to one of the tribes on the N.W. frontier of India.

pathetic (pá-thet′ik) [Gr. *pathētikos*], *a.* Affecting the feelings, esp. those of pity and sorrow. *n.* That which is pathetic; (*pl.*) the display of pathos; the study of pathetic emotions. **pathetically,** *adv.*

patho- [Gr. *pathos*, suffering], *comb. form.* **pathogenesis** (păth-ô-jen′é-sis), *n.* The origin and development of disease. **pathol′ogy,** *n.* The science of diseases, esp. of the body. **pathol′ogist,** *n.*

pathos (pā′thos), *n.* A quality or element in events or expression that excites emotion, esp. pity or sorrow.

-pathy [Gr. *-patheia*, as prec.], *suf.* Feeling; treatment of disease, as in *homœopathy, sympathy.*

patience (pā′shèns), *n.* The quality of being patient; calm endurance of pain or evil, fortitude; a card-game for one person. **patient,** *a.* Capable of bearing pain, suffering, etc., without fretfulness; not easily provoked; persevering. *n.* One who suffers; one under medical treatment. **patiently,** *adv.*

patois (păt′wa) [F.], *n.* A dialect spoken by the people of a district.

patriarch (pā′tri-ark) [Gr. *patria*, family, *archein*, to rule], *n.* The head of a tribe ruling by paternal right; (*R.-C. Ch.*) a bishop of the highest rank; a venerable old man; the oldest living person (in an assembly, order, etc.). **patriar′chal,** *a.* **pa′triarchate,** *n.* **patriarchy,** *n.* A patriarchal system of government.

patrician (pá-trish′án) [L. *patres*, senators], *a.* Noble, aristocratic. *n.* A member of the Roman aristocracy; a chief magistrate of a Roman province; a noble, a member of the highest class of society.

patrimony (păt′ri-mô-ni), *n.* An estate or right inherited from one's father; a church estate or endowment. **patrimonial** (-mô′ni-àl), *a.*

patriot (pā′tri-ót), *n.* One who loves his country and is devoted to its interests and independence. **patriotic** (-ot′ik), *a.* **pa′triotism,** *n.*

patristic (pá-tris′tik), *a.* Pertaining to the ancient Fathers of the Church.

patrol (pá-trōl′) [F. *patrouiller*, to dabble in the mud], *v.t.* To go the rounds of a camp, etc. *v.i.* To go round. *n.* The perambulation of a camp, town, etc., for security; the detachment of soldiers, police, firemen, etc., doing this; troops sent out to reconnoitre.

patron (pā′tròn) [L. *patrōnus*, from *pater*, father], *n.* One who supports or protects a person, cause, etc.; one who holds the gift of a benefice; a regular customer (at a shop). **patronage** (păt′rô-náj), *n.* Support, fostering encouragement, protection; right of presentation to a benefice or office; act of patronizing; support by customers (of a shop, etc.). **pat′ronize,** *v.t.*

patronymic (păt-rô-nim′ik), *a.* Derived from a father. *n.* A name so derived; a family name.

patten (păt′én) [F. *patin*], *n.* A mounted clog or overshoe.

patter (1) (păt′ér), *v.i.* To strike, with a quick succession of sharp sounds; to move with short quick steps. *n.* A quick succession of sharp, light sounds or taps.

patter (2) [PATERNOSTER], *v.t.* To say (one's prayers) in a mechanical, singsong way. *v.i.* To talk glibly. *n.* The patois or slang of a particular class, etc.; rapid speech introduced impromptu into a song, comedy, etc.

pattern (păt′érn) [as PATRON], *n.* A model serving as a guide; a sample or specimen; a decorative design for a carpet, wall-paper, etc.; hence type, style. *v.t.* To copy; to model (after); to decorate with a pattern.

patty (păt′i) [F. *pâté*], *n.* A little pie.

paucity (paw′si-ti) [L. *paucus*, few], *n.* Fewness.

paunch (pawnch) [L. *pantex, -ticem*], *n.* The belly; the first and largest stomach in ruminants. **paunchy,** *a.*

pauper (paw′pér) [L., poor], *n.* One without means of support, a destitute person. **pauperism,** *n.* **pauperize,** *v.t.* To reduce to pauperism.

pause (pawz) [Gr. *pauein*, to cease], *n.* A temporary cessation of action, speaking, etc.; a break for the sake of emphasis; (*Mus.*) a mark ⌒ or ⌣ over a note, etc., indicating that it is to be prolonged. *v.i.* To make a short stop; to wait.

pave (pāv) [L. *pavīre*, to ram], *v.t.* To make a surface upon, with stone, bricks, etc.; to cover with a pavement. **pave′ment,** *n.* A hard level covering of stones, bricks, wood-blocks, etc., a paved footway at the side of a street. **paviour,** *n.* One who lays pavements; a rammer for driving paving-stones. **paving,** *n.* **paving-stone,** *n.*

pavilion (pá-vil′yòn) [F. *pavillon*], *n.* A large tent of conical shape; a temporary structure for shelter, etc.; a building for spectators and players on a cricket-ground, etc.

paw (paw) [O.F. *powe*], *n.* The foot of a

quadruped having claws, as dist. from a hoof. *v.t.* To scrape or strike with the forefoot; to handle roughly or clumsily.

pawky (paw'ki) [Sc. and North.], *a.* Shrewd; humorous, arch. **pawkily**, *adv.*

pawl (pawl) [?], *n.* A hinged lever engaging with the teeth of a wheel to prevent it from running back; a bar for preventing the recoil of a windlass.

pawn (1) (pawn) [O.F. *paon*, med. L. *pedo*, *-dōnem*, foot-soldier], *n.* A piece of the lowest value in chess.

pawn (2) [O.F. *pan*, prob. from Teut.], *n.* A security for a debt or loan, a pledge; the state of being held as a pledge. *v.t.* To deliver or deposit as a pledge for repayment or for the performance of a promise. **pawnbroker**, *n.* One who lends money on the security of goods pawned. **pawnshop**, *n.* The place where this is carried on.

pay (1) (pā) [O.F. *paier*, L. *pācāre*, to appease], *v.t.* (*p.* and *p.p.* paid) To hand over what is due in discharge of a debt or for services or goods; to discharge (a bill, obligation, etc.); to defray the cost of; to expend (away); to compensate; to render (a compliment, visit, etc.). *v.i.* To make payment; to discharge a debt; to be remunerative. *n.* Payment, compensation; wages. **paying guest**, *n.* A boarder. **paymaster**, *n.* One who regularly pays wages, etc. **payable**, *a.* **pay-roll**, *n.* A list of employees. **payee** (pā-ē'), *n.* **payment**, *n.*

pay (2) [O. North. F. *peier*, L. *picāre*, from *pix picis*, pitch], *v.t.* (*p.* and *p.p.* payed) To coat or fill with hot pitch for water-proofing.

P.A.Y.E. [initials of Pay As You Earn], *n.* A device for collecting Income Tax on the weekly or other payments of salary or wages.

pea (pē), *n.* A leguminous plant, the seeds of which are used for food. **pea-pod**, *n.* The pericarp of the pea.

peace (pēs), *n.* [L. *pax*], *n.* A state of quiet; absence of civil disturbance; freedom from or cessation of war; a treaty reconciling two nations; a state of friendliness; calmness of mind. **peace-maker**, *n.* One who reconciles differences. **peace-offering**, *n.* A token of thanksgiving, etc.; a gift to procure peace or reconciliation. **peaceable**, *a.* Peaceful, quiet; disposed to peace. **peaceably**, *adv.* **peaceful**, *a.* In a state of peace; free from noise or disturbance; pacific, mild. **peacefulness**, *n.*

peach (1) (pēch) [L. *persicum*, Persian (apple)], *n.* A fleshy, downy fruit, the tree bearing it.

peach (2), *v.i.* To turn informer against an accomplice.

peacock (pē'kok) [A.-S. *pēa*, *pāwe*, L. *pāvo*], *n.* The male of the peafowl, a bird with gorgeous plumage and long tail expanding like a fan; (*fig.*) a vainglorious person. **peafowl**, *n.* **peahen**, *n.*

pea-jacket (pē'jăk-ĕt) [Dut.], *n.* A coarse, thick, loose, overcoat worn by seamen, etc.

peak (1) (pēk), *n.* A sharp top, esp. of a mountain; the projecting brim of a cap;

the upper after corner of a sail extended by a gaff; the upper end of a gaff. **peaked**, *a.*

peak (2) [?], *v.i.* To look sickly; to pine away. **peaky**, *a.*

peal (pēl) [APPEAL], *n.* A prolonged or resounding noise, as of thunder, bells, etc.; a set of bells tuned to each other; a series of changes rung on these. *v.i.* To sound a peal.

pear (pâr) [A.-S. *pere*], *n.* The fleshy fruit of the pear-tree.

pearl (pĕrl) [F. *perle*], *n.* A smooth, whitish iridescent concretion, found in the oyster and other bivalves, prized as a gem; something round and clear and resembling a pearl; the finest specimen of its kind; a small size of type [as this]. *a.* Pertaining to or made of pearls or mother-of-pearl. *v.t.* To set with pearls; to sprinkle with pearly drops; to strip barley into pearly grains. *v.i.* To fish for pearls. **pearly**, *a.* **pearling**, *n.* The process of removing the outer coat of barley, etc.

peasant (pez'ănt) [O.F. *paisant*], *n.* A countryman; a rustic labourer. *a.* Rustic, rural. **peasantry**, *n.* Peasants collectively.

pease (pēz) [A.-S. *pise*, L. *pisum*, Gr. *pison*], *n.* (*pl.* or *collect. sing.*) Peas. **peasecod**, *n.* A pea-pod.

peat (pēt) [M.E. *pete*], *n.* Decayed and partly carbonized vegetable-matter found in boggy places and used as fuel. **peaty**, *a.*

pebble (pebl) [A.-S. *papol*], *n.* A small stone rounded by the action of water; an agate; rock-crystal used for spectacles, etc. **pebbled**, **pebbly**, *a.*

peccadillo (pek-à-dil'ō) [Sp.], *n.* (*pl.* -does) A slight fault or offence.

peccant (pek'ănt) [L. *peccans*, *-antem*, sinning], *a.* Sinful; informal, wrong.

peccary (pek'à-ri) [Carib. *pakira*], *n.* A small S. American hog-like mammal.

peck (1) (pek) [O.F. *pek*], *n.* A measure of capacity, two gallons; a vessel used for measuring this.

peck (2), *v.t.* To strike with a beak or a pointed instrument; to pick up with the beak; (*colloq.*) to eat. *v.i.* To aim with a beak or pointed implement. *n.* A sharp stroke with or as with a beak; a mark made by this.

pectoral (pek'tò-răl) [L. *pectus*, breast], *a.* Pertaining to or for the breast. *n.* A pectoral fin.

peculate (pek'ū-lāt) [L. *peculāri*], *v.t.* To appropriate money, etc., entrusted to one's care. **pecula'tion**, *n.* **pec'ulator**, *n.*

peculiar (pē-kū'li-àr) [L. *peculiāris*, from *peculium*, private property], *a.* Belonging particularly and exclusively (to); one's own; particular, special; singular, odd. **peculi'arity**, *n.* The quality of being peculiar; a characteristic. **peculiarly**, *adv.*

pecuniary (pē-kū'ni-à-ri) [L. *pecūnia*, money], *a.* Relating to or consisting of money. **pecuniarily**, *adv.*

pedagogue (ped'à-gog) [Gr. *pais paidos*, boy, *agein*, to lead], *n.* A schoolmaster (usu. implying pedantry). **pedagog'ic**, **-al**, *a.*

pedal (ped'ál) [L. *pes pedis*, foot], *n.* A lever acted on by the foot. *v.i.* To work (a bicycle, sewing-machine, etc.) by pedals; to play on (an organ) by pedals. *v.i.* To play an organ or work a bicycle, etc., by pedals.

pedant (ped'ánt) [It. *pedante*, a schoolmaster], *n.* One who makes a show of learning, or lays undue stress on formulas; one with more book-learning than practical experience or common sense. **pedan'tic**, *a.* **ped'antry**, *n.*

peddle (pedl) [?], *v.i.* To travel about selling small wares; to busy oneself about trifles. *v.t.* To hawk; to retail. **peddling**, *a.* Trifling, insignificant.

pedestal (ped'ès-tál) [It. *piedestallo*], *n.* A base for a column, statue, etc.

pedestrian (pè-des'tri-án) [L. *pes pedis*, foot], *a.* Going or performed on foot; pertaining to walking; dull, commonplace. *n.* One who journeys or races on foot. **pedestrianism**, *n.*

pedigree (ped'i-grè) [F. *pié de grue* (L. *pes pedis*, foot, *de*, of, *grue*, L. *grus*, crane)], *n.* Genealogy, lineage; a genealogical table or tree. *a.* Pure-bred, having a known ancestry (of cattle, dogs, etc.).

pediment (ped'i-mènt), *n.* The triangular part surmounting a portico, in buildings in Grecian style; similar decoration over doorways, windows, etc.

pedlar (ped'lár) [?], *n.* A travelling hawker of small wares, usu. carried in a pack.

pedometer (pè-dom'e-tèr) [L. *pes, pedis*, foot], *n.* An instrument for measuring distance traversed on foot.

peel (1) (pèl) [F. *piller*, to rob], *v.t.* To strip the skin, bark, or rind off; to pillage. *v.i.* To lose the skin or rind, to become bare. *n.* Skin or rind; a long-handled shovel for taking bread from a baker's oven.

peel (2) (pèl) [O.F. *pel*, a palisade], *n.* A square fortified tower.

peep (pèp) [?], *v.i.* To look through a crevice; to look slyly or furtively; to appear cautiously, to come gradually into view. *n.* A furtive look, hasty glance, glimpse.

peer (1) (pèr) [L. *par*, equal], *n.* An equal in any respect; a noble, esp. a member of an hereditary legislative body (in Gt. Brit. comprising dukes, marquesses, earls, viscounts, and barons). **peerage**, *n.* The rank of peer; the body of peers; a book containing particulars of the nobility. **peeress**, *n.* **peerless**, *a.* Without an equal.

peer (2) [?], *v.i.* To peep, to pry (at, etc.); to appear, come into sight.

peevish (pè'vish) [?], *a.* Fretful, petulant; expressing discontent.

peg (peg) [M.E. *pegge*], *n.* A pin or bolt for holding parts of a structure or fastening articles together, hanging things on, marking etc.; a step, degree; an occasion, pretext, or topic for discourse, etc. *v.t.* To fix or fasten with a peg.

peignoir (pā'nwar) [F.], *n.* A loose robe worn by women during the toilet.

pejorative (pè'jòr-á-tiv) [L. *pejorare*, to make worse], *a.* Depreciatory.

Pekinese (pè-kin-èz'), *a.* Of or pertaining to Pekin, cap. of China. *n.* A small rough-coated Chinese dog.

pekoe (pek'ō) [Chin. *pek*, white, *ho*, down], *n.* A fine black tea.

pelagian, pelagic (pè-lāj'ián) [Gr. *pelagos*, sea], *a.* Inhabiting the deep sea. *n.* A pelagian animal.

pelargonium (pel-ár-gō'ni-ùm) [Gr. *pelargos*, stork], *n.* A genus of ornamental plants, the geraniums.

pelf (pelf) [?], *n.* Money, wealth (in contempt).

pelican (pel'i-kán) [Gr. *pelekan*], *n.* A large fish-eating water-fowl with an enormous pouch beneath the mandibles for storing fish when caught.

pelisse (pè-lès') [L. *pellicius*, of skin], *n.* A woman's long cloak; an outer garment for children.

pellet (pel'èt) [L. *pila*, ball], *n.* A little ball, esp. of something easily moulded; a small pill; a small shot.

pell-mell (pel-mel) [F. *pêle-mêle*], *adv.* In a confused manner, anyhow. *a.* Disorderly, promiscuous.

pellucid (pè-lū'sid) [L. *pellucidus* (*lucère*, to shine)], *a.* Limpid, transparent; clear in thought or style.

pelmet (pel'met) [?], *n.* A canopy from which curtains hang; a vallance.

pelt (1) (pelt) [O.F. *pel*, skin], *n.* A hide with the hair on, esp. of a sheep or goat; undressed fur; a raw skin. **peltry**, *n.* Furs in general.

pelt (2) [?], *v.t.* To assail by throwing missiles. *v.i.* To throw missiles; to keep on throwing, firing, etc. (at); to beat heavily (of rain).

pelvis (pel'vis) [L., basin], *n.* The lower portion of the great abdominal cavity; its bony walls.

pemmican (pem'i-kán) [Cree *pimikan*], *n.* Dried meat pounded, mixed with melted fat and pressed into cakes.

pen (1) (pen) [A.-S.], *n.* A small enclosure for cattle, poultry, etc. *v.t.* To enclose, confine.

pen (2) [L. *penna*, feather], *n.* A quill; an instrument for writing with ink; style of writing. *v.t.* To write, to compose and write. **penmanship**, *n.* The art of writing; style of writing. **pen-name**, *n.* A literary pseudonym.

penal (pè'nál) [L. *poena*, penalty], *a.* Pertaining to punishment; punishable, esp. by law. **penalize**, *v.t.* To make or declare penal; (*Sport*) to subject to a penalty or handicap; (*fig.*) to put under an unfair disadvantage.

penalty (pen'ál-ti), *n.* Legal punishment; a sum to be forfeited for non-performance or breach of conditions; a fine, a forfeit; (*Sport*) a handicap.

penance (pen'áns), *n.* Sorrow for sin evinced by voluntary suffering; an act of self-mortification undertaken as a satisfaction for sin, esp. one imposed by a priest.

Penates (pè-nā'tèz) [L.], *n.pl.* The Roman household gods.

penchant (pan-shan') [F.], *n.* A strong inclination or liking; a bias.

pencil (pen'sil) [O.F. *pincel*, L. *pèniculus*, brush], *n.* A small brush used by painters; a slip of graphite, crayon, etc., usu. enclosed in a casing of wood; (*Opt.*)

a system of rays diverging from or converging to a point. *v.t.* To paint, draw, write, or mark with a pencil.

pendant (pen'dănt) [F.], *n.* Anything hanging down or suspended, an earring, a locket, a tassel, etc.; a hanging chandelier, etc.; a tapering flag or pennant; a companion-piece, counterpart. **pen'dent**, *a.* Hanging; overhanging; (*fig.*) pending. **pending**, *a.* Depending, awaiting settlement, undecided. *prep.* During.

pendulous (pen'dū-lŭs), *a.* Hanging, suspended; swinging.

pendulum (pen'dū-lŭm), *n.* A body suspended from a fixed point and oscillating freely by the force of gravity.

penetrate (pen'ē-trāt) [L. *penetrāre*], *v.t.* To enter; to pierce; to permeate; to imbue (with); to affect the feelings of; (*fig.*) to discern by the intellect. *v.i.* To make way, to pass (into, etc.). **penetrable**, *a.* **penetrating**, *a.* Piercing; subtle, discerning. **penetra'tion**, *n.*

penguin (pen'gwin) [?], *n.* A swimming bird of the southern hemisphere, with rudimentary wings and scale-like feathers.

penicillin (pen-i-sil'in), *n.* A substance produced from the mould *Penicillium* with intense growth-inhibiting action against certain bacteria.

peninsula (pé-nin'sū-là) [L. *pœne*, almost, *insula*, island], *n.* A piece of land almost surrounded by water. **peninsular**, *a.* Pertaining to a peninsula.

penitent (pen'i-tĕnt) [L. *punīre*, to punish], *a.* Contrite, sorry. *n.* One who is penitent; one submitting to penance under a confessor. **penitence**, *n.* **peniten'tial**, *a.* **pen'itently**, *adv.* **peniten'tiary**, *a.* Penitential; pertaining to the reformatory treatment of criminals. *n.* A reformatory prison, a house of correction.

pennant (pen'ănt), *n.* A pennon; a long narrow streamer borne at a mast-head, a pendant.

penniless (pen'i-lĕs), *a.* Without money; destitute.

pennon (pen'ŏn) [O.F. *penon*], *n.* A small pointed or swallow-tailed flag, formerly borne as the ensign of a regiment of lancers; a long streamer carried by a ship.

penny (pen'i) [A.-S. *pening*], *n.* (*pl.* pennies, denoting coins; pence, denoting amount) A bronze coin, the 12th part of a shilling; (*Bibl.*) a denarius. **pennyweight**, *n.* Twenty-four grains or one-twentieth of an ounce troy. **pennywise**, *a.* Saving small sums at the risk of larger ones.

pensile (pen'sil, -sīl) [L. *pensus*, hanged], *a.* Hanging, pendulous.

pension (pen'shŭn) [L. *pensio*, payment], *n.* A periodical allowance for past services, to secure services when required, or to literary men, scientists, etc., to enable them to carry on their work; (pan-syon') a boarding-house or boarding-school, esp. on the Continent. *v.t.* To grant or pay a pension to. **pensionary**, *a.* and *n.* **pensioner**, *n.*

pensive (pen'siv) [F. *penser*, to think], *a.*

Thoughtful; serious, anxious; expressing sad thoughtfulness.

pent (pent), *a.* Penned in, confined.

pent- **penta-** [Gr. *pente*, five], *comb. form.*

pentagon (pen'tà-gŏn) [Gr. *gōnia*, angle], *n.* A plane figure having five sides and five angles. **pentag'onal**, *a.* **pentahe'dron** [Gr. *hedra*, base], *n.* A figure having five sides, esp. equal sides. **pentahedral**, *a.* **pentam'eter** [PENTA-, METRE], *n.* A verse of five feet; the iambic verse of ten syllables.

Pentateuch (pen'tà-tūk) [Gr. *teuchos*, book], *n.* The first five books of the Old Testament, usu. ascribed to Moses.

Pentecost (pen'tĕ-kost) [Gr. *pentēkostē*, fiftieth (day)], *n.* A solemn Jewish festival held on the fiftieth day from the second day of the Passover; Whit-sunday.

penthouse (pent'hous) [M.E. *pentice*], *n.* A roof or shed standing aslope against a building; (*Am.*) a private dwelling built on the roof of a skyscraper.

penult (pé-nŭlt') [L. *pœne*, almost, *ultimus*, last], *n.* The last syllable but one of a word. **penultimate**, *a.* and *n.*

penumbra (pé-nŭm'brà) [L. *pœne*, almost, *umbra*, shadow], *n.* The partly shaded zone around the total shadow caused by an opaque body intercepting light.

penury (pen'û-ri) [L. *pēnūria*], *n.* Extreme poverty, destitution. **penur'ious**, *a.* Niggardly, stingy; scanty.

peon (pē'ŏn) [Sp.], *n.* (*India*) A native constable; (*Mexico*) a labourer.

peony (pē'ô-ni) [Gr. *Paiōn*, god of healing], *n.* A plant with large globular terminal flowers.

people (pēpl) [L. *populus*], *n.* The persons composing a nation, community, or race; (*pl.* peoples) any body of persons; persons generally; one's family or tribe; retinue, workpeople, etc. *v.t.* To stock with inhabitants, to populate; to inhabit. **the people**: The populace, as dist. from the self-styled higher orders.

pepper (pep'er) [A.-S. *pipor*, of Oriental orig.], *n.* A pungent aromatic condiment made from the dried berries of the pepper-plant; applied also to plants of the genus *Capsicum*. *v.t.* To season with pepper; to besprinkle; (*fig.*) to season with pungent remarks; to pelt, to beat severely. **pepper-and-salt**, *n.* A cloth of black and white having a speckled appearance. **pepper-corn**, *n.* The dried berry of the pepper-tree, esp. as a nominal rent. **peppermint**, *n.* A pungent aromatic herb; an essential oil distilled from this; a lozenge flavoured with it. **peppery**, *a.* Having the qualities of pepper; (*fig.*) choleric, hot-tempered.

pepsin (pep'sin) [Gr. *pepsis*, digestion], *n.* A ferment in gastric juice, the chief agent in digestion. **peptic**, *a.* Promoting or pertaining to digestion; having good digestive powers.

per (pĕr) [L.], *prep.* By; through, by means of. **per annum**: Yearly; by the year. **per cent.**: By the hundred.

per- [prec.], *pref.* Through, completely; very, exceedingly; to the extreme.

peradventure (pĕr-àd-ven'tūr) [O.F. *par aventure*], *adv.* Perhaps, perchance.

perambulate (pĕr-ăm'bū-lāt) [L. *ambulāre*, to walk], *v.t.* To walk over or through; to survey. **perambula'tion**, *n.* **peram'-bulator**, *n.* A child's carriage propelled from behind.

perceive (pĕr-sēv) [O.F. *perceivre*], *v.t.* To apprehend, discern, understand; to have cognizance of by the senses. **perceivable**, *a.*

percentage (pĕr-sen'tåj), *n.* Rate or proportion for each hundred.

percept (pĕr'sept), *n.* That which is perceived, the mental product of perception. **percep'tible**, *a.* That may be perceived by the senses or intellect. **perceptibil'ity**, *n.* **percep'tibly**, *adv.* **percep'tion**, *n.* Act, process, or faculty of perceiving; intuitive apprehension, insight. **perceptive**, *a.* Having the faculty of perceiving.

perch (1) (pĕrch) [L. *perca*], *n.* A striped spiny-finned freshwater fish.

perch (2) [L. *pertica*, pole], *n.* A bar, twig, etc., used as a roost by birds; an elevated position; a land measure of 5½ yards. *v.i.* To alight or rest on or as on a perch. *v.t.* To place on a perch.

perchance (pĕr-chans') [O.F. *par chance*], *adv.* Perhaps, by chance.

percipient (pĕr-sĭp'i-ĕnt) [L. *percipiens*, perceiving], *a.* Perceiving, apprehending, conscious.

percolate (pĕr'kŏ-lāt) [L. *percōlāre*, strain], *v.i.* To pass through small interstices, to filter (through). *v.t.* To ooze through. **percola'tion**, *n.* **per'colator**, *n.* One who or that which strains or filters.

percuss (pĕr-kŭs') [L. *percussus*, p.p. of *percutere*], *v.t.* To strike quickly or tap forcibly, esp. to test or diagnose. **percussion** (pĕr-kŭsh'ŏn), *n.* Collision; the shock or sound of collision.

perdition (pĕr-dish'ŭn) [L. *perdere*, to destroy], *n.* Utter destruction, esp. in a future state; damnation.

perdurable (pĕr-dūr'åbl), *a.* Very lasting, or durable; permanent.

peregrination (per-ĕ-gri-nā'shŭn) [L. *peregrinus*, foreign], *n.* A travelling about; a sojourning in foreign countries. **peregrine**, *a.* Migratory, travelling abroad. *n.* A peregrine falcon, a widely distributed species used for hawking.

peremptory (per'emp-tŏr-i) [L. *peremptōrius*, destructive], *a.* Precluding question; absolute, decisive; imperious, dogmatic, dictatorial; determinate. **peremptorily**, *adv.*

perennial (pĕ-ren'i-ål) [L. *annus*, year], *a.* Lasting throughout the year; lasting long, never ceasing; (of plants) living for more than two years. *n.* A perennial plant.

perfect (pĕr-fĕkt) [L. *perfectus*], *a.* Complete in all its parts, qualities, etc., without defect; thoroughly versed, trained, skilled, etc.; of the best and most complete kind; entire, unqualified; (*Gram.*) expressing action completed. *v.t.* To finish or complete, to bring to perfection. **perfectible**, *a.* **perfec'tion**, *n.* Act of making or state of being perfect; supreme excellence; complete development; the highest degree, the extreme (of). **per'fectly**, *adv.*

perfervid (pĕr-fĕr'vid), *a.* Very fervid.

perfidy (pĕr'fi-di) [L. *perfidus*, treacherous], *n.* Violation of faith, allegiance, or confidence. **perfid'ious**, *a.* Treacherous, faithless. **perfidiousness**, *n.*

perforate (pĕr-fō-rāt) [L. *perforātus*, bored through (PER-, *forāre*, to bore)], *v.t.* To pierce; to make a hole through by boring. *v.i.* To penetrate (into or through). **perfora'tion**, *n.* **per'forator**, *n.*

perforce (pĕr-fōrs') [O.F. *par force*, by force], *adv.* Of necessity; compulsorily.

perform (pĕr-fôrm') [F. *former*, to form], *v.t.* To execute, accomplish; to fulfil; to represent, as on the stage; to render (music, etc.). *v.i.* To act a part; to play an instrument, etc. **performance**, *n.* **performer**, *n.*

perfume (pĕr-fūm') [L. *fūmāre*, to smoke], *v.t.* To fill with a scent. *n.* (pĕr'fūm) A substance emitting a sweet odour, fragrance, scent; fumes of something burning. **perfu'mer**, *n.* **perfumery**, *n.*

perfunctory (pĕr-fŭnk'tŏ-ri) [L. *functus*, performed], *a.* Done in a half-hearted manner; careless, superficial. **perfunctorily**, *adv.*

pergola (pĕr'gŏ-lå) [It.], *n.* A covered walk with climbing plants trained over posts.

perhaps (pĕr-hăps'), *adv.* It may be, by chance, possibly.

peri (pēr'i) [Pers. *parī*], *n.* A descendant of fallen angels, excluded from paradise till some penance is accomplished; a beautiful being, a fairy.

peri- [Gr., around, about], *pref.* **perianth** (per'i-ănth) [Gr. *anthos*, flower], *n.* A floral envelope. **pericar'dium** [Gr. *kardia*, heart], *n.* The membrane enveloping the heart. **per'icarp** [Gr. *karpos*, fruit], *n.* The seed-vessel or wall of the developed ovary of a plant. **pericra'nium**, *n.* The membrane investing the skull.

peridot (per'i-dot) [F.], *n.* A yellowish-green chrysolite; olivine.

perigee (per'i-jē) [Gr. *gē*, earth], *n.* The point in the orbit of the moon or of a planet nearest the earth.

perihelion (pĕr-i-hē'li-ŏn) [Gr. *hēlion*, sun], *n.* The part of the orbit of a planet, comet, etc., nearest the sun.

peril (per'il) [L. *periculum*], *n.* Danger, risk; exposure to injury or loss. *v.t.* To risk, to endanger. **perilous**, *a.* **perilously**, *adv.*

perimeter (pĕ-rim'ĕ-tĕr), *n.* The bounding line of a plane figure; its length; circumference.

period (pēr'i-ŏd) [Gr. *hodos*, way], *n.* A portion of time marked off by some recurring event, esp. an astronomical phenomenon, as the revolution of a planet round the sun; any specified or indefinite portion of time, an age, era, cycle; length of duration; a complete sentence; a full stop (.); an end, a limit; menstruation. **period'ic**, *a.* **period'ical**, *a.* Appearing at regular intervals. *n.* A magazine or other publication published at regular intervals. **periodic'ity**, *n.*

peripatetic (per-i-på-tet'ik) [Gr. *patein*, to walk], *a.* Walking about, itinerant; pertaining to the philosophy of Aristotle

(who walked about whilst teaching).
n. One who walks about; a follower of
Aristotle.

periphery (pê-rif'ê-ri) [Gr. *pherein*, to bear],
n. The outer surface; the perimeter or
circumference.

periphrasis (pê-rif'râ-sis) [Gr. *phrasis*, a
speech], *n.* Roundabout speaking or
expression, circumlocution. **periphrastic**
(-fràs'tik), *a.* Circumlocutory.

periscope (per'i-skōp), *n.* An apparatus
enabling persons inside a submarine,
trench, etc., to look about above the
surface.

perish (per'ish) [O.F.], *v.i.* To be destroyed,
to come to naught; to decay; to lose life
or vitality; to be lost eternally. **perish-
able,** *a.* Subject to rapid decay. *n.pl.*
Food-stuffs, etc., liable to rapid deterioration. **perishabil'ity,** *n.*

peristyle (per'i-stil) [Gr. *stulos*, pillar], *n.*
(*Arch.*) A row of columns about a
building, court, etc.; a court, etc., with
a colonnade around it.

peritoneum (per-i-tô-nē'úm) [Gr. *teinein,*
to stretch], *n.* A serous membrane lining
the abdominal cavity and enveloping all
the abdominal viscera. **peritoni'tis,** *n.*
Inflammation of the peritoneum.

periwig (per'i-wig), *n.* A peruke, wig.

periwinkle (1) (per'i-wingkl) [A.-S. *pine-
wincle, wine-wincle*], *n.* A small univalve
mollusc.

periwinkle (2) [A.-S. *perwince,* L. *pervinca*],
n. A trailing shrub with blue or white
flowers.

perjure (pêr'júr) [L. *jūrāre,* to swear], *v.t.*
To forswear (oneself). **perjured,** *a.*
Forsworn. **perjurer,** *n.* **perjury,** *n.* Act
of swearing falsely, the violating of an
oath.

perk (pêrk) [?], *v.t.* To make smart or
trim; to hold or prick up; to thrust
(oneself) forward. *v.i.* To bear oneself
saucily or jauntily. *a.* Pert, brisk.
perky, *a.* **perkily,** *adv.*

permanent (pêr'má-nènt) [L. *manens,*
remaining], *a.* Lasting, remaining, or
intended to remain in the same state,
etc. **permanence, -nency,** *n.* **permanently,** *adv.*

permeate (pêr'mê-āt) [L. *meātus,* passed],
v.t. To pass through the pores or
interstices of; to pervade, saturate.
v.i. To be diffused (in, through, etc.).
permeable, *a.* Yielding passage to
fluids; penetrable. **permeabil'ity,** *n.*
permea'tion, *n.* **per'meative,** *a.*

permit (pêr-mit') [L. *mittere,* to send], *v.t.*
To allow by consent; to give permission,
to authorize. *v.i.* To allow, admit (of).
n. (pêr'mit) A permission or warrant, a
written authority. **permis'sible,** *a.*
permission (-mish'ûn), *n.* The act of
permitting; leave or licence given. **permis'sive,** *a.* Permitting; allowing;
granting liberty.

permutation (pêr-mü-tā'shûn) [L. *mutāre,*
to change], *n.* (*Math.*) Change of the
order of a series of quantities; each of
the different arrangements, as regards
order, that can be made in this; trans-
mutation.

pernicious (pêr-nish'ûs) [L. *nex necis,*
death], *a.* Destructive, deadly, noxious.

pernickety (pêr-nik'ê-ti) [Sc.], *a.* Fastidious, over-particular; awkward to
handle, ticklish.

perorate (per'ô-rāt) [L. *ōrāre,* to speak],
v.i. To deliver an oration. *v.t.* To declaim. **perora'tion,** *n.* The concluding
part or winding up of an oration.

peroxide (pêr-ok'sid), *n.* The oxide of a
given base that contains the greatest
quantity of oxygen. **perox'idize,** *v.t.*
and *i.*

perpendicular (pêr-pên-dik'ū-lár) [L. *per-
pendiculum,* a plummet], *a.* At right
angles to the plane of the horizon;
upright, vertical; extremely steep (of a
hill, etc.); (*Geom.*) at right angles to a
given line or surface; applied to the style
of pointed architecture in England succeeding the Decorated. *n.* A perpendicular line; perpendicular attitude or
condition; an instrument for determining
the vertical.

perpetrate (pêr'pê-trāt) [L. *patrāre,* to
effect], *v.t.* To perform, commit; to be
guilty of. **perpetra'tion,** *n.* **per'pe-
trator,** *n.*

perpetual (pêr-pet'ū-ál) [L. *perpetuus*], *a.*
Eternal; always continuing, persistent.
perpetually, *adv.* **perpetuate,** *v.t.* To
make perpetual; to preserve from
oblivion. **perpetua'tion,** *n.* **perpetu'ity,**
n. The number of years' purchase to be
given for an annuity; endless duration.

perplex (pêr-pleks') [L. *plexus,* plaited], *v.t.*
To puzzle, bewilder, make anxious; to
confuse, to make difficult to understand;
to entangle. **perplexity,** *n.*

perquisite (pêr'kwi-zit) [L. *perquisītum*], *n.*
Emolument over and above regular
wages; anything to which one has a
prescriptive right after it has served its
purpose; a tip.

perry (per'i) [O.F. *peré*], *n.* A fermented
liquor made from pears.

persecute (pêr'sê-kūt) [L. *secūtus,* followed],
v.t. To pursue in a hostile or malicious
way; to afflict with suffering or loss of
life, esp. for adherence to a creed; to
harass, to importune. **persecu'tion,** *n.*
persecutor *n.*

persevere (pêr-sê-vēr') [L. *sevērus,* severe],
v.i. To persist in any undertaking or
course. **perseverance,** *n.* Persistence
in any design or undertaking; sedulous
endeavour. **perseveringly,** *adv.*

Persian (pêr'shán), *a.* Pertaining to
Persia, its inhabitants, or language. *n.*
A native of Persia; the Persian language;
a Persian cat; a kind of thin silk.

persiflage (pêr-si-flazh') [F.], *n.* Banter,
raillery; frivolous treatment of any
subject.

persimmon (pêr-sim'ôn) [Am. Ind.], *n.* A
plum-like fruit, the American date-plum.

persist (pêr-sist') [L. *sistere,* causal of
stāre, to stand], *v.i.* To continue steadfast in the pursuit of any design; to
remain, to endure. **persistence, -ency,** *n.*
persistent, *a.*

person (pêr'sôn) [L. *persōna,* a mask, a
personage], *n.* A human being, an

individual; the living human body; one of the three individualities in the Godhead, Father, Son, or Holy Spirit; (*Gram.*) one of the three relations of a subject or object of a verb. **in person:** By oneself; not by deputy. **personable,** *a.* Handsome, attractive. **personage,** *n.* A person of rank, distinction, or importance; a character in a play, etc. **personal,** *a.* (*Law*) appertaining to the person (applied to all property except land); (*Gram.*) denoting one of the three persons. **personal'ity,** *n.* Quality or state of being a person; individual existence; the sum of qualities, etc., that constitute individuality; a personage; (*pl.*) disparaging remarks. **per'sonally,** *adv.* In person; as regards oneself. **personalty,** *n.* (*Law*) Personal estate, movable property, as distinguished from real property.

personate (për'sŏ-nāt), *v.t.* To assume the character or act the part of; to impersonate. **persona'tion,** *n.*

personify (për-son'i-fī), *v.t.* To regard or represent (an abstraction) as possessing the attributes of a living being; to embody, to typify, in one's own person. **personifica'tion,** *n.*

personnel (për-sŏ-nel') [F.], *n.* The body of persons engaged in some service, esp. a public institution, military or naval enterprise, etc.

perspective (për-spek'tiv) [L. *perspectus,* p.p. of *perspicere* (PER-, *specere,* to look)], *n.* The art of representing solid objects on a plane exactly as they appear to the eye at a particular point; the apparent relation of visible objects; a representation of objects in perspective; a view, vista, prospect. *a.* Pertaining to perspective.

perspicacious (për-spi-kā'shůs) [L. *perspicax*], *a.* Quick-sighted; discerning. **perspicacity** (-kås'i-ti), *n.*

perspicuous (për-spik'ū-ůs), *a.* Free from obscurity or ambiguity, lucid. **perspicu'ity,** *n.*

perspire (për-spīr') [L. *spirāre,* to breathe], *v.i.* To sweat. *v.t.* To give out through the pores, to sweat. **perspira'tion,** *n.* **perspir'atory,** *a.*

persuade (për-swād') [L. *suādēre,* to advise], *v.t.* To influence or convince by argument, advice, entreaty, etc.; to induce; to try to influence, etc. **persuasible,** *a.* Capable of being persuaded. **persua'sion,** *n.* Act of persuading; power to persuade; a settled conviction; a religious sect. **persua'sive,** *a.* Able or tending to persuade. *n.* That which persuades, an inducement. **persuasively,** *adv.*

pert (përt) [obs. *apert*], *a.* Sprightly, lively; saucy. **pertly,** *adv.*

pertain (për-tān') [L. *tenēre,* to hold], *v.i.* To belong (to) as attribute, part, etc.; to relate or have reference (to).

pertinacious (për-ti-nā'shůs), *a.* Obstinate; stubborn, persistent. **pertinacity** (-nås'-i-ti), *n.*

pertinent (për'ti-nënt), *a.* Related to the matter in hand; relevant. **pertinence, -ency,** *n.*

perturb (për-tërb') [L. *turbāre,* to disturb], *v.t.* To disquiet, agitate; to throw into confusion. **perturba'tion,** *n.* **perturber,** *n.*

peruke (pë-rook') [F. *perruque*], *n.* A periwig.

peruse (pë-rooz'), *v.t.* To read, esp. with attention; to observe or examine carefully. **perusal,** *n.*

Peruvian (pë-roo'vi-ản), *a.* Pertaining to Peru. *n.* A native of Peru.

pervade (për-vād') [L. *vādere,* to go], *v.t.* To permeate, saturate; to be diffused throughout. **perva'sion,** *n.* **perva'sive,** *a.*

perverse (për-vërs'), *a.* Wilfully or obstinately wrong; unreasonable, untractable; peevish. **perversity,** *n.*

pervert (për-vërt') [L. *vertere,* to turn], *v.t.* To turn aside from the proper use; to misapply, misinterpret; to mislead, corrupt. *n.* (për'vërt) One who has forsaken his religion; a sexually deranged person. **perver'sion,** *n.* **perversive,** *a.* Tending to pervert.

peseta (pë-sā'tả) [Sp.], *n.* A Spanish silver coin worth about 9½*d.*

pessimism (pes'i-mizm) [L. *pessimus,* worst], *n.* The habit of taking a gloomy view of things; the doctrine that there is a predominant tendency towards evil. **pessimist,** *n.* and *a.* **pessimis'tic,** *a.*

pest (pest) [L. *pestis,* plague], *n.* Anything or anyone extremely hurtful or annoying. **pest-house,** *n.* A hospital for contagious diseases.

pester (pes'ter) [?], *v.t.* To bother, worry, annoy.

pestiferous (pes-tif'ër-ůs), *a.* Hurtful or noxious in any way; bearing social or moral contagion.

pestilence (pes'ti-lëns), *n.* Any contagious disease that is epidemic and deadly, the Black Death. **pestilent,** *a.* **pestilen'tial,** *a.*

pestle (pestl) [L. *pistillum*], *n.* An implement used in braying substances in a mortar. *v.* To pound with or use a pestle.

pet (pet) [?], *n.* An animal kept as a favourite or companion; a darling, a favourite; a fit of peevishness. *v.t.* To make a pet of; to fondle.

petal (pet'ăl) [Gr. *petalon,* a thin plate (of metal)], *n.* (*Bot.*) One of the divisions of a corolla consisting of several pieces.

petard (pë-tard') [F.], *n.* A conical iron case formerly used for blowing open gates, etc.

petition (pë-tish'ůn) [L. *petere,* to seek], *n.* An entreaty, request, prayer; a formal written supplication to persons in authority. *v.t.* To solicit; to address a formal supplication to. **petitionary,** *a.* **petitioner,** *n.*

petrel (pet'rël) [F. *pétre*], *n.* A small seabird, with long wings and great power of flight.

petrify (pet'ri-fī) [L. *petra,* stone], *v.t.* To convert into stone; to stupefy, as with fear, etc. *v.i.* To be converted into stone; to become stiffened, callous, etc. **petrifac'tion,** *n.* **petrifactive,** *a.*

petro- [Gr. *petra,* stone, rock], *comb. form.*

petrol (pet'rŏl), *n.* A refined form of petroleum used in motor-cars, etc.

petroleum (pĕ-trō'lĕ-ŭm) [L. *oleum*, oil], *n.* An inflammable oily liquid pumped from wells, used for lighting, heating, and the generation of mechanical power.

petticoat (pet'ĭ-kōt), *n.* A loose under-skirt worn by women and young children; (*pl*) skirts. **petticoat-government**, *n.* Government by women.

pettifog (pet'ĭ-fog) [?], *v.i.* To act (esp. of a lawyer) in a mean, quibbling, or shifty way. **pettifogger**, *n.* A petty, second-rate lawyer, one given to sharp practices.

pettish (pet'ish), *a.* Peevish, fretful; inclined to ill-temper. **pettishly**, *adv.*

pettitoes (pet'ĭ-tōz) [?], *n.pl.* The feet of a pig as food, pig's trotters.

petty (pet'ĭ) [F. *petit*], *a.* Trifling, insignificant; inferior, subordinate, on a small scale; mean. **petty officer**. A naval non-commissioned officer. **pettily**, *adv.*

petulant (pet'ū-lănt) [L. *petulans*], *a.* Given to fits of ill-temper; irritable. **petulance**, **-lancy**, *n.*

pew (pū) [O.F. *puie*, a platform], *n.* A box-like enclosed seat in a church; a long bench with a back, for worshippers.

pewit (pē'wit) [imit.], *n.* The lapwing; its cry.

pewter (pū'tẽr) [O.F. *peutre*], *n.* An alloy usually of tin and lead; vessels, esp. tankards made of this. *a.* Made of pewter. **pewterer**, *n.*

phaeton (fā'tŏn) [Gr. *Phaethōn*, who drove the chariot of the Sun for one day], *n.* A light four-wheeled open carriage.

phalanx (făl'ăngks) [Gr. *phalanx*], *n.* (*pl.* -xes, *Anat.* -ges (-jēz)) The close order in which the Greek army was drawn up; any compact body of troops or close organization of persons; (*Anat.*, also **phalange**) each of the small bones of the fingers and toes. **phalan'geal**, **-gian**, **phalan'giform**, *a.*

phantasm (făn'tăzm) [Gr. *phantasma*], *n.* A phantom; an optical illusion; a deception, a fantasy. **phantasmal**, **-mic**, *a.*

phantasmagoria (făn-tăz-mà-gôr'ĭ-à) [Gr. *agora*, assembly], *n.* An exhibition of optical illusions produced by a magic-lantern; (*fig.*) a series of phantasms, illusions appearing as in nightmare, frenzy, etc. **phantasmagorial**, **-goric** (-gor'ĭk).

phantom (făn'tŏm), *n.* An apparition, a ghost, spectre; an imaginary appearance; an empty show.

Pharisee (făr'ĭ-sē) [Heb. *pārūsh*, separated], *n.* One of an ancient exclusive Jewish sect who rigidly observed rites and ceremonies; (*fig.*) a self-righteous person, an unctuous hypocrite. **pharisa'ic**, **-al**, *a.* **pha'risaism**, *n.*

pharmaceutical (far-mà-sū'tĭ-kàl), *a.* Pertaining to or engaged in pharmacy. **pharmaceutics**, *n.* Pharmacy. **phar'macist**, *n.*

pharmaco- [Gr. *pharmakon*, drug], *comb. form.* Pertaining to chemistry or to drugs. **pharmacology** (far-mà-kol'ō-jĭ), *n.* The science of drugs and medicines. **pharmacol'ogist**, *n.* **pharmacopœ'ia** [Gr. *poiein*, to make], *n.* An official publica-

tion containing a list of drugs, formulas, doses, etc.

pharmacy (far'mà-sĭ), *n.* Art or practice of preparing, compounding, and dispensing drugs, for medicinal purposes; a chemist's shop; a dispensary.

pharynx (făr'inks) [Gr. *pharunx*], *n.* (*pl.* -ringes (fà-rin'jēz)) The canal opening from the mouth into the œsophagus and communicating with the nose. **pharyngal** (fà-ring'gàl), **pharyngeal** (-rin'jē-àl), *a.* **pharyngitis** (-jī-tis), *n.* Inflammation of the pharynx.

phase (fāz) *phasis [Gr. *phasis*], *n.* (*pl.* -ses) A particular aspect or appearance; a stage of development; (*Astron.*) a particular aspect of the illuminated surface of the moon or a planet.

pheasant (fez'ănt) [Gr. *Phasianos*, of the *Phasis*, a river of Colchis], *n.* A game bird noted for its brilliant plumage and delicate flesh. **pheasantry**, *n.* A place for rearing pheasants.

phenomenon (fē-nom'ē-nŏn) [Gr. *phaino-menon*], *n.* (*pl.* -ena) That which appears or is perceived by observation or experiment; an unusual appearance; (*Phil.*) that which is apprehended by the mind, as distinguished from real existence. **phenomenal**, *a.* Pertaining to phenomena, esp. as dist. from underlying realities or causes; of the nature of a phenomenon; (*colloq.*) extraordinary, prodigious.

phial (fī'àl) [Gr. *phialē*], *n.* A small glass bottle, esp. for medicine.

phil- [PHILO-], *comb. form.*

philander (fī-lăn'dẽr) [Gr. *anēr andros*, man], *v.i.* To make love in a trifling way; to flirt (with). **philanderer**, *n.*

philanthropy (fī-lăn'thrō-pĭ) [Gr. *anthrōpos*, man], *n.* Love of mankind; active benevolence. **philanthrop'ic**, *a.* **philan'thropist**, *n.* **philan'thropism**, *n.*

philately (fī'lăt'ē-lĭ) [F. *philatélie* (Gr. *ateleia*, freedom from toll, from *a-*, not, *telos*, toll, tax)], *n.* The collecting of postage stamps. **philatel'ic**, *a.* **philat'elist**, *n.*

-phile [Gr. *philos*, loving, dear], *suf.* A lover or friend of; as in *bibliophile*, *Germanophile*.

philharmonic (fil-hàr-mon'ĭk), *a.* Loving music. *n.* One fond of music.

philippic (fī-lip'ik) [Gr.], *n.* A declamation full of acrimonious invective (after the three orations of Demosthenes against Philip of Macedon).

Philistine (fil'is-tin, -tīn), *n.* One of an ancient race in S. Palestine; (*fig.*) a person of narrow or materialistic views or ideas; one deficient in liberal culture.

philo- [Gr. *philos*, loving], *comb. form.* Fond of, affecting; inhabiting.

philology (fī-lol'ō-jĭ) [Gr. *logos*, word, discourse], *n.* The science of language. **philol'ogist**, *n.* **philolog'ical**, *a.*

philosopher (fī-los'ō-fẽr) [Gr. *sophos*, wise], *n.* A lover of wisdom; one who studies natural or moral philosophy, investigates the principles of being or of knowledge, or regulates his conduct by the principles of philosophy. **philosoph'ic -al**, *a.* Pertaining or according to philosophy; devoted to or skilled in philosophy; calm, unimpassioned. **philosophize**, *v.t.* and *i.* **philosophy**, *n.* Love of wisdom; the knowledge or investigation of ultimate reality or of general principles of knowledge or existence; calmness and coolness of temper.

philtre (fĭl'tẽr) [Gr. *philtron*], *n.* A love-potion. *v.t.* To charm or excite with this.

phlegm (flem) [Gr. *phlegma, -matos*], *n.* Viscid mucus secreted in the air passages or stomach; (*fig.*) coolness, sluggishness, apathy. **phlegmatic** (fleg-măt'ĭk), *a.* Of a sluggish disposition; not easily excited.

phlogiston (flō-jĭs'tŏn) [Gr. *phlogistos*, burnt up], *n.* The principle of inflammability formerly supposed to be a necessary constituent of combustible bodies.

phlox (floks) [Gr., flame], *n.* A genus of N. American plants with clusters of showy flowers.

-phobe [Gr. *phobos*, fear], *suf.* Fearing; as in *Anglophobe*. **-phobia**, *suf.* Fear, morbid dislike; as in *Anglophobia*, *hydrophobia*.

phœnix (fē'nĭks) [Gr. *phoinix*], *n.* A fabulous Arabian bird, supposed to live for 500 years and to immolate itself on a funeral pyre, whence it rose again in renewed youth; (*fig.*) a person or thing of extreme rarity or excellence.

phon-, phono- [Gr. *phōnē*, sound], *comb. form.* Pertaining to sound or sounds.

phone (fōn), *v.t.* and *i.* To telephone. The telephone.

-phone [Gr. *phōnē*, sound, voice], *suf.* As in *dictaphone, telephone*.

phonetic (fō-net'ĭk) [Gr. *phōnētikos*, from *phōnein*, to speak], *a.* Pertaining to the voice; representing sounds, esp. by means of a character for each. *n.pl.* The science of articulate sounds. **phonetician** (-tĭsh'ǎn), *n.* A student of or one versed in phonetics.

phono- [PHON-], *comb. form.*

phonograph (fō'nō-gräf), *n.* An instrument for recording and reproducing sounds.

phonography (fō-nog'ra-fĭ), *n.* A system of shorthand invented by Pitman, in which each sound is represented by a distinct character; automatic recording and reproduction of sounds.

-phore [Gr. *phoros*, bearing], *suf.* As in *semaphore*. **-phorous**, *suf.* Bearing, -ferous.

phosphate (fos'fāt), *n.* A salt of phosphoric acid. (*pl.*) phosphates of calcium, iron, and alumina, etc., used as fertilizers. **phosphide**, *n.* A combination of phosphorus with another element or radical. **phosphite**, *n.* A salt of phosphorous acid.

phosphoresce (fos-fō-res'), *v.i.* To give out a light unaccompanied by perceptible heat or without combustion. **phosphorescence**, *n.* The emission of or the property of emitting light under such conditions. **phosphorescent**, *a.*

phosphorus (fos'fō-rŭs) [L., the morning-star, from Gr. *phōs*, light, *-phoros*, bringing], *n.* A yellowish non-metallic element, luminous in the dark.

photo-, phot- [Gr. *phōs phōtos*, light],

comb. form. Pertaining to light or to photography. **photo-chemical** (fō-tō-kem'ĭ-kǎl), *a.* Of, pertaining to, or produced by the chemical action of light. **photo-engraving**, *n.* Any process for producing printing-blocks by means of photography.

photogenic (fō-tō-jĕ'nĭk), *a.* Description of one who comes out well in photographs or cinematograph films.

photograph (fō-tō-gräf), *n.* A picture, etc., taken by photography. *v.t.* To take a picture of by photography. *v.i.* To practise photography; to appear in a photograph (well or badly). **photog'-rapher**, *n.* **photograph'ic**, *a.* **photog'-raphy**, *n.* The process of producing pictures of objects by the chemical action of light on certain sensitive substances. **photogravure'**, *n.* The process of producing an intaglio plate for printing by the transfer of a photographic negative to the plate and subsequent etching; a picture so produced. *v.t.* To reproduce by this process. **photomicrography** (fō-tō-mī-krog'-ra-fĭ), *n.* Making magnified photographs of microscopic objects.

phrase (frāz) [Gr. *phrazein*, to speak], *n.* An expression denoting a single idea or forming a distinct part of a sentence; style of expression, diction; idiomatic expression; (*Mus.*) a short passage forming part of a melody. *v.t.* To express in words or phrases. **phraseol'ogy**, *n.* Choice or arrangement of words; diction. **phraseolog'ical**, *a.*

phrenetic (frē-net'ĭk) [Gr. *phrenētikos*], *a.* Frenzied, frantic, fanatical. *n.* A frenzied person.

phrenic (fren'ĭk), *a.* Pertaining to the diaphragm.

phrenology (frē-nol'ō-jĭ) [Gr. *phrēn phrenos*, diaphragm, mind], *n.* The theory that the mental faculties, etc., are located in distinct parts of the brain denoted by prominences on the skull. **phrenol'-ogist**, *n.*

phthisis (thī'sĭs) [Gr. *phthiein*, to decay], *n.* A wasting disease, esp. pulmonary consumption. **phthisical, phthisicky**, *a.*

phylactery (fĭ-lǎk'tẽr-ĭ) [Gr. *phulaktēr*, a guard], *n.* A charm, or amulet worn as a preservative against disease or danger, esp. one containing passages from the Pentateuch worn by Jews.

-phyll [Gr. *phullon*], *suf.* Leaf; as in *chlorophyll*.

physic (fĭz'ĭk) [Gr. *phusikē*, of nature], *n.* The science or art of healing; the medical profession; medicine, a cathartic; (*pl.*) the sciences dealing with the phenomena of matter, esp. as affected by energy, and the laws governing these, excluding biology and chemistry. *v.t.* (*past and p.p.* **physicked**) To administer physic to, to purge. **physical**, *a.* Of or pertaining to matter; cognizable by the senses; pertaining to physics; material, bodily, as opp. to spiritual; medicinal. **physically**, *adv.* **physician** (fĭ-zĭsh'ǎn), *n.* One versed in the art of healing; a legally qualified practitioner. **physicist**, *n.* One versed in physics.

physio- [Gr. *phusis*, nature], *comb. form.* Pertaining to nature.

physiognomy (fiz-i-on'ŏ-mi) [Gr. *gnomvn*, interpreter], *n.* The art of reading character from features; the face as an index of character; cast of features; aspect, appearance, look (of a situation, event, etc.). **physiognomist** (-og'nŏ-mist), *n.*

physiography (fiz-i-og'rā-fi), *n.* The scientific description of the physical features of the earth; physical geography.

physiology (fiz-i-ol'ŏ-ji), *n.* The science of the vital phenomena and the organic functions of animals and plants. **physiolog'ic**, **-al**, *a.* physiol'ogist, *n.*

physique (fi-zēk') [F.], *n.* Physical structure or constitution of a person.

-phyte [Gr. *phuton*, plant], *suf.* Denoting a vegetable organism; as in *zoophyte*.

phyto- [as prec.], *comb. form.*

piano (1) (pē-a'nŏ) [It.], *adv.* (*Mus.*) Softly. *a.* Played softly.

piano (2) (pē-ăn'ŏ), **pianoforte** (pē-ăn-ŏ-fôr'ti) [It., earlier *piano e forte*, L. *plănus et fortis*, soft and strong], *n.* A musical instrument the sounds of which are produced on wire strings by blows given by means of keys. **pianist** (pē'ă-nist), *n.* A performer on the pianoforte.

piastre (pi-ăs'tẽr) [It. *piastra*, plate of metal], *n.* The Spanish dollar worth about 4*s.* 2*d.*; a small Turkish coin, value about 2*d.* to 6*d.*

piazza (pi-ăt'sä) [It.], *n.* A public square or market-place, esp. in Italian towns; a colonnaded walk.

pibroch (pē'broch) [Gael.], *n.* A series of variations, played on a bagpipe.

pica (pī'kå) [med. L.], *n.* A size of type, the standard of measurement in printing.

picador (pik'ā-dôr) [Sp.], *n.* In Spanish bull-fights, the horseman who rouses the bull.

picaresque (pik-ă-resk') [Sp. *picaron*], *a.* Describing the adventures of vagabonds, cheats, etc., esp. in a style of fiction originating in Spain.

picayune (pik-å-yoon') [Am.], *n.* and *a.* A small American coin; of insignificant value.

piccalilli (pik'å-lil-i) [?], *n.* A pickle of chopped vegetables with pungent spices.

piccaninny (pik'å-nin-i) [W. Ind., from Sp. *pequeño*, small], *n.* A little child, esp. of coloured race.

piccolo (pik'ŏ-lŏ) [It., small], *n.* A small flute, with the notes one octave higher than the flute.

pick (1) (pik) [M.E. *pikken*], *v.t.* To break or pierce with a pointed instrument; to make (a hole) thus; to strike at with something pointed; to remove extraneous matter from (the teeth, etc.) thus; to pluck, gather; to take up with a beak; to eat in little bits; to choose, select carefully; to find an occasion for (a quarrel); to open (a lock) with an implement other than the key; to pluck. *n.* Choice; the best (of). **picklock**, *n.* An instrument for opening a lock without the key; one who picks locks; a thief. **pickpocket**, *n.* One who steals from pockets. **picking**, *n.* (*in pl.*) Gleanings, odds-and-ends; pilferings.

pick (2), *n.* A pickaxe; any implement used for picking.

pick-a-back (pik'å-băk) [?], *adv.* On the back or shoulders, like a pack.

pickaxe (pik'ăks) [O.F. *picois*], *n.* A tool with a long iron head pointed at one end and chisel-edged at the other, fitted in the middle on a wooden shaft, used for breaking ground, etc. *v.* To break up with or to use a pickaxe.

picket (pik'ét) [F. *piquet*], *n.* A pointed stake forming part of a palisade, for tethering a horse to; a small body of troops as a guard or outpost; a man or men set by a trade union to watch a factory, etc., during labour disputes. *v.t.* To fortify with stakes, to fence in; to tether to a picket; to post as a picket; to set a picket at the gates of (a factory, etc.). *v.i.* To act as a picket.

pickle (pikl) [?], *n.* A liquid, as brine, vinegar, etc., for preserving fish, flesh, vegetables, etc.; (*pl.*) vegetables preserved in pickle; an embarrassing position; a troublesome child. *v.t.* To preserve in or treat with pickle.

picnic (pik'nik) [?], *n.* An outdoor pleasure-party on which provisions are taken. *v.i.* To go on a picnic.

picric (pik'rik) [Gr. *pikros*, bitter], *a.* Applied to an intensely bitter acid used in dyeing and explosives.

pictorial (pik'tôr'i-ål), *a.* Pertaining to, containing, or illustrated by pictures. **pictorially**, *adv.*

picture (pik'chữr) [L. *pictus*, painted], *n.* A painting, drawing, photograph, engraving, etc.; representing a person, scenery, etc., on a plane surface; a vivid description; a beautiful object or scene. *v.t.* To represent pictorially; to depict vividly; to imagine vividly. **the pictures**: A cinematographic show. **picturesque** (-esk'), *a.* Having those qualities that characterize a good picture; vivid (of language).

pidgin (pij'in) [Chinese *corr.* of English BUSINESS], *n.* Business, affair. **pidgin English**, *n.* Lingua franca of natives and Europeans in the Far East.

pie (1) (pī) [L. *pica*], *n.* A magpie.

pie (2) [?], *n.* A dish of meat, fruit, etc., baked with a paste over.

pie (3) *n.* (*Print.*) A confused mass of type.

piebald (pī'bawld), *a.* Parti-coloured, mottled, usu. black and white (of a horse or other animal).

piece (pēs) [O.F. *pece*], *n.* A distinct part, detached portion, fragment (of); a division, a section; a plot (of land); a short artistic composition or performance; a coin; a gun; a man at chess, draughts, etc. *v.t.* To add pieces to, to patch; to join together, reunite. **piece-work**, *n.* Work paid for by the job. **piecemeal**, *adv.* Piece by piece, part at a time; in pieces.

pied (pīd), *a.* Parti-coloured.

pier (pēr) [L. *petra*, stone], *n.* A mass of masonry supporting an arch, bridge, etc;

masonry between windows, etc.; a breakwater, jetty, landing-stage.

pierce (pērs) [?], *v.t.* To penetrate or transfix with (or of) a pointed instrument; (*fig.*) to affect deeply. *v.i.* To penetrate (into, through, etc.). **piercer,** *n.* piercing, *a.*

pierrot (pē'ĕr-ō) [F.], *n.* (*fem.* -rette (-ĕt')) A buffoon dressed in loose white costume and with the face whitened.

Pietist (pī'ĕ-tist), *n.* One who makes a display of strong religious feelings; one of a party of revivalists in the Lutheran Church in the 17th cent. **pietism,** *n.* pietis'tic, -al, *a.*

piety (pī'ĕ-ti) [L. *pietas*], *n.* The quality of being pious; reverence towards God.

pig (pig) [?], *n.* A swine, a hog, esp. when young; a greedy, filthy, obstinate, or annoying person; an oblong mass of metal as run from the furnace. **pig-headed,** *a.* Stupid; obstinate or perverse. **pig-iron,** *n.* Iron in pigs. **pigsty,** *n.* A pen for pigs; a dirty place, a hovel. **pigtail,** *n.* The tail of a pig; the hair of the head tied in a long queue; tobacco in a long twist. **piggish,** *a.* piggishly, *adv.*

pigeon (pij'ŏn) [O.F. *pijon*, from L. *pipire*, to chirp], *n.* A bird of the order *Columbæ*, a dove; a gull, a simpleton.

pigment (pig'mĕnt) [L. *pigmentum*], *n.* Colouring-matter used as paint or dye. **pigmen'tal,** pig'mentary, *a.* pigmenta'tion, *n.*

pike (1) (pīk) [F. *pique*, A.-S. *pīc*], *n.* A narrow, elongated lance-head fixed to a pole; a voracious freshwater fish. **pike-man,** *n.* A soldier armed with a pike. **pikestaff,** *n.* The wooden shaft of a pike.

pike (2), *n.* A toll-bar; a turnpike road.

pilaster (pi-lăs-tĕr) [L.], *n.* A rectangular column forming part of a wall.

pilchard (pil'chàrd) [?], *n.* A small seafish allied to the herring.

pile (1) (pīl) [L. *pīla*, pillar], *n.* A mass of things heaped together; a heap of combustibles for burning a dead body; a very large or massive building; a great quantity, a fortune; (*Elec.*) a form of battery. *v.t.* To heap up or together, to accumulate; to load.

pile (2) [L. *pīlum*, javelin], *n.* A sharp stake; a heavy timber driven into the ground, esp. under water, to form a foundation.

pile (3) [L. *pīlus*, hair], *n.* Soft hair, down; the nap of velvet, etc., or of a carpet.

pile (4) [L. *pīla*, ball], *n.* (*usu. in pl.*) Hæmorrhoids.

pilfer (pil'fĕr) [O.F. *pelfre*, **PELF**], *v.t.* To steal in small quantities.

pilgrim (pil'grim) [M.E. *pelegrim*], *n.* One who visits some holy place in performance of a vow, etc. *v.i.* To go on a pilgrimage; to wander as a pilgrim. **pilgrimage,** *n.* A pilgrim's journey; (*fig.*) the journey of human life.

pill (pil) [L. *pīla*, ball], *n.* A little medicinal ball to be swallowed whole; (*fig.*) something unpleasant which has to be put up with.

pillage (pil'áj) [F.], *n.* Act of plundering; plunder, the property of enemies taken

in war. *v.t.* To strip of money or goods by open force; to lay waste. *v.i.* To rob, ravage.

pillar (pil'ár) [L. *pīla*], *n.* An upright structure of considerable height to thickness, used for support, ornament, or as a memorial; a column, a post. *v.t.* To support, furnish, or adorn with pillars. **pillar-box,** *n.* A short hollow pillar in which letters are placed for collection.

pillion (pil'i-ŏn) [Celt. or Gael.], *n.* A cushion or seat for a woman to ride on behind a person on horseback or a motorcycle.

pillory (pil'ŏ-ri) [O.F. *pellori*], *n.* A wooden frame furnished with holes through which the head and hands of a person were put to expose him to public derision. *v.t.* To set in the pillory; to hold up to ridicule or execration.

pillow (pil'ō) [A.-S. *pyle*, *pylu*], *n.* A cushion filled with feathers or other soft material. *v.t.* To lay on or prop up with a pillow. *v.i.* To rest on a pillow. **pillow-case,** -slip, *n.* A cover of linen, etc., for drawing over a pillow.

pilot (pī'lŏt) [It. *pilota*], *n.* A steersman; one who conducts ships into or out of harbour or along particular coasts, channels, etc.; one qualified to fly an aeroplane or airship; (*fig.*) a guide, esp. in difficult circumstances. *v.t.* To act as pilot. **pilot-cloth,** *n.* A heavy blue woollen cloth. **pilot-jacket,** *n.* A pea-jacket. **pilotage,** *n.*

pimento (pi-men'tō) [Port. *pimenta*], *n.* Allspice; Jamaica pepper; the W. Indian tree producing it.

pimpernel (pim'per-nĕl) [O.F. *pimprenele*], *n.* A small annual plant with scarlet flowers that close in dark or rainy weather.

pimple (pimpl) [?], *n.* A small inflamed swelling on the skin. **pimpled,** -ply, *a.*

pin (pin) [A.-S. *pinn*], *n.* A short, slender, pointed piece of metal used for fastening parts of clothing, paper, etc., together; a peg of metal or wood; a hairpin; a ninepin, etc.; (*fig.*) anything of slight value. *v.t.* To fasten with a pin; to transfix; to make fast, to secure; to bind (down) to a promise or obligation. **pin-money,** *n.* An allowance to a wife for private expenses.

pinafore (pin'á-fôr), *n.* A sleeveless apron worn by children and women to protect the front of the dress.

pince-nez (pans-nā) [F.], *n.* A pair of eye-glasses held in place by a spring clipping the nose.

pincers (pin'sĕrz) [M.E. *pynsors*], *n.pl.* A tool for gripping, crushing, extracting nails, etc.; a nipping or grasping organ, as in crustaceans.

pinch (pinch) [O.North.F. *pinchier*], *v.t.* To nip or squeeze so as to cause pain; to remove by nipping; (*fig.*) to afflict, esp. with cold, hunger, etc. *v.i.* To nip or squeeze anything; (*fig.*) to be niggardly; to be straitened. *n.* A sharp nip or squeeze, as with the ends of the fingers; as much as can be taken between finger and thumb; (*fig.*) distress, a dilemma, stress. **at a pinch:** In an urgent case; if hard pressed.

pinchbeck (pinch'bek) [C. *Pinchbeck* (*c.* 1670–1732), inventor], *n.* An alloy of copper, zinc, etc., formerly used for cheap jewellery; (*fig.*) anything spurious.

Pindaric (pin-dăr'ik), *a.* Pertaining to the style of Pindar, the Greek lyric poet.

pine (1) (pīn) [A.-S. *pīn*, L. *pīnus*], *n.* A coniferous evergreen tree with needle-shaped leaves; timber from various coniferous trees; a pine-apple. **pine-apple,** *n.* The large multiple fruit of the ananas. **pine-needle,** *n.* The needle-shaped leaf of the pine.

pine (2) [A.-S. *pīn*, pain], *v.i.* To languish, waste away; to yearn (for, etc.).

pinion (1) (pin'yŏn) [L. *pinna*, feather], *n.* A wing-feather; a wing; the joint of a bird's wing remotest from the body. *v.t.* To cut the wing to prevent flight; to bind (the arms).

pinion (2) [L. *pinna*, pinnacle], *n.* The smaller of two cog-wheels in gear with each other; a cogged spindle.

pink (1) (pingk) [?], *n.* A plant largely cultivated in gardens; a pale rose colour; (*fig.*) the supreme excellence, the very height (of); a fox-hunter's scarlet coat. *a.* Of the colour of the garden pink, pale red or rose. **pinkish,** *a.* **pinky,** *a.*

pink (2) [M.E. *pinken*], *v.t.* To pierce, to stab; to make small round holes in for ornament.

pinnace (pin'ás) [F. *pinasse*], *n.* A man-of-war's boat with six or eight oars.

pinnacle (pin'ákl), *n.* A tapering turret on the top of a buttress, etc., or terminating an angle or gable; the apex, the culmination (of).

pint (pīnt) [F. *pinte*], *n.* A measure of capacity, the eighth part of a gallon or 34·659 cub. in.

pioneer (pī-ō-nēr') [F. *pionnier*], *n.* A soldier who clears and repairs roads, bridges, etc., for troops on the march; one who prepares or clears the way; an early leader. *v.t.* To act as pioneer to; to lead, conduct.

pious (pī'ŭs) [L. *pius*, orig. dutiful], *a.* Reverencing God; devout; dutiful.

pip (pip) [?], *n.* A disease in poultry, etc.; the seed of an apple, orange, etc.; a spot on a playing-card, domino, die, etc.

pipe (pīp) [A.-S.], *n.* A long tube; a musical wind-instrument formed of a tube; a boatswain's whistle; a signal on this; a shrill note of a bird, etc.; a tube with a bowl for smoking tobacco; a large cask for wine (usu. 105 gallons); (*pl.*) a bagpipe. *v.t.* To play on a pipe; to whistle; to utter in a shrill tone; to call or direct by a pipe or whistle; to trim with cord. *v.i.* To play on a pipe; to whistle. **pipe-clay,** *n.* A fine white clay used for making tobacco-pipes, and for cleaning military accoutrements.

piping (pī'ping), *n.* The action of one who pipes; a shrill whistling sound. **piping times:** Merry, prosperous times.

pipit (pip'it) [imit.], *n.* A lark-like bird.

pipkin (pip'kin) [?], *n.* A small earthen pot.

pippin (pip'in) [O.F. *pepin*, pip or seed], *n.* A name for several varieties of apples.

piquant (pē'kánt), *a.* Having an agreeably sharp taste; stimulating, racy, sparkling. **piquancy,** *n.*

pique (pēk) [F. *piquer*, to prick], *v.t.* To irritate; to stimulate or excite (curiosity, etc.); to plume or value (oneself on). *n.* Ill-feeling, irritation, resentment.

piquet (pi-ket') [?], *n.* A game of cards for two persons.

pirate (pī'rát) [Gr. *peiran*, to attempt], *n.* A robber on the high seas; a piratical ship; (*fig.*) one who infringes the copyright of another. *v.t.* To plunder; to publish (matter belonging to others) without permission or compensation. **piratic, -al,** *a.* **pi'racy,** *n.*

pirouette (pir-ŭ-et') [F.], *n.* A rapid whirling round on the point of one foot. *v.i.* To dance or perform a pirouette.

piscatory (pis'ká-tòr-i) [L. *piscātor*, fisher], *a.* Pertaining to fishers or fishing. **piscator'ial,** *a.*

piscina (pi-sē'-, -sī'ná) [L. *piscis*, fish], *n.* A perforated stone basin used in the R.-C. service to receive water for purifying the chalice, etc.

pistachio (pis-ta'shi-ō) [It.], *n.* The nut of a W. Asiatic tree; the flavour of its kernel.

pistil (pis'til) [L. *pistillum*, pestle], *n.* The female organ in flowering plants, comprising the ovary.

pistol (pis'tŏl) [F. *pistole*, orig. dagger, from *Pistoja*, where made], *n.* A small fire-arm for use with one hand. *v.t.* To shoot with a pistol.

piston (pis'tòn) [F., from It. *pistone*, as PESTLE], *n.* A solid cylinder exactly fitting a tube in which it can move to and fro, used in engines, pumps, musical wind-instruments, etc. **piston-rod,** *n.* A rod attaching a piston to machinery.

pit (pit) [A.-S. *pytt*], *n.* A hole in the ground, esp. of considerable depth to width; a coal mine; a hollow scar; the ground floor of the auditorium in a theatre, a cockpit. *v.t.* To match, to set in competition (against). **the pit:** The grave; hell. **pitfall,** *n.* A pit slightly covered so that animals may fall in; (*fig.*) a hidden danger. **pitman,** *n.* A collier.

pit-a-pat (pit'á-păt), *n.* A tapping, a flutter, a palpitation. *adv.* With this sound.

pitch (1) (pich) [A.-S. *pic*, from L. *pix*], *n.* A dark resinous substance obtained from tar. *v.t.* To coat or smear with pitch. **pitch-dark,** *a.* As dark as pitch, very dark. **pitch-pine,** *n.* A highly resinous pine.

pitch (2) [M.E. *pichen*], *v.t.* To fix or plant; to throw, to fling; to toss (hay) with a fork; (*Mus.*) to set to a particular keynote. *v.i.* To encamp; to fall headlong; to plunge at the bow or stern, as opp. to rolling. *n.* Height, intensity; point or degree of elevation or depression or slope; station taken up by a person for buying and selling, residence, etc.; (*Cricket*) the place in which the wickets are placed; (*Mus.*) the degree of acuteness or gravity of a tone. **pitched battle**: A battle for which both sides have made deliberate preparations. **pitchfork**, *n.* A large fork with a long handle for lifting hay, etc. *v.t.* To lift or throw with or as with a pitchfork.

pitcher (1) (pich'ér), *n.* One who or that which pitches, esp. the ball in games.

pitcher (2) [O.F. *picher*], *n.* A large vessel, usu. of earthenware, for holding and pouring out liquids.

pitchy (pich'i), *a.* Of the nature of or like pitch; dark, dismal.

piteous (pit'ē-ŭs), *a.* Exciting or deserving pity; lamentable, sad, mournful. **piteously**, *adv.*

pith (pith) [A.-S. *pitha*], *n.* A spongy substance in the stems and shoots of plants; the spinal cord; (*fig.*) the essence, the main substance; strength, vigour; cogency, pithy. **pithy**, *a.* Consisting of, like or abounding in pith; (*fig.*) forcible; condensed, sententious. **pithily**, *adv.*

pitiable (pit'i-ăbl), *a.* Deserving or calling for pity. **pitiful**, *a.* Full of pity, compassionate; calling for pity; contemptible. **pitiless**, *a.* Destitute of pity; unfeeling, hard-hearted.

pittance (pit'ăns) [?], *n.* A dole, an allowance, esp. of a meagre amount.

pity (pit'i), *n.* Compassion, sympathy; a subject for pity, a cause of regret, an unfortunate fact. *v.t.* To sympathize with, to commiserate.

pivot (piv'ŏt) [F.], *n.* A pin or bearing on which anything turns or oscillates; (*fig.*) that on which an important issue depends. *v.i.* To turn on a pivot; to hinge (upon). **pivotal**, *a.*

pixy (pik'si) [?], *n.* A fairy or elf.

placable (plā'kăbl, plăk'ăbl), *a.* That may be appeased; ready to forgive, complacent. **placabil'ity**, *n.* **placably**, *adv.*

placard (plăk'ard) [O.F.], *n.* A paper posted up in a public place, a poster. *v.t.* To post placards on; to announce by placards.

placate (plă-kāt') [L. *plācātus*, p.p. of *plācāre*], *v.t.* To appease, pacify, conciliate.

place (plās) [L. *platea* (*platus*, flat)], *n.* A particular portion of space; a spot, a locality; a city, town, etc.; a building; a residence with its surroundings; an open space in a town; a passage in a book; position in a definite order; room for a person; station in life, official position. *v.t.* To put in a particular place; to arrange in proper places; to appoint to a post; to find a situation for; to assign a definite date, position, etc., to, to locate. **place-hunter**, *n.* One seeking an appointment, esp. under Government. **placeman**, *n.* One holding such appointment.

placer (plā'sèr) [Am. Sp., from *plaza*, place], *n.* An alluvial or other deposit containing minerals; any mineral deposits not classed as veins.

placid (plăs'id) [L. *placēre*, to please], *a.* Gentle; calm, serene, unruffled. **placid'ity**, *n.* **placidly**, *adv.*

placket (plăk'ĕt) [F. *plaquer*, to lay on], *n.* The opening in a petticoat or skirt.

plagiarize (plā'ji-à-rīz) [L. *plagiāre*, to kidnap], *v.t.* To appropriate and give out as one's own (writings, inventions, etc.). **plagiarism**, *n.* **plagiarist**, *n.* **plagiary**, *n.* One who appropriates the writings or ideas of another and passes them off as his own; literary theft, plagiarism.

plague (plāg) [L. *plāga*, a stroke], *n.* A calamity; a pestilence. *v.t.* To visit with plague; to afflict with any evil; to tease, to annoy. **plaguy** (plā'gi), *a.* Vexatious, annoying. **plaguily**, *adv.*

plaice (plās) [O.F. *plaïs*], *n.* A flat-fish used for food.

plaid (plăd) [Gael.], *n.* A long rectangular outer garment of woollen cloth, usu. with a checkered pattern, worn by Highlanders. *a.* Like a plaid in pattern.

plain (plān) [L. *plānus*, flat], *a.* Clear, evident; free from difficulties; easy to understand; devoid of ornament; homely, unaffected; sincere, frank; ugly. *adv.* Plainly. *n.* A tract of level country. **plain-spoken**, *a.* Speaking or said without reserve. **plainly**, *adv.* **plainness**, *n.*

plaint (plānt) [L. *planctus*, lamentation], *n.* An accusation, a charge; (*poet.*) a lamentation. **plaintiff**, *n.* One who brings a suit against another, a prosecutor.

plaintive (plān'tiv), *a.* Expressive of sorrow or grief. **plaintively**, *adv.*

plait (plăt) [L. *plicitum*, folded], *n.* A braid of several strands, esp. a braided tress of hair; a flat fold, a doubling over, as of cloth. *v.t.* To braid, to form into plaits; to fold.

plan (plăn), *n.* A delineation by projection on a plane surface, a map on a large scale; a scheme; a project; an outline; method of procedure; habitual method, way, custom. *v.t.* To draw a plan of; to design; to scheme, devise.

plane (1) (plān) [Gr. *platanos*, from *platus*, broad], *n.* A spreading tree with broad angular leaves palmately lobed.

plane (2), *n.* A tool for smoothing boards, etc. *v.t.* To smooth or dress with a plane; to make flat and even.

plane (3) [L. *plānus*, flat], *a.* Level, flat, without depressions or elevations; extending in a plane. *n.* A level surface; an even surface extending uniformly in some direction; one of the supporting surfaces of this; level (of thought, existence, etc.).

plane (4) *n.* An aeroplane.

planet (plăn'ĕt) [Gr. *planan*, to lead astray, *planasthai*, to wander], *n.* A heavenly body revolving round the sun, or a satellite of one of these. **plan'etary**, *a.* Pertaining to the planets or the planetary system.

plank (plăngk) [L. *planca*], *n.* A long piece of sawn timber thicker than a board; (*fig.*) a principle of a political programme. *v.t.* To cover with planks.

plankton (plăngk'ton) [Gr.], *n.* (*Biol.*) Flora and fauna of low organization floating at any level of the ocean.

plant (plant) [A.-S. *plante*], *n.* Any vegetable organism; the tools, machinery, fixtures, etc., used in an industrial concern. *v.t.* To set in the ground for growth; to furnish or lay out with plants; to fix firmly; to settle, found, establish; to deliver (a blow, etc.).

plantain (1) (plăn'tăn) [O.F.], *n.* A low perennial weed with broad flat leaves.

plantain (2) [Sp.], *n.* A tropical American herbaceous tree closely akin to the banana; its fruit.

plantation (plăn-tā'shŭn) [L. *plantătio*], *n.* A quantity of trees, etc., that have been planted; a large estate for the cultivation of sugar, cotton, coffee, rubber, etc.; act of planting. **planter,** *n.* One who owns or works a plantation; a settler in a colony.

plaque (plak) [F.], *n.* A plate or tablet, of metal, porcelain, ivory, etc.

plash (plăsh) [A.-S. *plæsc*], *n.* A large puddle; a splash, the sound made by this. *v.t.* To cause (water) to splash; to sprinkle colouring-matter on (walls), in imitation of granite, etc. *v.i.* To dabble in water; to make a splash. **plashy,** *a.* Watery, marked as if with splashes of colour, etc.

plasma (plăz'má) [Gr. *plassein*, to mould], *n.* The viscous living matter of a cell, protoplasm; the part of the blood in which the red corpuscles float; plasmat'ic, **plas'mic,** *a.* plasmo-, *comb. form.*

plaster (plas'tĕr) [A.-S., Gr. *emplassein*, to daub on], *n.* A mixture of lime, sand, etc., for coating walls, etc.; calcined gypsum or sulphate of lime, mixed with water and moulded into ornaments, etc.; an adhesive application of some curative substance. *v.t.* To cover with plaster. **plaster of Paris:** Gypsum, esp. calcined.

plastic (plăs'tik) [Gr. *plastikos*], *a.* Having the power of giving form; capable of being moulded; pertaining to modelling or moulding; formative, causing growth; pliant, supple. **plastic'ity,** *n.* **plastics,** *n.pl.* A group of materials which, though stable at ordinary temperatures, are plastic at some stage of their manufacture and can be shaped by the application of heat and pressure.

plat, (plăt) *n.* A small plot or piece of a bed of flowering-plants.

plate (plăt) [O.F., flat], *n.* A flat, thin piece of metal; a plate used for engraving; a print taken from this; a sheet of glass or other material coated with a sensitized film for photography; a cast of a page of type, to be used for printing; a small shallow vessel, now usu. of crockery, for eating from; spoons, forks, knives, cups, dishes, etc., of silver or other metal; a shaped piece of metal or vulcanite, etc., to which artificial teeth are fixed for use; a cup or other article of gold or silver offered as a prize. *v.t.* To overlay with plates of metal for defence, ornament, etc.; to coat with a layer of metal; to make an electrotype or stereotype from (type). **plate-basket,** *n.* A receptacle for spoons, forks, etc. **plate-glass,** *n.* A superior glass used for mirrors, large windows, etc. **plating,** *n.* Act, art, or process of covering articles with a coating of metal; a coating of gold, silver, or other metal.

plateau (plá-tō') [F.], *n.* (*pl.* -eaux) A table-land, an elevated plain.

platform (plăt'fŏrm), *n.* A flat surface raised above the adjoining level; a raised flooring in a hall, etc.; a raised way beside the line at a railway station, etc.; a solid bed on which guns are mounted; a political programme.

platinum (plăt'i-nŭm) [Sp., dim. of *plata*, silver], *n.* A heavy ductile and malleable metal of a silver colour. **platinotype,** *n.* A photographic printing process in which a deposit of platinum gives a positive; a print with this.

platitude (plăt'i-tūd) [F.], *n.* Flatness, insipidity, triteness; a trite remark. **platitu'dinous,** *a.*

Platonic (1) (plá-ton'ik), *a.* Pertaining to Plato or to his philosophy.

platonic (2) *a.* Purely spiritual; with no element of sex.

platoon (plá-toon') [F. *peloton*], *n.* (*Mil.*) A subdivision of a company.

platter (plăt'ĕr), *n.* A large shallow dish, often of wood.

platy- [Gr. *platus*, broad], *comb. form.* Broad, flat. **platypus** (plăt'i-pŭs) [Gr. *platupous* (*pous* foot)], *n.* The ornithorhynchus or duckbill of Australia.

plaudit (plaw'dit) [L. *plaudere*, to applaud], *n.* (*usu. in pl.*) Praise, approval.

plausible (plaw'zibl), *a.* Apparently right, specious; using specious arguments. **plausibil'ity,** *n.*

play (plā) [A.-S. *plega*], *n.* Action engaged in for amusement; sport, exercise; playing in a game; style of this; style of execution (as on an instrument), gambling; a drama; conduct towards others (fair or unfair). *v.i.* To move about in a lively manner, to dance, shimmer, etc.; to act freely; to have freedom of movement; to perform a regular operation (of instruments, machinery, guns, etc.); to sport; to perform on a musical instrument; to gamble; to act a part (esp. on a stage). *v.t.* To put in action or operation; to engage in (a game); to make use of as implement in a game; to execute (a trick, etc.); to perform on (a musical instrument); to perform (a play) on the stage; to act (a character); to toy or trifle with. **play-bill,** *n.* A bill announcing or giving the cast of a play. **playhouse,** *n.* A theatre. **play-wright,** *n.* A dramatist. **player,** *n.* **play-ful,** *a.* Sportive; humorous.

plea (plē) [A.-F. *plee* (L. *placĕre*, to please)], *n.* A pleading, excuse, apology; a defence.

plead (plēd), *v.i.* To speak in support of a claim, or in defence against a claim; to argue for or against; to supplicate earnestly; to address a court on behalf of. *v.t.* To maintain by arguments; to allege in argument; to offer in excuse. **pleader,** *n.* One who pleads in a court of law; one who draws up pleas. **pleading,** *n.* Act of making a plea; imploring;

a written statement of a party in a suit at law.

pleasant (plez'ánt), *a.* Agreeable, affording gratification to the mind or senses. **pleasantly,** *adv.* pleasantness, *n.* **pleasantry,** *n.* Facetiousness; a joke, an amusing trick.

please (plēz) [M.E. *plese*, O.F. *plesir*, L. *placēre*], *v.t.* To afford pleasure to; to be agreeable to; to satisfy. *v.i.* To afford gratification; to like, think fit, prefer; (*ellipt.*) may it please you. if **you please**: If it is agreeable to you; with your permission.

pleasure (plezh'úr), *n.* Gratification of the mind or senses; enjoyment, delight; a source of gratification; choice, desire. *v.t.* To give pleasure to. **pleasure-ground,** *n.* A park or garden for outdoor entertainments. **pleasurable,** *a.* Giving pleasure.

pleat (plēt), *v.t.* To fold or double over, to crease. *n.* A flattened fold, a crease.

plebeian (plē-bē'án) [L. *plebs*, the common people], *a.* Pertaining to the common people; vulgar, low. *n.* One of the common people, esp. in ancient Rome.

plebiscite (pleb'i-sit) [L. *scītum*, decree], *n.* A direct vote of the whole body of citizens on a definite question, a referendum.

pledge (plej) [O.F. *plege*, from Teut.], *n.* Anything given by way of guarantee for repayment of money borrowed, or the performance of some obligation; a binding engagement. *v.t.* To give as security; to deposit in pawn; to engage solemnly; to drink a health to. **pledgeable,** *a.*

Pleiad (plī'ád) [Gr.], *n.* (*pl.* -ades (-á-dēz)) (*pl.*) A cluster of small stars in the constellation Taurus (seven discernible by the naked eye); (*fig., sing.*) a cluster of brilliant persons.

plenary (plē'ná-ri) [L. *plēnus*, full], *a.* Full, entire, absolute.

plenipotentiary (plen-i-pō-ten'shá-ri), *a.* Invested with full powers; absolute. *n.* An ambassador to a foreign court; with full powers.

plenitude (plen'i-tūd), *n.* Fullness; completeness, abundance.

plenty (plen'ti), *n.* Abundance; an ample supply; fruitfulness. **plenteous,** *a.* plentiful, *a.* plentifulness, *n.*

pleonasm (plē'ō-nàzm) [Gr. *pleonazein*, to abound], *n.* Redundancy of expression. **pleonas'tic,** *a.*

plesiosaurus (plē-si-ō-saw'rùs) [Gr. *plēsios*, near, *sauros*, lizard], *n.* An extinct marine reptile with long neck, small head, and four paddles.

plethora (pleth'ō-rà) [Gr. *plēthōrē*, fullness], *n.* Superabundance, esp. of blood. **plethoric** (plē-thor'ik), *a.* Of full habit of body; superabundant.

pleura (ploor'à) [Gr., side], *n.* (*pl.* -rae) A thin membrane covering the interior of the thorax and investing the lungs. **pleural,** *a.* **pleurisy,** *n.* Inflammation of the pleura, usu. attended with fever.

plexus (plek'sùs) [L. *plexus*, plaited], *n.* (*Anat.*) A network of veins, fibres, or nerves; a network, a complication. **solar**

plexus: A network of nerves behind the stomach.

pliable (plī'àbl) [L. *plicāre*, to bend], *a.* Easily bent; flexible, pliant; yielding readily to influence or argument. **pliabil'ity,** *n.* pliant, *a.*

pliers (plī'érz), *n.pl.* Small pincers for bending wire, etc.

plight (1) (plīt) [A.-S. *plihtan*], *v.t.* To pledge, promise, engage (oneself, one's faith, etc.).

plight (2) [A.-F. *plit*], *n.* Condition, state, esp. one of distress or disgrace.

plinth (plinth) [Gr. *plinthos*, brick], *n.* A square member forming the lower division of a column, etc.

pliocene (plī'ō-sēn) [Gr. *pleiōn*, more, *kainos*, new], *a.* Applied to the most modern tertiary deposits.

plod (plod) [?], *v.i.* To walk slowly and laboriously; to trudge; (*fig.*) to toil; to study with steady diligence. *v.t.* To make (one's way) thus. **plodder,** *n.* **plodding,** *a.*

plot (plot) [?], *n.* A small piece of ground; a plan of a field, estate, etc.; a scheme or stratagem; the plan of the story in a play, novel, etc. *v.t.* To make a map or diagram of; to lay out in plots; to plan, devise, contrive secretly. *v.i.* To form schemes against another, to conspire. **plotter,** *n.*

plough (plou) [A.-S. *plōh*], *n.* An implement for furrowing, and turning over the soil; the Great Bear. *v.t.* To turn up (ground) with a plough; to furrow or groove with a plough; to reject at an examination. **ploughman,** *n.* One who ploughs; a rustic. **ploughshare,** *n.* The blade of a plough.

plover (plùv'ér) [O.F. *pluvier*], *n.* A bird, esp. the golden, yellow, or green plover.

pluck (plùk) [A.-S. *pluccian*], *v.t.* To pull off or out, to pick; to twitch; to strip by pulling out feathers; to reject (at an examination). *n.* Act of plucking; a twitch; the heart, lights, and liver of an animal; courage, spirit. **plucky,** *a.* Having pluck, spirit, or courage.

plug (plùg) [Teut.], *n.* Something used to stop a hole or pipe; (*Elec.*) an appliance for connecting and disconnecting a circuit; a peg, bung; a cake of compressed tobacco. *v.t.* To stop with a plug; (*colloq.*) to popularize a song by getting it sung frequently.

plum (plùm) [A.-S. *plūme*, L. *prūnum*], *n.* A fleshy fruit containing a stone; a tree bearing it; a raisin as used in cakes, puddings, etc.; (*fig.*) the best part of anything; (*slang*) £100,000, a fortune.

plumage (ploo'máj), *n.* The feathers of a bird.

plumb (plùm) [L. *plumbum*, lead], *n.* A plummet used to test perpendicularity; a vertical position. *a.* Perpendicular, vertical; downright, sheer, perfect; level. *adv.* Vertically; correctly; completely. *v.t.* To adjust by a plumb-line; to make vertical; to measure the depth of with a plummet. **plumb-line,** *n.* The cord by which a plummet is suspended for testing perpendicularity; a vertical line.

plumb-rule, *n.* A mason's rule with a plumb-line attached.

plumbago (plŭm-bā'gō), *n.* A form of carbon, blacklead, graphite.

plumber (plŭm'ẽr), *n.* One who fits and repairs cisterns, pipes, drains, etc. **plumbing,** *n.*

plume (ploom) [L. *plūma*], *n.* A feather, esp. large or conspicuous; a tuft of feathers, or anything resembling this as ornament.

plummet (plŭm'ĕt) [O.F. *plommet*, dim. of *plomb*, lead], *n.* A weight attached to a line used for sounding or testing perpendicularity; a ball of lead for a plumb-line.

plump (1) (plŭmp) [Teut.], *a.* Well-rounded, fat, chubby; well-filled (of a purse).

plump (2) [Teut.], *v.i.* To fall suddenly and heavily; (*fig.*) to give all one's votes to one candidate. *v.t.* To fling or drop suddenly and heavily. *n.* A sudden plunge, a heavy fall; the sound of this *adv.* Suddenly and heavily; (*fig.*) flatly, bluntly. *a.* Downright, plain.

plumy (ploo'mi), *a.* Covered with feathers; adorned with plumes; feathery.

plunder (plŭn'dẽr) [G.], *v.t.* To pillage, rob, strip; to embezzle. *n.* Forcible or systematic robbery; spoil, booty. **plunderer,** *n.*

plunge (plŭnj) [O.F. *plunjer*], *v.t.* To force or thrust into water or other fluid; to immerse. *v.i.* To throw oneself, to dive (into); to rush impetuously (into a place, condition, etc.); to gamble recklessly, get heavily into debt. *n.* Act of plunging; a dive; a sudden and violent movement; (*fig.*) a risky step. **plunger,** *n.* One who plunges; a reckless gambler, a part of a machine working with a plunging movement.

pluperfect (ploo-pẽr'fĕkt) [L. *plūs quam perfectum*, more than perfect], *a.* (*Gram.*) Expressing action or time prior to some other past time.

plural (ploor'ăl) [L. from *plūs plūris*, more], *a.* Denoting or consisting of more than one. *n.* The form of a word which expresses more than one. **pluralism,** *n.* The holding of more than one benefice at the same time. **pluralist,** *n.*

pluri- [L. *plus*, *pluris*, more], *comb. form.*

plus (plŭs) [L., more], *n.* The sign of addition (+); a positive quantity.

plush (plŭsh) [F. *pluche*, L. *pilus*, hair], *n.* A cloth with a pile longer than that of velvet.

plutocracy (ploo-tok'ră-si) [Gr. *ploutos*, wealth], *n.* The rule of wealth; a ruling class of the rich; the wealthy classes. **plu'tocrat,** *n.* **plutocrat'ic,** *a.*

Plutonian (ploo-tō'ni-ăn) [Gr. *Ploutōn*, god of the infernal regions], *a.* Pertaining to Pluto or the lower regions; infernal, subterranean; (*Geol.*) igneous. **Pluton'ic,** *a.* Plutonian; pertaining to the theory that most geological changes have been caused by igneous agency.

pluvial (ploo'vi-ăl) [L. *pluvia*, rain], *a.* Pertaining to rain; rainy. **plu'vious,** *a.*

ply (1) (plī) [F. *pli*, fold, L. *plicāre*, to bend], *n.* A fold, plait, a strand of (a rope, etc.); a layer.

ply (2), *v.t.* To use or employ vigorously or with diligence; to work at; to pursue, urge; to supply (with). *v.i.* To go to and fro regularly; to be employed; to wait for custom.

pneumatic (nū-măt'ik) [Gr. *pneuma -matos*, wind], *a.* Pertaining to or actuated by air; containing or filled with air. *n.pl.* The science treating of the mechanical properties of air and other gases.

pneumonia (nū-mō'ni-à) [Gr. *pneumōn*, lung], *n.* Acute inflammation of the lungs.

poach (1) (pōch) [O.F. *pochier*, from *poche*, pocket], *v.t.* To cook (an egg) by dropping it, when divested of its shell, into boiling water.

poach (2) [?], *v.i.* To trespass on (another's lands) to take game, etc.; to take game by illegal methods; to intrude unfairly. *v.t.* To take (game, fish, etc.) from another's preserves. **poacher,** *n.* One who intrudes on preserves to take game.

pock (pok) [A.-S. *poc*], *n.* A pustule in an eruptive disease, as small-pox. **pockpitted, pocky,** *a.*

pocket (pok'ĕt) [M.E. *poket*, as F. *poche*], *n.* A small bag, esp. one inserted in the clothing or one to receive the balls at billiards; a measure for hops, etc.; a cavity in rock containing gold or other ore; (*fig.*) pecuniary means. *v.t.* To put into or keep in a pocket; to appropriate; to put up with; to repress (one's feelings); (*Billiards*) to drive (a ball) into a pocket. **pocket-money,** *n.* Money for occasional expenses.

pod (pod) [?], *n.* A long seed-vessel, esp. of leguminous plants. *v.t.* To shell (peas, etc.).

podge (poj) [?], *n.* A short and stout person. **podgy,** *a.*

poem (pō'ĕm) [Gr. *poiēma*, from *poiein*, to make], *n.* A metrical composition with beauty of thought and language, esp. of an imaginative kind.

poesy (pō'ė-si), *n.* The art of poetry; (*collect.*) metrical compositions.

poet (pō'ĕt), *n.* A writer of poems, esp. one possessing high powers of imagination and rhythmical expression. **poetas'ter,** *n.* An inferior poet; a pitiful versifier. **poetess,** *n.* **poet'ic, -al,** *a.* Pertaining to or suitable for poetry; having the finer qualities of poetry; expressed in or fit to be expressed in poetry. **poetics,** *n.* The theory or principles of poetry.

poetry (pō'ĕ-tri) [L. *poētria*, from *poēta*, POET], *n.* The art of the poet, the art which expresses the imagination and feelings in sensuous and rhythmical language; imaginative or creative power; a quality that powerfully stirs the imagination; (*collect.*) verse, poems.

pogrom (pō-grom') [Rus., destruction], *n.* An organized attack on a class of the population, esp. Jews.

poignant (poi'nànt) [O.F., from L. *pungere*, to prick], *a.* Sharp; pungent; piercing; bitter, painful. **poignancy,** *n.*

point (point) [L. *punctus*, pricked], *n.* A mark made by the end of anything sharp, a dot; a punctuation mark; a particular item, place, moment, etc.; stage in progress or increase, as in temperature, price of stocks, etc.; the precise moment for an event, etc., a unit in reckoning superiority, etc., a salient quality; a unit in the British food-rationing system; the essential matter, the aim, the exact object of discussion, the main purport, the gist, the sharp end of a tool, etc., the tip, a promontory, thread-lace made entirely with the needle, a tapering rail moving on a pivot for switching a train from one line to another; (fig.) pungency, effectiveness; (Print.) the unit of measurement for type-bodies, ·0138 in. v.t. To sharpen; to mark with points, to punctuate, to give force or point to; to fill (the joints of masonry) with mortar; to indicate, to direct (a finger at); to indicate the meaning of by a gesture. v.i. To direct attention to; to draw attention to game (of a pointer or setter); to aim (at or towards); to face (towards). point-blank, a. Fired horizontally; (fig.) direct, flat, plain. adv. With direct aim; (fig.) flatly, plainly. pointsman, n. A man in charge of the switches on a railway. pointed, a. Having a sharp point; penetrating, cutting; referring to some particular person or thing; emphasized. pointedness, n. pointer, n. One who or that which points; the index-hand of a clock; a rod for pointing on a blackboard, etc.; a dog trained to point at game. pointless, a. Having no point; dull, not apposite.

poise (poiz) [O.F. poise, from L. pendere, to weigh], v.t. To balance, to carry in equilibrium; to ponder. v.i. To be balanced or in equilibrium; to hover. n. Equipoise, equilibrium, a state of indecision, etc.

poison (poi'zòn), n. A substance that injures or kills an organism into which it is absorbed; a potion composed of this; anything noxious to health or morality; v.t. To put poison in or upon; to administer poison to; (fig.) to taint, vitiate, pervert. poisoner, n. poisonous, a.

poke (1) (pōk) [F. poche], n. A bag, a sack.

poke (2) [Teut.], v.t. To thrust, to push (against, etc.) with something pointed. v.i. (colloq.) To pry, search. n. A thrust, prod, nudge. poky, a. Cramped, stuffy (of a room, etc.).

poker (pō'kèr), n. An iron rod used to stir a fire; an instrument employed in poker-work; a gambling card-game.

polar (pō'lar), a. Pertaining to or situated near the poles; coming from the regions near the poles; pertaining to a magnetic pole. polar bear: A white arctic bear. polarity, n. In opposite directions, as the attraction and repulsion at opposite ends of the magnet.

pole (1) (pōl) [A.-S. pāl], n. A long slender piece of wood or metal, as a flagstaff, mast, support for tent, telegraph wires, etc.; the shaft of a large vehicle; a measure of length, 5½ yards.

pole (2) [Gr. polos, axis], n. One of the extremities of the axis on which the earth (or other sphere) revolves; one of the points where the projection of this pierces the celestial sphere and round which the stars appear to revolve; one of the two points where the attractive or repelling force is greatest in a magnet; a terminal of an electric battery, etc.; either of the polar regions. pole-star, n. A bright star within 1½° of the northern celestial pole.

Pole (3), n. A native of Poland.

poleaxe (pōl'ăks), n. An axe set on a long handle; one with a hammer at the back, used for slaughtering cattle. v.t. To kill with a poleaxe.

polecat (pōl'kăt) [?], n. A small carnivorous weasel-like mammal.

polemic (pó-lem'ik) [Gr. polemos, war], n. A controversy; a controversialist; (pl.) the art or practice of controversial discussion, esp in theology. polemical, a.

police (pó-lēs'), n. The executive administration concerned in the preservation of public order; a civil force for the maintenance of order, detection of crime, and apprehension of offenders; those belonging to this force. v.t. To control or maintain order in by means of police; to provide with police. police court: A court of summary jurisdiction. policeman, n. A member of a police force; a constable.

policy (1) (pol'i-si) [Gr. politeia, from polis, city], n. Prudence in managing or conducting, esp. State affairs; political wisdom, cunning statecraft; prudent conduct; a course of action or administration.

policy (2) [F. police], n. A document containing a contract of insurance.

policy (3), n. (Scots) Pleasure grounds around a large house or mansion.

poliomyelitis (pō'li-ō-mï-e-lï'tis) [Gr. polios, grey, meulos, marrow], n. (Path.) Inflammation of the grey matter of the spinal cord; infantile paralysis.

polish (1) (pol'ish) [L. polire], v.t. To make smooth or glossy, usu. by friction; (fig.) to refine, to free from coarseness. v.i. To take a polish. n. A smooth glossy surface; friction or a substance applied to impart a polish; refinement, elegance of manners.

Polish (2) (pō'lish), a. Pertaining to Poland or its inhabitants. n. The language of the Poles.

polite (pó-lït'), a. Refined in manners; courteous; well-bred; cultivated. politely, adv. politeness, n.

politic (pol'i-tik), a. Prudent and sagacious; judicious, expedient; scheming. n.pl. The science or art of civil government; political affairs or views. political, a. politician (-tish'-àn), n. One versed in politics, a statesman; one engaged in or devoted to party politics. polity, n. The form, system, or constitution of the civil government of a State; the State; a body politic; the form of organization of any institution.

polka (pōl'ká) [?], n. A lively dance; music for this.

poll (pōl) [M.E. polle], n. A human head, esp. the part on which the hair grows;

a register of persons, esp. those entitled to vote; the voting at an election, the number of voted polled. *a.* Polled; hornless. *v.t.* To remove the top of (trees, etc.); to crop the hair of; to cut off the horns of; to take the votes of. *v.i.* To give one's vote. **poll-tax,** *n.* One levied on every person. **poll-beast, -cow, -ox,** *n.* A polled beast, one of a hornless breed.

pollard (pol'ard), *n.* A tree with its top cut off so as to have a dense head of young branches. **polled,** *a.* Lopped.

pollen (pol'én) [L., fine flour], *n.* The fertilizing powder of flowers.

pollute (pŏ-lūt') [L. *pollūtus*, defiled], *v.t.* To make foul or unclean.

polo (pō'lō) [Tibetan], *n.* A game of Eastern origin resembling hockey but played on horseback.

polonaise (pol'ŏ-, pō'lŏ-nāz) [F., Polish], *n.* A bodice and short skirt in one piece; a slow dance of Polish origin; music for this.

polony (pŏ-lō'ni) [*Bologna*, Italy], *n.* A sausage of partly-cooked pork.

poltergeist (pol'tér-gīst) [G., noisy ghost], *n.* An alleged spirit which makes its presence known by noises and violence.

poltroon (pol-troon') [It. *poltrone*, from *poltro*, sluggard], *n.* An arrant coward; a dastard. **poltroonery,** *n.*

poly- [Gr. *polus*, many], *comb. form.* **polyanthus** [Gr. *anthos*, flower], *n.* (*pl.* -uses) A garden variety of primula. **polygamy** (pŏ-lig'à-mi) [Gr. *gamos*, marriage], *n.* The practice or condition of having a plurality of wives or husbands at the same time. **polyg'amist,** *n.* **polyg'amous,** *a.* **pol'yglot** [Gr. *glotta*, tongue], *a.* Expressed in or speaking many languages. *n.* A book, esp. the Bible, set forth in many languages. **polygon** [Gr. *gōnia*, angle], *n.* A figure of more than four angles or sides. **polyg'onal,** *a.* **polyg'ynous** [Gr. *gunē*, woman], *a.* Pertaining to or practising polygyny. **polygyny,** *n.* Plurality of wives. **polyhedron** [Gr. *hedra*, a base], *n.* (*pl.* -dra) A solid bounded by many plane sides.

polyp (pol'ip), *n.* An aquatic animal of low organization, the sea-anemone, etc. **polypus** (pol'i-pùs) [Gr. *pous podos*, foot], *n.* (*pl.* -pi) A tumour with ramifications growing in any of the mucous cavities; a polyp.

polysyllabic (pol-i-si-lăb'ik), *a.* Consisting of many syllables; characterized by polysyllables. **polysyllable,** *n.*

polytechnic (pol-i-tek'nik) [Gr. *technē*, art], *a.* Pertaining to or giving instruction in many arts. *n.* A school or educational institution for instruction in arts and science, esp. in their practical application.

polytheism (pol'i-thē-izm) [Gr. *theos*, god], *n.* The doctrine or worship of a plurality of gods. **polytheist,** *n.* **polytheis'tic,** *a.*

pomade (pŏ-mād', -mad') [F. *pommade*, from *pomme*, apple], *n.* Pomatum.

pomatum (pŏ-mā'tùm) [L. *pōmum*, apple], *n.* A perfumed ointment for dressing the hair.

pomegranate (pom'grăn-àt) [L. *grānāta*, seeded], *n.* The fruit of a N. African and W. Asiatic tree, with a thick, tough rind and acid red pulp enveloping numerous seeds; the tree.

pommel (pŭml) [O.F. *pomel*, L. *pōmum*, apple], *n.* A round ball on the hilt of a sword; the upward projection at the front of a saddle. *v.t.* To beat soundly, as with the handle of a sword; to beat with fists.

pomp (pomp) [Gr. *pompē*, procession], *n.* A pageant; splendour, display or parade.

pom-pom (pom'pom) [imit.], *n.* An automatic quick-firing gun.

pompon (pon-pon) [F.], *n.* An ornament as a tuft or soft ball worn on women's and children's hats and shoes, a soldier's shako, etc.

pompous (pom'pùs), *a.* Displaying pomp; ostentatious, pretentious. **pompos'ity,** *n.*

poncho (pon'chō) [S. Am. Sp., from native], *n.* A cloak or cape, with a slit through which the head passes.

pond (pond) [?], *n.* A body of still water, usu. artificial, a small lake.

ponder (pon'dér) [L. *ponderāre*, from *pondus -deris*, weight], *v.t.* To weigh carefully in the mind; to consider, to reflect upon. *v.i.* To deliberate, to muse (on, over, etc.).

ponderable (pon'dér-àbl), *a.* Capable of being weighed, having appreciable weight. **ponderabil'ity,** *n.* **pon'derous,** *a.* Very heavy; bulky, unwieldy; (*fig.*) dull; pompous, self-important.

poniard (pon'yàrd) [F. *poignard*, from *poing*, fist], *n.* A dagger. *v.t.* To stab with this.

pontiff (pon'tif) [L. *pontifex*, a chief priest in ancient Rome], *n.* The Pope. **pontif'-ical,** *a.* Pertaining to or befitting a pope: papal; pompous, dogmatic. *n.* A book containing the forms for rites and ceremonies to be performed by bishops; (*pl.*) the vestments and insignia of a pope or a bishop. **pontifically,** *adv.* **pontif'icate,** *v.t.* To celebrate (Mass, etc.) as a bishop. *v.i.* To officiate as a bishop, esp. at Mass. *n.* The dignity, office, or term of office of a pope.

pontoon (pŏn-toon') [F. *ponton*, from L. *pons pontis*, bridge], *n.* A buoyant structure supporting a floating bridge; a caisson; a barge or lighter; a gambling card-game.

pony (pō'ni) [O.F. *poulenet*, L. *pullus*, foal], *n.* A small breed of horse; (*slang*) £25.

poodle (poodl) [G. *pudeln*, to waddle], *n.* A small dog with long silky hair, often clipped in fanciful style.

pooh (poo) [imit.], *int.* An exclamation of contempt or impatience. **Pooh-bah,** *n.* (*facet.*) A person holding many offices (from a character in *The Mikado*).

pool (1) (pool) [A.-S. *pōl*], *n.* A small pond; a deep, still part of a stream; a puddle.

pool (2) [?], *n.* The receptacle for the stakes in certain games of cards; the collective amount of stakes, forfeits, etc.; a certain game on a billiard-table; a combination of companies, etc., for manipulating prices. *v.t.* To put (funds, risks, etc.) **into** a common fund.

poop (poop) [O.F. *pupe*, L. *puppis*], *n.* The stern of a ship; a deck over the after part of a spar-deck.

poor (poor) [O.F. *povre, poure,* L. *pauper*], *a.* Needy, indigent; lacking (in); barren; meagre, inadequate in quantity or quality; unhealthy, uncomfortable, inferior, paltry, contemptible, insignificant, meek; pitiable; used as a term of slight contempt or pity. **poor-box,** *n.* A money-box for charitable contributions. **poorhouse,** *n.* A workhouse. **poorly,** *adv.* With poor results; defectively; despicably. *a.* In delicate health; indisposed.

pop (pop) [imit.], *v.i.* To make a short, sharp explosive noise; to enter or issue forth quickly and suddenly; to dart. *v.t.* To push or thrust (in, out, up) suddenly; to cause (a thing) to pop; (*slang*) to pawn. *n.* A short, sharp, explosive noise. **pop-gun,** *n.* A small toy gun shooting a pellet with air compressed by a piston.

pope (pōp) [A.-S. *pāpa,* Gr. *pappas,* father], *n.* The bishop of Rome as the head of the R.-C. Church; (*fig.*) a person claiming or credited with infallibility; a priest in the Greek Church; a small freshwater fish. **popedom,** *n.* **popery,** *n.* The religion or ecclesiastical system of the Church of Rome (in a hostile sense).

popinjay (pop'in-jā) [O.F. *papingay*], *n.* A parrot; a mark like a parrot shot at by archers; (*fig.*) a conceited fop.

popish (pō'pish), *a.* Pertaining to the Pope or to popery, papistical.

poplar (pop'lar) [L. *pōpulus*], *n.* A large tree of rapid growth, having a soft, light wood.

poplin (pop'lin) [It. *papalina,* papal, because made at Avignon], *n.* A silk and worsted fabric with a ribbed surface.

poppy (pop'i) [A.-S. *popig*], *n.* A plant with large showy flowers chiefly scarlet, with a milky juice having narcotic properties.

populace (pop'ū-lás) [L. *populus,* people], *n.* The common people; the masses.

popular (pop'ū-lår), *a.* Esteemed by, pertaining to, or carried on by the people; suitable to the people, not expensive, not abstruse; prevailing among the people. **popular'ity,** *n.* **pop'ularize,** *v.t.* To make popular; to treat in a popular style. **populariza'tion,** *n.* **popularly,** *adv.*

populate (pop'ū-lāt), *v.t.* To furnish with inhabitants, to people; to inhabit. **popula'tion,** *n.* The inhabitants collectively; the state of a country with respect to the number of its inhabitants.

populous (pop'ū-lŭs), *a.* Full of people; thickly populated.

porcelain (pôr'slán) [It. *porcellana,* the sea-snail, porcelain], *n.* A fine kind of earthenware; ware made of this.

porch (pôrch), *n.* A covered structure before an entrance; a covered approach to a doorway.

porcupine (pôr'kū-pīn) [L. *porcus,* hog, *spina,* thorn], *n.* A rodent quadruped covered with erectile, quill-like spines.

pore (1) (pôr) [L. *porus,* passage], *n.* A minute opening in the skin for absorption, perspiration, etc.; an aperture in the cuticle of a plant.

pore (2) [?], *v.i.* To meditate or study patiently and persistently (over, upon, etc.).

pork (pôrk) [L. *porcus,* hog], *n.* The flesh of swine, esp. fresh, as food. **porker,** *n.* A pig raised for killing, esp. a young fattened pig. **porky,** *a.*

pornography (pôr-nog'rá-fi) [Gr. *pornē,* a harlot], *n.* Obscene literature, obscenity. **pornographic,** *a.*

porous (pôr'ŭs), *a.* Having pores or passages for fluids. **poros'ity,** *n.*

porphyry (pôr'fi-ri) [Gr. *porphuros,* purple], *n.* An igneous rock containing feldspar and quartz crystals; a rock quarried in Egypt having a purple ground-mass.

porpoise (pôr'pús) [O.F. *porpeis* (L. *porcus,* hog, *piscis,* fish)], *n.* A gregarious cetacean, about 5 ft. long, with a blunt snout.

porridge (por'ij), *n.* A soft food made by boiling meal till it thickens.

porringer (por'in-jèr), *n.* A small bowl for soup or porridge.

port (1) (pôrt) [A.-S., from L. *portus*], *n.* A harbour, haven.

port (2) [L. *porta*], *n.* A gate, esp. to a walled town or fortress; a port-hole. **port-hole,** *n.* An aperture in a ship's side for light and air.

port (3) [L. *portāre,* to carry], *n.* Carriage, mien, deportment.

port (4) [*Oporto*], *n.* A strong dark-red wine from Portugal.

port (5) [?], *n.* The larboard or left-hand side as one looks forward. *a.* Towards or on the larboard. *v.t.* To turn (the helm) to the left side of a ship. *v.i.* To turn to port (of a ship).

portable (pôr'tåbl), *a.* Capable of being easily carried, esp. about the person. **portabil'ity,** *n.*

portage (pôr'tåj), *n.* Act of carrying, carriage; cost of carriage.

portal (pôr'tål), *n.* A door, gate, gateway; an entrance of an imposing kind.

portcullis (pôrt-kŭl'is) [M.E. *porte-colys,* O.F. *porte coleïce*], *n.* A strong framework let down to close the entrance to a castle in case of assault.

Porte (pôrt) [F. *Sublime Porte,* sublime gate, trans. of Turkish name of chief Government office], *n.* The Turkish Government.

portend (pôr-tend') [L. *portendere,* to stretch], *v.t.* To indicate by previous signs, to presage; to be an omen of. **por'tent,** *n.* An omen, esp. of evil; a prodigy, a marvel. **porten'tous,** *a.*

porter (1) (pôr'tèr) [O.F. *portour,* from *porter,* to carry], *n.* One who carries parcels, etc., esp. one employed at a railway station; a dark-brown beer. **porterage,** *n.* Charge for carriage by a porter.

porter (2), *n.* A gatekeeper, doorkeeper.

portfolio (pôrt-fō'li-ō) [It. *portafogli* (*fogli,* leaves)], *n.* A portable case for holding papers, drawings, etc.; (*fig.*) the office of a minister of state.

portico (pŏr'tĭ-kō) [L. *porticus*, from *porta*, gate], *n.* A colonnade; a porch with columns.

portion (pŏr'shŭn) [L. *portio*], *n.* A part; a share, an allotment; a helping; a dowry. *v.t.* To divide, distribute; to allot, endow. **portionless.** *a.*

portly (pŏrt'lĭ), *a.* Dignified in mien or appearance; stout, corpulent.

portmanteau (pŏrt-măn'tō) [F.], *n.* (*pl.* -**eaux**) A long leather trunk for carrying apparel, etc., in travelling.

portrait (pŏr'trāt) [O.F. *pourtraict*, portrayed], *n.* A likeness of a person or animal; a vivid description. **portraitist,** *n.* A portrait-painter. **portraiture,** *n.* Portraits collectively; the art of painting portraits or describing vividly. **portray,** *v.t.* (*fig.*) To describe vividly.

Portuguese (pŏr-tū-gēz'), *a.* Pertaining to Portugal. *n.* A native or inhabitant (*also pl.*) of Portugal; the Portuguese language.

pose (1) (pōz) [F. *poser*, L. *pausāre*, to pause], *v.t.* To place, to cause to take a certain attitude; to affirm. *v.i.* To assume an attitude or character; to appear or set up (as). *n.* An attitude or position, esp. put on for effect.

pose (2), *v.t.* To puzzle, to cause to be at a loss.

position (pŏ-zĭsh'ŭn) [L. *positio*], *n.* The state of being placed, manner in which a thing is placed; posture; mental attitude, way of regarding anything; rank; a post, appointment; status, rank.

positive (pŏz'ĭ-tĭv), *a.* Definitely, authoritatively, or formally laid down; explicit; absolute, not relative; real, actual; certain, undoubted; confident, dogmatic; (*Gram.*) not comparative or superlative; (*Phot.*) exhibiting lights and shades in the same relations as in nature. **positively,** *adv.*

positivism (pŏz'ĭ-tĭv-ĭzm), *n.* The philosophical system of Comte (1798–1857), which recognizes only observed phenomena; the religious system based on this.

posse (pŏs'ĭ) [L., to be able], *n.* A body or force (of persons).

possess (pŏ-zes') [O.F. *possesser*, L. *possidēre*], *v.t.* To own, to have full power over, to control (oneself, one's mind, etc.); to occupy, dominate; to acquire, to hold. **possessed,** *a.* Dominated (by an idea, etc.); controlled (as by a devil), mad. **possession** (pŏ-zesh'ŭn), *n.* Act or state of possessing; holding or occupancy; that which is possessed; territory; (*pl.*) property, wealth. **possessive,** *a.* Of or pertaining to possession. **possessor,** *n.* One who possesses anything.

posset (pŏs'ĕt) [M.E. *possyt, poshote*, etym. doubtful], *n.* A drink made of hot milk curdled with ale, wine, etc. *v.t.* To curdle.

possible (pŏs'ĭbl) [L. *possibilis* (*posse*, to be able)], *a.* That may happen, be done, or exist; that is not contrary to the nature of things; tolerable, reasonable. **possibil'ity,** *n.* **pos'sibly,** *adv.* By any possible means; by a remote chance.

post (1) (pōst) [A.-S.], *n.* A piece of timber,

metal, etc., set upright; a stake, a stout pole. *v.t.* To fix on a post or in a public place; to fasten bills, etc., upon a wall, etc.

post (2) (pōst) [L. *positus*, p.p. of *pōnere*, to set], *n.* A fixed place; a military station; the troops at such station; a trading-place, a situation, appointment; system of letter-conveyance; a courier, messenger; a post-office, a dispatch of mails; (*collect.*) the letters, etc., taken from a post-office or letter-box or delivered at one time; a size of writing-paper, about 18¾ in. by 15¼ in; (*Mil.*) a bugle-call announcing nightfall, etc. *adv.* Express, with speed. *v.t.* To station, place in position; to transmit by post; to transfer (accounts) to a ledger, etc. *v.i.* To travel with post-horses; to hurry. **post-chaise,** *n.* A vehicle for travelling by post. **post-free,** *a.* Without charge for postage. **post-haste,** *a., adv.,* and *n.* Great expedition. **postman,** *n.* One who delivers letters brought by post. **postmaster,** *n.* The superintendent of a post-office. **post-office:** A place for the receipt and delivery of letters, etc.; the public postal department.

post- [L.], *pref.* After, behind, since. **post-classical** (pŏst-klăs'ĭ-kàl), *a.* Later than the classical times of Greece and Rome.

postage (pōs'tăj), *n.* The fee for conveyance of a letter, etc., by post. **postal,** *a.*

poster (pōs'tẽr), *n.* A large placard or advertising bill; one who posts this.

posterior (pos-tēr'ĭ-ôr) [L.], *a.* Coming or happening after; hinder. *n.* (*usu. in pl.*) The buttocks.

posterity (pos-ter'ĭ-tĭ), *n.* Those proceeding in the future from any person, descendants, succeeding generations.

postern (pōs'tẽrn) [O.F. *posterne* (L. *post,* after)], *n.* A small doorway.

posthumous (pos'tū-mŭs) [L. *postumus,* superl. of *post,* after], *a.* Born after the death of the father; happening after one's decease; published after the death of the author.

postilion (pŏ-stĭl'yŏn) [F. *postillon*], *n.* One who rides on the near horse of the leaders or of a pair drawing a carriage.

postmeridian (pŏst-mĕ-rĭd'ĭ-àn), *a.* Of or belonging to the afternoon; late.

post-mortem (pŏst-môr'tĕm) [L.], *a.* After death], *a.* Made or occurring after death. *n.* An examination of a dead body.

post-obit (pŏst-ob'ĭt) [L. *post,* after, *obitus,* decease], *a.* Taking effect after death. *n.* A bond securing payment of a sum of money to a lender on the death of a specified person.

postpone (pŏst-pōn') [L. *pōnere,* to put], *v.t.* To put off, defer, delay; to regard as of minor importance. **postponement,** *n.*

postscript (pōst'skrĭpt) [L. *scriptus,* written], *n.* A paragraph added to a letter after the signature.

postulate (pos'tū-lāt) [L. *postulātus,* demanded], *n.* A position assumed without proof as being self-evident; a fundamental assumption; an indispensable preliminary. *v.t.* To demand, claim, assume without proof, to take as self-evident; to stipulate.

posture (pos'tūr) [L. *positus*, from *ponere*, to put], *n.* Pose, attitude; situation, condition, state (of affairs, etc.).

posy (pō'zi), *n.* A motto or short inscription, esp. in a ring; a nosegay.

pot (pot) [A.-S. *pott*], *n.* A round vessel of earthenware or metal, usu. deep relatively to breadth, for holding. liquids, etc., used for cooking, drinking, etc.; the quantity this holds; a flower-pot, teapot, etc. *v.t.* To put into, plant, preserve in pots, etc. **pot-house,** *n.* A low public-house.

potable (pō'tábl) [L. *pōtāre*, to drink], *a.* Drinkable. *n.* Anything drinkable.

potash (pot'ãsh), *n.* Potassium carbonate in a crude form, orig. obtained from ashes of plants. **potassium** (pô-tãs'ĭ-ŭm), *n.* A bluish or pinkish white metallic element.

potation (pô-tā'shŭn) [L. *pōtāre*, to drink], *n.* The act of drinking; a draught; a beverage; (*usu. pl.*) tippling.

potato (pô-tā'tō) [Haitian *batata*], *n.* (*pl.* -toes) A plant with edible farinaceous tubers; a tuber of this.

poteen (pô-tēn') [Ir. *poitín*], *n.* Irish whisky illicitly distilled.

potent (pō'tĕnt) [L. *potens*, being able], *a.* Powerful; having great influence; cogent; strong, intoxicating. **potency,** *n.* **potently,** *adv.* **po'tentate,** *n.* One who possesses great power; a monarch, a ruler. **poten'tial,** *a.* Latent; existing in possibility not in actuality. **potential'ity,** *n.*

pother (poth'er) [?], *n.* Bustle, confusion.

potion (pō'shŭn), *n.* A drink, a draught, a dose.

potpourri (pō-pu-rē') [F., rotten pot], *n.* A mixture of dried and fragrant petals and spices; (*fig.*) a miscellany, medley.

potsherd (pot'shérd), *n.* A broken piece of earthenware.

pottage (pot'áj), *n.* A kind of soup; porridge.

potter (1) (pot'ér), *n.* A maker of pottery.

potter (2) (pot'ér) [?], *v.i.* To work in a trifling, ineffective way (at, in, etc.); to idle (about).

pottery (pot'ér-ĭ), *n.* Earthenware; its making; a place where it is made.

pottle (potl), *n.* A measure of four pints; a large tankard; a vessel for holding fruit.

pouch (pouch) [O.F. *poche*], *n.* A small bag; a detachable pocket.

poult (pōlt), *n.* A young partridge, turkey, etc. **poulterer,** *n.* One who deals in poultry.

poultice (pōl'tis), *n.* A soft composition for applying to sores or inflamed parts. *v.t.* To apply a poultice to.

poultry (pōl'tri), *n.* Domestic fowls, pullets, geese, ducks, turkeys, etc.

pounce (1) (pouns) [?], *n.* The claw of a bird of prey; an abrupt swoop. *v.i.* To sweep down or spring upon and seize.

pounce (2) (pouns) [F. *ponce*, pumice], *n.* A powder formerly used for drying ink. **pounce-box,** *n.* A box with perforated lid for scattering pounce.

pound (1) (pound) [A.-S. *pund*, L. *pondo*, rel. to *pendere*, to weigh], *n.* A measure of weight, 12 oz. troy or 16 oz. av.; an English money of account consisting of 20s., a sovereign.

pound (2) [A.-S. *pund*, enclosure], *n.* An enclosure for confining stray cattle, etc.; a pen. *v.t.* To confine in a pound.

pound (3) [A.-S. *pūnian*], *v.t.* To crush, pulverize, strike heavily; to pommel; to walk heavily along.

poundage (pound'áj), *n.* An allowance of so much in the pound; a payment or charge per pound weight.

pour (pôr) [?], *v.t.* To cause (liquids, etc.) to flow; to send (forth) in a stream or great numbers. *v.i.* To flow in a stream; to fall copiously (of rain); to rush in great numbers or in a constant stream.

pourboire (poor-bwar') [F., for drinking], *n.* A gratuity, a tip.

pour-parler (poor-par-lā) [F., to discuss], *n.* A preliminary discussion.

pout (pout) [M.E. *pouten*], *v.i.* To thrust out the lips in sullenness, etc.; to be prominent (of lips). *n.* A protrusion of the lips; a fit of sullenness. **pouter,** *n.* One who pouts; a variety of pigeon, from its way of inflating its crop.

poverty (pov'ér-ti) [O.F. *poverte*], *n.* State of being poor; want, destitution; inferiority.

powder (pou'dér) [F. *poudre*, L. *pulver*], *n.* Any dry substance in fine particles; dust; a medicine, cosmetic, etc., in the form of powder; gunpowder. *v.t.* To reduce to powder; to put powder on; to sprinkle with fine spots or figures. *v.i.* To become like powder; to use powder for the face or hair. **powder-monkey,** *n.* (*Naut.*) A boy formerly employed to bring powder from the magazine to the guns. **powdery,** *a.*

power (pou'ér) [O.F. *poër*, from L. *posse*, to be able], *n.* Ability to do; strength, energy; influence, authority (over); right or ability to control; political ascendancy; an influential State; the product obtained by multiplication of a number into itself; mechanical energy as dist. from hand-labour; any apparatus for applying energy to mechanism; the magnifying capacity of a lens. **powerful,** *a.* Having great strength or energy; mighty, potent.

practicable (prãk'ti-kábl), *a.* Capable of being done, etc., feasible. **practicabil'ity,** *n.* **practicably,** *adv.*

practical (prãk'ti-kál), *a.* Pertaining to, governed by practice, or derived from practice; experienced; pertaining to action not theory; such in effect, virtual. **practically,** *adv.* In a practical manner; virtually, in effect. **practical'ity,** *n.*

practice (prãk'tis), *n.* Customary action or procedure; habit; systematic exercise of any profession, etc.; professional connexion; actual performance as opp. to theory or intention.

practise (prãk'tis) [O.F. *practiser* (F. *pratiquer*), L. *practicus*, Gr. *praktikos*, from *prassein*, to do], *v.t.* To do or perform habitually; to exercise a profession, etc.; to instruct, to exercise, to drill (in a subject). *v.i.* To exercise oneself; to do a thing habitually. **prac-**

tised, *a.* **practitioner,** *n.* One who regularly practises any profession, esp. medicine.

præ-, pre- [L. *præ*, before], *pref.*

prætor (prē'tór) [L.], *n.* (*Rom. Hist.*) A magistrate in ancient Rome elected yearly. **prætorian,** *a.* Pertaining to a prætor or to a body-guard, esp. the imperial body-guard established by Augustus. *n.* A soldier in this.

pragmatic (prăg-măt'ik) [Gr. *pragma*, deed, from *prassein*, to do], *a.* Pertaining to the affairs of a State; pragmatical. **pragmat'ical,** *a.* Given to interfering in the affairs of others; relating to pragmatism. **prag'matism,** *n.* Officiousness; treatment of things with regard to causes and effects; the doctrine that our only test of the truth of human cognitions or philosophical principles is their practical results.

prairie (prâr'i) [F.], *n.* An extensive tract of level grass-land, usu. destitute of trees, esp. in the western U.S.A.

praise (prāz) [L. *pretium*, price, value], *v.t.* To express approval and commendation of; to extol, to glorify. *n.* Approbation, encomium; glorifying. **praisable,** *a.* **praiseworthy,** *a.*

prance (prans) [?], *v.i.* To spring or caper on the hind legs.

prank (prăngk) [?], *n.* A wild frolic; a practical joke; a gambol, a capricious action.

prate (prāt) [M.E. *praten*], *v.i.* To chatter, babble, cackle. *n.* Silly talk; unmeaning loquacity. **prater,** *n.*

prattle (prătl), *v.i.* To talk in a childish or foolish manner. *n.* Idle talk; a babbling sound.

prawn (prawn) [M.E. *prane, prayne*], *n.* A small crustacean like a large shrimp.

pray (prā) [O.F. *preier,* L. *precārī,* from *prex,* prayer], *v.t.* To beseech, to entreat, to supplicate; to petition for; to address devoutly and earnestly. *v.i.* To address God with adoration or earnest entreaty; to beseech or petition (for). **prayer** (1) (prā'ér), *n.* One who prays.

prayer (2) (prâr), *n.* Act of praying; a solemn petition, esp. to God; a prescribed formula of divine worship; a religious service. **prayerful,** *a.* Given to prayer; devout.

pre- [L. PRÆ-, before], *pref.*

preach (prēch) [O.F. *prechier,* L. *prædicāre*], *v.i.* To deliver a sermon or discourse on some religious subject; to give earnest advice, esp. in an obtrusive way. *v.t.* To proclaim, to expound in a public discourse; to teach or advocate thus. **preacher,** *n.*

preamble (prē-ăm'bl) [L. *ambulāre,* to walk], *n.* An introductory statement, esp. setting forth the reasons and intentions of a statute.

prebend (preb'énd) [L. *præbēre,* to grant], *n.* The stipend of a canon; the land or tithe yielding this; a prebendaryship. **prebendary,** *n.* The holder of a prebend.

precarious (prē-kâr'i-ús) [L. *precārius,* obtained by prayer, from *precārī,* to PRAY], *a.* Depending on the will of another or on chance; not well-established, doubtful.

precaution (prē-kaw'shún) [L. *præcautio*], *n.* Previous caution, prudent foresight.

precede (prē-sēd') [L. *cēdere,* to go], *v.t.* To go before in time, rank, importance; to walk in front of. *v.i.* To have precedence. **precedence** (prē-sē'déns), *n.* Act or state of preceding; priority; right to a higher position. **precedent** (prē-sē'dént), *a.* Going before in time, rank, etc. *n.* (pres'é-dént) Something serving as an example to be followed in a similar case; a necessary antecedent.

precentor (prē-sen'tór) [L. *cantor,* singer], *n.* The leader of a choir in a cathedral.

precept (prē'sept) [L. *præceptum*], *n.* An injunction respecting conduct; a maxim. **preceptor,** *n.* A teacher; the head of a preceptory. **precep'tory,** *n.* A subordinate community of the Knights Templars.

precession (prē-sesh'ún), *n.* Precedence in time or order. **precession of the equinoxes:** (*Astron.*) A slow westward motion of the equinoctial points along the ecliptic.

precinct (prē'sinkt) [PRE-, L. *cinctus,* girt], *n.* The space enclosed by the boundaries of a place, esp. a church; (*pl.*) the environs (of).

precious (presh'ús) [L. *pretiōsus,* from *pretium,* price], *a.* Of great price or value; highly esteemed, dear; affected, over-refined in manner, etc. **precios'ity,** *n.* Over-fastidiousness or affected delicacy, esp. in the use of words.

precipice (pres'i-pis), *n.* A vertical or very steep cliff.

precipitate (prē-sip'i-tāt) [L. *præcipitāre*], *v.t.* To throw headlong; to urge on eagerly, to hasten; (*Chem.*) to cause (a substance) to be deposited from a solution. *v.i.* To fall to the bottom of a vessel (of a substance in solution); to condense and be deposited in drops (of vapour). *a.* (-tát) Headlong; rushing with haste and violence; hasty, rash. *n.* A solid substance deposited from solution. **precipita'tion,** *n.*

precipitous (prē-sip'i-tús), *a.* Like a precipice, very steep; hasty, rash.

précis (prā-sē') [F.], *n.* An abstract, summary.

precise (prē-sīs') [L. *præcīsus*], *a.* Definite, exact; strictly observant of rule, punctilious. **precisian** (-sizh'án), *n.* A punctilious person. **precision** (prē-sizh'ún), *n.*

preclude (prē-klood') [L. *claudere,* to shut], *v.t.* To shut out, exclude; to prevent; to render inoperative. **preclu'sion,** *n.*

precocious (prē-kō'shús) [L. *coquere,* to cook], *a.* Developing before the normal time; prematurely developed intellectually; forward, pert. **precocity** (-kos'i-ti), *n.* State of being precocious.

preconceive (prē-kón-sēv'), *v.t.* To form an opinion of beforehand. **preconception,** *n.* **preconcert',** *v.t.* To agree by previous arrangement.

precursor (prē-kêrs'ór), *n.* A forerunner; one who precedes the approach of anything, a predecessor in office, etc.

predatory (pred'á-tór-i) [L. *prædātor,* plunderer], *a.* Plundering; addicted to pillage; living by preying on others (of animals).

predecease (prē-dē-sēs'), *n.* The death of

a person before some other. *v.t.* To die before (a particular person).

predecessor (prē'dĕ-ses-ŏr) [L. *dēcessor*, from *dēcēdere*, to go away], *n.* One who precedes another in any office, etc.; a thing preceding another thing; an ancestor.

predestinate (prē-des'ti-nāt) [L. *destināre*, to destine], **predestine**, *v.t.* To appoint beforehand by irreversible decree; to pre-ordain; to predetermine. *a.* (-nȧt) Ordained beforehand. **predestinarian**, *a.* Pertaining to predestination. *n.* A believer in this. **predestina'tion**, *n.* The act of God in foreordaining some to salvation and some to perdition.

predetermine (prē-dĕ-tẽr'min), *v.* To determine beforehand; to foreordain. **predeterminate**, *a.* **predetermina'tion**, *n.*

predicable (pred'i-kȧbl), *a.* Capable of being affirmed of something. *n.* Anything that may be predicated of something. **predicabil'ity**, *n.*

predicament (prē-dik'ȧ-mĕnt), *n.* That which is predicated, a category; a particular state, condition, etc., esp. an unpleasant one.

predicate (pred'i-kȧt) [L. *dicātus*, proclaimed], *v.t.* To affirm, to assert as a property, etc. (of a thing). *v.i.* To make an affirmation. *n.* (-kȧt) That which is affirmed or denied of the subject; (*Gram.*) the entire statement made about the subject. **predica'tion**, *n.* **predic'ative**, *a.*

predict (prē-dikt') [L. *dictus*, said], *v.t.* To tell beforehand; to prophesy. **prediction** (-dik'shŭn), *n.* Act of predicting; a prophecy.

predilection (prē-di-lek'shŭn) [L. *dilectio*, choice], *n.* A prepossession in favour of something, a preference, a partiality.

predispose (prē-dis-pōz'), *v.t.* To dispose or incline beforehand; to make liable to. **predisposition** (-zish'ŭn), *n.*

predominate (prē-dom'i-nāt), *v.i.* To be superior in strength, influence, or authority; to prevail. **predominance**, **-nancy**, *n.* predominant, *a.*

pre-em'inent, *a.* Eminent beyond others; superior to all others. **pre-eminence**, *n.*

pre-emp'tion, *n.* Act or right of buying before others.

preen (prēn) [?], *v.t.* To trim (feathers) with the beak (of birds).

pre-fab (prē-făb') [prefabricated], *n.* A house, bridge, etc., the component parts of which are constructed separately and assembled *in situ.*

preface (pref'ás) [L. *fārī*, to speak], *n.* An introduction; a preamble, prelude. *v.t.* To furnish with a preface; to introduce (with preliminary remarks, etc.). **preface'tor'ial**, **pref'atory**, *a.*

prefect (prē'fekt) [L. *præfectus*, an overseer], *n.* (*Rom. Ant.*) A governor, a chief magistrate; in France, the civil governor of a department; a school monitor. **prefector'ial**, *a.* **pre'fecture**, *n.* The office or jurisdiction of a prefect.

prefer (prē-fẽr') [L. *ferre*, to bear], *v.t.* To set before, to like better; to bring forward; to promote. **pref'erable**, *a.* **preferably**, *adv.* **preference**, *n.* Act of preferring one thing to another; choice;

favour displayed towards a person or country before others. **preferen'tial**, *a.* Giving, receiving, or constituting preference; favouring certain countries. **preferment**, *n.* Promotion.

prefigure (prē-fig'ŭr), *v.t.* To represent by antecedent figures; to picture to oneself beforehand. **prefigura'tion**, *n.*

prefix (prē-fiks'), *v.t.* To put in front of; to attach at the beginning. *n.* (prē'fiks) A letter or syllable put at the beginning of a word to modify the meaning.

pregnant (preg'nánt) [L. *prægnans*], *a.* Being with young; full of meaning, significant. **pregnancy**, *n.*

prehensile (prē-hen'sil) [L. *prehensus*, laid hold of], *a.* Grasping; adapted to seizing or grasping, as the tails of monkeys.

prehistoric (prē-his-tor'ik), *a.* Pertaining to time prior to that known to history.

prejudice (prej'ŭ-dis) [L. *præjūdicium*], *n.* Opinion formed without due consideration; damage arising from unfair judgment or action. *v.t.* To bias; to affect injuriously, esp. to impair the validity of a right, etc. **without prejudice:** (*Law*) without impairing any pre-existing right. **prejudicial** (-dish'ál). *a.* Causing prejudice or injury; detrimental.

prelate (prel'ȧt) [L. *lātus*, borne], *n.* A high ecclesiastical dignitary as archbishop, bishop, etc. **prelacy**, *n.* prelat'ic, *a.*

preliminary (prē-lim'i-nȧ-ri) [L. *limen*, threshold], *a.* Introductory. *n.* Something introductory; (*pl.*) preparatory arrangements, etc.

prelude (prel'ūd) [L. *lūdere*, to play], *n.* Something introductory or preparatory to that which follows. *v.t.* To perform or serve as a prelude to.

premature (prem'ȧ-tūr), *a.* Ripe or mature too soon; happening, etc., before the proper time.

premeditate (prē-med'i-tāt), *v.t.* To meditate on or plan and contrive beforehand. *v.i.* To deliberate previously. **premedita'tion**, *n.*

premier (prē'mi-ẽr), *n.* The prime minister of Great Britain or a British colony. *a.* Prime, first, chief. **premiership**, *n.*

première (prem'yâr) [Fr. *first*], *n.* The first public performance of a play or showing of a cinematograph film.

premise (prem'is) [L. *missus*, sent], *n.* A proposition from which another is inferred; (*pl.*) land, buildings, and appurtenances. *v.t.* (prē-miz') To put forward as preparatory; to lay down as an antecedent proposition or condition.

premium (prē'mi-ŭm) [L. *emere*, to buy], *n.* A reward; a sum paid in addition, a bonus; a fee for instruction in a profession, etc.; a payment made for insurance; selling price above nominal value.

premonition (prē-mō-nish'ŭn) [L. *monēre*, to warn], *n.* Previous warning or notice. **premon'itory**, *a.*

preoccupy (prē-ok'ū-pī), *v.t.* To take possession of beforehand or before another; to engross (the mind, etc.).

prepaid (prē-pād'), *a.* Paid in advance (as postage, etc.).

prepare (prē-pâr') [L. *parāre*, to make ready], *v.* To make ready; to bring into a suitable condition, to fit for a certain purpose. **prepara'tion,** *n.* **prepar'atory,** *a.* Tending or serving to prepare; introductory (to).

prepay (prē-pā'), *v.t.* To pay in advance. **prepayment,** *n.*

prepense (prē-pens') [O.F. *purpenser*], *a.* Premeditated, deliberate.

preponderate (prē-pon'dēr-āt) [L. *ponderāre*, to ponder], *v.i.* To be superior or to outweigh in power, influence, etc. **preponderance,** *n.* **preponderant,** *a.*

preposition (prep-ō-zish'un) [L. *positus*, put], *n.* A word used to express the relations of a word to another word. **prepositional,** *a.*

prepossess (prē-pō-zes'), *v.t.* To occupy beforehand; to bias (esp. favourably); to preoccupy (of an idea, etc.). **prepossessing,** *a.* Biasing; attractive.

preposterous (prē-pos'tēr-us) [L. *posterus*, coming after], *a.* Contrary to nature or common sense; foolish, absurd. **preposterously,** *adv.*

prerogative (prē-rog'ȧ-tiv) [L. *rogātus*, asked], *n.* An exclusive right vested in a particular person or body.

presage (pres'āj) [L. *sāgīre*, to perceive quickly], *n.* Something that foretells a future event; an omen; presentiment. *v.t.* (prē-sāj') To foreshadow, betoken; to forebode.

presbyter (prez'bi-tēr) [Gr. *presbuteros*, elder], *n.* An elder; a minister of a presbytery. **Presbyter'ian,** *n.* An adherent of Presbyterianism. *a.* Pertaining to Church government by presbyters; governed by presbyters; denoting a Church governed by elders, including ministers, all equal in rank. **Presbyterianism,** *n.* pres'bytery, *n.* A body of elders.

prescient (presh'i-ènt) [L. *sciens*, knowing], *a.* Foreknowing, far-seeing. **prescience,** *n.*

prescribe (prē-skrib') [L. *scribere*, to write], *v.t.* To lay down with authority; (*Med.*) to direct to be used as a remedy. *v.i.* To write directions for medical treatment. **prescrip'tion,** *n.* Act of prescribing; that which is prescribed; (*Law*) long-continued use or possession, as giving right or title. **prescriptive,** *a.* Acquired or authorized by long use.

presence (prez'éns), *n.* Quality or state of being present, situation face to face with a person or persons; approach to a person of high rank; mien, deportment.

present (1) (prez'ènt) [L. *præsentem*], *a.* Being in a place referred to; being in view, at hand, or under consideration; now existing; (*Gram.*) expressing what is actually going on. *n.* The present time; (*Gram.*) the present tense; (*pl.*) these writings, this document itself.

present (2) (prē-zent'), *v.t.* To introduce to the acquaintance or presence of; to exhibit, to offer to the sight; to point (a gun, etc.); to give in a ceremonious way. *n.* (prez'ènt) That which is presented, a gift. **presen'table,** *a.* Fit to be presented; of suitable appearance. **presenta'tion,** *n.* Act of presenting; a formal offering; a gift; a theatrical representation; a formal introduction

to a superior personage or a sovereign, act or right of presenting to a benefice.

presentiment (prē-zen'ti-ment), *n.* Vague anticipation of an impending event, esp. of evil, a foreboding.

presently (prez'ènt-li), *adv.* Soon, shortly; (old usage) at once, immediately.

presentment (prē-zent'mènt), *n.* Act of presenting; a theatrical representation, a likeness, semblance.

preserve (prē-zĕrv') [L. *servāre*, to keep], *v.t.* To keep safe, to save; to maintain in good condition; to keep intact or from decay or decomposition; to keep for private use by preventing poaching, etc. *n.* Fruit, etc., prepared with preservative substances; a place where game is preserved. **preserva'tion,** *n.* **preser'vative,** *a.* Having the power of preserving from injury, decay, or corruption. *n.* That which preserves. **preserver,** *n.*

preside (prē-zīd') [L. *sedēre*, to sit], *v.i.* To act as director, chairman, or president; to superintend. **pres'idency,** *n.* Office, jurisdiction, or term of office of a president. **president,** *n.* One who presides over a body of persons; the chief magistrate of the government in a modern republic. **presiden'tial,** *a.*

press (1) (pres) [L. *pressāre*], *v.t.* To push down against with steady force; to squeeze, crush, compress; to crowd upon; to urge. *v.i.* To exert pressure, bear heavily; to be urgent; to crowd. *n.* The act of pressing, urging, or crowding; a throng; urgency, hurry; a cupboard for storing things; an instrument for compressing any substance; newspapers, also journalists, collectively; **pressman,** *n.* One who works a printing-press; a journalist. **pressing,** *a.* Urgent, importunate.

press (2) [L. *præstāre* (*stāre*, to come forward, to stand)], *v.t.* To force into naval or military service. **press-gang,** *n.* A detachment of men employed to impress men.

pressure (presh'ür), *n.* Act of pressing; state of being pressed; a force steadily exerted by one body upon or against another; amount of this; (*fig.*) urgency, rush; straits, trouble; oppression; compulsion.

prestige (pres-tēzh') [L. *præstigium*, glamour], *n.* Influence derived from former fame, achievements, etc.

presto (pres'tō) [It.], *adv.* (*Mus.*) Quickly. *a.* Quick.

presume (prē-zūm') [L. *sūmere*, to take], *v.t.* To venture on without leave; to take for granted. *v.i.* To form overconfident or arrogant opinions; to behave with assurance. **presumable,** *a.* presumably, **presumedly,** *adv.* presuming, *a.* Presumptuous. **presumption** (-zŭmp'shun), *n.* presump'tive, *a.* Giving grounds for or based on presumption.

presumptuous (prē-zŭmp'tū-ús), *a.* Full of presumption; forward; venturesome.

pretend (prē-tend') [L. *tendere*, to stretch], *v.t.* To assume the appearance of; to feign; to simulate. *v.i.* To make believe; to put forward a claim (to). **pretence',**

n. A claim; a false profession; a pretext; show, ostentation; act of feigning. **pretender**, *n.* Assumption of a claim, true or false. **pretentious**, *a*

preter- [L. *præter*, past, beyond], *pref.* Beyond; beyond the range of; more than. **preterhuman** (prē-tēr-hū′mán), *a.* More than human, superhuman.

preterit (pret′ėr-it) [L. *præteritus*, gone by], *a.* (*Gram.*) Denoting completed action or existence in past time. *n.* The preterit tense.

preternatural (prē-tėr-năt′ū-rál), *a.* Beyond what is natural; out of the regular course of nature.

pretext (prē′tekst) [L. *textus*, woven], *n.* An excuse; an ostensible motive.

pretty (prit′i) [A.-S. *prœtig*, from *prœt*, trickery], *a.* Having beauty of a slight kind; attractive, but lacking in the perfect proportions of beauty. *adv.* Tolerably, moderately. **prettily**, *adv.* Daintily; pleasingly to the eye, ear, etc. **prettiness**, *n.*

prevail (prē-vāl′) [L. *valēre*, to be strong], *v.i.* To have the mastery or victory (over); to have or gain influence or effect (upon); to be in vogue. **prevalence**, *n.* Act of prevailing; superiority; frequency, currency. **prevalent**, *a.*

prevaricate (prē-văr′i-kāt) [L. *prævāricātus*, straddled, shuffled], *v.i.* To shuffle, quibble; to act evasively. **prevarication**, *n.*

prevent (prē-vent′) [L. *prævenīre*, to precede], *v.t.* To hinder, thwart; to go before, to precede. **preventable**, **-ible**, *a.* Capable of prevention. **preventative** [PREVENTIVE]. **prevention**, *n.* Act of preventing; obstruction. **preventive**, *a.* Tending to hinder. *n.* That which prevents; a medicine or precaution to ward off disease.

previous (prē′vi-ús) [L. *via*, way], *a.* Going before, prior (to). **previously**, *adv.* **previousness**, *n.*

prevision (prē-vizh′ún), *n.* Foresight.

prey (prā) [L. *præda*, booty], *n.* That which may be seized and devoured by animals; spoil, plunder. *v.i.* To take booty; to take food by violence.

price (prīs) [O.F. *pris*, L. *pretium*], *n.* The amount for which a thing is sold; estimation, value. *v.t.* To value, appraise; to ask the price of. **priceless**, *a.* Invaluable, inestimable.

prick (prik) [A.-S. *prica*], *n.* Act of pricking; state or sensation of being pricked; a puncture; a small mark made by or as by pricking; a pointed instrument. *v.t.* To puncture; to cause (the ears) to point upwards. *v.i.* To ride rapidly, to spur on. **prick-eared**, *a.* Having erect or pointed ears (of dogs, etc.).

prickle (prikl) [A.-S. *pricel*], *n.* A small, sharp point; a thorn-like growth. *v.t.* To give a pricking sensation to. *v.i.* To have such a sensation. **prickly**, *a.* Full of prickles; itching, stinging.

pride (prīd) [A.-S. *prýto*], *n.* Inordinate self-esteem; insolence, arrogance; sense of dignity, self-respect; generous elation or a source of this.

priest (prēst) [A.-S. *prēost*], *n.* One who officiates in sacred rites, esp. by offering sacrifice; a minister below a bishop and above a deacon. **priestcraft**, *n.* Priestly policy based on material interests. **priest-ridden**, *a.* Dominated or swayed by priests. **priesthood**, *n.* **priestly**, *a.*

prig (prig) [?], *n.* A conceited or didactic person; a thief. *v.t.* To steal. **priggish**, *a.* Conceited, affectedly precise, formal.

prim (prim) [?], *a.* Formal, affectedly proper, demure. **primly**, *adv.*

prima (prē′mà) [It.], *a.* First, principal. **prima donna** (don′à): A chief female singer in an opera.

primacy (prī′mà-si) [L. *primātus*], *n.* The dignity or office of a primate.

prima facie (prī-mà-fā′shi-ē) [L.], *adv.* At first sight, on the first impression.

primal (prī′mál) [L. *primus*, first], *a.* Primary, primitive; fundamental.

primary (prī′mà-ri), *a.* First in time, order, importance, or origin; radical, fundamental; chief; lowest in development, elementary. *n.* That which stands first in order, rank, or importance; a planet.

primate (prī′mát), *n.* The chief prelate in a national episcopal church, an archbishop. **primatial** (-mā′shàl), *a.*

primates (prī-mā′tēz), *n.pl.* The highest order of mammals, comprising man, monkeys, and lemurs.

prime (1) (prīm) [L. *primus*, first], *a.* First in time, rank, excellence, or importance; chief; first-rate; primary; in full vigour; divisible by no integral factors except itself and unity. *n.* Period or state of highest perfection; the best part.

prime (2) [?], *v.t.* To prepare (a gun) for firing; to supply (with information or with liquor); to lay the first coat of paint, etc., on.

primer (prī′mėr), *n.* An elementary reading book; a short introductory book; (prim′ėr) one of two sizes of type, great primer and long primer.

primeval (prī-mē′vál) [L. *ævum*, age], *a.* Belonging to the earliest ages, primitive.

priming (prī′ming), *n.* Act of preparing a fire-arm for discharge; the powder for a flint gun, or for connecting a blasting-charge with the fuse; a first layer of paint, etc.

primitive (prim′i-tiv), *a.* Pertaining to the earliest periods; ancient, original; (*Gram.*) radical, not derivative; plain, old-fashioned. **primitively**, *adv.*

primogeniture (prī-mō-jen′i-tūr) [F. *geniteur*], *n.* Seniority by birth amongst children of the same parents; the system under which, in cases of intestacy, the eldest son succeeds.

primordial (prī-môr′di-ál), *a.* First in order, primary; existing at or from the beginning. *n.* A first principle or element.

primrose (prim′rōz) [L. *prima rōsa*, early rose], *n.* A common British wild plant, flowering in early spring. *a.* Like a primrose; of a pale yellow colour; flowery.

prince (prins) [L. *princeps*], *n.* The ruler of a principality or small state; a son or grandson of a monarch. **prince of the Church:** A cardinal. **prince royal**, *n.* The eldest son of a sovereign. **princedom**, *n.* The rank or jurisdiction of a prince. **princelet**, **princeling**, *n.* A petty prince. **princely**, *a.* Pertaining to or befitting a prince; stately, dignified. **princess**, *n.*

principal (prin'si-pál), *a.* Chief, main; first in rank, authority, importance, etc. *n.* A president, governor, head of a college, etc.; a chief actor, the chief party; a person employing another as agent; a capital sum invested or lent. **principal'ity**, *n.* The territory or jurisdiction of a prince; the country from which he derives his title; (*pl.*) one of the orders of angels. **prin'cipally**, *adv.* Chiefly, mainly, for the most part.

principle (prin'sipl), *n.* A fundamental cause, doctrine or tenet; a comprehensive truth or proposition; a rule of action or conduct deliberately adopted; a law of nature.

print (print) [O.F. *preinte*, from *preint*, p.p. of *preindre*, L. *premere*, to press], *n.* A mark made by pressure, an impression, esp. from type; printed matter; an engraving, a newspaper, etc.; printed cloth; a positive image produced from a negative. *v.t.* To mark by pressure; to take an impression of, to stamp; to make copies of by pressure, as from inked types, etc.; to publish. *v.i.* To practise the art of printing; to publish. **printer**, *n.* One engaged in printing. **printing**, *n.* Act, process, or practice of impressing letters, etc., on paper, etc., the business of a printer. **printing-press**, *n.* A printing-machine.

prior (pri'ór) [L.], *a.* Former, preceding; earlier. *adv.* Previously. *n.* A superior of a monastic house next below an abbot. **prioress**, *n.* **prior'ity**, *n.* State of being prior (in time, rank, etc.). **priory**, *n.* A religious house governed by a prior or prioress.

prise (priz), *v.t.* To wrench; to force open with a lever.

prism (prizm) [Gr. *prisma*, from *prizein*, to saw], *n.* A solid having similar, equal, and parallel plane ends, its sides forming similar parallelograms; a transparent solid of this form used in optics. **prismat'ic**, *a.*

prison (priz'ón) [O.F. *prison*, L. *prensio*, from *prehendere*, to seize], *n.* A place of confinement for criminals; confinement, captivity, *v.t.* To imprison. **prisoner**, *n.* One confined in a prison; a captive.

pristine (pris'tin) [L. *pristinus*], *a.* Pertaining to an early state; ancient, primitive.

private (pri'vát) [L. *privātus*, set apart], *a.* Not public; secluded; confidential; not official; personal, one's own; secretive. *n.* A soldier in the ranks. **privacy** (pri'vá-si, priv'á-si), *n.*

privateer (pri-vá-těr'), *n.* A privately-owned ship commissioned for war; one who engages in privateering.

privation (pri-vā'shŭn), *n.* Deprivation or lack of what is necessary; want; negation (of). **pri'vative**, *a.* Causing or expressing privation or absence of a quality, etc., negative.

privet (priv'ét) [?], *n.* An evergreen, white-flowered shrub used for hedges.

privilege (priv'i-léj) [L. *privilēgium*], *n.* A benefit, right, or immunity; favour, a special advantage; an exemption pertaining to an office. *v.t.* To invest with a privilege. **privileged**, *a.*

privy (priv'i), *a.* Hidden, clandestine, private. *n.* A latrine, a necessary. **Privy council**: The private council of the British sovereign. **privily**, *adv.* Secretly, privately. **privity**, *n.* The state of being privy to (certain facts, etc.).

prize (1) (priz) [O.F. *pris*, price], *n.* The reward of merit or superiority in a competition, exhibition, etc. *v.t.* To value highly, to esteem. **prize-fight**, *n.* A boxing-match for stakes.

prize (2) [F. *prise*, a taking], *n.* That which is taken from an enemy in war, esp. a ship.

pro (prō) [L.], *prep.* For. pro and con [L. *pro et contra*]: For and against; on both sides.

pro- [L. *pro*, before, in front of, in favour of, in the place of, on account of], *pref.*

probability (prob-á-bil'i-ti), *n.* Quality of being probable; likelihood.

probable (prob'ábl), *a.* Having more evidence for than against, likely. **probably**, *adv.*

probate (prō'bát) [L. *probātus*, proven], *n.* The official proving or a certified copy of a will.

probation (prō-bā'shŭn), *n.* A proving or testing of character, ability, etc.; a period of trial; a method of dealing with young criminals; evidence, proof. **probational**, *a.* **probationary**, *a.* Undergoing probation. **probationer**, *n.* One on probation; an offender under probation.

probe (prōb), *n.* A surgical instrument for exploring cavities, wounds, etc., *v.t.* To search or examine (a wound, ulcer, etc.) with a probe; (*fig.*) to scrutinize thoroughly.

probity (prob'i-ti), *n.* Tried honesty, sincerity; rectitude.

problem (prob'lém) [Gr. *problēma*], *n.* A question proposed for solution, or involving doubt or difficulty. **problemat'ic**, **-al**, *a.* Doubtful, questionable. **problematically**, *adv.*

proboscis (prō-bos'is) [Gr. *proboskis*], *n.* (*pl.* -ides, -i-děz) The trunk of an elephant, snout of a tapir, etc.; the elongated mouth of some insects.

procedure (prō-sē'dyŭr), *n.* Act or manner of proceeding; a course of action.

proceed (prō-sēd') [L. *cēdere*, to go], *v.i.* To go on; to advance; to carry on a series of actions; to take steps; to issue, to originate; to take a degree. **proceeding**, *n.* Progress; a line of conduct, a transaction; (*pl.*) steps in the prosecution of an action at law; (*pl.*) the records of a learned society. **pro'ceeds**, *n.pl.* Material results, profits.

process (prō'ses) [L. *cessus*, gone], *n.* A course or method of proceeding; a progressive movement or state of activity; the course of proceedings in an action at law; a writ commencing this.

procession (prō-sesh'ŭn), *n.* A train of persons proceeding in formal march.

proclaim (prō-klām') [L. *clāmāre*, to cry

out], *v.t.* To announce or declare publicly or openly; to publish; to outlaw. **proclama'tion**, *n.*

proclivity (pró-kliv'ĭ-ti) [L. *clivus*, slope], *n.* Tendency, bent.

proconsul (pró-kon'sul), *n.* A governor, or viceroy of a dependency.

procrastinate (pró-krăs'ti-nāt) [L. *crastinus*, pertaining to to-morrow], *v.* To put off action; to be dilatory; to defer. **procrastina'tion**, *n.*

procreate (pró'krē-āt) [L. *creātus*, created], *v.t.* To generate, to beget. **procrea'tion**, *n.*

proctor (prok'tór), *n.* A University official maintaining order and discipline; one employed to manage another's cause, esp. in an ecclesiastical court. **proctor'ial**, *a.*

procumbent (pró-kŭm'bĕnt) [L. *cumbens*, lying down], *a.* Lying down on the face, prone.

procuration (prok-ū-rā'shŭn), *n.* Action on behalf of another, function of attorney, a proxy.

procurator (prok'ū-rā-tór), *n.* One who manages another's affairs, an agent, attorney.

procure (prŏk-ūr') [L. *cūrāre*, to see to], *v.t.* To obtain, to acquire, to gain. **procurable**, *a.*

prod (prod) [?], *v.t.* To poke with a pointed instrument.

prod– [PRO–, before vowels], *pref.*

prodigal (prod'ĭ-gǎl) [L. *agere*, to drive], *a.* Given to extravagant expenditure; lavish (of). *n.* A spendthrift. **prodigal'ity**, *n.* Extravagance; lavishness, waste. **prodigally**, *adv.*

prodigy (prod'ĭ-jĭ) [L. *prōdigium*, portent], *n.* Something wonderful or extraordinary; a person with extraordinary gifts or qualities; a monstrosity. **prodig'ious** prŏ-dij'ŭs), *a.*

produce (pró-dūs') [L. *dūcere*, to lead], *v.t.* To bring into view; to exhibit; to bring into existence; to yield, to manufacture; to cause; (*Geom.*) to continue (a line) in the same direction. *n.* (prŏd'ūs) That which is produced or yielded; result. **producible**, *a.*

product (prod'ŭkt), *n.* That which is produced by natural processes, labour, art, or mental application; effect, result; number resulting from multiplication. **produc'tion**, *n.* Act of producing, esp. as opposed to consumption; a product. **productive**, *a.* Producing; fertile.

proem (pró'ĕm) [Gr. *oimos*, way, or *oimē*, song], *n.* A preface, introduction, prelude.

profane (pró-fān') [L. *fānum*, temple], *a.* Not sacred, secular; irreverent, blasphemous. *v.t.* To treat with irreverence; to desecrate, pollute. **profanation** (prof-á-nā'shŭn), *n.* **profanity** (-făn'ĭ-ti), *n.* The use of profane language.

profess (pró-fes') [L. *fatēri*, to confess], *v.t.* To avow publicly; to affirm one's belief in or allegiance to; to teach (a subject) as a professor. *v.i.* To make protestations or show of. **profes'sedly**, *adv.* By profession; avowedly; ostensibly. **profession** (-fesh'ŭn), *n.* Act of professing; an avowal; a protestation, a pretence;

a vocation, esp. one involving high qualifications; the body of persons engaged in such a vocation. **professional**, *a.* Pertaining to a profession, as opp. to amateur. *n.* A member of a profession; sport, etc. **professionalism**, *n.* **professor**, *n.* One who makes profession, esp. of a religious faith; a public teacher in a University. **professor'iate**. **profes'sorship**, *n.* **professor'ial**, *a.*

proffer (prof'ĕr) [L. *offerre*, to offer], *v.t.* To offer or tender. *n.* An offer.

proficient (pró-fish'ĕnt), *a.* Skilled in any art, science, etc., expert. *n.* An adept, an expert. **proficiency**, *n.*

profile (pró'fīl) [L. *fīlāre*, to spin], *n.* An outline; a side view, esp. of the human face.

profit (prof'it) [*prōfectus*, advanced], *n.* Any benefit resulting from labour; excess of receipts over outlay, gain. *v.t.* To benefit, be of advantage to. *v.i.* To receive benefit or advantage (by or from). **profitable**, *a.* Yielding or bringing profit; beneficial, useful. **profiteer'**, *n.* One who, esp. at a time of national stress, makes undue profit at the expense of the public. **profiteering**, *n.* **profitless**, *a.*

profligate (prof'li-gāt) [L. *prōfligātus*, cast down], *a.* Abandoned to vice, dissolute; wildly extravagant. *n.* A profligate person. **profligacy**, *n.*

profound (pró-found') [L. *fundus*, bottom], *a.* Having great insight or knowledge; requiring great study, abstruse, deep; reaching to or coming from a great depth; very low (as an obeisance). *n.* An abyss; chaos. **profun'dity**, *n.*

profuse (pró-fūs') [L. *fūsus*, poured], *a.* Poured forth lavishly, copious; extravagant. **profu'sion**, *n.*

progenitor (pró-jén'i-tór) [L. *genitor*, a parent], *n.* An ancestor in the direct line; (*fig.*) an original.

progeny (proj'é-ni), *n.* Offspring, descendants.

prognosis (prog-nō'sis) [Gr. *gignōskein*, to know], *n.* (*pl.* -oses) An opinion as to the probable result, esp. of an illness.

prognostic (prog-nos'tik), *n.* An omen, a token; a forecast; (*Med.*) a symptom. *a.* Foreshowing. **prognosticate**, *v.t.* To foreshadow, presage, betoken. **prognostica'tion**, *n.*

programme (pró'grăm) [Gr. *programma* (*graphein*, to write)], *n.* A list of items of an entertainment, etc.; a plan of proceedings to be carried out.

progress (pró'grĕs, prog'rĕs) [L. *gressus*, walked], *n.* A going forward; movement onward, advance, development. *v.i.* (-grĕs') To advance; to be carried on; to develop. **progression** (-gresh'ŭn), *n.* Motion onward; regular or proportional advance. **progressional**, *a.* **progressive**, *a.* and *n.* A progressive person, esp. in municipal politics. **progressively**, *adv.*

prohibit (pró-hib'it) [L. *habēre*, to have], *v.t.* To forbid authoritatively, to prevent. **prohibi'tion**, *n.* Act of or order prohibiting. **prohib'itive**, *a.*

project (proj'ĕkt) [L. *jectus*, thrown], *n.* A scheme, design. *v.t.* (pró-jekt') To throw forward; to cause to jut out; to contrive, plan; (*Geom.*) to make a projection of. *v.i.* To jut out, protrude. **projec'tile**, *a.* Impelling forward; adapted to be projected. *n.* A missile, esp. from a heavy gun. **projec'tion**, *n.* Act or state of projecting, throwing, or impelling; a part that projects; act of planning; the geometrical projecting of a figure; the representation of the terrestrial or celestial sphere on a plane surface.

prolegomenon (prŏ-lĕ-gom'ĕ-nŏn) [Gr. *legein*, to say], *n.* (*usu. in pl.*, -ena) An introductory or preliminary discourse.

proletarian (prŏ-lĕ-tār'i-ăn) [L. *prōlĕtārius*, one of the lowest class], *a.* Pertaining to the common people. *n.* A member of the proletariat. **proletariat**, *n.* Those without property, the wage-earners, the labouring-classes.

prolific (prŏ-lif'ik) [L. *prōles*, offspring], *a.* Fruitful, productive; abounding (in).

prolix (prŏ-liks') [L. *liquĕre*, to flow], *a.* Wordy; tedious, diffuse. **prolix'ity**, *n.* Wordiness, diffuseness.

prologue (prŏ'log) [Gr. *logos*, speech], *n.* An introductory discourse, a poem introducing a play.

prolong (prŏ-long'), *v.t.* To lengthen, to extend in duration or distance. *n.* Act of lengthening; a lengthening in time or space.

promenade (prom-ĕ-nad') [L. *prōmināre*, to drive], *n.* A walk, drive, etc., for pleasure; a public walk. *v.i.* To take a walk, etc., for pleasure, exercise, or show.

prominent (prom'i-nĕnt) [L. *prominens*, projecting], *a.* Standing out, jutting; conspicuous; distinguished. **prominence**, *n.*

promiscuous (prŏ-mis'kū-ŭs) [L. *miscēre*, to mix], *a.* Mixed together in a disorderly manner; of different kinds mingled confusedly; indiscriminate; (*colloq.*) fortuitous. **promiscu'ity**, *n.*

promise (prom'is) [L. *missus*, sent], *n.* An engagement to do or forbear from doing; that which is promised; ground of expectation. *v.t.* To engage to do or not do; to give good grounds for expecting. *v.i.* To bind oneself by a promise. **promising**, *a.* Giving grounds for hope; favourable. **promissory**, *a.* Containing a promise, esp. a promise to pay money.

promontory (prom'ŏn-tŏr-i) [L. *mons*, mount], *n.* A headland. **promontoried**, *a.*

promote (prŏ-mōt') [L. *mōtus*, moved], *v.t.* To advance, to contribute to the increase or advancement of; to foster, encourage; to raise to a higher position; to organize and float (a company, etc.).

prompt (prompt) [L. *promptus*], *a.* Ready to act as occasion demands; done with alacrity. *v.t.* To instigate; to suggest to the mind, to inspire; to assist (actor, etc.) by suggesting the words forgotten. **promptitude**, *n.*

promulgate (prom'ŭl-gāt) [L. *prōmulgāre*], *v.t.* To make known to the public; to publish abroad. **promulga'tion**, *n.* **promulgator**, *n.*

prone (prŏn) [L. *prŏnus*], *a.* Leaning forward; lying with the face downward; prostrate; disposed, inclined.

prong (prong) [?], *n.* A forked instrument; one of the spikes of a fork.

pronominal (prŏ-nom'i-năl), *a.* Pertaining to or of the nature of a pronoun.

pronoun (prŏ'noun), *n.* A word used in place of a noun.

pronounce (prŏ-nouns') [L. *nuntiāre*, to announce], *v.* To utter articulately, formally, or rhetorically; to declare, to affirm. **pronounceable**, *a.* **pronounced**, *a.* Strongly marked, emphatic; conspicuous. **pronouncement**, *n.*

pronunciation (prŏ-nŭn-si-ā'shŭn), *n.* Act or mode of pronouncing words, etc.; art or act of public speaking.

proof (proof) [L. *probāre*, to prove], *n.* Act of proving, a test; demonstration; convincing evidence; state of having been proved; a standard degree of strength in spirit; a trial impression from type or an engraved plate. *a.* Proved, tested; impenetrable; of a certain degree of alcoholic strength. *v.t.* To make proof, esp. waterproof.

prop (prop) [?], *n.* A support, esp. a temporary one; a person supporting a cause. *v.t.* To support or hold up with or by a prop.

propagate (prop'á-gāt) [L. *prōpāgātus*, extended], *v.t.* To cause to multiply; to reproduce; to diffuse, disseminate; to transmit. *v.i.* To be reproduced or multiplied; to have offspring. **propagan'da**, *n.* Any organization or scheme for propagating doctrines, systems, etc.; effort directed to this end. **propagandist**, *n.* One devoted to or engaged in propaganda. **propaga'tion**, *n.* Act of propagating; dissemination. **propagator**, *n.*

propel (prŏ-pel') [L. *pellere*, to drive], *v.t.* To drive or cause to move forwards. **propellent**, *n.* That which propels, esp. an explosive. **propeller**, *n.* One who or that which propels; a rotating device with two to four blades for propelling a vessel through water or air.

propensity (prŏ-pen'si-ti) [L. *pensus*, hung], *n.* Natural tendency, inclination.

proper (prop'ĕr) [L. *proprius*, one's own], *a.* Belonging exclusively or peculiarly to; designating an individual, place, etc. (of nouns); correct, suitable, becoming, real, genuine. **properly**, *adv.* Suitably; justly, correctly, accurately; quite.

property (prop'ĕr-ti), *n.* Peculiar or inherent quality; that which is owned; possessions, an estate; ownership; (*pl.*) articles required for a play. **propertied**, *a.* Possessed of property, esp. land.

prophecy (prof'ĕ-si) [Gr. *prophēteia*], *n.* A prediction; prediction of future events; gift of prophesying.

prophesy (prof'ĕ-si), *v.t.* To predict, herald. *v.i.* To utter prophecies.

prophet (prof'ĕt), *n.* One who foretells future events, esp. under divine inspiration; a religious leader; (*fig.*) a preacher of a cause, etc. **prophetess**, *n.* **prophet'ic**, **-al**, *a.* Pertaining to prophecy; predictive, anticipative.

propinquity (prŏ-ping'kwi-ti) [L. *propin-*

quus, near], *n.* Nearness in time, space, or relationship; similarity.

propitiate (pró-pish'i-āt) [L. *propitius*, propitious], *v.t.* To appease; to render favourable. **propitia'tion**, *n.* Act of propitiating, atonement. **propitiatory**, *a.* Intended or serving to propitiate. *n.* A propitiation; the mercy-seat of the Jews. **propitious**, *a.* Favourable; disposed to be kind or gracious; auspicious.

proportion (pró-pōr'shŭn), *n.* Comparative relation of one part or thing to another; ratio, suitable adaptation of parts, etc.; a share; (*pl.*) dimensions; the rule by which from three quantities a fourth may be found bearing the same ratio to the third as the second to the first. *v.t.* To adjust in suitable proportion; to apportion. **proportional**, *a.* **proportionate**, *a.* In proportion (to). *v.t.* To make proportionate or proportional. **proportionately**, *adv.*

propose (pró-pōz') [F. *proposer*], *v.t.* To offer for consideration; to nominate for election to put forward, to intend. *v.i.* To make an offer, esp. of marriage. **proposal** (-pō'zàl), *n.*

proposition (prop-ō-zish'ŭn) [*prōpositio*], *n.* That which is propounded; an assertion; a formal statement of a theorem; a scheme proposed.

propound (pró-pound') [L. *pōnere*, to put], *v.t.* To set forth for consideration, to propose; (*Law*) to bring forward for probate.

proprietor (pró-prī'ê-tòr) [L. *proprietārius*], *n.* An owner, one who has the exclusive legal right to anything. **proprietary**, *a.* Pertaining to a proprietor. **proprietor'ial**, *a.* **propri'etorship**, *n.*

propriety (pró-prī'ê-ti) [F. *propriété*], *n.* Fitness, rightness; correctness of behaviour.

propulsion (pró-pŭl'shŭn), *n.* Act of propelling; an impulse.

prorogue (pró-rōg') [L. *prōrogāre*, to defer], *v.t.* To end the meetings of Parliament without dissolving. **proroga'tion**, *n.*

pros- [Gr.], *pref.* To; before, in addition.

prosaic (pró-zā'īk) [as PROSE], *a.* Pertaining to prose; unimaginative, dull.

proscenium (pró-sē'ni-ŭm) [Gr. *proskenion*], *n.* (*Theat.*) The part of a stage between the curtain and the orchestra.

proscribe (pró-skrīb') [L. *scrībere*, to write], *v.t.* To outlaw; to exile; to denounce as dangerous; to interdict. **proscrip'tion**, *n.* **proscriptive**, *a.*

prose (prōz) [L. *prōsa orātio*, straightforward discourse], *n.* Ordinary language, opp. to verse. *v.i.* To write or talk in a dull, tedious manner.

prosecute (pros'ê-kūt) [L. *secūtus*, followed], *v.t.* To follow up with a view to accomplish, to carry on (work, etc.); to take legal proceedings against. *v.i.* To act as a prosecutor against. *v.i.* To act as a prosecutor. **prosecu'tion**, *n.* Act of prosecuting; the instituting and carrying on of a suit; the prosecutors collectively. **pros'ecutor**, *n.* **prosecutrix**, *n.*

proselyte (pros-è-līt) [Gr. *prosēlutos*], *n.* A new convert. **proselytize**, *v.t.* and *i.*

prosody (pros'ó-di) [Gr. *prosōdia*], *n.* The science of versification.

prospect (pros'pekt), *n.* An extensive view; the way a house, etc., fronts; mental outlook; expectation. *v.* (pró-spekt') To explore, esp. for minerals; to promise (a good or poor yield). **prospec'tive**, *a.* Pertaining to the future; probable. **prospec'tor**, *n.* One who searches for minerals or mining sites.

prospectus (pró-spek'tŭs) [L., a look-out], *n.* A circular announcing the objects and plans of a commercial scheme, work, etc.

prosper (pros'pèr) [L. favourable], *v.t.* To make successful or fortunate. *v.i.* To thrive. **prosperous**, *a.* **prosper'ity**, *n.*

prostitute (pros'ti-tūt) [L. *statuere*, to place], *v.t.* To offer for lewd, base, or unworthy purposes; to devote to base uses. *a.* Prostituted. *n.* A woman who offers herself for hire. **prostitu'tion**, *n.*

prostrate (pros'trāt) [L. *strātus*, laid flat], *a.* Lying in a horizontal position, in a posture of humility; overcome, exhausted. *v.t.* To lay flat; to cast (oneself) down before; to overthrow; to reduce to physical exhaustion. **prostra'tion**, *n.*

prosy (prō'zi), *a.* Dull, tedious, tiresome. **prosily**, *adv.* **prosiness**, *n.*

prot- [PROTO-], *pref.* **protagonist** (pró-tăg'ó-nist) [Gr. *prōtagōnistēs* (*agōnistēs*, actor)], *n.* The leading character in a Greek play; an advocate, champion, etc.

protean (pró'tê-ăn, pró-tê'an) [*Proteus*, a Greek deity who could change his shape], *a.* Readily assuming different shapes or aspects; changeable.

protect (pró-tekt') [L. *tectus*, covered], *v.t.* To shield, or keep safe (from danger, etc.); to support (industries) against foreign competition by imposing duties on imports. **protec'tion**, *n.* Act of protecting; state of being protected; a covering, shield, or defence; a passport. **protectionist**, *n.* and *a.* **protective**, *a.*

protector (pró-tek'tòr), *n.* One who protects; one in charge during the minority, incapacity, etc., of a sovereign. **protec'torate**, *n.* Partial control of a weak State by a more powerful one, territory under such protection; the office of protector of a kingdom; the period of this.

protégé (prot-ă-zhā) [F.], *n.* (*fem.* -gée, -zhā) One under the protection of another.

proteid (pró'tēid), *n.* A protein.

protein (pró'tê-in) [Gr. *prōtos*, first], *n.* An unstable organic compound found in all organic bodies and forming an essential constituent of animal foods.

protest (pró-test') [L. *testāri*, to declare], *v.i.* To make a solemn affirmation; to make formal opposition. *v.t.* To affirm or declare formally; to make a formal declaration that payment of (a bill) has been demanded and refused. *n.* (pró'test) Act of protesting; a solemn declaration of opinion, usu. of dissent. **protesta'tion**, *n.* A solemn affirmation or declaration, esp. of dissent; a vow, promise.

Protestant (prot'ês-tànt), *n.* One of the party adhering to Luther, who (1529) protested against submission to the R.C. Church; a member of a Church upholding the principles of the Reformation. *a.* Pertaining to the Protestants.

proto- [Gr. *prōtos*, first], *comb. form.* Chief; earliest, original, primitive.

protocol (prō'tô-kol) [Gr. *protokollon*, the first leaf glued to a MS.], *n.* The original draft of an official document, esp. of a treaty; the etiquette of diplomacy.

proton (prō'ton), *n.* (*Elec.*) A particle of positive electricity having the same amount of electricity as the electron; the unit of mass of positive electricity.

protoplasm (prō'tô-plăzm) [Gr. *plasma*, a moulded thing], *n.* The substance constituting the living matter from which all living organisms are developed.

prototype (prō'tô-tīp), *n.* A primary type or model, an exemplar.

protract (prô-trăkt') [L. *tractus*, drawn], *v.t.* To extend; to prolong; to draw (a plan, etc.) to scale. **protractedly,** *adv.* Tediously. **protractile,** *a.* Capable of extension. **protraction,** *n.* **protractor,** *n.* An instrument for laying down angles on paper.

protrude (prô-trood') [L. *trūdere*, to thrust], *v.t.* To thrust forward; to cause to issue. *v.i.* To project. **protrusion,** *n.* **protrusive,** *a.*

protuberant (prô-tū'bér-ánt), *a.* Bulging out, prominent, **protuberance,** *n.*

proud (proud) [A.-S. *prūt*], *a.* Having inordinate self-esteem; haughty: having a due sense of dignity; feeling honoured, gratified; (*fig.*) grand, imposing; inspired by or inspiring pride, noble, grand (of deeds, etc.). **proudly,** *adv.*

prove (proov) [L. *probāre*, to test, to approve], *v.t.* (*p.p.* **proved,** proovd, **proven,** prō'vén) To make trial of; to put to a test. *v.i.* To be found by experience or trial; to turn out to be. **provable,** *a.* **provably,** *adv.* **prover,** *n.*

provenance (prov'é-náns) [F., from L. *prōvenīre*], *n.* Origin, source.

provender (prov'én-dér) [O.F.], *n.* Dry food for beasts, fodder.

proverb (prov'érb) [L. *verbum*, word], *n.* A short, pithy sentence, containing some proved truth. **prover'bial,** *a.* **proverbially,** *adv.*

provide (prô-vīd') [L. *vidēre*, to see], *v.t.* To procure or prepare beforehand; to equip (with); to stipulate. *v.i.* To make preparation or provision (for or against); to furnish means of subsistence (for). **provided, providing,** *conj.* On the condition (that).

providence (prov'i-déns), *n.* Foresight; economy, prudence; the care of God over His creatures; God or nature as exercising such care. **provident,** *a.* **providential** (-den'shál), *a.* Due to or effected by divine providence; lucky, opportune. **providen'tially,** *adv.* **prov'idently,** *adv.*

province (prov'ins) [L. *prōvincia*], *n.* Anciently, a territory outside Italy under a Roman governor; a large administrative division of a country; the territory under an archbishop; (*pl.*) districts at a distance from the metropolis; proper sphere of action, business, etc. **provincial** (-vin'shál), *n.* One who belongs to a province or the provinces; (*Eccles.*) the superior of an order, etc., in a province. **provincialism,** *n.* Quality of being

provincial; a mode of speech, etc., peculiar to the provinces. **provincially,** *adv.*

provision (prô-vizh'ún), *n.* Act of providing; a precautionary measure; a stipulation; (*pl.*) victuals. *v.t.* To provide with provisions. **provisional,** *a.* Provided for present need; temporary. **provisionally,** *adv.*

proviso (prô-vī'zō), *n.* A provisional condition, a stipulation.

provisory (prô-vī'zô-ri), *a.* Conditional; provisional. **provisorily,** *adv.*

provoke (prô-vōk') [L. *vocāre*, to call], *v.t.* To rouse; to stimulate to action, anger, etc.; to exasperate. **provocation** (provô-kā'shún), *n.* **provoc'ative,** *a.* **provoking,** *a.*

provost (prov'ôst) [A.-S. *prōfost*], *n.* The head of a college or a chapter; a cathedral dignitary corresponding to a dean; (*Sc.*) the chief magistrate in a burgh. **Provost-Marshal,** *n.* A commissioned officer, the head of the military police in a camp, etc.

prow (prou) [F. *proue*], *n.* The fore part of a vessel, the bow.

prowess (prou'es) [O.F. *prouesse*], *n.* Valour.

prowl (proul) [?], *v.* To rove about stealthily as in search of prey. *n.* Prowling.

proximate (prok'si-màt) [L. *proximus*, nearest], *a.* Next; immediately preceding or following. **proxim'ity,** *n.* Immediate nearness in place, time, relation, etc. **proximo** (prok'si-mō), *a.* In the month succeeding the present.

proxy (prok'si) [L. *procuratio*, management], *n.* One deputed to act for another; a document authorizing this; a vote given under this authority.

prude (prood) [F.], *n.* A person who affects great modesty or propriety. **prudery,** *n.* **prudish,** *a.*

prudent (proo'dènt) [L. *prūdens*], *a.* Discreet, circumspect, careful of consequences. **prudence,** *n.* **pruden'tial,** *a.* Worldly-wise, mercenary. **prudently,** *adv.*

prune (1) (proon) [F.], *n.* The dried fruit of various kinds of plum; the colour of this, dark reddish-purple.

prune (2) [O.F. *proignier*] *v.t.* To lop off superfluous branches, etc.; to free from anything superfluous. **pruning-hook,** **-knife, -shears,** *n.* Instruments of various forms for pruning trees, etc.

prunella (prû-nel'á) [?], *n.* A smooth dark woollen stuff used for the uppers of shoes and formerly for clergymen's gowns.

prurient (proor'i-ènt) [L. *prūriens*, itching], *a.* Disposed to lewd ideas; characterized by a morbid curiosity. **prurience -ency,** *n.* **pruriently,** *adv.*

Prussian (prúsh'án), *a.* Pertaining to Prussia. *n.* A native of Prussia. **Prussianism,** *n.* A characteristic of the Prussians, esp. excessive militarism. **Prussianize,** *v.t.* **prussic,** *a.* Derived from Prussian blue, applied to hydrocyanic acid.

pry (prī) [?], *v.i.* To look inquisitively; to search or inquire impertinently (into).

psalm (sam) [Gr. *psalmos*, from *psallein*, to sing to the harp], *n.* A sacred song or hymn. **psalmist,** *n.* A composer of psalms, esp. David. **psalmody,** *n.* Art or practice of singing psalms; psalms collectively. **psalmodist,** *n.* A composer or singer of psalms. **psalter** (sawl'tẽr), *n.* The Book of Psalms; a book containing the Psalms for use in divine service.

psaltery (sawl'tẽr-i), *n.* A mediæval stringed instrument, like the dulcimer but played by plucking.

pseud-, pseudo- [Gr., from *pseudēs*, false], *comb. form.* False, spurious; closely resembling.

pseudonym (sū'dō-nim)[Gr. *onoma*, name], *n.* An assumed name. **pseudon'ymous,** *a.*

psychedelic (sī-ki-del'ik), *a.* Releasing psychic energies that are normally repressed.

psychiatry (sī-kī'à-tri), *n.* (*Med.*) The study and treatment of mental diseases. **psychiatrist,** *n.* A specialist in this.

psychic (sī'kik), *a.* Pertaining to the human soul, spirit, or mind, or to phenomena that appear to be outside the domain of physical law. *n.* A spiritualistic medium. **psychical,** *a.*

psycho- [Gr. *psychē*, breath, life, soul], *comb. form.* Mental; psychical. **psychoanalysis** (sī-kō-àn-ăl'i-sis), *n.* Mental analysis applied as a therapeutic method in cases of mental or nervous disease. **psycho-an'alyst,** *n.*

psychology (sī-kol'ō-ji), *n.* The science of the human mind; a system of mental laws and phenomena. **psycholog'ical,** *a.* Pertaining or relating to psychology. **psychol'ogist,** *n.* **psychopath**(sī'kō-pàth), *n.* One suffering from mental derangement. **psychosis** (sī-kō'sis), *n.* Mental disturbance. **psychosomatic** (sī-kō-sō-măt'ik), *a.* Describing a physical disorder caused by an emotional state. **psychotherapy,** *n.* The treatment of mental or other diseases by psychological means.

ptarmigan (tar'mi-gàn)[Gael. *tarmachan*], *n.* A bird allied to the grouse.

pter-, pteri-, ptero- [Gr. *pteron,* feather, a wing], *comb. form.* Winged. **pterodactyl** (ter-ō-dăk'til) [Gr. *daktulos,* finger], *n.* An extinct winged reptile resembling a large bat.

ptomaine (tō'mān) [Gr. *ptōma,* corpse], *n.* An alkaloid possessing highly poisonous qualities derived from decaying animal and vegetable matter.

puberty (pū'bẽr-ti) [L. *pūber,* youth], *n.* The age at which persons become capable of begetting or bearing children. **pubes'-cence,** *n.* The state or age of puberty.

public (pŭb'lik)[L. *pūblicus,* from *populus,* people], *a.* Pertaining to the people as a whole; open to all; done, existing, or such as may be observed by all; open, notorious. *n.* The people in general; any particular section of the people. **public-house,** *n.* A house licensed for the retail of intoxicating liquors. **publican** (pŭb'li-kàn), *n.* (*Rom. Hist.*) A collector of the revenues; a keeper of a public-house. **publica'tion,** *n.* Act of making public, or of publishing a book, periodical, musical composition, etc.; a work published. **publicity** (-lis'i-ti), *n.* Openness, notoriety, the business of advertising. **pub'licly,** *adv.*

publish (pŭb'lish), *v.t.* To make public, to promulgate; to ask (the banns of marriage); to print and offer for sale. **publisher,** *n.* One who produces books, etc., and distributes them to the public.

pucker (pŭk ẽr)[?], *v.t.* To gather into small folds. *n.* A fold, a wrinkle.

pudding (pud'ing) [?], *n.* Animal or vegetable food baked or boiled with flour or other farinaceous basis or covering; a large sausage.

puddle (pŭdl) [A.-S. *pudd,* a ditch], *n.* A small muddy pool; clay and sand worked together to form a watertight lining.

puerile (pū'ẽr-īl)[L. *puer,* boy], *a.* Childish; suited for children, trivial. **pueril'ity,** *n.*

puerperal pū-ẽr'pẽr-ăl) [L. *puer,* boy, *-parus,* bringing forth], *a.* Pertaining to childbirth.

puff (puf)[imit.], *v.i.* To emit or expel air, etc., in short blasts; to breathe hard. *v.t.* To emit with a short sudden blast; to blow away thus; to praise in an exaggerated way. *n.* A short, sudden blast of breath, smoke, steam, etc.; a small amount emitted at one puff; a cake, tart, etc., of light consistency; a light pad or tuft for applying powder to the skin; (*fig.*)an exaggerated or misleading advertisement, etc. **puff-ball,** *n.* A fungus, the spore-case of which emits dry, dust-like spores. **puffiness,** *n.*

puffin (pŭf'in)[?], *n.* A sea-bird of the auk family.

pug (pŭg)[?], *n.* A dwarf variety of bulldog or mastiff; **pugnose,** *n.* A short squat nose.

pugilism (pū'jil-izm) [L. *pugil,* boxer], *n.* The art or science of fighting with the fists, boxing. **pugilist,** *n.* A boxer, a prize-fighter. **pugilis'tic,** *a.*

pugnacious (pŭg-nā'shus) [L. *pugnāre,* to fight], *a.* Inclined to fight; quarrelsome. **pugnacity** (-nās'i-ti), *n.*

puisne (pū'ni) [O.F. *puis,* after, *né,* born], *a.* Junior (applied to judges).

puissant (pū'i-sànt) [F.], *a.* Powerful, mighty. **puissance,** *n.*

pule (pūl)[?], *v.i.* To cry plaintively, to whine, whimper. **puling,** *a,* and *n.*

pull (pul) [A.-S. *pullian*], *v.t.* To draw towards; to haul, tug; to pluck; to row (a boat); (*Print.*) to take a proof. *v.i.* To give a pull; to tug; to strain against the bit (of a horse); to suck (at a pipe). *n.* Act of pulling; a draught, a swig; (*Print.*) a proof; (slang) unfair or illegitimate influence.

pullet (pul'ĕt) [O.F. *polete,* late L. *pulla,* hen], *n.* A young fowl.

pulley (pul'i) [O.F. *polie*], *n.* A wheel with a grooved rim, mounted in a block, for a cord to run over, for raising weights or increasing the effect of a force.

Pullman (pul'màn) [George M. *Pullman* (1831–97), designer], *n.* A Pullman car, a luxurious railway saloon or sleeping-car.

pull-over, *n.* A buttonless jersey pulled over the head.

pulmonary (pŭl'mō-nàr-i)[L. *pulmo-mōnis,* lung], *a.* Pertaining to or affecting the lungs.

pulp (pŭlp) [L. *pulpa*], *n.* Any soft, moist, coherent mass; the fleshy portion of a fruit; the mixture from which paper is made. *v.t.* To convert into pulp. **pulpy,** *a.* Resembling pulp.

pulpit (pul'pit) [L. *pulpitum*], *n.* An elevated stand for a preacher. *a.* Pertaining to preaching.

pulsate (pŭl'sāt) [L. *pulsātus*, beaten], *v.i.* To beat rhythmically, to throb. **pulsa'tion,** *n.* Action of pulsating; the movement of the pulse.

pulse (1) (pŭls) [L. *pulsus*, driven], *n.* The rhythmic beating of the arteries or heart; a beat of these; a pulsation, a vibration.

pulse (2) (pŭls) [L. *puls*, pottage of meal, etc.], *n.* Leguminous plants or their seeds.

pulverize (pŭl'vĕr-īz) [L. *pulvus*, dust], *v.t.* To reduce to fine powder; (*fig.*) to demolish.

puma (pū'má) [Peruv.], *n.* The cougar, a large feline carnivorous animal of N. and S. America.

pumice (pŭm'is) [L. *pūmex*], *n.* A porous kind of lava, used for cleansing and polishing.

pump (1) (pŭmp) [M.E. and G., *pumpe*, F. *pompe*], *n.* A machine for raising water or other liquid, or for exhausting or compressing air; act of pumping. *v.t.* To raise or remove or free from water with a pump; to put out of breath (usu. *in p.p.*); (*fig.*) to elicit information by artful interrogations. *v.i.* To work a pump.

pump (2) [?]. A light slipper.

pumpkin (pŭmp'kin) [Gr. *pēpon*], *n.* The large globular fruit of *Cucurbita pepo*; the plant bearing this.

pun (pŭn) [?], *n.* Use of a word in two different senses or of words similar in sound but different in meaning. *v.i.* To make a pun. **punster,** *n.* One addicted to pun-making.

punch (1) (pŭnch) [?], *n.* A tool for making holes, indenting, forcing bolts out of holes, etc.; a tool for stamping a die; a blow with the fist. *v.t.* To stamp, indent, or perforate with a punch; to strike with the fist.

punch (2) [Hindi *panch*, five (ingredients)], *n.* A beverage of wine or spirit, water or milk, lemons, sugar, spice, etc.

Punch (3) [short for *Punchinello*, It. *Policinello*, a character in Neapolitan low comedy], *n.* The chief character in the puppet-show of Punch and Judy; a grotesque hump-backed man; a short, fat fellow; a buffoon; a stout-built carthorse.

puncheon (pŭn'chŏn) [?], *n.* A large cask holding from 72 to 120 gallons.

punctilio (pŭngk-til'i-ō) [Sp. *puntillo*, dim. of *punto*, point], *n.* A nice point in conduct, etc.; precision in etiquette. **punctilious,** *a.* Precise; strictly observant of ceremony or etiquette.

punctual (pŭngk'tū-ál), *a.* Observant and exact in matters of time; done, etc., exactly at the proper time. **punctual'ity,** *n.* punc'tually, *adv.*

punctuate (pŭngk'tū-āt), *v.t.* To mark with stops, divide into sentences, clauses, etc. **punctua'tion,** *n.*

puncture (pŭngk'chŭr), *n.* A small hole made with something pointed; act of pricking. *v.t.* To make a puncture in;

to pierce or prick. *v.i.* To sustain a puncture (of a tyre, etc.).

pundit (pŭn'dit) [Hindi *pandit*, learned], *n.* A learned Hindu; any learned person or pretender to learning.

pungent (pŭn'jĕnt) [L. *pungens*, pricking], *a.* Sharply affecting the senses, esp. of smell or taste; pricking; keen, caustic. **pungency,** *n.*

Punic (pū'nik) [L. *Pūnicus*, Gr. *Phoinix*, Phœnician], *a.* Pertaining to the Carthaginians; (*fig.*) treacherous, faithless.

punish (pŭn'ish) [L. *pūnīre*], *v.t.* To inflict a penalty on; to chastise; to inflict pain or injury on, to maul. **punishable,** *a.* **punishment,** *n.* **punitive** (pū'ni-tiv), *a.* Awarding or inflicting punishment; retributive.

punkah (pŭng'kà) [Hind. *pankhā*], *n.* A large fan hung from the ceiling worked by a cord.

punt (pŭnt) [A.-S.], *n.* A shallow, flat-bottomed, square-ended boat propelled with a pole. *v.* To propel a punt thus.

punter (pŭn'tĕr), *n.* A petty backer of horses.

puny (pū'ni), *a.* Undersized, weak, poorly developed; petty. **puniness,** *n.*

pup (pŭp), *n.* A puppy. *v.i.* To bring forth pups.

pupa (pū'pá) [L.], *n.* (*pl.* **-pæ**) A chrysalis.

pupil (pū'pil) [L. *pūpillus*], *n.* One under the care of a teacher, a scholar; (*Law*) a ward; the circular opening of the iris through which rays of light pass to the retina. **pupilage** *n.* State of being a pupil; one's minority.

puppet (pŭp'ĕt) [L. *puppa*, a doll], *n.* A small image representing a human being, moved by wires in a mock drama; (*fig.*) a mere tool.

puppy (pŭp'i [?], *n.* A young dog; (*fig.*) a coxcomb, a fop. **-hood,** *n.*

pur- [L. *por-*, PRO-], *pref.*

purblind (pĕr'blīnd), *a.* Partially blind, near-sighted.

purchase (pĕr'chàs), *v.t.* To buy; to acquire at the expense of some sacrifice, exertion, etc. *n.* Act of buying; that which is bought; (*Mech.*) advantage gained by mechanism, leverage; an appliance furnishing this. **purchaser,** *n.*

pure (pūr) [L. *pūrus*], *a.* Unmixed, clear, clean; mere, absolute; innocent, unsullied, chaste; (of sciences) theoretical, not applied. **purely,** *adv.* **pureness,** *n.*

purgation (pĕr-gā'shŭn), *n.* Act of purging, purification; act of clearing oneself by oath or ordeal. **pur'gative,** *a.* Having the quality of cleansing. *n.* An aperient.

purgatory (pĕr'gà-tŏr-i), *n.* A place or state of spiritual purging, esp. one succeeding the present life (R.C. Church); any place of temporary suffering. *a.* Cleansing, purifying. **purgator'ial,** *a.*

purge (pĕrj) [L. *purgāre*], *v.t.* To cleanse or purify.

purify (pūr'i-fī), *v.t.* To make pure, to cleanse; to free from sin, pollution, etc.; to clear of corruptions. **purifica'tion,** *n.* **purificatory,** *a.*

purist (pūr'ist), *n.* One advocating or affecting purity, esp. in the choice of words. **purism,** *n.*

Puritan (pūr'ĭ-tăn), *n.* One practising or advocating extreme strictness in conduct or religion (usu. in deprecation), esp. a Protestant dissenter from the Eng. Church in the 16th or 17th cents. *a.* Pertaining to the Puritans. **puritan'ic, -al,** *a.* Pur'itanism, *n.*

purity (pūr'ĭ-ti), *n.* State of being pure; freedom from pollution or adulteration; innocence, chastity.

purl (1) (pĕrl) [?], *n.* An inversion of the stitches in knitting. *v.t.* To decorate with purl.

purl (2) [?], *n.* Hot spiced gin and beer.

purl (3) [Scand.], *v.i.* To flow with a soft gurgling or murmuring sound. *n.* A gentle murmur as of a stream.

purlieu (pĕr'lū) [O.F. *puralee*], *n.* The bounds within which one ranges; (*pl.*) outskirts, environs.

purloin (pĕr-loin') [O.F. *purloigner*], *v.t.* To steal.

purple (pĕrpl) [L. *purpura*], *a.* Of the colour of red and blue blended, the former predominating; (*fig.*) imperial. *n.* A purple pigment or dye; (*fig.*) imperial or regal power.

purport (Ŀĕr-pōrt') [L. *portāre*, to carry], *v.t.* To imply, signify; to profess. *n.* (pĕr'pŏrt) Meaning; object.

purpose (pĕr'pŏs) [L. *prŏpositus*], *n.* Aim, object, design; meaning; effect, result. *v.* To intend, to design. **purposely,** *adv.* Of set purpose, intentionally.

purr (pĕr) [imit.], *n.* A murmur as of a cat when pleased. *v.i.* To make this sound.

purse (pĕrs) [A.-S. *purs*, Gr. *bursa*, leather], *n.* A small bag for money; (*fig.*) money, resources. *v.* To wrinkle, to pucker. **purse-proud,** *a.* Proud of one's wealth. **purser,** *n.* An officer on board ship in charge of the provisions, pay, etc. **pursiness** [PURSY], *n.*

pursue (pĕr-sū') [L. *sequere*, to follow], *v.t.* To follow with intent to seize, gain, or obtain; to go in accordance with; to follow up, to prosecute; to attend persistently (of consequences, etc.) *v.i.* To follow, to go in pursuit; to proceed, continue. **pursuance,** *n.* **pursuant,** *a.* and *adv.* In accordance, conformable (to). **pursuer,** *n.* **pursuit,** *n.* Act of pursuing, a following; a prosecution, an endeavour to attain some end; any employment, occupation, business, or recreation that one follows persistently.

pursuivant (pĕr'swi-vănt) [O.F. *porsivant*], *n.* An attendant on a herald.

pursy (pĕr'si) [O.F. *polsif*], *a.* Short-winded; fat. **pursiness,** *n.*

purulent (pūr'ū-lĕnt) [L. *pūrulentus*], *a.* Consisting of or discharging pus. **purulence,** *n.*

purvey (pĕr-vā'), *v.t.* To provide, esp. provisions. *v.i.* To make provision; to act as purveyor. **purveyance,** *n.* The providing of provisions; provisions supplied; the old royal prerogative of impressing provisions, horses, etc. **purveyor,** *n.* A caterer, esp. on a large scale.

pus (pŭs) L.], *n.* The matter secreted from inflamed tissues, the product of suppuration.

push (push) [L. *pulsāre*, to pulsate], *v.t.* To press against with force; to urge forward, to impel, to drive, to carry on vigorously. *v.i.* To exert pressure (against, etc.); to press forward; to thrust or butt (against). *n.* Act of pushing, a thrust, shove; a vigorous effort, an onset; an exigency, a crisis; self-assertion. **pusher,** *n.* pushing, *a.* Enterprising, energetic.

pusillanimous (pū-si-lăn'ĭ-mŭs) [L. *pusillus*, petty, *animus*, soul], *a.* Destitute of firmness, fainthearted. **pusillanim'ity,** *n.* Cowardice.

puss (pus) [?], *n.* A cat; a hare.

pustule (pŭs'tūl) [L. *pustula*], *n.* A pimple containing pus; a small excrescence, a blister. **pustular,** *a.*

put (put) [late A.-S. *putian*], *v.t.* To place in some position; to bring into some particular condition; to present, to express, to state; to apply, to set.

putative (pū'tă-tiv) [L. *putāre*, to think], *a.* Reputed; commonly regarded as.

putrefy (pūtrĕ-fī) [L. *putrēre*, to be rotten], *v.i.* To become putrid, to rot; to fester. **putrefac'tion,** *n.* **putrefac'tive,** *a.* **putres'cent,** *a.* **putrescence,** *n.*

putrid (pū'trĭd), *a.* In a state of decomposition; tainted, foul. **putrid'ity,** **pu'tridness,** *n.*

putt (pŭt), *v.t.* (*Golf*) To strike the ball so as to get it into the hole. *n.* This stroke. **putter,** *n.* A short, stiff golf-club, used for putting.

puttee (pŭt'ĭ) [Hindi *patti*, bandage], *n.* A strip of cloth wound round the leg as a gaiter.

putty (pŭt'ĭ) [F. *potée*, potful], *n.* Whiting and linseed-oil used as a cement in glazing. *v.t.* To fix or fill up with putty.

puzzle (pŭzl) [?], *n.* A state of perplexity; a perplexing problem, toy, riddle, etc. *v.t.* To perplex, to mystify. *v.i.* To be bewildered. **puzzlement,** *n.*

pygmy (pig'mi) [Gr. *pugmaios*, dwarfish, from *pugmē*, length from elbow to knuckles], *n.* A dwarf, a small man, anything very diminutive. *a.* Dwarfish.

pyjamas (pi-ja'măz) [Pers. and Hind. *pāe*, by, *jāmah*, garment], *n.pl.* A sleeping-suit of a loose jacket and trousers.

pylon (pī'lŏn) [Gr. *pulē*, gate], *n.* An imposing gateway; a post or turret marking out the course in an aerodrome; a structure, usu. of steel, supporting an electric cable.

pylorus (pī-lōr'ŭs) [Gr. *pulŏros*, gatekeeper], *n.* The contracted end of the stomach leading into the small intestine.

pyramid (pĭr'ă-mid) [L. *pyramis -idis*], *n.* A solid body, or a monumental structure of masonry, with a square base and triangular sloping side meeting at the apex; a pile of this shape; a game played on a billiard-table with fifteen coloured balls and a cue-ball. **pyram'idal,** *a.*

pyre (pīr) [Gr. *pur*, fire], *n.* A funeral pile for burning a dead body; any pile of combustibles.

pyretic (pī-ret'ĭk) [Gr. *puretos*, fever], *a.* Relating to fever; remedial in fever. *n.* A pyretic medicine.

pyrites (pī-rī'tēz) [Gr. *purītēs*, pertaining to fire], *n.* One of two common sulphides, yellow or copper pyrites, or iron pyrites.

pyro- [Gr. *pur puros*, fire], *comb. form.*

pyrog′raphy, *n.* Poker-work.

pyrometer (pirom′it-ẽr), *n.* An instrument for registering high temperatures.

pyrotechnic (pir-ó-tek′nik) [Gr. *technē*, art], *a.* Pertaining to fireworks or their manufacture; resembling a firework show, brilliant, dazzling. *n.pl.* The art of making fireworks; a display of fireworks.

Pyrrhic (pi′rik) [Gr. *Purrhos*, Pyrrhus], *a.* Pertaining to Pyrrhus, esp. of a victory that is as costly as a defeat, like that of Pyrrhus, king of Epirus, over the Romans at Asculum (279 B.C.).

python (pi′thŏn) [Gr., from *puthō*, former name of Delphi], *n.* A gigantic serpent slain by Apollo near Delphi; a large non-venomous serpent that crushes its prey; a familiar spirit; one possessed by this, a soothsayer. **pythoness,** *n.* A woman having the gift of prophecy, a witch; the priestess of Apollo at Delphi who delivered the oracles.

pyx (piks) [Gr. *puxis*, a box], *n.* (*Eccles.*) The covered vessel in which the host is kept.

Q

qua (kwā) [L.], *conj.* In the character of, as.

quack (1) (kwăk) [imit.], *v.i.* To cry like a duck; to chatter, to brag. *n.* The cry of a duck.

quack (2) [short for *quacksalver*], *n.* A pretender to knowledge or skill, esp. in medicine; an ignorant practitioner, a charlatan. *a.* Pertaining to quacks or quackery. **quackery,** *n.*

quad (kwod) [abbr.], *n.* A quadrangle as of a college, etc.; a quadrat. *v.i.* To insert blocks (in a line of type).

quadr- [L. *quatuor*, four], *comb. form.*

Quadragesima (kwod-rà-jes′i-mà) [L. *quadrāgēsimus*, fortieth], *n.* The first Sunday in Lent (which consists of forty days).

quadrangle (kwod′răng-gẽl), *n.* A plane figure having four angles and four sides; four-sided court surrounded by buildings. **quadrangular,** *a.*

quadrant (kwod′rànt) [L. *quadrans*], *n.* The fourth part of the circumference of a circle, an arc of 90°; a quarter of a sphere; a quarter-circle graduated for taking angular measurements.

quadrate (kwod′rāt) [L. *quadrātus*, squared], *a.* Square, rectangular. *v.i.* (-rāt) To square, to match, to correspond.

quadrat′ic, *a.* Involving the second and no higher power of the variable or unknown quantity. *n.pl.* The part of algebra dealing with quadratic equations. *n.* Act of squaring or finding a square equal in area to a given curved figure.

quadrennial (kwod-ren′i-àl) [L. *annus*, year], *a.* Comprising or lasting four years; recurring every four years.

quadri- [L., *quatuor*, four], *comb. form.* Four.

quadriga (kwod-ri′gà) [L. *jugum*, yoke], *n.* (*pl.* -gæ) A Roman two-wheeled chariot drawn by four horses abreast.

quadrilateral (kwod-ri-lăt′ẽr-àl), *a.* Having four sides and four angles. *n.* A quadrangular figure or area.

quadrille (kwà-dril′) [Sp. *cuadrillo*, a squadron, *cuadra*, square], *n.* A square dance for four couples; music for this; a four-handed card-game fashionable in the 18th cent.

quadrillion (kwà-dril′yŏn), *n.* The number produced by raising a million to its fourth power, 1 followed by 24 ciphers; (*Am. and F.*) the fifth power of a thousand, 1 and 15 ciphers.

quadroon (kwod-roon′) [Sp. *cuarteron*, from *cuarto*, fourth], *n.* The offspring of a mulatto and a white; one of quarter negro and three-quarters white blood.

quadruped (kwod′rū-ped) [L. *quadrupes*, *pes pedis*, foot], *n.* A four-footed animal.

quadruple (kwod′rupl) [L. -*plus*, -fold], *a.* Fourfold; consisting of four parts; involving four members, units, etc., or quantity of. *n.* Four times as much or as many. *v.* To become or make fourfold as much; to increase or multiply fourfold. **quadru′plicate,** *a.* Fourfold. *v.t.* To make fourfold. **quadruplica′tion,** *n.*

quaff (kwaf) [?], *v.* To drink in large draughts; to drink copiously. *n.* A copious draught.

quagga (kwăg′à) [native], *n.* A S. African quadruped, intermediate between the ass and the zebra.

quagmire, *n.* A quaking bog, a marsh.

quail (1) (kwāl) [?], *v.i.* To shrink, be cowed, lose heart.

quail (2) [O.F. *quaille*], *n.* A small migratory bird allied to the partridge.

quaint (kwānt) [O.F. *cointe*, L. *cognitus*, known], *a.* Odd, pleasing by virtue of strangeness or fancifulness; whimsical, singular.

quake (kwāk) [A.-S. *cuacian*], *v.i.* To shake, quiver, to rock, vibrate. *n.* A tremulous motion, a shudder. **quaky,** *a.* **quakiness,** *n.*

Quaker (kwā′kẽr) [orig. applied in derision (1650)], *n.* A member of the Society of Friends. **Quakeress,** *n.* **Quakerism,** *n.*

qualify (kwol′i-fī) [L. *quālis*, such], *v.t.* To furnish with the requisite qualities, to make competent, fit, or legally capable (to be, do, etc.); to modify, to limit; to moderate, mitigate; to dilute. *v.i.* To become qualified or fit; to make oneself competent, suitable, etc. **qualifica′tion,** *n.* Act of qualifying or state of being qualified; modification, limitation of meaning, partial negation restricting completeness; any quality fitting a person or thing (for an office, etc.); a condition that must be fulfilled.

quality (kwol′i-ti), *n.* Relative nature or kind, distinguishing character; that which gives individuality; particular capacity, value, efficacy, degree of excellence. **qualitative,** *a.* Pertaining to quality, opp. to quantitative.

qualm (kwawm) [?], *n.* A sensation of nausea, fear, or uneasiness.

quandary (kwon′dàr-i) [?], *n.* A state of difficulty; an awkward predicament.

quantity (kwon′ti-ti) [L. *quantitas*, as prec.],

n. That property in virtue of which anything may be measured; extent, measure, volume, a number; (*pl.*) large quantities, abundance; the duration of a syllable. **quan'titative**, *a.* Pertaining to or concerned with quantity.

quantum (kwon'tŭm), *n.* A quantity, an amount; a share.

quarantine (kwor'ăn-tēn) [L. *quadrăginta*, forty], *n.* The period of isolation (usu. 40 days) imposed on ships coming from places infected with contagious disease; the enforced isolation of infected persons, ships, goods, houses, etc. *v.t.* To isolate or put in quarantine.

quarrel (1) (kwor'ĕl), *n.* A short, heavy square-headed arrow, formerly used with the cross-bow.

quarrel (2) [L. *querēla*, complaint], *n.* A breach of friendship; a noisy or violent dispute, a brawl; a cause of complaint or dispute. *v.i.* To fall out; to dispute violently, to wrangle; to take exception, find fault (with). **quarrelsome**, *a.* Inclined to quarrel, contentious; easily provoked.

quarry (1) (kwor'i) [L. *quadrāre*, to square], *n.* A place whence stone, slates, etc., are dug, blasted, etc. *v.t.* To dig or take from a quarry. **quarrier**, *n.* A workman employed in a quarry.

quarry (2) [L. *corium*, skin], *n.* Any animal pursued for prey, game.

quart (kwôrt), *n.* The fourth part of a gallon, two pints.

quartan (kwôr'tăn), *a.* Occurring every fourth day, applied to a fever; recurring every third, or inclusively, every fourth day.

quarter (kwôr'tėr), *n.* A fourth part of anything; three calendar months; 28 lb., 8 bushels, 25 cents., etc.; a limb, a haunch; one of the divisions of an heraldic shield; the fourth part of a period of the moon; a particular direction or region, locality; a division of a town; (*pl.*) allotted position or station, esp. for troops; place of lodging or abode; appointed stations of a crew; exemption from death to a surrendered enemy. *v.t.* To divide into four equal parts; to provide (esp. soldiers) with lodgings and food. **quarter-day**, *n.* The day beginning each quarter of the year (25th March, 24th June, 29th Sept., and 25th Dec.), on which payments are due, etc. **quarterdeck**, *n.* The upper deck from stern to main-mast, usu. assigned to officers and cabin passengers. **quartermaster**, *n.* A regimental officer who provides quarters, lays out camps, issues rations, clothing, ammunition, etc.; (*Nav.*) a petty officer in charge of the steering, stowage, etc. **quartering**, *n.* (*Her.*) The grouping of several coats of arms on a shield; one of the coats so quartered. **quarterly**, *a.* Occurring or done every quarter of a year. *adv.* Once in each quarter.

quartern (kwôr'tėrn), *n.* A quarter of various measures, as a pint, peck, or pound. **quartern-loaf**, *n.* A 4 lb. loaf.

quartet (kwôr-tek²), *n.* A musical composition for four voices or instruments.

quarto (kwôr'tō), *n.* A size obtained by folding a sheet twice, making eight pages (4to); a book, etc., having such pages. *a.* Having the sheet folded into four leaves.

quartz (kwôrts) [?], *n.* A mineral consisting of pure silica or silicon dioxide.

quash (kwosh) [L. *quassāre*], *v.t.* To annul, to make void; to put an end to, to suppress.

quasi (kwā'sī) [L., as if], *conj.* As if. *pref.* Apparent, not real; not quite, as *quasi-historical, quasi-public.*

quassia (kwosh'á) [after *Quassi*, a negro who used its bark in fever], *n.* A S. American and W. Indian tree yielding a bitter oil used as a tonic.

quaternary (kwá-tĕr'ná-ri) [L. *quaterni*, four at a time], *a.* Consisting of four; fourth in order; applied to the most recent strata or those above the tertiary. *n.* A set of four.

quartorzain (kăt'ôr-zān) [F. *quatorze*, fourteen], *n.* A stanza of fourteen lines, esp. an irregular sonnet.

quatrain (kwot'rān), *n.* A stanza of four lines, usu. rhyming alternately.

quatrefoil (kăt'ėr-foil), *n.* A figure in ornamental tracery divided by cusps into four foils; a leaf composed of four lobes.

quaver (kwā'vėr), *v.i.* To quiver, to vibrate; to sing or play with tremulous modulations. *n.* A rapid vibration of the voice, a trill; a shakiness in speaking; a note equal to half a crotchet.

quay (kē) [A.-F. *kaie*. O.F. *kay*], *n.* A landing-place, usu. of masonry, for loading or unloading ships. **quayage**, *n.* Charge for use of a quay.

quean (kwēn) [A.-S. *cwene*, woman], *n.* A slut, a hussy.

queasy (kwē'zi) [?], *a.* Sick at the stomach, affected with or tending to cause nausea; squeamish.

queen (kwēn) [A.-S. *cwēn*, cp QUEAN], *n.* The wife or widow of a king; a female sovereign; a court-card; the most powerful piece in chess; a fully-developed female bee. *v.t.* To make (a woman or pawn) into a queen. *v.i.* To act the queen; (*Chess*) to become a queen. **queendom, queenhood, queenship**, *n.* **queenly**, *a.*

queer (kwēr) [?], *a.* Odd; singular, droll; questionable, suspicious; out of sorts. **queerish**, *a.* **queerly**, *adv.*

quell (kwel) [A.-S. *cwellan*, to kill], *v.t.* To suppress, subdue; to allay.

quench (kwench) [A.-S. *cuencan*], *v.t.* To put out, esp. with water; to allay, to slake; to suppress. **quenchless**, *a.*

querist (kwēr'ist), *n.* One who queries, who asks questions, an inquirer.

quern (kwērn) [A.-S. *cweorn*], *n.* A simple, hand-mill for grinding corn or spices.

querulous (kwer'ū-lŭs) [L. *queri*, to complain], *a.* Discontented, peevish, fretful.

query (kwēr'i) [L. *quærere*, to ask], *n.* A question; a point to be answered; a mark of interrogation. *v.i.* To put a question; to express a doubt. *v.t.* To call in question.

quest (kwest), *n.* Act of seeking, a search; an expedition in pursuit of some object; the object of such enterprise.

question (kwes'chŏn), *n.* Act of asking, inquiry; an interrogative sentence; a problem, a subject under discussion; a difference, doubt, uncertainty. *v.t.* To interrogate, to examine by asking questions; to raise objections to. *v.i.* To ask a question; to doubt. **questionable,** *a.* Open to doubt or suspicion.

queue (kū) [F., from L. *cauda*, tail], *n.* A plaited tail hanging at the back of the head, a pigtail; a file of persons, vehicles, etc., waiting their turn.

quibble (kwibl) [?], *n.* An equivocation; a trivial or sophistical argument or distinction; a pun. *v.i.* To evade the point in question; to pun. **quibbler,** *n.*

quick (kwik) [A.-S. *cwic*], *a.* Alive, living; pregnant, ready, alert, prompt to feel or act; irritable, rash, precipitate, swift. *adv.* In a short space, at a rapid rate. *n.* Living persons; sensitive flesh, esp. under the nails. **quick-firer,** *n.* **quicklime,** *n.* Burned lime not yet slaked. **quicksand,** *n.* Loose wet sand easily engulfing persons, animals, etc. **quickset,** *a.* Composed of living plants, esp. hawthorn bushes (of a hedge). **quick'silver,** *n.* Mercury; (*fig.*) a mobile temperament. **quicken,** *v.t.* To give or restore life or animation to; to stimulate, inspire, refresh. *v.i.* To come to life; to move with increased rapidity. **quickly,** *adv.* **quickness,** *n.*

quid (kwid), *n.* A piece of tobacco for chewing; (*Slang*) a sovereign.

quiddity (kwid'i-ti) [L. *quidditas*], *n.* The essence of a thing; a quibble, a trifling subtlety.

quidnunc (kwid'nŭnk) [L., what now?], *n.* One who is curious to know or pretends to know everything that goes on; a gossip.

quiescent (kwi-es'ĕnt) [L. *quiescens*], *a.* At rest, inert, dormant; tranquil, calm. **quiescence,** *n.*

quiet (kwi'ĕt) [L. *quiĕtus*, p.p. of *quiescere,* to rest], *a.* In a state of rest; calm, placid, tranquil; silent, hushed; gentle; not glaring or showy; secluded. *n.* A state of rest; tranquillity; silence, stillness, peace. *v.t.* To bring to a state of rest; to soothe. **quietly,** *adv.* **quietness,** *n.*

quietus (kwi-ē'tŭs) [L.], *n.* A final settlement; (*fig.*) release from life, death.

quill (kwil) [?], *n.* The hollow stem of a feather; one of the large feathers of a bird's wing or tail; a pen, float, toothpick, etc., made from such; a spine of a porcupine. *v.t.* To wind on a quill.

quillet (kwil'ĕt) [?], *n.* A quibble, quirk.

quilt (kwilt) [L. *culcita*, cushion], *n.* A padded bed-cover, a counterpane. *v.t.* To cover with padded material; to stitch two pieces of cloth together with soft material between them.

quince (kwins) [L. *cydōnium*, from *Cydōnia,* in Crete], *n.* A hard, acid, yellowish fruit for flavouring and for preserves, etc.

quincunx (kwin'kŭngks) [L. *quinque,* five], *n.* An arrangement of five things in a square or rectangle, one being in the middle.

quinine (kwi-nēn') [Quichua *Kina*, bark], *n.* A bitter alkaloid obtained from cinchona bark, used as a febrifuge, tonic, etc.

quinquagesima (kwin-kwà-jes'i-mà) [L., fiftieth], *n.* The Sunday next before Lent, about fifty days before Easter.

quinque-, quinqui- [L. *quinque,* five], *comb. form.* **quinquelateral** (kwing-kwĕ-lăt'ĕr-ăl), *a.* Having five sides. *n.* A five-sided thing.

quinsy (kwin'zi) [Gr. *kunanchē* (*kun-, kuon,* dog, *anchein,* to throttle)], *n.* Inflammatory sore throat, esp. with suppuration of the tonsils.

quintain (kwin'tăn) [O.F. *quintaine*], *n.* A post, or a figure on a post, to be tilted at.

quintessence (kwin-tes'ĕns) [L. *quinta essentia,* fifth essence], *n.* The highest essence, that coming after the four elements forming the substance of the heavenly bodies; the pure essence of any substance. **quintessential** (quin-tĕ-sen'-shăl), *a.*

quintet (kwin-tet'), *n.* A musical composition for five voices or instruments; a group of five persons or things.

quintillion (kwin-til'yŏn), *n.* The fifth power of a million, 1 followed by 30 ciphers; (*F. and Am.*) the sixth power of a thousand, 1 followed by 18 ciphers.

quintuple (kwin'tūpl), *a.* Fivefold. *n.* A fivefold thing, group, etc. *v.* To multiply or increase fivefold.

quip (kwip) [L. *quippe,* forsooth], *n.* A sarcastic sally; a witty retort or saying.

quire (1) (kwīr) [O.F. *quaer* (F. *cahier*), L. *quaterni,* four each], *n.* Twenty-four sheets of paper; a pamphlet.

quire (2) [CHOIR].

quirk (kwĕrk) [?], *n.* An artful trick, a shift; a quibble.

quit (kwit), *v.t.* To renounce, abandon; to leave, depart from, to desist from; to, liberate. *v.i.* To leave, to depart. *a.* Clear; absolved; rid (of). **quittance,** *n.* A discharge from a debt or obligation; a receipt.

quite (kwit) [M.E. *quyt,* free], *adv.* Completely, entirely, to the fullest extent, perfectly; (*colloq.*) very, considerably.

quiver (1) (kwiv'ĕr) [O.F. *cuivre*], *n.* A portable case for arrows. **quiverful,** *n.*

quiver (2) (kwiv'ĕr) [imit.], *v.i.* To tremble with a rapid motion; to shake, shiver. *n.* A quivering motion.

quixotic (kwik-sot'ik) [Don *Quixote,* hero of Cervantes's romance], *a.* Extravagantly romantic; aiming at lofty but impracticable ideals. **quixotically,** *adv.* **quix'otism, -try,** *n.*

quiz (kwiz) [?], *n.* Something designed to puzzle or turn one into ridicule, a hoax; a question, test of knowledge; an odd-looking person. *v.t.* To banter, make fun of. *v.i.* To behave in a bantering or mocking way.

quoin (koin), *n.* A corner-stone; the external angle of a building, etc.

quoit (koit, kwoit) [?], *n.* A flattish circular ring of iron for throwing at a mark; (*pl.*) the game of throwing these.

quondam (kwon'dăm) [L., formerly], *a.* Having formerly been, sometime, former.

quorum (kwôr'ŭm) [L., of whom], *n.* The minimum number of a committee, etc., that must be present to transact business.

quota (kwō'tá) [L. *quota* (*pars*), how great

(a part)], *n.* A proportional share, part, or contribution.

quote (kwōt) [L. *quotāre*], *v.t.* To adduce or cite from (an author, etc.); to repeat the words of (a passage in a book, etc.); to name the current price of. **quotable,** *a.* **quota'tion,** *n.* Act of quoting; a passage quoted; a price quoted or current.

quoth (kwōth) [past of obs. *quethe,* A.-S. *cwethan,* to speak], *v.t. 1st and 3rd past.* Said, spoke.

quotidian (kwō-tĭd'ĭ-àn) [L. *quotĭdiē,* daily], *a.* Daily; recurring every day; common-place.

quotient (kwō'shènt) [L. *quotiens,* how many times], *n.* Result of dividing one quantity by another.

R

rabbet (răb'ĕt) [O.F. *rabat*], *v.t.* To cut a groove in the edge of a board so that it may receive the edge of another cut to fit it; to unite in this way. *n.* Such a groove or slot; a joint so made.

rabbi (răb'ī) [Heb. my master], *n.* A Jewish teacher of the law, esp. one ordained. **rabbin'ic, -al,** *a.* Pertaining to the rabbis, their opinions, learning, or language.

rabbit (răb'ĭt) [?], *n.* A burrowing rodent, allied to the hare.

rabble (răbl) [M.E. *rabel*], *n.* A noisy crowd, a mob; the common people. **rabblement,** *n.*

rabid (răb'ĭd) [L. *rabēre,* to rage], *a.* Mad, raging; excessively zealous or enthusiastic, unreasoning; affected with rabies. **rabid'ity,** *n.* **rabidly,** *adv.*

rabies (rā'bĭ-ēz), *n.* Madness arising from the bite of a rabid animal, hydrophobia.

race (1) (rās) [A.-S. *ræs*], *n.* A rapid current, esp. in the sea or a tidal river; the channel of a stream; a contest of speed between horses, runners, ships, vehicles, etc.; a course or career; a channel along which a piece of mechanism glides to and fro. *v.i.* To move swiftly; to go at full speed; to contend in a race (with); to atten draces. *v.t.* To cause to contend in a race; to contend against in speed.

race (2) [F. *race*], *n.* A group of persons, animals, or plants sprung from a common stock.

racial (rā'shàl), *a.* Pertaining or in regard to race or lineage. **racially,** *adv.*

rack (1) (răk) [Teut.], *v.t.* To stretch or strain; esp. on the rack; to torture, to injure; (*fig.*) to puzzle (one's brains); to extort (rent) to the utmost possible extent. *n.* A framework on which a victim was tortured, his wrists and ankles being tied to rollers which were turned so as to stretch him; a grating or framework of metal or wooden bars for holding fodder for cattle, etc. **rack-rent,** *n.* An exorbitant rent.

rack (2) [Scand.], *n.* Light vapoury clouds, cloud-drift.

racket (1) (răk'ĕt) [F. *raquette*], *n.* A bat with a network of catgut, with which

players at tennis, etc., strike the ball; (*pl.*) a game resembling tennis, played against a wall in a four-walled court.

racket (2) [?], *n.* A clamour, a din, a fuss; a frolic, uproarious gaiety, or dissipation. *v.i.* To make a din; to frolic, to live a gay life, to knockabout.

racoon (rā-koon') [Algonkin], *n.* A N. American carnivore allied to the bears.

racy (rā'sĭ), *a.* Having the characteristic qualities in high degree; strongly flavoured; lively, spirited. **racily,** *adv.* **raciness,** *n.*

Radar (rā'dar) [abbr. *Radio, Detection And Ranging*], *n.* (*Wire.*) The employment of reflected or retransmitted radio waves to locate the presence and position of objects.

radial (rā'dĭ-àl), *a.* Pertaining to, or resembling a ray or radii; extending from a centre, divergent. **radian,** *n.* An arc equal in length to the radius of its circle; the angle subtending such an arc.

radiant (rā'dĭ-ànt), *a.* Emitting rays of light or heat; issuing in rays; beaming (with joy, love, etc.); brilliant. **radiance,** *n.* **radiantly,** *adv.*

radiate (rā'dĭ-āt), *v.i.* To emit rays of light or heat; to send out or to issue in rays from a central point. *v.t.* To send forth in all directions, to disseminate. *a.* Having rays or parts diverging from a centre; radially arranged, marked, etc. **radia'tion,** *n.* Act of radiating; transmission of heat, light, etc., from one body to another without raising the temperature of the intervening medium. **ra'diator,** *n.* That which radiates; pipes, etc., charged with hot air, water, or steam for heating a building; (*Motor.*) a device for dissipating the heat absorbed by the cooling-water of the jacket.

radical (răd'ĭ-kàl) [L. *rădix -ĭcis,* root], *a.* Pertaining to the root or source; fundamental, original, basic; thorough-going, extreme; pertaining to the Radical party. *n.* One promoting extreme measures or holding advanced views. **radicalism,** *n.* **radically,** *adv.* Thoroughly, fundamentally.

radio- [RADIUS or RADIUM], *comb. form.* Radiate, pertaining to rays or radiation, or to radium.

radio (rā'dĭ-ō), *n.* and *a.* Pertaining to or transmitted by wireless telegraphy. **radioactive,** *a.* Having the property of emitting invisible rays that penetrate bodies opaque to light; radioactivity, *n.* **radiogram,** *n.* (*Rad.*) A wireless receiving set combining a gramophone. **radiotelegram,** *n.*

radiology, *n.* The branch of medical science concerned with radioactivity.

radio-therapy, *n.* The treatment of disease by radiation, by the use of radium.

radish (răd'ĭsh) [F. *radis*], *n.* A plant, the root of which is eaten as a salad.

radium (rā'dĭ-ùm) [L. *radius,* rod, spoke, ray], *n.* A highly radioactive metallic element resembling barium, obtained from pitchblende.

radius (rā'dĭ-ùs), *n.* (*pl.* -dii) The shorter. of the two long bones of the forearm; the straight line from the centre of a circle or sphere to any point in the circumference; the length of this; a radiating line, a spoke.

raffle (răfl) [F. *rafle*, a game with dice], *n.* A lottery in which persons each subscribe a like sum for an article to be disposed of by lot. *v.t.* To dispose of thus.

raft (raft) [Icel. *raptr*], *n.* Logs fastened together for floating; a flat framework of planks used as a substitute for a boat in shipwreck.

rafter (raf'tẽr) [A.-S. *ræfter*], *n.* A sloping piece of timber supporting a roof.

rag (răg) [Scand.], *n.* A fragment of cloth, tattered or shabby clothes; a remnant, a scrap; (*pl.*) tattered or shabby clothes. **ragamuffin**, *n.* A ragged, beggarly fellow. **ragtag and bobtail:** The riff-raff, the rabble. **ragtime**, *n.* Irregular syncopated time in music.

rage (rāj) [L. *rabēre*, to rage], *n.* Violent anger, fury; a violent desire (for); intense emotion, passion; an object of temporary enthusiasm. *v.i.* To storm, to be furious with anger; to be at the highest state of vehemence, intensity, or activity. **raging**, *a.* Acting with violence; furious, vehement.

ragged (răg'ĕd), *a.* Rough, shaggy; jagged or uneven; disjointed, irregular, imperfect; dissonant; worn into rags, tattered; shabby, miserable in appearance.

ragout (ra-goo') [F. *ragoûter*, to bring one's taste back], *n.* A highly-seasoned stew.

raid (rād) [A.-S. *rād*, road], *n.* A predatory incursion, a foray; a sudden invasion, descent, or attack. *v.t.* To make a raid upon.

rail (1) (rāl) [L. *rēgula*, rule], *n.* A bar of wood or metal or series of bars resting on supports, forming part of a fence, banisters, etc., one of a continuous line of bars, forming the track of a railway, tramway, etc.; the railway. *v.t.* To enclose or furnish with rails; to send by rail. **railroad, railway,** *n.* A road laid with a track formed of rails of iron or steel along which trains are driven. **railing,** *n.* A fence made of rails; materials for railings.

rail (2) [F. *railler*], *v.i.* To use abusive language; to scoff (at or against). **raillery,** *n.* Good-humoured ridicule, banter.

rail (3) [F. *râle*] *n.* A bird of the family *Rallidæ*.

raiment (rā'mĕnt), *n.* Dress, clothes.

rain (rān) [A.-S. *regn*], *n.* The moisture of the atmosphere falling in drops; a fall of such drops, a shower of anything. *v.i.* To fall in drops from the clouds; to fall in showers like rain. *v.t.* To pour down (rain); to send down in showers like rain. **rainbow,** *n.* A luminous arch showing the prismatic colours, appearing opposite the sun during rain. *a.* Many-coloured. **rainfall,** *n.* The amount of rain which falls in a particular district in a given period; a shower of rain. **rain-gauge,** *n.* An instrument for measuring the amount of rain falling on a given surface. **rainy,** *a.* Characterized by much rain; showery.

raise (rāz) [Icel. *reisa*], *v.t.* To cause to rise or to stand up, to set upright; to restore to life, to excite; to erect, construct; to

rear, to breed; to produce; to collect, to levy (money) etc.; to increase the amount of. **to raise a blockade** or **siege:** To relinquish the attempt to take a place by blockade or siege.

raisin (rāzn) [O.F. *raizin*], *n.* A dried grape.

raj (raj) [Hindi], *n.* Sovereignty, rule.

Rajah, Raja (ra'jà) [Hindi], *n.* An Indian king or prince, a title of a noble.

rake (1) (rāk) [A.-S. *raca*], *n.* A long-handled implement with a toothed crossbar, used for drawing loose material together, smoothing soil, etc.; a dissolute or immoral man, a libertine. *v.t.* To collect or search with a rake; to scrape, smooth, clean, etc. (soil) with a rake; to fire along the length of, to enfilade. **raking,** *n.* Act of using a rake; amount of ground or quantity of material raked; that which is raked together (*usu. in pl.*) **rakish** (1), *a.* Dissolute, given to debauchery.

rake (2) [?], *n.* Slope, esp. backward; projection of the stem or stern of a vessel beyond the extremities of the keel. *v.* To slope backwards. **rakish** (2), *a.* (*Naut.*) With masts sharply inclined; smart looking with a suggestion of the pirate.

rally (1) (răl'i) [F. *rallier*], *v.t.* To bring (disordered troops) together again; to reanimate, to pull together. *v.i.* To reassemble, esp. after a reverse or rout; to recover tone or spirit. *n.* Act of rallying; (*Lawn-tennis, etc.*) rapid return of strokes.

rally (2) (răl'i), *v.t.* To banter, chaff.

ram (răm) [A.-S.], *n.* A male sheep; a battering-ram; a battleship armed with a steel beak for cutting into a hostile vessel; such a beak; a rammer. *v.t.* To beat, drive, or force (down, into, etc.) by heavy blows. **ramrod,** *n.* A rod for forcing down the charge of a muzzle-loading gun.

ramble (rămbl) [?], *v.i.* To walk about aimlessly, to rove; to be incoherent in speech, writing, etc. *n.* A roaming about without a definite object, a stroll. **rambler,** *n.* One who rambles about; a variety of climbing-rose. **rambling,** *a.*

ramify (răm'i-fī) [L. *rāmus*, branch], *v.i.* To divide, to branch out, to send out offshoots. *v.t.* To cause to divide into branches, etc. **ramifica'tion,** *n.*

ramose (ra-mōs'), *a.* Branching; branched; full of branches.

ramp (rămp) [O.F. *ramper*, to climb], *v.i.* To rear on the hind-legs (of an heraldic lion); to rage, to storm; (*Arch.*) to ascend or descend to another level (of a wall). *n.* A slope leading from one level to another; a sloping part in the top of a hand-rail, etc.; an exorbitant charge, a swindle.

rampage (răm'pāj) [?], *v.i.* To dash about, to storm, rage, behave violently. *n.* Boisterous, excited, or violent behaviour. **rampageous** (-pā'jŭs), *a.*

rampant (răm'pãnt), *a.* Standing upright on the hind legs (of the heraldic lion); aggressive, wild, luxuriant (of weeds).

rampart (răm'pàrt) [F. *rempart*, from *remparer*, to fortify], *n.* An embankment round a fortified place; (*fig.*) a defence.

ramshackle (răm′shăkl), *a.* In a crazy state, tumbledown.

ranch (ranch) [Sp. *rancho*, mess, a party eating together], *n.* (*Am.*) A farm for rearing cattle and horses.

rancid (răn′sid) [L. *rancidus*], *a.* Having the taste or smell of stale oil or fat. **rancid′ity,** *n.*

rancour (răng′kŏr) [L. *rancor*], *n.* Inveterate spite, resentment, or enmity. **rancorous,** *a.*

random (răn′dom) [F. *randir*, to press forward], *n.* Great speed or impetuosity. *a.* Done without calculation or method; left to chance.

ranee (ra′nē) [Hindi], *n.* A Hindu queen.

range (rānj), *v.t.* To set in a rank or row; to arrange in definite order, etc.; to roam or sail along or about. *v.i.* To extend or reach; (*Ordnance*) to carry (a specified distance) in a particular direction; to rank; to vary (from one specified point to another); to roam, to rove, to sail (along, etc.). *n.* A row, rank, or series, a tract, esp. of grazing or hunting-ground; the area, scope, or sphere of power, variation, etc.; the extreme horizontal distance attainable by a gun or a projectile; the distance between a gun and the object aimed at; a shooting-ground; a cooking-stove or kitchen grate. **ranger,** *n.* A rover, a wanderer; the superintendent of a royal forest or park.

rank (1) (răngk) [F. *ranc* (now *rang*], *n.* A line, a row, esp. of soldiers ranged side by side; order, high station, dignity; relative position, degree of excellence, etc. *v.t.* To draw up in rank; to classify, to give a (specified) rank to. *v.i.* To hold a (specified) rank; to have a position (among, with, etc.). **rank and file:** common soldiers; (*fig.*) the lower orders. **ranker,** *n.* A commissioned officer promoted from the ranks.

rank (2) [A.-S. *ranc*], *a.* Luxuriant in growth, over-abundant; coarse, rancid, offensive; flagrant, arrant, utter; obscene. **rankly,** *adv.*

rankle (răngkl) [O.F. *rancler,* from *rancle,* sore], *v.i.* To fester (of a wound, etc.); to be inflamed, to irritate.

ransack (răn′săk) [Icel. *rann,* house, *sœkja,* to seek], *v.t.* To search thoroughly; to plunder.

ransom (răn′som) [O.F. *ranson*], *n.* Release in return for a payment; a sum paid for such release or for goods captured by an enemy. *v.t.* To redeem from captivity or obtain the restoration of (property) by payment; to hold to ransom; to release in return for a ransom.

rant (rănt) [M. Dut. *randten,* to dance about], *v.i.* To use loud, bombastic language; to declaim in a noisy fashion. *n.* Bombastic or violent declamation; inflated talk.

ranunculus (ra-nŭn′kū-lŭs) [L., dim. of *rāna,* frog], *n.* A genus of plants including the buttercup. **ranunculaceous,** *a.*

rap (răp) [imit.], *v.t.* To strike with a slight, sharp blow; to utter in an abrupt way. *v.i.* To strike a sharp blow, esp. at a door. *n.* A slight, sharp blow; a sound such as is made thus.

rapacious (ra-pā′shŭs) [L. *rapere,* to seize], *a.* Grasping, extortionate; predatory; living on food seized by force (of animals). **rapacity** (ra-păs′i-ti), *n.*

rape (1) (răp), *v.t.* To seize, to force (a woman). *n.* A carrying away by force; carnal knowledge of a woman against her will.

rape (2) (răp) [L. *răpum,* turnip], *n.* A plant allied to the turnip; a plant grown for its seed which yields oil, cole-seed.

rapid (răp′id) [L. *rapidus*], *a.* Very swift, done, acting, or moving in a very short time; descending steeply. *n.* (*usu. pl.*) A sudden descent in a stream. **rapid′ity,** *n.* **rapidly,** *adv.*

rapier (rā′pi-ér) [F. *rapiere*], *n.* A light, narrow sword, used in thrusting.

rapine (răp′in), *n.* Act of carrying off by force; plunder, spoliation.

rapparee (răp-á-rē′) [Ir. *rapaire*], *n.* An Irish freebooter of the 17th and 18th centuries.

rappee (ră-pē′) [F. *rape,* rasped], *n.* A coarse kind of snuff.

rapprochement (ra-prŏsh-man) [F.], *n.* Reconciliation, re-establishment of friendly relations, esp. between nations.

rapt (răpt) [L. *raptus* seized], *a.* Carried away by one's thoughts or emotions, enraptured, absorbed.

rapture (răp′tyŭr), *n.* Ecstasy, transport; (*pl.*) a fit of delight. **rapturous,** *a.* **rapturously,** *adv.*

rare (1) (râr) [L. *rārus*], *a.* Of sparse, thin, or porous substance, not dense; seldom occurring, not often met with, scarce, uncommon; singularly good, choice. **rarely,** *adv.* **rareness,** *n.*

rare (2) [A.-S. *hrēr*], *a.* (*Am.*) Underdone.

rarefy (râr′ē-fī) [L. *rārus,* rare -FY], *v.t.* To make rare or less dense and solid; to refine, to make less gross. *v.i.* To become less dense. **rarefac′tion,** *n.*

rarity (râr′i-ti) [F. *rarité,* L. *rāritas* as RARE (1)], *n.* Rareness; tenuity; a rare thing.

rascal (ras′kăl) [O.F. *rascaille,* rabble], *n.* A mean rogue, a tricky fellow, a knave, a scamp. *a.* Worthless, low. **rascal′ity,** *n.* **ras′cally,** *a.*

rash (1) (răsh) [Teut.], *a.* Hasty, precipitate, venturesome; thoughtless. **rashly,** *adv.*

rash (2) (răsh) [?], *n.* An eruption of spots on the skin.

rasher (răsh′ér) [?], *n.* A thin slice of bacon or ham for frying.

rasp (rasp) [O.F. *rasper*], *v.t.* To scrape or grate with a coarse, rough implement; to file with a rasp; (*fig.*) to irritate. *v.i.* To rub, to grate; to make a grating sound. *n.* A coarse file for scraping.

raspberry (raz′bér-i) [?], *n.* A garden shrub allied to the bramble; its fruit: (*Slang*) sound made with the mouth as a sign of disapproval.

rat (răt) [A.-S. *rœt*], *n.* A large rodent of the mouse family; one who deserts his party, a turncoat. *v.i.* To hunt or kill rats (esp. with dogs); to turn traitor.

ratafia (răt-á-fē′á) [F.], *n.* A cordial flavoured with the kernels of cherry, almond, etc.

ratchet (răch′ét) [?], *n.* A wheel or bar with inclined angular teeth, between which a pawl drops, permitting motion in one direction only; the pawl itself. **ratchet-wheel**, *n.* A wheel with toothed edge.

rate (1) (răt) [O.F., from L. *ratus*, thought judged], *n.* Proportional measure, ratio, comparative amount, degree, etc.; a standard; price, value, relative speed, etc.; a levy for local purposes. *v.t.* To estimate the relative worth, rank, etc., of. *v.i.* To be ranked (as). **at any rate:** In any case; even so. **ratepayer**, *n.* One who is liable to pay municipal rates. **rateable** (rā'tăbl), *a.* Liable to be rated, subject to assessment for municipal rates; proportional. **-rater**, *n.* (*in comb*) A ship or yacht of a specified rate. **rating** (1), *n.* Act of assessing; the grade of a seaman as stated in the ship's books.

rate (2) [?], *v.* To chide angrily, to scold, to storm (at). **rating** (2), *n.* A harsh reprimand.

rath (rath), **rathe** (rāth) [A.-S. *hrathe*], *adv.* Early soon.

rather (ra'thèr) [compar. of RATHE], *adv.* Sooner, more readily, preferably; with more reason, more properly, more accurately; in a greater degree; slightly, somewhat.

ratify (răt'i-fī) [L. *ratus*, rate], *v.t.* To confirm, to make valid. **ratifica'tion**, *n.*

ratio (rā'shi-ō) [L.], *n.* Relation of one quantity to another of the same kind.

ratiocinate (răsh-i-os'i-nāt) [L. *ratiōcinātus*], *v.i.* To reason or argue. **ratiocina'tion**, *n.*

ration (răsh'ŭn), *n.* Allowance of food for a given time, esp. in the army or navy; a portion of provisions, etc., allowed to one individual. *v.t.* To supply with rations; to put on fixed rations.

rational (răsh'ŏ-năl), *a.* Having the faculty of reasoning; agreeable to reasoning; based on what can be tested by reason. **rationalism** (răsh'ŏ-nà-lizm), *n.* The determination of questions of belief by the reason, rejecting supernatural revelation. **rationalist**, *n.* **rationalis'tic**, *a.* **rational'ity**, *n.* Quality of being rational; power of reasoning; reasonableness. **rationalize**, *v.t.* To render reasonable; (*Math.*) to clear (an equation, etc.) of radical signs.

ratline, ratling (răt'lin, -ling) [?], *n.* One of the small ropes extended across the shrouds on each side of a mast, forming rungs.

rattan (ra-tăn') [Malay *rōtan*], *n.* The pliable stem of certain E. Indian climbing palms; a walking-stick of this.

rattle (rătl) [M.E. *ratelen*], *v.i.* To make a rapid succession of sharp noises; to talk rapidly or foolishly; to run, ride, or drive rapidly. *v.t.* To cause to make a rattling noise; to utter, play, etc. (off, away), rapidly; to cause to move with a clatter; to drive fast. *n.* A rapid succession of sharp noises; an instrument with which such sounds are made; a rattling noise in the throat; empty talk, chatter; a chatterer; racket, boisterous gaiety; the tail of the rattlesnake; a plant having seeds that rattle in their cases. **rattlesnake**, *n.* An American snake, the tail of which is furnished with a rattle. **rattling**, *a.*

raucous (raw'kŭs) [L. *raucus*], *a.* Hoarse, rough in sound. **raucously**, *adv.*

ravage (răv'áj), *n.* Ruin, havoc; (*pl.*) devastating effects. *v.t.* To devastate; to pillage. *v.i.* To make havoc.

rave (rāv) [?], *v.i.* To be delirious, to talk wildly, or irrationally; to act furiously, to rage; to go into raptures (about).

ravel (răvl) [?], *v.t.* To entangle, confuse, involve; to untwist, to disentangle; to fray. *v.i.* To become tangled; to become unwoven; to fray (out).

raven (1) răvn) [A.-S. *hræfn*], *n.* A large, black, omnivorous bird of the crow family. *a.* Glossy black.

raven (2) (răvn) [O.F. *raviner*], *v.t.* To devour with voracity. *v.i.* To plunder; to prowl after prey; to be ravenous.

ravenous (răv'è-nŭs), *a.* Voracious, famished; furiously rapacious, eager for gratification. **ravenously**, *adv.*

ravine (ra-vēn') [F.], *n.* A long, deep hollow caused by a torrent, a gorge.

ravish (răv'ish) [F. *ravir*, L. *rapere*, to snatch], *v.t.* To enrapture, transport (with pleasure, etc.); to violate, to rape. **ravisher**, *n.* One who ravishes, rapes, or carries off by force. **ravishing**, *a.* Enchanting, charming, filling one with rapture. **ravishment**, *n.*

raw (raw) [A.-S. *hréaw*], *a.* Uncooked; not wrought or manufactured; untrained, inexperienced, immature, fresh; having the flesh exposed, galled; cold and damp, bleak.

ray (1) (rā) [L. *radius*], *n.* A beam of light proceeding from a radiant point; a straight line along which radiant energy is propagated; (*fig.*) a gleam, a vestige; one of a series of radiating lines. *v.* To radiate; to issue or shine forth in rays.

ray (2) [L. *raia*], *n.* A large cartilaginous fish allied to the sharks.

rayon (rā'on), *n.* Artificial silk made from cellulose.

raze (rāz) [F. *raser*, scraped], *v.t.* To erase, obliterate; to level with the ground, to destroy.

razor (rā'zŏr), *n.* A cutting instrument for shaving off hair.

re (1) (rā), *n.* The second note of a major scale, esp. of C major, D.

re (2) (rē) [L.], *prep.* In the matter of.

re- [L., back, again], *pref.* Back, back again; after; un-; mutually; again and again, anew; in opposition; off, away, down.

reach (1) (rēch) [A.-S. *ræcan*], *v.t.* To stretch out; to extend; to attain to, arrive at, to affect; to hand, to pass. *v.i.* To reach or stretch out the hand; to put forth one's powers, to be extended so as to touch, to have extent in time, space, etc.; to attain (to). *n.* Act or power of reaching; extent, range, attainment; a stretch of water between two bends.

react (rē-ăkt'), *v.i.* To act in response (to a stimulus, etc.); to have a reciprocal effect; to tend in an opposite manner. *v.t.* To act again. **reaction**, *n.* Reciprocal action; response to stimulation; chemical action of one substance upon another;

the force exerted upon the agent by a body acted upon; contrary action; action in an opposite direction, esp. in politics. **reactionary**, *a.* Tending towards re-action, retrograde, conservative. *n.* A reactionary person.

read (rĕd) [A.-S. *rǽdan*], *v.t.* (*past and p.p.* read, rĕd) To perceive and under-stand the meaning of (characters, sym-bols, significant features, etc.), to peruse; reproduce mentally, vocally, or instru-mentally (words, notes, etc., conveyed by symbols); to discover by observation, to explain; to see through; to ascertain or study by reading. *v.i.* To follow or interpret the meaning of a book, etc., to render written music (well, easily, etc.); to mean (in a certain way, etc.); to sound (well, ill, etc.) when perused or uttered. **readable**, *a.* Worth reading; legible. **reader**, *n.* One who reads, esp. much; book of selections for the use of students; one who corrects proofs, etc. **reading**, *a.* Addicted to reading, studious. *n.* The act, practice, or art of reading; literary research; a public recital at which selections are read aloud; an interpre-tation, a rendering.

readjust (rĕ-ăd-jŭst'), *v.t.* To arrange or adjust afresh.

ready (rĕd'ĭ) [A.-S. *geræde*], *a.* Prepared, fit for use or action; willing, about (to); prompt; expert, facile; handy, quickly available. *n.* The position in which a fire-arm is held before presenting and aiming; (*slang*) money, actual cash ready to be put down. **ready-made**, *a.* Not made to order (esp. of clothing). **readily**, *adv.* Without trouble, easily, willingly. **readiness**, *n.* State of being ready, pre-paredness; willingness, ease, aptitude, quickness in acting.

real (1) (rē'ăl) [L. *redlis*, from *rēs*, thing], *a.* Actually existing; not imaginary theoretical, or nominal; not counterfeit; Having substantial existence; (*Law*) con-sisting of lands or houses, opp. to personal. **really**, *adv.* In fact, in reality; (*colloq.*) I assure you.

real (2) (rā'ăl) [Sp.], *n.* (*pl.* reales, rä-a'lĕz) A Spanish silver coin worth about 2½d.

realism (rē'ă-lĭzm), *n.* The practice of representing objects, persons, scenes, etc., as they are or as they appear to the painter, novelist, etc., opp. to idealism and romanticism. **realist**, *n.* **realis'tic**, *a.*

reality (rē-ăl'ĭ-tĭ), *n.* The quality of being real, actuality, that which underlies appearances; the real nature (of). **realty** rē'ăl-tĭ), *n.* (*Law*) Real property.

realize (rē'ă-līz), *v.t.* To apprehend clearly and vividly; to bring into actual exis-tence, give reality to; to impress on the mind as real, to make realistic; to convert into money; to bring in, as a price. **realizable**, *a.* **realiza'tion**, *n.*

realm (rĕlm) [O.F. *realme*], *n.* A kingdom; (*fig.*) domain, region, sphere.

realtor (rē'ăl-tŏr), *n.* (*Am.*) An estate agent, dealer in land for development.

ream (rēm) [Arab, *rizmah*, bundle], *n.* 480 sheets or twenty quires of paper.

reap (rēp) [A.-S. *rīpan*], *v.t.* To cut with a scythe, etc., to gather in (a harvest). *v.i.* To perform the act of reaping; to receive the consequences of labour, deeds, etc. **reaper**, *n.* One who reaps; a reaping-machiner.

rear (1) (rēr) [A.S. *rǽran*], *v.t.* To raise, to elevate to an upright position; to build, to erect; to bring up, to breed, to edu-cate; to raise, to cultivate. *v.i.* To stand on the hind legs (of a horse).

rear (2) *n.* The back part, the hindmost division of an armed force; a position at the back. **rear-guard**, *n.* A body of troops protecting the rear of an army.

reason (rē'zòn) [O.F. *raisun*], *n.* That which is adduced to support or serves as a ground or motive; that which accounts for anything; the intellectual faculties, the logical faculty; judgment, sanity; the exercise of the rational powers. *v.i.* To use the faculty of reason; to argue with intention of per-suading; to reach conclusions by way of inferences. *v.t.* To debate or examine by means of the reason or reasons and inferences; to assume or prove by way of argument; to persuade or dissuade thus. **reasonable**, *a.* Endowed with or governed by reason; rational; sensible, proper; fair, not extortionate. **reason-ably**, *adv.* **reasoning**, *n.* The act of drawing conclusions from premises or of using the reason; argumentation.

reassure (rē-ă-shoor'), *v.t.* To assure again; to restore to confidence, give fresh courage to; to reinsure. **reassuring**, *a.*

rebate (rĕ-bāt'), *v.t.* To make a deduction from, to diminish; to make blunt. *n.* (rē'bāt) A deduction, a discount.

rebel (rĕb'ĕl) [L. *rebellis*, rebellious], *a.* Rebellious; pertaining to rebels. *n.* One who forcibly resists the established government or renounces allegiance thereto. *v.i.* (rĕ-bel') To engage in rebellion (against); to revolt (against authority or control); (*fig.*) to feel repugnance (against). **rebellion** (rĕ-bel'-yòn), *n.* Organized resistance to the established government; opposition to any authority. **rebellious**, *a.* Difficult to control.

rebound (rĕ-bound') [O.F. *rebondir*], *v.i.* To bound back, to recoil; to react. *n.* The act of rebounding, a recoil; reaction (of feeling, etc.).

rebuff (rĕ-bŭf') [It. *ribuffo* (*buffo*, puff)], *n.* A rejection, a check; a snub; a defeat. *v.t.* To give a rebuff to, to repel.

rebuke (rĕ-būk') [O.F. *rebuchier*], *v.t.* To reprove, to reprimand; to censure. *n.* Act of rebuking; a reproof. **rebukingly**, *adv.*

rebus (rē'bŭs) [L., able. pl. of *rēs*, thing], *n.* A picture or figure representing enig-matically a word or phrase.

rebut (rĕ-bŭt') [O.F. *rebouter*], *v.t.* To check, to repel; (*Law*) to refute by plea or argument.

recalcitrant (rĕ-kăl'sĭ-trănt) [L. *recalcitrans* (RE- *calcitrāre*, to strike with the heel)], *a.* Refractory, obstinately refusing submission. *n.* A recalcitrant person. **recalcitrance, -cy**, *n.*

recall (rĕ-kawl'), *v.t.* To call back; to bring to mind, to recollect; to renew; to annul,

to take back. *n.* A summons to return;
a signal calling back soldiers, a ship,
etc.; the power of revoking or annulling.
recant (rê-kănt′) [L. *recantāre*], *v.t.* To
retract, abjure; to disavow. *v.i.* To
renounce opinions or beliefs, esp. with
acknowledgment of error. **recanta′tion,** *n.*
recapitulate (rē-kà-pit′ū-lāt), *v.t.* To repeat
in brief, to sum up, to summarize.
recapitula′tion, *n.*
recede (rē-sēd′) [L. *cēdere*, to go], *v.i.* To
go back; to be gradually lost to view;
to incline or trend backwards or away;
to retreat.
receipt (rê-sēt′) [L. *recepta*, received], *n.*
Act or fact of receiving or being received; that which is received, esp.
money; a written acknowledgment of
money, etc., received; a recipe. *v.t.* To
give a receipt for.
receive (rê-sēv′) [L. *recipere*], *v.t.* To
obtain or take as a thing offered; to be
supplied with, to acquire; to welcome,
to entertain as guest; to accept stolen
goods. *v.i.* To hold a reception. **receivable,** *a.* **receiver,** *n.* One who receives,
esp. stolen goods; a part of a telephonic
or telegraphic apparatus for receiving
messages or current; an officer administering the property of bankrupts.
recent (rē′sênt) [L. *recens*], *a.* Pertaining
to time not long past, lately; late (of
existence); modern, newly begun. **re-
cency,** *n.* **recently,** *adv.*
receptacle (rê-sep′tàkl), *n.* That which
receives or contains; a vessel or place of
deposit.
reception (rê-sep′shŭn), *n.* Act of receiving;
state of being received; receipt, acceptance, admission; the receiving of guests,
new members of a society, etc.; a formal
welcome; an occasion of ceremonious
receiving of visitors; mental acceptance
or admission (of a theory, etc.). **recep′-
tive,** *a.* Having capacity to receive, esp.
impressions, ideas, etc. **receptiv′ity,** *n.*
recess (rê-ses′) [L. *recessus*], *n.* Suspension
of business, a vacation; a part that
recedes, a niche, an alcove; a secluded
part. **recession,** *n.* Slump in trade.
recessional, *n.* A hymn sung as clergy
retire after a service.
réchauffé (rā-shō-fā) [F. warmed up again],
n. A dish warmed up again; a rehash.
recherché (rê-shâr′shā) [F.], *a.* (*fem.* -chée)
Out of the common; choice.
recipe (res′i-pi), *n.* A formula for compounding medicines, dishes, cakes, etc.,
a receipt; a means for effecting some
result.
recipient (rê-sip′i-ênt), *a.* Receptive. *n.*
One who receives.
reciprocal (rê-sip′rō-kál) [L. *reciprocus*],
a. Acting or given in return, mutual;
interchangeable, complementary. **recip′-
rocally,** *adv.* **recip′rocate,** *v.i.* To move
backwards and forwards; to return an
equivalent. *v.t.* To give alternating or
backward-and-forward motion to; to
interchange; to give in return. **reciproca-
ca′tion,** *n.* Act of reciprocating; giving
and returning. **reciprocity** (res-i-pros′-
i-ti), *n.* State of being reciprocal; mutual
action or the principle of give-and-take,

esp. international interchange of commercial privileges.
recite (rê-sīt′), *v.t.* To repeat from memory;
to rehearse (facts, etc., in a legal document); to quote; to enumerate. *v.i.* To
give a recitation. **reciter,** *n.* One who
recites; a book of selections for reciting.
reci′tal, *n.* Act of reciting; an enumeration of facts or particulars, a story; a
public giving of recitations; a musical
performance, esp. by one person or of
the works of one person. **recita′tion,** *n.*
The delivery of a composition committed to memory; a composition intended for recital. **recitative** (res-i-tà-
tēv′), *n.* (*Mus.*) A style of rendering
vocal passages intermediate between
singing and speaking; a piece to be sung
in recitative.
reck (rek) [A.-S. *reccan*], *v.t.* To care, to
heed. **reckless,** *a.* Heedless; rash;
regardless, indifferent, neglectful (of).
reckon (rek′ŏn) [A.-S. *gerecenian*], *v.t.* To
count, calculate, compute; to account,
to esteem, to consider (to be). *v.i.* To
settle accounts with; to reply, to count,
to place dependence (upon). **reckoner,** *n.*
reckoning, *n.* Act of counting; a statement of accounts, a bill; a settling of
accounts; (*Naut.*) a calculation of a
ship's position.
reclaim (rê-klām′), *v.t.* To bring back from
error, etc.; to tame, civilize, bring under
cultivation; to demand back, to recall.
reclaimable, *a.* **reclamation** (rek-là-mā′-
shŭn), *n.*
recline (rê-klīn′) [L. *clīnāre*, to lean], *v.t.*
To lay or lean (one's body, head, etc.)
back. *v.i.* To assume a leaning or recumbent posture, to lie down or lean back.
recluse (rê-kloos′) [O.F. *reclus*, L. *reclusus*,
shut up], *a.* Retired from the world;
sequestered. *n.* One who lives apart
from the world, esp. a religious devotee.
recognition (rek-ŏg-nish′ŭn) [L. *recognitio*],
n. Act of recognizing or acknowledging;
avowal.
recognizance (re-kog′ni-zàns, rê-kog′ni-
zàns), *n.* (*Law*) A bond entered into before
a magistrate to perform a specified
act; a sum deposited as pledge for
this.
recognize (rek′ŏg-nīz) [L. *cognoscere*, to
know], *v.t.* To know again; to recall the
identity of; to acknowledge, to admit
the truth of. **recogniz′able,** *a.*
recoil (rê-koil′) [O.F. *reculer*], *v.i.* To start
or shrink back; to rebound; to retreat.
n. Act of recoiling; a rebound; the
feeling of shrinking back, as in fear or
disgust.
recollect (1) (rê-kó-lekt′), *v.t.* To gather
together again; to collect or compose
(one's thoughts, etc.); to rally, recover.
recollect (2) (rek-ó-lekt′), *v.t.* To recall to
memory, to remember. **recollec′tion,** *n.*
Act or power of re- calling to the mind;
a reminiscence; the period over which
one's memory extends.
recommend (rek-ó-mend′), *v.t.* To commend to another, esp. to represent as
suitable; to advise (a certain course of
action, etc.); to render acceptable (of
qualities). **recommenda′tion,** *n.*

recompense (rek'ŏm-pens) [L. *compensāre*, to compensate], *v.t.* To requite, to repay (a person, a service, an injury, etc.); to compensate (for), make up (for). *n.* Something given as a reward, compensation, requital, or satisfaction (for a service, injury, etc.).

reconcile (rek'ŏn-sīl) [L. *conciliāre*, to conciliate], *v.t.* To restore to friendship; to make acquiescent or submissive (to); to harmonize, make compatible (with); to settle (differences, etc.). **reconcilable**, *a.* **reconciliation** (-sil-i-ā'-shŭn), *n.* **reconcil'iatory**, *a.*

recondite (rek'ŏn-dīt) [L. *conditus*, hidden], *a.* Abstruse, little known, obscure.

reconnaissance (rē-kon'ă-săns), *n.* Act of reconnoitring, a preliminary survey to ascertain the position of the enemy, the strategic features, etc.; a detachment performing this duty.

reconnoitre (rek-ó-noi'tér) [F.], *v.t.* To make a preliminary examination or survey of. *v.i.* To make a reconnaissance. **reconnoitre,** *n.*

reconsid'er, *v.t.* To consider again; to review, to revise. **reconsidera'tion,** *n.*

record (rē-kôrd') [L. *recordāre* (*cor, cordis,* heart)], *v.t.* To set down permanent evidence of, to imprint deeply on the mind. *n.* (rek'ôrd) A written or other permanent account or statement; a register, a report, minutes of proceedings, a series of marks made by a recording instrument; a device used in a mechanical musical instrument to reproduce a tune, etc.; the past history of a person's career; a memento of a person, event, etc. **recorder** (rē-kôr'dèr), *n.* One who or that which records; a magistrate presiding over quarter-sessions; a musical wind-instrument.

recount (rē-kount'), *v.t.* To relate in detail, to narrate; (rē-kount') to count over again. *n.* A new count.

recoup (rē-koop') [F. *couper,* to cut], *v.t.* To indemnify (oneself) for a loss or expenditure; to compensate.

recourse (rē-kôrs') [L. *cursus,* course], *n.* Resorting to as for help; a source of help. **to have recourse to:** To go to for advice, help, etc.

recover (rē-kŭv'ér) [O.F. *recovrer*], *v.t.* To regain, win back; to retrieve; (*Law*) to obtain by legal process. *v.i.* To regain a former state, esp. after sickness, misfortune, etc.; (*Law*) to be successful in a suit. **recoverable,** *a.* **recovery,** *n.* Act of recovering or state of having recovered; restoration to health; (*Law*) the obtaining of the right to something by judgment of a court.

re-cover (rē-kŭv'ér), *v.t.* To cover again, to put a new covering on.

recreant (rek'rē-ănt) [O.F., yielding in trial by combat], *a.* Craven, cowardly. *n.* One who has begged for mercy, an apostate, a deserter.

recreate (rek'rē-āt) [L. *creātus,* created], *v.t.* To refresh after toil; to entertain, amuse. *v.i.* To take recreation. **recrea'tion,** *n.* **recrea'tional, rec'reative,** *a.*

recriminate (rē-krim'i-nāt), *v.i.* To bring counter-charges against. *v.t.* To accuse

in return. **recrimination,** *n.* **recrim'inatory,** *a.*

recrudesce (rē-krŭ-des') [L. *crūdescere,* to become raw], *v.i.* To break out, or become sore again. **recrudescence,** *n.* State of becoming sore again; a relapse, a breaking out again; a reappearance.

recruit (rē-kroot') [F. *recruter*], *v.t.* To enlist (soldiers or sailors); to supply (an army, etc.) with recruits, to replenish, to fill up gaps, etc.; to refresh, to reinvigorate. *v.i.* To seek to recover health; to act as a recruiting-officer. *n.* A newly enlisted man.

rectangle (rek'tăng'gel) [L. *rectus,* straight], *n.* A plane rectilinear quadrilateral figure with four right angles. **rectang'ular,** *a.* Shaped like a rectangle; placed at right angles.

rectify (rek'ti-fī), *v.t.* To set right, amend, adjust; to reform. **rectifica'tion,** *n.*

rectilinear,- lineal (rek-ti-lin'ē-ár, -ăl), *n.* Consisting of or bounded by straight lines.

rectitude (rek'ti-tūd), *n.* Uprightness, conformity to truth and justice.

rector (rek'tòr) [L., ruler], *n.* A parson whose tithes are not impropriate; the head of a religious institution, University, etc. **rectorship,** *n.* **rector'ial,** *a.* **rectory** (rek'tòr-i), *n.* The benefice of a rector with all its rights, property, etc.; the house of a rector.

rectum (rek'tŭm) [L., straight], *n.* (*Anat.*) The lowest portion of the large intestine.

recumbent (rē-kŭm'bĕnt) [L. *recumbens*], *a.* Lying down, reclining.

recuperate (rē-kū'pèr-āt) [L. *recuperātus*], *v.* To recover; to restore to health. **recupera'tion,** *n.* **recu'perative,** *a.*

recur (rē-kèr') [RE-, L. *currere,* to run], *v.i.* To go back to in thought, etc.; to come back to one's mind; to happen again or repeatedly. **recurrence** (rē-kŭr'ĕns), *n.* **recurrent,** *a.* Recurring at regular intervals.

recusant (rek'ū-zănt) [L. *recusans,* refusing], *a.* Obstinately refusing to conform, esp. to the Established Church. *n.* One who refuses to comply. **recusance, -cy,** *n.*

red (red) [A.-S. *read*], *a.* Of a bright warm colour, as blood, of the colour at end of the spectrum farthest from the violet; (*fig.*) Communistic, anarchistic. *n.* A red colour or pigment; (*fig.*) a Communist, an anarchist. **redbreast,** *n.* The robin. **red flag:** The symbol of revolution or of anarchism. **red-handed,** *a.* Having hands red with blood; (caught) in the very act. **red-hot,** *a.* Heated to redness; (*fig.*) excited, wildly enthusiastic. **red-letter day:** An auspicious or memorable day, because saints' days were so marked in the calendar. **redskin,** *n.* A N. American Indian. **red-tape,** *n.* Extreme adherence to official routine. *a.* Characterized by this. **redden,** *v.t.* To make red. *v.i.* To become red, esp. to blush. **reddish,** *a.* **redness,** *n.*

red- [RE-, before vowels], *pref.*

-red, *suf.* Condition, as in *hatred, kindred.*

redeem (rē-dēm') [L., *emere,* to buy], *v.t.* To buy back; (*Law*) to recover (mortgaged property), to buy off (an obligation, etc.); to perform (a promise); to ransom; to save, rescue; (Theol.) to deliver from sin and its penalty; to atone for. **redeemer,** n. One who redeems, esp. Christ, the Saviour of the world.

redemption (rĕ-demp'shŭn), n. Act of redeeming, state of being redeemed, esp. salvation by the atonement of Christ; ransom.

redirect (rĕ-di-rekt'), v.t. To direct again; to readdress. **rediscov'er,** v.t. To discover afresh.

redolent (red'ŏ-lĕnt) [L. olens, smelling], a. Giving out a strong smell; reminding one (of). **redolence,** n.

redouble (rĕ-dŭbl'), v. To increase by repeated additions, to intensify; to grow more intense, numerous, etc.

redoubt (rĕ-dout') [L. reductus, retired], n. A detached outwork enclosed by a parapet without flanking defences.

redoubtable (rĕ-dou'tăbl) [O.F. redouter, to fear], a. Formidable; valiant.

redound (rĕ-dound') [L. redundāre, to overflow], v.i. To have effect, to conduce (to one's credit, etc.); to recoil (upon).

redress (rĕ-dres') [F. redresser], v.t. To set right or straight again, to rectify; to amend, to make reparation for. n. Reparation; rectification.

reduce (rĕ-dūs') [L. dūcere, to bring]. v.t. To bring to a specified condition; to make conformable (to a rule, formula, etc.); to subdue, conquer, degrade, diminish; (Cook.) to boil down; (Math.) to change from one denomination to another. **reducible,** a. **reduc'tion,** n. Act of reducing; state of being reduced; a conquest; a diminution; (Arith.) process of finding an equivalent expression in terms of a different denomination.

redundant (rĕ-dŭn'dănt) [L. redundans, overflowing], a. Superfluous; using more words than are necessary; exuberant; copious. **redundance, -cy,** n. **redundantly,** adv.

reduplicate (rĕ-dū'pli-kāt), v.t. To redouble, to repeat; to repeat a letter or syllable to form a tense. **reduplica'tion,** n. Act of doubling or repeating; repetition of a syllable or other part of a word; a part repeated or doubled. **redu'plicative,** a.

re-echo (rĕ-ek'ō), v. To echo again; to return the sound, to resound; to reverberate.

reed (rĕd) [A.-S. hrēod], n. The long straight stem of certain water or marsh plants: a musical pipe of this; a thin strip of metal in a musical instrument producing the sound by a current of air. **reed-pipe,** n. A reeded organ-pipe; a musical pipe made of a reed. **reedy,** a. Abounding in reeds; like a reed.

reef (1) (rēf) [?], n. A ridge of rock, etc., at or near the surface of the sea; a vein of auriferous quartz.

reef (2) [Icel. rif], n. A part of a sail which can be rolled up in order to shorten sail. v.t. To reduce the extent of a sail by taking in a reef. **reefer,** n. A close-fitting double-breasted jacket.

reek (rēk) [A.-S. rēc], n. Smoke; fume; a foul or stale odour, a foul atmosphere. v.i. To emit smoke, vapour, or steam; to give off a disagreeable odour.

reel (1) (rēl) [A.-S. hrēol-, n. A rotatory frame on which thread, etc., can be wound; quantity wound on a reel; a bobbin. v.i. To wind on or take (off) a reel.

reel (2) [?], v.i. To stagger; to have a whirling sensation, to be dizzy. n. A lively Scottish dance; music for this.

re-enforce (rē-en-fôrs'), v.t. To give fresh or additional force or strength to; to reinforce.

reeve (rēv) [?], v.t. (past and p.p. rove, reeved) To pass (the end of a rope, etc.) through a ring, a hole in a block, etc.; to fasten (a rope, etc.) thus.

re-examine (rē-ĕg-zăm'in), v.t. To examine again.

refection (rĕ-fek'shŭn), n. A light meal, a repast. **refectory,** n. A hall where meals are taken in religious houses.

refer (rĕ-fĕr') [L. ferre, to bear], v.t. To trace back, assign (to a certain cause, etc.); to hand over (for consideration, etc.); to send (a person) for information; to commit (oneself) to another's favour, etc. v.i. To apply for information; to cite, allude, direct attention (to); to be concerned with. **ref'erable,** a. **referee',** n. One to whom a question is referred; an arbitrator, umpire. v.i. To act as a referee. **reference** (ref'ĕr-ĕns), n. Act of referring; relation; allusion, directing of attention (to); a note referring from one book to another or to a commentary, diagram, etc.; that which or one who is referred to; a testimonial. **referen'dum,** n. Submission of a political question to the whole electorate. **referen'tial,** a.

refine (rĕ-fin'), v.t. To clear from impurities, to clarify; to educate, polish to cultivate the manners, etc., of; to make more subtle or complex. v.i. To become pure or clear; to become polished in talk, manners, etc.; to affect subtlety of thought or language. **refined,** a. Freed from impurities; highly cultivated, elegant. **refinement,** n. Act or process of refining; state of being refined; elegance of taste, manners, language, etc., polish; elaboration (of luxury, etc.); affected subtlety.

refit (rĕ-fit'), v.t. To make fit for use again, to repair. n. Repairing or renewing, esp. a ship. **refitment,** n.

reflect (rĕ-flekt') [L. flectere, to bend], v.t. To turn (light, heat, sound, etc.) back; to mirror; to cause to accrue (of honour, disgrace, etc.). v.i. To throw back light, etc.; to think, ponder, meditate; to bring shame or discredit (upon). **reflection,** n. Act of reflecting; state of being reflected; that which is reflected; continued consideration, thought, meditation, etc.; censure, reproach. **reflective,** a. **reflector,** n. That which reflects.

reflex (rē'fleks) [L. reflexus, reflected], a. Turned backward; introspective; reactive; bent back; (Physiol.) produced independently of the will. n. A reflection; a reflex action. **reflexive,** a. (Gram.) Denoting action upon the agent; implying action by the subject upon itself or himself; referring back to the grammatical subject.

reform (rė-fôrm') [L. *formāre*, to form], *v.t.* To change from worse to better; to improve, mend, remedy. *v.i.* To amend one's habits, morals, conduct, etc. *n.* The act of reforming; an alteration for the better, improvement, correction of abuses, etc.

re-form (rē-fôrm'), *v.t.* To form again or anew.

reformation (ref-ôr-mā'shŭn), *n.* Act of reforming; state of being reformed; redress of grievances or abuses. the **Reformation:** The movement in the 16th cent. which resulted in the establishment of the Protestant Churches. **refor'- matory** *n.* An institution for the detention and reformation of juvenile offenders. **reformer,** *n.* One who effects or favours a reform; one who took a leading part in the Reformation.

refract (rė-frăkt') [L. *fractus*, broken], *v.t.* To deflect (a ray of light, etc.) from its direct course (of water, glass, etc.). **refraction,** *n.* The deflection that takes place when a ray of light, heat, etc., passes at any other angle than a right angle from the surface of one medium into another medium of different density. **refractory** (rė-frăk'tòr-i), *a.* Perverse, obstinate in opposition, unmanageable.

refrain (1) (rė-frān'), *n.* The burden of a song, a phrase frequently repeated.

refrain (2) [O.F. *refrener*, L. *frēnum*, curb], *v.t.* To hold back, restrain, curb. *v.i.* To forbear; to abstain (from an act, etc.).

refresh (rė-fresh'), *v.t.* To make fresh again; to revive or restore; to freshen up (one's memory). **refreshment,** *n.* That which refreshes, esp. (*pl.*) food or drink.

refrigerate (rė-frij'ér-āt) [L. *frīgus*, cold], *v.t.* To freeze or keep at a very low temperature in a refrigerator. **refrigerant,** *a.* Cooling, allaying heat. *n.* That which cools or refreshes. **refrigera'tion,** *n.* **refrig'erator,** *n.* An apparatus for keeping provisions in a frozen state in order to preserve their freshness.

refuge (ref'ūj) [L. *refugium*], *n.* Shelter from danger or distress; a place, person, course of action, etc., that protects from distress or calamity; a stronghold, a sanctuary; an expedient. **refugee',** *n.* One who flees to a place of refuge.

refulgent (rė-fŭl'jėnt) [L. *fulgens*, shining], *a.* Shining brightly, brilliant. **refulgence,** *n.*

refund (rė-fŭnd') [L. *refundere*, to pour back], *v.t.* To pay back, to reimburse. *v.i.* To make payment. *n.* (rē'fŭnd).

refuse (1) (rė-fūz') [O.F. *refuser*], *v.t.* To decline; to deny the request of; to fail to take. *v.i.* To decline to comply. **refusal,** *n.*

refuse (2) (ref'ūs), *a.* Rejected. *n.* That which is rejected as worthless; waste matter.

refute (rė-fūt') [L. *refūtāre*], *v.t.* To prove (a statement, etc.) false, to disprove; to rebut in argument, to confute. **refutable** (refū'-tabl), *a.* **refuta'tion,** *n.*

regain (rė-gān'), *v.t.* To recover possession of; to reach again; to gain anew.

regal (rē'găl) [L. *rēgālis*], *a.* Pertaining to or fit for a king. **regally,** *adv.*

regale (rė-gāl') [It. *regalare*], *v.t.* To entertain sumptuously. *v.i.* To feast.

regalia (rė-gā'li-à), *n.pl.* The insignia of royalty, esp. the emblems displayed at coronations.

regard (rė-gard') [F. *regarder*], *v.t.* To look at; to give heed to, pay attention to; to value, pay honour to, esteem; to consider (as); to concern, to relate to. *v.i.* To look; to pay attention. *n.* A look, a gaze; observant attention, consideration; kindly or respectful feeling; reference, relation; (*pl.*) good wishes. **regardful,** *a.* **regarding,** *prep.* Respecting, concerning. **regardless,** *a.* Heedless, careless, negligent.

regatta (rė-găt'à) [It., contention], *n.* A race-meeting at which boats contend for prizes.

regency (rē'jėn-si) [L. *regere*, to rule], *n.* The office or government of a regent; a body entrusted with this; the period of office of a regent.

regenerate (rė-jen'ér-āt), *v.t.* To change fundamentally; to impart fresh vigour or higher life to; (*Theol.*) to renew the heart of by the infusion of divine grace; to convert. *a.* Reformed, converted. **regenera'tion,** *n.* New birth as the consequence of baptism. **regen'erative,** *a.*

regent (rē'jėnt) [L. *regere*, to rule], *n.* One appointed to govern a kingdom in place of the sovereign. **regentship,** *n.*

regicide (rej'i-sīd) [L. *rex rēgis*, king, -CIDE], *n.* The killing or one who takes part in the killing of a king. **regici'dal,** *a.*

regime (rė-zhēm') [F. *régime*], *n.* Mode or prevailing system of government, social system, or general state of things.

regimen (rej'i-mėn) [L. *regere*, to rule], *n.* The systematic management of food, drink, exercise, etc., for the preservation or restoration of health.

regiment (rej'i-mėnt), *n.* The largest permanent unit of the army, comprising several companies or troops. **regimen'tal,** *a.* Pertaining to a regiment; stiffly formal. *n.pl.* Military uniform.

region (rē'jŭn) [L. *regio*, from *regere*, to rule], *n.* A large but indefinite tract having certain prevailing characteristics; a district, a sphere, a realm; one of the strata into which the atmosphere or the sea may be divided; the surroundings of a bodily organ. **regional,** *a.*

register (rej'is-tėr) [L. *regesta*, things recorded], *n.* An official record, authoritative list of names, facts, etc., as of births, marriages, deaths, persons entitled to vote, shipping, etc.; a book in which such is kept; registration; a recording indicator; a contrivance for regulating admission of air or heat to a room, ventilator, fire, etc.; musical compass. *v.t.* To enter or cause to be entered in a register; to record, to indicate (of an instrument). **registrable,** *a.* **registrar,** *n.* An official keeper of a register. **reg'istry,** *n.* An office where a register is kept.

regius (rē'ji-ŭs) [L., royal], *a.* Appointed by the sovereign (of certain professors at Oxford and Cambridge).

regnant (rėg'nănt), *a.* Ruling; prevalent.

regrate (rė-grāt') [O.F. *regrater*], *v.t.* To

deal in food-stuffs with the object of raising prices. **regrater,** *n.*

regress (rē'gres) [L. *regressus,* gone back], *n.* Passage back, return. *v.i.* (rē-gres') To move back, to return. **regression,** *n.* Reversion to type; the turning back of a curve.

regret (rē-gret') [O.F. *regrater*], *n.* Sorrow for a disappointment, loss, etc.; grief, repentance, remorse. *v.t.* To be distressed or sorry for; to regard with sorrow or remorse. **regretful,** *a.* **regrettable,** *a.*

regular (reg'ū-lår) [L. *rēgula,* rule], *a.* Conforming to rule, law, or principle; systematic, methodical, unvarying, normal; acting, happening, etc., in an orderly or habitual manner; duly authorized, properly qualified; *(Geom.)* having the sides and angles equal; belonging to the standing army. *n.* A person permanently employed or constantly attending; a soldier of a permanent army; one bound by religious or monastic rules. **regular'ity,** *n.* **reg'-ularize,** *v.t.* **regularly,** *adv.*

regulate (reg'ū-lāt), *v.t.* To adjust or order by rule; to subject to restrictions; to put or keep in good order. **regulable,** *a.* **regula'tion,** *n.* Act of regulating; state of being regulated; a prescribed rule.

rehabilitate (rē-hȧ-bil'i-tāt), *v.t.* To restore to a former rank, privilege, etc., to reinstate; to re-establish one's character. **rehabilita'tion,** *n.* Re-establishment of character; *(Med.)* the branch of occupational therapy which deals with the restoration of the maimed or unfit to a place in society.

rehearse (re-hèrs') [O.F. *rehercer,* to harrow again], *v.t.* To repeat; to relate, enumerate; to recite or practise (a play, etc.) before public performance. **rehearsal,** *n.* Act of rehearsing; a trial performance.

reign (rān) [L. *regnum*], *n.* Sovereignty, rule, sway; the period during which a sovereign reigns. *v.i.* To exercise sovereign authority, to prevail.

reimburse (rē-im-bèrs'), *v.t.* To repay (one who has spent money); to refund (expenses). **reimbursement,** *n.*

rein (rān) [O.F. *rene*], *n.* A long narrow strap attached to a bit for guiding an animal in riding or driving; means of restraint or control. *v.t.* To check, control; *(fig.)* to curb, restrain.

reindeer (rān'dēr) [Icel. *hreinn*], *n.* A subarctic domesticated deer.

reinforce (rē-in-fōrs'), *v.t.* To strengthen as by additional troops, ships, etc., adding to the size, thickness, etc.

reins (rānz) [L. *renes*], *n.pl.* The kidneys.

reinstate (rē-in-stāt'), *v.t.* To restore, to replace (in a former position, etc.). **reinstatement,** *n.* **reinvig'orate,** *v.t.* To reanimate; to give fresh vigour to.

reis (rās) [Port.], *n.pl.* A Portuguese and Brazilian money of account.

reit'erate (rē-it'ér-āt), *v.t.* To repeat again and again. **reitera'tion,** *n.* Repetition.

reject (rē-jekt') [L. *jectus,* thrown], *v.t.* To discard, cast off; to refuse to accept, grant, etc.; to repel; to vomit. *n.* (rē'jekt) Person or thing rejected. **rejec'tion,** *n.*

rejoice (rē-jois') [O.F. *rejoissant,* rejoicing], *v.t.* To gladden. *v.i.* To feel joy or gladness in a high degree; to make merry. **rejoicing,** *n.*

rejoin (rē-join'), *v.i.* To come together again; to retort; to answer a charge or pleading. **rejoinder,** *n.* An answer, esp. to a reply, a retort.

rejuvenate (rē-joo've-nāt) [L. *juvenis,* young], *v.* To make or become young again. **rejuvena'tion,** *n.* **rejuvenes'-cence,** *n.* A renewal of youth; state of this. **rejuvenescent,** *a.*

relapse (rē-lăps') [L. *lapsus,* slipped], *v.i.* To fall back into vicious ways, etc., or into illness after partial recovery; to fall away after conversion or recantation. *n.* A falling or sliding back into a former bad state.

relate (rē-lāt') [L. *relātus*], *v.t.* To tell, to recount; to bring into relation (with); to ascribe to as source or cause. *v.i.* To have regard (to); to refer (to). **related,** *a.* Connected by blood or marriage. **rela'tion,** *n.* Act of relating; that which is related; an account, story; respect; condition of being related; way in which a thing stands in regard to another; kinship; a kinsman or kinswoman. **relationship,** *n.* State of being related; connexion by blood, etc., kinship.

relative (rel'ȧ-tiv), *a.* Being in relation to something; involving, implying, or resulting from relation, comparative; not absolute; corresponding, related; relevant, having reference; *(Gram.)* referring or relating to another word or sentence, called the antecedent. *n.* A person connected by blood or marriage, a relation; a relative word. **rel'a-tively,** *adv.* In relation to something else; comparatively. **relativ'ity,** *n.* A theory enunciated by A. Einstein founded on the postulate that velocity is relative.

relax (rē-lăks'), *v.t.* To slacken, to loosen; to enfeeble, make languid; to mitigate; to relieve from strain or effort. *v.i.* To become less tense, rigid, or severe; to grow less energetic; to take relaxation. **relaxa'tion,** *n.*

relay (rē-lā') [O.F. *relais*], *n.* A supply of fresh horses, etc., to relieve others when tired.

re-lay (rē-lā'), *v.t.* To lay again.

release (rē-lēs'), *v.t.* To liberate; to deliver from pain, care, grief, or other evil; to free from penalty; *(Law)* to surrender (a right, claim, etc.). *n.* Liberation; discharge from liability, responsibility, etc.; *(Law)* surrender of property or right, and the instrument by which this is effected.

relegate (rel'ē-gāt) [L. *legātus,* sent], *v.t.* To consign or dismiss (usu. to an inferior position); to commit, or hand over (to). **relegable,** *a.* **relega'tion,** *n.*

relent (rē-lent') [L. *lentus,* soft], *v.i.* To become less harsh or severe; to yield. **relentless,** *a.* Merciless, obdurate.

relevant (rel'ē-vȧnt) [L. *levans,* raising], *a.* Pertinent, applicable, apposite. **rele-vance, -cy,** *n.*

reliable (rē-li'ȧbl), *a.* That may be relied

on, trustworthy. reliabil'ity, n. reli'ance, n. Confident dependence (upon), trust. reliant, a.

relic (rel'ik) [L. *reliquiæ*, remains], n. Some part remaining, a remnant, a scrap, a survival.

relict (rel'ikt) [L. *lictus*, left over], n. A widow.

relief (rė-lēf'), n. Alleviation of pain, etc.; that which alleviates; assistance given to people in distress; release from a post by a substitute; such a substitute; assistance in time of stress; those carrying this out; (*fig.*) anything that relaxes tension; the projecting of carved figures from a surface; a piece of sculpture, etc., carved thus; apparent projection due to drawing, colouring, and shading.

relieve (rė-lēv') [L. *levāre*, to raise], v.t. To alleviate, lighten, esp. pain, grief, discomfort, monotony, dullness, etc.; to release from a post, responsibility, etc.; to raise the siege of; to bring out or make conspicuous by contrast.

religion (rė-lij'ŭn) [L. *religiōnem*], n. Belief in a personal God entitled to worship and obedience; feelings, effects and practices resulting from such belief; a system of faith, doctrine, and worship. religious (rė-lij'ŭs), a. Imbued with religion; devout; pertaining to religion. n. One belonging to a monastic order. religiously, adv.

relinquish (rė-ling'kwish) [L. *linquere*, to leave], v.t. To forsake, abandon; desist from. relinquishment, n.

reliquary (rel'i-kwá-ri), n. A depository for relics.

relish (rel'ish) [O.F. *reles*, that left behind], n. Effect of anything on the palate, esp. a pleasing flavour; fondness, liking; a flavouring, a trace (of). v.t. To give agreeable flavour to; to partake of with pleasure; to enjoy. v.i. To have a pleasing taste; to taste or smack (of).

reluctant (rė-lŭk'tánt) [L. *luctans*, struggling], a. Resisting, disinclined (to); done or granted unwillingly. reluctance, n. reluctantly, adv.

rely (rė-li') [L. *ligāre*, to bind], v.i. To trust or depend (upon) with confidence.

remain (rė-mān') [L. *manēre*, to stay], v.i. To stay behind or be left over, to survive; to continue in a place or state; to last. n. (*usu. pl.*) That which remains behind; a corpse; writings published after one's death; relics. remainder, n. Anything left over, the rest, the residue; (*Law*) an interest in an estate after a prior interest is determined.

remand (rė-mand') [L. *mandāre*, to commit], v.t. To send back (to); to recommit in custody. n. Act of remanding; state of being remanded.

remark (rė-mark'), v.t. To take notice of, esp. with particular attention. n. Act of noticing; an observation, comment. remarkable, a. Worthy of special observation.

remedy (rem'ė-di) [L. *medēri*, to heal], n. That which cures a disease; that which counteracts or repairs any evil; redress. v.t. To cure, heal; to rectify, redress. reme'diable, a. remedial, a.

remember (rė-mem'bėr) [L. *memor*, mindful], v.t. To keep in or recall to mind, not to forget, to know by heart. remembrance, n. Act of remembering; memory; time over which memory extends; a keepsake, memento; (*pl.*) regards, greetings. remembrancer, n. An officer of the Exchequer who collects debts due to the sovereign.

remind (rė-mind'), v.t. To put in mind (of); to cause to remember. reminder, n.

reminiscence (rem-i-nis'éns) [L. *reminisci*, to remember], n. Act or power of remembering; that which is remembered; (*pl.*) a collection of recollections. reminiscent, a. Recalling past events; reminding or suggestive (of).

remiss (rė-mis'), a. Careless in the performance of duty, negligent; slack, languid.

remission (rė-mish'ŭn), n. Act of remitting; the discharge of a debt, penalty, etc.; pardon; diminution, relaxation.

remit (rė-mit') [L. *mittere*, to send, p.p. *missus*], v.t. To send back; to transmit (cash, etc.); to submit, to refer to a lower court; to defer, to slacken, to mitigate; to forgo, to discharge from (penalty, etc.); to forgive. v.i. To abate. remittal, n. A surrender; remission from one court to another. remittance, n. Act of remitting money; the sum so remitted.

remnant (rem'nánt), n. That which remains; the last part of a piece of cloth, etc.; a scrap, fragment.

remonstrance (rė-mon'stráns) [L. *monstrāre*, to show], n. Act of remonstrating; a formal protest. remonstrant, a. Expostulatory. n. One who remonstrates. remon'strate, v. remonstra'tion, n. remon'strative, a.

remorse (rė-môrs') [RE-, L. *morsus*, bitten], n. Pain caused by a sense of guilt. remorseful, a. remorseless, a.

remote (rė-mōt') [L. *mōtus*, moved], a. Distant in time or space; not related, different; least (*usu. in superl.*).

remove (rė-moov'), v.t. To move from or to a place; to take away, get rid of. v.i. To change one's place of abode. n. A degree of gradation; a dish removed to give place to another; a form in some schools; removal, departure. removable, a. removal, n. Act of removing; change of place or abode; dismissal.

remunerate (rė-mū'nėr-āt) [L. *mūnus*, gift], v.t. To reward, to pay for a service, etc.; to serve as recompense (for or to). remunera'tion, n. remu'nerative, a. Producing a due return; paying, profitable.

Renaissance (rė-nā'-sáns, ren'ā-sans), n. The revival of art and letters in the 14th–16th cents.; the period of this; the style of art developed under it.

renal (rē'nál) [L. *rén*, kidney], a. Pertaining to the kidneys.

renascent (rė-năs'ént) [L. *nascens*, being born], a. Coming into being again; pertaining to the Renaissance. renascence, n. Renewal, a springing into fresh life; the Renaissance.

rencounter (ren-koun'tėr), rencontre (ran kontr), n. An encounter, combat; an unexpected meeting. *v.i.* To clash; to meet an enemy unexpectedly.

rend (rend) [A.-S. *rendan*], *v.t.* (*past and p.p.* **rent**) To tear or wrench (off, apart, etc.); to separate with violence; (*fig.*) to cause anguish to. *v.i.* To be pulled apart.

render (ren'dẽr) [O.F. *rendre*], *v.t.* To give in return; to give up; to present, hand in; to express, represent, translate, execute; to make; to boil down; to give the first coat of plaster to. **rendering**, *n.* A return; a translation, interpretation, execution (of music, a dramatic part, etc.).

rendezvous (ron'dẽ-voo) [F., render or betake yourselves], *n.* A place agreed upon for meeting; a place of common resort. *v.i.* To meet or assemble at a rendezvous.

renegade (ren'ẽ-gãd) [Sp.], *n.* An apostate; a turncoat.

renew (rẽ-nū'), *v.t.* To make new or as good as new, to renovate; to grant a further period of (a lease, etc.). *v.i.* To become young or new again; to grow or begin again. **renewable**, *a.* **renew'al**, *n.*

rennet (ren'ét) [M.E., from *renne*, to run], *n.* A preparation from the stomach-membrane, used to coagulate milk.

renounce (rẽ-nouns') [L. *nuntius*, messenger], *v.t.* To reject formally, to repudiate.

renovate (ren'ó-vãt) [L. *novus*, new], *v.t.* To make new again; to restore, repair. **renova'tion**, *n.* **ren'ovator**, *n.*

renown (rẽ-noun') [A.-F. *renoun*, L. *renominãre*, to name again], *n.* Exalted reputation, celebrity. *v.t.* To make famous, **renowned** (rẽ-nound'), *a.* Eminent, celebrated.

rent (1) (rent), *n.* A tear, slit, or opening made by rending; a cleft, a chasm; (*fig.*) a schism.

rent (2) (rent) [O.F. *rente*], *n.* Periodical payment for the use of any kind of property, esp. land or tenements. *v.t.* To occupy or use in return for rent; to let for rent; to impose rent upon. *v.i.* To be let (at a certain rent). **rent-roll**, *n.* A schedule of a person's property and rents; total income from this source. **rental**, *n.* The total income from rents of an estate.

rentier (ron'ti-ã) [F.], *n.* A person drawing his income from investments.

renunciation (rẽ-nŭn-si-ã'shŭn), *n.* Act of renouncing; self-denial, self-resignation. **renunciatory**, *a.*

reoc'cupy, *v.t.* To occupy again.

rep (rep) [F. *reps*], *n.* A textile with a finely-corded surface.

repair (1) (rẽ-pâr') [L. *patria*, one's native land], *v.i.* To betake oneself, to resort (to). *n.* A place to which one goes often or which is much frequented; a resort.

repair (2) [L. *parãre*, to make ready], *v.t.* To restore to a good state; to renovate, mend; to set right, to make amends for. *n.* Restoration; good or comparative condition.

reparable (rep'á-rábl), *a.* Capable of being repaired or put right. **repara'tion**, *n.* Act of repairing or restoring; state of

being repaired; satisfaction for wrong or damage, compensation. **rep'arative**, *a.*

repartee (rep-àr-tē') [F. *repartir*, to start again], *n.* A smart or witty rejoinder.

repass (rē-pas'), *v.t.* To pass or go past again; to recross. *v.i.* To pass in the opposite direction.

repast (rẽ-past') [L. *pascere*, to feed], *n.* A meal; food; act of taking food. *v.i.* To feed, to feast (upon, etc.).

repatriate (rẽ-pã'tri-ãt) [L. *patria*, one's country], *v.* To restore to or to return to one's country. **repatria'tion**, *n.*

repay (rẽ-pã'), *v.t.* (*past and p.p.* **repaid**) To pay back, refund; to deal (a blow, etc.) in retaliation; to requite. **repay'ment**, *n.*

repeal (rẽ-pēl') [O.F. *apeler*, to appeal], *v.t.* To revoke, annul; to retract. *n.* Abrogation, revocation. **repealable**, *a.*

repeat (rẽ-pēt') [L. *petere*, to seek], *v.t.* To do, make, or say over again; to recite; to imitate. *v.i.* To recur; to strike the hours or quarters (of a watch). **repeatedly**, *adv.* **repeater**, *n.* One who or that which repeats, esp. a fire-arm, or a watch striking the hours and parts of hours when required.

repel (rẽ-pel') [L. *pellere*, to drive], *v.t.* To drive back; to repulse, keep at a distance; to tend to drive back, etc. **repel'lent**, *a.* Repelling or tending to repel; repulsive.

repent (rẽ-pent') [L. *pœnitĕre*, to make contrite], *v.i.* To feel regret for something, esp. to feel such sorrow for sin as leads to amendment; to be penitent or contrite. *v.t.* To feel contrition or remorse for. **repentance**, *n.* **repentant**, *a.*

repercussion (rẽ-pẽr-kŭsh'ón), *n.* Recoil, echo, reverberation.

repertoire (rep-ẽr-twar'), *n.* A stock of musical pieces, plays, etc., that a person or company is ready to perform.

repertory (rep'ẽr-tó-ri) [L. *parere*, to produce], *n.* A storehouse, a magazine, esp. of information, statistics, etc.; a repertoire.

repetition (rep-ẽ-tish'ŭn), *n.* Act of repeating; recital from memory; that which is repeated; a replica.

repine (rẽ-pīn'), *v.i.* To fret oneself, to murmur; to grumble.

replace (rẽ-plãs'), *v.t.* To put back again in place; to take the place of; to supersede, displace. **replaceable**, *a.*

replenish (rẽ-plen'ish) [L. *plēnus*, full], *v.t.* To fill again or completely; to stock abundantly. **replenishment**, *n.*

replete (rẽ-plēt') [L. *plētus*, filled], *a.* Completely filled; abundantly supplied (with). **repletion**, *n.*

replica (rep'li-ká) [It.], *n.* A duplicate by him who executed the original; an exact copy, a facsimile. **replica'tion**, *n.* A reply, rejoinder; an echo.

reply (rẽ-plī') [L. *plicãre*, to fold], *v.i.* To answer, orally, in writing, or by action. *v.t.* To return as in answer. *n.* Act of replying; a response.

report (rẽ-põrt') [L. *portãre*, to bring], *v.t.* To bring back as an answer; to describe, esp. as an eye-witness; to state; to prepare a record of; to take down (a speech, etc.); to announce, to certify; to give information against. *v.i.* To tender a report; to act as a reporter; to announce oneself. *n.* That which is reported; common talk, rumour; repute, accepted character; a loud, esp. explosive, noise. **reporter**, *n.* One who reports, esp. law proceedings, decisions of legislative debates, public meetings, etc. (esp. for a newspaper). *adv.* **reportorial** (-tôr'i-ăl), *a.*

repose (1) (rê-pōz') [L. *positus*, placed], *v.t.* To place, to put (confidence, etc., in). **reposal,** *n.*

repose (2) [L. *pausāre*, to pause], *v.t.* To refresh with rest; to cause to rest. *v.i.* To rest; to lie or be laid at rest. *n.* Rest, cessation of activity, etc.; sleep, tranquillity, composure.

repository (rê-poz'i-tôri) [L. *repositus*], *n.* A place where things are deposited for safety or preservation; a store, a warehouse.

repoussé (rê-poo'sā) [F. *pousser*, to push], *a.* Embossed by hammering from behind (of metal work).

reprehend (rep-rê-hend') [L. *prehendere*, to seize], *v.t.* To find fault with; to censure. **reprehensible,** *a.* **reprehension,** *n.*

represent (rep-rê-zent'), *v.t.* To bring before the mind by describing, imitating, etc.; to serve as a likeness of; to state (that), to make out (to be); to personate; to stand for, be an example of; to act for. **representa'tion,** *n.* Act of representing; a dramatic performance; a statement of arguments, etc.; the system of representing bodies of people. **represen'tative,** *a.* Serving or fitted to represent; typical; acting as agent, etc.; consisting of delegates, etc. *n.* One who or that which represents; an example; an agent, substitute, a person chosen by electors.

repress (rê-pres') [L. *pressus*, pressed], *v.* To restrain, put down, quell; to prevent from breaking out. **repression** (-presh'ûn), *n.* **repres'sive,** *a.*

reprieve (rê-prēv') [O.F. *repris*], *v.t.* To grant a respite to. *n.* Temporary suspension of a sentence on a prisoner; a respite.

reprimand (rep'ri-mand) [F. *reprimer*, to repress], *n.* A severe reproof, a rebuke. *v.t.* (-mand') To reprove severely, esp. publicly.

reprint (rê-print'), *v.t.* To print (a book, etc.) again. *n.* (rê'-) A new impression of a printed work without alteration.

reprisal (rê-pri'zăl) [O.F. *reprisaille*], *n.* Act of seizing by way of indemnification or retaliation.

reproach (rêprōch') [F. *reprocher*], *v.t.* To censure, to upbraid. *n.* Censure mingled with opprobrium or grief; a rebuke; shame, disgrace. **reproachable,** *a.* **reproachful,** *a.* Containing or expressing reproach; upbraiding; infamous.

reprobate (rep'rô-bāt) [L. *reprobātus*], *a.* Abandoned to sin, depraved. *n.* A wicked, depraved wretch. *v.t.* (-bāt) To condemn severely. **reproba'tion,** *n.*

reproduce (rê-prô-dūs'), *v.t.* To produce again; to copy. **reproduction** (-dŭk'-shŭn), *n.* **reproductive, -tory,** *a.*

reproof (rê-proof') [O.F. *reprove*], *n.* Censure, blame, reprehension. **reprove,** *v.t.* To rebuke, esp. to one's face, to chide.

reptile (rep'tĭl, -til) [L. *reptilis*], *a.* Creeping, crawling; (*fig.*) grovelling, servile. *n.* One of a class of animals comprising the snakes, lizards, turtles, crocodiles, etc., moving on the belly or on small, short legs. **reptilian** (-til'i-ăn), *a.* and *n.*

republic (rê-pŭb'lĭk) [L. *rēspublica*], *n.* A State or constitution in which the supreme power is vested in the people, a commonwealth. **republican,** *a.* Pertaining to or consisting of a republic. *n.* One who favours a republican form of government; member of the Republican Party in U.S.A. **republicanism,** *n.*

repudiate (rê-pū'di-āt) [L. *repudium*, divorce], *v.t.* To disown, to disclaim (a debt, etc.); to refuse to admit, accept, recognize, etc.; to cast off. **repudia'tion,** *n.*

repugnance (rê-pŭg'năns) [L. *pugnare*, to fight], *n.* Inconsistency, incompatibility, or opposition, of mind, statements, etc.; antipathy, aversion. **repugnant,** *a.*

repulse (rê-pŭls') [L. *pulsus*, driven], *v.t.* To drive back, esp. by force of arms; to rebuff, to snub; to defeat in argument. *n.* Act of repulsing; the state of being repulsed; a rebuff, failure, disappointment. **repul'sion,** *n.* Act of repulsing; the state of being repulsed; (*Phys.*) the tendency of certain bodies to repel each other; dislike, aversion. **repulsive,** *a.* Acting so as to repel; forbidding, repellent, disgusting.

reputable (rep'û-tăbl), *a.* Being in good repute; respectable, creditable. **reputation** (rep-û-tā'shŭn), *n.* The estimation in which one is generally held; good fame, credit, respectability; character, repute.

repute (rê-pūt') [L. *putāre*, to think], *v.t.* To deem, reckon. *n.* Reputation, fame. **reputed,** *a.* Generally regarded as (usu. with doubt).

request (rê-kwest'), *n.* An expression of desire or the act of asking; that which is asked for; state of being sought after. *v.t.* To ask (that); to address a request to.

requiem (rek'wi-êm) [L., rest], *n.* A Mass for the dead, the musical setting of this; a dirge.

requiescat (rek-wi-es'kăt) [L., let him rest], *n.* A wish for the repose of the dead.

require (rê-kwir') [L. *quærere*, to seek], *v.t.* To ask or claim as a right; to demand, to insist; to have need of, to depend upon for. *v.i.* To be necessary; an essential condition.

requisite (rek'wi-zit), *a.* Required by the nature of things, indispensable. *n.* That which is required. **requisi'tion,** *n.* Act of requiring or demanding as of right; a formal demand or request for the performance of a duty, etc.; an authoritative order; state of being put to use. *v.t.* To make a formal or authoritative demand for, esp. for military purposes; to call in for use.

requite (rê-kwit'), *v.t.* To repay, recompense; to give in return; to reward, to avenge. **requital,** *n.*

rescind (rĕ-sĭnd') [L. *scindere*, to cut], *v.t.* To annul, revoke, abrogate. **rescission** (-sĭzh'ŭn), *n.*

rescript (rĕ'skrĭpt) [L. *rescriptum*], *n.* An edict, decree, official announcement.

rescue (res'kū) [O.F. *rescoure*], *v.t.* To deliver from confinement, danger, etc.; to save. *n.* Deliverance. **rescuer**, *n.*

research (rĕ-sĕrch'), *n.* Diligent and careful inquiry; (*pl.*) systematic study of phenomena, etc.

resemble (rĕ-zĕmbl') [O.F. *resembler*], *v.t.* To be similar to; to have features, etc., like those of. **resemblance**, *n.*

resent (rĕ-zĕnt') [L. *sentire*, to feel], *v.t.* To regard as an insult; to feel or show displeasure at; to cherish bitter feelings about. *v.i.* To feel indignant. **resentful**, *a.* **resentment**, *n.*

reserve (rĕ-zĕrv') [L. *servāre*, to keep], *v.t.* To keep back for future use, to hold over, postpone; to retain; (*in p.p.*) to set apart for a certain fate, to destine. *n.* That which is reserved; (*Mil.*) troops kept for an emergency; state of being reserved; a limitation attached to a price, etc.; reticence, caution in speaking or action. **reserva'tion**, *n.* Act of reserving; that which is reserved; a clause by which something is reserved; a limitation, exception, or qualification. **reserved** (-zĕrvd'), *a.* Reticent, undemonstrative, distant; retained for a particular use. **reser'vist**, *n.* A member of the military or naval reserve.

reservoir (rez'ĕr-vwar), *n.* A receptacle in which anything, esp. fluid, may be stored; an artificial lake for the storage of water in large quantity.

reside (rĕ-zīd') [L. *sedēre*, to sit], *v.i.* To have one's home (at); to be in official residence; (of rights, etc.) to inhere. **res'idence**, *n.* Act or state of residing in a place; the place where one dwells. **Residency**, *n.* The official abode of a minister resident in colony, etc. **resident**, *a.* Residing; having quarters in connexion with one's duties. *n.* One who dwells permanently in a place; a minister residing at a foreign court. **residential** (-den'shăl), *a.* Suitable for or pertaining to residence.

residue (rez'ĭ-dū) [L. *residuus*, remaining], *n.* That which is left over; the remainder. **resid'ual**, *a.* **residuary**, *a.* Pertaining to a residue.

resign (rĕ-zīn') [L. *signāre*, to seal], *v.t.* To give up, relinquish, renounce, abandon; to yield, submit. *v.i.* To give up office, to retire (from). **resignation** (rez-ig-nā'-shŭn), *n.* Act of resigning; a document announcing this; state of being resigned, patience, submission. **resigned** (rĕ-zīnd'), *a.* **resignment**, *n.*

resilient (rĕ-zĭl'ĭ-ĕnt) [L. *saliens*, leaping], *a.* Leaping *or* springing back, recoiling, rebounding. **resilience**, *n.*

resin (rez'ĭn) [L. *rēsīna*], *n.* An amorphous inflammable vegetable substance secreted by plants, esp. the fir and pine. **resinous**, *a.* Pertaining to or resembling resin.

resist (rĕ-zĭst') [L. *sistere*, redupl. of *stāre*, to stand], *v.t.* To strive against, to act in opposition to; to withstand, repel, frustrate, to be proof against. *v.i.* To offer resistance. **resistance**, *n.* Act or power of resisting; refusal to comply; that which hinders or retards. **resistant**, *a.* and *n.* **resistible**, *a.* **resistive**, *a.* **resistless**, *a.*

resolute (rez'ŏ-loot) [L. *resolūtus*, loosened], *a.* Determined, constant in pursuing an object, firm. **resolutely**, *adv.* **resolu'tion**, *n.* Act or process of resolving anything into component parts; a proposition put forward for discussion and approval; a settled purpose; determination, firmness and boldness.

resolve (rĕ-zolv') [L. *solvere*, to loosen], *v.t.* To separate into the component parts; to disintegrate; to analyse mentally, to solve, explain, answer; to make up one's mind, to decide; to pass by vote a resolution that. *n.* A firm decision or determination; resoluteness. **resolvable**, *a.* **resolved** (-rĕ-zolvd'), *a.* Determined, resolute. **resolver**, *n.*

resonant (rez'ŏ-nănt) [L. *sonans*, sounding], *a.* Re-echoing, resounding; able to prolong or reinforce sound, esp. by vibration; prolonged or reinforced thus. **resonance**, *n.*

resort (rĕ-zôrt') [O.F. *resortir*, to come out], *v.i.* To go, betake oneself; to have recourse, to turn to (for aid, etc.). *n.* Act of frequenting a place; state of being frequented; place frequented; recourse; an expedient.

resound (rĕ-zound'), *v.i.* To ring, to re-echo (with); to be filled with sound (of a place); to be re-echoed or prolonged; to make a sensation (of events, etc.). *v.t.* To return the sound of; to spread the fame of.

resource (rĕ-sôrs') [F. *ressource*], *n.* A means of aid; an expedient; (*pl.*) means of support and defence; fertility in expedients, practical ingenuity. **resourceful**, *a.*

respect (rĕ-spekt') [L. *spectus*, looked], *n.* Relation, regard, reference; heed (to); particular, point; deferential regard, demeanour, or attention; (*pl.*) expressions of esteem. *v.t.* To esteem; to treat with consideration. **respectable**, *a.* Of good repute; of fair social standing, decent, passable; not mean, above the average. **respectabil'ity**, *n.* Quality or character of being respectable. **respectably**, *adv.* **respectful**, *a.* Showing respect. **respecting**, *prep.* In regard to, in respect of. **respective**, *a.* Relating severally to each; comparative, relative.

respire (rĕ-spīr') [RE-, L. *spīrāre*, to breathe], *v.* To breathe. **respirable**, *a.* Capable of being respired; fit to be breathed. **respira'tion**, *n.* Act or process of breathing; one act of inhaling and exhaling. **respirator** (res'pī-rā-tŏr), *n.* A contrivance worn over the mouth and nose to exclude injurious matter. **respira'tory**, *a.*

respite (res'pīt), *n.* A temporary intermission of labour, suffering, etc.; a reprieve. *v.t.* To relieve thus; to reprieve; to postpone, defer.

resplendent (rĕ-splen'dĕnt) [L. *splendens*, shining], *a.* Shining with brilliant lustre; gloriously bright. **resplendence**, *n.*

respond (rĕ-spond') [L. *spondēre*, to pledge], *v.i.* To answer; to react (to an external stimulus); to be responsive, to show sympathy (to). respondent, *a.* Giving response; responsive (to); in the position of defendant. *n.* One who answers, esp. in a suit at law, a defendant.

response (rĕ-spons') [as prec.], *n.* Act of answering; a reply, a retort; a versicle said or sung in answer to the priest. responsible, *a.* Liable; morally accountable for one's actions, able to discriminate between right and wrong; trustworthy; involving responsibility. responsibil'ity, *n.* State of being responsible, as for a person, trust, etc.; that for which one is responsible. responsive, *a.* Responding readily, impressionable.

rest (1) (rest) [A.-S.], *n.* Cessation from activity, repose; freedom from care, tranquillity; a period of such cessation or freedom; a prop, a support; (*Mus.*) an interval of silence, the sign indicating this. *v.i.* To cease from exertion, etc.; to repose; to be still; to be free from care, disturbance, etc., to be tranquil; to be supported or fixed, to be based, to lean, to stand (on); to rely (upon). *v.t.* To give repose to, to lay at rest; to place for support, to base. restful, *a.* Soothing; free from disturbance; quiet. restless, *a.* Never still, agitated, fidgety, unsettled, sleepless.

rest (2) [F. *reste*, L. *stāre*, to stand)], *n.* That which is left, the residue; the others. *v.i.* To remain, to continue (in a specified state).

restaurant (res'tô-ront, res-tō-ran) [F.], *n.* A place for refreshment; an eating-house.

restitution (res-ti-tū'shŭn) [L. *restitūtio*], *n.* Act of restoring; making good, reparation.

restive (res'tiv) [O.F. *restif*], *a.* Unwilling to go forward, unruly, refractory (of a horse).

restore (rĕ-stôr') [L. *stāre*, to stand], *v.t.* To bring back to a former state, to reconstruct; to replace; to reinstate; to bring into use again, to renew; to give back. restorable, *a.* restora'tion, *n.* Act of restoring; a restored building, etc.; the Restoration was the re-establishment of the Stuart line in 1660. restorative (res-tor'á-tiv), *a.* Tending to restore. *n.* Food, medicine, etc., for restoring strength, a tonic.

restrain (rĕ-strān') [L. *stringere*, to draw tight], *v.t.* To hold back, to curb; to keep under control, to hold in check. restraint, *n.* Act of restraining; state of being restrained; control, self-repression, reserve; limitation; abridgment of liberty.

restrict (rĕ-strikt'), *v.t.* To limit, confine, keep within bounds. restriction, *n.* restrictive, *a.*

result (rĕ-zŭlt') [L. *saltāre*, to leap], *v.i.* To follow as the consequence, to ensue; to have an issue, to end (in). *n.* Consequence, issue, effect; a quantity, etc., obtained from a calculation. resultant, *a.* Following as a result. *n.* That which results.

resume (rĕ-zūm') [L. *sūmere*, to take], *v.t.* To take back or again; to begin again;

to sum up, recapitulate. *v.i.* To continue after interruption.

résumé (rez'ū-mā), *n.* A summary, a recapitulation, abstract.

resumption (rĕ-zŭmp'shŭn), *n.* Act of resuming. resumptive, *a.*

resurgent (rĕ-sĕr'jĕnt) [L. *surgens*, rising], *a.* Rising again, esp. from the dead.

resurrection (rez-ŭ-rek'shŭn), *n.* A rising again, esp. that of Christ from the dead, and of all the dead at the Last Day; the future state; a springing again into life or prosperity.

resuscitate (rĕ-sŭs'i-tāt) [L. *resuscitātus*], *v.* To revive, to restore or be restored to vigour, usage, etc.; to come to life again. resuscita'tion, *n.*

retail (rē'tāl) [O.F. *retailler*, to cut off a piece], *n.* Sale of commodities in small quantities. *v.t.* (rĕ-tāl') To sell in small quantities; to recount, to re-tell. retailer, *n.*

retain (rĕ-tān') [L. *tenēre*, to hold], *v.t.* To hold possession of, to keep; to maintain, preserve; to engage the services of (esp. counsel); to hold back; to remember. retainer, *n.* One who or that which retains; an attendant; (*Law*) an agreement by which an attorney acts in a case; a preliminary fee paid (esp. to a counsel).

retaliate (rĕ-tăl'i-āt) [L. *tālio*, retaliation], *v.t.* To return evil for evil, to retort in kind. *v.i.* To return like for like, to make reprisals. retalia'tion, *n.* Act of retaliating. retaliative, -tory (rĕ-tăl'i-á-tiv, -tôr-i), *a.*

retard (rĕ-tard') [L. *tardus*, slow], *v.t.* To hinder, impede, to delay the growth, occurrence, etc., of. retarda'tion, *n.*

retch (rēch, rech) [A.-S. *hrǣcan*, from *hrāca*, spittle], *v.i.* To make an effort to vomit.

retention (rĕ-ten'shŭn), *n.* Act of retaining; state of being retained; power of retaining, esp. ideas in the mind. retentive, *a.*

reticent (ret'i-sĕnt) [L. *tacens*, being silent], *a.* Reserved, not disposed to communicate one's thoughts, counsel, etc.; taciturn. reticence, *n.*

reticule (ret'i-kūl) [L. *rēticulum*, a little net], *n.* A hand-bag. retic'ular, *a.* Having the form of a net or net-work.

retina (ret'i-nà) [med. L.], *n.* (*pl.* -nae) A net-like layer behind the eyeball in which the optic nerve terminates.

retinue (ret'i-nū), *n.* The attendants on a distinguished person; a suite.

retire (rĕ-tīr') [O.F. *retirer*], *v.i.* To withdraw, retreat, recede; to give up business, to resign one's office, withdraw from active service; to go to bed; to go into seclusion. *v.t.* To cause to resign; to order (troops) to retire; to withdraw (a bill, etc.) from circulation. retired, *a.* Private, withdrawn from society; having given up business, etc. retirement, *n.* retiring, *a.* Unobtrusive, unsociable.

retort (1) (rĕ-tôrt') [L. *retortus*, twisted back], *n.* A vessel with a long neck bent downwards used for distilling; a large receptacle used for the production of coal-gas.

M

retort (2), *v.t.* To turn or throw back, esp. to turn an argument, etc., against the author; to pay back in kind. *v.i.* To return an argument or charge. *n.* A sharp rejoinder, a repartee.

retouch (rē-tŭch'), *v.t.* To improve (a picture, etc.) by new touches. *n.* A second touch given to a picture, etc. **retrace** (rē-trās), *v.t.* To trace back to the source; to go over (one's track) again. **retraceable**, *a.*

retract (rē-trăkt') [L. *tractus*, drawn], *v.t.* To draw back or in; to recall, disavow. *v.i.* To shrink back; to recall a promise, etc. **retractile**, *a.* **retractil'ity**, *n.* **retracta'tion**, *n.* Act of retracting. **retrac'tion**, *n.* Act or process of drawing in; retraction. **retractive**, *a.* Serving to retract.

retreat (rē-trēt') [L. *retrahere*, to retract], *n.* Act of retiring, esp. before an enemy; state or period of retirement; a place of privacy or seclusion, a refuge. *v.i.* To retire, esp. before an enemy or from an advanced position; to withdraw to a place of privacy, seclusion, or security.

retrench (rē-trench'), *v.t.* To cut down, curtail, diminish; to pare down. *v.i.* To make economies. **retrenchment**, *n.*

retribution (ret-ri-bū'shŭn) [L. *tribuere*, to assign], *n.* A suitable return, esp. for evil; requital. **retrib'utive, -tory**, *a.*

retrieve (rē-trēv') [F. *trouver*, to find], *v.t.* To find and bring; to recover by searching; to re-establish (one's fortunes, etc.); to remedy. **retrievable**, *a.* **retriever**, *n.* A dog trained to fetch in game that has been shot.

retro- [L., behind, backwards], *pref.* Backwards, back; in return; behind. **retrocede** [CEDE], *v.t.* To cede back again; to restore (territory, etc.). *v.i.* (ret'rō-) To move backward; to recede. **retrograde** (ret'rō-grād) [L. *gradi*, to go], *a.* Going or directed backwards; reversed; declining, deteriorating; (of a planet) apparently moving from east to west. *v.i.* To move backward; to deteriorate, to recede.

retrogress (ret'rō-gres), *v.i.* To go backward, to degenerate. **retrogression** (-gresh'ŭn), *n.* **retrogressive** (-gres'iv), *a.*

retrospect (ret'rō-spekt) [L. *spectus*, looked], *n.* A looking back on things past; consideration of previous conditions, etc. **retrospec'tion**, *n.* **retrospective** (-spek'-tiv), *a.*

retroussé (rē-troo'sā) [F.], *a.* Turned up (of the nose).

return (rē-tĕrn'), *v.i.* To come or go back; to revert, to recur. *v.t.* To bring, convey, give, or send back; to repay; to say in reply; to report officially; to elect. *n.* Act of coming or going back, or of giving or sending back; an official report; act of electing, state of being elected; profits on labour, investments, etc. (*often in pl.*). **returning officer:** The presiding officer at an election.

reunion (rē-ū'nyŏn), *n.* Act of reuniting; state of being reunited; a social gathering. **reunite'**, *v.* To join again after separation; to reconcile.

reveal (rē-vēl') [L. *vēlāre*, from *vēlum*, veil],

v.t. To make known by supernatural means; to disclose, to betray.

réveille (rē-vel'i) [F. *réveillez*, awake], *n.* A morning signal by drum or bugle for soldiers to rise.

revel (rev'ĕl) [L. *revellāre*], *v.i.* To make merry, to carouse; to take unrestrained enjoyment (in). *n.* A carouse, a merry-making. **reveller**, *n.* **revelry**, *n.* Boisterous festivity.

revelation (rev-ē-lā'shŭn), *n.* Act of revealing, a disclosing of knowledge or information; that which is revealed, esp. by God to man; the Apocalypse.

revenge (rē-venj') [O.F *revenger*], *v.t.* To exact satisfaction for, to requite, retaliate; to avenge. *v.i.* To exact vengeance. *n.* Act of revenging; retaliation; a means of revenging; vindictiveness. **revengeful** *a.*

revenue (rev'ĕn-ū), *n.* Income; the annual income of a State; the department collecting this.

reverberate (rē-vĕr'bĕr-āt) [L. *verberātus*, beaten, from *verber*, a scourge], *v.t.* To re-echo, to reflect (sound, light, or heat). *v.i.* To be reflected; to resound, to re-echo; to recoil. **reverbera'tion**, *n.* **rever'beratory**, *a.*

revere (rē-vēr') [L. *verērī*, to fear], *v.t.* To regard with awe mingled with affection, to venerate. **rev'erence**, *n.* Act of revering, veneration; a bow, curtsy; a title given to the clergy. *v.t.* To regard or treat with reverence. **reverend**, *a.* Worthy of or entitled to reverence; a title given to clergymen. **reverent**, *a.* Feeling or expressing reverence. **reverential** (-en'shăl), *a.*

reverie (rev'ĕr-i) [F. *rêverie*, from *rêver*, to dream], *n.* A day-dream, an irregular train of thought; a delusion.

reverse (rē-vĕrs') [L. *versus*, turned], *a.* Turned backward, inverted; contrary. *n.* The contrary, the opposite; the back surface (of a coin, etc.); a check, a defeat. *v.t.* To turn in the contrary direction, the other way round, upside down, or inside out; to cause to have a contrary motion or effect; to revoke, annul. *v.i.* To change to a contrary condition, direction, etc. **reversal**, *n.* **reversible**, *a.* **rever'sion**, *n.* Return to a former condition, habit, etc.; the returning of an estate to the grantor or his heirs; the right of succeeding to an estate after the death of the grantee, etc.; a sum payable upon some event, as a death; right or expectation of succeeding to an office, etc. **reversioner**, *n.* One who holds the reversion to an estate. **reverso**, *n.* The left-hand page of an open book.

revert (rē-vĕrt') [L. *vertere*, to turn], *v.t.* To turn (esp. the eyes) back. *v.i.* To go back, return (to a previous condition, etc.); to recur, to turn to again; to come back to the possession of the former proprietor.

review (rē-vū'), *v.t.* To look back on, to go over in memory; to look over carefully and critically; to write a critical review of; to inspect. *v.i.* To write reviews. *n.* A reconsideration, a second view; a revision, esp. by a superior court; a critical account of a book, etc., a periodical containing such; a formal inspection of troops, etc. **reviewer**, *n.*

revile (rē-vīl'), *v.t.* To abuse, to vilify. *v.i.* To be abusive, to rail. **reviler**, *n.*

revise (rē-vīz') [L. *vīsus*, seen], *v.t.* To examine for emendation; to correct. *n.* A revision; a proof-sheet in which corrections have been embodied. **revisable**, *a.* **revision** (rē-vizh'ŭn), *n.* **reviser**, **revisor**, *n.*

revisit (rē-viz'it), *v.t.* To visit again.

revive (rē-vīv'), [L. *vivere*, to live], *v.i.* To return to life, health, vogue, etc.; to gain new life or vigour; to come back to the mind again. *v.t.* To bring back to life, etc.; to resuscitate, renew. **revival**, *n.* Act of reviving; state of being revived; return of life, vigour, etc.; a religious awakening. **revivalist**, *n.* **reviver**, *n.*

revivify (rē-viv'i-fī), *v.t.* To restore to life; to put new life into.

revoke (rē-vōk') [L. *vocāre*, to call], *v.t.* To cancel, to rescind; to take back. *v.i.* (*Cards*) To fail to follow suit when this is possible. *n.* Act of revoking at cards. **rev'ocable**, *a.* That may be revoked. **revoca'tion**, *n.*

revolt (rē-vōlt') [L. *volutāre*, freq. of *volvere*, to roll], *v.i.* To renounce allegiance, to rebel; to feel disgust or repugnance (at). *v.t.* To nauseate, disgust. *n.* A renunciation of allegiance; a rebellion, an insurrection; a change of sides. **revolting**, *a.* Causing disgust or abhorrence.

revolution (rev-ō-loo'shŭn), *n.* Act or state of revolving; a complete rotation or movement round a centre, the period of this; cycle of regular recurrence; a reversal of circumstances, relations, etc.; a fundamental change in government, esp. by force. **revolutionary**, *a.* Pertaining to or tending to produce a revolution in government. *n.* A revolutionist. **revolutionist**, *n.* An advocate of revolution; one who takes an active part in a revolution. **revolutionize**, *v.t.*

revolve (rē-volv') [L. *volvere*, to roll], *v.i.* To turn round; to rotate; to move in a circle or orbit; to roll along. *v.t.* To cause to rotate; to meditate on, ponder over. **revolver**, *n.* A pistol having a revolving breech by which it can be fired several times without reloading.

revue (rē-vū') [F.], *n.* A spectacular musical dramatic entertainment representing topical characters, events, etc.

revulsion (rē-vŭl'shŭn) [L. *vulsus*, pulled], *n.* A sudden or violent change or reaction, esp. of feeling.

reward (rē-wôrd') [A.-F. *rewarder*, O.F. *reguarder*, to regard], *v.t.* To repay, to recompense. *n.* That which is given in return for good or evil done or received; a recompense, requital.

reynard (ren'árd, rā'nàrd) [O.F. *Renart*], *n.* A proper name for the fox.

rhapsodic, -al (răp-sŏd'-ik, -ăl) [Gr. *rhapsōdos*], *a.* Pertaining to rhapsody; (*fig.*) irregular, disconnected; high-flown. **rhap'sodist**, *n.* An ancient Greek reciter of epic poems; any professional reciter; (*fig.*) one who uses high-flown or extravagant language. **rhapsodize**, *v.t.* and

i. **rhapsody**, *n.* (*Gr. Ant.*) An epic poem, or a portion of this for recitation; a high-flown, enthusiastic composition.

rhetoric (ret'ō-rik) [Gr. *rhētorikē technē*, rhetorical art], *n.* Art of effective speaking or writing; eloquence; the use of language for effect or display. **rhetor'ical**, *a.* Pertaining to rhetoric; designed for display, florid, affected, declamatory. **rhetorician** (-rish'án), *n.*

rheum (room) [Gr. *rheuma*, stream], *n.* The thin serous fluid secreted by the mucous glands as tears, saliva, or mucus. **rheumatic** (roo-măt'ik), *a.* Pertaining to, suffering from, or subject to rheumatism. **rheu'matism**, *n.* An inflammatory disease affecting the muscles and joints and attended by swelling and pain.

rhino- [Gr. *rhis rhinos*, nose], *comb. form.* Pertaining to the nose or nostrils.

rhinoceros (rī-nos'ér-ŏs) [Gr. *rhīnokerōs* (*kerōs*, horn)], *n.* A large pachydermatous quadruped of Africa and S. Asia, with one or two horns on the nose.

rhododendron (rō-dō-den'drŏn) [Gr. *rhodon*, rose, *dendron*, tree], *n.* An evergreen shrub akin to the azalea, with brilliant flowers.

rhomb (rom, *before a vowel* romb) [Gr. *rhombos*], *n.* An oblique parallelogram, with equal sides and angles. **rhombic**, *a.* **rhombo-** *comb. form.* **rhombus**, *n.* (*pl.* -bi) A rhomb.

rhubarb (roo'barb) [L. *rha barbarum*, foreign *Rha*, the Volga]. *n.* An herbaceous plant the leaf-stalks of which are used in cookery, and the roots of several Oriental species in the preparation of purgative medicines.

rhyme, rime (rīm) [Gr. *rhuthmos*, rhythm], *n.* A correspondence of sound in the final accented syllable or group of syllables of a line of verse with that of another line; poetry, verse; a word rhyming with another. *v.i.* To make rhymes, to versify; to rhyme with another word. **rhymer, rhymester**, *n.*

rhythm (rithm) [Gr. *rhuthmos*, from *rheein*, to flow], *n.* Movement characterized by regular alternation of strong and weak impulse, stress, sound, etc.; metrical movement; the flow of words. **rhyth'mic, -al**, *a.*

rib (rib) [A.-S. *ribb*], *n.* One of the bones extending outwards and forwards from the spine; a ridge, etc. analogous to this; a curved timber extending from the keel for supporting the side of a ship; a hinged rod forming part of an umbrella-frame; a ridge for stiffening a casting, etc.

ribald (rib'áld) [O.F. *ribaud*, a low ruffian], *n.* A coarse or indecent fellow. *a.* Scurrilous, coarse, licentious (of language). **ribaldry**, *n.*

ribbon (rib'ŏn) [O.F. *riban*], *n.* A narrow strip of silk, satin, etc., used as an ornament or as distinctive mark; a narrow strip of anything.

rice (rīs) [O.P. *riz*, Gr *oruza*], *n.* The white seeds of an E. Indian aquatic grass cultivated for food.

rich (rich) [A.-S. *rīce*], *a.* Wealthy, abounding (in resources, productions, etc.); fertile, well-filled; precious, costly; elaborate; high-flavoured, fat. **riches**, *n.* (*usu. as pl.*) Abundant possessions, opulence. **richly**, *adv.* In a rich manner; abundantly, thoroughly. **richness**, *n.*

rick (rik) [A.-S. *hréac*], *n.* A stack of corn, hay, etc. *v.t.* To make or pile into a rick.

rickets (rik'ĕts) [?], *n.* A disease of children consisting in the softening of the bones, bow-legs, and emaciation. **rickety**, *a.* Shaky, tumble-down, fragile.

ricochet (rik'ŏ-shā, -shet) [F.], *n.* A bounding or skipping of a stone, bullet, etc., over water or other flat surface; a hit so made. *v.i.* To bound in this manner.

rid (rid) [Icel. *rythja*], *v.t.* (*past* **ridded**, rid, *p.p.* rid) To free, to disencumber (of). **riddance**, *n.*

riddle (1) (ridl) [A.S. *rœdels*], *n.* An ambiguous question; a puzzle, conundrum, enigma.

riddle (2) [A.S. *hriddel*, from *hrid-*, to shake], *n.* A coarse sieve. *v.t.* To sift; to perforate with holes, as with shot. **riddlings**, *n.pl.* Screenings, siftings.

ride (rid) [A.-S. *rīdan*], *v.i.* (*past* **rode**, *p.p.* **ridden**) To sit and be carried along, as on a horse, cycle, conveyance, etc.; to practise horsemanship; to lie at anchor; to work (up). *v.t.* To sit on and be carried along by (a horse, etc.); to traverse on a horse, cycle, etc.; to tyrannize, to domineer (over). *n.* The act of riding, a journey on horseback or in or on a conveyance, a road for riding on. **ridable**, *a.* **rider**, *n.* One who rides, esp. on a horse; an additional clause, an opinion, recommendation, etc., added to a verdict; a subsidiary problem.

ridge (rij) [A.-S. *hrycg*], *n.* The long horizontal angle formed by the junction of two slopes; a long elevation of the earth's surface; a strip of ground thrown up by a plough. *v.t.* To form into ridges.

ridicule (rid'i-kūl) [L. *ridiculus*, laughable], *n.* Words or actions expressing contempt; derision, mockery. *v.t.* To laugh at, make fun of; to expose to derision. **ridic'ulous**, *a.*

riding (ri'ding) [A.-S. *thriding*], *n.* Each of the three divisions of Yorkshire.

rife (rīf) [A.-S. *rȳfe*], *a.* Occurring in great quantity; prevalent, common.

rifle (rifl) [O.F. *rifler*, to scrape], *v.t.* To plunder, pillage, strip; to snatch and carry off; to make spiral grooves in the barrel of a fire-arm to give a rotary motion to the projectile. *n.* A gun or musket having the barrel spirally grooved; (*pl.*) troops armed with rifles.

rift (rift) [Scand.], *n.* A cleft, a fissure; a wide crack made by splitting. *v.* To cleave, split, break open.

rig (rig) [?], *v.t.* To fit (a ship) with tackle; to dress or fit (up or out); to put together in a hasty way. *n.* The style of the masts and sails of a ship; the look of a person's clothes, etc.; an outfit. **rigger**, *n.* One who rigs vessels. **rigging**, *n.* The system of tackle supporting the masts and controlling the sails of a ship.

right (rīt) [A.-S. *riht*], *a.* Equitable, just, true, correct, fit, suitable; properly done, not mistaken, satisfactory; real; on the side towards the south when the face is to the sunrise. *adv.* In accordance with truth and justice, equitably; aright, exactly, correctly, well; very, to the full; to the right hand; all the way to. *n.* That which is just; equitable treatment; the cause having justice on its side; just claim or title, justification; that which one is entitled to; correct or satisfactory state; the right-hand side or part of anything; (*Polit.*) the Conservative party in political views. *v.t.* To set in an upright, correct, or proper position, to make right, to rectify; to do justice to. **right-about**, *n.* The opposite direction, the reverse. **rightful**, *a.* Just, equitable, fair; deserved, fitting. **rightly**, *adv.* Justly, fairly; honestly; accurately, properly.

righteous (ri'chŭs), *a.* Just, upright, morally good; deserved, fitting. **righteously**, *adv.* **righteousness**, *n.*

rigid (rij'id) [L. *rigidus*], *a.* Stiff, not pliant, unyielding; rigorous, stern, austere. **rigid'ity**, *n.*

rigmarole (rig'mà-rōl) [?], *n.* A long unintelligible story; loose disjointed talk.

rigor (rig'ŏr) [L.], *n.* A shivering attended with stiffening, premonitory of fever.

rigour (rig'ŏr) [L. *rigor*, from *rigēre*, to be stiff], *n.* Exactness in enforcing rules; inflexibility; austerity of life; sternness; inclemency of weather, etc., distress. **rigorous**, *a.*

rilievo (rē-lyā'vō) [It.], *n.* (*pl.* **-vi**, **-vē**) Raised or embossed work, relief.

rill (ril) [Teut.], *n.* A rivulet.

rim (rim) [A.-S. *rima*], *n.* An outer edge, esp. of a circular object; a ring or frame.

rime (rīm) [A.-S. *hrim*], *n.* Hoar-frost.

rimose, **-mous** (ri'mŏs, -mŭs) [L. *rima*, chink], *a.* Full of cracks, as the bark of trees.

rind (rind) [A.-S.], *n.* The outer coating of fruits, etc.; bark, peel, husk.

rinderpest (rin-dĕr-pest) [G. *rinder*, oxen, PEST], *n.* A malignant contagious disease attacking oxen, cattle-plague.

ring (1) (ring) [A.-S. *hring*], *n.* A circle, esp. one of gold worn on a finger; a concentric band of wood formed by the annual growth of a tree; a circular group of people, things, etc.; a circular arena; a combination of persons acting selfishly in concert. *v.t.* (*past and p.p.* **ringed**) To put a ring round; to encircle, hem in. **ring-dove**, *n.* A wood-pigeon. **ringleader**, *n.* The leader of a riot, mutiny, etc. **ringlet**, *n.* A curly lock of hair. **ringworm**, *n.* A contagious skin-disease, caused by a white fungus.

ring (2) [A.-S. *hringan*], *v.i.* (*past* **rang**, *p.p.* **rung**) To give a clear, vibrating, metallic sound; to re-echo, reverberate, continue to sound; to tingle (of the ears); to give a signal by ringing. *v.t.* To cause to ring; to sound on a bell, etc., by ringing. *n.* The sound of a bell or other resonant body; a set of bells; the quality of resonance; characteristic sound of a voice, etc.

rink (ringk) [?], *n.* A piece of ice marked off for curling; a floor for skating.

rinse (rins) [F. *rincer*], *v.t.* To cleanse, esp. with a second lot of clean water.

riot (rī'ŏt) [O.F. *riote*], *n.* An outbreak of lawlessness, a tumult, an uproar; unrestrained conduct, loose living, profligacy; revelry; (*fig.*) luxuriant growth. *v.i.* To take part in a riot. **rioter,** *n.* **riotous,** *a.*

rip (1) (rip) [Scand.], *v.t.* To tear or cut forcibly (out, off, up, etc.); to rend. *v.i.* To tear; to go along at a great pace. *n.* A rent, a tear.

rip (2) [?], *n.* A scamp, a rake.

riparian (ri-pâr'i-ăn) [L. *rīpa*, bank], *a.* Pertaining to the banks of a river.

ripe (rip) [A.-S. *rīpe*], *a.* Ready for gathering; mature, fully developed, mellow. **ripen,** *v.t.* and i.

riposte (ri-pŏst') [F. *riposte*, It. *risposta*, *repartee*], *n.* A quick reply, a retort, a repartee; a counterstroke.

ripple (ripl) [?], *v.i.* To run in small waves; to sound as water running over a rough surface, *n.* The ruffling of the surface of water; a wavelet (of water, hair, etc.); a sound as of rippling water.

rise (rīz) [A.-S. *rīsan*], *v.i.* (*past* **rose,** *p.p.* **risen,** rizn) To move upwards, to ascend, to soar; to get up, to become erect; to adjourn; to slope up; to come to the surface or into sight; to revolt. *n.* The act of rising; ascent, elevation; an upward slope; a knoll; source, origin; increase in price, power, rank, age, prosperity, height, salary, etc.; upward progress, advancement; the vertical part of an arch, step, etc.; appearance above the horizon (of the sun, etc.). **rising,** *n.* A mounting up; a resurrection; a revolt.

risible (riz'ibl) [L. *rīsus*, laughed], *a.* Inclined to laugh; exciting laughter. **risibil'ity,** *n.*

risk (risk) [F. *risque*], *n.* Hazard, chance of harm, loss, etc. *v.t.* To expose to hazard; to take the chances of. **risky,** *a.* Dangerous, hazardous; indelicate.

rissole (ris'ōl) [F.] *n.* A fried ball of minced meat, fish, etc., with breadcrumbs, etc.

rite (rīt) [L. *rītus*], *n.* A religious or solemn prescribed act; (*pl.*) ceremonies or forms of worship of any religion.

ritual (rit'ū-ăl), *a.* Pertaining to rites. *n.* A prescribed manner of performing divine service; performance of rites and ceremonies, esp. in an elaborate way; a book setting forth particular rites and ceremonies. **ritualism,** *n.* A system of ritual; exaggerated observance of ritual. **Ritualist,** *n.* **ritualis'tic,** *a.*

rival (rī'văl) [L. *rivālis*, originally one using the same brook, from *rivus*, brook], *n.* One's competitor for something; one striving to surpass another, an emulator. *a.* Being a rival, having the same claims or pretensions. *v.t.* To vie with, to emulate. **rivalry,** *n.*

rive (rīv) [Icel. *rīfa*], *v.* (*p.p.* **riven,** rivn) To tear or rend asunder; to wrench (off, etc.); to split; to be easily split.

river (riv'er) [A.-F. *rivere* L. *rivus*, stream], *n.* A large stream of water flowing overland in a channel to the sea, a lake, or another river; (*fig.*) an abundant stream,

a copious flow. **riverine** (-īn), *a.* Pertaining to or resembling a river; riparian.

rivet (riv'ét) [F. *river*, to clinch], *n.* A short bolt for fastening metal plates, etc., together. *v.t.* To join with rivets; to clinch; (*fig.*) to fix (attention, eyes, etc., upon). **riveter,** *n.*

rivulet (riv'ū-lět), *n.* A streamlet.

roach (rōch) [O.F. *roche*], *n.* A freshwater fish allied to the carp.

road (rōd) [A.-S. *rād*], *n.* A track for travelling on, a highway; route, course; a roadstead. **road-metal,** *n.* Broken stones for road-making. **roadstead,** *n.* A place where ships may ride at anchor at some distance from the shore.

roam (rōm) [?], *v.i.* To wander about without any definite purpose, to ramble.

roan (1) (rōn) [O.F.], *a.* Of a dark colour, with spots of grey thinly interspersed. *n.* A roan colour or animal, esp. a horse.

roan (2) [? *Rouen*, France], *n.* A soft flexible leather made of sheepskin tanned in a particular way.

roar (rōr) [A.-S. *rārian*], *v.i.* To make a loud, deep, hoarse. continued sound, as a lion, a person in rage, the sea, thunder, guns, etc.; to make a noise in breathing (of a diseased horse). *v.t.* To shout or utter with a roar. *n.* A loud, deep, continued sound as of a lion, etc.; a confused din resembling this; a burst of mirth. **roarer,** *n.* A broken-winded horse. **roaring,** *a.*

roast (rōst) [O.F. *rostir*, from Teut.], *v.t.* To cook by exposure to direct action of heat; to heat excessively. *v.i.* To dress meat by roasting; to be roasted. *n.* Roast meat. **roasting-jack,** *n.* A contrivance for turning a spit.

rob (rob) [O.F. *robber, rober*], *v.t.* To despoil of anything unlawfully; to plunder, deprive, strip (of). *v.i.* To commit robbery. **robber,** *n.* **robbery,** *n.* The act or practice of robbing.

robe (rōb) [O.F.], *n.* A long loose outer garment; a vestment of state, rank, or office. *v.t.* To invest with a robe; to clothe, to dress.

robin (rob'in) [fam. for *Robert*], *n.* A small warbler, the redbreast.

robot (rō'bot) [from Karl Capek's play *R.U.R.*], *n.* A man-like mechanism; (*fig.*) a mechanical, efficient person devoid of sensibility.

robust (rō-bŭst') [L. *rōbustus*], *a.* Strong, hardy, capable of endurance.

rochet (roch'ét) [O.F., from Teut.], *n.* A kind of surplice open at the sides, worn by bishops.

rock (1) (rok) [O.F. *roke*], *n.* The solid matter constituting the earth's crust; a mass of it, esp. forming a hill, islet, etc.; a detached block of stone; a hard sweetmeat. **rock-crystal,** *n.* The finest and most transparent kind of quartz. **rock-salt,** *n.* Salt found in stratified beds. **rockery,** *n.* A pile of rocks, stones, and earth, with places for Alpine and other plants.

rock (2) [A.-S. *roccian*], *v.t.* To move backwards and forwards; to swing, to lull to sleep; to cause to sway. *v.i.* To sway, to reel. **rocker,** *n.* One who or that which rocks; a curved piece on which a cradle, etc., rocks. **rocking-horse,** *n.* A wooden horse on rockers.

rocket (rok'ĕt) [F.], *n.* A name for some plants used for salads, etc.; a projectile firework used for display, signalling, conveying a line to stranded vessels, etc. *v.i.* To fly straight up or fast and high; a projectile containing its own propellant.

rocky (1) (rok'i), *a.* Full of rocks; consisting of or resembling rock; rugged, obdurate.

rocky (2), *a.* Unsteady, tottering.

rococo (rō-kō'kō) [F.], *n.* A florid, debased kind of ornamentation of the 17th and 18th cents. *a.* Debased, eccentric, quaint, antiquated.

rod (rod) [A.-S. *rodd*], *n.* A straight, slender stick, a wand; a bundle of twigs as an instrument of punishment; a fishing-rod; a slender bar of metal in machinery; a measure of 5½ yards.

rodent (rō'dĕnt) [L. *rōdens,* gnawing], *a.* Gnawing. *n.* An animal having two (or sometimes four) strong incisors and no canine teeth, comprising the squirrel, beaver, rat, etc.

rodeo (rō-dā'ō) [Sp.], *n.* A popular tournament featuring contests in horse-riding, shooting, etc.

rodomontade (rod-ō-mon-tād') [*Rodomont,* Saracen leader in 'Orlando Furioso'], *n.* Brag, bluster.

roe (1) (rō), **roe-deer** [A.-S. *rāha*], *n.* A small species of deer. **roebuck,** *n.* The male roe.

roe (2) [Teut.], *n.* The spawn of fishes, amphibians, etc.; the sperm or milt, called the soft roe.

rogation (rō-gā'shŭn) [L. *rogāre,* to ask], *n.* (*usu. in pl.*) A solemn supplication or litany.

rogue (rōg) [16th cent. cant], *n.* A knave, a scamp, a trickster, a swindler; a playful term for a child; a vicious elephant or horse. **roguery,** *n.* **roguish,** *a.*

roister (roi'stėr), *v.i.* To behave uproariously, to revel boisterously. **roisterer,** *n.* One who roisters.

role (rōl), *n.* A part taken by an actor; any function one is called on to perform.

roll (rōl) [O.F. *roler,* from L. *rotula,* dim. of *rota,* wheel], *v.t.* To send or cause to move along by turning over and over; to knead, flatten, or level with rollers; to wrap (up in); to form into a cylindrical shape. *v.i.* To move along by turning over and over and round and round; to revolve; to move or shift about with a rotary motion (of eyes, etc.); to reel, to move with a swaying motion. *n.* Anything rolled up; a small loaf; an official record, a register, esp. of names of solicitors, soldiers, schoolboys, etc.; a roller; a rolling gait; a peal of thunder, a continuous beating of a drum. **roll-call,** *n.* The act of calling over a list of names at muster. **roller,** *n.* One who or that which rolls; a cylindrical body turning on its axis; a long, swelling wave. **rolling-pin,** *n.* A wooden roller for rolling out dough, etc. **rolling stock.** The coaches, vans, locomotives, etc., of a railway.

rollick (rol'ik) [?], *v.i.* To frolic, revel, to

be boisterously merry. *n.* A frolic, a spree, an escapade.

roly-poly (rō'li-pō'li), *a.* Plump, podgy. *n.* A sheet of paste, spread over with jam, rolled up, and boiled.

Romaic (rō-mā'ik) [Gr. *Rōmaikos*], *n.* The vernacular language of modern Greece.

Roman (rō'mán), *a.* Pertaining to ancient Rome, its territory, or people; denoting numerals expressed in letters; ordinary upright printed letters used as dist. from italic or gothic; pertaining to the Roman Catholic Church. **Roman nose:** with high bridge, aquiline.

romance (rō-măns') [O.F. *romanz*], *n.* A mediæval tale of chivalry, usu. in verse; a prose story with characters, scenery, and incidents more or less remote from ordinary life; the atmosphere of imaginary adventure; an episode, love-affair, etc., having this character; a fiction, a fib. *a.* Pertaining to languages sprung from Latin or to the peoples speaking them. *v.i.* To tell extravagant stories; to make false or imaginary statements. **romancer,** *n.* A writer of romances; one who exaggerates. **romancist,** *n.* A writer of romances.

romanesque (rō-má-nesk'), *a.* Applied to the architecture that succeeded the Roman and lasted till the introduction of Gothic; Romance.

romantic (rō-măn'tik) [F. *romantique*], *a.* Pertaining to romance; imaginative, poetic, fanciful; unpractical; wild, picturesque (of scenery); pertaining to the movement in literature and art tending away from the sanity of classicism. **romanticism** (-sizm), *n.* The quality or state of being romantic; the reaction from classical to mediæval forms.

Romany (rom'á-ni) [native], *n.* A Gipsy; Gipsies; the Gipsy language.

romp (romp), *v.i.* To play roughly; to go rapidly (along) with ease. *n.* A child or girl fond of romping; rough or boisterous play.

rondeau (ron'dō) [F.], *n.* A poem in ten or thirteen lines, with only two rhymes, the opening words coming twice as a refrain.

rondel (ron'dĕl) [F.], *n.* A particular form of rondeau.

rondo (ron'dō) [It.], *n.* A musical composition having a principal theme which is repeated after each subordinate theme.

Röntgen rays (runt'gĕn rāz) [von *Röntgen* (1845–1923), discoverer], *n.pl.* A form of radiant energy penetrating most substances opaque to ordinary light, employed for photographing concealed objects.

rood (rood) [A.-S. *rōd*], *n.* A crucifix, esp. one on a screen; the fourth part of an acre.

roof (roof) [A.-S. *hrōf*], *n.* The upper covering of a building, vehicle, etc.; the palate; a covering, canopy; a house. *v.t.* To cover with a roof; to be the roof of; to shelter. **roof-tree,** *n.* The ridge-pole of a roof. **roofing,** *n.*

rook (1) (ruk) [A.-S. *hrōc*], *n.* A gregarious British bird of the crow family with glossy black plumage; (fig.) a cheat; a sharper. v.t. To cheat, to swindle; to charge extortionately. **rookery**, n. A clump of trees where rooks nest; a colony of rooks; a place frequented by sea-birds or seals for breeding; (fig.) a low neighbourhood densely populated. **rooky**, a.

rook (2) [Pers. rukh], n. The castle at chess.

room (rum) [A.-S. rūm], n. Space, accommodation, capacity; opportunity, scope; a portion of space enclosed by walls, floor and ceiling; (pl.) apartments, lodgings. **roomy**, a. Having ample room; spacious.

roost (roost) [A.-S. hrōst], n. A perch for birds, esp. fowls, to rest on; (fig.) a resting-place. v.i. To perch on or sleep on a roost. **rooster**, n. The domestic cock.

root (root) [A.-S.], n. The descending part of a plant which fixes itself in the earth and draws nourishment therefrom; the part of an organ or structure that is embedded; the fundamental part, that which supplies origin, sustenance, etc.; the elementary part of a word as dist. from its inflexional forms and derivatives; (Math.) the number that, multiplied by itself a specified number of times, yields a given quantity. v.i. To take root; to turn up the ground with the snout, etc.; to rummage (about, in, etc.). v.t. To cause to take root; (fig.) to fix firmly (to the spot); to pull (up) by the roots; to dig, turn, or grub (up) with the snout, beak, etc.; (Am.) to encourage noisily, to cheer for. **rootedly**, adv.

rope (rōp) [A.-S. rap], n. A stout cord of twisted fibres or wire; cordage over 1 in. in circumference; a series of things strung together in a line.. v.t. To tie, fasten, or enclose with rope. **rope-walk**, n. A long piece of ground where ropes are twisted.

rorqual (rôr'kwàl) [Norw. röyrkval, red whale], n. A whale with dorsal fins.

rosaceous (rō-zā'shŭs) [L. rosāceus, rose-coloured], a. Pertaining to the roses; rose-like. **rosarium**, n. A rose-garden.

rosary (rō'zȧ-ri) [L. rosārium, rose-garden], n. A rose garden; (R.-C. Ch.) a form of prayer in which 15 decades of aves, each decade preceded by a paternoster and followed by a gloria, are repeated; a string of beads by means of which account is kept of the prayers uttered.

rose (rōz) [A.-S., L. rosa], n. A prickly bush or climbing or trailing shrub bearing flowers from white and yellow to dark crimson; one of the flowers; a light crimson or pink colour or complexion; a rosette, ornament, or other object shaped like a rose; a perforated nozzle for a hose, etc.; erysipelas. a. Coloured like a rose. **rose-bud**, n. A flower-bud of a rose; (fig.) a young girl. **rose-coloured**, a. (fig.) Attractive, sanguine, optimistic. **rose-window**, n. A circular window filled with tracery branching from the centre. **rosewood**, n. A hard close-grained fragrant wood of a dark-red colour.

roseate (rō'zē-ȧt), a. Rose-coloured, rosy; (fig.) smiling, optimistic.

rosemary (rōz'mȧ-ri) [O.F. rosmarin (L. rōs, dew, marinus, marine)], n. An evergreen fragrant shrub of the mint family, etc.

roseola (rō-zē'ō-lȧ), n. German measles; a rose-coloured rash.

rosery (rō'zėr-i), n. A place where roses grow, a rose-plot, a rosarium.

rosette (rō-zet'), n. A rose-shaped ornament; a bunch of ribbons, etc., arranged concentrically.

rosin (roz'in), n. The resin left after the oil has been distilled from crude turpentine.

roster (ros'tėr) [Dut. rooster], n. A list showing the order of rotation in which turns of duty are to be performed.

rostrum (ros'trŭm) [L., beak], n. (pl. -tra) (Rom. Ant.) The beak of a war-galley; a platform in the Forum, hence, an orator's stand, a pulpit. **rostral**, a.

rosy (rō'zi), a. Resembling a rose; blooming; favourable. rosily, adv. **rosiness**, n.

rot (rot) [A.-S.], v.i. To decay, decompose, putrefy; to become morally corrupt. v.t. To cause to rot. n. Putrefaction, rottenness; dry-rot; a malignant liver-disease in sheep, etc.

rota (rō'tȧ) [L., wheel], n. A list of names, duties, etc., a roster. **rotal**, a. **ro'tary**, a. Rotating on its axis; characterized by rotation. **rotate'**, v.i. To revolve round an axis; to act in rotation. **rota'tion**, n. Act of rotating, rotary motion; alternation, regular succession. **ro'tatory**, a.

rote (1) (rōt) [?], n. Mere repetition of words, etc., without understanding.

rote (2) (rōt) [O.F., prob. from Celt.], n. A mediæval musical instrument like a fiddle.

rotor (rō'tor), n. (Elec.) the rotating part of an electric machine.

rotten (rŏt'én), a. Decomposed, decaying, tainted; unsound, liable to break, tear, etc.; morally corrupt; contemptible in quality.

rotund (rō-tŭnd') [L. rotundus, round], a. Sonorous; circular, spherical; plump. **rotunda**, n. A circular building, esp. with a dome. **rotun'dity**, n.

rouble (roobl) [Rus. ruble], n. The Russian monetary unit, a silver coin nominally worth about 2s. 0½d.

roué (roo'ā) [F., broken on the wheel], n. A rake, a debauchee.

rouge (roozh) [F.], n. A reddish cosmetic used on the cheeks or lips; red oxide of iron for polishing. v. To colour with rouge.

rough (rŭf) [A.-S. rūh], a. Having an uneven surface, not smooth, level, or polished; shaggy, of coarse texture; rude, lacking finish, crude; approximate, general. n. Rough ground; a hooligan; (collect.) rough or harsh experiences, hardships. v.t. To roughen; to shape (out) roughly. **rough-cast**, v.t. To form or compose roughly; to coat with coarse plaster. n. A rough model; a coarse plastering of lime and gravel, for outside walls, etc. **rough-rider**, n. A horse-breaker; an irregular horse-soldier. **rough-shod**, a. Shod with roughened shoes; (fig.) domineering. **roughen**, v.t. and i.

rouleau (roo-lō'), *n.* (*pl.* -**leaux**) A small roll, esp. a pile of coins done up in paper.

roulette (roo-let'), *n.* A game of chance played with a revolving disk.

round (round) [L. *rotundus*], *a.* Spherical, circular, cylindrical, or approximately so; convexly curved; evenly divisible by ten. *n.* A round object; a ladder-rung; a thick cut from the haunch (of beef); circumference; a circuit, a heat, a recurrent series, a bout. *adv.* So as to encircle. *prep.* On all sides of; in all directions from (in relation to the axis or centre). *v.t.* To make round or curved. **round-about**, *a.* Circuitous, indirect. *n.* A merry-go-round; a circuitous journey, etc.; place where traffic has to follow a circular course. **roundhead**, *n.* A term applied during the Civil War to the Parliamentarians. **round robin**: a petition with the signatures placed in a circle so that no name heads the list. **round-up**, *v.t.* To gather (pressed men, horses, etc.) together. *n.* A gathering together of such. **roundelay**, *n.* A simple song; a bird's song; a round dance. **roundish**, *a.* **roundly**, *adv.* Bluntly, straightforwardly. **roundness**, *n.*

rouse (1) (rouz) [?], *v.t.* To raise (game) from a covert; to wake; to provoke, to stir (up). *v.i.* To wake or be wakened; to start up; to be excited to activity, etc.

rouse (2), *n.* A bumper; a carouse.

rout (rout) [O.F. *route*, a troop], *n.* A crowd, a disorderly concourse; an utter defeat; a confused retreat; a large evening party. *v.t.* To defeat utterly and put to flight.

route (root, *Mil.* rout) [F.], *n.* A course or road.

routine (roo-tēn') [F.], *n.* A course of procedure regularly pursued; any regular habit or practice.

rove (rōv) [?], *v.i.* To ramble, to roam. *v.t.* To wander over, through, etc.; to draw out slivers of wool, cotton, etc., from a carding-machine before spinning into thread; to ravel out. *n.* Act of roving; a ramble. **rover**, *n.* A pirate, a freebooter; a wanderer; a senior Boy Scout.

row (1) (rō) [A.-S. *ráw*], *n.* A series of persons or things in a straight line; a rank.

row (2) (rō) [.-S. *rówan*], *v.t.* To propel by oars; to convey by rowing. *v.i.* To row a boat; to labour with an oar. *n.* A spell at rowing; an excursion in a row-boat. **rowlock** (rŭl'ŏk), *n.* A notch or device on the gunwale of a boat serving as a fulcrum for an oar. **rower**, *n.*

row (3) (rou) [?], *n.* (*colloq.*) A noisy disturbance, a din, tumult, quarrel.

rowan (rou'-, rō'ăn) [Scand.], *n.* The mountain-ash.

rowdy (rou'di) [?], *n.* A noisy or disorderly fellow. *a.* Rough, blackguardly. **rowdyism**, *n.*

rowel (rou'ĕl) [O.F. *rouel*], *n.* A spiked wheel on a spur.

royal (roi'ăl) [O.F. *roial*], *a.* Pertaining to or befitting a king or queen; princely; noble, majestic; surpassingly fine; a size of paper 20 × 25 in. for printing. **royalist**, *n.* An adherent or supporter of monarchical government. *a.* Supporting this; belonging to the Royalists. **royally**, *adv.* **royalty**, *n.* Office or dignity of a king or queen; royal rank or lineage; a royal person or persons; a share of profits paid to a landowner for the right to work a mine, to a patentee, to an author, etc.

rub (rŭb) [?], *v.t.* To apply friction to; to polish, scrape, graze; to slide or pass (a hand or other object) along, over, or against something; to take an impression of a design on paper laid over it; to remove by rubbing. *v.i.* To move along the surface of, to grate, chafe (against, on, etc.). *n.* The act or a spell of rubbing; (*fig.*) a hindrance, difficulty.

rubber (1) (rŭb'ĕr), *n.* One who or that which rubs; a part of a machine that rubs, grinds, polishes, etc.; india-rubber.

rubber (2) [?], *n.* A series of three games at whist, etc.; two games out of three, or that which decides the contest.

rubbish (rŭb'ish) [M.E. *robows*, A. F. *robeux*], *n.* Waste matter, refuse; trash. **rubbishy**, *a.*

rubble (rŭbl) [Scand.], *n.* Rough, broken fragments of stone, etc.; disintegrated rock, stones; masonry of irregular fragments of stone.

rubicund (roo'bi-kŭnd) [L. *rubicundus*], *a.* Ruddy, rosy.

rubric (roo'brik) [L. *rubrica*, from *ruber*, red], *n.* A title, chapter-heading, or direction printed in red, esp. in the Prayer Book, etc.

ruby (roo'bi) [O.F. *rubi*, L. *rubeus*, red], *n.* A precious stone of a red colour; a purplish red; a size of type between nonpareil and pearl. *a.* Of the colour of a ruby.

ruck (1) (rŭk) [?], *n.* A heap, a rick; a crowd, the common herd.

ruck (2) [Icel. *hrukka*], *n.* A crease, a fold. *v.t.* To wrinkle, to crease.

rucksack (ruk'săk) [G., back-sack], *n.* A valise carried on the back by straps.

rudder (rŭd'ĕr) [A.-S. *róther*], *n.* A solid piece hinged to the stern-post for steering a ship; an analogous implement for steering airships, etc.

ruddle (rŭdl), *n.* Red ochre for marking sheep.

ruddy (rŭd'i), *a.* Of a reddish colour; of a healthy complexion. **ruddiness**, *n.*

rude (rood) [L. *rudis*], *a.* Simple, crude, uncivilized, unrefined; rough; coarse in manners, uncivil, offensive, violent, robust. **rudeness**, *n.*

rudiment (roo'di-mĕnt) [L. *rudimentum*], *n.* A first principle of knowledge, etc. (*usu. in pl.*); (*pl.*) a beginning, a germ; a partially developed organ, structure, etc., a vestige. **rudimentary**, *a.*

rue (1) (roo) [Gr. *rhutē*, *n.* A shrubby evergreen plant, of fetid odour and acrid taste.

rue (2) [A.-S. *hréowan*], *v.t.* To grieve for, to regret, to repent of. **rueful**, *a.*

ruff (1) (rŭf) [O.F. *roffe*], *n.* Act of trumping at cards when one cannot follow suit. *v.i.* To trump.

ruff (2), *n.* A plaited collar or frill of linen; anything similarly puckered; a ruffle; a bird of the sandpiper family.

ruffian (rŭf'i-ăn) [O.F.], *n.* A low, lawless fellow, a bully, a desperado. *a.* Ruffianly. **ruffianism,** *n.* **ruffianly,** *a.*

ruffle (rŭfl) [M.E. *ruffelen*], *v.t.* To disorder, rumple, disarrange; to annoy, discompose. *v.i.* To grow turbulent, to flutter; to bluster (about). *n.* A frill of fine plaited or crimped lace, etc.; a ruff; a low, vibrating beat of the drum.

rug (rŭg) [Scand.], *n.* A heavy woollen wrap with a thick nap; a skin with the hair or wool left; a floor-mat.

Rugby (rŭg'bi) [School in Warwickshire], *n.* A football game (15 to each side) in which players are allowed to use their hands in carrying the ball and holding their opponents.

rugged (rŭg'ĕd) [Scand.], *a.* Full of inequalities, uneven, irregular.

ruin (roo'in) [L. *ruere*, to fall], *n.* Disaster, overthrow, downfall; a cause of destruction, etc., havoc; state of being ruined; the remains of a building, city, etc. *v.t.* To bring or reduce to ruin; to destroy, overthrow, subvert. **ruina'tion,** *n.* **ruinous,** *a.*

rule (rool) [L. *rēgula*], *n.* Act of ruling or state of being ruled, government, sway, control; that which is established as a principle; a line of conduct, an established custom, maxim, etc.; a graduated strip of wood, etc., used for linear measurement; (*Math.*) a prescribed formula for solving a problem. *v.t.* To govern, control, to restrain; to lay down as a rule; to mark with straight lines. *v.i.* To exercise supreme power over; to decide. **ruler,** *n.* One who rules; an instrument with straight edges used in drawing lines. **ruling,** *n.* An authoritative legal decision.

rum (rŭm) [?], *n.* A spirit distilled from fermented molasses or cane-juice. *a.* (*slang*) Strange, queer.

rumble (rŭmbl) [imit.], *v.i.* To make a low, heavy, continuous sound, as of thunder, heavy vehicles, etc. *n.* A rumbling sound; a seat behind the body of a carriage.

ruminant (roo'mi-nănt) [L. *rūminans*], *a.* Chewing the cud. *n.* An animal with a complex stomach serving for chewing the cud, as the ox, camel, deer, etc. **ruminate,** *v.i.* To chew over the cud; (*fig.*) to muse, to meditate. *v.t.* To ponder over. **rumina'tion,** *n.* **ru'minative,** *a.*

rummage (rŭm'ăj) [F. *arrumage*], *v.t.* To make a careful search in, to ransack. *v.i.* To make careful search. *n.* Act of rummaging, a search, esp. of a vessel by a customs officer; lumber, odds and ends.

rummer (rŭm'ĕr) [W. Flem.], *n.* A large glass or drinking cup.

rumour (roo'mŏr) [L. *rūmor*], *n.* Popular report, hearsay, common talk. *v.t.* To circulate as a rumour.

rump (rŭmp) [Scand.], *n.* The end of the backbone with the adjacent parts, the buttocks; (*fig.*) the tail-end of anything.

rumple (rŭmpl) [?], *v.t.* To wrinkle, crease.

rumpus (rŭm'pŭs) [?], *n.* An uproar, a row.

run (rŭn) [A.-S. *rinnan*], *v.i.* (*past* ran, run, *p.p.* run) To move or pass over the ground by using the legs more quickly than in walking, esp. so that both feet are never on the ground at once; to flee, to compete in a race; to move or travel rapidly; to go smoothly; to fuse, to melt; to drip, to emit liquid, etc. *v.t.* To cause to run, go, pass, penetrate, etc.; to drive, pursue, hunt; to press (hard) in a race, etc.; to follow or pursue (a course, etc.); to cast or mould; to smuggle; to expose oneself to. *n.* Act of running, a spell of running; a trip; a succession of demands (on a bank); a regular track (of certain animals); a grazing-ground; an enclosure for fowls.

runagate (rŭn'ă-gāt) [O.F. *renegat*], *n.* A renegade, a fugitive; a vagabond. **runaway,** *n.* A deserter, a fugitive; a bolting-horse.

rune (roon) [Icel.], *n.* A letter or character of the earliest Teutonic alphabet, used chiefly by the Scandinavians and Anglo-Saxons; (*fig.*) any mysterious mark. **runic,** *a.*

rung (rŭng) [A.-S. *hrung*], *n.* A step in a ladder; a rail in a chair, etc.; a floor-timber in a ship.

runnel (rŭnl) [A.-S. *rynel*], *n.* A little brook.

runner (rŭn'ĕr), *n.* One who runs; a messenger, a spy; a tout; a smuggler; that on which anything runs, slides, etc.; the blade of a skate or of a sleigh; a sliding loop on a strap, etc.; a creeping stem thrown out by a plant; a twining or climbing plant.

running (rŭn'ing), *n.* The act of the verb 'to run'; smuggling; power of running. *a.* Moving at a run; kept for a race. *adv.* In succession.

runt (rŭnt) [?], *n.* An ox of a small breed; any stunted animal; a dwarf.

runway, *n.* (*Aer.*) The prepared track on an aerodrome for the landing and take-off of aircraft.

rupee (ru-pē') [Hind.], *n.* An East Indian silver coin and money of account, nominally equal to 2s. 0d.

rupture (rŭp'tyŭr) [L. *ruptus*, broken], *n.* Act of breaking; state of being violently parted; a break, a breach; hernia. *v.t.* To burst, to separate by violence; to affect with hernia.

rural (roor'ăl) [L. *rus*, *rūris*, the country], *a.* Pertaining to the country; pastoral, agricultural; rustic. **ruralize,** *v.i.* and *t.* **rurally,** *adv.*

ruse (rooz) [F.], *n.* A stratagem, trick.

rush (1) (rŭsh) [A.-S. *risc*], *n.* A plant with long thin stems or leaves growing on wet ground; a stem of this plant; (*fig.*) something valueless. **rushlight,** *n.* A candle made of rush-pith dipped in tallow. **rushy,** *a.*

rush (2) [A.-F. *russher*, O.F. *reusser*], *v.t.* To urge or push with violence, to hurry; to take by sudden assault. *v.i.* To move precipitately. *n.* The act of rushing; an impetuous movement, dash, or onslaught.

rusk (rŭsk) [Sp. *rosca*, roll of bread], *n.* Bread or cake crisped and browned in the oven.

russet (rŭsĕt) [O.F. *rousset*, L. *russus*, red]. *a.* Of a reddish-brown colour; rustic, homely. *n.* A reddish-brown colour; a rough-skinned variety of apple.

russia (rŭsh'ä), a. Applied to a soft leather made from hides prepared with birch-bark oil.

Russian (rŭsh'án), a. Pertaining to Russia. n. A native of Russia; the Russian language.

rust (rŭst) [A.-S. rūst], n. The red incrustation formed on iron when exposed to moisture; a plant disease caused by parasitic fungi, blight. v.i. To contract rust; to be oxidated; to be attacked by blight; (fig.) to degenerate through idleness or disuse. v.t. To affect with rust. rusty, a. Of a rust colour; attacked by rust.

rustic (rŭstĭk) [L. rusticus], a. Rural; characteristic of country people, simple, unpolished, uncouth; of rude workmanship. rusticate, v.i. To retire to or dwell in the country. v.t. To suspend from residence at a University, as a punishment. rustica'tion, n. rusticity (-tis'-ĭ-ti), n.

rustle (rŭsl) [imit.], v. To make or cause to make a quick succession of small sounds like the rubbing of dry leaves. n. A rustling.

rut (?], n. A sunken track made by wheels of vehicles; a groove; (fig.) a settled habit.

ruth (rooth), n. Mercy, pity.

ruthless (rooth'lĕs), a. Pitiless, merciless, cruel. ruthlessness, n.

-ry, suf. As in poultry, yeomanry.

rye (rī) [A.-S. ryge], n. The seeds of a cereal allied to wheat; the plant bearing this. rye-grass, n. A grass cultivated for fodder.

S

Sabaoth (săb'ā-oth) Heb. cabāoth], n. Hosts, armies.

Sabbatarian (săb'á-târ'ĭ-ăn), n. A Jew who strictly observes the Sabbath; a Christian who is specially strict in the observance of Sunday. a. ·Inculcating such observance. Sabbatarianism, n.

Sabbath (săb'áth) [Heb. shābath, to rest], n. The seventh day of the week, the day of rest; Sunday. Sabba'tic, -al, a. Pertaining to or befitting the Sabbath; recurring in sevens.

sable (săbl) [O.F., from Slav.], n. A small carnivorous quadruped allied to the marten, the brown fur of which is very highly valued; its fur; black; (pl.) mourning garments. a. Black, dark, gloomy.

sabot (săb'ō) [F.], n. A wooden shoe worn by peasants in France, Belgium, etc. sabotage (sa-bō-tazh'), n. The operation of cutting shoes for railway-lines; malicious damage to a railway, machinery, etc.

sabre (sā'bĕr) [F.], n. A cavalry sword with a curved blade; (pl.) cavalry. v.t. To cut or strike down or kill with the sabre. sabretache (săb'ĕr-tăsh), n. A cavalry officer's leather pocket suspended from the sword-belt.

sac (săk) [F.], n. A pouch, a cavity or receptacle in an animal or vegetable.

saccharine (săk'á-rin) [Gr. sacchar-on,

sugar], n. An intensely sweet compound obtained from coal-tar. a. Pertaining to or having the qualities of sugar. sac-char'ic a.

sacerdotal (săs-ĕr-dō'tál) [L. sacer, holy, dōs dōtis, cogn. with dare, to give], a. Pertaining to priests; priestly.

sachem (sā'chĕm) [N.Am.Ind.], n. A chief of certain tribes of N.American Indians.

sachet (săsh'ā) [F.], n. A small ornamental bag for perfumes.

sack (1) (săk) [A.-S. sacc], n. A large, strong, oblong bag for holding corn, wool, etc.; the quantity this contains; a sack and contents; a sacque; (colloq.) dismissal. v.t. To put into sacks; (colloq.) to dismiss. sackcloth n. Sacking, esp. as token of mourning or penitence. sackful, n. sacking, n. Coarse stuff of which sacks are made.

sack (2) [?], v.t. To plunder or pillage (a place taken by storm); to loot. n. The pillaging of a captured place.

sack (3) (săk) [F. sec, dry], n. An old name for various dry white wines.

sackbut (săk'bŭt) [F. saquebote], n. A bass trumpet like the trombone; (Bibl.) a musical stringed instrument.

sacque (săk) [F.], n. A loose-fitting woman's gown; a coat hanging from the shoulders.

sacrament (săk'rá-mĕnt) [L. sacrāre, to make sacred], n. A religious rite instituted as an outward and visible sign of an inward and spiritual grace, as baptism and the eucharist; the consecrated elements. sacramen'tal, a. Pertaining to or constituting a sacrament; consecrated. sacramentalism, n. The doctrine of the spiritual efficacy of the sacraments. sacramentalist, n. sacramentar'ian, a. Relating to the sacraments. n. One holding extreme doctrines regarding the spiritual efficacy of the sacraments.

sacred (sā'krĕd). a. Dedicated to religious use or to a divinity; set apart, reserved; pertaining to religion, holy; sanctified, not to be profaned.

sacrifice (săk'ri-fĭs), n. The act of offering or surrendering a valued possession to a deity, as an act of propitiation, atonement, or thanksgiving; that which is so given up, a victim; the giving up of anything for the sake of someone or something else; the sale of goods at a loss; great destruction (of life, etc.). v.t. To offer to God or to a deity as a sacrifice; to surrender for the sake of another person, object, etc., to devote; to sell at a loss. sacrificial (-fish'ál), a.

sacrilege (săk'ri-lĕj), n. The profanation of sacred things, esp. larceny from a consecrated building. sacrilegious (-ij'ŭs), a.

sacrist (sā'krĭst), n. An officer in charge of a sacristy. sac'ristan, n. (săk-) A sacrist. sacristy, n. An apartment in a church in which the vestments, sacred vessels, books, etc., are kept.

sacrosanct (săk'rō-sănkt), a. Inviolable by reason of sanctity.

sad (săd) [A.-S. sœd, sated], a. Sorrowful, mournful; expressing or causing sorrow; lamentable; heavy (of bread). sadden, *v.* To make or become sad. **sadly,** *adv.* **sadness,** *n.*

saddle (sădl) [A.-S. *sadol*], *n.* A seat for a rider or a load on an animal, a cycle, agricultural machine, etc.; an object resembling a saddle; a joint of mutton, etc., including the loins. *v.t.* To put a saddle or a burden on. **saddle-bag,** *n.* A bag connected by straps to a saddle; carpeting woven in imitation of Persian saddle-bags. **saddler** (săd'lẽr), *n.* A maker or dealer in saddles and harness. **saddlery,** *n.*

Sadducee (săd'ū-sē) [Gr. *Saddoukaioi*], *n.* One of an ancient Jewish sect who adhered to the written law and denied the resurrection from the dead, etc.

sadism (sā'dizm) [Marquis de *Sade* (1740–1814) French writer], *n.* Sexual perversion characterized by cruelty.

safari (să-far'ĭ) [Ar. *ṣafar*, a journey], *n.* A hunting expedition.

safe (sāf) [O.F. *sauf*, L. *salvus*, uninjured], *a.* Free or secure from danger or evil; unharmed, sound; affording security; not risky; cautious, trusty; certain, sure; no longer dangerous, secure from escape. *n.* A receptacle for keeping things safe, a strong-box or strong-room; a cupboard for keeping meat, etc., in. **safe-conduct,** *n.* A passport, esp. in time of hostilities. **safeguard,** *n.* One who or that which protects; a precaution; a passport. **safely,** *adv.* **safety,** *n.* State of being safe, freedom from injury, danger, or risk; safe-keeping or custody.

saffron (săf'rŏn) [Arab. *za'farān*], *n.* A preparation from the flowers of the autumnal crocus, used for colouring and flavouring; this plant; the colour, deep orange; the meadow saffron. *a.* Deep yellow.

sag (săg) [Scand.], *v.i.* To sink or give way, esp. in the middle, under weight or pressure; to decline (of prices, esp. of stocks). *n.* Act or state of sagging; the amount of this.

saga (sa'gă) [Icel.], *n.* A mediæval prose narrative of contemporary events in Iceland or Norway; a story of heroic adventure.

sagacious (să-gā'shŭs) [L. *sagax*], *a.* Intellectually keen, perspicacious, shrewd, wise; sensible, quick-scented (of animals). **sagacity** (-găs'ĭ-tĭ), *n.*

sage (1) (sāj) [A.-F. *sauge*, L. *salvia*], *n.* A grey-leaved aromatic plant used in cookery. **sage-green,** *n.* A greyish green.

sage (2) [F., from L. *sapere*, to be wise], *a.* Wise, discreet, judicious, well-considered; solemn-looking. *n.* A man of great wisdom. **sagely,** *adv.*

sago (sā'gō) [Malay *săgu*], *n.* The soft inner portion of the trunk of several palms, the starch of which is separated and used as food.

sahib (sa'ĭb) [Hind.], *n.* The title used by East Indians in addressing Europeans.

sail (sāl) [A.-S. *segel*], *n.* A piece of canvas spread to catch the wind and so cause a ship to move in the water; (*collect.*) some or all of a ship's sails; a ship; an excursion by water; the arm of a windmill. *v.i.* To move by the action of wind upon sails; to be conveyed in a vessel by water; to set sail; to float (as a bird), to glide. *v.t.* To pass over in a ship, to navigate; to set afloat. **sailcloth,** *n.* Canvas, etc., for making sails; a kind of dress-material. **sailless,** *a.* **sailor,** *n.* A seaman, esp. one of the crew as dist. from an officer; one who sails (as 'a good sailor', *i.e.* one not liable to sea-sickness).

sainfoin (sān'foin) [F.], *n.* A leguminous fodder-plant resembling clover.

saint (sānt, *as pref.* sănt) [L. *sanctus*, made holy], *n.* A holy person; one of the blessed in heaven; one canonized by the Church. *v.t.* To canonize; to regard or address as a saint. **saint's day:** A day dedicated to the commemoration of a particular saint. **saintly,** *a.* **saintliness,** *n.* **sainted,** *a.* Canonized; gone to heaven; holy, pious.

sake (sāk) [A.-S. *sacu*], *n.* End, purpose; desire of obtaining; cause. **for the sake of:** Because of, out of consideration for.

sal (săl) [L.], *n.* Salt (used only with qualifying word). **sal-ammo'niac,** *n.* Ammonia. **sal volatile** (-vŏ-lăt'ĭ-lĭ): An aromatic solution of ammonium carbonate.

salaam (să-lam') [Arab.], *n.* A ceremonious salutation among Orientals. *v.i.* To make a salaam.

salacious (să-lā'shŭs) [L. *salax*], *a.* Lustful, lecherous. **salacity** (-lăs'ĭ-tĭ), *n.*

salad (săl'ăd) [O.F. *salade*, L. *salāta*, salted], *a.* A dish of vegetables prepared with dressing and eaten raw. **salad days:** The time of youth and inexperience.

salamander (săl-ă-măn'dẽr) [L. and Gr. *salamandra*], *n.* A lizard-like animal (also a genie) anciently believed to live in fire.

salame (sa-la'mi) [It.], *n.* A highly seasoned sausage.

salary (săl'ă-ri) [L. *salārium*, orig. salt-money given to soldiers], *n.* Fixed pay given periodically for work not of a manual or mechanical kind. **salaried,** *a.*

sale (sāl) [A.-S. *sala*], *n.* The act of selling; the exchange of a commodity; an auction; a disposal at reduced prices; demand, market. **saleable** *a.* **salesman, -woman,** *n.* A person employed to sell goods.

salient (sā'li-ĕnt) [L. *saliens*, leaping], *a.* Leaping, springing; pointing outwards; prominent, noticeable. *n.* A salient angle, esp. a portion of defensive works projecting towards the enemy.

saline (să-lin', sā'lin), *a.* Consisting of or partaking of the qualities of salt. **salinity** (să-lin'ĭ-tĭ), *n.*

saliva (să-li'vă) [L.], *n.* The secretions of the salivary and mucous glands into the mouth, spittle. **salivary,** *a.*

sallow (1) (săl'ō) [A.-S. *sealh*], *n.* A shrubby variety of willow; an osier.

sallow (2) [A.-S. *salu*], *a.* Of a sickly-yellowish or pale-brown colour. **sallowish,** *a.*

sally (săl'ĭ) [L. *salire*, to leap], *n.* A sudden rush of troops from within against besiegers; an issuing forth, an excursion; a flight of fancy or wit, a bantering remark. *v.i.* To rush out suddenly (of troops); to go (forth) on a journey, etc.

salmagundi (săl-mà-gŭn'dĭ) [F.], *n.* A dish of chopped meat, anchovies, eggs, oil, vinegar, etc.; a mixture, a medley.

salmon (săm'ŏn) [A.F. *saumoun*], *n.* A large silvery, pink-fleshed food-fish that ascends rivers to spawn. *a.* Salmon-coloured, pink. **salmon-trout,** *n.* A fish resembling the salmon but smaller.

salon (sa-lon) [F.], *n.* A reception room in France; reunion of eminent persons in it.

saloon (sà'loon'), *n.* A large room suitable for social receptions, entertainments, etc.; a large cabin on board ship; a saloon-carriage; a drinking-bar; a public room for some specified purpose (as *hairdressing-saloon*). **saloon-carriage,** *n.* A large railway-carriage without compartments.

salsify (săl'sĭ-fĭ) [F. *salsifis*], *n.* A composite plant, the purple goat's-beard, the root of which is eaten.

salt (sawlt) [L. *sal*], *n.* Chloride of sodium, used for seasoning and preserving food; that which gives flavour; relish, piquancy, wit; a salt-cellar; a sailor; a compound formed by the union of basic and acid radicals. *a.* Impregnated with salt, saline; cured with salt; living in salt water; pungent (of wit, etc.). *v.t.* To sprinkle, season, cure, or preserve with salt. **salt'cellar** [A.F. *saler*, O.F. *saliere*], *n.* A vessel for holding salt at table. **salt'pan,** *n.* A shallow depression in which sea-water is evaporated in order to obtain salt; a vessel in which brine is evaporated at salt-works. **salt water:** Sea-water. **salt-water,** *a.* Living in or pertaining to the sea. **saltiness,** *n.* **saltish,** *a.* **salts,** *n.pl.* Smelling-salts; various medicinal salts. **salty,** *a.*

salta'tion (săl-tā'shŭn) [L. *saltātio*, from *saltāre*], *n.* A bounding; an abrupt transition; a palpitation or beating. **saltator'ial, sal'tatory,** *a.*

saltire (săl'tir) [O.F. *sauteoir*, a stile], *n. Her.*) An ordinary in the form of a St. Andrew's cross or the letter X.

saltpetre (sawlt-pē'tĕr) [L. *sal petræ*, salt of the rock], *n.* Potassium nitrate, nitre.

salubrious (sà-lū'brĭ-ŭs) [L. *salus*, health], *a.* Promoting health. **salubrity,** *n.*

salutary (săl'ū-tăr-ĭ), *a.* Promoting good effects, beneficial, profitable.

salute (sà-lūt', -loot'), *v.t.* To greet with a gesture or words of welcome or respect; to accost (with a bow, kiss); to honour by the discharge of ordnance. *v.i.* To perform a salute. *n.* A gesture of welcome, homage, recognition, etc., a salutation; (*Mil. and Nav.*) a prescribed method of doing honour or paying a compliment or respect. **saluta'tion,** *n.* Act of saluting; that which is said or done in the act of greeting; a salute.

salvable (săl'vàbl) [L. *salvāre*, to save], *a.* Capable of being saved.

salvage (săl'vàj), *n.* The act of saving (a ship, goods, etc.) from shipwreck, capture, fire, etc.; compensation for such saving; property so saved. *v.t.* To save from wreck, etc.

salvation (săl-vā'shŭn), *n.* Act of saving; deliverance, preservation, esp. from sin and its consequences; that which delivers, etc. **Salvation Army** *n.* A religious organization working on military lines, esp. among the poorer classes. **Salvationist,** *n.* Member of this.

salve (sàlv) [A.-S. *sealf*], *n.* A healing ointment; anything that soothes. *v.t.* To anoint with a salve; to soothe, to make good.

salver (săl'vĕr) [F. *salve*], *n.* A tray on which visiting-cards, etc., are presented.

salvo (săl'vō) [It. *salva*, salutation], *n.* (*pl.* -vos) A discharge of guns, etc., esp. as a salute; (*fig.*) a volley of cheers, etc.

salvor (săl'vŏr), *n.* A person or ship effecting salvage.

Sam Browne (Sir *Samuel Browne* (1824–1901), the inventor], *n.* A military belt with a strap over the shoulder.

same (săm) [A.-S.], *a.* Identical; not other; similar in kind, quality, degree, etc.; just mentioned, aforesaid; unchanging, uniform. **all the same:** Nevertheless; notwithstanding. **sameness,** *n.*

samovar (săm'ō-var) [Rus.], *n.* A Russian tea urn.

samphire (săm'fir) [F. *herbe de St. Pierre* St. Peter's herb], *n.* A herb growing on sea-cliffs, the leaves of which are pickled.

sample (sampl), An example, a part taken as illustrating the whole, a specimen, pattern. *v.t.* To take samples of, to test. **sampler,** *n.* A piece of embroidered work done as a specimen of skill.

sanative (săn'à-tiv) [L. *sānāre*, to heal], *a.* Healing, curative. **sanator'ium,** *n.* (*pl.* -ia) A place to which people resort for the sake of their health; an institution for invalids. **san'atory,** *a.* Conducive to health.

sanctify (săngk'tĭ-fī) [L. *sanctus*, holy], *v.t.* To make holy; to set apart or observe as holy; to purify from sin; to make inviolable. **sanctifica'tion,** *n.*

sanctimony (săngk'tĭ-mō-nĭ), *n.* Affectation of piety, sanctimoniousness. **sancti-mo'nious,** *a.* Making a show of piety or saintliness.

sanction (săngk'shŭn) [L. *sanctio*], *n.* The act of ratifying, ratification, confirmation; a provision for enforcing obedience; anything that gives binding force to a law, etc.; countenance, support; (*n.pl.*) (*Polit.*) enforcement of a treaty, etc., by penalties. *v.t.* To give sanction to, to authorize, countenance, approve.

sanctity (săngk'tĭ-tĭ) [O.F. *sainctetê*], *n.* Holiness; spiritual purity, saintliness; inviolability.

sanctuary (săngk'tū-à-rĭ), *n.* A holy place; an inner shrine or most sacred part of a church; a place in which debtors and malefactors were free from arrest, a refuge; protection; a place where deer, birds, etc., are left undisturbed.

sanctum (săngk'tŭm), *n.* (*pl.* -ta) A sacred or private place; (*colloq.*) a private room.

sand (sănd) [A.-S.], *n.* Fragments of rock, flint, etc., reduced almost to powder; (*pl.*) tracts of sand, stretches of beach, submarine banks of sand. **sand-glass,** *n.* An hour-glass. **sand-paper,** *n.* A paper or thin cloth coated with sand, used for smoothing wood, etc. **sandpiper,** *n.* A popular name for several birds haunting sandy places. **sandstone,** *n.* Stone composed of an agglutination of grains of sand.

sandal (săn'dăl) [Gr. *sandalion*], *n.* A kind of shoe consisting of a sole fastened to the foot by straps.

sandalwood (săn'dăl-wud) [Gr. *sandalon*], *n.* The fragrant wood of various E. Indian trees, much used for cabinet work.

sandwich (sănd'wich) [after the 4th Earl of *Sandwich*], *n.* Two thin slices of bread and butter with meat, etc., between them. *v.t.* To insert between two things of a dissimilar kind.

sandy (săndi), *a.* Consisting of or abounding in sand; of the colour of sand, yellowish-red (of hair). **sandiness,** *n.* **sandyish,** *a.*

sane (săn) [L. *sănus*], *a.* Sound in mind; sensible, reasonable (of views). **sanely,** *adv.*

sangfroid (san-frwa) [F., cold blood], *n.* Coolness, calmness, composure in danger, etc.

sanguinary (săng'gwi-năr-i) [L. *sanguis -uinis*, blood], *a.* Attended with or delighting in bloodshed; bloodthirsty.

sanguine (săng'gwin), *a.* Having the colour of blood, ruddy; hopeful, cheerful, optimistic. *n.* Blood colour. **sanguin'eous,** *a.* Pertaining to or abounding in blood; of a blood colour; full-blooded, plethoric.

Sanhedrin (săn'ē-drin), *n.* The supreme court of justice and council of the Jewish nation, down to A.D. 425.

sanitary (săn'i-tăr-i), *a.* Relating to the preservation of health; hygienic. **sanitate,** *v.t.* To improve the sanitary condition of. *v.i.* To carry out sanitary measures. **sanita'tion,** *n.*

sanity (săn'i-ti) [L. *sănitas*, from *sănus*, sane], *n.* Saneness; reasonableness; moderation.

sans (sănz, san) [F.], *prep.* Without. **sansculotte** (san-ku-lot') [F., without breeches], *n.* Applied by the aristocrats to the republicans in the French Revolution. *a.* Republican, revolutionary. **sans-culottism,** *n.*

Sanskrit (săn'skrit) [Sansk.], *n.* The ancient language of the Hindu sacred writings, the oldest of the Indo-European group.

sap (1) (săp) [A.-S. *sæp*], *n.* The watery juice of living plants; (*fig.*) strength, vigour. *v.t.* To exhaust the vitality of. **sapling,** *n.* A young tree. **sappy,** *a.*

sap (2) [*sappa*, spade], *v.t.* To undermine; to render unstable by wearing away the foundation; (*fig.*) to destroy insidiously. *v.i.* To make an attack or approach by digging trenches or undermining. *n.* The act of sapping; a trench; undermining or subversion of faith, etc.

sapient (să'pi-ènt) [L. *sapiens*, being wise], *a.* Wise, sage (usu. ironical). **sapience,** *n.* Wisdom, seeming sageness.

saponaceous (săp-ô-nă'shŭs) [L. *săpe -pōnis*, soap], *a.* Soapy; resembling or containing soap.

sapper (săp'ėr), *n.* One who saps; an officer or private of the Royal Engineers.

sapphic (săf'ik), *a.* Pertaining to Sappho, a Lesbian poetess (*c.* 600 B.C.); applied to a stanza or metre used by her. *n.pl.* Sapphic verses or stanzas.

sapphire (săf'ir) [Gr. *sappheiros*], *n.* A transparent blue variety of precious stone; an intense and lustrous blue. *a.* Sapphire-blue.

saraband (săr'ă-bănd) [Sp. *zarabanda*, from Moorish], *n.* A slow and stately Spanish dance; music for this.

Saracen (săr'ă-sèn) [? Arab.], *n.* A nomad Arab in the times of the later Greeks and Romans; a Moslem at the time of the Crusades. **Saracenic** (-sen'ik), *a.*

sarcasm (sar'kăzm) [Gr. *sarkazein*, to tear flesh], *n.* A taunting or wounding remark, bitter irony or invective. **sarcas'tic,** *a.* **sarcastically,** *adv.*

sarcenet (sar'sê-net) [O.F.], *n.* A thin, fine silk used chiefly for linings, ribbons, etc.

sarco- [Gr. *sarx sarkos*, flesh], *comb. form.*

sarcoma (sar-kō'mă), *n.* (*Path.*) A tumour of fatty tissue.

sarcophagus (sar-kof'ă-gŭs) [Gr. *phagein*, to eat], *n.* (*pl.* **-gi,** **-jī**) A stone coffin.

sard (sard), *n.* A precious stone, a variety of cornelian.

sardine (sar-dēn) [F., of *Sardinia*], *n.* A fish caught off Brittany and Sardinia, and cured and preserved in oil.

sardius (sar'di-ŭs) [Gr. *sardios*, from Sardis], *n.* A precious stone mentioned in Scripture, perhaps the sard or the sardonyx.

sardonic (sar-don'ik) [Gr. *Sardonios*, Sardinian], *a.* Unnatural, insincere; sneering, malignant, bitterly ironical.

sardonyx (sar'dō-niks), *n.* A variety of onyx, white chalcedony alternating with layers of sard.

sari (sa'rē) [Hind.], *n.* A Hindu woman's dress.

sark (sark) [A.-S. *serc*], *n.* (*Sc.*) A shirt.

sarsaparilla (sar-să-pă-ril'ă) [Sp. *zarza*, bramble, *parra*, vine], *n.* The dried roots of smilax, used as a tonic.

sarsen (sar'sen), *n.* A sandstone boulder found on the Wiltshire downs.

sartorial (sar-tôr'i-ăl) [L. *sartor*, tailor], *a.* Pertaining to a tailor or tailoring.

sash (1) (săsh) [Arab. *shåsh*, muslin], *n.* An ornamental band or scarf, often worn as a badge or part of a uniform.

sash (2), *n.* A frame holding the glass of a window. *v.t.* To furnish with sashes.

sassafras (săs'ă-frăs) [Sp. *sasafras*], *n.* A small N. American laurel; its root used as an aromatic stimulant.

Sassenach (săs'ė-năch) [Gael. and Ir.], *n.* A Saxon, an Englishman. *a.* English.

Satan (să'tăn) [Heb., enemy, adversary], *n.* The arch fiend, the devil. **satan'ic,** *a.* Pertaining to or having the qualities of Satan; devilish, infernal. **sa'tanism,** *n.* A diabolical disposition or conduct; Satan-worship.

satchel (săch'ėl) [L. *saccellus*], *n.* A small bag suspended by a strap over one shoulder.

sate (săt), *v.t.* To satisfy the appetite or desire of; to surfeit, to cloy.

sateen (să-tēn'), *n.* A glossy woollen or cotton fabric made in imitation of satin.

satellite (săt'ė-līt) [L. *satelles*, guard, attendant], *n.* A secondary planet revolving round a primary one; an obsequious follower.

satiate (sā'shi-āt) [L. *satiātus*], *v.t.* To satisfy the desire or appetite of; to sate.

satiety (sà-tī'ĕ-ti), *n.* The state of being sated; excess of gratification producing disgust.

satin (săt'in) [L. *sēta*, silk], *n.* A silken fabric with a highly-finished glossy surface on one side. *a.* Made of or resembling this, esp. in smoothness. **satinet** (săt-i-net'), *n.* A thin satin; imitation satin. **satiny**, *a.*

satire (săt'īr) [L. *lanx satura*, full dish, medley], *n.* A composition in which wickedness or folly or individual persons are held up to ridicule; ridicule, sarcasm, irony, or invective used for the chastisement of vice or folly. **satiric, -al** (-tir'ik, -ál), *a.* **sat'irist**, One who writes, or employs satire. **satirize**, *v.t.*

satisfy (săt'is-fī) [L. *satis*, enough], *v.t.* To supply or gratify to the full; to content, to please (*usu. in p.p.*); to pay (a debt, etc.); to comply with; to be sufficient for; to convince. *v.i.* To give satisfaction; to make payment, to atone. **satisfaction** (-făk'shŭn), *n.* Act of satisfying; state of being satisfied; contentment, fulfilment of an obligation; compensation, amends. **satisfactory**, *a.* Giving satisfaction, adequate; relieving the mind from doubt; atoning. **satisfying**, *a.*

satrap (săt'-ràp) [Gr. *satrapēs*, O.Pers. *khsatra*, province, *pa-*, to protect], *n.* A governor of a province of ancient Persia; a despotic ruler of a dependency. **satrapy**, *n.*

saturate (săt'ū-rāt) [L. *saturātus*, cloyed], *v.t.* To soak or imbue thoroughly; to charge (a body, fluid, etc.) with another substance, fluid, electricity, etc., so that it will hold no more. **saturation** (-rā'shŭn), *n.*

Saturday (săt'ŭr-dā) [A.-S. *Sœter-dœg*, day of Saturn], *n.* The seventh day of the week.

saturnine (săt'ŭr-nīn) [L. *Saturnus*, a deity], *a.* Dull, phlegmatic, gloomy, morose.

satyr (săt'ĭr) [Gr. *saturos*], *n.* An ancient Greek sylvan deity represented with the legs of a goat, budding horns and goat-like ears, identified by the Romans with the fauns; a lascivious or brutish man.

sauce (saws) [F.], *n.* A liquid preparation taken with foods as a relish; anything that gives piquancy; impudence, cheek. *v.t.* To make piquant or pungent; to be impudent. **sauce-boat**, *n.* A table-vessel for holding sauce. **sauce-pan**, *n.* A metal pot with a long handle, for boiling or stewing. **saucer**, *n.* A shallow china vessel for holding a cup on. **saucy**, *a.* Pert, insolent to superiors, cheeky; smart, piquant.

sauerkraut (sou'er-krout) [G.], *n.* Chopped, salted white cabbage.

saunter (sawn'tér) [?], *v t.* To wander about idly; to walk leisurely (along). *n.* A stroll; a sauntering gait.

saurian (saw'ri-àn) [Gr. *saura*, lizard], *a.* Pertaining to the lizards. *n.* A lizard or lizard-like creature, esp. one of the extinct forms.

sausage (sos'åj) [F. *saucisse*], *n.* Pork or other meat minced, seasoned, and stuffed into a length of animal's gut as food.

sauté (sō'tā) [F.], *a.* Lightly fried.

savage (săv'åj) [L. *silva*, wood], *a.* Wild; uncivilized, brutal, cruel, furious. *n.* A human being in a primitive state; a brute, a barbarian. **savagery**, *n.*

savanna (sà-văn'à) [Sp. *sabana*], *n.* An extensive treeless plain covered with low vegetation, esp. in tropical America.

savant (sa-van) [F., knowing], *n.* A man of learning, esp. an eminent scientist.

save (sāv) [L. *salvus*, safe], *v.t.* To preserve, rescue, or deliver; to keep undamaged or from being spent or lost; to spare, to exempt (*with double object*); to obviate, to prevent; to take advantage of. *v.i.* To be economical. *prep.* Except, not including. *conj.* Unless. **saving**, *a.* Preserving from danger, loss, waste, etc.; frugal; expressing a reservation, stipulation, etc. *n.* Act of economizing; an economy (*usu. in pl.*); an exception, reservation. *prep.* Save, except; with due respect to.

saveloy (săv'ĕ-loi) [F. *cervelas*], *n.* A highly-seasoned dried sausage of salted pork.

saviour (sā'vyŭr) [L. *salvātor*], *n.* One who preserves, rescues, or redeems. **the Saviour:** Christ, the Redeemer of mankind.

savory (sā'vò-ri) [O.F. *savereie*], *n.* An aromatic plant used in cookery.

savour (sā'vòr) [L. *sapere*, to taste], *n.* Flavour, relish; characteristic quality. **savoury**, *a.* Having a pleasant savour; palatable. *n.* A savoury dish.

savoy (sà-voi') [district in France], *n.* A hardy variety of cabbage with wrinkled leaves.

saw (1) (saw) [A.-S. *saga*], *n.* A thin-bladed steel cutting-instrument with a toothed edge. *v.t.* To cut, form, or make with a saw. *v.i.* To use a saw; to make motions of one sawing. **sawdust**, *n.* Small fragments of wood produced in sawing. **sawyer**, *n.* One employed in sawing.

saw (2) (saw) [A.-S. *sagu*], *n.* A saying, a proverb, a familiar maxim.

saxifrage (săk'si-frāj) [F., from L. *saxum*, rock, *frag-*, root of *frangere*, to break], *n.* An Alpine or rock plant with mossy foliage and small flowers, formerly esteemed good for stone in the bladder.

Saxon (săk'sòn), *n.* One of a Teutonic race from northern Germany who conquered England in the 5th and 6th cents.; an Anglo-Saxon; the old Saxon or Anglo-Saxon language; a native of modern Saxony. *a.* Pertaining to any of these, their country, or language; Anglo-Saxon.

saxophone (săk'sò-fōn) [A. *Sax*, inventor], *n.* (*Mus.*) A brass instrument with single reed.

say (sā) [A.-S. *secgan*], *v.t.* (*past and p.p.* said, sed) To utter in words, to speak; to repeat; to tell, affirm, allege; to suppose, to assume; to decide. *v.i.* To speak, to talk, to answer. *n.* What one says or has to say, a statement; one's turn to speak. **saying,** *n.* That which is said; a maxim, an adage, a saw.

scab (skăb) [Scand.], *n.* An incrustation formed over a sore in healing; a contagious, mange-like skin-disease in horses, cattle, and sheep; a fungoid plant-disease; a workman who refuses to join in a strike, a blackleg. *v.i.* To form a scab. **scabby,** *a.*

scabbard (skăb'ărd) [A.-F *escaubers,* pl.], *n.* The sheath of a sword or similar weapon.

scabrous (skā'brŭs) [L. *scabrōsus*], *a.* Rough, rugged; scurfy; thorny; (*fig.*) approaching the indelicate.

scaffold (skăf'ŏld) [O.F. *escadafault*], *n.* A temporary structure of poles and platforms for use in building or repairing a house, etc.; a temporary platform for the execution of criminals. *v.t.* To furnish with a scaffold; to support. **scaffolding,** *n.* A scaffold for builders, shows, etc.; materials for scaffolds.

scald (skawld) [L. *calidus,* hot], *v.t.* To burn with hot liquid or vapour; to clean with boiling water. *n.* An injury from hot liquid or vapour.

scale (1) (skāl) [A.-S. *scealu*], *n.* One of the thin plates covering the skin of fishes and reptiles; a modified leaf, hair, feather, husk, etc., resembling this; an incrustation; a small flake of metal. *v.t.* To strip the scales off. *v.i.* To form or come off in scales. **scaly,** *a.* **scaliness,** *n.*

scale (2) (skāl) [O.F. *escale,* cup], *n.* The dish of a balance; (*pl.*) a simple balance. *v.t.* To amount to in weight.

scale (3) (skāl) [L. *scāla,* ladder], *n.* Anything graduated for use as a measure, or as a scheme for classification, gradation, etc.; a basis for a numerical system in which the value of a figure depends on its place in the order; a system of correspondence between different magnitudes, relative dimensions; (*Mus.*) all the tones of a key arranged in order according to pitch. *v.t.* To climb by a ladder; to draw to proper proportions. *v.i.* To be commensurable. **scaling-ladder,** *n.* A ladder used in storming.

scalene (skă-lēn') [Gr. *skalēnos*], *a.* Having no two sides equal (of triangles); having the axis inclined to the base (of a cone or cylinder).

scallop (skol'-, skăl'ŏp) [O.F. *escalope*], *n.* A bivalve mussel with an undulating margin; a single shell of this worn as a pilgrim's badge or used as a dish; (*pl.*) an ornamental undulating edging. *v.t.* To cut or indent an edge.

scalp (skălp) [Scand.], *n.* The top of the head; the skin of this with the hair belonging to it. *v.t.* To tear or take the scalp from; (*fig.*) to criticize savagely. **scalpel** (skăl'pĕl) [L. *scalpere,* to scrape], *n.* A small knife used in dissecting.

scamp (skămp) [?], *n.* A worthless fellow, a knave, a rogue. *v.t.* To do in a careless manner.

scamper (skăm'pĕr) [L. *campus,* field], *v.i.* To run rapidly or impulsively. *n.* A hasty run; a hurried tour.

scan (skăn) [L. *scandere,* to climb], *v.t.* To count or test the feet or syllables of (a line of verse); to scrutinize. *v.i.* To be metrically correct.

scandal (skăn'dăl) [Gr. *skandalon,* stumbling-block], *n.* Indignation at some act, esp. publicly expressed; reproach, shame, malicious gossip, a defamatory statement. **scandalize,** *v.t.* To offend by improper or outrageous conduct, to shock. **scandalmonger,** *n.* One who disseminates scandal. **scandalous,** *a.*

Scandinavian (skăn-di-nā'vi-ăn), *a.* Pertaining to Scandinavia (Norway, Sweden, Denmark, and Iceland), its language, or literature. *n.* A native of Scandinavia.

scanning (skăn'ing), *n.* (*Television*) The continuous traversing of a picture by a beam of light or of electrons, for the purpose of transmitting the image.

scansion (skăn'shŭn), *n.* The act of scanning verse; a system of scanning.

scant (skănt) [Icel. *skamt,* short], *a.* Not full, large, or plentiful; not enough; deficient. **scanty,** *a.* **scantily,** *adv.* **scantiness,** *n.*

scantling (skănt'ling) [O.F. *escantillon*], *n.* A specimen, a small quantity; a rough draft or sketch; a beam less than 5 in. in breadth and thickness; the sectional measurement of timber, the measurement of stone in all three dimensions; a trestle for a cask.

scapegoat (skāp'gŏt), *n.* One made to bear blame due to another (from the scapegoat of Leviticus xvi). **scapegrace,** *n.* A graceless, good-for-nothing person.

scaph-, scapho [Gr. *skaphe,* a boat], *comb. form.* Boat-shaped.

scapula (skăp'ū-là) [L.], *n.* (*pl.* -læ) The shoulder-blade. **scapular,** *a.* Pertaining to this. *n.* (*R.-C. Ch.*) A vestment consisting of two strips of cloth worn across the shoulders and hanging down the breast and back.

scar (1) (skar) [L. and Gr. *eschara*], *n.* A mark left by a wound, burn, etc. *v.* To mark with a scar or form a scar.

scar (2) (skar) [Icel. *sker*], *n.* A crag, cliff.

scarab (skăr'ăb) [L. *scarabœus*], *n.* An ancient Egyptian sacred beetle; an amulet shaped like this.

scaramouch (skăr'à-mouch) [It. *scaramuccia,* a braggart in old comedy], *n.* A poltroon and braggart.

scarce (skăr) [L. *carptus,* plucked)], *a.* Infrequent, rare, uncommon; not plentiful. *adv.* Hardly, scarcely. **scarcely,** *adv.* Hardly, barely, only just; with difficulty. **scarcity,** *n.* Rareness; a dearth (of); a famine.

scare (skăr) [?], *v.t.* To frighten, alarm, strike with or drive (away) through fear. *n.* A sudden fright, a panic. **scarecrow,** *n.* A rude figure set up to frighten birds away from crops; (*fig.*) a shabby person, a guy.

scarf (1) (skarf) [?], *n.* (*pl.* **scarfs, scarves**) A long strip of material worn round the neck, etc.; a neck-tie.

scarf (2) [?], *n.* A joint made by bevelling or notching so that the thickness is not increased, and then bolting or strapping together.

scarify ((skăr'ĭ-fī) [Gr. *skariphos*, pencil], *v.t.* (*Surg.*) To make slight incisions in; (*fig.*) to pain, to criticize mercilessly. **scarifica'tion**, *n.*

scarlatina (skar-là-tē'nà) [It. *scarlattina*], *n.* Scarlet fever.

scarlet (skar'lĕt) [Pers. *saqalāt*], *n.* A bright red colour tending towards orange; cloth or dress of this colour. *a.* Of a scarlet colour; dressed in scarlet. **scarlet fever:** An infectious fever characterized by red patches on the skin. **scarlet runner:** A trailing bean with scarlet flowers.

scarp (skarp) [It. *scarpa*], *n.* A nearly perpendicular slope; (*Fort.*) the interior slope of the ditch.

scathe (skāth) [A.-S. *scathan*], *n.* Harm, injury. *v.t.* To hurt, injure, destroy. **scatheless**, *a.* **scathing**, *a.* Very bitter or severe, withering (of sarcasm, etc.).

scatter (skăt'ér) [M.E. *scateren*], *v.t.* To throw loosely about, send broadcast; to strew, disperse, rout, diffuse. *v.i.* To disperse; to be routed; to be dissipated or diffused. **scatter-brain**, *n.* A giddy, heedless person. **scattered**, *a.* Irregularly situated; widely apart.

scavenger (skăv'ĕn-jĕr) [A.-F. *scavage*, inspection], *n.* A street-cleaner; an animal feeding on carrion, etc.; any one willing to do 'dirty work' or delighting in filth. **scavenge**, *v.t.* and *i.*

scenario (shā-na'ri-ō) [It.), *n.* A sketch or outline of the scenes and main points of a play.

scene (sēn) [Gr. *skēnē*, tent, stage], *n.* A stage, the theatre, the place where anything occurs or is exhibited or in which the action of a story, etc., is supposed to take place; a hanging or device on a stage; a division of a play; an exhibition of feeling or passion; a landscape, a view. **sce'nery**, *n.* The various accessories used on the stage; picturesque views presented by natural features. **sce'nic**, **-al**, *a.* Pertaining to the stage, theatrical; picturesque, arranged for effect.

scent (sent) [L. *sentire*, to perceive], *v.t.* To perceive by smell; to recognize the odour of; (*fig.*) to begin to suspect; to hunt (out) by smelling; to perfume. *v.i.* To exercise sense of smell. *n.* Odour, esp. of a pleasant kind, or that left by an animal which can be followed by hounds; a perfume; the sense of smell, esp. the power of recognizing or tracing things by smelling; a clue. **scentless**, *a.* Odourless; having no sense of smell.

sceptic (skep'tĭk) [Gr. *skeptesthai*, to examine], *n.* One who doubts the truth of Christianity or of any revealed religion; an incredulous person. **sceptical**, *a.* Pertaining to a sceptic; given to doubting or questioning, incredulous. **scepticism** (-sizm), *n.*

sceptre (sep'tér) [Gr. *skēptein*, to prop], *n.* A staff borne by a sovereign as a symbol of authority; (*fig.*) royal authority. **sceptred**, *a.* Invested with royal authority.

schedule (shed'ūl) [L. *scheda*, strip of papyrus], *n.* A list, catalogue, or inventory appended to a document. *v.t.* To enter in a schedule, to make a schedule or list of.

schematic (skē-măt'ĭk) Gr. *schēma -atos*, shape], *a.* Pertaining to a scheme.

scheme (skēm), *n.* A plan, project, proposed method of doing something; an underhand design; a table of proposed events, etc., a syllabus; a representation, diagram, or systematic arrangement of facts, principles, etc. *v.t.* To plan, contrive, plot. *v.i.* To form plans. **scheming**, *a.* Given to plotting or forming schemes.

schism (sizm) [Gr. *schizein*, to split], *n.* A split or division in a community, esp. separation into two Churches; the sin of causing such division. **schismat'ic**, *a.* and *n.*

schist (shist), *n.* A rock tending to split easily. **schistose**. **-tous**, *a.*

schiz-, **schizo-**, *comb. form.* **schizophrenia** (skit-zō-frē'niă), *n.* (*Path.*) A form of insanity characterized by a loss of contact with reality.

scholar (skol'ár) [L. *scholāris*], *n.* A learned person, esp. in literature; (*Univ.*) an undergraduate on the foundation of a college; a disciple; (*pop.*) a pupil, a student. **scholarly**, *a.* Befitting a scholar; learned. **scholarship**, *n.* High attainments in literature, etc.; instruction; education, free or at reduced fees, granted to a successful candidate after examination; emoluments so granted.

scholastic (skō-lăs'tĭk), *a.* Pertaining to school, schools, Universities, etc., academic, pedantic; given to logical subtleties. **scholasticism**, *n.* The philosophy of the mediæval schoolmen.

scholiast (skō'lĭ-ăst), *n.* A commentator, esp. one who annotated the classics.

school (1) (skool) [Dut., cp. SHOAL (2)], *n.* A shoal of fish, porpoises, etc.

school (2) [Gr. *scholē*, leisure, philosophy], *n.* An institution for education, esp. one for instruction of a more elementary kind; the building of this; the body of pupils; the body of disciples of a philosopher, artist, system of thought, etc.; (*pl.*) the mediæval Universities; scholasticism; (*Univ.*) any of the branches of study with separate examinations taken for honours; (*fig.*) any circumstances serving to discipline or instruct. *v.t.* To instruct, to educate; to discipline. **schoolboy**, **-girl**, *n.* A boy or girl attending a school. **schoolhouse**, *n.* A building used as a school; the headmaster's house or chief boarding-house at a public school. **schoolmaster**, **-mistress**, *n.* A chief or assistant teacher in a school. **schooling**, *n.* Instruction in school; **schooldays**; a reproof.

schooner (skoo'ner) [Clydesdale *scoon*, to skim along], *n.* A two- or three-masted vessel with fore-and-aft rigging.

schottische (shŏ-tēsh') [G., Scottish], *n.* A dance resembling a polka; the music for it.

sciatic (sī-ăt'ĭk) [Gr. *ischias*, pain in the loins], *a.* Pertaining to the hip or the sciatic nerve or sciatica. **sciatica**, *n.* Neuralgia of the hip and thigh; pain in the great sciatic nerve.

science (sī'ĕns) [L. *scire*, to know], *n.* Systematized knowledge; a department of this, a system of facts and principles concerning any subject; the pursuit of knowledge, the principles governing its acquirement; exceptional skill due to knowledge and training. **scientif′ic**, *a.* Pertaining to, used, or engaged in science; done according to the principles of science, systematic, exact; skilful, expert (esp. of pugilism, etc.). **scientifically**, *adv.* **scientist**, *n.*

scilicet (si′li-sĕt) [L. (*scire licet*, it is permitted to know)], *adv.* To wit, namely.

scimitar (sim′i-tàr) [It. *scimitarra*], *n.* A short Oriental curved sword, broad towards the point.

scintilla (sin-til′à) [L.], *n.* A spark; an atom. **scin′tillate**, *v.i.* To emit sparks; to sparkle, twinkle. **scintilla′tion**, *n.*

sciolist (si′ō-list) [L. *sciolus*, smatterer, dim of *scius*, knowing], *n.* One who knows many things superficially. **sciolism**, *n.*

scion (si′ŏn) [F.], *n.* A shoot, esp. for grafting or planting; a descendant, a child.

scissile (sis′il) [L. *scindere*, to cut], *a.* That may be cut. **scission**, *n.*

scissors (siz′ŏrz), *n.pl.* Two blades pivoted together for cutting objects placed between them, usu. **pair of scissors**.

scler-, sclero- [Gr. *skleros*, dry, hard], *comb. form.* **sclerosis** (skle-rō′sis), *n.* (*Path.*) Morbid thickening of a tissue.

scoff (skof) [Scand.], *n.* An expression of contempt or mockery; a gibe, a taunt. *v.i.* To speak in derision, to mock or jeer (at). *v.t.* To drink greedily.

scold (skōld) [Teut.], *v.i.* To find fault noisily or angrily. *v.t.* To chide thus; to rate, to rail at. *n.* A noisy, nagging woman; a scolding. **scolding**, *a.* and *n.*

sconce (skons) [O.F. *esconse*, dark-lantern], *n.* A candle-holder fixed to a wall; the socket of a candlestick; a detached fort.

scone (skon, skōn) [G. *schon*, fine], *n.* A soft thin cake cooked on a griddle.

scoop (skoop) [?], *n.* A short-handled shovel for lifting and moving loose material such as coal, grain, sugar, etc. *v.t.* To ladle (out), hollow (out), or lift (up) with a scoop.

scoot (skoot), *v.i.* To dart off, scurry away. **scooter**, *n.* A toy vehicle, like a roller-skate for one foot, with a handle for guiding it.

scope (skōp) [Gr. *skopos*, a watcher, a mark], *n.* Range of action or observation, outlook, sphere, etc.; opportunity, vent. **-scope**, *suf.* Denoting an instrument of observation, etc., as in *microscope*, *spectroscope*. **-scopic**, *suf.* Pertaining to this or to observation, etc. **-scopy**, *suf.* Observation by the instrument, etc., specified.

scorbutic (skŏr-bū′tik) [L. *scorbūtus*, scurvy], *a.* Pertaining to scurvy. *n.* One affected with scurvy.

scorch (skŏrch) [L. *cortex*, bark], *v.t.* To injure or discolour by burning the outside of, to singe, parch, shrivel (up). *v.i.* To be parched, singed, or dried up with heat; (*slang*) to go at an excessive rate of speed. *n.* A burn caused by scorching.

score (skōr) [A.-S. *scor*], *n.* A notch on a tally; a reckoning, an account, a debt; (*fig.*) anything laid up against one, a grudge; the points made by a player or side in certain games; a copy of a musical work in which all the parts are shown; twenty, a set of twenty; (*pl.*) large numbers; category, head, reason; a remark in which one scores off another. *v.t.* To mark with notches, lines, etc.; to groove; to enter in a score. *v.i.* To keep a score; to win points, advantages, etc. **scorer**, *n.*

scoria (skōr′i-à) [Gr. *skōria*, refuse], *n.* (*pl.* -iæ) Cellular lava or ashes; the refuse of fused metals, dross.

scorn (skŏrn) [O.F. *escorne*], *n.* Contempt; derision; a subject or object of extreme contempt. *v.t.* To hold in extreme contempt or disdain, to regard as paltry or mean. **scorner**, *n.* **scornful**, *a.*

scorpion (skŏr′pi-ŏn) [Gr. *skorpios*], *n.* One of the *Arachnida*, with claws like a lobster and a sting in the jointed tail; (*Bibl.*) a whip armed with points of iron; (*Astron.*) Scorpio.

scot (1) (skot) [A.-S. *sceot*], *n.* An assessment, a tax. **scot-free**, *a.* Free from payment, untaxed; unhurt, safe.

Scot (2), *n.* A native of Scotland; (*pl.*) a Gaelic tribe that migrated to Scotland from Ireland in the 5th or 6th cent.

Scotch (1) (skoch), *a.* Pertaining to Scotland, its people, language, or literature. *n.* The people of Scotland; the Scottish dialect or dialects of English; Scotch whisky. **Scotchman, Scotsman, -woman**, *n.* **Scotice** (skot′i-si), *adv.* In the Scottish manner. **Scots**, *a.* Scottish. **Scottish**, *a.*

scotch (2) (skoch) [M.E. *scocche*], *v.t.* To cut with narrow incisions; to disable.

scotch (3), *n.* A wedge. *v.t.*

scoundrel (skoun′drĕl) [?], *n.* An unprincipled person, a rascal, a villain. *a.* Base, villainous. **scoundrelism**, *n.* **scoundrelly**, *a.*

scour (1) (skour) [EX-, L. *cūrāre*, to cure], *v.* To clean or polish by friction; to flush or clear out. **scourer**, *n.*

scour (2) [EX-, L. *currere*, to run], *v.i.* To rove, to range; to search about. *v.t.* To move rapidly over, esp. in search.

scourge (skĕrj) [EX-, L. *corium*, hide], *n.* A whip with thongs; (*fig.*) any means of inflicting punishment or suffering. *v.t.* To whip with a scourge; to afflict, to harass.

scout (skout) [F. *écouter*, to listen], *n.* One sent out to bring in information; a Boy Scout; (*Oxf. Univ.*) a college servant. *v.i.* To act as a scout. *v.t.* To treat with contempt. **Boy Scout:** A member of a voluntary organization for training boys on semi-military lines.

scow (skou) [Dut.], *n.* A flat-bottomed boat.

scowl (skoul) [Scand.], *v.i.* To frown, to look sullen. *n.* An angry frown; a look of ill-temper or discontent.

scrabble (skrăbl), *v.i.* To make unmeaning marks; to scrawl.

scrag (skrăg) [Scand.], *n.* Anything thin or shrivelled; a lean, bony piece of meat, esp. neck of mutton. **scragged, scraggy**, *a.*

scram, *v.i.* (*Am.*) To go away, to make oneself scarce.

scramble (skrămbl) [?], *v.i.* To climb or move along by clambering, or on all fours; to struggle (for, after, etc.) in a rough-and-tumble manner. *v.t.* To prepare (eggs) by breaking into a pan and stirring up during cooking. *n.* The act of scrambling; a rough or unceremonious struggle for something. **scrambler**, *n.* (*Wire.*) A device to obtain secrecy in wireless telephone conversations.

scrap (skrăp), *n.* A small detached piece, a bit; a newspaper cutting; waste, esp. discarded metal; (*pl.*) odds-and-ends, leavings. *v.t.* To make scrap of; to discard as worn out. **scrappy**, *a.*

scrape (skrāp) [A.-S. *screpan*, to scratch], *v.t.* To rub with something rough or sharp; to abrade or smooth thus; to erase; to draw or rub along with a scraping noise; to collect or amass with difficulty or by small amounts. *v.i.* To rub something with a rough or sharp instrument; to abrade, smooth, or clean something thus; to get through by a close shave; to be parsimonious. *n.* Act, sound, or effect of scraping; an awkward bow; an awkward predicament. **scraper**, *n.* One who scrapes; an instrument for scraping; a miser.

scratch (skrăch) [?], *v.t.* To tear, mark or scrape with something sharp, as nails, claws, etc.; to wound slightly; to obliterate, to score (out); to expunge (esp. from a list of competitors). *v.i.* To use the nails or claws in marking, hollowing out, etc. *n.* A mark made by or as by scratching; a sound, act, or spell of scratching; a mark from which competitors start in a race or a fight; one most heavily handicapped. *a.* Got together at haphazard, nondescript.

scrawl (skrawl) [?], *v.* To write or mark clumsily or illegibly, to scribble. *n.* A piece of hasty, clumsy, or illegible writing.

scream (skrēm) [Scand.], *v.i.* To make a shrill, piercing, prolonged cry; to hoot or laugh loudly. *v.t.* To utter in a screaming tone. *n.* A loud, shrill, prolonged cry.

scree (skrē) [Icel. *skritha*, landslide], *n.* Loose fragments of rock on a steep slope.

screech (skrēch) [Scand.], *v.i.* To scream out with a harsh, shrill voice, to shriek. *n.* A shrill, harsh cry, as of terror or pain. **screech-owl**, *n.* An owl that screeches instead of hooting.

screed (skrēd), *n.* A long harangue or tirade; a piece, a fragment.

screen (skrēn) [O.F., *escren*], *n.* A partition, esp. in a church between the choir and the nave; a light, movable, covered framework used to shelter from draughts, excess of heat, light, etc.; anything serving to shelter, protect, or conceal; a sheet on which cinematographic pictures, etc., are projected; a coarse sieve. *v.t.* To shelter or protect, to shield; to sift. **screenings**, *n.pl.* Small stuff or refuse separated by screening.

screw (1) (skroo) [?], *n.* A cylinder with a spiral ridge round its outer surface used for fastening boards, etc., together, for conveying motion to part of a machine, bringing pressure to bear, etc.; a screw-propeller; a turn of a screw, a twist; a twisted-up package; (*slang*) a miser; pay, wages. *v.t.* To fasten, tighten, or compress with a screw; to turn round or twist; (*fig.*) to oppress, esp. by exactions; to contort, to distort. *v.i.* To turn as a screw; to swerve. **screw-driver**, *n.* A tool for turning screws.

screw (2), *n.* A broken-down or vicious horse.

scribble (skribl) [L. *scribere*, to write], *v.* To write hastily or illegibly or without regard to correctness. *n.* Hasty or careless writing; a scrawl. **scribbler**, *n.*

scribe (skrīb), *n.* A writer, a secretary, a copyist; (*Bibl.*) a keeper of official records, a commentator or interpreter of sacred law among the ancient Jews.

scrimmage (skrim'ăj), *n.* A confused or rough-and-tumble struggle; a scrummage.

scrimp (skrimp) [Scand.], *v.t.* To make small or scant; to limit, to skimp. **scrimpy**, *a.*

scrip (1) (skrip), *n.* A list of names, a schedule; a provisional certificate of stock.

scrip (2) [A.-S. *scripp*], *n.* A small bag, a wallet.

script (skript) [L. *scriptum*], *n.* A piece of writing; (*Theat., Radio*) typescript or scenario for a play, talk, etc.; handwriting as dist. from print; type in imitation of writing.

scripture (skrip'tyŭr), *n.* A sacred writing, esp. the Bible. **scriptural**, *a.* Pertaining to the Scriptures; **Holy Scripture** or **The Scriptures**: The Bible.

scrivener (skriv'ĕnĕr), *n.* One who drew up contracts, etc., a notary; a financial agent, a moneylender.

scrofula (skrof'ū-lă) [L.], *n.* A constitutional state tending to the development of glandular swellings and consumption; king's evil. **scrofulous**, *a.*

scroll (skrōl) [O.F. *escroue*, from Teut.], *n.* A roll of paper or parchment; a spiral ornament, as a volute, the head of a violin, etc.; a flourish.

scrub (skrŭb) [M.E. *scrobben*], *v.t.* To rub hard with something coarse and rough for cleaning or scouring. *n.* Undergrowth, stunted trees; a paltry, stingy person. **scrubby**, *a.* Mean, insignificant; covered with brushwood; unshaven.

scruff (skrŭf) [Icel.], *n.* The nape or back of the neck.

scrum, scrummage (skrŭm'ăj), *n.* (*Rugby Football*) A regular struggle in which the forwards grapple in a compact mass, the ball being in the middle.

scruple (skroopl) [L. *scrūpus*, sharp stone], *n.* A weight of twenty grains (apoth.); a tiny fraction, a particle; (*fig.*) conscientious doubt or hesitation. *v.i.* To have scruples, to doubt, to be reluctant (to do, etc.). **scru'pulous**, *a.* Influenced by scruples; cautious, punctilious, precise.

scrutator (skroo-tā'tŏr), *n.* One who scrutinizes, a close inquirer.

scrutiny (skroo'ti-ni) [L. *scrūtārī*, to search

carefully], *n.* Close observation or investigation; an official examination of votes. **scrutineer'**, *n.* One who acts as examiner in a scrutiny of votes. **scru'-tinize,** *v.t.* To examine narrowly.

scud (skŭd) [Norw.], *v.i.* To run or fly swiftly; (*Naut.*) to run fast before a gale with little or no sail spread.

scuffle (skŭfl) [Scand.], *v.i.* To fight in a rough-and-tumble way. *n.* A confused fight or struggle.

scull (skŭl) [?], *n.* One of a pair of short oars; one who sculls a boat. *v.t.* To propel (a boat) by sculls. **sculler,** *n.* One who sculls; a boat rowed with sculls.

scullery (skŭl'ĕr-i) [L. *scutellārius,* dish-keeper], *n.* A place where dishes, etc., are washed up.

scullion (skŭl'i-ŏn), *n.* A boy who cleans pots, etc., a kitchen drudge.

sculpture (skŭlp'chŭr) [L. *sculpere,* to carve], *n.* The art of carving, wood or stone into representations of natural objects; a carved figure; (*collect.*) carved work. *v.t.* To represent in or by sculpture; to ornament with sculpture. **sculptor, -tress,** *n.* One who sculptures. **sculptural,** *a.*

scum (skŭm) [Dan. *skum*], *n.* Impurities that rise to the surface of liquid; esp. in fermentation or boiling; froth, foam; (*fig.*) refuse, offscourings. **scummy,** *a.*

scupper (skŭp'ĕr) [?], *n.* A hole through a ship's side to carry off water from the deck.

scurf (skĕrf) [A.-S.], *n.* Flakes thrown off by the skin, esp. of the head; loose scaly matter adhering to a surface. **scurfy,** *a.*

scurrilous (skŭr'i-lŭs) [L. *scurra,* buffoon], *a.* Using or expressed in low, abusive, or indecent language. **scurril'ity,** *n.*

scurry (skŭr'i) [?], *v.i.* To hurry, to scamper. *n.* An act or the noise of scurrying.

scurvy (skĕr'vi), *a.* Mean, paltry, contemptible. *n.* A diseased condition of the blood due to deficiency of vegetables. **scurvily,** *adv.*

scut (skŭt) [cp. Icel. *skott*], *n.* A short tail, as of a hare, rabbit, or deer.

scutch (skŭch) [Scand.], *v.t.* To dress (cotton, flax, etc.) by beating.

scutcheon (skŭch'ŏn), *n.* An escutcheon; a frame for a keyhole; a nameplate.

scuttle (1) (skŭtl) [A.-S. *scutel,* dish], *n.* A receptacle for carrying or holding coals.

scuttle (2) [O.F. *escoutilles,* hatches], *n.* A hatchway on board ship; the lid or hatch covering this. *v.t.* To cut holes through the bottom or sides of (a ship); to sink by cutting such holes.

scuttle (3), *v.i.* To hurry along, to scurry, *n.* A hasty flight, a bolt.

scythe (sīth) [A.-S. *sithe*], *n.* A long curved blade with a crooked handle used for mowing or reaping. *v.t.* To cut with a scythe.

se- [L., away from, apart], *pref.* As *secede.*

sea (sē) [A.-S. *sǣ*], *n.* The body of salt water covering most of the earth, the ocean; a definite part of this; a very large lake; the swell or motion of the sea, a great wave. **sea-anemone,** *n.* A

popular name for a zoophyte. **sea-breeze,** *n.* A breeze blowing from the sea, usually by day in alternation with a land-breeze at night. **sea-captain,** *n.* The captain of a vessel, as dist. from a military officer; a great admiral. **sea-coast,** *n.* **seafarer,** *n.* A sailor, a seaman. **seafaring,** *a.* Following the occupation of a sailor. *n.* The occupation of a sailor. **sea-girt,** *a.* Surrounded by the sea. **sea-green,** *n.* A faint bluish-green. *a.* Of this colour. **sea-gull,** *n.* **sea-kale,** *n.* An indigenous plant grown as a culinary vegetable. **sea-king,** *n.* A viking or piratical Scandinavian chieftain. **sea-legs,** *n.pl.* Ability to walk on deck in a storm. **sea-level,** *n.* A level continuous with that of the surface of the sea at mean tide. **sea-lion,** *n.* A large-eared seal. **seaman,** *n.* (*pl.* **-men**) A sailor, esp. one below the rank of officer; a person able to navigate a ship. **seamanlike, seamanly,** *a.* seamanship, *n.* **seamew,** *n.* A sea-gull. **sea-piece,** *n.* A picture representing a scene at sea. **seaport,** *n.* A town with a harbour on the coast. **sea-room,** *n.* Room to handle a ship without danger of running ashore or of collision. **seashore,** *n.* The margin of the sea; the space between high- and low-water mark. **sea-sick,** *a.* Suffering from sea-sickness. **sea-sickness,** *n.* Nausea and vomiting, brought on by the motion of a ship. **seaside,** *n.* A place or district close to the sea, esp. a watering-place. *a.* Bordering on the sea. **sea-term,** *n.* A word or phrase peculiar to seamen. **sea-urchin,** *n.* A sea animal. **sea-wall,** *n.* A wall for protecting land against encroachment by the sea. **sea-way,** *n.* A ship's progress; a clear way for a ship at sea. **seaweed,** *n.* Any alga or other plant growing in the sea. **seaworthy,** *a.* In a fit state to go to sea (of a ship). **seaworthiness,** *n.* **sea-wrack,** *n.* Coarse seaweed.

seal (1) (sēl) [A.-S. *seolh*], *n.* A carnivorous amphibious marine mammal; various allied mammals, as sea-bear, sea-lion, etc. *v.i.* To hunt seals.

seal (2) (sēl) [L. *sigillum*], *n.* A stamp having a device for making an impression on wax; a piece of wax or other material stamped with this; the impression made thus; a seal affixed to a document in lieu of this; anything regarded as authenticating, ratifying, or guaranteeing. *v.t.* To affix a seal to; to stamp with a seal. **sealing-wax,** *n.* A composition of shellac and turpentine with a pigment, used for sealing letters, etc.

Sealyham (sē'li-hăm) [village in Wales], *n.* A breed of Welsh terrier.

seam (sēm) [A.-S.], *n.* A visible junction between two parts of things, as pieces of cloth sewn together; a crack, a fissure; a wrinkle on the face, a scar; a thin stratum of coal. *v.t.* To join together by a seam; to mark with a seam, scar, etc. **seamstress, sempstress,** *n.* A woman whose occupation is to sew. **seamy,** *a.* Showing the seams; applied to the disreputable or worst side of life, etc.

séance (sā-*ans*) [F.], *n.* A session; a

meeting for exhibiting or investigating spiritualistic manifestations.

sear, sere (sēr) [A.-S. *sēar*], *a.* Dried up, withered. *v.t.* To scorch the surface of; to cauterize; to brand. **seared,** *a.* Hardened, insensible, callous.

search (sĕrch) [M.E. *serchan*], *v.t.* To go over and examine to find something; to explore, to look for. *v.i.* To make inquiry or investigation. *n.* The act of seeking, looking, or inquiring; investigation, quest, examination. **searchlight,** *n.* A powerful light concentrated into a beam that can be turned in any direction. **searching,** *a.* Penetrating, thorough, close. *n.* Examination; minute inquiry.

season (sē'zŏn) [L. *serere*, to sow], *n.* One of the four divisions of the year, spring, summer, autumn, winter; a period of time; the period when something is in vogue, plentiful, at its best, etc.; a favourable opportunity; seasoning. *v.t.* To mature, acclimatize, inure, or harden; to give a relish to by addition of condiments, etc.; to add zest to; to mitigate, to qualify (justice with mercy, etc.). *v.i.* To become habituated, accustomed, etc.; to become hard and dry (of timber). **seasonable,** *a.* Occurring or done at the proper time, opportune. **seasonably,** *adv.* **seasonal,** *a.* **seasoning,** *n.* Anything added to food to make it more palatable; relish.

seat (sēt) [M.E. *sete*], *n.* That on which one may sit, a chair, bench, stool, etc.; the part of this on which one sits, or of a machine, etc., on which another part or thing is supported; location, site, situation; a country residence; the right of sitting, esp. in a legislative body; posture of sitting. *v.t.* To cause to sit down, to place on a seat; to assign seats to; to provide with a seat or seats.

sebaceous (sē-bā'shŭs) [L. *sēbum*, tallow], *a.* Fatty; made of, containing, conveying, or secreting fatty matter.

secant (sē'kănt) [L. *secans*, cutting], *a.* Cutting; dividing into two parts. *n.* (*Math.*) A straight line intersecting a curve.

secede (sē-sēd') [SE-, L. *cedere*, to go], *v.i.* To withdraw from fellowship, association, or communion. **seceder,** *n.* One who secedes.

seclude (sē-klood') [SE-, L. *claudere*, to shut], *v.t.* To shut up or keep (a person, place, etc.) apart or away; to cause to be solitary. **seclu'sion,** *n.* **seclu'sive,** *a.*

second (sek'ŏnd) [L. *secundus*], *a.* Immediately following the first; next in value, authority, rank, or position; other, supplementary, subordinate, derivative. *n.* The next after the first; another or an additional person or thing; one who supports another, esp. in a duel, pugilistic encounter, etc.; the sixtieth part of a minute; (*colloq.*) a very short time; (*pl.*) goods of second quality, esp. coarse flour, or bread made from this; a lower part added to a melody when arranged for two voices or instruments. *v.t.* To forward, promote, support; (*Mil.*, sē-kŏnd') to retire (an officer) temporarily, without pay, in order that he may take some appointment. **second childhood:** Senile dotage. **second-hand,** *a.* Not original; not new; dealing in second-hand goods. **second-rate,** *a.* Of inferior quality, size, value, etc. **second sight:** The power of seeing things at a distance in space or time as if they were present. **secondary,** *a.* and *n.* A deputy. **secondarily,** *adv.* **seconder,** *n.* **secondly,** *adv.* In the second place.

secret (sē'krĕt) [L. *sēcrētus*, reserved], *a.* Concealed, kept private, not to be revealed; occult, mysterious; given to secrecy, reticent; secluded, private. *n.* Something to be concealed or kept back from general knowledge; a mystery, or the key to one; secrecy. **secrecy,** *n.* The state of being secret, concealment; secretiveness; solitude, seclusion. **secretly,** *adv.*

secretary (sek'rē-tăr-ĭ) [L. *sēcrētārius*, a confidential officer], *n.* One conducting the correspondence, keeping the records, etc., of a company, society, etc.; one employed to assist in literary work, correspondence, etc.; a minister in charge of a Government department. **secretary-bird,** *n.* A S. African bird preying on snakes, etc. **secretar'ial,** *a.* **secretariat,** *n.* **secretaryship,** *n.*

secrete (sē-krēt'), *v.t.* To conceal, to hide; to separate from the blood, etc., by secretion. **secretion,** *n.* The act of concealing. **secre'tive,** *a.* Given to secrecy, reserved; promoting or causing secretion. **secretively,** *adv.*

sect (sekt) [L. *secta*], *n.* A body of persons who have separated from a larger body, esp. a Church; a religious denomination (as regarded by opponents); the adherents of a particular philosopher, school of thought, etc. **sectar'ian,** *a.* and *n.* **sectarianism,** *n.* **sec'tary,** *n.* A member of a sect; a Dissenter.

section (sek'shŭn) [L. *secāre*, to cut], *n.* Separation by cutting; that which is cut off, a part; a division of a book, chapter, etc.; the sign [§] indicating such a division; a thin slice of any substance prepared for microscopic examination; a cutting of a solid figure by a plane, the figure so produced; a vertical plan of a building, etc., as it would appear upon an upright plane cutting through it. **sectional,** *a.*

sector (sek'tŏr), *n.* (*Geom.*) A portion of a circle between two radii; a mathematical rule consisting of two hinged arms marked with sines, tangents, etc.; (*Mil.*) a section of a battle front. **sector'ial,** *a.* (*Zool.*) Adapted for cutting like scissors. *n.* A sectorial tooth.

secular (sek'ū-lăr) [L. *sœculum*, generation, age], *a.* Pertaining to the present world, or to things not spiritual or ecclesiastical; temporal, profane; lasting, occurring in, or accomplished during a century or a very long time. *n.* An R.C. parish priest not a Regular. **sec'ularize,** *v.t.*

secure (sē-kūr') [SE-, L. *cūra*, care], *a.* Free from danger or apprehension; safe from attack; reliable, certain, sure (of); in safe keeping. *v.t.* To make safe or secure; to fasten, to close, enclose, or confine securely; to make safe against loss; to get possession of. **securable,** *a.* **securely,** *adv.* **security,** *n.* The state of being or feeling secure; safety; certainty, over-confidence; that which secures; a pledge, a forfeitable guarantee; one who becomes surety for another; a document constituting evidence of debt or of property, a bond, etc.

sedan (sê-dăn') [town in France], *n.* A covered chair for one person, carried by two men by means of a pole on each side; an enclosed motor-car.

sedate (sê-dāt') [L. *sēdātus*, tranquil], *a.* Composed, calm, staid, not impulsive. **sedately,** *adv.* **sedateness,** *n.* sed'ative, *a.* Allaying nervous irritability, soothing. *n.* A sedative medicine, influence, etc.

sedentary (sed'ĕn-tá-ri) [L. *sedēre*, to sit], *a.* Accustomed, inclined, or obliged by occupation, to sit a great deal; involving much sitting.

sedge (sej) [A.-S. *secg*], *n.* A coarse grass-like plant growing in or near water.

sediment (sed'i-mĕnt) [L. *sedimentum*], *n.* The matter which subsides to the bottom of a liquid; dregs. **sedimentary,** *a.*

sedition (sê-dish'ŭn) [L. *seditio*], *n.* Agitation or disorder in a State, not amounting to insurrection; conduct tending to promote treason. **seditious** (sê-dish'ŭs), *a.*

seduce (sê-dūs') [SE-, L. *dūcere*, to lead], *v.t.* To lead astray, to entice from rectitude or duty. **seducer,** *n.* **seduc'tion,** *n.* Act of seducing, esp. of persuading a woman to surrender her chastity; state of being seduced; an enticement, a tempting or attractive quality. **seductive,** *a.*

sedulous (sed'ū-lŭs) [L. *sēdulus*], *a.* Assiduous, persevering in business or endeavour; industrious, diligent. **sedu'lity, sedulousness,** *n.*

see (1) (sē) [A.-S. *sēon*], *v.t.* (*past* **saw,** *p.p.* **seen**) To perceive by the eye; to discern, observe, look at; to understand, apprehend, have an idea of; to witness, to experience; to imagine; to call on, to receive; to escort (a person home, etc.); (*Poker, etc.*) to accept (a challenge). *v.i.* To have or exercise the power of sight; to comprehend; to inquire (into); to consider carefully; to take heed; to give attention; to make provision for; to look out. **seeing,** *conj.* Inasmuch as, since, considering (that). **seer,** *n.* One who foresees, a prophet.

see (2) (sē) [L. *sedēre*, to sit], *n.* The diocese or jurisdiction of a bishop or archbishop. **Holy See:** The Papacy.

seed (sēd) [A.-S. *sæd*], *n.* The mature fertilized ovum of a flowering plant, containing the embryo germ; (*collect.*) seeds, esp. in quantity for sowing; the germ from which anything springs; first principle, beginning or source; (*Bibl.*) offspring, descendants. *v.t.* To sow with seed. **seed-pearl,** *n.* A small seed-like pearl. **seed-time,** *n.* The season for sowing. **seedling,** *a.* Raised from seed; *n.* A plant reared from seed. **seedy,** *a.* Full of seed; going to seed; shabby.

seek (sēk) [A.-S. *sēcan*], *v.t.* (*past and p.p.* **sought,** sawt) To go in search of;

to ask, to solicit (a thing of a person); to pursue as an object; to resort to. *v.i.* To make search or inquiry (after or for); to try (to do).

seem (sēm) [A.-S. *sēman*, to conciliate], *v.i.* To give the impression of being, to be apparently though not in reality; to be evident or apparent (*impers.*). **seeming,** *a.* Apparent, not real; apparent and perhaps real. *n.* Appearance, semblance, esp. when false. **seemingly,** *adv.*

seemly (sēm'li), *a.* Becoming, decent; suited to the occasion. **seemliness,** *n.*

seersucker (sēer'sŭk'ĕr) [Pers.], *n.* A light fabric with a crinkled weave.

see-saw (sē'saw), *n.* A game in which two persons sit one on each end of a board balanced in the middle and move alternately up and down; to act in a vacillating manner.

seethe (sēth) [A.-S. *sēothan*], *v.t.* (*past* **seethed, sod,** *p.p.* **seethed, sod, sodden**) To boil; to prepare by boiling or steeping. *v.i.* To be in a state of ebullition; to bubble over.

segment (seg'mĕnt) [L. *segmentum*], *n.* A portion cut or marked off, a section, a division, esp. one of a natural series (as of a limb between the joints, a fruit or plant organ divided by clefts, etc.).

segregate (seg'rè-gāt) [L. *sēgregātus,* set apart], *v.t.* To separate from others, to isolate. **segrega'tion,** *n.*

seine (sān, sēn) [F.], *n.* A large fishing-net with floats at the top and weights at the bottom. *v.* To catch or fish with this.

seismic, seismal (sīz'mik, -mál) [Gr. *seism-as,* earthquake], *a.* Pertaining to earthquakes. **seismograph,** *n.* An instrument for recording the period, extent and direction of the vibrations of an earthquake. **seismol'ogy** [-LOGY], *n.* The study or science of earthquakes. **seismotic** (-mot'ĭk), *a.* Seismic.

seize (sēz) [O.F. *seisir, saisir,* to put in possession of], *v.t.* To grasp suddenly, to snatch, to take possession of by force; to grasp mentally, to comprehend; (*Law*) to seise; to impound, confiscate. *v.i.* To lay hold (upon). **seizure,** *n.* Act of seizing; a sudden attack, as of a disease.

seldom (sel'dŏm) [A.-S. *seldan*], *adv.* Rarely, not often.

select (sê-lekt') [L. SE-, L. *lectus,* chosen], *a.* Chosen, picked out, choice; exclusive; more valuable. *v.t.* To choose, to pick out (the best, etc.). **selection,** *n.* Act of selecting; right or opportunity of selecting, choice; that which is selected. **selective,** *a.* **selectivity,** *n.* (*Wire.*) The efficiency of a wireless receiver in separating the different broadcasting stations. **selectness,** *n.* **selector,** *n.*

selen- [Gr. *Selēnē,* the moon], *comb. form.* Pertaining to selenium or to the moon. **selenol'ogy** [-LOGY], *n.* The branch of astronomy treating of the moon. **selonolog'ical,** *a.*

self (self (A.-S.), *n.* (*pl.* **selves,** *selvz*) The individuality of a person or thing, as the object of reflexive consciousness or action; one's individual person, private interests, etc.; a flower of a uniform or the original wild colour. *a.* Same; unmixed (of colour); self-coloured; of one piece or the same material. **selfish**, *a.* Attentive only to one's own interests; not regarding the feelings of others; actuated by or proceeding from self-interest. **selfishly**, *adv.* **selfishness**, *n.* **selfless**, *a.* Having no regard for self, unselfish.

self- *comb. form.* Expressing (1) direct or indirect reflexive action, as in *self-command*; (2) action performed independently, or without external agency, as in *self-acting, self-fertilization*; (3) action or relation to the self, as in *self-conscious, self-suspicious*; (4) uniformity, naturalness, etc., as in *self-coloured, self-glazed*. **self-acting** [2], *a.* Acting of itself, automatic. **self-assumed** [2], *a.* Independently assumed by oneself. **self-centred** [3], *a.* Interested solely in oneself and one's own affairs, egotistic. **self-command** [1], *n.* Self-control. **self-complacent** [1], *a.* Pleased with oneself. **self-conscious** [3], *a.* Conscious of one's actions, behaviour, situation, etc., esp. as observed by others. **self-contained** [1], *a.* Reserved, not communicative; [2] complete in itself. **self-defence** [1], *n.* The act of defending one's own person, property, or reputation. **the art of self-defence:** Boxing. **self-evident** [3], *a.* Obvious of itself, not requiring proof or demonstration. **self-help** [1], *n.* The act or practice of attaining one's ends without help from others.

self-love [1], *n.* Undue regard for oneself or one's own interests; selfishness; conceit. **self-made** [1], *a.* Successful, wealthy, etc., through one's own exertions. **self-possessed** [1], *a.* Calm, imperturbable, having presence of mind. **self-preservation** [1], *n.* Preservation of oneself from injury; the instinct impelling one to this. **self-regard** [1], *n.* Consideration or respect for oneself. **self-reliant** [3], *a.* Relying on oneself, independent of outside aid. **self-respect** [1], *n.* Due regard for one's character and position; observing a worthy standard of conduct. **self-righteous** [3], *a.* Pharisaical. **selfsame** [4], *a.* Exactly the same, absolutely identical. **self-seeker** [3], *n.* One selfishly pursuing his own interests. **self-sufficient, -sufficing** [3], *a.* Capable of fulfilling one's own desires, etc., without aid; conceited, overbearing. **self-will** [3], *n.* Obstinacy. **self-willed**, *a.*

sell (sel) [A.-S. *sellan*], *v.t.* To dispose of (property) for money; to be a regular dealer in; to surrender or betray for a price; *(slang)* to disappoint, to cheat. *v.i.* To be a shopkeeper or dealer; to be purchased, to find purchasers. **seller**, *n.*

seltzer (selt'sẽr) [corr. of *Selters*, town of Nassau], *n.* An effervescing mineral water.

selvage, selvedge (sel'vĕj) [SELF, EDGE], *n.* The edge of cloth woven so as not to unravel; a narrow strip of different material woven at the edge.

semantics (se-măn'tiks) [Gr. *semantikos*, significant], *n.pl.* The study of the meanings of words as distinct from their derivations.

semaphore (sem'à-fôr) [Gr. *sēma*, sign, *pherein*, to bear], *n.* An apparatus for signalling by means of oscillating arms or flags or the arrangement of lanterns, etc.

semblance (sem-blàns) [O.F.], *n.* External appearance, seeming; an image.

semen (sē'mĕn) [L., seed], *n.* The fertilizing fluid of males.

semi- [L.], *pref.* Half; partially, imperfectly. **semibreve** (sem'i-brēv), *n.* (*Mus.*) A note equal to half a breve, a whole note. **semi-chorus**, *n.* One sung by only a half or portion of the choir; a chorus to be rendered thus. **semicircle**, *n.* A half circle. **semicolon**, *n.* A punctuation mark (;) intermediate between the period and the comma. **semidetached**, *a.* Partially detached (chiefly of houses built in pairs).

seminal (sem'i-nàl), *a.* Pertaining to semen or reproduction; propagative.

seminary (sem'i-nàr-i) [L. *sēminārium*, seed-plot], *n.* A place of education, a college.

semiquaver, *n.* (*Mus.*) A note of half the duration of a quaver.

Semite (sē'mīt), *n.* A descendant of Shem; a member of Hebrew, Phœnician, Aramæan, Assyrian, Arab, or Abyssinian race reputed to be descended from Shem. **Semitic** (sē-mit'ik), *a.* Pertaining to the Semites or their languages. *n.* One of this group of languages.

semitone (sem'i-tōn), *n.* (*Mus.*) An interval equal to half a major tone on the scale.

semolina (sem-ö-lē'nà) [It. *semolino*, fine bran], *n.* The hard grains of wheat left after bolting.

sempiternal (sem-pi'tẽr'nàl) [L. *sempiternus*], *a.* Everlasting, eternal.

sempstress [SEAM (1)].

senary (sē'nà-ri) [L. *sēni*, six each], *a.* Containing six units; by sixes.

senate (sen'àt) [L. *senātus*], *n.* An assembly performing legislative or administrative functions; a State council; an upper legislative house in various national parliaments; the governing body of certain Universities; (*fig.*) any venerable deliberative or legislative body. **senator**, *n.* A member of a senate. **senator'ial**, *a.*

send (send) [A.-S. *sendan*], *v.t.* (*past and p.p.* sent) To cause to go, pass, or be transmitted to some destination; to propel, hurl, cast; to cause to befall, to grant, bestow, inflict; to bring about. *v.i.* To dispatch a messenger.

senescent (sē-nes'ĕnt) [L. *senescens*], *a.* Growing old. **senescence**, *n.*

seneschal (sen'ĕ-shàl) [O.F., from Teut.], *n.* An officer in wealthy houses in the Middle Ages who superintended feasts and domestic ceremonies; a steward.

senile (sē'nīl) [L. *senīlis*], *a.* Pertaining to old age. **senility** (-nil'i-ti), *n.*

senior (sē'nyôr) [L. older, comp. of *senex*, old], *a.* Older, elder; higher in rank or service. *n.* One older or higher in rank, service, etc., than another. **seniority** (-ni-or'i-ti), *n.*

senna (sen'à) [Arab. *sanā*], *n.* The dried, purgative leaflets of several species of cassia.

señor (sen-yor'), *n.* (*fem.*, *-ora*, *-orita*, -yō-rē'tà), *n.* The Spanish form of address, equivalent to Mr. Mrs., Miss, sir, madam, etc.

sensation (sen-sā'shùn), *n.* Mental state or affection resulting from the excitation of an organ of sense; a state of excited feeling or interest; the thing or event exciting this. **sensational,** *a.* **sensationally** *adv.* **sensationalism** *n.* The employment of sensational methods.

sense (sens) [F., *sens,* L. *sensus,* feeling, from *sentīre,* to feel], *n.* One of the five faculties by which sensation is received (sight, hearing, touch, taste, smell); the faculty of sensation, perception, or sensitiveness; bodily feeling; intuitive comprehension, appreciation; conviction (of); sound judgment, sagacity, good mental capacity; meaning; general feeling, consensus of opinion; (*pl.*) normal command of the senses, sanity. **senseless,** *a.* **senselessness,** *n.*

sensible (sen'sibl), *a.* Perceptible by the senses; acting with or characterized by good sense, judicious, reasonable; having perception (of). **sensibil'ity,** *n.* Capacity to see, feel, or receive impressions; acute susceptibility, over-sensitiveness. **sensibly,** *adv.*

sensitive (sen'si-tiv), *a.* Of or depending on the senses, sensory; readily or acutely affected by external influences; impressible, excitable. **sensitive plant:** A mimosa, the leaves of which shrink from the touch. **sensitively,** *adv.*

sensual (sen'sū-àl), *a.* Pertaining to or affecting the senses, carnal as dist. from spiritual or intellectual; voluptuous, lewd. **sen'sualism, sensua'lity,** *n.* **sensualist,** *n.* **sensually,** *adv.*

sensuous (sen'sū-ùs), *a.* Pertaining to or readily affected through the senses; abounding in sensible images. **sensuously,** *adv.* **sensuousness,** *n.*

sentence (sen'tèns), *n.* A series of words expressing a complete thought; a penalty (or its declaration) upon a condemned person, a verdict; a maxim, a proverb. *v.t.* To pronounce judgment on; to condemn. **sententious,** *a.* Abounding in pithy sentences or maxims; terse; affectedly formal. **sententiously,** *adv.*

sentient (sen'shi-ènt), *a.* Having the power of sense-perception; having sense of feeling. **sentience,** *n.*

sentiment (sen'ti-mènt), *n.* Mental feeling; or the sum of the higher feelings excited by æsthetic, moral, or spiritual ideas; a thought, etc., of sensibility. **sentimen'tal,** *a.* Swayed by feeling, emotional, mawkish. **sentimentalism, -tal'ity,** *n.* **sentimen'talist,** *n.* **sentimentally,** *adv.*

sentinel (sen'ti-nèl) [O.F. *sentinelle*], *n.* One who keeps watch to prevent surprise, a soldier on guard.

sentry (sen'tri), *n.* A sentinel.

separate (sep'à-rāt) [L. *sēparātus,* p.p. of *sēparāre*], *v.t.* To disunite, to keep apart; to break up into parts, to disperse; to be between or the boundary of. *v.i.* To part, to be disconnected; to disperse. *a.* (sep'à-ràt) Disconnected, considered apart; distinct. **separabil'ity,** *n.* **separ-**

able, *a.* **separably,** *adv.* **separately,** *adv.* **separateness,** *n.* **separa'tion,** *n.* Act of separating or state of being separated; partial divorce. **sep'arator,** *n.*

sepia (sē'pi-à) [L. and Gr.], *n.* A dark brown pigment prepared from the cuttle-fish; a cuttle-fish.

sepoy (sē'poi) [Hind. *sipāh,* army], *n.* A native soldier in the former British Indian army.

sepsis (sep'sis) [Gr.], *n.* Putrefaction; infection from a festering wound, blood-poisoning.

sept (sept) [O.F.], *n.* A clan, a family, esp. in Ireland.

September (sep-tem'bėr) [L., *septem,* seven], *n.* The ninth month of the year (the seventh of the ancient Roman year).

septenary (sep'tè-nàr-i), *a.* Consisting of or relating to seven; by sevens; lasting seven years. *n.* A set of seven.

septet (sep-tet'), *n.* A group of seven, esp. singers, instruments, etc.; a musical composition for seven performers.

septic (sep'tik) [Gr. *sēptos,* rotten], *a.* Causing or tending to promote putrefaction, not aseptic. *n.* A septic substance. **septicæmia** (-sē'mi-à), *n.* Blood-poisoning caused by the absorption of putrid matter.

septuagenarian (sep-tū-à-jè-nâr'i-àn), *n.* A person of 70 years of age, or between 69 and 80. Of such an age. **Septuages'-ima** *n.* The third Sunday before Lent (about seventy days before Easter).

Septuagint (sep'tū-à-jint), *n.* A Greek version of the Old Testament and Apocrypha (*c.* 3rd cent. B.C.), traditionally made by seventy persons.

sepulchre (sep'ùl-kėr) [L. *sepelīre,* to bury], *n.* A tomb, esp. one hewn in rock; a burial-vault. **sepul'chral,** *a.* Pertaining to burial, the grave, or to monuments to the dead; dismal, funereal.

sequel (sē'kwèl) [L. *sequī,* to follow], *n.* That which follows; a succeeding part, a continuation; the upshot, consequence (of an event, etc.).

sequence (sē'kwèns), *n.* Succession, the process of coming after in space, time, etc.; a consecutive series. **sequent, sequen'tial** *a.*

sequester (sè-kwes'tėr) [L. *sequestrāre,* to surrender], *v.t.* To set apart, to seclude; (*Law*) to separate (property, etc.) from the owner until some case is decided or claim paid; to confiscate. **sequestrate** *v.t.* (*Law*) To sequester. **sequestra'tion** *n.* **se'questrator** *n.*

sequin (sē'kwin) [It. *zecchino,* Arab. *sikka,* die], *n.* A Venetian gold coin; a disk of metal, jet, etc., used as a trimming for dresses, etc.

seraglio (sè-ra'lyō) [It. *serraglio,* enclosure], *n.* A walled palace; a harem.

seraph (ser'àf) [Heb. *serāphīm,* pl., from Arab. *sharaf,* high], *n.* (*pl.* **-aphs -aphim**) An angel of the highest order. **seraph'ic,** *a.*

sere (sēr) [O.F. *serre,* grasp, lock], *n.* The pawl of a gun-lock holding the hammer at half or full cock.

serenade (ser-è-nād') [F. *sérénade*], *n.* Music played or sung in the open at night, esp. by a lover beneath his lady's window. *v.i.* To perform a serenade.

serene (sĕ-rēn') [L. *serēnus*], *a.* Calm and clear (of the sky); undisturbed. *n.* **serenely** *adv.* Calmly, quietly, deliberately. **serenity** (sĕ-ren'i-ti), *n.*

serf (sĕrf) [L. *servus*, slave], *n.* A feudal labourer attached to an estate; a slave. **serfdom** *n.*

serge (sĕrj) [F.], *n.* A strong twilled cloth, usu. of worsted.

sergeant (*Law*) **serjeant** (sar'jĕnt) [O.F. *sergant*, L. *servīre*, to serve], *n.* (*Mil.*) A non-commissioned officer ranking next above corporal; a police-officer next below an inspector; a serjeant-at-law. **serjeant-at-law**, *n.* Formerly a member of the highest order of barristers, abolished in 1877. **sergeant-major**, *n.* The chief sergeant of a regiment, or of a squadron of cavalry, or of a battery of artillery.

serial (sēr'i-ăl), *a.* Pertaining to or consisting of a series. *n.* A story or publication appearing in periodical parts. **serially**, *adv.* **seria'tim**, *adv.* In regular order; one point, etc., after the other.

series (sēr'ēz) [L. *serere*, to join together], *n.* (*pl. unchanged*) A number, set, or continued succession of things; a sequence, a row.

serif (ser'if), *n.* (*Typo.*) One of the fine cross-lines at the top or bottom of a letter.

serious (sēr'i-ùs) [L. *serius*], *a.* Grave, sedate, not frivolous; momentous; in earnest, sincere. **serio-**, *comb. form.* **serio-comic**, *a.* Mingling the serious and the comic. **seriousness**, *n.*

sermon (sĕr'mòn) [L. *sermo*, speech, discourse], *n.* A discourse founded on a text of Scripture in exposition of doctrine or instruction in religion; a moral reflection; a serious exhortation. **sermoner**, *n.* **sermonize**, *v.*

serous (sēr'ùs), *a.* Pertaining to serum; thin, watery; like whey. **seros'ity**, *n.*

serpent (sĕr'pent) [L. *serpere*, to creep], *n.* A reptile with an elongated scaly body and no limbs, a snake; a treacherous, insinuating person; an old-fashioned wind-instrument. **serpentine**, *a.* Pertaining to or resembling a serpent; coiling, sinuous; wily, treacherous. *n.* A variegated rock susceptible of a high polish.

serrate (ser'āt) [L. *serra*, a saw], *a.* Notched like a saw, serrated. *v.t.* (sĕ-rāt') To give a saw-like edge to (*usu. in p.p.*). **serra'tion**, *n.*

serried (ser'ĕd) [F. *serré*, closed], *a.* Closepacked, in compact order (esp. of soldiers).

serum (sēr'ùm) [L., whey], *n.* The thin, transparent part that separates from the blood in coagulation, a constituent of milk, lymph.

servant (sĕr'vánt) [F., serving], *n.* An employee, esp. in a household, a domestic; a devoted follower.

serve (sĕrv) [L. *servus*, slave], *v.t.* To act as servant to, to be useful to, render service to; to be subsidiary to; to satisfy, to suffice; to perform (a function, etc.);

to carry out the duties of; to treat (well, ill, etc.); to set on table; to supply (a person with); to send (a ball, etc.). *v.i.* To be employed, to perform the duties of at a function, etc.; to suffice, to avail; to be suitable; to deliver the ball in certain games.

service (1) (sĕr'vis), *n.* Act of serving; work done for another; a benefit conferred on some one; the state of being a servant; a department of State, etc., the organization, or the persons employed; willingness to act; use; a liturgical form or act for worship; a musical setting of this; legal delivery or publication (of a writ, summons, etc.); a set of dishes, etc., required for a meal; act of serving the ball at tennis, etc.

service (2) [M.E. *serves*, L. *sorbus*], *n.* The service-tree, a European tree, with small pear-like fruit.

serviceable (sĕr'vis-ábl), *a.*l Able or wiling to render service; useful, fit for service.

serviette (sĕr-vi-et') [F.], *n.* A table-napkin.

servile (sĕr'vil), *a.* Pertaining to or befitting a slave; abject, cringing; dependent. **servility** (-vil'i-ti), *n.*

servitor (sĕr'vi-tòr), *n.* A male servant or attendant. **servitorship**, *n.*

servitude (sĕr'vi-tūd), *n.* The condition of a slave, bondage.

servo control (sĕr'vō), *n.* A mechanical means of reinforcing or replacing physical effort in working the controls of an aircraft or vehicle.

sesame (ses'á-mi) [Gr. *sesamon*], *n.* An E. Indian annual herb with oily seeds.

sesqui- [L. more by one half], *comb. form.* **sesquipedalian** (-dā'li-án), *a.* Manysyllabled (of words); given to using long words.

session (sesh'ùn) [L. *sedēre*, to sit], *n.* The act of being assembled; a sitting or meeting of a court, council, etc., for business; the period during which such meetings are held. **sessional**, *a.*

sestet (ses-tet') [L. *sextus*, sixth], *n.* (*Mus.*) A composition for six instruments or voices; the last six lines of a sonnet.

set (1) (set) [A.-S. *settan*, casual of *sittan*, to sit], *v.t.* To place, to put; to fix; to plant (*usu.* out); to put or station in a specified or right position, state, etc.; to dispose for use, display, etc.; to attach, join; to determine, appoint, settle; to cause to sit; to apply (oneself, etc., to), to cause (to work, etc.); to offer (an example, task, etc.); to compose (type); (*Mus.*) to adapt (words) to music; (*Naut.*) to spread (sail). *v.i.* To become solid or firm, to congeal; to take shape; to move or tend in a definite direction; to mature (of flowers, etc.); to point (of a dog); to pass below the horizon. *a.* Fixed, unyielding; determined, intent (on); stationary; prescribed; regular, in due form.

set (2) (set) [O.F. *sette*], *n.* A number of similar or related things or persons, a group; a number of things forming a whole; a group of games counting as a unit, as in lawn-tennis; the way a dress, etc., sits; bend, bias; the act of pointing at game (by a setter). **set off,** *n.* A counterpoise, a counter-claim; an embellishment.

settee (sė-tē') [?], *n.* A long seat with a back; a short sofa for two.

setter (set'ėr), *n.* One who or that which sets; a dog trained to point at game.

setting (set'ing), *n.* The action of one who or that which sets; the result of this; solidification; the framing in which a jewel, etc., is set; the environment of a thing, event, etc.; the music to which words are fitted.

settle (1) (setl) [A.-S. *setl*], *n.* A long, high-backed bench with arms.

settle (2) [A.-S. *setlan*], *v.t.* To place in a permanent position, to establish; to cause to become fixed; to determine; to colonize; to cause to subside; to deal with, dispose of, do for, to pay (an account); to secure property, etc. (on); to arrange, adjust (a dispute, etc.). *v.i.* To sit down, to alight; to cease from agitation, etc.; to become motionless, permanent or established, to become a colonist (in); to sink to the bottom; to become clarified; to resolve (upon); to adjust differences. **settlement,** *n.* Act of settling; state of being settled; a subsidence; a place newly settled; a community of persons living together; the conveyance of property or creation of an estate to make provision for some person or object; the property so settled. **settler,** *n.* A colonist; a knock-down blow, a decisive argument.

seven (sevn) [A.-S. *seofon*], *n.* The sum of one and six, 7 or vii. *a.* Consisting of one more than six. **seven-fold,** *a.* and *adv.* **seventeen,** *n.* The sum of seven and ten, 17 or xvii. *a.* Consisting of seven and ten. **seventeenth,** *a.* and *n.* **seventh,** *a.* Coming next after the sixth. *n.* The next after the sixth; a seventh part. **seventhly,** *adv.*

seventy (sevn'ti), *n.* Seven times ten, 70 or lxx. *a.* Consisting of or amounting to seven times ten. **seventieth,** *a.* and *n.*

sever (sev'ėr) [O.F. *sevrer*], *v.t.* To part, disjoin; to divide, cleave, sunder; to keep distinct. *v.i.* To separate, part. **severable,** *a.* **severance,** *n.*

several (sev'ėr-ȧl), *a.* Separate, distinct, individual; not shared with others; consisting of a number. *n.* An indefinite number, more than two but not many. **severally,** *adv.* **severalty,** *n.* (*Law*) Exclusive tenure or ownership.

severe (sė-vēr') [L. *severus*], *a.* Rigorous, austere, merciless; hard to endure; bitter, painful; grave, sedate; unadorned, restrained. **severely,** *adv.* **severity** (-ver'i-ti), *n.*

sew (sō) [A.-S. *siwian*], *v.t.* (*p.p.* sewn, sewed) To unite by thread worked through and through with a needle; to make, mend, attach, etc., thus.

sewer (sū'ėr) [O.F. *seuwiere*, sluice], *n.* A channel or tunnel for carrying off drainage and liquid refuse. **sewerage,** *n.*

sex (seks) [F. *sexe*, L. *sexus*], *n.* The quality of being male and female. **sexless,** *a.* **sexlessness,** *n.*

sex-, sexi- [L. *sex*, six], *comb. form.* Containing six; six-fold. **sexagenarian**

(sek-sȧ-jė-nâr'i-ȧn) [L. *sexāgēnī*, sixty each], *n.* Sixty years of age or between 59 and 70. *n.* A sexagenarian person.

Sexagesima (sek-sȧ-jes'i-mȧ), *n.* The second Sunday before Lent (about the sixtieth day before Easter).

sextant (sek'stȧnt), *n.* The sixth part of a circle; an instrument for measuring angular distances or altitudes.

sexton (sek'stȯn), *n.* A sacristan, a caretaker of a church.

sexual (sek'sū-ȧl), *a.* Pertaining to sex, the sexes or the distinction of sexes; pertaining to generation. **sexual'ity,** *n.* sexually, *adv.*

shabby (shăb'i), *a.* Ragged, threadbare; clothed thus, mean, despicable. **shabbily,** *adv.* **shabbiness,** *n.*

shackle (shăkl) [A.-S. *sceacul*], *n.* A fetter, handcuff; the bow of a padlock; a coupling link; (*pl.*) impediments. *v.t.* To chain, fetter; to restrain, impede, hamper.

shad (shăd) [A.-S. *sceadda*], *n.* A deep-bodied food-fish of the herring family.

shade (shād) [A.-S. *scæd*], *n.* Obscurity caused by the interception of light; gloom, darkness; a secluded retreat; the darker part of a picture; a screen for protecting from light; a glass cover; a gradation of colour; (*fig.*) a small amount, something unreal or delusive; a spectre; (*pl.*) Hades. *v.t.* To shelter or screen; to obscure, to darken; to show gradations of colour or effects of light and shade; to cause to blend with another colour. **shadeless,** *a.* **shadily,** etc. [SHADY[. **shading,** *n.*

shadow (shăd'ō), *n.* Shade; a patch of shade; the dark figure projected on the ground, etc., by the interception of light; obscurity; shelter; something unreal; a phantom. *v.t.* To cloud; to set (forth) dimly, to adumbrate; to spy upon. **shadowy,** *a.*

shady (shā'di), *a.* Sheltered from the sun; casting shade; of equivocal honesty. **shadily,** *adv.* **shadiness,** *n.*

shaft (shaft) [A.-S. *sceaft*], *n.* The slender stem of a spear, arrow, etc.; anything resembling this, as a ray (of light), a dart (of lightning, ridicule, etc.); a column between the base and the capital; a large axle; a well-like excavation, as in a mine. **shafting,** *n.* A system of shafts for the transmission of power.

shag (shăg) [A.-S. *sceacga*], *n.* A rough coat of hair; cloth having a coarse nap; strong tobacco cut into fine shreds; the crested cormorant. **shaggy,** *a.* Rough-haired, hairy; tangled, unkempt; overgrown, scrubby, rugged.

shagreen (shȧ-grēn'), *n.* A leather with a granular surface prepared without tanning from the skins of horses, asses, sharks, etc., usu. dyed green.

shah (sha) [Pers.], *n.* The sovereign of Persia.

shake (shāk) [A.-S. *sceacan*], *v.t.* (*past* shook, shuk, *p.p.* shaken) To move forcibly or rapidly to and fro; to cause to quiver; to shock, convulse, agitate; to brandish; to impair, to shatter; to trill. *v.i.* To move quickly to and fro or up and down, to tremble, to shiver; to make

trills. *n.* Act of shaking; a jerk, shock, concussion; state of being shaken, vibration, trembling; a trill.

shako (shăk'ō) Hung. *csako*], *n.* A military flat-topped cylindrical hat, with a peak in front, and a pompom, or plume.

shaky (shā'ki), *a.* Liable to shake, rickety, tottering; (*fig.*) of doubtful integrity. solvency, etc. **shakily,** *adv.* **shakiness,** *n.*

shale (shāl) [G. *schale*], *n.* A laminated rock resembling soft slate, often containing bitumen. **shaly,** *a.*

shall (shăl) [A.-S. *sceal*, past of *sculan*, to owe], *v.aux.* (*2nd sing.* **shalt,** *past and subj.* **should,** shud, shouldst, shouldest) Used to express simple futurity or a conditional statement (*now only in 1st pers.*); to express a command, intention, promise, permission, etc. (*in 2nd and 3rd pers.*); to express future or conditional obligation, duty, etc., or to form a conditional antecedent clause, etc. (*in any person*).

shalloon (shà-loon') [F. *Châlons*-sur-Marne], *n.* A light worsted fabric used for linings, etc.

shallop (shăl'ŏp) [F. *chaloupe*], *n.* A light open boat.

shallot (shà-lot') [O.F. *eschalote*, corr. of *Ascalon*, Palestine], *n.* A plant allied to garlic.

shallow (shăl'ō) [M.E. *schalowe*], *a.* Not having much depth; (*fig.*) superficial, trivial. *n.* A shallow place, a shoal. *v.* To become or make shallow or shallower.

sham (shăm), *v.* To feign, to pretend. *n.* An imposture, a false pretence, a fraud, *a.* Feigned, counterfeit.

shamble (shămbl) [?], *v.i.* To walk in an awkward or unsteady manner. *n.* A shuffling gait. **shambling,** *a.*

shambles (shămblz) [A.-S. *scamel*], *n.pl.* A slaughter-house; a meat market; (*fig.*) a place of carnage or execution.

shame (shām) [A.-S. *sceamu*], *n.* A painful feeling due to consciousness of guilt, degradation, humiliation, etc.; the instinct to avoid this, decency, decorum; a state of ignominy; a disgrace. *v.t.* To make ashamed; to bring shame on; to disgrace. **shamefaced, shamefast** [A.-S. *scamfœst* (FAST (1))], *a.* Bashful, modest, retiring. **shameful,** *a.* shamefully, *adv.* **shameless,** *a.*

shampoo (shăm-poo') [Hind. *chămpnā*], *v.t.* To massage the body of after a hot bath; to wash and rub the head of. *n.* The act of shampooing.

shamrock (shăm'rok) [Ir. *seamrog*]. *n.* A trefoil forming the national emblem of Ireland.

shandrydan (shăn'dri-dăn) [?], *n.* A kind of hooded chaise; (*fig.*) a ramshackle conveyance.

shandygaff (shăn'di-găf) [?], *n.* A mixture of beer and ginger-beer.

shanghai (shăng-hi') [Chinese city], *v.t.* To kidnap a sailor when drugged.

shank (shăngk) [A.-S. *sceanca*], *n.* The leg from knee to ankle; the shin-bone; the part of a tool connecting the acting part with the handle.

shanty (shăn'ti) [?], *n.* A rude hut.

shape (shāp) [A.-S *scieppan*], *v.t.* To form, to construct; to mould, to fashion; to adapt, adjust, make conform (to); to regulate. *v.t.* To take shape, come into shape; to become adapted (to). *n.* The outward form or appearance; concrete form, embodiment, realization; kind, sort; an appearance, an apparition; a pattern, a mould. **shapeable,** *a.* **shapeless,** *a.* Having no regular form; lacking in symmetry. **shapely,** *a.* Well-proportioned; having beauty or regularity. **shapeliness,** *n.*

shard (shard) [A.-S. *sceard*], *n.* A potsherd; the wing-case of a beetle. *v.t.* and *i.* To break or flake off.

share (1) (shâr) [A.-S. *scearu*, from *sceran*, to shear], *n.* A part detached from a common amount; a part to which one has a right or which one is obliged to contribute, an allotted part; one of the equal parts into which the capital of a company is divided. *v.t.* To divide into portions, to apportion; to give away a portion of; to partake of, to participate in. *v.i.* To have a share (in), to participate. **sharer,** *n.*

share (2) (shâr), *n.* A plough-share; a blade of a cultivator, etc.

shark (shark) [?], *n.* A large and voracious sea-fish with lateral gill openings and an inferior mouth armed with formidable teeth; (*fig.*) a rapacious person; a swindler.

sharp (sharp) [A.-S. *scearp*], *a.* Having a keen edge or fine point; peaked, angular, abrupt; clean-cut; acid, sour; shrill, piercing; sarcastic, severe, painful; acute, keen-witted; vigilant, penetrating; unscrupulous, dishonest; quick, brisk, impetuous; (*Phon.*) voiceless; (*Mus.*) above the true pitch, esp. a semitone higher. *adv.* Punctually; at a sharp angle; above the true pitch. *n.* (*Mus.*) A note a semitone above the true pitch; the sign (♯) indicating this. *v.i.* To swindle. **sharp-cut,** *a.* Clearly outlined, well-defined. **sharpshooter,** *n.* A skilled marksman. **sharpen,** *v.* **sharpener,** *n.* **sharper,** *n.* A swindler, a rogue. **sharply,** *adv.* **sharpness,** *n.*

shatter (shăt'ér), *v.t.* To break up at once into many pieces, to smash; to destroy, ruin. *v.i.* To break into fragments.

shave (shāv) [A.-S. *sceafan*], *v.t.* To remove hair from (the skin) with a razor, etc.; to pare thin slices off; to pass by closely, to brush past, to graze. *v.i.* To shave oneself. *n.* Act of shaving or process of being shaved; a thin slice; a narrow escape or miss. **shaving,** *n.* A thin slice pared off.

Shavian (shā'vi-àn) [G. B. *Shaw* (1856–1950)], *a.* Of or in the manner of G. B. Shaw.

shawl (shawl) [Pers. *shāl*], *n.* A loose wrap for the upper part of the person.

shawm (shawm) [Gr. *kalamos*, reed], *n.* An ancient clarionet-like wind instrument.

she (shē) [A.-S. *sēo*], *pron.* (*obj.* **her,** *poss.* **her, hers**) The female person, animal, etc., referred to. *a.* Female (as *she-cat, she-devil,* etc.).

sheaf (shēf) [A.-S. *scēaf*], *n.* (pl. **-ves**) A quantity of things bound together lengthwise, esp. a bundle of wheat, oats, barley, etc.

shear (shēr) [A.-S. *sceran*], *v.t.* (*past* sheared, *p.p.* shorn, sheared) To cut with shears; to remove nap, wool, etc., by clipping; (*fig.*) to fleece. *v.i.* To use shears, *n.* (*pl.*) A large cutting-instrument like scissors. **shearer**, *n.* **shearling**, *n.* A sheep that has been once shorn.

sheath (shēth) [A.-S. *scœth*], *n.* A case for a blade or tool, a scabbard; (*Nat. Hist.*) an envelope investing tissue, membrane, etc. **sheathe** (shēth), *v.t.* To put into a sheath; to protect by a casing; to hide. **sheathing**, *n.* That which sheathes, esp. a metal covering for a ship's bottom.

sheave (shēv) [M.E. *schīve*], *n.* The grooved wheel in the block or pulley over which the rope runs.

shed (1) (shed) [A.-S. *scēadan*, to separate], *v.t.* To let fall, to drop, to spill; to throw off, diffuse. *v.i.* To cast off seed, a covering, etc. *n.* The ridge of a hill; a divide, a watershed.

shed (2), *n.* A slight building for storing, use as a workshop, etc.

sheen (shēn) [A.-S. *scēne*], *n.* Brightness, lustre, glitter. **sheeny**, *a.*

sheep (shēp) [A.-S. *scēap*], *n.* (*pl. unchanged*) A gregarious ruminant animal reared for its flesh and wool; sheepskin; (*fig.*) a timid, unoriginal person. **sheepfold**, *n.* A pen for sheep. **sheep-run**, *n.* A large tract of land for pasturing sheep. **sheep's eye**, *n.* (*usu. in pl.*) A bashful or diffident look or glance. **sheepish**, *a.* Like a sheep; bashful, timid. **sheepishly**, *adv.*

sheer (1) (shēr) [Icel. *skœrr*], *a.* Pure, simple, mere, absolute, downright; perpendicular, unbroken by a ledge or slope. *adv.* Vertically, plumb; entirely.

sheer (2) (shēr) [Dut. *scheren*, to shear], *v.i.* (*Naut.*) To deviate from a course. *n.* The upward curvature of a vessel toward the bow and stern.

sheers (shērs), *n.pl.* An apparatus consisting of two masts secured at the top, for hoisting heavy weights.

sheet (shēt) [A.-S. *scēte*], *n.* A thin, flat, broad piece of anything; a rectangular piece of linen or cotton used on a bed; a piece of metal in a thin sheet, a piece of paper of a regular size, reckoned as the 24th of a quire; a newspaper; a broad expanse; (*Naut.*) a rope attached to the clew of a sail. *v.t.* To cover or shroud in a sheet; to form into sheets. **sheet-anchor** [*shoot-anchor*, one to be shot out], *n.* A large anchor for use in emergencies; (*fig.*) a last refuge. **sheet-lightning**, *n.* Lightning in wide extended flashes. **sheeting**, *n.*

sheikh (shēk, shek) [Arab.], *n.* The head of a Bedouin family, clan, or tribe.

shekel (shek'él) [Heb. *shegel*], *n.* A Hebrew weight of nearly ½ oz.; a silver coin, worth about 2*s.* 4*d.*; (*pl.*) money, riches.

sheldrake (shel'drāk) [A.-S. *scild*, shield], *n.* A large wild duck with vivid plumage.

shelf (shelf) [A.-S. *scylfe*], *n.* (*pl. -ves*) A horizontal board or slab for standing vessels, books, etc., on.

shell (shel) [A.-S. *scell*], *n.* A hard outside covering, as of a nut, egg, animal, etc., a husk; the framework or walls of a house, ship, etc.; an inner coffin; a hollow projectile containing a bursting-charge, missiles, etc.; (*fig.*) mere outer form or semblance. *v.t.* To strip or break off the shell from; to take out of the shell; to cover with a shell; to throw shells at, to bombard. **shellfish**, *n.* Any aquatic mollusc or crustacean having a shell. **shelly**, *a.*

shellac (shě-lăk'), *n.* Resin purified and melted into thin plates. *v.t.* To varnish with this. **shellacking**, *pres.p.*

shelter (shel'tér) [A.-S. *scildtrume*], *n.* Anything that shields from danger, heat, wind, etc.; security; a place of safety. *v.t.* To shield from injury, danger, etc.; to protect, to conceal, to screen. *v.i.* To take shelter (under).

shelve (1) (shelv), *v.t.* To place on a shelf; to fit with shelves; (*fig.*) to put aside, to defer indefinitely. **shelving**, *n.*

shelve (2), *v.i.* To slope gradually.

shepherd (shep'érd), *n.* One who tends sheep; (*fig.*) a pastor. *v.t.* To tend as a shepherd; to gather together. **shepherdess**, *n.*

sherbet (shér'bĕt) [Pers.], *n.* An oriental cooling drink, made of diluted fruit juices.

sheriff (sher'if) [SHIRE, REEVE], *n.* The chief Crown officer of a shire.

sherry (sher'i) [*Xeres*], *n.* A Spanish white wine from Xeres or S. Spain.

Shetland (shet'lånd) [islands of N.E. Scotland], *n.* A Shetland pony, a very small variety of horse with flowing mane and tail.

shibboleth (shĭb'ō-lĕth) [Heb.], *n.* A word used as a test (*see* Judges xii.); (*fig.*) a criterion, a watchword; discredited doctrine.

shield (shēld) [A.-S. *scild*], *n.* A broad piece of defensive armour to protect the body, a buckler; a screen or metal plate used as a protection in tunnelling, machinery, gun-firing, etc.; a shield-like part in an animal or a plant; an escutcheon bearing a coat of arms; (*fig.*) defence, a defender. *v.t.* To screen with a shield.

shieling (shē'ling), **shiel** (shēl) [Icel. *skjōl*, shelter], *n.* (*Sc.*) A hut used by shepherds, sportsmen, etc.; a cottage.

shift (shift) [A.-S. *sciftan*, to divide], *v.t.* To move from one position to another; to change (one thing) for another. *v.i.* To move or be moved about; to change place, position, form, state, etc.; to resort to expedients, to manage, contrive; to prevaricate. *n.* A change of place, form, or character; a substitution of one thing for another; a vicissitude; a change of clothing; a relay of workmen; a chemise; an expedient; a dodge, evasion. **shifty**, *a.* **shiftily**, *adv.* **shiftiness**, *n.*

shillelagh (shi-lā'lå) [place in co. Wicklow, Ireland], *n.* An oak or blackthorn cudgel.

shilling (shil'ing) [A.-S. *scilling*], *n.* A British silver coin and money of account, one-twentieth of a pound sterling.

shilly-shally (shil'i-shăl'i), *v.i.* To act in an

irresolute manner; to be undecided. *n.* Irresolution, hesitation, trifling.

shimmer (shim´ẽr) [A.-S. *scymrian*], *v.i.* To emit a faint or tremulous light; to glimmer, beam, glisten faintly. *n.* A faint or tremulous light.

shin (shin) [A.-S. *scinu*], *n.* The forepart of the human leg between the ankle and knee. *v.i.* (*colloq.*) To climb.

shine (shīn) [A.-S. *scinan*], *v.i.* (*past and p.p.* **shone**, shon) To emit or reflect light; to glow; to be brilliant, eminent, or animated. *v.t.* To make bright, to polish. **shiny**, *a.* **shininess**, *n.*

shingle (1) (shing´gl) [L. *scindere*, to split], *n.* A thin piece of wood used as a roof-covering. *v.t.* To cut (woman's) hair closely.

shingle (2) [Scand.], *n.* Coarse rounded gravel on the seashore. **shingly**, *a.*

shingles (shing´gẽlz) [L. *cingulum*, girth], *n.pl.* A cutaneous disease which spreads like a girdle.

shinty (shin´ti) [?], *n.* A game resembling hockey.

ship (ship) [A.-S. *scip*], *n.* A large sea-going vessel, esp. one with three or more square-rigged masts. *v.t.* To put on board or to convey in a ship; to engage for service on board a ship; to fix (a rudder, etc.) in the proper place. *v.i.* To embark on a ship; to engage as a sailor. **shipboard**, *n.* The deck or side of a ship. **shipmate**, *n.* One who serves or sails in the same ship. **shipshape**, *adv.* In a seaman-like manner, in good order. *a.* Well-arranged, trim. **shipwreck**, *n.* The loss of a ship, by foundering, striking a rock, etc.; (*fig.*) destruction, ruin. *v.t.* To cause to suffer shipwreck; to ruin. *v.i.* To suffer shipwreck; to be ruined. **shipyard**, *n.* A place where ships are built. **shipment**, *n.* The act of shipping; goods shipped, a consignment. **shipper**, *n.* One who ships or sends goods by a common carrier. **shipping**, *a.* Pertaining to ships. *n.* The act of putting on board ship; ships collectively, esp. of a country or port.

-ship [A.-S. *-scipe*], *suf.* Denoting state, condition, the quality of being so-and-so; status, office; skill in the capacity specified; as in *friendship*, *judgeship*, *ladyship*, *marksmanship*.

shire (shīr) [A.-S. *scīr*], *n.* An English county.

shirk (shẽrk) [?], *v.t.* To get out of unfairly. *v.i.* To avoid the performance of work or duty.

shirr (shẽr), *v.t.* (*Cook.*) To bake eggs in a buttered dish.

shirt (shẽrt) [A.-S. *scyrte*], *n.* A loose undergarment of linen, etc., extending from the neck to the thighs, worn by men. **shirting**, *n.* Material for shirts.

shittim (shit´im) [Heb.], *n.* A hard wood (prob. acacia).

shiver (1) (shiv´ẽr), *n.* A small fragment, a sliver. To break into shivers.

shiver (2) [M.E. *chiveren*], *v.i.* To tremble, as with fear, cold, or excitement. *n.* An act or movement of shivering. **the shivers:** A feeling of horror. **shivery**, *a.*

shoal (1) (shōl), *a.* Shallow. *n.* A shallow,

a submerged sand-bank. *v.t.* To become shallower. **shoaly**, *a.*

shoal (2) [A.-S. *scolu*], *n.* A large number, a crowd, esp of fish moving together.

shock (1) (shok) [O.H.G. *scoc*], *n.* A violent collision of bodies, a violent onset; a sudden and violent emotion or sensation, prostration caused by such; a sudden and violent sensation produced on the nerves by a discharge of electricity. *v.t.* To give a violent sensation of disgust, horror, or indignation to; to jar. **shock absorber**, *n.* (*Motor.*) An apparatus to neutralize the shock of axle-springs on recoil. **shock troops**, *n.pl.* (*Mil.*) Selected soldiers employed on tasks requiring exceptional endurance and courage. **shocking**, *a.*

shock (2) [Teut.], *n.* A collection of sheaves of grain; a thick bushy mass of hair. *a.* Shaggy. *v.i.* To collect sheaves into shocks.

shoddy (shod´i) [?], *n.* Fibre obtained from old cloth torn to pieces and shredded; inferior cloth made from a mixture of this with new wool, etc.; anything inferior or sham. *a.* Made of shoddy; not genuine, trashy.

shoe (shoo) [A.-S. *scēō*], *n.* An outer covering for the foot, etc., not coming up to the ankles; a metal rim or plate nailed to the hoof of a horse; anything resembling a shoe in form or function. *v.t.* (*past and p.p.* **shod**) To furnish (esp. a horse) with shoes.

shoot (shoot) [A.-S. *scēotan*], *v.i.* (*past and p.p.* **shot**) To dart or rush (out, etc.) swiftly; to sprout, to extend in growth; to protrude, jut out; to discharge a missile; to hunt game, etc., thus. *v.t.* To propel, let fly, discharge; to cause (a weapon) to discharge a missile; to wound, kill, or hunt thus. *n.* A young branch or sprout; an inclined plane, a chute, a rapid; a place where rubbish can be shot; a shooting-party, or expedition. **shooting**, *n.* Act of discharging fire-arms or arrows, land rented for shooting game; the right to shoot over an estate, etc. **shooting-box**, *n.* A lodge for use during the shooting season.

shop (shop) [A.-S. *sceoppa*, stall], *n.* A building in which goods are sold by retail; a building in which a manufacture, craft, or repairing is carried on; (*fig.*) one's business, or talk about this. *v.i.* To visit shops for purchasing goods. **shopkeeper**, *n.* The owner of a shop, a retail tradesman. **shoplifter**, *n.* One who steals from a shop under pretence of purchasing. **shop-walker**, *n.* One employed in a large shop to direct customers, etc. **shopping**, *n.* **shoppy**, *a.*

shore (1) (shōr) [A.-S from *sceran*, to shear], *n.* The land on the borders of the sea, a lake, etc.

shore (2) [?], *n.* A prop; a support for a building or vessel on the stocks. *v.t.* To support with shores.

short (shört) [A.-S. *sceort*], *a.* Not long in time or space; not tall: brief; deficient, scanty, in want (of); abrupt, curt; crumbling or breaking easily; not prolonged, unaccented (of vowels and syllables); not in hand (of stocks, etc.). *adv.*

Abruptly, at once; so as to be short or deficient. *n.* A short syllable, vowel, or mark (˘); (*pl.*) knickers worn for games, etc. **short-coming,** *n.* A failure or performance of duty, etc.; a falling short of supply, etc. **shorthand,** *n.* A system of contracted writing used for reporting, etc. **short-handed,** *a.* Short of workmen, helpers etc. **shorthorn,** *n.* One of a breed of cattle with short horns. **shortage,** *n.* A deficiency; the amount of this. **shorten,** *v.t.* To make short in time, extent, etc.; to reduce the amount of (sail spread). *v.i.* To contract. **shortening,** *n.* **shortly,** *adv.*

shot (shot), *n.* A solid missile for a fire-arm, a bullet; the act of shooting; the distance reached by a missile, the range of a fire-arm, bow, etc.; a marksman; an attempt to guess, etc. *v.i.* (*p.p.* **shotted**) To load or weight with shot. **shot-gun,** *n.* A light gun for firing small-shot. **shot silk:** Silk with warp and weft of different colours.

shoulder (shōl'dėr) [A.-S. *sculdor*], *n.* The part of the body at which the arm, fore-leg, or wing is attached to the trunk; anything resembling a shoulder; (*pl.*) the upper part of the back. *v.t.* To push with the shoulder; to jostle; to take on one's shoulders. **shoulder-blade, -bone,** *n.* The scapula.

shout (shout) [?], *n.* A loud and sudden call of joy, triumph, or the like. *v.i.* To utter a loud cry or call; to speak at the top of one's voice. *v.t.* To utter with a shout; to say at the top of one's voice.

shove (shŭv) [A.-S. *scūfan*], *v.* To push forcibly along; to push against, to jostle. *n.* A strong push.

shovel (shŭvl) [A.-S. *scofl*], *n.* A wide blade with a handle for shifting loose material. *v.t.* To shift or gather together with a shovel. **shovelful,** *n.*

show, shew (shō) [A.-S. *scēawian*], *v.t.* (*past and p.p.* **shown, showed**) To cause or allow to be seen, to exhibit, expose, reveal; to bestow, offer; to make clear, explain, prove. *v.i.* To become visible or noticeable, to appear; to have a specified appearance. *n.* The act of showing; outward appearance; display, parade; a spectacle, a display, entertainment, exhibition. **showman,** *n.* The manager or proprietor of a circus, etc. *n.* **showy,** *a.* **showily,** *adv.*

shower (shou'ėr) [A.-S. *scūr*], *n.* A short fall of rain, hail, etc., or of bullets or other missiles. *v.t.* To discharge or deliver in a shower. *v.i.* To fall in a shower. **showery,** *a.*

shrapnel (shrăp'nėl) [inventor], *n.* Bullets enclosed in a shell with a charge for bursting and spreading.

shred (shred) [A.-S. *screade*], *n.* A rag, a fragment, a bit. *v.t.* To tear or cut into shreds. **shreddy,** *a.*

shrew (shroo) [A.-S. *scrēawa*, shrew-mouse], *n.* A bad-tempered, scolding woman, a virago; a shrew-mouse. **shrew-mouse,** *n.* A small nocturnal insectivorous mammal. **shrewish,** *a.*

shrewd (shrood) [M.E. *schrewed*, cursed], *a.* Astute, discerning. **shrewdly,** *adv.*

shriek (shrēk), *v.i.* To utter a sharp, inarticulate cry; to scream, to screech, as in a sudden fright. *v.t.* To utter with a shriek. *n.* A sharp, shrill, inarticulate cry.

shrievalty (shrē'vál-ti), *n.* The office or jurisdiction of a sheriff; the tenure of this.

shrift (shrift) [A.-S. *scrift*], *n.* Confession to a priest; absolution.

shrike (shrīk) [A.-S. *scrīc*], *n.* A bird feeding on insects and small birds; the butcher bird.

shrill (shril) [Teut.], *a.* High-pitched and piercing in tone, sharp; importunate. **shrilly,** *adv.*

shrimp (shrimp) [A.-S.], *n.* A slender long-tailed edible crustacean; a dwarfish person.

shrine (shrīn) [A.-S. *scrīn*], *n.* A casket in which sacred relics are deposited; a tomb, altar, etc., of special sanctity; a place hallowed by its associations.

shrink (shringk) [A.-S. *scrincan*], *v.i.* (*past* **shrank,** *p.p.* **shrunk,** *part.a.* **shrunken**) To grow smaller, to shrivel; to give way; to flinch. *v.t.* To make smaller. **shrinkage,** *n.* **shrinkingly,** *adv.*

shrive (shrīv) [L. *scrībere*, to write], *v.t.* (*past* **shrove,** *p.p.* **shriven**) To receive the confession of, impose penance on, and absolve; to confess (oneself) and receive absolution.

shrivel (shrivl) [Scand.], *v.* To contract, wither, become wrinkled.

shroud (shroud) [A.-S. *scrūd*], *n.* A winding sheet; anything that covers or conceals; (*pl.*) ropes extending from the lower mast-heads to the ship's sides to steady the masts.

Shrovetide (shrōv'tīd), *n.* The period before Lent. **Shrove Tuesday:** The day before Ash Wednesday.

shrub (1) (shrŭb) [Arab. *sharāb*], *n.* A drink composed of sweetened fruit-juice with spirit.

shrub (2) (shrŭb) [A.-S. *scrybb*], *n.* A woody plant smaller than a tree with branches proceeding directly from the ground. **shrubbery,** *n.* A plantation of shrubs. **shrubby,** *a.*

shrug (shrug) [Scand.], *v.* To draw up (the shoulders) to express dislike, doubt, etc. *n.* This gesture.

shudder (shŭd'ėr) [Teut.], *v.i.* To shiver suddenly as with fear; to quake. *n.* A sudden shiver or trembling.

shuffle (shŭfl), *v.t.* To shift to and fro or from one to another; to mix (up); to throw into disorder; to put aside, to throw (off or on). *v.i.* To change the relative positions of cards in a pack; to prevaricate; to move with a dragging gait. *n.* The act of shuffling; a general change of position; a prevarication. **shuffler,** *n.* **shufflingly,** *adv.*

shun (shŭn) [A.-S. *scunian*], *v.t.* To avoid, eschew, keep clear of.

shunt (shŭnt), *v.t.* To turn (a train) on to a side track. *v.i.* To turn off on to a side track (of a train, etc.). **shunter,** *n.*

shut (shŭt) [A.-S. *scyttan*], *v.t.* To close by means of a door, lid, cover, etc.; to bar (out), to keep from entering or participating in. *v.i.* To become closed; to come together (of teeth, scissor-blades, etc.). **shutter,** *n.* A cover for fastening over a window to exclude light, burglars, etc.; a device for cutting off light to a photographic lens.

shuttle (shŭtl) [A.-S. *scyttel*], *n.* A contrivance used by weavers for passing the thread of the weft between the threads of the warp; the sliding holder carrying the lower thread in a sewing-machine. **shuttlecock,** *n.* A cork stuck with feathers which is struck to and fro in the game of battledore and shuttlecock.

shy (1) (shī) [A.-S. *scēoh*], *a.* Timid; bashful, coy; cautious, suspicious; watchful (of), elusive. *v.i.* To start aside suddenly (of a horse). *n.* The act of shying. **shyly,** *adv.*

shy (2) [?], *v.* To fling, to throw. *n.* The act of shying.

Siamese (sī-à-mēz'), *a.* Pertaining to Siam. *n.* A native of Siam; the language.

sibilant (sib'ĭ-lànt) [L. *sibilans*, hissing], *a.* Hissing. *n.* A letter with a hissing sound, as *s* or *z.* **sibilate,** *v.* **sibila'tion,** *n.*

sibyl (sib'il) [Gr. *Sibulla*], *n.* A prophetess, a sorceress; a gipsy, an old hag. **sibylline** (si-bil'in), *a.* Pertaining to a sibyl; prophetic, oracular, mysterious.

sic (sik) [L.], *adv.* Thus, so (after a doubtful word to indicate that it is quoted exactly).

siccative (sik'à-tiv) [L. *siccus*, dry], *a.* Drying, causing to dry.

sick (sik) [A.-S. *sēoc*], *a.* Ill, in bad health, inclined to vomit; feeling disturbed; pining (for, etc.). **sicken,** *v.i.* To grow ill, to show symptoms of illness. *v.t.* To make sick; to affect with nausea. **sickening,** *a.* **sickly,** *a.* Habitually indisposed, invalid; languid, weakly-looking; mawkish. *adv.* In a sick manner. **sickness,** *n.*

sickle (sikl) [A.-S. *sicol*], *n.* A long curved blade on a short handle, for reaping, lopping, etc., a reaping-hook.

side (sīd) [A.-S], *n.* A bounding surface or line, as of a building, room, natural object, etc., esp. dist. from the top and bottom, or the ends; the part to left or right; direction right or left in relation to a person or thing; one of two opposing parties, views, or causes. *v.i.* To put oneself on the side of. *a.* Situated at or on the side; being from or towards the side, oblique, indirect. **side-arms,** *n.pl.* Weapons as swords or bayonets carried at the side. **side-light,** *n.* Light admitted from the side; an incidental illustration (of a subject, etc.), **side-track,** *v.t.* To shunt; (*fig.*) to shelve, to defer indefinitely. **sidelong,** *adv.* Obliquely; laterally. *a.* Oblique, sideways, *adv.* **siding,** *n.* The act of taking sides; a short line of metals beside a railway line used for shunting and joining this at one end.

sidereal (sī-dēr'ĭ-àl) [L. *sidus-deris*, star], *a.* Pertaining to the stars; starry.

sidle (sīdl), *v.i.* To go or move sideways.

siege (sēj) [L. *sedes*, seat], *n.* The process of besieging or the state of being besieged; the operations to compel a fortified place to surrender. **siege-train,** *n.* Artillery, etc., carried by an army for siege purposes.

sienna (si-en'à) [(earth of) *Siena*], *n.* A brownish-yellow pigment composed of a native clay coloured with iron and manganese.

sierra (si-er'à) [Sp., from L. *serra*, saw], *n.* A long serrated mountain-chain.

siesta (si-es'tà) [Sp., from L. *sexta hora,* sixth hour], *n.* A short midday sleep.

sieve (siv) [A.-S. *sife*], *n.* An instrument for separating the finer particles of substances from the coarser by means of meshes through which the former pass.

sift (sift) [A.-S. *siftan*], *v.t.* To separate into finer and coarser particles with a sieve, to sprinkle (flour, etc.) as with a sieve; to examine minutely.

sigh (si) [A.-S. *sīcan*], *v.i.* To draw a deep, long respiration, as in grief; to yearn (for). *n.* The act or sound of sighing.

sight (sit) [A.-S. *gesihth*], *n.* The faculty or act of seeing; range of vision; point of view, estimation; visibility; a display, a show; a strange object; a device on a fire-arm, etc., enabling one to direct it accurately. *v.t.* To get sight of, to espy; to adjust the sights of; to aim by means of sights. **sightless,** *a.* Wanting sight, blind. **sightly,** *a.* Pleasing to the eye, not unsightly.

sign (sin) [L. *signum*], *n.* A mark expressing a particular meaning; a symbol; a symptom or proof (of); a secret formula, a gesture by which confederates recognize each other; a device displayed as a token of a trade, esp. by inn-keepers; one of twelve ancient divisions of the zodiac. *v.t.* To mark with a sign or signature, initials. *v.i.* To write one's name as signature. **signpost,** *n.* A mark of direction at cross-roads, etc.; a post supporting a sign.

signal (sig'nàl), *n.* A sign conveying information, esp. to persons at a distance. *v.t.* To convey by signals. *v.i.* To make signals. *a.* Distinguished from the rest, noteworthy. **signal-box,** *n.* A room or hut from which railway signals are operated. **signalize,** *v.t.* To make remarkable.

signature (sig'nà-chŭr), *n.* The name, initials, or mark of a person written with his own hand; a distinguishing letter or number at the bottom of the first page of each sheet of a book, a significant mark, sign, or stamp. **signature tune,** *n.* (*Theat.*) A distinctive piece of music played at the beginning and end of a variety turn or of a band's performance. **signatory,** *a.* Bound by signature. *n.* One who signs, esp. as representing a State.

signet (sig'nèt , *n.* A small seal. **signet-ring,** *n.* A finger-ring set with a seal.

signify (sig'ni-fi), *v.t.* To make known, to communicate, announce; to be a sign of, to denote, to matter. *v.i.* To be of consequence. **signif'icance, -icancy,** *n.* The quality of being significant, expressiveness; real import; moment, consequence. **signif'icant,** *a.*

signor (sē'nyōr), **-nora** (-nyōr'à), **-norina** (-nyò-rē'nà) [It.], *n.* Italian form of address corresponding to Mr., Mrs., and Miss.

silage (sī'làj) [ENSILAGE].

silence (sī'lĕns) [L. *silentium*], *n.* The state of being silent, taciturnity, stillness; secrecy; absence of mention, oblivion. *v.t.* To make silent, esp. by conclusively refuting; to stop from sounding; to compel to cease firing. **silencer,** *n.* A device for reducing or muffling noise. **silent,** *a* Not making any sound, noiseless, still; not pronounced (of a letter). **silently,** *adv.*

silhouette (sil-u-et') [Etienne de *Silhouette* (1709–67)], *n.* A portrait in profile in black on a white ground; an outline as seen against the light or as a shadow.

silica (sil'i-ka) [L. *silex*, flint], *n.* A hard crystalline silicon dioxide, occurring in sand, flint, quartz, etc. **silicate,** *n.* A salt of silicic acid. **siliceous** (-lish'ŭs), **silicic** (-lis'ik), *a.* silici-, silico-, *comb. form.* **sil'icon,** *n.* A non-metallic element next to oxygen the most abundant of the elements.

silk (silk) [A.-S. *seolc*], *n.* A fine, soft, glossy fibre spun by the larvæ of certain moths and by some spiders; cloth made of silk; garments made of this. *a.* Made of silk, silken. **silkworm,** *n.* The larva of *Bombyx mori* which encloses its chrysalis in a cocoon of silk. **silken,** *a.* **silky,** *a.* Like silk, glossy; silken.

sill (sil) [A.-S. *syll*], *n.* A block forming a basis or foundation, esp. a slab of timber or stone at the foot of a door or window.

silly (sil'i) [A.-S. *sælig*, fortunate], *a.* Foolish, weak-minded; unwise, imprudent; imbecile. **sillily,** *adv.* **silliness,** *n.*

silo (sī'lō), *n.* Pit or air-tight chamber for ensilage.

silt (silt) [Norw. *sylta*, salt-marsh], *n.* Fine sediment deposited by water. *v.t.* To choke with silt.

silver (sil'vĕr) [A.-S. *seolfor*], *n.* A precious metal of a lustrous white colour; utensils made of this; silver coin. *a.* Made of or resembling silver; soft and clear in tone. *v.t.* To coat with silver or with tin-foil amalgamated with quicksilver; to give a silvery lustre to. **silver fir:** A tall species of fir with silvery bark. **silver-gilt,** *a.* Silverware gilded. **silver plate:** Silverware. **silver-side,** *n.* The upper and choice part of a round of beef. **silver'-ware,** *n.* Articles of silver, esp. table utensils. **silvery,** *a.*

Simia (sim'i-à) [L., ape], *n.* (*pl.* -*miæ*). A genus of anthropoid apes containing the orang-utan. **simian,** *a.* and *n.* **simioid,** *a.*

similar (sim'i-làr) [L. *similis*, like], *a.* Like resembling (each other); alike; (*Geom.*) made up of the same number of parts arranged in the same manner. **similar'ity,** *n.* **similarly,** *adv.* **simile** (sim'i-li), *n.* A comparison of two things which have some strong point of resemblance, esp. a poetical figure. **simil'itude,** *n.* Likeness, outward appearance; comparison, metaphor, counterpart.

simmer (sim'ĕr) [?], *v.i.* To boil gently; to be just below boiling-point.

simnel (sim'nĕl) [L. *simila*, the finest wheat flower], *n.* A rich cake eaten on Mid-Lent Sunday, Easter, and Christmas Day.

simony (sī'mŏ-ni) [*Simon* Magus (Acts viii,

18)], *n.* The buying or selling of ecclesiastical preferment.

simper (sim'pĕr) [Scand.], *v.i.* To smile in an affected manner. *n.* An affected smile or smirk.

simple (simpl) [L. *simplex*, onefold], *a.* Consisting of only one thing; not subdivided, elementary; not complex, elaborate, adorned, or sumptuous; plain, of low degree; trifling; unaffected, artless, sincere; clear; silly, ignorant; mere. *n.* Something not mixed; a medicinal herb or a medicine made from it. **simpleton,** *n.* A silly, gullible, or feeble-minded person. **simplicity** (-plis'i-ti), *n.* **sim'plify,** *v.t.* To make simple or simpler. **simplifica'tion,** *n.* **simply,** *adv.*

simulacrum (sim-ū-lā'-krŭm) [L. *similis*, similar], *n.* (*pl.* -**cra**) An image; a mere pretence, a sham.

simulate (sim'-ū-lāt), *v.t.* To assume the likeness of; to counterfeit, to put on, to mimic. **simula'tion,** *n.* **sim'ulative,** *a.* **simulator,** *n.*

simultaneous (sim-ŭl-tā'nĕ-ŭs), *a.* Happening or done at the same time. **simultaneously,** *adv.*

sin (sin) [A.-S. *synn*], *n.* Transgression of duty, morality, or the law of God; wickedness, a transgression. *v.i.* To commit sin; to offend (against). **sinful,** *a.* **sinfully,** *adv.* **sinfulness,** *n.* **sinner,** *n.*

since (sins) [A.-S. *siththan*], *adv.* After or from a time specified or implied till now; at some time after such a time and before now; before now, ago. *prep.* From the time of; throughout the time after. *conj.* From the time that or when; inasmuch as; because.

sincere (sin-sēr') [L. *sincērus*], *a.* Being in reality as in appearance; not feigned, honest, frank. **sincerity** (-ser'i-ti), *n.*

sine (sīn) [L. *sinus*, curve], *n.* (*Trig.*) The straight line drawn from one extremity of an arc perpendicular to the diameter passing through the other extremity.

sinecure (sī'nĕ-kūr) [L. *sine cura*, without care], *n.* Any paid office with few or no duties attached.

sinew (sin'ū) [A.-S. *sinu*], *n.* A tendon, a fibrous cord connecting muscle and bone; (*pl.*) muscles; strength **sinewy,** *a.*

sing (sing) [A.-S. *singan*], *v.i.* (*past* **sang,** *p.p.* **sung**) To utter words in a tuneful manner, to make vocal melody; to emit sweet sounds; to compose poetry. *v.t.* To utter in a tuneful melodious manner; to celebrate in verse; to accompany, greet, acclaim, etc., with singing.

singe (sinj) [A.-S. *sengan*], *v.t.* To burn slightly; to burn the surface or tips of, to scorch. *n.* A slight burn.

single (sing'gl) [L. *singulī*, one by one], *a.* Consisting of one only; individual, separate, unaided; unmarried; not compound or complicated. *n.* A single round, game, a hit for one run, etc. *v.t.* To pick out from among others. **single-handed,** *a.* Done without assistance. *adv.* Without assistance. **single-minded,** *a.* Free from duplicity. **single-stick,** *n.* A long stick for fencing. **singlet** (sing'glĕt), *n.* An under-shirt, a vest. **singly,** *adv.*

singsong (sing'song), *a.* Sung, recited, etc.

monotonous, *n.* Monotonous cadencely. or rhythm; an impromptu concert.

singular (sing'gū-làr), *a.* Single, standing alone, strange, remarkable, distinguished; peculiar, odd; (*Gram.*) denoting or referring to one only. *n.* The singular number. **singular'ity,** *n.* singularity, *adv.*

sinister (sin'is-tèr) [L., left], *a.* (*Her.*) On the left side (of a shield, etc.), the side to the right of the observer; inauspicious; ill-looking, malignant.

sink (singk) [A.-S. *sincan*], *v.i.* (*past* **sank,** *p.p.* **sunk,** *part.a.* **sunken**) To descend, to fall gradually; to disappear below the surface or the horizon; to decline to a lower level of health, morals, etc.; to droop, despond; to become shrunken or hollow. *v.t.* To cause to sink; to submerge, to send below the surface; to excavate. *n.* A basin or trough for receiving waste water, etc.; a receptacle for filth (*usu. fig.*). **sinker,** *n.* One who or that which sinks; a weight used to sink a fishing-line, net, etc. **sinking-fund,** *n.* A fund set aside for the reduction of a public debt.

Sinn Fein (shin-fān') [Gael., ourselves], *n.* An Irish national party formed in 1905. **Sinn Feiner,** *n.* A member of Sinn Fein.

sinology (si-nol'ō-ji), *n.* Knowledge of the Chinese language, literature, etc. **sinol'ogist,** **sin'ologue,** *n.*

sinuate (sin'ū-àt) [L. *sinuātus*, curved], *a.* Bending, winding in and out. **sin'uous,** *a.* Bending in and out; winding.

sinus (sī'nùs), *n.* A cavity, esp. in bone or tissue.

sip (sip) [A.-S. *sypian*], *v.* To drink in small quantities. *n.* A very small draught of liquid. **sippet,** *n.* A small piece of toast or bread served with soup, mince, etc.

siphon (sī'fòn) [Gr. *siphōn*, pipe], *n.* A curved tube having one branch longer then the other, used for conveying liquid over the edge of a cask, etc.; a siphon-bottle. *v.* To convey or flow by a siphon.

sir (sèr), *n.* A term of courteous or formal address to a man; a title prefixed to the names of baronets and knights.

sirdar (sèr'dar) [Hind], *n.* (*E.Ind.*) A chieftain; commander-in-chief.

sire (sir), *n.* A title used in addressing a king; a father; the male parent of a beast.

siren (sī'rèn) [L. Gr. *seirēn*], *n.* (*Gr. Myth.*) A sea-nymph, half-woman and half-bird, who lured sailors to shipwreck by singing; a seductive woman; a sweet singer; an apparatus for producing a loud sound from steam or compressed air; such an apparatus for sounding a warning, etc. *a.* Bewitching, fascinating. **siren suit,** *n.* A suit in one piece and closed with a zip fastening.

sirloin (sèr'loin) [O.F., *sur*, over, *longe*, loin], *n.* The upper part of the loin of beef.

sirocco (si-rok'ō) [It., Arab. *sharq*, east], *n.* A hot oppressive wind blowing from northern Africa.

sirrah (sir'à), *n.* Sir (in anger or contempt).

siskin (sis'kin) [Teut.], *n.* A small migratory song-bird allied to the goldfinch.

sister (sis'tèr) [A.-S. *sweoster*], *n.* A female born of the same parents as another; a female member of the same society, community, etc., esp. of a religious community; a qualified sick-nurse. **sister-in-law,** *n.* A husband's or wife's sister; a brother's wife. **sisterhood,** *n.* The state of being a sister; a community of women. **sisterlike, -ly.** *a.*

sit (sit) [A.-S. *sittan*], *v.i.* To set oneself or be in a resting posture on the buttocks; to be in a resting posture (of birds and beasts); to cover eggs, to brood; to be situated; to fit (of clothes); to pose (for one's portrait); to hold a session, to occupy a seat on a deliberative body, in judgment, etc., to encamp (before). *v.t.* To set, to place (oneself) in a seat, to hold a sitting position on (a horse, etc.). **sitting,** *a.* and *n.* The action of the verb; a session; the time one sits; a seat in a church; a clutch of eggs for hatching. **sitting-room,** *n.* A parlour; room or space for persons sitting.

site (sit) [L. *situs*], *n.* Situation; ground on which a building stands, has stood, or will stand.

situated, **situate** (sit'ū-ā-tèd, -àt), *a.* Placed or being in a specified situation, condition, or relation. **situa'tion,** *n.* The place in which something is situated; position of affairs, esp. a critical juncture; a paid office, esp. of a domestic servant.

sitz-bath (sits'bath), *n.* A bath in which one sits; a bath taken thus.

six (siks) [A.-S.], *a.* One more than five. *n.* This number, the symbol representing it, 6, vi. **sixain,** *n.* A six-line stanza. **sixfold,** *a.* and *adv.* **sixpence,** *n.* An English silver coin of the value of six pennies. **sixpenny,** *a.* Worth or priced at sixpence. **sixshooter,** *n.* A six-chambered revolver. **sixteen',** *a.* Consisting of six and ten. *n.* This number, the symbol representing it, 16, xvi. **sixteenmo,** *n.* Sextodecimo. **sixteenth,** *a.* and *n.* **sixth,** *a.* Next in order after the fifth; being one of six equal parts. *n.* A sixth paft; the sixth form in a school. **sixthly,** *adv.* **sixty,** *a.* Ten times six, *n.* This number, the symbol representing it, 60, lx. **six'tieth,** *a.* and *n.*

sizar (sī'zàr), *n.* A student at Cambridge University or Trinity College, Dublin, who pays reduced fees.

size (1) (sīz), *n.* Measurement, extent; a standard grade of garments and other things according to relative dimensions. *v.t.* To arrange according to size; to cut to a required size. **sized,** *a.* (*usu. in comb.* as *small-sized*).

size (2) [It. *sisa*], *n.* A gelatinous solution used to glaze surfaces, stiffen fabrics, etc. *v.t.* To treat with size. **sizy,** *a.* **siziness,** *n.*

sizzle (sizl) [imit.], *v.i.* To make a hissing noise as of frying.

skate (1) (skāt) [Icel. *skata*], *n.* A fish with a long, pointed snout.

skate (2) [Dut. *schaats*], *n.* A steel blade or runner attached under the boot to enable one to glide over ice. *v.i.* To move over ice, etc., on skates.

skein (skān) [O.F. *escaigne*], *n.* A quantity

of yarn, etc., wound in a coil, folded over, and knotted.

skeleton (skel'ĕ-tòn) [Gr., a mummy], *n.* The supporting or protective framework of an animal or vegetable body, comprising bones, cartilage, shell, and other rigid parts; the supporting framework of any structure; the nucleus (of an organization); an outline or rough draft.

skep (skep) [Icel. *skeppa*], *n.* A basket of wicker, wood, etc.; a straw or wicker beehive.

skerry (sker'ĭ) [Icel. *sker*], *n.* A rocky islet.

sketch (skech) [Gr. *schedios*, off-hand], *n.* A rough, unfinished, or tentative delineation; a preliminary study, an outline; a play, or literary or musical composition, etc., of a slight character. *v.t.* To make a sketch of; to present in outline. *v.i.* To make a sketch or sketches. **sketchy,** *a.* **sketchily,** *adv.*

skewbald (skū'bald), *a.* Piebald with white and another colour than black.

skewer (skū'ér), *n.* A pin for holding meat together. *v.t.* To fasten or pierce with a skewer.

ski (shē, skē) [Norw.], *n.* (*pl.* **skis**) A long narrow snow-shoe. *v.i.* To progress on skis. **ski-ing,** *pres.p.*

skid (skid) [?], *n.* A drag or other device acting as a brake; a slip on muddy ground. *v.t.* To check or brake with a skid. *v.i.* (of wheels or vehicles) To slip sideways; to revolve rapidly without progressing.

skiff (skif) [F. *esquif*], *n.* A small light boat.

skill (skil) [Icel. *skil*, discernment], *n.* Familiar knowledge of any art or science combined with dexterity; expertness. **skilful,** *a.* **skilled,** *a.*

skillet (skil'ét) [O.F. *escuellette*], *n.* A metal pan or kettle, with a long handle, for boiling water, etc.

skilly (skil'ĭ) [?], *n.* Thin broth or gruel.

skim (skim), *v.t.* To clear or take the scum, cream, etc., from the surface of a liquid; to touch lightly or nearly touch; to read superficially. *v.i.* To pass lightly and rapidly over or along a surface. **skim-milk,** *n.* Milk from which the cream has been skimmed.

skimp (skimp) [Scand.], *v.t.* To stint (a person, provisions, etc.). *v.i.* To be stingy.

skin (skin) [Icel. *skinn*], *n.* The natural outer covering of an animal body; the hide; the outer layer of a fruit, etc. *v.t.* To strip the skin from, to flay, to peel.

skinny, *a.* Consisting only of skin, very lean.

skip (skip) [Scand.], *v.i.* To move about by shifting rapidly from one foot to another; to gambol; to pass rapidly from one thing to another; to make omissions. *n.* A light leap or spring, esp. from one foot to the other.

skipper (skip'er) [Dut. *schipper*], *n.* The master of a merchant vessel.

skirl (skérl) [Sc., shrill], *v.i.* To make a shrill noise like that of the bagpipes; to shriek.

skirmish (skér'mish) [O.F. *eskermir*, to fence], *n.* A fight between small parties;

a desultory combat; a light contest. *v.i.* To fight in a slight, desultory, or preliminary way.

skirt (skért) [Icel. *skyrta*, shirt], *n.* The part of a garment hanging below the waist; a woman's outer garment like a petticoat; a border, margin; (*pl.*) the outer parts. *v.t.* To lie or go along or by the edge of; to border. *v.i.* To lie on the border or outskirts.

skit (skit) [?], *n.* A lampoon, burlesque.

skittish (skit'ish) [?], *a.* Easily frightened (of horses); capricious, coquettish, lively.

skittle (skitl) [Dan. *skyttel*], *n.* One of the pins thrown at in ninepins; (*pl.*) the game of ninepins.

skulk (skŭlk) [Dan.], *v.i.* To lurk; to lie concealed, to move about furtively; to sneak away. **skulker,** *n.*

skull (skŭl) [M.E. *skulle*], *n.* The bony case enclosing the brain, the cranium. **skullcap,** *n.* A brimless cap fitting closely to the head.

skunk (skŭngk) [Algonkin *segongw*], *n.* A N. American weasel which when irritated ejects a fetid secretion; (*fig.*) a low fellow.

sky (skī) [Icel.], *n.* The apparent vault of heaven, the upper region of the atmosphere; a climate; (*pl.*) the celestial regions. **sky-high,** *a.* or *adv.* Very high. **sky-lark,** *n.* A lark that flies singing high into the air. *v.i.* (*slang*) To lark, to play practical jokes, etc. **skylight,** *n.* A window set in a roof. **skyey,** *a.* **skyward,** *a.* and *adv.*

slab (slăb) [?], *n.* A thin, flat, regularly-shaped piece of anything.

slack (slăk) [A.-S. *sleac*], *a.* Not drawn tight; limp, careless, not zealous, eager, or active. *adv.* In a slack manner; insufficiently. *n.* The part of a rope that hangs loose; small coal; (*pl.*) trousers. *v.* To slacken. **slack-water,** *n.* The interval between the flux and the reflux of the tide. **slacken,** *v.i.* To become slack. **slacker,** *n.*

slag (slăg) [Scand.], *n.* The dross separated in the reduction of ores; volcanic scoria. **slaggy,** *a.*

slake (slāk) [A.-S. *slacian*], *v.t.* To quench, satisfy, appease; to mix (lime) with water.

slam (slăm) [imit.], *v.t.* To shut suddenly with a loud noise; to put (a thing down) thus. *n.* A noise as of the violent shutting of a door; winning every trick in whist, bridge, etc.

slander (slan'dér) [O.F. *esclander*], *n.* A false report maliciously uttered; defamation. *v.t.* To defame falsely. **slanderer,** *n.* **slanderous,** *a.*

slang (slăng), *n.* Words or language used colloquially but not regarded as correct English; the special language of a class, jargon. *v.t.* To use slang to; to abuse. **slangy,** *a.*

slant (slant) [?], *v.i.* To slope; to incline from the vertical or horizontal. *v.t.* To cause to slant. *a.* Sloping, oblique. *n.* A slope; inclination from the vertical or horizontal.

slap (slăp) [imit.], *v.t.* To strike with the open hand, to smack. *n.* Such a blow. *adv.* Suddenly, plump, bang.

slash (slăsh) [O.F. *esclachier*], *v.t.* To cut by striking violently at random; to make gashes in, to slit. *v.i.* To strike (at) violently and at random with a knife, sword, etc.; to lash (out at). *n.* A long cut, slit, or incision; a slashing cut.

slat (slăt) [?], *n.* A thin narrow strip of wood, used in Venetian blinds, crates, etc.

slate (slāt) [O.F. *esclater*, to break to pieces], *n.* A fine-grained laminated rock easily splitting into thin slabs; a piece of this for use as a roofing-tile, writing-tablet, etc. *v.t.* To cover or roof with slates; to criticize savagely, to abuse, to berate. **slaty,** *a.*

slattern (slăt'ĕrn), *n.* An untidy or sluttish woman. **slatternly,** *a.*

slaughter (slaw'tĕr) [Icel. *slātr*], *n.* Wholesale or indiscriminate killing, carnage; the killing of beasts for market. *v.t.* To kill wantonly, to massacre; to kill for the market.

Slav (slav, slăv) [L. *Slavus, Sclavus,* or Gr. *sklabos, sklabēnos*], *n.* One of an Aryan race comprising the Russians, Poles, Serbo-Croatians, Bulgarians, Slovenes, etc. *a.*

slave (slāv) [L. *sclavus*], *n.* One who is the property of another; one entirely under the influence (of) or a helpless victim (to); a drudge; a mean, abject person. *v.i.* To toil like a slave.

slaver (1) (slāv'ĕr), *n.* One who deals in slaves; a slave-ship. **slavery,** *n.*

slaver (2) (slăv'ĕr) [Icel. *slafra*], *v.i.* To let saliva flow from the mouth, to dribble. *n.* Saliva dribbling from the mouth.

slavish (slā'vish), *a.* Pertaining to or characteristic of a slave; servile, ignoble; devoid of originality; consisting in drudgery. **slavishly,** *adv.*

slay (slā) [A.-S. *slēan*], *v.t.* (*past* **slew,** *p.p.* **slain**) To put to death, to kill. **slayer,** *n.*

sled (sled), **sledge** (1) (slej) [M.E. *slede*], *n.* A vehicle on runners used on snow or ice; a sleigh; a toboggan.

sledge (2) [A.-S. *slecge*], *n.* The heavy two-handed hammer of a blacksmith.

sleek (slēk) [Icel. *slīkr*], *a.* Smooth, glossy; (*fig.*) unctuous, smooth-spoken. *v.t.* To make (hair, etc.) sleek; **sleekly,** *adv.* **sleekness,** *n.*

sleep (slēp) [A.-S. *slǣpan*], *v.i.* (*past and p.p.* **slept**) To take rest in sleep, to be asleep; to be inactive or in abeyance; to spin so as to seem motionless (of a top). *v.t.* To rest in (sleep); to lodge. *n.* A state of rest in which consciousness is almost entirely suspended. **sleeper,** *n.* One who sleeps; a wooden beam or other support for rails on a railway, etc. **sleepless,** *a.* **sleeplessness,** *n.* **sleepy,** *a.* Inclined to sleep, drowsy; indolent, habitually inactive; (of pears, etc.) beginning to decay. **sleepily,** *adv.* **sleepiness,** *n.*

sleet (slēt) [Teut.], *n.* Hail or snow mixed with rain. *v.i.* To snow or hail with rain. **sleety,** *a.*

sleeve (slēv) [A.-S. *slȳf*], *n.* The part of a garment that covers the arm; a cylindrical sheath. **sleeved,** *a.* Having sleeves.

sleigh (slā), *n.* A vehicle mounted on runners for driving over snow or ice.

sleight (slīt) [Icel. *slœgth*], *n.* Dexterity, skill in manipulating things; a trick.

slender (slen'dĕr) [O.F. *esclendre*], *a.* Small in width as compared with length; slim; slight, scanty, meagre; feeble.

sleuth (slooth), *n.* A track as known by the scent. **sleuth-hound,** *n.* A bloodhound.

slice (slīs) [O.F. *esclice,* slit], *n.* A broad thin piece cut off; a part, share; an implement for slicing. *v.t.* To cut (*usu.* up) into broad, thin pieces; to cut (off) slices from; to divide.

slick (slik), *a.* Smooth, sleek; (*fig.*) oily, smooth of speech; adroit, specious.

slide (slīd) [A.-S. *slīdan*], *v.i.* (*past and p.p.* **slid**) To move smoothly along a surface, to glide, esp. over ice without skates; to pass (away, into, etc.) gradually or imperceptibly. *v.t.* To cause to move along smoothly. *n.* A thing or part that slides into place; a surface, groove, etc., on which a part slides; a shute; ice on which persons slide; act of sliding; a smooth and easy passage.

slight (slīt) [M.Dut. *slicht*], *a.* Inconsiderable; small in amount, intensity, etc.; paltry, superficial; slim; frail, weak. *n.* An act of disrespect or neglect. *v.t.* To treat as of little importance, to disregard; to put a slight upon. **slightingly,** *adv.* **slightly,** *adv.*

slim (slim) [M.Dut. *slim,* sly], *a.* Slender, thin, of slight build; (*colloq.*) cunning, crafty. **slimness,** *n.*

slime (slīm) [A.-S. *slīm*], *n.* A soft, viscous substance, esp. moist and sticky earth. *v.t.* To smear or cover with slime. **slimy,** *a.* Consisting of, like, covered with, or abounding in slime; slippery; (*fig.*) repulsively mean or obsequious. **slimily,** *adv.*

sling (sling) [Icel. *slyngva*], *v.t.* (*past and p.p.* **slung**) To hurl, esp. from a sling; to suspend in a swing or so as to swing; to hoist by a sling. *v.i.* To hurl missiles with a sling; to move swiftly or violently. *n.* A short leather strap with a string at each end for hurling a small missile by hand; a band or loop for suspending, hoisting, or transferring anything; a band for supporting an injured limb.

slink (slingk) [A.-S. *slincan*], *v.i.* (*past and p.p.* **slunk**) To sneak away in a furtive or cowardly manner.

slip (slip) [M.E. *slippen*], *v.i.* To slide, to glide, esp. unintentionally, to miss one's footing; to pass unnoticed, furtively, or quickly; to commit a small mistake or oversight; to go (along) swiftly. *v.t.* To cause to move in a sliding manner; to let loose, to unleash. *n.* Act or state of slipping; an unintentional error, a lapse; a garment easily slipped on or off, a pillow-case; a leash for a dog; an inclined plane on which vessels are built, etc.; a narrow strip of paper, etc.; a cutting for planting or grafting. **slipshod,** *a.* Down at heel; careless, slovenly. **slipper,** *n.* One who or that which slips or lets slip; a loose shoe for indoors. **slippery,** *a.* So smooth, muddy, etc., as to cause slipping; elusive, shifty, cunning. **slippy,** *a.* Quick, wide-awake.

slit (slit) [A.-S. *slítan*], *v.t.* To cut lengthways; to cut into strips. *n.* A long cut or narrow opening.

sliver (sliv′ér), *n.* A piece of wood, etc., torn off, a splinter. *v.t.* To tear into long, thin pieces.

slobber (slob′ér) [Dan. *schlubbre*, to slaver], *v.i.* To let saliva run from the mouth.

sloe (slō) [A.-S. *slā*], *n.* The wild plum; the blackthorn bearing it.

slog (slog) [?], *v.* To hit vigorously and at random; to work doggedly. *n.* A vigorous stroke.

slogan (slō′gán) [Gael. *sluagh*, host, *gairm*, outcry], *n.* The war-cry of the old Highland clans; a political catchword; a catchy advertising phrase or word.

sloop (sloop) [Dut. *sloep*], *n.* A fore-and-aft rigged vessel with one mast; (*Nav.*) a steam- or petrol-driven patrol boat.

slop (1) (slop) [A.-S. *sloppe*], *n.* Liquid carelessly thrown about; (*pl.*) dirty water; liquid food, weak liquors. *v.t.* To spill or allow to overflow; to make sloppy. *v.i.* To overflow the side of a vessel. **sloppy,** *a.* Wet, splashed, covered with puddles; (*fig.*) slovenly, done carelessly; maudlin. **sloppily,** *adv.*

slop (2), *n.* (*Usu. pl.*) Ready-made clothing, etc.

slope (slōp), *n.* An inclined direction, an incline, ground whose surface makes an angle with the horizon. *v.i.* To be inclined, to lie obliquely, to slant. *v.t.* To place or form with a slope.

slot (1) (slot) [?], *n.* A depression or opening for some part to fit into; an oblong aperture in a slot-machine. *v.t.* To make a slot in.

slot (2), *n.* The track of a deer.

sloth (slōth) [A.-S. *slǽwth*], *n.* Laziness, sluggishness; a S. American arboreal mammal. **slothful,** *a.*

slouch (slouch) [Icel. *slōkr*], *n.* An ungainly drooping attitude or movement; a downward bend of the hat-brim; an awkward fellow. *v.i.* To droop or hang down carelessly; to stand or move in a negligent or ungainly way.

slough (1) (slou) [.-S. *slōh*], *n.* A bog, quagmire.

slough (2) (slŭf) [M.E. *sloh*], *n.* The cast skin of a snake; dead tissue separating from living, a scab. *v.t.* To cast off (a skin, dead tissue, etc.). **sloughy** (slŭf′i), *a.*

sloven (slŭv′én) [M.E. *sloveyn*], *n.* One who is careless of dress or negligent of cleanliness. **slovenly,** *a.*

slow (slō) [A.-S. *sláw*], *a.* Not quick, moving at a low speed; taking a long time; not hasty, behind the right time; stupid, dull; tedious. *adv.* Slowly. *v.i.* To slacken speed, to go slower (*usu.* up or down). *v.t.* To reduce the speed of. **slowly,** *adv.* **slowness,** *n.*

slow′worm (slō′wẽrm) [A.-S. *slā-wyrm*], *n.* A small limbless lizard, the blind-worm.

sludge (slŭj) [?], *n.* Mud, mire, slush.

slue (sloo) [?], *v.* To turn or swing (round, etc.) as on a pivot. *n.* Such a twist.

slug (slŭg) [Scand.], *n.* A shell-less in-

vertebrate destructive to plants; a roughly-shaped bullet or lump of metal.

sluggard, *n.* A person habitually lazy.

sluggish, *a.* Habitually lazy, inactive; inert, torpid.

sluice (sloos) [L. *exclūsa*, floodgate], *n.* A waterway with a valve controlling the level of a body of water; a flood-gate. *v.t.* To flood or drench by means of a sluice; to let out by a sluice.

slum (slŭm) [?], *n.* A low, dirty back street.

slumber (slŭm′bér) [M.E. *slumeren*], *v.i.* To sleep, esp. lightly. *n.* Light sleep. **slumberous,** *a.*

slump (slŭmp) [Scand.], *v.i.* To sink suddenly; to collapse (of prices, prosperity, interest in a matter, etc.). *n.* A heavy decline, a collapse (of prices, etc.).

slur (slẽr) [M.Dut. *sleuren*, to trail], *v.t.* To speak slightingly of; to pass lightly over; to pronounce indistinctly. *v.i.* To speak or articulate indistinctly; to pass lightly or slightingly (over). *n.* A stain, a disparagement; a slurring in pronunciation or singing.

slush (slŭsh) [?], *n.* Liquid mud, sludge; half-melted snow; (*slang*) piffle. **slushy,** *a.*

slut (slŭt) [Scand.], *n.* A dirty, slovenly woman, a slattern. **sluttish,** *a.*

sly (slī) [Icel. *slœgr*], *a.* Crafty, stealthily artful; underhand; knowing, arch. **slyly,** *adv.*

smack (1) (smăk) [A.-S. *smæc*], *n.* A slight taste or flavour; a trace or dash (of); a smattering. *v.i.* To have a taste or flavour (of).

smack (2) [M.Dut. *smacke*], *n.* A one-masted vessel used in fishing, etc.

smack (3) (onomat.], *n.* A smart report as a crack of a whip, etc.; a blow with the flat of the hand, a slap; a loud kiss. *v.t.* To slap, to separate (the lips) with a sharp noise, to crack (a whip).

small (smawl) [A.-S. *smæl*], *a.* Deficient or relatively little in size, power, number, etc.; trifling, petty; of low degree, unpretentious; paltry, mean. *adv.* Quietly, humbly. *n.* The slender part of anything, especially of the back. **small-arms,** *n.pl.* Portable fire-arms, as rifles, pistols, etc. **small beer:** Beer of a mild, light quality; (*fig.*) trivial matters. **small hours:** The time from midnight till 3 or 4 a.m. **smallpox,** *n.* A contagious, feverish disease, characterized by eruptions on the skin.

smart (smart) [A.-S. *smeortan*], *v.i.* To feel or give a sharp pain, to rankle. *adv.* Smartly. *n.* A sharp pain, a stinging sensation; a feeling of irritation; distress. *a.* Stinging, severe, poignant; lively, brisk; acute, ingenious; quick at repartee; shrewd; spruce, stylish. **smarten,** *v.* **smartly,** *adv.*

smash (smăsh), *v.t.* To break to pieces violently, to shatter; (*fig.*) to rout, to crush. *v.i.* To break to pieces; to crash (into). *n.* A breaking to pieces; a collapse; a disaster; bankruptcy, ruin. *adv.* With a smash.

smatter (smăt′ér) [?], *v.i.* To have a slight knowledge of. *n.* A smattering. **smattering,** *n.* A slight superficial knowledge.

smear (smēr) [A.-S. *smerien*], *v.t.* To daub with anything sticky; to blur. *v.i.* To make a smear; to be blurred; (*fig.*) to besmirch someone's name, to make crafty and unpleasant insinuations. *n.* A mark made by smearing. **smeary,** *a.*

smell (smel) [M.E. *smel*], *n.* The sense by which odours are perceived; the sensation or act of smelling; scent, odour; a stench. *v.t.* (*past and p.p.* **smelt**) To perceive or inhale the odour of; to detect by means of scent; to trace by the scent. *v.i.* To affect the sense of smell, to give out an odour (of); to smack (of); to have the sense of smell. **smelly,** *a.* Malodorous.

smelt (1) (smelt) [Teut.], *v.t.* To fuse (an ore) so as to extract the metal; to extract (metal) from ore thus. **smelter,** *n.*

smelt (2) [A.-S.], *n.* A small food-fish allied to the salmon.

smilax (smī'lăks) [Gr.], *n.* A genus of climbing shrubs, some of which yield sarsaparilla.

smile (smīl) [M.E. *smīlen*], *v.i.* To express pleasure, amusement, or contempt by an instinctive movement of the lips and cheeks; to look gay or favourable (of the weather, fortune, etc.). *n.* The act of smiling; a cheerful or favourable expression. **smilingly,** *adv.*

smirch smērch), *v.t.* To soil, stain, defile.

smirk (smērk) [A.-S. *smercian*], *v.i.* To smile affectedly, to simper, *n.* A simper.

smite (smīt) [A.-S. *smītan*], *v.t.* (*past* **smote,** *p.p.* **smitten**) To deal a severe blow to; to inflict disaster upon. *v.i.* To strike, knock, come (on, against, etc.) with force.

smith (smith) [A.-S.], *n.* One who works in metals, one who forges iron with the hammer. **smithy** smith'i), *n.* A blacksmith's shop.

smock (smok) [A.-S. *smoc*], *n.* A smockfrock; a chemise. **smock-frock,** *n.* A coarse outer shirt-like garment formerly worn by farm labourers. **smocking,** *n.* Honeycomb ornamentation in gathers, as on a smock.

smoke (smōk) [A.-S. *smoca*], *n.* Volatile products escaping as visible vapour from a burning substance; (*fig.*) anything unsubstantial; the act of smoking. *v.i.* To emit smoke; to inhale and exhale tobacco smoke. *v.t.* To colour, cure, destroy, cleanse, etc., with smoke; to use (tobacco) in smoking. **smoke-screen,** *n.* A dense volume of smoke to conceal a ship, the movements of troops, etc., from the enemy. **smoke-stack,** *n.* A funnel, esp. on a steamer. **smokable,** *a.* **smoker,** *n.* **smoky,** *a.*

smooth (smooth) [A.-S. *smethe*], *a.* Having an even surface, free from roughness; or impediments; not harsh; not hairy; equable, pleasant; polite, flattering. *v.t.* To make smooth; to free from harshness, discomforts, etc.; to soften, to cloak (over). **smooth-faced,** *a.* Beardless; having a suave appearance. **smoothly,** *adv.* **smoothness,** *n.*

smother (smŭth'ĕr) [A.-S. *smorian*, to stifle], *n.* A stifling cloud of dust, smoke, etc. *v.t.* To suffocate, to stifle; to keep from being divulged. *v.i.* To be suffocated. **smothery,** *a.*

smoulder (smōl'dĕr) [M.E. *smolder*, smoke], *v.i.* To burn in a smothered way without flame; (*fig.*) to exist in a suppressed condition.

smudge (smŭj) [M.E. *smogen*], *v.t.* To blur (writing, drawing, etc.); to make a smear on; (*fig.*) to soil, defile, sully. *n.* A dirty mark, a smear, blur.

smug (smŭg) [Teut.], *a.* Trim in dress, bearing, etc.; self-satisfied. **smugly,** *adv.*

smuggle (smŭgl) [L.G. *smuggeln*], *v.t.* To import or export illegally without paying the duties; to introduce clandestinely. **smuggler,** *n.* **smuggling,** *n.*

smut (smŭt) [Teut.], *n.* A particle of soot, etc., a smudge made by this; a disease of corn due to parasitic fungi; obscene language. *v.t.* To mark with smut; to infect with smut; to tarnish. **smutty,** *a.*

snack (snăk), *n.* A slight meal.

snaffle (snăfl) [Teut.], *n.* A bridle-bit with a joint in the middle and without a curb. *v.t.* (*colloq.*) To steal, to take.

snag (snăg) [Scand.], *n.* A jagged projection, esp. of a tree-stump; an unexpected difficulty.

snail (snāl) [A.-S. *snœgl*], *n.* A slow-moving mollusc feeding on vegetation; (*fig.*) a sluggish person.

snake (snāk) [A.-S. *snaca*], *n.* A serpent; a snake-like lizard or amphibian; (*fig.*) a treacherous person. **snaky,** *a.*

snap (snăp) [Teut.], *v.t.* To bite, try to bite, or snatch (at); to make a sharp, quick sound; to break suddenly; to speak sharply. *v.t.* To snatch; (*fig.*) to take (up) in the midst of a speech, etc.; to cause (a whip, the fingers, etc.) to make a sharp crack; to break with such a noise; to shut (to) thus; to photograph instantaneously. *n.* Act of snapping; the sound produced by this; a spring catch; a snapshot; (*colloq.*) dash, go. *a.* Done, taken, etc., suddenly. **snapshot,** *n.* An instantaneous photograph. *v.t.* To photograph thus. **snapper,** *n.* **snappish,** *a.* Given to snapping or biting, spiteful, irascible. **snappy,** *a.*

snare (snâr) [A.-S. *snear*], *n.* A trap; (*fig.*) a trick by which one is brought into difficulty, defeat, sin, etc. *v.t.* To catch in a snare; to entrap, inveigle.

snarl (snarl) [M.Dut. *snarren*, to trawl], *v.i.* To growl as an angry dog; to speak in a harsh, surly, or savage manner. *n.* A sharp-toned growl; a savage remark.

snatch (snăch) [M.E. *snacchen*], *v.t.* To seize suddenly, eagerly, or without permission.

sneak (snēk) [A.-S. *snīcan*, to creep], *v.i.* To creep, slink, or steal (about, away, off, etc.); to behave in a mean or underhand way; to tell tales. *v.t.* (*slang*) To steal. *n.* One who sneaks. **sneakingly,** *adv.*

sneer (snēr) [M.E. *sneren*], *v.i.* To show contempt by a smile or grin; to jibe. *n.* An expression of contempt or derision.

sneeze (snēz) [M.E. *snesen*], *v.i.* To eject air through the nostrils audibly and convulsively. *n.* The act of sneezing.

snib (snib) [Sc.], *n.* A bolt or catch. *v.t.* To fasten with this.

sniff (snif) [M.E. *sneven*], *v.i.* To draw air audibly up the nose. *v.t.* To smell, to perceive by sniffing. *n.* Act of sniffing; that which is sniffed in.

snigger (snig'ér) [imit.], *v.i.* To laugh in a half-suppressed manner. *n.* A suppressed laugh.

snip (snip) [Teut.], *v.t.* To clip, as with shears. **snippet**, *n.* A small bit snipped off; (*pl.*) scraps (of news, etc.).

snipe (snip) [Icel. *snipa*], *n.* A long-billed marsh- and shore-bird.

snivel (sniv'ėl) [M.E. *snevelen*], *v.i.* To run at the nose; to cry with snuffling; to be affectedly tearful. *n.* Audible or affected weeping. **sniveller**, *n.*

snob (snob), *n.* A person who apes gentility, truckles to those of higher social position, or regards the wealthy with respect; a cobbler. **snobbery, snobbishness**, *n.* **snobbish**, *a.*

snood (snood) [A.-S. *snōd*], *n.* A hairribbon or fillet; a crocheted net to contain a woman's back hair.

snooker (snoo'kér) [?], *n.* A game resembling pool played on a billiard-table.

snooze (snooz) [?], *v.i.* To take a short sleep. *n.* A short sleep, a nap.

snore (snōr) [?], *v.i.* To breathe with a hoarse noise in sleep. *n.* Act or sound of snoring.

snort (snôrt) [imit.], *v.i.* To force air violently and loudly through the nostrils. *n.* Act or sound of snorting.

snout (snout) [A.-S. *snytan*, to blow the nose], *n.* The projecting nose of a beast; a nozzle.

snow (snō) [A.-S. *snāw*], *n.* Watery vapour frozen into crystals and falling to the ground in flakes; a fall of this. *v.i.* (*impers.*) Snow to fall. *v.t.* To sprinkle or block (up) with snow; to scatter down as snow. **snow-blind**, *a.* Blinded, usu. temporarily, through the glare of light from snow. **snow-drift**, *n.* A mass of snow accumulated by the wind. **snowdrop**, *n.* A bulbous plant with a white flower appearing in early spring. **snowwhite**, *a.* **snowy**, *a.*

snub (snŭb) [Icel. *snubba*, to chide], *v.t.* To check or rebuke with sarcasm or contempt, to slight. *n.* An act of snubbing, a check.

snuff (1) (snŭf) [Teut.], *v.t.* To draw in through the nostrils. *v.i.* To sniff; to take snuff. *n.* A sniff; finely powdered tobacco. **snuffy**, *a.*

snuff (2) [?], *n.* The charred part of a wick. *v.t.* To trim (a wick, candle, etc.) by removing this. **snuffers**, *n.pl.* A scissorlike instrument for trimming away snuff.

snuffle (snŭfl), *v.i.* To breathe noisily as when the nose is obstructed; to talk through the nose.

snug (snŭg) [Teut.], *a.* Lying close and comfortable; cosy, compact, well secured. **snugly**, *adv.*

so (sō) [A.-S. *swā*], *adv.* and *conj.* In such a manner or to such an extent, degree, etc. (with *as*); in the manner or to the extent, intent, etc. (with *that* or *but*); provided (that); extremely, very; therefore, accordingly; (*ellipt.*) thus, this, that, as follows; in such a case. **so-and-so**, *n.*

An indefinite person or thing. **so-called**, *a.* Usually called thus (with implication of doubt). **so-so**, *a.* Middling, mediocre. *adv.* Indifferently.

soak (sōk) [A.-S. *socian*], *v.t.* To suck (in or up); to steep, to wet thoroughly. *v.i.* To lie in liquid so as to become permeated. *v.t.* To get money by an extortionate charge or demand. **soaking**, *a.* and *n.*

soap (sōp) [A.-S. *sāpe*], *n.* An unctuous compound of a fatty acid and soda or potash, used for washing. *v.t.* To rub or wash with soap. **soapy**, *a.* (*fig.*) Unctuous, flattering. **soapiness**, *n.*

soar (sōr) [F. *essorer*], *v.i.* To fly aloft, to float at a great height (of a bird, etc.); (*fig.*) to rise intellectually or morally.

sob (sob) [M.E. *sobben*], *v.i.* To catch the breath in a convulsive manner, as in weeping. *n.* A convulsive catching of the breath, as in weeping.

sober (sō'bér) [L. *sōbrious*], *a.* Not drunk; temperate in the use of alcoholic liquors; well-balanced, self-possessed, sedate; quiet (of colours, etc.). *v.t.* To make sober. *v.i.* To become calm or quiet. **soberly**, *adv.* **sobri'ety**, *n.*

sobriquet (sō'bri-kā) [F.], *n.* A nickname.

sociable (sō'shàbl) [L. *socius*, companion], *a.* Fit or inclined to associate or be companionable; of a friendly character (of a party, etc.). **sociabil'ity**, *n.* **sociably**, *adv.*

social (sō'shàl), *a.* Pertaining to society or to the mutual relations of man; living in communities, companionable, convivial. *n.* A sociable gathering. **social'ity**, *n.* **so'cialize**, *v.t.* **socially**, *adv.*

Socialism (sō'shà-lizm), *n.* The doctrine that society should be based on the subordination of the individual to the interests of the community. **Socialist**, *n.* and *a.* **Socialistic**, *a.*

society (sò-sī'é-ti), *n.* A social community; mankind regarded as a community; social organization, civilization; the upper classes of a community; a body of persons associated for some common object; companionship, fellowship.

sociology (sō-si-ol'ó-ji), *n.* The science of the evolution and constitution of human society. **sociological**, *a.* **sociologist**, *n.*

sock (sok) [A.-S. *socc*], *n.* A short stocking; a removable inner sole; the light shoe worn by classic comic actors (L. *soccus*), hence (*fig.*) comedy.

socket (sok'ét) [O.F. *soket*], *n.* A hollow adapted for receiving and holding another part or thing. **socketed**, *a.*

Socratic (sō-krăt'ik), *a.* Pertaining or according to Socrates, Greek philosopher (*d.* B.C. 399).

sod (sod) [Teut.], *n.* Turf, sward; a piece of this.

soda (sō'dà) [It.], *n.* Carbonate or bicarbonate of sodium, esp. in the crystalline form used in washing, etc.; (*colloq.*) soda-water. **soda-water**, *n.* An effervescent drink composed of water charged with carbonic acid.

sodality (sò-dăl'i-ti) [L. *sodālis*, comrade] *n.* A fellowship, esp. (*R.-C. Ch.*) a charitable association.

sodden (sodn) [p.p. of SEETHE], a. Soaked, saturated; heavy, doughy (of bread); stupid with drink. v.t. To soak, to saturate, esp with drink.

sodium (sō'di-ŭm), n. A silver-white metallic element, the base of soda.

sofa (sō'fà) [Arab. *suffah*], n. A long stuffed couch with raised back and ends.

soffit (sof'it) [It. *soffita*, ceiling], n. The under surface of a cornice, balcony, arch, etc.

soft (soft) [A.-S. *sŏfte*], a. Yielding easily to pressure, easily moulded or cut, pliable, plastic; mild, delicate; smooth to the touch; not hot or cold; genial; not glaring (of colours, etc.); low-toned; free from mineral salts (of water); concilia- tory; impressionable, sympathetic; weak, effeminate; silly, spoony; (*Phon.*) not guttural or explosive, sibilant (as *c* in *cede* or *g* in *gem*), voiced (as *b*, *d*, and *g*). adv. Softly, gently, quietly. int. Gently; Hush! **soften** (sofn), v.t. To make soft or softer; to mitigate, tone down. v.i. To become soft or softer. **softish**, a. **softly**, adv. **softy**, n. A silly, weak-minded person.

soil (1) (soil) [A.-F.], n. The ground, esp. the top stratum whence plants derive their mineral food; land, country.

soil (2) [A.-F., *soyler*], v.t. To make dirty; to tarnish, pollute.

soirée (swa'rā) [F.], n. An evening party for social intercourse, discussion, etc., and music.

sojourn (soj'ŭrn) [O.F. *sojourner*], v.i. To stay (in, among) temporarily. n. A temporary stay.

sol (sol), n. The fifth tone of the diatonic scale.

solace (sol'ås) [O.F. *solaz*], n. Comfort in grief, etc., consolation, compensation. v.t. To comfort or console.

solan (goose) (sō'làn) [Icel. *sūla*], n. The gannet.

solar (sō'làr) [L. *sol*, the sun], a. Pertaining to or proceeding from the sun.

solatium (sô-lā'shi-ŭm) [L]. n. (pl. **-tia**) Compensation for suffering or loss.

solder (sol'-, sō'dèr) [L. *solidāre*, to make firm], n. A fusible alloy for uniting less fusible metals. v.t. To unite with solder.

soldier (sōl'jèr) [L. *soldārius*], n. A man engaged in military service; a man of military experience; an able commander. **soldier-like, -ly**, a. and adv. **soldiery**, n. Soldiers collectively; a body of soldiers.

sole (1) (sōl) [A.-S., L. *solea*], n. The flat underside of the foot; the part of a boot, etc., under the foot. v.t. To furnish (a boot, etc.) with a sole.

sole (2), n. A flat-fish highly esteemed as food.

sole (3) [L. *sōlus*], a. Single, only, unique; (*Law*) unmarried. **solely**, adv.

solecism (sol'è-sizm) [Gr. *soloikos*, speaking incorrectly], n. A deviation from correct idiom or grammar; an impropriety.

solemn (sol'ĕm) [L. *sōlemnis*], a. Performed with or accompanied by rites or due formality; impressive; grave, momen- tous; formal, pompous. **solem'nity**, n. Impressiveness; affected gravity or for- mality; a rite or ceremony. **solemnize**

solemniza'tion, n. (sol'ĕm-nīz), v.t. To celebrate with for- malities or ceremonies; to make solemn.

solicit (sô-lis'it) [L. *sollicitāre*], v. To make earnest request for or persistent appeals to, to importune. **solicitant**, a. and n. **solicita'tion**, n.

solicitor (sô-lis'i-tôr), n. A legal practi- tioner authorized to advise clients and prepare causes for barristers. **Solicitor- General**, n. A law officer of the British Crown, advising and representing it in legal matters.

solicitous (sô-lis'i-tùs), a. Anxious, appre- hensive; eager (to). **solicitude**, n.

solid (sol'id) [L. *solidus*], a. Dense, com- pact; not hollow, broken, or porous; firm, unyielding; sound, not flimsy; (*fig.*) real, reliable; homogeneous; feeling or acting unanimously; (*Geom.*) cubic. n. A rigid, compact body. **solidar'ity**, n. Cohesion; community of interests, feel- ings, responsibilities, etc. **solid'ify**, v. **solidifiable**, a. **solidifica'tion**, n **solid'ity**, n. **solidly**, adv.

soliloquy (sô-lil'ô-kwi) [L. *sōlus*, alone, *loqui*, to speak], n. A talking to oneself; a monologue. **soliloquize**, v.i. **solilo- quist**, n.

solitaire (sol-i-târ'), n. A gem set singly; a game played by one person.

solitary (sol'-i-tår-i) [L. *sōlus*, alone], a. Lonely, not gregarious; living, passed, or spent alone; unfrequented, secluded; individual. n. A recluse. **solitude**, n. Seclusion; a lonely place.

solo (sō'lō) [It.], n. A composition for a single instrument or voice; a kind of whist, a call in this game. **soloist**, n.

solstice (sol'stis) [L. *sōlstitium*, a standing of the sun], n. The time (about 21 June and 22 Dec.) when the sun is farthest from the equator (N. in summer, S. in winter), and seems to stand for a little before moving back. **solstitial** (-stish'ål), a. Pertaining to the solstice.

soluble (sol'ŭbl) [L. *solvere* to solve], a. Capable of being dissolved or solved. **solubil'ity**, n.

solution (sô-lū'shŭn) L. *solvere*, to solve], n. The liquefaction of a body by mixture with a liquid; the combination so pro- duced; the act or process of solving a problem, the correct answer; separation, disintegration.

solve (solv), v.t. To resolve or find an answer to (a problem, etc.); to put an end to. **solvable**, a.

solvent (sol'vènt), a. Having the power to dissolve; able to pay all claims. n. A liquid that can dissolve a substance. **solvency**, n.

somatic (sô-măt'ik) [Gr. *sōma*, body], a. Pertaining to the body, corporeal, physical.

sombre (som'bèr) [F.], a. Dark, gloomy.

sombrero (som-brâr'ō) [Sp., from *sombra*, shade], n. A wide-brimmed hat.

some (sŭm) [A.-S. *sum*], a. An indetermin- ate quantity of; a certain, a particular but not definitely known or specified (person or thing). adv. About, approxi- mately. pron. A particular but unde- termined part or quantity; certain not definitely known or unspecified ones. **somebody,** *n.* Some person; a person of consequence. **somehow,** *adv.* In some indeterminate way; in some way or other. **something,** *n.* Some indeterminate or unspecified thing; some quantity or portion if not much. *adv.* In some degree. **sometime,** *adv.* Once, formerly, at one time. *a.* Former, late. **sometimes,** *adv.* At some times. **somewhat,** *adv.* To some extent, rather. *n.* A certain amount or degree; something **somewhere,** *adv.* In some unknown or unspecified place; in some place or other. **-some** [A.-S. *-sum*], *suf.* Forming adjectives, full of, as in *gladsome, troublesome, winsome.*

somersault, somerset (sŭm'ĕr-sawlt, -set) [O.F. *sombresaut*], *n.* A leap in which one turns heels over head and alights on one's feet.

somnambulism (som-năm'bū-lizm) [L. *somnus,* sleep, *ambulāre,* to walk], *n.* The act of walking in sleep; the mental affection causing this. **somnambulist,** *n.*

somniferous (som-nif'ĕr-ŭs), *a.* Causing or inducing sleep.

somnolent (som'nō-lĕnt), *a.* Sleepy, drowsy; inducing sleep. **Somnolence,** *n.*

son (sŭn) [A.-S. *sunu*], *n.* A male child in relation to a parent; *(fig.)* a descendant. **son-in-law,** *n.* The husband of one's daughter. **sonship,** *n.*

sonata (sō-na'tà) [It.], *n.* An instrumental composition in three or four movements in different rhythms.

song (song) [A.-S. *sang*], *n.* Musical utterance, singing; a melodious cry, as of a bird; a musical composition accompanied by words; a short poem suitable for singing. **songster,** *n.* One skilled in singing. **songstress,** *n.*

sonnet (son'ĕt) [F., It. *sonetto*], *n.* A poem of fourteen iambic pentameter lines with a definite rhyme-scheme. **sonneteer,** *n.* A writer of sonnets.

sonorous (sō-nôr'ŭs) [L. *sonor, sonōris,* sound], *a.* Resonant; sounding rich or full; high-sounding, impressive. **sonor'ity, sonorousness,** *n.*

sonsy (son'si) [Sc. from Gael. *sonas,* good fortune]. Happy-looking, buxom.

soon (soon) [A.-S. *sōna*], *adv.* In a short time from now or after a specified time, early; quickly, readily, willingly.

soot (sut) [A.-S. *sōt*], *n.* A black substance rising from burning fuel. **sooty,** *a.*

sooth (sooth) [A.-S. *sōth*], *n.* Truth, reality.

soothe (sooth) [A.-S. *gesōthian,* to assent to, as prec.], *v.t.* To calm; to soften, mitigate; to humour.

soothsayer (sooth'sā-ĕr), *n.* A prognosticator, a diviner.

sop (sop) [A.-S. *sopp*], *n.* Any food steeped in milk, gravy, etc.; *(fig.)* something given to pacify. **soppy,** *a.* **soppiness,** *n.*

sophism (sof'izm) [Gr. *sophos,* wise], *n.* A specious but fallacious argument. **sophist,** *n.* A fallacious reasoner, a quibbler. **sophis'tic, -al,** *a.* **sophisticate,** *v.t.* To obscure with sophistry; to mislead thus; to garble (a text) in order to support one's arguments; to adulterate

to deprive of simplicity, to make artificial. **sophistica'tion,** *n.* **sophistry** (sof'is-tri), *n.*

sophomore (sof'ō-môr) [Gr. *sophisma,* wisdom], *n.* (*Am.*) A student in his second year at high school or college.

soporific (sō-pō-rif'ik) [L. *sopor,* sleep], *a.* Causing or tending to cause sleep. *n.* A soporific medicine.

soprano (sō-pra'nō) [It.], *n.* A female or boy's voice of the highest kind; a singer having such a voice; a part for such voices.

sorcerer (sôr'sĕr-ĕr) [L. *sortiāre,* to cast lots], *n.* One who uses magic, a wizard. **sorceress,** *n.* **sorcery,** *n.*

sordid (sôr'did) [L. *sordes,* filth], *a.* Mean, ignoble, vile; niggardly. **sordidly,** *adv.* **sordidness,** *n.*

sore (sôr) A.-S. *sār*], *a.* Tender and painful to the touch; aggrieved, vexed; touchy; grievous, heavy. *adv.* Sorely, severely, intensely. *n.* A place on the body where the surface is bruised, broken, or inflamed; *(fig.)* a subject that excites resentment, remorse, etc. **sorely,** *adv.*

sorites (sō-rī'-tēz) [Gr. *sōros,* heap], *n.* A series of syllogisms so connected that the predicate of one forms the subject of that which follows.

sorrel (sor'ĕl) [O.F. *sorel*], *a.* Of a reddish or yellowish-brown. *n.* This colour; a horse of this colour; a herb allied to the dock.

sorrow (sor'ō) [A.-S. *sorg*], *n.* Mental pain from loss, disappointment, etc., grief, sadness; something causing this; mourning, lamentation. *v.i.* To grieve; to lament. **sorrowful,** *a.*

sorry (sor'i), *a.* Feeling grief for some loss, etc., regretful; paltry, despicable. **sorrily,** *adv.*

sort (sôrt) [L. *sortem,* nom. *sors,* lot, chance], A number (of things, etc.) having the same or similar qualities; way, manner. *v.t.* To separate into sorts, classes, etc.; to select from a number. *v.i.* To consort, to agree or accord (with).

sortie (sôr'ti) [F., gone out], *n.* A sally, as from a besieged place.

sortilege (sôr'ti-lĕj) [O.F.], *n.* Divination by drawing lots.

sot (sot) [M.E.], *n.* An habitual drunkard. **sottish,** *a.*

sou (soo) [F.], *n.* A French copper coin, the five-centime piece.

soubrette (soo-bret') [F.], *n.* (*Theat.*) A waitingmaid.

soufflé (soo'flā) [F.], *n.* A light dish of beaten whites of eggs, etc.

sough (sŭf, sou) [A.-S. *swōgan*], *v.i.* To make a murmuring, sighing sound, as the wind. *n.* This sound.

soul (sōl) [A.-S. *sāwel*], *n.* The spiritual, the moral and emotional, or intellectual part of a person; consciousness; the vital principle and mental powers possessed by living creatures; *(fam.)* a person. **soulful,** *a.* Rich in the spiritual, emotional, or higher intellectual qualities. **soulless,** *a.*

sound (1) (sound) [A.-S. *sund*], *a.* Whole, free from injury, defect, or decay;

healthy; based on truth or reason, correct; solvent; thorough. **soundness**, *n.*

sound (2) [L. *sonus*], *n.* The sensation produced through the organs of hearing; that which causes this sensation; a specific tone or note. *v.i.* To give out sound. *v.t.* To cause to sound; to give a signal for by sound; to make known, proclaim; to test by sound. **soundproof**, *a.* Impenetrable to sound. **sounding** (1), *a.* Making or giving out sound; sonorous, noisy; (*fig.*) imposing, highflown. **sound barrier**, *n.* The shock wave produced when a moving body attains the speed of sound, *i.e.* 764 miles per hour. **sound track**, *n.* (*Cinema.*) The portion at the side of a picture film which bears the recording of the accompanying sound.

sound (3) [A.-S. *sund*], *n.* A narrow passage of water connecting two seas; the swimming-bladder of a fish.

sound (4) (sound) [F. *sonder*], *v.t.* To measure the depth of with a sounding-line or rod; to test; to endeavour to discover (intentions, feelings, etc.). *v.i.* To use the line and lead to ascertain the depth of water. **sounding** (2), *n.* The act of measuring depths; (*pl.*) a part of the sea where the bottom can be reached by sounding.

soup (soop) [F. *soupe*], *n.* A liquid food made from meat, fish, or vegetables.

sour (sour) [A.-S. *sūr*], *a.* Sharp to the taste, tart; rancid; harsh of temper, morose. **sourish**, *a.*

sourdough (sour'dō), *n.* (*Canadian*) An old timer.

source (sôrs) [O.F. *sorse*, as SURGE], *n.* The spring from which a stream of water proceeds; original, first cause.

souse (sous) [O.F. *souse*, sauce], *n.* Pickle made with salt; anything preserved in pickle, esp. the ears, feet, etc., of swine; plunging into water. *adv.* With sudden descent, plump. *v.t.* To pickle; to plunge into or drench thoroughly with water, etc.

soutane (soo-tan') [F.], *n.* A priest's cassock.

south (south) [A.-S. *sūth*], *n.* The cardinal point of the compass directly opposite to the north; a southern region; a wind from the south. *a.* Situated in or facing the south; coming from the south (of the wind). *adv.* Towards or from the south. **south-east** *n.* and *a.* The point of the compass midway between south and east. **southeaster**, *n.* A S.E. wind. **south-easterly**, *a.* and *adv.* **south-eastern**, *a.* **southerly** (sŭth'ĕr-li), *a.* and *adv.* **southern** (sŭth'ĕrn), *a.* **southerner**, *n.* An inhabitant or native of the south, esp of the Southern States of U.S.A. **southernmost**, *a.* **southmost**, *a.* **southward** (south'wård), *adv.* and *a.* **southwards**, *adv.* **south-west**, *n.* and *a.* **southwester**, **sou'wester**, *n.* A wind from the S.W.; a waterproof hat with a wide brim hanging behind.

souvenir (soo've-nēr) [F., to remember], *n.* A keepsake, a memento.

sovereign (sov'răn) [O.F. *soverain*], *a.* Supreme; royal; efficacious (as a remedy). *n.* A supreme ruler, a king, an emperor;

an English gold coin, value 20*s.* **sovereignty**, *n.*

Soviet (sov'yet) [Rus., council], *n.* A council elected by workers and inhabitants of a district; a council elected by a number of these; the all-Russian congress of delegates from these last.

sow (1) (sō) [A.-S. *sāwan*], *v.t.* (*past* **sowed**, *p.p.* **sown**, **sowed**) To scatter (seed) for growth; to scatter over, to cover thickly with; to disseminate. *v.i.* To scatter seed for growth. **sower**, *n.* **sowing**, *n.*

sow (2) (sou) [A.-S. *sugu*, *sū*], *n.* A female pig; the main channel for molten iron; a block of iron solidified in this.

soya bean (soi'ya bēn) [Chin. *shi-yu*], *n.* A nutritious bean used as a source for making margarine; the flour made from this bean.

spa (spa) [town in Belgium], *n.* A mineral spring; a place where there is such a spring.

space (spās) [L. *spatium*], *n.* Continuous extension or any portion of this; location beyond the earth's atmosphere; an interval between points, etc.; an interval of time. *v.t.* To put the proper spaces between (words, lines, etc.). **spacial**, *a.* **spacing**, *n.* **spacious** (spā'shŭs), *a.* Having ample room; capacious, roomy.

spade (spād) [A.-S. *spœdu*, *spadu*], *n.* An implement for digging worked with both hands and one foot; a playing-card of a black suit; (*pl.*) this suit. *v.t.* To dig with or use a spade.

span (spăn) [A.-S. *spannan*], *v.t.* To extend from side to side of; to measure with one's hand expanded. *n.* The space from the end of the thumb to the end of the little finger when extended; nine inches; a brief space; the space from end to end of a bridge, etc.; a yoke or team of oxen, etc. **spanner**, *n.* An instrument for tightening or loosening nuts, a wrench.

spandrel (spăn'drĕl) [?], *n.* The space between the shoulder of an arch and the rectangular moulding enclosing it.

spangle (spăng'gĕl) [dim. from A.-S. *spang*, a metal clasp], *n.* A small disk of glittering metal, etc.; any small sparkling object. *v.t.* To adorn with spangles.

Spaniard (spăn'yård) [Sp. *Español*], *n.* A native of Spain.

spaniel (spăn'yĕl) [Sp. *Español*], *n.* A dog with large drooping ears, long silky coat, and a gentle disposition.

Spanish (spăn'ish), *a.* Pertaining to Spain. *n.* The Spaniards; their language.

spank (spăngk) [?], *v.t.* To strike with the open hand, to slap. *v.i.* To move briskly along. *n.* A slap, a smack.

spanner (SPAN).

spar (1) (spar) [M.E. *sparre*], *n.* A pole, esp. used as a mast, boom, etc.

spar (2) [A.-S. *spœr*], *n.* A lustrous crystalline mineral.

spar (3), *v.i.* To move the arms about as in boxing.

spare (spăr) [A.-S. *spœr*], *a.* Meagre, scanty, frugal; kept in reserve, available for an emergency, etc. *v.t.* To use frugally; to refrain from using; to dispense with; to refrain from punishing, injuring, etc. **sparely**, *adv.* sparingly, *adv.*

spark (spark) [A.-S. *spearca*], *n.* An incandescent particle thrown off from a burning substance; a flash of wit, a particle of energy; a gay young fellow. *v.i.* To give out sparks; to sparkle. **sparkish**, *a.* Gay, gallant.

sparkle (sparkl), *n.* A gleam, glitter, brilliance. *v.i.* To emit sparks; to glisten, glitter, twinkle; to bubble (of some wines). **sparkling**, *a.* Glittering; lively; bubbling.

sparrow (spăr'ō) [A.-S. *spearwa*], *n.* A small brownish-grey bird. **sparrowhawk**, *n.* A small hawk.

sparse (spars) [L. *sparsus*, scattered], *a.* Thinly scattered, not dense. **sparsity**, *n.*

Spartan (spar'tàn), *n.* A native of Sparta; one of great hardihood or endurance. *a.* Pertaining to Sparta or the Spartans; like a Spartan.

spasm (spăzm) [Gr. *spasmos*], *n.* A convulsive and involuntary muscular contraction, movement, etc. **spasmod'ic**, *a.*

spat (1) (spăt) [?], *n.* The spawn of shellfish.

spat (2), *n.* A short gaiter.

spate (spăt) [?], *n.* A heavy flood, especially in a mountain stream.

spatial (spā'shàl) [SPACE], *a.* Of or relating to space.

spatter (spăt'ér), *v.t.* To scatter (water, etc.) about; to splash with water, mud, etc.; (*fig.*) to defame. *n.* A sprinkling, a pattering. **spatterdash**, *n.* A legging for protecting against mud.

spavin (spăv'in) [O.F. *esparvin*], *n.* A disease in horses affecting the hock-joint.

spawn (spawn) [L. *expandere*, to expand], *v.t.* To deposit or produce eggs (of fish, etc.). *n.* The eggs of fish, frogs, and molluscs. **spawner**, *n.*

speak (spēk) [.-S *sprecan*], *v.i.* (*past* spoke, spake, *p.p.* spoken) To utter words; to talk, converse; to deliver a speech; to be highly expressive. *v.t.* To utter articulately; to tell, declare; to talk in a language. **speaker**, *n.* One who speaks, esp. delivers a speech; an officer presiding over a deliberative assembly (esp. the House of Commons). **speakership**, *n.* **speaking**, *a.* Animated, vivid (of a likeness).

spear (spēr) [A.-S *spere*], *n.* A weapon with a pointed head on a long shaft. *v.t.* To pierce or capture with a spear. **spearmint**, *n.* The garden mint.

special (spesh'ăl) [L. *speciālis*], *a.* Particular, not ordinary or general; for a particular purpose. *n.* A person or thing designed for a special purpose, etc.; a special train, constable, edition of a newspaper, etc. **specialist**, *n.* One who devotes himself to a particular branch of a profession, etc. **specialism**, *n.* **special'ity**, *n.* A special characteristic, a peculiarity; a special occupation, commodity, etc. **specialize**, *v.t.* **specializa'tion**, *n.*

specie (spē'shē) [L. in *speciē*, in kind], *n.* Coin as dist. from paper money.

species (spē'shēz) [L., appearance, sort], *n.* (*Nat. Hist.*) A group of organisms (subordinate to a genus); a group of individuals having certain common attributes; a kind, sort.

specific (spé-sif'ik), *a.* Clearly specified, explicit, precise; pertaining to a species; special. *n.* An efficacious medicine, etc. **specifically**, *adv.* **specifica'tion**, *n.* Act of specifying; a detailed statement of particulars, description of an invention, etc. **specify** (spes'i-fī), *v.t.* To mention expressly; to include in a specification.

specimen (spes'i-mèn) [L.], *n.* Something illustrating or typifying the nature of a whole or a class, an example, an instance.

specious (spē'shùs) [L. *speciōsus*], *a.* Apparently right, plausible; showy.

speck (spek) [A.-S. *specca*], *n.* A small stain or blemish; a minute particle of rottenness, etc. *v.t.* To mark with specks.

speckle (spekl), *n.* A small spot, stain, or patch of colour, etc.

spectacle (spek'tàkl) [L. *spectāculum*], *n.* A show, a pageant; a sight; (*pl.*) lenses mounted in a light frame for assisting the sight. **spectac'ular**, *n.*

spectator (spek-tā'tòr) [L.], *n.* One who looks on.

spectre (spek'tèr) [L. *spectrum*, a vision], *n.* An apparition, a ghost. **spectral**, *a.* Ghostlike, pertaining to ghosts or to the spectrum.

spectroscope (spek'trò-skōp), *n.* An instrument for forming and analysing the spectra of rays emitted by bodies. **spectroscop'ic**, *a.*

spectrum (spek'trùm) [L.], *n.* (*pl.* **spectra**) An image produced by the decomposition of rays of light by means of a prism.

speculate (spek'ū-lāt) [L. *speculātus*, beheld], *v.i.* To pursue an inquiry or form conjectures, to theorize; to make investments, etc., on the chance of profit. **specula'tion**, *n.* Act or practice of speculating; a mental inquiry, series of conjectures; a speculative investment or undertaking; a card-game. **spec'ulative**, *a.*

speech (spēch) [A.-S. *spǽc*], *n.* The faculty or act of uttering words; that which is spoken; an oration; the language of a nation, etc. **speechifier**, *n.* One who makes long and empty speeches. **speechless**, *a.* Silent through emotion; dumb.

speed (spēd) [A.-S. *spēd*], *n.* Rapidity, rate of motion. *v.i.* (*past and p.p.* sped) To move rapidly, to hasten; to prosper, to fare (well, ill, etc.).). *v.t.* To promote, to cause to succeed; to cause to go fast, to urge; (*past and p.p.* speeded) to regulate the speed of. **speedboat**, *n.* (*Naut.*) A light boat driven at great speed by a motor engine. **speedway**, *n.* A racing track for motor cycles. **speedwell**, *n.* A flowering herb. **speedy**, *a.* **speedily**, *adv.*

spell (1) (spel) [A.-S. *spel*], *n.* A charm, an incantation; occult power. **spellbound**, *a.* Under the influence of a spell.

spell (2) [O.F. *espeler*], *v.t.* (*past and p.p.*

spelt) To say or write the letters of a word; to form a word (of letters); (*fig.*) to mean, portend. **speller,** *n.* **spelling,** *n.*

spell (3) [A.-S. *spelian*], *n.* A turn of work; a short period.

spelt (spelt) [A.-S.], *n.* A variety of wheat cultivated in S. Europe.

spelter (spel'tèr) [Teut.], *n.* (*Comm.*) Zinc.

spencer (1) (spen'sèr) [3rd Earl *Spencer* (1782–1845)], *n.* A short jacket.

spend (spend) [A.-S. *spendan*], *v.t.* (*past and p.p.* spent) To pay out (money); to use up; to squander, waste; to wear out. **spendthrift,** *a.* Prodigal, wasteful, *n.* A prodigal person.

sperm (spèrm) [Gr. *sperma*], *n.* The male seminal fluid of animals; a whale yielding spermaceti, a cachalot.

spermaceti (spèr-mà-sē'ti), *n.* A white, fatty, brittle substance obtained from the sperm-whale.

spermatic ((spèr-măt'ik), *a.* Consisting of, pertaining to, or conveying sperm or semen.

spermology (spèr-mó'lò-gi), *n.* The branch of botany dealing with seeds.

spew (spū) [A.-S. *speowan*], *v.* To vomit; to cast out with abhorrence.

sphere (sfēr) [Gr. *sphaira*, ball], *n.* A solid bounded by a surface every part of which is equally distant from the central point within; a ball, a globe, a heavenly body; (*fig.*) field of action, influence, etc., scope range. **spheral,** *a.* **Spherical,** pertaining to spheres. **spherical,** *a.* Sphere-shaped, globular; relating to spheres. **sphericity (sfè-ris'i-ti),** *n.* **spher'oid,** *n.* A body nearly spherical. **spheroi'dal,** *a.*

sphinx (sfingks) [Gr.], *n.* (*Gr. Ant.*) A winged monster, half woman and half lion, said to have proposed a riddle to the people of Thebes; (*Egypt. Ant.*) a figure with the body of a lion and a human or animal head; (*fig.*) a taciturn or enigmatic person.

spice (spis) [L. *speciēs*, kind], *n.* Any aromatic and pungent vegetable seasoning; (*fig.*) a flavour, a trace. *v.t.* To season with spice. **spicy,** *a.*

spick-and-span (spik'ànd-spàn'), *a.* New and fresh, fresh and smart.

spider (spi'dèr) [A.-S.], *n.* An eight-legged insect that spins webs to catch its prey. **spidery,** *a.*

spigot (spi'gòt) [?], *n.* A peg for stopping a faucet or the vent-hole in a cask; a faucet.

spike (spik) [Scand. *spik*], *n.* A pointed piece of metal, a sharp point; a large nail; a flower cluster along a common axis. *v.t.* To fasten or furnish with spikes; to sharpen to a point; to pierce; to plug the touch-hole (of a cannon) with a spike.

spikenard (spik'nard) [O.F. *spiquenard*], *n.* A herb related to valerian; an ancient and costly aromatic ointment prepared from this.

spill (1) (spil) [?], *n.* A slip of paper or wood used to light a lamp, etc.

spill (2) [A.-S. *spillan*], *v.t.* (*past and p.p.* spilt, spilled) To suffer to fall or run out of a vessel; to shed. *v.i.* To run

or fall out (of liquid). *n.* A fall, esp. from a vehicle or saddle.

spillikin (spil'i-kin), *n.* A pin of bone, wood, etc., used in certain games.

spin (spin) [A.-S. *spinnan*], *v.t.* (*past* spun, span, *p.p.* spun) To draw out and twist (wool, cotton, etc.) into threads; to make (yarn, etc.) thus; to produce threads (of spiders, etc.); to make (a top, etc.) rotate rapidly. *v.i.* To draw out and twist cotton, etc., into threads; to whirl round. *n.* The act or motion of spinning, a whirl; (*colloq.*) a run, ride, etc., at a brisk pace. **spinner,** *n.* One who spins; a machine for spinning thread; a spider.

spinach (spin'åj) [Arab. *aspanātch*], *n.* An annual herb with succulent leaves cooked as food.

spinal (spi'nål), *a.* Pertaining to the spine. **spinal column:** The backbone.

spindle (spindle) [A.-S. *spinl*], *n.* A rod in a spinning-wheel for twisting and winding the thread; a rod which revolves or on which anything revolves. *v.i.* To grow into a long slender stalk, etc. **spindle-legged,** *a.* Having long, thin legs.

spindrift (spin'drift), *n.* Fine spray from the surface of water.

spine (spin) [L. *spina*, thorn, backbone], *n.* The backbone. **spines'cent,** *a.* (*Bot.*) Tending to be spinous; thorny. **spinous,** **spiny,** *a.*

spinet (spin'èt) [It. *spinetta*], *n.* An obsolete musical instrument, similar to the harpsichord.

spinnaker (spin'à-kèr) [?], *n.* A large jib-shaped sail carried opposite the main-sail.

spinney (spin'i), *n.* A small wood with undergrowth, a copse.

spinous [SPINE].

spinster (spin'stèr) [SPIN, -STER], *n.* An unmarried woman. **spinsterhood,** *n.*

spiral (spir'ål), *a.* Forming a spire, spiral, or coil; continually winding as the thread of a screw. *n.* A spiral curve, spring, or other object. **spirally,** *adv.*

spire (spir) [A.-S. *spir*], *n.* A tapering structure, the tapering portion of a steeple, etc. *v.i.* To shoot up like a spire.

spirit (spir'it) [L. *spīritus*, from *spīrāre*, to breathe], *n.* The immaterial part of man, the soul, this disembodied, a ghost; a sprite, an elf, a fairy; vigour of mind; vivacity, ardour, enthusiasm; disposition; mental attitude, mood; (*usu. pl.*) distilled alcoholic liquors. *v.t.* To animate, to inspirit; to convey (away) secretly and rapidly. **spirits of wine:** Pure alcohol. **spirit-level,** *n.* An instrument for determining the horizontal by an air-bubble in a tube containing alcohol. **spirited,** *a.* Full of spirit, animated, lively, courageous. **spiritless,** *a.*

spiritual (spir'i-tū-ål), *a.* Pertaining to or consisting of spirit; incorporeal; pertaining to the soul; derived from God, pure, holy, inspired; not lay or temporal. **spiritual'ity,** *n.* Unworldliness.

spiritualism (spir'i-tū-à-lizm), *n.* A system of professed communication with departed spirits; (*Phil.*) the doctrine that the spirit exists as distinct from

matter. **spiritualist**, *n.* **spiritualis'tic**, *a.*
spirituous (spir'i-tū-ŭs), *a.* Containing
spirit, alcoholic.

spit (1) (spit) [A.-S. *spitu*], *n.* A rod on
which meat for roasting is rotated before
a fire; a point of land extending into the
sea.

spit (2) [A.-S. *spittan*], *v.t. (past and p.p.*
spat) To eject (saliva, etc.) from the
mouth; to utter in a violent or spiteful
way. *v.i.* To eject saliva from the
mouth; to make a spitting noise. *n.*
Spittle, saliva; spitting. **spitfire**, *n.* An
irascible person. **spittle**, *n.* Saliva.
spittoon', *n.* A receptacle for spittle.

spite (spit), *n.* Ill-will, malice; a grudge.
v.t. To thwart maliciously; to vex. **in
spite of:** Notwithstanding. **spiteful**, *a.*

spiv (spiv) [?], *n.* A petty black-market
dealer; a cheaply over-dressed and lazy
man who battens on those who work.

splash (splăsh), *v.t.* To bespatter with
water, mud, etc. *v.i.* To dash liquid
about; to be dashed about in drops, to
dabble, to plunge; to make one's way
(along, etc.) thus. *n.* A spot or patch
of liquid, colour, etc. **splash-board**, *n.*
A guard to protect the occupants of a
vehicle from mud. **splashy**, *a.*

splay (splā), *v.t.* To form (an opening, etc.)
with oblique sides. **splay-foot**, *n.* A
broad, flat foot turned outwards.

spleen (splēn) [Gr. *splēn*], *n.* A soft
vascular organ in vertebrates; (*fig.*)
spitefulness, ill-temper; melancholy.
spleenish, *a.*

splendid (splen'did) [L. *splendēre*, to
shine], *a.* Magnificent, glorious, illustrious; brilliant; fine, first-rate. **splendour**, *n.*

splenetic (splé-net'ik), *a.* Pertaining to
the spleen; peevish, ill-tempered.

splice (splis) [Dut. *splitsen*, to splice], *v.t.*
To unite (two ropes, etc.) by inter-
weaving; to unite (timbers, etc.) by
fitting the ends together. *n.* A union of
ropes, timbers, etc., by splicing.

splint (splint) [M.Dut. *splinte*], *n.* A thin
piece of wood, etc., used to keep the
parts of a broken bone together. *v.t.*
To secure or support with splints.

splinter (splin'tèr), *n.* A thin piece broken,
split, or shivered off. *v.* To split, or
rend into splinters.

split (split) [M. Dut. *splitten*], *v.t. (past
and p.p.* **split**) To break, cleave or
divide longitudinally or with the grain;
to divide (votes) between different
candidates. *v.i.* To be divided longitudinally; to go to pieces; to divide into
opposed parties. *n.* The act or result
of splitting; a crack, rent, fissure; a
rupture, a schism.

splutter (splŭt'èr) [imit.], *v.* To sputter.
n. A noise, a fuss. **splutterer**, *n.*

spoil (spoil) [L. *spolia*, booty], *v.t. (past
and p.p.* **spoilt, spoiled**) To mar, impair
the goodness, usefulness, etc., of; to
injure by over-indulgence; to plunder.
v.i. To decay, deteriorate. *n.* Plunder,
booty. **spoiler**, *n.*

spoke (spōk) [A.-S. *spáca*], *n.* One of the
members connecting the hub with the
rim of a wheel; a rung of a ladder. **spoke-
shave**, *n.* A small plane with a handle
at each end.

spokesman (spōks'mản), *n.* One who
speaks for another or others.

spoliation (spō-li-ā'shŭn) [L. *spoliåre*, to
spoil], *n.* Robbery, pillage, the act or
practice of plundering. **spoliator**, *n.*

spondee (spon'dē) [Gr. *spondeios*], *n.* A
metrical foot of two long syllables.
sponda'ic, *a.*

sponge (spŭnj) [A.-S., Gr. *spongos*], *n.* A
marine animal with pores in the body-
wall; its soft, elastic skeleton used as an
absorbent; a parasite. *v.t.* To wipe or
cleanse with a sponge; to obliterate.
spongy, *a.* **sponger**, *n.* One who or that
which sponges; a mean parasite.

sponsor (spon'sŏr) [L.], *n.* One who undertakes to be responsible for another; a
godparent. **sponsorship**, *n.*

spontaneous (spon-tā'nė-ŭs) [L. *sponte*, of
one's own accord], *a.* Arising, done,
acting, etc., without external cause;
voluntary; instinctive, automatic, involuntary; self-originated. **spontane'ity**, *n.*
spontan'eously, *adv.*

spook (spook) [Dut.], *n.* A ghost.

spool (spool) [M. Dut. *spoele*], *n.* A small
cylinder for winding thread on.

spoon (1) (spoon) [A.-S. *spōn*, chip], *n.* A
utensil for conveying liquid food to the
mouth, etc.; an oar, golf-club, bait, etc.,
shaped like a spoon. **spoon'meat**, *n.*
Liquid food. **spoonful**, *n.*

spoon (2) [?], *n.* A silly fellow; a mawkish
lover. *v.i.* To indulge in foolishly
demonstrative love-making. **spoony**, *a.*

spoonerism (spoo'nėr-izm) [W. A. *Spooner*
(1844–1930)], *n.* Accidental or facetious
transposition of the initial letters or
syllables of words, *e.g.* "I have in my
breast a half-warmed fish."

spoor (spoor) [Dut.], *n.* The track of a
wild animal. *v.i.* To follow a spoor.

sporadic (spó-răd'ik) [Gr. *speirein*, to sow],
a. Scattered, occurring here and there.
sporadically, *adv.*

spore (spōr), *n.* (*Biol.*) A minute organic
body that develops into a new individual.

sporran (spor'ản) [Gael.], *n.* A fur pouch
worn by Highlanders in front of the kilt.

sport (spōrt), *n.* Amusement; fun, jest; a
game, pastime, hunting, shooting,
fishing, racing, running, etc. *v.i.* To
play, to divert oneself; to trifle, to jest.
v.t. To display ostentatiously. **sporting**,
a. **sportive**, *a.* Gay, frolicsome, playful.
sportiveness, *n.* **sportsman**, *n.* One skilled
in or devoted to sports, one who faces
good or bad luck with equanimity.
sportsmanlike, *a.* **sportsmanship**, *n.*

spot (spot) [M.E.], *n.* A small mark, a
speck; a particular locality. *v.t.* To
mark with spots. *v.i.* To become or be
liable to be marked with spots. **spotted
fever:** Cerebro-spinal meningitis. **spotless**, *a.* **spotty**, *a.*

spouse (spouz) [L. *sponsus*, promised], *n.*
A husband or wife. **spousal**, *a.* Pertaining to marriage.

spout (spout) [M.E. *spouten*], *v.t.* To pour
out with force; to utter in a declamatory
manner. *v.i.* To issue forcibly or

copiously, to declaim. *n.* A short pipe or channelled projection for carrying off water from a gutter, conducting liquid from a vessel, etc.; a continuous jet of water. spouter, *n.*

sprain (sprān) [O.F. *espreindre*], *v.t.* To wrench muscles or ligaments so as to injure without dislocation. *n.* Such a twist or wrench or the injury due to it.

sprat (sprăt) [A.-S. *sprott*], *n.* A small food-fish of the herring tribe.

sprawl (sprawl) [A.-S. *spreawlian*], *v.i.* To lie or stretch out the limbs in a careless posture; to straggle.

spray (sprā) [Teut.], *n.* Liquid flying in small, fine drops; a small branch used as a decoration; an ornament resembling a sprig of leaves, flowers, etc. *v.t.* To throw or apply in the form of spray; to treat with a spray.

spread (spred) [A.-S. *sprædan*], *v.t.* (*past and p.p.* spread) To extend by opening, unrolling, flattening out, etc.; to diffuse, disseminate; to cover the surface of. *v.i.* To be extended in length and breadth; to be scattered or disseminated. *n.* Act of spreading; breadth, extent, expansion; diffusion; a feast.

spree (sprē) [?], *n.* A lively frolic.

sprig (sprig) [?], *n.* A small branch; an ornament resembling this; a small brad, a scion, a young fellow. spriggy, *a.*

sprightly (sprīt'li), *a.* Lively, spirited, gay.

spring (spring) [A.-S. *springan*], *v.i.* (*past* sprang, *p.p.* sprung) To leap, bound, jump; to rise, as from a source, to originate, to appear; to warp (of wood, etc.). *v.t.* To cause to move, act, etc., suddenly by releasing a spring; to cause (a mine) to explode; to develop (a leak). *n.* A leap; a recoil, a rebound; the starting of a plank, seam, leak, etc.; elastic force; an elastic body or structure, usu. of bent or coiled metal; an issue of water from the earth; (*fig.*) an origin; the first of the four seasons (about 21st March–22nd June); (*fig.*) the early part, youth. spring-board, *n.* A springy board giving impetus in diving, etc. spring tide: A high tide occurring a day or two after the new or the full moon. springtime, *n.* The season of spring. springy, *a.* Elastic, like a spring.

springbok (spring'bok) S. Afr. Dut.], *n.* A S. African gazelle.

springe (sprinj), *n.* A noose, a snare for small game.

sprinkle (spring'kěl), *v.* To scatter in small drops.

sprint (sprint) [?], *v.* To run at one's topmost speed. *n.* A short run thus.

sprit (sprit) A.-S. *spréot*, pole], *n.* A small spar set diagonally to the top outer corner of a sail. spritsail, *n.*

sprite (sprit), *n.* A fairy, an elf.

sprocket (sprok'ĕt) [?], *n.* One of the teeth on a wheel engaging with a chain. sprocket-wheel, *n.* A wheel set with sprockets.

sprout (sprout) [A.-S. *sprūtan*], *v.i.* To shoot forth, to germinate. *v.t.* To cause to put forth sprout or to grow. *n.* A new shoot on a plant; (*pl.*) Brussels sprouts.

spruce (1) (sproos) [?], *a.* Neat, trim, smart. *v.t.* To smarten (up). sprucely, *adv.* spruceness, *n.*

spruce (2) [G. *sprossen*, sprouts], *n.* Sprucefir, a pine of the genus *Picea*.

spry (sprī) [?], *a.* Active, sharp, wide-awake.

spud (spŭd) [M.E. *spuddle*], *n.* A short spade for cutting up weeds by the root; a potato.

spume (spūm) [L. *spūma*], *n.* Froth, foam. *v.i.* To froth.

spunk (spŭngk) [Ir. *sponc*, tinder], *n.* Mettle, pluck; touchwood, tinder.

spur (spěr) [A.-S. *spura*], *n.* An instrument worn on a horseman's heel having a point or a rowel; (*fig.*) incentive, stimulus; a spur-shaped projection, as on a cock's leg. *v.t.* To prick with spurs; to urge, incite; to furnish with spurs.

spurious (spūr'i-ŭs) [L. *spurius*], *a.* Not genuine, false, counterfeit.

spurn (spěrn) [A.-S. *spornan*], *v.t.* To thrust away; to reject with disdain.

spurt (1) (spěrt) [A.-S. *spryttan*], *v.i.* To gush out in a jet. *v.t.* To force out thus. *n.* A forcible gush or jet of liquid.

spurt (2) [Icel. *sprettr*], *n.* A sudden vigorous effort, esp. in racing. *v.i.* To make a spurt.

sputnik (sput'-nik) [R.], *n.* An earth-satellite; the first one put into orbit 4 Oct., 1957.

sputter (spŭt'ěr), *v.i.* To emit saliva in scattered particles, to splutter; to speak in an excited way.

sputum (spū'tŭm) [L.], *n.* (*pl.* -ta) Spittle; matter expectorated.

spy (spī), *v.t.* To see, to discover, esp. by close observation; to explore secretly. *v.i.* To act as a spy; to pry. *n.* One sent secretly into an enemy's territory to obtain information.

squab (skwob) [Swed.], *a.* Fat, short, squat. *adv.* With a heavy fall; plump. *n.* A short, fat person; a young pigeon.

squabble (skwobl) [Swed.], *v.i.* To engage in a petty quarrel, to wrangle. *n.* A petty or noisy quarrel.

squad (skwod) [It. *squadra*, square], *n.* An organized group of soldiers; a small party of people.

squadron (skwod'rŏn), *n.* A main division of a cavalry regiment; a detachment of several warships.

squalid (skwol'id) [L. *squālēre*, to be dirty], *a.* Dirty, poverty-stricken. squalor, *n.*

squall (skwawl) [Icel. *skvala*], *v.* To scream discordantly. *n.* A harsh, discordant scream; a sudden, violent gust or succession of gusts, esp. accompanied by rain, etc. squally, *a.*

squander (skwon'děr) [?], *v.t.* To spend wastefully; to dissipate.

square (skwâr) [EX-, L. *quadrāre*, to make square], *n.* A rectangle with equal sides; any surface, area, etc., of this shape; an instrument for laying out and testing right angles; the product of a quantity multiplied by itself; (*fig.*) order, proper proportion; equity, fairness. *a.* Rectangular; at right angles (to), broad with straight sides; (*fig.*) fair, honest in proper order; even, settled absolute; full. *v.t.* To make square or rectangular; (*fig.*) to bring into conformity (with); to make even, to settle. *v.i.* To be at right angles (with); (*fig.*) to agree, to harmonize; to put oneself in a fighting attitude. **square dance,** *n.* A form of old English folk-dance, taken to U.S.A. and reintroduced to Gt. Britain in 1951. **square-rigged,** *a.* Having the principal sails extended by horizontal yards suspended from the middle. **square root:** The quantity that, multiplied by itself, will produce the given quantity. **squarely,** *adv.*

squash (skwosh) [?], *v.t.* To crush, to press flat or into pulp. *n.* A thing or mass squeezed to pulp. **squashy,** *a.*

squat (skwot) [O.F. *esquatir,* to flatten]; *v.i.* To sit on the haunches; to crouch, to settle on land without any title. *a.* Short, dumpy; in a squatting position, **squatter,** *n.* One who settles without a title, esp. on public land; (*Austral.*) one who leases pasturage from the Government.

squaw (skwaw) [N. Am. Ind. *squa*], *n.* A N. American Indian woman or wife.

squawk (skwawk), *v.i.* To utter a loud, harsh cry. *n.* Such a cry.

squeak (skwēk) [Scand.], *v.i.* To utter a sharp, shrill cry; to break secrecy. *n.* A sharp, shrill sound; (*colloq.*) a narrow escape. **squeaky,** *a.*

squeal (skwēl) [M. Swed. *sqvæla*], *v.i.* To utter a more or less prolonged shrill cry. *n.* A shrill cry.

squeamish (skwē'mish) [A.-F. *escoymous*], *a.* Easily disgusted or offended; fastidious, excessively nice, prudish.

squeeze (skwēz) [A.-S. *cwiesan*], *v.t.* To press closely, esp. between two bodies or with the hand; to extract (juice, etc.) thus; to force (oneself into, out of, etc.). *v.i.* To press, to push, to force one's way (into, etc.). *n.* The act of squeezing; pressure; a close embrace; a throng. **squeezable,** *a.*

squelch (skwelch) [?], *v.t.* To crush; to silence, to discomfit.

squib (skwib) [?], *n.* A firework emitting sparks and exploding; a petty lampoon.

squid (skwid) [Scand.], *n.* A cuttle-fish.

squill (skwil) [L. *squilla*], *n.* A plant resembling the bluebell; its bulb used as an expectorant, diuretic, etc.

squint (skwint) [?], *v.t.* To look with the eyes differently directed. *a.* Looking obliquely or askance. *n.* An affection of the eyes causing the axes to be differently directed; a stealthy or oblique look.

squire (skwir), *n.* A country gentleman: the chief landowner in a place; a beau; (*Hist.*) an attendant on a knight. *v.t.* To attend as a squire. **squireen, squireling,** *n.* A petty squire.

squirm (skwėrm) [?], *v.i.* To writhe about, to climb (up) by wriggling; (*fig.*) to display embarrassment, etc. *n.* A wriggling movement.

squirrel (skwir'él) [Gr. *skiouros*], *n.* A brown bushy-tailed rodent quadruped living chiefly in trees.

squirt (skwėrt) [Teut.], *v.t.* To eject in a jet from a narrow orifice. *n.* A syringe; a jet (of liquid).

stab (stăb) [Scand.], *v.t.* To wound with a point; to plunge (a weapon into). *v.i.* To aim a blow with a pointed weapon (at). *n.* A blow or thrust with a pointed weapon; a wound inflicted thus.

stable (1) (stăbl) [L. *stâre,* to stand], *a.* Firmly fixed, established; resolute, not changeable. **stabil-ity,** *n.* **sta'bilize,** *v.t.* **stably,** *adv.*

stable (2), *n.* A building for horses or cattle; (*fig.*) the race-horses belonging to a particular stable. *v.t.* To put or keep in a stable. *v.i.* To lodge in a stable. **stabling,** *n.* Accommodation in a stable.

stabilize [STABLE (1)].

staccato (stá-ka'tō) [It.], *adv.* (*Mus. direction*). With each note sharply distinct.

stack (stăk) [Icel. *stakkr*], *n.* A regular pile of corn, hay, straw, etc., usu. with a thatched top; an orderly pile or heap; a chimney, a smoke-stack. *v.t.* To pile in a stack.

stadium (stā'di-ŭm) [Gr. *stadion*], *n.* (*pl.* -dia) (*Gr. Ant.*) A measure of about 202 yds.; an enclosure for foot-racing and other sports.

staff (staf) [A.-S. *stæf*], *n.* (*pl.* **staffs,** *Mus., etc.,* **staves,** stāvz) A stick; a support; a rod used as an emblem of office, as a handle, a flagstaff, in surveying, etc.; (*Mil.*) a body of officers assisting an officer in command; a body working under a manager, etc.; (*Mus.*) a set of five lines on or between which a note is written.

stag (stăg) [A.-S. *stagga*], *n.* The male of the red deer and other large deer. **staghound,** *n.* A large hound used for hunting stags. **stag party,** *n.* (*colloq.*) A party for men only.

stage (stāj) [O.F. *estage*], *n.* An elevated platform; a raised platform on which theatrical performances take place; the theatre, the drama, the profession of an actor, actors collectively; a regular stopping-place on a route: the distance between two such; a definite portion of a journey. *v.t.* To put on the stage. **stage-coach,** *n.* A coach running regularly for conveyance of passengers, etc. **stage-effect,** *n.* Theatrical effect. **stagefright,** *n.* Nervousness in facing an audience. **stage-struck,** *a.* Smitten with intense desire to become an actor. **stagewhisper,** *n.* An aside.

stagger (stăg'ér) [Icel. *stakra*], *v.i.* To move unsteadily, to totter, to reel; to waver, to hesitate. *v.t.* To cause to reel or hesitate; to shock with surprise, etc. *n.* A staggering movement.

stagnate (stăg'nāt) [L. *stagnum,* pool], *v.i.* To cease to flow; to be without current; to become sluggish or inert. **stag'nant,** *a.* stagnancy, stagna'tion, *n.* The state of being stagnant.

staid (stād), *a.* Sober, steady, sedate. **staidly,** *adv.*

stain (stān) [M.E. *steinen*], *v.t.* To discolour, to soil; to blemish (a reputation, etc.). *v.i.* To cause discoloration; to take stains. *n.* A discoloration; a blot, a blemish. **stainer,** *n.* **stainless,** *a.*

stair (stār) [A.-S. *stæger*], *n.* One of a series of steps; a flight of stairs. **staircase,**

n. A flight of stairs with banisters, supporting structure, etc.

stake (stāk) [A.-S. *staca*], *n.* A pointed stick set in the ground as a support, part of railing, etc.; anything wagered on a contingency, etc.; (*pl.*) money competed for; (*fig.*) anything contended for. *v.t.* To fasten, support, mark off, or protect with stakes; to wager.

stalactite (stăl′ăk-tīt) [Gr. *stalaktos*, dripping], *n.* A deposit of carbonate of lime, hanging like an icicle. **stalac′tiform**, **stalactit′ic**, *a.*

stalagmite (stăl′ăg-mīt) [Gr. *stalagmos*, dripping], *n.* A deposit of the same material as in a stalactite on the floor or walls of a cave. **stalagmit′ic**, *a.*

stale (stāl) [O.F. *estâler*, to make water], *a.* Not fresh, musty; kept too long; (*fig.*) trite. *v.i.* To urinate (of a horse).

stalemate (stāl-māt) [?], *n.* (*Chess*) The position when the king, not actually in check, is unable to move without placing himself in check, and there is no other piece that can be moved. *v.t.* To subject to a stalemate; (*fig.*) to bring to a standstill.

stalk (1) (stawk) [A.-S. *stealcan*], *v.i.* To walk with high, pompous steps; to go stealthily, to steal (up to game) under cover. *v.t.* To pursue stealthily. *n.* The act of stalking game; a pompous gait. **stalker**, *n.* **stalking-horse**, *n.* A horse behind which a sportsman conceals himself; a mask, a pretence.

stalk (2) (stawk) [M.E. *stalke*, A.-S. *stœla*], *n.* The stem of a plant. **stalky**, *a.*

stall (stawl) [A.-S. *steal*], *n.* A compartment for a horse, ox; a booth; a bench, table, etc., for the sale of goods; a finger-stall; a canopied seat in a choir for a clergyman, chorister, etc.; a canonry; a theatre seat in front of the pit. *v.t.* To keep in a stall (esp. cattle for fattening); to furnish with stalls; (*Motor.*) to render or become unable to proceed (of a vehicle); (*Aer.*) to lose air speed necessary for control of a plane.

stallion (stăl′yŏn) [O.F. *estalon*], *n.* An uncastrated male horse.

stalwart (stawl′wĕrt) [A.-S. *stœlwyrthe*], *a.* Sturdy; stout, resolute.

stamen (stā′mĕn) [L.], *n.* The pollen-bearing male organ of a flower. **stam′-inal**, **stamin′eous**, *a.*

stamina (stăm′i-nà), *n.* Strength, power of endurance.

stammer (stăm′ĕr) [M.E. *stameren*, A.-S *stamm*, *stamor*, stammering], *v.* To speak haltingly, with nervous hesitation or repetitions of the same sound; to stutter. *n.* A stammering utterance or vocal affection.

stamp (stămp) [A.-S. *stempen*], *v.t.* To mark with a dye, pattern, etc.; to affix a stamp to; to impress; (*fig.*) to imprint; to bring (the foot) down heavily; to crush, pulverize, or extinguish by downward force or pressure. *v.i.* To strike the foot forcibly on the ground. *n.* Act of stamping; an instrument for stamping designs, etc.; the mark made by this; an official mark showing that duty has been paid; a postage-stamp for affixing to

letters, receipts, etc.; a label certifying genuineness, etc. **stamp-duty**, *n.* A duty imposed on certain legal documents.

stampede (stăm-pēd′) [Sp. *estampar*, to stamp], *n.* A sudden fright causing horses or cattle to scatter and run; a sudden panic. *v.i.* To take part in a stampede. *v.t.* To cause to do this.

stanch (stanch) [O.F. *estancher*], *v.t.* To stop the flow of (blood from a wound). *a.* Loyal, constant, trustworthy (in this sense also **staunch**). **stanchless**, *a.* **stanchly**, *adv.* **stanchness**, *n.*

stanchion (stan′shŏn) [O.N.F. *estanchon*], *n.* A pillar, etc., supporting a structure; a vertical bar for confining cattle in a stall.

stand (stănd) [A.-S. *standan*], *v.i.* (*past and p.p.* **stood**, stud) To be erect upon the feet; to be in a specified state, position, rank, etc.; to have a specified height; to stop, to remain immovable, firm, or constant, to persist; to remain valid or unimpaired; to lie stagnant; to become a candidate. *v.t.* To set in an erect or a specified position; to endure without complaining; to undergo (a trial, etc.). *n.* A halt, a state of inactivity, a standstill; the act of standing stationary, esp. with firmness; resistance; a small support; a place where cabs stand for hire; an erection for spectators. **stand-by**, *n.* A thing or person to be confidently relied upon. **standpoint**, *n.* A point of view. **standstill**, *n.* A stoppage, a cessation of progress. **standing**, *a.* Erect; not cut down; not temporary; stagnant. *n.* The act of one that stands; station; relative position; repute, estimation; duration, existence. **standing orders:** Orders regulating the procedure, etc., of a deliberative assembly.

standard (stăn′dàrd), *n.* A flag as a distinctive emblem; a measure established as a criterion; any type, fact, thing, etc., serving as a criterion; degree of excellence required; comparative degree of excellence. *a.* Recognized as a standard for imitation, comparison, etc. **standardize**, *v.t.* **standardiza′tion**, *n.*

stannary (stăn′à-ri) [L. *stannum*, tin], *n.* A tin-mine, tin-works; a tin-mining district. *a.* Pertaining to tin-mines, etc.

stanza (stăn′zà) [It.], *n.* A group of rhymed lines in a definite scheme.

staple (1) (stāpl) [A.-S. *stapul*], *n.* A metal loop to receive part of a fastening or to hold a wire, etc.

staple (2) [O.F. *estaple*], *n.* The principal commodity of any country, etc.; the chief substance of anything; raw material. *a.* Marketable; chief, principal. *v.t.* To classify (wool, etc.) according to staple. **stapler**, *n.*

star (star) [A.-S. *steorra*, Gr. *astēr*], *n.* A celestial body, esp. one of those so distant that their relative position in the heavens appears constant; an object resembling a star, esp. used as an emblem or ornament; an asterisk (*); a prominent person, esp. an actor or singer. *v.t.* To spangle with stars; to put an asterisk against. *v.i.* To appear as a star (of an actor, etc.). **starfish**, *n.* A prickly-skinned sea animal with five or more rays. **starry**, *a.*

starboard (star'bôrd) [A.-S. *stéobord* (*stéor*, rudder)], *n.* The right-hand side of a vessel looking forward. *v.t.* To put or turn (the helm) to starboard.

starch (starch) [A.-S. *stercan*, to stiffen], *n.* A white, tasteless, vegetable compound used as a soluble powder to stiffen linen, etc.; (*fig.*) stiffness, formality. *v.t.* To stiffen with starch. **starchy**, *a.* Stiff, precise, prim.

stare (stâr) [A.-S. *starian*], *v.i.* To look with eyes fixed and wide open; (*fig.*) to be prominent. *v.t.* To affect by staring. *n.* A staring gaze.

stark (stark) [A.-S. *stearc*], *a.* Rigid, stiff; inflexible; downright, sheer. *adv.* Wholly, absolutely.

starling (star'ling), *n.* A small black and brown speckled bird.

start (start) [M.E. *sterten*], *v.i.* To make a sudden involuntary movement; to move abruptly (aside, etc.); to wince; to become loose, etc. (of rivets, etc.); to set out, to make a beginning. *v.t.* To cause to start, to rouse; to set going. *n.* A sudden involuntary movement, as of fear, surprise, etc.; a spasmodic effort; the beginning of a journey, enterprise, etc.; a starting-place. **starter**, *n.* **starting-point**, *n.* A point of departure.

startle (startl), *v.t.* To cause to start; to alarm. **startling**, *a.* Surprising, alarming.

starve (starv) [A.-S. *steorfan*, to die], *v.i.* To perish or suffer severely from hunger; to be in great want; to suffer severely from cold; to die, to perish. *v.t.* To cause to perish or be extremely distressed by lack of food or by cold; to make inefficient through lack of expenditure. **starva'tion**, *n.* **starveling**, *a.* and *n.*

state (stât) [L. *status*], *n.* Condition, mode of existence, situation; a commonwealth, a nation, the body politic; civil government; pomp, splendour. *a.* Of or pertaining to the State or body politic; reserved for ceremonial occasions. *v.t.* To set forth, to determine, to specify. **statable**, *a.* **stately**, *a.* Grand, dignified, imposing. **stateliness**, *n.* **statement**, *n.* Act of stating; that which is stated, a formal account. **statesman**, *n.* One versed in the art of government; one taking a leading part in the administration of the State. **statesmanlike**, *a.* **statesmanship**, *n.*

static (stăt'ik) [Gr. *statikos*], *a.* Pertaining to bodies at rest. **statics**, *n.pl.* That branch of dynamics which treats of the relations between forces in equilibrium. **statically**, *adv.*

station (stâ'shûn) [L. *statio*, from *stâre*, to stand], *n.* The place where a person or thing stands, an appointed place; police, coastguard, military, etc., headquarters; a place at which railway-trains stop; position, standing, rank, esp. high rank. *v.t.* To assign to or place in a particular station, to post.

stationary (stâ'shô-når-ï), *a.* Remaining in one place; fixed; not changing in character, condition, etc.

stationer (stâ'shô-nêr), *n.* One who sells paper, pens, writing-materials, etc. **stationery**, *n.*

statistics (stà-tis'tiks), *n.pl.* Numerical facts arranged and classified; (*as sing.*) the science of collecting and applying statistics. **statis'tically**, *adv.* **statistician** (-tish'ån), *n.*

statue (stăt'ū), *n.* A representation of a person or animal sculptured or cast. **statuary**, *a.* and *n.* **statuesque** (-esk'), *a.* **statuette** (-et'), *n.*

stature (stăt'ûr), *n.* The natural height of a body.

status (stâ'tûs), *n.* Relative standing, rank, or position in society.

statute (stăt'ūt), *n.* A law enacted by a legislative body; an ordinance intended as a permanent law. **statute-book**, *n.* A book in which statutes are published. **statutory**, *a.*

stave (stāv), *n.* A curved strip forming the side of a cask, etc.; a verse. *v.t.* (*past and p.p.* **staved**, **stove**) To break a hole in (a cask, boat, etc.); to stop, avert, or ward (off). **staves**, *pl.* [STAFF and STAVE].

stay (1) (stā) [L. *stâre*, to stand], *v.i.* To continue in a specified place or state; to remain; to tarry; to last out (in a race, etc.). *v.t.* To hinder; to postpone, suspend. *n.* The art of staying or dwelling; continuance in a place, etc.; a check.

stay (2) [O.F. *estayer*, to prop], *n.* A support, a prop; (*pl.*) a corset. *v.t.* To support.

stay (3) (stā) [?], *n.* A rope supporting a mast or spar. **to miss stays**: To fail in tacking.

stead (sted) [A.-S. *stede*], *n.* Place or room which another had or might have had.

steadfast (sted'fåst) [A.-S. *stedefæst*], *a.* Firm, resolute, unwavering.

steady (sted'ï), *a.* Firmly fixed; acting in a regular way, constant. *v.t.* To make steady. *v.i.* To become steady. **steadily**, *adv.*

steak (stāk) [Icel. *steik*, from *steikja*, to roast], *n.* A slice of beef for broiling.

steal (stēl) [A.-S. *stelan*], *v.t.* (*past* **stole**, *p.p.* **stolen**) To take without right or permission; to secure covertly or insidiously. *v.t.* To take anything feloniously; to go or come furtively.

stealth (stelth), *n.* Furtiveness; secret procedure. **stealthy**, *a.*

steam (stēm) [A.-S], *n.* Water in the form of vapour or the gaseous form to which it is changed by boiling. *v.i.* To give off steam; to rise in or move by the agency of steam. *v.t.* To treat with steam for the purpose of softening, etc., to cook by steam. **steam-gas**, *n.* Superheated steam. **steamship**, *n.* A ship propelled by steam. **steamer**, *n.* A vessel propelled by steam; a steam fire-engine; a vessel for steaming food. **steamy**, *a.*

stearin (stē'à-rin) [Gr. *stear*, fat], *n.* The chief and more solid component of animal and vegetable fats.

steed (stēd) [A.-S. *stéda*], *n.* A horse, esp. a war-horse.

steel (stēl) [A.-S. *style*], *n.* Iron combined

with carbon hardened by cooling; a rod for sharpening knives. *v.t.* To point or face with steel; to harden (the heart). **steely**, *a.* **steeliness**, *n.*

steelyard (stēl'yard), *n.* A balance with unequal arms in which a weight is moved along the longer.

steep (1) (stēp) [A.-S. *stēap*], *a.* Sharply inclined, sloping at a high angle; exorbitant (of prices). *n.* A steep slope; a precipice.

steep (2) [Icel. *steypa*, to pour out metals], *v.t.* To soak in liquid; to wet or imbue thoroughly.

steeple (stēpl) [A.-S. *stȳpel*], *n.* A lofty structure rising above a roof; a church tower with a spire. **steeplechase**, *n.* A horse-race across country. **steeple-jack**, *n.* One who climbs steeples to do repairs.

steer (1) (stēr) [A.-S. *stēoran* (*stēor*, rudder)], *v.t.* To guide (a ship or conveyance) by a rudder, wheel, etc.; to direct (one's course) thus. *v.i.* To direct one's course by this means; to be steered (easily, etc.). **steerage**, *n.* The part of a ship allotted to passengers travelling at the lowest rate. **steersman**, *n.* One who steers.

steer (2) [A.-S. *stēor*], *n.* A young ox, a castrated bullock.

stele (stē'lē) [Gr.], *n.* (*Ant.*) An upright slab for sepulchral or other purposes.

stellar (stel'ár) [L. *stella*, star], *a.* Pertaining to stars. **stellate**, *a.* Star-shaped, radiating.

stem (1) (stem) [A.-S.], *n.* The ascending axis of a tree or other plant; the slender stalk of a flower, etc.; an analogous part, as between the body and foot of a wine-glass, etc.; the part of a word to which case-endings, etc., are affixed; the stock or a branch of a family; the upright piece at the fore end of a vessel. **from stem to stern**: From one end of the ship to the other.

stem (2) [Icel. *stemma*.], *v.t.* To check, hold back; to make headway against.

stench (stench), *n.* A foul smell, a stink.

stencil (sten'sil) [?], *n.* A thin plate out of which patterns have been cut, for painting through the spaces on to a surface.

stenograph (sten'ó-gräf) [Gr. *stenos*, narrow], *n.* A character used in shorthand. **stenog'rapher**, *n.* A shorthand writer, shorthand typist. **stenograph'ic**, *a.* stenography, *n.* Shorthand; the art of writing in shorthand.

Stentor (sten'tor, -tòr) [Gr. *Stentōr*, herald in Trojan war], *n.* A person with a loud, strong voice. **stentorian** (-tòr'i-án), *a.*

step (step) [A.-S. *steppan*], *v.i.* To lift and set down a foot or the feet alternately, to walk; to dance slowly or with dignity. *v.t.* To perform or measure by stepping; (*Naut.*) to insert the foot of (a mast) in a step. *n.* A single complete movement of one leg in the act of walking, dancing, etc.; the distance traversed; a short distance; action taken towards some end; a single stair in a flight of stairs; a degree in rank; a socket for the end of a mast, shaft, etc. **step-ladder**, *n.* A ladder with flat treads or rungs. **stepping-stone**, *n.* A raised stone in a stream or

swamp for crossing; (*fig.*) a means to an end.

step- [A.-S. *steop*, orphaned], *pref.* A prefix used to express relation only by the marriage of a parent, as **stepbrother, -sister.** **stepchild**, *n.* The child of one's husband or wife by a former marriage. **stepfather, -mother,** *n.* The later husband or wife of one's parent.

steppe (step) [Rus. *stepe*], *n.* A vast plain devoid of forest, esp. Russia and Siberia.

-ster (A.-S. *-estre*, as in L. *minister*], *suf.* Denoting an agent, as in *maltster*, *songster*; or a female agent, as in *spinster*.

stereo- [Gr. *stereos*, stiff, solid], *comb. form.*

stereoscope (ster'ē-ō-skōp), *n.* A binocular instrument for blending into one two pictures taken at slightly divergent angles. **stereoscopic, -al** (-skop'ik, -ál), *a.* Giving the effect of solidity. **ster'eotype**, *n.* A printing plate cast from a mould taken from movable type. *v.t.* To take a stereotype of; (*fig.*) to fix in unchangeable form.

sterile (ster'īl) [L. *sterilis*], *a.* Barren, unfruitful. **sterility** (stē-ril'i-ti), *n.* **ster'ilize**, *v.t.* **sterilizer**, *n.*

sterling (stēr'ling) [?], *a.* Of standard value, genuine, pure (of coins and precious metals); (*Fin.*) applied specially to the English pound.

stern (1) (stērn) [A.-S. *styrne*], *a.* Severe, grim; harsh, strict; ruthless, resolute. **sternly**, *adv.* **sternness**, *n.*

stern (2) [Icel. *stjörn*, steering], *n.* The hind part of a ship; the rump of an animal. **stern-chase**, *n.* A chase in which one vessel follows the other straight behind. **stern-sheets**, *n.pl.* The place in a boat between the stern and the aftermost thwart. **sternmost**, *a.*

sternum (stēr'núm) [Gr. *sternon*], *n.* The breast-bone.

sternutation (stēr-nū-tā'shún) [L. *sternuere*, to sneeze], *n.* The act of sneezing, a sneeze. **sternu'tative**, *a.*

stertorous (stēr'tor-ús) [L. *stertere*, to snore], *a.* Characterized by deep snoring.

stet (stet) [L.], *v.t.* (*Print.*) Let it stand (cancelling a previous correction).

stethoscope (steth'ó-skōp) [Gr. *stēthos*, breast], *n.* An instrument used in auscultation of the chest.

stevedore (stē'vē-dōr) [Sp. *estivador*], *n.* One who loads or unloads ships.

stew (stū) [O.F. *estuve*, hot-house], *v.t.* To cook by boiling slowly. *v.i.* To be cooked thus; (*fig.*) to be stifled by a close atmosphere. *n.* Meat, etc., cooked by stewing; (*fig.*) a state of mental agitation.

steward (stū'árd) [A.-S. *stigweard*, a styward], *n.* A person employed to manage the affairs, estate, or household, etc., of another, or the service of provisions, etc., in a college, club, on shipboard, etc. **stewardess**, *n.* **stewardship**, *n.*

stick (stik) [M.E. *steken*, to pierce, A.-S. *stician*, to stick], *v.t.* (*past and p.p.* **stuck**) To thrust the point of (in, etc.); to fix (into); to thrust (out or up); to protrude; to fix on a point; to pierce, stab; to cause to adhere to; to set (type). *v.i.* To be inserted (into); to protrude, project, or stand (up, etc.); to adhere; to be inseparable; to persist, persevere; to be hindered or checked; to be perplexed; to have misgivings, to hesitate (at). *n.* A slender piece of wood, a rod, wand, staff, baton, walking-cane; anything resembling this; a drum-stick, fiddle-stick, etc.; (*fig.*) an awkward or stupid person. **sticking-plaster,** *n.* An adhesive plaster for wounds, etc. **sticky,** *a.* Tending to stick, adhesive; glutinous. **stickily,** *adv.* **stickiness,** *n.* **stuck-up,** *a.* Erect; (*fig.*) conceited, giving oneself airs.

stickle (stikl) [?], *v.i.* To contend pertinaciously for some trifle. **stickler,** *n.*

stickleback (stikl'băk) [A.-S. *sticel*, prickle], *n.* A small spiny-backed fish.

stiff (stif) [A.-S. *stíf*], *a.* Rigid, not pliant, flexible, or working freely; obstinate, stubborn; not graceful; awkward, formal, precise; difficult; high (of prices); viscous. **stiff-necked,** *a.* Stubborn, self-willed. **stiffen,** *v.* To make or become stiff or stiffer. **stiffener,** *n.* **stiffening,** *n.* **stiffness,** *n.*

stifle (stifl) Icel. *stífla*], *v.* To smother, to suffocate. **stiflingly,** *adv.*

stigma (stig'mà) [Gr., a brand], *n.* (*pl.* -mas) A mark branded on slaves, criminals, etc.; a mark of infamy; (*pl.* **stigmata**) (*R.-C. Ch.*) marks miraculously developed on the body, corresponding to the wounds of Christ. **stigmat'ic,** *a.* **stigmatize,** *v.t.* To mark with a brand of disgrace, etc.

stile (stil) [A.-S. *stígan*, to climb], *n.* A series of steps over a fence, etc.

stiletto (sti-let'ō) [It.], *n.* A small dagger; a pointed instrument for making eyelet-holes, etc.

still (1) (stil) [A.-S. *stille*], *a.* At rest; motionless; calm; silent, hushed; not effervescent. *adv.* Now, then, or for the future, as previously; yet; nevertheless, all the same. *v.t.* To quiet, to silence, to appease. **stillness,** *n.*

still (2) [L. *stillāre*, to drip], *n.* A vessel or apparatus employed in distillation, esp. of spirituous liquors. *v.t.* To distil. **still-room,** *n.* A room for distilling; a store-room for liquors.

stilt (stilt) [Swed. *stylta*], *n.* A pole having a rest for the foot, used in pairs, to raise a person in walking; a shore-bird related to the plover. **stilted,** *a.* Bombastic, inflated (of literary style, etc.).

Stilton (stil'tòn), *n.* A rich, white cheese, orig. made at Stilton, Hunts.

stimulant (stim'ū-lànt) [L. *stimulans*, pricking], *a.* Serving to stimulate. *n.* Anything that stimulates or produces a transient increase of vital energy, esp. alcohol. **stimulate,** *v.t.* To rouse to action or greater exertion; to spur on; to excite organic action. *v.i.* To act as a stimulus. **stimula'tion,** *n.* **stim'ulative,** *a.* **stimulus,** *n.* (*pl.* -uli) That which stimulates; an incitement.

sting (sting) [A.-S. *stingan*], *v.t.* (*past and p.p.* **stung**) To wound with a sting; (*fig.*) to cause acute pain to. *v.i.* To have or use a sting; to have an acute and smarting pain. *n.* A sharp-pointed organ, often conveying poison, with

which certain insects, scorpions, and plants are armed; any acute pain, smart, etc.

stingo (sting'gō), *n.* Strong ale.

stingy (stin'ji), *a.* Close-fisted, niggardly. **stingily,** *adv.* **stinginess,** *n.*

stink (stingk) [A.-S. *stincan*], *v.i.* (*past* **stank**, **stunk**, *p.p.* **stunk**) To emit a strong, offensive smell; to have an evil reputation. *n.* A strong, offensive smell.

stint (stint) [A.-S. *styntan*], *v.t.* To give scantily or grudgingly. *n.* Limit, scarcity; allotted quantity of work.

stipend (sti'pĕnd) [L. *stipendium*], *n.* A salary, esp. of a clergyman. **stipen'diary,** *a.* Performing services for a stipend. *n.* One receiving a stipend, esp. a magistrate.

stipple (stipl) [Dut. *stippel*], *v.* To engrave, paint, or draw by means of dots. *n.* This method; work produced thus. **stippler,** *n.*

stipulate (stip'ū-lāt) [L. *stipulus*, firm, fast], *v.t.* To specify as essential to an agreement. *v.i.* To settle terms. **stipula'tion,** *n.* **stip'ulator,** *n.*

stir (stēr) [A.-S. *styrian*], *v.t.* To cause to move, to disturb; to bestir (oneself, etc.); to rouse (up), to excite, animate. *v.i.* To move, not to be still. *n.* Agitation, commotion, bustle; a movement; the act of stirring. **stirabout,** *n.* Porridge. *a.* Active, bustling. **stirring,** *a.* Moving; animating, exciting.

stirrup (stir'ŭp) [A.-S. *stírāp*], *n.* An iron loop suspended from the saddle by a strap as a rider's foot-rest. **stirrup-cup,** *n.* A parting cup on horseback.

stitch (stich) [A.-S. *stice*], *n.* A sharp pain in the side; a single pass of the needle in sewing; a single turn of wool, etc., round a needle in knitting; the link of thread, wool, etc., thus inserted. *v.* To sew.

stiver (stiv'ér) [Dut.], *n.* Any small coin.

stoat (stōt) [M.E. *stot*], *n.* The ermine, esp. in its summer coat; the weasel.

stock (stok) [A.-S. *stocc*], *n.* The main stem of a tree or other plant; a family, a line of descent, a post, stump; the principal supporting part of anything, the handle, base, body, etc.; liquor from bones, etc., as a basis for soup; the aggregate of goods, etc., kept on hand; the beasts on a farm (live stock) or implements of husbandry and produce (dead stock); (*Finance*) money lent to a government; the capital of a corporate company; (*pl.*) the shares of such capital; (*pl.*) a frame in which the ankles (and sometimes wrists) of petty offenders were formerly confined; (*pl.*) a framework on which a vessel rests during building; a cravat. *a.* Kept in stock; habitually used, permanent. *v.t.* To provide with goods, live stock, etc.; to keep in stock; to furnish with a handle, butt, etc. **stock-broker,** *n.* One engaged in the purchase and sale of stocks on commission. **stockdove,** *n.* The European wild pigeon. **stock exchange:** The place where stocks or shares are bought and sold. **stockfish,** *n.* Cod, ling, etc., split open and dried in the sun without salting. **stock-in-trade,** *n.* Goods, tools,

and other requisites of a trade, etc.
stock-jobber, *n.* An intermediary between buying and selling stock-brokers.
stock-man, *n.* (*Austral.*) One in charge of live stock. **stock-rider,** *n.* (*Austral.*) A herdsman in charge of stock. **stock-still,** *a.* Motionless. **stock-yard,** *n.* An enclosure with pens for cattle at market, etc. **stocky,** *a.* Thick-set, short and stout.

stockade (stŏ-kād') [Sp. *estacada*], *n.* A line or enclosure of stakes. *v.t.* To fortify with a stockade.

stocking (stok'ing), *n.* A close-fitting covering for the foot and leg. **stocky,** etc. [STOCK].

stodgy (stoj'i) [?], *a.* Heavy, indigestible (of food); dull, matter-of-fact (of books, etc.).

stoep (stoop) [S. Afr. Dutch], *n.* A sort of veranda.

Stoic (stŏ'ik) [Gr. *Stoikos*, from *stoa*, with ref. to the porch where Zeno taught], *n.* A philosopher of the Greek school holding that virtue is the highest good, and that the passions and appetites should be rigidly subdued. **stoical,** *a.* **stoically,** *adv.* **stoicism,** *n.*

stoke (stŏk) [Dut. *stoken*, to make fire], *v.t.* To tend (a furnace). **stoker,** *n.* One who attends to a furnace.

stole (stŏl) [Gr.], *n.* A narrow band of silk, etc., worn over both shoulders by priests, and by deacons over the left shoulder; a necklet of fur, etc., worn by women.

stolid (stol'id) [L. *stolidus*], *a.* Dull, impassive, stupid. **stolid'ity,** *n.* **stolidly,** *adv.*

stomach (stŭm'ak) [Gr. *stoma*], *n.* A digestive cavity formed by a dilatation of the alimentary canal; the belly; (*fig.*) appetite, inclination. *v.t.* To accept as palatable; (*fig.*) to put up with. **stomachic** (stŏ-mäk'ik), *a.* Pertaining to the stomach; aiding digestion. *n.* A stomachic medicine.

stone (stŏn) [A.-S. *stān*], *n.* A small piece of rock, a pebble, cobble; material for building, paving, etc.; a millstone, grindstone, tombstone, etc.; a gem; the disease calculus; a testicle; the seed of a grape, etc., the kernel in stone-fruit; a hailstone; a measure of weight of 14 lb. *a.* Made of stone; like a stone. *v.t.* To pelt with stones; to free (fruit) from stones. **stone age:** The period in which primitive man used implements of stone. **stone-blind,** *a.* Perfectly blind. **stone-cold,** *a.* Quite cold. **stone-dead,** *a.* Dead as a stone. **stone-deaf,** *a.* Quite deaf. **stone-fruit,** *n.* A fruit with seeds covered by a hard shell, as peaches, plums, etc. **stone-mason,** *n.* One who dresses stones or builds with stone. **stone-ware,** *n.* Pottery made from clay and flint or a hard siliceous clay. **stone-work,** *n.* Masonry. **stony,** *a.* Pertaining to, made or consisting of, abounding in or resembling stone; (*fig.*) hard, cruel; impassible; obdurate; (*slang*) destitute of money. **stonily,** *adv.*

stooge (stooj) [?], *n.* A decoy, a confederate; a butt.

stook (stuk) [Teut.], *n.* A bundle of sheaves set up.

stool (stool) [A.-S. *stōl*], *n.* A seat without a back, for one person; a low bench. **stool pigeon,** *n.* (*colloq.*) a decoy.

stoop (stoop) [A.-S. *stūpian*], *v.t.* To bend the body downward and forward; to incline forward habitually; (*fig.*) to bring oneself down (to). *v.t.* To incline (the head, shoulders, etc.) downward and forward. *n.* Act of stooping; an habitual inclination of the shoulders, etc.

stop (stop) [A.-S. *stoppian*], *v.t.* To close, stanch, plug (up); to fill a crack or cavity; to impede; to cause to cease moving, working, etc.; to prevent the doing of; to keep back, suspend. *v.i.* To come to an end, to come to rest; to cease or desist (from); (*colloq.*) to stay, sojourn; to punctuate. *n.* Act of stopping, state of being stopped, a cessation, interruption; a punctuation mark; a block, etc., used to stop the movement of something; (*Mus.*) the pressing down of a string, closing of an aperture, etc., effecting a change of pitch; a key, etc., employed in this; a set of pipes in an organ having tones of a distinct quality. **stoppage,** *n.* **stopper,** *n.* One who or that which stops; a stopple. *v.t.* To close with a stopper. **stopple,** *n.* That which stops or closes, the mouth of a vessel, a stopper, plug, bung, etc.

store (stŏr) [L. *staurāre*, to restore], *n.* A stock, an abundant supply, abundance; a place where things are laid up, a storehouse, warehouse; a large establishment where articles of various kinds are sold; (*pl.*) articles kept on hand for special use. *v.t.* To accumulate or lay (up or away) for future use; to stock (with); to deposit in a warehouse. **storehouse,** *n.* A place where things are stored up, a warehouse, granary, etc. **storage,** *n.* Act of storing; price paid or space reserved for this.

storey [story (2)].

stork (stŏrk) [A.-S. *storc*], *n.* A long-necked, long-legged wading-bird allied to the heron.

storm (stŏrm) [A.-S.], *n.* A violent atmospheric disturbance, a tempest; a violent agitation of society, the mind, etc., a tumult, commotion; a direct assault on a fortified place. *v.i.* To rage (of wind, rain, etc.); to bluster, fume, behave violently. *v.t.* To take by storm. **storming-party,** *n.* A party told off to lead an assault. **stormy,** *a.* Characterized by storms; tempestuous; (*fig.*) violent, passionate.

story (1) (stŏr'i) [L. *historia*], *n.* A narrative of actual or fictitious events, a tale; the plot or incidents of a novel, play, etc.; an account of an incident, etc.; a falsehood. **storied,** *a.* Adorned with scenes from or celebrated in story.

story (2), *n.* A set of rooms on the same floor. **storied,** *a.* (*usu. in comb.*, as *three-storied*).

stoup (stoop) [Icel. *staup*], *n.* A basin for holy water.

stout (stout) [O.F. *estout*], *a.* Strong, sturdy, well-built, vigorous, intrepid;

corpulent, bulky. *n.* A malt liquor, strong porter. **stoutish,** *a.* stoutly, *adv.* **stoutness,** *n.*

stove (stōv) [A.-S. *stofa*], *n.* An apparatus in which fuel is burned for heating, cooking, etc. *v.t.* To heat, dry, etc., in a stove. **stove-pipe,** *n.* A pipe for conducting smoke from a stove.

stow (stō) [A.-S. *stōwigan*], *v.t.* To put in a suitable or convenient place; to pack away. **stowaway,** *n.* One who hides in a vessel so as to get a free passage. **stowage,** *n.*

strabismus (strå-biz'mŭs) [Gr. *strabos*, crooked], *n.* (*Path.*) Squinting, a squint.

straddle (strådl), *v.i.* To stand or stride with the legs wide apart. *v.t.* To stand or sit astride of thus.

strafe (straf) [G. *strafen*, to punish], *v.t.* To punish severely; to do a serious injury to.

straggle (strägl) [?], *v.i.* To wander away from the direct course; to get dispersed; to spread irregularly (of plants, etc.). **straggler,** *n.*

straight (strāt) [A.-S. *streht*, stretched], *a.* Not curved or crooked; upright, not deviating from truth or fairness, correct, right; level; unobstructed; reliable, authoritative. *n.* A straight part, piece, or stretch of anything. *adv.* In a straight line; without deviation; immediately. **straight-edge,** *n.* An implement having one edge straight, used as a ruler, etc. **straightforward,** *a.* Upright, honest, frank. **straighten,** *v.t.* **straightway,** *adv.* Forthwith, at once.

strain (1) (strān) [O.F. *estraindre*], *v.t.* To stretch tight; to exert to the utmost; to weaken or injure by excessive effort; to force beyond due limits; to embrace; to make artificial or uneasy; to purify by passing through a colander or other strainer; to remove (solids) by straining (out). *v.i.* To exert oneself; to pull or tug (at); to be filtered, to percolate. *n.* Act of straining, a violent effort, a pull, tension; a distortion or change of structure, caused by excessive effort or tension; impulse; a song, melody; spirit, manner, style. **strainer,** *n.*

strain (2) [A.-S. *strēon*], *n.* Race, stock, family, breed; natural tendency or disposition.

strait (strāt) [A.F. *estreit*], *a.* Narrow, confined, restricted. *n.* A narrow passage of water between two seas; a trying position. **straiten,** *v.t.*

strake (strāk), *n.* A continuous line of planking or plates from stem to stern of a vessel.

strand (1) (strånd) [A.-S.], *n.* A shore or beach. *v.* To run aground. **stranded,** *a.* Brought to a standstill or into straits, esp. from lack of funds.

strand (2) (strånd) [O.N.F. *estran*], *n.* One of the twists of which a rope is composed.

strange (strānj) [O.F. *estrange*], *a.* Foreign; not well known, new; unusual, extraordinary, queer, surprising; fresh or unused (to), unacquainted. **strangely,** *adv.* **strangeness,** *n.* **stranger,** *n.* A foreigner; a visitor; a person unknown (to one); one ignorant or unaccustomed (to).

strangle (sträng'gĕl) [Gr. *strangalē*, halter], *v.t.* To kill by compressing the windpipe, to throttle.

strangulate (sträng'gū-lāt), *v.t.* To strangle; to compress a blood-vessel, intestine, etc. **strangulation,** *n.*

strap (sträp) [A.-S. *stropp*], *n.* A long, narrow strip of leather, usu. with a buckle. *v.t.* To fasten or to beat with a strap; to strop. **strapper,** *n.* One who uses a strap; a tall, strapping person. **strapping,** *a.* Tall, lusty, strong muscular.

strata, *pl.* [STRATUM].

stratagem (strät'å-jěm) [Gr. *stratos*, army, *agein*, to lead], *n.* An artifice or manœuvre for deceiving an enemy.

strategic, -al (strå-tē'jik, -tej'ik, -ål), *a.* Pertaining to, used in, or of the nature of strategy. **strategics,** *n.* **strategy** (strät'ĕ-ji), *n.* The art of war, generalship. **strat'egist,** *n.*

strath (sträth) [Gael. *srath*], *n.* A wide valley through which a river runs.

stratify (strät'i-fī), *v.t.* To form or arrange in strata. **stratifica'tion,** *n.*

stratocracy (strå-tok'rå-si) [Gr. *stratos*, an army], *n.* Military government, government by a military class.

strato cruiser, *n.* (*Aer.*) An aircraft for flying in the stratosphere.

stratosphere (strät'ō-sfēr), *n.* [*Meteor*] The upper layer of atmosphere.

stratum (strā'tŭm) [L.], *n.* (*pl.* -ta) A bed or layer spread out horizontally, esp. by the action of water.

stratus (strā'tŭs) [L.], *n.* (*pl.* -ti) A continuous horizontal sheet of cloud.

straw (straw) [A.-S. *strēaw*], *n.* The dry, ripened stalks of wheat, rye, oats, etc.; (*fig.*) anything worthless; a straw-hat. **strawberry,** *n.* A low, stemless perennial plant; its fleshy red fruit. **strawberry-tree,** *n.* An evergreen arbutus.

stray (strā) [O.F. *estraier*], *v.i.* To wander, to go wrong, to lose one's way. *n.* Any domestic animal that has gone astray; a waif. *a.* Gone astray; straggling; occasional.

streak (strēk) [Scand.], *n.* A long narrow mark of a distinct colour from the ground. *v.t.* To mark with streaks. **streaky,** *a.* **streakily,** *adv.*

stream (strēm) [A.-S.], *n.* A body of flowing water or other fluid; a brook; a steady flow, a current; a moving throng etc. *v.i.* To flow, move, or issue in a stream; to wave in the wind. **streamer,** *n.* A long narrow ribbon, a pennon. **streamlet,** *n.* **stream-lined,** *a.* Shaped in order to cause the minimum of air resistance. **streamy,** *a.*

street (strēt) [L. *strāta* (*via*), paved (way)], *n.* A road in a town with houses on one side or both.

strength (strength), *n.* The quality of being strong; muscular force; firmness; amount of the whole number (of an army, etc.). **strengthen,** *v.t.* To make strong or stronger. *v.i.* To increase in strength.

strenuous (stren'ū-ŭs) [L. *strēnuus*], *a.* Energetic, ardent; eagerly persistent. **strenuously,** *adv.*

streptococcus (strep-tŏ-kok'ŭs) [Gr. *streptos*, twisted; *kokkus*, a grain], *n.* (*Bacter*.) A genus of bacteria consisting of chains of spherical organisms.

stress (stres) [O.F. *estrecier*], *n.* Constraining or impelling force; pressure, violence; weight, importance; emphasis. *v.t.* To lay the stress or accent on; to subject to force.

stretch (strech) [A.-S. *streccan*], *v.t.* To draw out; to extend; to tighten; to straighten; to strain; to exaggerate. *v.i.* To be extended in length or breadth; to reach; to admit of being drawn out; to extend one's body or limbs. *n.* Act of stretching, state of being stretched; extent, reach; a sweep or tract (of land, water, etc.). **stretcher,** *n.* One who or that which stretches; a litter for carrying a disabled person; a cross-piece for a rower to press his feet against.

strew (stroo) [A.-S. *strēowian,* as STRAW], *v.t.* (*p.p.* strewn, strewed). To scatter, to spread; to cover by scattering or by being scattered over.

strict (strikt) [L. *strictus*], *a.* Enforcing or observing rules precisely; severe, stringent; precise. **strictly,** *adv.* **strictness,** *n.* **stricture,** *n.* A censure.

stride (strid) [A.-S. *strīdan*], *v.i.* (*past* strode, *p.p.* stridden, strid) To walk with long steps. *v.t.* To pass over in one step; to bestride. *n.* A long step, the distance covered by this.

strident (strī'dĕnt) [L. *strīdens,* creaking], *a.* Sounding harsh, grating.

strife (strif) [O.F. *estrif*], *n.* Contention, conflict, hostile struggle.

strike (strik) [A.-S. *strīcan,* to go], *v.t.* (*past* struck, *p.p.* struck, stricken) To hit; to deliver, to inflict (a blow, etc.); to afflict (*usu. in p.p.*), to drive (a ball, etc.) with force; to produce, make, effect, etc., by a stroke, to ignite (a match); to mint (a coin), to blind, deafen, etc.; to make (a bargain); to notify by sound (of clocks); to thrust (into); to hook (a fish); to occur suddenly to the mind of; to lower (sails, tent, etc.); to surrender by lowering (a flag); to leave off (work), esp. to enforce a demand; to determine (an average, etc.); to assume (an attitude). *v.i.* To hit; to dash (against, etc.); to be driven on shore, a rock, etc.; to sound (the time) by a stroke (of a bell, etc.); to lower a flag, etc., in surrender; to take root; to leave off work to enforce a demand; to happen (upon); to enter (a track). *n.* The act of striking for an increase of wages, etc. **striker,** *n.* One who or that which strikes, esp. a workman on strike. **striking,** *a.* Surprising, forcible, impressive, noticeable.

string (string) [A.-S. *streng*], *n.* Twine, a fine line thinner than cord; a length of this; a piece of wire, catgut, etc., in a piano or stringed instrument; a cord upon which anything is strung, a series of things or persons connected together or following in close succession. *v.t.* (*past and p.p.* strung) To furnish with strings; to fasten the string on (a bow); (*fig.*) to make (nerves, etc.) tense (*usu. in p.p.*); to thread on a string. **stringy** (string'ĭ),

a. Consisting of strings or small threads, fibrous; ropy, viscous.

stringent (strin'jĕnt) [L. *stringens,* drawing tight], *a.* Strict, binding, rigid; tight, unaccommodating. **stringency,** *n.*

strip (1) (strip) [A.-S. *strȳpan*], *v.t.* To pull or remove the covering from, to skin, peel; to despoil, plunder. *v.i.* To take off one's clothes; to come away in strips; to have the thread torn off (of a screw). **strip-tease,** *n.* (*Theat.*) A turn in which an actress partially undresses herself.

strip (2) [foll.], *n.* A long, narrow piece. **comic strip** [COMIC].

stripe (strīp) [?], *n.* A long, narrow distinctive band; a chevron. *v.t.* To mark with stripes.

stripling (strip'ling), *n.* A lad.

strive (striv), *v.i.* (*past* strove, strŏv, *p.p.* striven, striv'ĕn) To endeavour, earnestly to struggle; to vie, to emulate; to quarrel (with each other).

stroke (strōk) [A.-S. *strāc*], *n.* Act of striking, a blow; act of stroking, a gentle rub; a sudden attack (of disease, etc.); a mark of a pen, pencil, etc.; a stroke-oar. *v.t.* To pass the hand over the surface of caressingly; to act as stroke for (a boat). **stroke-oar,** *n.* The aftermost oarsman in a boat who sets the time for the rest.

stroll (strōl) [?], *v.i.* To walk idly, to saunter. *n.* A leisurely ramble. **stroller,** *n.*

strong (strong) [A.-S. *strang*], *a.* Able to exert great force, muscular, capable; forcible, energetic; having great powers of resistance or endurance; robust, hale, tough; having great resources, etc.; having a specified number of men, etc.; having a powerful effect on the senses; (*Gram.*) forming inflexions by internal vowel-change. **stronghold,** *n.* A fortress, a refuge. **strongly,** *adv.*

strop (strop), *n.* A strip of leather for sharpening razors on. *v.t.* To sharpen on a strop.

strophe (strof'ĭ, strŏ'fĭ) [Gr.], *n.* The first part of an ode (consisting of strophe, antistrophe, and epode).

structure (strŭk'chŭr) [L. *structus,* built], *n.* A combination of parts, as a building, machine, organism, etc., esp. the framework; the manner in which a complex whole is constructed, or its arrangement. **structural,** *a.*

struggle (strŭgl) [Scand.], *v.i.* To put forth great efforts, esp. against difficulties; to strive (to); to contend (with or against). *n.* An act or spell of struggling; a strenuous effort; a confused fight.

strum (strŭm) [imit.], *v.* To play carelessly on a stringed instrument.

strumpet (strŭm'pĕt) [?], *n.* A prostitute.

strut (strŭt) [M.E. *strouten,* prob. Scand.], *v.t.* To brace with a strut; to walk with a pompous, conceited gait. *n.* Such a gait; a beam inserted in a frame-work to keep other members apart, a brace.

strychnine (strik'nin) [Gr. *struchnos,* nightshade], *n.* A highly poisonous alkaloid used in medicine as a stimulant, etc.

stub (stŭb) [A.-S. *stybb*], *n.* A stump, end, or remnant of anything. *v.t.* To grub

up by the roots; to clear of stubs.
stubby, *a.* Containing stubs; short and thick.

stubble (stŭbl) [O.F. *estouble*], *n.* The stumps of wheat, barley, etc., left in the ground after harvest; (*fig.*) short, bristly hair.

stubborn (stŭb'ŏrn) [M.E. *stoburn*], *a.* Unreasonably obstinate; intractable, refractory. **stubbornness**, *n.*

stucco (stŭk'ō) [It.], *n.* Fine plaster for coating walls or moulding. *v.t.* To coat with stucco.

stud (1) (stŭd) [A.-S. *studu*, a post], *n.* A large-headed nail, head of a bolt, etc., esp. as an ornament; an ornamental button. *v.t.* To set with studs or ornamental knobs; to bestrew.

stud (2) [A.-S. *stōd*], *n.* A number of horses kept for racing, breeding, etc.

studding sail (stŭnsl) [?], *n.* An additional sail set with a square sail in light winds.

student (stū'dĕnt) [L. *studium*, zeal, whence *studens*], *n.* A person engaged in study, esp. at an institution for higher education or technical training; a studious person.

studio (stū'di-ō) [It.], *n.* The working-room of a sculptor, painter, photographer, etc.

studious (stū'di-ŭs), *a.* Devoted to study; diligent, anxious (to do something); observant (of); studied, deliberate.

study (stŭd'ĭ), *n.* Application to books, etc., the pursuit of knowledge; a piece of work done for practice or as a preliminary; a room devoted to study, literary work, etc.; a reverie; earnest endeavour, watchful attention; the object of this. *v.t.* To apply the mind to for the purpose of learning; to investigate; to consider attentively. *v.i.* To apply oneself to study, esp. to reading; to meditate, to cogitate, to muse; to be assiduous, diligent, or anxious (to do). **studied**, *a.* Deliberate, premeditated, intentional.

stuff (stŭf) [O.F. *estoffe*], *n.* The material of which anything is made; a woollen fabric as opp. to silk or linen; (*fig.*) nonsense, trash. *v.t.* To cram, to pack, to stop (up); to fill (a fowl, etc.) with seasoning; (*fig.*) to fill with notions, nonsense, etc. *v.i.* To cram oneself with food. **stuffing**, *n.* Material with which anything is filled; seasoning for a fowl, etc. **stuffy**, *a.* Ill-ventilated, close; narrow-minded. **stuffiness**, *n.*

stultify (stŭl'ti-fī) [L. *stultus*, foolish], *v.t.* To render absurd; to cause to appear ridiculous. **stultifica'tion**, *n.*

stumble (stŭmbl) [M.E. *stumblen*], *v.i.* To trip in walking or to have a partial fall; to act, move, or speak blunderingly; to come (upon) by chance. *n.* An act of stumbling. **stumbling-block**, *n.* An impediment, a cause of difficulty, etc.

stumer (stū'mer), *n.* A cheque that has no money to back it.

stump (stŭmp) [Icel. *stumpr*], *n.* Any part left when the rest of a tree, branch, limb, tooth, etc., has been cut away, amputated, destroyed, or worn out, a stub; (*Cricket*) one of the three posts of a wicket. *v.i.* To walk stiffly or noisily, as on

wooden legs; to make stump-speeches. *v.t.* To go about (a district) making stump-speeches; to put out (the batsman) at cricket while he is out of the crease. **stump-orator**, *n.* One who makes stump-speeches. **stump-speech**, *n.* A speech from a tree-stump or an improvised platform; an electioneering speech.

stun (stŭn) [A.-S. *stunian*], *v.t.* To daze with noise; to render senseless with a blow. **stunner**, *n.* One who or that which stuns; (*slang*) something first-rate. **stunning**, *a.* (*slang*) Wonderfully good, fine, etc.

stunt (stŭnt), *n.* A difficult or absurd feat done to attract notice; an advertising device; (*Aer.*) a feat of aerobatics.

stupefy (stū'pė-fī) [L. *stupēre*, to be amazed], *v.t.* To make stupid or senseless; to deprive of sensibility. **stupefac'tion**, *n.*

stupendous (stū-pen'dŭs), *a.* Astounding in magnitude, force, etc., amazing, astonishing.

stupid (stū'pĭd), *a.* Stupefied; dull of apprehension, wit, or understanding; senseless. **stupid'ity**, **stupidness**, *n.*

stupor (stū'pŏr), *n.* A dazed condition, torpor, deadened sensibility.

sturdy (1) (stĕr'dĭ) [O.F. *estourdi*, astounded], *a.* Robust, lusty, hardy. **sturdily**, *adv.* **sturdiness**, *n.*

sturdy (2) [O.F. *estourdie*, giddiness], *n.* A disease in sheep characterized by giddiness.

sturgeon (stĕr'jŏn) [O.H.G. *sturjo*], *n.* A large fish characterized by bony scales, valued as a delicacy, and yielding caviare and isinglass.

stutter (stŭt'er), *v.i.* To keep hesitating or spasmodically repeating in the articulation of words. *v.t.* To utter thus. *n.* This act or habit.

sty (1) (stī) [A.-S. *stigo*], *n.* A pen for swine; a mean or filthy habitation.

sty (2) [prob. A.-S. *stigend*, rising], *n.* An inflamed swelling on the edge of the eyelid.

Stygian (stij'i-ăn), *a.* Pertaining to the river Styx; (*fig.*) gloomy, dark.

style (stīl) [L. *stilus*, *stylus*], *n.* A pointed instrument used for writing on wax; an etching-needle, a graver, a blunt-pointed surgical instrument; manner of writing, expressing ideas, doing, etc., as dist. from the matter expressed or done; kind, make; the general characteristics of literary diction or artistic expression, distinguishing a particular people, person, period, etc.; (*colloq.*) fashion, distinction; mode of address, title, description. *v.t.* To designate, to describe formally by name and title. **stylish**, *a.* Fashionable, smart, showy. **stylishness**, *n.* **stylist**, *n.* A writer having a good style. **stylis'tic**, *a.*

stylite (stī'līt), *n.* A mediæval recluse who lived on the top of a pillar.

stylus (stī'lŭs), *n.* A pointed instrument for writing by means of carbon paper.

stymie (stī'mi) [?], *n.* (*Golf*) The position when an opponent's ball lies between the player's ball and the hole. *v.t.* To hinder by a stymie.

styptic (stip'tĭk) [Gr. *stuphein*, to contract],

a. That stops bleeding. *n.* A preparation that arrests bleeding.

suasion (swā'zhŭn) [L. *suādēre*, to persuade], *n.* Persuasion. **suasive** (swā'siv), *a.*

suave (swäv, swav) [F.], *a.* Agreeable, bland, polite. **suavity** (swăv'i-ti), *n.*

sub- [L. *sub-*, pref., *sub*, prep., under], *pref.* Under; from below upward; denoting inferior position; slightly; (*Chem.*) less than normal; (*Math.*) denoting the inverse of a ratio.

subacid (sŭb'ăs'id), *a.* Slightly acid or sour. *n.* A subacid substance.

subaltern (sŭb'ăl-tẽrn) [L. *alternus*, alternate], *a.* Subordinate; of inferior rank. *n.* (*Mil.*) An officer below the rank of captain.

subconscious (sŭb-kon'shŭs), *a.* Slightly or partially conscious.

subdivide (sŭb-di-vīd'), *v.* To divide again or into smaller parts. **subdivision** (-vizh'ŭn), *n.*

subdue (sŭb-dū') [O.F. *subduz*], *v.t.* To conquer, vanish, overcome; to tame; to tone down, soften. **subdu'able,** *a.*

sub-edit (sŭb-ed'it), *v.t.* To prepare matter (esp. newspaper matter) for the press. **sub-editor,** *n.*

subjacent (sŭb-jā'sẽnt) [L. *jacens*, lying], *a.* Underlying; lower in position.

subject (sŭb'jĕkt) [L. *subjectus*, p.p. of *subjicere* (SUB-, *jacere*, to cast)], *a.* Being under the power of another; liable, disposed (to); dependent, conditional. *n.* One under the dominion or political rule of a person or State, one owing allegiance to a sovereign; that which is treated, as the topic under consideration, a body for dissection, etc.; the cause or occasion (for); (*Log.*) that member of a proposition about which something is predicated; (*Gram.*) the nominative of a sentence. *v.t.* (sŭb-jekt') To reduce to subjection (to); to expose, to make liable. **subject-matter,** *n.* The object of consideration, discussion, etc. **subjec'tion,** *n.* **subjec'tive,** *a.* Concerned with or proceeding from the consciousness as opp. to objective or external things; due to the individual mind, fanciful. **subjectiv'ity,** *n.* **subjec'tivism,** *n.* The doctrine that human knowledge is purely subjective, and therefore relative.

subjoin (sŭb-join'), *v.t.* To add at the end, to append, to affix.

subjugate (sŭb'jŭ-gāt) [L. *jugātus*, brought under the yoke], *v.t.* To subdue, bring into subjection, enslave. **subjuga'tion,** *n.*

subjunctive (sŭb-jŭnk'tiv) [L. *subjunctīvus* (*junctus*, joined)], *a.* Denoting the mood of a verb expressing condition, hypothesis, or contingency. *n.* The subjunctive mood.

sublease (sŭb'lēs), *n.* A lease held by a subtenant. **sublet** (sŭb-let'), *v.t.* To let to another, the person letting being the tenant.

sublimate (sŭb'li-māt), *v.t.* To convert (a solid) to the state of vapour and to solidity again; (*fig.*) to refine, purify. *n.* The product of sublimation. **sublima'tion,** *n.*

sublime (sŭ-blīm') [L. *sublīmis*], *a.* Of the

most lofty or exalted nature, inspiring awe; (*iron.*) indifferent to criticism (of conceit, etc.), elevated. *a.* Exalted; high in excellence; elevated in manner. **sublimity** (-lim'i-ti), *n.*

sublunary (sŭb-lū'när-i) [L. *luna*, the moon], *a.* Situated beneath the moon, pertaining to this world, mundane.

submarine (sŭb-má-rēn'), *a.* Situated, acting, or growing beneath the surface of the sea. *n.* (sŭb'má-rēn) A vessel that may be submerged, esp. one employed in war.

submerge (sŭb-mẽrj') [L. *mergere*, to dip], *v.t.* To put under water, etc., to flood, inundate; to overwhelm. *v.i.* To sink under water, etc. **submergence,** *n.* **submersible,** *a.* and *n.* **submersion,** *n.*

submit (sŭb-mit') [L. *mittere*, to send], *v.t.* To yield or surrender (oneself); to present or refer for consideration; to put forward deferentially. *v.i.* To yield, to give in; to be submissive. **submission** (-mish'ŭn), *n.* Act of submitting; state of being submissive; compliance, resignation, meekness. **submissive,** *a.*

suborder (sŭb-ôr'dẽr), *n.* (*Zool. and Bot.*) A subdivision of an order.

subordinate (sŭ-bôr'di-nát), *a.* Inferior in order, rank, power, etc.; subject, subsidiary (to). *n.* A person working under another; an inferior. *v.t.* (-nāt) To make subordinate; to treat as of secondary importance; to make subservient (to). **subordina'tion,** *n.*

suborn (sŭ-bôrn') [L. *ornāre*, to incite], *v.t.* To procure by underhand means, esp. bribery, to commit a crime. **suborna'tion,** *n.* **suborner,** *n.*

subpœna (sŭb-pē'ná) [L., under penalty], *n.* A writ commanding a person's attendance in a court of justice. *v.t.* To serve with this.

subscribe (sŭb-skrīb'), *v.t.* To write (one's name, etc.) at the end of a document; to sign (a document, promise, etc.); to contribute (a sum to a fund, etc.); to publish by securing subscribers beforehand. *v.i.* To write one's name at the end of a document; (*fig.*) to assent (to an opinion, etc.); to engage to pay a contribution; to receive and pay for a newspaper, book, etc. **subscriber,** *n.* **subscription** (-skrip'shŭn), *n.*

subsection (sŭb-sek'shŭn), *n.* A subdivision of a section.

subsequent (sŭb'sē-kwẽnt) [L. *sequens*, following], *a.* Coming immediately after in time or order; following, succeeding. **subsequence,** *n.* **subsequently,** *adv.*

subserve (sŭb-sẽrv'), *v.t.* To serve as a means or instrument in promoting (an end, etc.). **subservient,** *a.* Useful as a means; obsequious, servile. **subservience,** *n.*

subside (sŭb-sīd') [L. *sīdere*, to settle], *v.i.* To sink, to settle (of lees, etc.); to collapse; (*fig.*) to settle down, become tranquil. **subsidence** (sŭb'si-dẽns), *n.*

subsidiary (sŭb-sid'i-á-ri), *a.* Auxiliary, supplemental; pertaining to a subsidy; tributary.

subsidy (sŭb'si-di) [L. *sedēre*, to sit], *n.* A tax to defray special expenses; a sum paid by one government to another; a

State contribution to a commercial or charitable undertaking of public benefit.

subsidize, v.t.

subsist (sŭb-sist´) [L. *sistere*], v.i. To exist, remain in existence; to live, to find sustenance, be sustained (on); to inhere. **subsistence**, n. **subsistent**, a.

subsoil (sŭb´soil), n. The stratum of earth immediately below the surface-soil.

substance (sŭb´stăns) [L. *substantia*], n. That of which a thing consists; matter, material; the essence, gist, or main purport; that which is real, solidity, firmness; property, resources. **substantial** (-stăn´shăl), a. **substantiate**, v.t. To make real; to establish, prove, make good (a statement, etc.). **substantia´tion**, n.

substantive (sŭb´stăn-tiv) [L. *substantīvus*], a. Expressing real existence; having substance or reality; independently existent, not merely implied. n. A noun or clause used as a noun. **substantival** (-tī´văl), a. **substantively**, adv.

substitute (sŭb´sti-tūt) [L. *substitūtus*], n. A person or thing serving for another. v.t. To put in the place of another person or thing. **substitu´tion**, n. **substra´tum** [SUB-, STRATUM], n. (pl. -ta) That which underlies anything; subsoil; ground or basis. **substruc´ture**, n. An understructure or foundation.

subten´ant, n. One holding land, etc., from a tenant. **subtenancy**, n. **subtend´** [L. *tendere*, to stretch], v.t. To extend under or be opposite to (of a chord relatively to an arc, or side of a triangle to an angle).

subter- [L., under, less than], pref. **subterfuge** (sŭb´-tĕr-fūj) [L. *fugere*, to flee], n. A shift, an evasion, a prevarication. **subterranean, -terraneous** (sŭb-tē-rā´nē-ăn, -ŭs) [L. *terra*, earth], a. Underground. **sub-title** (sŭb-titl), n. A subsidiary title to a book, etc.; a half-title.

subtle (sŭtl) [L. *subtilis*, finely woven], a. Rarefied, delicate, hard to seize, elusive; making fine distinctions, discerning; skilful, artful, insidious. **subtlety** (sŭtl´ti), n. **subtly** (sŭt´li), adv.

subtract (sŭb-trăkt´) [L. *tractus*, drawn], v.t. To take away (a part) from the rest, to deduct. **subtrac´tion**, n. **subtractive**, a. **sub´trahend**, n. The number to be subtracted from another.

suburb (sŭb´ŭrb) [L. *urbs*, city], n. An outlying part of a city or town. **suburban**, a. and n.

subvene (sŭb-vēn´) [L. *venīre*, to come], v.i. To happen so as to aid or effect a result. **subven´tion**, n. A grant in aid, a subsidy. **subvert** [L. *vertere*, to turn], v.t. To overthrow, destroy; to corrupt, pervert. **subversion**, n. **subversive**, a. **subvertible**, a.

subway (sŭb´wā), n. An underground passage, conduit, etc.

suc- [SUB-], pref. (before c).

succedaneum (sŭk-sē-dā´nē-ŭm) [L.], n. (pl. -nea) That which is used instead of something else, a substitute. **succedaneous**, a.

succeed (sŭk-sēd´) [L. *cēdere*], v.t. To come after (in time or order), to be subsequent to; to take the place previously occupied

by. v.i. To follow in time or order; to be the heir or successor (to); to be successful, to attain a desired object.

success (sŭk-ses´), n. The act of succeeding, favourable result, attainment, esp. of worldly prosperity. **successful**, a. **successor**, n. One who follows another in an office, etc.

succession (sŭk-sesh´ŭn), n. A following in order; a series of things in order; the act or right of succeeding to an office or inheritance; the order in which persons so succeed. **successional**, a.

successive (sŭk-ses´iv), a. Following in order, consecutive. **successively**, adv.

succinct (sŭk-sinkt´) [L. *cinctus*, girt], a. Compressed into few words, concise. **succinctly**, adv.

succour (sŭk´ŏr) [L. *currere*, to run], v.t. To come to the aid of; to relieve in distress, etc. n. Aid in time of difficulty or distress.

succulent (sŭk´ū-lĕnt) [L. *succulentus*], a. Juicy; thick and fleshy (of plants, stems, etc.). **succulence**, n. **succulently**, adv.

succumb (sŭ-kŭm´) [L. *cumbere*, to lie], v.i. To cease to resist, to give way; to die.

such (sŭch) [A.-S. *swylc*], a. Of that or the like kind or degree (as); of the kind or degree mentioned or implied; so great, intense, etc. (as or that); so. pron. Such a person or thing (as); the same.

suck (sŭk) [A.-S. *sūcan*], v.t. To draw into the mouth by the action of the lips and lungs; to drink in, acquire; to draw liquid from with the mouth; to dissolve thus. v.i. To draw liquid, milk, nourishment, etc., in by suction. n. An act or spell of sucking, suction. **sucker**, n. One who or that which sucks; the piston of a suction-pump; a tube for suction; (Bot.) a shoot from a root; (colloq.) a dupe, a simpleton. **sucking**, a. Not yet weaned.

suckle (sŭkl), v.t. To give suck to. **suckling**, n. A child or animal not yet weaned.

suction (sŭk´shŭn) [L. *suctus*, sucked], n. Act or process of sucking; the production of a vacuum in a confined space causing fluid to enter, or a body to adhere to something.

sudation (sū-dā´shŭn) [L. *sūdātio*, a sweating], n. Sweating, sweat. **su´datory**, a. Exciting perspiration.

sudden (sŭdn) [L. *subitus*], a. Happening unexpectedly; instantaneous, abrupt. **suddenly**, adv. **suddenness**, n.

sudoriferous (sū-dŏ-rif´er-ŭs) [L. *sūdor*, sweat], a. Causing perspiration. n. A sudorific drug.

suds (sŭdz) [lit., things sodden], n.pl. Soapy water forming a frothy mass.

sue (sū) [O.F. *suir*, to follow], v.t. To prosecute or pursue a claim by legal process; to entreat. v.i. To take legal proceedings (for); to make petition (to or for).

suède (swād) [F., Swedish], n. Undressed kid.

suet (sū´ĕt) [O.F. *seu*], n. The hard fat about the kidneys of oxen, etc. **suety**, a.

suf- [SUB-], pref. (before f).

suffer (sŭf´ĕr) [L. *ferre*, to bear], v.t. To undergo (something unpleasant or unjust); to endure, support (unflinchingly, etc.); to put up with; to allow. *v.i.* To undergo pain, injury, etc.; to undergo punishment, to be executed. **sufferable,** *a.* **sufferance,** *n.* Toleration, allowance, tacit permission; patience, submissiveness. **sufferer,** *n.* **suffering,** *n.*

ffice (sŭ-fīs') [L. *facere*, to make], *v.i.* To be enough, to be sufficient (for or to do, etc.). *v.i.* To be enough for, to satisfy. **sufficiency** (-fĭsh'ĕn-sĭ), *n.* The quality of being sufficient; an adequate supply (of); competence. **sufficient,** *a.* Enough, adequate, sufficing (for). *n.* Enough, a sufficiency.

suffix (sŭf'ĭks) [L. *fixus* fixed], *n.* A letter or syllable appended to a word. *v.t.* (sŭ-fĭks') To add as a suffix, to append.

suffocate (sŭf'ō-kāt) [L. *suffocātus*, throttled], *v.i.* To kill by choking; to smother, to stifle. *v.i.* To be or feel suffocated. **suffoca'tion,** *n.*

suffragan (sŭf'rȧ-gȧn) [F.], *a.* Assisting (of an assistant bishop). *n.* A suffragan or auxiliary bishop.

suffrage (sŭf'rȧj) [L. *suffrāgium*], *n.* A vote; approval, consent; the right to vote, esp. in parliamentary elections. **suffragette** (-jet'), *n.* A female agitator for women suffrage. **suffragist,** *n.* An advocate of extension of the suffrage.

suffuse (sŭ-fūz') [L. *fūsus*, poured], *v.t.* To overspread, as from within. **suffu'sion,** *n.*

sugar (shug'ȧr) [Arab. *sakkar*], *n.* A sweet, crystalline substance obtained from the sugar-cane, beet, and other plants; a substance resembling sugar, esp. in taste; (*fig.*) flattering or mitigating words. *v.t.* To sweeten or sprinkle with sugar; (*fig.*) to render palatable. **sugarcane,** *n.* A very tall grass, with jointed stems, from the juice of which sugar is made. **sugar-plum,** *n.* A sweetmeat. **sugar-tongs,** *n.pl.* A pair of small tongs for lifting lumps of sugar at table. **sugary,** *a.* Like or containing sugar; (*fig.*) flattering, unctuous.

suggest (sŭ-jest') [L. *suggestus,* brought under], *v.t.* To cause (an idea) to arise in the mind; to propose (a plan, etc.) for consideration. **suggestible,** *a.* That may be suggested. **suggestion,** *n.* Act of suggesting; a hint, prompting. **suggestive,** *a.* **suggestively,** *adv.*

suicide (sū'ĭ-sĭd) [L. *sui,* of oneself, *cedere,* to kill], *n.* The act of intentionally taking one's own life; one who takes his own life intentionally. **suici'dal,** *a.*

suit (sūt) [F. *suite,* from L. *secūtus,* followed], *n.* The act of suing, request; courtship; a legal prosecution; one of the four sets in a pack of cards; a set of outer clothes, or of other articles used together. *v.t.* To adapt, to make fitting (to); to meet the desires of; to befit, be appropriate to. *v.i.* To agree, correspond (with); to be convenient. **suitable,** *a.* Suited, fitting, becoming. **suitabil'ity,** *n.* **suitably,** *adv.* **suitor** (sū'tŏr), *n.* A petitioner; a lover; (*Law*) a party to a suit. **suite** (swēt) [F.], *n.* A retinue; a set (of rooms, furniture, etc.).

sulfa drugs (sŭl'fȧ), *n.pl.* Collective name given to sulphonamides.

sulk (sŭlk) [A.-S. *solcen,* slothful], *v.i.* To be sulky. *n.pl.* A fit of sulkiness. **sulky,** *a.* Sullen, ill-humoured, resentful.

sullen (sŭl'ĕn) [O.F. *solain*], *a.* Persistently ill-humoured, morose, cross; dismal, baleful. *n.pl.* The sulks. **sullenness,** *n.*

sully (sŭl'ĭ) [A.-S. *sylian,* from *sol,* mud], *v.t.* To soil, to tarnish; to defile. *v.i.* To be soiled or tarnished. *n.* A blemish.

sulph-, sulpho- [SULPHUR], *comb. form.* **sulphate** (sŭl'fāt), *n.* A salt of sulphuric acid. **sulphide,** *n.* A compound of sulphur with an element or radical. **sulphite,** *n.* A salt of sulphurous acid. **sulphonamides,** *n.pl.* (*Chem.*) A group of drugs used in medicine on account of their powerful antibacterial action.

sulphur (sŭl'fŭr) [L.], *n.* A pale-yellow non-metallic element used in the manufacture of gunpowder, matches, vitriol, etc., brimstone. *a.* Pale-yellow. **sul'phurate,** *v.t.* To impregnate with or subject to the action of sulphur. **sulphureous** (-fūr'ē-ŭs), *a.* Consisting of or having the qualities of sulphur; sulphur-coloured. **sulphuret'ted,** *a.* Saturated or combined with sulphur. **sulphuric** (-fūr'ĭk), *a.* Derived from or containing sulphur, esp. in its highest combining quality. **sulphuric acid:** Oil of vitriol. **sulphurous** (sŭl'fū-rŭs), *a.* Containing sulphur in any degree; sulphureous. **sulphury,** *a.*

sultan (sŭl'tȧn) [Arab.], *n.* A Mohammedan sovereign, esp. of Turkey. **sultana** (-ta'nȧ), *n.* The wife, mother, or daughter of a sultan; a kind of raisin grown in Smyrna. **sul'tanate,** *n.* **sultanic** (-tăn'ĭk), *a.*

sultry (sŭl'trĭ), *a.* Very hot and close; oppressive. **sultrily,** *adv.*

sum (sŭm) [L. *summa,* fem. super. of *superus,* higher], *n.* The aggregate, the total; substance, essence; a particular amount of money; an arithmetical problem. *v.t.* To add or combine into one total (*usu.* up); to put in a few words (*usu.* up). *v.i.* To recapitulate (*usu.* up).

summary (sŭm'ȧ-rĭ), *a.* Abridged, concise; done briefly or unceremoniously. *n.* A condensed statement, an epitome. **summarily,** *adv.* **summarize,** *v.t.* To make or be a summary of.

summer (sŭm'ĕr) [A.-S. *sumor*], *n.* The season when the sun shines most directly upon a region, the warmest season. *a.* Pertaining to or used in summer. **summer-house,** *n.* A light building in a garden, for shade, etc. **summer-time,** *n.* The official time (1 hr. earlier than Greenwich Mean Time) during the summer months in Great Britain. **summery,** *a.*

summit (sŭm'ĭt), *n.* The highest point, the top; utmost elevation.

summon (sŭm'ŏn) [L. *monēre,* to warn], *v.t.* To command to attend, esp. in court; to call upon (to surrender, etc.); to call (up courage, etc.). **summoner'** *n.* **summons,** *n.* (*pl.* -ses) Act of summoning; an authoritative call to appear before a court or judge.

sumpter (sŭmp'tĕr) [O.F. *sommetier,* pack-horse driver], *n.* A baggage-horse; a driver of this.

sumptuary (sŭmp′tū-ăr-ĭ), *a.* Pertaining to expenditure. **sumptuary law:** One restraining luxury, etc.

sumptuous (sŭmp′tū-ŭs), *a.* Costly, showing lavish expenditure; magnificent.

sun (sŭn) [A.-S. *sunne*], *n.* The heavenly body round which the earth revolves and which gives light and heat to all the planets; the light or warmth of this, sunshine, a sunny place; a fixed star that has satellites; a chief source of light, honour, etc. *v.t.* To expose to the rays of the sun. *v.i.* To sun oneself. **sunbeam,** *n.* A ray of sunlight. **sun-blind,** *n.* A window shade. **sunbonnet,** *n.* A large, light, shady bonnet. **sunburn,** *n.* Tanning or inflammation of the skin due to exposure to the sun. **sundew,** *n.* A low, hairy, insectivorous bog-plant. **sundown,** *n.* Sunset. **sunflower,** *n.* A plant with large yellow-rayed flowers. **sunlight,** *n.* **sunlit,** *a.* **sunny,** *a.* Bright with or warmed by sunlight; (*fig.*) cheery, genial. **sunrise, -rising,** *n.* The first appearance of the sun above the horizon; the time of this. **sunset, -setting,** *n.* The disappearance of the sun below the horizon; the time of this. **sunshade,** *n.* A parasol, awning, etc., used against the sun. **sunshine,** *n.* The light of the sun; the space illuminated by this. **sunshiny,** *a.* **sunspot,** *n.* A dark patch sometimes seen on the surface of the sun. **sunstroke,** *n.* A cerebral affection due to exposure to the hot sun.

sundæ (sŭn′dā), *n.* A kind of ice-cream containing nuts, etc.

Sunday (sŭn′dĭ) [A.-S. *sunnan dæg*, day of the sun], *n.* The first day of the week.

sunder (sŭn′dẽr) [A.-S. *sundrian*], *v.t.* To separate; to keep apart.

sundry (sŭn′drĭ) [A.-S. *syndrig*], *a.* Several, various. *n.pl.* Matters or miscellaneous articles, too trifling or numerous to specify.

sup (sŭp) [A.-S. *sūpan*], *v.* To take (liquid) in successive sips; to take supper. *n.* A mouthful (of liquor, soup, etc.).

sup- [SUB-], *pref.* (*before p*).

super- [L.] *super*, prep., orig. compar. of SUB-], *pref.* Over, above; on the top of; excessive, more than, transcending; besides; of a higher kind.

superable (sū′pẽr-ăbl) [L. *superābilis*], *a.* That may be overcome, conquerable.

superabound (sū-pẽr-à-bound′), *v.i.* To be more than enough. **superabun′dance,** *n.* **superabundant,** *a.* **superadd′,** *v.t.* To add over and above. **superannuate,** *v.t.* To dismiss or disqualify on account of age; to pension off. **superannua′tion,** *n.*

superb (sū-pẽrb′) [L. *superbus*], *a.* Grand, majestic, stately; (*colloq.*) first-rate. **superbly,** *adv.*

supercargo, *n.* An officer in a merchant-ship who superintends sales, etc.

supercilious (sū-pẽr-sil′ĭ-ŭs) [L. *cilia*, eye-brows (with alln. to raising the eye-brows)], *a.* Overbearing, haughtily indifferent, disdainful. **superciliousness,** *n.*

supererogation (sū-pẽr-er-ò-gā′shŭn) [L. *superērogāre*, to pay out beyond what is expected], *n.* Performance of more than duty requires. **supererog′atory,** *a.* **superex′cellent,** *a.* Of outstanding excellence.

superficies (sū-pẽr-fish′ĭ-ēz) [L. *facies*, face], *n.* A surface; its area. **superficial** (-fish′ăl), *a.* Pertaining to or lying on the surface; not penetrating deep; shallow. **superficial′ity,** *n.* **superficially,** *adv.*

superfine (sū′pẽr-fīn), *a.* Exceedingly fine, of extra quality; over-refined.

superfluous (sū-pẽr′floo-ŭs) [L. *fluere*, to flow], *a.* More than is necessary or sufficient, superabundant. **super′fluity,** *n.* **super′fluously,** *adv.* **superhu′man,** *a.* Beyond what human beings are ordinarily capable of. **superincum′bent,** *a.* Lying or resting on something. **superintend′,** *v.t.* To have or exercise the management or oversight of; to direct, control. **superintendence,** *n.* **superintendent,** *n.*

superior (sū-pẽr′ĭ-ôr), *a.* Upper, of higher position, grade, excellence, etc.; greater relatively (to); of wider application (of a class, etc.); situated near the top; above being influenced by or amenable (to). *n.* A person superior to one or to others, one's better, the head of a religious house. **superior′ity,** *n.*

superlative (sū-pẽr′là-tiv), *a.* Raised to the highest degree, consummate, supreme; (*Gram.*) expressing the highest degree. *n.* The superlative degree; a word or phrase in the superlative. **superlatively,** *adv.*

superman (sū′pẽr-măn), *n.* A hypothetical superior being, esp. one advanced in intellect and morals; an overman.

supernal (sū-pẽr′năl) [M.F. *supernel*], *a.* Of a loftier kind or region; celestial, divine, lofty.

supernatural (sū-pẽr-năch′răl), *a.* Existing by, due to, or exercising powers above the forces of nature, outside the sphere of natural law. **supernaturalism,** *n.* Belief in the supernatural. **supernaturally,** *adv.* **supernu′merary,** *a.* Being in excess of a prescribed or customary number. *n.* A supernumerary person or thing, esp. (*Theat.*) a person appearing on the stage without a speaking part.

superscribe [L. *scribere,* to write], *v.t.* To write over; to add an inscription to. **superscrip′tion,** *n.*

supersede (sū-pẽr-sēd′) [SUPER-, L. *sedēre,* to sit], *v.t.* To put a person or thing in the place of, to set aside, to annul; to take the place of, supplant.

super-sonic (sū-pẽr-son′ik), *a.* Pertaining to sound waves with such high frequency that they are inaudible. **super-sonic boom,** *n.* The sound heard when a jet-plane passes the sound-barrier.

superstition (sū-pẽr-stish′ŭn) [L. *superstitio,* standing over, amazement], *n.* Credulity regarding the supernatural or the mysterious; unreasoning dread of the unknown; belief in omens, charms, etc. **superstitious,** *a.*

superstructure, *n.* The top part of a building; a structure raised on some other structure.

supervene (sū-pẽr-vēn′) [L. *vēnīre,* to come], *v.i.* To happen as something additional. **superven′tion,** *n.*

supervise (sū'pér-viz) [L. *visus*, seen], *v.t.* To have oversight of, to superintend. **supervision** (-vizh'ŭn), *n.* su'pervisor, *n.*

supine (sū-pīn') [L. *supīnus*], *a.* Lying with the face upward; listless, careless. *n.* (sū'pĭn) (*Lat. Gram.*) A verbal noun formed from a p.p. stem.

supper (sŭp'ér) [O.F. *soper*], *n.* The last meal of the day.

supplant (sŭ-plant') [L. *planta*, sole of foot], *v.t.* To take the place of or oust, esp. by treachery. **supplanter**, *n.*

supple (sŭpl) [L. *plicāre*, to fold], *a.* Pliant, easily bent; yielding, submissive, obsequious. **suppleness**, *n.*

supplement (sŭp'li-mènt) [L. *plēre*, to fill], *n.* An addition; an addition to a book or newspaper. *v.t.* (-ment') To make additions to; to complete by additions. **supplemen'tal, -ary,** *a.*

suppliant (sŭp'li-ánt) [F., entreating], *a.* Entreating, supplicating; expressing entreaty. *n.* A humble petitioner. **sup'pliance,** *n.* **suppliantly,** *adv.*

supplicate (sŭp'li-kāt), *v.t.* To ask for earnestly and humbly; to address in earnest prayer. *v.i.* To beseech. **supplicant,** *n.* A suppliant. **supplica'tion,** *n.* **sup'plicatory,** *a.*

supply (sŭ-plī') [L. *plēre*, to fill], *v.t.* To furnish, to provide; to serve instead of. *n.* Act of supplying things needed; that which is supplied; necessary stores or provisions (*often in pl.*); (*pl.*) money granted to meet the expenses of government.

support (sŭ-pōrt') [L. *portāre*, to carry], *v.t.* To bear the weight of, to sustain, to keep from yielding, to give endurance to; to provide for; to advocate, defend, second; to bear out, substantiate, corroborate; to endure, put up with; to be able to carry on; to represent (a character, etc.). *n.* Act of supporting, state of being supported; one who or that which supports; aid; subsistence, livelihood. **supportable,** *a.* **supporter,** *n.* One who or that which supports or maintains; (*Her.*) a figure on each side of a shield.

suppose (sŭ-pōz'), *v.t.* To assume by way of argument or illustration; to believe; to take to be the case, to surmise; to require as a condition, to imply. **supposable,** *a.* **supposedly,** *adv.* **supposi'tion,** *n.*

suppositions (sŭ-poz-i-tish'ŭs) [L. *suppōnere*, to substitute], *a.* Substituted, not genuine.

suppress (sŭ-pres') [L. *pressus*, pressed], *v.t.* To put down, subdue, quell; to keep back, stifle, repress, conceal. **suppressible,** *a.* **suppression** (-presh'ŭn), *n.* **suppressive,** *a.*

suppurate (sŭp'ū-rāt) [L. *suppūrāta*, pus], *v.i.* To generate pus, to fester. **suppura'tion,** *n.* **sup'purative,** *a.*

supra- [L. *suprā*, abl. of *superus*, higher], *pref.* Above, over, super-; beyond. **supracostal** (sū-prá-kos'tál) [L. *costa*, a rib], *a.* Lying or situated above or outside the ribs. *n.* **supramun'dane,** *a.* Celestial; above the world.

supreme (sū-prēm') [L. *suprēmus*], *a.* Highest in authority, power, degree, or

importance; extreme, greatest possible; last, final. **supremacy** (sū-prem'á-si), *n.*

sur- [O.F., from L. SUPER-], *pref.* Super-, as in *surcingle, surface, surfeit.*

surcease (sér-sēs') [A.-F. *sursise,* L. *supersedēre,* to supersede], *n.* Cessation. *v.i.* To cease.

surcharge (sûr-charj'), *v.t.* To overload, overfill; to put an extra charge on; to impose payment of (a sum) or on (a person) for amounts disallowed by an auditor. *n.* An excessive burden or charge; an overcharge; an amount surcharged; over-printing on a postage- or revenue-stamp, a stamp so treated.

surcingle (sér'singl) [L. *cingula,* belt], *n.* A girth for holding a saddle or blanket on a horse's back; the girdle of a cassock.

surcoat (sér'kōt), *n.* A loose robe worn over armour; an outer jacket.

surd (sérd) [L. *surdus,* deaf], *a.* (*Math.*) Not capable of being expressed in rational numbers; (*Phon.*) uttered with the breath and not with the voice. *n.* An irrational quantity; (*Phon.*) a surd consonant, as *p, f, s.*

sure (shoor) [O.F. *sur*], *a.* Certain, confident; free from doubts (of); confidently trusting (that); infallible, stable; safe, reliable; unquestionably true. **surely,** *adv.* Securely; certainly (often by way of asseveration or to deprecate doubt). **sureness,** *n.* **surety,** *n.* One undertaking responsibility for payment of a sum, discharge of an engagement, etc., a guarantor; a pledge deposited as security.

surf (sérf) [?], *n.* The swell of the sea breaking on rocks, etc.; the foam of this. **surfy,** *a.*

surface (sér'fás), *n.* The exterior part of anything that has length and breadth, the outside; (*fig.*) that which is apparent at first view.

surfeit (sér'fét) [O.F. *sorfait*], *n.* Excess, esp. in eating and drinking; satiety, nausea. *v.* To feed to excess, to cloy.

surge (sérj) [L. *surgere*], *v.i.* To swell, to heave (of waves). *n.* A large wave, a billow, a heaving and rolling motion.

surgeon (sér'jŏn) [O.F. *cirurgeon*], *n.* A medical practitioner treating injuries, deformities, etc., by mechanical procedure; a general practitioner; a medical officer. **surgeonship,** *n.* **surgery,** *n.* Treatment of injuries, diseases, etc., by manual operation; a consulting-room or dispensary. **surgical,** *a.*

surly (sér'li), *a.* Churlish, rude, gruff, uncivil. **surlily,** *adv.* **surliness,** *n.*

surmise (sûr-mīz') [L. *missus,* sent], *n.* A supposition on slight evidence, a conjecture. *v.* To guess; to suspect, to suppose.

surmount (sûr-mount'), *v.t.* To overcome, vanquish; to cap (*usu. in p.p.*); to surpass. **surmountable,** *a.*

surname (sér'nām), *n.* A family name, a name added to the Christian name. *v.t.* To call by a surname; to give a surname to.

surpass (sûr-pas'), *v.t.* To excel, to go beyond. **surpassable,** *a.* **surpassing,** *a.* Excellent in an eminent degree.

surplice (sér'plis) [L. *pellicius,* pelisse)], *n.* A loose white vestment worn by the clergy and choristers.

surplus (sĕr'plŭs), *n.* That beyond what is used or required; balance in hand. **surplusage,** *n.*

surprise (sŭr-prīz') [L. *prehensus,* taken], *n.* A taking unawares; emotion excited by something unexpected, astonishment, an event exciting this. *v.t.* To come or fall upon suddenly and unexpectedly, to attack unawares; to strike with astonishment, to be different from expectation; to shock (*usu. in p.p.*); to disconcert. **surprisal.** *n.* surprising, *a.* **surprisingly,** *adv.*

surrealism (sŭ-rē'á-lizm) [F.], *n.* (*Art*) An artistic and literary movement of the 20th century which sought to express the subconscious activities of the mind by presenting images with the chaotic incoherence of a dream.

surrender (sŭ-ren'dĕr), *v.t.* To yield up to another; to give up possession of; to yield (oneself) to any influence, habit, etc. *v.i.* To yield, esp. to an enemy in war; to submit; to appear in court in discharge of bail, etc. *n.* Act of surrendering or state of being surrendered.

surreptitious (sŭr-ép-tish'ŭs) [L. *surreptīcius*], *a.* Done by stealth or fraud; clandestine. **surreptitiously,** *adv.*

surrogate (sŭr'ŏ-gát) [L. *surrogātus,* elected as substitute], *n.* A deputy, esp. of a bishop or his chancellor.

surround (sŭ-round') [L. *undāre,* to flow], *v.t.* To lie or be situated all round, to encompass, invest, enclose. **surroundings,** *n.pl.* Things around a person or thing, environment.

surtax (sĕr'tăks), *n.* An additional tax on higher incomes.

surveillance (sŭr-vā'lăns) [F.], *n.* Oversight, close watch, supervision.

survey (sŭr-vā') [O.F. *veeir,* to see], *v.t.* To take a general view of; to examine closely and ascertain the condition, value, etc., of; to determine the boundaries, extent, position, contours, etc., of (a tract of country, etc.). *n.* (sĕr'vā) Act or process of surveying; a general view; a careful scrutiny; a department carrying on the surveying of land, etc.; a map, etc., recording the results of this. **surveying,** *n.* **surveyor,** *n.*

survive (sŭr-vīv') [L. *vīvere,* to live], *v.t.* To outlive, outlast; to be alive after. *v.i.* To be still alive or in existence. **survival,** *n.* Act of surviving; a person, thing, custom, etc., surviving into a new state of things. **survivor,** *n.*

sus- [SUB-], *pref.* (before *p, t,* and sometimes *c*).

susceptible (sŭ-sep'tibl) [L. *susceptus,* taken up], *a.* Admitting (of); capable of being affected, liable (to); impressionable. **susceptibil'ity,** *n.* susceptibly, *adv.* **susceptive,** *a.* Readily receiving impressions, susceptible.

suspect (sŭs-pekt') [L. *suspectus,* suspicious], *v.t.* To imagine to exist, to surmise; to be inclined to believe guilty; to doubt, to mistrust. *v.i.* To be suspicious. *a.* Suspected, under suspicion; doubtful. *n.* A suspected person.

suspend (sŭs-pend') [L. *pendere,* to hang], *v.t.* To hang up; to sustain (of the particles of a body, fluid, etc.); to intermit, to defer. **suspender,** *n.* One who or that which suspends; (*pl.*) attachments to hold up socks, etc.; (*Am.*) braces.

suspense (sŭs-pens'), *n.* A state of uncertainty, apprehensive expectation. **suspen'sion,** *n.* **suspension-bridge,** *n.* A bridge sustained by flexible supports passing over a tower at each extremity. **suspensory,** *a.* Having power to suspend; uncertain, doubtful.

suspicion (sŭs-pish'ŭn), *n.* The act or feeling of one who suspects; doubt, mistrust; (*fig.*) a very slight amount. **suspicious,** *a.* Inclined to suspect; entertaining suspicion.

sustain (sŭs-tān') [L. *tenēre,* to hold], *v.t.* To bear the weight of, to hold up; to stand, to undergo without yielding; to suffer; to enable to bear, to encourage, keep up; to maintain, to establish by evidence; to confirm, bear out. **sus'tenance,** *n.* That which sustains; food, subsistence. **sustenta'tion,** *n.* Support, maintenance.

sutler (sŭt'ler) [Dut. *zoetelaar*], *n.* One who follows an army and sells provisions, liquor, etc.

suttee (sŭ-tē') [Sansk. *satī,* virtuous wife], *n.* A Hindu custom by which the widow was burnt on the funeral pyre with her dead husband; a widow so burnt. **sutteeism,** *n.*

suture (sū'tyŭr) [L. *sūtūra*], *n.* The junction of two parts as if by sewing, esp. of the bones of the skull; the uniting of the edges of a wound by stitching.

suzerain (sū'zė-rān, -rin) [F.], *n.* A lord paramount; a State having sovereignty or control over another. **suzerainty,** *n.*

svelte (svelt) [F.], *a.* Slender, lissom.

swab (swob) [Dut. *zwabber,* drudge], *n.* A mop for cleaning floors, gun-bores, etc.; an absorbent pad used by surgeons in operations, etc. *v.t.* To wipe or clean with a swab.

swaddle (swodl) [A.-S. *swethel,* swaddling-band], *v.t.* To swathe in a bandage or wraps. **swaddling-bands, -clothes,** *n.pl.*

swag (swăg) [Scand.], *n.* A burglar's booty; (*Austral.*) a bundle.

swagger (swăg'ér), *v.i.* To walk (about) with an air of defiance or superiority; to talk in a blustering or hectoring manner. *n.* A swaggering walk or behaviour; bluster, self-conceit.

swain (swān) [Icel. *sveinn*], *n.* A rustic; a country gallant; a male lover.

swallow (1) (swol'ō) [A.-S. *swalewe*], *n.* A small, swift, migratory bird. **swallowtail,** *n.* A deeply-forked tail; a dress-coat.

swallow (2) [A.-S. *swelgan*], *v.t.* To take through the throat into the stomach; to engulf, to consume (up); (*fig.*) to accept with credulity; to put up with; to recant. *v.i.* To perform the action of swallowing.

swamp (swomp) [Dut. *zwamp*], *n.* A tract of wet, spongy land, a marsh. *v.t.* To cause (a boat) to be filled with water. **swampy,** *a.*

swan (swon) [A.-S.], *n.* A large, web-footed aquatic bird noted for its grace in the water. **swansdown,** *n.* Down obtained from a swan; a thick cotton cloth with a nap on one side. **swan-song,** *n.* The song traditionally believed to be sung by a dying swan; (*fig.*) the last work, esp. of a poet.

swank (swăngk), *v.i.* (*colloq.*) To show off, to bluster. *n.* Swagger. **swanky,** *a.*

swap (swop) [?], *v.* To exchange, to barter. *n.* An exchange, a barter.

sward (swôrd) [A.-S. *sweard,* skin], *n.* Land covered with thick short grass; turf.

swarm (swôrm) [A.-S. *swearm*], *n.* A large number of insects, people, etc.; (*pl.*) great numbers; a cluster of honey-bees seeking a new home with a queen-bee. *v.i.* To collect together, to leave or go (out of) a hive in a swarm (of bees); to throng, to be exceedingly numerous; (of places) to be thronged or overcrowded (with); to climb (up a tree, etc.) by embracing it with arms and legs.

swarthy (swôr'thĭ) [A.-S. *sweart*], *a.* Dark or dusky in complexion. **swarthiness,** *n.*

swashbuckler (swosh'bŭ-klẽr), *n.* A bully, a bravo.

swastika (swos'ti-ká) [Sansk., fortunate], *n.* A fylfot or gammadion.

swath (swawth) [A.-S. *sweth,* track], *n.* A row of grass, corn, etc., cut and left lying; the space cut in one course.

swathe (swăth) [M.E. *swathen*], *v.t.* To bind or wrap in a bandage, cloth, etc. *n.* A bandage.

sway (swā) [Scand.], *v.i.* To move backwards and forwards, to oscillate irregularly; to waver, to vacillate. *v.t.* To cause to oscillate, vacillate, or incline to one side; to bias; to control, rule. *n.* Rule, dominion, control; the act of swaying, a swing.

swear (swâr) [A.-S. *swerian*], *v.i.* (*past* swore, sware, *p.p.* sworn, swôrn). To affirm solemnly invoking God or some other sacred person or object, to take an oath; to use profane language; to give evidence or to promise on oath. *v.t.* To utter or affirm with an oath; to cause to take oath, to administer an oath to, to bind by an oath; to utter profanely. **swearer,** *n.*

sweat (swet) [A.-S. *swat*], *n.* The moisture exuded from the skin, perspiration; moisture resembling this; act or state of sweating; (*fig.*) labour, toil, a spell of exercise; drudgery; a state of anxiety. *v.i.* To perspire; to exude (of moisture); (*fig.*) to be in a flurry, panic, etc.; to toil, drudge; to carry on business by sweating employees. *v.t.* To emit as sweat; to cause to sweat by exertion; to employ at starvation wages; to bleed, to subject to extortion; to wear away (coins). **sweater,** *n.* One who or that which sweats or causes to sweat; a thick woollen jersey. **sweaty,** *a.*

Swede (swēd), *n.* A native or inhabitant of Sweden; a Swedish turnip. **Swe'dish,** *a.* Pertaining to Sweden or its inhabitants. *n.* The language of the Swedes.

sweep (swēp) [A.-S. *suăpan,* to swoop], *v.t.* (*past and p.p.* swept) To clean or gather (up) with a broom; to carry (along, etc.) with powerful force; to move swiftly and powerfully over, to range, to scour; to pass over swiftly (of the eyes); to rake, enfilade; to dredge (a river bottom); to propel with sweeps; to cause to move with a sweeping motion. *v.i.* To glide along with a strong, continuous or stately motion, to range unchecked (of the eye); to extend continuously (of a curve, etc.). *n.* The act of sweeping; a clearance, a riddance; a sweeping motion, curve, piece of road, etc.; the range or compass of a sweeping motion, etc.; a long oar; a chimney-sweeper. **sweepstakes,** *n.* A transaction in which a number of persons stake sums on an event, the total amount being divided among the winning betters. **sweeper,** *n.* **sweeping,** *a.* That sweeps; wide-ranging, comprehensive. *n.pl.* Things collected by sweeping; (*fig.*) rubbish. **sweepingly,** *adv.*

sweet (swēt) [A.-S. *swēte*], *a.* Having a taste like that of honey or sugar; pleasing to the senses; fragrant; refreshing; not salt; (*fig.*) agreeable, delightful; charming, lovable, dear. *n.* A sweetmeat; (*pl.*) sweet dishes. **sweetbread,** *n.* The pancreas of a calf or sheep as food. **sweetheart,** *n.* A lover, male or female. *v.i.* To be love-making. **sweetmeat,** *n.* An article of confectionery consisting principally of sugar, a fruit candied with sugar. **sweet-oil,** *n.* Olive oil. **sweet-pea,** *n.* An annual leguminous climbing plant, with showy flowers. **sweet-potato,** *n.* A tropical climbing plant with an edible root. **sweetwilliam,** *n.* A perennial species of pink with clusters of showy and fragrant flowers. **sweeten,** *v.* **sweetening,** *n.* **sweeting,** *n.* A sweet variety of apple. **sweetish,** *a.* **sweetly,** *adv.* **sweetness,** *n.*

swell (swel) [A.-S. *swellan*], *v.i.* (*p.p.* swollen, swŏ'lĕn, **swelled**) To increase in bulk, volume, strength, or intensity; to expand; to rise in altitude; (*fig.*) to be puffed up, to be inflated with anger, etc. *v.t.* To increase the size of; to inflate, to puff up. *n.* The act or effect of swelling; a succession of long, unbroken waves in one direction; a bulge; (*Mus.*) an increase followed by a decrease in the volume of sound; a contrivance in an organ for effecting this; (*colloq.*) a person of importance, a showy or fashionable person. *a.* Characterized by display, smart, dandified; (*Am.*) just right, desired. **swelling,** *n.* Act of expanding or state of being swollen or augmented; (*Path.*) an unnatural enlargement of a part.

swelter (swel'tẽr) [A.-S. *sweltan*], *v.i.* To be hot and oppressive, to cause faintness (of the weather, etc.); to be overcome with heat. **sweltry,** *a.*

swerve (swẽrv) [A.-S. *sweorfan,* to rub], *v.i.* To turn to one side, to deviate. *n.* Act of swerving.

swift (swift) [A.-S.], *a.* Fleet, rapid, speedy, prompt; soon over, sudden. *adv.* Swiftly. *n.* A long-winged insectivorous bird resembling the swallow. **swiftly,** *adv.* **swiftness,** *n.*

swig (swig) [?], *v.* To drink in large draughts. *n.* A deep draught of liquor.

swill (swil) [A.-S. *swilian,* to wash], *v.t.*

To rinse; to drink greedily. *v.i.* To drink to excess. *n.* A rinsing; hog-wash.

swim (swim) [A.-S. *swimman*], *v.i.* (*past* swam, *p.p.* swum) To float; to move through water by the motion of the hands and feet, fins, etc.; to glide along; to be drenched (with water); to feel dizzy. *v.t.* To pass by swimming; to compete in (a race); to cause (a horse, boat, etc.) to swim; to float (a ship, etc.). *n.* Act or spell of swimming; a run frequented by fish. **swimmer**, *n.* **swimmingly**, *adv.* Smoothly, easily, without impediment.

swindle (swindl) [G. *schwindeln*, to be dizzy], *v.* To cheat; to defraud grossly. *n.* Act or process of swindling; a gross imposition, a fraudulent scheme; (*colloq.*) a deception, a fraud. **swindler**, *n.*

swine (swīn) [A.-S. *swín*], *n.* (*pl. unchanged*) A hoofed omnivorous mammal, a pig, a hog; (*fig.*) a greedy or debased person. **swine-herd**, *n.* One who tends swine. **swinish**, *a.*

swing (swing) [A.-S. *swingan*], *v.i.* (*past* swung, *p.p.* swung) To move to and fro, as a suspended body, to sway, hang freely, oscillate; to turn on a pivot; to go with a rhythmical motion; to be hanged. *v.t.* To cause to move to and fro or to turn or move round, as on a pivot. *n.* Act or state of swinging; a swinging or oscillating motion, gait, or rhythm; the sweep of a moving body; unrestrained liberty; a suspended seat in which one can swing to and fro, a spell of swinging in this; (*Mus. Dancing*) a style of jazz in which the basic melody and rhythm persist through individual interpretations of the theme. **swing-boat**, *n.* A boat-shaped car for swinging in. **swing-bridge**, *n.* A draw-bridge turning horizontally.

swinge (swinj) [A.-S. *swengan*], *v.t.* To beat, thrash. *n.* **swingeing**, *a.* Thumping; huge.

swipe (swīp) [A.-S. *swipian*], *v.* To hit with great force. *n.* A hard blow, esp. at cricket; (*pl.*) thin beer.

swirl (swėrl) [Scand.], *v.i.* To form eddies, to whirl about. *n.* A whirling motion, an eddy.

swish (swish) [imit.], *v.i.* To make a whistling sound in cutting through the air. *a.* (*colloq.*) Smart, elegant.

Swiss (swis), *a.* Pertaining to Switzerland or its inhabitants. *n.* A native or the people of Switzerland.

switch (swich) [M.Dut. *swick*], *n.* A flexible twig or rod; a tress of hair tied up at one end; a mechanism for diverting vehicles from one line to another, transferring electric current from one wire to another, etc. *v.t.* To lash with a switch; to shift (a train, etc.) from one line to another; to turn (on or off) with a switch.

switchback, *n.* A railway on which the vehicles are carried over a series of ascending inclines by the momentum of previous descents. **switch-board**, *n.* A board from which electric or telephonic circuits are controlled.

swivel (swivl), *n.* Mechanism allowing two parts to revolve independently; a support allowing free horizontal rotation.

swoon (swoon) [A.-S. *swogan*], *v.i.* To faint. *n.* Act of swooning, a faint.

swoop (swoop) [A.-S. *swápan*, to rush], *v.i.* To descend upon prey, etc., suddenly, to come (down) upon. *n.* A sudden plunge as of a bird of prey on its quarry.

sword (sôrd) [A.-S. *sweord*], *n.* A long blade fixed in a hilt used for cutting or thrusting; (*fig.*) the power of the sword; war, death. **sword-arm**, *n.* The right arm. **sword-fish**, *n.* A sea-fish allied to the mackerel, having the upper jaw prolonged into a formidable sword-like weapon. **sword-play**, *n.* Fencing; (*fig.*) repartee. **swordsman**, *n.* One who carries a sword; one skilled in the use of the sword.

sybarite (sib′à-rīt), *n.* An inhabitant of Sybaris, an ancient Greek colony in S. Italy, noted for effeminacy; an effeminate and luxurious person.

sycamore (sik′à-môr), *n.* A medium-sized tree allied to the maple and plane.

sycophant (sik′ō-fànt) [Gr. *sukophantēs*], *n.* A servile flatterer, a parasite. **sycophancy**, *n.* **sycophan′tic**, *a.*

syenite (sī′ē-nīt) [*Syene*, Egypt], *n.* a granular igneous rock.

syl- [SYN], *pref.* (*before l*).

syllable (sil′abl) [Gr. *sullabē*], *n.* A word or part of a word containing one vowel sound and uttered at a single effort; (*fig.*) the least particle of speech. *v.t.* To articulate, to utter. **syllab′ic**, *a.* Pertaining to or consisting of a syllable or syllables; having each syllable distinct.

syllabus (sil′à-bùs), *n.* A summary, abstract, etc., giving the principal heads of a course, etc.

syllogism (sil′ō-jizm) [Gr. *logos*, reason)], *n.* A form of argument consisting of a general statement, an instance, and a conclusion deduced from these. **syllogis′tic**, *a.*

sylph (silf) [? Gr. *silphē*, some beetle], *n.* A fabulous being inhabiting the air; a graceful and slender girl.

sylvan (sil′vàn) [L. *silva*, wood], *a.* Pertaining to a forest; growing in woods; rural. **sylviculture**, *n.* Forestry.

sym- [SYN], *pref.* (*before b, m,* or *p*).

symbol (sim′bòl) [Gr. *sumbolon*, token], *n.* An object typifying something, a type, an emblem; a character accepted as representing some thing, idea, process, etc., as the letters of the alphabet; those representing the elements, mathematical signs, etc. **symbol′ic, -al**, *a.* **sym′bolism**, *n.* **sym′bolize**, *v.t.* To typify; to represent by symbols; to treat as symbolic, to make representative of something.

symmetry (sim′ē-tri) [Gr. *metron*, measure], *n.* Due proportion of the several parts of a body, congruity, harmony; arrangement so that opposite parts are similar in shape and size. **symmet′ric, -al**, *a.* **symmetrize**, *v.t.* To make symmetrical.

sympathy (sim′pà-thi) [Gr. *pathein*, to suffer], *n.* The quality of being affected with the same feelings as another, or of sharing emotions, etc.; fellow-feeling, accord (with); compassion (for) **sym-**

pathet'ic, *a.* Pertaining to sympathy; having sympathy with another; being in agreement, concordant. **sympathetically,** *adv.* **sympathize,** *v.i.* To have or express sympathy with another; to be of the same disposition, opinion, etc.

symphony (sim'fō-ni) [Gr. *phōnē*, sound], *n.* A complex composition for an orchestra. **symphonic** (-fon'ik), **symphonious** (-fō'ni-ús), *a.*

symposium (sim-pō'zi-ŭm) [Gr. *posis*, drink], *n.* (*pl.* -ia) (*Gr. Ant.*) A convivial party with music, dancing, etc.; a collection of contributions by various authors on a particular subject.

symptom (simp'tŏm) [Gr. *sumptōma*, a chance, a casualty], *n.* A perceptible change in the appearance or functions of the body indicating disease; an indication. **symptomat'ic,** *a.*

syn- [Gr. *sun.* prep. with], *pref.* With; together; alike. **synæresis** (si-nēr'ē-sis) [Gr. *hairein*, to take], *n.* The contraction of two vowels or syllables into one.

synagogue (sin'ȧ-gog) [Gr. *agein*, to bring], *n.* A Jewish congregation for religious instruction and observances; a place of meeting for this.

synchronism (sing'krō-nizm) [Gr. *chronos*, time], *n.* Concurrence of two or more events in time, simultaneousness; a tabular arrangement of historical events or personages according to date. **synchronal, sychronous,** *a.* **synchronis'tic,** *a.* **synchronize,** *v.i.* To concur in time, to happen at the same time. *v.t.* To cause to agree in time.

syncopate (sing'kō-pāt) [Gr. *koptein*, to strike], *v.t.* To contract (a word) by omitting one or more letters from the middle; (*Mus.*) to begin (a note or tone) on an unaccented and continue with an accented beat. **syncopa'tion,** *n.*

syncope (sing'kō-pē), *n.* The elision of a letter or syllable from the middle of a word; (*Path.*) fainting, swooning. **syncopize,** *v.t.* To syncopate.

syndic (sin'dik) [Gr. *dikē*, justice], *n.* An officer invested with varying powers in different places and times.

syndicalism (sin'di-kȧ-lizm), *n.* The economic doctrine that workers should participate in the management and profits of the industry, and that the workers in different trades should federate to bring this about. **syndicalist,** *n.*

syndicate (sin'di-kȧt), *n.* A body of syndics, esp. at Cambridge; an association formed to promote some special interest.

syne (sin) [Sc.], *adv.* Long ago.

synecdoche (si-nek'dō-ki) [Gr. *ek*, out, *dechesthai*, to receive], *n.* A rhetorical figure by which a part is put for the whole or the whole for a part.

synod (sin'ŏd) [Gr. *hodos*, way], *n.* An ecclesiastical council. **synod'ic, -al,** *a.* Pertaining to a synod.

synonym (sin'ō-nim) [Gr. *onuma*, name], *n.* A word having the same meaning as another of the same language. **synonym'ic,** *a.* Pertaining to synonymy. **synon'ymous,** *a.* Expressing the same thing by a different word or words; conveying the same idea.

synopsis (si-nop'sis) [*opsis*, seeing], *n.* (*pl.* -ses, sēz) A general view, a conspectus, a summary. **synop'tic,** *a.* Of the nature of a synopsis. *n.* One of the synoptic gospels, viz., those of Matthew, Mark, and Luke; these evangelists.

syntax (sin'tăks) [Gr. *tascein*, to arrange], *n.* The part of grammar that deals with the arrangement of words in sentences. **syntac'tic,** *a.* Pertaining to, or according to the rules of syntax. **syntactically,** *adv.*

synthesis (sin'thē-sis) [Gr. *thesis*, putting], *n.* (*pl.* -ses, -sēz) The putting of things together, combination, composition; the building up of a complex whole, the process of forming concepts, theories, etc.; (*Gram.*) the formation of compound words; (*Surg.*) the union of broken parts. **synthet'ic, -al,** *a.* Pertaining to or consisting in synthesis. **syn'thesize,** *v.t.*

Syriac (sir'i-ăk), *a.* Pertaining to Syria or its language. *n.* The language of the ancient Syrians, western Aramaic. **Syrian,** *a.* and *n.*

syringa (si-ring'gȧ) [Gr. *surinx*, reed], *n.* A genus of plants containing the lilacs (*esp.*) mock-orange.

syringe (si-rinj'), *n.* A cylindrical instrument, a piston used to draw in and eject liquid, a squirt. *v.t.* To water, spray, or cleanse with a syringe.

syrup (sir'ŭp) [Arab. *sharāb*], *n.* A saturated solution of sugar in water, usu. with fruit-juice, etc.; treacle. **syrupy,** *a.*

system (sis'těm) [Gr. *sustēma*], *n.* Organization, method; a co-ordinated body of principles, facts, theories, etc.; a method of classification; a co-ordinated arrangement of things or parts, for working together; any organic structure taken as a whole, as the animal body, the universe, etc. **systemat'ic,** *a.* Methodical; done, etc., on a regular plan, not haphazard. **sys'tematize,** *v.t.* **systematiza'tion,** *n.*

systole (sis'tō-lē) [Gr. *sustellein*, to draw together], *n.* The contraction of the heart impelling the blood outwards, alternating with diastole. **systol'ic,** *a.*

T

Taal (tal) [Dut., language], *n.* S. African Dutch.

tab (tăb) [?], *n.* A small flap, tag, etc.

tabard (tăb'ȧrd) [O.F.], *n.* A garment worn over armour; a herald's sleeveless coat blazoned with the arms of the sovereign.

tabby (tăb'i) [Arab. *utābi*], *n.* Silk or other stuff with a watered surface; a brindled cat, esp. a female.

tabernacle (tăb'ėr-năkl) [L. *tabernāculum*, tent], *n.* A movable booth, used as a habitation, temple, etc.; a tent-like structure used by the Jews as a sanctuary before their settlement in Palestine; a receptacle for the consecrated elements or the pyx; (*Arch.*) a canopy, esp. over a niche, tomb, etc. *v.i.* To sojourn.

table (tābl) [L. *tabula*], *n.* A flat surface resting on supports, used for serving meals upon, working, playing games,

Tableau 399 Talk

etc.; food served upon it, fare, cuisine; the company sitting at a table; a list of numbers, references, etc., arranged systematically; a flat surface, a plateau. **table-cloth,** *n.* A cloth for covering a table, esp. at meal-times. **table d'hôte** (tabl dŏt) [F., host's table], *n.* (*pl.* **tables-**) A common table for guests at an hotel, with meal at fixed price. **table-land,** *n.* A plateau. **table-talk,** *n.* Familiar conversation, miscellaneous chat.

tableau (tăb'lō) [F.], *n.* (*pl.* **-eaux**) A picture; a vivid representation or effect. **tableau vivant:** (*pl.* **tableaux vivants**) A motionless group representing some scene or event.

tablet (tăb lėt), *n.* A thin flat piece of wood, ivory, etc., for writing on; a small slab, esp. used as a memorial.

taboo (tá-boo') [Maori *tapu*], *n.* A custom among Polynesians of prohibiting the use of certain persons, places, or things. *a.* Banned, prohibited.

tabular (tăb'ū-lár), *a.* In the form of a table; formed in thin plates; arranged in or computed from tables. **tabulate,** *v.t.* To reduce to or arrange (figures, etc.) in tabular form. **tab'ulator,** *n.*

tacit (tăs'it) [L. *tacēre*, to be silent], *a.* Implied but not expressed. **tacitly,** *adv.* **taciturn** (tăs i-tẽrn), *a.* Habitually silent, reserved. **tacitur'nity,** *n.* **taciturnly,** *adv.*

tack (tăk) [O.F. *tache*, peg], *n.* A small, flat-headed nail; a long stitch for temporary fastening; the course of a ship as determined by the position of her sails; the act of changing direction to take advantage of a side-wind, etc. *v.t.* To fasten with tacks; to append (to). *v.i.* To change the course of a ship by shifting the position of the sails. **hard tack,** *n.* Ship's biscuit. **tacky,** *a.* Sticky. **tackiness,** *n.*

tackle (tăkl) [Teut.], *n.* Ropes, pulleys, etc., for lifting or for working spars, sails, etc.; a windlass with its ropes, etc.; the gear for carrying on any particular work or sport. *v.t.* To grapple with; to set to work vigorously upon.

tact (tăkt) [L. *tactus*, touch], *n.* An intuitive sense of what is fitting, adroitness in doing the proper thing. **tactful,** *a.* **tactless,** *a.*

tactics (tăk'tiks) [Gr. *taktos*, ordered], *n.* The art of manoeuvring armed forces, esp. in contact with the enemy; (*pl.*) devices to attain some end. **tactical,** *a.* **tactician** (-tish'án), *n.*

tactile (tăk'tĭl) [L. *tactus*, touch], *a.* Of, pertaining to, or perceived by the sense of touch.

tadpole (tăd'pōl), *n.* The larva of a frog or toad before the gills and tail disappear.

tael (tāl) [Malay *tahil*], *n.* A Chinese weight of 1½ oz., and a former silver monetary unit (about 5s. 10d.).

tafferel (tăf'ẽr-ėl) [Dut. *tafereel*], *n.* The upper part of a ship's stern.

taffeta (tăf'è-tà) [Pers. *tâftan*, to twist], *n.* A light, thin, glossy silk fabric.

taffrail (tăf'rāl, -rál), *n.* The rail round a ship's stern.

tag (tăg) [Scand.], *n.* Any small appendage,

as a metal point at the end of a lace, a loop, a label, etc.; a well-worn quotation.

tail (1) (tāl) [A.-S. *tœgl*], *n.* The hindmost part of an animal extending beyond the body; a prolongation of or a pendant or appendage to anything; a retinue, a queue. *v.i.* To fall behind or drop (away or off) in a scattered line. **tailboard,** *n.* The board at the back of a cart, wagon, etc. **tail-end,** *n.* The fag-end. **tail-piece,** *n.* An ornamental design at the end of a chapter, etc.

tail (2) (tāl), *n.* Limitation of or limited ownership; an estate of inheritance limited to a person and the heirs of his body.

tailor (tā'lór) [O.F. *tailleor*], *n.* One who cuts out and makes men's outer clothes. *v.i.* To work as a tailor. **tailor-made,** *a.* Made by a tailor (of women's outer clothes). **tailoress,** *n.*

taint (tānt) [F. *teint*, stained], *n.* A trace of decay, disease, etc.; infection; a stain, blemish, disgrace.

take (tāk) [A.-S. *tacan*], *v.t.* (*past* **took**, tuk, *p.p.* **taken**) To lay hold of, to grasp, catch, arrest, gain possession of, win, etc.; to carry off, away, or with one, to conduct, withdraw, extort, etc.; to receive, procure, acquire, consume; to adopt, select, submit to; to ascertain by inquiry; to understand, consider, infer; to be infected with; to experience; to bear in a specified way; to perform (an action, etc.); to photograph. *v.i.* To derogate, detract; to have a desired effect; to come out well (in a photograph), to please, to be attracted or inclined (to), to betake oneself (to). *n.* That which is taken; amount taken at one catch or in one season. **take-off,** *v.i.* To parody, to mimic; (*Aer.*) to begin flight. **taking,** *a.* Pleasing, alluring. *n.* The act of one that takes; capture; state of agitation; (*pl.*) money taken; receipts.

talbot (tawl'bŏt) [?], *n.* A large variety of hound, formerly used for hunting.

talc (tălk) [Arab. *talq*], *n.* A fibrous, greasy magnesium silicate occurring in prisms and plates, used as a lubricator, etc. **talcky,** *a.*

tale (tāl) [A.-S. *talu*, story], *n.* An account, a story, true or fictitious; a total, a reckoning.

talent (tăl'ėnt) [Gr. *talanton*, balance], *n.* A weight and denomination of money in ancient Greece, Rome, Assyria, etc.; a particular aptitude or faculty; superior mental capacity; persons of talent. **talented,** *a.* Endowed with talents or ability.

talisman (tăl'iz-mán) [Arab. *tilsam*, Gr. *telesma*, payment], *n.* An amulet, a magical figure to which wonderful effects were ascribed.

talk (tawk) [M.E. *talken*], *v.i.* To utter words; to converse; to have the power of speech. *v.t.* To express in speech; to discuss; to speak (a specified language); to affect by talking. *n.* Chat; a subject of conversation; gossip. **talkative,** *a.* Given to talking. **talker,** *n.* **talking,** *a.* That talks; able to talk.

tall (tawl) [Celt.], *a.* Above the average height; having a specified height. **talliness,** *n.*

tallow (tăl'ō) [M.E. *talgh*], *n.* A substance composed of the harder fats, used for candles, soap, etc. **tallow-chandler,** *n.* One who makes or deals in candles. **tallowy,** *a.*

tally (tăl'i) [F. *taille*, notch], *n.* A stick in which notches are cut for keeping accounts; such a notch, a reckoning, an account; a counterpart, a duplicate (of); a tag for identification. *v.t.* To score as on a tally, to record. *v.i.* To correspond (with).

tally-ho (tăl'i-hō') [F. *taïaut*], *int.* and *n.* The huntsman's cry to hounds.

talon (tăl'ŏn) [F. heel], *n.* A claw, esp. of a bird of prey.

tamable (tā'măbl), *a.* Capable of being tamed. **tamabil'ity,** *n.*

tamale (tȧ-ma'li) [Sp.], *n.* A Mexican dish of meat and maize highly seasoned.

tamarind (tăm'ȧ-rind) [Arab. *tamr*, ripe date, *Hind*, India], *n.* A tropical tree; its pulpy leguminous fruit, used in cooling beverages.

tamarisk (tăm'ȧ-risk) [L.], *n.* An evergreen shrub with slender feathery branches.

tambour (tăm'bȯr) [F., drum], *n.* A drum; a circular frame for embroidery; a cylindrical stone, as part of a column. *v.* To embroider with or on a tambour.

tambourine (tăm-bȯ-rēn'), *n.* A small drum-like instrument, a hoop with parchment stretched across one head and loose jingles in the sides.

tame (tām) [A.-S. *tam*], *a.* Domesticated, not wild; tractable; subdued; dull; insipid. *v.t.* To make tame; to domesticate; to humble. **tamely,** *adv.* **tamer,** *n.*

Tamil (tăm'il) [native name], *n.* A language spoken in S. India and Ceylon.

tam-o'-shanter (tăm-ŏ-shăn'tèr) [Burns's poem *Tam o' Shanter*], *n.* A cap fitted closely round the brows but wide and full above.

tamper (tăm'pèr), *v.i.* To meddle (with); to alter documents, etc., illegitimately; to adulterate; to employ bribery.

tampion (tăm'pi-ȯn) [O.F.], *n.* A stopper for the mouth of a gun.

tan (tăn) [O.H.G. *tanna*, fir, oak], *n.* Bark bruised and broken and used for tanning hides; its yellowish-brown colour; bronzing of the complexion. *a.* Tan-coloured. *v.t.* To convert (hide) into leather; to brown by exposure to the sun; to subject (sails, artificial marble, etc.) to a hardening process; to flog. *v.i.* To become sunburned. **tan-yard,** *n.* A tannery. **tanner,** *n.* **tannery,** *n.* **tanning,** *n.* A flogging.

tandem (tăn'dém) [L., at length], *adv.* With two horses harnessed one behind the other. *n.* A vehicle with two horses so harnessed; a cycle for two riders one behind the other.

tang (1) (tăng) [M.E., sting], *n.* A strong taste or flavour, a twang; a distinctive quality.

tang (2) [Icel. *tangi*], *n.* A projecting piece,

as the shank of a chisel, etc., inserted into the haft. *v.t.* To furnish with a tang.

tang (3) [imit.], *v.i.* To make a ringing, twanging noise.

tangent (tăn'jĕnt) [L. *tangere*, to touch], *n.* A straight line meeting a curve without intersecting it (even if produced).

tangible (tăn'jibl), *a.* Perceptible by touch; definite, not visionary. **tangibil'ity,** *n.* **tangibly,** *adv.*

tangle (tăng'gĕl) [Scand.], *v.t.* To intertwine in a confused mass; to entangle, entrap; to complicate. *v.i.* To become knotted together or intertwined. *n.* A confused mass of threads, etc.; a state of confusion; various kinds of seaweed. **tangly,** *a.*

tango (tăng'gō) [Am. Sp.], *n.* A dance of a complicated kind for couples.

tank (tăngk) [Port, *tanque*], *n.* A large cistern for holding liquid, gas, etc.; a reservoir for water; the part of a loco-motive-tender containing water for the boiler; a heavily armoured motor-vehicle on wheels which run over endless chains, first used by the British in attacking at Flers, Sept. 1916. **tanker,** *n.* A tank-vessel, a steamer fitted with tanks for carrying oil.

tankard (tăng'kård) [M.Dut. *tanckaert*], *n.* A large metal drinking-vessel.

tanner (tăn'ér) [?], *n.* (*colloq.*) Sixpence.

tannic (tăn'ik), *a.* Pertaining to or derived from tan. **tannin,** *n.* Tannic acid, an astringent obtained from oak-bark, etc.

tansy (tăn'zi) [O.F. *tanasie*, Gr. *athanasia*, immortality], *n.* A yellow-flowered perennial herb with bitter, aromatic leaves.

tantalize (tăn'tȧ-līz) [Tantalus in Gr. mythology], *v.t.* To torment by holding out some desirable object and continually disappointing by keeping it out of reach.

tantamount (tăn'tȧ-mount) [A.-F. *tant amunter*, to amount to so much], *a.* Equivalent (to) in value or effect.

tantrum (tăn'trŭm) [?], *n.* A burst of ill-temper, a fit of passion.

Taoiseach (tē'shach) [Ir.], *n.* The Prime Minister of Eire.

tap (1) (tăp) [F. *taper*], *v.t.* To strike gently; to apply leather to the heel of (a shoe). *v.i.* To strike a gentle blow. *n.* A light or gentle blow, the sound of this.

tap (2) [A.-S. *tœppa*], *n.* A cock for drawing fluid through; a faucet; a bung for a cask, etc.; liquor of a particular brew or quality. *v.t.* To pierce (a cask, etc.); to let out or draw off (a liquid) thus; (*Surg.*) to draw (fluid) from a person's body; to intercept (a message). **tap-root,** *n.* The main root of a plant. **tapster,** *n.* One who serves liquor in a bar.

tape (tāp) [A.-S. *tœppe*], *n.* A narrow woven strip used for tying things together, in dressmaking, book-binding; at a winning-post, etc.; a tape-measure; a strip on which messages are recorded by a recording telegraph. **tape-measure,** *n.* A marked tape or strip of metal for measuring. **tape-worm,** *n.* A parasitic worm infesting the alimentary canal of vertebrates.

taper (tā′pér) [A.-S. *tapor*], *n.* A small
wax-candle; a feeble light; tapering
form. *v.i.* To become gradually smaller
towards one end. *v.t.* To make taper.

tapestry (tăp′és-tri) [F. *tapis*, a carpet], *n.*
A heavy textile fabric with designs
applied by stitches across the warp. *v.t.*
To hang with or as with tapestry.
tapestried, *a.*

tapioca (tăp-i-ō′kà) [Tupi-Guarani *tipioka*,
cassava-juice], *n.* A starchy, granular,
farinaceous food prepared from cassava.

tapir (tā′pir) [Tupi-Guarani *tapīra*], *n.* A
hoofed herbivorous mammal allied to
the rhinoceros, with a short, flexible
proboscis.

tapis (tà-pē , tăp′is) [F.], *n.* A table-
covering. **to be on the tapis:** To be
under consideration; to be rebuked by
an employer, etc.

tar (1) (tar) [A.-S. *teoru*], *n.* A thick,
dark, oily liquid produced by the dry
distillation of organic bodies and bituminous minerals. *v.t.* To cover with
tar. tarry (1), *a.*

tar (2), *n.* (*colloq.*) A sailor.

tarantella (tăr-àn-tel′à) [*Taranto*, S. Ital.
town], *n.* A rapid Neapolitan dance in
triplets for one couple; the music for this.
taran′tula, *n.* A large venomous spider
of S. Europe.

tardy (tar′di) [L. *tardus*], *a.* Slow, sluggish;
behindhand, dilatory; reluctant. tardily,
adv.

tare (1) (târ) [M.E.], *n.* The common
vetch.

tare (2) [Arab. *tarhah*, rejected], *n.* An
allowance for the weight of boxes, etc.,
in which goods are packed; the weight
of a vehicle without fuel, load, or equipment.

target (tar′gĕt) [dim. of A.-S. *targe*], *n.*
A mark to be fired at, a bull's eye; any
person or thing made the object of
attack, a butt; the aim, sum of money,
etc., to be reached by a combined effort;
a small round shield.

tariff (tăr′if) [Arab. *ta′rīf*, information], *n.*
A table of import or export duties; a duty
on any particular kind of goods; a law
imposing such; a table of charges.

tarn (tarn) [Icel. *tjörn*], *n.* A small
mountain lake.

tarnish (tar′nish) [F. *ternir*], *v.t.* To
diminish or destroy the lustre of; to
sully, to stain. *v.i.* To lose lustre. *n.*
Loss of lustre, a blemish.

tarpaulin (tar-paw′lin), *n.* A waterproofed
canvas-cloth; a sailor's tarred or oiled
hat.

tarpon (tar′pòn) [?], *n.* A large and powerful game-fish of the herring family.

tarradiddle (tăr′-à-didl) [?], *n.* A lie, a fib.

tarry (tăr′i) [M.E. *tarien*, A.-S. *tergan*, to
vex], *v.i.* To remain behind; to linger,
to delay.

tart (1) (tart) [A.-S. *teart*], *a.* Sharp to
the taste, acid; (*fig.*) biting, cutting.
tartly, *adv.* tartness, *n.*

tart (2) [O.F. *tarte*], *n.* A pie containing
fruit; a piece of pastry with jam, etc.
tartlet, *n.*

tart (3) *n.* [?]. A prostitute.

tartan (tar′tàn), *n.* A woollen fabric cross-
barred with stripes of various colours
the pattern, or a plaid, on this. *a.*
Consisting, made of, or like tartan.

tartar (1) (tar′tár) [Arab. *durd*, dregs], *n.*
Impure tartrate of potassium deposited
from wines; cream of tartar; calcium
phosphate deposited on the teeth. tar-
tareous (-târ′é-ús), tartaric (-tăr′ik), *a.*

Tartar (2) (tar′tár), Tatar (ta′tár) [Pers.],
a. Pertaining to Tartary or the races
comprising Turks, Cossacks, and Kirghis
Tartars. *n.* A native of Tartary or a
member of this group of races; (*fig.*) a
person of an intractable temper or more
than one's match.

Tartarus (tar′tà-rús), *n.* (*Gr. Myth.*) A
deep abyss below Hades where the
Titans were confined; the abode of the
wicked. Tartarean (-târ é-àn), *a.*

Tartuffe (tar′tuf) [character in Molière's
play], *n.* A hypocritical pretender.

tasimeter (tăs′i-mē-tèr) [Gr. *tasis*, stretch],
n. An electrical appliance for measuring
very small variations of pressure,
moisture, etc.

task (task) [O.F. *tasche*], *n.* A definite
amount of work imposed; work undertaken voluntarily. *v.t.* To impose a
task upon; to overtax. task force, *n.*
(*Nav.*) A temporary naval attack unit
organized for a specific action. task-
master, *n.* One who imposes a task.

tassel (tăs′ĕl) [O.F. *tasel*], *n.* A pendent
ornament composed of a tuft of threads,
cords, silk, etc.

taste (tāst) [O.F. *taster*], *v.t.* To try or
perceive the flavour of by taking into
the mouth; to eat a little of. *v.i.* To
partake (of); to have experience (of);
to have a flavour (of). *n.* Flavour; the
sense by which this is perceived; the
mental faculty of apprehending and
enjoying the beautiful and the sublime
or of appreciating degrees of artistic
excellence; manner, style, as directed
by this; a predilection (for). tastable,
a. tasteful, *a.* Having, characterized
by, or done with good taste. tasteless, *a.*
taster, *n.* One employed to test teas,
liquors, etc., by tasting. tasty, *a.* Savoury, toothsome. tastily, *adv.*

tat (tăt) [Scand.], *v.t.* To make by knotting.
v.i. To make tatting. tatting, *n.* Knotted
work or lace used for edging, etc.

tatter (tăt′ér) [Teut.], *n.* A rag; a hanging
shred. tatterdema′lion, *n.* A ragged
fellow.

tattle (tătl) [imit.], *v.i.* To chatter, gossip;
to tell tales. *n.* Idle talk. tattler, *n.*
One who tattles, a gossip.

tattoo (1) [tà-too′) [Dut. *taptoe*, signal for
closing tavern taps], *n.* The beat
of drum recalling soldiers to their
quarters.

tattoo (2) [Tahitian *tatan*], *v.t.* To mark
(the skin) by pricking and inserting
pigments. *n.* A mark or pattern so
produced.

taunt (tawnt) [?], *v.t.* To reproach sarcastically or contemptuously. *n.* A
bitter reproach.

taut (tawt) [M.E. *togt*], *a.* Tight, tense,
not slack; in good order, trim.

tauto- [Gr., *to auto*, the same], *comb. form.*

o

tautology (taw-tol'ŏ-jĭ), *n.* Repetition of the same thing in different words. **tautolog'ic**, -al, *a.*

tavern (tăv'ĕrn) [L. *taberna*], *n.* A public-house, an inn.

taw [?], *n.* A game at marbles.

tawdry (taw'drĭ) [*St. Audrey* (*Etheldrida*), whose fair was held on 17th Oct.], *a.* Showy without taste; gaudy. *n.* Tasteless finery. **tawdrily**, *adv.*

tawny (taw'nĭ), *a.* Brownish-yellow, tan-coloured. **tawniness**, *a.*

taws (tawz) [A.-S. *tawian*, to prepare], *n.* (*Sc.*) A leather strap with the end cut into strips, used for punishing.

tax (tăks) [L. *taxăre*, to tax], *n.* A compulsory contribution to meet the expenses of the public service; (*fig.*) a heavy demand, strain, etc. *v.t.* To impose a tax on; to charge (with an oversight, etc.); (*Law*) to fix amounts of (costs); **taxable**, *a.* **taxa'tion**, *n.*

taxi (tăk-sĭ), *n.* A motor-cab.

taxidermy (tăk'sĭ-dĕr-mĭ) [Gr. *taxis*, arrangement, DERM], *n.* The art of mounting the skins of animals so that they resemble the living forms. **taxidermist**, *n.*

taximeter (tăk'sĭ-mē-tèr) [F. *taximètre*], *n.* An instrument fitted in a cab for registering distances.

tea (tē) [Chin.], *n.* The dried and prepared leaves of a small evergreen shrub of the camellia family; the tea-plant; a decoction of tea-leaves for drinking; a light afternoon or evening meal at which tea is served. **tea-fight**, *n.* (*colloq.*) A tea party. **tea-garden**, *n.* A garden where refreshments are served to the public. **tea-gown**, *n.* A woman's loose gown. **tea-rose**, *n.* A rose with scent supposed to resemble tea.

teach (tēch) [A.-S. *tǣcan*], *v.t.* (*past and p.p.* taught, tawt) To instruct or train in; to impart information concerning (a subject), to give lessons in; to educate; to explain, show, make known. *v.i.* To perform the duties of a teacher; to give instruction. **teachable**, *a.* That may be taught (of a subject, etc.); apt to learn. **teacher**, *n.* **teaching**, *n.*

teak (tēk) [Malayalam *tekka*], *n.* A large E. Indian tree yielding a heavy durable timber; this timber.

teal (tēl) [M.E. *tele*], *n.* A small freshwater duck.

team (tēm) [A.-S. *tēam*], *n.* Two or more horses, oxen, etc., harnessed together; a number of persons working together, forming a side in a game, etc. **teamster**, *n.* One in charge of a team.

tear (1) (târ) [A.-S. *teran*], *v.t.* (*past* tore, tôr, *p.p.* torn, tôrn). To pull forcibly apart, to rend; to make (a rent, wound, etc.) thus. *v.i.* To pull violently (at); to part on being pulled; to rush or act with violence. *n.* A rent.

tear (2) (tēr) [A.-S. *tēar*], *n.* A drop of the saline liquid moistening the eyes or flowing in strong emotion, etc. **teardrop**, *n.* **tearful**, *a.* **tearless**, *a.*

tease (tēz) [A.-S. *tæsan*, to pluck], *v.t.* To separate the fibres of; to comb or card (wool or flax); to annoy, irritate, vex;

to importune (to do something). *n.* One who teases or irritates.

teasel (tēzl), *n.* A plant with large burs covered with stiff, hooked awns, used for raising a nap on cloth; a machine for this purpose.

teat (tēt) [A.-S. *tit*], *n.* The nipple of the female breast through which milk is drawn; a projection or appliance resembling this.

technic (tek'nik) [Gr. *technē*, art], *a.* Technical. *n.* Technique. **technical**, *a.* Pertaining to the mechanical arts or to any particular art, science, business, etc. **technical'ity**, *n.* A technical term, expression, etc. **technique** (tek-nēk'), *n.* Mode of artistic performance; mechanical skill in art.

technician (tek-nish'àn), *n.* One skilled in the technical side of a subject.

technology (tek-nol'ŏ-jĭ), *n.* The science of the industrial arts.

tectonics (tek-ton'iks) [Gr. *tekton*, carpenter], *n.pl.* The art of constructing buildings, vessels, etc., for use and beauty.

ted (ted) [A.-S.], *v.t.* To turn over and spread (hay) so as to expose to the sun and air. **tedder**, *n.* An implement that does this.

teddy-bear (ted'ĭ bâr) [Pres. Theodore (Teddy) Roosevelt (1858–1919)], *n.* A stuffed toy bear.

tedious (tē'di-ùs) [L. *tædium*], *a.* Tiresome, monotonous, fatiguing. **tedium**, *n.*

tee (tē) [?], *n.* A mark for quoits, curling-stones, etc.; (*Golf*) a small eminence from which the ball is played at the commencement of each hole. *v.t.* To put the ball on this.

teem (1) (tēm) [A.-S. *tyman*], *v.* To bring forth (offspring); to be prolific; to overflow.

teem (2) (tēm) [Icel. *tōmr*, empty], *v.t.* To pour out (esp. molten metal); to empty. *v.i.* To pour (down) as rain, etc.

-teen (A.-S. *-tȳne, tien*, TEN], *suf.* Denoting the addition of ten (in numbers 13–19).

teens (tēnz), *n.pl.* The years of one's age from 13 to 19. **teen-ager** (tēn'āj'ér), *n.* A girl in her teens.

-teenth, *suf.* Forming ordinal numbers from the cardinals 13–19.

teethe (tēth), *v.i.* To cut or develop teeth. **teething**, *n.*

teetotal (tē-tō'tàl), *a.* Pertaining to, or advocating total abstinence from intoxicants. **teetotalism**, *n.* **teetotaller**, *n.*

teetotum (tē-tō'tùm), *n.* A spinning-top used in a game of chance.

tegument (teg'ū-mènt) [L. *tegere*, to cover], *n.* A protective covering or membrane in animals. **tegumen'tal**, **tegumen'tary**, *a.*

tele- (Gr. *tēle*, far off], *comb. form.*

telegram (tel'ē-grăm), *n.* A communication sent by telegraph.

telegraph (tel'ē-grăf), *n.* An apparatus for transmitting messages to a distance, esp. by electricity; a board on which the names of horses in a race, cricket-scores, etc., are displayed. *v.t.* To transmit (a message) by telegraph; to signal in any way. *v.i.* To send a message by telegraph; to signal (to, etc). **teleg'raph-**

ist, *n.* One who works a telegraph.
telegraph'ic, *a.* teleg'raphy, *n.*

teleology (tel-ê-ol'ô-ji) [Gr. *telos teleos,*
end], *n.* The doctrine of final causes.
teleolog'ic, *a.*

telepathy (tê-lep'à-thi), *n.* Communictaion
between minds at a distance, thought-
transference, mind-reading. telepath'ic,
a. telep'athist, *n.*

telephone (tel'ê-fôn), *n.* An instrument for
transmitting sounds (esp. speech) to
distances by electrical agency. telephonic
(fon'ik), *a.* teleph'onist, *n.* teleph'ony, *n.*

telephotography, *n.* Photographing objects
beyond the limits of ordinary vision.

telephoto lens, *n.* A lens for telephotography.

teleprinter, *n.* A telegraphic apparatus
with keyboard transmitter and type-
printing receiver whereby messages are
received in printed form.

telescope (tel'ê-skôp), *n.* An optical instrument for increasing the apparent size of
distant objects. *v.t.* To drive or force
(sections, trains, etc.) into each other,
like the sections of a telescope. tele-
scopic (-skop'ik), *a.*

televise (tel'-e-viz), *v.t.* To transmit by
television.

television, *n.* The transmission and reception of moving visual images by radio.

tell (tel) [A.-S. *tellan*], *v.t.* (*past and p.p.*
told, tôld) To relate, recount; to express
in words, to inform; to assure; to bid,
direct; to distinguish, ascertain. *v.i.*
To give information or an account (of).
teller, *n.* One who tells; one who numbers, esp. one appointed to count votes
in the House of Commons; a bank
official who receives or pays out money.
telling, *a.* Having marked effect. tell-
tale, *a.* Given to conveying information.
n. One who tells tales, esp. about the
private affairs of others.

tellural (tê-lûr'ál) [L. *tellus-lûris,* the earth],
a. Pertaining to the earth. tellurian, *n.*
An inhabitant of the earth. telluric, *a.*

temerarious (tem-ê-râr'i-ûs) [L. *temere,*
rashly], *a.* Reckless, headstrong; careless, done at random. temerity (tê-
mer'i-ti), *n.*

temper (tem'pêr) [L. *tempus,* time, season],
v.t. To mix in due proportion; to harden
(steel, etc.) by heating and cooling; to
modify, tone down, mitigate. *n.* Disposition of mind; composure, self-
command; irritation, passion; state of a
metal as regards hardness and elasticity;
condition or consistency (of a plastic
mixture).

temperament (tem'pêr-à-ment), *n.* Individual character, natural disposition.
temperamen'tal, *a.*

temperance (tem'pêr-àns), *n.* Moderation,
self-restraint, esp. in the indulgence of
the appetites; moderation in the use of
intoxicants; total abstinence.

temperate (tem'pêr-àt) , *a.* Self-restrained;
abstemious; mild (of climate). tem-
perately, *adv.*

temperature (tem'pêr-à-tyùr), *n.* Degree
of sensible heat or cold, esp. as registered
by the thermometer.

tempest (tem'pêst) [L. *tempestas,* weather],
n. A violent storm, esp. with heavy
rain, hail, or snow; (*fig.*) violent tumult.
tempes'tuous, *a.*

Templar (tem'plàr), *n.* A member of a
religious and military order, founded in
the 12th cent., protecting pilgrims to
the Holy Land; a lawyer or student
having chambers in the Temple, London.

temple (1) (temp'êl) [L. *templum*], *n.* An
edifice dedicated to the service of some
deity; the ancient seat of Jewish worship at Jerusalem; a place of public
Christian worship.

temple (2) [L. *tempus,* time], *n.* The flat
portion of the head between forehead
and ear. temporal *a.*

templet (tem'plêt) [L. *templum,* a small
timber], *n.* A pattern used as a guide in
shaping, turning, or drilling.

tempo (tem'pô) [It.], *n.* (*Mus.*) Quickness
or rate of movement, time.

temporal (tem'pô-rál), *a.* Pertaining to
this life; secular. temporal'ity, *n.* Tem-
poralness; (*pl.*) the revenues of a religious
corporation or an ecclesiastic.

temporary (tem'pô-rà-ri), *a.* Lasting or
intended only for a time or a special
occasion. temporarily, *adv.* temporize,
vi. To pursue a procrastinating or time-
serving policy; to yield to the requirements of the occasion; to trim.

tempt (tempt) [L. *tenêre,* to hold], *v.t.*
To incite or entice (to); to attract,
allure, invite. temptation, *n.* tempter, *n.*

ten (ten) [A.-S. *tiên, tyn*], *n.* The sum of
one and nine; 10, x. *a.* One more than
nine. tenfold, *a.* and *adv.* tenpenny, *a.*
Priced or sold at tenpence. tenth, *a.* and
n. tenthly, *adv.*

tenable (ten'âbl) [L. *tenêre,* to hold], *a.*
Capable of being held against attack.
tenabil'ity, *n.*

tenacious (tê-nâ'shùs), *a.* Holding fast;
obstinate, unyielding; sticky; tough. ten-
acity (tên-ás'i-ti), *n.*

tenant (ten'ánt), *n.* A person holding a
land or tenement from a landlord. *v.t.* To
hold as tenant; to occupy. tenancy, *n.* The
holding of lands, etc.; the period of such
holding. tenantry, *n.* (*collect.*) Tenants.

tench (tench) [L. *tinca*], *n.* A freshwater
fish of the carp family.

tend (1) (tend) [L. *tendere,* to stretch], *v.i.*
To move or hold a course (in a certain
direction, etc.); to have a bent or inclination, to conduce (to). tendency, *n.* Bent,
drift, disposition.

tend (2), *v.t.* To watch, look after, take
charge of. *v.i.* To attend, to wait (upon).

tender (1) (ten'dêr), *n.* One who tends; a
car attached to a locomotive carrying
the supply of fuel, etc.; a vessel attending
a larger one, to supply provisions, carry
despatches, etc.

tender (2), *v.t.* To present for acceptance,
offer in payment. *v.i.* To make a
tender. *n.* An offer for acceptance; an
offer to do certain work, or supply
certain articles, at a certain rate.

tender (3) [L. *tener*], *a.* Easily impressed,
etc., delicate, fragile, frail; sensitive,
sympathetic; fond; considerate (of).
tenderness, *n.*

tendon (ten'dôn) [L. *tendere,* to stretch], *n.*

One of the strong cords forming the termination or connexion of a muscle.

tendril (ten'dril) [?], *n.* A leafless organ by which a plant clings for support.

tenement (ten'è-mènt) [O.F., L. *tenēre*, to hold], *n.* An apartment used by one family; a dwelling-house; permanent property that may be held, as lands, houses, etc. **tenement-house,** *n.* A house let out in tenements.

tenet (ten'èt, tē'net) [L., he holds], *n.* An opinion, doctrine, etc., held by a person or school.

tennis (ten'is) [O.F. *tenez*, hold], *n.* A game played by striking a ball to and fro with rackets over a net in a walled court; lawn-tennis.

tenon (ten'òn) [F.], *n.* The projecting end of a piece of timber fitted for insertion into a mortise, etc.

tenor (ten'òr) [L., a holding on], *n.* A settled course or direction; general drift (of thought, etc.); (*Law*) the exact purport, an exact copy; the highest of male chest voices between baritone and alto; one with a tenor voice. *a.* Pertaining to or adapted for the tenor part.

tense (1) (tens) [L. *tempus*, time], *n.* (*Gram.*) A form taken by a verb to indicate the time, and also the continuance or completedness, of an action.

tense (2) [L. *tensus*, stretched], *a.* Stretched tight, strained. **tensely,** *adv.* **ten'sile,** *a.* Pertaining to tension; capable of extension. **tension** (ten'shùn), *n.* The act of stretching, state of being stretched; strain, effort; mental stress or excitement; the expansive force of a gas or vapour. **tensity,** *n.*

tent (tent) [L. *tentus*], *n.* A portable shelter consisting of flexible material stretched over a pole or poles. *v.t.* To lodge in a tent. *v.i.* To encamp in a tent. **tent-peg,** *n.* A peg fixed in the ground for fastening down the ropes stretching a tent.

tentacle (ten'tàkl), *n.* A long slender feeler or arm, as of a cuttle-fish. **tentac'ular,** *a.*

tentative (ten'tà-tiv), *a.* Consisting or done as a trial, experimental. *n.* An experiment, a conjecture. **tentatively,** *adv.*

tenter (ten'tèr) [L. *tendere*, to stretch], *n.* A frame or machine for stretching cloth; a tenter-hook. **tenter-hook,** *n.* One of a set of hooks used in stretching cloth on the tenter. **on tenter-hooks:** In a state of suspense.

tenuity (tė-nū'i-ti) [L. *tenuis*, thin], *n.* Thinness; rarity; meagreness. **tenuous,** *a.* Thin, slender, minute; rarefied, overrefined.

tenure (ten'ūr), *n.* Act, manner, or right of holding property; period of holding.

tepid (tep'id) [L. *tepēre*, to be warm], *a.* Moderately warm; lukewarm. **tepid'ity,** *n.*

teratology (ter-à-tol'ō-ji) [Gr. *teras*, monster], *n.* The branch of biology dealing with monsters and malformations.

tercentenary (tẽr-sèn-tē'nà-ri) [L. *ter*, thrice], *a.* Comprising 300 years. *n.* A 300th anniversary.

terebinth (ter'è-binth) [Gr. *terebinthos*], *n.* The turpentine-tree; its resin.

teredo (tèr-ē'dō) [Gr. *teirein*, to bore], *n.* A mollusc that bores into submerged timber, the ship-worm.

tergiversate (tẽr'ji-vèr-sāt) [L. *tergum*, back, *versāri*, to turn], *v.i.* To practise evasions, to equivocate; to change sides. **tergiversa'tion,** *n.*

term (tẽrm) [L. *terminus*], *n.* A limit, a boundary; a limited period; a period, esp. during which instruction is regularly given or courts are in session; an appointed date; a word having a definite meaning; (*pl.*) expressions used; (*pl.*) conditions, price, rate of payment; relative position; one of the parts of a mathematical expression connected by the plus or minus sign. *v.t.* To designate, denominate.

termagant (tẽr'mà-gànt) [M.E. *Tervagant*, name of a supposed Saracen deity], *n.* A shrewish, abusive woman. *a.* Violent, boisterous, shrewish.

terminal (tẽr'mi-nàl), *a.* Pertaining to or forming a boundary or terminus. *n.* That which terminates; a limit; an end, esp. one of the free ends of an electrical conductor. **terminally,** *adv.*

terminate (tẽr'mi-nàt) [L. *terminātus*, ended], *v.t.* To bound; to form the end of; to put an end to. *v.i.* To stop, to end (in, etc.). *a.* Limited, bounded. **terminable,** *a.* Capable of being terminated; having a given term or period. **termina'tion,** *n.*

terminology (tẽr-mi-nol'ō-ji), *n.* The science of the correct use of terms; (*collect.*) the terms used in any art, science, etc.

terminus (tẽr'mi-nùs), *n.* (*pl.* -ni) A boundary, limit; the station at the end of a railway or important branch.

termite (tẽr'mīt) [L. *termes*, wood-worm], *n.* A white ant.

tern (tẽrn) [Scand.], *n.* A gull-like sea-bird with narrow, sharp-pointed wings.

Terpsichorean (tẽrp-si-kò-rē'àn) [Gr. *Terpsichorē*, Muse of dancing], *a.* Pertaining to dancing.

terra (ter'à) [L.], *n.* Earth. **terra-cotta,** *n.* A hard, unglazed pottery; a statue or figure in this; its brownish-orange colour. **terra firma:** Dry land.

terrace (ter'às) [It. *terrazza*], *n.* A raised level space or bank; a row of houses; (*Geol.*) an ancient shore-line. *v.t.* To form into or furnish with terraces.

terrain (te-rān'), *n.* A region, an extent of land of a definite geological character; a tract of country which is the scene of military operations.

terrapin (ter'à-pin) [Algonkin], *n.* A N. American freshwater tortoise, highly esteemed for food.

terraqueous (ter-ā'kwē-ùs), *a.* Consisting of land and water, as the globe.

terrestrial (tė-res'tri-àl) [L. *terra*, earth], *a.* Pertaining to or existing on the earth; pertaining to this world; consisting of land; living on the ground, not aquatic, arboreal, etc.

terrible (ter'ibl) [L. *terribilis*], *a.* Causing terror; awful, appalling, shocking; (*colloq.*) excessive. **terribly,** *adv.*

terrier (1) (ter'i-ẽr), *n.* A small active dog with an instinct for digging.

terrier (2) [F.], *n.* A book or roll in which lands are described by ownership, site, boundaries, acreage, etc.

terrific (tẽ-rif'ik) [L. *terrēre*, to frighten], *a.* Causing terror; frightful. **ter'rify**, *v.t.* To strike with terror, to frighten.

territorial (ter-i-tôr'i-ȧl), *a.* Pertaining to territory; of or pertaining to the Territorial Army; limited to a given district. *n.* A member of the Territorial Army. Territorial Army: A voluntary military force for British home defence.

territory (ter'i-tôr-i), *n.* The extent of land within the jurisdiction of a particular sovereign or state; a large tract of land; (*U.S.*) a division of the country not yet granted full State rights.

terror (ter'ôr), *n.* Extreme fear; an object of fear; (*colloq.*) an exasperating nuisance. **terrorist**, *n.* One who rules or advocates rule by intimidation. **terrorism**, *n.* **terrorize**, *v.t.*

terse (tẽrs) [L. *tersus*, wiped], *a.* Concise, pithy.

tertian (tẽr'shȧn) [L. *tertius*, third], *a.* Occurring or recurring every third day, esp. of a fever or ague, the paroxysms of which recur thus.

tertiary (tẽr'shȧ-ri), *a.* Of the third order, rank, or formation.

tessellated (tes-ȇ-lā'tĕd) [L. *tessellātus*], *a.* Composed of chequered squares, inlaid. **tessella'tion**, *n.*

test (test) [L. *testum*], *n.* A critical trial or examination; a means of trial; judgment, discrimination; a vessel used in refining gold and silver. *v.t.* To put to the test, to prove by experiment; to try severely.

testament (tes'tȧ-mĕnt) [L. *testāri*, to testify], *n.* A writing by which a person disposes of his property after death, a will; one of the two main divisions of the Scriptures; (*colloq.*) a copy of the New Testament. **testamen'tary**, *a.*

testate (tes'tȧt , *a.* Having made and left a will. **testa'tor**, **testatrix**, *n.*

tester (tes'tẽr [L. *testa*, head], *n.* A canopy, esp. over a four-post bedstead; a shilling of Henry VIII; (*colloq.*) a sixpence.

testicle (tes'tikl) [L. *testiculus*], *n.* Each of two glands which secrete the seminal fluid in males.

testify (tes'ti-fī) [L. *testis*, witness], *v.i.* To bear witness; to give evidence. *v.t.* To attest; to affirm or declare; to serve as proof of.

testimonial (tes-ti-mō'ni-ȧl), *n.* A certificate of character, qualifications, etc.; a gift as a token of esteem and acknowledgement of services, etc.

testimony (tes'ti-mō-ni) [L. *testis*, witness], *n.* A solemn declaration or statement; evidence, proof.

testudinal (tes-tūd'i-nȧl) [L. *testūd-o*, *-inis* tortoise], *a.* Pertaining to the tortoise.

testy (tes'ti) [A.-F. *testif*], *a.* Irritable, peevish, petulant. **testily**, *adv.*

tetanus (tet'ȧ-nŭs) [L., from Gr. *tetanos*, from *teinein*, to stretch], *n.* A disease marked by spasms with rigidity, as in lock-jaw.

tetchy (tech'i) [?], *a.* Fretful, touchy.

tête-à-tête (tāt'a-tāt') [F., head to head], *a.* Private, confidential. *adv.* In close confabulation. *n.* A private interview.

tether (teth'ẽr) [M.E. *tedir*], *n.* A halter preventing a grazing animal from moving too far; (*fig.*) scope. *v.t.* To confine with a tether.

tetra- [Gr., from *tettares*, four], *comb. form.* **tetrachord** (tet'ra-kôrd), *n.* A scale series of half an octave, esp. as used in ancient music.

tetragon (tet'ra-gòn) [Gr. *tetragōnon*], *n.* A plane figure having four angles. **tetrahedron** (-hē'dròn) [Gr. *hedra*, base], *n.* A solid figure bounded by four plane, esp. equilateral, triangular faces. **tetrahedral**, *a.* tetram'eter, *n.* A verse consisting of four measures.

tetrarch (tet'rark) [Gr. *archein*, to rule], *n.* A governor of the fourth part of a province under the Roman empire; a tributary prince. **tetrarchate**, **tetrarchy**, *n.*

Teuton (tū'tòn) [L. *Teutoni*, *Teutonēs*], *n.* One of an ancient German tribe dwelling near the Elbe; a member of any Teutonic race. **Teuton'ic**, *a.* Of the German peoples, including Scandinavians, Anglo-Saxons and Germans.

text (tekst) [L. *textus*, style], *n.* The original words of an author; a passage of Scripture, esp. as the theme of a discourse; a topic; text-hand. **text-book**, *n.* A standard book for a particular branch of study. **text-hand**, *n.* Large hand-writing.

textile (tek'stil, -stīl) [L. *texere*, to weave], *a.* Woven; suitable for or pertaining to weaving. *n.* A woven fabric. **textor'ial**, *a.* Pertaining to weaving.

textual (tek'stū-ȧl), *a.* Pertaining to or contained in the text. **textually**, *adv.*

texture (teks'chŭr), *n.* The arrangement of threads in a woven fabric; the disposition of the constituent parts of any structure or material.

-th, *suf.* Forming abstract names, as *filth*, *wealth*; forming ordinal numbers, as *fifth*, *fiftieth*.

thaler (ta'lẽr), *n.* A German silver coin nominally worth about 3s.

than (*th*ȧn, *th*ȧn) [A.-S.], *conj.* Used after adjectives and adverbs expressing comparison, such as *better*, *worse*, etc., to introduce the second member of a comparison.

thanat-, **thanato-** [Gr. *thanatos*, death], *comb. form.* **thanatism** (thȧn'ȧ-tizm), *n.* The doctrine of annihilation at death.

thane (thān) [A.-S. *thegen*], *n.* (*A.-S. Hist.*) A freeman holding land by military service.

thank (thȧngk) [A.-S. *thanc*, thought, grace], *n.* (*now pl.*) An expression of gratitude; a formula of acknowledgment. *v.t.* To express gratitude; to make acknowledgment to for a gift, etc. **thank-offering**, *n.* An offering made as an expression of gratitude. **thankful**, *a.* **thankfulness**, *n.* **thankless**, *a.* **thanksgiving**, *n.* Act of returning thanks or expressing gratitude; a form of words expressive of this; a thank-offering.

that (*thăt*, *thət*) [A.-S. *thæt*], *a.* (*pl.* those, *thōz*). The person or thing specifically designated or implied; (correlated with *this*) the less obvious of two things; such (usu. followed by *as*). *pron.* The person or thing specifically designated or implied; who or which. *adv.* In such a manner, to such a degree. *conj.* Introducing a clause stating a fact or supposition; so that, in order that; implying result, consequence, etc.; because, since.

thatch (*thăch*) [A.-S. *thæc*], *n.* A roof-covering of straw, rushes, etc. *v.t.* To cover with this. **thatcher**, *n.*

thaumaturge (*thaw'mȧ-tẽrj*) [Gr. *thauma*, *-atos*, wonder, *-ergos*, working], *n.* A worker of miracles, a magician or conjurer. **thaumatur'gic**, *a.* **thaumaturgy**, *n.*

thaw (*thaw*) [A.-S. *thāwian*], *v.i.* To become liquid (of ice, snow, etc.); to become so warm as to melt ice, etc. (of weather); (*fig.*) to unbend, to become genial *v.i.* To melt; (*fig.*) to infuse geniality into. *n.* Act of thawing or state of being thawed; warm weather that thaws.

the (*thē*, *thĕ*) [A.-S.], *a.* Applied to a person or thing or persons or things mentioned or definitely understood, and to a singular noun to denote a species; prefixed to adjectives used absolutely, giving them the force of a substantive; before nouns expressing a unit to give distributive force (as '4*d.* the pint'); emphatically (*thē*) to express the chief of several (as '*the* Duke of Wellington'). *adv.* Used before adjectives and adverbs in the comparative degree, to that extent, by so much.

theatre (*thē'ȧ-tẽr*) [Gr. *theatron*], *n.* A play-house; a hall for lectures, demonstrations, etc.; the room in a hospital used for operations; (*fig.*) the drama, the stage; the scene of an action, etc. **theat'rical**, *a.* theatricals, *n.pl.* Dramatic performances, esp. private.

theft (*theft*) [A.-S. *thiefth*], *n.* Act of thieving or stealing; that which is stolen.

theism (*thē'izm*) [Gr. *theos*, god], *n.* Belief in a righteous God supernaturally revealed, as opp. to Deism. **theist**, *n.* **theis'tic**, *a.*

theme (*thēm*) [Gr. *thema*], *n.* A subject on which a person writes or speaks; a short essay; (*Mus.*) a melodic subject usu. developed with variations. **thematic** (*thē-măt'-ik*), *a.*

themselves (*thĕm-selvz'*), *pron.* The emphatic and reflexive form of the third plural personal pronoun.

then (*then*) [A.-S. *thanne, thonne, thœnne*], *adv.* At that time; soon after, next; at another time. *conj.* Therefore; this being so, accordingly. *a.* Of or existing at that time.

thence (*thens*) [M.E. *thennes*], *adv.* From that place, source, or time; for that reason. **thenceforth, thenceforward**, *adv.* From that time onward.

theo- [Gr. *theos*, god], *comb. form.* **theocracy** (*thē-ok'rȧ-si*) [Gr. *theokratia*], *n.* Government by the immediate direction of God or through a sacerdotal class; a State so governed.

theodolite (*thē-od'ō-līt*) [?], *n.* A portable surveying-instrument for measuring angles.

theology (*thē-ol'ō-ji*), *n.* The science of God, His relations to the universe, etc.; the science of religion, esp. Christianity. **theologian** (*-lō'ji-ăn*), **theological** (*-loj'i-kăl*), *a.* **theol'ogize**, *v.t.*

theorem (*thē'-ō-rém*) [Gr. *theōrein*, to behold], *n.* A proposition to be proved; a principle to be demonstrated by reasoning; a rule expressed by symbols.

theoretic, -al (*thē-ō-ret'ik*, *-ăl*), *a.* Pertaining to or founded on theory, not practical, speculative. **theoretically**, *adv.* **theoretics**, *n.* The speculative parts of a science. **theoretician** (*-tish'ăn*), *n.*

theory (*thē'ō-ri*), *n.* Supposition or generalization explaining something; mere hypothesis; speculation, abstract knowledge; an exposition of the general principles of a science, etc. **theorist**, *n.* One given to forming theories. **theorize**, *v.i.* **theoriza'tion**, *n.*

theosophy (*thē-os'ō-fi*) [Gr. *sophos*, wise], *n.* A form of speculation, mysticism, or philosophy aiming at the knowledge of God by means of intuition, contemplation, or direct communion. **theos'ophist, theos'ophism**, *n.*

therapeutic (*ther'ȧ-pū'tik*) [Gr. *therapeuein*, to wait on (also to heal) from *theraps*, servant], *a.* Pertaining to the healing art; curative. *n.pl.* The branch of medical science dealing with the treatment of disease. **therapy**, *n.* **Therapeutics**.

there (*thâr*, *thèr*) [A.-S. *thær, thĕr*], *adv.* In or at that place, point, or stage; to that place, thither, frequently used before the verb in interrogations, negative sentences, etc. *n.* That place. *int.* Expressing direction, confirmation, triumph, alarm, etc. thereabout', -bouts', *adv.* Near that place, degree, etc. **thereaf'ter**, *adv.* After that; according to that. **thereat'**, *adv.* At that place; thereupon; on that account. **thereby**, *adv.* In consequence of that; thereabouts. **therefore'**, *adv.* For that reason, consequently. **therefrom**, *adv.* From this or that time, place, etc.

therein', *adv.* In that or this time, place, respect, etc. **thereof** (*-ov'*), *adv.* Of that or it. **thereon'**, *adv.* On that or it. **thereto** (*-too'*), *adv.* To that or this; besides, over and above. **thereupon'**, *adv.* In consequence of that; immediately after that. **therewith** (*-with'*), *adv.* With that; thereupon. **therewithal** (*-wi-thawl'*), *adv.* With all this, besides.

therm (*thẽrm*) [Gr. *thermē*, heat], *n.* The unit of heat, being the quantity of heat required to raise 1 lb. of water from 60° F. to 61° F. The Mean British Thermal Unit is $\frac{1}{180}$ part of the quantity of heat required to raise the temperature of 1 lb. of water from 32° F. to 212° F. **thermal**, *a.* Pertaining to heat.

thermionics (*ther-mi-on'iks*), *n.pl.* (*Phys.*) The science dealing with the emission of electrons from hot bodies. **thermionic valve**, *n.* (*Wire.*) A vacuum tube in which wireless waves are converted into vibrations audible in a wireless set.

thermo- [Gr. *thermos*, warm], *comb. form.*

thermometer (thẽr-mom'ẽ-tẽr), *n.* An instrument for measuring temperature. **thermomet'ric, -al,** *a.*

thesis (thē'sis) [Gr.], *n.* (*pl.* **theses, -sēz**) A proposition advanced or maintained; a dissertation submitted by a candidate for a degree.

Thespian (thes'pi-án), *a.* Pertaining to Thespis, traditional Greek dramatic poet; relating to tragedy or the drama. *n.* An actor.

thew (thū) [A.-S *thēaw*, habit], *n.* (*usu.* in *pl.*) Muscles, sinews; strength. **thewed,** *a.*

they (thā) [A.-S. *thā*], *pron.* (*obj.* **them,** *poss.* **their,** *absol.* **theirs**) The plural of the third personal pronoun (*he, she,* or *it*).

thick (thik) [A.-S. *thicce*], *a.* Having extent or depth from one surface to the opposite; set or planted closely, crowded together, abounding (with), following in quick succession; dense, turbid, cloudy, foggy; indistinct (of articulation). **thickhead,** *n.* A blockhead. **thick-headed,** *a.* **thick-set,** *a.* Planted or growing close together; solidly built. **thick-skinned,** *a.* Not sensible to taunts, reproaches, etc. **thicken,** *v.* **thicket** [A.-S. *thiccet*], *n.* A thick growth of small trees, bushes, etc. **thickness,** *n.* State of being thick; extent from upper surface to lower, the dimension that is neither length nor breadth.

thief (thēf) [A.-S. *thēof*], *n.* (*pl.* **thieves**) One who steals, esp. without violence. **thieve** (A.-S. *gethēofian*), *v.i.* To practise theft; to be a thief. *v.t.* To take by theft. **thievery, thievishness,** *n.* thievish. *a.*

thigh (thī) [A.-S. *thēoh*], *n.* The thick, fleshy portion of the leg between the hip and knee.

thimble (thimbl) [A.-S. *thȳmel*, thumbstall], *n.* A metal cap worn to protect the finger in sewing; a ferrule. **thimblerig,** *n.* Sleight-of-hand trick with a pellet and three thimbles.

thin (thin) [A.-S. *thynne*], *a.* Of little thickness, slender; not dense; scanty, meagre; lean, not plump; easily seen through. *adv.* Thinly. *v.t.* To make thin or less crowded. *v.i.* To become thin or thinner; to waste away. **thin-skinned,** *a.* Sensitive, easily offended. **thinly,** *adv.* **thinnish,** *a.*

thing (thing) [A.-S.], *n.* Any object or thought; an inanimate object as dist. from a living being; an affair, circumstance, etc.; a person regarded with commiseration; (*pl.*) clothes, belongings. **the thing:** The conventional thing (to do, etc.).

think (thingk) [A.-S. *thencan*], *v.t.* (*past and p.p.* **thought,** thawt) To examine in the mind, to reflect, to ponder (over, etc.); to consider, be of opinion, to intend. *v.i.* To exercise the mind, to reason; to meditate, cogitate. **thinkable,** *a.* **thinker,** *n.* **thinking,** *a.* and *n.*

third (thẽrd) [A.-S. *thridda*], *a.* Coming next after the second. *n.* One of three equal parts (of anything); the sixtieth

part of a second of time or angular measurement; (*Mus.*) an interval between a tone and the next but one on the regular scale. **third-class, -rate,** *a.* Of the class coming next to the second; inferior. **thirdly,** *adv.*

thirst (thẽrst) [A.-S. *thurst*], *n.* Uneasiness or suffering caused by want of drink; desire for drink; (*fig.*) eager longing. *v.i.* To feel thirst (for or after). **thirsty,** *a.*

thirteen (thir-tēn') [A.-S. *thrēotēnc*], *a.* Consisting of one more than twelve. *n.* Ten and three; 13, xiii. **thirteenth,** *a.* and *n.*

thirty (thẽr'ti) [A.-S. *thritig, thrittig*], *a.* Consisting of three times ten. *n.* Thrice ten; 30, xxx. **thirtieth,** *a.* and *n.* Tenth after the twentieth.

this (*this*) [A.-S. *thes*], *a.* or *pron.* (*pl.* **these,** *thēz*) Used to denote the person or thing that is present or near or already mentioned, implied, or familiar.

thistle (thisl) [A.-S. *thistel*], *n.* A plant of the aster family with prickly stems, etc.; the Scottish national emblem.

thither (*thith'*ẽr) [A.-S. *thider*], *adv.* To that place; to that end, point, or result.

thole (thōl) [A.-S. *thol*], *n.* A pin in the gunwale of a boat serving as fulcrum for the oar, also called **thole pin.**

thong (thong) [A.-S. *thwang*], *n.* A strip of leather used as a whip-lash, reins, etc.

thorax (thōr'āks) [Gr.], *n.* (*pl.* **thoraces,** thō-rā'sēz) The part of the trunk between the neck and the abdomen; the middle division of the body of insects. **thoracic** (-răs'ik), *a.*

thorn (thôrn) [A.-S.], *n.* A spine, a prickle; a thorny shrub or tree; (*fig.*) an annoyance. **thornback,** *n.* The British skate (fish). **thorn-bush,** *n.* **thorny,** *a.*

thorough (thûr'ō), *a.* Complete, perfect, not superficial. **thoroughbred,** *a.* Of pure breed; mettlesome. *n.* A thoroughbred animal, esp. a horse. **thoroughfare,** *n.* An unobstructed road or street. **thoroughly,** *adv.* **thoroughness,** *n.*

thorp, thorpe (thôrp) [A.-S.], *n.* A village, a hamlet (esp. in place-names).

thou (*thou*) [A.-S. *thū*], *pron.* (obj. **thee,** *thē*) The second personal pronoun singular, denoting the person spoken to.

though (thō) [M.E. *thogh*, A.-S. *thēah, thēh, thāh*], *conj.* Notwithstanding that; even if; supposing that; (*ellipt.*) and yet; however.

thought (thawt) [A.-S. *thōt*], *n.* Act or process of thinking; reflection, meditation; solicitude; the faculty of thinking or reasoning; that which is thought; an idea, a reflection, a conclusion; (*pl.*) one's views, ideas, opinions, etc. **thought-reader** *n.* One who perceives by telepathy what is passing in another person's mind. **thought-reading,** *n.* **thoughtful,** *n.* **thoughtfully,** *adv.* **thoughtless,** *a.* **thoughtlessly,** *adv.*

thousand (thou'zánd) [A.-S. *thūsend*], *a.* and *n.* Ten hundred, 1000, M.; a great many. **thousandfold,** *a.* and *adv.* **thousandth,** *a.* and *n.*

thrall (thrawl) [Icel. *thrǽll*], *n.* A serf; bondage, thraldom, *a.* In thrall. *v.t.* To enthral, to enslave. **thraldom,** *n.*

thrash (thrăsh), **thresh** (thresh) [A.-S.

therscan], *v.t.* To beat out the grain from (corn, etc.); to beat soundly, esp. with a stick or whip; to defeat, conquer.

thread (thred) [A.-S. *thrǽd*], *n.* A slender cord; a single filament of cotton, silk, wool, etc.; anything resembling this; a thin seam or vein; the spiral on a screw. *v.t.* To pass a thread through the eye of; to string (beads, etc.) on a thread; (*fig.*) to pick (one's way) through; to streak (the hair) with grey, etc.; to cut a thread on (a screw). **threadbare**, *a.* Worn so that the thread is visible, having the nap worn off; (*fig.*) trite, hackneyed. **thready,** *a.*

threat (thret) [A.-S. *thréat*], *n.* A declaration of intention to inflict punishment, injury, etc., a menace. **threaten,** *v.t.* To use threats to; to announce intention (to inflict injury, etc.). *v.i.* To use threats; to have a threatening appearance.

three (thrē) [A.-S. *thréo, thrī*], *a.* Consisting of one more than two. *n.* One more than two; the figure representing this, 3, iii. **three-decker,** *n.* A vessel carrying guns on three decks; a pulpit in three stories. **threepence** (threp-éns), *n.* The sum of three pence. **threepenny,** *a.* **three-ply,** *a.* Having three strands, thicknesses, etc. **three-quarter,** *a.* Of three-fourths the usual size or number; showing three-fourths of the face, or going down to the hips (of portraits). **three-score,** *a.* Sixty. *n.* The age of sixty. **threefold,** *a.* and *adv.*

threnody (thren'ō-di) [Gr. *thrēnos,* dirge, ODE], *n.* A song of lamentation; a poem on the death of a person.

thresh [THRASH].

threshold (thresh'ōld) [A.-S. *therscold*], *n.* The stone or plank at the bottom of a doorway; (*fig.*) an entrance, a beginning.

thrice (thrīs) [M.E. *thries*], *adv.* Three times.

thrift (thrift), *n.* Frugality; economical management; the sea-pink. **thriftless,** *a.* **thriftlessness,** *n.* **thrifty,** *a.* Frugal, careful, economical. **thriftily,** *adv.*

thrill (thril) [A.-S. *thyrlian*], *v.t.* To affect with emotion so as to give a sense as of vibrating or tingling; to go through one (of emotion). *v.i.* To vibrate or quiver through, etc. (of emotion); to have a shivering or tingling sense of emotion. *n.* Wave of emotion. **thriller,** *n.* A sensational detective or mystery novel. **thrilling,** *a.*

thrive (thriv) [Icel. *thrīfa,* to seize], *v.i.* (*past,* **throve, thrived,** *p.p.* **thriven, thrived**) To prosper, to be successful; to grow vigorously.

throat (thrōt) [A.-S. *throte*], *n.* The front part of the neck; the gullet, the pharynx, the windpipe, etc.

throb (throb) [M.E. *throbben*], *v.i.* To beat rapidly or forcibly (of the heart or pulse); to quiver. *n.* A strong pulsation, a palpitation.

throe (thrō) [Icel. *thrā*], *n.* A violent pain, a pang.

thrombosis (throm-bō'sis) [Gr. *thrombos,* a clot], *n.* (*Path.*) Local coagulation of the blood in the heart or a blood vessel.

throne (thrōn) [Gr. *thronos,* seat, support], *n.* A royal seat, a chair of State for a sovereign, bishop, etc.; (*fig.*) sovereign power.

throng (throng) [A.-S. *thringan,* to crowd], *n.* A close multitude of persons or living things, a crowd. *v.i.* To crowd or press together; to come in multitudes.

throstle (throsl) [A.-S.], *n.* The songthrush.

throttle (throtl), *n.* The windpipe, the throat; a throttle valve. *v.t.* To strangle; to shut off (the flow of steam in a steamengine). **throttle-valve,** *n.* A valve regulating the supply of steam to a cylinder.

through (throo) [A.-S. *thurh*], *prep.* From end to end or side to side of, between the sides or walls of; in the midst of, throughout; by means or fault of, on account of. *adv.* From end to end or side to side, from beginning to end; to a final issue. *a.* Going through or to the end, proceeding right to the end or destination. **throughout,** *adv.* Right through, in every part. *prep.* Right through, from beginning to end of.

throw (thrō) [A.-S. *thrāwan,* to twist, to hurl], *v.t.* (*past* **threw,** throo, *p.p.* **thrown,** thrōn) To fling, hurl, cast, esp. to a distance with some force; to cause to fall, to prostrate; to drive, to impel; to make (a cast) with dice; to turn quickly or suddenly (the eyes, etc.); to cast off (the skin, as a snake); to bring forth (young, of rabbits, etc.); to twist, to wind into threads. *v.i.* To hurl a missile (at, etc.); to cast dice. *n.* Act of throwing, a cast; distance to which a missile is thrown; the extent of motion (of a crank, etc.). **to throw back:** To reflect, as light, etc.; to revert (to ancestral traits).

thrum (thrum) [A.-S. *tungethrum*], *n.* The fringe of warp-threads left when the web has been cut off, one of such threads; a tassel; (*pl.*) coarse yarn.

thrush (1) (thrush) [A.-S. *thrysce*], *n.* A common genus of birds, the song-thrush or throstle.

thrush (2) [Scand.], *n.* A disease of the mouth and throat; an inflammatory affection of the frog in the feet of horses.

thrust (thrust) [M.E. *thrusten,* Icel. *thrysta*], *v.t.* To push suddenly or forcibly; to stab. *v.i.* To make a sudden push or stab (at); to force or squeeze (in, etc.). *n.* A sudden or violent push; an attack with a pointed weapon, a stab; horizontal outward pressure, as of an arch against its abutments.

thud (thud) [?], *n.* A dull sound as of a blow on something soft. *v.i.* To make a thud; to fall with a thud.

thug (thug) [Hindi.], *n.* A cut-throat, a violent ruffian.

thumb (thum) [A.-S. *thūma*], *n.* The short thick digit of the hand. *v.t.* To handle awkwardly; to soil or mark with the thumb; (*colloq.*) to hail a passing vehicle by raising the hand with thumb extended. **thumb-nut,** *n.* A nut with wings for screwing up with the thumb. **thumb-screw,** *n.* A screw for turning with the finger and thumb; an old instrument of torture for compressing the thumb. thumb-stall, *n.* A covering for an injured thumb.

thump (thŭmp) [imit.], *v.t.* To strike with something giving a dull sound. *v.i.* To knock, to hammer (on, at, etc.). *n.* A blow giving a dull sound; the sound.

thunder (thŭn'dẽr) [A.-S. *thunor*], *n.* The sound following a flash of lightning; a loud noise; a vehement denunciation or threat. *v.i.* To make the noise of thunder; to make strong denunciations, etc. *v.t.* To emit or utter as with the sound of thunder. thunderbolt, *n.* A flash of lightning; a missile formerly believed to be discharged in this; (*fig.*) an irresistible force, a daring denunciation, etc. thunder-clap, -peal, *n.* thunder-cloud, *n.* A cloud from which lightning and thunder are produced. thunder-storm, *n.* A storm with thunder. thunder-struck, *a.* Struck by lightning; amazed, astounded. thunderous, thundery, *a.*

thurible (thūr'ĭbl) [L. *thūribulum*, from *thūs thūris*, frankincense], *n.* A censer. thurifer, *n.* One who carries a censer.

Thursday (thẽrz'dā, -dĭ) [A.-S. *Thūres dœg*, Thor's day, after *dies Jovis*, Jupiter's day], *n.* The fifth day of the week.

thus (thŭs) [A.-S.], *adv.* In the way indicated or about to be indicated; accordingly; to this extent.

thwart (thwŏrt) [M.E., from Icel. *thvert*], *a.* Transverse, oblique. *n.* A transverse plank in a boat serving as seat for a rower. *v.t.* To cross, to frustrate.

thy (thī) [A.-S. *thīn*, gen. of *thū*, THOU], *pron.* and *a.* (*before vowels usu. and absolutely* thine) Of or pertaining to thee (the poss. corresp. to THOU).

thyme (tīm) [Gr. *thumos*], *n.* A pungent aromatic herb used in cookery.

thyroid (thī'roid) [Gr. *thureos*, shield], *a.* Shield-shaped; applied esp. to the thyroid gland, a large ductless organ consisting of two lobes situated on each side of the larynx and the upper part of the windpipe, and to a large cartilage in the larynx, the Adam's apple.

thyself (thī-self'), *pron.* A reflexive and emphatic form used after or instead of 'thou'.

tiara (ti-a'rà) [L. and Gr.], *n.* The head-dress of the ancient Persian kings; the triple crown worn by the Pope, hence, the papal dignity; a jewelled headband worn by women.

tibia (tib'i-à) [L.], *n.* The shin-bone, an ancient flute. tibial, *a.*

tic (tik) [F.], *n.* An habitual convulsive twitching of muscles, esp. of the face; facial neuralgia.

tick (1) (tik) [A.-S.], *n.* Various parasitic insects.

tick (2) [L. *thēca*], *n.* A case for the filling of mattresses; the material for this, ticking.

tick (3), *n.* (*colloq.*) Credit, trust.

tick (4) [M.E. *tek*, a light touch], *v.i.* To make a small regularly recurring sound like that of a watch. *v.t.* To mark (off) with a tick. *n.* The sound made by a watch or clock; a tiny mark used in checking items.

ticket (tik'ĕt) [G. *stecken*, to stick], *n.* A

card, etc., entitling the holder to admission, to conveyance by train, etc., or to some privilege; a price or other label; (*slang*) the correct thing; the principles or programme of a political party. *v.t.* To put a ticket on. ticket of leave: A licence to a prisoner to be at large under certain restrictions.

tickle (tikl), *v.t.* To touch lightly so as to cause a sensation usu. producing laughter; (*fig.*) to please, gratify, amuse. *v.i.* To feel the sensation of tickling. *n.* Act or sensation of tickling. tickler, *n.* ticklish, *a.*

tide (tīd) [A.-S. *tīd*, time, hour], *n.* Time, season; the alternate rise and fall of the sea; (*fig.*) a rush of water, a torrent; the tendency of events. to tide over: To surmount difficulties by the help of circumstances. ti'dal, *a.* Pertaining to the tides; periodically rising and falling as the tides.

tidings (tī'dingz), *n.pl.* News, intelligence, a report.

tidy (tī'di), *a.* Orderly, neat, trim; (*colloq.*), pretty large. *v.t.* To make tidy, to put in order.

tie (tī) [A.-S. *tiegan*], *v.t.* (*pres.p.* tying) To fasten with a cord, etc., to secure, to bind; to draw into a knot or bow; to unite; to confine, restrict. *v.i.* To be exactly equal (with) in a score. *n.* Something used to tie or hold things together; a neck-tie; an obligation; an equality of votes, score, etc.; a match between any pair of a number of players or teams. tie-beam, *n.* A horizontal beam connecting rafters.

tier (tēr) [O.F. *tire*], *n.* A row, esp. one of several placed one above another.

tierce (tērs) [L. *tertius*, third], *n.* A cask of 42 gallons, one-third of a pipe; a sequence of three cards of the same suit; (*Fencing*) the third position for guard, parry, or thrust.

tiercel (tēr'sĕl), *n.* A male falcon.

tiff (tif) [Scand.], *n.* A fit of peevishness, a slight quarrel.

tiffany (tif'à-ni) [orig. a Twelfth Night dress], *n.* A kind of thin silk-like gauze.

tiffin (tif'in), *n.* (*Ang.-Ind.*) A light meal between breakfast and dinner.

tiger (tī'gẽr) [L. and Gr. *tigris*], *n.* A large Asiatic carnivorous feline mammal, tawny with black stripes; the jaguar, the cougar, etc.; a liveried groom. tiger-cat, *n.* A wild cat. tiger-lily, *n.* A lily with orange-spotted flowers. tigerish, *a.* tigress, *n.*

tight (tīt) [Scand.], *a.* Compactly put together, not leaky; fastened, held, or fitting closely; tense, taut; neat, trim; parsimonious; not easily obtainable (of money); (*colloq.*) awkward, difficult. *adv.* Tightly. *v.* Tighten. tightly, *adv.* tightness, *n.* tights, *n.pl.* Tight-fitting clothes worn by acrobats, etc.

tike (tīk) [Scand.], *n.* A cur; a low fellow.

tile (tīl) [A.-S. *tigele*], *n.* A thin slab used for covering roofs, paving floors, etc. *v.t.* To cover with tiles; (*Freemasonry*) to secure against intrusion. tiler, *n.* One who makes or lays tiles; (*Freemasonry*) the door-keeper of a lodge. tiling, *n.*

till (1) (til) [*til*, goodness], *v.t.* To cultivate. **tillage**, *n.* **tiller**, *n.*

till (2) [Icel. *til*], *prep.* Up to the time of, until. *conj.* Up to the time when.

till (3) [A.-S. *tyllan*, to draw], *n.* A money-drawer in a counter.

tiller (til'êr) [M.E. *tillen*], *n.* The lever by which a rudder is turned.

tilt (1) (tilt) [A.-S. *teld*], *n.* A covering for a cart; an awning over the stern-sheets of a boat.

tilt (2) (tilt) [A.-S. *tealt*, unsteady], *v.i.* To heel over, to be in a slanting position; to charge with a lance. *v.t.* To raise at one end, to tip, to incline; to aim (a lance). *n.* A slanting position; a charge with the lance, a tournament. **tilt-yard**, *n.* A place for tilting.

tilth (tilth), *n.* Tillage, cultivation; the depth of soil tilled.

timber (tim'bêr) [A.-S.], *n.* Wood suitable for building, carpentry, etc.; (*collect.*) trees, esp. those yielding such wood; a piece of prepared wood, esp. one of the ribs of a ship. *v.t.* To furnish or construct with timber. **timber-yard**, *n.* A yard where timber is stored. **timbered**, *a.* Wooded. **timbering**, *n.*

timbre (tanbr) [F.], *n.* The quality of tone distinguishing particular voices, instruments, etc.

timbrel (tim'brêl), *n.* An ancient instrument like the tambourine.

time (tim) [A.-S. *tima*], *n.* Duration or continuous existence, a particular portion of this, esp. for a specific purpose, available, or at one's disposal; a period having certain characteristics, an epoch, an era; a particular moment or hour; a date an occasion; (*Gram.*) the relation of a verb as regards past, present, or future; (*Mus.*) the relative duration of a note or rest; rate or style of movement, rhythm. *v.t.* To adapt to the time or occasion; to regulate as to time; to ascertain or mark the duration or rate of. **time-expired**, *a.* Applied to soldiers whose period of service is completed. **time-fuse**, *n.* A fuse arranged to ignite a charge at a certain time. **time-honoured**, *a.* Of venerable age. **timekeeper**, *n.* A clock or watch; a person who records time, esp of workmen. **time lag**, *n.* The interval that elapses between cause and result. **timepiece**, *n.* A clock or watch. **time-server**, *n.* One who suits his conduct, etc., to those in power. **time-table**, *n.* A list of the times of departure and arrival of trains, etc.; a record of times of employees, lessons, etc. **time-worn**, *a.* Antiquated, dilapidated **timely**, *a.* Seasonable, opportune, premature.

timid (tim'id) [L. *timēre*, to fear], *a.* Easily frightened, shy. **timid'ity**, *n.* Habitual shyness or cowardice. **timidly**, *adv.*

timorous (tim'ŏ-rŭs), *a.* Fearful, timid. **timorously**, *adv.*

tin (tin) [A.-S.], *n.* A lustrous white metal easily beaten into thin plates; a container or utensil made of thin plates of iron coated with tin; (*slang*) money. *v.t.* To coat with tin; to preserve (meat, fruit, etc.) in tins. **tinfoil**, *n.* A tin-like alloy beaten into foil for wrapping. **tinman**,

tinsmith, *n.* One who makes or deals in articles of tin or tin-plate. **tin-plate**, *n.* Iron-plate coated with tin *v.t.* To coat with tin. **tinware**, *n.* (*collect.*) Utensils of tin or tin-plate. **tinner**, *n.* **tinny**, *a.*

tincture (tink'chêr) [L. *tinctūra*], *n.* A solution of some principle, used in medicine; a tinge, a tint; a slight flavour (of). *v.t.* To imbue with a tint, to tinge; to flavour.

tinder (tin'dêr) [A.-S. *tendan*, to kindle], *n.* Any combustible substance used to kindle fire from a spark.

tine (tin) [A.-S. *tind*], *n.* The prong or spike of an antler, fork, harrow, etc.

tinge (tinj) [L. *tingere*], *v.t.* To colour slightly, to stain (with); (*fig.*) to modify the qualities of. *n.* A tint; (*fig.*) a flavour.

tingle (ting'gêl) [omit.], *v.i.* To feel a stinging, prickly sensation; to give this sensation.

tinker (ting'kêr) [M.E. *tinken*, to ring], *n.* An itinerant mender of pots, kettles, pans, etc.; a rough-and-ready worker, a botcher. *v.t.* To mend pots, etc.; to patch up in a clumsy, makeshift, or ineffective manner.

tinkle (ting'kêl), *v.i.* To make a succession of sounds as of a bell. *v.t.* To cause to tinkle, to ring. *n.* Such a sound.

tinsel (tin'sêl) [O.F. *estincelle*], *n.* Brass or other lustrous substance used in strips or spangles to give a sparkling effect to dresses, hangings, etc.; a fabric adorned with this; cloth of silk and silver; superficial brilliancy. *a.* Gaudy, showy.

tint (tint), *n.* A colour produced by admixture with another, esp. white; a slight tinge (of another colour); an effect of shading obtained by a series of parallel lines. *v.t.* To give a tint to; to tinge. **tinty**, *a.* Inharmoniously tinted.

tintinnabulum (tin-ti-năb'ū-lŭm) [L.], *n.* (*pl.* -la) A bell for fitting to harness, etc.; a tinkling or jingling of bells, plates, etc. **tintinnabular**, *a.* **tintinnabula'tion**, *n.*

tiny (ti'ni) [?], *a.* Very small.

-tion [L. *-tiōnem*, accus, sing. of nouns in *-tio*, cp. *-ion*], *suf.* Denoting action or condition, as *mention, expectation, vacation.*

tip (1) (tip) [M.E. *typ*], *n.* The point or end, esp. of a small or tapering thing; a small piece forming a point or end as a ferrule. *v.t.* To put a tip on; to form the tip of. **tipstaff**, *n.* A metal-tipped staff carried by a sheriff's officer; a sheriff's officer. **tiptoe**, *adv.* On the tips of the toes. *v.i.* To walk or stand on tiptoe. **tip-top**, *n.* The highest point, the very best. *a.* Of the very best.

tip (2) [M.E. *tippen*], *v.t.* To cause to lean; to overturn; to discharge (the contents of a cart, etc.) thus; to tap, touch; (*colloq.*) to give a small gratuity to. *v.i.* To lean over, to tilt; to upset. *n.* A small present in money; private information, esp. for betting.

tippet (tip'êt) [A.-S. *tœppet*], *n.* An outer covering for the neck and shoulders, worn by women, footmen, and by judges when robed.

tipple (tip'êl), v.i. To drink alcoholic liquors habitually. n. Strong drink; one's favourite beverage. **tippler**, n.

tipster (tip'stér), n. One who supplies tips about races, etc.

tipsy (tip'si) [?], a. Fuddled, partially intoxicated. **tipsily**, adv.

tirade (ti-rād') [It. tirata], n. A vehement speech or harangue, esp. of censure.

tire (1) (tīr) [A.-S. tȳrigan], v.t. To exhaust the strength of by toil; to fatigue, weary. v.i. To become weary or exhausted. **tireless** (1), a. Unwearied. tiring, a.

tire (2), tyre (tīr) [?], n. A band of metal, rubber, etc., placed round the rim of a wheel. **tireing**, n. **tireless** (2), a. **tire-smith**, n.

tiresome (tīr'sòm), a. Fatiguing; wearisome, tedious, annoying.

'tis (tiz) [short for IT IS].

tissue (tish'ū) [L. textus, woven], n. Any gauzy woven fabric; (Biol.) a fabric of cells and their products, the elementary substance of plant and animal organs; (fig.) a fabrication. **tissue-paper**, n. A thin unsized paper.

tit (1) (tit) [Icel. tittr], n. A titmouse or other small bird; a small horse. **titbit**, n. A dainty morsel. **titlark**, n. A small bird, the meadow-pipit. **titmouse**, n. (pl. -mice) A small insectivorous bird.

tit (2) [?], n. A tap, a slight blow. **tit for tat:** Retaliation.

Titan (tī'tàn) [Gr.], n. (Gr. Myth.) One of the giant deities; a person of superhuman strength or genius. **Titanesque** (-nesk'), **Titan'ic**, a.

tithe (tīth) [A.-S. tēodha], n. The tenth part of anything; a tax of one-tenth, esp. for the support of the clergy and Church. v.t. To impose tithes upon. **tithable**, a. **tither**, n. **tithing**, n. The taking or levying of tithes.

titillate (tit'i-lāt) [L. titillāre, to tickle], v.t. To tickle; to excite pleasurably. **titilla'tion**, n.

titivate (tit'i-vāt) [?], v. To dress up, to adorn, make smart.

title (tītl) [L. titulus], n. A name or designation, as of a book, poem, etc.; the contents of a title page, or a part of this; the distinguishing formula at the head of a statute, etc.; a division of a document as arranged for reference; a personal appellation denoting office, nobility, distinction, etc.; (Law) the right to ownership of property; a title-deed. **title-deed**, n. A legal instrument proving a person's right to property. **title page:** The page at the beginning of a book giving the title, author's name, etc. **title-rôle**, n. The character from whose name the title of a play is taken. **titled**, a. Bearing a title of nobility.

Titoism (tē'tō-izm([Marshal Tito], n. The theory of Communism practised in Yugoslavia, owning no allegiance to the Bolshevist Communism of Russia.

titter (tit'ér) [M.E. titeren], v.i. To giggle. n. A restrained laugh.

tittle (titl) [M.E. titel], n. A particle, an iota.

tittle-tattle (titl'tătl), n. Gossip. v.i. To gossip.

titular (tit'ū-làr), a. Existing in name only, holding a title without the office or duties attached. **titularly**, adv. Nominally. **titulary**, a.

to (tò, too) [A.-S.], prep. In a direction towards; as far as; no less than in comparison with, etc.; concerning; in the relation of, for, as; preceding the indirect object; the sign of the infinitive mood, expressing purpose, consequence, etc., limiting the meaning of adjectives, or forming verbal nouns. adv. Toward the condition or end required.

toad (tōd) [A.-S. tādige], n. A tailless amphibian like a frog; (fig.) a repulsive person. **toad-eater**, n. A sycophant. **toadstool**, n. An umbrella-shaped fungus. **toady**, n. A toad-eater. v.t. To fawn upon. **toadyism**, n.

toast (tōst) [L. tostus, parched], n. A slice of bread browned at the fire; a drinking or a call for drinking a health; the person or other object of this; a woman often toasted. v.t. To brown (bread), cook (bacon, etc.), or warm (the feet, etc.) at an open fire; to drink to the health or in honour of. **toast-master**, n. An official who announces the toasts at public dinners. **toasting-fork**, n. A fork to hold bread for toasting.

tobacco (tò-băk'ō) [Sp. tabaco], n. An American plant with narcotic leaves; the leaves dried and prepared for smoking. **tobacco-pipe**, n. A pipe used in smoking tobacco. **tobacconist**, n. A dealer in tobacco.

toboggan (tò-bog'àn) [Algonkin], n. A long low sled used for sliding down snow-covered slopes. v.i. To slide on a toboggan.

tocsin (tok'sin) [O.F. toquer, to touch, signal], n. An alarm-bell; the ringing of this.

to-day (tò-dā') [A.-S. todæge, for or on (this) day], adv. On, during, or at the present day. n. This day.

toddle (todl), v.i. To walk with short unsteady steps, as a child; to saunter. n. A toddling walk; a stroll. **toddler**, n.

toddy (tod'i) [Hind. tādi, from tār, palm], n. A juice obtained from certain palms and fermented; spirits and hot water sweetened.

to-do (tò-doo'), n. Ado, commotion.

toe (tō) [A.-S. tā, cp. Dut. teen, G. zehe, Icel. tā, Dan. taa], n. One of the five digits of the foot, the part of a boot, etc., covering the toes.

toffee, toffy (tof'i), n. A sweetmeat of boiled sugar or molasses and butter.

toga (tō'gă) [L.], n. A loose flowing robe, the outer garment of an ancient Roman citizen.

together (tò-geth'ér) [A.-S. tōgædere], adv. Conjointly, unitedly; in the same place or at the same time; into union; without cessation.

toggle (togl) [?], n. (Naut.) A pin put through a loop in a rope for securing this.

toil (1) (toil) [A.-F. toiler, to strive], v.i. To labour painfully; to move or progress laboriously. n. Hard and unremitting labour, drudgery. **toiler**, n. **toilsome**, a.

toil (2) [F. toile, cloth], n. A net or snare.

toilet (toi'lĕt), *n.* Act or process of dressing; dress, style of dress; a dressing-table with looking-glass, etc.; a water-closet. **toilet-cover**, *n.* A cloth for a toilet-table. **toilet-service**, **-set**, *n.* A set of utensils for a toilet-table.

Tokay (tō-kā'), *n.* A rich wine made at Tokay in Hungary from white grapes.

token (tōk-ĕn) [A.-S. *tācen*], *n.* A sign or symbol representing or recalling something, event, etc.; an indication, symptom; a keepsake; a piece of metal like a coin, formerly issued privately and representing money. **token payment**, *n.* A small payment made to indicate the acknowledgment of a debt.

tolerate (tol'ér-āt) [L. *tolerāre*], *v.t.* To permit by not preventing or forbidding; to abstain from judging harshly or condemning; to sustain, endure (pain, toil, etc.). **tolerable**, *a.* Endurable, supportable; fairly good. **tolerance**, *n.* **tolerant**, *a.* **tolera'tion**, *n.* Act of tolerating; the spirit of tolerance; recognition of the right of private judgment, esp. in religious matters.

toll (1) [tōl] [A.-S.], *n.* A tax charged for the use of a road, bridge, market, etc.; a portion of grain taken by a miller as compensation for grinding. **toll-bar, -gate,** *n.* A bar across a road to stop passengers till toll is paid.

toll (2) [M.E. *tollen*], *v.t.* To cause (a bell) to sound slowly; to give out (a knell, etc.) with a slow, measured sound. *v.i.* To sound or ring (of a bell) with slow, regular strokes. *n.* A tolling or a stroke of a bell.

tom (tom) [short for *Thomas*], *n.* A male animal, esp. a tom-cat. **tomboy**, *n.* A romping girl, a hoyden. **tom-cat**, *n.* A male cat. **tom-fool**, *n.* A ridiculous fool, a trifler. **tom-foolery**, *n.* **tom-tit**, *n.* A small bird, esp. a titmouse.

tomahawk (tom'ȧ-hawk) [Algonkin], *n.* A N. American Indian battle-axe.

tomato (tȯ-ma'tō) [Mex. *tomatl*], *n.* (*pl.* -toes) The pulpy edible fruit of a trailing plant of the nightshade family, orig. S. American; the plant itself.

tomb (toom) [Gr. *tumba*], *n.* A grave; a sepulchral monument. *v.t.* To bury, to entomb. **tombstone**, *n.* A stone memorial over a grave.

tome (tōm) [F.], *n.* A volume.

tommy (tom'i), *n.* A British private soldier (from *Tommy Atkins*); (*slang*) food, provisions. **tommy-gun**, *n.* (*Mil.*) A short-barrelled, quick-firing firearm.

to-morrow (tȯ-mor'ō), *n.* The next day after to-day. *adv.* On or during this.

tom-tom (tom'tom) [Hindi, *tam-tam*], *n.* A native drum used in India, Africa, etc.

-tomy (Gr. *-tomia*, from *temnein*, to cut], *suf.* Used of surgical operations, as in *tracheotomy.*

ton (1) (tŭn), *n.* A measure of weight, 20 cwt.

ton (2) (ton) [F., *tone*], *n.* The prevailing fashion or mode. **tonish**, *a.*

tonal (tō'nȧl), *a.* Pertaining to tone or tonality. **tonal'ity**, *n.* (*Mus.*) Character or quality of a tone.

tone (tōn) [L. *tonus*, Gr. *tonos*], *n.* Sound, with reference to pitch, quality, and volume; a musical sound; modulation of the voice; timbre; (*fig.*) mood, prevailing sentiment, spirit; syllabic stress; degree of luminosity of a colour; the general effect of a painting, photographic print, etc.; healthy general condition. *v.t.* To give tone or quality to; (*Mus.*) to tune. *v.i.* To harmonize in colour; to receive a particular tone or tint. **to tone down:** To subdue, to soften; to become emphatic.

tongs (tongz) [A.-S. *tange*, sing.], *n.pl.* An implement used for grasping coals, etc.

tongue (tŭng) [A.-S. *tunge*], *n.* A fleshy muscular organ in the mouth, used in tasting, swallowing, and (in man) speech; the clapper of a bell, the pin in a buckle, a piece of leather at the front of a laced shoe, a projecting edge for fitting into a groove in matchboard, a long low promontory, a long narrow inlet, or other tongue-shaped thing or part; (*fig.*) speech, the voice, manner of speech; a language. **tongue-tied**, *a.* Impeded in speech; prevented from speaking freely.

tonic (ton'ik), *a.* Invigorating, bracing; of or pertaining to tones; (*Phonet.*) denoting a voiced sound; stressed. *n.* A tonic medicine; (*Mus.*) the key-note.

to-night (tȯ-nīt'), *n.* The present night. *adv.* On or during this.

tonnage (tŭn'aj), *n.* The carrying capacity of a vessel expressed in tons; the aggregate freightage of a number of vessels, esp. of a country's merchant marine; a duty on ships.

tonneau (ton'ō, tȯ-nō') [F., cask], *n.* The part of a motor-car containing the back seats.

tonsil (ton'sil) [L. *tonsilla*, a sharp stake], *n.* Either of two organs in the hinder part of the mouth. **tonsilli'tis**, *n.* Inflammation of the tonsils.

tonsorial (ton-sōr'i-ȧl) [L. *tonsor*, barber], *a.* Pertaining to a barber or his art.

tonsure (ton'shŭr), *n.* The shaving of the crown or of the whole head on admission to the priesthood, etc.; (*fig.*) admission into Holy orders.

tontine (ton-tēn') [Lorenzo *Tonti*, It. banker, *c.* 1653], *n.* A form of annuity in which the shares of subscribers who die are added to the profits shared by the survivors.

too (too), *adv.* More than enough; as well, also, in addition; moreover; (*colloq.*) superlatively.

tool (tool) [A.-S. *tōl*], *n.* A simple implement, esp. one used in manual work; (*fig.*) anything used in one's occupation; a person employed as an instrument, a cat's-paw. *v.t.* To impress designs on (a book-cover. etc.). **tooling**, *n.* Designs impressed, etc., on a book-cover.

toot (toot) [imit.], *v.i.* To make a noise like that of a horn; to give out such a sound. *v.t.* To sound (a horn, etc.).

tooth (tooth) [A.-S. *tōth*], *n.* (*pl.* **teeth**) One of the hard structures growing in the mouth and used for mastication; an artificial tooth; a tooth-like projection or part. *v.t.* To furnish with teeth; to indent. **toothache**, *n.* Pain in the teeth.

toothpick, *n.* A pointed instrument for removing particles of food from between the teeth. **toothless,** *a.* **toothsome,** *a.* Palatable, pleasing to the taste.

top (1) (top) [A.-S.], *n.* The highest part of anything; the upper side or surface; the head of a page in a book; the upper end or head of a table; the highest position, rank, etc.; the culmination, the height; (*Naut.*) a platform round the head of a lower mast. *v.t.* To remove the top of (a plant, etc.); to put a top on; to surmount; to surpass. *a.* Being on or at the top or summit; highest in position, degree, etc. **top-boot,** *n.* A boot having high tops. **top-coat,** *n.* An overcoat. **top-dress,** *v.t.* To manure on the surface, as distinguished from digging or ploughing in. **top-dressing,** *n.* **top-gallant,** *a.* Applied to the mast, rigging, and sail next above the topmast. **top-hamper,** *n.* The light upper sails and rigging; tackle encumbering the deck. **top-hat,** *n.* A tall silk hat. **top-heavy,** *a.* Having the upper part too heavy for the lower. **top-knot,** *n.* An ornamental bow worn on the top of the head; a tuft growing on the head. **topmast, s.** The mast next above the lower mast. **topsail,** (topsl), *n.* A square sail next above the lowest sail on a mast; a fore-and-aft sail above the gaff. **topmost,** *a.* Highest, uppermost. **topping,** *a.*

top (2) [A.-S. *topp*], *n.* A toy made to rotate with great velocity on a point underneath, by the rapid unwinding of a string, etc.

topaz (tō′păz) [Gr. *topazos*], *n.* A transparent or translucent variously coloured gem.

tope (tōp) [?], *v.i.* To drink alcoholic liquors excessively or habitually, to tipple. **toper,** *n.*

topic (top′ĭk) [Gr. *topikos*, local], *n.* The subject of a discourse, literary composition, etc. **topical,** *a.* Pertaining to a topic, or consisting of allusions, esp. to current or local topics. **topically,** *adv.*

topography (tō-pog′ră-fĭ) [Gr. *topos*, place], *n.* The detailed description of particular places; the features of a district. **topographer,** *n.* **topographic, -al,** *a.*

topple (top′pĕl), *v.i.* To totter and fall; to project as if about to fall.

topsy-turvy (top-sĭ-tĕr′vĭ), *adv.* and *a.* Upside down; in a disordered condition.

toque (tōk) [F.], *n.* A small, brimless, close-fitting headdress.

tor (tôr) [A.-S. *torr*], *n.* A prominent hill.

torch (tôrch) [F. *torche*, from L. *tortus*, twisted], *n.* A light made of twisted hemp, etc., soaked in oil, for carrying in the hand; any light for carrying.

torment (tôr′mĕnt) [L. *tormentum*, from *torquēre*, to twist], *n.* Extreme pain or anguish; a source or cause of this. *v.t.* (tôrment′) To subject to torment, to afflict, vex. **tormentor,** *n.* One who or that which torments.

tornado (tôr-nā′dō) [Sp. *tronada*, thunderstorm], *n.* (*pl.* -does) A storm of extreme violence, usu. having a rotary motion with electric discharges.

torpedo (tôr-pē′dō) [L. *torpēre*, to be numb],

n. (*pl.* -does) A long, cigar-shaped explosive engine propelled under water or through the air; an electric ray, a sea-fish having an electrical apparatus for killing its prey. *v.t.* To attack, blow up, or sink with a torpedo. **torpedo-boat,** *n.* A small swift vessel fitted for firing torpedoes.

torpid (tôr′pĭd), *a.* Having lost the power of motion; benumbed; dormant; sluggish, inactive. **torpid′ity, torpor,** *n.*

torque (tôrk) [L. *torquēre*, to twist], *n.* A twisted necklace; (*Mech.*) the movement of a system of forces causing rotation.

torrent (tor′ĕnt) [L. *torrens*, parching], *n.* A violent rushing stream; a flood (of abuse, passion, etc.). **torrential** (tŏ-ren′shăl), *a.*

torrid (tor′id), *a.* Dried up with heat, parched, very hot. **torrid′ity, n.**

torsion (tôr′shŭn) [L. *torquēre*, to twist], *n.* Act of twisting or state of being twisted; the force with which a body tends to return to its original state after being twisted.

torso (tôr′sō) [It., stump], *n.* (*pl.* -sos) The trunk of a statue without the head and limbs.

tort (tôrt) [F., wrong], *n.* (*Law*) A private or civil wrong. **tortious** (tôr′shŭs), *a.*

tortoise (tôr′tŭs, -toiz) [Late L. *tortuca*], *n.* A terrestrial or freshwater turtle.

tortuous (tôr′tū-ŭs), *a.* Twisting, crooked; (*fig.*) roundabout, devious.

torture (tôr′chĕr), *n.* The infliction of extreme physical pain; excruciating pain or anguish. *v.t.* To subject to torture; (*fig.*) to distort; to pervert the meaning of (a statement, etc.). **torturer,** *n.*

Tory (tôr′ĭ) [Ir., a moss-trooper], *n.* Orig. one of the party opposed to the exclusion of James II from the throne; a Conservative. *a.* Pertaining to the Tories. **Toryism, n.**

-tory [-ORY, cp. -TOR], *suf.* Forming nouns and adjectives, as *factory, oratory, perfunctory.*

toss (tos) [Norw. *tossa*], *v.t.* To throw up with the hand; to pitch, fling; to throw back (the head) with a jerk; to throw about, to cause to rise and fall, to agitate. *v.i.* To tumble about, to be agitated; to throw oneself from side to side. *n.* Act of tossing; state of being tossed. **toss-up,** *n.* The tossing up of a coin to decide a wager, etc., by seeing which way it falls; an even chance.

tot (1) (tot) [Scand.], *n.* Anything small or insignificant; a small child; a dram of liquor.

tot (2) [L., so many], *n.* A sum in addition. *v.* To add or mount (up).

total (tō′tăl) [L. *tōtus*, entire], *a.* Complete, comprising the whole or everything; absolute, thorough. *n.* The total sum; the aggregate. **totalitarian** (tō-tăl-ĭ-tār′ĭ-ăn), *a.* (*Polit.*) Permitting no rival parties or policies; controlling the entire national resources of trade, national wealth and manpower. **total′ity, n.** **totally,** *adv.* **totalizator** (tō-tăl-ĭ-zā′tŏr), *n.* (*Sport*) A contrivance for showing the total amounts of bets staked on a race in order to divide the whole among those betting on the winner.

totem (tō′tĕm) [Algonkin], *n.* A natural object taken by primitive peoples as a badge on account of supposed relationship; an image of this. **to′temism**, *n.*

totter (tot′ẽr), *v.i.* To stagger; to be on the point of falling. **tottery**, *a.*

toucan (too′kăn) [Braz. *tucana*], *n.* A tropical American bird with an enormous beak.

touch (tŭch) [O.F. *tuchier*, *tochier*], *v.t.* To meet the surface of, to be in or come into contact with; to cause (two objects) to come into contact; to reach, to attain; to meddle; to injure slightly; to compare with; to relate to; to treat of hastily; to tap, to play upon lightly, to put (in) fine strokes with the brush, etc.; to affect, esp. with tender feeling; to rouse, to irritate. *v.i.* To come into contact (of two or more objects); to deal with (usu. with *on*) in a slight manner; to call (at a port, etc.). *n.* Act of touching; contact; the sense by which contact, pressure, etc., are perceived; a slight effort, a light stroke with brush or pencil; a twinge; a minute quantity; characteristic impress; (*Football*) the part of the field outside the touch-lines and between the goal-lines. **touch-hole**, *n.* The priming hole or vent of a gun. **touch-lines** (*Football*). The two longer or side boundaries of the field. **touch-stone**, *n.* A stone used for testing the purity of gold and other alloys; (*fig.*) a criterion. **touching**, *a.* Affecting, moving, pathetic. *prep.* Concerning, with regard to. **touchwood**, *n.* Tinder.

touchy (tŭch′ĭ), *a.* Apt to take offence, irascible, irritable. **touchiness**, *n.*

tough (tŭf) [A.-S. *tōh*], *a.* Flexible without being brittle; able to endure hardship; stiff, tenacious; stubborn; laborious, difficult. **toughen**, *v.* **toughish**, *a.*

tour (toor) [F.], *n.* A journeying from place to place; an extended excursion; a circuit. *v.i.* To make a tour. **tourist**, *n.*

tournament (toor′nà-mĕnt) [O.F. *torneiement*], *n.* A contest or pageant in which mounted knights contested; a contest in which a number of persons take part.

tourney (toor′nĭ), *n.* A tournament. *v.i.* To engage in a tournament.

tourniquet (toor′ni-ket), *n.* An instrument for compressing an artery.

tousle (touzl), *v.t.* To pull about; to rumple, dishevel.

tout (tout) [A.-S. *tōtian*, to peep out], *v.i.* To solicit custom obtrusively; to spy (esp. on horses training). *n.* One employed to tout.

tow (1) (tō) [A.-S. *togian*], *v.t.* To pull (a boat, etc.) through the water by a rope, etc.; to drag behind one. *n.* **tow-boat,** *n.* A tug.

tow (2) [?], *n.* The coarse broken part of hemp or flax after heckling, etc. **towy,** *a.*

toward -wards (to-wôrd′, -z, tôrd, -z) [A.-S. *tōweard*], *prep.* In the direction of; as regards; for, for the purpose of; about.

towel (tou′ĕl) [O.F. *toaille*], *n.* A cloth for drying oneself on, etc.

tower (tou-er) [M.E. *tour*, A.-S. *torr*, L. *turris*], *n.* A lofty building, circular, square, or polygonal, frequently of several stories; (*fig.*) a place of defence, a protection. *v.i.* To rise to a great height, to soar. **towering,** *a.* Very high; (*fig.*) violent (of passion, etc.).

town (toun) [A.-S. *tūn*], *n.* A collection of dwelling-houses larger than a village; the people of a town; the chief town of a district. **town-clerk,** *n.* The clerk to a municipal corporation; the keeper of the town records. **town-council,** *n.* The governing body in a town. **town hall:** A building for transaction of municipal business, meetings, etc. **town planning,** *n.* The regulating of the laying-out or extension of a town with a view to securing the greatest advantages for public health, amenities, etc. **townsfolk,** *n.pl.* (*collect.*) The people of a town.

tox-, toxi-, toxio- [Gr. *toxikon* (*pharmakon*), poisonous (drug for arrows), from *toxa*, arrows], *comb. form.* Pertaining to poison. **toxic** (tok′sĭk), *a.* Pertaining to poison; poisonous. **toxico′logy** [-LOGY], *n.* The branch of medicine treating of poisons and their antidotes. **toxin,** *n.* A poisonous compound causing a particular disease.

toxophilite (tok-sof′i-līt) [Gr. *toxon*, bow, -PHIL, -ITE], *n.* One skilled in or devoted to archery. *a.* Pertaining to archery.

toy (toi) [?], *n.* A plaything; something of an amusing or trifling kind, not for actual use. *v.i.* To trifle, to dally. **toy spaniel,** etc. A pigmy variety of dog.

tra- [TRANS], *pref.* As in *tradition*, *travesty*.

trace (1) (trās) [as TRAIT], *n.* One of the two straps by which a vehicle is drawn.

trace (2) [F., from L. *tractus*, drawn], *n.* A track, a footprint, rut, etc. (*usu. in pl.*); a sign of something that has been; a minute quantity. *v.t.* To follow the traces of; to note the vestiges of; to ascertain the course of; to pursue one's way along; to mark or sketch out; to copy (a drawing, etc) on transparent paper, etc., laid upon it. **traceable,** *a.* **tracery,** *n.* Ornamental open-work in Gothic windows; any decoration resembling this. **tracing-paper, -cloth, -linen,** *n.* A transparent paper or linen used for tracing drawings, etc.

trachea (trà-kē′à) [Gr. *tracheia*, rough], *n.* (*pl.* -cheæ) The windpipe; (*Bot.*) a duct.

tracheot′omy [-TOMY], *n.* The operation of making an opening into the windpipe.

track (trăk) [O.F. *trac*], *n.* A series of marks left by the passage of a person, animal, or thing, a trail; a path, esp. one beaten by use; the route followed by ships; a racing-path; a line of railway. *v.t.* To follow the track of; to follow out (the course of anything); to tow. **tracker,** *n.* **trackless,** *a.* Pathless; untravelled, leaving no track.

tract (1) (trăkt) [L. *tractus*, drawn], *n.* An area of land or water of a considerable extent; (*Anat.*) the region of an organ or system.

tract (2) [L. *tractāre*, to treat], *n.* A pamphlet, esp. on religion or morals.

tractable (trăk′tàbl), *a.* That may be easily managed or controlled; docile. **tractabil′ity,** *n.* **tractably,** *adv.*

traction (trăk'shŭn) [*trahere*, to draw], *n.* Act of drawing something along a surface; state of being so drawn.

tractor (trăk'tôr), *n.* A self-propelling vehicle capable of drawing other vehicles, farm implements, etc.

trade (trād), *n.* A business or occupation, etc., dist. from agriculture, unskilled labour, the professions, etc.; commerce; the amount of business done in a particular year, place, etc.; persons in a particular trade; (*colloq.*) a deal, a bargain (in business or politics); (*pl.*) the trade-winds. *v.i.* To barter, to traffic, to deal (in); to carry on business (with); to carry merchandise (between, etc.). *v.t.* To sell or exchange in commerce. **to trade on:** To take advantage of. **trade-mark,** *n.* A registered symbol used to guarantee genuineness. **tradesman,** *n.* A retail dealer; a craftsman. **trade-union,** *n.* An organized body of workmen in any trade, formed for the promotion and protection of their common interests. **trade-unionism,** *n.* **trade-unionist,** *n.* **trade-wind,** *n.* A wind blowing from the north or south toward the thermal equator and deflected in a westerly direction by the easterly rotation of the earth; (*pl.*) these and the anti-trades. **trader,** *n.* One engaged in trade; a vessel employed in trade.

tradition (tră-dish'ŭn) [L. *trădere*, to hand over], *n.* The handing down of opinions, customs, etc., to posterity, esp. by oral communication; a belief, custom, etc., so handed down; principles, maxims, etc., derived from the usage and experience of artists, dramatists, actors, etc. **traditional,** *a.* **traditionally,** *adv.*

traduce (tră-dūs') [L. *dūcere*, to lead], *v.t.* To defame, to misrepresent. **traducer,** *n.*

traffic (trăf'ik) [F. *trafique*], *n.* The exchange of goods, trade, commerce; transportation by road, rail, steamer, etc.; the passage of persons, vehicles, etc., on a road, etc., amount of this. *v.i.* To trade, to have business (with). *v.t.* To barter. **trafficator,** *n.* (*Motor.*) A device for showing to which side the driver is going to turn. **trafficker,** *n.*

tragedy (trăj'ĕ-di) [Gr. *tragōidia*], *n.* A drama dealing with a lofty theme of a sad or terrible kind, usu. with an unhappy ending; a calamitous event. **tragedian** (tră-jē'di-ăn), *n.* A writer of tragedies; an actor in tragedy. **tragedienne,** *n.* A tragic actress. **trag'ic, -al,** *a.* Of the nature of tragedy; lamentable, calamitous.

trail (trāl) [M.E. *trailen*], *v.t.* To drag along behind, esp. along the ground; to carry (a rifle) in a horizontal position. *v.i.* To be dragged along behind, to hang down loosely or grow to some length along the ground, over a wall, etc. *n.* Anything trailing behind a moving thing; the end of a gun-carriage resting on the ground; a track left by an animal, etc.; the scent followed in hunting; a beaten track through wild country.

trailer, *n.* A vehicle drawn by another; (*Cinema.*) a short film giving advance publicity of a film.

train (trān) [F.], *n.* That which is trailed, trailing part of a gown, the long tail-feathers of a bird, etc.; a retinue, a suite; a long series of persons or things; a line of railway carriages or trucks drawn by an engine; a trail of combustible material leading fire to a charge; process, orderly succession. *v.t.* To instruct, to drill, to accustom (to perform certain acts); to prepare by diet and exercise (for a race, etc.); to bring (a plant) into a desired shape, etc.; to aim (a gun upon). *v.i.* To prepare oneself or come into a state of efficiency for (a contest); to go by train. **trainer,** *n.* One who trains, esp. one who prepares men or horses for races. **training,** *a.*

train-oil (trān'oil) [M.Dut. *traen*, resin], *n.* Oil from the blubber or fat of whales.

traipse (trāps), *v.i.* To trudge.

trait (trā) [F.], *n.* A distinguishing or peculiar feature; a stroke, a touch (of).

traitor (trā'tôr) [L. *trădere*, to hand over], *n.* One who violates his allegiance; one guilty of treason or treachery. **traitorous,** *a.* **traitress,** n.

trajectory (tră-jek'tôr-i) [L. *jectus*, thrown], *n.* The path described by a projectile, etc., under the action of given forces.

tram (trăm) [L. G. *traam*, balk, beam], *n.* A line of beams or rails, a pair of which form a tramway; a tramway; a tram-car; a four-wheeled truck used in coalmines. **tramway,** *n.* A street railway on which cars are drawn usu. by electricity.

trammel (trăm'el) [M.F. *tramail*], *n.* A net for fish or birds; a fetter used in teaching a horse to amble; anything restraining freedom or activity (usu. *pl.*). *v.t.* To confine, hamper, restrict.

tramp (trămp) [Scand.], *v.i.* To walk or tread heavily; to go on foot. *v.t.* To trample; to traverse on foot. *n.* An act of tramping, the tread of persons marching; a journey on foot; a vagrant; a freight-vessel having no regular line.

trample (trăm'pĕl), *v.t.* To tread under foot; to crush thus; to treat with contemptuous indifference. *v.i.* To tread heavily or in contempt (on).

trampoline (trăm'-pō-lin), *n.* A net extended beneath trapeze acrobats, etc., in case of their falling.

trance (trans), *n.* A state of insensibility with suspension of some of the vital functions, catalepsy; ecstasy, rapture.

tranquil (trăng'kwil) [L. *tranquillus*], *a.* Calm, peaceful, serene. **tranquil'lity,** *n.* **tran'quillize,** *v.t.* **tranquillizer,** *n.* A sedative drug.

trans- [L., across, cross-wise; beyond through; into another state or place], *pref.*

transact (trăn-săkt') [L. *actus*, acted], *v.t.* To do, perform, carry out. *v.i.* To do business, to conduct matters (with). **transac'tion,** *n.* The management or carrying out of a piece of business, etc.; an affair, a proceeding; (*pl.*) the reports of the proceedings of learned societies.

transcend (trăn-send') [L. *scandere*, to climb], *v.* To rise above, surpass, exceed; to pass or be beyond the range (of human understanding, etc.). **transcendent,** *a.* Surpassing, supremely excellent; beyond the sphere of knowledge or experience. **transcendence, -dency,** *n.* **transcenden'tal** (-den'tăl), *a.* Beyond the sphere of experience; explaining matter and the universe as products of mental conception; abstruse, vague. **transcen-den'talism,** *n.* **transcendentalist,** *n.*

transcribe (trăn-skrīb') [TRANS-, L. *scrībere*], *v.t.* To copy in writing. **tran'script,** *n.* A written copy. **transcrip'tion,** *n.*

transept (trăn'sept) [L. *sēptus*, enclosed], *n.* Either of the transverse arms extending north and south in a cruciform church.

transfer (trăns-fĕr') [L. *ferre*, to bear], *v.t.* To shift from one place or person to another; to make over the possession of; to convey (a design) from one surface to another, as in lithography. *n.* (trăns'-fĕr) The removal of a thing from one person or place to another; (*Law*) act of conveying a right, property, etc., thus, the deed by which this is effected; that which is transferred. **transferable,** *a.* **transferee,** *n.* **trans'ference,** *n.*

transfiguration (trăns-fĭg-ū-rā'shŭn) [L. *transfigūrāre*, to change the figure of], *n.* A change of form or appearance, esp. that of Christ on the Mount (Matt. xvii. 1–9); a festival on 6 Aug. in commemoration of this. **transfigure,** *v.t.* To change the outward appearance of.

transfix (trăns-fĭks') [L. *transfixus*], *v.t.* To pierce through, to impale.

transform (trăns-fôrm'), *v.t.* To change the form or appearance of, to meta-morphose; to change in disposition, character, etc. **transformation,** *n.* Act of transforming; state of being transformed, a metamorphosis. **transformer,** *n.* (*Elec.*) A contrivance for producing by means of an electric current one of different strength and potential.

transfuse (trăns-fūz') [L. *fūsus*, poured], *v.t.* To cause to pass from one vessel, etc., into another; (*Med.*) to transfer (blood) from the veins of one to those of another. **transfu'sion,** *n.*

transgress (trăns-gres') [L. *gressus*, walked], *v.t.* To break, to infringe. *v.i.* To offend by violating a rule, to sin. **transgression,** (-gresh'ŭn), *n.* **transgressor,** *n.*

transient (trăn'sĭ-ĕnt), *a.* Not lasting; momentary, brief. **transience, -ency,** *n.*

transistor (trăn-zĭs'-tŏr), *n.* (*Elec.*) A device for giving power and current amplification.

transit (trăn'sĭt), *n.* Act of passing; conveyance; a route; the passage of a heavenly body over the meridian of a place or across the disk of another. **tran-sition** (-sĭzh'ŭn), *n.* Passage or change from one place, state, or action to another; a change in architecture, literature, etc., from one key to another, or from the major to the relative minor. **transitional,** *a.*

transitive (trăn'sĭ-tĭv), *a.* (*Gram.*) Expressing an action passing over from a subject to an object (of verbs).

transitory (trăn'sĭ-tŏr-ĭ), *a.* Lasting but a short time, not durable.

translate (trăn-slāt') [L. *translātus*], *v.t.* To render the sense of in another language; (*fig.*) to express in clearer terms;

to remove from one office to another. **translatable,** *a.* **transla'tion,** *n.* **translator,** *n.*

translucent (trăns-lū'sĕnt) [L. *lūcens*, shining], *a.* Allowing light to pass through but not transparent. **translucence -cency,** *n.*

transmigrate (trănz-mī'grāt), *v.i.* To pass from one body into another (of the soul); to migrate. **transmigrant,** *a.* and *n.* **transmigra'tion,** *n.*

transmit (trănz-mĭt') [L. *mittere*, to send], *v.t.* To send or transfer from one person or place to another; to act as a medium for, to conduct. **transmissible,** *a.* **transmission** (-mĭsh'ŭn), *n.* **transmitter,** *n.*

transmute (trănz-mūt') [L. *mūtāre*, to change], *v.t.* To change from one form to another; to transform (into). **transmuta'tion,** *n.* Act of transmuting; (*Alch.*) the change of base metals into gold or silver.

transom (trăn'sŏm) [M.E. *traunsum*], *n.* A horizontal strengthening bar across a window, doorway etc.

transparent (trăns-pâr'ĕnt) [L. *pārens*, appearing], *a.* Transmitting rays of light without diffusion, so that objects may be distinctly seen through; plain, evident; sincere. **transparence,** *n.* **transparency,** *n.* **transparently,** *adv.*

transpire (trăn'spīr') [L. *spīrāre*, to breathe], *v.t.* To emit through the excretory organs (of the skin or lungs), to exhale. *v.i.* To pass off as vapour (of perspiration, etc.); (*fig.*) to leak out, become known. **transpira'tion,** *n.* **transpir'atory** (-spīr'ă-tŏr-ĭ), *a.*

transplant (trăns-plant'), *v.t.* To remove and plant or establish in another place; (*Surg.*) to transfer (living tissue) from one part or person to another. **trans-planta'tion,** *n.*

transport (trăns-pôrt') [L. *portāre*, to carry], *v.t.* To carry from one place to another; to remove (a criminal) to a penal colony; (*chiefly in p.p.*) to carry away by powerful emotion, to entrance. *n.* (trăns'pôrt) Conveyance from one place to another; a transport ship, one carrying troops, munitions of war, etc.; (*fig.*) rapture; ecstasy. **transportable,** *a.* That may be transported; involving transportation (of an offence). **trans-porta'tion,** *n.* Act of transporting; state of being transported; conveyance; carriage from one place to another; banishment to a penal colony.

transpose (trăns-pōz'), *v.t.* To cause to change places, to change the natural order of; (*Mus.*) to write or play in a different key. **transpo'sal, transposi'tion,** *n.* Act of transposing; state of being transposed.

transubstantiate (trăn-sŭb-stăn'shĭ-āt), *v.t.* To change the substance of. **transub-stantia'tion,** *n.* A change of essence; conversion of the substance of the bread and wine in the eucharist into the body and blood of Christ.

transverse (trănz-vĕrs') [L. *vertere*, to turn], *a.* Lying or acting across or in a cross direction. **transversal,** *a.* Transverse; running or lying across.

trap (trăp) [A.-S. *treppe*], *n.* A contrivance

for catching animals; an ambush, a stratagem; a device for releasing a bird or propelling an object to be shot at; trap-ball, the device used in this; a contrivance in a drain, etc., for preventing the return of foul gas; a two-wheeled vehicle; a trap-door. *v.t.* To catch in a trap; to furnish (a drain) with a trap. *v.i.* To catch animals in traps; to be impeded (of gas, etc., in a pipe). **trap-door,** *n.* A door in a floor or roof opening like a valve. **trapper,** *n.* One who traps animals, esp. for furs.

trapeze (trá-pēz') [Gr. *trapezion*], *n.* A suspended bar on which gymnasts perform.

traps (trăpz) [F. *drap*, cloth], *n.* One's personal belongings; luggage.

Trappist (trăp'ist), *n.* A member of a Cistercian order, following the strict rule of La Trappe (French monastery founded in 1140).

trash (trăsh) [?], *n.* Any waste matter, rubbish; loppings of trees; a rubbishy production of any kind. *v.t.* To lop. **trashy,** *a.*

trauma (traw'má) [Gr., wound], *n.* An external injury; the morbid condition produced by this. **traumat'ic,** *a.* Pertaining to the cure of wounds. *n.* A medicine for wounds.

travail (trăv'ăl) [O.F. *travailler*, to toil], *n.* Painful toil, exertion, or effort; the pangs of childbirth. *v.i.* To toil painfully; to suffer the pangs of childbirth.

travel (trăv'el), *v.i.* To make a journey, esp. to distant lands; to move (along, etc., of machinery); to move through space; to make journeys as a commercial traveller. *n.* Act of travelling; (*pl.*) an account of travelling; length of stroke of a piston, etc. **travelled,** *a.* **traveller,** *n.*

traverse (trăv'ĕrs), *n.* Anything crossing something else; a gallery between opposite sides of a church, etc.; a zigzag line described by a ship owing to contrary winds; act of travelling across; the sideways travel of part of a machine; (*Law*) a denial of a formal allegation by the opposite party; the horizontal sweep of a gun. *v.t.* To travel across; to lie across or through; to examine or discuss thoroughly; to thwart, to bring to naught; (*Law*) to deny (a plea or allegation).

travesty (trăv'ĕs-ti) L. *vestire*, to clothe], *n.* A burlesque imitation. *v.t.* To make a travesty of, to misrepresent absurdly.

trawl (trawl) [?], *n.* A net for dragging along the sea-bottom; a trawl-line. *v.i.* To fish with a trawl. **trawl-net,** *n.* **trawler,** *n.* One who trawls; a fishing-vessel using a trawl-net.

tray (trā) [A.-S. *trig*], *n.* A flat shallow vessel for carrying small articles on.

treacherous (trech'ĕr-ŭs) [O.F. *trecheur*, traitor], *a.* Disloyal, perfidious; deceptive, illusory. **treacherously,** *adv.* **treachery,** *n.*

treacle (trēkl) [L. *thēriaca*, an antidote against bites or poison], *n.* A syrup drained from sugar in refining.

tread (tred) [A.-S. *tredan*], *v.i.* (*past*

trod, trod, trode, trōd, *p.p.* trodden, trodn) To set the foot on the ground; to walk; (*fig.*) to deal (cautiously, etc.); to copulate (of a male bird). *v.i.* To step on; to crush with the feet; to trample on; to dance (a measure, etc.). *n.* Act or manner of walking; a footstep; the flat part of a step, a piece of rubber, metal, etc., placed on this to reduce wear or noise; the part of a wheel that bears upon the ground, of a sole that rests on the ground; (*fig.*) wearisome monotony or routine.

treadle (tredl) [A.-S. *tredel*], *n.* A lever worked by the foot giving motion to a lathe, etc.

treason (trē'zòn) [M.E. *trayson*], *n.* A violation of allegiance by a subject against his sovereign or Government; an act of treachery. **treason-felony,** *n.* Act of attempting to depose the sovereign, intimidating Parliament, or stirring up foreign invasion. **treasonable,** *a.*

treasure (trezh'ûr) [Gr. *thēsauros*], *n.* Precious metals in any form, or gems; a quantity of these hidden away or kept for future use; accumulated wealth; anything highly valued; a hoard; a person greatly valued. *v.t.* To lay (up) as valuable; to prize. **treasure trove** (trōv) [A.-F. *tresor trove*, treasure found]; Gold, silver, etc., found in the earth or private place, the owner thereof being unknown. **treasurer,** *n.* One who has charge of a treasury or of funds. **treasury,** *n.* A place in which treasure is stored or where the public revenues are kept; a Government Department in charge of the public revenue; the officers of this.

treat (trēt) [L. *tractāre*, to handle], *v.t.* To act or behave towards; to deal with for a particular result, to apply a particular process to; to handle or present (a subject, etc.) in a particular way; to supply with food, drink, or entertainment at one's expense; to discuss; to arrange terms (with). *n.* An entertainment; an unusual pleasure. **treatise** (trē'tiz), *n.* A literary composition discussing some particular subject. **treatment,** *n.* Act or manner of treating a subject, behaving towards a person, applying remedies, etc. **treaty,** *n.* An agreement formally concluded and ratified between different States; negotiation.

treble (treb'ĕl), *a.* Triple, threefold; soprano. *n.* A soprano voice, singer, or part. *v.t.* To multiply by three or become threefold. **trebly,** *adv.*

tree (trē) [A.-S. *treo*], *n.* A perennial woody plant with a single trunk; a genealogical table; a gibbet; a cross of crucifixion; a timber beam or framework; a boot-last.

trefoil (trē'foil) [L. *folium*, leaf], *n.* A plant with three leaflets or three-lobed leaves; a three-lobed ornament in window-tracery, etc.

trek (trek) [Dut. *trekken*], *v.i.* (*S. Afr.*) To travel by ox-wagon; to journey, esp. in search of a new settlement. *n.* A journey with a wagon; a day's march. **trekker,** *n.*

trellis (trel'ĭs) [O.F. *trelis*], *n.* Open-work of strips of wood crossing each other and nailed together.

tremble (trĕm'bĕl) [F. *trembler*], *v.i.* To shake involuntarily; to be in a state of fear or agitation; to be alarmed (for); to totter. *n.* Act or state of trembling; fear. tremblingly, *adv.*

tremendous (trĕ-men'dŭs) [L. *tremendus*], *a.* Of overpowering magnitude, violence, etc.; dreadful; extraordinary.

tremor (trem'ŏr) [L. from *tremere*, to tremble], *n.* A trembling, quivering; a thrill.

tremulous (trem'ū-lŭs), *a.* Trembling, shaking, quivering; irresolute.

trench (trench) [O.F. *trenche*], *n.* A long narrow furrow in the earth; a long narrow ditch with a parapet formed by the excavated earth to cover troops. *v.t.* To cut trenches in (ground, etc.); to turn over (ground) by cutting a successive series of trenches and filling in with the excavated soil.

trenchant (tren'chănt) [O.F., cutting], *a.* Sharp, keen; biting, incisive.

trencher (tren'chĕr) [A.-F. *trenchour*], *n.* A wooden plate for use at table, now for cutting bread upon; (*fig.*) the pleasures of the table; a trencher-cap. trencher-cap, *n.* A college cap, with a flat top, a mortar-board.

trend (trend) [A.-S. *trendan*], *v.i.* To extend in a particular direction; to incline; to have a general tendency. *n.* Bent, inclination.

trepan (trĕ-păn') [Gr. *trupanon*, borer], *n.* A surgeon's cylindrical saw for removing portions of the skull. *v.t.* To perforate with a trepan.

trepidation (trep-ĭ-dā'shŭn) [L. *trepidus*, agitated], *n.* A state of alarm, or agitation.

trespass (tres'păs) O.F. *trespas*, L. *passāre*, to pass], *n.* A transgression, an offence; (*Law*) a wrongful act involving injury to another. *v.i.* To commit an illegal intrusion (upon the property or rights of another; (*fig.*) to encroach or make undue claims (upon). trespasser, *n.*

tress (tres) [F. *tresse*], *n.* A plait of hair; (*pl.*) hair.

trestle (tres'ĕl) [O.F. *trestel*], *n.* A movable frame for supporting a table, etc.; a framework of timber or iron for supporting the horizontal portion of a bridge.

tret (tret) [?], *n.* An allowance to purchasers of goods for damage or deterioration during transit.

trews (trooz), *n.pl.* (*Sc.*) Trousers, esp. made of tartan.

tri- [L., three], *pref.* Three; triple.

triad (trī'ăd) [Gr. *trias triados*], *n.* A collection of three.

trial (trī'ăl), *n.* Act or process of trying or testing; an examination, an experiment; that which tests strength, endurance, etc.; hardship, suffering, etc.; the judicial examination and determination of the issues in a cause between parties.

triangle (trī'ănggĕl), *n.* A figure bounded by three lines; anything of this shape; a steel rod bent into a triangle and sounded by striking with a steel rod.

triangular, *a.* Having the shape of a triangle; three-cornered. triangulate, *v.t.* To divide into triangles, esp. (an area) in surveying. triangula'tion, *n.*

tribal (trī'băl), *a.* Belonging or pertaining to a tribe. tribalism, *n.*

tribe (trīb) [L. *tribus*], *n.* A group of people ethnologically related and forming a community; a clan or group of clans; a group of plants or animals.

tribulation (trib-ū-lā'shŭn) [L. *tribulāre*, to oppress], *n.* Severe affliction, suffering, distress.

tribunal (trī-bū'năl) [L. *tribus*, a tribe], *n.* A court of justice; a board of arbitrators; a judgment-seat.

tribune (trib'ūn), *n.* (*Rom. Hist.*) One of the representatives elected by the people to protect them against the patriancis, a civil, fiscal, or military officer; a platform for speaking from.

tributary (trib'ū-tăr-ĭ) [L. *tributus*, paid; given], *a.* Paying or subject to tribute; subsidiary, contributory. *n.* A tributary person or State; a stream flowing into another.

tribute (trib'ūt), *n.* Money or other valuables paid by one State to another in token of submission, etc.; the state of being obliged to pay this; (*fig.*) a gift or offering (of praise, etc.).

trice (trīs) [M.Dut. *trisen*], *v.t.* (*Naut.*) To haul; to tie (up). *n.* An instant.

triceps (trī'seps) [L. *-seps*, from *caput*, head], *n.* The large muscle at the back of the upper arm.

trick (trik) [O.F. *trique*], *n.* An artifice, a stratagem; a practical joke; a feat of dexterity or sleight of hand; a knack; a mannerism, a personal peculiarity; (*Cards*) the whole number of cards played in one round; a round. *v.t.* To cheat, to delude; to inveigle (into, out of, etc.); to deck (out or up). trickster, *n.* trickery, *n.* tricky, *a.* trickily, *adv.* tricksy, *a.* Playful, sportive.

trickle (trik'ĕl) [M.E. *triklen*], *v.i.* To flow in drops or in a small stream. *n.* A trickling; a rill.

tricolour (trī'kŏ-lŏr), *n.* A flag having three colours, esp. in three colours divided vertically, as that of France of blue, white, and red.

tricycle (trī-sikl), *n.* A three-wheeled cycle. tricyclist, *n.*

trident (trī'dĕnt) L. *dens*, tooth], *n.* A three-pronged implement, sceptre, or spear, esp. the emblem of Neptune as god of the sea, and of Britannia as ruling the waves.

triennial (trī-en'ĭ-ăl) [L. *annus*, year], *a.* Lasting for three years; happening every three years.

trier (trī'ĕr), *n.* One who tries or tests in any way; a person appointed to determine whether a challenge to a juror is well founded.

trifle (trī'fĕl) [O.F. *truffe*, mockery], *n.* A thing of no importance; a small amount of money, etc.; a light confection of cake, jam, wine, etc. *v.i.* To act with levity; to jest. *v.t.* To waste or fool away (time). trifler, *n.* trifling, *a.* Trivial, worthless.

triforium (trī-fôr′i-ùm) [L. *foris*, door], *n.*
(*pl.* -ia) An arcade over the arches of
the nave, choir, or transepts in a large
church.

trigger (trig′ėr) [Dut. *trekken*, to pull], *n.*
A catch for releasing the hammer of a
gun-lock, or a spring.

trigonometry (trig-ô-nom′ė-tri) [Gr. *tri-
gōnon*, triangle], *n.* The branch of
mathematics treating of triangles, with
their application to astronomy, navigation, surveying, etc. **trigonomet′ric,
-al,** *a.*

trill (tril) [imit.], *v.i.* To give forth a
sound with a tremulous vibration. *n.*
A tremulous or quavering sound; a
rapid alternation of two notes a tone
or semitone apart.

trillion (tril′yòn), *n.* The product of a
million raised to the third power; (*Am.
and F.*) a million million. **trillionth,** *a.*

trilogy (tril′ô-ji), *n.* (*Gr. Ant.*) A series of
three plays, novels, etc., each complete
in itself, but connected by the story or
theme.

trim (trim) **[A.-S.** *trymian*, to make firm],
v.t. To put in good order; to remove
irregularities, superfluous, or unsightly
parts from; to decorate (with trimmings,
etc.); to adjust (a ship) by arranging the
cargo, ballast, sails, etc. *v.i.* To adopt
a middle course between parties, opinions,
etc. *a.* Properly adjusted, in good
order; neat, tidy. *n.* State of fitness,
esp. of a ship or her cargo, ballasts, masts,
etc. **trimly,** *adv.* **trimmer,** *n.* One who
trims between parties, esp. in politics.
trimming, *n.* Material sewn on a garment for ornament.

trinity (trin′i-ti) [L. *trīnitas*], *n.* A union
of three; the threefold state; the union of
three persons (the Father, the Son, and
the Holy Ghost) in one Godhead. **Trini-
tarian,** *a.* Of or pertaining to the doctrine
of the Trinity.

trinket (tring′kėt) [?], *n.* A small personal
ornament or fancy article of no great
value.

trio (trē′ō) [It.], *n.* A set of three; a
musical composition for three voices or
instruments.

triolet (trē′ô-let), *n.* A poem of eight lines
with two rhymes arranged *abaaabab.*

trip (trip) [O.F. *treper*], *v.i.* To step
lightly; to go evenly (of rhythm); to
stumble so as nearly to fall; to err. *v.t.*
To cause to fall; to detect in a fault,
etc.; (*Naut.*) to loosen (an anchor) from
the bottom. *n.* A light nimble step; a
short excursion; a stumble; a mistake.
tripper, *n.* One who trips, or who trips
up another; an excursionist.

tripartite (trī-par′tīt) [L. *partītus*, divided],
a. Divided into three parts; having
three copies; made between three parties.

tripe (trīp) [F.], *n.* A part of the stomach of
ruminating animals prepared for food.

triphthong (trif′thong), *n.* A combination
of three vowels forming one sound.
triphthongal (-thong′gàl), *a.*

triplane (trī′-plān), *n.* An aeroplane with
three supporting planes.

triple (trip′el) [L. *triplus*], *a.* Consisting of
three, threefold; multiplied by three.
v.t. To treble. **triplet,** *n.* A set of three;
each of three children at a birth; three
verses rhyming together. **trip′licate,** *a.*
Threefold; a document corresponding to
two others of the same kind. *v.t.* To
make triplicate, to treble.

tripod (trī′pod) [Gr. *pous podos*, foot], *n.*
A three-legged stand, stool, support for
a camera, etc.

tripos (trī′pós) [L. *tripus*], *n.* (*pl.* -ses)
(*Camb. Univ.*) The examination for
honours, the successful candidates being
arranged in three grades.

triptych (trip′tik) [Gr. *ptuchē*, fold], *n.* A
picture, carving, etc., on three hinged
panels.

trireme (trī′rēm) [L. *rēmus*, oar], *n.* (*Class.
Ant.*) A war-galley with three benches
of oars.

trisect (trī-sekt′) [L. *sectus*, cut], *v.t.* To
divide into three equal parts. **tri-
section** (-sek′shùn), *n.*

trisyllable, *n.* A word of three syllables.
trisyllab′ic, *a.*

trite (trīt) [L. *trītus*, rubbed], *a.* Commonplace, hackneyed, stale.

triturate (trit′ū-rāt) [L. *trītūrātus*, rubbed],
v.t. To rub down to a fine powder.
triturable, *a.* **tritura′tion,** *n.*

triumph (trī′ùmf) [L. *triumphus*, Gr.
thriambos, hymn to Bacchus], *n.* (*Rom.
Ant.*) A pageant in honour of a victorious
general; state of being victorious; victory; exultation for success. *v.i.* To
enjoy a triumph; to gain a victory; to
exult. **trium′phal,** *a.* Pertaining to a
triumph. **triumphant,** *a.* Victorious;
exultant.

triumvir (trī-ùm′vėr) [L. *trium*, of three,
vir, man], *n.* Any one of three united in
office. **triumvirate,** *n.* The office of a
triumvir; a group of triumvirs.

triune (trī′ùn), *a.* Three in one. **triunity,** *n.*

trivet (triv′ėt) [A.-S. *trefet* (L. *pēs pedis*,
foot)], *n.* A three-legged stand, esp.
for supporting cooking-vessels at a fire.

trivial (triv′i-àl) [L. *triviālis*, ordinary], *a.*
Of little value or importance, trifling;
commonplace. **trivial′ity,** *n.* **trivially,**
adv.

trochee (trō′kė) [Gr. *trochaios*, running], *n.*
A metrical foot of two syllables, long and
short. **trochaic** (trô-kā′ik), *a.* and *n.*

troglodyte (trog′lô-dīt) [Gr. *trōglē*, cave,
duein, to enter], *n.* A cave-dweller.

Trojan (trō′jàn) [L. *Trōjānus*], *a.* Pertaining to ancient Troy. *n.* An inhabitant of ancient Troy; (*fig.*) a
plucky person.

troll (1) (trōl) [G. *trollen*, to roll], *v.t.* To
reel out (a song) in a careless manner;
to pass round. *v.i.* To fish by trailing
or spinning a revolving bait, esp. behind
a boat; to sing in a free and easy way.

troll (2) [Icel.], *n.* (*Scand. Myth.*) A
familiar and impish dwarf.

trolley (trol′i), *n.* A low four-wheeled
truck; a grooved wheel on a pole used
for conveying current to the motor on
electric tramways, etc. **trolley bus,** *n.*
Such a tramcar running free without
rails.

trollop (trol′óp) [?], *n.* A careless, slovenly
woman, a slattern.

trombone (trom-bōn') [It.], *n.* A powerful brass wind-instrument with a sliding tube.

troop (troop) [F. *troupe*], *n.* An assemblage, a crowd, a company; a band of performers, a troupe; *(Mil.)* the unit of cavalry formation; *(pl.)* soldiers. *v.i.* To come together, to assemble; to move in a troop. **troop-ship**, *n.* A transport for soldiers. **trooper**, *n.* A cavalry-soldier, esp. a private; a troop-ship.

trope (trōp) [Gr. *tropos*, turn], *n.* A figurative use of a word.

trophy (trō'fi) [Gr. *tropaion*, from *tropē*, defeat], *n.* Any captured thing preserved as a memorial of victory; an ornamental group of symbolical objects placed on a wall, etc. **trophied**, *a.*

tropic (trop'ik) [Gr. *tropē*, turning, solstice], *n.* Either of the two parallels of latitude at 23° 27' N. *(Cancer)* or S. *(Capricorn)* of the equator; *(pl.)* the region between these. *a.* Pertaining to the tropics, tropical. **tropical**, *a.*

troposphere (trō'pō-sfēr), *n.* *(Meteor.)* The hollow sphere of atmosphere surrounding the earth.

trot (trot) [F. *trotter*], *v.i.* To move at a steady rapid pace; to run with short brisk strides. *v.t.* To cause to trot; to cover (a distance) by trotting. *n.* The pace or motion of a horse, etc. in trotting; a brisk steady pace; an old woman. **trotter**, *n.* A horse trained for fast trotting; *(pl.)* animals' feet as food.

troth (trōth) [A.-S. *trēowth*, truth], *n.* Faith, fidelity, truth.

troubadour (troo'bà-door) [Prov. *trobador*], *n.* One of a class of Provençal lyric poets of the 11th cent.

trouble (trŭbl) [L. *turba*, crowd], *v.t.* To annoy, to molest; to distress; to inconvenience. *v.i.* To be disturbed; to take pains. *n.* Affliction, worry, perplexity, misfortune; exertion, inconvenience. **troublesome**, *a.* Giving trouble.

trough (trof) [A.-S. *trog*], *n.* A long, narrow, open vessel for holding water, fodder, etc., for animals, washing ore, etc.; a narrow depression (in land, the sea, etc.).

trounce (trouns) [O.F. *trons*], *v.t.* To beat severely. **trouncing**, *n.*

troupe (troop), *n.* A company of actors, performers, etc.

trouser (trou'zẽr) [? Ir. *triubhas*], *n.* A two-legged outer garment reaching from the waist to the ankles, worn by men *(usu. in pl.)*. **trousering**, *n.* Cloth for making trousers.

trousseau (troo'sō) [F., bundle], *n.* *(pl.* -eaux) The general outfit of a bride.

trout (trout) [A.-S. *truht*], *n.* A fresh-water game-fish allied to the salmon. **troutlet**, *n.*

trow (trō, trou) [A.-S. *trūwian*], *v.* To think, to suppose, to believe.

trowel (trou'ĕl) [L. *trua*, ladle], *n.* A tool used by masons for spreading mortar; a tool used in digging up plants.

troy (troi) [? *Troyes*, town S.E. of Paris], *n.* A system of weights (12 oz. av. to 1 lb.) used for gold, silver, and gems, also called **troy weight.**

truant (troo'ầnt) [A.-F. *truaunt*], *a.* Shirking. *n.* One who neglects duty; a loiterer; one who stays away from school without leave.

truce (troos) [A.-S. *trēow*], *n.* A temporary cessation of hostilities; an armistice.

truck (1) (trŭk) [A.-S. *troquier*, from O.F. *troque*, barter], *v.* To exchange; to peddle, hawk. *n.* Exchange of commodities; commodities suitable for barter; intercourse, dealings.

truck (2) [Gr. *trochos*, wheel], *n.* A strong vehicle for conveying heavy goods; a lorry; an open railway wagon; a low barrow for moving luggage, etc.; a frame and set of wheels for supporting a railway carriage, etc.; a small wooden disk at the top of a mast or flagstaff.

truckle (trŭkl) [Gr. *trochalia*, pulley], *v.i.* To give way obsequiously; to cringe. **truckle-bed**, *n.* A low bed on castors for rolling under another.

truculent (trŭk'ū-lẽnt) [L. *trux*, savage], *a.* Ferocious, violent. **truculence**, **-lency**, *n.* **truculently**, *adv.*

trudge (trŭj) [F. *trucher*, to beg], *v.* To travel on foot with labour and fatigue. *n.* A walk of this kind.

trudgeon (trŭj'ŏn) [J. *Trudgeon* (fl. 1860-70)], *n.* A swimming stroke, with the hands brought over the head alternately.

true (troo) [A.-S. *trēowe*], *a.* Conformable to fact, not false; not deceptive or spurious, genuine; legitimate, rightful; corresponding to type; in perfect tune (of a voice, etc.); loyal, constant; honest.

truffle (trŭfl) [O.F. *trufle*], *n.* A fleshy fungus used for seasoning, etc.

truism (troo'izm), *n.* A self-evident truth; an obvious statement, a platitude. **tru'ly**, *adv.* Sincerely, in accordance with truth, accurately; genuinely; honestly, loyally.

trump (1) (trŭmp) [O.F. *trompe*], *v.t.* To impose (a thing) upon. **to trump up:** To fabricate, concoct. **trumpery**, *n.* Worthless finery; rubbish.

trump (2) [F. *triomphe*, a card-game], *n.* Any card of a suit ranking for the time being above the others; *(colloq.)* a good fellow; *(fig.)* an infallible expedient.

trump (3), *n.* Trumpet call, as in "the last Trump" or end of the world (I Cor. xv, 52).

trumpet (trŭm'pĕt), *n.* A musical wind instrument, usu. of brass, with a cup-shaped mouthpiece; a thing resembling this, as a funnel, an ear-trumpet; a sound of a trumpet. *v.t.* To proclaim by or as by a trumpet. *v.i.* To make a loud sound (esp. of the elephant). **trumpeter**, *n.* One who sounds a trumpet, esp. a cavalryman.

truncate (trŭng'kāt) [L. *truncatum*, mutilated], *v.t.* To cut the top or end from. *a.* Cut short; terminating abruptly. **trunca'tion**, *n.*

truncheon (trŭn'chŏn) [O.F. *tronçon*], *n.* A short club; a staff of authority.

trundle (trŭndl) [L.G. *tröndeln*], *n.* A small broad wheel; a truck. *v.* To roll.

trunk (trŭngk) [L. *truncus*, stem], *n.* The main stem of a tree; the body of an animal apart from the limbs, head, and tail; main body of anything; a trunk-line; a chest for packing clothes, etc., in for travel; the proboscis of an elephant. **trunk-line,** *n.* The main line of a railway, telephone-system, etc.

trunnion (trŭn'yŏn) [F. *trognon*], *n.* A cylindrical projection from the side of a cannon, two of which serve as supports.

truss (trŭs) [O.F. *trusser*], *v.t.* To support or brace with a truss; to fasten (the wings of a fowl, etc.) before cooking. *n.* A supporting and strengthening structure in a roof, bridge, etc.; a padded belt worn round the body for preventing or compressing a hernia; a bundle of hay or straw.

trust (trŭst) [M.E.], *n.* Confident reliance on or belief in a person or thing; firm expectation (that); that on which reliance is placed; commercial credit; property held in trust; the legal relation between such property and the holder; (*Comm.*) a combination of a number of businesses for the purpose of defeating competition, creating a monopoly, etc. *v.t.* To place confidence in, to reply upon; to believe, to have a confident expectation; to entrust; to give credit to. *v.i.* To have trust or confidence. **trustee'**, *n.* One to whom property is committed in trust for the benefit of another; one of a body managing an institution. **trusteeship**, *n.* trustful, *a.* Full of trust; confiding. **trustless,** *a.* Not worthy of trust. **trustworthy,** *a.* Deserving of confidence. **trusty,** *a.* Trustworthy; not liable to fail in time of need.

truth (trooth) [A.-S. *trēowthu*], *n.* State or quality of being true; conformity to fact or reality; a fact, a verity; honesty, veracity; fidelity; true religion. **truthful,** *a.* Habitually speaking the truth, conformable to truth. **truthless,** *a.*

try (trī) [F. *trier*], *v.t.* (*past and p.p.* tried) To test; to find out by experiment or experience; to attempt; to strain; to afflict; to investigate (a charge, etc.) judicially, to subject (a person) to judicial trial. *v.i.* To endeavour, to make an attempt. *n.* An attempt; (*Football*) the right to try to kick a goal. **triable,** *a.*

tryst (trist, trīst) [O.F.V. *triste,* a watching-station in hunting], *n.* An appointment; a rendezvous. *v.i.* To agree to meet; to appoint (a time or place) for meeting. **trysting-day,** *n.* **trysting-place,** *n.*

Tsar (tsar, zar) [Rus. *tsari,* L. *Cæsar*], *n.* The title of the former Emperors of Russia. **Tsarevitch,** *n.* The son of a Tsar. **Tsarevna** (-ev'na), *n.* The daughter of a Tsar. **Tsarina** (-ê'na), **Tsaritza** (-it'sa), *n.* The wife of a Tsar.

tsetse (set'si) [native], *n.* A S. African fly, the bite of which is often fatal to cattle, horses, etc.

tub (tŭb) [M. Dut. *tobbe*], *n.* An open wooden (usu. round) vessel; a small cask; a bath in a tub; a clumsy boat. *v.t.* To place in a tub; to bathe in a tub. *v.i.* To take a bath in a tub; to row in a tub.

tube (tūb) [L. *tubus,* a trumpet], *n.* A long hollow cylinder, a pipe; a cylindrical case of thin flexible metal for holding pigment, etc.; an underground tubular electric railway. *v.t.* To furnish with or enclose in a tube. **tubing,** *n.*

tuber (tū'bĕr) [L., hump], *n.* A short, thick part of an underground stem, set with modified buds, as in the potato; a truffle.

tubercle (tū'bĕrkl), *n.* A small prominence; a small granular tumour formed within an organ tending to set up degeneration. etc. **tuber'cular, -lous,** *a.* **tuberculo'sis,** *n.* A diseased condition characterized by the presence of tubercles in the tissues, esp. consumption.

tuberose (tū'bĕr-ōs), *a.* Tuberous. *n.* (*incorr. pron.* tūb'rōz) A bulbous plant with fragrant white flowers. **tuberous,** *a.* Having prominent knobs or excrescences; like or bearing tubers.

tubular (tū'bū-lår), *a.* Tube-shaped; having or consisting of a tube.

tuck (tŭk) [M.E. *tukken*], *v.t.* To fold in or roll up the loose ends of; to cover up closely; to gather into small compass. *n.* A horizontal fold in a dress, etc.

tucker (tŭk'ér), *n.* One who or that which tucks; a frilling round the top of a woman's dress.

-tude [L. *-tūdo*], *suf.* Forming abstract nouns, as *altitude, beatitude, fortitude.*

Tuesday (tūz'dā, -di) [A.-S. *Tiwes dæg,* day of *Tiw,* the god of war], *n.* The third day of the week.

tuft (tŭft) [F. *touffe*], *n.* A cluster of hairs, threads, feathers, etc., bound at one end. **tufted, tufty,** *a.*

tug (tŭg) [M.E. *toggen*], *v.t.* To pull with great effort; to haul, to tow. *v.i.* To pull violently (at). *n.* Act or a spell of tugging; a vigorous pull; a small powerful steam-vessel for towing others.

tuition (tū-ish'ŭn) [L. *tuēri,* to watch], *n.* Instruction, esp. in a particular subject.

tulip (tū'lip) [Turk. *tulbend,* turban], *n.* A bulbous plant of the lily family, with gorgeous bell-shaped flowers. **tulip-tree,** *n.* A large N. American tree of the magnolia family.

tulle (tool, tul) [Toul, in France], *n.* A fine silk net, used for veils, etc.

tumble (tŭmb'ĕl) [M.E. *tumblen,* freq. from A.-S. *tumbian*], *v.i.* To fall suddenly or violently; to roll about; to perform acrobatic feats. *v.t.* To toss forcibly, to push (down, etc.); to cause to fall; to rumple. *n.* A fall; an acrobatic feat, a somersault. **tumble-down,** *a.* Dilapidated. **tumbler,** *n.* One who or that which tumbles; an acrobat; a variety of pigeon; a stemless drinking-glass; a spring-latch in a lock.

tumbrel (tŭm'brĕl) [O.F.], *n.* A two-wheeled covered cart for ammunition, etc.; a dung-cart.

tumid (tū'mid) [L. *tumēre,* to swell], *a.* Enlarged, distended; (*fig.*) pompous, bombastic. **tumescent** (-mes'ènt), *a.* **tumid'ity,** *v.t.*

tumour (tū'mŏr), *n.* A morbid swelling on some part of the body.

tumult (tū'mŭlt), *n.* The commotion of a multitude, esp. with confusion of sounds;

a confused outbreak; riot; excitement. **tumultuary, tumultuous,** *a.*

tumulus (tū'mū-lùs), *n.* (*pl.* -lī) A mound of earth, usu. sepulchral; a barrow. **tumular,** *a.*

tun (tŭn) [A.-S. *tunne*], *n.* A large cask; a wine-measure, 252 galls.

tune (tūn) [A.-F. *tun*], *n.* A melodious succession of musical tones, a melody; correct intonation; proper adjustment of an instrument for this; (*fig.*) concord, frame of mind, mood. *v.t.* To put in tune; (*fig.*) to adjust, attune. **tunable,** *a.* **tuneful,** *a.* Melodious, musical. **tuneless,** *a.* Not in tune; inharmonious; (*fig.*) silent. **tuner,** *n.* One who tunes musical instruments. **tuning-fork,** *n.* A two-pronged steel instrument giving a fixed note when struck.

tungsten (tŭng'stèn) [Swed. *tung,* heavy, *sten,* stone], *n.* A heavy, greyish metallic element.

tunic (tū'nĭk) [L. *tunica*], *n.* A short-sleeved body-garment; a surcoat worn over armour; a military coat.

tunnel (tŭn'él) [O.F. *tonnel*], *n.* An underground passage, artificial or burrowed by an animal. *v.* To make a tunnel through (a hill, etc.); to shape like a tunnel.

tunny (tŭn'ĭ) [Gr. *thunnos*], *n.* A large Mediterranean sea-fish.

tup (tŭp) [M.E. *tuppe*], *n.* A ram.

Turanian (tū-rā'nĭ-àn) [*Turan,* mythical founder of the Turkish race], *a.* Applied to certain Asiatic languages that are neither Aryan nor Semitic, e.g. Turkish.

turban (tèr'bàn) [Turk. *tulbend*], *n.* An Oriental head-dress consisting of a scarf wound round the cap; a woman's head-dress imitating this.

turbid (tèr'bid) [L. *turba,* crowd], *a.* Muddy, thick; (*fig.*) disturbed. **turbid'ity,** *n.*

turbine (tèr'bin, -bĭn) [L. *turbo,* wheel, top], *n.* A water-wheel or motor enclosed in a case and acted upon by a flowing stream, steam, or air; a vessel propelled by a turbine.

turbot (tèr'bòt), *n.* A large flat-fish.

turbulent (tèr'bū-lènt) [L. *turba,* crowd], *a.* Disturbed, tumultuous; insubordinate. **turbulence,** *n.*

tureen (tū-rēn') [F. *terrine,* earthenware pot], *n.* A deep covered dish for soup.

turf (tèrf) [A.-S.], *n.* Surface earth filled with the matted roots of grass, etc.; a sod; growing grass. *v.t.* To cover or line with turfs. **turfy,** *a.*

turgid (tèr'jid) [L. *turgēre,* to swell], *a.* Bloated, morbidly distended; (*fig.*) pompous, bombastic. **turges'cent,** *a.* Swelling. **turgescence,** *n.* **turgid'ity,** *n.*

Turk (tèrk), *n.* One of the Mohammedan race ruling in Turkey; (*fig.*) a troublesome person, esp. a boy. **Turkish,** *a.*

turkey (tèr'ki) [from belief that it came from Turkey], *n.* A large gallinaceous bird, allied to the pheasant, orig. from America.

turmeric (tèr'mĕ-rik) [F. *terre-merite*], *n.* An E. Indian plant of the ginger family; a dye-stuff, stimulant, and condiment made from this.

turmoil (tèr'moil) [?], *n.* Commotion, tumult.

turn (tèrn) [A.-S. *turnian,* L. *tornus,* lathe, Gr. *tornus*], *v.t.* To cause to move round, to give a rotary motion to; to cause to go, look, etc., in a different direction; to invert, reverse; to revolve in the mind; to change in form, condition, nature, etc ; to go round; to blunt (a knife-edge, etc.); to cause to ferment; to nauseate; to shape in a lathe or on a wheel; (*fig.*) to round (a sentence, etc.). *v.i.* To rotate, revolve, move round or about; to change front; to change in posture, attitude, or position; to be changed in nature, form, condition, etc.; to become sour; to become unsettled or infatuated; to become nauseated; to result. *n.* Act of turning, rotary motion; a revolution; state of being turned; a change of direction, a deflexion; a bend, a corner; a single coil of rope, etc.; a vicissitude; a short stroll; a spell (of doing something), an occasion or time (for doing something) coming in succession; alternation, rotation; (*fig.*) mould, character, temper. **turn-coat,** *n.* One who deserts his party or principles. **turncock,** *n.* One who turns water on or off from a main. **turner,** *n.* One who turns articles in a lathe; a variety of tumbler-pigeon. **turnery,** *n.* turning, *n.* Act of one who or of that which turns; the point where a road meets another; such a road. **turning-point,** *n.* The decisive point. **turnkey,** *n.* One in charge of the keys of a prison, a warder. **turn-out,** *n.* A turning out for duty; a quitting of employment; a strike; a large party; a showy equipage; a quantity manufactured in a given time. **turn-over,** *n.* An upset; a tart made by turning over half the crust; the amount of money turned over in a business in a given time. **turnpike,** *n.* A gate set across a road to stop carriages, etc., from passing till the toll is paid; a road on which toll-gates were established. **turn-stile,** *n.* A post with revolving arms at the entrance to an enclosure, building, etc., allowing persons to pass only after the toll is paid. **turn-table,** *n.* A rotating platform for shifting rolling-stock from one lines of rails to another.

turnip (tèr'nip) [L. *nāpus*], *n.* A plant with a fleshy globular root used as a vegetable and for feeding sheep.

turpentine (tèr'pèn-tin) [TEREBINTH], *n.* An oil resin exuding from several coniferous trees; oil or spirit of turpentine.

turpitude (tèr'pi-tūd) [L. *turpis,* base], *n.* Baseness, depravity.

turquoise (tèr'koiz, -kwoiz) [O.F., Turkish], *n.* A bluish-green precious stone.

turret (tŭr'ét) [F. *tour,* tower], *n.* A small tower on a building; a revolving, cylindrical, armoured tower on a warship or fort. **turreted,** *a.*

turtle (1) (tèrtl) [L. *turtur*], *n.* The common wild dove, the turtle-dove.

turtle (2) (tèrtl), *n.* A marine tortoise, with flippers used in swimming; a reptile used for soup; turtle-soup.

Tuscan (tŭs'kàn), *a.* Pertaining to Tuscany, or to the simplest of the five classic orders of architecture, a Roman modification of Doric. *n.* A native, or the language, of Tuscany; the Tuscan order.

tusk (tŭsk) [A.-S. *tusc*], *n.* A long pointed protruding tooth as in the elephant; a spike, as in a harrow, lock, etc.

tussle (tŭsl), *v.i.* To struggle, to scuffle (with or for); to tousle. *n.* A struggle, a scuffle.

tussock (tŭs'ŏk) [?], *n.* A tuft or hillock of growing grass; a lock of hair, etc.

tut (tŭt) [instinctive], *int.* An exclamation of impatience, rebuke, or contempt.

tutelage (tū'tě-lǎj) [L. *tutus*, looked after], *n.* Guardianship; state of being under a guardian; the period of this. **tutelar,** **-lary,** *a.* Having the care of a person or thing, protective.

tutor (tū'tŏr), *n.* A private teacher; (*Univ.*) an officer directing studies of undergraduates in college. *v.t.* To act as a tutor to; to teach, train. **tutorage,** *n.* **tutor'ial,** *a.* tutorship, *n.*

tuxedo (tŭk-zē'dō), *n.* (*Am.*) A dinner-jacket.

twaddle (twodl), *v.i.* To talk unmeaningly. *n.* Unmeaning talk, silly chatter, nonsense. **twaddler,** *n.*

twain (twān) [A.-S. *twegen*], *a.* Two. *n.* A pair. **in twain:** In two, asunder.

twang (twăng), *v.i.* To make a ringing sound as by plucking the string of an instrument; to speak with a nasal sound. *n.* Such a ringing metallic sound; a nasal tone.

tweak (twēk) [A.-S. *twiccian*], *v.t.* To pinch and twist or pull with a sudden jerk, to twitch. *n.* A sharp pinch or pull, a twitch.

tweed (twēd) [TWILL, through Sc. *tweel*], *n.* A twilled woollen fabric used for outer garments.

tweezer (twē'zẽr) [F. *étui*, a small case for instruments], *n.* (*in pl.*) Small pincers for plucking out hairs, etc.

twelfth (twelfth) [A.-S. *twelfta*], *a.* Next after the eleventh. *n.* One of twelve equal parts.

twelve (twelv) [A.-S. *twelf*], *a.* Consisting of the sum of two and ten. *n.* The sum of two and ten, 12, xii. **twelve-month,** *n.* A year.

twenty (twen'ti) [A.-S. *twentig*], *a.* Twice ten, 20, xx. *n.* The number of twice ten. **twentieth,** *a.* and *n.*

twerp (twẽrp) [?], *n.* (*colloq.*) A contemptible fellow.

twice (twīs), *adv.* Two times; doubly.

twiddle (twidl) [?], *v.* To twirl idly; to fiddle with.

twig (1) (twig) [A.-S.], *n.* A small shoot, a branchlet. **twiggy,** *a.*

twig (2) [? Ir. *tuigim*, I understand], *v.t.* To comprehend; to notice.

twilight (twī'līt) [A.-S. *twi-*, two], *n.* The diffused light a little before sunrise and after sunset; obscurity; (*fig.*) indistinct perception of knowledge. *a.* Pertaining to the twilight; dim, shady.

twill (twil) [A.-S. *twilic*, two threaded], *n.* A fabric in which the weft- and warp-threads produce diagonal ribs or lines.

twin (twin) [A.-S. *getwinne*], *a.* Being one of two born at a birth; similar, or closely related; double, twofold. *n.* One of

two produced at a birth; an exact counterpart.

twine (twīn) [A.-S. *twīn*, twisted thread], *v.t.* To twist; to coil round, to embrace; to form by interweaving. *v.i.* To be interwoven; to entwine; to meander. *n.* A twist, a coil; act of twining or entwining; a tangle; strong string made of two or three strands.

twinge (twinj) [A.-S. *twengan*], *v.t.* To affect with a sharp, sudden pain. *n.* A sharp, sudden, shooting pain; a pang, as of remorse or sorrow.

twinkle (twing'kěl) [A.-S. *twinclian*], *v.i.* To gleam fitfully, to sparkle; to appear and disappear in rapid alternation; to blink. *n.* A tremulous gleam, a sparkle; a wink; a rapid tremulous movement. **twinkling,** *n.* A twinkle; the time of this, an instant.

twirl (twẽrl) [A.-S. *thweran*, to turn], *v.t.* To cause to rotate rapidly, to spin; to whirl (round); to twist, to curl (the moustache, etc.).

twist (twist) [A.-S. *twist*, rope], *v.t.* To wind a thread, etc., round another; to make spiral by turning the ends in opposite directions. *v.i.* To be turned round and round upon itself; to move in a winding or irregular path; to writhe. *n.* Act or manner of twisting or state of being twisted; a quick or vigorous turn; a sharp bend; (*fig.*) a peculiar tendency, a bent; strong silk thread or cotton yarn made from twisted strands; twisted tobacco.

twit (twit) [A.-S. *ætwitan* (AT, *witan*, to blame)], *v.t.* To reproach, taunt, upbraid.

twitch (twich) [M.E. *twicchen*], *v.t.* To pull with a sudden or sharp jerk. *v.i.* To move with a spasmodic jerk. *n.* A sudden pull; a sudden involuntary contraction of a muscle.

twitter (twit'ẽr), *v.i.* To utter short, tremulous, intermittent notes; to chirp. *n.* Such a succession of sounds, a chirping; (*colloq.*) a state of excitement.

two (too) [A.-S. *twegen*], *a.* One more than one, 2, ii. *n.* The sum of one and one. **two-edged,** *a.* Having an edge on both sides; cutting both ways. **two-faced,** *a.* Deceitful, insincere. **twofold,** *a.* Double. *adv.* Doubly. **twopence** (tŭp'ĕns), *n.* The sum of two pence.

-ty [F. *-té*], *suf.* Forming abstract nouns as *bounty, cruelty*; [A.-S. *-tig*, cogn. with TEN], as in *fifty, twenty.*

tycoon (tī-koon') [Jap. *taikun*, great prince], *n.* A financial, commercial or shady political magnate.

tympanum (tim'pǎ-nŭm) [Gr. *tumpanon*, drum], *n.* (*pl.* **-na**) The middle ear; the ear-drum; (*Arch.*) a triangular arch, usu. recessed, in a pediment.

type (tīp) [L. *typus*, Gr. *tupos*, stamp, character], *n.* A distinguishing mark, a symbol, emblem, a representative specimen of a class of things; (*Art*) a model or guide to later artists; a piece of metal or hard wood bearing a letter or character for printing with; (*collect.*) a set or quantity of these. *v.t.* To typewrite **type-founder,** *n.* One who casts types type-foundry, *n.* type-setter, *n.* A compositor. typewriter, *n.* A machine for producing printed characters as a substitute for handwriting; (*incorr.*) a typist. typewrite, *v.* To write with this. typewriting, *n.* typewritten, *a.*

typhoid (tī'foid), *a.* Pertaining to or resembling typhus. *n.* An infectious fever characterized by red spots on the chest and abdomen, severe intestinal irritation, inflammation, diarrhœa, etc., enteric.

typhoon (tī-foon') [Arab. *tūfān*, cogn. with foll.], *n.* A violent cyclonic hurricane occurring in the China Seas. typhon'ic, *a.*

typhus (tī'fŭs) [Gr. *tuphos*, smoke, stupor], *n.* A contagious fever marked by an eruption of dark purple spots, great prostration, stupor and delirium. ty'phous, *a.*

typic (tip'ik), *a.* Figurative, typical. typical, *a.* Of the nature of or serving as a type; emblematic or characteristic (of); embodying the characters of a group, class, etc. typically, *adv.* typify (tip'i-fī), *v.t.* To represent by a type; to prefigure; to exemplify. typifica'tion, *n.*

typist (tī'pist), *n.* One who works on a typewriter.

typography (tī-pog'rȧ-fī), *n.* The art of printing; the arrangement, character, or appearance of printed matter. typographer, *n.* typograph'ic, *a.* typographically, *adv.*

tyrannicide (ti-răn'i-sīd), *n.* The act of killing a tyrant; one who does this. tyrannici'dal, *a.*

tyrannize (tĭr'ȧ-nīz), *v.i.* To act the tyrant; to rule oppressively (over). *v.t.* To rule (a person, etc.) despotically. tyrannous, *a.* tyranny, *n.* Arbitrary or despotic exercise of power; an oppressive act, the office or rule of a tyrant; the period of this; harshness, severity.

tyrant (tī'rȧnt) [L. *tyrannus*, Gr. *turannos*], *n.* An oppressive or cruel master; a despot, an autocrat, esp. when a usurper. tyran'nical, *a.* Acting like or characteristic of a tyrant; despotic, imperious.

tyro (tīr'ō) [L. *tiro*, a newly enlisted soldier], *n.* A beginner, a novice.

Tyrolese (tĭr-ō-lēz'), *a.* Pertaining to Tyrol. *n.* A native of Tyrol.

U

ubiquity (ū-bik'wi-ti) [L. *ubīque*, everywhere], *n.* The quality or state of being everywhere or in many places at the same time, omnipresence. ubiquitous, *a.*

udder (ŭd'ẽr) [A.-S. *ūder*], *n.* The milk-secreting organ of a cow, ewe, etc.

ugly (ŭg'li) [Icel. *uggr*, fear], *a.* Unpleasing to the sight; ungraceful, not comely; morally repulsive, suggesting evil; threatening, formidable. ugliness, *n.*

Uhlan (oo'-, ū'lȧn) [G. and Pol. *ulan*, Turk. *oglān*, son], *n.* A German cavalry-man armed with a lance.

Uitlander (oo'it-lan-dẽr) [Dut.], *n.* A non-Dutch immigrant into the Transvaal.

ukelele (ū-ke-lā'li) [Hawaiian], *n.* A small 4-stringed musical instrument resembling a guitar.

ulcer (ŭl'sẽr) [L. *ulcus*, sore], *n.* An open sore accompanied by a secretion of pus or other discharge; (*fig.*) a source of corruption. ulcerate, *v.t.* To affect with an ulcer. *v.i.* To become ulcerous. ulcera'tion, *n.* ulcerous, *a.*

-ule [L. *-ulus*], dim. suf. As in *globule*, *pustule*.

ullage (ŭl'ij) [L. *oculus*, an eye, an orifice], *n.* The quantity that a cask wants of being full.

ulna (ŭl'nȧ) [L., elbow], *n.* (*pl.* -næ) The larger and longer of the two bones of the fore-arm.

ulster (ŭl'stẽr) [prov. of Ireland], *n.* A long, loose overcoat, usu. with a belt.

ulterior (ŭl-tēr'i-ȯr) [L., comp. of *ulter*, whence], *a.* Lying beyond or on the other side of any boundary; more distant; not at present under consideration; not yet disclosed.

ultimate (ŭl'ti-mȧt), *a.* Last, final; incapable of further analysis; fundamental, primary; most remote. ultimately, *adv.* ultima'tum, *n.* A final proposal, the rejection of which may involve war; anything final, essential, or fundamental. *ultimo*, *adv.* Last month.

ultra- [L., beyond; excessively; beyond the normal, reasonable, etc.], *pref.* ultra-conservative (ŭl'trȧ-kȯn-sẽr'vȧ-tiv), *a.* Extravagantly conservative.

ultramarine (ŭl-trȧ-mȧ-rēn'), *a.* Situated or being beyond the sea. *n.* A deep-blue pigment; the colour of this.

ultramontane (ŭl-trȧ-mon'tȧn), *a.* Being or lying beyond the mountains, esp. the Alps, esp. on the Italian side; hence, supporting the absolute power and infallibility of the Pope.

ultramundane (ŭl-trȧ-mŭn'dȧn), *a.* External to the world or the solar system; pertaining to another life.

ultra-violet rays, *n.pl.* (*Phys.*) Active rays belonging to that portion of the spectrum which is beyond violet. They are used therapeutically.

umbel (ŭm'bel) [L.], *n.* An inflorescence in which the flower-stalks spring and spread from one point, as in parsley. umbellate, umbellif'erous, *a.*

umber (ŭm'bẽr) [L. *umbra*, shadow], *n.* A dark-brown pigment. *a.* Of the colour of umber, dusky.

umbilical (ŭm-bil'i-kȧl) [L. *umbilicus*, navel], *a.* Pertaining to or situated near the navel; central. umbilicus, *n.* The navel; a navel-shaped depression, as at the axial base of some univalve shells. umbil'iform, *a.*

umbles (ŭmblz) [L. *lumbus*, loin], *n.pl.* The entrails of a deer.

umbra (ŭm'brȧ) [L., shadow], *n.* (*pl.* -bræ) The part of the shadow of a planet or moon in which the light of the sun is entirely cut off.

umbrage (ŭm'brȧj), *n.* A sense of injury, offence. umbrageous (-brā'jŭs), *a.* Shady, shaded.

umbrella (ŭm-brel'ȧ) [It. *ombrella*], *n.* A light, circular folding screen on a stick for protection of the person against rain or sun.

umpire (ŭm'pīr) [M.E. *nompere*, peerless], *n.* A person chosen to enforce rules and settle disputes, a referee; (*Law*) a third person called in to settle a disagreement between arbitrators. *v.* To act as umpire.

umpteen (ŭmp-tēn'), *a.* (*colloq.*) Any number.

un- [A.-S.], *pref.* (1) Giving a negative sense to adjectives, adverbs, and nouns; (2) used with verbs to denote reversal or annulment of the action of the simple verb (sometimes ambiguous, thus *un-rolled* may mean 'not rolled', or 'opened out after having been rolled up'). Since there is no limit to the use of this prefix the meaning of words not given in the following selection can be ascertained by reference to the simple verb, adjective, etc.

unaccount'able, *a.* Not accountable or responsible; inexplicable.

unanimous (ū-năn'ī-mŭs) [L. *ūnus*, one, *animus*, mind], *a.* Being all of one mind; formed, held or expressed with one accord. **unanim'ity,** *n.* **unan'imously,** *adv.*

unap'petizing, *a.* Unpleasant to the palate; not enticing (of food). **unassu'ming,** *a.* Not arrogant or presuming; modest. **unawares,** *adv.* Without warning; by surprise, unexpectedly; undesignedly. **unbal'ance,** *v.t.* To throw off one's balance. **unbalanced,** *a.* Not balanced; not brought to an equality of debit and credit; unsteady, erratic. **unbear'able,** *a.* Not to be borne, intolerable. **unbelief',** *n.* The withholding of belief; incredulity; scepticism; disbelief (in, esp. divine revelation). **unbeliever,** *n.* **unbelieving,** *a.* **unbend',** *v.t.* To straighten; to relax from exertion, constraint, etc.; untie. **unblush'ing,** *a.* Shameless, barefaced, impudent. **unbosom** (-buz'ŭm), *v.t.* To disclose (one's feelings, etc.). *v.i.* To disclose one's secret feelings, opinions, or intentions; to open one's heart. **unbowed** (-boud'), *a.* Not bowed; (*fig.*) unconquered. **uncalled for:** Not necessary; not asked for, gratuitous, impertinent. **uncan'ny,** *a.* Weird, mysterious; incautious. **unceasing** (-sē'sing), *a.* Not ceasing, incessant, continual. **uncer'tain,** *a.* Not sure; doubtful; not certainly or precisely known; not to be relied on; fickle, capricious. **unchris'tian,** *a.* Heathen; not according to or befitting the spirit of Christianity.

uncial (ŭn'shàl) [L. *uncia*, inch, ounce], *a.* Denoting a kind of writing resembling modern capitals used in MSS. of the 4th-8th cents. *n.* An uncial letter or MS.

uncircumcised (ŭn-sêr'kŭm-sīzd), *a.* Not circumcised; not Jewish; (*fig.*) heathen, profane.

uncle (ŭnkl) [A.-F., L. *avunculus*], *n.* The brother of one's father or mother; the husband of one's aunt; (*slang*) a pawn-broker.

unclean (ŭn-klēn'), *a.* Foul, dirty; unchaste; not ceremonially clean. **uncleanly** (-klen'li), *a.* **uncom'mon,** *a.* Not common, unusual, remarkable, extraordinary. **uncon'scious,** *a.* Not con-

scious, ignorant, unaware (of); temporarily deprived of consciousness; not perceived by the mind. **unconsidered** (-kŏn-sid'ẽrd), *a.* Not taken into consideration. **uncork',** *v.t.* To take the cork out of; (*fig.*) to give vent to (one's feelings, etc.).

uncouth (ŭn-kooth') [A.-S. *uncūth* (*cūth*, p.p. of *cunnan*, to know)], *a.* Awkward, clumsy; outlandish, odd, ungainly. **uncouthness,** *n.* **uncover** (-kŭv'ẽr), *v.t.* To remove a covering from; to make known, to disclose. *v.i.* To take off the hat in salutation. **uncreated** (-krē-ā'tĕd), *a.* Not yet created; existing independently of creation. **uncrossed** (-krost'), *a.* Not crossed (as a cheque); not opposed.

unction (ŭnk'shŭn) [L. *unctio*, from *ungere*, to anoint], *n.* Act of anointing with oil in consecration or for medical purposes; that which is used in anointing, an unguent or ointment; (*fig.*) anything soothing or ingratiating; a quality in speech conveying deep fervour; effusive emotion, gush; relish; (*Theol.*) grace. **unctuous,** *a.* Greasy, soapy to the touch; full of unction; (*fig.*) hypocritically or affectedly fervid. **unctuously,** *adv.*

uncut', *a.* Not cut; having the margins untrimmed (of a book).

under (ŭn'dẽr) [A.-S.], *prep.* Below; at the foot of; beneath the surface of; (*fig.*) beneath the disguise of; inferior to; subject or subservient to; governed or directed by; on condition or pain of; by virtue of; in the time of; attested by; sown with. *adv.* In a lower or subordinate place, condition, or degree. *a.* Lower, inferior, subordinate.

under-, *pref.* Under, below (the substantive to which it is prefixed); beneath, lower than, subordinate; insufficiently, incompletely, immaturely. Only a selection of compounds with this prefix is given; others can be explained by reference to the simple adjective, noun, or verb. **underbid',** *v.t.* To bid less than (as at an auction). **underbred',** *a.* Not thoroughbred; ill-bred. **un'derclothes,** *n.pl.* Clothes worn under others, esp. next to the skin. **un'derclothing,** *n.* **un'dercurrent,** *n.* A current running below the surface; (*fig.*) a secret or unapparent tendency or influence. **undercut',** *v.t.* To cut under (coal, etc.) so as to remove it easily; to cut away the material beneath (a carved design); to offer lower terms than a competitor. *n.* (ŭn'-dẽr'kŭt) A blow upward; the under side of a sirloin, the tenderloin. **underdone** (-dŭn'), *a.* Insufficiently cooked. **underfoot',** *adv.* Under the feet; beneath. *v.t.* To under-pin. **undergo',** *v.t.* (*past* -went, *p.p.* -gone) To experience, to pass through, to suffer; to bear up against. **undergrad'uate,** *n.* A member of a University who has not yet taken a degree. **un'derground,** *a.* Situated below the surface of the earth. *n.* An underground railway. *adv.* (-ground') Below the surface of the earth. **un'dergrowth,** *n.* Small trees or shrubs growing under large ones. **underhand',** *adv.* Secretly, not openly; slyly, by fraud; with the hand underneath (of bowling). *a.* (ŭn'dẽr-hǎnd), Clandestine; sly, unfair. **underlie'**, *v.t.* (*past* -lay, *p.p.* -lain) To lie under or beneath; to be the basis or foundation of. **underline'**, *v.t.* To mark with a line underneath, esp. for emphasis. **underling** (ŭn'dẽr-ling), *n.* An inferior agent or assistant. **under-men'tioned**, *a.* Mentioned below or later. **undermine'**, *v.t.* To dig an excavation under; to render unstable by digging away the foundation of; (*fig.*) to injure by underhand means; to wear away (one's strength, etc.) by imperceptible degrees. **un'dermost**, *a.* Lowest in place, position, rank, etc. **underneath'**, *adv. and prep.* Beneath, below. **underpay'**, *v.t.* (*past and p.p.* -paid) To pay inadequately. **underpin'**, *v.t.* To support (a wall, etc.) by propping up with timber, masonry, etc. **underproof'**, *a.* Containing less alcohol than proof spirit. **undersell'**, *v.t.* To sell cheaper than. **the un'dersigned:** The person or persons signing a document etc. **understand** (ŭn-dẽr-stand'), *v.t.* (*past and p.p.* -stood) To know or perceive the meaning of; to comprehend fully; to take as meant or implied, to assume; to supply (a word, explanation, etc.) mentally. *v.i.* To have or exercise the power of comprehension; to be told; to hear. **understanding**, *a.* Intelligent; sensible. *n.* Act of one who understands; comprehension; the power or faculty of apprehension or of drawing inferences; discernment; accord; an informal agreement. **understrapper**, *n.* An inferior or subordinate agent. **un'derstudy**, *v.t.* To study (a part) in order to play it if the usual actor is unable; to study the acting of (an actor) thus. *n.* One who studies a part or actor thus. **undertake** (ŭn-dẽr-tāk'), *v.t.* (*past* -took, *p.p.* -taken) To take upon oneself, to enter upon (a task, enterprise, etc.); to engage oneself; to guarantee, to answer for it (that). *v.i.* To promise, to be guarantee (for). **un'dertaker**, *n.* One who undertakes; a tradesman who manages funerals. **underta'king**, *n.* Act of one who undertakes any business; that which is undertaken, a task, enterprise, agreement, stipulation. **undertone** (ŭn'dẽr-tōn), *n.* A low or subdued tone, esp. in speaking; a subdued colour. **un'derwear**, *n.* Clothes worn underneath others, underclothing. **un'derwood**, *n.* Undergrowth. **un'derworld**, *n.* The infernal regions; (*colloq.*) the criminal classes of society. **un'derwrite**, *v.t.* To execute and deliver a policy of marine insurance; to engage to buy all the stock in (a new company, etc.) not subscribed for; to subscribe. *v.i.* To act as an underwriter, to practise marine insurance. **underwriter**, *n.* **underwriting**, *n.* **undig'nified**, *a.* Not dignified; not consistent with one's dignity. **undiplomatic** (ŭn-dip-lō-mǎt'ik), *a.* Not diplomatic. **undistinguished**, *a.* Pos-

sessing no distinguishing mark or characteristic; not famous. **undone** (-dŭn'), *a.* Not done; unfastened; ruined, destroyed. **undoubted** (ŭn-dou'tĕd), *a.* Not called in question; unsuspected. **undoubtedly**, *adv.* Without doubt. **undress'**, *v.t.* To divest of clothes, to strip; to take the bandages, etc., from (a wound, etc.). *v.i.* To undress oneself. *n.* Ordinary dress, opp. to full dress or uniform; negligent attire. *a.* Pertaining to everyday dress; (*fig.*) commonplace. **undulate** (ŭn'dū-lāt) [L. *unda*, wave], *a.* Wavy, bending in and out or up and down. *v.i.* (-lāt) To have a wavy motion; to rise and fall (of water). **undula'tion**, *n.* Act of undulating; a wavy or sinuous form or motion, a gentle rise and fall. **undula'tory**, *a.* **unearth** (ŭn-ẽrth') *v.t.* To dig up or bring out of the earth; (*fig.*) to bring to light, to find out. **unearth'ly**, *a.* Not of this world, supernatural; weird, ghostly. **unequiv'ocal**, *a.* Not equivocal, not ambiguous; plain, manifest. **U.N.E.S.C.O.** [initials of United Nations Educational Scientific and Cultural Organization], *n.* (*Polit.*) A United Nations body seeking to promote peace through the means indicated in its title. **uneven** (ŭn-ē'ven), *a.* Not level or smooth; not uniform, regular, or equable; not divisible by 2 without a remainder, odd. **unexpired** (-ĕkspīrd'), *a.* Not having come to an end or termination. **unfet'tered**, *a.* Freed from restraint; without control. **unfit'**, *a.* Not fit (to do, to be, for, etc.); improper, unsuitable. *v.t.* To make unfit or unsuitable; to disqualify. **unfrock'**, *v.t.* To deprive of the character and privileges of a priest. **unfun'ded**, *a.* Not funded, floating (of a debt, etc.). **ungainly** (ŭn-gān'li) [M.E. *ungenliche*], *a.* Clumsy, awkward. **unglazed** (-glāzd'), *a.* Deprived of glazing; not furnished with glass (of window-frames, pictures, etc.). **ungroun'ded**, *a.* Unfounded, baseless. **ungual** (ŭng'gwǎl) [L. *unguis*, nail, claw], *a.* Pertaining to, or having a nail, claw, or hoof. **unguarded** (ŭn-gar'dĕd), *a.* Not guarded; careless; incautiously said or done. **unguent** (ŭng'gwĕnt) [L. *unguens -ntis*, anointing], *n.* Any soft composition used as an ointment or for lubrication. **un'guen'tary**, *a.* **unhallowed** (ŭn-hǎl'ōd, *a.* Profaned, desecrated; not consecrated. **unhand'**, *v.t.* To take the hand or hands off; to let go from one's grasp. **unhan'dy**, *a.* Not handy; clumsy, awkward. **unhoped** (-hōpt'), *a.* Not hoped for; unexpected, beyond hope. **uni-** [L. *ūnus*, one], *comb. form.* **uniarticulate** (ū-ni-ar-tik'ū-lāt), *a.* Single-jointed. **unicorn** (ū'ni-kõrn) [L. *ūnicornis*], *n.* A fabulous animal like a horse, with a long, straight, tapering horn. **uniform** (ū'ni-fôrm) [*uni-*, -FORM], *a.* Having always one and the same form, appearance, character, etc., always the same, homogeneous; conforming to one rule or standard. *n.* A dress of the same kind and appearance as that worn by other members of the same body. **uniformity**, *n.* Quality or state of being uniform; consistency, sameness. **uniformly**, *adv.*

unify (ū'ni-fī), *v.t.* To make a unit of; to regard as one; to reduce to uniformity. **unifica'tion**, *n.*

unilateral (ū-ni-lăt'ĕr-ăl), *a.* Applied by one side or party only.

unilluminated (ŭn-i-lū'mi-nă-tĕd), *a.* Not illuminated; dark; ignorant. **unimaginable** (-măj'i-năbl), *a.* That cannot be imagined; inconceivable. **unimaginative**, *a.* Lacking in imagination. **unintelligent**, *a.* Not showing intelligence; dull, stupid. **unintel'ligible**, *a.* Not understandable; meaningless. **uninten'tional**, *a.* Done without intent or design.

union (ū'nyŏn) [L. *uniō -nis*, from *ūnus*, one], *n.* Act of uniting; state of being united; junction, coalition; agreement, concord; a combination forming a whole, a confederation, a league; two or more parishes consolidated for administration of the Poor Laws; a workhouse established by this; (*Gt. Brit.*) a device emblematic of union borne in the upper corner next the staff of a flag; this used as a flag, called a **union jack** or **union flag**. **unionism**, *n.* The principle of combining, esp. the system of combination among workmen engaged in the same occupation or trade, and (*Polit.*) the principles of the Unionist party. **unionist**, *n.* A member of a trade-union; a promoter of trade-unionism; a member of a political party absorbed in the Conservative party.

unique (ū-nēk') [L. *ūnicus*], *a.* Having no like or equal; unmatched, unparalleled. **uniquely**, *adv.* **uniqueness**, *n.*

unison (ū'ni-zŏn) [L. *sonus*, sound], *n.* Coincidence of sounds, unity of pitch; an interval of one or more octaves; act or state of sounding together at the same pitch; concord, agreement, harmony. *a.* Sounding together; coinciding in pitch. **unisonal, -nant**, *a.*

unit (ū'nit), *n.* A single person, thing, or group, regarded as one and individual; a quantity adopted as a standard, the number one. **Unitarian** (-tăr'i-ăn), *n.* A member of a Christian body that rejects the doctrine of the Trinity. *a.* Pertaining to the Unitarians. **Unitarianism**, *n.* u'nitary, *a.* Pertaining to a unit; of the nature of a unit, whole, integral.

unite (ū-nit') [L. *ūnitus*, united], *v.t.* To join together so as to make one; to combine, to amalgamate. *v.i.* To become one; to become consolidated, to combine, to agree, to co-operate. **unitedly**, *adv.*

unity (ū'ni-ti) *n.* State of being one or individual, oneness; state of being united, union; structural coherence; concord, agreement, harmony; a thing forming a coherent whole; the number one.

universal (ū-ni-věr'săl) [L. *universus*, combined into one whole], *n.* Pertaining to the whole world or all persons or things in the world or in the class under consideration; unlimited, general. *n.* A universal proposition or concept; a general idea. **universally**, *adv.*

universe (ū'ni-věrs), *n.* All created things viewed as constituting one system or whole, the cosmos; all mankind.

university (ū-ni-věr'si-ti) [A.-F. *universite*, a school for universal knowledge], *n.* An institution for instruction and examination in the higher branches of knowledge with the power to confer degrees; the members of this collectively.

unkempt (ŭn-kempt') [M.E. *kempt*, p.p. of *kemben*, A.-S. *cemban*, to comb], *a.* Uncombed; rough, unpolished. **unkind'**, *a.* Not kind; harsh, hard, cruel. **unknown** (-nōn'), *a.* Not known; untold, incalculable, inexpressible; (*Math.*) unascertained (of quantities, etc.). **unlatch** (-lăch'), *v.t.* To unfasten the latch of (a door, etc.).

unless (ŭn-les'), *conj.* If it be not the case that; except when.

unlettered (ŭn-let'ĕrd), *a.* Illiterate. **unlike'**, *a.* Not like; dissimilar; improbable. **unlikely**, *a.* Improbable; unpromising. *adv.* Improbably. **unlimited**, *a.* Not limited; indefinite, unmeasured, unnumbered; unrestrained. **unload'**, *v.t.* To discharge the load from; to discharge (a load); to withdraw the charge from (a gun); (*Stock Exch.*) to sell heavily. *v.i.* To discharge a load or freight; (*Stock Exch.*) to sell stock, etc., freely. **unlock'**, *v.t.* To unfasten the lock of; (*fig.*) to disclose. **unlooked-for** (-lukt'fôr), *a.* Unexpected. **unluck'y**, *a.* Not lucky or fortunate; unsuccessful; disastrous; ill-omened. **unmask'**, *v.t.* To remove the mask from; to expose. *v.i.* To reveal oneself. **unmeaning**, *a.* Having no meaning; senseless. **unmen'tionable**, *a.* Not fit to be mentioned; *n.pl* (*facet.*) Trousers. **unmind'ful**, *a.* Not mindful, heedless (of). **unmit'gated**, *a.* Not mitigated; unqualified, unconscionable. **unmoor'**, *v.t.* To loose the moorings of. *v.i.* To weigh anchor. **unmoun'ted**, *a.* Not on horseback; not mounted (of a drawing, gem, etc.). **unnat'ural**, *a.* Contrary to nature, monstrous, inhuman; artificial, strained; affected. **unnecessary** (-nes'ĕ-săr-i), *a.* Not necessary; needless, superfluous. **unnerve'**, *v.t.* To deprive of nerve, strength, or resolution. **unno'ted**, *a.* Not heeded. **unnum'bered**, *a.* Not marked with numbers; countless. **unpar'alleled**, *a.* Not paralleled; unequalled, unprecedented. **unpick'**, *v.t.* To loosen, take out, or open, by picking; to remove the stitches from. **unpleasant** (-plez'ănt), *a.* Not pleasant; disagreeable. **unpolled** (-pōld'), *a.* Not polled, not having registered one's vote. **unpo'sted**, *a.* Not posted (of a letter, etc.); not posted up; without information. **unprecedented** (-pres'ĕ-děn-tĕd), *a.* Being without precedent, unparalleled. **unprofessional** (-prō-fesh'ŏ-năl), *a.* Not pertaining to one's profession; contrary to the rules or etiquette of a profession; not belonging to a profession. **unprogres'sive**, *a.* Not progressive, conservative. **unques'tionable**, *a.* Not to be questioned or doubted, indisputable. **unques'tioned,** *a.* Not called in question, not doubted; having no questions asked, not interrogated. **unquestioning,** *a.* Not doubting; implicit. **unrav'el,** *v.t.* To separate the threads of; to disentangle; (*fig.*) to solve, to clear up (the plot of a play, etc.). *v.i.* To be disentangled; to be opened up or revealed. **unready** (-red'i), *a.* Not ready; not prompt to act, etc. **unremit'ting,** *a.* Not relaxing; incessant, continued. **unrest',** *n.* Restlessness, agitation, disquiet, uneasiness, unhappiness. **unrighteous** (-rī'chŭs), *a.* Not righteous, not just; contrary to justice or equity; evil, wicked, sinful.

UNRRA (ŭn'ra) [initials of United Nations Relief and Rehabilitation Administration], *n.* (*Polit.*) A body authorized by the Atlantic Charter to organize relief, etc., to peoples freed from enemy occupation after the war of 1939–45.

unruffled (-rŭfld'), *a.* Calm, tranquil, not agitated or perturbed. **unru'ly,** *a.* Not submitting to restraint; lawless, turbulent, ungovernable. **unruliness,** *n.* **unsan'itary,** *a.* Unhealthy. **unsa'voury,** *a.* Unattractive, repellent, disgusting. **unscalable** (-skā'lábl), *a.* That cannot be climbed. **unscathed** (-skā*th*d), *a.* Not harmed, uninjured. **unscrew',** *v.t.* To withdraw or loosen (a screw); to unfasten thus. **unscru'pulous,** *a.* Having no scruples of conscience; unprincipled. **unseal',** *v.t.* To break or remove the seal of; to open. **unseat',** *v.t.* To remove from one's seat; to throw from one's seat on horseback; to deprive of a seat in the House of Commons. **unsee'ing,** *a.* Blind; unobservant, unsuspecting. **unseen',** *a.* Not seen; invisible; not seen previously (as a piece to be translated). **unsel'fish,** *a.* Regarding or prompted by the interests of others rather than one's own. **unsettle** (-setl'), *v.t.* To change from a settled state or position; to make uncertain; to derange, to disturb. **unsettled,** *a.* **unshapely** (-shāp'li), *a.* Misshapen. **unsheathe** (-shē*th*'), *v.t.* To draw from its sheath. **unsightly** (-sit'li), *a.* Unpleasing to the sight, ugly. **unskilled** (-skild'), *a.* Not possessing skill or special knowledge; produced without or not requiring special skill or training. **unslum'bering,** Sleepless, vigilant. **unsophis'ticated,** *a.* Simple, artless, free from artificiality, inexperienced; not corrupted or adulterated, pure, genuine. **unsound',** *a.* Not sound; weak, decayed; unreliable; diseased; ill-founded, not valid, fallacious. **unsports'manlike,** *a.* Unbecoming a sportsman. **unstable** (-stābl'), *a.* Inconstant, irresolute; wavering. **unsteady** (-sted'i), *a.* Not steady, not firm; changeable; unstable, precarious; irregular in habits. **unstop',** *v.t.* To free from obstruction; to remove the stopper from, to open. **unstring',** *v.t.* (*past and p.p.* -**strung**) To take away or to loosen the string or strings of; to relax the tension of (nerves, etc.); to remove (pearls, etc.) from a string. **unsubstantial**

(-stăn'shál). *a.* Not substantial; not very solid; unreal. **unsuited** (-sū'tĕd), *a.* Not suited, not fit or adapted (for or to). **unsworn',** *a.* Not sworn; not bound by an oath. **untangle** (-tăngl'), *v.t.* To disentangle. **untaught** (-tawt'), *a.* Not instructed, illiterate; ignorant. **unten'antable,** *a.* Not in suitable condition for a tenant. **untenanted,** *a.* **unten'der,** *a.* Not tender, unkind. **unten'dered,** *a.* Not offered. **unthinkable,** *a.* Incapable of being thought or conceived; (*colloq.*) highly improbable. **unthinking,** *a.* Heedless, careless; done without thought or care. **untie** (-tī'), *v.t.* To undo (a knot); to unfasten. **untied,** *a.*

until (ŭn-til'), *prep.* Till.

unto (ŭn'tu), *prep.* To.

untold (ŭn-tōld'), *a.* Not told or communicated; not counted, innumerable. **untoward** (-tō'árd), *a.* Unlucky, awkward; froward, perverse, refractory. **untroubled** (-trŭbld'), *a.* Not disturbed by care, sorrow, business, etc.; calm, unruffled. **untrue',** *a.* Not in accordance with facts, false; disloyal, inconstant; not conforming to the correct standard. **untruth',** *n.* Contrariety to truth; a lie; want of veracity; faithlessness. **unu'sual,** *a.* Not usual; uncommon, strange, remarkable. **unut'terable,** *a.* Unspeakable, inexpressible, indescribable. **unvalued** (-văl'ūd), *a.* Not esteemed; not appraised. **unvarnished** (-var'nisht), *a.* Plain, simple. **unveil** (-vāl'), *v.t.* To remove a veil or covering from, esp. with public ceremony; (*fig.*) to reveal, to disclose. *v.i.* To take one's veil off; to be revealed. **unvera'cious,** *a.* Untruthful. **unversed** (-vĕrst'), *a.* Not versed or skilled (in). **unwarrantable** (-wor'án-tábl), *a.* Not defensible or justifiable, inexcusable; improper, illegitimate. **unwell',** *a.* Not well; sick, indisposed. **unwieldy** (-wĕl'di), *a.* That cannot be easily wielded; bulky, ponderous, clumsy. **unwil'ling,** *a.* Not willing; averse, reluctant, undesirous (of, to, for, etc.); involuntary. **unwise** (-wīz'), *a.* Not wise, without judgment; foolish. **unwished** (-wisht'), *a.* Not desired; not sought (for). **unwit'ting,** *a.* Unconscious, unintentional, inadvertent. **unwittingly,** *adv.* **unwonted** (-wŏn'tĕd), *a.* Not accustomed. **unworthy** (-wĕr'*th*i), *a.* Not worthy, not deserving (of); not becoming, not seemly, discreditable. **unwritten** (-rit'ĕn), *a.* Not written; traditional. **unyoke** (-yōk'), *v.t.* To loose from or as from a yoke.

up (ŭp) [A.-S. *ŭp*], *adv.* To a higher place, degree, amount, pitch, etc.; to a capital, university, or a place farther north; to or in an erect position, out of bed, in the saddle; under arms; in a state of proficiency; above the horizon; so as to be level with; completely, entirely, effectually. *prep.* In an ascending direction, towards the higher part of or the interior of. *a.* Moving, sloping, or directed, towards a higher or more central part; towards the capital. *n.* That which is up.

up- [as prec.], *pref.*

upas (ū'păs) [Malay, poison], *n.* The upas-tree; its poisonous sap; (*fig.*) corrupting or pernicious influence. **upas-tree,** *n.* A Javanese tree the juice of which contains a virulent poison.

upbraid (ŭp-brād') [A.-S. *upbregdan*, to lay hold of], *v.t.* To charge; to reproach (with); to reprove severely. *v.i.* To chide.

upbringing (ŭp'bring-ing), *n.* Bringing up, education. **upheave** (-hēv'), *v.t.* To lift up from beneath. *v.i.* To heave up. **upheaval,** *n.* **uphill** (ŭp'hil), *a.* Leading or going up a hill; (*fig.*) difficult, arduous. *adv.* (ŭp-hil') In an ascending direction, upwards.

uphold (ŭp-hōld'), *v.t.* (*past and p.p.* **upheld**) To hold up, keep erect; to support, sustain, maintain; to defend; to approve, countenance. **upholder,** *n.*

upholster (ŭp-hōl'stér) [upholder or repairer], *v.t.* To furnish with curtains, carpets, etc.; to furnish (chairs) with cushions, coverings, etc. **upholsterer,** *n.* **upholstery,** *n.*

upkeep (ŭp'kēp), *n.* Maintenance. **upland** (ŭp'lǎnd), *n.* The higher part of a district. *a.* Pertaining to the uplands. **uplift'**, *v.t.* To lift up, to raise. *n.* (ŭp'lift) An exaltation; an upheaval.

upon (ŭ-pon'), *prep.* and *adv.* On.

upper (ŭp'ér), *a.* Higher in place, rank, dignity, etc. *n.* The part of a boot or shoe above the sole. **upper hand:** Superiority, mastery. **uppermost,** *a.* Highest in place, etc.; predominant.

uppish (ŭp'ish), *a.* Self-assertive.

upraise (ŭp-rāz'), *v.t.* To raise up; to lift. **uprear** (-rēr'), *v.t.* To rear up.

upright (ŭp'rīt, *predicatively*, -rīt'), *a.* Erect, perpendicular; righteous, honest. *adv.* Erect, vertically. *n.* An upright part of a structure; an upright piano, etc. **uprightly,** *adv.*

uprising (ŭp-rīz'ing), *n.* Act of rising, esp. from bed; an insurrection, a riot.

uproar (ŭp'rôr) [Dut. *oproer* (UP-, *roeren*, to stir)], *n.* A noisy tumult; bustle and clamour. **uproarious,** *a.*

uproot (ŭp-rōot'), *v.t.* To tear up by the roots; to unsettle completely.

upset (ŭp-set'), *v.t.* To overturn; to put out of one's normal state, to put out of sorts. *v.i.* To be overturned. *n.* (ŭp'set) The act of upsetting; the state of being upset. **upset price:** The reserve price at auction.

upshot (ŭp'shot), *n.* The final issue, result, or conclusion (of a matter).

upside-down (ŭp'sid-doun') [M.E. *up so down*, up as it were down], *adv.* and *a.* With the upper part under; (*fig.*) in complete disorder.

upstairs, *adv.* In or to an upper story. **up'start,** *n.* One who rises suddenly from a humble position to wealth or power. **upstroke** (ŭp'strōk), *n.* An upward line in writing.

upward (ŭp'wård), *a.* Directed or moving towards a higher place. **upwards,** *adv.* Towards a higher place, in an upward direction.

uranium (ūrā'ni-ŭm), *n.* A rare, heavy, white, metallic element found in pitchblende, etc.

Uranus (ūr'à-nŭs) [Gr. *ouranos*, heaven], *n.* (*Gr. Myth.*) The most ancient of the Greek gods; a planet between Saturn and Neptune, discovered by Sir Wm. Herschel (1781).

urban (ĕr'bàn) [L. *urbs*, city], *a.* Pertaining to, or situated or living in, a city or town. **urban district,** *n.* A district comprising a small town or towns not incorporated as a borough.

urbane (ĕr-bàn'), *a.* Courteous, polite, suave. **urbanity** (-bǎn'i-ti), *n.*

urchin (ĕr'chin) [M.E. *urchon*, L. *ēricius*, from *ĕr*, hedgehog], *n.* A roguish, mischievous boy; a sea urchin.

urethra (ū-rē'thrà) [Gr. *ourēthra*], *n.* The duct by which urine is discharged from the bladder. **urethral,** *a.*

urge (ĕrj) [L. *urgēre*], *v.t.* To drive, impel, force onwards; to importune, to insist on. **urgency,** *n.* Quality or state of being urgent; pressure of necessity. **urgent,** *a.*

urine (ūr'in) [L. *ūrīna*], *n.* A pale-yellow fluid secreted from the blood by the kidneys, stored in the bladder, and discharged through the urethra. **uric,** *a.*

urn (ĕrn) [L. *urna*], *n.* A vase with a foot and a swelling body; (*fig.*) something in which the remains of the dead are preserved.

Ursa Major (er'sà mā'jòr) [L., she-bear], *n.* The constellation of the Great Bear. **Ursa Minor,** *n.* The Little Bear. **ursine** (ĕr'sin) [L. *ursus*, bear], *a.* Pertaining to or resembling a bear.

Ursuline (er'sū-lin) [St. Ursula], *n.* One of an order of nuns founded in 1537.

use (ūs) [L. *ūsus*], *n.* Act of using; state of being used; employment in a purpose; occasion or liberty to use; quality of serving a purpose, utility, custom, wont, usage; ritual peculiar to a church, diocese, or country; (*Law*) enjoyment of lands and tenements held in trust. *v.t.* (ūz) To employ, to apply to a purpose; to turn to account; to treat in a specified way; to wear out; to make a practice of; (*usu. in p.p.*) to accustom, habituate. *v.i.* (*usu. in past*) To be accustomed, to be wont, to make it one's constant practice (to). **usage** (ū'zåj), *n.* Manner of using, treatment; customary practice. **useful** (ūs'fúl), *a.* Of use, serving a purpose; beneficial, advantageous. **usefulness,** *n.* **useless,** *a.* Not of use; unavailing, ineffectual. **uselessness,** *n.* **user** (ū'zér), *n.* One who uses; (*Law*) continued use or enjoyment of a thing.

usher (ŭsh'ér) [L. *ostiàrius* (*ostium*, door)], *n.* A doorkeeper (esp. in a court or public hall), one who introduces strangers or walks before a person of rank; an assistant in a school *v.t.* To introduce, to bring or show (in).

U.S.S.R. [initials of Union of Soviet Socialist Republics], *n.* (*Polit.*) The Communist governing body of the Soviet republic of Russia.

usual (ū'zhŭ-àl), *a.* Customary, habitual, common, ordinary. **usually,** *adv.*

usufruct (ū'zū-frŭct) [L. *ūsusfructus* (USE, *fructus*)], *n.* Right to the use of another's property without waste or destruction of it.

usurer (ū'zhŭr-ėr) [L. *ūsūra*, use, interest], *n.* One who lends money at exorbitant interest. **usur'ious**, *a.* Exacting exorbitant interest; pertaining to or of the nature of usury. **usury** (ū'zhŭ-ri), *n.*

usurp (ū-zėrp') [L. *ūsurpāre*, to employ, acquire], *v.t.* To seize or take posssession of without right. **usurpa'tion**, *n.* **usurp'er**, *n.*

ut (ut) [L.], *n.* The first or key note in Guido's musical scale (see GAMUT).

utensil (ū-ten'sil) [L. *ūtensilis*, fit for use], *n.* An implement, an instrument, esp. one used in domestic work.

uterine (ū'ter-īn) [L. *uterus*, womb], *a.* Pertaining to the womb, born of the same mother but not the same father. **uterus**, *n.* The womb.

utilitarian (ū-til-i-târ'i-àn), *a.* Pertaining to utility or to utilitarianism. *n.* An advocate of utilitarianism. **utilitarianism**, *n.* The ethical doctrine that actions are right in proportion to their usefulness or as they tend to promote happiness, the doctrine of 'the greatest happiness of the greatest number'.

utility (ū-til'i-ti) [L. *ūtilitas*], *n.* Usefulness, serviceableness, that which is useful. **utiliza'tion**, *n.* **u'tilize**, *v.t.* To make use of, to turn to account.

utmost (ŭt'mōst) [A.-S. *ūtemest*], *a.* Being at the farthest point or extremity, extreme, greatest, ultimate. *n.* The utmost extent or degree.

Utopia (ū-tō'pi-à) [Gr. *ou*, not, *topos*, place, nowhere, title of Sir Thomas More's book (1516) describing a perfect social and political system], *n.* A state of ideal perfection. **Utopian**, *a.* Ideal; highly desirable but impracticable. *n.* An ardent but visionary reformer.

utter (1) (ŭt'ėr) [A.-S. *uttera*], *v.t.* Complete, perfect, entire, unconditional. **utterly**, *adv.* **uttermost**, *a.*

utter (2) [M.E. *uttren*], *v.t.* To give forth audibly; to put notes, base coin, etc., into circulation. **utterance**, *n.* Act of uttering; vocal expression, speech.

uvula (ū'vū-là) [dim. of L. *uva*, a bunch of grapes], *n.* (*pl.* -læ) A fleshy body hanging over the root of the tongue.

uxorious (ŭk-sôr'i-ùs) [L. *uxor*, wife], *a.* Excessively or foolishly fond of one's wife, doting. **uxorial**, *a.*

V

vacant (vā'kànt) [L. *vacāre*, to be empty], *a.* Empty, unoccupied; at leisure; unintelligent, silly. **vacancy**, *n.* State of being vacant, emptiness; mental vacuity, inanity; empty space; an unfilled post or office. **vacate** (và-kāt'), *v.t.* To give up occupation or possession of; to annul **vaca'tion**, *n.* The act of vacating; a period of cessation of business or studies, a holiday.

vaccinate (văk-si-nāt) [L. *vacca*, cow], *v.t.* To innoculate with vaccine or virus, to procure immunity from disease, esp.

smallpox. **vaccina'tion**, *n.* **vaccine** (văk'sin), *a.* Pertaining to, or obtained from cows; pertaining to vaccination. *n.* The virus of cowpox prepared for use in vaccination; any agent used for inoculation.

vacillate (văs'i-lāt) [L. *vacillāre*], *v.i.* To sway to and fro; to waver between opinions; to be irresolute. **vacilla'tion**, *n.*

vacuous (văk'ū-ùs), *a.* Empty, void; vacant; unintelligent, blank. **vacuity** (và-kū'i-ti), *n.*

vacuum (văk'ū-ùm), *n.* A space completely devoid of matter; a vessel from which the air has been exhausted. **vacuum cleaner**, *n.* An appliance for removing dirt by suction.

vagabond (văg'à-bònd) [L. *vagārī*, to wander], *a.* Wandering about; nomadic; drifting, aimless. *n.* A wanderer, esp. an idle or disreputable one, a vagrant; a rogue. **vagabondage**, *n.*

vagary (và-gâr'i), *n.* A whimsical idea, a freak. **vagarity** (-gǎr'i-ti), *n.*

vagrant (vā'grànt), *a.* Without a settled home; itinerant, strolling; unrestrained. *n.* A wanderer, a vagabond, a tramp, esp. one without visible means of subsistence. **vagrancy**, *n.*

vague (vāg), *a.* Doubtful, ambiguous, indefinite. **vaguely**, *adv.* **vagueness**, *n.*

vain (vān) [L. *vānus*], *a.* Empty, unreal, worthless, unavailing; unprofitable; fallacious; proud of petty things, conceited, self-admiring; foolish. **vainglor'y**, *n.* Excessive vanity; pride, boastfulness. **vainglorious**, *a.* vainly, *adv.*

valance (văl'àns) [? *Valence*, France], *n.* The hanging round the frame of a bedstead, etc.

vale (1) (vāl) [L. *vallis*], *n.* A valley.

vale (2) (vā'lē) [L.], *int.* and *n.* Farewell.

valediction (văl-ē-dik'shùn), *n.* A bidding farewell; an adieu. **valedic'tory**, *a.* Bidding farewell; pertaining to or of the nature of a farewell. *n.* A parting oration.

valentine (văl'én-tīn), *n.* A sweetheart chosen on St. Valentine's day (14 Feb.), when birds were supposed to begin to mate; an amatory or satirical letter or picture sent to one of the opposite sex on this day.

valerian (và-lēr'i-àn) [late L. *valēriana*], *n.* An herbaceous plant with clusters of pink or white flowers; a preparation from this used as a mild stimulant, etc.

valet (văl'ét, -ā) [F.], *n.* A man-servant who attends on his master's person.

valetudinarian (văl-ē-tū-di-nâr'i-àn) [L. *valētūdo -dinis*, health], *a.* Sickly; seeking to recover health; morbidly anxious about one's health. *n.* An invalid.

Valhalla (văl-hǎl'à) [Icel. *valhöl*, hall of the slain], *n.* The palace where the souls of heroes slain in battle were carried by the valkyries; a final resting-place of the great men of a nation.

valiant (văl'yànt, -i-ànt) [O.F. *valant*, being worth], *a.* Brave, courageous, intrepid. **valiantly**, *adv.*

valid (văl'id) [L. *validus*], *a.* Well-grounded, sound, cogent; binding. **validate**, *v.t.* To make valid, to confirm. **valid'ity**, *n.*

valise (vă-lēs´) [F.], *n.* A case for holding a traveller's clothes, etc., a small portmanteau.

valkyrie (văl´kir-i) [Icel. *valkyrja*, chooser of the slain], *n.* One of twelve maidens of Valhalla who selected those destined to be slain in battle and conducted their souls to Valhalla.

valley (văl´i), *n.* A depression in the earth's surface bounded by hills; a large vale; any hollow between elevations of a surface.

valour (văl´ôr) [L.], *n.* Courage, esp. in fighting; prowess. **valorous**, *a.*

value (văl´ū) [F., fem. of *valu*, p.p. of *valoir*, to be worth], *n.* Worth; the desirability of a thing, the qualities that are the basis of this; market price; an equivalent; estimation; signification. *v.t.* To estimate the value of, to appraise; to rate highly, to prize. **val´uable**, *a.* Having great value, costly; capable of being appraised; estimable. **valua´tion**, *n.* Act of valuing; estimation of the value of a thing; estimated worth. **val´uator, valuer**, *n.* One who values, an appraiser. **valueless**, *a.*

valve (vălv) [L. *valva*, leaf of folding door], *n.* A contrivance for permitting or preventing passage of a fluid, as water, gas or steam; (*Wire.*) a vacuum tube employed to control the direction and strength of a current. **valvular**, *a.* Acting as a valve; containing valves; valve-like.

vamp (vămp) [M.F. *avant-pied*], *n.* The part of a boot upper in front of the ankle seams; (*fig.*) a patch for appearance's sake; (*Mus.*) an improvised accompaniment; (*colloq.*) an adventuress. *v.t.* To furbish (up); to fascinate, to exploit men; (*Mus.*) to improvise an accompaniment to.

vampire (văm´pir) [Serbian *vampir*], *n.* A ghost of some outcast, supposed to leave the grave at night and suck the blood of sleeping persons; (*fig.*) one who preys upon others; a blood-sucking bat.

van (1) (văn), *n.* The vanguard; the foremost division of an army or fleet; (*fig.*) leaders, the forefront.

van (2) [Caravan], *n.* A large covered vehicle for furniture, etc.; a closed railway-carriage for luggage or the guard.

vandal (văn´dăl) [L. *Vandalus*], *n.* One of a Teutonic race that overran Gaul, Rome, etc., in the 5th cent., destroying works of art; (*fig.*) one who destroys or dislikes a work of art. **vandalism**, *n.*

vandyke (văn-dik´) [Sir A. *Van Dyck* (1599–1641)], *n.* A picture by him; points forming an ornamental border. *a.* Pointed, esp. a beard.

vane (văn) [A.-S. *fana*, small flag], *n.* A weathercock; a device on an axis turned by a current, as in a meter.

vanguard (văn´gard), *n.* The troops who march in the front of an army, an advance-guard.

vanilla (vă-nil´á) [Sp. *vainilla*, small pod], *n.* A genus of orchids, of tropical Asia and America, bearing fragrant flowers; the fruit of some species; an extract from this as a flavouring.

vanish (văn´ish) [L. *êvânescere*], *v.i.* To disappear suddenly; to become imperceptible, to pass away.

vanity (văn´i-ti), *n.* Quality or state of being vain; empty pride; ostentation; futility, unreality; that which is unreal or deceptive.

vanquish (văn´kwish) [L. *vincere*], *v.t.* To conquer, to subdue; to refute. **vanquisher**, *n.*

vantage (van´tàj), *n.* Advantage; a situation, etc., favourable to success; (*Lawntennis*) the point scored by either side after deuce. **vantage-ground**, *n.* Superiority of position or place.

vapid (văp´id) [L. *vapidus*], *a.* Insipid, flat, spiritless. **vapid´ity**, *n.*

vapour (vā´pôr) [L. *vapor*], *n.* Moisture in the air, light mist; the gaseous form of a substance that is normally liquid or solid; (*fig.*) a vain imagination. *v.i.* To give out vapour; to brag, to bluster. **vaporize**, *v.* To turn or be turned into vapour.

variable (vâr´i-ăbl), *a.* Capable of varying; changeable, fickle; able to be varied or adjusted; (*Math.*) quantitatively indeterminate; (*Biol.*) tending to variation. **variabil´ity**, *n.* **variably**, *adv.*

variance (vâr´i-áns), *n.* State of being variant; difference of opinion, dissension; (*Law*) disagreement between the allegations and proof or between the writ and the declaration. **variant**, *a.* Showing variation, differing, tending to vary. *n.* A variant form, reading, type, etc.

variation (vâr-i-ā´shŭn), *n.* Act, process, or state of varying; alteration, deviation, mutation; (*Gram.*) inflexion.

varicose (văr-i-kōs) [L. *varix*, a dilatation of a vein], *a.* Permanently dilated (of veins); intended for the cure of such veins.

variegate (vâr-i-gāt) [L. *variegâtus*, composed of different colours], *v.t.* To diversify in colour; to dapple, to chequer. **variega´tion**, *n.*

variety (vă-rī´é-ti), *n.* Quality or state of being various; diversity, versatility; a collection of diverse things; a kind, a sort; (*Biol.*) an individual or group differing from type, a sub-species.

variorum (vâr-i-ôr´ŭm), *a.* With notes of various readings, etc., by commentators.

various (vâr´i-ùs) [L. *varius*], *a.* Differing from each other; several; uncertain, not uniform.

varlet (var´lĕt) [O.F. *vaslet*], *n.* A page, esp. one preparing to be a squire; a menial, a knave.

varnish (var´nish) [F. *vernis*], *n.* A thin resinous solution for giving a hard, shiny coating to wood, etc.; any lustrous appearance on leaves, of pottery, etc.; (*fig.*) superficial polish. *v.t.* To cover with varnish; (*fig.*) to gloss over.

vary (vâr´i), *v.t.* (*past and p.p.* varied) To alter in appearance, form, or substance; to modify. *v.i.* To be altered in any way, to differ, to be of different kinds.

vascular (văs´kū-lâr) [L. *vas*, vessel], *a.* Of, consisting of, or containing ducts; containing or rich in blood-vessels.

vase (vaz, Am. văz) [L. *vasum*], *n.* A

vessel of pottery, etc., of various forms but usu. circular and ornamental.

vaseline (văs'é-lēn), *n.* Protected trade name of an unctuous substance used as ointment and lubricant.

vassal (văs'ăl) [F.], *n.* One holding land by feudal tenure; a slave; a low wretch. *a.* Servile. **vassalage,** *n.*

vast (vast) [L. *vastus*], *a.* Of great extent, huge, boundless; very great in numbers, amount, etc. **vastly,** *adv.* **vasty,** *a.*

vat (văt) [A.-S. *fæt*], *n.* A large tank or other vessel used in brewing and in many operations in which substances are boiled or steeped. *v.t.* To put into or treat in a vat.

Vatican (văt'i-kán), *n.* The palace of the Pope on the Vatican Hill, Rome; (*fig.*) the papal government.

vaticinate (và-tis'i-nāt) [L. *vāticinārī*, to predict], *v.* To prophesy. **vaticina'tion,** *n.* **vatic'inator,** *n.*

vaudeville (vōd'vil) [F., *Vau* (*Val*) *de Vire*, Valley of the Vire, where it may have originated], *n.* A variety entertainment.

vault (1) (vawlt) [O.F.], *n.* An arched roof or chamber, esp. underground; a cellar; a place of interment under a church or in a cemetery; (*fig.*) the sky. *v.t.* To cover with a vault.

vault (2), *v.i.* To leap, to spring, esp. from the hands or with a pole. *v.t.* To leap over thus. *n.* Such a leap.

vaunt (vawnt) [F. *vanter*], *v.i.* To boast, to brag. *v.t.* To boast of. *n.* A boast. **vauntingly,** *adv.*

veal (vēl) [O.F. *veel*, L. *vitellus*, calf], *n.* The flesh of a calf as food.

vedette (vė-det') [L. *vidēre*, to see], *n.* A mounted sentinel in advance of an outpost; (*Nav.*) a small scouting vessel.

veer (vēr) [F. *virer*], *v.i.* To change its direction (of the wind); to change about in opinion, etc.

vegetable (vej'ė-tåbl) [L. *vegetāre*, to quicken], *n.* A plant used for culinary purposes or for feeding cattle. *a.* Pertaining to or resembling a plant or made of or pertaining to culinary vegetables; applied to the kingdom or division of organic nature comprising plants. **veg'etal,** *a.* Pertaining to or of the nature of plants; common to plants and animals (of the functions of nutrition, growth, etc.). **vegetarian** (-tár'i-án), *n.* One who lives on vegetable food, and usu. eggs, milk, etc. *a.* Pertaining to vegetarians. **vegetarianism,** *n.* **veg'etate,** *v.i.* To grow in the manner of a plant; (*fig.*) to live an idle, monotonous life. **vegeta'tion,** *n.* **vegetative,** *a.*

vehement (vē'ė-mėnt) [L. *vehemens*], *a.* Proceeding from or exhibiting intense fervour; ardent, passionate, impetuous. **vehemence,** *n.*

vehicle (vē'ikl) [L. *vehere*, to carry], *n.* Any kind of carriage or conveyance for use on land, having wheels or runners; a liquid medium for pigments, medicinal substances, etc.; an agent or medium for the transmission of thought, feeling, etc. **vehicular** (vē-hik'-), *a.*

veil (vāl) [L. *vēlum*], *n.* A semi-transparent piece of muslin, etc., concealing or shading the face; a drapery for concealing or protecting an object; (*fig.*) a disguise, a pretext. *v.t.* To cover with a veil; to hide, to disguise.

vein (vān) [L. *vēna*], *n.* A tubular vessel conveying blood to the heart; (*loosely*) any blood-vessel; a rib in an insect's wing or a leaf; a fissure in rock filled with material deposited by water, a seam; a streak of different colour in wood, marble, etc.; a distinctive trait; particular mood. *v.t.* To fill or cover with, or as with veins. **veiny,** *a.*

veldt (felt) [Dut. *veld*, field], *n.* (*S. Afr.*) Open treeless country suitable for pasturage.

vellum (vel'úm), *n.* A fine parchment orig. made of calf-skin.

velocity (vė-los'i-ti) [L. *vēlox*, swift], *n.* Swiftness, rapid motion; rate of motion.

velure (vel'ûr) [F., L. *villus*, shaggy hair], *n.* Velvet, or fabric resembling this.

velvet (vel'vét), *n.* A closely woven silken fabric with a cut pile on one side; the furry skin over growing antlers. *a.* Velvety. **velvety,** *a.* **velveteen',** *n.* A cotton velvet or cotton fabric with a velvet-pile; (*pl.*) a gamekeeper.

venal (vē'nál) [L. *vēnus*, sale], *a.* Ready to be bribed or to sacrifice honour or principle for sordid considerations; mercenary. **venal'ity,** *n.*

vend (vend) [L. *vendere*], *v.t.* To sell. **vender, vendor,** *n.* **vendible,** *a.*

vendetta (ven-det'å) [It.], *n.* A blood-feud (often carried on for generations), esp. in Corsica, Sardinia, and Sicily; this practice.

veneer (vė-nēr') [G. *furniren*, to inlay], *v.t.* To cover with a thin layer of fine wood; to put a superficial polish on, to gloss over. *n.* A thin layer of superior wood; (*fig.*) superficial polish.

venerable (ven'ér-åbl) [L. *venerābilis*], *a.* Worthy of veneration; rendered sacred; applied as a title to archdeacons, and to one who has attained the first degree in canonization (*R.-C. Ch.*).

venerate (ven'ér-āt) [L. *venerātus*, adored], *v.t.* To regard or treat with profound deference, to revere. **venera'tion,** *n.*

venetian (vė-nē'shàn), *a.* Pertaining to Venice, in N. Italy. *n.* A native of Venice; (*pl.*) a heavy kind of tape or braid used in venetian blinds. **venetian blind:** A window blind made of slats of wood arranged so as to turn.

vengeance (ven'jåns) [F. *venger*, to avenge], *n.* Punishment in return for an injury, retribution; chief, evil. **vengeful,** *a.* Vindictive, revengeful.

venial (vē'ni-ál) [L. *venia*, pardon], *a.* That may be pardoned or excused.

venison (ven'zòn) [L. *venari*, to hunt], *n.* The flesh of the deer as food.

venom (ven'óm) [L. *venēnum*, poison], *n.* Poison secreted by serpents, etc.; (*fig.*) spite, malignity. **venomous,** *a.*

vent (vent) [L. *findere*, to cleave], *n.* A hole for the passage of air, water, etc., an outlet; free play, utterance, etc. *v.t.* To give vent to; to utter, to pour forth.

ventilate (ven'ti-lāt) [L. *ventus*, wind], *v.t.* To supply with fresh air; (*fig.*) to give publicity to. **ventila'tion,** *n.* **ventilator,** *n.*

ventral (ven'trăl) [L. *venter*, stomach], *a.*
Situated on the anterior surface (of
fins).

ventriloquism (ven-tril'ŏ-kwizm) [L. *venter*,
stomach, *loqui*, to speak], *n.* The act or
art of producing sounds that appear to
come from elsewhere than the person
speaking. ventriloquist, *n.* ventriloquy, *n.*

venture (ven'chûr), *n.* The undertaking
of a risk, a hazard; a risky undertaking;
a commercial speculation; that which is
risked. *v.t.* To adventure; to expose to
risk, to hazard, to stake. *v.i.* To dare;
to have the presumption (to). venturesome, venturous, *a.*

venue (ven'û) [F., arrival], *n.* (*Law*) The
place or country where a crime is alleged
to have been committed.

veracious (vē-rā'shŭs) [L. *vērus*, true], *a.*
Habitually truthful; characterized by
truth and accuracy. veracity (-ăs'i-ti), *n.*

veranda (vē-răn'dà) [port. *varanda*], *n.* A
light gallery with a roof on pillars, along
the outside of a house.

verb (vērb) [L. *verbum*, word], *n.* That
part of speech which predicates, a word
that asserts something in regard to
something else (the subject). verbal, *a.*
Pertaining to words; respecting words
only, not ideas, etc.; literal; (*Gram.*)
pertaining to a verb; spoken, not written.
verbally, *adv.* verba'tim, *adv.* Word for
word.

verbena (vēr-bē'nà) [L.], *n.* A large genus
of plants, of which the common vervain
is the type.

verbiage (vēr'bi-ăj), *n.* The use of many
words without necessity, wordiness.
verbose (-bōs'), *a.* Using or containing
more words than are necessary. ver-
bosity (-bos'i-ti), *n.*

verdant (vēr'dànt) [L. *viridis*, green], *a.*
Green; covered with growing grass; fresh,
flourishing; (*slang*) easily taken in.
verdancy, *n.*

verdict (vēr-dikt) [L. *vērē*, truly, [DICTUM],
n. The decision of a jury in a trial;
decision, judgment.

verdigris (vēr-dē-gris) [A.-F. *vert de Grece*,
green of Greece], *n.* A green crystalline
substance formed on copper by the action
of dilute acetic acid; greenish rust on
copper, etc.

verdure (vēr-dyûr), *n.* Greenness of vegetation or foliage.

verge (1) (vērj) [L. *virga*, rod], *n.* The
extreme edge; the grass-edging of a bed;
a rod or staff of authority, esp. one
carried before a bishop; a spindle in a
watch, loom, etc. verger, *n.* An officer
carrying the verge before a bishop or
other dignitary; a church official acting
as usher.

verge (2) [L. *vergere*, to incline], *v.i.* To
approach, come near, border (on).

veridical (vē-rid'ĭ-kăl) [L. *vērus*, true,
dicere, to say], *a.* Truthful, veracious.

verify (ver'ĭ-fī), *v.t.* To confirm or to
inquire into the truth of, to authenticate;
(*Law*) to affirm under oath. verifiable, *a.*
verifica'tion, *n.*

verily (ver'i-lĭ), *adv.* In very truth,
assuredly.

verisimilitude (ver-i-si-mil'i-tūd) [L. *vērus*,

true, *similis*, like], *n.* The appearance
of or resemblance to truth; probability,
likelihood.

veritable (ver'i-tàbl), *a.* Real, genuine;
actual, true. veritably, *adv.*

verity (ver'i-ti) [L. *vēritas*], *n.* Truth; a
true statement; a fact.

verjuice (vēr'joos) [F. *vert*, green, JUICE],
n. An acid liquid expressed from
crab-apples, etc.

vermicelli (vēr-mi-sel'ĭ) [It.], *n.* A wheaten
paste in the form of long slender rods
like spaghetti.

vermicide (vēr'mi-sīd) [L. *vermis*, worm], *n.*
A medicine that kills worms. vermicidal,
a. vermic'ular, *a.* Pertaining to a worm;
resembling the motion or track of a
worm; worm-eaten in appearance; vermiform. vermiform, *a.* Worm-shaped.

vermilion (vēr-mil'yŏn) [F.], *n.* A brilliant
red pigment; the colour of this. *a.* Of a
beautiful red colour.

vermin (vēr'min) [L. *vermis*, a worm], *n.*
A collective name for mischievous,
noxious, or offensive animals, birds,
insects, etc. verminate, *v.i.* To breed
vermin, to become infested with parasites. verminous, *a.*

vermuth (vēr'mooth) [G. *wermuth*, worm-
wood], *n.* A liqueur flavoured with
wormwood.

vernacular (vēr-năk'û-làr) [L. *vernāculus*,
pertaining to home-born slaves], *a.* Belonging to the country of one's birth (of
language, idiom, etc.). One's native
tongue, idiom, or dialect.

vernal (vēr'năl) [L. *vernus*, pertaining to
spring], *a.* Pertaining to, prevailing,
done, or appearing in spring.

vernier (vēr'mi-ér) [Pierre *Vernier* (d. 1637),
inventor], *n.* A movable scale for
measuring fractions of the divisions of
the scale on a measuring instrument.

veronica (vē-ron'i-kà) [Gr. *Berenikē*,
woman's name], *n.* A herb with blue,
purple, or white flowers; the speedwell.

versatile (vēr'sà-til) [L. *versare*, to turn], *a.*
Readily applying oneself to new subjects,
etc., many-sided; inconstant. versatility (-til'i-ti), *n.*

verse (vērs), *n.* A metrical line consisting
of a certain number of feet; (*pop.*) a
stanza; metrical composition as dist.
from prose; a division of a chapter of
the Bible. versicle, *n.* A short verse,
esp. one of a series recited in divine
service by the minister alternately with
the people. ver'sify, *v.t.* To turn (prose)
into verse; to narrate in verse. *v.i.* To
make verses. versifica'tion, *n.* versifier,
n. A rhymster.

versed (vērst), *a.* Skilled, experienced, proficient (in); (*Trig.*) reversed (of sines).

version (vēr'shŭn), *n.* A translation; act
of translating; the rendering of a
passage into another language; an
account or description of something
from one's point of view. ver'so, *n.* A
left-hand page of a book; the reverse
of a coin or medal.

verst (vērst) [Rus. *versta*], *n.* A Russian
measure of length, nearly two-thirds of
a mile.

vertebra (vēr'tē-brà) [L.], *n.* (*pl.* -bræ)

One of the bony segments of the spine. **vertebral,** a. **vertebrata,** n.pl. A division of animals comprising those with a backbone. **vertebrate,** a. and n.

vertex (vĕr'teks) [L., whirlpool], n. (pl. -tices, -ti-sēz) The highest point, the apex; the zenith. **vertical,** a. Pertaining to, or situated at the highest point; situated at or passing through the zenith; perpendicular to the plane of the horizon.

vertigo (vĕr'ti-gō), n. Dizziness; a feeling as if one were whirling round. **vertiginous** (-tij'i-nŭs), a.

verve (vĕrv) [F.], n. Spirit, energy.

very (ver'i) [L. verus, true], a. Real, true, genuine, self-same. adv. In a high degree; greatly, extremely, exceedingly.

vesper (ves'pėr) [L.], n. The evening star, Venus; (fig.) evening; (pl.) the sixth of the seven canonical hours, the evening service. a. Pertaining to the evening or to vespers.

vessel (ves'ĕl) [L. vascellum], n. A hollow receptacle, esp. for holding liquids, a ship; (Anat.) a duct in which blood or other fluids are conveyed.

vest (vest) [L. vestire, to clothe], n. A waistcoat; a singlet. v.t. To invest or endow (with authority, etc.); to confer an immediate fixed right of possession of (property in a person). v.i. (of property, right, etc.) To come or take effect (in a person). **vested,** a. Robed; (Law) held by or fixed in a person, not subject to contingency.

vesta (ves'tà) [L.], n. (Rom. Myth.) The goddess of the hearth and the hearth-fire. **vesta,** n. A wax match igniting by friction. **vestal,** a. Pertaining to Vesta or to her priestesses, the vestal virgins, who were vowed to perpetual chastity; (fig.) pure, chaste. n. A woman of spotless chastity; a nun.

vestibule (ves'ti-būl) [L. vestibulum], n. A hall or lobby next the outer door of a house.

vestige (ves'tij) [L. vestigium, footstep], n. A sign, a mark or trace of something no longer present or in existence; a particle.

vestment (vest'mĕnt), n. A garment, esp. a robe of state or office.

vestry (ves'tri), n. A room in a church in which the vestments are kept; a meeting of the ratepayers of a parish or of their representatives for dealing with parochial business. **vestryman,** n. A member of a vestry.

vesture (ves'tyûr), n. (poet.) Dress, apparel; a covering.

vetch (vech) [L. vicia], n. A p'ant of the bean family used for forage.

veteran (vet'ėr-án) [L. vetus, old], a. Grown old or experienced, esp. in the military service; pertaining to veterans. n. One who has had long experience in any occupation, esp. a soldier.

veterinary (vet'ėr-i-nár-i) [L. veterinárius], a. Pertaining to treatment of the diseases of domestic animals. n. A veterinary surgeon.

veto (vē'tō) [L., I forbid], n. The power or right of forbidding or negativing; the act of exercising such right; any authori-

tative prohibition or refusal. v.t. To refuse approval to (a Bill, etc.); to prohibit.

vex (veks) [L. vexáre], v.t. To cause trouble to, to irritate. **vexa'tion,** n. Act of vexing or state of being vexed; irritation, annoyance, trouble; that which causes this. **vexatious,** a. **vexed** (vekst), a. Annoyed, worried; much debated or contested.

via (vī-à) [L.], adv. By way of, through.

viable (vī'-à-bėl), a. Able to survive, capable of separate existence.

viaduct (vī'à-dŭkt) [L. dúcere, to lead)], n. A bridge composed of a considerable number of arches.

vial (vī'ál), n. A small cylindrical phial or glass vessel for liquids.

viand (vī'ánd) [L. vivere, to live], n. (pl.) Articles of food.

vibrate (vī'brăt, vi-brăt') [L. vibrātus, shaken], v.i. To move to and fro rapidly; to thrill, quiver, throb. v.t. To cause to swing, oscillate, or quiver. **vibrant,** a. Vibrating, tremulous; resonant. **vibra'-tion,** n. Act of vibrating; oscillation.

vicar (vik'ár) [L. vicárius], n. A parish priest who receives a stipend, not the tithes. **vicar apostolic** (R.-C. Ch.) A titular bishop. **vicar-general,** n. An officer appointed by a bishop as his assistant. **vicarage,** n. The benefice of a vicar; his residence. **vicarious** (vi-kâr'i-ŭs), a. Deputed, delegated; performed, done, or suffered for or instead of another.

vice (1) [vīs] [L. vitium], n. An evil practice or habit; gross immorality, depravity; a fault, a defect.

vice (2) [F. vis, screw], n. An instrument with two jaws between which an object may be clamped securely; (fig.) a grip, a grasp.

vice- [L., by change], pref. Denoting one acting as deputy of another or one next in rank.

vicegerent (vis-jer'ĕnt) [L. gerens, carrying on], n. An officer exercising delegated authority, a deputy. **vicegerency,** n.

viceregal (vis-rē'gál), a. Viceroyal. **vice-reine** (-rān) [F., queen], n. The wife of a viceroy.

viceroy (vis'roi) [F. roi, king], n. A ruler acting with royal authority in a colony, dependency, etc. **viceroyal,** a.

vice versa (vī'sė vėr'sà), adv. The relation being inverted, the other way round.

vicinage (vis'i-náj) [F. voisin, neighbour], n. Neighbourhood, vicinity. **vicin'ity,** n. The neighbourhood, the surrounding district; proximity.

vicious (vish'ŭs), a. Characterized by some vice; imperfect, corrupt; contrary to moral principles; depraved; spiteful. **viciously,** adv. **viciousness,** n.

vicissitude (vi-sis'i-tūd) [L. vicissim, by turns], n. A change of condition, circumstances, fortune, etc.

victim (vik'tim) [L. victima], n. A living creature sacrificed to some deity, or destroyed or injured in pursuit of some object; a dupe. **victimize,** v.t. To make a victim of; to swindle. **victimiza'tion,** n.

victor (vik'tŏr) [L. victus, conquered], n.

One who conquers in battle or wins in a contest.

victoria (vik'tōr'i-à) [Queen *Victoria* (1819–1901)], *n.* A four-wheeled carriage for two persons with a falling top. victorian, *a.* Pertaining to or flourishing in the reign of Victoria. *n.* A person, esp. a writer, flourishing then.

victory (vik'tō-rǐ) [L. *victoria*], *n.* The defeat of an enemy or opponent. victorious (-tōr'i-ŭs), *a.* Having conquered in battle or any contest; triumphant.

victual (vitl) [L. *victuālis*, pertaining to nourishment], *n.* (*usu. in pl.*) Food, provisions. *v.* To supply with or lay in provisions. victualler, *n.* One who supplies victuals, esp. an innkeeper.

vide (vī'dē) [L., see], *v. imper.* See (in reference to a passage in a book, etc.).

videlicet (vi-dē'li-sět) [L. *vidēre licet*, it is allowable to see], *adv.* Namely, to wit (abbrev. to viz.).

vie (vī) [M.E. *envien*], *v.i.* To strive for superiority; to be equal or superior (with or in). vying, *a.*

view (vū) [F. *voir*, to see], *n.* A look; range of vision; power of seeing; a scene, a prospect; a picture of this; a mental survey; manner of looking at things; judgment, opinion; intention, design. *v.t.* To examine with the eye; to survey intellectually; to consider, to form a mental impression of.

vigil (vij'il) [L., awake], *n.* Keeping awake during hours of rest, watchfulness; the eve of a festival; (*pl.*) nocturnal devotions. vigilance, *n.* State of being vigilant. vigilant, *a.*

vignette (vin-yet') [F.], *n.* (*Arch.*) An ornament of tendrils and vine-leaves; an ornamental flourish; an engraving without a definite border; head-and-shoulders portrait with a background shading off gradually.

vigour (vig'ōr) [L. *vigor*], *n.* Active strength or energy; vital force, robustness; exertion of strength; forcibleness. vigorous, *a.*

viking (vī'king) [Icel. *vīkingr*], *n.* A pirate, esp. a Scandinavian warrior of the 8th-10th cent.

vile (vīl) [L. *vilis*, base], *a.* Worthless, depraved, villainous, odious; abominable. vilely, *adv.* vileness, *n.* vilify (vil'i-fī), *v.t.* To traduce, to defame. vilifica'tion, *n.* Defamation, abuse.

villa (vil'à) [L., farm-house], *n.* A country house; a suburban house.

village (vil'āj), *n.* A small assemblage of houses. *a.* Rustic, countrified. villager, *n.* An inhabitant of a village.

villain (vil'àn) [O.F. *vilein*, servile], *n.* A person guilty or capable of crime; a scoundrel; (*Hist.*) a feudal serf. villainage, *n.* villainous, *a.* Characteristic of a villain; depraved, vile. villainously, *adv.* villainy, *n.*

vim (vim) [L., acc. of *vis*], *n.* Energy, vigour.

vinaigrette (vin-à-gret') [F.], *n.* An ornamental bottle or perforated case for holding aromatic vinegar, a smelling-bottle.

vindicate (vin'di-kāt) [L. *vindicāre*, to lay claim to], *v.t.* To maintain (a claim, etc.)

against attack or denial; to defend; to prove to be valid, to establish, justify. vindica'tion, *n.* vin'dicative, *a.* vindicator, *n.* vindicatory, *a.* Tending to vindicate or justify; punitory.

vindictive (vin-dik'tiv), *a.* Revengeful; characterized or prompted by revenge.

vine (vīn) [L. *vinum*, wine], *n.* A slender climbing plant, esp. the grape-vine. vinery, *n.* A greenhouse for vines. vineyard (vin'yàrd), *n.* A plantation of grape-vines. vin'iculture, *n.* The cultivation of grape-vines. vinous (vī'nŭs), *a.* Pertaining to, or having the qualities of wine.

vinegar (vin'ė-gàr) [L. *vinum*, wine, O.F. *aigre*, keen], *n.* An acid liquid obtained by acetous fermentation from wine, etc.; (*fig.*) anything sour. vinegarish, vinegary, *a.*

vintage (vin'tàj), *n.* The yield of a vine-district for a particular season; the season of gathering grapes; wine. vintner, *n.* A wine-merchant.

viol (vī'ól) [F. *viole*], *n.* A mediæval stringed musical instrument; a violoncello. viola (1) (vē'ō-, vī'ō-là) [It.], *n.* The alto or tenor violin.

viola (2) (vī'ō-là [L., violet], *n.* A plant of the genus containing the violet and pansy.

violate (vī'ō-lāt) [L. *violātus*, injured], *v.t.* To infringe, break, or disobey (a law, obligation, duty, etc.); to profane, desecrate; to outrage. violable, *a.* viola'tion, *n.* violator, *n.*

violence (vī'ō-lens), *n.* State or quality of being violent; injury, outrage; vehemence, impetuosity of feeling, action, etc. violent, *a.* Vehement, impetuous, furious; intense, immoderate; not natural (of death). violently, *adv.*

violet (vī'ō-lět), *n.* The sweet violet, the dog violet, and some other species of the genus *Viola*, with small blue, purple, or white flowers. *a.* Of the colour of violet.

violin (vī-ō-lin'), *n.* A musical instrument with four strings, played with a bow. violinist, *n.*

violoncello (vē-ō-lon-chel'ō), *n.* A large and powerful violin played while rested on the ground between the legs. violoncellist, *n.*

viper (vī'pér) [L. *vīpera*], *n.* A venomous snake, the only poisonous British snake; (*fig.*) a mischievous or malignant person. viperine, viperish, viperous, *a.*

virago (vi-rā'gō) [L.], *n.* An impudent, turbulent woman; a termagant.

virelay (vir'ė-lā) [O.F. *virelai*], *n.* An old form of French verse with two rhymes to a stanza and a refrain.

virgin (vĕr'jin) [L. *virgo -ginis*], *n.* A maiden; a member of an order of women under vows of chastity; Virgo, one of the ancient zodiacal constellations. *a.* Being or befitting a virgin; pure, chaste; maidenly, modest; untried, not brought into cultivation. virginal, *a.* Pertaining to or befitting a virgin; chaste, maidenly. virginity (-jin'i-ti), *n.*

viridescent (vir-i-des'ént) [L. *viridis*, green], *a.* Greenish; becoming slightly green.

viridescence, *n.* virid′ity, *n.* Greenness, the colour of fresh vegetation.

virile (vir′il) [L. *vir*, man], *a.* Pertaining to man or the male sex; masculine, manly. viril′ity, *n.*

virtu (vir-too′) [It.], *n.* Love of or taste for the fine arts. virtuo′so, *n.* A connoisseur of articles of virtu; a skilled exponent of some fine art. virtuos′ity, *n.*

virtue (ver′tū) [L. *virtus*], *n.* Moral excellence, goodness, rectitude; conformity with morality or duty; chastity, esp. in women; inherent power or efficacy. **virtual,** *a.* Being such in essence though not in name; equivalent in effect. virtually, *adv.* virtuoso, etc. [VIRTU]. virtuous, *a.* Morally good; chaste. virtuously, *adv.* virtuousness, *n.*

virulent (vir′ū-lent) [L. *virus*, slime, poison], *a.* Extremely poisonous; (*fig.*) extremely bitter or malignant. virulence, *n.* virulently, *adv.*

virus (vir′ŭs), *n.* A morbid poison, esp. the germ in contagious disease; (*fig.*) any moral taint or corrupting influence; malignity.

vis (vis) [L.], *n.* (*Mech.*) Force, energy.

visage (viz′āj) [L. *visus*], *n.* The face, the countenance. visaged, *a.* Having a visage or look of a particular type.

vis-à-vis (vē-za-vē′) [F.], *adv.* Face to face, opposite to. *n.* A person facing another; a carriage for two sitting *vis-à-vis.*

viscera (vis′ēr-a) [L., pl. of *viscus*], *n.pl.* The internal organs of the great cavities of the body, esp. the intestines. visceral, *a.*

viscid (vis′id) [L. *viscidus*], *a.* Sticky; semifluid in consistency. viscid′ity, *n.* viscous, *a.*

viscount (vi′kount), *n.* A noble ranking next below an earl, and above a baron. viscountcy, *n.* viscountess, *n.*

visé (vē′zā) [F. viser, to inspect], *n.* An official endorsement on a passport showing that it has been examined and found correct.

visible (viz′ibl) [L. *visibilis*], *a.* Perceptible by the eye; in view, conspicuous. visibil′ity, *n.* State of being visible. visibly, *adv.*

vision (vizh′ŭn), *n.* Act or faculty of seeing, sight; that which is seen; a supernatural or prophetic apparition; a creation of the imagination. visional, *a.* visionary, *a.* Existing in a vision or in the imagination only; unreal.

visit (viz′it) [L. *visere*, to behold], *v.t.* To go or come to see; to come upon, to afflict (of diseases, etc.); to bless. *v.i.* To call on or visit people; to keep up friendly intercourse. *n.* Act of visiting; a call; a stay or sojourn (with or at). visita′tion, *n.* Act of visiting; a formal or official visit for the purpose of inspection, correction, etc.; a divine dispensation, esp. a chastisement or affliction. visiting-book, *n.* One in which calls received or intended are entered. visiting-card, *n.* A small card, bearing one's name, etc. visitor, *n.* One who makes a call; one who visits a place; an inspecting officer.

visor (viz′ôr), *n.* The movable part of a helmet defending the face; a mask.

vista (vis′tȧ) [It.], *n.* A long view shut in at the sides.

visual (vizh′ū-ȧl), *a.* Pertaining to or used in sight or seeing. visualize, *v.t.* To make visible; to give a visible form to (an idea, etc.).

vital (vi′tȧl) [L. *vita*, life], *a.* Pertaining to, necessary to, supporting, or affecting life; indispensable. *n.pl.* The organs essential to life, as the heart, brain, etc. vital′ity, *n.* vi′talize, *v.t.* To give life to; to animate. vitally, *adv.*

vitamin (vi-tȧ-min), *n.* One of a group of substances, found in very small amounts in fresh vegetables, which are essential to normal metabolism.

vitiate (vish′i-āt) [L. *vitium*, an end practice (1)], *v.t.* To impair the quality of; to corrupt; to render ineffectual. vitia′tion, *n.*

vitreous (vit′rē-ŭs) [L. *vitrum*, glass], *a.* Consisting of, resembling, or obtained from glass. vitreos′ity, *n.* vitric, *a.* Of or like glass. vitrify, *v.t.* To convert into glass or a glassy substance by heat and fusion. vitrifica′tion, *n.*

vitriol (vit′ri-ol) [L. *vitreolus*], *n.* Sulphuric acid, or any salt of this, a sulphate; (*fig.*) malignancy, caustic criticism, etc. vitriol′ic, *a.*

vituperate (vi-tū′pēr-āt), *v.t.* To upbraid, to abuse, rail at. vitupera′tion, *n.* vituperative, *a.*

vivacious (vi-vā′shŭs) [L. *vivere*, to live], *a.* Lively, animated, gay; (*Bot.*) living through the winter, perennial. vivac′ity, *n.* Animation, charm.

viva voce (vi′vȧ-vō′sē) [L., with the living voice], *adv.* and *a.* By word of mouth, orally.

vivid (viv′id), *a.* Lively; very bright, brilliant; clear, highly coloured.

vivify (viv′i-fi), *v.t.* To give life to; to enliven.

viviparous (vi-vip′ȧ-rŭs) [L. *vivus*, alive, *parere*, to produce], *a.* Bringing forth young alive.

vivisection (viv-i-sek′shŭn), *n.* The dissection of or experimentation on living animals. viv′isect, *v.t.* To dissect (a living animal). vivisector, *n.*

vixen (vik′sen) [A.-S. *fyxen*], *n.* A she-fox; (*fig.*) a shrewish woman; a scold. vixenish, *a.*

vizier (vi-zēr′) [Arab. *wazir*, counsellor], *n.* A high officer of State in Mohammedan countries.

vocable (vō′kȧbl) [L. *vocāre*, to call], *n.* A word.

vocabulary (vō-kȧb′ū-lȧr-i), *n.* A list of words used in a language, science, book, etc.; the stock of words at one's command.

vocal (vō′kȧl), *a.* Pertaining to the voice; having a voice; uttered or produced by the voice; (*Phon.*) not surd; (*Gram.*) having the character of a vowel. vocal′ic, *a.* Pertaining to or consisting of vowel sounds. vo′calist, *n.* A singer. vo′cally, *adv.*

vocation (vō-kā′shŭn), *n.* A call to follow a particular career, or undertake a duty, occupation, etc.; one's calling. **vocational**, *a*.

vocative (vŏk'ā-tiv), *a*. Pertaining to or used in addressing a person or thing. *n*. The case of a noun used in addressing a person or thing.

vociferate (vŏ-sĭf'ĕr-āt), *v.t*. To bawl, to shout. **vociferation**, *n*. **vociferous**, *a*. **vociferously**, *adv*.

vodka (vod'kà) [Rus.], *n*. A strong spirituous liquor distilled from rye, used in Russia.

vogue (vōg) [F.], *n*. Fashion prevalent at any particular time; currency; popular acceptance, usage.

voice (vois) [L. *vox*], *n*. The sound in speaking, singing, etc.; the faculty of vocal utterance, language; one's opinion, one's right to express this, one's choice or vote; one expressing the will or judgment of others; (*Phon.*) sound produced by the breath acting on the vocal cords; (*Gram.*) the verb-form expressing the relation of the subject to the action. *v.t*. To give utterance to, to express. **voiced**, *a*. Sonant.

void (void) [O.F.], *a*. Empty; having no holder or occupant; free from; ineffectual; null, invalid. *n*. An empty space. *v.t*. To nullify; to evacuate. **voidable**, *a*.

volatile (vol'à-tĭl) [L. *volāre*, to fly], *a*. Readily evaporating; (*fig.*) lively, sprightly; changeable. **volatil'ity**, *n*.

volcano (vol-kā'nō) [L. *volcānus*], *n*. A mountain from the top of which lava, cinders, gases, etc., are ejected. **volcan'ic**, *a*. Pertaining to or produced by a volcano.

vole (vōl) [Icel. *vŏllr*, field], *n*. A mouse-like rodent; the water-rat.

volition (vŏ-lĭsh'ŭn) [L. *volitio*], *n*. Exercise of the will; the power of willing.

volley (vol'ĭ) [F. *volée*, flight], *n*. A flight of missiles; the missiles thus discharged; (*fig.*) a noisy outburst or emission of many things at once; a return of the ball at tennis, etc., before it touches the ground. *v.t*. To discharge or return in a volley. *v.i*. To fly in or discharge a volley; to fire together (of guns).

volplane (vol'plān), *v.i*. (*Aeroplane*) To fly downwards at a high angle.

volt, (vōlt)**n.** The unit of electromotive force.

volta- (Alessandro *Volta* (1745–1827), It. physicist], *comb. form.* **voltage**, *n*. Electromotive force as measured or expressed in volts. **volta'ic**, *a*. Pertaining to electricity produced by chemical action or contact, galvanic. **voltaism** (vōl'tà-izm), *n*.

voluble (vol'ŭbl) [L. *volvere*, to roll], *a*. Fluent, glib, garrulous. **volubil'ity**, *n*. **volubly**, *adv*.

volume (vol'ūm), *n*. A book, esp. as forming one of a set; a tome; a roll or scroll constituting a book; a rounded, swelling mass, a coil (*usu. in pl.*); mass, bulk; (*Mus.*) fullness or roundness of tone. **volu'minal**, *a*. Pertaining to volume. **volu'minous**, *a*. Consisting of many volumes; producing many books (of a writer); of great bulk.

voluntary (vol'ŭn-tàr-ĭ) [L. *voluntas*, free will], *a*. Proceeding from one's own free will, not under constraint; spontaneous; willing; subject to the will (of muscles, movements, etc.); supported by voluntary action (of a church, school, etc.). *n*. An organ solo played in a church. **voluntarily**, *adv*. **voluntariness**, *n*.

volunteer (vol-ŭn-tēr'), *n*. One who enters into any service of his own free will. *a*. Voluntary. *v.i*. To offer one's services voluntarily.

voluptuary (vŏ-lŭp'tū-àr-ĭ), *n*. One given to luxury or sensual pleasures. *a*. Pertaining to sensual pleasure.

voluptuous (vŏ-lŭp'tū-ŭs) [L. *voluptas*], *a*. Pertaining to, contributing to, or producing sensuous or sensual gratification.

volute (vŏ-lūt') [L. *volūtus*, rolled], *n*. A spiral scroll used in Ionic, Corinthian, and Composite capitals.

vomit (vom'it) [L. *vomitus*], *v.i*. To eject from the stomach by the mouth; to disgorge. *v.i*. To eject the contents of the stomach by the mouth. *n*. Matter ejected thus; an emetic.

voodoo (voo'doo) [Creole F.], *n*. A system of magic worship practised by Creoles and Negroes, esp. in Haiti.

voracious (vŏ-rā'shŭs) [L. *vorāre*, to devour], *a*. Greedy in eating; gluttonous. **voracity**, *n*.

-vorous, *suf*. Feeding on, living on, as *carnivorous, herbivorous*.

vortex (vôr'tĕks) [L.], *n*. (*pl.* vortices, -ti-sēz). A rotating mass of fluid, a whirlpool. **vortic'ity**, *n*. **vortig'inous**, *a*.

votary (vō'tà-rĭ) [L. *votum*, wish, vow], *n*. One consecrated by a vow or devoted to some particular service, study, etc. **votaress**, *n*.

vote (vōt), *n*. A formal expression of choice in regard to the election of a candidate, etc.; that by which this is expressed, as a ballot, ticket, etc.; that which is voted; aggregate votes; the suffrage. *v.i*. To give one's vote; to express one's approval (for). *v.t*. To give one's vote for; to enact by a majority. **voter**, *n*.

votive (vō'tiv), *a*. Given or dedicated in fulfilment of a vow.

vouch (vouch) [L. *vocāre*, to call], *v.t*. To uphold by assertion, proof, etc., to confirm. *v.i*. To give testimony, to answer (for). **voucher**, *n*. One who or that which vouches for; a document confirming or establishing something.

vouchsafe (vouch-sāf'), *v.t*. To concede. *v.i*. To deign, to condescend (to).

vow (vou),*n*. A solemn promise undertaking a sacrifice, obligation, etc. *v.t*. To promise or affirm solemnly; to dedicate by a vow. *v.i*. To make a vow.

vowel (vou'ĕl), *n*. A sound able to be sounded alone; a letter representing this, esp. *a, e, i, o, u*.

voyage (voi'àj) [L. *via*, way], *n*. A journey by water, esp. to a distance. *v.i*. To make a voyage. **voyager**, *n*. **voyageur** (vwa-ya-zhĕr') [F.], *n*. A trafficker between the Hudson Bay and North-West Companies' trading-posts; a Canadian boatman.

Vulcan (vŭl'kàn), *n*. (*Rom. Myth.*) The god of fire and metal-working. **vulcanic**, **-ism**, etc. [VOLCANIC, -ISM, etc.] **vul-**

canite, *n.* Vulcanized rubber, ebonite. **vulcanize**, *v.t.* To treat (india-rubber) with sulphur at a high temperature to increase its strength and elasticity.

vulgar (vŭl'gàr) [L. *vulgus*, the common people], *a.* Pertaining to or characteristic of the people, common, low, boorish; in common use. **vulgarian**, *a.* Vulgar. *n.* A rich person with low ideas, manners, etc. **vulgarism**, *n.* **vulgar'ity**, *n.* **vulgarize**, *v.t.* **vulgarly**, *adv.* **Vulgate**, *n.* The Latin translation of the Bible made by St. Jerome, 383–405.

vulnerable (vŭl'-nèr-àbl) L. *vulnerāre*, to wound], *a.* Capable of being wounded; liable to injury, attack, etc. **vulnerabil'ity**, *n.*

vulpine (vŭl'pĭn, -pĭn) [L. *vulpes*, fox], *a.* Characteristic of a fox; crafty, cunning.

vulture (vŭl'tyŭr) [L. *vultur*], *n.* A large falconoid bird feeding chiefly on carrion; (*fig.*) a rapacious person. **vulturine**, *a.*

W

wabble, wobble (wobl) [M.E. *quappen*, to palpitate], *v.i.* To go unsteadily, to stagger.

wad (wod) [Scand.], *n.* A small, compact mass of soft material; a felt or paper disk keeping the charge in place in a cartridge. **wadding**, *n.* A fibrous material usu. of cotton or wool, used for stuffing garments, cushions, etc.

waddle (wodl) [freq. of WADE], *v.i.* To walk with a swaying motion and with short, quick steps. *n.* A waddling gait.

waddy (wod'ĭ) [native], *n.* An Australian war-club with a thick head.

wade (wād) [A.-S. *wadan*], *v.i.* To walk through water, snow, mud, etc.; to make one's way with difficulty. *v.t.* To pass through or across by wading. **wader**, *n.* One who wades; a high waterproof boot; a long-legged bird that wades, as the stork, heron, etc.

wafer (wā'fèr) [A.-F. *wafre*], *n.* A thin, sweet biscuit; (*R.-C. Ch.*) a disk of unleavened bread, used in the Eucharist; a disk for sealing letters. *v.t.* To seal or attach with a wafer.

waft (waft), *v.t.* To convey through the air; to carry lightly along.

wag (wăg) [A.-S. *wegan*, to carry], *v.t.* To shake lightly and quickly, esp. in play, reproof, etc. *v.i.* To oscillate; (*fig.*) to keep going. *n.* An act of wagging, a shake; a wit, a joker. **waggery**, *n.* Facetiousness, jocularity. **Waggish**, *a.*

wage (wāj) [O.F.], *n.* Fixed periodical pay for labour (*usu. in pl.*); recompense, requital. *v.t.* To engage in, to carry on.

wager (wā'jèr) [low L. *wadiāre*, to pledge], *n.* Something hazarded on the event of a contest, etc.; a bet. *v.* To stake, to bet.

waggle (wăgl), *v.* To wag quickly and frequently. *n.* A short, quick wagging.

wagon (wăg'ŏn), *n.* A strong four-wheeled vehicle for heavy loads; an open railway truck. **wagon-roof**, *n.* A semi-cylindrical ceiling. **wagoner**, *n.* One who drives a wagon; the constellation Auriga. **wagon-**

ette', *n.* A four-wheeled pleasure carriage with two seats facing each other.

wagtail (wăg'tāl), *n.* A small black and grey or white or yellow bird.

waif (wāf) [O.F., from Norse], *n.* A person or thing found astray or ownerless; a forsaken or unowned child.

wail (wāl) [Icel. *væla*], *v.t.* To lament loudly over, to bewail. *v.i.* To lament; to make a plaintive sound (as the wind). *n.* A loud, high-pitched lamentation, a plaintive cry.

wain (wān) [A.-S. *wægn*], *n.* A wagon.

wainscot (wān'skŏt) [Dut. *wagenschot*, a grained oak-wood], *n.* A wooden lining of the walls of rooms. *v.t.* To line with this. **wainscoting**, *n.*

waist (wāst) [M.E. *wast*], *n.* That part of the human body below the ribs and above the hips; (*fig.*) the middle, contracted part of anything; the part of a ship between the quarter-deck and forecastle. **waistcoat** (wes'kŭt), *n.* A garment, usu. without sleeves, extending from the neck to the waist.

wait (wāt) [O.F. *waiter*], *v.i.* To remain inactive or in the same place until some certain time, to tarry; to be in a state of watchfulness or readiness; to attend at table. *v.t.* To wait for, to bide; to postpone, defer. *n.* Act of waiting; delay, watching, ambush; (*pl.*) a band of singers performing in the streets at Christmas-time. **waiter, waitress**, *n.* An attendant on the guests at a restaurant, etc. **waiting-room**, *n.* A room where persons can rest while waiting.

waive (wāv) [A.-F. *weiver*], *v.t.* To forgo, to relinquish, to refrain from using.

wake (1) (wāk) [A.-S. *wacan*, to arise], *v.i.* (*past and p.p.* woke, waked) To be aroused from sleep, a trance, or death; to be awake, to be unable to sleep; to be roused or to rouse oneself from inaction, etc. *v.t.* To rouse from sleep, to awake; to revive, to raise from the dead; to stir (up); to disturb; to hold a wake over. *n.* The feast of the dedication of a church; a merry-making held in connexion with this; (*Ir.*) the watching of a dead body, prior to burial.

wake (2) (wāk) [Icel. *vökr*, a hole in ice], *n.* The track left by a vessel passing through water.

wakeful (wāk-fŭl), *a.* Not disposed to sleep, restless; disturbed; watchful.

waken (wākn), *v.t.* To rouse from sleep or to action. *v.i.* To wake.

walk (wawk) [A.-S. *wealcan*, to roll], *v.i.* To go along on the feet without running; to go at the ordinary pace; to show itself (of a ghost); to be off, to be dismissed. *v.t.* To walk over, on, or through; to cause to walk. *n.* Act of walking; the pace of one who walks; a stroll, the route chosen for this; a foot-path, promenade, etc.; a hawker's round; (*fig.*) one's occupation. **walk-over**, *n.* An easy success. **walkie-talkie**, *n.* (*Wire.*) A portable combined transmitter and receiver. **walking-stick**, *n.* A stick carried in walking.

wall (wawl) [L. *vallum*], *n.* A continuous structure of stone, brick, etc., forming an enclosure, an internal partition of a building, etc.; a rampart (*usu. in pl.*); a cliff, a mountain-range, etc.; the enclosing sides of a cavity. *v.t.* To furnish, enclose, or defend with a wall. **wall-flower**, *n.* A sweet-smelling plant with yellow, brown, and crimson flowers; (*slang*) a lady without a partner at a dance. **wall-paper**, *n.* Paper, usu. decorative, for the walls of rooms.

wallaby (wol′á-bi) [Austral.], *n.* One of the smaller species of kangaroo.

wallet (wol′ét) [?], *n.* A bag for carrying necessaries for a journey; a pocket-book; a small case for papers, tools, etc.

wall-eye (waw′li) [Icel. *vagl.* beam, *eyythr*, eyed], *n.* An affection of the eye due to opacity of the cornea or to squinting; an eye with a very light-coloured iris; a large, glaring eye. **wall-eyed,** *a.*

wallop (wol′úp) [O.F. *waloper*], *v.i.* To boil with a noisy bubbling. *v.t.* To thrash, to flog. *n.* (*Slang*) Thin beer. *a.* walloping, *n.* A thrashing. *a.* Big, whopping.

wallow (wol′ō) [A.-S. *wealwian*], *v.i.* To tumble about in mire, water, etc.; (*fig.*) to revel grossly (in vice). *n.* Act of wallowing; a place in which animals wallow.

walnut (wawl′nŭt) [A.-S. *wealh,* foreign NUT], *n.* A tree bearing a nut enclosed in a green fleshy covering; the fruit or timber of this.

walrus (wawl′rŭs) [Scand.], *n.* A large, amphibious, long-tusked, seal-like mammal of the Arctic.

waltz (wawlts) [G. *walzen,* to revolve], *n.* A dance in triple time in which the partners whirl round each other; the music for this. *v.i.* To dance a waltz; to trip. **waltzer,** *n.*

wampum (wom′pŭm) [N. Am. Ind.], *n.* Small shell beads used by the Indians as money or ornaments.

wan (won) [A.-S. *wann,* black], *a.* Sickly in hue, pallid, worn. **wanness,** *n.*

wand (wond) [Icel. *vöndr*], *n.* A long, slender rod.

wander (won′dér) [A.-S. *wandrian*], *v.i.* To ramble about without any definite object, to rove, roam; to go astray; to get lost; to talk or think senselessly, to be delirious. *v.t.* To traverse in a random way. **wanderer,** *n.* **wandering,** *a.* and *n.*

wane (wān) [A.-S. *wanian*], *v.i.* To diminish as the illuminated portion of the moon; to decrease in power, etc., to decline. *n.* Act or process of waning, decrease.

wangle (wăng′gél), *v.t.* To manipulate, to employ cunningly; to falsify.

want (wont) [Icel. *vant*], *n.* Lack, deficiency, need (of); privation, poverty; a longing for something that is required for happiness, etc.; that which is so desired. *v.t.* To be without; to need, to require; to crave, to desire the presence or assistance of. *v.i.* To be in need; to be deficient (in); to be lacking. **wanting,** *a.* Absent, lacking; (*colloq.*) daft. *prep.* Without, less, save.

wanton (won′tŏn) [M.E. *wantoun*], *a.*

Sportive, playful; wild, unruly, luxuriant; licentious; heedless, reckless. *n.* A lewd person, esp. a woman; a trifler. *v.i.* To sport, to frolic; to act or grow unrestrainedly. **wantonness,** *n.*

war (wôr) [O.F. *werre*], *n.* A contest carried on by force of arms between nations or parties in the same State; a state of hostilities; hostile operations, armed attack; the military art, strategy; (*fig.*) active enmity, strife. *v.i.* To make or carry on war; to contend; to be in opposition, to be inconsistent. **war-cry,** *n.* A name or phrase formerly shouted in charging, etc.; a watchword; a party cry. **war-head,** *n.* The explosive head of a torpedo, aerial bomb, etc. **war-horse,** *n.* A charger; (*fig.*) a veteran. **warlike,** *a.* Fit or ready for war; fond of war, martial; threatening war, hostile. **war-paint,** *n.* Paint put on the body by savages before going into battle; (*fig.*) full dress. **warship,** *n.* An armed ship for use in war.

warble (wôrbl) [O.F. *werbler*], *v.i.* To sing in a continuous quavering or trilling manner (of birds); to make such a sound (of streams); to sing or utter thus. *n* Act or sound of warbling. **warbler,** *n.* One of a family of small birds, comprising the nightingale, hedge-sparrow, robin, etc.

ward (wôrd) [A.-S. *weard,* watchman], *n.* Watch, guard, act of guarding; confinement, custody; guardianship; a person under guardianship; an administrative or electoral division of a town or city; a separate division of a hospital, etc.; a projection in a lock preventing the turning of any but the right key. *v.t.* To turn aside, to keep (off). **ward-room,** *n.* A room on a warship for commissioned officers below the rank of commander. **wardship,** *n.* Guardianship, tutelage.

-ward, -wards (A.-S. *-weard,* from *weorthan,* to become], *suf.* Expressing direction as in *backward, forward, outwards,* etc.

warden (wôr′dén) [A.-F. *wardein*], *n.* A keeper, a guardian; a governor or president; a watchman.

warder (wôr′dér), *n.* A keeper, a jailer. **wardress,** *n.*

wardrobe (wôr′drōb) [O.F. *warderobe*], *n.* A cabinet, cupboard, etc., where clothes are hung; a person's stock of wearing apparel.

ware (1) (wâr) [A.-S. *waru*], *n.* Manufactured articles, esp. pottery; (*pl.*) articles of merchandise. **warehouse,** *n.* A building in which goods are stored; a wholesale or large retail store. *v.t.* To deposit (furniture, bonded goods, etc.) in a warehouse. **warehouseman,** *n.* One who keeps or is employed in a warehouse.

ware (2) (wâr) [A.-S. *warian,* to guard], *a.* Conscious, aware; cautious. *v.t.* (*imper.*) Beware! Keep clear of!

warfare (wôr′fâr), *n.* A state of war, hostilities; (*fig.*) conflict, strife.

warlock (wôr′lok) [A.-S. *wærloga,* traitor], *n.* A wizard, a sorcerer.

warm (wôrm) [A.-S. *wearm*], *a.* Being at a rather high temperature; ardent, zealous, cordial; emotional, amorous;

excited, vehement; violent, brisk, lively (of a skirmish, etc.); predominantly red or yellow (of colours); fresh (of scent); well off; unpleasant, uncomfortable. *v.t.* To make warm; to excite. *v.i.* To become warm, animated, sympathetic, or enthusiastic. warm-hearted, *a.* Having affectionate, kindly, or susceptible feelings. warming-pan, *n.* A closed metal pan with a long handle for holding live coals, formerly used to warm a bed; (*fig.*) a person who holds a post till another is qualified for filling it. warmly, *adv.* warmth, *n.*

warn (wôrn) [A.-S. *wearnian*], *v.t.* To inform beforehand; to caution or put on one's guard against; to admonish. warning, *n.* Act of cautioning against danger, etc.; previous notice, esp. to quit one's service; that which warns.

warp (wôrp) [A.-S. *wearp*], *n.* The threads running the long way of a woven fabric; a rope used in towing; state of being twisted, a distortion in timber, etc.; a perversity of mind or disposition. *v.t.* To twist out of shape; to make crooked, distort, bias; (*Naut.*) to tow or move with a line attached to a fixed point; To run (yarn) off for weaving. *v.i.* To become twisted or crooked; to turn aside; to become perverted.

warrant (wor'ănt) [O.F. *warant*], *v.t.* To give assurance for, to guarantee; to justify. *n.* Authorization; sanction; anything that attests or bears out a statement, etc., a voucher; an instrument giving power to arrest a person, levy a distress, etc.; a certificate of office. warrant-officer, *n.* An officer next below a commissioned officer, acting under a warrant. warrantable, *a.* Defensible; old enough to be hunted (of deer). warrantor, *n.* (*Law*) warranty, *n.* A warrant, an authorization; (*Law*) a vendor's undertaking that the thing sold is his and is fit for use, etc.

warren (wor'ĕn) [O.F. *warenne*], *n.* A ground where rabbits live and breed.

warrior (wor'i-ôr), *n.* A man experienced in war, a distinguished soldier.

wart (wôrt) [A.-S. *wearte*], *n.* A small hard excrescence on the skin; a spongy growth on the hinder pastern of a horse. wart-hog, *n.* A large-headed African hog with warty excrescences on the face. warty, *a.*

wary (wâr'i), *a.* Cautious, watchful, etc.; circumspect; characterized by caution. warily, *adv.* wariness, *n.* Caution.

was (woz), wast, were (wĕr), wert [A.-S. *wæs, wære, wæs, wæron* (*wæran, wærun*), *wesan*, infin. (see also BE, AM)], past tense of the v. TO BE.

wash (wosh) [A.-S. *wascan*], *v.t.* To cleanse with water, etc.; to purify; to moisten, or dash against (as dew, waves, etc.); to separate the early parts from (ore); to cover with a thin coat of colour or metal. *v.i.* To cleanse (oneself); to wash clothes; to stand washing without being injured; to sweep along, etc. (of water). *n.* Act or operation of washing; state of being washed; a quantity of linen, etc., washed at one time; the

motion of a body of water; waste kitchen-stuff used as food for pigs; slops; a cosmetic, a lotion; a thin coating of colour or metal. washhouse, *n.* A building furnished for washing clothes in, a laundry. washleather, *n.* Chamois leather. wash-out, *v.t.* (*colloq.*) To cancel. *n.* A failure. washstand, *n.* A piece of furniture for holding the ewer, basin, etc., for the toilet. washer, *n.* One who or that which washes; a washerwoman; a ring of metal, rubber, leather, etc., for placing beneath a nut to tighten a joint. washerwoman, *n.* A laundress. washing, *n.*

wasp (wosp) [A.-S. *wæps*], *n.* A predatory insect with black and yellow stripes and a powerful sting; (*fig.*) a spiteful or irritable person.

wassail (wosl) [A.-S. *wæs hăl*, be thou of good health], *n.* A festive occasion, a carouse; spiced liquor prepared for a wassail. wassailer, *n.*

waste (wāst) [L. *vastus*, vast], *a.* Desolate, unoccupied, untilled, devastated; unproductive; dismal, cheerless; superfluous. *v.t.* To devastate; to wear away gradually; to use up unnecessarily or lavishly, to squander. *v.i.* To dwindle, to wither. *n.* Act of squandering, or throwing away to no purpose; state or process of being wasted, gradual diminution of substance, strength, etc.; food, etc., rejected as superfluous, useless, or valueless; a wilderness, a dreary scene, a void. waste-pipe, *n.* A discharge-pipe for used or superfluous water. wastage, *n.* Loss by use, decay, leakage, etc. wasteful, *a.* Extravagant, using recklessly or unnecessarily. wastefully, *adv.* wastrel, *n.* An abandoned child, a waif; a profligate; a wasteful person.

watch (woch) [A.-S. *wacian*, to watch], *n.* Act or state of watching; vigil, look out, waiting in a state of expectancy, dread, etc.; a watchman, a guard; a division of the night; a small timepiece for carrying on the person; the period during which each division of a ship's crew is alternately on duty; either half into which the officers and crew are divided, taking duty alternately. *v.i.* To be on the watch, to be vigilant or expectant; to act as a guard (over); to keep vigil. *v.t.* To observe closely, to keep one's eyes on; to look out for, to await. watch-case, *n.* The metal case enclosing the works of a watch. watch-dog, *n.* A dog kept to guard premises. watch-fire, *n.* A camp-fire, a signal-fire. watch-house, *n.* A house occupied by a watch or guard; a lock-up. watchmaker, *n.* watchmaking, *n.* watchman, *n.* A guard, a sentinel, esp. a member of a former street patrol; one who guards a building, etc., at night. watch-night, *n.* The last night of the year. watch-spring, *n.* The mainspring of a watch. watch-tower, *n.* A tower of observation. watchword, *n.* A password; a motto or phrase symbolizing the principles of a party, etc. watcher, *n.* watchful, *a.* Vigilant, observant, wary.

water (waw'tėr) [A.-S. *wæter*], *n.* A colourless, transparent liquid, destitute of taste and smell, a compound of hydrogen and oxygen; a sea, lake, river (*often in pl.*); tears, sweat, urine, and other animal secretions; the transparency or lustre of a diamond, pearl, etc. *v.t.* To apply water to; to irrigate; to furnish with water for drinking; to overflow with water (of the mouth, eyes, etc.); (*Comm.*) to increase (nominal capital) by issue of stock without corresponding increase of assets; (*in p.p.*) to give an undulating sheen to (silk, etc.). *v.i.* To secrete, shed, or run with water (of the mouth, eyes, etc.); to take in water; to drink (of cattle, etc.). **water-cart,** *n.* A wheeled tank for carrying water or for watering the streets. **water-closet,** *n.* A privy with a water-supply for flushing. **water-colour,** *n.* A pigment ground up with water and mucilage; a water-colour painting; the art of painting in watercolours. **watercourse,** *n.* A stream; a channel for conveyance of water. **watercress,** *n.* A creeping aquatic plant eaten as salad. **waterfall,** *n.* A steep descent of a river, a cascade. **waterfowl,** *n.* (*sing. or collect. pl.*) A bird that frequents rivers, lakes, etc. **water-hen,** *n.* The moor-hen. **watering-place,** *n.* A place where water may be procured for cattle, etc.; a place to which people resort to drink mineral waters or for bathing, a spa, a seaside resort. **watering-pot,** *n.* A vessel with a perforated nozzle for sprinkling water on plants. **wateringtrough,** *n.* A drinking-trough for horses or cattle. **waterish,** *a.* **water-level,** *n.* The level of the sea used as datum. **water-lily,** *n.* A plant with large floating leaves and white or coloured flowers. **water-line,** *n.* The line up to which the hull of a vessel is submerged in the water. **waterlogged,** *a.* Soaked or flooded (of a vessel) with water so as to lie like a log. **waterman,** *n.* A boatman plying for hire; a (good or bad) oarsman. **water-mark,** *n.* A mark indicating the level to which water rises; the limits of the rise and fall of the tide. **watermark,** *n.* A translucent design stamped in paper in the manufacture. **water-mill,** *n.* A mill driven by the agency of water. **water-proof,** *a.* Impervious to water. *n.* Cloth rendered impervious to water; a coat or other garment of this. *v.t.* To render water-proof. **water-rat,** *n.* A large aquatic vole. **water-shed,** *n.* A ridge between two river-basins or drainage-systems. **waterside,** *n.* The margin of a river, lake, or the sea. **waterspout,** *n.* A phenomenon in which a whirling column of water descends towards the sea, sometimes connecting sea and cloud. **water-supply,** *n.* A system for storing and supplying water; the amount of water stored for the use of a house, works, etc. **watertight,** *a.* So tightly fitted as to retain or exclude water. **water wave,** *n.* A wave in the hair made when it is wet. **waterway,** *n.* A navigable channel; a fairway. **water-wheel,** *n.* A wheel moved

by water and turning machinery. **waterworks,** *n.pl.* (*usu. as. sing.*) An establishment for the collection and distribution of water for use of communities. **watery,** *a.* Containing much water; sodden; thin, transparent, like water; rainy-looking; consisting of water; tasteless.

watt (wot) [James *Watt* (1736–1819), engineer], *n.* The unit of electric power or rate of work, the rate when the electromotive force is one volt and the intensity of current one ampere.

wattle (wotl) [A.-S. *watel*], *n.* A hurdle of wicker-work; the fleshy lobe under the throat of the turkey, etc.; one of various species of acacia, the bark of which is used in tanning. *v.t.* To interlace, to plait. **wattle-work,** *n.* Wicker-work.

wave (wāv) [A.-S. *wafian*], *v.i.* To move to and fro as a flag in the wind, to flutter, to undulate; to be wavy; to signal (to) by waving. *v.t.* To cause to move to and fro, to brandish; to make wavy; to indicate by a waving signal. *n.* A moving ridge or long curved body of water, esp. one on the surface of the sea that breaks on the shore; (*poet.*) the sea; an undulation; act or gesture of waving; an intensity of some force, influence, emotion, etc. **wave length,** *n.* (*Wire.*) The space intervening between the maximum positive points of two successive waves; the number by which transmitting stations can be found. **wavelet,** *n.* **wavy,** *a.* **waviness,** *n.*

waver (wā'vėr) [freq. of WAVE], *v.t.* To flicker, to quiver; to falter, hesitate, vacillate. **waverer,** *n.*

wax (1) (wăks) [A.-S. *weax*], *n.* A yellow, plastic substance excreted by bees, beeswax; any substance resembling beeswax, as vegetable wax, bee-bread, sealing-wax, etc. *a.* **Waxen.** *v.t.* To smear or treat with wax. **wax-cloth,** *n.* A floor-cloth. **waxwork,** *n.* Modelling in wax in imitation of living persons, fruit, flowers, etc.; (*pl.*) an exhibition of wax figures. **waxes.** *a.* Made or consisting of wax; resembling wax. **waxy,** *a.* (*colloq.*) Cross, ill-tempered.

wax (2) (wăks) [A.-S. *weaxan*], *v.i.* To increase gradually (esp. of the moon between new and full); to grow in numbers, strength, etc.; to become gradually.

way (wā) [A.-S. *weg*], *n.* A road, path, track; distance traversed; course or route between two places; direction; method or manner of doing something; a usual mode of action, an idiosyncrasy; one's line of business, sphere, range; relation, point; condition; onward movement, progress, headway (esp. of a ship); (*pl.*) the framework over which a ship is launched. **way-bill,** *n.* A list of passengers in a public conveyance or of goods sent by a common carrier. **wayfarer,** *n.* A traveller, esp. a pedestrian. **waylay,** *v.t.* To wait in the way of with a view to rob, etc.; to lie in wait for. **way-leave,** *n.* A right of way over the land of another. **wayside,** *n.*
-ways [A.-S. *weges*, gen. of prec.], *suf.*

Forming adverbs as *always, lengthways, straightway.*

wayward (wā′wàrd), *a.* Perverse, froward, freakish, obstinate.

wayzgoose (wāz′goos) [?], *n.* A printers' annual outing.

we (wē) [A.-S. Dut.], *nom. pl. of 1st pers. pron.* The plural of I; used by a sovereign, editor, writer of an unsigned article, etc.

weak (wēk) [A.-S. *wāc*], *a.* Deficient in strength; feeble, infirm, easily fatigued; feeble-minded, lacking resolution or power of resistance, easily led; fragile, brittle, pliant; unreliable; deficient in quantity, weight, etc.; inadequate, trivial; unconvincing; (*Gram.*) inflected by the addition of *-ed, -d,* or *-t* to the stem in forming the past tense and p.p. (of verbs). **weak-kneed,** *a.* Giving way easily; lacking in resolution. **weaken,** *v.* To make or become weak or weaker. **weakling,** *n.* A feeble person. **weakly,** *adv.* In a weak manner. *a.* Not strong; infirm, sickly. **weakness,** *n.* Quality or state of being weak; a particular defect, one's weak point.

weal (1) (wēl) [A.-S. *wela*], *n.* A healthy or prosperous state.

weal (2) [A.-S. *walu*], *n.* A ridge made by a rod or whip on the flesh.

weald (wēld) [M.E. *weeld, wald*], *n.* A tract of open forest land.

wealth (welth), *n.* Riches, large possessions, affluence; a profusion, great plenty (of). **wealthy,** *a.* Rich.

wean (wēn) [A.-S. *wenian,* to accustom], *v.t.* To accustom (a child or animal) to deprivation of the breast; to estrange from a habit, indulgence, etc. *n.* (*Sc.*) A child.

weapon (wep′ŏn) [A.-S. *wæpen*], *n.* A thing used to inflict bodily harm; anything used for attack or defence.

wear (1) (wâr) [A.-S. *werian*], *v.t.* (*past* wore, *p.p.* worn) To carry on the person, to have on; to maintain, to exhibit; to waste, impair, or alter by rubbing or use; to fatigue or weary; to produce (a hole, etc.) by attrition. *v.i.* To be consumed, diminished, effaced, altered, etc., by rubbing or use; to be exhausted; to stand continual use (well, badly, etc.); to endure, to last; to pass gradually (away. etc.). *n.* Act of wearing; state of being worn; fashion, vogue; damage by attrition, use, etc. **wearable,** *a.* **wearer,** *n.*

wear (2), *v.t.* (*past and p.p.* wore) To bring (a ship) about tack by putting the helm up. *v.i.* To come round thus (of a ship).

weary (wēr′i) [A.-S. *wērig*], *a.* Tired, exhausted; dispirited, sick (of); tiresome, irksome. *v.t.* To tire, to fatigue; to make weary or impatient (of). *v.i.* To become tired or fatigued; to become weary (of); (*Sc.*) to yearn. **wearily,** *adv.* **weariness,** *n.* **wearisome,** *a.* Tedious, tiresome, causing weariness.

weasel (wē′zél) [A.-S. *wesle*], *n.* A small British quadruped related to the stoat.

weather (weth′ér) [A.-S. *weder*], *n.* State of the atmosphere with reference to temperature, clouds and rain, wind,

electrical conditions, etc. *v.t.* To encounter and pass through (bad weather) in safety; to get to windward of (a cape, etc.) in spite of inclement weather; to expose (corn, etc.) to the weather; (*usu.* in *p.p.*) to disintegrate or discolour (rock, masonry, etc.) by this. *v.i.* To stand the effects of weather; to disintegrate, etc. through exposure. **weatherbeaten,** *a.* Seasoned by exposure to storms. **weather-boarding,** *n.* Boards fastened together and overlapping so as to throw off rains. **weatherbound,** *a.* Detained by bad weather. **weathercock,** *n.* A revolving vane to show the direction of the wind; (*fig.*) an inconstant person. **weather-glass,** *n.* A barometer. **weatherwise,** *a.* Skilful in forecasting the weather. **weatherly,** *a.* Presenting such lateral resistance to the water as to make little leeway (of a ship). **weathermost,** *a.* Farthest to windward.

weave (wēv) [A.-S. *wefan*], *v.t.* (*past* wove, *p.p.* woven, wove) To form (yarns, etc.) into a fabric by interlacing; to produce (cloth, etc.) thus; (*fig.*) to interweave (details) into a story, theory, etc. *v.i.* To make fabrics by interlacing threads, etc. **weaver,** *n.* One who weaves; a finch-like bird of warm climates, constructing nests of woven grass.

web (web) [A.-S.], *n.* A woven fabric; a cobweb or similar structure woven by caterpillars; a large roll of paper from the mill; membrane between the toes of swimming-birds, etc. **web-foot,** *n.* One with the digits connected by a web. **webfooted, -toed,** *a.* **webbed,** *a.* **webbing,** *n.* A strong woven band used for girths, seat-bottoms, etc.

wed (wed) [A.-S. *weddian*], *v.t. past and p.p.* **wedded**) To marry; to give in marriage. *v.i.* To marry. **wedded,** *a.* Married; pertaining to matrimony; intimately united. **wedding,** *n.* A marriage ceremony with the accompanying festivities. **wedding-day,** *n.* The day of a marriage or its anniversary.

wedge (wej) [A.-S. *wecg*], *n.* A tapering piece of wood or metal used for splitting wood, rocks, etc., for exerting pressure, etc., forming one of the mechanical powers; anything in the shape of a wedge. *v.t.* To cleave, fix, or fasten with a wedge; to crowd or push (in), as a wedge forces its way.

wedlock (wed′lok) [A.-S. *wedlāk*], *n.* Matrimony, the married state.

Wednesday (wenz′dā, -di) [A.-S. *Wōdnes dæg,* Woden's day], *n.* The fourth day of the week.

wee (wē) [M.E., a bit], *a.* Very small, tiny.

weed (wēd) [A.-S. *wēod*], *n.* A useless or troublesome wild plant; (*fig.*) any useless intrusive thing; a leggy horse; (*colloq.*) a cigar. *v.t.* To clear (ground) of weeds; to sort out useless or inferior elements, etc. **the weed:** Tobacco. **weedy,** *a.* Full of weeds; (*fig.*) lanky and weakly.

weeds (wēdz) [A.-S. *wœde,* garment], *n.pl.* Mourning worn by a widow.

week (wēk) [A.-S. *wice*], *n.* A period of seven days, esp. from Sunday to Saturday inclusively; the six working days, excluding Sunday. **weekday**, *n.* Any day except Sunday. **week-end**, *n.* The days ending one and beginning the following week (usu. Saturday-Monday); *v.i.* To make a holiday, etc., on these. **week-ender**, *n.* Happening, issued, or done once a week or every week; lasting a week; reckoned by the week. *adv.* Once a week; week by week. *n.* A weekly periodical.

ween (wēn) [A.-S. *wēnan*], *v.i.* To be of opinion; to think, fancy.

weep (wēp) [A.-S. *wēpan*], *v.i.* (*past and p.p.* wept) To shed tears; (*fig.*) to drip, to exude. *v.t.* To lament, to bewail; to exhaust with weeping. **weeping-ash**, **-willow**, *n.* An ash or willow with delicate pendulous branches.

weevil (wē´vil) [A.-S. *wifel*], *n.* A small beetle feeding on grain, nuts, etc. **weevilled**, **weevilly**, *a.*

weft (weft) [A.-S. *wefan*, to weave], *n.* The threads passing through the warp from selvedge to selvedge, the woof; a web.

weigh (wā) [A.-S. *wegan*, to carry], *v.t.* To find the weight of; to be equivalent to in weight; (*fig.*) to ponder, to estimate the relative value of; to raise (an anchor). *v.i.* To have a specified weight; to be weighed; (*fig.*) to have influence; to be oppressive (upon); to start on a voyage. **weigh-bridge**, *n.* A machine with a platform on which carts, etc., are weighed.

weight (wāt), *n.* Heaviness, ponderosity, esp. as expressed in terms of some standard unit; a scale of units of weight; a piece of metal of known weight used with scales for weighing; a heavy mass used for mechanical purposes, as in a clock; a heavy load, a burden, pressure; importance, consequence. *v.t.* To attach a weight to, to burden (*lit. and fig.*); to load, to adulterate. **weighty**, *a.*

weir (wēr) [A.-S. *wer*], *n.* A dam across a stream for raising the level of the water above it; stakes, nets, etc., set in a stream to catch fish.

weird (wērd) [A.-S. *wyrd*], *n.* Fate, destiny. *a.* Pertaining to this; unearthly, uncanny; strange. **weirdness**, *n.*

welcome (wel´kŏm) [A.-S. *willa*, pleasure, *cuma*, comer], *a.* Admitted or received with pleasure; producing satisfaction; gladly permitted (to do, etc.). *n.* A kind or cordial reception or entertainment of a new-comer; a willing acceptance of an offer. *v.t.* To greet (a new-comer) cordially; to entertain with kindness; to receive with pleasure.

weld (weld), *v.t.* To unite (pieces of metal) by hammering after they have been softened by heat; to make thus; (*fig.*) to unite into a coherent mass. *n.* A joint or junction by welding.

welfare (wel´fâr), *n.* Prosperity, health, well-being, success. **welfare worker**, *n.* A person paid to look after the welfare of factory workers, etc.

welkin (wel´kin) [A.-S. *wolcnu*, clouds], *n.* (*poet.*) The sky, the vault of heaven.

well (1) (wel) [A.-S. *wel*], *adv.* (*comp.* better, *superl.* best) In a good manner, properly, satisfactorily; happily, fortunately, successfully; fully, perfectly, sufficiently; heartily; with kindness, on good terms; justly, fairly, befittingly. *a.* (*predicative only*) In good health; in a satisfactory state of circumstances. *int.* Expressing astonishment, resignation, etc.; often introductory to resuming one's discourse. **well-advised**, *a.* Prudent, judicious, wise. **well-being**, *n.* Welfare. **well-bred**, *a.* Of good manners; of pure stock. **well-found**, *a.* Well-appointed. **well-meaning**, *a.* Having good intentions. **wellnigh**, *adv.* Almost, nearly. **well-read**, *a.* Having wide knowledge gained from books. **well-spoken**, *a.* Speaking well, eloquent; of good disposition. **well-to-do**, *a.* In good circumstances, prosperous. **well-wisher**, *n.* A person who wishes well to one.

well (2) (wel) [A.-S. *wella*], *n.* A shaft bored in the ground to obtain water, oil, etc.; a hole more or less resembling this; a space in the middle of a building enclosing the stairs or a lift or for light and ventilation; (*fig.*) a source. *v.i.* To spring (forth) as a fountain. **well-sinker**, *n.* One who digs or sinks wells.

welladay (wel-â-dā´) **wellaway** (-wā´) [A.-S. *wā lā wā*, woe, lo! woe], *int.* An exclamation of sorrow or despair.

wellington (wel´ing-tŏn) [after the first Duke (1769–1852)], *n.pl.* A boot, usu. rubber, coming to the knee.

Welsh (welsh) [A.-S. *wælisc*, foreign], *a.* Pertaining to Wales or its inhabitants. *n.* The language of the Welsh; the Welsh people. *v.* To cheat on a racecourse by making off without paying. **welsher**, *n.* One who welshes. **welsh rarebit**, properly **rabbit**: Cheese melted and spread over toasted bread.

welt (welt) [M.E. *welte*], *n.* A strip of leather between the upper and the sole of a boot for sewing them together.

welter (1) (wel´tẽr) [M.E. *weltren*], *v.i.* To roll, to tumble about; to wallow. *n.* A turmoil, a confusion.

welter (2) [?], *a.* (*Horse-racing, etc.*) Heavy-weight.

wen (wen) [A.-S. *wenn*], *n.* An indolent tumour, usu. occurring on the neck; (*fig.*) an abnormal growth.

wench (wench) [A.-S. *wencel*, infant], *n.* A girl or young woman.

wend (wend) [A.-S. *wendan*, to turn], *v.t.* To go or direct (one's way). *v.i.* To go.

werwolf (wẽr´wulf) [A.-S. *werewulf*], *n.* A person turned or supposed to have the power of turning himself into a wolf.

Wesleyan (wes´li-ân), *a.* Of or belonging to the Church founded by John Wesley (1703–91). *n.* A member of this.

west (west) [A.-S.], *adv.* At or towards the quarter opposite the east, or where the sun sets at the equinox. *n.* The cardinal point exactly opposite the east; the region lying opposite to the east; a wind blowing from the west. *a.* Being, lying, or living in the west; blowing from the west. **west-south-west**, *a.*, *n.*, and *adv.* **westering**, *a.* Passing to the west (of the sun). **westerly**, *a.* Being in, situated, or directed towards the west; blowing from the west. *adv.* Towards the west.

western, *adv. n.,* and *a.* **Western Powers,** *n.pl.* (*Polit.*) A loose term for the European Powers and U.S.A., contrasted with the U.S.S.R. **westerner,** *n.* **westing,** *n.* Distance travelled or amount of deviation towards the west. **westward,** *a.* and *adv.*

wet (wet) [A.-S. *wǣt*], *a.* Moistened, soaked, covered with, or containing water or other liquid; rainy; allowing sale of alcohol, opp. to prohibitionist. *n.* Wetness, moisture; rain. *v.t.* To make wet; to moisten, drench, or soak with liquid. **wet-nurse,** *n.* A woman employed to suckle a child not her own. **wettish,** *a.*

wether (weth′ĕr) [A.-S.], *n.* A castrated ram.

wey (wā) [A.-S. *wǣge,* weight], *n.* A weight varying with different articles (of wool, 182 lb.; oats and barley, 48 bushels; cheese, 224 lb.; salt, 40 bushels).

whack (wăk) [imit.], *v.t.* To strike heavily, to thwack. *n.* A heavy blow, a thwack; (*slang*) a share. **whacking,** *n.* A thrashing.

whale (wāl) [A.-S. *hwœl*], *n.* A large marine fish-like mammal. *v.i.* To engage in whale-fishing. **whalebone,** *n.* A horny, elastic substance occurring in long, thin plates, found in the palate of certain whales. **whaler,** *n.* A whale-man; a ship employed in whaling. **whaling-gun,** *n.* A gun for firing harpoons at whales. **whale-oil,** *n.* Oil obtained from the blubber of whales; spermaceti.

wharf (wôrf) [A.-S. *hwerf,* bank, dam], *n.* (*pl.* **-ves**) A landing-place for cargoes, a quay, a pier. *v.t.* To moor at a wharf; to deposit goods on a wharf. **wharfage,** *n.* **wharfinger** (whôr′fin-jer), *n.* One who owns or has charge of a wharf.

what (wot) [A.-S. *hwœt,* neut. of *hwā,* WHO], *pron.* (*interrog.*) Which thing or things (often used ellipt.); (*rel.*) that which, those which, the things that; how much! (as an exclamation). *a.* Which thing, kind, amount, etc. (in questions); how great, remarkable, ridiculous, etc. (exclamatory); (*rel.*) such as, as much or as many as, any that. *adv.* (*interrog.*) To what extent, in what respect? **whate'er** (-âr), *pron.* (*poet.*) Whatever. **whatev′er,** *pron.* Anything soever that; all that which. *a.* No matter what (thing or things). **whatnot,** *n.* A piece of furniture with shelves for ornaments, books, etc.

whatsoever (wot-sō-ev′ĕr), **-soe′er** (-âr′), *pron.* and *a.* (*poet.*) Whatever.

wheat (wēt) [A.-S. *hwǣte*], *n.* An annual cereal grass the grain of which is ground into flour for bread. **wheat-ear,** *n.* An ear of wheat. **wheaten,** *a.*

wheatear (wēt′ĕr), *n.* The stone-chat or whitetail.

wheedle (wēdl) [?], *v.t.* To gain over, to persuade by coaxing or flattery; to cajole; to obtain from thus. **wheedlingly,** *adv.*

wheel (wēl) [A.-S. *hwēol*], *n.* A circular frame or solid disk turning on its axis;

a machine consisting principally of a wheel, as a spinning-wheel, potter's wheel, steering-wheel, etc.; an old instrument of torture for breaking the limbs; act of wheeling, a revolution. *v.t.* To move (a wheeled vehicle) in some direction; to cause to turn on a pivot. *v.i.* To turn or swing round thus; to change direction; to gyrate; to ride a cycle. **wheelbarrow,** *n.* A barrow on a single wheel, with two handles. **wheel-house,** *n.* A shelter for the steersman. **wheelwright,** *n.* A man who makes wheels, etc.

wheeze (wēz) [A.-S. *hwēsan*], *v.i.* To breathe with an audible sound, as in asthma. **wheezy,** *a.*

whelk (welk) [A.-S. *wiloc*], *n.* A marine spiral-shelled sea-snail used for food.

whelp (welp) [A.-S. *hwelp*], *n.* A pup; a cub; an offensive or ill-bred youth.

when (wen) [A.-S. *hwœnne*], *adv.* (*interrog.*) At what or which time? (*rel.*) at which (time), at the time that, at whatever time; as soon as; at or just after; and then; while (often ellipt. with pres.p.). *pron.* What or which time. **whenever, whene'er,** *adv.* At whatever time. **whensoever,** *adv.* At which time soever.

whence (wens) [A.-S. *hwanan*], *adv.* (*interrog.*) From what place or which, where from? how? (*rel.*) from which place, source, etc.; wherefore; (*ellipt.*) to or at the place from which. *pron.* What or which place.

where (wâr) [A.-S. *hwǣr*], *adv.* (*interrog.*) At or in what place, case, circumstances, etc.; whither, in what direction; (*rel.*) in which (place or places), in or to the direction, etc., in which. *pron.* What or which place. **whereabouts,** *adv.* Near what or which place roughly. *n.* (wâr′-) The approximate locality. **whereas** (-ăz′), *conj.* The fact or case being that, considering that; when in reality. **whereat** (-ăt′), *adv.* At which. **whereby,** *adv.* By which means. **where′fore,** *adv.* For what reason? why? on which account. *n.* The reason why. **wherein** (-in′), *adv.* In what place, respect, etc., in which thing, place, respect, etc. **whereof** (-ov′), *adv.* Of what? of which or whom. **whereon** (-on′), *adv.* On which or what. **wheresoev′er,** *adv.* In or to what place soever. **whereto** (-too′), *adv.* To what place or end. **whereupon′,** *adv.* Upon which; in consequence of or immediately after which. **where'er** (*poet.*), **where′er** (-âr′), *adv.* At, in, or to whatever place. **wherewith** (-with′), *adv.* With what? with which. **wherewithal** (-awl′), *adv.* Wherewith. *n.* (wâr′-) The necessary means, esp. money.

wherry (wer′i) [?], *n.* A light shallow rowing-boat for plying on rivers. **wherryman,** *n.*

whet (wet) [A.-S. *hwœt,* keen], *v.t.* To sharpen by rubbing on a stone; (*fig.*) to excite, stimulate. **whetstone,** *n.* A piece of stone for sharpening cutlery.

whether (weth′ĕr) [A.-S. *hwœther*], *pron*

NOTE: In certain words beginning with **wh** the **w** is not sounded; in all others modern English usage (but not Scots, Irish, Welsh or American) drops the **h,** which is now little better than a pedantic affectation.

Which of the two? *conj.* Introducing an indirect question in the form of an alternative clause followed by an alternative *or, or not,* or *or whether,* or with the alternative unexpressed.

whey (wā) [A.-S. *hwæg*], *n.* The watery part of milk that remains after the curds have been separated. **wheyey,** *a.*

which (wich) [A.-S. *hwilc, whilc*], *pron. (interrog.)* What person, thing, person(s) or thing(s) of a definite number; *(rel.)* representing in a clause a noun in the principal sentence. *a. (interrog.)* What (person, etc.) of a definite number; *(rel.)* used with a noun defining an indefinite antecedent. **whichev'er, whichsoev'er,** *a.* and *pron. (emphat.)* Which (person or thing) of two or more.

whiff (wif) [imit.], *n.* A sudden expulsion of smoke, etc., a puff, a light gust of odour. *v.* To puff or blow lightly.

whig (wig) [obs. *whiggamor,* Sc. nickname for buyers of corn at Leith], *n.* A member of the political party opposed to the Court party or Tories; a Liberal. **whiggery, whiggism,** *n.* whiggish, *a.*

while (wīl) [A.-S. *hwīl*], *n.* A space of time, esp. during which something happens. *conj.* During the time that, as long as, at the same time as; whereas. **whilst,** *conj.* While.

whim (wim) [Icel. *hvima,* to wander with the eyes], *n.* A sudden fancy, a caprice. **whimsical,** *a.* Full of whims; odd-looking, curious, fantastic. whimsical'ity, *n.*

whimbrel (wim'brĕl) [imit. of cry], *n.* A small curlew.

whimper (wim'pĕr), *v.i.* To cry with a low, whining voice; to whine. *v.t.* To utter in such a tone. *n.* A low, querulous cry.

whin (win) [Scand.], *n.* Furze, gorse. **whinchat,** *n.* A small bird, the stone-chat.

whine (wīn) [A.-S. *hwīnan*], *v.i.* To make a plaintive, long-drawn cry; to complain in a peevish way. *v.t.* To utter with a whine or peevishly. *n.* A whining cry; a mean or unmanly complaint.

whinny (win'i), *v.i.* To neigh gently; act or sound of this.

whinstone (win'stōn) [?], *n.* A very hard unstratified rock, as basalt or quartzose sandstone.

whip (wip) [Teut.], *v.t.* To snatch, to jerk (away, etc.); to lash, flog; to urge (on) with a whip; to beat (cream, etc.) into a froth; to fish (a stream) by casting a line over the water; to bind closely with twine, etc.; to oversew (a seam) with close stitches. *v.i.* To move or start suddenly, to dart (out, in, etc.). *n.* A lash tied to a handle or rod for driving horses, etc., or for punishing persons; a coachman or driver; a whipper-in; a M.P. appointed unofficially to summon the members of his party to divisions, etc.; a summons sent out thus. **whip-cord,** *n.* A hard twisted cord for making a whip. **whip-hand,** *n.* The hand holding

the whip; *(fig.)* the advantage. **whip-top,** *n.* A top kept spinning with a whip. **whipper,** *n.* **whipper-in,** *n.* A man employed to assist the huntsman by looking after the hounds. **whipper-snapper,** *n.* A presuming, insignificant person.

whippet (wip'ĕt) [?], *n.* A racing-dog, a cross between the greyhound and terrier.

whir (wĕr) [M.E. *whirr*], *v.i.* To move or fly quickly with a whizzing sound. *n.* This sound.

whirl (wĕrl) [Icel. *hvirfla*], *v.t.* To swing round and round, or cause to fly round, with great velocity; to carry (along) rapidly; to hurl. *v.i.* To turn round and round rapidly, to spin; to travel rapidly in a circular course; to move along swiftly; to be giddy. *n.* A whirling motion. **whirlpool,** *n.* An eddy or vortex. **whirlwind,** *n.* A funnel-shaped column of air moving spirally round an axis and progressing. **whirligig,** *n.* A child's spinning toy; a merry-go-round; *(fig.)* a rotation.

whisk (wisk) [Scand.], *v.t.* To sweep or flap (away or off); to carry off suddenly; to wave about quickly; to beat up (eggs, etc.). *v.i.* To move swiftly or suddenly. *n.* A whisking movement; a small brush for flapping away flies, dust, etc.; an instrument for beating up eggs, etc. **whisker,** *n.* Hair growing on the cheeks of a man, or on the upper lip of a cat or other animal. **whiskered,** *a.* Having whiskers.

whisky (wis'ki) [Gael. *uisge (beatha),* water (of life), usquebaugh)], *n.* An ardent spirit distilled from barley, rye, etc.

whisper (wis'pĕr) [O. Northumbrian, *hwisprian*], *v.i.* To speak in a low voice so as not to be overheard; to converse privately; to plot. *v.t.* To tell or bid in a whisper; to disseminate thus. *n.* A whispering tone or voice; a whispered remark; an insinuation, a rumour. **whispering,** *n.*

whist (wist) [WHISK, in alln. to the sweeping up of the cards], *n.* A card game, usu. for four, played with the full pack of 52 cards.

whistle (wisl) [A.-S. *hwistlan* (imit.)], *v.i.* To make a shrill musical sound by forcing the breath through the lips or with an instrument; to emit such a sound (of an engine, birds, a flying missile, the wind, etc.). *v.t.* To emit (a tune, etc.) by whistling; to signal to thus. *n.* A whistling sound or note; an instrument for producing such.

whit (wit) [A.-S. *wiht*], *n.* A jot, an iota.

white (wīt) [A.-S. *hwīt*], *a.* Being of the colour produced by reflection of all the visible rays in sunlight as of pure snow, common salt, etc.; pale, light-complexioned, bloodless, colourless; pure, stainless; innocent; silvery or hoary, as from age. *n.* A white colour; a member of one of the paler races, a Euro-

---

NOTE: In certain words beginning with **wh** the **w** is not sounded; in all others modern English usage (but not Scots, Irish, Welsh or American) drops the **h,** which is now little better than a pedantic affectation.

pean; a white part of anything; (*pl.*) white clothes; superior flour. **whitebait**, *n.* The fry of several kinds of fish. **white frost:** Hoar-frost. **white heat:** The degree of heat at which bodies become incandescent; (*fig.*) a high pitch of passion, etc. **white-hot**, *a.* **white lead:** Carbonate of lead, esp. used as basis of white oil-paint. **white-livered**, *a.* Cowardly. **white metal:** A cheap alloy imitating silver. **whitesmith**, *n.* A tinsmith; one who finishes or galvanizes ironwork. **whitethorn**, *n.* The hawthorn. **whitethroat**, *n.* A small warbler. **whitewash**, *n.* A mixture used for whitening walls, ceilings, etc.; (*fig.*) a false colouring given to one to counteract disreputable allegations. *v.t.* To cover with whitewash; (*fig.*) to clear from imputations; to clear a bankrupt of his debts by judicial process. **whiten**, *v.t.* and *i.* **whiteness**, *n.* **whitening**, *n.* Act of making white; state of becoming white; whiting for whitewashing, etc. **whitish**, *a.*

whither (with'ẽr) [A.-S. *hwider*], *adv.* (*interrog.*) To what or which place, where; (*rel.*) to which; wheresoever. **whithersoev'er**, *adv.* To what place soever.

whiting (wī'ting), *n.* Fine chalk prepared for use in whitewashing, polishing, etc.; a small sea-fish, used for food.

whitlow (wit'lō) [*quick-flaw*, a flaking off of the skin round the quick], *n.* An inflammatory tumour, esp. on a finger.

Whitsun (wit'sŭn) [from the white garment commonly worn at this festival], *a.* Pertaining to Whitsuntide. **Whitsuntide**, *n.* Whit-Sunday (the 7th Sunday after Easter) and the following days.

whittle (witl) [A.-S. *thwitan*, to pare], *v.t.* To trim, shave, or cut slices off with a knife; to reduce, pare away.

whity (wī'ti), *a.* Whitish (as in *whitybrown*, between white and brown).

who (hoo) [A.-S. *hwā*], *pron.* (*obj.* whom, hoom, *poss.* whose, hooz) (*interrog.*) What or which person or persons? (*rel.*) that (identifying the subject or object in a relative clause with that of the principal clause). **whoev'er, whoe'er** (-âr') (*poet.*), **whosoev'er**, *pron.* (*obj.* whomever, etc.) Any one, no matter who.

whole (hōl) [A.-S. *hāl*, HALE], *a.* Sound, in good health; unimpaired, intact; composed of units, not fractional. *n.* A thing complete in all its parts, units, etc.; the entirety; a complete system, an organic unity. **whole-hearted**, *a.* Done or intended with all one's heart; cordial, sincere. **whole-length**, *a.* Exhibiting the whole figure (of a portrait). **whole meal:** Flour not deprived of a portion of its constituents by bolting. **wholesale**, *n.* The sale of goods in large quantities as dist. from retail. *a.* Buying or selling thus.

wholesome (hōl'sŏm), *a.* Tending to promote health; promoting moral or

mental health, not morbid; clean; healthy, sound.

wholly (hōl'li), *adv.* Entirely, completely; totally, exclusively.

whoop (hoop) [M.E. *houpen*], *v.t.* To cry out loudly in excitement, encouragement, exultation, etc.; to hallo. *v.t.* To urge (on) or to mock at with loud cries. *n.* The cry "whoop"; a loud shout of excitement, encouragement, etc.; the sound made in whooping-cough. **whooping-cough**, *n.* An infectious disease, esp. of children, characterized by a violent cough.

whore (hōr) [Icel. *hōra*, adulteress], *n.* A prostitute, a courtezan. *v.i.* To patronize prostitutes. **whoredom**, *n.* **whoremonger**, *n.* A fornicator.

whorl (wôrl), *n.* A ring of leaves, sepals, or other organs on a plant; one turn of a spiral.

whortleberry (wẽrtl'bẽr-i) [A.-S. *horta*, BERRY], *n.* The bilberry.

why (wī) [A.-S. *hwī*], *adv.* (*interrog.*) For what reason? (*rel.*) on account of which. *n.* The reason, explanation, or purpose of anything. *int.* Expressing surprise, etc.

wick (wik) [A.-S. *wice*], *n.* A piece of fibrous material used in a candle or lamp to convey the melted grease or oil to the flame.

wicked (wik'ĕd) [obs. *wikke*, cogn. with WEAK], *a.* Sinful, addicted to evil or vice: immoral, depraved; mischievous. **wickedness**, *n.*

wicker (wik'ẽr) [Scand.], *n.* Twigs or osiers plaited. *a.* Made of this. **wickerwork**, *n.* and *a.*

wicket (wik'ĕt) [A.-F. *wiket*], *n.* A small door, esp. one close to or forming part of a large one; (*Cricket*) a set of three stumps surmounted by two bails at which the bowler directs the ball; the ground on which this is set up.

wide (wīd) [A.-S. *wīd*], *a.* Having great relative extent from side to side, broad; far-extending; spacious; not restricted, free, liberal, comprehensive; considerably distant from a mark, point, purpose, etc. *adv.* Widely; to a great distance, extensively; far from the mark. *n.* (*Cricket*) A ball bowled too far to the side. **wide-awake**, *a.* Alert, wary; knowing. *n.* A soft felt hat with a broad brim. **widespread**, *a.* Widely disseminated. **widen**, *v.* **widish**, *a.*

widgeon (wij'ŏn) [L. *vipio*, a small crane], *n.* A migratory wild duck.

widow (wid'ō) [A.-S. *widwe*], *n.* A woman who has lost her husband by death and remains unmarried. *v.t.* To bereave of a husband. **widower**, *n.* A man who has lost his wife by death and remains unmarried. **widowhood**, *n.*

width (width), *n.* Extent from side to side, breadth.

wield (wēld) [A.-S. *wealdan*, to govern], *v.t.* To have the management of; to sway; to use or employ. **wieldable**, *a.* **wielder, wieldy**, *a.* Manageable.

NOTE: In certain words beginning with wh the w is not sounded; in all others modern English usage (but not Scots, Irish, Welsh or American) drops the h, which is now little better than a pedantic affectation.

wife (wīf) [A.-S. *wīf*], *n.* A married woman, esp. in relation to her husband. **wife-hood,** *n.* **wifely,** *a.*

wig (wig), *n.* A periwig, a false head of hair, worn to conceal baldness, as a disguise, or (by judges, livery servants, etc.) as part of an official costume. **wigged,** *a.* **wigging,** *n.* A reprimand, a scolding.

wight (wīt) [as WHIT], *n.* A person.

wigwam (wig'wom) [Algonkin, *weekouomut*, in his house], *n.* A N. Am. Indian hut or tent.

wild (wīld) [A.-S. *wilde*], *a.* Living in a state of nature; not tamed or cultivated (of animals and plants); savage; irregular, desert, uninhabited; disorderly in conduct, lawless, reckless, rash; ill-considered, imprudent, extravagant; ungoverned; stormy, furious; anxiously eager; mad (with); excited (about); shy, easily startled. *n.* A desert. **wildfowl,** *n.* (*collect.*) Birds pursued as game, esp. waterfowl. **wildish,** *a.* **wildly,** *adv.* **wildness,** *n.*

wilderness (wil'dér-nès), *n.* An uninhabited or uncultivated land; a waste, a scene of disorder.

wile (wīl) [A.-S. *wil*], *n.* A trick, a stratagem. *v.t.* To entice, to cajole (into, etc.).

wilful (wil'fùl), *a.* Intentional, deliberate; done of one's own free will, not accidental; due to malice; self-willed, perverse. **wilfully,** *adv.* **wilfulness,** *n.*

will (1) (wil) [A.-S. *willan*], *v.t.* (*past and cond.* would, wud, *2nd sing.* wouldest, **wouldst,** *colloq. neg.* won't, wônt, **wouldn't,** wudnt), *v.t.* To desire, wish, choose, want (a thing, that, etc.); to consent (to); to resolve, to determine; to direct or cause (a hypnotized person) to act in a specified way; to bequeath by will. *v.i.* To exercise will-power. *v.aux.* (*in 2nd and 3rd pers., or in 1st pers. in reported statement*) To be about or going to; (*in 1st pers.*) to intend, have a mind to; to be certain or probable, must. **willing,** *a.* Not averse or reluctant (to); cheerfully acting, given, etc. **willingly,** *adv.* **willingness,** *n.* **would-be,** *pref.* Desirous, vainly aspiring to be.

will (2) (wil) [A.-S. *willa*], *n.* The mental power by which one initiates or controls one's activities; exercise of this power, a choice, an intention, a fixed purpose; determination, energy of character; that which is willed or determined upon; arbitrary disposal; disposition towards others; the legal declaration of one's intentions as to disposal of his property after death. **will-power,** *n.*

will-o'-the-wisp (wil'ò-thè-wisp'), *n.* An ignis fatuus.

willow (wil'ò) [A.-S, *welig*], *n.* A tree or shrub with long, slender, pliant branches, usu. growing near water; a cricket-bat made from its wood. **willowy,** *a.* Graceful, like a willow.

willy nilly (wil'ĭ-nil-ĭ) [*will he, nill he*], *adv.* Willingly or unwillingly; inevitably. *a.* Vacillating.

wilt (wilt) [?], *v.i.* To wither, to droop; to lose freshness. *v.t.* To cause to wilt.

wily (wī'lĭ), *a.* Using or full of wiles; cunning, crafty. **wilily,** *adv.* **wiliness,** *n.*

wimple (wimpl) [A.-S. *winpel*], *n.* A covering for the head, formerly worn by women and still by some nuns.

win (win) [A.-S. *winnan*, to fight], *v.t.* (*past and p.p.* won, wŭn) To gain or achieve by struggling, superiority, toil, etc., to earn; to be victorious in; to reach; to charm (*in pres.p.*); to persuade, to gain over. *v.i.* To be successful in a fight, contest, wager, etc.; to make one's way by effort (to, etc.). *n.* (*colloq.*) A success, a victory. **winner,** *n.* **winning,** *a.* That wins; attractive, charming. *n.pl.* Amount won. **winning-post,** *n.* A post making the end of a race.

wince (wins), *v.i.* To shrink or recoil, as from trouble or a blow. *n.* Act of wincing.

wincey (win'sĭ) [?], *n.* A cotton cloth with wool filling.

winch (winch) [A.-S. *wince*], *n.* A windlass; a crank turning an axle, etc.

wind (1) (wind, *poet.* wīnd) [A.-S.], *n.* Air in motion, a breeze, a gale; (*collect.*) wind-instruments; breath; lung power; a part near the stomach a blow on which causes temporary inability to breathe; (*fig.*) meaningless talk; flatulence; scent carried on the wind; a hint or indication (of). *v.t.* (wīnd, *past and p.p.* wound) To sound (a horn, etc.) by blowing; (wind, *past and p.p.* winded) to perceive the presence of by scent; to put out of breath; to enable to recover breath by resting, etc. **wind-bag,** *n.* A bag inflated with wind; (*fig.*) a man of mere words, a long-winded speaker. **windfall,** *n.* Something blown down by the wind; (*fig.*) unexpected good fortune. **wind-gauge,** *n.* An instrument for showing the force or pressure of the wind. **wind-hover** (wind'hŭv-èr), *n.* The kestrel. **wind-instrument,** *n.* A musical instrument in which the tones are produced by the vibration of an air-column forced into the pipes, reeds, etc., by a bellows or the mouth. **windjammer,** *n.* A merchant sailing ship. **windmill,** *n.* A mill driven by the action of the wind on sails; (*fig. pl.*) chimeras. **windpipe,** *n.* The breathing passage, the trachea. **wind-screen,** *n.* (*Motor.*) A glass screen in front of the driver. **windward,** *n.* The direction from which the wind blows. *a.* Lying in or directed towards this. *adv.* In this direction. **windy,** *a.*

wind (2) (wīnd) [A.-S. *windan*], *v.t.* (*past and p.p.* wound, wound) To turn, go, or be twisted in a spiral or tortuous course or shape; to meander; to proceed circuitously, to insinuate oneself (into, etc.), *v.t.* To cause to turn spirally, to wrap, twine, or coil; to entwine; to pursue (one's course) in a sinuous way; to hoist by means of a windlass, etc. to wind up: To coil up; (*fig.*) to put ready for activity; to conclude; to arrange the final settlement of the affairs of (a business, etc.); to go into liquidation. **winding-engine,** *n.* A hoisting engine. **winding-sheet,** *n.* The sheet in which a corpse is wrapped.

windlass (wind´lås) [M.E. *windelas*], *n.* A cylinder on an axle turned by a crank used for hoisting or hauling.

window (win´dō) [Icel. *vindauga*], *n.* An opening in a building, vehicle, etc., with the glazed framework filling it, for the admission of light and air. window-sash, *n.* A frame in which panes of glass for windows are set.

wine (win) [L. *vīnum*], *n.* The fermented juice of grapes, or of certain fruits in imitation of this. wineglass, *n.* A small glass for drinking wine from. wine-press, *n.* An apparatus in which grapes are pressed; the place in which this is done.

wing (wing) [M.E. *wingè, wengè*], *n.* One of the organs of flight in birds, insects, etc.; a supporting part of a flying-machine; (*Aer.*) R.A.F. unit of 3 squadrons; (*fig.*) flight, power of flight; a part of a building, army, bone, etc., projecting laterally; (*Theat., pl.*) the sides of the stage. *v.t.* To furnish with wings; to traverse on wings; to wound in the wing. wing-case, sheath, *n.* The horny cover protecting the wings of coleopterous insects.

wink (wingk) [A.-S. *wincian*], *v.i.* To close and open (of an eye); to give a sign or signal by such a motion; to blink; (*fig.*) to twinkle. *v.t.* To close and open (an eye or the eyes). *n.* Act of winking esp. as a signal; a hint.

winkle (wing´kél) [A.-S. *wine-wincla*], *n.* An edible sea-snail, a periwinkle.

winnow (win´ō) [A.-S. *windwian*], *v.t.* To separate and drive the chaff from (grain); (*fig.*) to sift, sort; to analyse thoroughly.

winsome (win´sŏm) [A.-S. *wynn*, joy], *a.* Winning, charming, attractive.

winter (win´tér) [A.-S.], *n.* The cold season of the year; (*fig.*) a period of inactivity, a cheerless state of things. winter-garden, *n.* A large conservatory for plants. winter-green, *n.* A small ever-green shrub, the berries of which furnish a strong-smelling oil used medicinally. wintry, *a.*

wipe (wīp) [A.-S. *wipian*], *v.t.* To rub with something soft in order to clean or dry. *v.i.* To strike (at). *n.* The act of wiping; a sweeping blow.

wire (wīr) [A.-S. *wīr*], *n.* Metal drawn out into a thread of uniform diameter; such a rod, thread, or strand of metal; (*fig.*) the telegraph, a telegraphic message. *v.t.* To apply wire to, to fasten, bind, stiffen or snare with wire. (*colloq.*) to telegraph to. *v.i.* To send a telegram. wiredraw, *v.t.* (*p.p.* -drawn) To draw (metal) into wire; (*fig.*) to over-refine (an argument, etc.). wire-haired, *a.* Having stiff, wiry hair. wire-puller, *n.* (*fig.*) A politician, etc., working behind the scenes. wireworm, *n.* A larva destructive to roots of vegetables, etc. wireless, *a.* Without a wire, *n.* Wireless telegraphy; an instrument for receiving such messages, music, etc.; the pro-grammes, etc., thus transmitted; radio. *v.i.* (*colloq.*) To communicate with by this. wiry, *a.* wiriness, *n.*

wisdom (wiz´dŏm), *n.* Quality or state of being wise; knowledge and experience, with ability to make use of them rightly, sagacity, common sense.

wise (1) (wīz) [A.-S. *wīs*], *a.* Having the power of discerning rightly, sagacious, sensible, discreet; experienced, under-standing. wisely, *adv.*

wise (2) [A.-S.], *n.* Manner, way, guise.

-wise [WISE (2)], *suf.* Forming adverbs of manner, as *lengthwise, likewise, otherwise.*

wiseacre (wī´să-kér) [M.H.G. *wizago*, a prophet], *n.* One pretending to learning or wisdom. wisecrack, *n.* (*colloq.*) A smart but not profound epigram, a slick witty comment.

wish (wish) [A.-S. *wȳscan*], *v.t.* To have a strong desire or craving (that, etc.), to want; to express a desire concerning; to invoke, to bid. *v.i.* To have a strong desire (for). A desire, a longing, an aspiration; an expression of this, a petition, invocation; that which is desired. wishful, *a.* wish-bone, *n.* The merrythought.

wisp (wisp) [M.E.], *n.* A small bunch of straw, hay, etc. wispy, *a.*

wistaria (wis-tār´i-à) [Caspar *Wistar* (1761-1818)], *n.* A climbing shrub with lilac-coloured flowers.

wistful (wist´fŭl) [?], *a.* Full of vague yearnings, sadly longing; pensive.

wit (1) (wit) [A.-S. *witan*], *v.* (*1st sing.* wot, *2nd sing.* wottest, *past.* wist: *no other parts used*) To know (esp. in the infin. "to wit", namely). witting, *a.* wittingly, *adv.* Knowingly, intentionally.

wit (2), *n.* Intelligence, sense (*often in pl.*); the power of perceiving other relations between apparently incongruous ideas; a person distinguished for this power. witticism, *n.* A witty saying, a jest. witless, *a.* witty, *a.* wittily, *adv.*

witch (wich) [A.-S. *wicca* (masc.)], *n.* A woman dealing with evil spirits or prac-tising sorcery; a fascinating woman; an old and ugly hag. *v.t.* To bewitch, to fascinate. witchcraft, *n.* The practices of witches; sorcery, magic. witchery, *n.* witching, *a.*

witenagemot (wit´é-nà-gé-mōt) [A.-S., meeting of wise men], *n.* The Anglo-Saxon parliament.

with (with) [A.-S. *wither*, against], *prep.* In the company of or association; having, possessed of, characterized by; in the possession or care of; by the means, use, or aid of; by the addition of; because of; in regard to, in respect of, concerning; in opposition to, against.

withal (wi-thawl´), *adv.* With the rest, in addition, at the same time, moreover.

withdraw (with-draw´), *v.t.* (*past* -drew, *p.p.* -drawn) To draw back or apart; to remove, retract. *v.i.* To retire; to go apart or aside. withdrawal, *n.*

withe (with, with), *n.* A tough, flexible branch used in binding; a tie made of osiers, twigs, straw, etc.

wither (with´ér) [M.E. *widren*], *v.t.* To shrivel and dry (up); to cause to lose freshness, soundness, or vigour. *v.i.* To become dry and wrinkled; to dry and shrivel (up); to fade away, languish, droop. withering, *a.*

withers (with'èrz) [A.-S. *wither*, against], *n.pl.* The ridge between the shoulder-blades of a horse.

withershins (with'èr-shinz) [Icel. *vithr*, against, A.-S. *wither*, *sinni*, movement], *adv.* In the contrary direction, esp. opposite to the direction of the sun, anti-clockwise.

withhold (with-hōld'), *v.t.* (*past and p.p.* -held) To keep from action, to hold back, to refuse to grant.

within (wi-thin'), *adv.* Inside, in or to the inner part or parts; internally; indoors. *prep.* In or to the inner part of, inside; in the range or compass of; not beyond; in no longer a time than.

without (wi-thout'), *adv.* In, at, or to the outside, outside; externally; out of doors. *prep.* Not having, destitute of, free from; outside of; out of the compass or range of, beyond.

withstand (with-stănd'), *v.t.* (*past and p.p.* -stood) To resist, to oppose.

witness (wit'nés), *n.* Attestation of a fact, etc., testimony, evidence; one who has seen or known an incident, one present at an event; one who gives evidence in a law-court; one who testifies to the genuineness of a signature. *v.t.* To see or know by personal presence, to be a spectator of; to attest, to sign as witness; (*fig.*) to show, to prove. *v.i.* To give evidence; to serve as evidence (against, for, etc.). **witness-box,** *n.* An enclosure in a law-court for witnesses.

wizard (wiz'árd) [M.E. *wisard*], *n.* A sorcerer, a magician; (*fig.*) one who works wonders. **wizardry,** *n.*

wizen (wizn) [A.-S. *wisnian*], *v.* To wither, dry up, shrivel. *a.* Wizened.

woad (wōd) [A.-S. *wād*], *n.* A plant yielding a blue dye.

woe (wō) [A.-S. *wā*, int.], *n.* Sorrow, calamity, overwhelming grief. **woebe-gone,** *a.* Overcome with woe, sorrowful-looking. **woeful,** *a.* **woefully,** *adv.*

wold (wōld) [A.-S. *weald*], *n.* A tract of open country, esp. downland.

wolf (wulf) [A.-S. *wulf*], *n.* (*pl.* wolves) A greyish, carnivorous quadruped, allied to the dog, preying on sheep, etc., and hunting in packs; (*fig.*) a rapacious, greedy, or cruel person. *v.t.* To devour ravenously, to gulp greedily. **wolf-hound,** *n.* A large powerful dog of Russian or Irish breed. **wolf's-bane,** *n.* A species of aconite. **wolfish,** *a.* **wolf-ishly,** *adv.*

wolverine (wul'vér-ēn), *n.* A small N. American carnivorous animal, the glutton or carcajou.

woman (wum'án) [A.-S. *wifman*], *n.* (*pl.* women, wim'ĕn), *n.* An adult human female, womankind, the female sex, a lady-in-waiting. **womenfolk,** *n.* One's womenkind; women collectively. **woman-kind,** *n.* Women collectively, the female sex; the women of one's household. **womanhood,** *n.* **womanish,** *a.* Having the character or qualities of a woman, effeminate. **womanly,** *a.* Having the qualities becoming a woman, truly feminine. *adv.* In the manner of a woman.

womb (woom) [A.-S. *wamb*], *n.* The uterus; (*fig.*) the place where anything is brought into existence.

wombat (wom'băt) [Austral. *womback*], *n.* A nocturnal marsupial resembling a small bear.

wonder (wŭn'dĕr) [A.-S. *wundor*, a portent], *n.* A strange or marvellous thing, event, etc., a prodigy, the emotion excited by the unexpected, extraordinary, or inexplicable; surprise mingled with admiration. *v.i.* To be struck with surprise; to feel doubt or curiosity (about, etc.). **wonderful,** *a.* Exciting wonder or admiration, astonishing, strange. **wonderfully,** *adv.* **wonderland,** *n.* A fairyland.

wont (wŏnt) [M.E. *woned*, accustomed], *a.* Used, accustomed (to); using or doing habitually. *n.* Custom, habit, use. *v. aux.* To be accustomed or used (to). **wonted,** *a.* Customary, habitual, usual.

woo (woo) [A.-S. *wōgian*, in], *v.* To court, to solicit in marriage; to coax, to importune. **wooer,** *n.*

wood (wud) [A.-S. *wudu*], *n.* A large and thick collection of growing trees, a forest (*often in pl.*); the fibrous, solid substance of a tree; timber. **woodbine,** *n.* The wild honeysuckle. **woodblock,** *n.* A die cut in wood for striking impressions from; a woodcut. **woodcock,** *n.* A game-bird related to the snipe. **wood-craft,** *n.* Skill in anything pertaining to life in the woods. **woodcut,** *n.* An engraving on wood, a wood-block; a print from this. **wood-cutter,** *n.* One who cuts timber; an engraver on wood. **wooded,** *a.* **wooden,** *a.* Made of wood; (*fig.*) stiff, clumsy, ungainly, spiritless. **wood-engraving,** *n.* The art of cutting wood-blocks; an impression or print from one of these. **woodland,** *n.* Wooded country. *a.* Pertaining to this, sylvan. **wood-lark,** *n.* A European lark smaller than the skylark. **wood-louse,** *n.* A wingless creeping insect infesting decayed wood. **woodpecker,** *n.* A bird living in woods and tapping trees to discover insects. **wood-pigeon,** *n.* The ringdove, a European pigeon whose neck is nearly encircled by a ring of whitish feathers. **woodwork,** *n.* Things made of wood; the part of a building composed of wood. **woody,** *a.* Abounding in woods.

woof (woof) [A.-S. *ōwef*], *n.* The threads that cross the warp, the weft; cloth; texture.

wool (wul) [A.-S. *wull*], *n.* The fine, soft hair forming the fleece of sheep, etc., used as the raw material of cloth; under-fur or down, resembling this; the hair of a Negro; woollen yarn, worsted. **woollen,** *a.* Made or consisting of wool. *n.* Cloth made of wool; (*pl.*) woollen goods. **wool-gathering,** *a.* (*fig.*) In a brown study, absent-minded. *n.* Inattention. **wool-pack,** *n.* A bale of wool, formerly 240 lb.; (*fig.*) a fleecy cloud. **Woolsack,** *n.* The seat of the Lord Chancellor in the House of Lords (a large, square cushion, without back or arms). **woolly,** *a.* Consisting of, or resembling, or naturally covered with wool; fleecy.

word (wĕrd) [A.-S.], *n.* An articulate

sound uttered or written, printed, etc.; expressing an idea and forming part, or the whole, of a sentence; discourse, talk; news, a message; an order, an injunction; a password, watchword, motto; one's promise; (*pl.*) terms expressive of anger or reproach. *v.t.* To express in words, to phrase. **the Word:** The Scriptures, or any part of them. **wordy,** *a.* Verbose, prolix; consisting of words, verbal.

work (wĕrk) [A.-S. *weorc*], *n.* Exertion of energy (physical or mental), effort; labour, toil; an undertaking, task; materials used in this; occupation; an action, performance, achievement; product of nature, art, or labour; a large engineering structure, a fortification; a book, a literary, musical, or other artistic production; (*pl.*) a manufactory; building operations, esp. under a public authority; the mechanism (of a watch, etc.); (*Theol.*) moral duties or the performance of meritorious acts, as opp. to grace. *v.i.* (*past and p.p.* worked, wrought (rawt)). To exert physical or mental energy, to labour, to be employed or occupied (at, in, etc.); to be in continuous activity, to act, operate; to take effect, to exercise influence; to ferment. *v.t.* To exert energy in or upon; to employ, to keep busy; to carry on, to manage; to effect, to produce as a result; to mould, to fashion; to solve; to excite. **workaday,** *a.* Pertaining to or suitable for workdays, everyday, ordinary. **worker,** *n.* **worker-bee,** *n.* A partially developed female bee doing the work of the hive. **workhouse,** *n.* A public establishment for paupers. **working,** *a.* Engaged in work, esp. manual labour. *n.* Act of labouring; operation, mode of operation; a mine or quarry, disused or in which work is going on; fermentation, movement. **workman,** *n.* Any man employed in manual labour, an operative. **workmanlike,** *a.* Done in the manner of a good workman. **workmanship,** *n.* Skill or finish shown in making something or in the thing made; the result of working or making. **workshop,** *n.* A room or building in which a handicraft or other work is carried on.

world (wĕrld) [A.-S. *weoruld*], *n.* The universe, everything; a system of things, a cosmos; the earth with its lands and seas; a celestial body; a large division of the earth; mankind, human society, the public; fashionable people; human affairs, social life; a particular class of people, animals, or things, a realm, domain, sphere; a vast quantity (of); the present state of existence; secular interest as opp. to spiritual; the unregenerate portion of mankind. **worldling,** *n.* A worldly person. **worldly,** *a.* Pertaining to the material world; earthly, secular, not spiritual. **worldly-wise,** *a.* Wise in the things of this world.

worm (wĕrm) [A.-S. *wyrm*, cogn. with L. *vermis*], *n.* An invertebrate creeping animal with a long limbless segmented body; an intestinal parasite; a grub, caterpillar, maggot, etc.; (*fig.*) a poor

grovelling creature; a spiral part or thing. *v.i.* To crawl or progress with a worm-like motion; (*fig.*) to work stealthily. *v.t.* To insinuate (oneself); to draw out by craft and perseverance. **worm-cast,** *n.* A cylindrical mass of earth voided by an earth-worm. **worm-eaten,** *a.* Gnawed or bored by worms. **wormy,** *a.*

wormwood (wĕrm'wud) [A.-S. *wermōd*], *n.* A perennial herb having bitter and tonic properties; (*fig.*) bitterness, gall, mortification.

worry (wŭr'ĭ) [A.-S. *wyrgan*], *v.t.* To pull about with the teeth (of dogs); to harass, bother, persecute, or wear out with importunity, etc. *v.i.* To bite, pull about, etc. (of dogs); to be unduly anxious, to fret. *n.* Act of worrying; a worrying person; care, anxiety, vexation, fret (*often in pl.*). **worrier,** *n.*

worse (wĕrs) [A.-S. *wyrs*], *a.* (*comp. of* BAD) More bad; (*predicatively*) in a poorer state of health, position, or circumstances. *adv.* More badly; into a poorer state; less. *n.* A worse thing; loss, defeat. **worsen,** *v.*

worship (wĕr'shĭp), *n.* Act of paying divine honour to God, esp. in religious services; act or feeling of adoration or loving or admiring devotion or submissive respect; deference, respect (used as a title of respect in addressing magistrates, mayors, etc.). *v.t.* To pay divine honours to; to perform religious service to; to reverence, adore, treat as divine. *v.i.* To take part in a religious service. **worshipful,** *a.*

worst (wĕrst) [A.-S. *wyrst*], *a.* Bad in the highest degree. *adv.* Most badly, *n.* The most bad, evil, severe, or calamitous part, state, etc. *v.t.* To get the better of, to defeat, to best.

worsted (wĕrs'tĕd) [*Worsted* (now Worstead), Norfolk], *n.* Woollen yarn used for stockings, carpets, etc. *a.* Made of worsted.

wort (wĕrt) [A.-S. *wyrt*], *n.* A plant, a herb (*usu.* in *comb.,* as *soapwort*); an infusion of malt for fermenting into beer.

worth (wĕrth) [A.-S. *wyrth*, value], *a.* Equal in value to; deserving; having property to the value of. *n.* That which a person or thing is worth, the equivalent of anything, esp. in money; merit, desert. **worthless,** *a.*

worthy (wĕr'thĭ), *a.* Having worth, estimable; deserving of honour, respectable; fit, suitable, adequate. *n.* A person of note in his time, locality, etc. **worthily,** *adv.* **worthiness,** *n.*

wound (woond) [A.-S. *wund*], *n.* An injury (esp. a cut to the flesh of an animal or the substance of plants; (*fig.*) any hurt or pain to feelings, reputation, etc. *v.t.* To inflict a wound on.

wrack (răk), *n.* Seaweed thrown upon the shore; a cloud-rack; wreck, ruin.

wraith (rāth/ [?], *n.* The double of a living person; an apparition.

wrangle (răng'gĕl) [A.-S. *wrang*], *v.i.* To dispute or quarrel angrily or peevishly, to brawl. *n.* An angry or noisy quarrel, an altercation. **wrangler,** *n.* One who wrangles; *(Camb. Univ.)* one placed in the first class in the mathematical tripos.

wrap (răp) [?], *v.t.* To fold or arrange so as to cover something; to muffle, surround, or conceal in soft material; to enfold thus; *(in p.p.)* to absorb, to engross (with *up*). *n.* A cloak, shawl, rug, etc. **wrapper,** *n.* That in which anything is wrapped, a covering for a book, or for a newspaper for posting; a woman's loose outer garment. **wrapping,** *n.*

wrath (rawth), *n.* Deep or violent anger, indignation. **wrathful,** *a.*

wreak (rēk) [A.-S. *wrecan*], *v.t.* To carry out, to inflict, to execute.

wreath (rēth) [A.-S. *wrǽth*], *n.* A ring of flowers or leaves tied or twisted together, a garland; this in wood, stone, etc.; a circlet of twisted silk, etc.; a curl (of cloud, smoke, etc.). **wreathe** (rēth), *v.t.* To form (flowers, etc.) into a wreath.

wreck (rek) [A.-S. *wrǽc*, expulsion], *n.* Destruction, ruin, esp. of a ship; a vessel seriously crippled or shattered; the remains of anything dilapidated or worn-out; wreckage. *v.t.* To destroy (a vessel) by collision, driving ashore, etc.; to ruin. *v.i.* To suffer shipwreck. **wreckage,** *n.* The debris from a wreck. **wrecker,** *n.* One who causes shipwreck with intent to plunder; a person or ship employed in recovering a wreck.

wren (ren) [A.-S. *wrenna*], *n.* A small bird with a short erect tail and short wings. **Wren,** *n.* A member of the Womens Royal Naval Service, W.R.N.S.

wrench (rench) [A.-S. *wrenc*], *n.* A violent twist or sideways pull; a sprain; *(fig.)* pain or distress caused by a parting, loss. etc.; a tool for twisting screws, nuts, etc, *v.t.* To wrest or twist with force; to strain, to sprain; *(fig.)* to distort.

wrest (rest) [A.-S. *wrǽstan*], *v.t.* To twist, to turn aside violently; to pull or extort forcibly; *(fig.)* to pervert, deflect from its natural meaning. *n.* A violent wrench or twist; a turning implement.

wrestle (res'ĕl), *v.i.* To contend by grappling with and trying to throw one's opponent; *(fig.)* to struggle, to strive vehemently. *v.t.* To contend with a wrestling-match. *n.* A bout at wrestling. **wrestler,** *n.*

wretch (rech) [A.-S. *wrecca*, an outcast], *n.* A miserable, unfortunate, despicable, or vile person. **wretched** (rech'ĕd), *a.* Miserable, sunk in deep affliction or distress; calamitous, pitiable; worthless, paltry.

wriggle (rig'ĕl), *v.i.* To twist the body to and fro with short motions; to move with contortions or twistings. *n.* A wriggling motion.

wright (rīt) [A.-S. *wyrht*, work], *n.* One in some mechanical business, an artificer, a workman (esp. in comb, as *wheelwright*).

wring (ring) [A.-S. *wringan*], *v.t. (past and p.p.* wrung) To twist and squeeze; to turn, forcibly; to press (water, etc., out) thus; *(fig.)* to distress; to extort.

wrinkle (1) (ring'kĕl), *n.* A small furrow caused by the contraction of a flexible surface. *v.* To fold or contract into furrows, creases, or ridges. **wrinkly,** *a.*

wrinkle (2), *n.* A useful bit of information, a bright idea, a tip.

wrist (rist) [A.-S.], *n.* The joint uniting the hand to the forearm.

writ (rit) [A.-S. *gewrit*, a writing], *n.* A writing; a written command issued by a court in the name of the sovereign.

write (rīt) [A.-S. *writan*], *v.t. (past* wrote, writ, *p.p.* written, writ) To form words in letters or symbols, with a pen, etc., on paper or the like; to set (down), to record, to convey by writing, to produce as an author. *v.i.* To trace letters or symbols representing words on paper, etc.; to write or send a letter; to compose books, etc., as an author. **writer,** *n.* One who writes; an author, journalist, etc.; a clerk; *(Sc.)* a solicitor. **writing,** *n.* Act of one who writes; that which is written; a literary composition, a legal instrument.

writhe (rīth) [A.-S. *writhan*], *v.i.* To twist or roll the body about, as in pain; to squirm. *v.t.* To twist or distort (the limbs, etc.).

wrong (rong) [A.-S. *wrang*, a wrong thing] *a.* Not morally right, wicked; not the right (one, etc.); not according to reality; out of order, not suitable, etc.; false, mistaken. *adv.* Wrongly, unjustly. *n.* That which is wrong; an injustice, trespass, or injury, hurt or pain; error. *v.t.* To treat unjustly, to do wrong to. **wrongdoer,** *n.* **wrongdoing,** *n.* **wrongheadedness,** *n.* **wrongful,** *a.* Injurious, unjust, wrong. **wrongfully,** *adv.* wrongly, *adv.*

wroth (rōth), *a. (poet.)* Angry, wrathful.

wry (rī) [A.-S. *wrigian*], *a.* Twisted, distorted, skew; showing distaste, disgust. etc. **wry-mouthed,** *a.* Having a distorted or cynical expression. **wryneck,** *n.* A bird allied to the woodpeckers, which twists its head round as on a pivot; stiffneck.

wych-hazel (wich), *n.* A N. American shrub the bark and leaves of which are used medicinally.

X

x (eks), *n. (Alg.,* x) The first unknown quantity or variable. **X-rays,** *n.* Röntgen rays.

xanthous (zăn'thŭs), *a. (Ethn.)* Of the fair-haired type.

xiphoid (zif'oid) [Gr. *xiphos*, sword, [-OID] *a.* Sword-shaped.

xyl-, xylo- [Gr. *xulon*, wood], *comb. form.*

Y

-y [L. *-ius*], *suf.* Forming (1) abstract nouns, etc., as in *memory, remedy;* (2) [A.-S. *-ig*] adjectives as in *mighty, trusty;* (3) diminutives and pet names, as *horsy, sonny;* (4) [F. *-é*], forming nouns as *army, treaty.*

yacht (yot) [Dut.], *n.* A light sailing-vessel, esp. for racing; a vessel propelled by sails or power used for pleasure cruising, as a state vessel, etc. *v.i.* To cruise about in a yacht. **yachting,** *n.* **yachtsman,** *n.* One who keeps or sails a yacht.

yahoo (ya-hoo') [coined by Swift in "Gulliver's Travels"], *n.* One of a race of brutes in human shape; a brutish or degraded person.

yak (yăk) [Tibetan *gyak*], *n.* A long-haired ruminant from Central Asia.

yam (yăm) [W. Afr. native], *n.* The fleshy edible tuber of a tropical climber; the plant.

Yankee (yăng'ki) [Am. Ind., corr. of F. *Anglais*, the English], *n.* An inhabitant of New England; an American. *a.* Pertaining to America.

yard (1) (yard) [A.-S. *gyrd*, stick], *n.* The British standard of length, 3 ft. or 36 in.; a spar slung on a mast to extend a sail. **yard-arm,** *n.* Either half of a sail-yard from centre to end. **yard-measure,** *n.* A tape or stick, three feet in length, used for measuring.

yard (2) (yard) [A.-S. *geard*], *n.* A small piece of enclosed ground, esp. adjoining a house; such an enclosure used as a dockyard, graveyard, timber-yard, etc.

yarn (yarn) [A.-S. *gearn*], *n.* Any spun fibre prepared for weaving, rope-making, etc.; (*colloq.*) a long or rambling story, esp. one of doubtful truth. *v.i.* To tell or spin yarns.

yarrow (yăr'ō) [A.-S. *gœruwe*], *n.* Milfoil, a perennial herb with white flowers.

yaw (yaw) [Icel. *jaga*, to hunt], *v.i.* To steer out of the direct course, to move unsteadily (of a ship).

yawl (yawl) [Dut. *jol*], *n.* A ship's jolly-boat; a small sailing-vessel cutter-rigged with a jigger-mast.

yawn (yawn) [A.-S. *gănian*], *v.i.* To gape, to stand wide open; to open the mouth through drowsiness, boredom, etc. *n.* The act of yawning.

ye (1) (yē, yė) [A.-S. *gē*], pron., *2nd pers. pl.* The nominative of YOU.

ye (2) (*thē*) Old form of definite article *the*.

yea (yā) [A.-S. *gēa*], *adv.* Yes; truly, indeed; not only so but also. *n.* An affirmative.

year (yĕr) [A.-S. *gēar*], *n.* The period of time occupied by the revolution of the earth round the sun; 365 days, divided into 12 months; (*pl.*) age, length or time of life, old age. **yearling,** *n.* An animal more than one and less than two years old. **yearly,** *a.* Happening or recurring once a year or every year; lasting a year. *adv.* Annually; by the year.

yearn (yĕrn) [A.-S. *giernan*], *v.i.* To feel a longing desire, tenderness, etc. (for). **yearning,** *a.* and *n.*

yeast (yĕst) [A.-S. *gist*], *n.* A growth of fungus cells developed in contact with saccharine liquids and producing alcoholic fermentation; (*fig.*) mental or moral ferment. **yeasty,** *a.* Containing or resembling yeast; (*fig.*) frothy; empty, superficial.

yell (yel) [A.-S. *gellan*], *v.i.* To cry out with a loud, sharp cry as in rage, terror, or uncontrollable laughter. *v.t.* To utter

or express thus. *n.* Such a shout, esp. a war-cry of savages, students, etc.

yellow (yel'ō) [A.-S. *geolo, geolu*], *a.* Of the colour of gold, brass, sulphur, or lemon; (*fig.*) jaundiced, jealous. *n.* This colour; a yellow pigment, dye, etc. *v.* To make or turn yellow. **yellow-hammer** [A.-S. *amore*], *n.* A bunting with yellow head, neck, and breast.

yelp (yelp) [A.-S. *gilpan*, to boast], *v.i.* To utter a sharp, quick cry, as a dog. *n.* Such a cry.

yeoman (yōmán) [M.E. *yeman*], *n.* (*pl.* **-men**) A freeholder not ranking as one of the gentry; a farmer, a small land-owner; a member of the yeomanry. **yeoman's service:** Good service, hearty support. **yeomanly,** *a.* **yeomanry,** *n.* (*collect.*) Yeomen; a British force of volunteer cavalry.

-yer, *suf.* Denoting an agent, as in *lawyer*, *sawyer*.

yes (yes) [A.-S. *gise*], *adv.* As you say; indicating affirmation or consent, or that the speaker hears and understands.

yester- [A.-S. *geostra*, as in (acc.) *geostran dæg*, yesterday], *pref.* Pertaining to that preceding this. **yesterday,** *n.* The day immediately before to-day; (*fig.*) time in the immediate past. *adv.* On or during yesterday.

yet (yet) [A.-S. *git*], *adv.* Still, up to this or that time; by this or that time, so soon as the present, in addition, further; eventually; even (*with compar.*). *conj.* Nevertheless, but still.

yew (ū) [A.-S. *iw*], *n.* A dark-leaved ever-green tree with spreading branches and durable timber; its wood.

Yiddish (yid'ish) [G. *jüdisch*, Jewish], *n.* A language spoken by Jews of E. Europe and N. America, based on a Hebraicized Middle German, with an admixture of Polish, French and English.

yield (yēld) [A.-S. *gieldan*, to pay], *v.t.* To produce, to bring forth; to give up, surrender, relinquish. *v.i.* To give a return, to repay; to give way, to assent, to comply; to make submission (to). *n.* That which is yielded; output, return. **yielding,** *a.* Compliant.

yoke (yōk) [A.-S. *geoc*], *n.* Gear fitting over the necks of two draught animals and attaching them to a plough, etc.; a frame for carrying a pair of buckets sus-pended from the shoulders; a frame or cross-bar for some similar purpose, a tie-beam, tie-rod, etc.; a part of a garment made to support the rest; (*fig.*) a bond, a tie; a pair of draught animals, esp. oxen; servitude, submission. *v.t.* To put a yoke upon; to couple, join, link; to enslave.

yokel (yō'kĕl), *n.* A rustic, a country bumpkin.

yolk (yōk) [A.-S. *geolca*, YELLOW], *n.* The yellow part of an egg. **yolked, yolky,** *a.*

yon, yonder (yon'dèr) [A.-S. *geon*], *a.* That over there; being at a distance, but in the direction indicated, *adv.* Over there; at a distance but within view.

yore (yòr) [A.-S. *gēar*, YEAR], *n.* Long ago, old time. **of yore:** Formerly.

you (ū, yū) [A.-S. *ēow*; sing. THOU, *obj.*

THEE, poss. YOUR. YOURS], 2nd pers. pron. sing. and pl. (with pl. v.) The person, persons, or things, etc., addressed; (reflex.) yourself, yourselves; (indef.) anyone.

young (yŭng) [A.-S. geong], a. Being in the early stage of life or development; of recent beginning, newly produced, etc.; vigorous, fresh; raw, inexperienced; characteristic of youth. n. Offspring, esp. of animals. **youngster**, n. A young person, a child, a lad.

your (ūr, yùr, yŏr) [A.-S. ēower, gen. pl. of YE], a. Pertaining or belonging to you. **yours**, pron. That or those belonging or pertaining to you. a. (predicatively) Belonging to you; at your service. **yourself** (-self'), pron. (pl. -selves) You, you alone; you in particular or in your normal condition, health, etc. (also used reflexively).

youth (ūth) [A.-S. geoguth], n. (pl. youths, ūthz) State of being young; the period of life following infancy, youthfulness, the vigour, inexperience, etc., of this period; a young man; young people. **youthful**, a. **youthfully**, adv.

yule (ūl) [A.-S. gēola], n. Christmas time the festival of Christmas. **yule-tide**, n.

Z

zany (zā'ni) [It. Giovanni, John], n. A buffoon who mimicked the clown; a simpleton.

zeal (zēl) [L. zēlus], n. Ardour, earnestness, enthusiasm. **zealot** (zel'ŏt), n. One full of or carried away by zeal; a fanatical partisan. **zealous** (zel'ùs), a. **zealously**, adv.

zebra (zēbrá) [Afr. native], n. A striped ass-like mammal allied to the horse, from S. Africa.

Zend (zend) [a commentary], n. The ancient Iranian language; the Zend-Avesta, a collection of the sacred scriptures of the Parsees or Zoroastrians.

zenith (zen'ith) [Arab. samt, way, road], n. The point in the heavens directly overhead to an observer; (fig.) the highest or culminating point.

zephyr (zef'ir) [L. zephyrus], n. The west wind personified; any gentle breeze; light worsted or woollen yarn; a shawl or other garment made of this.

zero (zēr'ō) [Arab. cipr, cipher], n. (pl. -oes) The figure 0, a cipher, nil; the point on a scale from which positive or negative quantities are reckoned; the lowest point.

zest (zest) [O.F., the woody skin dividing the kernel of a walnut], n. A flavouring; piquancy, relish; keen enjoyment.

zigzag (zig'zăg) [G. zickzack, redupl. from zacke, tooth], a. Having sharp alternate turns or angles. n. A zigzag line, path, pattern, etc. adv. In a zigzag course or manner.

zinc (zingk) [G. zink], n. A bluish-white metallic element used in alloys, as roofing-material, for printing-blocks, etc. v.t. To coat or cover with zinc. **zincblende**, n. Native sulphide of zinc.

zip, zip fastener (zip) [imit.], n. A fastening device with interlocking teeth which opens or closes with a single motion.

zither (zith'ér), n. A simple musical instrument with strings plucked by the fingers.

zodiac (zō'di-ăk) [Gr. zōdiakos, pertaining to animals], n. The zone or broad belt of the heavens, extending about 8° to each side of the ecliptic, which the sun traverses during the year, anciently divided by twelve equal parts called the signs of the zodiac which orig. corresponded to the zodiacal constellations bearing the same names, but now, through the precession of the equinoxes, coincides with the constellations bearing the names next in order. **zodi'acal**, a. Pertaining to the zodiac.

zone (zōn) [Gr. zōnē, girdle], n. A girdle, a belt; a well-marked stripe encircling an object; one of the five great divisions of the earth (two temperate, two frigid, and one torrid) bounded by circles parallel to the equator; any well-defined belt or tract of land.

zoo- [Gr. zōon, animal], comb. form. Pertaining to animals or to animal life.

zoo (zoo), n. A collection of living wild animals, a zoological garden.

zoology (zō-ol'ò-ji), n. The natural history of animals, the branch of biology dealing with the structure, physiology, classification, habits, and distribution of animals. **zoological** (zō-ò-log'i-kál), a. **zoologist** (zō-ol'ò-jist), n.

zoophyte (zō'ò-fīt), n. An invertebrate animal resembling a plant, as a coral, sea-anemone, sponge, etc.

Zoroastrian (zor-ò-ăs'tri-án), a. Pertaining to Zoroaster or his religious system set forth in the Zend-Avesta, the ancient Persian religion still held by the Parsees, or fire-worshippers. n. A follower of Zoroaster. **Zoroastrianism**, n.

Zouave (zoo-av') [N. Afr. zuawa, a Kabyle tribe], n. A soldier in a French infantry corps. orig. composed of Kabyles and still wearing an Oriental uniform; a short, round-fronted jacket, usu. sleeveless, worn by women.

Zulu (zoo'loo) [native], n. A member of a tribe of Bantu race inhabiting South-East Africa.

zymotic (zī-mot'ik) [Gr. zumē, leaven], a. Pertaining to or produced by fermentation; applied to epidemic, endemic, or contagious diseases produced by the multiplication of germs introduced from without.

FOREIGN PHRASES AND WORDS IN ENGLISH USE

Many foreign words, etc., that have become semi-naturalized are given in the main body of the Dictionary

à bas [F.]. Down! down with!

ab initio [L.]. From the beginning.

ab origine [L.]. From the commencement.

ab ovo [L.]. From the egg, from beginning.

absit omen. Let there be no ill omen.

ab urbe condita or A.U.C. [L.]. From the building of the city (Rome), 754 B.C.

ad astra [L.]. To the stars.

à demi [F.]. By halves.

ad hoc [L.]. For this particular purpose, specially.

ad infinitum [L.]. To infinity.

ad nauseam [L.]. So as to disgust or nauseate.

ad rem [L.]. To the point

adsum [L.]. I am present.

ad unguem [L.]. To a nicety, exactly.

ad usum [L.]. According to the custom (of).

ad valorem [L.]. According to value.

advocatus diaboli [L.]. The devil's advocate.

ætatis suæ [L.]. Of his (or her) age.

affaire d'honneur [F.]. An affair of honour, a duel.

à fond [F.]. To the bottom, thoroughly.

à jamais [F.]. For ever.

à la [F.]. According to; in the style of.

à la carte [F.]. By the bill of fare.

à la mode [F.]. In fashion.

al fresco [It.]. In the open air.

allons! [F.]. Come, let us be off!

Alma Mater [L., fostering mother]. One's school, college, or university.

alter ego [L.]. One's second self.

alter idem [L.]. Another exactly similar.

amende honorable [F.]. Public apology, public amends.

a mensa et toro [L.]. From bed and board.

à merveille [F.]. Admirably, perfectly.

amicus curiæ [L.]. A friend of the court, an adviser with no personal interest.

amour-propre [F.]. Self-esteem, vanity.

anno Domini [L.]. In the year of our Lord.

anno mundi [L.]. In the year of the world.

annus mirabilis [L.]. A year of wonders.

ante bellum [L.]. Before the war.

ante meridiem [L.]. Before noon.

à outrance [F.] To the end, to extremities.

à pied [F.]. On foot.

à plaisir [F.]. At pleasure, at will.

a posteriori [L.]. From effect to cause; inductive.

a priori [L.]. From cause to effect; deductive.

à propos de bottes [F., with regard to boots]. Irrelevantly.

arbiter elegantiarum [L.]. A judge in matters of taste.

Arcades ambo [L.]. Two of similar tastes, etc.

argumentum ad hominem [L.]. An appeal to personal interests, etc.

ars est celare artem [L.]. The art is to conceal art.

ars longa, vita brevis [L.]. Art is long, life short.

artium magister [L.]. Master of Arts.

assez bien [F.]. Moderately well.

à tout prix [F.]. At any price.

à travers [F.]. Across, through.

au contraire [F.]. On the contrary.

au courant de [F.]. Fully informed about.

audi alteram partem [L.]. Hear the other side.

au fait [F.]. Familiar, well-acquainted with.

au fond [F.]. At bottom.

au gratin [F.]. (Cooked) with breadcrumbs or grated cheese.

au naturel [F.]. In its natural state.

au pied de la lettre [F.]. Literally, precisely.

au revoir [F.]. Till we meet again.

au sérieux [F.]. Seriously.

aut Cæsar aut nullus [L.]. Either Cæsar or nobody; either first or nowhere.

aux armes! [F.]. To arms!

avant-propos [F.]. Preface, preliminary remarks.

ave, atque vale [L.]. Hail! and farewell!

ave Imperator, morituri te salutant [L.]. Hail Cæsar (or Emperor)! Those who are about to die salute thee.

a vinculo matrimonii [L.]. From the marriage bond, complete divorce.

à votre santé! [F.]. To your health!

Bachelier ès lettres, sciences [F.]. Bachelor of Letters, of Science.

ballon d'essai [F.]. A feeler.

beau sabreur [F.]. A dashing cavalryman.

beaux esprits [F.]. Men of wit.

beaux yeux [F.]. Fine eyes, good looks.

bel esprit [F.]. A brilliant mind, man of parts.

ben trovato [It.]. Well invented.

ben venuto [It.]. Welcome.

bête noire [F.]. A bugbear, one's aversion.

bien aimé [F.]. (*fem.* aimée) Well-beloved.

bien entendu [F.]. To be sure, of course.

bis dat qui cito dat [L.]. He gives twice who gives speedily.

blague [F.]. Humbug.

bona fide [L.]. In good faith.

bonjour [F.]. Good day.

bon marché [F.]. A cheap shop; a bargain.

bon mot [F.]. A witty saying.

bonne-bouche [F.]. A dainty morsel.

bon soir [F.]. Good evening.

bon ton [F.]. Fashion, good style.

bon vivant [F.]. One fond of good living.

bon voyage [F.]. A pleasant journey, farewell.

ça ira [F.]. That will go, that's the thing.

canaille [F.]. The rabble.

carpe diem [L.]. Enjoy the day, seize the present opportunity, improve the time.

casus belli [L.]. A ground of war.

casus fœderis [L.]. A case provided for by treaty.

cause célèbre [F.]. A notable case or trial.

cave canem [L.]. Beware of the dog.

caveat actor (emptor, viator) [L.]. Let the doer (purchaser, traveller) beware.

cead mile failte [Ir.]. A hundred thousand welcomes.

cedant arma togæ [L.]. Let arms yield to the gown; let violence give place to law.

cela va sans dire [F.]. That goes without saying.

ce n'est que le premier pas qui coûte [F.]. It is only the first step that is troublesome.

c'est-à-dire [F.]. That is to say.

ceteris paribus [L.]. Other things being equal.

chacun à son goût [F.]. Every one to his taste.

chef-d'œuvre [F.]. A masterpiece.

chemin de fer [F.]. A railway.

cherchez la femme [F.]. Look for the woman, there's a woman at the bottom of it.

che sarà, sarà [It.]. What will be, will be.

ci-devant [F.]. Formerly, of a past time.

circa [L.]. About.

cogito, ergo sum [L.]. I think, therefore I exist.

comme il faut [F.]. As it should be, correct.

communiqué [F.]. An official report.

compos mentis [L.]. Sound of mind.

compte rendue [F.]. An official report.

con amore [It.]. With affection, with zeal.

con spirito [It.]. With animation.

consummatum est [L.]. It is finished.

corpus delicti [L.]. The substance of the offence.

coup de grâce [F.]. A finishing stroke.

coup de main [F.]. A sudden attack, enterprise, or undertaking.

coup d'état [F.]. A stroke of policy; a sudden, esp. unconstitutional, change of government.

coup d'œil [F.]. A rapid glance.

coûte que coûte [F.]. Cost what it may.

crème de la crème [F.]. The very best.

cucullus non facit monachum [L.]. The cowl does not make the monk.

cui bono? [L.]. For whose advantage?

cum grano salis [L.]. With a grain of salt; with some allowance.

cum privilegio [L.]. With privilege.

d'accord [F.]. Agreed; in time.

dame d'honneur [F.]. A maid of honour.

de bonne grâce [F.]. With good will, willingly.

de die in diem [L.]. From day to day.

de facto [L.]. In reality, actually.

défense de fumer [F.]. Smoking not allowed.

de gustibus non est disputandum [L.]. There is no disputing about tastes.

Dei gratia [L.]. By the grace of God.

déjeuner à la fourchette [F.]. Luncheon.

de jure [L.]. By right.

delenda est Carthago [L.]. Carthage must be utterly destroyed.

delineavit [L.]. He (or she) drew it.

de luxe [F.]. Luxurious

de minimis non curat lex [L.]. The law does not concern itself with trifles.

de mortuis nil nisi bonum [L.]. Let nothing be said of the dead but what is good.

de novo [L.]. Anew.

Deo gratias [L.]. Thanks be to God.

Deo volente [L.]. God willing.

de profundis [L.]. Out of the depths.

de proprio motu [L.]. On one's own initiative.

de rigueur [F.]. According to strict etiquette.

dernier ressort [F.]. A last resource.

de trop [F.]. Superfluous, not wanted.

deus ex machina [L.]. A god from the machine (in the Gr. theatre) a romantic *dénouement.*

dies iræ [L.]. The Day of Judgment.

dies non [L.]. A day when business is not transacted.

Dieu et mon droit [F.]. God and my right.

Dieu vous garde! [F.]. God protect you!

dis aliter visum [L.]. The gods have decided otherwise.

disjecta membra [L.]. Scattered remains.

divide et impera [L.]. Divide and govern.

dolce far niente [It.]. Sweet idleness.

Domine, dirige nos [L.]. O Lord direct us (the motto of the City of London).

Dominus illuminatio mea [L.]. The Lord is my light (the motto of Oxford Univ.).

Dominus vobiscum [L.]. The Lord be with you.

dulce, domum [L.]. Sweet is the strain of "Homeward".

dulce et decorum est pro patria mori [L.]. It is sweet and glorious to die for one's country.

dum spiro, spero [L.]. While I breathe, I hope.

ecce homo [L.]. Behold the man!

ecce signum [L.]. Behold the proof.

édition de luxe [F.]. A sumptuous edition.

editio princeps [L.]. A first printed edition.

embarras de richesse [F.]. A superfluity of anything wanted or desirable.

en arrière [F.]. In the rear, behind.

en avant [F.]. Forward.

en bloc [F.]. In the mass.

en déshabillé [F.]. In undress; in one's true colours.

en effet [F.]. Substantially, in effect.
en famille [F.]. With one's family, at home.
enfant terrible [F.]. A precocious youngster.
en fête [F.]. In festivity.
en garçon [F.]. As a bachelor.
en grand tenue [F.]. In full dress.
en masse [F.]. In a body.
en passant [F.]. By the way.
en pension [F.]. On boarding-house terms.
en rapport [F.]. In sympathy with.
en règle [F.]. In order, as it should be.
en revanche [F.]. In return, as compensation.
en route [F.]. On the way.
en suite [F.]. In a set, in succession.
entente cordiale [F.]. A good understanding.
entre nous [F.]. Between ourselves, in confidence.
e pluribus unum [L.]. One out of or composed of many. (Motto of the U.S.A.)
errare est humanum [L.]. To err is human.
esprit de corps [F.]. Animating spirit of a collective body; pride in one's school, regiment, etc.
et similia [L.]. And the like.
et tu Brute! [L.]. And thou too Brutus (the last words of Cæsar).
ex animo [L.]. Heartily, sincerely.
ex cathedra [L.]. From the chair, with authority.
exceptio probat regulam [L.]. The exception proves the rule.
exempli gratia [L.]. By way of example.
exeunt omnes [L.]. All go out.
ex gratia [L.]. As an act of favour.
ex hypothesi [L.]. According to the hypothesis.
ex nihilo nihil fit [L.]. Out of nothing, nothing comes.
ex officio [L.]. By virtue of one's office.
ex parte [L.]. From one side only.
experientia docet [L.]. Experience teaches.
experto crede [L.]. Believe one who has tried it.
ex post facto [L.]. After the deed is done.
ex proprio motu [L.]. Of one's own initiative.
ex tempore [L.]. At the time, off-hand.
extra muros [L.]. Outside the walls.

facile princeps [L.]. The acknowledged chief.
facilis descensus Averno [L.]. The descent to hell is easy.
façon de parler [F.]. Manner of speaking.
factum est [L.]. It is done.
fait accompli [F.]. An accomplished fact.
far niente [It.]. Doing nothing.
faute de mieux [F.]. In default of something better.
faux pas [F.]. A blunder, a slip.
fecit [L.]. He (or she) made or drew it.
festina lente [L.]. Don't be impetuous.
fiat justitia ruat cœlum [L.]. Let justice be done though the heavens should fall.
fiat lux [L.]. Let there be light.
fidei defensor [L.]. Defender of the faith.
fi donc! [F.]. For shame!
fidus Achates [L.]. Faithful Achates (companion of Æneas); a true friend.
fille de chambre [F.]. A chamber-maid.
finis coronat opus [L.]. The end crowns the work.

floreat [L.]. May (it) flourish.
force majeure [F.]. Superior power, circumstances not under one's control.
fortiter in re, suaviter in modo [L.]. Acting forcibly yet in gentle fashion.

garde du corps [F.]. A body-guard.
gardez bien [F.]. Take good care, be careful.
gaudeamus igitur [L.]. Therefore, let us rejoice.
gens d'affaires [F.]. Business people.
gens de lettres [F.]. Literary men.
gloria in excelsis Deo [L.]. Glory to God in the highest.
gloria Patri [L.]. Glory be to the Father.
grâce à Dieu [F.]. Thanks be to God.
gradatim [L.]. Step by step.
gradus ad Parnassum [L.]. A step to Parnassus; aid in writing Latin poetry.
grande passion [F.]. A serious love-affair.

hic et ubique [L.]. Here and everywhere.
hic labor, hoc opus est [L.]. This is the labour, this the toil.
hinc illæ lacrimæ [L.]. Hence these tears; this is the cause of the trouble.
hoc genus omne [L.]. All this sort of (people, etc.).
hodie mihi, cras tibi [L.]. It is my turn to-day, yours to-morrow.
homme de bien [F.]. A man of worth.
homme d'esprit [F.]. A wit, a genius.
homo sum; humani nihil a me alienum puto [L.]. I am a man, and I consider nothing that concerns mankind a matter of indifference.
honi soit qui mal y pense [F.]. Shame be to him who thinks evil of it (motto of the Order of the Garter).
honoris causa or gratia [L.]. For the sake of honour, honorary.
horæ subsecivæ [L.]. Leisure hours.
horresco referens [L.]. I shudder as I tell the story.
horribile dictu [L.]. Horrible to tell.
horribile visu [L.]. Horrible to see.
hors concours [F.]. Not for competition.
hors de combat [F.]. Disabled.
hôtel garni [F.]. Furnished apartments.
humanum est errare [L.]. To err is human.

ich dien [G.]. I serve (Prince of Wales's motto).
ici on parle français [F.]. French is spoken here.
idée fixe [F.]. A fixed idea, monomania.
il faut de l'argent [F.]. Money is necessary.
il n'y a pas de quoi [F.]. There is no need, don't mention it.
il va sans dire [F.]. It goes without saying.
in æternum [L.]. For ever.
in articulo mortis [L.]. At the moment of death.
in camera [L.]. In the judge's chamber, not in open court.
in capite [L.]. In chief, (holding) directly from the Crown.
in commendam [L.]. (Holding a vacant benefice) in trust for the successor.
inconnu [F.]. (fem. -nue) Unknown.
in curia [L.]. In open court.
in Deo speravi [L.]. In God have I trusted.
in esse [L.]. In actual being.

in excelsis [L.]. In the highest.
in extenso [L.]. At full length.
in extremis [L.]. At the point of death.
in flagrante delicto [L.]. In the very act.
in forma pauperis [L.]. As a pauper.
infra dignitatem (infra dig.) [L.]. Beneath one's dignity.
in hoc signo vinces [L.]. By this sign thou shalt conquer (motto of Constantine the Great).
in infinitum [L.]. For ever.
in initio [L.]. In the beginning.
in loco [L.]. In the place (of).
in loco parentis [L.]. In the place of a parent.
in medias res [L.]. Into the very midst of the business.
in memoriam [L.]. To the memory of.
in nomine [L.]. In the name (of).
in pace [L.]. In peace.
in partibus infidelium [L.]. In the countries of unbelievers.
in petto [It.]. Within the breast, in reserve.
in posse [L.]. In possibility, potentially.
in propria persona [L.]. In one's own person.
in puris naturalibus [L.]. In a state of nature; naked.
in re [L.]. In the matter of.
in sæcula sæculorum [L.]. For ever and ever.
in situ [L.]. In (its original or proper) position.
in statu quo [L.]. In the same state as.
in tenebris [L.]. In the dark, in doubt.
inter alia [L.]. Among other things.
in toto [L.]. Entirely.
in transitu [L.]. On the way, en route.
in vacuo [L.]. In a vacuum, in empty space.
invenit [L.]. He (or she) devised this.
in vino veritas [L.]. Drunkenness makes a man let out the truth.
ipse dixit [L.]. He himself has said it; a mere assertion.
ipsissima verba [L.]. The identical words.
ipso facto [L.]. By the fact itself.

jacta alea est [L.]. The die is cast.
jam satis! [L.]. Enough now of this!
je ne sais quoi [F.]. I know not what, something indefinable.
je suis prêt [F.]. I am ready.
jeune premier [F.]. A stage lover.
jeunesse dorée [F.]. The gilded youth.
jubilate Deo [L.]. Oh be joyful in the Lord.
jure divino [L.]. By divine law.
jus civile [L.]. Civil law.
jus divinum [L.]. Divine law.
jus et norma loquendi [L.]. The law and rule of speech.
jus gentium [L.]. The law of nations.
juste milieu [L.]. The golden mean.
j'y suis et j'y reste [F.]. Here I am and here I stay.

labor omnia vincit [L.]. Labour overcomes all difficulties.
lares et penates [L.]. Household gods.
lasciate ogni speranza, voi ch' entrate [It.]. All hope abandon ye who enter here.
laus Deo [L.]. Praise be to God.
le beau monde [F.]. The world of fashion, society.

le pas [F.]. Precedence.
les absents ont toujours tort [F.]. The absent are always wrong.
les convenances [F.]. The proprieties.
l'État, c'est moi [F.]. The State! I am the State.
le tout ensemble [F.]. The general effect.
lever de rideau [F.]. A curtain-raiser.
lex talionis [L.]. The law of retaliation.
l'homme propose et Dieu dispose [F.]. Man proposes and God disposes.
licet [L.]. It is permitted, it is legal
l'inconnu [F.]. The unknown.
lite pendente [L.]. During the trial.
litera scripta manet [L.]. The written word remains.
locus sigilli [L.]. The place of the seal.
locus standi [L.]. Recognized place or position authorizing appearance in court, etc.
loquitur [L.]. He (or she) speaks.
lucus a non lucendo [L.]. Lucus (a grove) is derived from lucere (to shine) because it is dark; (fig.) anything inconsequent and absurd.
lusus naturæ [L.]. A freak of nature.
lux in tenebris [L.]. Light in darkness.
lux mundi [L.]. The light of the world.

magna est veritas et prævalet [L.]. Truth is great and all-powerful.
magnum bonum [L.]. A great good.
magnum opus [L.]. A great undertaking, the great work of a man's life.
maître d'hôtel [F.]. A house steward; head waiter.
mal à propos [F.]. Unseasonably.
mala fide [L.]. In bad faith, treacherously.
mal de mer [F.]. Sea-sickness.
mal entendu [F.]. Misunderstood.
manet [L.]. (pl. manent) He (or she) remains.
manu forti [L.]. With the strong hand.
manu propria [L.]. With one's own hand.
mardi gras [F.]. Shrove Tuesday.
marque de fabrique [F.]. A trade-mark.
mauvaise honte [F.]. False shame.
mauvais sujet [F.]. A worthless fellow.
mauvais ton [F.]. Bad style.
mea culpa [L.]. By my fault.
mens sana in corpore sano [L.]. A sound mind in a sound body.
meum et tuum [L.]. Mine and thine.
mi-carême [F.]. Mid-Lent.
mirabile dictu [L.]. Wonderful to relate.
mirabile visu [L.]. Wonderful to see.
miserere mei [L.]. Have mercy upon me.
mon Dieu! [F.]. Good heavens! gracious!
more suo [L.]. In his usual way.
mors janua vitæ [L.]. Death is the gate of life.
motu proprio [L.]. Of his own accord.
moyen âge [F.]. The Middle Ages.
multum in parvo [L.]. Much in little.
mutatis mutandis [L.]. The necessary changes being made.

necessitas non habet legem [L.]. Necessity knows no law.
negatur [L.]. It is denied.
nemine contradicente [L.]. (Nem. con.) No one contradicting.
nemine dissentiente [L.]. No one dissenting.

nemo me impune lacessit [L.]. No one provokes me with impunity.

ne plus ultra [L.]. Nothing further; perfection.

nihil ad rem [L.]. Nothing to the purpose.

nihil tetigit quod non ornavit [L.]. He touched nothing without embellishing it.

nil admirari [L.]. To be astonished at nothing.

nil desperandum [L.]. Never despair.

n'importe [F.]. It is of no consequence.

noblesse oblige [F.]. Rank imposes obligations.

nolle prosequi [L.]. To be unwilling to prosecute.

nolo episcopari [L.] I do not wish to be a bishop (formal reply to offer of bishopric).

non compos mentis [L.]. Not of sound mind, mentally deranged, lunatic.

non est inventus [L.]. (He) is not to be found.

non mi ricordo [It.]. I do not remember.

non multa, sed multum [L.]. Not many things, but much.

non nobis [L.]. Not unto us.

non placet [L.]. A formula expressing a negative vote.

non possumus [L., we cannot]. A statement of inability or a refusal to act.

non sequitur [L., it does not follow]. An illogical inference; an irrelevant conclusion.

nota bene [L.]. Note well.

nous avons changé tout cela [F.]. We have changed all that.

nous verrons [F.]. We shall see.

nouveau riche [F.]. (pl. nouveaux riches) A newly-rich man, a parvenu.

nulli secundus [L.]. Second to none.

obit [L.]. He (or she) died.

obiter dictum [L.]. A thing said incidentally.

odium theologicum [L.]. Hatred among theologians.

œuvres [F.]. Works.

omnia mutantur, nos et mutamur in illis [L.]. All things are subject to change, and we change with them.

omnia vincit amor [L.]. Love conquers all things.

onus probandi [L.]. The burden of proving.

ora e sempre [It.]. Now and always.

ora et labora [L.]. Pray and work.

ora pro nobis [L.]. Pray for us.

orate pro anima [L.]. Pray for the soul (of).

O! si sic omnia! [L.]. O if only all had been (spoken or acted) thus!

O tempora! O mores! [L.]. Alas for the times and the manners!

otium cum dignitate [L.]. Dignified leisure.

pace [L.]. By leave of, with the consent of.

pallida mors [L.]. Pale Death.

palmam qui meruit ferat [L.]. Let him bear the palm who has deserved it.

panem et circenses [L.]. Bread and the circus-games; food and amusement.

parbleu! [F.]. An exclamation of surprise, etc.

par excellence [F.]. Pre-eminently.

par exemple [F.]. For instance.

pari passu [L.]. At the same rate or pace.

parole d'honneur [F.]. Word of honour.

parturiunt montes, nascetur ridiculus mus [L.]. The mountains are in labour and the result will be a ridiculous mouse.

pas de deux [F.]. A dance for two.

pas possible! [F.]. Impossible!

pas seul [F.]. A dance for one person.

pax Romana [L.]. The peace of the Roman Empire.

pax vobiscum [L.]. Peace be with you.

peine forte et dure [F.]. Very severe punishment (a kind of judicial torture).

per aspera ad astra [L.]. Through rough ways to the stars; through suffering to renown.

per contra [L.]. On the contrary.

per fas aut nefas [L.]. Through right or wrong.

per mare, per terras [L.]. By sea and land.

per mensem [L.]. Monthly.

per saltum [L.]. At a leap.

per se [L.]. By itself.

persona grata [L.]. An acceptable person.

petitio principii [L.]. Begging the chief point, begging the question.

pièce de résistance [F.]. The most substantial dish at a meal.

pied-à-terre [F.]. A footing, a temporary lodging.

pis aller [F.]. A makeshift.

plein air [F.]. The open air.

poco curante [It.]. Indifferent, apathetic.

poeta nascitur, non fit [L.]. The poet is born, not made.

post hoc, ergo propter hoc [L.]. After this, therefore on account of this.

post obitum [L.]. After death.

pour ainsi dire [F.]. So to speak.

pour encourager les autres [F.]. To encourage the others.

pour faire rire [F.]. To raise a laugh.

pour prendre congé (P.P.C.) [F.]. To take leave.

preux chevalier [F.]. A brave knight.

prima facie [L.]. At first sight.

primus inter pares [L.]. First among equals.

pro aris et focis [L.]. For our altars and hearths.

probatum est [L.]. It has been proved.

pro bono publico [L.]. For the public good.

pro forma [L.]. As a matter of form.

pro patria et rege [L.]. For country and king.

proprio motu [L.]. Of one's own accord.

pro rata [L.]. In proportion.

pro tanto [L.]. For so much, to that extent.

pro tempore [L.]. For the time being.

Punica fides [L.]. Punic faith, treachery.

quære [L.]. Inquire.

quæritur [L.]. It is asked.

quæ vide [L.]. Which (things) see.

quantum libet [L.]. As much as you like.

quantum sufficit [L.]. As much as suffices.

quelque chose [F.]. Something; a trifle.

que voulez-vous? [F.]. What would you have?

quem deus vult perdere, prius dementat [L.]. Whom a god means to destroy he first makes mad.

quid pro quo [L.]. Something in return.

quid rides? [L.]. Why do you laugh?

quién sabe? [Sp.]. Who knows?

qu'importe? [F.]. What does it matter?

qui s'excuse, s'accuse [F.]. He who excuses himself accuses himself.

quis separabit? [L.]. Who shall separate us? (the motto of the Order of St. Patrick).

qui va là? [F.]. Who goes there?

quocunque modo [L.]. In whatever manner.

quod dixi, dixi [L.]. What I have said, I have said.

quod erat demonstrandum (Q.E.D.) [L.]. Which was to be proved.

quod erat faciendum (Q.E.F.) [L.]. Which was to be done.

quod vide (q.v.) [L.]. Which (thing) see.

quo jure? [L.]. By what right?

quo modo? [L.]. By what means?

quot homines, tot sententiæ [L.]. As many minds as men, so many men, so many minds (sometimes incorr. quoted TOT HOMINES, etc.).

quo vadis? [L.]. Whither goest thou?

raison d'être [F.]. The reason for a thing's existence.

rara avis [L.]. A rare bird; a prodigy.

reculer pour mieux sauter [F.]. To retire in order to advance better.

reductio ad absurdum [L.]. Proof by demonstrating the absurdity of the contrary.

répondez s'il vous plaît (R.S.V.P.) [F.]. Please reply.

requiescat in pace (R.I.P.) [L.]. May he rest in peace.

res angusta domi [L.]. Matters straitened at home, poverty.

res judicata [L.]. An issue that has been settled in a court.

resurgam [L.]. I shall rise again.

revenons à nos moutons [F.]. Let us return to our sheep, let us come back to our subject.

ruat cœlum [L.]. Let the heavens fall.

rus in urbe [L.]. Country in town.

sal Atticum [L.]. Attic salt, wit.

sans doute [F.]. Doubtless.

sans pareil [F.]. Unequalled.

sans peur et sans reproche [F.]. Without fear and without blame.

sans souci [F.]. Free from care.

sauve qui peut [F.]. Save himself who can.

savoir faire [F.]. Tact, skill.

savoir vivre [F.]. Good breeding.

scandalum magnatum [L.]. The defamation of exalted personages.

sculpsit [L.]. He engraved or carved this.

semper eadem [L. pl.]. (sing. idem) Always the same.

semper fidelis [L.]. Always faithful.

semper paratus [L.]. Always ready.

Senatus Populusque Romanus (S.P.Q.R.) [L.]. The Roman Senate and People.

se non è vero, è ben trovato [It.]. If it is not true, it is cleverly invented.

servus servorum Dei [L.]. The servant of the servants of God (a title of the Pope).

sic transit gloria mundi [L.]. So earthly glory passes away.

sic vos non vobis [L.]. So you do not (labour) for yourselves.

s'il vous plaît [F.]. If you please.

si monumentum requiris, circumspice [L.]. If you seek his memorial look around you. (In St. Paul's Cathedral, of the architect, Sir Christopher Wren.)

sine cura [L.]. Without charge or office.

sine die [L.]. Without any day (being fixed).

sine qua non [L.]. An indispensable condition.

si vis pacem, para bellum [L.]. If you want peace be ready for war.

solvitur ambulando [L.]. It is proved as you go along.

spolia opima [L.]. The richest spoils.

statim [L.]. At once.

status quo ante [L.]. The same state as before.

Sturm und Drang [G.]. Storm and stress.

suaviter in modo, fortiter in re [L.]. Gentle in manner, resolute in execution.

sub judice [L.]. Under consideration.

sub pœna [L.]. Under penalty (of).

sub rosa [L.]. Under the rose, confidentially.

sub silentio [L.]. Without notice being taken.

succès d'estime [F.]. A success with more credit than profit.

suggestio falsi [L.]. A suggestion of something that is untrue.

sui generis [L.]. Of its (his, or her) own kind.

sui juris [L.]. Of his (or her) own right.

sunt lacrimæ rerum [L.]. There are tears for mortal things.

suppressio veri suggestio falsi [L.]. The suppression of the truth is the suggestion of a falsehood.

sursum corda [L.]. Lift up your hearts.

suum cuique [L.]. To each his own.

tabula rasa [L.]. A smooth tablet ("a clean slate").

tædium vitæ [L.]. Weariness of life.

tant mieux [F.]. So much the better.

tant pis [F.]. So much the worse.

tantum quantum [L.]. Just as much as (is required).

tempora mutantur, nos et mutamur in illis [L.]. The times are changed and we with them.

tempus fugit [L.]. Times flies.

terminus ad quem [L.]. The goal.

terminus a quo [L.]. The starting-point.

terra incognita [L.]. An unknown land.

tertium quid [L.]. A third something.

teste [L.]. By the evidence (of).

timeo Danaos et dona ferentes [L.]. I fear the Greeks even when they offer gifts.

toties quoties [L.]. As often as.

toujours perdrix [F.]. Always partridge, too much of a good thing.

tour de force [F.]. A feat of strength or skill.

tout à coup [F.]. Suddenly.

tout à fait [F.]. Wholly, entirely.

tout à l'heure [F.]. Instantly.

tout de suite [F.]. Immediately.

tout ensemble [F.]. The general effect.

tria juncta in uno [L.]. Three things combined in one (motto of the Order of the Bath).

tu quoque [L.]. You also.

ubique [L.]. Everywhere.
ultimus Romanorum [L.]. The last of the Romans (used by Brutus of Cassius).
ultra vires [L.]. Beyond one's (legal) powers.
urbi et orbi [L.]. To the city and the world.
ut infra [L.]. As (mentioned) below.
uti possidetis [L.]. As you now have in your possession.
ut supra [L.]. As (mentioned) above.

vade in pace [L.]. Go in peace.
væ victis! [L.]. Woe to the vanquished!
vanitas vanitatum, et omnia vanitas [L.]. Vanity of vanities, all is vanity.
veni Creator Spiritus [L.]. Come, Holy Spirit, Creator.
veni, vidi, vici [L.]. I came, I saw, I conquered.
verbatim et literatim [L.]. Word for word and letter for letter.
verbum satis sapienti (verb. sap.) [L.]. A word is enough to the wise.
via media [L.]. A middle course.
vide ut supra [L.]. See as above.
vi et armis [L.]. By force and arms.
vigilate et orate [L.]. Watch and pray.

virginibus puerisque [L.]. For maidens and boys.
vis inertiæ [L.]. The power of inertness.
visum visu [L.]. To see and to be seen.
vita brevis, ars longa [L.]. Life is short, but art is long.
vivat rex (regina)! [L.]. Long live the king (queen)!
vive la République! [F.]. Long live the Republic!
vive l'Empereur! [F.]. Long live the Emperor.
vogue la galère [F.]. Row the galley, happen what may.
voilà [F.]. See there, there it is.
voilà tout [F.]. That's all.
vox et praeterea nihil [L.]. A voice and nothing more.
vox (pl. voces) populi [L.]. The voice of the people, popular feeling.
vox populi vox Dei [L.]. The voice of the people is the voice of God.

Weltgeist [G.]. The world-spirit.
Weltschmerz [G.]. World-sorrow, pessimism.

Zeitgeist [G.]. The spirit of the age.

PRONUNCIATION OF PROPER NAMES

The accepted English pronunciation of certain proper names is shown in this list. For Key to Pronunciation see p. 4

Abercrombie, ăb' ẽr krŭm bĭ
Abergavenny, ăb ẽr gen' ĭ, ăb ẽr gà ven' ĭ
Abernethy, ăb ẽr nẽ' thĭ
Aberystwith, ăb ẽr ĭst' wĭth
Abiathar, à bī' à thar
Abinger, ăb' ĭn jẽr
Aboukir, a book kẽr'
Abruzzi, a broo t' zē
Abydos, à bī' dos
Acapulco, a ka pool' kō
Aceldama, à sel' dà má
Acheron, ăk' ẽr ŏn
Acheson ăch' ē son
Achilles, à kĭl' ēz
Achitophel, à kĭt'ó fel
Achonry, ăk' ŏn rĭ
Aconcagua, a kon ka' gwa
Acre, ā' kẽr, a' kẽr
Actæon, ăk tē' ŏn
Adalbert, ăd' ál bẽrt
Addis Ababa, ăd ĭs ăb' à bà
Adelphi, à del' fī
Aden, ā' dẽn, a' dẽn
Adirondacks, ăd ĭ ron' dăks
Adonais, ăd ŏ nā'ĭs
Adrianople, ā dri à nopl'
Ægean, ê jē'án
Ægeria, ê jēr' ĭ à

Ægina, ē jĭ' nà
Æneas, ē nē' ás
Æneid, ē' nē ĭd, ē nē' ĭd
Æolus, ē' ŏ lŭs
Æschylus, ēs'-, es' kĭ lŭs
Æsculapius, ēs-, es kŭ lā' pĭ ŭs
Afghanistan, ăf găn ĭ stan'
Agamemnon, ăg à mem' nŏn
Agatha, ăg' à thà
Agenor, à jē' nŏr
Agincourt, aj' ĭn kŏrt
Agonistes, ăg ŏ nĭs' tēz
Agra, a' grà
Agricola, à grĭk' ó là
Agrippina, ăg rĭ pī' nà
Agulhas, a gool' yas
Ahasuerus, a hăz ū ēr' ŭs
Ahriman, a' rĭ mán
Aida, a ē' dá
Aiglon, ā glon
Aino, ī' nŏ
Aisne, ān
Aix-la-Chapelle, āks la shà pel'
Aix-les-Bains, āks lā ban
Ajaccio, a ya' chŏ
Ajalon, ăj' à lon
Alabama, ăl à băm' à
Aladdin, à lăd' ĭn

Alamo, a' la mō
Alaric, ăl' à rĭk
Albani, ăl ba' nĭ
Albania, ăl bā' nĭ á
Albany, awl'-, ăl' bà nĭ
Albemarle, ăl' bê marl
Albigenses, ăl bĭ jen' sēz
Albuquerque, al boo kẽr' kĕ
Alcantara, al kăn' ta ra
Alcazar, ăl ka' zar
Alcester, awls' tẽr
Alcott, awl' kot
Aldebaran, ăl deb' à rán
Aldeburgh, old' brú
Aldrich, awl' drich, -drĭj
Alençon, a lan'son'
Aleppo, à lep' ŏ
Alethea, ăl ê thē' à
Aleutian, ăl ĭ oo' shĭ án, à lū' shàn
Alfonso, ăl fon'sŏ
Algeciras, ăl jê sēr' às
Algiers, ăl jẽrz'
Algonkin, ăl gong' kĭn
Alhambra, ăl hăm' brà
Ali Baba, a' lĭ ba' ba
Alighieri, a lē gyãr' ŏ
Allahabad, ăl à hà bad'
Alleghany, ăl' ê gā nĭ
Alleyn, Alleyne, ăl' én

Alma Tadema, äl' mä täd' ē mä
Alnwick, än' ik
Alonzo, ȧ lon' zō
Aloysius, äl ō is'-, -ish'i ús
Alphonso, äl fon' sō
Alsace-Lorraine, äl säs'-, al sas' lō rän'
Althæa, äl thē' ȧ
Amadis, äm' ȧ dis
Amalfi, ȧ mäl' fi
Amaryllis, äm ȧ ril'is
Amery, ā' mėr i
Amiens, äm' i enz
Amlwch, äm' luk
Amory, ā' mō ri
Amos, ā' mos
Amphion, äm fi' ȯn
Amphitrite, äm fi tri' ti
Amphitryon, äm fit' ri ȯn
Ampthill, äm' til
Amritsar, äm rit' sár
Amyas, äm' i ás
Anacreon, ȧ nák' rē ȯn
Anam, ȧ nam'
Ancona, äng kō' nä
Andalusia, än dȧ lū'shä
Andaman, än' dȧ män
André, än' drä
Androcles, än' drō klēz
Andromeda, an drom' ē dä
Andronicus, än drō ni' kus, (Shak.) än dron' i kús
Aneurin, ȧ noi' rin
Angelica, än jel' i kä
Angelina, än jē li' nä
Angevin, än' jē vin
Angora, äng gōr' ȧ
Ankara, äng' kȧ ra
Annaly, än' ȧ li
Annecy, an sē'
Annesley, änz' li
Anstruther (place) än'stėr, (baronet) än' strū thėr
Anthony, än' tȯ ni
Antietam, än tē' tám
Antigua, an tē' gwa
Antilles, än til' ēz
Antiochus, än ti' ȯ kús
Antoine, an twan'
Antoinette, än tȯ net', an twa net'
Antrobus, än' trō bús
Anubis, ȧ nū' bis
Anzio, än' zi ō
Aphrodite, äf rȯ dī' tē
Apollyon, ȧ pol' i on, -yȯn
Appalachian, äp ȧ lāch'i án
Appomattox, äp ō mät' oks
Aquarius, ȧ kwär' i ús
Aquila, äk' wi lä
Aquinas, ȧ kwī' nás
Araby, är' ȧ bi
Aramis, a ra mēs'
Aran, är' án
Arbuthnot, ar búth' not, ar' búth not
Arcadia, ar kā' di ȧ
Archangel, ark än' jél
Archdall, arch' däl
Archimedes, ar ki mē' dēz
Arcturus, ark tūr' ús
Ardagh, ar' da
Ardennes, ar den'

Ardingly, ar ding li'
Arditi, ar dē' ti
Areopagitica, är ē op ȧ jit' i kä
Ares, ār' ēz
Arethusa, är ē thū' sȧ
Argentina, ar jėn tē' nä
Argentine, ar' jėn tēn, -tīn
Argyll, ar gīl'
Ariadne, ä i ȧd' ni
Arian, är' i án
Aristophanes, är is tof' ȧ nēz'
Aristotle, är' is totl
Arius, ȧ rī' ús, är' i ús
Arizona, är i zō' nä
Arkansas, ar' kán saw
Arkansas City, ar kän' zás sit' i
Arles, arlz
Armageddon, ar mȧ ged' ȯn
Armagh, ar ma'
Armenia, ar mē' ni ȧ
Armida, ar mē' dä
Artaxerxes, ar täk zėrk' sēz
Artemis, ar' tē mis
Arundel är' ún del; Arundelian, ar ún dē' li än
Aryan, är'-, är' yán
Asaph, ā' sáf
Ascalon, äs' kȧ lȯn
Ascham, äs' kám
Ashanti, ȧ' shan'-, -shän' ti
Ashburnham, äsh' búr näm
Ashburton, äsh' búr tȯn
Assheton, äsh' tȯn
Assiniboia, äs sin i boi' ȧ
Assiniboine, äs sin' i boin
Assisi, a sē' zi
Assuan, äs u an'
Astarte, äs tar' ti
Astolat, äs' tȯ lät
Asturias, as toor' ē äs
Asuncion, a sun si on'
Atalanta, ät ȧ län' tȧ
Athene, ȧ thē' nē
Athenry, äth ėn ri'
Athlumney, äth' lúm ni
Athol, äth' ȯl
Atropos, ät'rȯ pos
Attila, ät' i lä
Auchinleck, aw'kin lek
Audubon, ō du bon'
Augean, aw jē' án
Aurungzebe, awrúng zäb'
Austerlitz, ou' stėr lits
Ava, a' vä
Avalon, äv' ȧ lon
Aventine, äv' ėn tin, -tīn
Avignon, a vē nyon'
Avon, ā' von
Ayers, ārz
Ayesha, i' ē shä
Aylesbury, ālz' bėr i
Aylmer, āl' mėr
Aylwin, āl' win
Ayscough, äs' kū
Azof, a zōf', ä' zov
Azores, ȧ zōrz'

Baal, bā' äl
Babel, bā' bėl
Babylon, bäb' i lon
Bacchus, bäk' ús
Bach, bach

Badajoz, ba da hōth'
Baden-Powell, bä dėn pou'él
Bagehot, bäj' ȯt
Baggallay, bäg' ȧ li
Bagot, bäg' ȯt
Bahamas, bȧ ha' mȧz
Bahia, ba ē' ȧ
Bajazet, bäj ȧ zet'
Balaclava, bäl ȧ kla' vȧ
Balboa, bal bō' ȧ
Balcarres, bäl kär'is
Baleares, bäl ē är' ēz, ba lā a' rēz; Balearic, bäl ē är' ik
Baliol, bā' li ȯl
Ballater, bäl'ȧ tėr
Balliol, bäl' i ȯl
Balmerino, bäl me' ri nō
Balmoral, bäl mor' ál
Balthazar, bäl thä' zár
Baluchistan, bȧ loo chi stan'
Balzac, bäl' zäk, bal zak'
Bamfylde, bäm'fēld
Bancroft, bän' kroft
Banff, bamf
Bangalore, bäng gȧ lōr'
Bangor, bäng' gȯr
Banquo, bäng' kō, -kwō
Baptiste, ba tēst'
Barabbas, bȧ räb' ás
Barbados, bar bä'dōz
Barbarossa, bar bȧ ros' ȧ
Barbauld, bar' bawld
Barbizon, bar bē zon'
Barcelona, bar si lō' na
Barclay, bar' kli
Barham, bar' ám
Barnardiston, bar när dis' tȯn
Barnave, bar nav'
Baroda, ba rō' dä
Barraclough, bär ȧ klúf'
Barth, bart
Bartholdi, bar tōl dē'
Bartimeus, bar ti mē' ús
Bartolozzi, bar tō lot' si
Barttelot, bar' tē lȯt
Baruch, bär'úk
Barwick, bär' ik
Bashan, bā' shán
Basil, bäz'-, bäz' il
Basque, bask
Bassanio, bȧ sa' ni ō
Bastia, bas tē' a
Batavia, bȧ tä' vē a
Bathsheba, bäth shē' ba, bäth' shē bȧ
Baugh, baw
Bayard, bī' ėrd, ba yar'
Bayeux, ba yėr'
Bayreuth, bī roit'
Beaconsfield, (place) bek' ȯnz-, (name) bē' kȯnz-fēld
Beattie, bē' ti, bā' ti
Beaucaire, bō kár'
Beauchamp, bē chám
Beauclerc, bō' klár, -klėrk
Beauclerk, bō' klark
Beaufort, bō' fȯrt
Beauharnais, bō ar nä'
Beaujolais, bō zhō lā'
Beaulieu, bū' li
Beauly, bū' li

Beaumaris, bō mâr' is
Beaumont, bō' mont
Beaune, bōn
Beauregard, bō' rē gard
Beauvais, bō vā'
Bechstein, bech' shtīn
Bechuanaland, bech ū a' nä
  länd
Beddgelert, beth gel' ėrt
Bedel, bē dėl
Beelzebub, bē el' zē bŭb
Beerbohm, bēr' bōm
Beersheba, bē ėr shē' bä,
  bėr shē ba
Beethoven, bā' tō vėn
Behring, bā' ring
Beira, bī' rä
Beirut, bā root'
Belial, bē' li ăl, bēl' yăl
Belisha, be lī' shä
Belknap, bel' năp
Bellerophon, bē ler' ō fon
Bellew, bel' ū, bē lū'
Bellini, bel lē' nē
Belvoir, bē' vėr
Benares, be na' rēz
Benbecula, ben bek' ū lä
Ben Cruachan, ben kroo'
  chän
Benes, ben' esh
Bengal, ben gawl'
Benguela, ben gä' lä
Benin, ben in'
Ben Machdhui, ben mach
  doo' i
Ben Nevis, ben nev' is,
  -nē' vis
Bentham, ben' tăm
Beowulf, bā' ō wulf
Berengaria, ber ėn gâr' i ä
Berenice, ber ē nī' sī
Beresina, ber ā zē' nä
Bergerac, bėr zhē rak'
Berkeley, bark' li
Berkshire, bark' shir
Berlioz, bėr li ōs'
Bermuda, bėr mū' dä
Bernadotte, bėr nä dot'
Bernhardt, bėr' nart, bėr
  nar'
Bernina, bėr nē' na
Bertie (title and surname),
  bar' ti
Bertillon, bėr ti yon'
Bertrand, bėr tran'
Berwick, ber' ik
Besant (1) [Annie], bes' ănt
Besant (2) [Sir Walter], bē
  zănt'
Bessborough, bez' bŏ rō
Bethany, beth' ȧ ni
Bethesda, bē thez' dä
Bethlehem, beth' lē hėm
Bethphage, beth' fȧ ji, -fāj
Bethsaida, beth sā' i dä
Bethune (1), bē' ton, bē thŭn'
Bethune (2) [F.], bā tun'
Betwys-y-Coed, bet' us i koid
Beulah, bū' lä
Bewick, bū' ik
Beyrout [BEIRUT]
Bianca, bi ăng' kä
Biarritz, bi a ritz'
Bicester, bis' tėr

Bideford, bid' ē fôrd
Bigelow, big' ē lō
Bihar, bē har'
Bingen, bing' ėn
Bingham, bing' ăm
Bingley, bing' li
Birkbeck (family), bėr' bek
Birnam, bėr' năm
Bisley, biz' li
Bismarck, bis' mark
Bispham, bisp' ăm, bis' făm
Bizet, bē zā'
Blackstone, blăk' stōn
Blair-Atholl, blâr âth' ōl
Blantyre, blăn tīr'
Blavatsky, bla vat' ski
Blenheim, blen' im
Blennerhassett, blen ėr häs'
  ėt
Bligh, blī
Bloemfontein, blum'fŏn tān
Blois, blwa
Blondin, blon' din
Blount, blŭnt
Blücher, bloo' chėr
Blyth, blī, blīth
Boadicea, bō ȧ di sē' ä
Boanerges, bō ȧ nėr' jēz
Boccaccio, bō ka' chō
Bœotia, bē ō' shi ä
Boethius, bō ē' thi ûs
Bogota, bō gō ta'
Bohn, bōn
Boileau-Despréaux, bwa lō'
  dä prä ō'
Bois de Boulogne, bwa dē
  bu loin'
Boleyn, bul' ėn, bŭl' en
Bolingbroke, bŭl' in bruk
Bolitho, bō li' thō
Bolivar, bō lē' var
Bolivia, bō liv' i ä
Bolsover, bol' sō vėr
Bombay, bom bā'
Bonaparte, bō nä part
Bonheur, bon ėr'
Bonifacio, bon ē fa' chō
Boötes, bō ō' tēz
Bordeaux, bôr dō'
Boreas, bôr' ē ăs
Borgia, bôr' jä
Bosanquet, bō' sän ket
Boscawen, bos' kō en, -ka
  wen
Boscobel, bos' kō bel
Bosnia, boz' ni ȧ
Bosporus, bos' pŏ rūs
Bossuet, bō' swä
Botha, bō' tä
Bothwell, both' wel
Botticelli, bot i chel' i
Boucicault, boo si kō'
Boughton, baw-, bou' ton
Boulogne, bu loin'
Bourbon, boor' bŏn
Bourchier, bou' chėr
Bourke, bėrk
Bourne, bôrn, bėrn, boorn
Bovary, bō va rē'
Bow, bō
Bowen, bō' ėn
Bowie, bō' i
Bowland, bō' länd, bol' änd
Bowles, bōlz

Bowring, bou' ring
Bowyer, bō' yėr
Brabançonne, bra ban son'
Brabantio, bra băn' shi ō
Brabazon, brăb' ȧ zŏn
Brabourne, brā' bûrn
Braemar, brä mar'
Braganza, bra gan' zä
Braham, brā' ăm
Brahms, bramz
Brasenose, brāz' nōz
Brazil, brȧ zil'
Breadalbane, brē dawl' bȧn
Brechin, brech' in, brē' chin
Breda, brä da'
Bremen, brem' ėn
Brentano, bren ta' nō
Brescia, brā' sha
Breslau, brez' lou
Brian Boru, brī ȧn bō roo'
Briançon, brē an son'
Bridlington, brid' ling tŏn,
  bėr' ling tŏn
Brindisi, brin' dē zē
Broglie, brō' i
Broke, bruk
Bromley, brŭm' li
Bromwich, brom'ich
Brooklyn, bruk' lin
Brough, brŭf
Broughall, brŭfl
Brougham, broo' ăm, broom
Broughton, braw'-, brou'
  tŏn
Bruges, broozh
Brunehild, broo' nē hilt
Brunel, bru nel'
Bryn-Mawr (Wales), brin
  mour', (Penn.) - mar'
Buccleugh, bŭ kloo'
Bucentaur, bū sen' tôr
Buchan, bŭk' ȧn
Buchanan, bŭ kăn' ȧn
Bucharest, bū kȧ rest'
Budapest, boo' dȧ pest
Buddha, bud' ȧ
Buenos Ayres, bō nås âr' iz,
  bwä' nōs îr' es
Buffon, bŭf' ŏn, bu fon'
Bulawayo, boo lä wä' ō
Bulgaria, bul gâr' i ä
Bunsen, bun' sėn
Buonarroti, bwō na ro' tē
Burdett, bûr det'
Burghclere, bėr' klâr
Burghersh, bėr' gėrsh
Burleigh, bėr' li
Burnett, bûr net'
Burroughs, bûr' ōz
Bury (town and Albemarle
  family), ber' i; (viscount)
  bûr' i
Bysshe, bish

Caaba, ka' ȧ bä
Cabot, kăb' ŏt
Cabul [KABUL]
Cadillac, ka dē yak'
Cadiz, kā'diz
Cadogan, kȧ dŭg' ȧn
Cadwaladr, kȧd wol' ȧ dėr
Cædmon, kăd' mŏn
Caen, kan
Cæsarea, ses ȧ rē' ä

Cagliostro, ka lyos' trō
Caiaphas, kī' ȧ fȧs, kā' yȧ fȧs
Caillard, kī'ar
Cairo, kīr' ō
Caius (pers. name), kā' ŭs; (the Cambridge college) kēz
Calabria, kȧ lā' brī ȧ
Calais, kăl' ȧs, kăl' ā
Calchas, kal' kȧs
Calderon, kawl' der ŏn, kal dä rŏn'
Calhoun, kȧ hoon'
California, kăl i fôr' ni a
Caligula, kȧ lig' ū lȧ
Callahan, kăl' ȧ hän
Callao, ka la' ō, kal ya' ō
Calliope, kȧ lī' ŏ pē
Calypso, kȧ lĭp' sō
Cambyses, kăm bī' sēz
Camelot, kăm' ē lot
Camilla, kȧ mil' ȧ
Camille, kȧ mēl'
Camoens, kăm' ō ens
Campagnia, kam pa' nya
Campbell, kăm' bel
Campden, kăm' dĕn
Campeggio, kăm pej' ō
Canaan, kā' năn
Canberra, kăn' ber ȧ
Candace, kăn' dȧ sē
Candide, kaɴ dēd'
Cannes, kan, kăn
Canopus, kȧ nō' pŭs
Canossa, kȧ nos' ȧ
Canova, kȧ nō' vȧ
Canton, kăn ton'
Canute [ᴄɴᴜᴛ] kȧ nūt'
Capek, chä' pek
Capell, kā' pĕl
Capernaum, kȧ pĕr' nȧ ŭm
Capet, kȧ' pä'
Caprera, ka prâr' a
Capri, ka' prē
Capua, kăp' ū ȧ
Capulet, kăp' ū let
Carabas, kăr' ȧ bäs, ka ra ba' zä'
Caracalla, kăr ȧ kăl' ȧ
Caractacus, kȧ răk' tȧ kŭs
Carew, kâr' i, kȧ roo'
Caribbean, kăr i bē' ȧn
Carlyon, kar lī' ŏn
Carmichael, kar mī' kȧl
Carnegie, kar neg' i
Carnot, kar nō'
Carnwath, karn' woth
Carolina, kăr ō lī' na
Carrara, kar ra' rȧ
Carrousel, kăr oo zel'
Carruthers, kȧ rŭth' ērz
Cartagena, kar tȧ jē' nȧ
Carteret, kar' tēr et
Cartier, kar tyä'
Caruso, kȧ roo' zō
Carysfort, kăr' is fôrt
Casabianca, ka za byang' ka
Casa Guidi, ka' za gwē' dē
Casaubon, kȧ saw' bŏn
Casimir, kăs' i- mēr
Cassandra, kȧ săn' drȧ
Cassilis, kăslz
Cassiopeia, kăs i ŏ pē' yä
Cassivelaunus, kăs i vē law' nŭs

Castellammare, kas tel la ma' rä
Castile, kăs' tēl'
Castlereagh, kăsl rā'
Catalan, kăt' ȧ lȧn
Cathay, kȧ thā'
Catullus, kȧ tŭl' ŭs
Caucasus, kaw' kȧ sŭs
Cavalleria Rusticana, ka va lā rē' a rus tē ka' na
Cavan, kăv' ȧn
Cavanagh, kăv' ȧ nä
Cavendish, kăn' dish, kăv' ȧn dish
Cavour, ka voor'
Cawnpore, kawn pōr'
Cayenne, kā en', kī en'
Cecil, ses' il, sis' il
Cecilia, sē sĭl' i ȧ
Cecily, ses' i li
Cedric, sed' rik, ked' rik
Celebes, sel' e bēz
Celestine, sel' ĕs tīn, sē les' tin
Cellini, chē lē' nē
Cenci, chen' chē
Cephas, sē' fȧs
Cerberus, sēr' bēr ŭs
Ceres, sēr' ēz
Cervantes, sēr văn' tēz
Cetewayo, set i-, kech wa' yō
Cetinje, tset' in yä
Ceuta, sū' tȧ
Ceylon, sē lon'
Cezanne, sā zăn'
Chalmers, chaw'-, cha'-, chäl mērz
Chaloner, chăl' ŏ nēr
Chambery, shan bā rē
Chambord, shan bōr'
Chamonix, sha mō nē
Champagne, shăm pān'
Champ-de-Mars, shan dē mar'
Champlain, shăm plän'
Champs-Elysées, shan zā lē zä'
Chandos, shăn' dos
Chantilly, shan ti yē'
Charlemagne, shar le măn'
Charlemont, sharl' mont
Charleroi, shar le rwa'
Charmian, shar' mi ȧn
Charon, kâr' ŏn
Charteris, char' tērz
Chartres, shartr
Charybdis, kȧ rib' dis
Chateaubriand, sha tō brē aɴ'
Chauncey, chan'-, chawn' si
Chautauqua, sha taw' kwä
Chavannes, sha văn'
Chaworth, cha' wŏrth
Cheetham, chēt' ȧm
Cheltenham, chelt' năm
Cherbourg, sher boor'
Cherubini, kȧ roo bē' nē
Chesham Bois, che' shăm bois
Chetwode, chet' wud
Chetwynd, chet' wind
Chevalier, she val yä'
Cheviot, chev' i ŏt
Cheyenne, shi en'
Cheyne, chä' ni
Chicago, shi ka' gō

Chichele, chich' ē li
Chiene, shĕn
Chile, chi' li
Chillon, shē yon'
Chimborazo, chim bō ra' zō
Chinchilla, chin chē' lyä
Chingachgook, chin gach' guk
Chippewa, chip' ē wa
Chiron, kīr' ŏn
Chisholm, chiz' ŏm
Chiswick, chiz' ik
Chloe, klō' ē
Cholmeley, Cholmondeley, Cholmley, chŭm' li
Chopin, shō paɴ'
Chriemhild, krēm' hil dē
Cicely, sis' ē li
Cicero, sis' ēr ō
Cid, sid
Cilicia, si lish' i ȧ
Cimabue, chē ma boo' ä
Cincinnati, sin si nă' ti
Circe, sēr' sē
Cirencester, sis' i tēr, sīr' ĕn ses tēr
Clanricarde, klăn rik' ȧrd
Claude, klŏd
Claverhouse, klā' vers, klăv' ers, klăv' ēr ŭs
Cleckheaton, klek' ē tòn
Cleishbotham, klēsh' both ȧm
Clementine, klem' ĕn tin, -tin
Cleopatra, klē ō pä' trä
Clerk, klark
Clerkenwell, klark' ĕn wel
Clogher, klŏ' ēr
Clonfert, klon fērt'
Clough, klŭf
Clytemnestra, klī tĕm nes' trä
Cnut, kē nūt'
Coblentz, kō blents
Cochin-China, kō' chin chī' nä
Cochrane, koch' răn
Cockburn, kō' bērn
Cœur de Lion, ker dē lē' òn
Coke, kōk, kuk
Colborne, kōl' bŏrn
Colchester, kōl' chĕs tēr
Colclough, kōk' li
Colenso, kō len'zō
Coleridge, kōl' rij
Coliseum, kol i sē' ŭm
Cologne, kō lōn'
Colombia, ko lom' bia
Colombo, ko lŭm' bō
Colon, kō lon'
Colorado, kol ō ra' dō
Colquhoun, kō hoon'
Colville, kol' vil
Compton, kŭmp' tòn
Connaught, kon' awt
Connecticut, kō net' i kŭt
Constable, kun' stȧbl
Conybeare, kŏn' i bär
Conyngham, kŭn' ing ȧm
Copernicus, kō pēr' ni kŭs
Cophetua, kō fet' ū ȧ
Coplestone, kopl' stòn
Coquelin, kok laɴ'
Corday, kŏr dā'
Cordoba, kŏr' dō ba
Corfu, kŏr foo'

Coriolanus, kŏ ri ò lā′ nŭs
Corkran, kok′ răn
Corneille, kŏr ni′ yĕ
Corot, kó rŏ′
Correggio, kor rej′ ŏ
Corunna, kò rŭn′ á
Costa Rica, kos′ tá rē′ ká
Cotopaxi, kŏ tŏ păk′ si
Couch, kooch
Courtenay, kŏrt′ ni
Courthope, kŏrt′ ŏp
Coventry, kŭv′ ĕn tri
Coverley, kŭv′ ĕr li
Cowen, kŏ-, kou′ ĕn
Cowper, koo′-, kou′ pĕr
Cozens, kŭz′ ĕnz
Creagh, krā
Crécy, kre′ si
Creighton, krī′ tòn
Crespigny, krep′ i ni
Cressida, kres′ i dá
Crichton, krī′ tòn
Crimea, krī mē′ á
Crœsus, krē′ sŭs
Cromartie, krŭm′ ár ti
Crombie, krŭm′ bi
Cromwell, krom′wĕl
Cronje, kron′ yĕ
Crowninshield, grŭn′ sel
Cruickshank, kruk′ shăngk
Culebra, koo lā′ bra
Culloden, kŭl od′ ĕn
Culpeper, kul′ pĕp ĕr
Curteis, Curtois, kĕr′ tis
Cuvier, ku vyā
Cuyp, koip
Cuzco, kus′ kŏ
Cybele, sib′ ĕ lē
Cyclopes, si klŏ′ pēz
Cymbeline, sim′ bē lēn
Cymmrodorion, kim rŏ dŏr′
  i ŏn
Cymry, kim′ri, kum′ ri
Cyrene, si rē′ nē
Czech, chek

Dacre, dā′ kĕr
Dædalus, ded′ á lŭs
Daguerre, dá gâr′
Dahomey, da hŏ′ mā
Dalgetty, dăl′ gĕ ti
Dalhousie, dăl hoo′ zi
Dalmeny, dăl mā′ ni
Dalrymple, dăl rimpl′, dăl′
  rimpl
Dalzell, Dalziel, dē el′
Damien, da myăn′
Damocles, dăm′ ò klēz;
  Damoclean, dăm ò klē′ án
Dana, dā′ ná
Dante, dăn′ ti
Danton, dan toń
Daphne, dăf′ nē
Daphnis, dăf′ nis
Darfur, dar′ fur
Darien, dăr′ i ĕn
Darius, dá rī′ ŭs
Darjeeling, dar jē′ ling
Daudet, dŏ dā′
Daventry, dăv′ ĕn tri
da Vinci, da vin′ chi
Deak, dā ak′
Dealtry, dawl′ tri
Dease, dēs

Death, dĕ ăth′
Debussy, dĕ bus ē′
Deccan, dek′ăn
Decies, dē′ shēz
Delacroix, de la krwa′
Deland, dĕ lănd′
Delano, del′ á nŏ
De la Pasture, dĕ lăp′ á tūr
De la Poer, dĕ la poor′
De la Rey, dĕ la rā′
De la Warr, del′ á war
Delhi, del′ i
Delilah, dĕ lī′ lá
De L'Isle, dĕ lil′
Delphi, del′ fī
Democritus, dĕ mok′ ri tŭs
Demosthenes, dĕ mos′ thē
  nēz
Denbigh, den′ bi
Denderah, den′ dĕr á
d'Eon, dā on′
Deptford, det′fŏrd
Derby, dar′ bi
Dering, dēr′ ing
De Ros, de roos′
Desart, des′ árt
De Saumarez, dĕ sŏ′ má rez
Descartes, dā kart′
Desdemona, dez dĕ mŏ′ ná
Desiré, dā zē rā′
des Moines, dĕ moin′
De Valera, de văl ē rá
Devereux, dev′ ēr oo, -ooks
Dewar, dā ár′
Deyncourt, dān′ kûrt
Diana, dī ăn′ á
Diaz, dē′ as
Diderot, dēd rŏ′
Dieppe, dĕ ep′
Dijon, dē zhoń′
Dinant, dē nan′
Diocletian, dī ò klē′shán
Diogenes, dī oj′ ē nēz
Diomed, dī′ò med
Dionysius, dī ò nish′ i ŭs
Dionysus, dī ò nī′ sŭs
Disraeli, diz rā′ li
Dives, dī′ vēz
Dobell, dŏ bel′
Dolce, dŏl′ chā
Dolgelly, dol geth′ li
Dolores, dò lŏr′ ēs
Domenichino, dŏ mā nē kē′
  nŏ
Dominica, dom i nē′ ká
Domitian, dò mish′i án
Domvile, dŭm′ vil
Donati, dŏ na′ tē
Donegal, don ē gawl′
Don Giovanni, don jŏ va′ ni
Donizetti, don i zet′ i
Don Juan, don joo′ án
Donne, don, dŭn
Donoghue, dŭn′ ò hoo
Donoughmore, dŭn′ ò mŏr
Don Quixote, don kwik′ sŏt
Doré, dŏ rā′
Doris, dŏr′ is, dor′ is
d'Orsay, dŏr′ sā
Dostoevski, dos tò ef′ ski
Dotheboys, doo′ the boiz
Douay, (place) doo′ ā,
  (bible) dou′ á
Dougall, doo′ gál

Douglas, dŭg lás
Dreyfus, drā fus′
Drogheda, dro′ hŏ dá
Dryburgh, drī′ bŭ rŏ
Drysdale, driz′ dál
Dudevant, dud van′
Dulcinea, dŭl sin′ ē á
Dulles, dŭl′ ĕs
Dulwich, dŭl′ ij, -ich
Dumas, du ma′
Dumfries, dŭm frēs′
Dunalley, dŭn ăl′ i
Dundalk, dŭn dawk′
Dundas, dŭn dăs′
Dundee, dŭn dē′
Dunedin, dŭn ē′ din
Dunfermline, dŭn fĕrm′-,
  fĕr′ lin
Dunglass, dŭn glas′
Dunmore, dŭn mŏr′
Dunnottar, dŭn not′ ár
Dunsany, dŭn sā′ ni
Dunisinane, dŭn si năn′
Duplessis, du plē sē′
Du Quesne, Duquesne, du
  kān′
Durazzo, du rad′ zŏ
Durban, dēr′ bán
Durham, dûr′ hăm
Durrant, dû rant′, dûr′ ánt
Dusé, doo′ zā
Dvořák, dvŏr′ zhăk
Dyak, dī′ ăk
Dymoke, dim′ ŏk
Dynevor, din′ ē vór
Dysart, dī′ zárt

Eaux, ŏ
Ebbw, eb′ ŏ
Ebury, ē′ bŭ ri
Ecclefechan, ekl fech′ án
Ecuador, ek wá dŏr′
Edinburgh, edn′ bŭ rŏ
Egalité, ā ga lē tā
Egeria, ē jēr′ i á
Egerton, ej′ ĕr tòn
Eifel, ī′ fel
Eikon Basilike, i′ kon bá sil′
  i kē
Eileen, i′ lēn
Einstein, īn′ stīn
Eire, âr′ ē
Elcho, el′ kŏ
Eleanor, el′ē nór, el′ ē a nór
Electra, ē lek′ trá
Eleusis, ē lū′ sis
Elgin, el′ gin
Eli, ē′ lī
Elia, ē′ li á
Elibank, el′ i bănk
Elijah, ē lī′ já
Elinor, el′ i nór
Elisha, ē lī′ shá
Ellesmere, elz′ mēr
Elphinstone, el′ fin stòn
Elsinore, el si nŏr′
Elwes, el′ wiz
Ely, ē′ li
Emile, ā mēl′
Emmaus, ē mā′ ŭs
Endymion, en dim′ i ŏn
Engadine, en gá dēn′
Enid, ē′ nid

Enniskillen, en is kil′ ĕn
Eutebbe, en teb′ i
Eŏthen, ĕ ŏ′ thĕn
Ephesus, ef′ e sŭs
Ephraim, ĕ′ frā im
Epicurus, ep i kūr′ ŭs
Erasmus, ĕ răz′ mŭs
Erebus, er′ ĕ bŭs
Erin, ĕr′-, er′ in
Ernani, ĕr na′ ni
Eros, ĕr′ os
Escorial, es kŏr′ i ăl
Esmonde, ez′ mŏnd
Este, es′ tā
Esterhazy, es′ tĕr ha zĕ
Esther, es′ tĕr
Etienne, ā tyen′
Euclid, ū′ klid
Eugene, ū jēn′, ū′ jēn
Eugéne, u zhăn′
Eugénie, u zhā nĕ′
Eulenspiegel, oi′ lĕn spē gĕl
Eunice, ū′ nis, ū ni′ sĕ
Euphemia, ū fē′ mi ă
Euphrates, ū frā′ tēz
Euphrosyne, ū fros′ i nĕ
Euphues, ū′ fū ēz
Euripides, ū rip′ i dēz
Europa, ū rō′ pá
Eurydice, ū rid′ i sĕ
Eusebius, ū sē′ bi ŭs
Euterpe, ū tĕr′ pĕ
Evangeline,   ĕ văn′ je lēn,
  -lin, -lin
Eveline, ev′ĕ lēn, -lin
Evelyn, ĕv′ lin, ev′ lin
Evesham, ĕv′ shăm
Ewart, ū′ ărt
Excalibur, ek skăl′ i bŭr
Eyam, ĕ′ ăm
Eyck, ik
Eylau, i′ lou
Eyre, âr
Ezekiel, ĕ zĕ′ kyĕl, -ki ĕl

Faed, fād
Fagin, fā′ gin
Falconbridge, faw′ kŏn brij
Falconer, fawk′ nĕr
Falkland, fawk′ lănd
Farnese, far nĕ′ sā
Faroe, fâ′ rō
Farquhar, far′ kwăr, -kár
Farquharson, far′ kár sŏn
Fatima, făt′ i mă
Faust, foust
Faversham, fev′ĕr shăm
Fawcett, fos′ ĕt, faw′ sĕt
Feilden, fēl′ dĕn
Feilding, fēl′ ding
Fénelon, fā nĕ lon′
Fenwick, fen′ ik
Fermanagh, fĕr măn′ a
Ferrara, fē ra′ ra
ffolkes, fōks
Fichte, fich′ tĕ
Fidelio, fē dā′ li ŏ
Fiennes, fīnz
Fiesole, fi ā′ zŏ lā
Figaro, fē ga rō′
Fiji, fē′ jē
Fildes, fildz
Findlater, find′ lā tĕr
Findlay, fin′ li

Finistère, fin is târ′
Finisterre, fin is târ′
Firdausi, fēr dou′ sĕ
Fiume, fū′ mā
Flaubert, flō bâr′
Flotow, flō′ tō
Foch, fosh
Foljambe, foo′ jăm
Folkestone, fōk′ stŏn
Fontainebleau, fon tān blŏ′
Fontenoy, fou′ tĕ noi
Fors Clavigera, fŏrz klâ vij′
  ĕr á
Fortescue, fŏr′tĕs kū
Foscari, fos′ ka rē
Fouché, foo shā′
Foulis, foulz
Fowey, foi
Francesca, frän ses′ kă, fran
  ches′ ka
François, fran swa′
Frankenstein, frăng′ kĕn stīn
Frederica, fred ĕr ē′ kă
Freiburg, frī′ burg
Freischütz, frī′ shuts
Fremantle, frē măntl′
Freud, froid
Frobisher, frob′ ish ĕr, frŏ′
  bish ĕr
Froebel, fru′ bel
Frontenac, fron′ tĕ năk
Frome, froom
Froude, frood
Fuchs, fuks
Fujiyama, foo jē ya′ ma
Furneaux, fĕr′ nŏ

Gabriel, gā′ bri ĕl
Galahad, găl′ á hăd
Galapagos, ga la′ pá gŏs
Galashiels, găl á shēlz′
Galata, găl′ a ta
Galatea, găl á tē′ á
Galatia, gă lā′ shi á
Galbraith, găl brāth′
Galen, gā′ len
Galileo, găl i lē′ ŏ
Gallagher, găl′ á hĕr
Gallipoli, gă lip′ ŏ li
Galsworthy, gawlz′ wĕr′ thi
Galway, gawl′ wā
Gamaliel, gă mā′ li ĕl
Ganymede, găn′ i mēd
Garibaldi, gar i boi′ di
Garonne, ga ron′
Gatun, ga toon′
Gautama, gaw′-, gou′ ta ma
Gawain, gaw′ wān
Geddes, ged′ is
Geikie, gē′ ki
Gelert, gel′ ĕrt
Geneva, je nĕ′ vá
Genevieve, jen′ ĕ vēv
Genevra, jē nev′ rá
Genghis Khan, jen′ gis kan′
Gennesaret, ge nes′ á ret
Genoa, jen′ ŏ á
Genseric, jen′ sĕr ik
Geoffrey, jef′ ri
Geoghegan, gā′ găn
Geraint, ge rīnt′
Geraldine, jer′ ăl din
Gerald, jer′ ăld
Geronimo, jē ron′ i mŏ

Gethsemane, geth sem′ á nĕ
Gettysburg, get′ iz bĕrg
Ghana, ga′ ná
Ghent, gent
Ghirlandajo, gēr lan da′ yŏ
Giacomo, ja′ kŏ mŏ
Gibraltar, jib rol′ tár
Giddens, gid′ ĕnz
Gide, zhēd
Giffard, jif′ ărd, gif′ árd
Giffen, gif′ ĕn
Gifford, gif′ ŏrd, jif′órd
Gigli, jē′ lyē
Gil Bias, zhēl blas
Gilboa, gil bŏ′ á
Gilchrist, gil′ krist
Gilkes, jilks
Gilles, gil′ is
Gillespie, gi les′ pi
Gilroy, gil roi′
Gilzean, gi lēn′
Ginevra, ji nev′ rá
Giordano, jŏr da′ nŏ
Giotto, jot′ ŏ
Giovanni, jŏ va′ nē
Girard, ji rard′, zhē rar″
Girolamo, zhē rŏ′ la mŏ
Gironde, ji rond′, zhē rond″
Giuseppe, joo sep′ ā
Gizeh, gē′ zĕ
Gladstone, glăd′ stŏn
Glamis, glamz
Glenlivet, glen liv′ ĕt
Glenmuick, glen mik′
Gloag, glōg
Gloriana, glŏr ri ă′ ná
Gloucester, glos′ tĕr
Gluck, gluk
Godalming, god′ ăl ming
Godiva, gŏ di′ vá
Godoy, gŏ dol′
Goethe, gĕr′ tĕ
Goliath, go li′ áth
Gomorra, gŏ mor′ á
Gorky, gŏr′ ki
Goschen, gŏ′ shĕn
Gotha, gŏ′ ta
Gotham, got′ ăm
Gouda, gou′ da
Gough, gŭf, gof
Goulburn, gool′ bŭrn
Gounod, goo nŏ′
Gourley, goor′ li
Gower, gou′ ĕr, gŏr
Graeme, grăm
Graham, Grahame, grā′ ăm
Granada, grá na′ dá
Granard, grăn′ árd
Greaves, grăvz
Greenough, grē′ nŏ
Greenwich, grin′ ij
Greig, greg
Grenada (W. Indies), grĕ
  ná′ dá
Grenada [U.S.A.], grĕ na′ dá
Grenoble, gre nŏbl′
Greuze, grĕrz
Greville, grevl′
Grieg, grĕg
Grimaldi, grē mal′ dē
Grosvenor, grŏv′ nŏr
Gruyers, groo′ yâr
Guadalquivir, gwa dal kwiv′
  ĕr

Ω

Guadeloupe, gwa de loop'
Guaira, gwär' a
Guatemala, gwa tä ma' la
Guayaquil, gwī ä kēl'
Gudrun, good' run
Guedalla, gwe da'lä
Guelph, gwelf
Guernsey, gẽrn' zi
Guglielmo, gool yēl' mō
Guiana, gē a' na
Guilford, gil' fōrd
Guillaume, gē yōm'
Guinevere, gwin' ē vēr
Guinness, gin' ēs
Guise, gēz
Guizot, gē zō'
Gujarat, goo jä rat'
Gustavus, gus ta'vŭs
Gwatkin, gwot' kin
Gwydyr, gwi' dẽr
Gye, jī

Haakon, hō' kon
Haarlem, har' lem
Habsburg, hăbz' burg
Haden, hā' dĕn
Hades, hā' dēz
Hafiz, ha' fiz
Haggai, hăg' ā ī
Hague, hāg
Haidarabad, hī dä rä bad'
Rainault, hä' nolt
Haiti, hā' ti
Hakluyt, hăk' loot
Haldane, hawl' dän
Halkett, hăk' ĕt
Halsbury, hawlz' bri
Hambro, hăm' bō rō
Hamilcar, hă mil' kar
Hamish, hä' mish
Hampden, hămp' dĕn
Handel, hăn' del
Hardicanute, har dī kă nŭt'
Hardinge, har' ding
Harlech, har' lech
Harlem, har' lĕm
Hartlepool, hart'll pool
Harwich, hăr' ij
Haughton, hō' tŏn
Haussa, hou'sa
Havana, ha va' na
Havre, avr
Hawaii, ha wī' ē
Hawarden (place), har' dĕn
Hawarden (title), hä' wōr dĕn
Haweis, haw' is
Haworth, haw' wōrth
Haydn, hădn, hīdn
Hebe, hē' bē
Hebrides, heb' rĭ dēz
Heidelberg, hī' dĕl bẽrg
Heine, hī' nē
Heinrich, hīn' rich
Helicon, hel' ĭ kŏn
Hellas, hel' ăs
Hellespont, hel' ĕs pont
Héloise, ă lō ēz'
Helvetia, hel vē' shi ă
Hemans, hĕm' ănz
Heneage, hĕn' ĕj
Hengest, heng' gest
Hennessey, hen' ē si
Henri, an rē'
Henriques, hen rē' kēs

Hepburn, heb' ŭrn
Herculaneum, hẽr kū lä' nē
  ŭm
Hercules, hẽr' kū lēz
Hereford, her' ē fōrd
Hereward, her'ē wôrd
Hermes, hẽr'mēz
Hermione, hẽr mī' ō nē
Herod, her' ŏd
Herodotus, hē rod' ō tŭs
Herries, her' is
Herschel, hẽr' shĕl
Hertford, har' fōrd
Hervey, har' vi
Hesperides, hes per'ĭ dēz
Hesse (personal name), hes
Hesse (place name), hes' ē
Heytesbury, hāts' bŭ ri
Hiawatha, hī ă woth' ă
Hildebrand, hil' dē brănd
Himalaya, him ä lā' ya
Hispaniola, his pa nyō' la
Hobart, hŭb' ärt; (place) hō'
  bart
Hobbema, hob' ē ma
Hoboken (N. Y.), hō' bō kĕn
Hoboken (Belgium), ho bō
  kĕn
Hohenstaufen, hō ĕn stou'
  fĕn
Hohenzollern, hō ĕn tsol' ẽrn
Holbeach, hōl' bēch
Holbein, hōl' bīn
Holborn, hō' bŭrn
Holinshed, hol' inz hed, -in
  shed
Holmes, hōmz
Holyhead, hol' ĭ hed
Holyoake, hol' ĭ ōk
Holyoke, hōl' yōk
Holyrood, hol' ĭ rood
Home, hūm
Honduras, hon dūr' ăs
Honiton, hon' ĭ tŏn
Honolulu, ho nō loo' lu
Hopetoun, hōp' tŏn
Horace, hor' ăs
Horatio, hō rā' shi ō
Hortense, ōr tans'
Hosea, hō zē' ă
Hough, hŭf
Houghton, haw'-, hou' tŏn
Houyhnhnm, win' im
Houston, hoos' tŏn
Hudibras, hū' dĭ brăs
Hueffer, huf' ẽr
Hugessen, hū' jē sĕn
Hughenden, hū' ĕn dĕn
Huish, hū' ish
Humboldt, hŭm' bōlt
Hunstanton, hŭn' stŏn
Huron, hū' ron
Hyades, hī' ă dēz
Hyderabad, hī de rä băd'
Hyères, i är'
Hyndman, hīnd' măn
Hypatia, hī pā' shi ă
Hyperion, hī pēr' ĭ ŏn, hī
  pẽr ī' ŏn

Iago, ē a' gō, ya' gō
Ian, ē' an
I'Anson, ī' ăn sŏn
Ibsen, ĭb' sĕn

Icolmkill, ĭ kōm kil'
Idaho, ī' dă hō
Iddesleigh, idz' lī
Ightham, ī tăm
Illinois, il ĭ noi', -noiz'
Imogen, ĭm' ō jĕn
Inchiquin, inch' kwin
Indiana, in dĭ ăn' ă
Indianapolis, in dĭ ă năp' ō
  lis
Indonesia, in dō nē' zĭ ă
Inez, ē' nēz, ī' nēz
Inge, ing
Ingelow, in' jē lō
Innes, in' ĕs
Innisfail, in' ĭs fāl
Inveraray, in vēr är' ĭ
Inverness, in vẽr nes'
Iona, ī ō' nă
Iowa, ī' ō wă
Iphigenia, if ĭ jē nī' ă
Iran, ē răn'
Iraq, ē răk
Irawadi, ir a wo' di
Irene, ī rē' nē
Iroquois, ir ō kwoi'
Isaiah, ī zī' ă, ī zā' yă
Iseult, ē soolt'
Isham, ish' ăm
Isis, ī' sis
Islay, ī' lă, is' lă
Isleworth, izl' wôrth
Islip, īz' lĭp
Ismail, is ma ēl'
Ismay, is' mā'
Isolde, ĭ sōld'
Issacher, is' ă kẽr
Ivan, ī' van, ē van
Iveagh, ī' vă
Ixion, ĭk sī' ŏn

Jacobi, Jacoby, jăk' ō bi
Jacobus, ja kō' bŭs
Jaeger, yā' ger
Jaipur, jī poor'
Jairus, jā ir' ŭs
Jameson, Jamesone, Jamie-
  son, jim' ĭ sŏn
Janet, jăn' ĕt, (Am.) jă net'
Janiculum, jă nik' ū lŭm
Japheth, jā' fĕth
Jaques, jāks
Jarndyce, jarn' dĭs
Java, jä' vă
Jeaffreson, jef' ẽr sŏn
Jehoshafat, jē hosh' ă făt
Jekyll, jek' ll
Jena, yā' nă
Jephtha, jĕf' thă
Jeremiah, jer ē mi' ă
Jerome, jē rōm', jer' ŏm
Jervaulx, jẽr' vō
Jervis, jär' vis, jẽr' vis
Jervoix, jẽr' vis
Jessica, jes' ĭ kă
Jethro, jeth' rō, jē' thrō
Jeune, joon
Jevons, jev' ŏnz
Jeyes, jāz
Joachim, jō' ă kim, yō' a
  chĭm
Job, jōb
Jocelyn, jos' lin
Jodhpur, jōd poor'

Johannesburg, jō hăn' ĕs burg

Johnstone, jon' stón

Jolliffe, jol' if

Josephine, jō' zĕ fēn

Joubert (1) (F.], zhoo bâr

Joubert (2) [Dut.], you' bĕrt

Joule, joul

Jowett, jou' ĕt

Juarez, ju a' rĕz

Jules, zhul

Juliana, joo li ăn' à

Julienne, zhu lyen'

Jungfrau, yung' frou

Justine, zhus tēn'

Kabul, ka' bul

Kalahari, ka la ha' rē

Kalamazoo, kăl à má zoo'

Kalevala, ka' lä va la

Kamchatka, kăm chăt' kà

Kansas, kăn' zàs

Kant, kant, kănt

Karachi, kà ra' chē

Karakoram, ka rà kôr' àm

Kashmir, kăsh mēr'

Kauffman, Kaufmann, kawf' man

Kavanagh, kăv' à nà

Kazan, ka zan'

Kearny, kar' ni

Kearsage, kēr' sarj

Keble, kēbl

Kedleston, kel' sòn, ked' lĕs tòn

Keighley, kēth' li

Keightley, kēt' li

Kekewich, kek' wich

Kennard, kĕ nard'

Kentucky, ken tŭk' i

Kenya, kē' nyà

Keogh, kyō

Ker, Kerr, kar

Kernahan, kēr' nà hàn

Keswick, kez' ik

Keynes, kēnz

Khartoum, kar toom'

Khayyam, kĭ yam'

Kiev, kē' ĕf

Kikuyu, kē koo' yoo

Kilima-Njaro, kil i man ja' rō

Kilmorey, kil mŭr' i

Kincairney, kin kar' ni

Kincardine, kin kar' din

Kingscote, kingz' kùt

Kinnead, ki nârd'

Kinnear, ki nēr'

Kinnoul, ki nool'

Kinross, kin ros'

Kinsale, kin säl'

Kintyre, kin tīr'

Kirghiz, kîr gez'

Kirkcaldy, kîr kaw' di

Kirkcudbright, kîr koo' bri

Knollys, Knowles, nōlz

Knyvett, niv' ĕt

Korea, kò rē' à

Kossuth, kos' uth, kosh' ut

Krakatoa, kra ka tō' à

Krupp, krup

Kubelik, koo' bĕ lik

Kuch Behar, kuch bā har'

Kumassi, ku măs' i

Kurdistan, koor dis tan'

Kynaston, kin' às tòn

Kyoto, kyō' tō

Kyrle, kĕrl

Labouchere, lăb oo shâr'

Labrador, lăb rà dôr'

La Bruyère, la bru yâr'

Lacedæmon, lăs ĕ dē' mòn

Ladislaus, lăd' is laws

Ladoga, là dō ga

Laertes, là ēr' tēz

Lafayette, la fā yet'

La Fontaine, la fon tān

Lagado, là ga' dō

Lagos, lā' gos

La Guaira, la gwīr' à

Lahore, là hôr'

Laing, lăng

L'Allegro, la le' grō

Lamech, lā' mĕk

Langrishe, lăng' rish

Laocoon, lā ok' ō òn

Laodicea, lā ō di sē' à

Lao-tsze, la' ot zēr

Lathom, lā' thòm

Laughlin, laf' lin

Laughton, law' tòn

Lausanne, lō zan'

Lavengro lăv' ĕn grō

Lea, lē

Leamington, lem' ing tòn

Leander, lē ăn' dēr

Leathers, lĕ' thĕrz, leth' erz

Lechmere, lēch' mēr

Leda, lē' dá

Legh, lē

Lehigh, lē' hī

Lehmann, lā' mán

Leibnitz, līp' nits

Leicester, lea' tēr

Leigh, lē, lī

Leighton, lā' tòn

Leila, lē' là

Leinster, len' stēr

Leipzig, līp' sīk

Leith, lēth

Leitrim, lē' trim

Leland, lē' lánd

Lely, lē' li

Lemesurier, lè mezh' ùr ēr

Lemprière, lem prēr'

Lemuel, lem' ū ĕl

Lenin, len' ēn

Leningrad, len' in grăd

Lennox, len' ocks

Leominster lem' stēr

Leonardo, lā ō nar' dō

Leonidas, lē on' i dās

Leonora, lā ō nôr' à

Le Queux, lē kū'

Lerwick, lēr' wik

Le Sage, lē sazh'

Lesbia, lez'bi à

L'Estrange, lè stränj'

Letitia, lē tish' à

Levant, lē vănt'

Leven, lē' vēn

Leveson, loo' sòn

Levey, Levy, lev' i

Lewes, lū' is

Leyden, lī' dĕn

Lhasa, lās' à

Lie, lē

Liège, li äzh'

Ligonier, lig' ò nēr

Lilith, lil' ith

Lille, lēl

Lillibulero, lil i bu lâr' ō

Lima, lē' má

Lincoln, ling' kòn

Linlithgow, lin lith' gō

Lisbon, liz' bon

Liskeard, lis kard'

Lisle, lēl, līl

Lismore, liz môr'

Listowell, lis' tōl

Liszt, list

Lithuania, lith ū ā' ni à

Livingstone, liv' ing stòn

Llanberis, hlăn ber' is

Llandudno, hlăn did' nō

Llanelly, hlăn eth' li

Llangollen, hlăn goth' lĕn

Llewelyn, hloo el' in

Lloyd, loid

Lochiel, loch ēl'

Lochinvar, loch in var'

Lodore, lō dôr'

Lohengrin, lō' ĕn grin

Lombardy, lom'-, lŭm' bàr di

Lopez, lō' pās

Lorelei, lōr' ĕ lī

Lorraine, lō rān'

Los Angeles, los ăng' ge lĕz

Lothario, lō thâr' i ō

Lothrop, lō' thrŭp

Lough, lŭf

Louis, (Fr.) loo'i, (Am.) loo'b

Louisa, loo ē' zà

Louisburg, loo' is bērg

Louisiana, loo ē zi ăn' à

Louisville, loo' is vil

Lourdes, loord

Louvre, loovr

Lovat, lŭv' àt

Lowe, lō

Lowell, lō' ĕl

Lowestoft, lōs' toft

Loyola, loi ō' la

Lucerne, loo sērn'

Lucia, lū' shi à

Lucknow, lŭk' nou

Lucretia, lū krē' shi à

Lugard, lu gard'

Luigi, loo ē' jē

Luke, look

Lusitania, lū si tā' ni à

Luther, loo' thēr

Lutwyche, lŭt' wich

Lutyens, lŭt' yenz

Lutzen, lut' sĕn

Luxemburg, lŭk sém bērg

Luxor, lŭx' sòr

Lycidas, lis' i dàs

Lydgate, lid' gàt

Lyly, lī' i

Lym, lim

Lyons, lī' ònz

Lysaght, li' sat

Lysander, li sän' dēr

Lyveden, liv' dĕn

Macalister, mà kăl' is tēr

Macao, má ka' ō

Macbeth, măk beth'

McCorquodale, má kôr' kò dàl

M'Crea, má krā
Maccullagh, má kŭl' á
M'Culloch, má kŭl' och
Macdona, mác dŭn' á
M'Evoy, măk' é voi
M'Gee, má gē'
MacGillivray, má gil' i vrā
M'Gillycuddy, ma gil' i kŭd i, mag' li kŭd' i
Machell, mă' chĕl
Machiavelli, ma kē a vel' i
M'Ilwraith, mak il räth'
MacIvor, má kī' vŏr
Mackarness, măk' á nĕs
Mackay, má kī'
Mackie, măk' i
Mackinac, măk' i nŏ
Maclachlan, má klawch' lán
Maclagan, má klăg' án
Maclaren, má klăr' ĕn
Maclean, má klān'
Maclear, má klēr'
Macleay, má klā'
Macleod, McLeod, ma kloud'
Macmahon, mák man'
Macnamara, măk ná ma' rá
M'Naught, măk nawt'
McNeill, mák nēl'
Macquoid, má koid'
Macready, má krē' di
Macrorie, má krŏr' i
Madeira, má dēr' á
Madeleine, măd è lān'
Madras, má dras'
Maeterlinck, mā' tér link
Mafeking, mă' fé king
Magdalen [Oxf.], Magdalene [Camb.], mawd' lin
Magdalen (Mary) măg' de lén
Magellan, má jel' án
Maggiore, ma jŏr' ā
Maginn, má gin'
Magrath, má gra'
Maguire, má gwīr'
Mahan, man, má han'
Mahoon, má hoon'
Mahony, ma' ni
Mahratta, má răt' á
Mainwaring, măn' ér ing
Majendie, măj' én di
Malabar, măl' á bar
Malacca, má lăk' á
Malachi, măl' á ki
Malaga, măl' á ga
Malcolm, măl' kóm
Maldive, măl' dīv
Malet, măl' ét
Malmesbury, mamz' bŭ ri
Malory, măl' ó ri
Malvolio, măl vō' li ō
Manasseh, ma năs' é
Manchu, măn choo'
Manchuria, măn choor' i á
Mandalay, măn' dá lā
Mandeville, măn' dè vil
Manhattan, măn hăt' án
Manitoba, măn i tō' bá
Manitou, măn' i tu
Marat, ma ra'
Marazion, măr á zī' ón
Marconi, mar kō' ni
Margherita, mar gá rē' ta
Marie, ma rē'
Marino, ma rē nō

Marion, măr' i ón
Marischall, mar' shál
Marjoribanks, marsh' bănks
Marlborough, mawl' bó ró
Marmora, mar' mó rá
Marquesas, mar kā' sas
Marseilles, mar sālz'
Martinique, mar ti nēk'
Marylebone, măr' i bŭn
Mascagni, mas ká nyē
Masham (1) [name], [măsh' ám: (2) [place in Yorks], măs' ám
Massachusetts, măs a choo' sets
Matabele, măt á bē' lē
Matapan, ma ta pan'
Mathers, măth' ĕrz
Matheson, măth' é sŏn
Maugham, mawm
Maunsell, măn' sél
Maupassant, mō pa san'
Mauretania, maw rē tā' ni á
Maurice, mor' is, mó rēs'
Mauritius, maw rish' ŭs
Maya, ma' ya
Mayer, mī' ér
Mayo, mā' ō
Mazzini, mat sē' nē
Meagher, ma' ér
Meath, mēth
Medea, mē dē' á
Medici, med' i chē, mā' dē chē
Medina, me dē' ná
Medusa, mē dū' sá
Meerut, mēr' ŭt
Meiklejohn, mikl' jon
Melanesia, mel á nē' shá
Melchizedec, mel kiz' é dek
Menai, men' ī
Mendelssohn, men' del sŏn
Mendoza, men dō' zá
Menzies, ming' is
Meopham, mep' ám
Mercator, mér kā' tór
Mersey, mér' zi
Merthyr Tydfil, mér' thir tĭd' vil
Mesopotamia, mes ó pó tā' mi á
Messalina, mes á lē' ná
Messina, mé sē' ná
Methuen, meth' ū én
Methuselah, mē thū' sé lá
Metternich, met' ér nich
Meux, mŭks, mū
Meyer, mī' ér
Meyerbeer, mī' ér bâr
Meyrick, mer' ik
Miami, mī ăm' i
Micah, mī' ká
Micawber, mi kaw' bér
Michelangelo, mī kěl án' jé lō
Michigan, mish' i gán
Midas, mī' dás
Miguel, mē gāl'
Milan, mi lán'
Millais, mi lā'
Millard, mi lard'
Milwaukee, mil waw' ki
Mirabeau, mir' á bō
Mississippi, mis i sip' i
Missouri, mi soor' i, -zoor' i
Mivart, mī' vart

Mobile, mō bēl'
Modona, mod' é ná
Mohammed, mó hăm' éd
Mohican, mó hē'kán, mō'i kan
Molière, mō lyâr'
Moltke, molt' kē
Moluccas, mó lŭk' áz
Molyneux, mŭl' i nicks, -nŭks, -nŭ
Mombasa, mom ba'sa
Monaco, mon'á kō, mó na' kō
Monaghan, mon' á han
Monck, mŭnk
Moncrieff, mon krēf'
Monckton, mŭnk' tón
Monro, Monroe, mŭn rō'
Monson, mŭn' són
Montague, mon'-, mŭn' tá gū
Montana, mon ta'ná
Montcalm, mont kam'
Monteagle, mŭn tēgl'
Monte Cristo, mon' ti kris' tŏ
Montenegro, mon tē nē' grō
Monterey, mon te rā'
Montessori, mon tē sōr' i
Montevideo, mon te vidā' ō
Montfort, mont' fôrt
Montgomery, mont-, mŭnt gŭm' ér i
Montmorency, mont mó ren' si
Montpellier, mon pel yā'
Montreal, mon' tri awl
Monzie, mó nē'
Morant, mó rant'
Moray, mŭr' i
Mordaunt, môr' dŭnt
Morrell, mŭr' él
Moscow, mos' kō
Moulton, mōl' tón
Mowbray, mō' bri
Mozambique,, mō zăm bēk'
Mozart, mō' zart
Mozley, mōz' li
Muir, mūr
Müller, mul' ér, mil' ér
Muncaster, mŭn' ká stér
Munich, mū' nik
Murat, mū ra'
Murchison, mér' chi són

Naaman, nā' á mán
Nagasaki, na ga sa' kē
Nagpur, nag poor'
Nansen, nan' sén
Naomi, nā' ō-, nā ō' mi
Naphtali, năf' tá li
Napier, nā' pi ér, nā pēr'
Narcissus, nar sis' ŭs
Narragansett, năr á găn'set
Naseby, năz' bi
Nasmyth, nā' smith
Nassau, năs' aw
Natal, ná tăl'
Nathaniel, ná thăn' i él
Nausicaa, naw sik' ā á
Navajo, năv' á hō
Navarre, na var'
Neanderthal, nā an' dér tal
Neave, nēv
Nebuchadnezzar, neb ū kăd nez' ár
Nehemiah, nē hē mī' á

Neil, Neill, nĕl
Neilson, nĕl' sŏn
Nepal, nĕ pawl'
Nepean, nĕ pēn'
Nerissa, nĕ ris' à
Neuchâtel nĕr sha tel'
Nevada, nĕ va' dà
Newburgh, nū' bŭr ŭ
Newfoundland, nū fŭnd land'
Newnes, nūnz
New Orleans, nū ŏr' lè ănz,
  ŏr lēnz
Newquay, nū' ki
Ney, nā
Niagara, nī ăg' à rà
Nicaragua, nik à ra' gwa
Nice, nēs
Nietzsche, nē' chĕ
Niger, nī' jĕr
Nineveh, nin' e vi
Niobe, nī' ŏ bē
Nippon, ni pon'
Nobel, nō bel'
Nollekens, nol' è kĕnz
Nordau, nŏr' dou
Northcote, nôrth' kŏt
Norwich, nor' ich, -ij
Nyassa, nī ăs' à, nya' sa

Obadiah, ŏ bà dī' à
Ober-Ammergau, ŏ bĕr a'
  mĕr gou
Oberon, ŏ' bĕr ŏn, ob' ĕr ŏn
O'Callaghan, ŏ kăl' à hăn
Oceana, ŏ sē' à nà, ŏ shē ăn' à
Ochterlony, och tĕr lŏ' ni
Octavia, ok tā' vi à
Odéon, ŏ dā on'
O'Donoghue, ó dŭn' ó hoo
Odysseus, ŏ dis' ūs
Odyssey, ŏd' i si
Œdipus, ē' di pŭs, ed' i pŭs
Ogilvy, ŏgl' vi
O'Hagan, ŏ hā' gàn
Ohio, ŏ hī' ŏ
Oklahoma, ŏ klà hŏ' mà
Olivier, ŏ liv' i ĕr
Ollivier, ŏ lē vyā'
Olympus, ŏ lim' pŭs
Omagh, ŏ ma'
Omaha, ŏ' mà haw
Omar, ŏ' már
Onions, ŭn' yŭnz
Ontario, on tār' i ŏ
Ophelia, ŏ fē' li à, -fēl' yà
Ophir, ŏ' fir
Orestes, ó res' tēz
Orinoco, or i nŏ' kŏ
Orion, ó rī' ón
Orlando, ôr lăn' dŏ
Orleans, ôr' lè ănz
Ormonde, ôr' mŏnd
Orpheus, ôr' fūs
Osage, ŏ' sàj
Osbourne, oz' bŭrn
O'Shaughnessy, ŏ shaw' nĕ
  si, ŏ shawch' nĕ si
O'Shea, ŏ shā'
Osiris, ó sir' is
Ossian, osh'àn
Oswego, os wē' gŏ
Ottawa, ot' à wà
Ouida, wē' dà
Ouless, oo' lĕs

Ouseley, ooz' li
Outram, oo' trăm
Ovid, ov' id

Paderewski, pa dĕ rev' ski
Padua, păd' ū à
Paganini, pa ga nē' nē
Paget, păj' it
Palermo, pá lĕr' mŏ
Palestrina, pa lás trē' nà
Falgrave, pawl' grăv
Pallas, păl' ás
Pall Mall, păl măl
Palmas, păl' màs
Palmer, pal mĕr
Palmerston, pa' mĕr stŏn
Pamela (1) [Richardson],
  păm' è là; (2) [Sidney],
  pá mē' là
Panama, păn à ma'
Pandora, păn dŏr' à
Pantagruel, păn tăg' ru el
Paolo, pa' ŏ lŏ
Papua, pa' pu à
Paracelsus, păr à sel' sùs
Paraguay, păr à gwā', pa ra
  gwī
Paris, pă' ris
Parnassus, par năs ùs
Parsifal, par' si fal
Parthenope, par then' ŏ pē
Pasteur, pas tur'
Paterson, păt' ĕr sòn
Patiala, pŭt i à' la
Pauncefote, pawns' fut
Pavia, pa vē' a
Peary, pēr' i
Pedro, pē drŏ
Pegasus, peg' à sùs
Peking, pē king'
Pelion, pē' li ón
Pelissier, pè lē syā'
Peloponnesus, pel ó pó nē'
  sùs
Pembroke, pem' bruk
Penang, pĕ năng'
Penelope, pe nel' ó pē
Penmaenmawr, pen mā' ĕn
  mour
Pennefather, pen' i fa thĕr
Pennycuick, pen' i kuk
Penobscot, pe nob' skŏt
Penrhyn, pen' rin
Penrith, pen' rith
Pepys, pēps
Perdita, pĕr' di tà
Pernambuco, per nam boo' kŏ
Perowne, pé rŏn'
Perseus, pĕr' sŭs
Peru, pè roo'
Perugia, pe roo' ja
Peshawar, pĕ shawr'
Peto, pē' tŏ
Petra, pē' trà
Petrarch, pē' trark
Petre, pē' tĕr
Petrie, pe' tri
Pharaoh, fâr' ŏ
Philadelphia, fil à del' fi à
Philemon, fī lē' mòn
Philippe, fē lēp'
Philippine, fil' i pin, -pīn
Phineas, fin' è ăs
Phœbe, fē' bē

Piedmont, pēd' mont
Pierre, pyâr
Pierrepont, pĕr' point
Pietermaritzburg, pē ter ma'
  ritz berg
Pinero, pi nâr' ŏ
Piozzi, pē ot'si
Piræus, pī rē' ùs
Pirie, pir' i
Pitcairn, pit' kârn
Pitti, pit' ē
Pizarro, pi zar' ŏ
Plantagenet, plăn tăj' è net
Pleydell, pled' él
Plinlimmon, plin lim' ón
Pliny, plin' i
Pleiades, plī' à dēz
Plumptre, plŭmp' tĕr
Plutarch, ploo' tark
Poe, pó
Poincaré, pwan ka rā'
Pole, pool
Pole Carew, pool kâr' i
Polk, pŏk
Pollux, pol' ûks
Polwarth, pol' wòrth
Pomona, pó mŏ' nà
Pompadour, pom pa door'
Pompeii, pŏm pā' yē
Ponsonby, pŭn' sòn bi
Pontefract, pon' tè frăkt
Pontiac, pon' tī àk
Popocatepetl, pó pŏ kà tā
  petl', -tā' petl
Portia, pôr' shī à
Porto Rico, pôr' tŏ rē' kŏ
Port Said, pôrt săd
Postlewaite, posl' thwāt
Potomac, pó tŏ' măk
Potosi, pŏ tŏ sē'
Poughkeepsie, pŏ kip' si
Poulett, paw' let
Powell, pou' él, pŏ' él
Powerscourt, poorz' kôrt
Powhatan, pou à tăn'
Powlett, paw' let
Powys, pŏ' is, pou' is
Praed, prăd
Prague, prag
Pretyman, prit' i măn
Probyn, prob' in
Procrustes, prŏ krŭs' tēz
Prometheus, prŏ mē' thûs
Proserpine, pros' ĕr pīn, -pin
Prospero, pros' pĕr ŏ
Prothero, proth' ĕr ŏ
Prowse, prouz
Psyche, sī' kē
Ptolemy, tol' è mi
Puccini, poo chē' nē
Pueblo, pweb' lŏ
Puget, pū' jēt
Pugh, pū
Pugin, pū' jin
Pulteney, pŏlt' nē
Punjab, pŭn jab'
Pusey, pū' zi
Pushkin, push' kin
Pwll-heli, puthl-, puhl hā' lē
Pygmalion, pig mā' lē on
Pyramus, pir' à mŭs
Pyrenees, pir' è nēz
Pytchley, pīch' li
Pythagoras, pi thăg' ó răs

Quebec, kwē bek'
Queenstown, kwēnz' toun, -tón
Queux, kū
Quichua, kēch' wa
Quiller-Couch, kwil' ēr kooch
Quirinal, kwir' i nál
Quito, kē' tō

Rabelais, ra bē lā'
Rachel (1), rā' chel; (2) [F.], ra shel'
Raeburn, rā' burn
Ralegh, Releigh, raw' li, ra' li
Ralph, rälf, räf, raf
Rameses, răm' ē sēz
Ranelagh, răn' e lä
Ranfurly, răn' fŭr li
Rangoon, răng goon'
Raoul, ra ul', roul
Raphael, răf' á ĕl
Rappahannock, răp á hăn' ŏk
Rashleigh, rash' li
Rasselas, răs' ĕ lăs
Rathlin, răth' lin
Rathmines, răth mīnz
Rawalpindi, raw ál pin' dē
Rayleigh, rā' li
Reading, red' ing
Reay, rā
Reith, rēth
Rembrandt, rem' brănt
Renaud, Renault, rē nō'
Rensselaer, ren'sē lēr
Renwick, ren' ik
Réunion, rā oo nē on'
Reuter, roi' tēr
Reykjavik, rā' kyá vēk
Rhodes, rōdz
Rhodesia, rō dē' zyá, -syá
Rialto, ri ál' tō, rē al' tō
Richelieu, rēsh' ē lū, rēsh lyēr'
Riddell, ridl
Rievaulx, riv' ērz
Rigi, rē' gē
Rigoletto, rē gō let' ō
Rio de Janeiro, rē' ō dē zha nār' ō
Rio Grande, rē' ō gran' di
Riordan, rēr' dán
Ripon, rip' ón
Riviera, rē vyár' a
Roanoke, rō' á nōk
Robartes, rō barts'
Robeson, rō' bē sŏn
Robespierre, rō' bēs pēr
Rochdale, roch' dāl
Rockefeller, rok' ē fel ēr
Rodriguez, rō drē gās
Roget, rō zhá
Rolleston, rōl' stŏn
Romford, rŭm' fŏrd
Romilly, rom' li, -i li
Romney, rŭm' ni
Romola, rom' ó lä
Romsey, rŭm' zi
Romulus, rom' ū lŭs
Röntgen, runt' gén
Roosevelt, rōz' velt
Rosa, rō zá
Rosalind, roz' á lind
Rosamund, roz' á mŭnd
Rosetta, rō zet' á

Rosinante, roz i năn' ti
Rosselti, rō sĕt' i
Rosse, ros
Rossini, rō sē' nē
Rotherhithe, roth' ēr hīth
Rothes, roth' ēz
Rothesay, roth' sā
Rothschild, roths' chīld
Rothwell, roth' wĕl
Rotorua, rot ō roo' a
Rouen, roo'an
Rouse, roos
Rousseau, roo sō'
Rowan, rō' án
Rowena, rō ē' nä
Rowland, rō' lånd
Rowley, rou' li
Roxburgh, roks' bŭ ru, -bŭrg
Rubaiyat, roo bī yat'
Rudolph, roo' dŏlf
Ruislip, rīz' lip
Ruthven, riv' ĕn, ruth' ven

Sabrina, sä brī' ná
Sacharissa, săk á ris' á
Sacheverell, sä shev' ēr el
Sagittarius, săj i tár' i ŭs
Sahara, sä ha' rá
Saint Albans, sănt awl' bánz
St. Clair, sin' klär
St Gothard, sánt goth' árd
Saint Helena, sănt ē lē' ná
St. John (pers. name), sin' jón
St. Leger, (pers. name), sil' ēn jēr; (horse-race), sánt lej' ēr
St. Maur, sē' mór, sănt mawr'
St. Neots, sănt nē' óts
Saint-Saens, săn sans'
Sala, sa' lä
Saladin, săl' á din
Salamanca, săl á măng' ká
Salisbury, solz' bŭ ri
Salome, sá lō' mē
Salonika, sa lō nē' ká
Saltoun, sawl' tun
Salzburg, salts' boorgh
Samarkand, sa mar kánd'
Samoa, sá mō á
Sancho, săn' chō
Sandes, Sandys, sănds
Sanquhar, săng' kér
San Remo, san rä' mō
San Salvador, san sal va dōr'
Santa Cruz, sán' tá krooz
Santa Fé, săn' tá fä
Santiago, san tē a' gō
Sappho, săf' ō
Saratoga, sä rá tō' gá
Sardanapalus, sar dá ná pä' lŭs
Sargasso, sar găs' ō
Saskatchewan, săs kăch' ē won
Savonarola, săv ó nä rō' lä
Savoy, sá voi'
Scafell, skaw' fĕl
Scarborough, skar' brō
Schenectady, skē nek' tá di
Scheveningen, skä' vén ing én
Schiehallion, shē häl' i òn
Schiller, shil' ēr
Schlegel, shlä' gĕl

Schmidt, shmit
Schofield, skō' fēld
Schopenhauer, shō' pēn hou ér
Schreiner, shrī' nēr
Schubert, shoo' bērt
Schuylkill, skool' kil
Sclater, slä'tēr
Scone, skon, skōn
Scrymgeour, skrim' jēr
Scutari, skoo' tá rē
Scylla, sil' á
Sean, shawn
Searle, sĕrl
Seattle, sē ätl'
Sebastopol, sē băs' tō pol
Sedan, sē dän'
Seine, sän
Selous, sē loo'
Semele, sem' ē lē
Semiramis, sē mir' á mis
Semphill, sem' pil
Seneca, sen' ē kä
Senegal, sen ē gawl'
Seoul, sä ool'
Sergeant, Serjeant, sar' jént
Seton, Setoun, sē' tón
Seville, sev' il
Sèvres, sävr
Seward, sū' ård
Sewell, sū' ĕl
Seychelles, sä shel'
Seymour, sē' mór
Shairp, sharp
Shanghai, shăng hī'
Shechem, shē' kém
Sheila, shē' lá
Shenandoah, shen án dō' á
Sheraton, sher' á tón
Sherbourne, shēr' bŭrn
Shiloh, shī' lō
Shostakovich, shos ta ko vich
Shrewsbury, shrōz' bēr i
Siam, sī äm'
Sidebotham, sīd' bot óm
Siegfried, sēg' frēd
Sienkiewicz, shen kyä' vich
Sierra Leone, si er' á lē ō' ni
Sierra Nevada, si er' á nē va' dá
Sikh, sik
Silesia, sī lē' shi á
Siloam, sī lō' ám
Silvanus, sil vä' nŭs
Silvester, sil ves' tér
Simplon, sim' plon
Sinai, sī' ni, -ná ī
Singapore, sing gá pōr'
Sioux, soo
Sirius, sir' i ŭs
Sistine, sis' tēn, -tin
Skager-Rack, skäg' ēr răk
Skiddaw, skid' aw
Skrine, skrēn
Slidell, sli del'
Sligo, slī' gō
Slough, slou
Smyth, smith, smith
Socrates, sok' rá tēz
Sofia, sō fē' yá
Solent, sō' lént
Somaliland, sō ma' li lănd
Somers, sŭm' ērz
Somerset, sŭm' ēr set

Somervell, sŭm' ĕr vel
Sondes, sondz
Sorel, só rel'
Sotheby, sŭth' ĕ bi
Sousa, soo' zà
Southey, sŭth' ĭ, sou' thi
Southwark, suth' àrk
Spa, spa
Speight, spāt
Spinoza, spi nō' zà
Staël, sta' ĕl
Stalbridge, stawl' brij
Stamboul, stăm bool'
Stanhope, stăn' óp
Stalin, sta' lin
Stéphanie, stä fa nē'
Stephens, stē' vĕnz
Stephenson, stē' vĕn sŏn
Steyne, stīn, stăn
Stoke Poges, stōk pō' jes
Stothard, stoth' àrd
Stoughton, stō' tŏn, stou' tŏn
Stourton, stēr' tŏn
Stowe, stō
Stowell, stō' ĕl
Strachan, Strahan, (Eng.)
  strawn; (Scots.) stra' chàn
Strachey, strā' chi
Stranraer, străn rar'
Strathallan, străth ăl' àn
Strathcona, străth kō' nà
Stratheden, străth ē' dĕn
Strathmore, străth mōr'
Stratton, străt' ŏn
Strauss, strous
Streatham, stret' ăm
Stuyvesant, sti' ve sànt
Styx, stiks
Suakin, swa' kĕn
Sudeley, sūd' li
Sue, sū
Suetonius, sū ē tō' nĭ ŭs
Suez, soo ez'
Sumatra, soo ma' trà
Susanna, soo zăn' à
Susquehanna, sŭs kwĕ hăn' à
Sutro, soo' trō
Suwanee, su wa' nē, swa nē
Swahili, swa hīl' ĭ
Sweyn, swān
Swiney, swin' ĭ
Symonds, sim' ondz
Symons, sim' ŏnz
Synge, sing
Syracuse, sĭr' à kūs

Tacoma, tà kō' mà
Taft, taft
Taliesin, tăl' ĭ ā sin
Talleyrand, tăl' ĭ rând
Talmage, tăl' măj
Tammany, tăm' à ni
Tampico, tăm pē' kō
Tancred, tăng' krĕd
Tanganyika, tăn gà nē' kà
Tangier, tăn jēr'
Tangye, tăng' ĭ
Tannhäuser, tan' hoi zĕr
Tantalus, tăn' tà lŭs
Tara, ta' rà
Tasmania, tăz mā' ni à
Tauchnitz, touch' nits
Tecumseh, tē kŭm' sĕ

Teheran, tā hé ran'
Teignmouth, tin' mŭth
Tenerife, ten ĕr ēf'
Tennessee, ten ĕ sē'
Teresa, tē rē' zà
Terpsichore, tĕrp sik' ŏ rē
Tetrazzini, tā trat sē' nē
Thaddeus, thăd' ĕ ŭs
Thais, thā' is
Thame, tăm
Thames, temz
Thebes, thēbz
Theobald, thē' ŏ bawld
Theodora, thē ŏ dōr' à
Thérèse, tā räz'
Thermopylæ, thĕr mop' ĭ lē
Theseus, thē' sūs
Thesiger, thes' ĭ jĕr
Thessalonica, thes à lŏ nī' kà
Thisbe, thiz' bē
Thomas, tom' às
Thompson, tom' sŏn
Thoreau, tho' rō, tho rō'
Thorold, thŭr' ŏld
Thucydides, thū sid' ĭ dēz
Thule, thūl' lē
Thynne, thin
Tiberius, tī bēr' ĭ ŭs
Tibet, tĭ bet', tib' ĕt
Tibullus, tĭ bŭl' ŭs
Tichborne, tich' bŭrn
Ticonderoga, tī kon dē rō' gà
Tientsin, tē ent sēn
Tiflis, tē' flēs', tif' lis
Tighe, tī
Timbuktu, tim bŭk' too
Timon, tī' mŏn
Tintagel, tin tăj' ĕl
Titania, tī tān' ĭ à
Titian, tish' àn
Titicaca, tit ē ka' kà
Tobago, tŏ bā' gō
Tobolsk, tŏ bolsk'
Todmorden, tod' mŏr dĕn
Tokay, tŏ kā'
Tokio, tō' kĭ ō
Toledo, tŏ lē' dō
Tollemache, tol' mash
Tolstoy, tol stoi'
Topeka, tŏ pē' kà
Torquay, tŏr kē'
Totnes, tot' nēz
Towcester, tōst' ĕr
Townshend, toun' zend
Toynbee, toin' bē
Trafalgar, trà fàl' gàr
Tralee, trà lē'
Transvaal, trănz' val
Traquair, trà kwâr'
Travers, trăv' ĕrz
Trebizond, treb' ĭ zond
Trefusis, trē fū' sis
Tregelles, trē gel' ĕs
Treloar, trē lōr'
Trevelyan, trē vel' yàn
Treves, trēvz
Trevithick, trev' ĭ thik
Trevor, trē' vŏr, trev' ŏr
Trinidad, trin ĭ dăd'
Tripoli, trip' ŏ li
Trocadéro, trō ka dā rō'
Trollope, trol'óp
Troubridge, troo' brij
Tschaikovsky, chī kof' skē

Tuileries, twē' lér iz
Tullibardine, tŭl ĭ bar' dēn
Tulloch, tŭl' ŏch
Tunbridge, tŭn' brij
Turkestan, tĕr kĕ stan'
Tuscarora, tŭs kà rōr' à
Tussaud, tu sō'
Tutankhamen, too tăn' kà
  mén
Tuxedo, tŭk sē' dō
Tybalt, tib' ălt
Tyndale, tin'dăl
Tynemouth, tin' mŭth
Tyrconnel, tir kon' ĕl
Tyrol, tir' ŏl
Tyrone, tī rōn'
Tyrwhitt, tir' it
Tytler, tīt' lér

Uig, oo' ĭg
Uist, oo' ist
Ukraine, ū krān,
Ulick, ū' lik
Ulloa, ool yō' a
Ulysses, ū lis' ēz
Upsala, up sa' la
Ural, ūr' àl
Uranus, ūr' à nŭs
Uriah, ū rī' à
Urquhart, ĕr' kàrt
Ursula, ĕr' sū là
Uruguay, ū' ru gwā, ū ru gwī
Ushant, ŭsh' ànt
Utah, ū' taw
Utrecht, ū' trekt
Uttoxeter, uk' sĕ tĕr, ŭt tok'
  sĕ tér

Valparaiso, văl pà rī' so, -zō
Vanbrough, văn' broo
Vancouver, văn koo' vĕr
Van Dyck, văn dīk'
Vansittart, văn sit' àrt
Vassar, vas' àr
Vaughan, vawn
Vaux, vō, vōks
Vauxhall, vawks-, voks hawl'
Vavasour, văv' sŭr
Vega, vā' gà
Veitch, vēch
Velazquez, ve lăs' kez
Venezuela, ven ē zwē' là
Venice, ven' is
Verdi, vâr dē'
Vermont, vĕr mont'
Veronica, vē ron' ĭ kà
Versailles, vĕr sălz'
Verulam, ver' u lăm
Vespasian, ves pā' zhĭ àn
Vichy, vish' ĭ, vē shē'
Vigo, vē-, vī' gō
Viola, vī' ŏ là, vē ō' là
Virgil, vĕr' jil
Vladivostock, vla dē vos tok'
Volpone, vol pō' nē
Voltaire, vol târ'
Vosges, vōzh
Vyvyan, viv' ĭ àn

Wabash, waw' băsh
Waddington, wod' ing tŏn
Wagga wagga, wog'à wog'à
Wagner, vag' nĕr, wăg' nĕr
Waldegrave, wol' grăv

Walford, wol' fôrd
Walloon, wǎ loon'
Walmesley, wawmz' li
Walsingham, wol' sing ăm
Waltham, wol' tăm
Walworth, wol' wôrth
Warham, wôr' ăm
Warkworth, wawk' wôrth
Warre, wôr
Warwick, wor' ik
Wauchope, waw' chŏp
Waugh, waw
Weber, vā' bĕr
Wednesbury, wenz' bŭ ri
Weimar, vi' mar
Weir, wēr
Welles, welz
Wellesley, welz' li, wez' li
Welwyn, wel' in
Wemyss, wēmz
Weobley, web' li
Wesley, wes' li
Whewell, hū' ĕl
Whitefield, wit' fēld
Whitelock, wit' lok
Whytham, wīt' ăm
Widnes, wid' nez
Wilhelmina, wil hel mē' nǎ

Willard, wi lard'
Willesden, wilz' dĕn
Winchelsea, winchl' sē
Windsor, win' zôr
Winstanley, win' stan li
Wisconsin, wis kon' sin
Wishart, wish' ărt
Witwatersrand, vit' va tĕrz rant
Wodehouse, wud' hous
Wolcott, wul' kŏt
Wollaston, wul' ă stŏn
Wollstonecraft, wul' stŏn krăft
Wolseley, wulz' li
Wolsey, wul' zi
Wombwell, woom' wel
Woolwich, wul' ich, -ij
Worcester, wus' tĕr
Wortley, wĕrt' li
Wrensfordsley, renz' li
Wrey, rā
Wrotham, root' ăm
Wrottesley, rots' li
Wroughton, raw' tŏn
Wycherley, wich' er li
Wykeham, wik' ăm
Wymondham, wind' ăm

Wyndham, wind' ăm
Wyoming, wī ō' ming

Xanadu, zăn' ă doo
Xavier, za' vi êr
Xenophon, zen' ŏ fŏn

Yeats, yāts, yĕts
Yeovil, yŏ' vil
Yerburgh, yar' bŭ rŭ
Yerkes, yĕr' kĕz
Yosemite, yŏ sem' i tē
Ypres, ēpr
Yucatan, ū kă tan'

Zachariah, zăk ă ri' ă
Zambesi, zam bē' zi
Zante, zan' tă
Zarathustra, za ră thoos' tră
Zechariah, zek ă ri' ă
Zephaniah, zef ă ni' ă
Zeus, zūs
Zola, zō' lă
Zoroaster, zō rŏ ăs' tĕr
Zouche, zoosh
Zurich, zū' rik

ABBREVIATIONS IN COMMON USE

Initials indicating Associates, Fellows and Members of learned and other bodies are too numerous to be included in this Concise List

A., Academy, Academician; America; Associate; (*Cinema*) programme for adults only; (*Mil.*) administration.

A, (*Chem.*) Argon.

a., Acre; adjective; alto; *anno* (in the year); *ante* (before).

@, For, at, to (in quoting prices).

A1, First-class (ship in Lloyd's register).

A.A., Associate in Arts; Automobile Association; Army Act; anti-aircraft.

A.A.A., Amateur Athletic Association.

A.A.F., Auxiliary Air Force.

A.A.G., Assistant-Adjutant-General.

A.B. [L. *Artium Baccalaureus*], Bachelor of Arts; able-bodied seaman.

A.B.A., Amateur Boxing Association.

abbr., Abbreviated, abbreviation.

A.B.C., The alphabet; Aerated Bread Company; a railway guide.

A.B.C.A., Army Bureau of Current Affairs.

ab init. [L. *ab. initio*], From the beginning.

abl., Ablative.

abor., Aborigines, aboriginal.

Abp., Archbishop.

abr., Abridged, abridgment.

A.B.S., Able-bodied seaman.

A.C., Aero Club; Alpine Club; [L. *Ante Christum*], before Christ; Alternating Current; Army, Air Council; Army Corps.

a/c., Account.

A.C.A., Associate of the Institute of Chartered Accountants.

Acad., Academy, Academician.

A.C.C., Army Catering Corps.

A/CC., Aircraft carrier.

acc., Acceptance, accepted; accusative; account.

accel. [It. *accelerando*], (*Mus.*) With gradually increasing velocity.

acct., Account, accountant.

A.C.G., Assistant Chaplain-General.

A.C.G.B., Arts Council of Great Britain (successor (1945) to C.E.M.A.).

A.C.I.G.S., Assistant Chief of the Imperial General Staff.

A.C.M., Air Chief Marshal.

A.D. [L. *anno Domini*], In the year of our Lord.

a.d., After date; [L. *ante diem*], before the day.

ad., Advertisement.

adag., (*Mus.*) *Adagio*

A.D.C., Aide-de-camp.

A.D. Corps, Army Dental Corps.

ad eund. [L. *ad eundem gradum*], (Admitted) to the same degree.

ad inf. [L. *ad infinitum*], To infinity; without limit.

ad int. [L. *ad interim*], In or for the meantime.

Adj., Adjutant.

adj., Adjective.

Adj.-Gen., Adjutant-General.

ad lib. [L. *ad libitum*], At pleasure; to any desired extent.

Adm., Admiral, Admiralty

adv., Adverb, adverbially; [L. *adversus*], against; advocate.

ad val. [L. *ad valorem*], According to the value.

advert., advt., Advertisement.

Æ, (*Shipping*) 3rd class at Lloyd's.

A.E.A., Air Efficiency Award.

Æn., Æneid.

æsth., Æsthetics.

æt., ætat. [L. *ætatis*], In the year of his age, aged.

A.E.U., Amalgamated Engineers' Union.

A.F., Admiral of the Fleet; Army Form.

A.F.A., Associate of the Faculty of Actuaries; Amateur Football (*also* Fencing) Association.

A.F.C., Air Force Cross; Australian Flying Corps.

aff., Affirmative, affirming.

afft., Affidavit.

A.F.M., Air Force Medal.

A.F.S., Auxiliary Fire Service.

Afr., Africa, African.

Ag [L. *argentum*], (*Chem.*) Silver.

A.G., Adjutant-General, Accountant-General, Agent-General (of Colonies); Attorney-General; [G. *Aktiengesellschaft*], joint-stock or limited-liability company.

agr., agric., Agriculture, agricultural, agriculturist.

agt., Against; agent.

A.H. [L. *anno Hegiræ*], In the year of the Hegira (A.D. 622), the Mohammedan era.

A.H.S. [L. *anno humanæ salutis*], In the year of human salvation.

A.I.D., Army Intelligence Department.

A.I.G., Assistant-Inspector-General.

A.K.C., Associate of King's College, London.

Al, (*Chem.*) Aluminium.

al. [L. *alias*], Otherwise; under another name.

Ala., Alabama.

Alas., Alaska.

Alb., Albanian; Albert.

Ald., Alderman.

Alex., Alexander.

Alf., Alfred.

Alg., Algernon; Algiers; algebra.

all' otta. [It. *all' ottava, all' 8va*], (*Mus.*) An octave above that written.

A.L.S., Associate Fellow of the Linnean Society; autograph letter signed.

Alt. [F. *Altesse*], Highness.

alt., Alternate, alternating; altitude.

Alta., Alberta, Canada.

Alum., Alumnus.

A.M. [L. *Artium Magister*], Master of Arts (also M.A.); Albert Medal; [L. *anno mundi*], In the year of the world; Air Ministry; Air Marshal; associate member.

a.m. [L. *ante meridiem*], Before noon.

Am., America, American.

A.M.D., Army Medical Department.

A.M.D.G. [L. *ad majorem Dei Gloriam*], To the greater Glory of God.

Amer., America, American.

A.M.G.O.T., Allied Military Government of Occupied Territories.

A.M.O., Administrative Medical Officer; Air Ministry Order.

amp., Ampere, electrical unit.

A.M.S., Army Medical Services.

an. [L. *anno*], In the year; [*annum*], as in *per an.*

anal., Analogy, analogous; analysis; analytic, analytical.

anat., Anatomy, anatomical, anatomist.

anc., Ancient.

An. Dom. [A.D.].

Angl. [L. *anglice*], In English.

Ann. [L. *annales*], Annals; [L. *anni*], years; [L. *anno*], in the year; annual.

annot., Annotated.

anon., Anonymous.

A.N.S., Army Nursing Service.

ans., Answer.

Ant., Antony; Antigua.

ant., Antiquities; antonym.

anthrop., Anthropology, anthropological.

antiq., Antiquary, antiquarian.

A.N.Z.A.C., Australian and New Zealand Army Corps.

A.O., Army Order.

a/o., Account of.

A.O.C. [L. *anno orbis conditi*], in the year of the Creation; [R.A.O.C.].

A.O.D., Army Ordnance Department; Ancient Order of Druids.

A.O.F., Ancient Order of Foresters.

A.O.H., Ancient Order of Hibernians.

aor., Aorist.

A.O.S., Ancient Order of Shepherds.

A. P., Associated Presbyterian; Associated Press; armour-piercing.

a.p., Above proof.

Ap., Apostle; April.

aph., Aphorism.

A.P.M., Assistant Provost Marshal.

A.P.O., Army Post Office.

Apoc., Apocalypse.

Apocr., Apocrypha.

apog., Apogee.

App., Apostles.

app., Appendix; apparently.

appr., Apprentice.

appro., Approbation, approval.

approx., Approximate, approximately, approximation.

Apr., April.

A.P.R.C. [L. *anno post Romam conditam*], In the year after the building of Rome (754 B.C.).

A.P.S., Aborigines Protection Society; Army Postal Service.

aq. [L. *aqua*], Water

A.Q.M.G., Assistant-Quartermaster-General.

A.R. [L. *anno regni*], In the year of the reign.

A.R.A., Associate of the Royal Academy; Amateur Rowing Association.

Arab., Arabia, Arabian, Arabic.

arach., Arachnology.

archæol., Archæology, archæological.

Arch., Archibald; archaic, archaism; archery; archipelago; architect, architecture, architectural.

Archbp. [ABP.].

Archd., Archdeacon; Archduke.

arg., (*Her.*) Argent.

Arg. Rep., Argentine Republic.

A.R.I.B.A., Associate of the Royal Institute of British Architects.

arith., Arithmetic, arithmetical, arithmetician.

Ariz., Arizona.

Ark., Arkansas.

Arm., Armenian; Armoric.

A.R.P., Air Raid Precautions.

A.R.R. [L. *anno regni regis* or *reginæ*], In the year of the King's (or Queen's) reign.

arr., Arranged; arrival, arrivals, arrive, arrived, arrives.

A.R.R.C., Association (or Associate) of the Royal Red Cross.

art., Article; artificial; artillery.

As., Asia, Asian, Asiatic.

As, (*Chem.*) Arsenic.

A.S., Academy of Science; assistant secretary.

A.S. [L. *anno salutis*], In the year of salvation.

A.-S., Anglo-Saxon.

a./s., Account Sale.

A.S.R.S., Amalgamated Society of Railway Servants.

ass., Assistant.

Ass.-Com.-Gen., Assistant Commissary-General.

assoc., Associate, association.

asst., Assistant.

Assyr., Assyria, Assyrian.

astr., Astronomy, astronomer.

astrol., Astrology.

astron., Astronomy.

A/T, Anti-tank.

at., Atomic.

A.T.A.S., Air Transport Auxiliary Service.

A.T.C., Art Teachers' Certificate (South Kensington); Air Training Corps.

At.-Gen., Attorney-General.

Ath., Athabasca; athletic.

Athen., Athenian.

Atl., Atlantic.

atm. pr., Atmospheric pressure.

ats., (*Law*) At the suit of.

atty., Attorney.

at. wt. Atomic weight.

A.U. [L. *anno urbis*], In the year of the city [A.U.C.]; (*Phys.*) Ångström unit.

Au., Augustus.

Au, (*Chem.*) [L. *aurum*], Gold.

A.U.C. [L. *ab urbe condita*, or *anno urbis conditæ*], From the year of the building of the City [Rome, in 754 B.C.].

Aud.-Gen., Auditor-General.

Aug., August; Augustan; Augustus; augmentative.

Aus., Austria, Austrian.

Austral., Australia, Australian, Australasia, Australasian.

auth., Authentic; author, authoress; authority, authorized.

auxil., Auxiliary.

A.V. (*Bib.*), Authorized version; artillery volunteers.

av., Average; avoirdupois.

a.v. [L. *annos vixit*], (He or she) lived (so many) years.

a/v., Ad valorem.

avdp., Avoirdupois.

A.V.M., Air Vice-Marshal.

a.w., Atomic Weight.

ax., Axiom, axiomatic.

az., (*Her.*) Azure.

B., Bachelor; Baron; black (of pencils); Baptist; battle.

b., Born; brother; (*Naut.*) blue sky; (*Cricket*) bowled, bye, byes; (*Mus.*) bass.

B, (*Chem.*) Boron.

B.A., Bachelor of Arts; British Academy; British

America; British Association; Buenos Aires.

Ba, (*Chem.*) Barium.

Bab., (*Bot.*) Babington.

Bach., Bachelor.

B.Agr., Bachelor of Agriculture.

bal., Balance.

Ball., Balliol College, Oxford.

Balt., Baltimore.

B. & F.B.S., British and Foreign Bible Society.

B. & S., (*colloq.*) Brandy and soda.

B.A.O., Bachelor of Obstetrics.

bap., Baptized.

B.A.O.R., British Army of the Rhine.

bar., Barometer; barley-corn; barrel; (*Naut.*) barque.

B. Arch., Bachelor of Architecture.

barr., Barrister.

Bart., Baronet; Bartholomew.

Bart's., St. Bartholomew's Hospital.

batt., Battalion; battery.

Bav., Bavaria, Bavarian.

BB, Very black (of pencils).

BBB, Extremely black (of pencils).

B.B.C., British Broadcasting Corporation.

B.C., Before Christ; Board of Control; Borough Council; British Columbia.

B.Ch. [L. *Baccalaureus Chirurgiæ*], Bachelor of Surgery.

B.Ch.D., Bachelor of Dental Surgery.

B.Chir. [B.CH.].

B.C.L. [L. *Baccalaureus Civilis Legis*], Bachelor of Civil Law; [L. *Baccalaureus Canonicæ Legis*], Bachelor of Canon Law.

B.Comm., Bachelor of Commerce.

B.D., Bachelor of Divinity.

Bd. [G. *Band*], A volume.

bd., Board; bond; bound.

bdle., Bundle.

Bdr., Brigadier; bombardier.

B.D.S., Bachelor of Dental Surgery.

bds., (*Bookbinding*) Boards; bonds.

B.E., Bachelor of Engineering; Board of Education.

Be, (*Chem.*) Beryllium.

b.e., Bill of exchange.

Beds., Bedfordshire.

B.E.F., British Expeditionary Force.

Belg., Belgium, Belgian, Belgic.

B.E.M., British Empire Medal.

B.Eng., Bachelor of Engineering.

Beng., Bengal.

Benj., Benjamin.

Berks, Berkshire.

B. ès L. [F. *Bachelier ès Lettres*], Bachelor of Letters and Arts.

B. ès S. [F. *Bachelier ès Sciences*], Bachelor of Science.

b.f., Beer firkin.

bg., Bag; being.

B'ham, Birmingham.

B'head, Birkenhead.

b.h.p., Brake horse-power.

B.Hond., British Honduras.

B.Hy., Bachelor of Hygiene.

Bi, (*Chem.*) Bismuth.

Bib., Bible, biblical.

bibl. [L. *bibliotheca*], Library.

bibliog., Bibliographer, bibliographic, bibliographical, bibliography.

B.I.F., British Industries Fair.

biog., Biographer, biographic, biographical, biography.

biol., Biology, biological.

B.I.S., Bank of International Settlements.

bis., Bissextile.

Bisc., Biscayan.

bk., Bank; book; barque.

bkg., Banking.

bkrpt., Bankrupt.

bkt., Basket.

B.L., Black letter; British Legion; Bachelor of Law; breech-loader.

B/L, Bill of lading.

bl., Bale; barrel.

bldg., Building.

B.Litt., Bachelor of Letters.

blk., Black; block.

B.LL., Bachelor of Laws.

B.L.R., Breech-loading rifle.

B.M., Bachelor of Medicine; [L. *Beata Maria*], the Blessed Virgin; [L. *beatæ memoriæ*], of blessed memory; Brigade Major; British Museum; (*Survey.*) bench mark; [L. *bene merenti*], to the well-deserving; bronze medallist (Bisley).

B.M.A., British Medical Association.

B.M.E., Batchelor of Mining Engineering

B.M.J., British Medical Journal.

B.Mus., Bachelor of Music.

Bn., Battalion.

B.N.C., Brasenose College, Oxford.

b.o., Branch office; buyer's option.

B.O.A.C., British Overseas Airways Corporation.

Bodl., Bodleian.

B. of E., Board of Education; Bank of England.

B. of H., Board of Health.

B. of T., Board of Trade.

Boh., Bohem., Bohemia, Bohemian.

Bol., Bolivia, Bolivian.

Bo'ness, orig. Borrowstounness (Linlithgowshire).

B.O.P., Boy's Own Paper.

bor., Borough.

bot., Botany, botanical, botanist; bought; bottle.

B.P., British public; British pharmacopœia; Baden-Powell.

b.p., Below proof (of spirits); boiling point; bill of parcels; bills payable; [L. *bonum publicum*], the public good.

Bp., Bishop.

B.P.B., Bank post bills.

bpl., Birthplace.

Bp. Suff., Bishop Suffragan.

bque., (*Naut.*) Barque.

B.R., British Railways.

Br., British.

Br, (*Chem.*) Bromine.

br., (*Naut.*) Brig.

b.r., Bills receivable.

Braz., Brazil, Brazilian.

Br. Col., British Columbia.

B.R.C.S., British Red Cross Society.

Brd., Board.

Brec., Breconshire.

Bret., Breton.

brev., Brevet, breveted; (*Printing*) brevier.

brig., Brigade, brigadier.

Brig.-Gen., Brigadier-General.

Brit., Britain, British, Britannia, Britannica, Britannicus.

Brit. Mus., British Museum.

Britt. [L. *Britanniarum*], Of all the Britains (on coins).

bro., brother.

bros., brothers.

Brum, (*slang*) Brummagem (Birmingham).

Brux.[F. *Bruxelles*], Brussels.

B.S., Bachelor of Surgery; Blessed Sacrament.

b.s., Balance sheet, bill of sale.

B.S.A., Birmingham Small Arms Co.; British South Africa.

B.Sc., Bachelor of Science.

B.Sc.(Econ.), Bachelor of Science in the Faculty of Economics.

B.Sc.(Eng.), Bachelor of Science in the Faculty of Engineering.

B.S.T., British Summer Time.

Bt., Baronet; bought.

B.Th., Bachelor of Theology.

B.Th.U., British Thermal Unit.

B.T.U., (*Elec.*) Board of Trade unit, or kilowatt hour.

bu., Bushel.

Bucks, Buckinghamshire.

B.U.F., British Union of Fascists.

bul., Bulletin.

Bulg., Bulgaria, Bulgarian.

bull., Bulletin.

B.U.P., British United Press.

bur., Buried.

burg., Burgess; burgomaster.

bus., Bushel.

b.v. [L. *bene vale*], Farewell.

B.V.M. [L. *Beata Virgo Maria*], The Blessed Virgin Mary.

B.W., Board of Works.

B.W.G., Birmingham wire gauge.

B.W.I., British West Indies.

C, 100; (*Chem.*) Carbon.

C., Catholic; centigrade; Chancellor; Chancery; Church; common metre (of hymns); congress; contralto; conservative; (*Mus.*) counter-tenor; Court; caught; chapter.

c., Cent; centigramme; centime; (*Naut.*) cloudy; constable; cubic; (*Elec.*) current.

c., Circa, circiter, circum (about); calorie(s).

c. & b., (*Cricket*) Caught and bowled.

C.A., Chartered Accountant; Chief Accountant; commercial agent; Confederate Army; Controller of Accounts; County Alderman; Croquet Association.

Ca, (*Chem.*) Calcium.

ca., Cases; cathode.

Cæs., Cæsar.

Cal., California; (*Pharm.*) calomel.

cal., Calendar; calibre.

cal. [It.] (*Mus.*) *Calando*.

cam., Camouflage.

Camb., Cambridge.

Cambs, Cambridgeshire.

Camd. Soc., Camden Society.

Can., Canada.

can., Canon; (*Mus.*) *canto*, *cantoris*.

Cant., Canterbury; (*Relig.*) canticles; canto.

Cantab. [L. *Cantabrigiensis*], Of Cambridge.

Cantuar. [L. *Cantuaria*], Canterbury; [L. *Cantuariensis*], of Canterbury (signature of the Archbishop of Canterbury).

cap., Capital, capital letter; [L. *capitulum*], little chapter; [L. *caput*], head; section; chapter; foolscap.

Capt., Captain.

Car. [L. *Carolus*], Charles; Carolina.

car., Carat.

Card., Cardinal.

cash., Cashier.

cat., Catalogue, catalogued,

cataloguing, cataloguer (*Med.*) [L. *cataplasma*], a poultice; catechism.

Cath., Catherine; Catholic; Cathedral.

caus., Cause, causation, causative.

Cav., Cavalry.

cav., (*Law*) Caveat.

C.B., Cape Breton; Cavalry Brigade; Chief Baron; (*Law*) Common Bench Reports and Scott's Reports; Companion of the Order of the Bath; (*Mil.*) confined to barracks; County borough.

Cb, (*Chem.*) Columbium.

C.B.E., Commander of the Order of the British Empire.

C.C., Caius College (Cambridge); Chamber of Commerce; Chess Club; Circuit Court; City Council; City Councillor; Civil Court; Common Councilman; Consular Clerk; County Commmissioner; County Councillor; County Council; County Clerk; Cricket Club; Cycling Club; Crown Clerk; Curate-in-charge.

c.c. [F. *compte courant*], Account current; cubic centimetre; cubic contents.

C.C.A., Chief Clerk of the Admiralty.

C.C.C., Corpus Christi College (Oxford); Central Criminal Court.

C.C.P., Code of Civil Procedure; Court of Common Pleas; Chief Commissioner of Police.

C.C.S., Casualty Clearing Station.

C.D., Coast Defence(s); Civil Defence; *Corps Diplomatique*.

Cd, (*Chem.*) Cadmium.

Cd., Command Paper (to 1918 inclusive).

c.d. [L. *cum dividendo*], With dividend.

c.d.v., Carte-de-visite.

C.E., Chief Engineer; Church of England; Civil Engineer.

Ce, (*Chem.*) Cerium.

cel., Celebrated.

Cels., Celsius.

Celt., Celtic.

C.E.M.A., Council for the Encouragement of Music and the Arts (see A.C.G.B.).

cent., Centigrade; central; century.

cert., certif., Certificate, certificated; certify; certainty.

Cestr. [L. *Cestriensis*], Of Chester (Bishop of Chester's signature).

cet. par. [L. *ceteris paribus*], Other things being equal.

C.F., Chaplain to the Forces.

cf., Calf; [L. *confer*], compare.

c.f.i., Cost, freight, and insurance.

C.G., Coast-Guard; Captain-General; Captain of the Guard; Coldstream Guards; Commissary-General; Consul-General.

cg., Centigram.

C.G.H., Cape of Good Hope.

C.G.M., Conspicuous Gallantry Medal.

C.G.S., centimetre-gramme-second (combined unit of length, mass and time).

C.G.T., Confédération Générale du Travail (the French T.U.C.). Compagnie Générale Transatlantique.

C.H., Captain of the Horse; Companion of Honour; Court House; Custom House.

Ch., China, Chinese; Church.

ch., Chairman; chaldron; champion (of dogs); chapter; chief; child; (*Knitting*) chain; choir organ; (of horses) chestnut.

Chamb., Chamberlain.

Chanc. Ex., Chancellor of the Exchequer.

Chap., Chaplain; chapter.

Chas., Charles.

Ch.B. [L. *Chirurgiæ Baccalaureus*], Bachelor of Surgery.

chbrs., Chambers.

Ch. Ch., Christ Church (Oxford).

chem., Chemical, chemist, etc.

Chesh., Cheshire.

chev., (*Her.*) Chevron; chevalier; knight.

Chi., Chicago.

Chin., China, Chinese.

Ch.M. [L. *Chirurgiæ Magister*], Master of Surgery (Edinburgh University).

chmn., chn., Chairman.

chp., Championship.

chq., Cheque.

Chr., Christ, Christian; Christopher.

Chr. Coll. Cam., Christ's College, Cambridge.

Chron., Book of Chronicles.

chron., Chronicle, chronological, chronologically, chronology.

C.H.U., Centigrade heat unit.

C.I., Channel Isles.

Cicestr. [L. *Cicestriensis*], Of Chichester (Bishop of Chichester's signature).

C.I.D., Criminal Investigation Department; Committee of Imperial Defence.

C.I.E., Companion (of the Order) of the Indian Empire.

Cie. [F. *compagnie*], Limited company.

c.i.f., Cost, insurance, and freight.

C.I.G.S., Chief of Imperial General Staff.

C.-in-C., Commander-in-Chief.

circ., Circa, circiter, circum (about).

cit., Citation, cited; citizen; citrate.

civ., Civil, civilian.

C.J., Chief Justice.

ck., Cask.

Cl, (*Chem.*) Chlorine.

cl., Centilitre; class; clause; clergyman; cloth.

Cla., Clare College, Cambridge.

clar., (*Printing*) Clarendon type; Clarencieux King-of-Arms; clarinet, clarinetist.

class., Classic, classical, classification.

cld., (*Shipping*) Cleared; coloured.

Clerg., Clergyman, clergy.

clk., Clerk.

C.M., Certificated Master or Mistress; [L. *Chirurgiæ Magister*], Master of Surgery; Church Missionary; common metre (of hymns); corresponding member.

c.m., Causa mortis (by reason of death).

cm., Centimetre.

C.M.B., Central Midwives Board.

Cmd., Command Paper (from 1919 inclusive).

cmdg., Commanding.

C.M.G., Companion of (the Order of) St. Michael and St. George.

cml., Commercial.

C.M.S., Church Missionary Society.

C.O., Colonial Officer; Crown Office; Commanding Officer; Criminal Office; conscientious objector.

Co, (*Chem.*) Cobalt.

Co., Colon; Company; County.

c/o, Care of; (*Stock Exchange*) carried over.

coad., Coadjutor.

C.O.D., Cash on delivery; collect on delivery.

cod., Codex. **codd.,** Codices.

C. of E., Church of England.

co-ed., Co-educational.

cog., Cognate.

Col., Colonel; Colossians; Columbia District (U.S.A.).

col., Colonial, colony; coloured; column.

coll., Colleague, colleagues;

collection, collector; college, collegiate.

collab., Collaborated, collaborator.

collat., Collateral, collaterally.

collect., Collective, collectively.

colloq., Colloquial, colloquially, colloquialism.

Colo., Colorado.

Coloss., Colossians.

col. p. [It. *colla parte*], (*Mus.*) Adapt to the principal part.

Col.-Sergt., Colour-Sergeant.

col. vo. [It. *colla voce*], (*Mus.*) Adapt to the principal voice.

Com., Commander; commission, commissioner; committee.

com., Comic, comedy; common, commoner, commonly; commune, community; communicate, communicated, communication.

comb., Combine, combined, combining.

Comdr., Commander.

Comdt., Commandant.

Com.-in-Chf., Commander-in-Chief.

Comm., Commodore.

comm., Commentary; commerce; commercial; commonwealth.

Commy., Commissary.

Comp., Comparative, compare, comparison; compilation, compile, compiled, compiler; composer, composition; compositor; compound, compounded.

Com. Serj., Common Serjeant.

Con., Consul.

con., Conclusion; conversation.

con. [L. *conjunx*], Consort; [L. *contra*], in opposition to.

conch., Conchology.

con esp. [It. *con espressione*], (*Mus.*) With expression.

conf., Conference.

conf. [L. *confer*], Compare.

cong., Congregation, congregational, congregationalist, congregationist; congress, congressional.

conj., Conjugation; conjunction, conjunctive.

Conn., Connecticut.

cons., Consonant; consolidated (stocks); constable; constitution, constitutional; consul.

Cons.-Gen., Consul-General.

Consols, Consolidated; (Funds).

constr., Construction; construe, construed.

cont., Containing, contents;

continent, continental; continue, continued.

cont. bon. mor. [L. *contra bonos mores*], Contrary to good manners.

contd., Continued.

contg., Containing.

contr., Contract, contracted; contraction; contrary.

conv., Convent; convention; conversation.

Co-op., Co-operative Society.

Cop., Copernican.

cop., Copper.

C.O.P.E.C., Conference on Politics, Economics and Christianity.

Copt., Coptic.

Cor., (*Bib.*) Corinthians; Cornelia, Cornelius; coroner.

cor., Corpus; correction, corrective; (*Mus.*) cornet; correlative.

Corn., Cornish; Cornwall.

coroll., Corollary.

Corp., Corporal; Corpus Christi College, Cambridge.

corr., Correspond, correspondence, correspondent, corresponding; corrupt, corrupted, corruption.

Corr. Fel., Mem., Sec., Corresponding Fellow, Member, Secretary.

cort., Cortex.

C.O.S., Charity Organization Society.

cos., Cosine.

co. sa. [It. *come sopra*], (*Mus.*) As above.

cosec., Cosecant.

cosmog., Cosmography.

Coss. [L. *consules*], Consuls.

cot., Cotangent.

Cott. MSS., Cottonian Manuscripts.

Cox, Coxswain.

C.P., Chief Patriarch; civil power; Clerk of Peace; Code of Procedure; College of Preceptors; Common Pleas; Common Prayer; [L. *Congregatio Passionis*], Passionist Fathers; Court of Probate; Cape Province (of South Africa).

cp., Compare.

c.p. Candle-power.

C.P.C., Clerk of the Privy Council.

Cpl., Corporal.

C.P.M., Common particular metre (of hymns).

C.P.O., (*Nav.*) Chief Petty Officer.

C.P.R., Canadian Pacific Railway.

C.P.R.E., Council for the Preservation of Rural England.

C.P.S., [L. *Custos Privati Sigilli*], Keeper of the Privy Seal.

C.R. [L. *Carolus Rex*], King Charles; [L. *Custos Rotulorum*], Keeper of the Rolls.

Cr, (*Chem.*) Chromium.

Cr., Credit, creditor; Crown.

cr., Created; crown (size of paper).

C.R.A. (Officer) Commanding Royal Artillery.

craniol., Craniology.

craniom., Craniometry.

C.R.E. (Officer) Commanding Royal Engineers.

cresc., Crescendo.

crim. con., (*Law*) Criminal conversation (adultery).

crit., Critic, critical, criticized.

crystal., Crystallography.

C.S., Civil Service; Civil Servant; Clerk of Session; Clerk to the Signet; Common Serjeant; Court of Session; [L. *Custos Sigilli*], Keeper of the Seal.

Cs, (*Chem.*) Cæsium.

cs. [L. *communis*], Common.

C.S.C., Conspicuous Service Cross.

C.S.I., Companion of (the Order of) the Star of India.

C.S.M., Company Serjeant-Major.

C.S.O., Chief Signal Officer-Chief Staff Officer.

C.SS.R. [L. *Congregatio Sanctissimi Redemptoris*], Redemptorist Fathers.

C.T., Certificated Teacher.

Ct., Count; Court.

ct., Cent.

C.T.C., Cyclists' Touring Club.

ctge., Cartage.

ctl., Cental.

cto., (*Mus.*) Concerto.

cts., Centimes, cents.

Ctss., Countess.

Cu [L. *cuprium*], (*Chem.*) Copper.

C.U., Cambridge University.

cub., Cubic.

cuj. [L. *cujus*], Of which.

cujusl. [L. *cujuslibet*], Of any.

Cumb., Cumberland.

cum. div. [C.D.], With dividend.

cur., Currency, current.

C.V.O., Commander of (the Royal) Victorian Order.

C.W., Canada West.

C.W.B., Central Welsh Board (Education).

c.w.o., Cash with order.

C.W.S., Co-operative Wholesale Society.

cwt., Hundredweight.

cyc., Cyclopædia, cyclopædic.

Cym., Cymric.

D, Deacon; (*Polit.*) democrat, democratic; [L. *Deus*], God; doctor; [L. *Dominus*], Lord; Duke; 500.

d., Dale; daughter; day; dead, died; deceased; degree; [L. *denarius*], penny; deserted, deserter; diopter; dollar; dose; drama; dorsal; (*Naut.*) drizzling.

δ [L. *deleatur*], Delete.

Da., Danish.

D.A.A.G., Deputy-Assistant-Adjutant-General.

D.A.G., Deputy-Adjutant-General.

dag., decagram.

Dak., Dakota.

dal., decalitre.

Dan., Daniel, Danish.

D.A.Q.M.G., Deputy-Assistant-Quartermaster-General.

dat., Dative.

dau., Daughter.

Dav., David.

D.B., Domesday Book.

d.b., Day-book.

D.B.E., Dame Commander of (the Order of) the British Empire.

dbk., Drawback.

D.B.S.T., Double British Summer Time.

D.C., Deputy-Consul; District Court; District of Columbia; [It. *da capo*], (*Mus.*) repeat; Direct Current.

D.C.L., Doctor of Civil Law.

D.C.L.I., Duke of Cornwall's Light Infantry.

D.C.M., Distinguished Conduct Medal; District Court Martial.

D.Cn.L., Doctor of Canon Law.

D.C.S., Deputy Clerk of Session.

D.D. [L. *Divinitatis Doctor*], Doctor of Divinity.

D.d. [L. *Deo dedit*], Gave to God.

dd., Delivered.

d.d., Days after date (bills of exchange); [L. *dono dedit*], gave as a gift.

D.D.D. [L. *dat, dicat, dedicat*], He gives, devotes, and dedicates; [L. *dono dedit dedicavit*], He gave and consecrated as a gift.

D.D.S., Doctor of Dental Surgery.

deb., Debenture.

Dec., December.

dec., Declaration; declension; declination, decoration, decorative; deceased.

de d. in d. [L. *de die in diem*], From day to day; continuously.

def., Defendant; defined, definite, definition.

deg., Degree.

Del., Delaware.

del., Delegate; [L. *delineavit*], he (or she) drew it.

dele. [L. *deleatur*], Omit, δ.

Dem., Democrat, Democratic; (*Paper*) demy.

demob., Demobilization.

demon., Demonstrative.

Den., Denmark.

dent., Dental, dentist, dentistry.

dep., Departs; deposed; deputy.

dép [F. *département*], Department, province; [F. *député*], deputy.

der., deriv., Derivative, derived, derivation.

dept., Department.

Det., Detective.

Deut., Deuteronomy.

Devon., Devonshire, Devonian.

D.F., Dean of Faculty; [F.D.].

D.F.C., Distinguished Flying Cross.

D.F.M., Distinguished Flying Medal.

dft., Defendant; draft.

D.G., Director-General; Dragoon Guards; [L. *Dei gratia*], by the grace of God; [L. *Deo gratias*], thanks to God.

dg., Decigram.

D.Hy., Doctor of Hygiene.

D.I., District Inspector.

Di, (*Chem.*) Didymium.

d.i. [G. *das ist*], That is.

dial., Dialect, dialectal, dialectic, dialectical; dialogue.

diam., Diameter.

dict., dictionary.

dif., Differ, difference.

dim. [L. *dimidius*], One half; diminutive; (*Mus.*) diminuendo.

dioc., Diocesan, diocese.

dipl., Diploma, diplomat, diplomatic, diplomatist.

disc., discipline; discount; distribute, distributed (of type).

disc., Discovered, discoverer.

disp., Dispensary.

dist., Distance; distinguish, distinguished; district.

disy., Dissyllable.

div., Divide, divided; dividend; divine; division, devisor; divers, diverse.

divde. [F. *dividende*], Dividend.

D.L., Deputy-Lieutenant.

D.L.I., Durham Light Infantry.

D.Lit., Doctor of Literature.

D.Litt., Doctor of Letters [cp. LITT.D.].

D.L.O., Dead Letter Office (Returned Letter Office).

D.M., Deputy Master; Doctor of Medicine (Oxford); [It. *destra mano*], (*Mus.*) with the right hand.

D.M.D., Doctor of Dental Medicine.

D.M.I., Director of Military Intelligence.

D.Mus., Doctor of Music.

D.N. [L. *Dominus noster*], Our Lord.

D.N.B., Dictionary of National Biography.

do., Ditto, the same.

doc., Doctor; document.

dol., Dollar, dollars.

D.O.M. [*Deo optimo maximo*], To God the best and greatest; [*Domino omnium magister*], The Lord master of all, motto of the Benedictines.

dom., Domestic; dominion.

Dom. Proc. [L. *Domus procerum*], (*Law*) The House of Lords.

Dor., Doric.

D.O.R.A., Defence of the Realm Act; (following the first World War).

Dors., Dorsetshire.

dow., Dowager.

D.O.W.B., Department of Works and Buildings.

doz., Dozen.

D.P. Displaced persons (after second World War; [DOM. PROC.].

D.Ph., Doctor of Philosophy.

D.R. (*Naut.*), Dead reckoning; district registry.

Dr., Debtor; Doctor.

dr., Drachma, dram; drawer.

dram. pers., Dramatis personæ, characters of the play.

d.s., Days after sight, day's sight.

D.S.C., Distinguished Service Cross.

D.Sc., Doctor of Science.

D.S.M., Distinguished Service Medal.

D.S.O., Distinguished Service Order.

d.s.p. [L. *decessit sine prole*], Died without issue.

d.t., Delirium tremens.

D.Th., Doctor of Theology.

dub. [L. *dubitante*], Doubting; [L. *dubius*], dubious.

Dubl., Dublin.

Dunelm. [L. *Dunelmensis*], Of Durham (signature of the Bishop of Durham).

Dur., Durham.

Dut., Dutch.

D.V. [L. *Deo volente*], God willing.

d.v.p. [L. *decessit vita patris*], Died during his (or her) father's life.

dwt. [L. *denarius*], Pennyweight, 24 grains troy.

dyn., Dynamics.

D.Z., Doctor of Zoology.

E, (*Chem.*) Erbium.

E., Earl; east; Eastern (London postal district);

Edward; second-class merchant ship at Lloyd's; engineer, engineering; English.

e., Eccentricity of eclipse; co-efficient of elasticity; electro-motive force of cell.

ea., Each.

E. & O.E., Errors and omissions excepted.

E.B., Encyclopædia Britannica.

Ebor. [L. *Eboracum*], York; [L. *Eboracensis*], of York (signature of the Archbishop of York).

E.b.S., East-by-South.

E.C., Eastern Central (London postal district); Established Church.

Eccles., Ecclesiastes, ecclesiastical, ecclesiology.

Ecclus., Ecclesiasticus.

Ecl., Eclogues.

E.C.O., European Coal Organization.

econ., Economical, economics, economy, economist.

Ecua., Ecuador.

ed., Edition, editor.

Edin., Edinburgh.

edit., Edited, edition.

eds., Editors, editions.

educ., Educated.

E.E., Early English; errors excepted.

E.E. & M.P., Envoy Extraordinary and Minister Plenipotentiary.

e.g. [L. *exampli gratia*], For example.

E.G.M., Empire Gallantry Medal.

Egyptol., Egyptologist, Egyptology.

E.H.P., Electrical horsepower.

E.I., East India, East Indian; East Indies.

E.I.C., East India Company.

ejusd. [L. *ejusdem*], Of the same.

elec., Electrical, electricity; electuary.

elem., Elementary.

Eliz., Elizabeth.

ellipt., Elliptical, elliptically.

Elz., Elzevir.

E.M., Earl Marshal; [L. *Equitum Magister*], Master of the Horse; Edward Medal.

Em., Emmanuel; Emily; Emma.

embry., Embryology.

E.M.D.P., Electromotive difference of potential.

E.M.F., Electromotive force.

Emm., Emmanuel College, Cambridge.

Emp., Emperor, Empire, Empress.

ency., Encyclopædia, encyclopædian, encyclopædic, encyclopædist, etc.

E.N.E., East-north-east.

Eng., England, English.

eng., Engineer, engineering; engraved, engraver, engraving.

E.N.S.A., Entertainments National Service Association.

entom., Entomology.

Ent. Sta. Hall, Entered at Stationers' Hall.

Env. Extr., Envoy Extraordinary.

Ep., Epistle.

E.P.D., Excess Profits Duty.

Eph., Ephesians; Ephraim.

Epiph., Epiphany.

episc., Episcopal.

E.P.T., Excess Profits Tax.

Eq., Equator, equatorial.

equiv., Equivalent.

Er, (*Chem.*) Erbium.

E.R., East Riding (of Yorkshire); [L. *Eduardus Rex*], King Edward; Queen Elizabeth.

E.R.A., Engine-room artificer.

Erasm., Erasmus.

erron., Erroneous, erroneously.

eschat., Eschatology, eschatological.

E.S.E., East-south-east.

esp., Especially.

Esq., Esquire.

ess., Essence, essences.

est., Established; estimated.

Esth., Esther.

et al. [L. *et alibi* [, and elsewhere.

etc. [L. *et cetera*], And the rest.

ethno., ethnol., Ethnology.

et seq. [L. *et sequens*], (*pl.*) **et sqq.** [*et sequentes* or *sequentia*], And the following.

E.T.U., Electrical Trades Union.

etym., Etymological, etymologically, etymologist, etymology.

Euc., Euclid.

euphem., Euphemism, euphemistic, euphemistical.

Eur., Europe, European.

Evang., Evangelical, evangelist.

ex., Examined; example; exchanged; executed; executive.

Exc., Excellency.

exc., Excellent; except, excepted, exception.

Exch., Exchange; Exchequer.

excl., exclam., Exclamation, exclamatory.

ex div., Without next dividend.

ex. gr. [L. *exempli gratia*], For example.

ex int., Without next interest.

Exod., Exodus.

Exon. [L. *Exoniensis*], Of Exeter (signature of the Bishop of Exeter).

exor., Executor.

exp., Export, exportation, exported; expression.

ext., External, externally; extinct; extract.

Ez., Ezra.

Ezek., Ezekiel.

F, (*Chem.*) Fluorine.

F., Fahrenheit; (*R.-C. Ch.*) Father; (*Univ.*) Fellow; felon; (*Naut.*) fog; folio; formula, formulæ; French; Friday.

f., Farthing; fathom; feet; fem.; francs; furlongs; [L. *forte*], (*Mus.*) loud.

F.A., Football Association.

F.A.A., Fleet Air Arm.

f.a.a., (*Marine Insurance*) Free of all average.

fac., facs., Facsimile.

Fahr., Fahrenheit.

fam., Familiar, familiarly; family.

F.A.N.Y., First Aid Nursing Yeomanry.

F.A.O., Food and Agriculture Organization (of United Nations).

far., Farad, faradaic; farriery; farthing.

f.a.s., Free alongside ship.

fasc. [L. *fasciculus*, bundle], A single part or number (of serial publication).

F.B.I., Federation of British Industries; Federal Bureau of Investigation (U.S.A.).

F.C., Football Club; Free Church of Scotland.

f.c. [L. *fidei-commissum*], Bequeathed in trust.

fcap., Foolscap.

f.co., Fair copy.

fcp., Foolscap.

F.D. [L. *fidei defensor*], Defender of the Faith.

Fe [L. *ferrum*], (*Chem.*) Iron.

Feb., February.

fec. [L. *fecit*], He (or she) made it.

Fed., Federalist, federation.

fem., Feminine.

Ferd., Ferdinand.

Feud., Feudal.

F.F. (*Naut.*) thick fog.

ff. [L. *fecerunt*], They made it; [G. *folgende Seiten*], following pages, following.

ff. [It. *fortissimo*], (*Mus.*) Louder than forte, very loud.

fff. [It. *fortississimo*], (*Mus.*) As loud as possible.

F.G., Foot Guards.

f.g., (*Leather*) fine grain; (*Paper*) friction glazed.

f.g.a., Free of general average.

F.I.A.T., [It. *Fabbrica Ital-*

iana Automobile, Torino], The Italian Automobile Factory, Turin.

fict. [L. *fictilis*], Made of pottery.

F.I.D., Field Intelligence Department.

Fid. Def. [L. *fidei defensor*], Defender of the Faith.

fi. fa. [L. *fieri facias*, That you cause it to be done]. A writ.

fig., Figurative, figure.

Fin., Finland, Finnish.

fin. [L. *ad finem*], At the end.

Fin. Sec., Financial Secretary.

fir., Firkin, firkins.

Fl., Flanders, Flemish.

fl., Florin; [L. *flores*], flowers; [L. *floruit*], flourished; fluid.

f.l. [L. *falsa lectio*], A false reading.

Fla., Florida.

Flem., Flemish [FL.].

flor. [L. *floruit*], He (or she) flourished.

F.L.S., Fellow of the Linnean Society.

F.M., Field Marshal. Foreign Mission.

fm., Fathom.

F.M.D., Foot-and-mouth disease.

F.O., Field Officer; Foreign Office; Flying Officer.

fo., Folio.

f.o.b., Free on board.

fol., foll., Following.

for., Foreign.

f.o.r., Free on rail.

fort., Fortification, fortified.

F.P., Fine paper (edition of books); fire-plug; field punishment.

f.p., Foot-pound.

fp. [It. *forte piano*], (*Mus.*) Loud and soft.

f.p.a., Free of particular average.

f.p.c., For private circulation.

Fr., France, French; [G. *Frau*], Mrs., wife; Friar; Father (priest); Friday; [It. *Fratelli*], Brothers.

fr., Franc; [G. *frei*], free; from.

Fras., Francis.

F.R.C.P., Fellow of the Royal College of Physicians.

F.R.C.S., Fellow of the Royal College of Surgeons.

Fred., Frederic, Frederick.

freq., Frequent, frequently, frequentative.

Fri., Friday.

Fris., Frisia, Frisian.

Frl. [G. *Fräulein*], Miss.

F.R.S., Fellow of the Royal Society.

frs., Francs.

F.S., Fleet Surgeon.

f.s. [F. *faire suivre*], To be forwarded.

F.T., Free Trade, Free-trader.

Ft., Fort.

ft., Faint; (*Paper*) flat; foot, feet; fortified.

F.T.C.D., Fellow of Trinity College, Dublin.

fur., Furlong.

fut., Future.

f.v. (L. *folio verso*), On the back of the page.

F.W.A., Factories and Work-shops Acts.

G., German, Germany; grand; gulf; (*Nav.*) gunnery.

g., Acceleration of gravity.

g. [F. *gauche*], Left; genitive; guinea, guineas; (*Naut.*) gloomy; gram; [F. *gros*, fem. *-se*], big.

G.A., (*Insce.*) General average; General Assembly; Golfing Association.

Ga, (*Chem.*) Gallium.

Ga., Gallic; Georgia.

Gabr., Gabriel.

Gael., Gaelic.

Gai., Gaius.

Gal., Galatians.

gal., Gallon, gallons.

galv., Galvanic, galvanism.

Gaz., Gazette, gazetteer.

G.B., Great Britain.

G.B. & I., Great Britain and Ireland.

G.B.E., Knight (*or* Dame) Grand Cross of (the Order of) the British Empire.

G.B.S., George Bernard Shaw.

G.C., George Cross; Gentleman Cadet; Golf Club; Grand Chancellor; Grand Chapter; Grand Conductor.

G.C.B., Knight Grand Cross of (the Order of) the Bath.

G.C.C., Gonville and Caius College, Cambridge.

g.c.f., (*Math.*) Greatest common factor.

G.C.I.E., Grand Commander of (the Order of) the Indian Empire.

g.c.m., (*Math.*) Greatest common measure.

G.C.M.G., Knight Grand Cross of St. Michael and St. George.

G.C.S.I., Knight Grand Commander of the Star of India.

G.C.V.O., Knight Grand Cross of the (Royal) Victorian Order.

Gdns., Gardens.

Gds., Guards regiments.

Ge, (*Chem.*) Germanium.

g.e., (*Bookbinding*) Gilt edges.

Gell., Gellius.

Gen., General; Genesis; Geneva.

gen., Gender; general, generally; generic; genitive; genus.

geneal., Genealogy.

gent., Gentleman.

gen. t., General title.

Geo., George.

geod., Geodesy.

Geoff., Geoffrey.

geog., Geographer, geographical, geography.

geol., Geological, geologist, geology.

geom., Geometer, geometrical, geometry.

Ger., German, Germany.

ger., Gerund, gerundive.

Ges., [G. *Gesellschaft*], A limited company or society.

G.F.S., Girls' Friendly Society.

G.G., Grenadier Guards.

g.gr., Great gross (144 dozen).

G.H.Q., General Head-quarters.

Gib., Gibraltar.

Gk., Greek.

Gl, (*Chem.*) Glucinum.

Glam., Glamorganshire.

Glos., Gloucester, Gloucestershire.

G.M., George Medal; General Manager; Gold Medallist (Bisley); Grand Master.

gm., Gram.

G.M.B., Good Merchantable Brand.

G.M.I.E., Grand Master of (the Order of) the Indian Empire.

G.M.K.P., Grand Master of the Knights of St. Patrick.

G.M.M.G., Grand Master of (the Order of) St. Michael and St. George.

G.M.S.I., Grand Master of (the Order of) the Star of India.

G.M.T., Greenwich Mean Time.

G.O., General order; (*Mus.*) grand organ.

G.O.C., General Officer Commanding.

G.O.M., Grand Old Man (W. E. Gladstone).

Goth., Gothic.

gov., Governor, government.

Gov.-Gen., Governor-General.

G.P., (*Med.*) General paralysis; general practitioner; Graduate in Pharmacy.

gp., Group.

g.p., (*Print.*) Great primer.

G.P.I., General paralysis of the insane.

G.P.O., General Post Office.

G.Q.C., Grand Quartier Général, G.H.Q. of the French army.

G.R. [L. *Georgius Rex*], King George; Grand Recorder;

General Reserve; Grand Registrar.

Gr., Grand; Greece, Grecian, Greek.

gr., Grain, grains; gram, grams; Groschen.

gram., Grammar, grammarian, grammatical.

Greg., Gregory.

grm., Gramme, grammes.

gro., Gross.

G.S., General Secretary; Golfing Society; General Staff.

g.s., Grandson.

G.S.N., General Steam Navigation.

G.S.O., General Staff Officer.

gt., Gilt; great; (*Pharm.*) [L. *gutta*], drop.

g.t., (*Bookbinding*) Gilt top.

Gt. Br. [C.B.], Great Britain.

guar., Guarantee, guarantor.

gun., Gunnery.

Gustav., Gustavus.

gymn., Gymnastics, gymnasium.

H, (*Chem.*) Hydrogen.

H., (*Naut.*) Harbour, hoy; hydrant; hard (of pencils); (*Mech.*) total energy.

h., (*Naut.*) Hail; (*Min.*) hardness; height; hour, hours; hundred; husband.

H.A., Hockey Association.

h.a. [L. *hoc anno*], This year; [L. *hujus anni*], this year's.

Hab., Habakkuk.

hab., Habitat.

hab. corp. [L. *habeas corpus*, you may have the body], A writ.

H.A.C., Honourable Artillery Company.

Hag., Haggai.

h. & c., Hot and cold (water).

Hants., Hampshire.

Har., Harold.

Harl. MSS., Harleian Manuscripts.

Harv., Harvard [H.U.].

HB, Hard and black (of pencils).

H.B. & K., (*Bot.*) Humboldt, Bonpland and Kunth.

H.B.M., Her (or His) Britannic Majesty.

H.C., Habitual criminal; Heralds' College; High Church, High Churchman; House of Commons; House of Correction; Hunterian Club.

h.c.f., (*Math.*) Highest common factor.

H.Comm., High Commissioner.

hdbk., Handbook.

hdkf., Handkerchief.

hdqrs., Headquarters.

H.E., His Eminence; His Excellency.

He, (*Chem.*) Helium.

h.e., High explosive.
Heb., Hebrew, Hebrews.
hectog., Hectogram.
hectol., Hectolitre.
Hel., Helvetia (Switzerland).
her., Herald, heraldry.
herp., Herpetology.
Herts., Hertfordshire.
H.F., Home Forces; high frequency.
hf., half.
hf.-bd., (*Bookbinding*) Half-bound.
hf.-cf., Half-calf.
hf.-cl., Half-cloth.
hf.-mor., Half-morocco.
hf.-vel., Half-vellum.
Hg., [L. *hydrargyrum*], (*Chem.*) Mercury.
H.G., His (or Her) Grace; Horse Guards; High German.
H.H., His (or Her) Highness; His Holiness (the Pope).
HH, Extra hard (of pencils).
hhd., Hogshead.
HHH, Very hard (of pencils).
Hib., Hibernian.
H.I.H., His (or Her) Imperial Highness.
Hil., Hilary.
H.I.M., His (or Her) Imperial Majesty.
Hind., (*Urdu*) Hindu, Hindustan, Hindustani.
hist., Historian, historic, historical, history.
H.K., House of Keys, Isle of Man.
H.L., House of Lords.
hl., h.l., Hectolitre.
H.L.I., Highland Light Infantry.
H.M., Her (or His) Majesty; Home Mission
Hm., Hectometer; handmade (of paper); (*Hymns*) Hallelujah metre; Head Master; Head Mistress.
H.M.A.S., Her Majesty's Australian Ship.
H.M.C., Her Majesty's Customs; Head Masters' Conference.
H.M.C.S., Her Majesty's Canadian Ship.
H.M.F., Her Majesty's Forces.
H.M.I., Her Majesty's Inspector.
H.M.O.W., Her Majesty's Office of Works.
H.M.S., Her Majesty's Service; Her Majesty's Ship.
H.M.S.O., Her Majesty's Stationery Office.
H.M.T., Her Majesty's Trawler.
H.O., The Home Office.
ho., House.
Hon., Honourable, Honorary.
hor., Horizon.
horol., Horology.

hort., Horticultural, horticulture.
Hos., Hosea.
hosp., Hospital.
how., Howitzer.
H.P., Half-pay; high-pressure; high-priest; house-physician; hot-pressed (of paper).
h.p., Horse-power.
h.p.n., Horse-power nominal.
H.Q., Headquarters.
H.R.H., His (or Her) Royal Highness.
H.S., Honorary Secretary; Home Secretary; house-surgeon.
H.S.H., His (or Her) Serene Highness.
h.t., (*Elec.*) High tension.
Hum. [L. *humaniora*], The humanities.
Hun., Hungarian, Hungary.
Hunts, Huntingdonshire.
h.w., (*Cricket*) Hit wicket.
H.W.M., High-water mark.
Hy., Henry.
Hyb., Hybrid.
hyd., Hydrostatics.
hyp., Hypothesis, hypothetical.
hypoth., Hypothesis, hypothetical.

I, (*Chem.*) Iodine; (*Elec.*) moment of inertia.
I. [L. *Imperator*], Emperor; Intelligence (Army); [L. *Imperatrix*], Empress; Idaho; [G. *Ihr*], your; Ireland; island.
i. [L. *id*], That.
Ia., Iowa.
ib., ibid. [L. *ibidem*], In the same place.
I. C. [L. *Iesus Christus*], Jesus Christ.
i/c., In charge.
Icel., Iceland, Icelandic.
ichth., icthyol., Ichthyology.
I.C.I., Imperial Chemical Industries.
icon., Iconographic, iconography.
I.D., Intelligence Department.
id. [L. *idem*], The same.
I.D.B., (*S. Afr.*) Illicit diamond buyer, *or* buying.
i.e. [L. *id est*], That is.
Ill., Illinois.
ill. [L. *illustrissimus*], Most distinguished.
illus., Illustrated, illustration.
I.L.O., International Labour Office (Geneva).
I.L.P., Independent Labour Party.
imit., imitation, imitated.
imp., Imperative; imperfect; imperial; impersonal; imported, importer; *imprimatur* (let it be printed).

imper., Imperative.
imperf., Imperfect; imperforate (of stamps).
impers., Impersonal.
Imp.Inst., Imperial Institute.
In, (*Chem.*) Indium.
in., Inch, inches.
inc., Incorporated.
incl., Including, inclusively.
incog., Incognito.
incor., Incorporated.
incr., Increased, increasing.
Ind., India, Indian, Indiana.
ind., Independent; index; indication.
indecl., (*Gram.*) Indeclinable.
indic., (*Gram.*) Indicative.
indiv., Individual.
Indo-Eur., Indo-European.
Indo-Ger., Indo-Germanic.
Ind. T., Indian Territory.
in. f., In fine, finally.
inf., Infantry; infinitive.
inf. [L. *infra*], Below.
infin., Infinitive.
infra dig. [L. *infra dignitatem*], Beneath one's dignity.
in lim. [L. *in limine*], At the outset.
in pr. [L. *in principio*], in the beginning.
I.N.R.I. [L. *Iesus Nazarenus Rex Iudœorum*], Jesus of Nazareth, King of the Jews.
Ins., Inspector.
ins., insce., Insurance.
Ins.-Gen., Inspector-General.
Insp., Inspector.
inst., Institute, institution; instant (of this month).
instr., Instrument, instrumental.
int., Interest; interior; interjection; interpreter; intransitive.
int. al. [L. *inter alia*], among other things.
intens., Intensive, intensative.
inter., Intermediate; interrogation mark.
interj., Interjection.
internat., International.
interrog., Interrogation, interrogative, interrogatively.
intrans., Intransitive.
in trans., In transit.
introd., Introduction, introductory.
inv. [L. *invenit*], He (or she) designed it; invented, inventor; invoice.
I.O., Intelligence Officer.
I.O.F., Independent Order of Foresters.
I.o.M., Isle of Man.
I.O.G.T., Independent Order of Good Templars.
Ion., Ionic.
I.O.O.F., Independent Order of Oddfellows.

I.O.R., Independent Order of Rechabites.

IOU, I owe you.

I.O.W., Isle of Wight.

ipecac., Ipecacuanha.

I.Q., Intelligence Quotient.

i.q. [L. *idem quod*], The same as.

I.R., Inland Revenue.

Ir, (*Chem.*) Iridium.

Ir., Ireland, Irish.

Iran., Iranian, Iranic (Persian).

Ire., Ireland.

I.R.O., Inland Revenue Office.

iron., Ironically.

irreg., Irregular, irregularly.

Is., Isaiah.

Isl., Island, isle, islands, isles.

I.S.O. (Companion of the) Imperial Service Order.

Isth., Isthmus.

It., Italian, Italy.

I.T.A., Independent Television Authority.

ital., Italics.

I.W., Isle of Wight.

I.W.T., Inland Water Transport.

I.W.W., International Workers of the World.

I.Y., Imperial Yeomanry.

J., Judge, justice; Jew, Jewish; (*Elec.*) joule.

J., (*Phys.*) Joule's mechanical equivalent of heat.

J.A., Judge-Advocate.

J./A., Joint Account.

Jac. [L. *Jacobus*], James.

J.A.G., Judge-Advocate-General.

Jam., Jamaica.

Jan., January.

Jap., Japan, Japanese.

Jas., James.

Jav., Javanese.

J.C., Jesus Christ; Julius Cæsar; [L. *Juris-Consultus*], Jurisconsult; Justice-Clerk.

J.C.D. [L. *Juris Civilis Doctor*], Doctor of Civil Law.

J.D., Junior Deacon; Junior Dean; [L. *Jurum Doctor*] Doctor of Laws.

Jer., Jeremiah.

Jes., Jesus.

JHS [IHS].

J.H.U., Johns Hopkins University.

JJ., Justices.

Jn., Junction.

Jno., John.

jnr., Junior.

Jo., Joel.

joc., Jocular, jocose.

Joh., St. John's College, Cambridge.

Jon., Jonathan.

Jos., Joseph.

Josh., Joshua.

jour., Journal; journey; journeyman.

J.P., Justice of the Peace.

jr., Junior [JUN.].

jt., Joint.

jtly., Jointly.

J.U.D. [L. *Juris utriusque Doctor*], Doctor of both Civil and Canon Law.

Jud., Judith.

jud., Judicial; *judicium*; judgment.

Judg., Book of Judges.

Jul., Julius, Julian.

Jun., Junius.

jun., Junior.

junc., Junction.

Jun. Opt., Junior Optime.

jurisp., Jurisprudence.

K, (*Astron.*) The solar constant; [L. *kalium*], (*Chem.*) potassium; (*Elec.*) capacity.

K., King, Kings; (*Assaying*) carat.

k., (*Meteor.*) Cumulus.

k, (*Astron.*) Gauss's constant.

kal., Kalends.

Kan., Kansas.

K.B., Knight of the Bath; King's Bench; Knight Bachelor.

K.B.E., Knight Commander of (the Order of) the British Empire.

K.C., King's College: King's Counsel; Kennel Club.

K.C.B., Knight Commander of (the Order of) the Bath.

K.C.I.E., Knight Commander of (the Order of) the Indian Empire.

K.C.L., King's College, London.

K.C.M.G., Knight Commander of (the Order of) St. Michael and St. George.

K.C.S.I., Knight Commander of the Star of India.

K.C.V.O., Knight Commander of the Royal Victorian Order.

Keb. Coll., Keble College, Oxford.

Ken., Kentucky.

K.G., Knight of (the Order of) the Garter.

k.g, Kilogramme.

K.G.C., Knight Grand Cross.

K.i.H., K.I.H., Kaisar-i-Hind Medal.

kil., Kilderkin.

kilo., Kilogram.

K.K.K., Ku-Klux-Klan.

kl., Kilolitre.

km., Kilometre.

Knt., Knight.

k.o., (*Boxing*) Knock-out.

K.O.S.B., King's Own Scottish Borderers.

K.O.Y.L.I., King's Own Yorkshire Light Infantry.

K.P., Knight of (the Order of) St. Patrick.

K.P.M., King's Police Medal.

Kr, (*Chem.*) Krypton.

kr., Kreutzer.

K.R.C., Knight of the Red Cross.

K.R.R., King's Royal Rifles.

K.R.R.C., King's Royal Rifle Corps.

K.S.I., Knight of the Star of India.

K.T., Knight of the Order of the Thistle; Knight Templar.

Kt., Knight.

Kt. Bach., Knight Bachelor.

κ.τ.λ. [Gr. *kai ta loipa*], And the rest, etc.

kv., Kilovolt.

kw., (*Elec.*) Kilowatt (100 watts).

Ky., Kentucky.

L., 50, 50th.

L., Lady; lake; Latin; (*Theat.*) left; [L. *liber*]; book; Liberal; licentiate; (*Bot.*) Linnæus; lira, lire; [F. *livre*], pound; [L. *locus*], place; London.

l., League; length; line; link; litre; left; (*Naut.*) lightning.

L.A., Law Agent; Legislative Assembly; local Authority.

La, (*Chem.*) Lanthanum.

La., Louisiana.

lab., (*Polit.*) Labour; Labrador; laboratory.

Lab.M., Labour Member (of Parliament).

L.A.M. [L. *Liberalium Artium Magister*], Master of the Liberal Arts; London Academy of Music.

Lam., Lamentations; (*Bot.*) Lamarck.

Lancs, Lancashire.

lang., Language.

Lap., Lapland.

L.A.S., Lord-Advocate of Scotland.

Lat., Latin.

lat., Latitude.

L.B. [L. *Litterarum Baccalaureus*], Bachelor of Letters; Local Board.

lb. [L. *libra*, -*bræ*], Pound, pounds.

l.b., (*Cricket*) Leg-bye.

l.b.w., (*Cricket*) Leg before wicket.

L.C., Letter of credit; Lord Chamberlain; Lord Chancellor; Lower Canada.

l.c. [L. *loco citato*], In the place cited; lower case (of type).

L.C.C., London County Council, *or* Councillor.

L.Ch., L.Chir., Licentiate in Surgery.

L.C.J., Lord Chief Justice.

l.c.m., Least common multiple.

L.Cpl., Lance-corporal.

l/cr., Letter of credit.

Ld., Lord.

Ldg., (Nav.) Leading.

Ldp., Lordship.

£E., Egyptian pounds (1 : 0 : 6½).

L.E.A., Local Education Authority.

lect., Lecture.

Leg., Legislative, legislature.

leg., Legal; [It. legato], (Mus.) in a smooth and connected manner.

Leics., Leicestershire.

Lev., Leviticus.

lex., Lexicon.

lexicog., Lexicographer, lexicographical, lexicography.

L.F., Low frequency.

L.F.B., London Fire Brigade.

L.G., (Comm.) Large grain; Life Guards.

L.G.B., Local Government Board.

L. Ger., Low German.

L. Gr., Low Greek.

l.h., Left hand.

L.H.C., Lord High Chancellor.

L.H.D. [L. Litterarum Humaniorum Doctor], Doctor of Humane Letters.

L.H.T., Lord High Treasurer.

L.I., (Mil.) Light infantry; Long Island (U.S.A.).

Li, (Chem.) Lithium.

Lib., (Pol.) Liberal.

lib., Librarian, library.

Lieut., Lieutenant.

Lieut.-Col., -Gen., -Gov., Lieutenant-Colonel, -General, -Governor.

lin., Lineal, linear.

Lincs, Lincolnshire.

Linn., Linnæan, Linnæus (Carl von Linné).

liq., Liquid, liquor.

lit., Literal, literally, literary, literature; litre.

Lit.D. [L. Literarum Doctor], Doctor of Letters.

litho., Lithography.

Lit.Hum. [L. Literæ Humaniores], Final school of classics at Oxford.

Litt.D. [L. Literarum Doctor], Doctor of Letters (Camb. and T.C.D.).

liturg., Liturgy, liturgical.

L.J. (pl. L.JJ.), Lord Justice.

L.L., Late Latin; law Latin, low Latin; Lord-Lieutenant.

ll., Leaves; (Print.) lines; [L. leges], laws.

LL.B. [L. Legum Baccalaureus], Bachelor of Laws.

LL.D., [L. legum Doctor], Doctor of Laws.

LL.JJ., Lords Justices.

L. Ω, (Elec.) The legal ohm.

loc. cit. [L. loco citato], In the place cited.

loco., (Rail.) Locomotive.

log., Logarithm; logic.

long., Longitude.

loq. [L. loquitur], He (or she) speaks.

L.P. Large paper (copy of a book); Lord Provost.

l.p., (Print.) Long primer; low pressure.

L.P.M., Long particular metre.

L'pool, Liverpool.

L.P.S., Lord Privy Seal.

L.P.T.B., London Passenger Transport Board.

L.R.A.M., Licentiate of the Royal Academy of Music.

L.R.B., London Rifle Brigade.

L.R.C., London Rowing Club.

L.R.C.M., Licentiate of the Royal College of Music.

L.R.C.P., Licentiate of the Royal College of Physicians.

L.R.C.S., Licentiate of the Royal College of Surgeons.

L.R.C.V.S., Licentiate of the Royal College of Veterinary Surgeons.

L.R.F.P.S., Licentiate of the Royal Faculty of Physicians and Surgeons.

L.S., Linnean Society; [L. locus sigilli], the place of the seal.

l.s., Left side.

L.S.A., Licentiate of the Society of Apothecaries.

L.S.B., London School Board.

l.s.c. [L. loco supra citato], In the place above cited.

L.s.d. [L. libræ, solidi, denarii], Pounds, shillings and pence.

L.T., Low tension.

£T. [It. lira Turca], Turkish pound (approx. 18s. 2d.).

Lt., Lieutenant.

L.T.A., Lawn Tennis Association; London Teachers' Association.

L.T.C.L., Licentiate of Trinity College (of Music), London.

Lt.-Col., Lieutenant-Colonel.

Lt. Comm., (Nav.) Lieutenant Commander.

Ltd., Limited.

Lt.-Gen., Lieutenant-General.

Lt. Inf., Light Infantry.

Luth., Lutheran.

L.V., (Elec.) Legal volt.

l.w., (Wire.) Long wave.

L.W.L., Load-water-line.

LXX, The Septuagint; 70.

lyr., Lyric, lyrical, lyrist.

M, 1000.

M. [L. magister], Master;

majesty; magistrate; [G.] mark; Marquess; [L. medicinæ], (Med.) of medicine; member; middle; militia; [F.], Monsieur.

m., Male; married; masculine; (Cricket) maiden over; (Mech.) mass meridian; [L. meridies], noon; metre, metres; mile, miles; (Med.) minim; minute, minutes; (Naut.) mist; month, months; moon.

M.A., [L. Magister Artium], Master of Arts; Military Academy.

ma., (Elec.) Milliampere.

Maced., Macedonia, Macedonian.

Mad., Madam.

Mag., Magyar.

mag., Magazine; magnetism.

Magd., Magdalen College, Oxford; Magdalene College, Cambridge.

Maj., Major.

Maj.-Gen., Major-General.

Mal., Malachi; Malayan.

Man., Manitoba; Manila.

man., Manual.

Manch., Manchester.

Manit., Manitoba.

M.A.P., Ministry of Aircraft Production.

mar., Maritime; married.

Marg., Margaret.

masc., Masculine.

Mass., Massachusetts.

mat., Matins.

math., Mathematical, mathematician, mathematics.

Matric., Matriculation.

Matt., St. Matthew.

Max., Maximilian.

max., Maxim; maximum.

M.B., [L. Medicinæ Baccalaureus], Bachelor of Medicine.

M.B.E., Member of (the Order of) the British Empire.

M.C., Master Commandant; Master of the Ceremonies; Member of Congress; Member of Council; the Military Cross.

M/C, Manchester.

M.C.C., Marylebone Cricket Club; Middlesex County Council.

M.Ch. [L. Magister Chirurgiæ], Master of Surgery.

M.Ch.D., Master of Dental Surgery.

M.C.L., Master of Civil Law.

M.C.S., Malayan Civil Service.

M.D. [L. Medicinæ Doctor], Doctor of Medicine; Middle Dutch; mentally deficient; [F. main droite, It. mano destra], (Mus.) with the right hand.

Md., Maryland.

m.d., Month's date.

Mdlle, Mademoiselle.

Mdme, Madame.

M.D.S., Master of Dental Surgery.

mdse., (*Am.*) Merchandise.

M.E., Mechanical Engineer; Methodist Episcopal; Military Engineer; Mining Engineer; Middle English; Most Excellent.

Me., Maine (U.S.A.).

Me [*F. maître*], Advocate.

mech., Mechanical, mechanics.

med., Medical, medicine; mediæval; medium; medalist.

Medit., Mediterranean.

med. jur., Medical jurisprudence.

mem., Memento, memorandum; memoir.

mensur., Mensuration.

mer., Meridian, meridional.

Mert., Merton College, Oxford.

Messrs., Messieurs.

met., Metronome; metropolitan.

metaph., Metaphysical, metaphysician, metaphysics, metaphor, metaphorical.

meteor., Meteorological, meteorology.

Meth., Methodist.

meton., Metonymy.

metrop., Metropolis, metropolitan.

Mex., Mexican, Mexico.

mf. [*It. mezzo-forte*], (*Mus.*) Moderately loud.

M.F.B., Metropolitan Fire Brigade.

mfd., Manufactured; (*Elec.*) microfarad.

mfg., Manufacturing.

M.F.H., Master of Foxhounds.

mfr., Manufacture, manufacturer.

M.G., Machine gun.

Mg, (*Chem.*) Magnesium.

mg., Milligram, -grams.

Mgr. (*pl.* **Mgrs.**), (*R.-C.Ch.*) Monsignor.

M.H., Ministry of Health.

M.H.K., Member of the House of Keys (Isle of Man).

mho., (*Elec.*) Unit of conductivity.

M.H.R., Member of the House of Representatives.

M.Hy., Master of Hygiene.

M.I., Mounted Infantry; Military Intelligence (department).

Mic., Micah.

Mich., Michaelmas; Michigan.

micros., Microscopy.

mid., Middle; Midlands.

Mid. Lat., Middle Latin.

min., Mineralogy; minim; minimum, minima; minister, ministerial; minor; minute, minutes.

M.I.N.A., Member of the Institute of Naval Architects.

Minn., Minnesota.

Min. Plen., Minister Plenipotentiary.

Min. Res., Minister Resident.

M.Ir., Middle Irish.

misc., Miscellaneous, miscellany.

Miss., Mission, missionary; Mississippi.

Mk., Mark (German coin).

Mkt., Market.

M.K.W., Military Knight of Windsor.

M.L., Licentiate in Midwifery; Mediæval Latin; Middle Latin; Ministry of Labour; Licentiate in Medicine.

Mlle, Mademoiselle.

MM., Majesties; messieurs; 2000.

M.M., The Military Medal.

mm., Millimetre, -metres.

Mme, Madame.

Mn, (*Chem.*) Manganese.

M.O., Money Order; Medical Officer.

Mo, (*Chem.*) Molybdenum.

Mo., Missouri.

mo., Month, months.

mob., Mobile.

mod., Moderate; modern.

Mods., (*Oxf. Univ.*) Moderations.

M.o.F., Ministry of Food.

M.O.H., Medical Officer of Health.

M.o.I., Ministry of Information.

mol. wt., Molecular weight.

Mon., Monday; Monmouthshire.

Mons., Monsieur (it is regarded as an insult in France to use this abbreviation).

Mont., Montana.

Mor., Morocco.

morph., Morphology.

M.P., Member of Parliament; Methodist Protestant; Metropolitan Police; military police.

m.p., Melting point.

mp [It. *mezzo-piano*], (*Mus.*) Rather softly.

M. Pens., Ministry of Pensions.

m.p.g., **m.p.h.**, Miles per gallon, per hour.

M.R., Master of the Rolls; Municipal Reformer.

Mr., Mister.

M.R.C.P., Member of the Royal College of Physicians.

M.R.C.S., Member of the Royal College of Surgeons.

M.R.I., Member of the Royal Institution.

Mrs., Missis, Mistress.

MS. (*pl.* **MSS**), Manuscript.

M.S., Master of Science; Master of Surgery.

m.s., Month's sight (comm.).

M.S.A., Member of the Society of Arts.

M.S.C., Medical Staff Corps.

M.Sc., Master of Science.

m.s.l., Mean sea-level.

M.S.M., Meritorious Service Medal.

M.T., Motor Transport; mechanical transport.

Mt., Mount; mountain.

M.T.B., (*Nav.*) Motor Torpedo boat.

mtg., Meeting.

mth., Month.

Mt. Rev., Most Reverend.

Mts., Mountains.

mus., Museum; music, musical, musician.

Mus.B., Mus.Bac. [L. *Musicæ Baccalaureus*], Bachelor of Music.

Mus.D., **Mus.Doc.** [L. *Musicæ Doctor*], Doctor of Music.

Mus.M. [L. *Musicæ Magister*], Master of Music (Cambridge).

M.V., Motor Vessel.

m.v. [It. *mezza voce*], (*Mus.*) With half the full power of the voice.

M.V.O., Member of the Royal Victorian Order.

M.W., Most Worshipful; Most Worthy.

M.W.B., Metropolitan Water Board.

M.Y., Motor Yacht.

myth., Mythological, mythology.

Mx., Middlesex.

N, (*Chem.*) Nitrogen.

N., (*Polit.*) Nationalist; (*Nav.*) navigating, navigation; Norse; north, northern; Northern London postal district; (*Mag.*) symbol of magnetic flux.

n., Name; nephew; neuter; new; noon; note, notes; nominative; noun.

Na [L. *natrium*], (*Chem.*) Sodium.

N.A., Nautical Almanac; North America.

n/a., (*Banking*) No advice, no account; non-acceptance.

N.A.A., National Artillery Association.

N.A.A.F.I., Navy, Army, and Air Force Institutes.

Nap., Napoleon.

Nat., Natal; Nathaniel; national.

nat., Natural, naturalist.

nat. hist., Natural history.

N.A.T.O., North Atlantic Treaty Organization.

nat. ord., Natural order.

nat. phil., Natural philosophy.

naut., Nautical.

nav., Naval; navigation.

N.B., New Brunswick; North Britain (Scotland).

N.B. [L. *nota bene*], Mark well.

Nb, (*Chem.*) Nobium.

n.b., (*Cricket*) No ball.

N.C., North Carolina.

N.C.O., Non-commissioned officer.

N.C.U., National Cyclists' Union.

N.C.W., National Council of Women.

n.d., No date.

N. Dak., North Dakota.

N.E., New edition; New England (U.S.A.); north-east; North-Eastern London postal district.

Ne, (*Chem.*) Neon.

N/E., (*Banking*) No effects.

Nebr., Nebraska.

N.E.D., New English Dictionary (now known as the Oxford English Dictionary [O.E.D.]).

neg., negative, negatively.

Neh., Nehemiah.

nem. con. [L. *nemine contar dicente*], No one contradicting.

nem. diss. [L. *nemine dissentiente*], No one dissenting.

N. Eng., New England (U.S.A.).

Nep., Neptune.

Neth., Netherlands.

neut., Neuter.

Nev., Nevada.

N.F., Newfoundland; Norman-French.

n/f., No funds.

N.F.S., National Fire Service.

N.F.U., National Farmers' Union.

N.Gr., New Greek.

N.H., New Hampshire.

N.Heb., New Hebrides.

N.H.I., National Health Insurance.

Ni, (*Chem.*) Nickel.

N.I., Northern Ireland; Naval Intelligence.

Nicar., Nicaragua.

N.I.D., Naval Intelligence Department.

ni. pri., *Nisi prius.*

N.J., New Jersey (U.S.A.).

n. l., (*Print.*) New line.

N. Lab., National Labour Party.

N. lat., North latitude.

N.L.C., National Liberal Club.

N.L.F., National Liberal Federation.

N.L.I., National Lifeboat Institution.

N. Mex., New Mexico.

N.N.E., North-north-east.

N.N.W., North-north-west.

N.O., Natural order; New Orleans.

No. [It. *Numero*], (*pl.* **Nos.**) Number.

n.o., (*Cricket*) Not out.

nol. pros. [L. *nolle prosequi*], To be unwilling to prosecute.

nom., nomin., Nominative.

Non-Coll., Non-Collegiate.

non-com—, Non-com- missioned.

Noncon., Nonconformist.

non obst. [L. *non obstante*], Notwithstanding.

non pros. [L. *non prosequitur*], He does not prosecute.

non seq. [L. *non sequitur*], It does not logically follow.

Nor., Norman; Norway, Norwegian.

Norf., Norfolk.

north., Northern.

Northants, Northampton- shire.

Northumb., Northumber- land.

Norvic. [L. *Norvicensis*], Of Norwich (Bishop of Norwich's signature).

Norw., Norway, Norwegian.

Nos. [see **NO.**], Numbers.

Notts, Nottinghamshire.

Nov., November.

N.P., New Providence; Notary-Public.

n.p., (*Print.*) New paragraph.

N.P.A., Newspaper Proprietors' Association.

N.R., North Riding (of Yorks).

nr., Near.

N.R.A., National Rifle Association.

N.S., National Society; New School; New Series; new side; new style; Nova Scotia; Numismatic Society.

n.s., Not specified.

n/s., (*Banking*) Not sufficient (money to meet a cheque).

N.J.C. [F. *Notre Seigneur Jesus-Christ*], Our Lord Jesus Christ.

N.S.L., National Sunday League.

N.S.P.C.C., National Society for the Prevention of Cruelty to Children.

N.S.W., New South Wales.

N.T., New Testament; New Translation; Northern Territory (Australia).

n.u., Name unknown.

Num., Numbers.

num., Numeral.

numis., Numismatics.

N.U.R., National Union of Railwaymen.

N.U.T., National Union of Teachers.

nux vom., Nux vomica.

N.V., New Version.

N.W., North Wales; north-west; North-Western London postal district.

N.W.T., North-Western Territory.

N.Y., New York (State).

N.Y.C., New York City.

N.Z., New Zealand.

O, (*Chem.*) Oxygen.

O., Ohio; old; Order; officer, Officers; (*Naut.*) overcast; owner.

o/a., On account.

O.A.S., On Active Service.

Ob., Oboe.

ob. [L. *obiit*], He (or she) died.

Obad., Obadiah.

obb. (*Mus.*) *Obbligato.*

O.B.E., Officer of (the Order of) the British Empire.

obj., Object, objection, objective.

obl., Oblique, oblong.

obs., Observation, observatory; obsolete.

ob. s.p. [L. *obiit sine prole*], Died without issue.

obstet., Obstetrics.

O.C., Officer commanding; Old Carthusian.

o/c, Overcharge.

occ., Occasionally.

Oct., October.

oct., Octavo.

O.C.T.U., Officer Cadets Training Unit.

O/D., Overdraft.

o/d., (*Banking*) On demand.

O.Dan., Old Danish.

O.E.D., Oxford English Dictionary.

O.F., Odd Fellows; Old French; (*Print.*) old face type.

off., Official, officinal.

O.F.M. [L. *Ordo Fratrum Minorum*], Order of Friars Minor.

O.F.S., Orange Free State.

O. Gael., Old Gaelic.

O.H.G., Old High German.

O.H.M.S., On Her (His) Majesty's Service.

O.Ir., Old Irish.

O.K., (*colloq.*) All right, very well; quite correct.

Okla., Oklahoma.

Ol., Olympiad.

O.L.G., Old Low German.

O.M. (Member of the) Order of Merit.

o.m., Old measure (of hymns).

O.N., Old Norse.

O.N.F., Old Norman-French.
onomat., Onomatopœia.
Ont., Ontario (Upper Canada).
O.P., (*Mil.*) observation post; old prices; [L. *Ordinis Prœdicatorum*], Order of Preachers, or Dominicans.
o.p., (*Theat.*) Opposite the prompt side; optime; overproof (of spirits); **out of print** (of books).
op. cit. [L. *opere citato*], In the work cited.
opt., Optative; optical, optician, optics; optime.
O.R., (*Mil.*) Other Ranks.
orat., Orator, oratorical, oratorically.
orch., Orchestra.
ord., Ordained, order, ordinal, ordinance, ordinary.
Ordn., Ordnance.
Ore., Oregon (U.S.A.).
org., Organ, organic, organism, organized.
orig., Origin, original, originally, originate.
ornith., Ornithological, ornithology.
Os, (*Chem.*) Osmium.
O.S., Old Saxon (language); Ordnance Survey; old school; old series; old side; old style; outsides (of paper); ordinary seaman.
o.s., Only son.
O.S.B., Order of St. Benedict.
O.S.F., Order of St. Francis.
O.Sl., Old Slavonic.
o.s.t., Ordinary spring tides.
O.T., Old Testament.
O.T.C., Officers' Training Corps.
O.Teut., Old Teutonic.
O.U., Oxford University.
O.U.D.S., Oxford University Dramatic Society.
Ox., Oxford.
Oxon, Oxfordshire; [L. *Oxonia*], Oxford; [L. *Oxoniensis*], of Oxford (Bishop of Oxford's signature).
oz., Ounce, ounces.

P, (*Chem.*) Phosphorus; car park.
p., Pastor; [L. *Pater*, F. *Père*], Father; president; prince; proconsul; (*Mech.*) pressure; priest; (*Polit.*) progressive; page; participle; (*Naut.*) passing showers; past; perch; pipe; pole; [F. *pied*], foot.
p. [It. *piano*], (*Mus.*) Soft.
p. [It. *poco*], A little, somewhat.
Pa., Pennsylvania.
p.a. [F. *per amitié*], By favour; [L. *per annum*], yearly.
P./A., Power of attorney.

p.a.c., (*Mil.*) Passed Advance Class (at Ordnance College).
paint., Painting.
Pal., Palestine.
palæog., Palæography.
palæont., Palæontology.
pam., Pamphlet.
Pan., Panama.
P. & O., Peninsular and Oriental (Steam Navigation Company).
par., Paragraph; parallel; parenthesis; parish.
Para., Paraguay.
Parl., Parliament, parliamentary.
part., Participle.
pass., Passive.
Pata., Patagonia.
path., Pathology.
Pat. Off., Patent Office.
Patr., Patron.
P.A.Y.E., Pay As You Earn (payment of Income Tax on salaries, wages, etc., as earned).
Pb [L. *plumbum*], (*Chem.*) Lead.
P.B. [L. *Pharmacopœia Britannica*], British Pharmacopœia; Plymouth Brethren; Prayer Book; Primitive Baptists; provisional battalion.
P.C., Parish Council; Parish Councillor; Perpetual Curate; Police Constable; Privy Council; Privy Councillor.
p.c., Post card; per cent.
p/c., Petty cash; prices current.
P.C.C., Prerogative Court of Canterbury.
P.C.S., Principal Clerk of Session (Scotland).
P.D., Postal District; (*Elec.*) potential difference.
Pd, (*Chem.*) Palladium.
pd., Paid.
P.D.A.D., Probate, Divorce, and Admiralty Division.
P.E., Presiding Elder; Protestant Episcopal.
Ped., (*Mus.*) Pedal.
P.E.N., Poets, Playwrights, Essayists, Editors and Novelists club.
P.E.I., Prince Edward Island.
pen., Peninsula.
Penit., Penitentiary.
Pent., Pentecost.
per., Period.
P.E.P., Political Economic Planning (club).
per cent [L. *per centum*], By the hundred.
perf., Perfect; perforated (of stamps).
perig., Perigee.
per proc. [L. *per procurationem*], On behalf of.
Pers., Persia, Persian.

pers., Person, personal, personally.
persp., Perspective.
Pet., Peter.
petrol., Petrology.
P.F., Procurator Fiscal.
Pf. [It. *piu forte*], (*Mus.*) A little louder.
Pfg. (*pl. -ge*), Pfennig.
P.G., Paying guest, *i.e.,* boarder.
phar., Pharmacopœia.
pharm., Pharmaceutical, pharmacy.
pharmacol., Pharmacology.
Ph.B. [L. *Philosophiœ Baccalaureus*], Bachelor of Philosophy.
Ph.D. [L. *Philosophiœ Doctor*], Doctor of Philosophy.
Phil., Philadelphia; (Epistle to the) Philippians.
phil., Philosophical, philosopher, philosophy.
Philat., Philately.
philol., Philological, philology.
Phil. Soc., **Philological Society.**
Phil. Trans., Philosophical Transactions of the Royal Society of London.
phon., Phonetic, phonetics, phonology.
phonog., Phonography.
phot., Photographic, photography.
phr., Phrase.
phren., Phrenological, phrenology.
phys., Physical, physician, physics.
physiol., Physiological, physiologist, physiology.
pinx. [L. *pinxit*], He (or she) painted it.
pizz., (*Mus.*) Pizzicato.
pk., Peck, pecks.
pkg., Package.
P.L. [L. *Pharmacopœia Londinensis*], London Pharmacopœia; Poet Laureate.
pl., Place; plate, plates; plural.
P.L.A., Port of London Authority.
Plen., Plenipotentiary.
plf., Plaintiff.
P.L.M., Paris Lyon Méditerranée (French rly.).
plup., Pluperfect.
P.M., Past Master; Paymaster; Postmaster; postmortem.
p.m. [L. *post meridiem*], Afternoon.
pm., Premium, premolar.
P.M.G., Paymaster-General; Postmaster-General.
P.M.O., Principal Medical Officer.
p.n., Promissory note.
P.N.E.U., Parents' National Education Union.

pneum., Pneumatic, pneumatics.

pnxt. [L. *pinxit*], He (or she) painted it.

P.O., Petty Officer; postal order; post office; Province of Ontario.

P.O.D., Pay on delivery; Post Office Department; Post Office Directory.

poet., Poetic, poetical, poetry.

pol. econ., Political economy.

pol., Political, politics.

Poly., Polytechnic.

P.O.O., Post office order.

P.O.P., (*Phot.*) Printing out paper.

pop., Popular, population.

por., Portrait.

Port., Portugal, Portuguese.

pos., Positive.

P.O.S.B., Post Office Savings Bank.

poss., Possession, possessive.

pot., Potential.

P.O.W., Prisoner(s) of War.

PP. [L. *Patres*], Fathers.

P.P., Parish priest; Past President.

pp., Pages.

pp [It. *pianissimo*], (*Mus.*) Very soft.

p.p., Past participle; *per procurationem*, on behalf of; post paid.

p.p. [It. *più piano*], (*Mus.*) More softly.

p.p.c. [F. *pour prendre congé*], To take leave.

ppp [It. *pianissimo*], (*Mus.*) As softly as possible.

P.P.U., Peace Pledge Union.

P.Q., Previous question; Province of Quebec.

Pr., Priest; printer.

pr., Pair, pairs; pounder of guns, *e.g.* 60 pr.

P.R., Porto Rico; proportional representation; prize ring.

P.R.A., President of the Royal Academy.

preb., Prebend, Prebendary.

prec., Preceding; precentor.

pref., Preface; preference; preferred; prefix, prefixed.

prelim., Preliminary.

prep., Preparatory; preposition.

Pres., President.

pres., Present.

pres. part., Present participle.

Presb., Presbyterian.

pret., Preterit.

P.R.I., President of the Royal Institute (of Painters in Water-colours).

P.R.I.B.A., President of the Royal Institute of British Architects.

prim., Primary, primate, primitive.

Prin., Principal.

prin., Principally, principles.

print., Printing.

priv., Private, privative.

Priv. Doz. [G.], *Privatdozent* (a recognized teacher not on the regular staff).

P.R.O., Public Records Office; Public Relations Officer.

pro., Professional.

Prob., (*Law*) Probate Division.

prob., Probable, probably; problem.

proc., Proceedings; proctor.

Prof., Professor.

Prog., Progressive.

prol., Prologue.

prom., Promontory.

pron., Pronoun; pronounced.

prop., Proposition.

propr., Proprietor; proprietary.

props., (*Theat.*) Properties.

pros., Prosody.

Prot., Protestant.

pro tem. [L. *pro tempore*], For the time being.

Prov., Provence, Provençal; Proverbs; province; Provost.

prov., Provincial; provisionally.

prox. [L. *proximo*], Next month.

prox. acc. [L. *proxime accessit*], He (or she) came next.

P.R.S., President of the Royal Society.

Pruss., Prussia, Prussian.

P.S., Permanent Secretary; [L. *postscriptum*], postscript; Privy Seal; (*Theat.*) prompt side.

Ps., Psalm, Psalms.

p.s., (*Mil.*) Passed School (of Instruction).

p.s.a., (*Mil.*) Passed Artillery College (School of Artillery).

p.s.c., (*Mil.*) Passed Staff College.

pseud., Pseudonym, pseudonymous, -ly.

psych., Psychic, psychical.

psychol., Psychological, psychology.

P.T., Post town; pupil teacher.

Pt, (*Chem.*) Platinum.

Pt., (*Geog.*) Point; port.

pt., Part; payment; pint, pints; (*Math.*) point.

Pte., (*Mil.*) Private.

ptg., Printing.

P.T.O., Please turn over; Public Trustee Office.

pub., Public; publican; publicly; publish, published, publisher, publishing.

pub. doc., Public document.

pud., Pudding.

p.v., Post village; priest vicar.

P.V.O., Principal Veterinary Officer.

P.V.-P., Past Vice-President.

P.W.D., Public Works Department.

P.W.R., Police War Reserve.

pwt. [DWT].

P.X., Please exchange.

pyrotech., Pyrotechnical, pyrotechnics.

Q., Quart; queen; question; (*Elec.*) coulomb; quire; (*Naut.*) squalls.

q., Quasi; query; quintal.

q. [L. *quære*], Inquire.

Q.A.B., Queen Anne's Bounty.

Q.B., Queen's Bench.

Q.C., Queen's College, Oxford; Queens' College, Cambridge; Queen's Counsel.

q.d. [L. *quasi dicat*], As if one should say; [L. *quasi dictum*], as if said.

q.e. [L. *quod est*], Which is.

Q.E.D. [L. *quod erat demonstrandum*], Which was to be proved.

Q.E.F. [L. *quod erat faciendum*], Which was to be done.

Q.E.I. [L. *quod erat inveniendum*], Which was to be found out.

Q.F., Quick-firing (of guns).

Q.H.P., Queen's Honorary Physician.

q.l. [L. *quantum libet*], As much as you please.

Q'l'd., Qld., Queensland, Australia.

Q.M., Quartermaster.

Q.M.G., Quartermaster-General.

Q.M.S., Quartermaster-Sergeant.

qr., Quarter, quarters (weight); quire, quires.

Q.S., Quarter-Sessions.

q.s. [L. *quantum sufficit*], A sufficient quantity.

qt., Quantity; quart, quarts.

qu., Question.

quad., Quadrant.

quant. suff. [Q.S.].

quart., Quarterly.

Que., Quebec.

Queensl., Queensland.

quot., Quotation, quoted; quotient.

q.v. [L. *quod vide*], Which see; [L. *quantum vis*], as much as you will.

qy., Query.

R., Radical; radius; railway; rabbi; (*Thermom.*) Réaumur; republican; [L. *rex*], King; (*Theat.*) right side; river; royal; rupee.

r., Rare; residence, resides;

rises; rod; rood; recipe; (*Naut.*) rain.

r., (*Math.*) Radius vector of co-ordinates.

R°, Radius of a circle in degrees of arc; **R′,** in minutes; **R″,** in seconds.

Ra, (*Chem.*) Radium.

R.A., Rear-Admiral; Royal Academy; Royal Academician; Royal Artillery.

R.A.A., Royal Academy of Arts.

R.A.A.F., Royal Australian Air Force.

R.A.C., Royal Automobile Club.

R.A.Ch.D., Royal Army Chaplains' Department.

rad. [L. *radix*], Root.

R.A.D.A., Royal Academy of Dramatic Art.

Radar [*see* Dictionary].

R.-Adm., Rear-Admiral.

R.A.E.C., Royal Army Educational Corps.

R.A.F., Royal Air Force.

R.A.M., Royal Academy of Music.

R.A.M.C., Royal Army Medical Corps.

R.A.O.C., Royal Army Ordnance Corps.

R.A.P.C., Royal Army Pay Corps.

R.A.S.C., Royal Army Service Corps.

R.A.V.C., Royal Army Veterinary Corps.

R.B., Rifle Brigade.

Rb, (*Chem.*) Rubidium.

R.C., Roman Catholic.

r.-c., Right of centre (of stage).

R.C.A.F., Royal Canadian Air Force.

R.C.I., Royal Colonial Institute.

R.C.N., Royal Canadian Navy.

R.D., Royal Dragoons; Rural Dean.

R./D., (*Banking*) Refer to drawer.

Rd., Road.

R.D.C., Rural District Council.

R.D.Y., Royal Dockyard.

R.E., Reformed Episcopal; Royal Engineers; Royal Exchange.

Réaum., Réaumur (thermometer).

rec., Receipt; recipe; record, recorded, recorder.

recd., Received.

rect., Rectified.

Ref., The Reformation.

ref., Refer, referred, referee, reference; reformed, reformer.

refl., Reflection, reflective, reflectively; reflex, reflexive, reflexively.

Reg., Regent; [L. *Regina*], Queen.

reg., Register, registrar, registry; regular, regularly.

regd., Registered.

Reg.-Gen., Registrar-General.

regl., Regimental.

Reg. Prof., Regius Professor.

Regr., Registrar.

regt., Regiment.

rel., Relative, relatively; religion, religious; [L. *reliquiæ*], relics.

rem., Remark, remarks.

R.E.M.E., Corps of Royal Electrical and Mechanical Engineers.

rep., Report, reporter; representative; republic, republican.

repr., Representing.

res., Reserve; residence, resident; resides; resigned.

resp., Respondent.

rest., Restored.

ret., Retired.

retd., Returned.

Rev., Revelations; Reverend; review.

rev., Revenue; reverse; revise, revised, revision; revolution.

Rev. Stat., Revised Statutes.

Rev. Ver., Revised Version (of the Bible).

R.F. [F. *République française*], French Republic.

rf., (*Mus.*) [RINF.].

R.F.A., Royal Field Artillery.

R.G.A., Royal Garrison Artillery; Royal Guernsey Artillery.

R.H., Royal Highness.

Rh, (*Chem.*) Rhodium.

R.H.A., Royal Horse Artillery.

rhet., Rhetoric, rhetorical.

R.H.G., Royal Horse Guards.

R.H.S., Royal Horticultural Society; Royal Humane Society.

R.I., Rhode Island; Royal Institute of (Painters in Water-colours); Royal Institution.

R.I.B.A., Royal Institute of British Architects.

R.I.C., Royal Irish Constabulary.

rinf. [It. *rinforzando*], (*Mus.*) With additional emphasis.

R.I.P. [L. *Requiescat* or -*cant in pace*], May he (she) or they rest in peace.

riten. [It. *ritenuto*], (*Mus.*) Slower.

Riv., River.

R.L.O., Returned Letter Office.

R.L.S., Robert Louis Stevenson.

Rly., Railway.

R.M., Resident Magistrate;

Royal Mail; Royal Marines.

rm., Ream.

R.M.A., Royal Marine Artillery; Royal Military Academy (Woolwich); Royal Military Asylum.

R.M.C., Royal Military College (Sandhurst).

R.Met.S., Royal Meteorological Society.

R.M.L.I., Royal Marine Light Infantry.

R.N., Royal Navy.

R.N.A.S., Royal Navy Air Service.

R.N.D., Royal Naval Division.

R.N.L.I., Royal National Lifeboat Institution.

R.N.R., Royal Naval Reserve.

R.N.V.R., Royal Naval Volunteer Reserve.

R.O., Receiving office, receiving officer; recruiting officer; relieving officer; returning officer; Royal Observatory.

ro., Rood.

R.O.C., Royal Observer Corps.

Roffen. [L. *Roffensis*], Of Rochester (the Bishop of Rochester's signature).

Rom., Roman; romance; (Epistle to the) Romans.

rom., (*Print.*) Roman or ordinary type, opp. to italic, etc.

R.P., Reformed Presbyterian; [F. *Révérend Père*], Reverend Father; (*Print.*) reprint; reply paid (telegram).

R.P.D., Regius Professor of Divinity.

r.p.m., Revolutions per minute.

rr. [L. *rarissime*], Very rarely.

R.R.C., Royal Red Cross (medal).

R.S., Recording Secretary; Revised Statutes; Royal Society.

Rs., Rupees.

r.s., (*Theat.*) Right side.

R.S.A., Royal Scottish Academy, Royal Scottish Academician; Royal Society of Antiquaries.

R.S.M., Regimental Sergeant-Major; Royal School of Mines; Royal Society of Medicine.

R.S.O., Railway sub- or sorting-office.

R.S.P.C.A., Royal Society for the Prevention of Cruelty to Animals.

R.S.S. [L. *Regiæ Societatis Socius*], Fellow of the Royal Society.

R.S.V.P. [F. *répondez s'il vous plaît*], Please reply.

R.T., Received text.

Rt. Hon., Right Honourable.

R.T.R., Royal Tank Regiment.

Rt. Rev., Right Reverend.

R.T.S., Religious Tract Society.

R.T.Y.C., Royal Thames Yacht Club.

R.U., Rugby Union.

Ru, (*Chem.*) Ruthenium.

r.u.e., (*Theat.*) Right upper entrance.

Rum., Rumania, Rumanian.

Rus., Russia, Russian.

R.V., Revised Version (of the Bible); Rifle Volunteers.

R.W., Right Worshipful.

Rx., Rix-dollar.

Rx., Tens of rupees.

Ry., Railway.

R.Y.S., Royal Yacht Squadron.

S, (*Chem.*) Sulphur.

S., Sabbath; Saint; Saturday; Saxon; Signor; Socialist; south, southern; Southern London postal district; sun; Sunday.

S., Second, seconds; section; shilling, shillings; singular; (*Naut.*) snow; son; substantive; succeeded.

$, Dollar, dollars.

S.A., Salvation Army; South Africa; South America; South Australia.

s.a. [L. *sine anno*], Without date.

Sab., Sabbath.

S.A.I. [F. *Son Altesse Impériale*], His (or Her) Imperial Highness.

Salop, Shropshire.

Sam., Samaritan; Samuel.

S. Amer., South America.

Sansk., Sanskrit.

S.A.R. [F. *Son Altesse Royale*], His (or Her) Royal Highness; South African Republic.

Sar., Sardinia, Sardinian.

Sarum, Of Salisbury (the Bishop of Salisbury's signature).

Sask., Saskatchewan.

Sat., Saturday.

Sax., Saxon, Saxony.

Sb [L. *stibium*], (*Chem.*) Antimony.

S.C., South Carolina; Special Constable; Staff College; Supreme Court.

Sc., Science, scientific; Scots, Scottish.

Sc, (*Chem.*) Scandium.

sc., Scene; scruple.

sc. [L. *sculpsit*], He (or she) engraved it; *scilicet.*

s.c., (*Print.*) Small capitals; (*Mil.*) student at the Staff College.

Scan., Scandinavia, Scandinavian.

scan. mag. [L. *scandalum magnatum*], Defamation of exalted persons.

s. caps., (*Print.*) Small capitals.

Sc.B. [L. *Scientiæ Baccalaureus*], Bachelor of Science.

Sc.D. [L. *Scientiæ Doctor*], Doctor of Science.

sch., School; schooner.

sci., Science, scientific.

scil. [L. *scilicet*], Namely, being understood.

S.C.M., State Certified Midwife; Students' Christian Movement.

Scot., Scotch, Scotland, Scottish.

Scp., Script.

scr., Scruple (weight).

Scrip., Scriptural, Scripture.

sculp., Sculptor, sculptural, sculpture.

sculps. [L. *sculpsit*], He (or she) engraved it.

S./D., Sea-damaged (grain trade).

s.d. [L. *sine die*], Indefinitely.

S. Dak., South Dakota.

S.D.F., Social Democratic Federation.

S.D.U.K., Society for the Diffusion of Useful Knowledge.

S.E., South-east; South-Eastern postal district of London; [F. *Son Éminence*], His Eminence; [F. *Son Excellence*], His Excellency.

S/E, Stock Exchange.

Se, (*Chem.*) Selenium.

sec., Secant; second; secretary.

sec. [L. *secundum*], According to.

sec. art. [L. *secundum artem*], According to art.

sec. leg. [L. *secundum legem*], According to law.

sec. nat. [L. *secundum naturam*], Naturally.

sec. reg. [L. *secundum regulam*], According to rule.

sect., Section.

S.E.D., Scottish Education Department.

sel., Selected, selection.

Selw., Selwyn College, Cambridge.

sem., Semicolon.

semp. [It. *sempre*], (*Mus.*) Always, throughout.

Sen., Senate, senator; senior.

sen. [It. *senza*], (*Mus.*) Without.

Sept., September; Septuagint.

seq. [L. *sequens*], The following; [L. *sequente*], and

in what follows; [L. *sequitur*], It follows.

seqq. [L. *sequentes, sequentia*], The following (*pl.*); [L. *sequentibus*], in the following places.

ser., Series.

Serb., Serbia, Serbian.

sess., Session.

sfz. [It.], (*Mus.*) Sforzando, *sforzato.*

S.G., Solicitor-General; specific gravity.

Sgt., Sergeant.

Shak., Shakespeare.

S.H.A.P.E., Supreme Headquarters Allied Powers Europe.

Shet., Shetland Islands.

s.h.v. [L. *sub hac voce or hoc verbo*], Under this word.

S.I., Sandwich Islands; Seine-Inférieure; Staten Island (N.Y.).

Si, (*Chem.*) Silicon.

Sib., Siberia, Siberian.

Sig., Signor.

sig., Signature.

S.I.M., Sergeant Instructor of Musketry.

sin., (*Math.*) Sine.

sin. [It. *sinistra*], (*Mus.*) The left hand.

sing., Singular.

S.J., Society of Jesus (Jesuits).

S.J.A.A., St. John Ambulance Association.

S.J.A.B., St. John Ambulance Brigade.

S.L., Serjeant-at-law.

Slav., Slavic, Slavonian, Slavonic.

sld., Sailed.

s.l.p. [L. *sine legitima prole*], Without lawful issue.

S.M. [F. *Sa Majesté*, G. *Seine Majestät*, It. *Sua Maestà*, Sp. *Su Magestad*], His (or Her) Majesty; Senior Magistrate; Sergeant-Major; Staff-Major; short metre (of hymns).

S.M.D., Short metre double (of hymns).

S.M.I. [F. *Sa Majesté Impériale*], His (or Her) Imperial Majesty.

Smith. Inst., Smithsonian Institution (Washington, U.S.A.).

S.M.O., Senior Medical Officer.

S./N., Shipping note.

Sn [L. *stannum*], (*Chem.*) Tin.

s.n. [L. *sine nomine*] Without name.

S.N.O., Senior Naval Officer.

S.O., Stationery Office; suboffice; (*Mil.*) staff officer.

s.o., Seller's option.

Soc., Society.

social., Sociology.

Sol., Solomon.

sol., Solicitor; solution.

Sol.-Gen., Solicitor-General.

sop., Soprano.

Soph., Sophocles.

S.O.S., Saving of Souls.

sov., Sovereign.

Sp., Spain, Spanish.

sp., Species; specimen; spirit.

S.P.C.K., Society for Promoting Christian Knowledge.

spec., Special, specially; specific, specifically, specification; spectrum, spectra.

S.P.G., Society for the Propagation of the Gospel.

sp. gr., Specific gravity.

S.P.Q.R. [L. *Senatus populusque Romanus*], The Senate and people of Rome.

sq., Square.

sq. ft., Square feet.

sq. in., Square inches.

sq. m., Square miles; square metre.

sqq. [SEQQ].

sq. yd., Square yard.

Sr, (*Chem.*) Strontium.

S.R. & O., Statutory Rules and Orders.

S.S. [F. *Sa Sainteté*], His Holiness; Secretary of State; steamship; Straits Settlements; Sunday School.

SS., Saints; [L. *Sanctissimus*], Most Holy.

ss. [L. *semi, semissus*], (*Med.*) One half.

s.s., Screw steamer; [It. *senza sordini*], (*Mus.*) without mutes.

S.S.A., Secretary of State for Air.

S.S.C., Solicitor before the Supreme Court.

S.S.E., South-south-east.

S.S.W., South-south-west.

St., Saint; strait, straits; street.

s.t., Short ton.

st., Stanza; (*Print.*) stet; stone (weight).

Sta. [It. *santa*], Female saint; station.

Staffs., Staffordshire.

stat., Statuary; statute, statutory; [L. *statim*], immediately.

S.T.B. [L. *Sacræ Theologiæ Baccalaureus*], Bachelor of Theology.

S.T.D. [L. *Sacræ Theologiæ Doctor*], Doctor of Theology.

Ste. [F. *sainte*], Female saint.

Stet [L.] (*Printing.*) Let it stand (annulling a correction).

stg., Sterling.

Sth., South.

stip., Stipend, stipendiary.

Stk., Stock.

Stn., Station.

S.T.P. [L. *Sacræ Theologiæ Professor*], Professor of Sacred Theology.

sub., Subaltern; subscription; substitute; suburb, suburban.

subj., Subject, subjective, subjectively; subjunctive.

Sub.-Lt., (*Nav.*) Sub-lieutenant.

suf., suff., Suffix.

Suff., Suffolk.

Sult., Sultan.

Sun., Sunday.

sup., Superior; supine.

sup., [L. *supra*], Above.

super., Superfine.

superl., Superlative.

supp., Supplement.

supr., Supreme.

supt., Superintendent.

surg., Surgeon, surgery, surgical.

Surg.-Gen., Surgeon-General.

surv., Surveyor; surviving.

sus. per coll. [L. *suspensio per collum*], Hanging by the neck.

s.v. [L. *sub voce*], Under the word, heading, etc.

s.v.p. [F. *s'il vous plaît*], If you please.

S.W., South Wales; south-west; South-Western London postal district.

Swed., Swedish, Sweden.

S.W.G., Standard wire gauge.

Sx., Sussex.

S.Y., Steam yacht.

syl., Syllable.

syn., Synonym, synonymous.

Syr., Syria, Syriac, Syrian.

syst., System.

T., Temperature; tenor; Territorial; Territory; Testament; Tuesday.

t. [F. *tome*], Volume; ton, tons; town, township; [L. *tempore*], in the time of; (*Naut.*) thunder; tun, tuns.

Ta, (Chem.) Tantalum.

T.A.A., Territorial Army Association.

Tal., Talmud, Talmudic.

Tam., Tamil (language).

tan., Tangent.

Tasm., Tasmania, Tasmanian.

Tb, (*Chem.*) Terbium; Tuberculosis.

T.B., (*Nav.*) Torpedo boat.

T.B.D., (*Nav.*) Torpedo-boat destroyer.

T.C., Town Councillor.

T.C.D., Trinity College, Dublin.

T.C.F., Touring Club de France.

T.C.O., Trinity College, Oxford.

T.D., Territorial Decoration.

Te, (*Chem.*) Tellurium.

tech., Technical, technically.

technol., Technological, technology.

tel., Telephone.

telg., Telegram.

temp., Temperature; temporary.

temp. [L. *tempore*], In the time of.

Tenn., Tennessee.

Ter., Terrace.

terat., Teratology.

term., Terminology.

Test., Testament.

Teut., Teuton, Teutonic.

Tex., Texan, Texas.

text.rec. [L. *textus receptus*], The received text.

t.g., Type genus.

T.H., Transport House.

Th., Thomas, Thursday.

Th, (*Chem.*) Thorium.

theat., Theatrical.

Theo., Theodore.

theol., Theologian, theological, theology.

theor., Theorem.

theoret., Theoretic, theoretical, theoretically.

theos., Theosophical, theosophist, theosophy.

therap., Therapeutic, -ics.

thermom., Thermometer, thermometric.

Thess., Thessalonians; Thessaly.

Thos., Thomas.

thro', Through.

Thurs., Thursday.

T.H.W.M., Trinity high-water mark.

Ti, (*Chem.*) Titanium.

Tim., Timothy.

tinct., Tincture.

Tit., Titus.

tit., Title.

Tl, (*Chem.*) Thallium.

T.L.S., Territorial Long Service Medal.

T.N.T., Trinitrotoluene (*explosive*).

T.O., Telegraph Office; turn over.

Toc H, Talbot House society.

tonn., Tonnage.

topog., Topography.

torp., Torpedo.

Tr., Translate, -lated, -lation, -lator; trustee.

tr/, (*Print.*) Transpose.

trag., Tragedy, tragic.

trans., Transactions; transitive; translated, -lation, -lator.

transf., Transferred.

Treas., Treasurer, treasury.

Trees., Trustees.

T.R.H., Their Royal Highnesses.

trig., trigon., Trigonometry.

Trin., Trinity College, Cambridge.

Trin. H., Trinity Hall, Cambridge.

Trip., Tripos.

Trs., Trustees.

Truron, [L. *Truronensis*], Of Truro (signature of the Bishop of Truro).

T.T., Teetotaller; telegraphic transfers.

t.t.l., To take leave.

T.U., Trade Union.

T.U.C., Trades Union Congress.

Tues., Tuesday.

Turk., Turkey, Turkish.

T.V., Television.

T.V.A., Tennessee Valley Authority (U.S.A.).

T.V.R., (*Elec.*) Temperature variation of resistance.

Typ., Typographer, typographical, typography.

U, (*Chem.*) Uranium.

U. (*Polit*). Unionist.

U./a., Underwriting account (marine).

U.A.R., United Arab Republic

U.C., University College; Upper Canada.

u.c., (*Print.*) Upper case; [It. *una corda*], (*Mus.*) on one string.

U.C.H., University College Hospital.

U.C.L., University College, London.

U.D.C., Urban District Council.

U.F.C., United Free Church of Scotland.

U.K., United Kingdom.

Ukr., Ukraine.

ult. [L. *ultimo*], Last month.

U.N., United Nations.

U.N.A., United Nations Association.

unabr., (*Bibliog.*) Unabridged.

U.N.E.S.C.O., United Nations Educational, Scientific and Cultural Organization.

Unit., Unitarian, Unitarianism.

Univ., University.

univ., Universal.

unm., Unmarried.

unop., Unopposed.

unpubl., Unpublished.

U.N.R.R.A., United Nations Relief and Rehabilitation Administration.

U.P., United Presbyterian.

u.p., Under proof (of spirits).

np., Upper.

Uru., Uruguay.

U.S., United Service; United States.

u.s. [L. *ubi supra*], In the place above mentioned; [L. *ut supra*] as above.

U.S.A., United States of

America; United States Army.

U.S.C., United States of Colombia.

U.S.M., United States Marines.

U.S.N., United States Navy.

U.S.S., United States Senate; United States ship; United States steamer.

U.S.S.R., (Russian) Union of Soviet Socialist Republics.

Ut., Utah.

ut dict. [L. *ut dictum*], As directed.

ut sup. [L. *ut supra*], As above.

U/w., Underwriter.

u.x. [L. *uxor*], Wife.

V, (*Chem.*) Vanadium; (*Elec.*) volt.

V., Five; (*Math.*) potential energy; Vice; Viscount; Volunteers.

v., (*Math.*) Vector; (*Phys.*) velocity; ventral; verb; verse.

v., Versus (against); [L. *vide*], see; (*Mus.*) violin; voice.

V.A., Vicar-Apostolic; Vice-Admiral; (Royal Order of) Victoria and Albert; Volunteer Artillery.

Va., Virginia.

v.a. [L. *vixit annos*], Lived (so many) years.

V.A.D., Voluntary Aid Detachment.

V.-Adm., Vice-Admiral.

V. & A. Mus., Victoria and Albert Museum.

var., Variety; (*Math.*) variant.

var. lect. [L. *vario lectio*], Variant reading.

Vat., Vatican.

vaud., Vaudeville.

vb., Verb.

V.C., Vice-Chairman; Vice-Chancellor; Vice-Consul; Victoria Cross.

V.D., Volunteer Decoration; Venereal disease.

v.d., (*Bibliog.*) Various dates.

V.D.H., Valvular Disease of the Heart.

Ven., Venerable.

Venet., Venetian.

Venez., Venezuela.

verb. sap., or sat. [L. *verbum satis sapienti*], A word is enough for a wise man.

Vet., Veterinary Surgeon.

V.G., Vicar-General.

V.H.C., Very highly commended.

V.H.F., (*Radio*) Very high frequency.

Vic., Vict., Victoria.

vid. [L. *vide*], See.

vil., Village.

Visct., Viscount, Viscountess.

viz. [L. *videlicet*], Namely.

v.l. [L. *varia lectio*], A variant reading.

V.O., (Royal) Victorian Order.

V°, Verso.

voc., Vocative.

vocab., Vocabulary.

vol., Volume; volunteer.

V.-P., Vice-President.

v.r., Verb reflective.

V.R.I. [L. *Victoria Regina et Imperatrix*], Victoria Queen and Empress.

V.S., Veterinary Surgeon.

v.s. [F. *vieux style*], Old style; [L. *vide supra*], see above; [It. *volta subito*], (*Mus.*) turn over quickly.

V.T. [L. *Vetus Testamentum*], Old Testament.

v.t., Verb transitive.

Vt., Vermont (U.S.A.).

Vulg., Vulgate.

vulg., Vulgar, vulgarly.

vv., Verses; (*Mus.*) violins.

V.W., Very worshipful.

V.y., (*Bibliog.*) Various years.

W [G. *Wolfram*], (*Chem.*) Tungsten.

W., Wales; warden; Wednesday; Welsh; west; western; Western London postal district; Wesleyan.

w., Week, weeks; (*Naut.*) wet dew; wife.

W.A., Western Australia.

Wadh., Wadham College, Oxford.

W. Afr., West Africa.

Wal., Walloon.

W. & M., (*King*) William and (Queen) Mary.

War., Warwickshire.

Wash., Washington.

W.B., Way-bill.

w.b., (*Shipping*) Water ballast.

W.C., Western Central London postal district.

w.c., Water-closet; without charge.

W.D., War Department; Works Department.

W.E.A., Workers' Educational Association.

Wed., Wednesday.

Wes., Wesleyan.

w.f., (*Print.*) Wrong fount.

w.g., Wire gauge.

whf., Wharf.

W.I., West Indies, West Indian, Women's Institute.

Wilts., Wiltshire.

Wind. I., Windward Islands.

Winton [L. *Wintoniensis*], Of Winchester (the Bishop of Winchester's signature).

W.I.R., West India Regiment.

Wisc., Wisconsin.

Wm., William.

W.N.W., West-north-west.
W.O., War Office.
Wor., Worshipful.
W.P., Weather permitting.
W.P.B., Waste-paper basket.
W.R., West Riding (Yorks).
W.R.A.C., Women's Royal Army Corps.
W.R.A.F., Women's Royal Air Force.
W.R.N.S., Women's Royal Naval Service.
W.S., Writer to the Signet.
W.S.W., West-south-west.
W/T., Wireless telegraphy.
W. Va., West Virginia.
W.V.S., Women's Voluntary Service.
Wyo., Wyoming (U.S.A.).

X., Christ.
x.c., (*Comm.*) Ex (without) coupon.

xcp., Without coupon.
x.d., Ex (without) dividend.
Xe, (*Chem.*) Xenon.
x.i., Ex interest, without next interest.
Xmas, Christmas.
Xn., Christian.
x.n., ex (without the right to) new shares.
Xopher, Xpher, Christopher.
Xt., Christ.

Y, (*Chem.*) Yttrium.
Y., Year, years.
Y./A., York Antwerp rules (marine insur.).
Y.B., Year-book.
Yb, (*Chem.*) Ytterbium, yttrium.
Y.C., Yale College (U.S.A.).
yd., Yard, yards.
Yeo., Yeomanry.
yest., yesty., Yesterday.
Y.H.A., Youth Hostels Association.

Y.L.I., Yorkshire Light Infantry.
Y.M.C.A., Young Men's Christian Association.
Yorks, Yorkshire.
Yks., Yorkshire.
yr., Year; younger; your.
Yt, (*Chem.*) Yttrium.
Y.W.C.A., Young Women's Christian Association.

Z, (*Mag.*) Symbol for reluctance.
Zach., Zachary.
Zech., Zechariah.
Zeph., Zephaniah.
Zn, (*Chem.*) Zinc.
zoochem., Zoochemical, zoo-chemistry.
zoogeog., Zoogeographical, zoogeography.
zool., Zoological, zoologist, zoology.
Zr, (*Chem.*) Zirconium.
Z.S., Zoological Society.

BRITISH AND METRIC WEIGHTS AND MEASURES

BRITISH

MEASURES OF LENGTH

12	inches = 1 foot.
3	feet = 1 yard = 36 inches.
5½	yards = 1 pole = 16½ feet = 198 inches.
40	poles = 1 furlong = 220 yards = 660 feet.
8	furlongs = 1 mile = 1,760 yards = 5,280 feet.
3	miles = 1 league = 5,280 yards = 15,840 feet.

Nautical and Geographical Measure

6	feet = 1 fathom.
100	fathoms = 1 cable.
120	fathoms = 1 cable length.
2,027·3	yards = 1·152 miles = 1 nautical (or geographical) mile.
3	nautical miles = 1 nautical league = 3·456 ordinary miles.

Surveying Measure

1	link = 7·92 inches.
100	links = 1 chain = 66 feet = 22 yards.
80	chains = 1 mile = 5,280 feet.

MEASURES OF AREA

144	square inches = 1 square foot.
9	square feet = 1 square yard = 1,296 square inches.
30¼	square yards = 1 square pole (*Note:* 30¼ = 5½ × 5½).
40	square poles = 1 rood = 1,210 square yards.
4	roods = 1 acre = 4,840 square yards.
16	square poles = 1 square chain = 484 square yards (= 22 × 22).
10	square chains = 1 acre = (22 × 220 yards).
640	acres = 1 square mile.

MEASURES OF CAPACITY

1,728	cubic inches = 1 cubic foot.
27	cubic feet = 1 cubic yard.
40	cubic feet = 1 shipping ton.

Liquid and Dry Measure

4	gills = 1 pint (20 avoirdupois oz. of water).
2	pints = 1 quart.
2	quarts = 1 pottle.
4	quarts = 1 gallon (10 avoirdupois lb. of water).
2	gallons = 1 peck.
4	pecks = 1 bushel = 8 gallons. Bushel of Barley, 47 lb.; beans, 63 lb.; oats, 40 lb.; peas, 64 lb.; rye, 53 lb.; wheat, 60 lb.
8	bushels = 1 quarter.
5	quarters = 1 wey or load
2	weys = 1 last.
4½	gallons = 1 pin.
9	gallons = 1 firkin.

2	firkins = 1 kilderkin.
4	firkins = 1 barrel = 36 gallons.
54	gallons = 1 hogshead ale.
63	gallons = 1 hogshead wine.
84	gallons = 1 puncheon.
126	gallons = 1 pipe or butt.
2	pipes = 1 tun.

Apothecaries' Fluid Measure

60	minims = 1 drachm = ·216 cubic inches.
8	drachms = 1 ounce = 437½ grains (1 ounce avoirdupois of water).
20	ounces = 1 pint = 8,750 grains.

MEASURES OF WEIGHT

Avoirdupois Weight

16	drams = 1 ounce = 437½ grains.
16	ounces = 1 pound = 7,000 grains.
14	pounds = 1 stone.
2	stones = 1 quarter = 28 pounds.
4	quarters = 1 hundredweight (cwt.) = 112 pounds.
20	cwts. = 1 ton = 2,240 pounds.

Troy Weight

24	grains = 1 pennyweight (dwt.).
20	dwts. = 1 ounce = 480 grains.
12	ounces = 1 pound = 5,760 grains

Apothecaries' Weight

20	grains = 1 scruple (written ℈).
3	scruples = 1 drachm (written ℥).
8	drachms = 1 ounce = 480 grains (written ℥).
12	ounces = 1 pound = 5,670 grains.

METRIC

Measures of Length

10 millimetres = 1 centimetre = ·3937 inch.

10	centimetres = 1 decimetre.
10	decimetres = 1 metre = 39·370113 inches.
10	metres = 1 decametre.
100	metres = 10 decametres = 1 hectometre = 109·36 yards.
1,000	metres = 10 hectometres = 1 kilometre = ·62138 mile.
10,000	metres = 10 kilometres = 1 myriametre = 6·2138 miles.

Measures of Capacity

1,000 cubic centimetres (1 cubic decimetre) = 1 litre = 61·024 cubic inches. The tenth, hundredth, and thousandth of a litre are called decilitre, centilitre, and millilitre respectively, while ten, a hundred, and a thousand are decalitres, hectolitres, and kilolitres respectively.

Measures of Weight

The weight of 1 cubic centimetre of distilled water at 4° Centigrade (39·2° F.) is 1 gramme. As with the other units, the tenth hundredth, and thousandth are the deci-, centi-, and milli-gramme respectively, while ten, a hundred, and a thousand are called deca-, hecto-, and kilo-gramme respectively.

1 gramme = 15·43235 grains.
1 kilogramme = 2·20462 lb. avoirdupois.

Measures of Area

1	square metre = 10·7644 square feet.
100	square metres = 1 square decametre = 1 are.
10,000	square metres = 1 square hectometre = 1 hectare = 11,960·46 square yards = 2·471 acres.
100	hectares = 247·1169 acres.